ELEMENTS OF Literature

FOURTH COURSE

with Readings in World Literature

We have not even to risk the adventure alone,
for the heroes of all time have gone before us.

—from "The Monomyth" by Joseph Campbell

HOLT, RINEHART AND WINSTON

A Harcourt Education Company

Austin • Orlando • Chicago • New York • Toronto • London • San Diego

CREDITS

EDITORIAL

Project Director: Kathleen Daniel
Managing Editor: Richard Sime
Executive Editor: Laura Mongello
Editorial Staff: Robert Schirmer, Leora Harris, Robert Hoyt, Kathryn Rogers, Christopher LeCluyse
Editorial Support: Laurie Muir, Dan Hunter
Editorial Permissions: Ann B. Farrar, Sacha Frey

Research and Development: Joan Burditt

Index: Robert Zolnerzak

PRODUCTION, DESIGN, AND PHOTO RESEARCH

Director: Athena Blackorby
Design Coordinator: Betty Mintz
Program Design: Kirchoff/Wohlberg, Inc.
Electronic Files: Banta Digital
Design/Production: Joseph Padial/Carol Marunas
Photo Research: PhotoSearch, Inc.
Photo Resources Coordinator: Mary Monaco
Manufacturing: RR Donnelley & Sons Company, Willard, Ohio

COVER

Cover artist: Greg Geisler
Photo credits: Front cover: (Oseberg Viking Ship), Ulf Sjostedt/FPG International; (Red Giants and M87), Julian Baum/Photo Researchers, Inc. Back cover: (button), Ken Marschall Collection.
Quotation on Cover: from "The Monomyth" by Joseph Campbell, courtesy of Princeton University Press.

Acknowledgments appear on pages 1074–1077, which are an extension of the copyright page.

Printed in the United States of America
ISBN 0-03-067282-1 2 3 4 5 6 048 03 02

PROGRAM AUTHORS

Kylene Beers wrote the Reading Matters section of the book and developed the accompanying *Reading Skills and Strategies* component. A former middle school teacher, Dr. Beers has turned her commitment to helping readers having difficulty into the major focus of her research, writing, speaking, and teaching. A clinical associate professor at the University of Houston, Dr. Beers is also currently the editor of the National Council of Teachers of English journal *Voices from the Middle*. She is the author of *When Kids Can't Read: The Reading Handbook for Teachers Grades 6–12* and co-editor of *Into Focus: Understanding and Creating Middle School Readers*. She has served on the review boards of the *English Journal* and *The ALAN Review*. Dr. Beers is a recipient of the NCTE Richard W. Halle Award. She currently serves on the board of directors of the International Reading Association's Special Interest Group on Adolescent Literature.

Robert E. Probst established the pedagogical framework for the 1997, 2000, and current editions of *Elements of Literature*. Dr. Probst is Professor of English Education at Georgia State University. He has taught English in Maryland and been Supervisor of English for the Norfolk, Virginia, Public Schools. He is the author of *Response and Analysis: Teaching Literature in Junior and Senior High School* and has contributed chapters to such books as *Literature Instruction: A Focus on Student Response; Reader Response in the Classroom; Handbook of Research on Teaching the English Language Arts; Transactions with Literature;* and *For Louise M. Rosenblatt*. Dr. Probst has worked on the National Council of Teachers of English Committee on Research, the Commission on Reading, and the Commission on Curriculum. He has also served on the board of directors of the Adolescent Literature Assembly and is a member of the National Conference on Research in Language and Literacy.

Robert Anderson wrote the introductions to "The Drama Collection" and "William Shakespeare." He also wrote biographies and instructional materials for *I Never Sang for My Father* and *Julius Caesar*. Mr. Anderson is a playwright, novelist, screenwriter, and teacher. His plays include *Tea and Sympathy; Silent Night, Lonely Night; You Know I Can't Hear You When the Water's Running;* and *I Never Sang for My Father*. His screenplays include *The Nun's Story* and *The Sand Pebbles*. Mr. Anderson has taught at the Writers' Workshop at the University of Iowa, the American Theater Wing Professional Training Program, and the Salzburg Seminar in American Studies. He is a past president of the Dramatists' Guild, a past vice president of the Authors' League of America, and a member of the Theater Hall of Fame.

John Malcolm Brinnin wrote the *Elements of Literature* essays on poetry, biographies of the poets, and instructional materials on individual poems. Mr. Brinnin is the author of six volumes of poetry, which received many prizes and awards. He was a member of the American Academy and Institute of Arts and Letters. He was also a critic of poetry and a biographer of poets and was for a number of years director of New York's famous Poetry Center. His teaching career, begun at Vassar College, included long terms at the University of Connecticut and Boston University, where he succeeded Robert Lowell as Professor of Creative Writing and Contemporary Letters. Mr. Brinnin's books include *Dylan Thomas in America: An Intimate Journal* and *Sextet: T. S. Eliot & Truman Capote & Others*.

John Leggett wrote the *Elements of Literature* essays on the short story, biographies of the short-story writers, and instructional materials on individual short stories. Mr. Leggett is a novelist, a biographer, and a former teacher. He went to the Writers' Workshop at the University of Iowa in the spring of 1969, expecting to work there for a single semester. In 1970, he assumed temporary charge of the program, and for the next seventeen years he was its director. Mr. Leggett's novels include *Wilder Stone; The Gloucester Branch; Who Took the Gold Away?; Gulliver House;* and *Making Believe*. He also wrote the highly acclaimed biography *Ross and Tom: Two American Tragedies*.

SPECIAL CONTRIBUTORS

Janet Burroway wrote an *Elements of Literature* essay on nonfiction and instructional materials on individual nonfiction selections. Ms. Burroway is a novelist and teacher who has also written children's books and a popular textbook called *Writing Fiction.* Ms. Burroway has taught at the University of Sussex, England; the University of Illinois; and the Writers' Workshop at the University of Iowa. She is currently Robert O. Lawton Distinguished Professor at Florida State University in Tallahassee. Her novels include *The Buzzards* (nominated for the Pulitzer Prize), *Raw Silk* (nominated for the National Book Award), *Opening Nights,* and *Cutting Stone.*

Richard Cohen wrote *Elements of Literature* essays on nonfiction and instructional material on individual selections. Mr. Cohen is an educational writer and editor as well as a novelist. Mr. Cohen has written a college creative-writing textbook, *Writer's Mind: Crafting Fiction,* and the novels *Domestic Tranquility, Don't Mention the Moon,* and *Say You Want Me.* A graduate of the University of Michigan, he has taught creative writing at the University of Wisconsin, Madison.

David Adams Leeming wrote the introductions "Greek Drama: Out of Ritual" and "The Myth of Oedipus," as well as instructional material on *Antigone.* He also wrote the introduction to the Bible and instructional material on the selections in "Traditions! Readings in World Literature." Dr. Leeming was for many years a Professor of English and Comparative Literature at the University of Connecticut. He is the author of several books on mythology, including *Mythology: The Voyage of the Hero; The World of Myth;* and *Encyclopedia of Creation Myths.* For several years Dr. Leeming taught English at Robert College in Istanbul, Turkey. He also served as secretary and assistant to the writer James Baldwin in New York and Istanbul. He has published two biographies, *James Baldwin* and *Amazing Grace: A Biography of Beauford Delaney.*

WRITERS

The writers prepared instructional materials for the text under the supervision of Dr. Probst and the editorial staff.

Ellen Ashdown
Educational writer and editor
Tallahassee, Florida

Elaine Goldenberg
Educational writer and editor
Cambridge, Massachusetts

Phyllis Goldenberg
Educational writer and editor
Miami, Florida

Lynn Hovland
Former teacher
Educational writer and editor
Berkeley, California

Carole Lambert
Journalist and educational writer and editor
Waterville, Maine

Carroll Moulton
Former teacher
Educational writer and editor
Southampton, New York

Pam Ozaroff
Educational writer and editor
Newton Center, Massachusetts

Mairead Stack
Educational writer and editor
New York, New York

Diane Tasca
Educational writer and editor
Palo Alto, California

REVIEWERS AND CONSULTANTS

Reviewers assisted in choosing selections and evaluated instructional materials. Consultants assisted in securing student active-reading models and provided advice on current pedagogy.

Special Consultant
Baird Neville
Communications Arts High School
San Antonio, Texas

Doug Bader
Cloverhill High School
Midlothian, Virginia

Pat Baker
Central High School
Grand Rapids, Michigan

Barbara Beeson
Elkhart Central High School
Elkhart, Indiana

Debra Blunier
Eureka High School
Eureka, Illinois

Gary Breese
Torrance High School
Torrance, California

Marilyn Buehler
North High School
Phoenix, Arizona

Lory Butcher
Oakmont High School
Roseville, California

Joan Cooper
Washington High School
Indianapolis, Indiana

Diana Crawford
Belfry High School
Belfry, Kentucky

Beverly Davenport
Boone High School
Orlando, Florida

Jerome Evans
Crenshaw High School
Los Angeles, California

Kathryn S. Falkenberg
Brush High School
Cleveland, Ohio

Sally Finley
Belle Vernon High School
Belle Vernon, Pennsylvania

Ann Freelove
Oakmont High School
Roseville, California

Jason Gallman
Ben Davis High School
Indianapolis, Indiana

Marianne Gardner
Putman City West High School
Oklahoma City, Oklahoma

Hannah Goolsby
Bowie High School
Arlington, Texas

Faith Greenfield
Edison Senior High School
Miami, Florida

John Hagadorn
Midlothian High School
Midlothian, Virginia

Donna Hopewell
Rosewood High School
Goldsboro, North Carolina

Louise Jones
San Angelo Central High School
San Angelo, Texas

Julie Joslin
West Rowan High School
Mount Ulla, North Carolina

Janet Kerley
Southeast High School
Bradenton, Florida

Marianne King
Park High School
Cottage Grove, Minnesota

Michele Kloss
Eastmont Senior High School
East Wenatchee, Washington

Kathleen Luedke
David Crockett High School
Austin, Texas

Beverly Masters
Muncie Central High School
Muncie, Indiana

Debbie Miller
Design and Architecture Senior High School
Miami, Florida

Vivian Nida
Putman City West High School
Oklahoma City, Oklahoma

Margaret Oberender
Westwood High School
Austin, Texas

Mike Owens
Plum Senior High School
Pittsburgh, Pennsylvania

Frank Pool
Travis High School
Austin, Texas

Andre Prenoveau
Westerville North High School
Westerville, Ohio

Kay Price-Hawkins
English/Language Arts Consultant
Abilene, Texas

Gayle Rainey
Longmont High School
Longmont, Colorado

Mike Romeo
West Orange High School
West Orange, New Jersey

Merle Singer
Parkway North High School
St. Louis, Missouri

Bridgett S. Sisson
Marian High School
Omaha, Nebraska

Shirley Stewart
Warren High School
Downey, California

Veda Kay Waheed
Ellison High School
Killeen, Texas

Karen Wilkerson
Center Grove High School
Greenwood, Indiana

Nancy Zuwiyya
Binghamton High School
Binghamton, New York

FIELD-TEST PARTICIPANTS

The following teachers participated in field-testing of prepublication materials for the series.

Janet Blackburn-Lewis
Western Guilford High School
Greensboro, North Carolina

Dana E. Bull
F. J. Turner High School
Beloit, Wisconsin

Maura Casey
Skyline High School
Oakland, California

Deborah N. Dean
Warner Robins Middle School
Warner Robins, Georgia

Gloria J. Dolesh
Friendly High School
Fort Washington, Maryland

Christina Donnelly
Parkdale High School
Riverdale, Maryland

Kay T. Dunlap
Norview High School
Norfolk, Virginia

Joseph Fitzgibbon
West Linn High School
West Linn, Oregon

Paul Garro
Communications Arts High School
San Antonio, Texas

Suzanne Haffamier
Agoura High School
Agoura, California

Robert K. Jordan
Land O' Lakes High School
Land O' Lakes, Florida

Terry Juhl
Bella Vista High School
Fair Oaks, California

Elizabeth Keister
Blair Middle School
Norfolk, Virginia

Jane S. Kilgore
Warner Robins High School
Warner Robins, Georgia

Janet S. King
Reading High School
Reading, Pennsylvania

Cheryl L. Lambert
Milford Mill Academy
Baltimore, Maryland

Sarah A. Long
Robert Goddard Middle School
Seabrook, Maryland

Donna J. Magrum
Rogers High School
Toledo, Ohio

Nancy Maheras
Western High School
Las Vegas, Nevada

Mara Malone
Central High School
Baton Rouge, Louisiana

Margaret E. McKinnon
Roger L. Putnam Vocational-Technical High School
Springfield, Massachusetts

Lourdes J. Medina
Pat Neff Middle School
San Antonio, Texas

Joan Mohon
Todd County Central High School
Elkton, Kentucky

Terrence R. Moore
John Muir High School
Pasadena, California

Gayle C. Morey
Countryside High School
Clearwater, Florida

Beverly Mudd
Western High School
Las Vegas, Nevada

Jan Nichols
Apollo High School
Glendale, Arizona

Jeffrey S. Norton
Lewis and Clark High School
Spokane, Washington

Barbara Powell
Todd County Central High School
Elkton, Kentucky

Gloria S. Pridmore
Morrow High School
Morrow, Georgia

Dee Richardson
Moore High School
Moore, Oklahoma

Carole A. Scala
Southwest Middle School
Orlando, Florida

Barbara A. Slaughter
Lewis and Clark High School
Spokane, Washington

Barbara B. Smith
Dr. Phillips 9th Grade Center
Orlando, Florida

Sister Eileen Stephens, CSJ
Cathedral Preparatory Seminary
Elmhurst, New York

Sally Thompson
Andrew Jackson Middle School
Suitland, Maryland

Blanca M. Valledor
G. Holmes Braddock Senior High School
Miami, Florida

Charla J. Walton
John C. Fremont Junior High School
Las Vegas, Nevada

William Ward
Roger L. Putnam Vocational-Technical High School
Springfield, Massachusetts

Lynn White
Tascosa High School
Amarillo, Texas

Noretta M. Willig
Baldwin High School
Pittsburgh, Pennsylvania

Deborah K. Woelflein
Merrimack High School
Merrimack, New Hampshire

STUDENT CONTRIBUTORS

The following students wrote annotations for the active-reading models (Dialogue with the Text).

Melissa Bender
Torrance High School
Torrance, California

Sara Hunter
Southeast High School
Bradenton, Florida

Paula Stoller
Eureka High School
Eureka, Illinois

Contents in Brief

The Poetry Collections

The Drama Collection

William Shakespeare

Traditions! Readings in World Literature

Resource Center

CONTENTS

The Short-Story Collections

Collection I

Hard Choices

Language/Grammar Links

COMMUNICATIONS WORKSHOPS

Collection 2

Hearts That Love

COMMUNICATIONS WORKSHOPS

Language/Grammar Links

Collection 3

Exiles, Castaways, and Strangers

COMMUNICATIONS WORKSHOPS

Language/Grammar Links

Collection 4

Breakthroughs

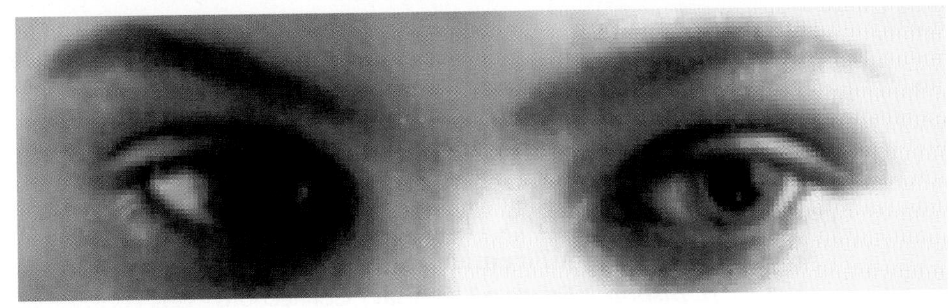

The Nonfiction Collections

Collection 5

Becoming Myself

Collection 6

Being There!

COMMUNICATIONS WORKSHOPS

Language/Grammar Links

Collection 7

Making a Point

The Poetry Collections

Collection 8

How to Live

COMMUNICATIONS WORKSHOPS

Collection 9

Can This Be Love?

Collection 10

Dreams—Lost and Found

COMMUNICATIONS WORKSHOPS

The Drama Collection

Collection 11

Doing the Right Thing

William Shakespeare

Collection 12

Ambition or Honor?

Traditions!
Readings in World Literature

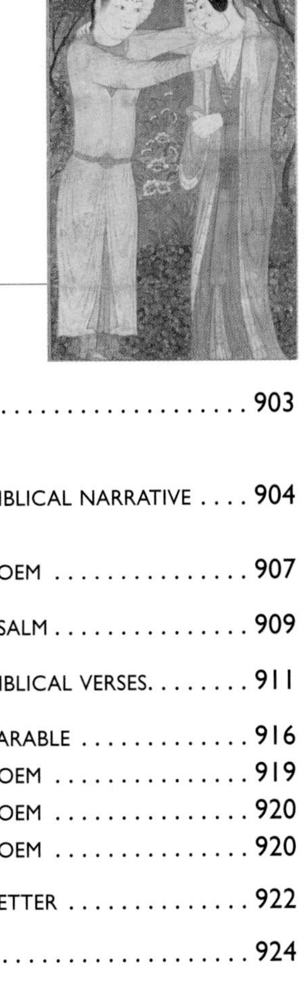

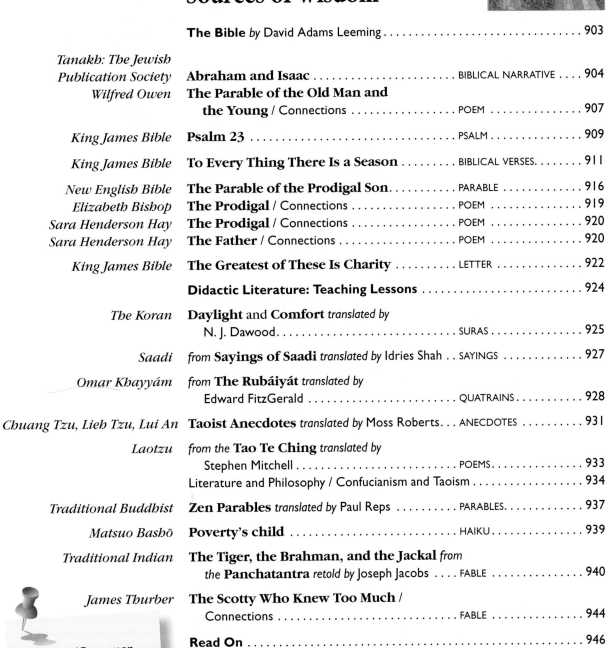

Collection 13
Sources of Wisdom

Language/Grammar Link

Collection 14

Finding Our Heroes

COMMUNICATIONS WORKSHOPS

Language/Grammar Links

Resource Center

SELECTIONS BY GENRE

Short Story

Nonfiction

Article, Editorial, and Feature

Autobiography

Biography

Essay and Photo Essay

Journal and Diary

Letter

Oral History

Other Nonfiction

Review

Speech

Poetry

Anecdote

Biblical Narrative, Psalm, and Verse

Drama

Epic

Fable and Legend

Musical

Parable

Parody

Sayings

Sura

World Literature

FEATURES

Elements of Literature

Interviews with Authors

Extending the Theme

Writer's Workshops

Reading for Life

Learning for Life

Across the Curriculum

Student Models

Skills

Reading Skills and Strategies

Language / Grammar Links

Vocabulary / Spelling

Speaking and Listening Workshops

Sentence Workshops

Elements of Literature on the Internet

To the Student

Discover more about the stories, poems, and essays in *Elements of Literature* by logging on to the Internet. At **go.hrw.com** we help you complete your homework assignments, learn more about your favorite writers, and find facts that support your ideas and inspire you with new ones. Here's how to log on:

1. Start your Web browser and enter **go.hrw.com** in the location field.

2. Note the keyword in your textbook.

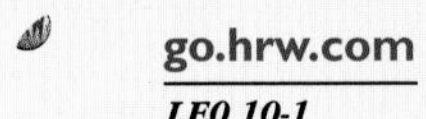

3. In your Web browser, enter the keyword and click on GO.

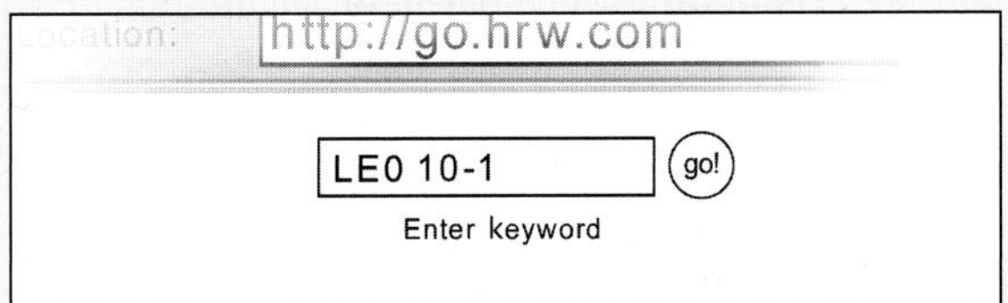

Now that you've arrived, you can peek into the palaces and museums of the world, listen to stories of exploration and discovery, or view fires burning on the ocean floor. As you move through *Elements of Literature,* use the best online resources at **go.hrw.com.**

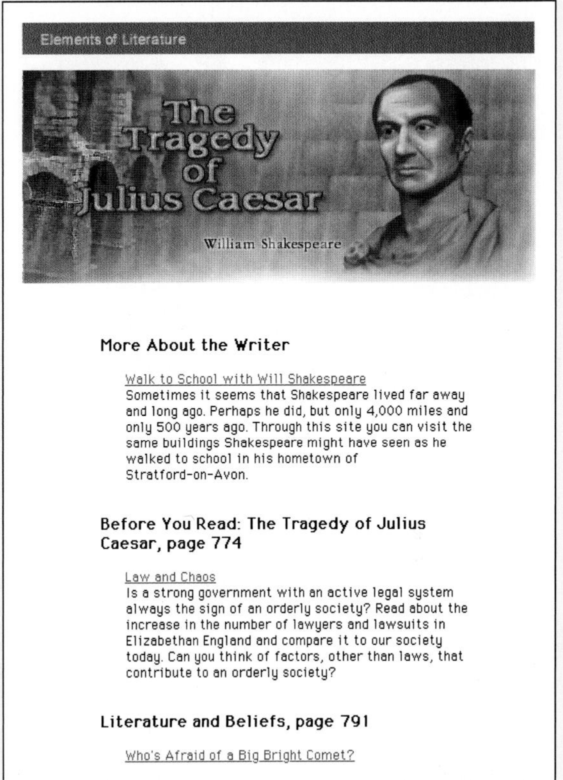

Elements of Literature
The Tragedy of Julius Caesar
William Shakespeare
More About the Writer
Walk to School with Will Shakespeare
Sometimes it seems that Shakespeare lived far away and long ago. Perhaps he did, but only 4,000 miles and only 500 years ago. Through this site you can visit the same buildings Shakespeare might have seen as he walked to school in his hometown of Stratford-on-Avon.
Before You Read: The Tragedy of Julius Caesar, page 774
Law and Chaos
Is a strong government with an active legal system always the sign of an orderly society? Read about the increase in the number of lawyers and lawsuits in Elizabethan England and compare it to our society today. Can you think of factors, other than laws, that contribute to an orderly society?
Literature and Beliefs, page 791
Who's Afraid of a Big Bright Comet?

Enjoy the Internet, but be critical of the information you find there. Always evaluate your sources for credibility, accuracy, timeliness, and possible bias.

Web sites accessed through **go.hrw.com** are reviewed regularly. However, online materials change continually and without notice. Holt, Rinehart and Winston cannot ensure the accuracy or appropriateness of materials other than our own. Students, teachers, and guardians should assume responsibility for checking all online materials. A full description of Terms of Use can be found at **go.hrw.com.**

Building a Foundation for Success in Literature

A Foundation for Reading

Reading Matters *By Dr. Kylene Beers*

Improving Your Comprehension

Think-Aloud
Retelling
Re-reading and Rewording
Summarizing Narrative Text
Summarizing Expository Text
Key Words

Improving Your Reading Rate

Reading Rate and Homework
Figuring Out Your Reading Rate
Reading Rate Reminders

A Foundation for Test Taking

Test Smarts

Test Smarts Lesson 1

Using Context to Understand Specialized or Technical Terms

Test Smarts Lesson 2

Inferring Causes and Effects

Test Smarts Lesson 3

Identifying Facts and Opinions

Test Smarts Lesson 4

Answering Inference Questions on Reading Tests

Test Smarts Lesson 5

Analyzing a Writing Prompt

Reading Matters

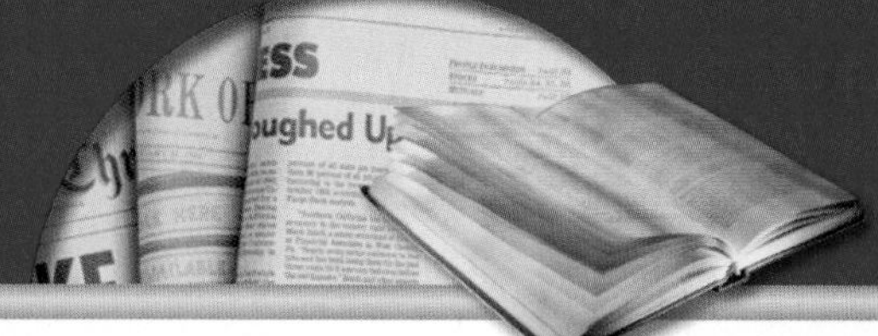

When the Text Is Tough

Remember the reading you did back in first, second, and third grades? Big print. Short texts. Easy words. Now in high school, however, the texts you read are often filled with small print, long chapters, and complicated plots or topics. Also, you now find yourself reading a variety of material—from your driver's ed handbook to college applications, from notes passed in the hall to graffiti printed on the wall, from job applications to income tax forms, from e-mail to e-zines, from classics to comics, from textbooks to checkbooks.

Doing something every day that you find difficult and tedious isn't much fun—and that includes reading. So, this section of this book is designed for you, to show you what to do when the text gets tough. Let's begin by looking at some *reading* matters—because, after all, reading *matters*.

Reading Up Close

◆ *How to Use This Section*

- **This section is for you.** Turn to it whenever you need to remind yourself about what to do when the text gets tough. Don't wait for your teacher to assign this section for you to read. It's your handbook. Use it.
- **Read the sections that you need.** You don't have to read every word. Skim the headings and find the information you need.
- **Use this information to help you with reading for other classes,** not just for the reading you do in this book.
- **Don't be afraid to *re-read* the information** you find in Reading Matters. The best readers constantly re-read information.
- **If you need more help, then check the index.** The index will direct you to other pages in this book with information on reading skills and strategies.

Improving Your Comprehension

Have you seen the re-runs of an old weekly television show called *Lost in Space*? Perhaps you saw the more recent movie version of it that played in theaters? If so, you probably remember the robot that constantly tried to warn the young boy, Will Robinson, when danger was near by waving his robot arms and announcing loudly, "Danger approaching, Will Robinson!" Then, Will would look up from whatever he was doing, notice whatever evil was moments away, and take evasive action. But until the robot warned him, Will would ignore all warning signs that danger was at hand.

Wouldn't it be nice if when we were reading, something would warn us as we were about to enter a dangerous area—a part of the text that we might not understand. Perhaps our own little robots could pop up in books saying "Danger, dear reader! Misunderstandings approaching!" Then we'd know to slow down, pay attention, and carefully study the text we were reading.

Actually, those signs do appear, but not as arm-waving robots in the margins of books. Instead, the signs appear in our minds, as we are reading. However, unless we are paying attention, we often read on past them, not noticing the warnings they offer. What we need to do is learn to recognize the danger signs, so, like Will Robinson, we know when to look up and take action.

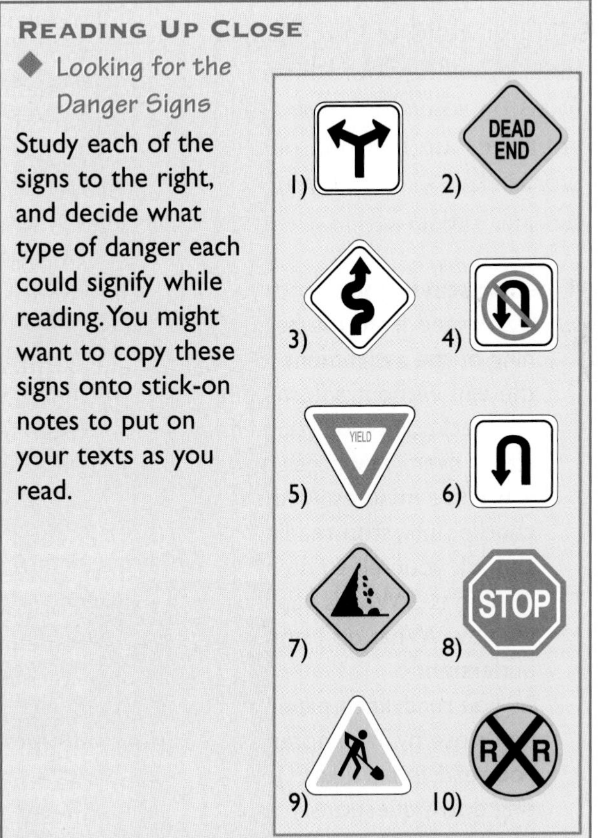

Reading Up Close

◆ *Looking for the Danger Signs*

Study each of the signs to the right, and decide what type of danger each could signify while reading. You might want to copy these signs onto stick-on notes to put on your texts as you read.

1 DANGER SIGN #1
You can't remember what you read.

This happens to all readers occasionally. You read something, and your attention wanders for a moment, but your eyes don't quit moving from word to word. In a few minutes, you realize you are several pages beyond the last point where you can remember thinking about what you were reading. Then, you know you need to back up and start over.

Forgetting what you've read is a danger sign only if it happens to you frequently. If you constantly complete a reading assignment but don't remember anything that you've been reading, then you probably are in the bad habit of letting your mind focus on something else while your eyes are focusing on the words. That's a habit you need to break.

Tips for staying focused:

1. Don't read from the beginning of the assignment to the end without pausing. Set up checkpoints for yourself, either every few pages or every five minutes. At those checkpoints, stop reading and ask yourself some basic questions—What's happening now? What do I not understand?
2. As you read, keep paper and pen close by. Take notes as you read, in particular jotting down questions you have about what confuses you, interests you, or perhaps surprises you.

READING UP CLOSE

◆ *Measure Your Attention Quotient*

Take the following survey to see what your Attention Quotient is. The lower the score, the less you pay attention to what you are reading.

When I read, I . . .

1. let my mind wander
- 1 most of the time
- 2 sometimes
- 3 almost never

2. forget what I'm reading
- 1 most of the time
- 2 sometimes
- 3 almost never

3. get confused and stay confused
- 1 most of the time
- 2 sometimes
- 3 almost never

4. discover I've turned lots of pages and don't have a clue as to what I've read
- 1 most of the time
- 2 sometimes
- 3 almost never

5. rarely finish whatever I'm supposed to be reading
- 1 most of the time
- 2 sometimes
- 3 almost never

DANGER SIGN #2

You don't "see" what you are reading.

The ability to visualize—or see in your mind—what you are reading is important for comprehension. To understand how visualizing makes a difference, try this quick test. When you get home, turn on a television to a program you enjoy. Then, turn your back to the television set. How long will you keep "watching" the program that way? Probably not long. Why not? Because it would be boring if you couldn't see what was happening. The same is true with reading: If you can't "see" in your mind what is happening on the page, then you probably will tune out quickly. You can improve your ability to visualize the text by practicing the following:

1. **Read a few sentences; then pause and describe what is happening on the page.** Forcing yourself to actually describe the scene will take some time at first, but will help in the long run.
2. **As you are reading, make a graphic representation of what is happening on a sheet of paper or a stick-on note.** For instance, if two characters are talking, draw two stick figures with arrows pointing between them to show yourself that they are talking.
3. **Discuss a scene or a part of a chapter with a buddy.** Talk about what you "saw" as you were reading.
4. **Read aloud.** If you are having trouble visualizing the text, it might be because you aren't really "hearing" it. Try reading a portion of your text aloud, using good expression and phrasing. As you hear the words, you may find it easier to see the scenes.

READING UP CLOSE

◆ Visualizing What You Read

Read this scene from "Where Have You Gone, Charming Billy?" (p. 198) and discuss what you see.

> "The platoon of twenty-six soldiers moved slowly in the dark, single file, not talking. One by one, like sheep in a dream, they passed through the hedgerow, crossed quietly over a meadow, and came down to the rice paddy. There they stopped. Their leader knelt down, motioning with his hand, and one by one the other soldiers squatted in the shadows, vanished in the primitive stealth of warfare. For a long time they did not move. Except for the sounds of their breathing, the twenty-six men were very quiet...."

DANGER SIGN #3

You constantly answer "I don't know" to questions at the end of reading selections.

If you consistently don't know the answers to questions about what you've been reading, then you probably would benefit from the following strategies.

Think-Aloud. Comprehension problems don't appear only after you *finish* reading. Confusion occurs *as* you read. Therefore, don't wait until you complete your reading assignment to try to understand the text; instead, work on comprehending while reading by becoming an active reader.

Active readers **predict, connect, clarify, question,** and **visualize** as they read. If you don't do those things, then you need to pause while you read to

- make predictions,
- make connections,
- clarify in your own thoughts what you are reading,
- question what you don't understand, and
- visualize the text and observe key details.

Use the Think-Aloud strategy to practice your active-reading skills. Read a selection of text aloud to a partner. As you read, pause to make comments and ask questions. Your partner's job is to tally your comments and classify each according to the list above.

READING UP CLOSE

◆ *One Student's Think-Aloud*

Here's Jarred's Think-Aloud for "Everyday Use," by Alice Walker (p. 70).

Page 70, 1st sentence: "What in the world is this talking about when it says they made the yard so wavy? How do you make a yard wavy?" **(Questioning)**

Page 70, 5th sentence: "Okay, I get it. It's not a grass yard, but like clay and sand." **(Clarifying)**

Page 72, top of 2nd column: "Maggie and Dee remind me of my two sisters. My older sister thinks she is so much better than the other one." **(Connecting)**

Page 72 bottom and top 73: "I can just imagine what Dee and her boyfriend look like with their bright clothes and long hair." **(Visualizing)**

Retelling. While the Think-Aloud strategy keeps you focused as you read, the Retelling strategy helps you after reading. Read the tips for retelling on this page, and then practice retelling small portions of your reading assignments. You might ask a friend to listen to you retell what you have read, or you might record yourself as you retell a selection.

READING UP CLOSE

◆ Evaluate Your Retelling

Listen to your retelling and ask yourself

1. Does my retelling make sense?
2. Does it have enough information?
3. Is the information in the correct order?
4. Could a drawing or a diagram help my retelling?
5. If someone listening to my retelling hadn't read the text, what would that person visualize?
6. To improve my next retelling, should I focus on characters, sequence of events, amount of detail, or general conclusions?

Retelling Prompts for Fiction

1. State what text you are retelling.
2. Give characters' names, and explain who they are.
3. Sequence the events using words like *first, second, third, then, later, next,* or *last.*
4. Identify the conflict in the story.
5. Explain the resolution of the conflict.
6. Tell what you enjoyed or did not enjoy about the text.

Retelling Prompts for Informational Texts

State what text you are retelling, and identify the structure of the text.

- If the structure is a **sequence** (the water cycle), use words like *first, second, third, then, later, afterwards, following that, before,* and *last.*
- If the structure is **comparison and contrast** (the differences between World War I and World War II), use words such as *by comparison, by contrast, on the other hand, yet, but, however, nevertheless, conversely, then again,* or *in opposition.*
- If showing **cause-and-effect relationships**, use words like *reason, motive, basis,* and *grounds* to discuss **causes**, and use words like *outcome, consequence, result,* and *product* to discuss **effects**.

Re-reading and Rewording. The best way to improve your comprehension is simply to **re-read.** The first time you read something, you get the basic idea of the text. The next time you read it, you revise your understanding. Try thinking of your first reading as a draft—just like the first draft of an essay. As you revise your essay, you are improving your writing. As you revise your reading, you are improving your comprehension.

Sometimes, as you re-read, you find some specific sentences or even passages that you just don't understand. When that's the case, you need to spend some time closely studying those sentences. One effective way to tackle tough text is to **reword** the text:

1. On a sheet of paper, write the sentences that are confusing you.
2. Leave a few blank lines between each line you write.
3. Then, choose the difficult words and reword them in the space above.
4. While you wouldn't want to reword every line of a long text—or even of a short one—this is a powerful way to help you understand key sentences.

READING UP CLOSE

◆ *One Student's Rewording*

After tenth-grader Katie read "Distillation" (p. 133) she copied a few sentences she didn't understand. After re-reading them, she reworded them, using a thesaurus and a dictionary. Later she explained that "rewording helps me understand what the author is trying to say."

street *gave in* *started*
1. "When the ~~pavement~~ leveled off, he ~~yielded~~ for a moment, ~~broke into a~~
smiling *calling on what was left* *jumble* *pushed*
~~smile~~, and then ~~summoning reserves~~ from the ~~labyrinth~~ of his will ~~lunged~~
hard *stirred up*
forward ~~furiously~~, as if ~~galvanized~~ by his victory, and reached full speed at
same time *started to fall over.*
the ~~moment~~ the wagon ~~began to descend.~~" (page 136)

Over and over, *sliced* *top of sky to where sky meets*
2. "~~Repeatedly~~, bright bolts of lightning ~~tore~~ the sky from ~~zenith to~~
land and made *explosions*
~~horizon and set off~~ ~~detonations~~ that seemed to come from deep in the earth." (page 139)

Summarizing Narrative Text. Understanding a long piece of text is easier if you can summarize chunks of it. If you are reading a **narrative,** or story, then use a strategy called **Somebody Wanted But So (SWBS)** to help you write summaries of what you are reading. SWBS is a powerful way to think about the characters in a story and note what each did, what conflict each faced, and what the resolution was. As you write an SWBS statement for different characters within the same story, you are forcing yourself to rethink the story from different **points of view.** By analyzing point of view in this way, you get a better understanding of the impact of the author's choice of narrator.

Here are the steps for writing SWBS statements:

1. Write the words *Somebody, Wanted, But,* and *So* at the top of four columns.
2. Under the *Somebody* column, write a character's name.
3. Then, under the *Wanted* column, write what that character wanted to do.
4. Next, under the *But* column, explain what happened that kept the character from doing what he or she wanted.
5. Finally, under the *So* column, explain the eventual outcome.
6. If you're making an SWBS chart for a long story or novel, you might need to write several statements at different points in the story.

READING UP CLOSE

◆ *One Student's SWBS Chart*

Here's Josh's SWBS chart for "With All Flags Flying" (p. 309). He's written an SWBS statement for the grandfather, up to the first break on page 313. You write another for the same character from page 313 to the end. Then, write an SWBS statement for Clara and Mr. Pond.

Somebody	Wanted	But	So
The grandfather	wanted to go to an old folks' home instead of living with his daughter,	but Clara wants him to stay with her,	so he's going to have to convince her to let him have his way.

Summarizing Expository Text. If summarizing the information in **expository,** or informational, texts is difficult, try a strategy called GIST.

Steps for GIST:

1. Divide the text you want to summarize into three or four sections.
2. Read the first section.
3. Draw twenty blank lines on a sheet of paper.
4. Write a summary of the first section of text using exactly twenty words—one word for each blank.

5. Read the next section of text. In your next set of twenty blanks, write a new summary statement that combines your first summary with whatever you want to add from this second section of text. It's important to note that even though you've now got two sections of text to cover, you still have only twenty blanks to fill, not forty.
6. Repeat this one or two more times depending on how much more text you have. When you are finished, you have a twenty-word statement that gives you the gist, or overall idea, of what the entire text is about.

READING UP CLOSE

◆ *One Student's GIST*

After reading "Reading a Map" (p. 170), Tony wrote the following GIST statements.

GIST #1 (for the section called "Understand the different types of maps")
Physical maps show landscape, while political maps show nations, states, and cities, and special maps like road maps show highways.

GIST #2 (for the first section plus the next called "Learn to use map features")
Physical, political, and special maps all use features like distance scales, legends, locator maps, and a compass rose for directions.

Now you try creating a GIST summary for the information found in the first two columns of "Reading a Science Article" (p. 92).

Key Words. Sometimes you don't want to write a summary or outline of what you've been reading. Sometimes you just want to jot down some key words to remind you about a specific topic. To keep your key words organized, don't forget your ABCs. Just make yourself a copy of a page filled with boxes, as in the following example. You can use your computer to make this page or just grab a pencil and notebook paper. Once your boxes are drawn, all you have to do is decide what information to include.

For instance, Amy uses her Key Word chart while reading "Two Kinds" on page 95. She puts "Mother" in blue at the top of the page and "Ni kan" in red. As she reads the story and thinks of words to describe each character, she puts those key character-description words in the correct box in the correct color. So, she writes "demanding" in blue (because she thinks that word describes Mother) in the *C–D* box. She writes "angry" in red (because this word is for Ni kan) in the *A–B* box. Amy's completed Key Word chart can serve as a starting point for writing a comparison-contrast essay.

Reading Up Close

◆ *Using a Key Word Chart*

Here is Amy's partially filled-out Key Word chart for "Two Kinds." Read the story, and find more key words to describe the two main characters.

A-B	C-D	E-F	G-H	I-J	K-L
angry (Mother)	demanding (Ni Kan)				

M-N	O-P	Q-R	S-T	U-V-W	X-Y-Z

Kwan used his Key Word chart in history class as he was reading the chapter on World War II. He used it to keep up with countries (*Allies* written in black, *Axis* in blue), military leaders, and major battles.

Improving Your Reading Rate

If your reading concerns are more about getting through the words than figuring out the meaning, then this part of Reading Matters is for you.

If you think you are a slow reader, then reading can seem overwhelming. But you can change your reading rate—the pace at which you read. All you have to do is practice. The point isn't to read so fast that you just rush over words—the I'mgoingtoreadsofastthat-allthewordsruntogether approach. Instead, the goal is to find a good pace that keeps you moving comfortably through the pages. Why is it important to establish a good reading rate? Let's do a little math to see why your silent reading rate counts.

MATH PROBLEM!

If you read 40 words per minute (WPM) and there are 400 words on a page, then how long will it take you to read 1 page? 5 pages? 10 pages? How long will it take if you read 80 WPM? 120 WPM? 200 WPM?

As you figure out the problem, you see that it takes 100 minutes to read 10 pages at the slowest pace and only 20 minutes at the fastest pace. See the chart for all the times:

	1 page @400 words/page	5 pages @400 words/page	10 pages @400 words/page
40 WPM	10 minutes	50 minutes	100 minutes
80 WPM	5 minutes	25 minutes	50 minutes
120 WPM	3 minutes	17 minutes	34 minutes
200 WPM	2 minutes	10 minutes	20 minutes

Reading Rate and Homework

Now, assume that with literature homework, science homework, and social studies homework, in one night you have 40 pages to read. If you are reading at 40 WPM, you are spending over 6 *hours* just reading the information; but at 120 WPM you spend only about 2–1/4 hours. And at 200 WPM you'd finish in 1 hour and 20 minutes.

Reading Up Close

◆ Tips on Varying Your Reading Rate

- Increasing your rate doesn't matter if your comprehension goes down.
- Remember that your rate will vary as your purpose for reading varies. You'll read more slowly when you are studying for a test than when you are skimming a text.

Figuring Out Your Reading Rate

To determine your silent-reading rate, you'll need three things: a watch with a second hand, a book, and someone who will watch the time for you. Then, do the following:

1. Have your friend time you as you begin reading to yourself.
2. Read at your normal rate. Don't speed just because you're being timed.
3. Stop when your friend tells you one minute is up.
4. Count the number of words you read.
5. Repeat this process several more times using different passages.
6. Then, add the number of words together and divide by the number of times you timed yourself. That's your average rate.

Example

1st minute	180 words
2nd minute	215 words
3rd minute	190 words
	585 words ÷ 3 = 195 WPM

Reading Rate Reminders

You can improve your reading rate by doing the following:

1. **Make sure you aren't reading just one word at a time, with a pause between each word.** Practice phrasing words in your mind as you read. For instance, look at the sample sentence and pause only where you see the slash marks. One slash (/) means pause a bit. Two slashes (//) mean pause longer.

> Jack and Jill/ went up the hill/ to fetch a pail of water.// Jack fell down/ and broke his crown/ and Jill came tumbling after.//

Now read it pausing after each word:

> Jack/ and/ Jill/ went/ up/ the/ hill/ to/ fetch/ a/ pail/ of/ water.// Jack/ fell/ down/ and/ broke/ his/ crown/ and/ Jill/ came/ tumbling/ after.//

Hear the difference? Word-at-a-time reading is much slower than phrase reading. You can hear good phrasing by listening to a book on tape.

2. **Make sure you aren't sounding out each word.** At this point in school, you need to be able to recognize whole words and save the sounding-out strategy for words you haven't seen before. In other words, you ought to be able to read *material* as "material" and not "ma-ter-i-al," but you might need to move more slowly through *metacognition* so that you read that word as "met-a-cog-ni-tion."

3. **Make sure when you are reading silently that you really are reading silently.** Don't move your lips or read very softly when reading. These habits slow you down. Remember, if you need to slow down (for instance, the information you are reading is confusing you), then reading aloud to yourself is a smart thing to do. But generally, silent reading means reading silently!

4. **Don't use your finger to point to words as you read.** If you find that you always use your finger to point to words as you read (instead of just occasionally, when you are really concentrating), then you are probably reading one word at a time. Instead, use a bookmark to help yourself stay on the right line and practice your phrase reading.

5. **As you practice your fluency, remember that the single best way to improve your reading rate is simply to read more!** You won't get better at what you never do. So start reading more, and remember these tips. Soon, you'll find that reading too slowly isn't a problem any more.

Test Smarts

SELECTION TEST
Choice: A Tribute to Dr. Martin Luther King, Jr.
Alice Walker

LESSON 1 Using Context to Understand Specialized or Technical Terms

On many reading tests, you may be asked to find the meaning of a specialized or technical term in a reading passage in order to test your vocabulary and ability to reason. If you do not already have the word in your vocabulary, consider its **context**—that is, look at how the word is used in the sentence in order to figure out the meaning.

Read the following passage, and use the Thinking It Through steps below to figure out the answer to the reading question.

> Researchers continue to be fascinated by the behavior of humpback whales. But what do we really know about these gentle giants? Researchers have made interesting observations about female whales' behavior after calving. After giving birth, a mother lifts her newborn to the surface of the water for the calf's first breath of air. The calf, whose lungs have yet to be inflated, would sink without its mother's assistance.

In this passage, *calving* refers to—
A. whale birth
B. whale breathing
C. whale identification
D. whale research

Thinking It Through: Using Context to Understand Specialized or Technical Terms

■ Use the following steps to find the meanings of specialized terms.

1. **Read the question and the answer choices, and then read the passage again.** Re-reading the passage with the question and answer choices in mind might help you find the writer's explanation of the specialized or technical term.
2. **Look at the word's context for clues to the word's meaning.** In the third sentence, *calving* is mentioned as a behavior that is typical of female whales.
3. **Cross out the answers that do not seem correct.** Choice **C** and choice **D** can be eliminated because neither is an activity typical of female whales.
4. **Review the context of the specialized or technical term again, and make an educated guess at the word's meaning.** Choices **A** and **B** are both possibilities. In the passage, however, a newborn whale is referred to as a *calf.* This suggests that *calving* is the process of having a calf, or giving birth to a baby whale. Choice **A** must be the correct answer.

Practice

Directions. Read the passage below. On a separate sheet of paper, list the numbers *1* through *5*. Then, for each numbered item, write the letter of the correct response.

The Galileo space probe has been a great source of information about space and space exploration. Space probes are sent into outer space to collect data on the solar system. At first, Galileo was intended to observe only one planet—Jupiter—and its moons.

Galileo was initially supposed to be launched from a shuttle, with a powerful rocket boosting the probe into orbit. However, plans changed after the explosion of the space shuttle Challenger. The original trajectory of Galileo had to be changed because the booster rocket would no longer be carried by a shuttle. Galileo's new travel path relied on gravity assists from Earth and Venus to propel Galileo toward Jupiter.

Then, after Galileo was already in orbit, its strongest antenna failed to open, and engineers had to rethink their plans again. They sensitized a system of orbiting deep-space communication satellites, and relied on data compression and a smaller antenna onboard Galileo so that other, less powerful satellites could still relay computerized images back to Earth.

During its journey, Galileo observed Venus, Earth, and the asteroids Gaspra and Ida. It recorded new information about Jupiter's atmosphere and also witnessed a surprising cosmic event—a comet's collision with Jupiter.

Galileo's instruments also revealed that one of Jupiter's moons, Ganymede, had its own magnetosphere. This is the first moon in the solar system that scientists have found to have its own magnetic field.

1. From the passage, you can tell that the word *trajectory* refers to the space probe's—
- **A.** path
- **B.** cost
- **C.** equipment
- **D.** discoveries

2. In this passage, the term *gravity assists* means—
- **F.** forces that helped the space probe on its way
- **G.** obstacles in the space probe's path
- **H.** forces that pulled the space probe off course
- **J.** obstacles stemming from the space probe's construction

3. In this passage, the words *data compression* refer to—
- **A.** making the data more sensitive
- **B.** enhancing data to get more detail
- **C.** making data more compact to ease transmission
- **D.** flattening data to make it easier to see

4. In this passage, the word *cosmic* refers to—
- **F.** Earth
- **G.** outer space
- **H.** scientific research
- **J.** Jupiter's moons

5. According to the passage, having a *magnetosphere* means having—
- **A.** underground water
- **B.** pockets of magnesium
- **C.** its own weather
- **D.** a magnetic field

LESSON 2 Inferring Causes and Effects

Reading tests often measure your ability to infer, or make an educated guess about, causes or effects not directly stated in a reading passage. Because inference reading passages will seldom include clue words or phrases such as *because* or *as a result,* you must figure out the cause-and-effect relationship within them yourself.

Here is a typical reading passage and test question:

Before Shakespeare wrote the majority of his plays, he was an actor in a theater group. Elizabethan theater convention, which he knew through his experience as an actor, played an important role in the development and "shape" of his plays. In Shakespeare's day, theater groups had only limited rehearsal time, and this forced playwrights to keep scenes simple and straightforward. With a trained eye one can see how the scenes in his plays were affected; there were usually only three or fewer characters per scene.

From this passage, we can infer that Elizabethan playwrights allowed only three or fewer actors onstage because—

A. women were not allowed to perform onstage
B. Shakespeare began as an actor
C. actors probably liked being part of a crowd onstage
D. scenes needed to be simple so actors could rehearse them quickly

Thinking It Through: Inferring Causes and Effects

Use the following steps to answer cause-and-effect inference test questions like the sample question above.

1. **Skim the passage once for a general understanding; then re-read it carefully.** Keep in mind that most of these questions are designed to measure your reading comprehension, not your reading speed.
2. **Locate key words and phrases in the sample answers that match similar words or ideas in the reading passage.** Answers **A** and **C** contain information that is not contained in the reading passage. The passage does not mention the nonparticipation of women or the size of the stage. Both answers **B** and **D,** however, refer to information that is contained in the passage.
3. **Apply your knowledge to the remaining answers.** Shakespeare (**B**) did, in fact, begin his career as an actor, but this had no effect on the number of actors who normally performed in a scene. The correct answer is **D.**

Practice

Directions. Read the passage below. On a separate sheet of paper, list the numbers *1* through *5*. Then, for each numbered item, write the letter of the correct response.

On hot, sunny days, distant road surfaces may appear wet. Cars in the distance seem to be driving through shimmering water, yet as you approach, the "water" vanishes. Your mind is not playing tricks on you; this occurrence is an atmospheric phenomenon known as a mirage. People associate the word <u>mirage</u> with thirsty desert travelers who are beguiled by a distant patch of water, only to have it "disappear" as they approach.

These fleeting flickers are actually reflections of the bright sky on the ground. Light rays from the sky pass downward through layers of relatively cool air before hitting the hotter and less dense layer of air nearest the pavement. When the rays encounter the less dense air, they change speed and direction. Bent, or refracted upward, they meet the eye of the viewer at an oblique angle.

Because the light rays come from below, a "copy" of the object appears below the object itself. The sky seems to be displaced onto the pavement—the "water" is just a distorted reflection of the sky.

Under these same conditions, distant objects on the horizon appear to have upside-down mirror images, or inverted doubles. The right-side-up image reaches the eye of the viewer in the normal way, while the refraction generates an upside-down image that shimmers beneath the original.

1. What accounts for the mirage phenomenon that occurs under some atmospheric conditions?
- **A.** At great distances sky is reflected in water.
- **B.** There are actually two images being reflected.
- **C.** Refracted light rays reach the viewer's eyes before other rays.
- **D.** Refracted light rays reach the viewer's eyes at an angle.

2. What effect does air density have on light rays passing through?
- **F.** The light rays change speed.
- **G.** The light is reflected.
- **H.** The light rays pass downward.
- **J.** The light comes from below.

3. From the passage, which is most directly responsible for the mirage phenomenon?
- **A.** desert sand
- **B.** refracted light
- **C.** reflections in water
- **D.** distant roads

4. Which of the following would be the best title for this passage?
- **F.** What You See Is What You Get
- **G.** Can You Believe Your Eyes?
- **H.** Distant Roads
- **J.** Desert Travelers

5. What is the main idea of the final paragraph?
- **A.** Mirages disappear when you approach them.
- **B.** Inverted images have little in common with mirages.
- **C.** Distant objects sometimes appear wet.
- **D.** Inverted images and mirages are formed under the same conditions.

Test Smarts

LESSON 3 Identifying Facts and Opinions

Standardized tests often include questions designed to check your ability to distinguish between facts and opinions. Here is a typical reading passage and multiple-choice question.

Many students work hard in unskilled and part-time jobs. For the most part, their parents support them in the endeavor, eager for their children to take on the responsibilities of work and of balancing their own budgets. But students should be learning valuable skills for their futures as well. To acquire such career skills, students would benefit more from volunteering or taking internships (paid or unpaid) than from working regular jobs.

For students who have a clear career direction but lack experience, internships are wonderful opportunities to learn while on the job. Internships give them valuable experience and the chance to decide whether a field is really right for them. Students also get the opportunity to make contacts and create impressions on potential employers. In the long run, working for free will have a much greater payoff.

Which of these is a fact in the passage?

A. Students will benefit more from internships than from a part-time job.

B. Internships are a wonderful opportunity to learn while on the job.

C. Many parents support their children's decision to work.

D. In the long run working for free should have a greater payoff.

Thinking It Through: Answering Fact-and-Opinion Questions

■ Use the following steps to answer fact-and-opinion questions.

1. **Read each statement carefully.**
2. **Look for clue words that signal an opinion.** Words such as *should, must, always,* and *never* signal an opinion. **D** is an opinion, indicated by the writer's use of the term *should.*
3. **Continue through all the answer choices.** For remaining answer choices, ask yourself, "Can this statement be proved true?" **A** is an opinion: The writer's claim about the benefits of working for free cannot be proved. **B** is also an opinion: The writer's belief—that interning is a "wonderful opportunity"—can be supported with evidence; however, it can never be definitively proved, since you cannot prove that something is "wonderful." **C,** however, is fact: Even though the writer does not support this statement with evidence, it is a fact that *can* be proved with relevant evidence. Therefore, **C** is the correct answer.

Practice

Directions. Read the passage below. On a separate sheet of paper, list the numbers *1* through *5*. Then, for each numbered item, write the letter of the correct response.

How much of today's journalism could be considered yellow journalism? Too much, if you ask this writer. Yellow journalism, which first appeared around the turn of the nineteenth century, is the practice of using sensationalistic stories to sell newspapers. Newspaper owners realized that news that shocked readers also increased sales. The downside to this practice, then and now, is that it is inconsistent with some basic ethical principles in journalism, and it is potentially harmful to readers.

Part of a journalist's job is to give a fair, unbiased account of the news. This is a worthy if difficult goal to achieve, and reporters should strive toward it. In trying to engage readers' emotions, however, reporters are probably not eager to present all sides of a story and are more likely to use biased, emotional appeals. Does today's journalism do this? Watch the latest evening news programs, and tell me how many balanced stories you see.

Furthermore, modern news executives have noticed that people like to watch shows that exhibit gloomy crime statistics and make dire predictions about the future. Unfortunately, too much of a bad thing is also bad for us. Excessive presentation of such themes has led to misunderstandings about the current state of society. Statistics show that crime has dropped over the last several years. However, the public believes crime is worse than ever.

1. Which of the following is a fact in this passage?
- **A.** "Unfortunately, too much of a bad thing is also bad for us."
- **B.** "How much of today's journalism could be considered yellow journalism? Too much, if you ask this writer."
- **C.** "Yellow journalism . . . is the practice of using sensationalistic stories to sell newspapers."
- **D.** "[Yellow journalism] . . . is potentially harmful to readers."

2. Which of the following is an opinion in this passage?
- **F.** "Newspaper owners realized that news that shocked readers also increased sales."
- **G.** "This [giving unbiased news accounts] is a worthy if difficult goal to achieve, and reporters should strive toward it."
- **H.** "Statistics show that crime has dropped over the last several years."
- **J.** "However, the public believes crime is worse than ever."

3. Which of the following is a fact from this passage?
- **A.** Journalists give unbiased accounts of the news.
- **B.** Sensationalistic stories help sell newspapers.
- **C.** Crime statistics are always gloomy.
- **D.** The public believes statisticians.

4. Which of the following is an opinion that can be inferred from this passage?
- **F.** Modern news executives should be more responsible in their choices.
- **G.** The authorities should fight crime harder.
- **H.** Gloomy news shows can enrage us.
- **J.** Yellow journalism first appeared around the turn of the nineteenth century.

5. Which of the following is an opinion presented in this passage?
- **A.** Evening news programs are well written.
- **B.** Crime doesn't pay.
- **C.** Crime statistics have dropped in recent years.
- **D.** Journalists should always try to be unbiased in their reporting.

LESSON 4 Answering Inference Questions on Reading Tests

Reading tests often include questions that check your ability to make inferences from a reading passage. Here is a typical reading passage and inference test question.

During my summers off from college, I worked on my uncle's dairy farm trying to gain an understanding of the community I would be serving later. My unofficial farm motto was, "Nature will take its course." Given veterinary technology, the statement was a little archaic, but I had always accepted it as an inevitable truth.

One day, in the summer of my junior year, we noticed a heifer that was close to giving birth. When her labor began, we called the local veterinarian, and I worked with him to make the mother-to-be comfortable.

When the calf finally began to emerge, however, it was backward. The vet assured us the heifer would make it through, but he added that nothing else was certain. . . .

What can you infer about the narrator before the incident with the calf?

A. The narrator did not like working with cattle.
B. The narrator would rather be at school than on the farm.
C. The narrator's views were fairly passive.
D. The narrator was a controlling person.

Thinking It Through: Answering Inference Questions

- Use the following steps to answer inference test questions like the one above.

1. **Skim the passage once for a general understanding; then, re-read it carefully.** Keep in mind that most of these questions are designed to measure your reading comprehension, not your reading speed.
2. **Locate key words and phrases in the answer choices that match related words and phrases in the reading passage.** You may be able to eliminate some answers right away. Choice **A** refers to a dislike of cattle; no words or phrases in the passage indicate this is the case. Choice **B** indicates a preference for school over farming, but nothing in the passage indicates this preference. Choice **D** refers to control; although the passage refers to veterinary technology, the narrator does not seem to feel it has the ability to control nature's course. Choice **C** is the best answer; the narrator's motto "Nature will take its course" supports the idea that he or she would tend to be passive in the face of nature.
3. If possible, **confirm you answer by considering your prior knowledge about the subject of the passage.**

Practice

Directions. Read the passage below. On a separate sheet of paper, list the numbers *1* through *5*. Then, for each numbered item, write the letter of the correct response.

Until I decided to join a Shakespearean drama group, I wouldn't have dreamed of purposely making a fool of myself in front of a crowd of people. I fancied myself a serious scholar and did my best to look the part. Naturally, I had hoped the drama group would choose Romeo and Juliet for its production, but instead I found myself trapped in an altogether different play. I was cast as a pompous "fool" character. Struggling with the embarrassment of acting foolish, I accepted suggestions from the other cast members and gradually learned to relax within my slapstick role, but only in their company. Even after our last rehearsal, I had serious qualms about opening night.

The next evening, I stood in the shadows with my shiny purple cape draped over my shoulders and my slightly lopsided goatee glued firmly in place. When my cue came, I stumbled into the spotlight and spoke my first line. The audience giggled. I clowned through an entire speech. They roared. Soon the entire room was charged with laughter.

That night, everything I'd learned during the previous weeks came together. I realized how important it was to allow myself to have fun. I became more accepting of my own foolishness and rediscovered the sense of humor I had lost somewhere in adolescence. I never took up that old role of the overly serious scholar again.

1. What can you infer from the narrator's statement "I found myself trapped in an altogether different play"?
- **A.** The narrator was moved to another drama group.
- **B.** The play was a comedy.
- **C.** The play was a different kind of love story.
- **D.** The play was not one of Shakespeare's works.

2. From the information in the passage, what can you infer about the narrator's thoughts about the play that was selected?
- **F.** The narrator was happy with the choice.
- **G.** The narrator had mixed feelings about the choice.
- **H.** The narrator had hoped to be cast as the lead.
- **J.** The narrator had hoped to act in a tragedy.

3. You can tell from the passage that before the play, the narrator's personality would be best described as
- **A.** easygoing
- **B.** outgoing
- **C.** rude
- **D.** formal

4. What can you infer about the setting in the beginning of the second paragraph?
- **F.** The narrator is backstage during opening night.
- **G.** The narrator is at a costume party.
- **H.** The narrator is backstage during a dress rehearsal.
- **J.** The narrator is dreaming about the play.

5. Given the information in the passage, what can you infer about the audience's reaction to the narrator?
- **A.** The audience was making fun of the narrator.
- **B.** The audience was laughing at the narrator's clothes.
- **C.** The audience found the narrator convincing and humorous.
- **D.** The audience found the narrator offensive.

LESSON 5 Analyzing a Writing Prompt

A writing test normally begins with a set of directions, called a **prompt**, for which you are asked to write a response. A prompt usually specifies the topic and form you should use, along with the audience and purpose for which you should write.

In order to be successful on a writing test, you must analyze the prompt to understand *exactly* what you are being asked to write. If you misread or misunderstand a prompt, your score will not be as high as it could be—no matter how well written your response is. Looking for key words or phrases in the prompt—such as *write* or *explain*—will help you be successful. Also, be aware that words and phrases such as *think about* and *include* are actually clues to the required information. Here is an example of a typical writing prompt.

> Your high-school class president is planning a party for the end of the school year. She has asked all of her classmates to suggest a theme for the party. Think about what theme you think would be the most interesting, and write a letter to persuade her to choose your idea. Remember to include reasons to support your opinion.

Thinking It Through: Analyzing a Prompt

- The following steps will help you analyze writing prompts.

1. **Read through the entire prompt.** Start by getting a general idea of what is being asked of you.
2. **Re-read the prompt, noticing key words and phrases that signal four specific requirements for your writing:**
   - the ***topic:*** the specific subject you are asked to address
   - the ***form:*** for example, a letter or an essay
   - the ***purpose:*** the reason for writing—for example, to inform or persuade
   - the ***audience:*** the intended reader of your writing—for example, another student, a reader of a local newspaper, or a teacher
3. **Jot down, underline, or highlight the required elements signaled by the key words or phrases you discovered.**
   Topic: theme for the end-of-year party
   Form: a letter
   Purpose: to persuade
   Audience: your class president
4. **Write your response.** In this case, you would write a letter [**form**] to persuade [**purpose**] your class president [**audience**] to accept your theme for the end-of-the-year party [**topic**].

Practice

Directions. The graphic organizer below shows ways to help you analyze writing prompts. Copy the graphic organizer onto your own paper. Then, complete the activity below.

- Read through the entire prompt to get a general idea of what is being asked.
- Re-read the prompt for key words and phrases that signal four specific requirements for the writing as defined below.
- Jot down the required elements signaled by the key words and phrases.

PROMPTS

1. Career counseling can help students plan their career paths. Consider the career resources available at your school and how adequate they are. Consider additional career services that would be helpful to you. Write an essay to persuade your school board members to offer additional services that you believe would be valuable to students.

2. What classes are missing from your high school's curriculum? If you had the opportunity, what new elective classes would you recommend? Write a letter to your superintendent to persuade him or her to add one elective class to the curriculum. Remember to include your thoughts about how the class would benefit a wide range of students.

3. Do students in your school have enough input in school extracurricular programs? Write an article for a school newspaper explaining how your school and its students would benefit from a new extracurricular activity designed by students themselves.

4. Should students be more involved in issues of local and national interest? Think about a particular issue where student voices and actions could have an impact. Write an editorial for your school newspaper persuading students that they should take a more active part in the issue. Include how bringing student initiative to the issue would be beneficial to the country or community and to the students themselves.

Specific Requirements for Your Writing	Prompt 1	Prompt 2	Prompt 3	Prompt 4
1. Topic: the specific subject you are asked to address				
2. Form: the shape and structure of the writing—for example, a letter or an essay				
3. Purpose: the reason for writing—for example, to inform or persuade				
4. Audience: the intended reader of your writing—for example, another student, a reader of a local newspaper, or a teacher				

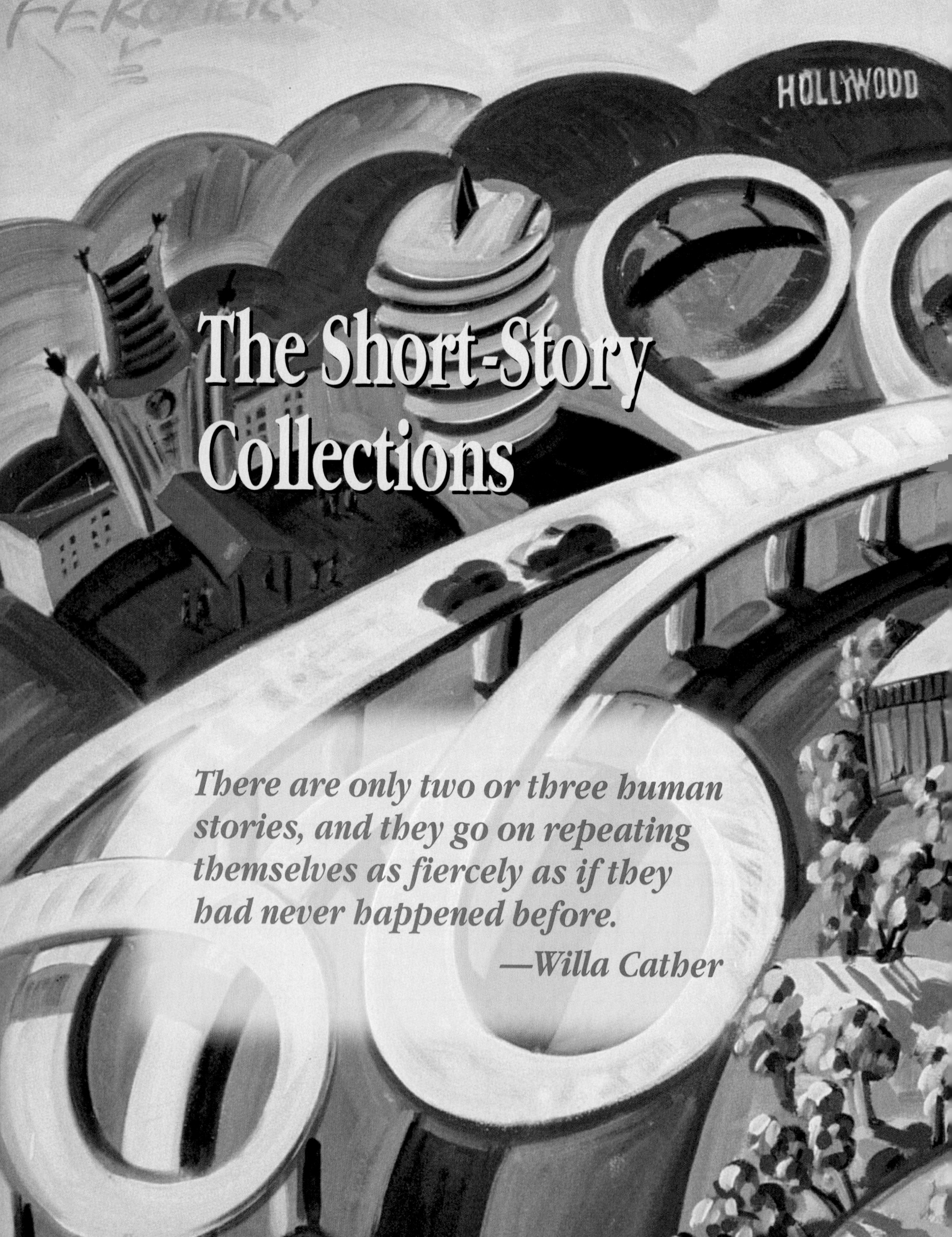

The Short-Story Collections

There are only two or three human stories, and they go on repeating themselves as fiercely as if they had never happened before.

—Willa Cather

Olive Hill (1987)
by Frank Romero
(1941–   ).
Oil on canvas.

Private collection.

Photo ©1995 by Jill Krementz.

A WRITER ON STORYTELLING

A CONVERSATION WITH RAY BRADBURY

Reading and writing are so closely linked that it's almost impossible to do one without the other. As you work through this book, you will be both a reader and a writer. Before you begin, see what Ray Bradbury, a down-to-earth writer of fantasy, has to say about how and why he writes. (Bradbury's story "The Pedestrian" begins on page 173.)

Ray Bradbury: My field is myself, as it should be for any writer. I wouldn't have given the same answer years ago. I've only stumbled on it in recent years. We're all on a voyage of self-discovery when we move into any of the art fields. . . .

Q: Do you write every day?

Bradbury: Every day of my life except weekends . . .

Q: Do you have to do much revision?

Bradbury: I do a first draft as passionately and as quickly as I can. I believe a story is valid only when it is immediate and passionate, when it dances out of your subconscious. If you interfere in any way, you destroy it. There's no difference between a short story and life. Surprise is where creativity comes. . . . Let your characters have their way. Let your secret life be lived. Then at your leisure, in the succeeding weeks, months, or years, you let the story cool off, and then, instead of rewriting, you relive it. If you try to rewrite, which is a cold exercise, you'll wind up with all kinds of Band-Aids on your story, which people can see.

Q: How do you feel a story coming on?

Bradbury: You get . . . I say "you," I mean "I." . . . I get tremendously excited. I remember the time I read a line in a poem by Robert Hillyer or the time I read a line in an essay by Aldous Huxley and then sprang immediately to my typewriter and wrote a short story. . . .

—*Writer's Digest,* February 1967

Reading Skills and Strategies

Reading a Short Story: Making Meanings

You might think that reading a story is a passive activity, but something mysterious happens as you read. The words on a page enter your mind and interact with whatever else happens to be there—your experiences, thoughts, memories, hopes, and fears. If a character says, "I had to run away. I had no choice," you might say, "Yeah, I know what that feels like." Another reader, however, may say, "What is he talking about? You always have a choice." We all make our own meaning depending on who we are. Here are some of the ways we do that:

1. **We connect with the text.** We might think, "This reminds me of something," or "I once did that."
2. **We ask questions.** We ask about unfamiliar words, or about what might happen next, or about a character's motivation.
3. **We make predictions.** We may not realize that we are making predictions as we read, but if we've ever been surprised by something in a story, that means we had predicted something else.
4. **We interpret.** We figure out what each part of a story means and how the parts work together to create meaning.
5. **We extend the text.** We extend the meaning of a story to the wider life around us, including other stories, films, and actual life.
6. **We challenge the text.** We might feel that a character is not realistic or that the plot is poor or that we don't like the writing.

How to Own a Word

Learning from Context

One strategy we use when we're confronted with an unfamiliar word is the use of **context clues.** That is, we try to get the word's meaning (or a very good idea of it) from the words surrounding the unfamiliar word. We also use the knowledge we already have in our heads.

In the following story, a group of boys approaches some pheasants, but the birds don't "flush." Here is how a reader who is not sure what *flush* means guesses (almost correctly) that the word must mean "to fly away." (It means, in this context, "to fly up suddenly, as if from a hiding place.")

What does *flush* mean?

Some of them lifted their heads and turned them from side to side, but they were blindfolded with ice and didn't flush.

- lifted their heads — The pheasants know someone is nearby.
- and turned them from side to side, — They are trying to find out who or what it is and whether they should fly away.
- blindfolded with ice — They can't see anything, so they don't move?

***Flush* might mean "to fly up or away."**

Extending your store of words. *Flush* is a word with **multiple meanings.** If the context is card playing, *flush* has one meaning. If the context is a display of emotion, it has another meaning. If the context is carpentry, *flush* has yet another meaning. Do you know all three of these meanings?

Apply the strategy on the next page.

READING SKILLS AND STRATEGIES

Dialogue with the Text

The notes that follow show the thoughts of one reader as she read this story for the first time. For your first reading, cover her responses with a sheet of paper, and write your own responses in your notebook. Then compare your responses with hers.

They stood looking at each other, each expecting the other to do something.

What Happened During the Ice Storm

Jim Heynen

One winter there was a freezing rain. "How beautiful!" people said when things outside started to shine with ice. But the freezing rain kept coming. Tree branches glistened like glass. Then broke like glass. Ice thickened on the windows until everything outside blurred. Farmers moved their livestock into the barns, and most animals were safe. But not the pheasants. Their eyes froze shut.

Some farmers went ice-skating down the gravel roads with clubs to harvest pheasants that sat helplessly in the roadside ditches. The boys went out into the freezing rain to find pheasants too. They saw dark spots along a fence. Pheasants, all right. Five or six of them. The boys slid their feet along slowly, trying not to break the ice that covered the snow. They slid up close to the pheasants. The pheasants pulled their heads down between their wings. They couldn't tell how easy it was to see them huddled there.

Dialogue with the Text

Why does this winter matter?

I like this imagery.

What do pheasants have to do with anything? But the eyes freezing shut does create a picture.

OK, here are pheasants again, but I still don't see the reason for it.

Who are these boys? Friends of the narrator? Bystanders or participants?

Dialogue with the Text

These boys are in conflict. Don't they want to kill the pheasants? Why can't they bring themselves to do it?

WOW! I can really see this!

Oh, my gosh! This isn't what I expected. I like this ending better than the boys killing the pheasants. It's not as realistic, but it does have an emotional appeal.

Melissa Bender

—Melissa Bender
Torrance High School
Torrance, California

The boys stood still in the icy rain. Their breath came out in slow puffs of steam. The pheasants' breath came out in quick little white puffs. Some of them lifted their heads and turned them from side to side, but they were blindfolded with ice and didn't flush. The boys had not brought clubs, or sacks, or anything but themselves. They stood over the pheasants, turning their own heads, looking at each other, each expecting the other to do something. To pounce on a pheasant, or to yell "Bang!" Things around them were shining and dripping with icy rain. The barbed-wire fence. The fence posts. The broken stems of grass. Even the grass seeds. The grass seeds looked like little yolks inside gelatin whites. And the pheasants looked like unborn birds glazed in egg white. Ice was hardening on the boys' caps and coats. Soon they would be covered with ice too.

Then one of the boys said, "Shh." He was taking off his coat, the thin layer of ice splintering in flakes as he pulled his arms from the sleeves. But the inside of the coat was dry and warm. He covered two of the crouching pheasants with his coat, rounding the back of it over them like a shell. The other boys did the same. They covered all the helpless pheasants. The small gray hens and the larger brown cocks. Now the boys felt the rain soaking through their shirts and freezing. They ran across the slippery fields, unsure of their footing, the ice clinging to their skin as they made their way toward the blurry lights of the house.

Collection 1

HARD CHOICES

WRITING FOCUS: Persuasive Essay

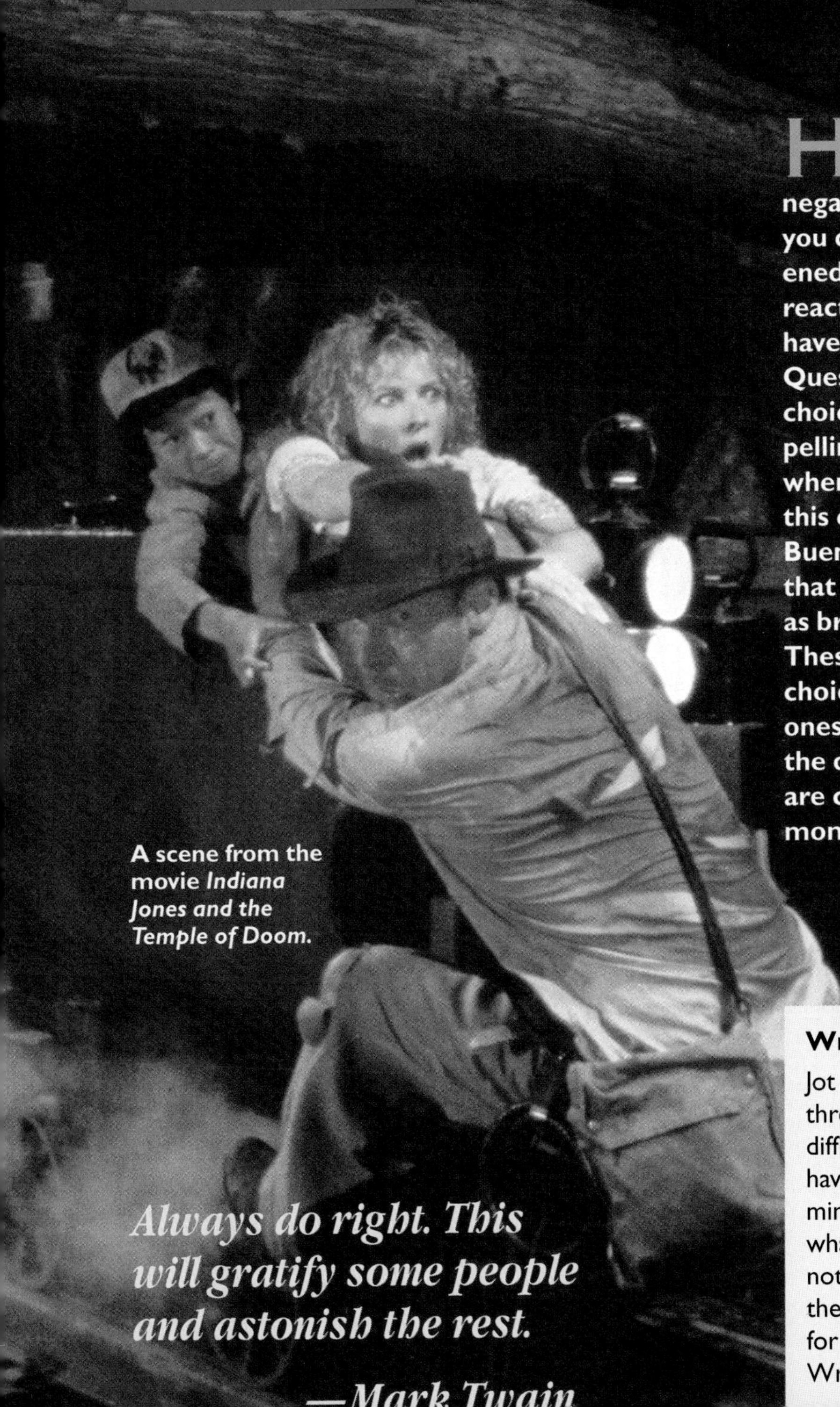

How would you make a decision if all the possible choices had negative consequences? How would you deal with a bully who threatened you in school? How would you react if friends expected you to behave in ways that aren't "you"? Questions like these involve difficult choices—the kind that make compelling plots in fiction—as you'll see when you read the short stories in this collection. From outer space to Buenos Aires, these stories show that choices are as essential to life as breathing and communicating. These stories also reveal that some choices—perhaps the hardest ones—can force you to look beyond the decision itself to the person you are choosing to be at a particular moment.

A scene from the movie *Indiana Jones and the Temple of Doom.*

Always do right. This will gratify some people and astonish the rest.

—Mark Twain

Writer's Notebook

WORK IN PROGRESS

Jot down two or three examples of difficult choices that you have had to face. Freewrite for a minute or two about the choices and what they meant to you. Keep your notes. You might want to return to them when you're looking for a subject for the essay you'll write for the Writer's Workshop on page 85.

Before You Read

THE COLD EQUATIONS

Make the Connection

No Easy Way Out

No one gets through life without having to make hard decisions. Think of all the choices we have to make in life—as students, parents, friends, teachers, voters, jurors, politicians, lawyers, law enforcers, journalists, scientists, business people, builders, doctors.

Quickwrite

What kinds of choices might we have to make in life that would have difficult consequences—no matter what we decide to do? Freewrite about such a choice. How would you make a decision when faced with such a hard choice?

Elements of Literature

Suspense: What Next?

Suspense can be an important element in stories that force characters to make hard decisions. In literature, as in life, suspense is our uncertainty about future events. It's a feeling of keen tension. We feel that *something* is going to happen to someone we care about, and we fear it may be bad.

As you read this story, think about *why* you feel suspense. What are you afraid will happen?

Suspense is a feeling of anxious curiosity about what is going to happen next in a story.

For more on Suspense, see the Handbook of Literary Terms.

Reading Skills and Strategies

Monitoring Your Reading: Questioning

Good readers keep questioning as they read—whether they're reading a detective story or a serious novel. As you read "The Cold Equations," write in your notebook any questions you have about what is going to happen *next.* Can you predict how this suspenseful tale will end? Also note your questions about the characters' actions, their unusual setting, and any passages that strike you as especially important or controversial. You may even have questions about Godwin's science.

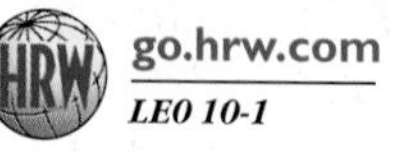

go.hrw.com
LEO 10-1

The Cold Equations

Tom Godwin

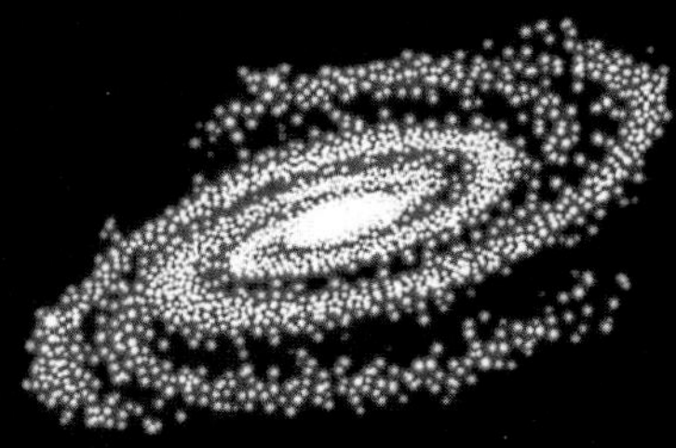

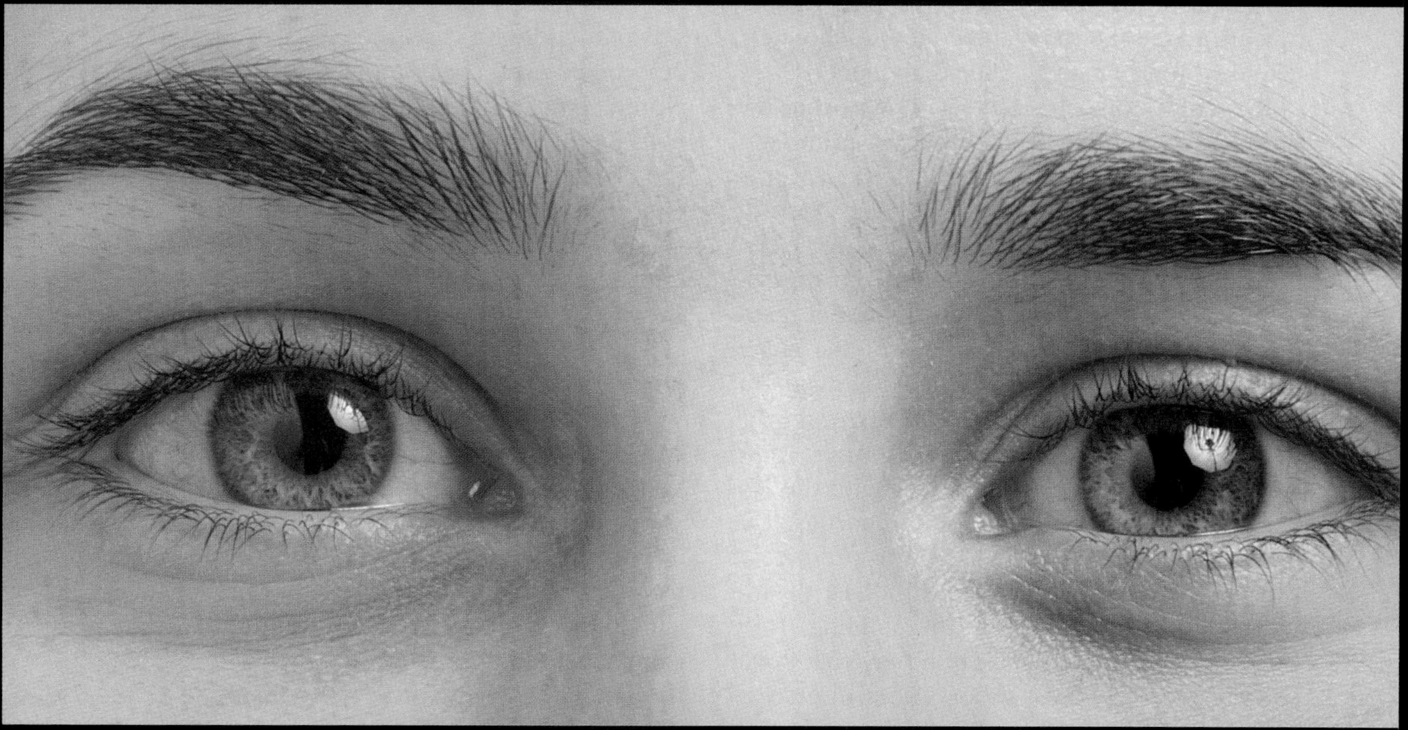

It was the law, and there could be no appeal.

He was not alone.

There was nothing to indicate the fact but the white hand of the tiny gauge on the board before him. The control room was empty but for himself; there was no sound other than the murmur of the drives—but the white hand had moved. It had been on zero when the little ship was launched from the *Stardust*; now, an hour later, it had crept up. There was something in the supply closet across the room, it was saying, some kind of a body that radiated heat.

It could be but one kind of a body—a living, human body.

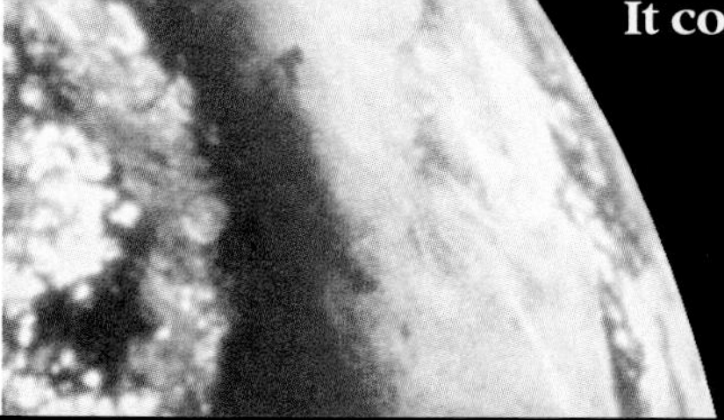

He leaned back in the pilot's chair and drew a deep, slow breath, considering what he would have to do. He was an EDS pilot, inured to the sight of death, long since accustomed to it and to viewing the dying of another man with an objective lack of emotion, and he had no choice in what he must do. There could be no alternative—but it required a few moments of conditioning for even an EDS pilot to prepare himself to walk across the room and coldly, deliberately, take the life of a man he had yet to meet.

He would, of course, do it. It was the law, stated very bluntly and definitely in grim Paragraph L, Section 8, of Interstellar Regulations: *"Any stowaway discovered in an EDS shall be jettisoned immediately following discovery."*

It was the law, and there could be no appeal.

It was a law not of men's choosing but made imperative by the circumstances of the space frontier. Galactic expansion had followed the development of the hyperspace drive, and as men scattered wide across the frontier, there had come the problem of contact with the isolated first colonies and exploration parties. The huge hyperspace cruisers were the product of the combined genius and effort of Earth and were long and expensive in the building. They were not available in such numbers that small colonies could possess them. The cruisers carried the colonists to their new worlds and made periodic visits, running on tight schedules, but they could not stop and turn aside to visit colonies scheduled to be visited at another time; such a delay would destroy their schedule and produce a confusion and uncertainty that would wreck the complex interdependence between old Earth and the new worlds of the frontier.

Some method of delivering supplies or assistance when an emergency occurred on a world not scheduled for a visit had been needed, and the Emergency Dispatch Ships had been the answer. Small and collapsible, they occupied little room in the hold of the cruiser; made of light metal and plastics, they were driven by a small rocket drive that consumed relatively little fuel. Each cruiser carried four EDSs, and when a call for aid was received, the nearest cruiser would drop into normal space long enough to launch an EDS with the needed supplies or personnel, then vanish again as it continued on its course.

The cruisers, powered by nuclear converters, did not use the liquid rocket fuel, but nuclear converters were far too large and complex to permit their installation in the EDSs. The cruisers were forced by necessity to carry a limited amount of bulky rocket fuel, and the fuel was rationed with care, the cruiser's computers determining the exact amount of fuel each EDS would require for its mission. The computers considered the course coordinates, the mass of the EDS, the mass of pilot and cargo; they were very precise and accurate and omitted nothing from their calculations. They could not, however, foresee and allow for the added mass of a stowaway.

The *Stardust* had received the request from one of the exploration parties stationed on Woden, the six men of the party already being stricken with the fever carried by the green kala midges and their own supply of serum destroyed by the tornado that had torn through their camp. The *Stardust* had gone through the usual procedure, dropping into normal space to launch the EDS with the fever serum, then vanishing again in hyperspace. Now, an hour later, the gauge was saying there was something more than the small carton of serum in the supply closet.

He let his eyes rest on the narrow white door of the closet. There, just inside, another man lived and breathed and was beginning to feel assured that discovery of his presence would now be too late for the pilot to alter the situation. It *was* too late; for the man behind the door it was far later than he thought and in a way he would find it terrible to believe.

There could be no alternative. Additional fuel would be used during the hours of deceleration to compensate for the added mass of the stow-

Words to Own

inured (in·yoord') *v.* used as *adj.:* accustomed (to something difficult or painful).

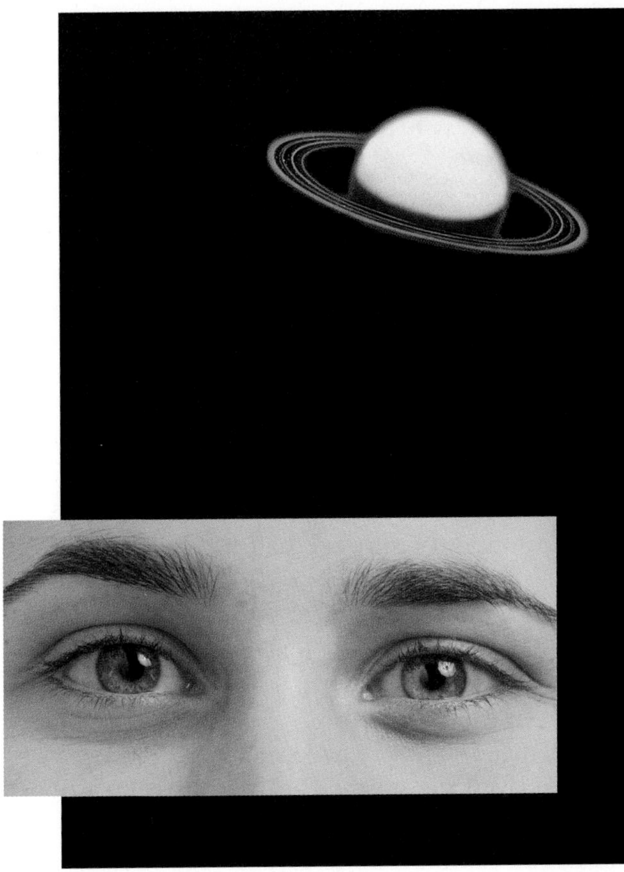

away, infinitesimal increments of fuel that would not be missed until the ship had almost reached its destination. Then, at some distance above the ground that might be as near as a thousand feet or as far as tens of thousands of feet, depending upon the mass of ship and cargo and the preceding period of deceleration, the unmissed increments of fuel would make their absence known; the EDS would expend its last drops of fuel with a sputter and go into whistling free fall. Ship and pilot and stowaway would merge together upon impact as a wreckage of metal and plastic, flesh and blood, driven deep into the soil. The stowaway had signed his own death warrant when he concealed himself on the ship; he could not be permitted to take seven others with him.

He looked again at the telltale white hand, then rose to his feet. What he must do would be unpleasant for both of them; the sooner it was over, the better. He stepped across the control room to stand by the white door.

"Come out!" His command was harsh and abrupt above the murmur of the drive.

It seemed he could hear the whisper of a furtive movement inside the closet, then nothing. He visualized the stowaway cowering closer into one corner, suddenly worried by the possible consequences of his act, his self-assurance evaporating.

"I said *out!*"

He heard the stowaway move to obey, and he waited with his eyes alert on the door and his hand near the blaster at his side.

The door opened and the stowaway stepped through it, smiling. "All right—I give up. Now what?"

It was a girl.

He stared without speaking, his hand dropping away from the blaster, and acceptance of what he saw coming like a heavy and unexpected physical blow. The stowaway was not a man—she was a girl in her teens, standing before him in little white gypsy sandals, with the top of her brown, curly head hardly higher than his shoulder, with a faint, sweet scent of perfume coming from her, and her smiling face tilted up so her eyes could look unknowing and unafraid into his as she waited for his answer.

Now what? Had it been asked in the deep, defiant voice of a man, he would have answered it with action, quick and efficient. He would have taken the stowaway's identification disk and ordered him into the air lock. Had the stowaway refused to obey, he would have used the blaster. It would not have taken long; within a minute the body would have been ejected into space—had the stowaway been a man.

He returned to the pilot's chair and motioned her to seat herself on the boxlike bulk of the drive-control units that were set against the wall beside him. She obeyed, his silence making the smile fade into the meek and guilty expression of a pup that has been caught in mischief and knows it must be punished.

WORDS TO OWN

increments (in′krə·mənts) *n.:* small increases.

"You still haven't told me," she said. "I'm guilty, so what happens to me now? Do I pay a fine, or what?"

"What are you doing here?" he asked. "Why did you stow away on this EDS?"

"I wanted to see my brother. He's with the government survey crew on Woden and I haven't seen him for ten years, not since he left Earth to go into government survey work."

"What was your destination on the *Stardust*?"

"Mimir. I have a position waiting for me there. My brother has been sending money home all the time to us—my father and mother and me—and he paid for a special course in linguistics I was taking. I graduated sooner than expected and I was offered this job in Mimir. I knew it would be almost a year before Gerry's job was done on Woden so he could come on to Mimir, and that's why I hid in the closet there. There was plenty of room for me and I was willing to pay the fine. There were only the two of us kids—Gerry and I—and I haven't seen him for so long, and I didn't want to wait another year when I could see him now, even though I knew I would be breaking some kind of a regulation when I did it."

I knew I would be breaking some kind of a regulation. In a way, she could not be blamed for her ignorance of the law; she was of Earth and had not realized that the laws of the space frontier must, of necessity, be as hard and relentless as the environment that gave them birth. Yet, to protect such as her from the results of their own ignorance of the frontier, there had been a sign over the door that led to the section of the *Stardust* that housed the EDSs, a sign that was plain for all to see and heed: UNAUTHORIZED PERSONNEL KEEP OUT!

"Does your brother know that you took passage on the *Stardust* for Mimir?"

"Oh, yes. I sent him a spacegram telling him about my graduation and about going to Mimir on the *Stardust* a month before I left Earth. I already knew Mimir was where he would be stationed in a little over a year. He gets a promotion then, and he'll be based on Mimir and not have to stay out a year at a time on field trips, like he does now."

There were two different survey groups on Woden, and he asked, "What is his name?"

"Cross—Gerry Cross. He's in Group Two—that was the way his address read. Do you know him?"

Group One had requested the serum: Group Two was eight thousand miles away, across the Western Sea.

"No, I've never met him," he said, then turned to the control board and cut the deceleration to a fraction of a gravity, knowing as he did so that it could not avert the ultimate end, yet doing the only thing he could do to prolong that ultimate end. The sensation was like that of the ship suddenly dropping, and the girl's involuntary movement of surprise half lifted her from her seat.

"We're going faster now, aren't we?" she asked. "Why are we doing that?"

He told her the truth. "To save fuel for a little while."

"You mean we don't have very much?"

He delayed the answer he must give her so soon to ask, "How did you manage to stow away?"

"I just sort of walked in when no one was looking my way," she said. "I was practicing my Gelanese on the native girl who does the cleaning in the Ship's Supply office when someone came in with an order for supplies for the survey crew on Woden. I slipped into the closet there after the ship was ready to go just before you came in. It was an impulse of the moment to stow away, so I could get to see Gerry—and from the way you keep looking at me so grim, I'm not sure it was a very wise impulse. But I'll be a model criminal—or do I mean prisoner?" She smiled at him again. "I intended to pay for my keep on top of paying the fine. I can cook and I can patch clothes for everyone and I know how to do all kinds of useful things, even a little bit about nursing."

There was one more question to ask:

"Did you know what the supplies were that the survey crew ordered?"

"Why, no. Equipment they needed in their work, I supposed."

Why couldn't she have been a man with

some ulterior motive? A fugitive from justice hoping to lose himself on a raw new world; an opportunist seeking transportation to the new colonies where he might find golden fleece for the taking; a crackpot with a mission. Perhaps once in his lifetime an EDS pilot would find such a stowaway on his ship—warped men, mean and selfish men, brutal and dangerous men—but never before a smiling, blue-eyed girl who was willing to pay her fine and work for her keep that she might see her brother.

He turned to the board and turned the switch that would signal the *Stardust*. The call would be futile, but he could not, until he had exhausted that one vain hope, seize her and thrust her into the air lock as he would an animal—or a man. The delay, in the meantime, would not be dangerous with the EDS decelerating at fractional gravity.

A voice spoke from the communicator. "*Stardust*. Identify yourself and proceed."

"Barton, EDS 34GII. Emergency. Give me Commander Delhart."

There was a faint confusion of noises as the request went through the proper channels. The girl was watching him, no longer smiling.

"Are you going to order them to come back after me?" she asked.

The communicator clicked and there was the sound of a distant voice saying, "Commander, the EDS requests . . ."

"Are they coming back after me?" she asked again. "Won't I get to see my brother after all?"

"Barton?" The blunt, gruff voice of Commander Delhart came from the communicator. "What's this about an emergency?"

"A stowaway," he answered.

"A stowaway?" There was a slight surprise to the question. "That's rather unusual—but why the 'emergency' call? You discovered him in time, so there should be no appreciable danger, and I presume you've informed Ship's Records so his nearest relatives can be notified."

"That's why I had to call you, first. The stowaway is still aboard and the circumstances are so different—"

"Different?" the commander interrupted, impatience in his voice. "How

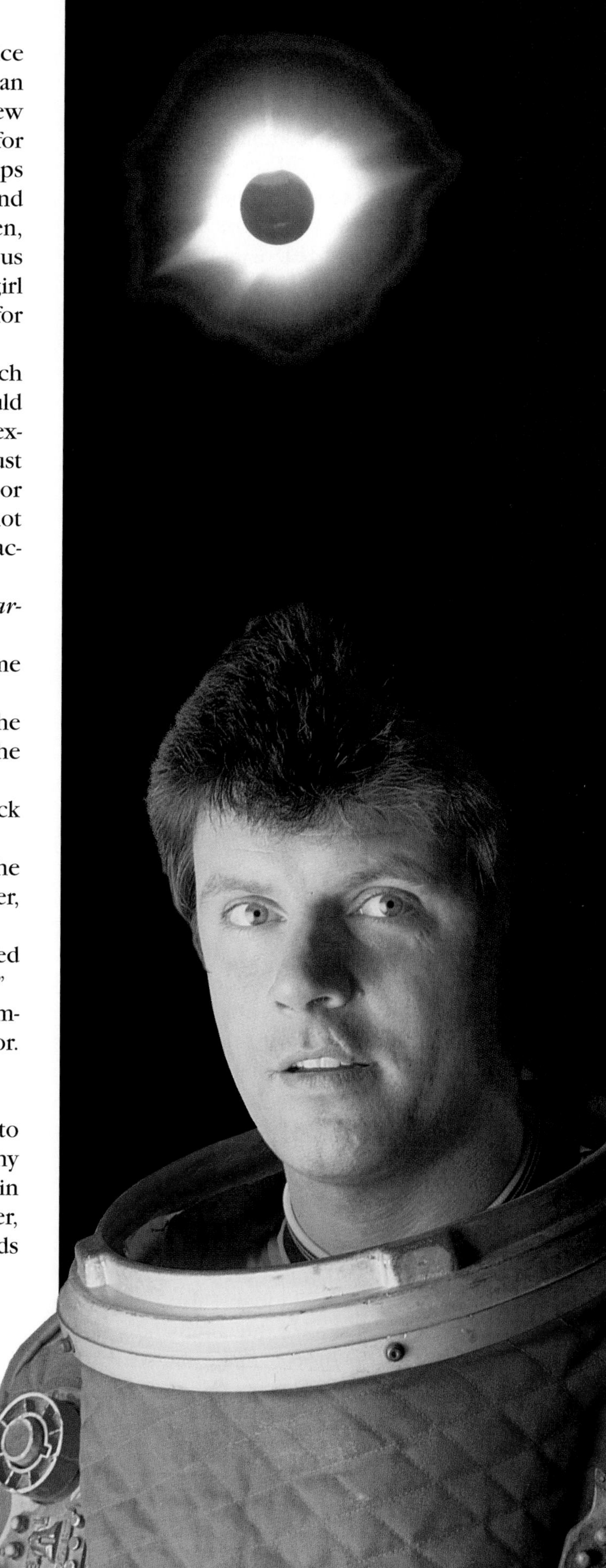

can they be different? You know you have a limited supply of fuel; you also know the law as well as I do: 'Any stowaway discovered in an EDS shall be jettisoned immediately following discovery.'"

There was the sound of a sharply indrawn breath from the girl. *"What does he mean?"*

"The stowaway is a girl."

"What?"

"She wanted to see her brother. She's only a kid and she didn't know what she was really doing."

"I see." All the curtness was gone from the commander's voice. "So you called me in the hope I could do something?" Without waiting for an answer he went on, "I'm sorry—I can do nothing. This cruiser must maintain its schedule; the life of not one person but the lives of many depend on it. I know how you feel but I'm powerless to help you. You'll have to go through with it. I'll have you connected with Ship's Records."

The communicator faded to a faint rustle of sound, and he turned back to the girl. She was leaning forward on the bench, almost rigid, her eyes fixed wide and frightened.

"What did he mean, to go through with it? To jettison me . . . to go through with it—what did he mean? Not the way it sounded . . . he couldn't have. What did he mean—what did he really mean?"

Her time was too short for the comfort of a lie to be more than a cruelly fleeting delusion.

"He meant it the way it sounded."

"No!" She recoiled from him as though he had struck her, one hand half raised as though to fend him off and stark unwillingness to believe in her eyes.

"It will have to be."

"No! You're joking—you're insane! You can't mean it!"

"I'm sorry." He spoke slowly to her, gently. "I should have told you before—I should have, but I had to do what I could first; I had to call the *Stardust*. You heard what the commander said."

"But you can't—if you make me leave the ship, I'll *die*."

"I know."

She searched his face, and the unwillingness to believe left her eyes, giving way slowly to a look of dazed horror.

"You know?" She spoke the words far apart, numbly and wonderingly.

"I know. It has to be like that."

"You mean it—you really mean it." She sagged back against the wall, small and limp like a little rag doll, and all the protesting and disbelief gone. "You're going to do it—you're going to make me die?"

"I'm sorry," he said again. "You'll never know how sorry I am. It has to be that way and no human in the universe can change it."

"You're going to make me die and I didn't do anything to die for—I didn't *do* anything——"

He sighed, deep and weary. "I know you didn't, child. I know you didn't."

"EDS." The communicator rapped brisk and metallic. "This is Ship's Records. Give us all information on subject's identification disk."

He got out of his chair to stand over her. She clutched the edge of the seat, her upturned face white under the brown hair and the lipstick standing out like a blood-red cupid's bow.

"Now?"

"I want your identification disk," he said.

She released the edge of the seat and fumbled at the chain that suspended the plastic disk from her neck with fingers that were trembling and awkward. He reached down and unfastened the clasp for her, then returned with the disk to his chair.

"Here's your data, Records: Identification Number T837——"

"One moment," Records interrupted. "This is to be filed on the gray card, of course?"

"Yes."

"And the time of execution?"

"I'll tell you later."

"Later? This is highly irregular; the time of the subject's death is required before——"

He kept the thickness out of his voice with

Words to Own

recoiled (ri·koild') *v.:* drew back in fear, surprise, or disgust.

an effort. "Then we'll do it in a highly irregular manner—you'll hear the disk read first. The subject is a girl and she's listening to everything that's said. Are you capable of understanding that?"

There was a brief, almost shocked silence; then Records said meekly, "Sorry. Go ahead."

He began to read the disk, reading it slowly to delay the inevitable for as long as possible, trying to help her by giving her what little time he could to recover from her first horror and let it resolve into the calm of acceptance and resignation.

"Number T8374 dash Y54. Name, Marilyn Lee Cross. Sex, female. Born July 7, 2160." *She was only eighteen.* "Height, five-three. Weight, a hundred and ten." *Such a slight weight, yet enough to add fatally to the mass of the shell-thin bubble that was an EDS.* "Hair, brown. Eyes, blue. Complexion, light. Blood type O." *Irrelevant data.* "Destination, Port City, Mimir." *Invalid data.*

He finished and said, "I'll call you later," then turned once again to the girl. She was huddled back against the wall, watching him with a look of numb and wondering fascination.

"They're waiting for you to kill me, aren't they? They want me dead, don't they? You and everybody on the cruiser want me dead, don't you?" Then the numbness broke and her voice was that of a frightened and bewildered child. "Everybody wants me dead and I didn't *do* anything. I didn't hurt anyone—I only wanted to see my brother."

"It's not the way you think—it isn't that way at all," he said. "Nobody wants it this way; nobody would ever let it be this way if it was humanly possible to change it."

"Then why is it? I don't understand. Why is it?"

"This ship is carrying kala fever serum to Group One on Woden. Their own supply was destroyed by a tornado. Group Two—the crew your brother is in—is eight thousand miles away across the Western Sea, and their helicopters can't cross it to help Group One. The fever is invariably fatal unless the serum can be had in time, and the six men in Group One will die unless this ship reaches them on schedule. These little ships are always given barely enough fuel to reach their destination, and if you stay aboard, your added weight will cause it to use up all its fuel before it reaches the ground. It will crash then, and you and I will die and so will the six men waiting for the fever serum."

It was a full minute before she spoke, and as she considered his words, the expression of numbness left her eyes.

"Is that it?" she asked at last. "Just that the ship doesn't have enough fuel?"

"Yes."

"I can go alone or I can take seven others with me—is that the way it is?"

"That's the way it is."

"And nobody wants me to have to die?"

"Nobody."

"Then maybe—— Are you sure nothing can be done about it? Wouldn't people help me if they could?"

"Everyone would like to help you, but there is nothing anyone can do. I did the only thing I could do when I called the *Stardust*."

"And it won't come back—but there might be other cruisers, mightn't there? Isn't there any hope at all that there might be someone, somewhere, who could do something to help me?"

She was leaning forward a little in her eagerness as she waited for his answer.

"No."

The word was like the drop of a cold stone and she again leaned back against the wall, the hope and eagerness leaving her face. "You're sure—you *know* you're sure?"

"I'm sure. There are no other cruisers within forty light-years; there is nothing and no one to change things."

She dropped her gaze to her lap and began twisting a pleat of her skirt between her fingers, saying no more as her mind began to adapt itself to the grim knowledge.

It was better so; with the going of all hope would go the fear; with the going of all hope would come resignation. She needed time and she could have so little of it. How much?

The EDSs were not equipped with hull-cooling units; their speed had to be reduced to a moderate level before they entered the atmosphere. They were decelerating at .10 gravity, approaching their destination at a far higher speed than the computers had calculated on. The *Stardust* had been quite near Woden when she launched the EDS; their present velocity was putting them nearer by the second. There would be a critical point, soon to be reached, when he would have to resume deceleration. When he did so, the girl's weight would be multiplied by the gravities of deceleration, would become, suddenly, a factor of paramount importance, the factor the computers had been ignorant of when they determined the amount of fuel the EDS should have. She would have to go when deceleration began; it could be no other way. When would that be—how long could he let her stay?

"How long can I stay?"

He winced involuntarily from the words that were so like an echo of his own thoughts. How long? He didn't know; he would have to ask the ship's computers. Each EDS was given a meager surplus of fuel to compensate for unfavorable conditions within the atmosphere, and relatively little fuel was being consumed for the time being. The memory banks of the computers would still contain all data pertaining to the course set for the EDS; such data would not be erased until the EDS reached its destination. He had only to give the computers the new data—the girl's weight and the exact time at which he had reduced the deceleration to .10.

"Barton." Commander Delhart's voice came abruptly from the communicator as he opened his mouth to call the *Stardust*. "A check with Records shows me you haven't completed your report. Did you reduce the deceleration?"

So the commander knew what he was trying to do.

"I'm decelerating at point ten," he answered. "I cut the deceleration at seventeen fifty and the weight is a hundred and ten. I would like to stay at point ten as long as the computers say I can. Will you give them the question?"

It was contrary to regulations for an EDS pilot to make any changes in the course or degree of deceleration the computers had set for him, but the commander made no mention of the violation. Neither did he ask the reason for it. It was not necessary for him to ask; he had not become commander of an interstellar cruiser without both intelligence and an understanding of human nature. He said only, "I'll have that given to the computers."

The communicator fell silent and he and the girl waited, neither of them speaking. They would not have to wait long; the computers would give the answer within moments of the asking. The new factors would be fed into the steel maw° of the first bank, and the electrical impulses would go through the complex circuits. Here and there a relay might click, a tiny cog turn over, but it would be essentially the electrical impulses that found the answer; formless, mindless, invisible, determining with utter precision how long the pale girl beside him might live. Then five little segments of metal in the second bank would trip in rapid succession against an inked ribbon and a second steel maw would spit out the slip of paper that bore the answer.

The chronometer on the instrument board read 18:10 when the commander spoke again.

"You will resume deceleration at nineteen ten."

She looked toward the chronometer, then quickly away from it. "Is that when . . . when I go?" she asked. He nodded and she dropped her eyes to her lap again.

"I'll have the course correction given to you," the commander said. "Ordinarily I would never permit anything like this, but I understand your position. There is nothing I can do, other than what I've just done, and you will not deviate from these new instructions. You will complete your report at nineteen ten. Now—here are the course corrections."

°**maw:** huge, all-consuming mouth.

WORDS TO OWN

paramount (par′ə·mount′) *adj.:* supreme; dominant.

The voice of some unknown technician read them to him, and he wrote them down on the pad clipped to the edge of the control board. There would, he saw, be periods of deceleration when he neared the atmosphere when the deceleration would be five gravities—and at five gravities, one hundred ten pounds would become five hundred fifty pounds.

The technician finished and he terminated the contact with a brief acknowledgment. Then, hesitating a moment, he reached out and shut off the communicator. It was 18:13 and he would have nothing to report until 19:10. In the meantime, it somehow seemed indecent to permit others to hear what she might say in her last hour.

He began to check the instrument readings, going over them with unnecessary slowness. She would have to accept the circumstances, and there was nothing he could do to help her into acceptance; words of sympathy would only delay it.

It was 18:20 when she stirred from her motionlessness and spoke.

"So that's the way it has to be with me?"

He swung around to face her. "You understand now, don't you? No one would ever let it be like this if it could be changed."

"I understand," she said. Some of the color had returned to her face and the lipstick no longer stood out so vividly red. "There isn't enough fuel for me to stay. When I hid on this ship, I got into something I didn't know anything about and now I have to pay for it."

She had violated a man-made law that said KEEP OUT, but the penalty was not for men's making or desire and it was a penalty men could not revoke. A physical law had decreed: *h amount of fuel will power an EDS with a mass of m safely to its destination;* and a second physical law had decreed: *h amount of fuel will not power an EDS with a mass of m plus x safely to its destination.*

EDSs obeyed only physical laws, and no amount of human sympathy for her could alter the second law.

"But I'm afraid. I don't want to die—not now. I want to live, and nobody is doing anything to help me; everybody is letting me go ahead and acting just like nothing was going to happen to me. I'm going to die and nobody *cares*."

"We all do," he said. "I do and the commander does and the clerk in Ship's Records; we all care and each of us did what little he could to help you. It wasn't enough—it was almost nothing—but it was all we could do."

"Not enough fuel—I can understand that," she said, as though she had not heard his own words. "But to have to die for it. *Me* alone . . ."

How hard it must be for her to accept the fact. She had never known danger of death, had never known the environments where the lives of men could be as fragile and fleeting as sea foam tossed against a rocky shore. She belonged on gentle Earth, in that secure and peaceful society where she could be young and gay and laughing with the others of her kind, where life was precious and well guarded and there was always the assurance that tomorrow would come. She belonged in that world of soft winds and a warm sun, music and moonlight and gracious manners, and not on the hard, bleak frontier.

"How did it happen to me so terribly quickly? An hour ago I was on the *Stardust,* going to Mimir. Now the *Stardust* is going on without me and I'm going to die and I'll never see Gerry and Mama and Daddy again—I'll never see anything again."

He hesitated, wondering how he could explain it to her so she would really understand and not feel she had somehow been the victim of a reasonlessly cruel injustice. She did not know what the frontier was like; she thought in terms of safe, secure Earth. Pretty girls were not jettisoned on Earth; there was a law against it. On Earth her plight would have filled the newscasts and a fast black patrol ship would have been racing to her rescue. Everyone, everywhere, would have known of Marilyn Lee Cross, and no effort would have been spared to save her life. But this was not Earth and there were no patrol ships; only the *Stardust,* leaving them behind at many times the speed of light. There was no one to help her; there would be no Marilyn Lee Cross smiling from the newscasts tomorrow. Marilyn Lee Cross would be but a poignant memory for an EDS pilot and a name on a gray card in Ship's Records.

"It's different here; it's not like back on Earth," he said. "It isn't that no one cares; it's that no one can do anything to help. The frontier is big, and here along its rim the colonies and exploration parties are scattered so thin and far between. On Woden, for example, there are only sixteen men—sixteen men on an entire world. The exploration parties, the survey crews, the little first colonies—they're all fighting alien environments, trying to make a way for those who will follow after. The environments fight back, and those who go first usually make mistakes only once. There is no margin of safety along the rim of the frontier; there can't be until the way is made for the others who will come later, until the new worlds are tamed and settled. Until then men will have to pay the penalty for making mistakes, with no one to help them, because there is no one *to* help them."

"I was going to Mimir," she said. "I didn't know about the frontier; I was only going to Mimir and *it's* safe."

"Mimir is safe, but you left the cruiser that was taking you there."

She was silent for a little while. "It was all so wonderful at first; there was plenty of room for me on this ship and I would be seeing Gerry so soon. I didn't know about the fuel, didn't know what would happen to me. . . ."

Her words trailed away, and he turned his attention to the viewscreen, not wanting to stare at her as she fought her way through the black horror of fear toward the calm gray of acceptance.

Woden was a ball, enshrouded in the blue haze of its atmosphere, swimming in space against the background of star-sprinkled dead blackness. The great mass of Manning's Continent sprawled like a gigantic hourglass in the Eastern Sea, with the western half of the Eastern Continent still visible. There was a thin line of shadow along the right-hand edge of the globe, and the Eastern Continent was disappearing into it as the planet turned on its axis. An hour before, the entire continent had been in view; now a thousand miles of it had gone into the thin edge of shadow and around to the night that lay on the other side of the world. The dark blue spot that was Lotus Lake was approaching the shadow. It was somewhere near the southern edge of the lake that Group Two had their camp. It would be night there soon, and quick behind the coming of night the rotation of Woden on its axis would put Group Two beyond the reach of the ship's radio.

He would have to tell her before it was too late for her to talk to her brother. In a way, it would be better for both of them should they not do so, but it was not for him to decide. To each of them the last words would be something to hold and cherish, something that would cut like the blade of a knife yet would be infinitely precious to remember, she for her own brief moments to live and he for the rest of his life.

He held down the button that would flash the grid lines on the viewscreen and used the known diameter of the planet to estimate the distance the southern tip of Lotus Lake had yet to go until it passed beyond radio range. It was approximately five hundred miles. Five hundred miles; thirty minutes—and the chronometer read 18:30. Allowing for error in estimating, it would not be later than 19:05 that the turning of Woden would cut off her brother's voice.

The first border of the Western continent was already in sight along the left side of the world. Four thousand miles across it lay the shore of the Western Sea and the camp of Group One. It had been in the Western Sea that the tornado had originated, to strike with such fury at the camp and destroy half their prefabricated buildings, including the one that housed the medical supplies. Two days before, the tornado had not existed; it had been no more than great gentle masses of air over the calm Western Sea. Group One had gone about their routine survey work, unaware of the meeting of air masses out at sea, unaware of the force the union was spawning. It had struck their camp without warning—a thundering, roaring de-

Literature and Science

Inner Space

A frontier as exciting and demanding as outer space is being explored here on Earth. "Inner space" is dark and airless. It is freezing cold in some places, boiling hot in others. It is full of strange life forms, including giant creatures more than one hundred feet long. Inner space is the ocean, which has an average depth of 2.4 miles and, by volume, makes up about 99.5 percent of Earth's habitable space. On the ocean floor scientists have found deposits of rare minerals, heat-resistant bacteria useful in medicine, and geological information that provides clues about the planet's history. Bony fishes, shimmering gelatinous animals, and thousands of yet unclassified species live in the vast middle depths. Aquanauts in submersibles make some underwater research journeys, but in recent years sophisticated robots have ventured into regions too dangerous for humans. These robots have sensors, video cameras, sonars, and tools for collecting samples. Looking through a robot's eyes, geologists may stumble on a "black smoker," a geyser belching water with a temperature of 350 degrees Celsius. Marine biologists may get their first glimpse of a type of siphonophore (a kind of sea creature similar to jellyfish) that has long stinging tentacles and many stomachs. Discoveries like these happen every day, and each new find helps us protect and learn from Earth's fascinating inner space.

(Background) Giant tube worms in the Galápagos deep-water vents.

struction that sought to annihilate all that lay before it. It had passed on, leaving the wreckage in its wake. It had destroyed the labor of months and had doomed six men to die and then, as though its task was accomplished, it once more began to resolve into gentle masses of air. But, for all its deadliness, it had destroyed with neither malice nor intent. It had been a blind and mindless force, obeying the laws of nature, and it would have followed the same course with the same fury had men never existed.

Existence required order, and there was order; the laws of nature, irrevocable and immutable. Men could learn to use them, but men could not change them. The circumference of a circle was always pi times the diameter, and no science of man would ever make it otherwise. The combination of chemical A with chemical B under condition C invariably produced reaction D. The law of gravitation was a

Words to Own

annihilate (ə·nī′ə·lāt′) *v.:* destroy; demolish.
irrevocable (ir·rev′ə·kə·bəl) *adj.:* irreversible; incapable of being canceled or undone.
immutable (im·myo͞ot′ə·bəl) *adj.:* unchangeable; never changing or varying.

rigid equation, and it made no distinction between the fall of a leaf and the ponderous circling of a binary star system. The nuclear conversion process powered the cruisers that carried men to the stars; the same process in the form of a nova would destroy a world with equal efficiency. The laws *were,* and the universe moved in obedience to them. Along the frontier were arrayed all the forces of nature, and sometimes they destroyed those who were fighting their way outward from Earth. The men of the frontier had long ago learned the bitter futility of cursing the forces that would destroy them, for the forces were blind and deaf; the futility of looking to the heavens for mercy, for the stars of the galaxy swung in their long, long sweep of two hundred million years, as inexorably controlled as they by the laws that knew neither hatred nor compassion. The men of the frontier knew—but how was a girl from Earth to fully understand? *h amount of fuel will not power an EDS with a mass of m plus x safely to its destination.* To him and her brother and parents she was a sweet-faced girl in her teens; to the laws of nature she was *x,* the unwanted factor in a cold equation.

She stirred again on the seat. "Could I write a letter? I want to write to Mama and Daddy. And I'd like to talk to Gerry. Could you let me talk to him over your radio there?"

"I'll try to get him," he said.

He switched on the normal-space transmitter and pressed the signal button. Someone answered the buzzer almost immediately.

"Hello. How's it going with you fellows now—is the EDS on its way?"

"This isn't Group One; this is the EDS," he said. "Is Gerry Cross there?"

"Gerry? He and two others went out in the helicopter this morning and aren't back yet. It's almost sundown, though, and he ought to be back right away—in less than an hour at the most."

"Can you connect me through to the radio in his copter?"

"Huh-uh. It's been out of commission for two months—some printed circuits went haywire and we can't get any more until the next cruiser stops by. Is it something important—bad news for him, or something?"

"Yes—it's very important. When he comes in, get him to the transmitter as soon as you possibly can."

"I'll do that; I'll have one of the boys waiting at the field with a truck. Is there anything else I can do?"

"No, I guess that's all. Get him there as soon as you can and signal me."

He turned the volume to an inaudible minimum, an act that would not affect the functioning of the signal buzzer, and unclipped the pad of paper from the control board. He tore off the sheet containing his flight instructions and handed the pad to her, together with pencil.

"I'd better write to Gerry too," she said as she took them. "He might not get back to camp in time."

She began to write, her fingers still clumsy and uncertain in the way they handled the pencil, and the top of it trembling a little as she poised it between words. He turned back to the viewscreen, to stare at it without seeing it.

She was a lonely little child trying to say her last goodbye, and she would lay out her heart to them. She would tell them how much she loved them and she would tell them to not feel bad about it, that it was only something that must happen eventually to everyone and she was not afraid. The last would be a lie and it would be there to read between the sprawling, uneven lines: a valiant little lie that would make the hurt all the greater for them.

Her brother was of the frontier and he would understand. He would not hate the EDS pilot for doing nothing to prevent her going; he would know there had been nothing the pilot could do. He would understand, though the understanding would not soften the shock and pain when he learned his sister was gone. But the others, her father and mother—they would not

Words to Own

ponderous (pän′dər • əs) *adj.:* heavy and slow-moving.

understand. They were of Earth and they would think in the manner of those who had never lived where the safety margin of life was a thin, thin line—and sometimes nothing at all. What would they think of the faceless, unknown pilot who had sent her to her death?

They would hate him with cold and terrible intensity, but it really didn't matter. He would never see them, never know them. He would have only the memories to remind him; only the nights of fear, when a blue-eyed girl in gypsy sandals would come in his dreams to die again. . . .

He scowled at the viewscreen and tried to force his thoughts into less emotional channels. There was nothing he could do to help her. She had unknowingly subjected herself to the penalty of a law that recognized neither innocence nor youth nor beauty, that was incapable of sympathy or leniency. Regret was illogical—and yet, could knowing it to be illogical ever keep it away?

She stopped occasionally, as though trying to find the right words to tell them what she wanted them to know; then the pencil would resume its whispering to the paper. It was 18:37 when she folded the letter in a square and wrote a name on it. She began writing another, twice looking up at the chronometer, as though she feared the black hand might reach its rendezvous before she had finished. It was 18:45 when she folded it as she had done the first letter and wrote a name and address on it.

She held the letters out to him. "Will you take care of these and see that they're enveloped and mailed?"

"Of course." He took them from her hand and placed them in a pocket of his gray uniform shirt.

"These can't be sent off until the next cruiser stops by, and the *Stardust* will have long since told them about me, won't it?" she asked. He nodded and she went on: "That makes the letters not important in one way, but in another way they're very important—to me, and to them."

"I know. I understand, and I'll take care of them."

She glanced at the chronometer, then back to him. "It seems to move faster all the time, doesn't it?"

He said nothing, unable to think of anything to say, and she asked, "Do you think Gerry will come back to camp in time?"

"I think so. They said he should be in right away."

She began to roll the pencil back and forth between her palms. "I hope he does. I feel sick and scared and I want to hear his voice again and maybe I won't feel so alone. I'm a coward and I can't help it."

"No," he said, "you're not a coward. You're afraid, but you're not a coward."

"Is there a difference?"

He nodded. "A lot of difference."

"I feel so alone. I never did feel like this before; like I was all by myself and there was nobody to care what happened to me. Always, before, there were Mama and Daddy there and my friends around me. I had lots of friends, and they had a going-away party for me the night before I left."

Friends and music and laughter for her to remember—and on the viewscreen Lotus Lake was going into the shadow.

"Is it the same with Gerry?" she asked. "I mean, if he should make a mistake, would he have to die for it, all alone and with no one to help him?"

"It's the same with all, along the frontier; it will always be like that so long as there is a frontier."

"Gerry didn't tell us. He said the pay was good, and he sent money home all the time because Daddy's little shop just brought in a bare living, but he didn't tell us it was like this."

"He didn't tell you his work was dangerous?"

"Well—yes. He mentioned that, but we didn't understand. I always thought danger along the frontier was something that was a lot of fun; an exciting adventure, like in the three-D shows." A wan smile touched her face for a moment. "Only it's not, is it? It's not the same at all, because when it's real you can't go home after the show is over."

"No," he said. "No, you can't."

Her glance flicked from the chronometer to the door of the air lock, then down to the pad and pencil she still held. She shifted her position slightly to lay them on the bench beside her, moving one foot out a little. For the first time he saw that she was not wearing Vegan gypsy sandals, but only cheap imitations; the expensive Vegan leather was some kind of grained plastic, the silver buckle was gilded iron, the jewels were colored glass. *Daddy's little shop just brought in a bare living. . . .* She must have left college in her second year, to take the course in linguistics that would enable her to make her own way and help her brother provide for her parents, earning what she could by part-time work after classes were over. Her personal possessions on the *Stardust* would be taken back to her parents—they would neither be of much value nor occupy much storage space on the return voyage.

"Isn't it——" She stopped, and he looked at her questioningly. "Isn't it cold in here?" she asked, almost apologetically. "Doesn't it seem cold to you?"

"Why, yes," he said. He saw by the main temperature gauge that the room was at precisely normal temperature. "Yes, it's colder than it should be."

"I wish Gerry would get back before it's too late. Do you really think he will, and you didn't just say so to make me feel better?"

"I think he will—they said he would be in pretty soon." On the viewscreen Lotus Lake had gone into the shadow but for the thin blue line of its western edge, and it was apparent he had overestimated the time she would have in which to talk to her brother. Reluctantly, he said to her, "His camp will be out of radio range in a few minutes; he's on that part of Woden that's in the shadow"—he indicated the viewscreen—"and the turning of Woden will put him beyond contact. There may not be much time left when he comes in—not much time to talk to him before he fades out. I wish I could do something about it—I would call him right now if I could."

"Not even as much time as I will have to stay?"

"I'm afraid not."

"Then——" She straightened and looked toward the air lock with pale resolution. "Then I'll go when Gerry passes beyond range. I won't wait any longer after that—I won't have anything to wait for."

Again there was nothing he could say.

"Maybe I shouldn't wait at all. Maybe I'm selfish—maybe it would be better for Gerry if you just told him about it afterward."

There was an unconscious pleading for denial in the way she spoke and he said, "He

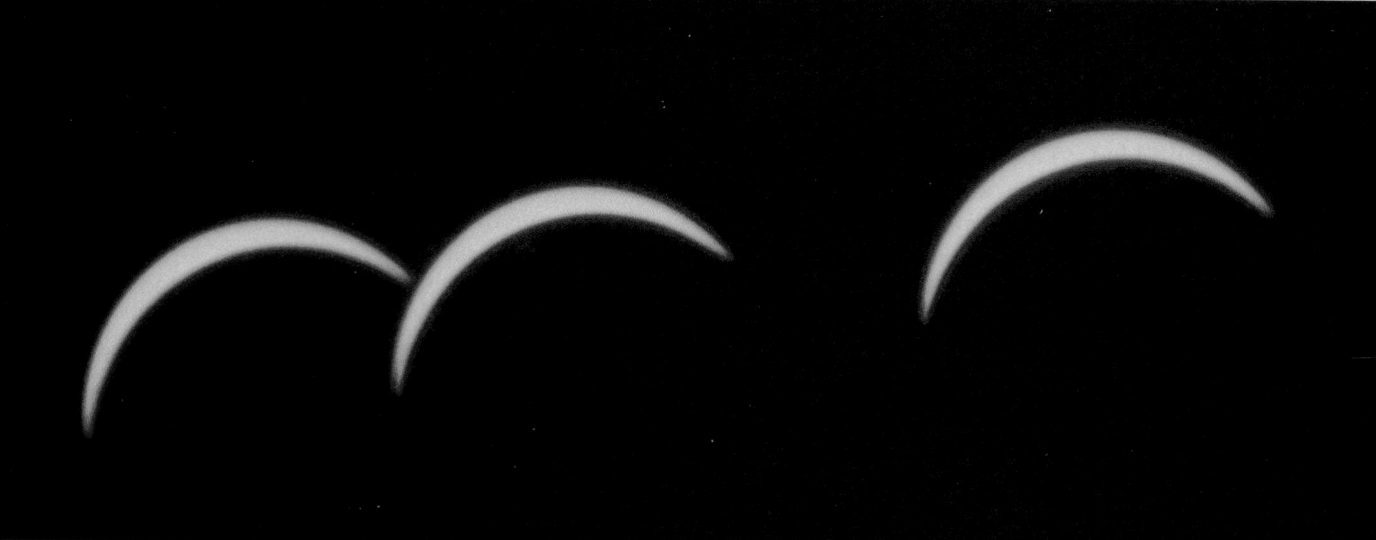

wouldn't want you to do that, to not wait for him."

"It's already coming dark where he is, isn't it? There will be all the long night before him, and Mama and Daddy don't know yet that I won't ever be coming back like I promised them I would. I've caused everyone I love to be hurt, haven't I? I didn't want to—I didn't intend to."

"It wasn't your fault," he said. "It wasn't your fault at all. They'll know that. They'll understand."

"At first I was so afraid to die that I was a coward and thought only of myself. Now I see how selfish I was. The terrible thing about dying like this is not that I'll be gone but that I'll never see them again; never be able to tell them that I didn't take them for granted; never be able to tell them I knew of the sacrifices they made to make my life happier, that I knew all the things they did for me and that I loved them so much more than I ever told them. I've never told them any of those things. You don't tell them such things when you're young and your life is all before you—you're so afraid of sounding sentimental and silly. But it's so different when you have to die—you wish you had told them while you could, and you wish you could tell them you're sorry for all the little mean things you ever did or said to them. You wish you could tell them that you didn't really mean to ever hurt their feelings and for them to only remember that you always loved them far more than you ever let them know."

"You don't have to tell them that," he said. "They will know—they've always known it."

"Are you sure?" she asked. "How can you be sure? My people are strangers to you."

"Wherever you go, human nature and human hearts are the same."

"And they will know what I want them to know—that I love them?"

"They've always known it, in a way far better than you could ever put in words for them."

"I keep remembering the things they did for me, and it's the little things they did that seem to be the most important to me, now. Like Gerry—he sent me a bracelet of fire rubies on my sixteenth birthday. It was beautiful—it must have cost him a month's pay. Yet I remember him more for what he did the night my kitten got run over in the street. I was only six years old and he held me in his arms and wiped away my tears and told me not to cry, that Flossy was gone for just a little while, for just long enough to get herself a new fur coat, and she would be on the foot of my bed the very next morning. I believed him and quit crying and went to sleep dreaming about my kitten coming back. When I woke up the next morning, there was Flossy on the foot of my bed in a brand-new white fur coat, just like he had said she would be. It wasn't until a long time later that Mama told me Gerry had got the pet-shop owner out of bed at four in the morning and, when the man got mad about it, Gerry told him he was either going to go down and sell him the white kitten right then or he'd break his neck."

"It's always the little things you remember people by, all the little things they did because they wanted to do them for you. You've done the same for Gerry and your father and mother; all kinds of things that you've forgotten about, but that they will never forget."

"I hope I have. I would like for them to remember me like that."

"They will."

"I wish——" She swallowed. "The way I'll die—I wish they wouldn't ever think of that. I've read how people look who die in space—their insides all ruptured and exploded and their lungs out between their teeth and then, a few seconds later, they're all dry and shapeless and horribly ugly. I don't want them to ever think of me as something dead and horrible like that."

"You're their own, their child and their sister. They could never think of you other than the way you would want them to, the way you looked the last time they saw you."

"I'm still afraid," she said. "I can't help it, but I don't want Gerry to know it. If he gets back in time, I'm going to act like I'm not afraid at all and——"

The signal buzzer interrupted her, quick and imperative.

"Gerry!" She came to her feet. "It's Gerry now!"

He spun the volume control knob and asked, "Gerry Cross?"

"Yes," her brother answered, an undertone of tenseness to his reply. "The bad news—what is it?"

She answered for him, standing close behind him and leaning down a little toward the communicator, her hand resting small and cold on his shoulder.

"Hello, Gerry." There was only a faint quaver to betray the careful casualness of her voice. "I wanted to see you——"

"Marilyn!" There was sudden and terrible

apprehension in the way he spoke her name. "What are you doing on that EDS?"

"I wanted to see you," she said again. "I wanted to see you, so I hid on this ship——"

"You *hid* on it?"

"I'm a stowaway. . . . I didn't know what it would mean——"

"Marilyn!" It was the cry of a man who calls, hopeless and desperate, to someone already and forever gone from him. "What have you done?"

"I . . . it's not——" Then her own composure broke and the cold little hand gripped his shoulder convulsively. "Don't, Gerry—I only wanted to see you; I didn't intend to hurt you. Please, Gerry, don't feel like that——"

Something warm and wet splashed on his wrist, and he slid out of the chair to help her into it and swing the microphone down to her level.

"Don't feel like that. Don't let me go knowing you feel like that——"

The sob she had tried to hold back choked in her throat, and her brother spoke to her. "Don't cry, Marilyn." His voice was suddenly deep and infinitely gentle, with all the pain held out of it. "Don't cry, Sis—you mustn't do that. It's all right, honey—everything is all right."

"I——" Her lower lip quivered and she bit into it. "I didn't want you to feel that way—I just wanted us to say goodbye, because I have to go in a minute."

"Sure—sure. That's the way it'll be, Sis. I didn't mean to sound the way I did." Then his voice changed to a tone of quick and urgent demand. "EDS—have you called the *Stardust*? Did you check with the computers?"

"I called the *Stardust* almost an hour ago. It can't turn back; there are no other cruisers within forty light-years, and there isn't enough fuel."

"Are you sure that the computers had the correct data—sure of everything?"

"Yes—do you think I could ever let it happen if I wasn't sure? I did everything I could do. If there was anything at all I could do now, I would do it."

"He tried to help me, Gerry." Her lower lip was no longer trembling and the short sleeves of her blouse were wet where she had dried her tears. "No one can help me and I'm not going to cry anymore and everything will be all right with you and Daddy and Mama, won't it?"

"Sure—sure it will. We'll make out fine."

Her brother's words were beginning to come in more faintly, and he turned the volume control to maximum. "He's going out of range," he said to her. "He'll be gone within another minute."

"You're fading out, Gerry," she said. "You're going out of range. I wanted to tell you—but I can't now. We must say goodbye so soon—but maybe I'll see you again. Maybe I'll come to you in your dreams with my hair in braids and crying because the kitten in my arms is dead; maybe I'll be the touch of a breeze that whispers to you as it goes by; maybe I'll be one of those gold-winged larks you told me about, singing my silly head off to you; maybe, at times, I'll be nothing you can see, but you will know I'm there beside you. Think of me like that, Gerry; always like that and not—the other way."

Dimmed to a whisper by the turning of Woden, the answer came back:

"Always like that, Marilyn—always like that and never any other way."

"Our time is up, Gerry—I have to go now. Good——" Her voice broke in midword and her mouth tried to twist into crying. She pressed her hand hard against it and when she spoke again the words came clear and true:

"Goodbye, Gerry."

Faint and ineffably poignant and tender, the last words came from the cold metal of the communicator:

"Goodbye, little sister . . ."

She sat motionless in the hush that followed, as though listening to the shadow-echoes of the words as they died away; then she turned away from the communicator, toward the air lock,

Words to Own

apprehension (ap'rē·hen'shən) *n.:* dread; fear of a future event.

ineffably (in·ef'ə·blē) *adv.:* indescribably; inexpressibly.

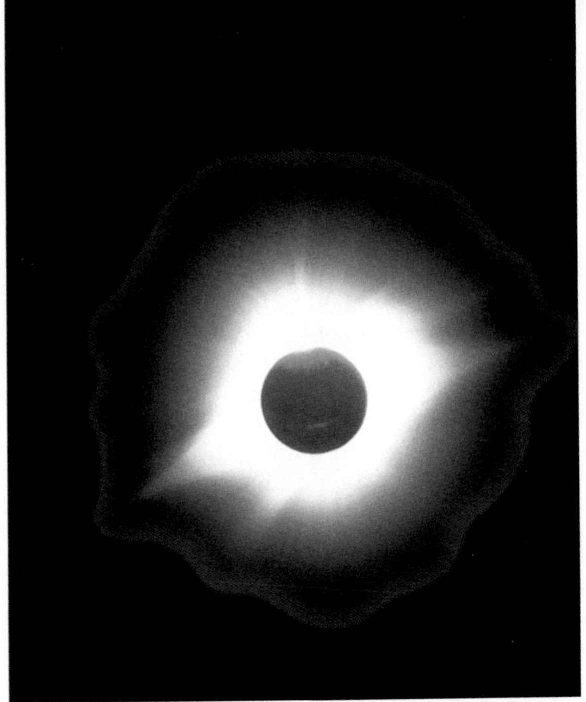

and he pulled down the black lever beside him. The inner door of the air lock slid swiftly open to reveal the bare little cell that was waiting for her, and she walked to it.

She walked with her head up and the brown curls brushing her shoulders, with the white sandals stepping as sure and steady as the fractional gravity would permit and the gilded buckles twinkling with little lights of blue and red and crystal. He let her walk alone and made no move to help her, knowing she would not want it that way. She stepped into the air lock and turned to face him, only the pulse in her throat to betray the wild beating of her heart.

"I'm ready," she said.

He pushed the lever up and the door slid its quick barrier between them, enclosing her in black and utter darkness for her last moments of life. It clicked as it locked in place and he jerked down the red lever. There was a slight waver of the ship as the air gushed from the lock, a vibration to the wall as though something had bumped the outer door in passing; then there was nothing and the ship was dropping true and steady again. He shoved the red lever back to close the door on the empty air lock and turned away, to walk to the pilot's chair with the slow steps of a man old and weary.

Back in the pilot's chair he pressed the signal button of the normal-space transmitter. There was no response; he had expected none. Her brother would have to wait through the night until the turning of Woden permitted contact through Group One.

It was not yet time to resume deceleration, and he waited while the ship dropped endlessly downward with him and the drives purred softly. He saw that the white hand of the supply-closet temperature gauge was on zero. A cold equation had been balanced and he was alone on the ship. Something shapeless and ugly was hurrying ahead of him, going to Woden, where her brother was waiting through the night, but the empty ship still lived for a little while with the presence of the girl who had not known about the forces that killed with neither hatred nor malice. It seemed, almost, that she still sat, small and bewildered and frightened, on the metal box beside him, her words echoing hauntingly clear in the void she had left behind her:

I didn't do anything to die for. . . . I didn't do anything. . . .

MEET THE WRITER

A Sci-Fi Pioneer

Tom Godwin (1915–1980) lived for many years in various small towns in the Mojave Desert—a harsh environment that the average urbanite or suburbanite might consider as alien as outer space. Godwin began publishing science-fiction stories in magazines in the early 1950s. He also published three novels: *The Survivors; The Space Barbarians,* which describes warfare on the planet Ragnarok; and *Beyond Another Sun.* His best-known work by far, however, is "The Cold Equations."

Connections AN EDITORIAL

Lunar Legacy

When Neil Armstrong set foot on the moon twenty-five years ago today, the nation responded ecstatically. It was not just that American astronauts had beaten Soviet cosmonauts to the moon in the Cold War's most visible symbolic struggle.° Their feat implied that the same combination of heroism, determination, technical wizardry, and managerial genius would soon conquer other worlds and a host of earthly ills as well.

But how fast the dream dissipated! The space agency that put astronauts on the moon later blew up the shuttle Challenger and gained a reputation for incompetence rather than omnipotence. Space budgets shriveled. NASA lowered its sights. Instead of venturing onward to Mars, astronauts now cling close to home, working only in low earth orbit. It is as if, critics say, Columbus's epic voyage to the New World had been followed with boat trips around the harbor.

The space agency's fall from grace should not be exaggerated. The mythology of the lunar achievement makes it easy to forget that three astronauts were incinerated in a fire on the launch pad and three others almost lost in an explosion on the way to the moon. But in that race for national supremacy, losses were tolerated that today might prove crippling.

Historians in coming centuries will have to judge whether the moon landing was a "giant leap for mankind," as Mr. Armstrong proclaimed on taking his first step, or merely the most extreme and daring example of an exploit on the order of climbing Mount Everest or reaching the poles. As of now, it has not led to much—a few follow-up landings, a momentary reputation as the world's top technical power, and some genuine scientific gains in determining the moon's age, composition, and likely origin. But more might have been learned at a fraction of the cost by sending an armada of automated devices.

The moon program, born of Cold War desperation, had nowhere to go after its success. Once the Soviets had been vanquished, why run another lap? In subsequent years, space operations have proved far more expensive and far less useful than enthusiasts once imagined, thus difficult to justify without an overriding political goal.

In the end it was the sheer strangeness of the experience—man on the moon!—that caused it to endure in memory with a romance that cannot quite be blown away by hardheaded analysis. Perhaps the most memorable image to emerge from the moon program was that of astronauts bobbing around the lunar surface or planting an American flag.

But a far more important image was the sight of the Earth seen from afar—a radiant blue-and-white sphere, beautiful and vulnerable, shimmering against the dark background of space. The lunar landing that some thought would launch mankind on its way as a spacefaring species instead highlighted the fragility and isolation of home.

—from *The New York Times*, July 20, 1994

° *The Cold War was the state of hostility and the struggle for global dominance between the United States and the Soviet Union. It lasted roughly from the end of World War II, in 1945, until the collapse of the Soviet Union, in 1991. The race to land a person on the moon was one aspect of the Cold War.*

Apollo 11 (7/20/69). Edwin "Buzz" Aldrin, on lunar surface, next to solar-wind composition.

Making Meanings

First Thoughts

1. How did you think the story would end? Why?

Reading Check

Summarize the main events of this story in a paragraph. Open with a note describing the **setting,** and then tell who the **characters** are and what their **problem** is. Be sure to explain how the problem is resolved.

Shaping Interpretations

2. What would you say is the source of this story's **suspense**—that is, what questions keep you turning the pages? Refer to the notes you took while reading.
3. This story **contrasts** life on Earth with life on the space frontier. In what important ways are these **settings** different? Do you find Godwin's space frontier believable? Why or why not?
4. What do you think is the most important passage in this story, and why?
5. Find the passage toward the middle of the story that explains its **title.** What are the "cold equations"? What other **images** of coldness can you find in the story?
6. The title of the story seems to imply that the more technology influences our lives, the less room there is for human choice and emotions. How does the story illustrate that idea? Do you agree, or not? Why?

Connecting with the Text

7. How believable are Marilyn's choice to stow away and her later responses to her fate? If you were in her situation, how do you think you would react? Be sure to check your Quickwrite notes.

Extending the Text

8. "The Cold Equations" was written in 1954, at a time when technology was far less advanced than it is now. Today we are living in what, to Tom Godwin in 1954, was the future (though not as far in the future as the story is set). Do you think the technological "future" is turning out to be as cold and harsh as Godwin expected? Explain your answer with specific examples from your own experience. You might organize your thoughts in a chart like this:

What Godwin Predicted	Today's Reality

Challenging the Text

9. The story says on page 11 that Barton would have immediately carried out the regulation to eject the stowaway if it had been a man. What do you think of this attitude?

CHOICES: Building Your Portfolio

Writer's Notebook

1. Collecting Ideas for a Persuasive Essay

Finding a topic. This story may have made you think about problems or issues such as the role of technology in our lives or the conflicts involved in obeying difficult rules. With a partner or small group, brainstorm a list of school, local, national, or world problems. These should be debatable issues or situations that you think need fixing. On your list, check off the issues that you've had some personal experience with. You may have worked in a day care center, for example, or helped in a local political campaign. (Save your list for use with the Writer's Workshop on p. 85.)

WORK IN PROGRESS

Issues for Persuasive Essay

Technology—good or bad?
✓ *Bikes for borrowing*
Teenage violence
Helping the elderly
✓ *Laws for teenage drivers*
✓ *Medical care for elderly—hard choices (my grandfather)*
stereotyping

Creative Writing

2. Changing the Ending

You are a researcher in the year 2196. You discover some pages of an ancient textbook containing a short story called "The Cold Equations." However, the final pages are missing. The last bit of text you can read is Marilyn's "I'm ready" on page 27. Write a plausible resolution for the story that is different from the present ending. Suppose you are an optimistic researcher. Is it possible to find a happy ending?

Evaluating a Story

3. Letter to the Editor

For "The Cold Equations" to succeed, the writer must convince us, first, that Marilyn could actually have been able to stow away on the ship, and, second, that Barton had no choice but to eject her. Is the story airtight, or are there leaks in it? Suppose you are reading this story in a magazine, and you want to write a letter to the editor, commenting on its credibility. Write the letter, including specific details to support your evaluation. You might find the notes you took while reading useful.

Science Research/ Critical Thinking

4. Godwin's Science

Godwin imagines a technological future in which space travel is as common as airplane travel is today. Yet he imagines that the EDS will not have the smallest amount of extra fuel for unforeseen emergencies. Is this realistic? Go back to the text to find other aspects of Godwin's technological future. Formulate any questions you have. The notes you took while reading may help. Then, do some research to determine how scientifically accurate Godwin is. You might check the library or up-to-date databases or the Internet. Present your results to the class.

Current Events/ Speaking

5. A Political Decision

Read the editorial about the NASA space program (see *Connections* on page 28), and prepare a two-minute speech offering your view of the value of space exploration. Outline your talk, limiting it to two or three key ideas. At the end, ask your audience for feedback. How compelling were your opinions and your presentation?

GRAMMAR LINK **MINI-LESSON**

Language Handbook HELP

See Agreement of Subject and Verb, pages 1022–1024.

Technology HELP

See Language Workshop CD-ROM. *Key word entry: subject-verb agreement.*

They Always Agree—Subject and Verb

Probably the most common error people make in their writing and speaking has to do with subject-verb agreement. The rule is simple: **Singular subjects take singular verbs; plural subjects take plural verbs.** The trick is to find the subject and determine its **number**.

1. The number of the subject is not changed by a phrase following the subject.

   EXAMPLE:

   The dials in the EDS control room were flashing.

2. Singular subjects joined by *or* or *nor* take a singular verb.

   EXAMPLE:

   Neither Barton nor his supervisor wants to carry out the rules.

3. When a singular subject and a plural subject are joined by *or* or *nor,* the verb agrees with the subject nearer the verb.

   EXAMPLE:

   Neither Barton nor his supervisors want to eject the girl.

Try It Out

➤ Identify the subjects below and determine their number. Then decide which verb choice is correct.

1. Marilyn or her brother is/are going to die.
2. Neither Barton nor his supervisors was/were willing to make an exception to the rule.
3. The men on the EDS team is/are obliged to eject Marilyn.

➤ When you proofread your writing, always check the subject of each sentence, and be sure the verb agrees with it in number. There's only one situation in which you can leave such errors uncorrected: when you're writing dialogue for a character who's careless about the rules.

VOCABULARY **HOW TO OWN A WORD**

WORD BANK

inured
increments
recoiled
paramount
annihilate
irrevocable
immutable
ponderous
apprehension
ineffably

Meet the Glossary and Check a Dictionary

A **glossary** is a mini-dictionary containing specialized vocabulary that is often included at the back of a textbook. (Your science and history textbooks probably have glossaries.) Become familiar with the glossary in this book (see pages 1065–1073). There you'll find the **pronunciation, part of speech,** and **definition** for each Word to Own as it is used in the selection. Now check a **dictionary** to see what additional information you can discover about each word in the Word Bank. Does the word have other meanings besides those listed in the glossary? Can the word function as a different part of speech? Does the dictionary list any **synonyms** (words that have the same meaning)? Compile all the information you gather, and write an example sentence using each word in the Word Bank.

Elements of Literature

PLOT: The Story's Framework *by* John Leggett

"What Happened?"

This cartoon is funny, but it actually shows the "nuts and bolts" plot elements of any story. **Plot** is a series of related events—it's what happens between "Once upon a time" and "happily ever after." The plot of a story includes characters who experience some problem or conflict (maybe a dragon), which is solved in some way (maybe by a Superman). A complete story, of course, fills in the interesting details. Let's see how in another example.

A Character with a Problem

Once upon a time, there was a rock star who had been changed into an ugly, deformed wombat by an irate parent.

We've just stated the **basic situation** of a story. We have a main character, and he has a problem.

The wombat, still human behind his claws and fur, was desperately lonely in his mansion. People ran off screaming at the sight of him. Would anyone ever love him?

We've just learned the single most important fact about our character's inner life. He wants love. As you will see, his struggle to win someone's love despite his claws and fur will be the central **conflict** of the story. This conflict is **external** because it involves the beast and another person. The conflict also becomes **internal** as the beast struggles to adjust to people's understandable reactions to his appearance.

The Plot Thickens: Complications

One dark and stormy night, there came a knock at the mansion door. It was a shoehorn salesman, drenched and lost, seeking shelter.

A new factor has been added, which gives the main character a new problem to deal with. This is a **complication**. If it weren't for the beast's worry that the salesman will go hysterical when he sees his host's furry face, the visitor's arrival wouldn't be a problem at all. The beast could simply let him in for the night and let him out the next morning.

Now the beast must deal with a whole chain of

complications triggered by the visitor's arrival. They include

- the arrival of the salesman's beautiful daughter
- the daughter's terror at the sight of the huge furry wombat
- the daughter's illness, which is cured by the beast, an expert in herbal medicine
- the beast's growing love for the daughter
- the attempts of nearby villagers to free the daughter from the beast

Complications tend to come in a series. Each event is usually linked to what happened before and what happens afterward by bonds of cause and effect. The reader's excitement builds incident by incident as the plot thickens with complications.

The High Point: The Climax

Eventually, the high point of the plot is reached. In our story this might happen when the villagers break down the mansion's doors and try to rescue the daughter (who at this point realizes she loves the wombat for his kind heart and doesn't want to be rescued, which is another complication). The young woman's change of heart is the **climax** of the plot, the most exciting moment, when something happens that will determine the outcome of the conflict. After the climactic moment comes the **resolution,** when the story is closed.

The now-repentant villagers cheered the wedding of the rock star and his bride. From then on, the shoehorn salesman and the couple lived happily ever after, touring the world and occasionally giving free concerts on the village green.

> "What happens next?" is the single most important question readers ask about stories.

"Happily Ever After," Sort Of

A good resolution solves the conflict, but especially in modern fiction, it doesn't necessarily solve everything in the characters' lives. The conclusion of a story may even open up new questions, prolonging our pleasure by giving us something to think, talk, and write about after we close the book.

Although "they lived happily ever after" is very gratifying, such an ending can sound unrealistic, except in a fairy tale. A more modern resolution to our story would suggest "they lived happily ever after, sort of" and hint at what's behind the "sort of."

The Most Important Question in Fiction

Not every story depends on a full-fledged plot that marches along as methodically as our example does. Many modern short stories focus not so much on plot as on revelation of character. Such stories often drop us right into the middle of the action at the start.

Even in modern fiction, however, the question "What happens next?" is the single most important question readers ask about stories—and no matter how the world changes or what new media are invented, people will never stop asking it: "And then what happens? And then? And then. . . ?"

Before You Read

THE BASS, THE RIVER, AND SHEILA MANT

Make the Connection

Fish, or Cut Bait!

This may be a story about a search for love (or a quest for a fish). Consider the problems of a young man who's searching for both—and who will always think about the one that got away.

Quickwrite

Think back to some time when you had to give up one thing for something else. Write down what happened. Did you make the right choice? Do you have some regrets?

Elements of Literature

Conflict Inside and Out

A showdown with another person or a struggle with nature puts us in opposition to something outside of ourselves. That **external conflict** is often the heart of adventure stories or mysteries. The most difficult struggles, however, may be those within us. The **internal conflict** between two sides of our personalities, between competing desires, forces us to choose, and that choice can be agonizing. In this story, a boy is caught up in both external and internal conflicts—watch to see how he deals with them.

In an **external conflict,** a character struggles against an outside force—nature, another person, a machine, or even a whole society. An **internal conflict** takes place when a character struggles mentally to resolve opposing needs, desires, or emotions.

For more on Conflict, see pages 32–33 and the Handbook of Literary Terms.

Reading Skills and Strategies

Understanding Cause and Effect

A **cause** is *why* something happens. An **effect** is the *result* of some event or action. As you read this story, think about the causes behind the narrator's behavior. Think about the effects of the girl's words and actions. Tuning in to cause-and-effect relationships—the "why's" between one moment and the next—can help you understand what happens in a plot, and why it happens.

go.hrw.com

LEO 10-1

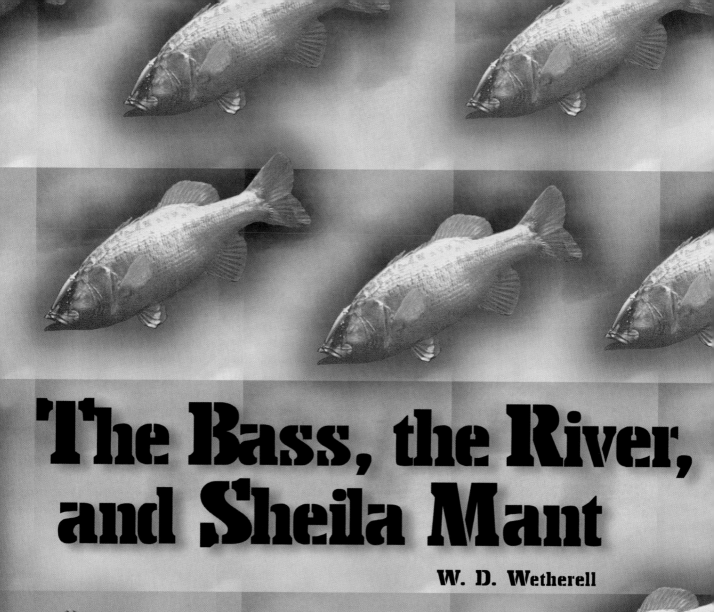

The Bass, the River, and Sheila Mant

W. D. Wetherell

I never made the same mistake again.

There was a summer in my life when the only creature that seemed lovelier to me than a largemouth bass was Sheila Mant. I was fourteen. The Mants had rented the cottage next to ours on the river; with their parties, their frantic games of softball, their constant comings and goings, they appeared to me denizens of a brilliant existence. "Too noisy by half," my mother quickly decided, but I would have given anything to be invited to one of their parties, and when my parents went to bed I would sneak through the woods to their hedge and stare enchanted at the candlelit swirl of white dresses and bright, paisley skirts.

Sheila was the middle daughter—at seventeen, all but out of reach. She would spend her days sunbathing on a float my Uncle Sierbert had moored in their cove, and before July was over I had learned all her moods. If she lay flat on the diving board with her hand trailing idly in the water, she was pensive, not to be disturbed. On her side, her head propped up by her arm, she was observant, considering those around her with a look that seemed queenly and severe. Sitting up, arms tucked around her long, suntanned legs, she was approachable, but barely, and it was only in those glorious moments when she stretched herself prior to entering the water that her various suitors found the courage to come near.

These were many. The Dartmouth heavyweight crew would scull[1] by her house on their way upriver, and I think all eight of them must have been in love with her at various times during the summer; the coxswain[2] would curse them through his megaphone, but without effect—there was always a pause in their pace when they passed Sheila's float. I suppose to these jaded twenty-year-olds she seemed the incarnation of innocence and youth, while to me she appeared unutterably suave, the epitome[3] of sophistication. I was on the swim team at school, and to win her attention would do endless laps between my house and the Vermont shore, hoping she would notice the beauty of my flutter kick, the power of my crawl. Finishing, I would boost myself up onto our dock and glance casually over toward her, but she was never watching, and the miraculous day she was, I immediately climbed the diving board and did my best tuck and a half for her and continued diving until she had left and the sun went down and my longing was like a madness and I couldn't stop.

It was late August by the time I got up the nerve to ask her out. The tortured will-I's, won't-I's, the agonized indecision over what to say, the false starts toward her house and embarrassed retreats—the details of these have been seared from my memory, and the only part I remember clearly is emerging from the woods toward dusk while they were playing softball on their lawn, as bashful and frightened as a unicorn.

Sheila was stationed halfway between first and second, well outside the infield. She didn't seem surprised to see me—as a matter of fact, she didn't seem to see me at all.

"If you're playing second base, you should move closer," I said.

She turned—I took the full brunt of her long red hair and well-spaced freckles.

"I'm playing outfield," she said, "I don't like the responsibility of having a base."

"Yeah, I can understand that," I said, though I couldn't. "There's a band in Dixford tomorrow night at nine. Want to go?"

One of her brothers sent the ball sailing over the left-fielder's head; she stood and watched it disappear toward the river.

"You have a car?" she said, without looking up.

I played my master stroke. "We'll go by canoe."

I spent all of the following day polishing it. I turned it upside down on our lawn and rubbed

1. **scull** (skəl): row, as in a rowboat.
2. **coxswain** (käk′sən): person steering a racing shell and calling out the rhythm of the strokes for the crew.
3. **epitome** (ē·pit′ə·mē): embodiment; one that is representative of a type or class.

WORDS TO OWN

denizens (den′ə·zənz) *n.:* inhabitants or occupants.
pensive (pen′siv) *adj.:* dreamily thoughtful.

every inch with Brillo, hosing off the dirt, wiping it with chamois[4] until it gleamed as bright as aluminum ever gleamed. About five, I slid it into the water, arranging cushions near the bow so Sheila could lean on them if she was in one of her pensive moods, propping up my father's transistor radio by the middle thwart[5] so we could have music when we came back. Automatically, without thinking about it, I mounted my Mitchell reel on my Pfleuger spinning rod and stuck it in the stern.

I say automatically, because I never went anywhere that summer without a fishing rod. When I wasn't swimming laps to impress Sheila, I was back in our driveway practicing casts, and when I wasn't practicing casts, I was tying the line to Tosca, our springer spaniel, to test the reel's drag, and when I wasn't doing any of those things, I was fishing the river for bass.

Too nervous to sit at home, I got in the canoe early and started paddling in a huge circle that would get me to Sheila's dock around eight. As automatically as I brought along my rod, I tied on a big Rapala plug, let it down into the water, let out some line, and immediately forgot all about it.

It was already dark by the time I glided up to the Mants' dock. Even by day the river was quiet, most of the summer people preferring Sunapee or one of the other nearby lakes, and at night it was a solitude difficult to believe, a corridor of hidden life that ran between banks like a tunnel. Even the stars were part of it. They weren't as sharp anywhere else; they seemed to have chosen the river as a guide on their slow wheel toward morning, and in the course of the summer's fishing, I had learned all their names.

I was there ten minutes before Sheila appeared. I heard the slam of their screen door first, then saw her in the spotlight as she came slowly down the path. As beautiful as she was on the float, she was even lovelier now—her white dress went perfectly with her hair, and complimented her figure even more than her swimsuit.

4. **chamois** (sham′ē): soft leather used for polishing.
5. **middle thwart:** brace across the middle of a canoe.

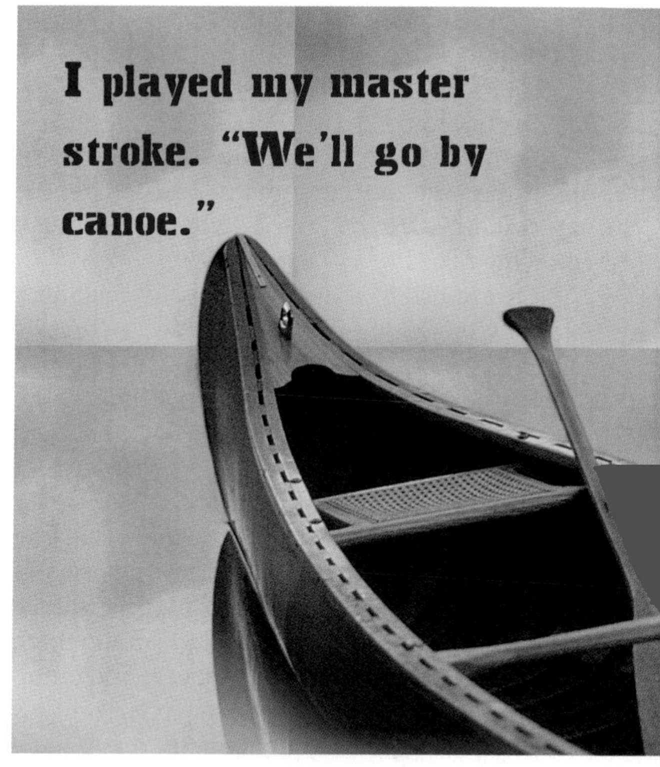
I played my master stroke. "We'll go by canoe."

It was her face that bothered me. It had on its delightful fullness a very dubious expression.

"Look," she said. "I can get Dad's car."

"It's faster this way," I lied. "Parking's tense up there. Hey, it's safe. I won't tip it or anything."

She let herself down reluctantly into the bow. I was glad she wasn't facing me. When her eyes were on me, I felt like diving in the river again from agony and joy.

I pried the canoe away from the dock and started paddling upstream. There was an extra paddle in the bow, but Sheila made no move to pick it up. She took her shoes off and dangled her feet over the side.

Ten minutes went by.

"What kind of band?" she said.

"It's sort of like folk music. You'll like it."

"Eric Caswell's going to be there. He strokes number four."

"No kidding?" I said. I had no idea whom she meant.

WORDS TO OWN

dubious (do͞o′bē · əs) *adj.:* doubtful; not sure.

"What's that sound?" she said, pointing toward shore.

"Bass. That splashing sound?"

"Over there."

"Yeah, bass. They come into the shallows at night to chase frogs and moths and things. Big largemouths. *Micropterus salmoides,"*[6] I added, showing off.

"I think fishing's dumb," she said, making a face. "I mean, it's boring and all. Definitely dumb."

Now I have spent a great deal of time in the years since wondering why Sheila Mant should come down so hard on fishing. Was her father a fisherman? Her antipathy toward fishing nothing more than normal filial rebellion? Had she tried it once? A messy encounter with worms? It doesn't matter. What does is that at that fragile moment in time I would have given anything not to appear dumb in Sheila's severe and unforgiving eyes.

She hadn't seen my equipment yet. What I *should* have done, of course, was push the canoe in closer to shore and carefully slide the rod into some branches where I could pick it up again in the morning. Failing that, I could have surreptitiously dumped the whole outfit overboard, written off the forty or so dollars as love's tribute. What I actually *did* do was gently lean forward, and slowly, ever so slowly, push the rod back through my legs toward the stern where it would be less conspicuous.

6. ***Micropterus salmoides:*** the scientific name for a largemouth bass.

"I think fishing's dumb," she said, making a face. "I mean, it's boring and all. Definitely dumb."

It must have been just exactly what the bass was waiting for. Fish will trail a lure sometimes, trying to make up their mind whether or not to attack, and the slight pause in the plug's speed caused by my adjustment was tantalizing enough to overcome the bass's inhibitions. My rod, safely out of sight at last, bent double. The line, tightly coiled, peeled off the spool with the shrill, tearing zip of a high-speed drill.

Four things occurred to me at once. One, that it was a bass. Two, that it was a big bass. Three, that it was the biggest bass I had ever hooked. Four, that Sheila Mant must not know.

"What was that?" she said, turning half around.

"Uh, what was what?"

"That buzzing noise."

"Bats."

She shuddered, quickly drew her feet back into the canoe. Every instinct I had told me to pick up the rod and strike back at the bass, but there was no need to—it was already solidly hooked. Downstream, an awesome distance downstream, it jumped clear of the water, landing with a concussion heavy enough to ripple the entire river. For a moment, I thought it was gone, but then the rod was bending again, the tip dancing into the water. Slowly, not making

Words to Own

antipathy (an·ti′pə·thē) *n.:* feeling of hatred; powerful and deep dislike.

filial (fil′ē·əl) *adj.:* pertaining to or due from a son or a daughter.

surreptitiously (sur′əp·tish′əs·lē) *adv.:* stealthily; sneakily.

conspicuous (kən·spik′yo͞o·əs) *adj.:* obvious or easy to see.

concussion (kən·kush′ən) *n.:* powerful shock or impact.

any motion that might alert Sheila, I reached down to tighten the drag.

While all this was going on, Sheila had begun talking, and it was a few minutes before I was able to catch up with her train of thought.

"I went to a party there. These fraternity men. Katherine says I could get in there if I wanted. I'm thinking more of UVM or Bennington.[7] Somewhere I can ski."

The bass was slanting toward the rocks on the New Hampshire side by the ruins of Donaldson's boathouse. It had to be an old bass—a young one probably wouldn't have known the rocks were there. I brought the canoe back into the middle of the river, hoping to head it off.

"That's neat," I mumbled. "Skiing. Yeah, I can see that."

"Eric said I have the figure to model, but I thought I should get an education first. I mean, it might be a while before I get started and all. I was thinking of getting my hair styled, more swept back? I mean, Ann-Margret?[8] Like hers, only shorter."

She hesitated. "Are we going backward?"

We were. I had managed to keep the bass in the middle of the river away from the rocks, but it had plenty of room there, and for the first time a chance to exert its full strength. I quickly computed the weight necessary to draw a fully loaded canoe backward—the thought of it made me feel faint.

"It's just the current," I said hoarsely. "No sweat or anything."

I dug in deeper with my paddle. Reassured, Sheila began talking about something else, but all my attention was taken up now with the fish. I could feel its desperation as the water grew shallower. I could sense the extra strain on the line, the frantic way it cut back and forth in the water. I could visualize what it looked like—the gape of its mouth, the flared gills and thick, vertical tail. The bass couldn't have encountered many forces in its long life that it wasn't capable of handling, and the unrelenting tug at its mouth must have been a source of great puzzlement and mounting panic.

Me, I had problems of my own. To get to Dixford, I had to paddle up a sluggish stream that came into the river beneath a covered bridge. There was a shallow sandbar at the mouth of this stream—weeds on one side, rocks on the other. Without doubt, this is where I would lose the fish.

"I have to be careful with my complexion. I tan, but in segments. I can't figure out if it's even worth it. I wouldn't even do it probably. I saw Jackie Kennedy[9] in Boston, and she wasn't tan at all."

Taking a deep breath, I paddled as hard as I could for the middle, deepest part of the bar. I could have threaded the eye of a needle with the canoe, but the pull on the stern threw me off, and I overcompensated—the canoe veered left and scraped bottom. I pushed the paddle down and shoved. A moment of hesitation . . . a moment more. . . . The canoe shot clear into the deeper water of the stream. I immediately looked down at the rod. It was bent in the same tight arc—miraculously, the bass was still on.

The moon was out now. It was low and full enough that its beam shone directly on Sheila there ahead of me in the canoe, washing her in a creamy, luminous glow. I could see the lithe, easy shape of her figure. I could see the way her hair curled down off her shoulders, the proud, alert tilt of her head, and all these things were as a tug on my heart. Not just Sheila, but the aura she carried about her of parties and casual touchings and grace. Behind me, I could feel the strain of the bass, steadier now, growing weaker, and this was another tug on my heart, not just the bass but the beat of the river and the slant of the stars and the smell of the night, until finally it seemed I would be torn apart between longings, split in half. Twenty yards

7. **UVM or Bennington:** University of Vermont or Bennington College, Bennington, Vermont.

8. **Ann-Margret** (1941–): movie star, very popular at the time of this story.

9. **Jackie Kennedy** (1929–1994): First Lady during the administration of President John F. Kennedy; greatly admired by the public for her dignity and sense of style.

WORDS TO OWN

luminous (lo͞o • mə′nəs) *adj.:* glowing; giving off light.

ahead of us was the road, and once I pulled the canoe up on shore, the bass would be gone, irretrievably gone. If instead I stood up, grabbed the rod, and started pumping, I would have it—as tired as the bass was, there was no chance it could get away. I reached down for the rod, hesitated, looked up to where Sheila was stretching herself lazily toward the sky, her small breasts rising beneath the soft fabric of her dress, and the tug was too much for me, and quicker than it takes to write down, I pulled a penknife from my pocket and cut the line in half.

With a sick, nauseous feeling in my stomach, I saw the rod unbend.

"My legs are sore," Sheila whined. "Are we there yet?"

Through a superhuman effort of self-control, I was able to beach the canoe and help Sheila off. The rest of the night is much foggier. We walked to the fair—there was the smell of popcorn, the sound of guitars. I may have danced once or twice with her, but all I really remember is her coming over to me once the music was done to explain that she would be going home in Eric Caswell's Corvette.

"Okay," I mumbled.

For the first time that night she looked at me, really looked at me.

"You're a funny kid, you know that?"

Funny. Different. Dreamy. Odd. How many times was I to hear that in the years to come, all spoken with the same quizzical, half-accusatory tone Sheila used then. Poor Sheila! Before the month was over, the spell she cast over me was gone, but the memory of that lost bass haunted me all summer and haunts me still. There would be other Sheila Mants in my life, other fish, and though I came close once or twice, it was these secret, hidden tuggings in the night that claimed me, and I never made the same mistake again.

WORDS TO OWN

quizzical (kwiz′i·kəl) *adj.:* puzzled; questioning.

MEET THE WRITER

An Eye for Detail

W. D. Wetherell (1948–) lives in New Hampshire. He was born in Mineola, New York, and earned a bachelor's degree at Hofstra University, on Long Island. Like many writers, he has worked at various jobs—he has been a magazine editor, a movie extra, a teacher, a journalist, and a tour guide. Wetherell's works have won numerous awards, including the O. Henry Award, the Drue Heinz Literature Prize, and a fellowship in fiction from the National Endowment for the Arts. "The Bass, the River, and Sheila Mant" won the 1983 PEN Syndicated Fiction Prize. After reading this story, you won't be surprised to learn that Wetherell has also written essays about nature and fishing.

In one essay, he relates a "fish story" with an ending quite different from the one you just read. In the Pacific Northwest, his wife asked him to take a photograph of her and the fish she had caught.

"And I did, and as I focused the lens, the fog lifted, and behind her I saw the snowbanks and glacier and cliffs that framed the pond, revealing themselves only now when the moment was perfect. I held the camera steady until the beauty of the water and the woman and the trout came together, then—the moment captured—I crossed over the logs and took my wife by the hand."

MAKING MEANINGS

First Thoughts

1. What choice would *you* have made if you had been this narrator?

Shaping Interpretations

2. How does the story's **title** suggest all the narrator's **external** and **internal conflicts**? What do you think of the title?
3. What do you think is the story's **climax**?
4. What mistake has the narrator never repeated? What are the "secret, hidden tuggings in the night" that he mentions?

Reading Check

Make a cause-and-effect list of the **main events** in this story. The first and last events are listed:

Narrator asks Sheila out.

↓

Sheila says he's a funny kid.

Challenging the Text

5. A reader objects to the character of Sheila Mant, saying she is portrayed as a stereotypical "airhead." How would you respond?
6. Another reader says the boy isn't believable. How would you respond?

CHOICES: Building Your Portfolio

Writer's Notebook

1. Collecting Ideas for a Persuasive Essay

WORK IN PROGRESS

Using an experience. Look back at the issues you listed in your Writer's Notebook for the exercise on page 30. Zero in now on a specific incident related to one of those issues or to another issue of interest to you. Perhaps this story made you think of issues involving dating, or even stereotyping. Jot down all the details you can recall about your experience. Keep your notes for possible use in the Writer's Workshop on page 85.

Personal Narrative

2. A Choice Effect

Use the experience you wrote about in your Quickwrite as the basis for a narrative about your own experience making a choice. (If you wish, disguise the names in your story.) Tell what you decided, what happened as a result, what you did next, and what the final effect was. Will your narrative be funny, or serious?

Evaluating a Story

3. Thumbs Up? Thumbs Down?

In a review that might be published in a school magazine, tell whether you would recommend this story to other students. Rate the story on a scale from zero (worst) to ten (best). Give at least three reasons for your rating. Think about the believability of the characters and the plot, the story's message, and the story's language.

Language Link MINI-LESSON

See Me, Hear Me—Using Imagery

Handbook of Literary Terms HELP

See Imagery.

An **image** describes something so that we think we can **see, smell, taste, touch,** or **hear** it. Below are three general statements that W. D. Wetherell *could* have used in "The Bass, the River, and Sheila Mant." Following each one is the sentence the author actually wrote. Notice how Wetherell's imagery (underscored) makes each statement come alive.

1. I would look at the dancers moving in the candlelight.

   Wetherell: "I would . . . stare enchanted at the candlelit swirl of white dresses and bright, paisley skirts."

2. The stars seemed to follow the river as morning approached.

   Wetherell: "They [the stars] seemed to have chosen the river as a guide on their slow wheel toward morning."

3. The line came off the spool with a snap.

   Wetherell: "The line, tightly coiled, peeled off the spool with the shrill, tearing zip of a high-speed drill."

Try It Out

1. Find at least four other passages in this story where the writer uses imagery to help you see, hear, smell, taste, or even feel something.
2. Write a detailed description of the mental picture you formed after reading each of Wetherell's passages. Use words that are different from his. Share your mental pictures with your classmates.

A tip for writers: Imagery is a key element in any writing. When you revise your writing, try to bring clarity and vividness to it by adding images that evoke color, sound, taste, smell, or tactile sensations. Remember that imagery is used not only in fiction and poetry but also in historical and scientific writings.

Vocabulary HOW TO OWN A WORD

Word Bank

denizens
pensive
dubious
antipathy
filial
surreptitiously
conspicuous
concussion
luminous
quizzical

Vocabulary Resource File

By now, you've studied a number of words. You might want to create a Vocabulary Resource File—something you can refer to when you're writing and at a loss for words. Put each entry on an index card. Note the word, its definition, and two or three sentences that show how the word can be used. Make out a card for each word in this Word Bank. The first one is done for you. (The words could also be filed on a computer.)

denizens (noun)

Definition: inhabitants or occupants

Examples:

Whales and octopuses are denizens of the deep.

The rock star entertained the denizens of the discothèque.

My father, mother, brother, and I are the denizens of my house.

Note: A denizen is not a monster. That's what I always thought. It has a monsterlike sound—like a dragon or dinosaur.

Before You Read

The Book of Sand

Make the Connection

What's Real?

We take for granted that reality is dependable—that gravity will continue to keep us from floating away, that time always moves forward, that an object can exist in only one place at a time. However, what if one of our dependable realities suddenly changed? Jorge Luis Borges loved to play with puzzles and reality. "The Book of Sand," like much of his work, invites you to join in his game.

Quickwrite

Jot down at least two more dependable realities of daily life—things we take for granted, that we expect will never change. Circle one, and briefly describe what you imagine the world would be like if that reality no longer existed, or shifted slightly.

go.hrw.com
LEO 10-1

Elements of Literature

Resolution: So, How Does It End?

In years past, stories were expected to provide us with neat **resolutions** to all their **conflicts**. In these stories, we end up knowing exactly what happens to all the main characters and how the various mysteries and difficulties are untangled. (In French, the resolution of a story is called the *dénouement*, which means "untying of the knot.")

In contrast, many modern stories end right in the midst of the action, and some end by opening up new questions for the reader to consider. Readers who dislike these endings complain that they are "left hanging," but others enjoy the challenge of figuring out for themselves what happens. After all, life itself hardly ever has neat endings.

> The **resolution** comes at the end of a story and reveals the characters' final situation. In modern stories the resolution is often inconclusive or omitted altogether.
>
> *For more on Plot, see pages 32–33 and the Handbook of Literary Terms.*

Reading Skills and Strategies

Making Predictions: Guessing Ahead

Part of the pleasure of reading comes from making predictions about what will happen next. A **prediction** is a type of inference, a guess based on evidence. In a story that presents a mystery or puzzle, we read carefully, looking for clues. We base our predictions on the characters and their situations and on our own experiences and knowledge about life. As a story unfolds, we may adjust our predictions to fit new events and information. Sometimes despite our careful reading, a writer still surprises us. Those are often the stories we remember best.

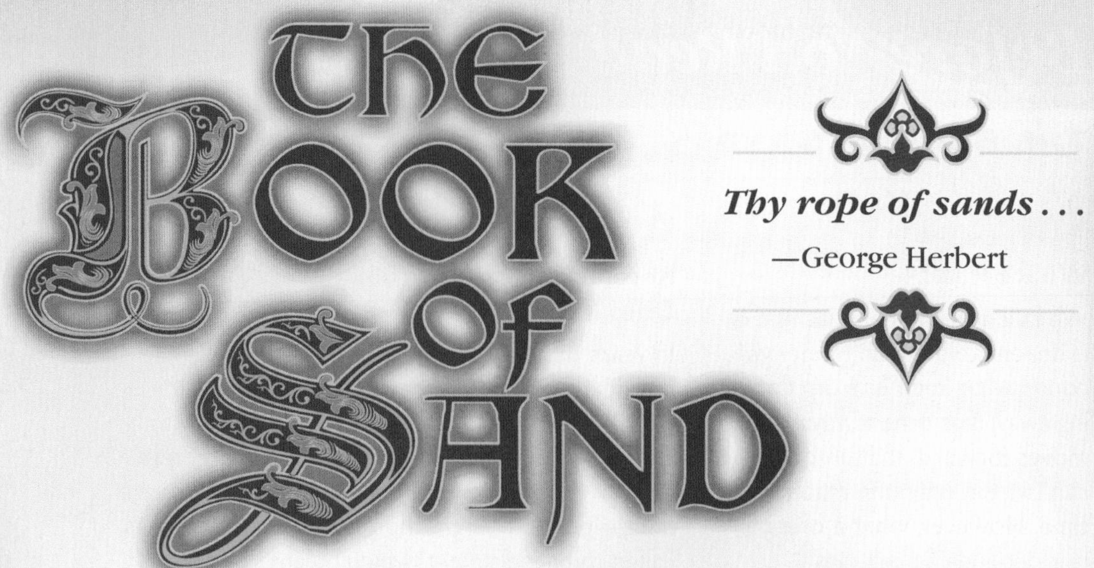

Thy rope of sands . . .

—George Herbert

The Book of Sand

Jorge Luis Borges

translated by Norman Thomas Di Giovanni

The line is made up of an infinite number of points; the plane, of an infinite number of lines; the volume, of an infinite number of planes; the hypervolume, of an infinite number of volumes. . . . No, unquestionably this is not—*more geometrico*—the best way of beginning my story. To claim that it is true is nowadays the convention of every made-up story. Mine, however, *is* true.

I live alone in a fourth-floor apartment on Belgrano Street, in Buenos Aires. Late one evening, a few months back, I heard a knock at my door. I opened it and a stranger stood there. He was a tall man, with nondescript features—or perhaps it was my myopia[1] that made them seem that way. Dressed in gray and carrying a gray suitcase in his hand, he had an unassuming look about him. I saw at once that he was a foreigner. At first, he struck me as old; only later did I realize that I had been misled by his thin blond hair, which was, in a Scandinavian sort of way, almost white. During the course of our conversation, which was not to last an hour, I found out that he came from the Orkneys.[2]

I invited him in, pointing to a chair. He paused awhile before speaking. A kind of gloom emanated from him—as it does now from me.

"I sell Bibles," he said.

Somewhat pedantically, I replied, "In this house are several English Bibles, including the first—John Wycliffe's. I also have Cipriano de Valera's, Luther's—which, from a literary viewpoint, is the worst—and a Latin copy of the Vulgate. As you see, it's not exactly Bibles I stand in need of."

After a few moments of silence, he said, "I don't only sell Bibles. I can show you a holy book I came across on the outskirts of Bikaner.[3] It may interest you."

He opened the suitcase and laid the book on a table. It was an octavo volume, bound

1. **myopia** (mī·ō′pē·ə): nearsightedness.

2. **Orkneys:** group of islands to the north of Scotland.

3. **Bikaner** (bē·kə·nir′): city in northwest India.

WORDS TO OWN

infinite (in′fə·nit) *adj.:* endless.

pedantically (pi·dant′i·klē) *adv.:* with undue attention to trivial points of scholarship.

in cloth. There was no doubt that it had passed through many hands. Examining it, I was surprised by its unusual weight. On the spine were the words "Holy Writ" and, below them, "Bombay."

"Nineteenth century, probably," I remarked.

"I don't know," he said. "I've never found out."

I opened the book at random. The script was strange to me. The pages, which were worn and typographically poor, were laid out in double columns, as in a Bible. The text was closely printed, and it was ordered in versicles.[4] In the upper corners of the pages were Arabic numbers. I noticed that one left-hand page bore the number (let us say) 40,514 and the facing right-hand page 999. I turned the leaf; it was numbered with eight digits. It also bore a small illustration, like the kind used in dictionaries—an anchor drawn with pen and ink, as if by a schoolboy's clumsy hand.

It was at this point that the stranger said, "Look at the illustration closely. You'll never see it again."

I noted my place and closed the book. At once, I reopened it. Page by page, in vain, I looked for the illustration of the anchor. "It seems to be a version of Scriptures in some Indian language, is it not?" I said to hide my dismay.

"No," he replied. Then, as if confiding a secret, he lowered his voice. "I acquired the book in a town out on the plain in exchange for a handful of rupees and a Bible. Its owner did not know how to read. I suspect that he saw the Book of Books as a talisman.[5] He was of the lowest caste; nobody but other untouchables could tread his shadow without contamination. He told me his book was called the Book of Sand, because neither the book nor the sand has any beginning or end."

The stranger asked me to find the first page.

I laid my left hand on the cover and, trying to put my thumb on the flyleaf, I opened the book. It was useless. Every time I tried, a number of pages came between the cover and my thumb. It was as if they kept growing from the book.

"Now find the last page."

Again I failed. In a voice that was not mine, I barely managed to stammer, "This can't be."

Still speaking in a low voice, the stranger said, "It can't be, but it *is*. The number of pages in this book is no more or less than infinite. None is the first page, none the last. I don't know why they're numbered in this arbitrary way. Perhaps to suggest that the terms of an infinite series admit any number."

Then, as if he were thinking aloud, he said, "If space is infinite, we may be at any point in space. If time is infinite, we may be at any point in time."

His speculations irritated me. "You are religious, no doubt?" I asked him.

"Yes, I'm a Presbyterian. My conscience is clear. I am reasonably sure of not having cheated the native when I gave him the Word of God in exchange for his devilish book."

I assured him that he had nothing to reproach himself for, and I asked if he were just passing through this part of the world. He replied that he planned to return to his country in a few days. It was then that I learned that he was a Scot from the Orkney Islands. I told him I had a great personal affection for Scotland, through my love of Stevenson and Hume.

"You mean Stevenson and Robbie Burns,"[6] he corrected.

While we spoke, I kept exploring the infinite book. With feigned indifference,

4. versicles: short verses.
5. talisman: something thought to have special or magical powers; a charm.

6. Robert Louis Stevenson (1850–1894) and Robert Burns (1759–1796) were famous and very popular Scottish writers. David Hume (1711–1776) was a Scottish philosopher.

Literature and Art

Impossible Worlds: An Artist's View

Dutch graphic artist M.C. Escher (1898–1972) often conjured up strange, "Borges-like" worlds filled with visual puzzles and illusions. What, for example, do you see happening in *Reptiles?* How does the lithograph seem to bring a two-dimensional sketch to life?

Reptiles by M.C. Escher.

I asked, "Do you intend to offer this curiosity to the British Museum?"

"No. I'm offering it to you," he said, and he stipulated a rather high sum for the book.

I answered, in all truthfulness, that such a sum was out of my reach, and I began thinking. After a minute or two, I came up with a scheme.

"I propose a swap," I said. "You got this book for a handful of rupees and a copy of the Bible. I'll offer you the amount of my pension check, which I've just collected, and my black-letter Wycliffe Bible. I inherited it from my ancestors."

"A black-letter Wycliffe!" he murmured.

I went to my bedroom and brought him the money and the book. He turned the leaves and studied the title page with all the fervor of a true bibliophile.

"It's a deal," he said.

It amazed me that he did not haggle. Only later was I to realize that he had entered my house with his mind made up to sell the book. Without counting the money, he put it away.

We talked about India, about Orkney, and about the Norwegian jarls who once ruled it. It was night when the man left. I have not seen him again, nor do I know his name.

I thought of keeping the Book of Sand in the space left on the shelf by the Wycliffe, but in the end I decided to hide it behind the volumes of a broken set of *The Thousand and One Nights.* I went to bed and did not sleep. At three or four in the morning, I turned on the light. I got down the impossible book and leafed through its pages. On one of them I saw engraved a mask. The upper corner of the page carried a number,

Words to Own

bibliophile (bib′lē·ə·fīl′) *n.:* book lover or collector.

which I no longer recall, elevated to the ninth power.

I showed no one my treasure. To the luck of owning it was added the fear of having it stolen, and then the misgiving that it might not truly be infinite. These twin preoccupations intensified my old misanthropy. I had only a few friends left; I now stopped seeing even them. A prisoner of the book, I almost never went out anymore. After studying its frayed spine and covers with a magnifying glass, I rejected the possibility of a contrivance of any sort. The small illustrations, I verified, came two thousand pages apart. I set about listing them alphabetically in a notebook, which I was not long in filling up. Never once was an illustration repeated. At night, in the meager intervals my insomnia granted, I dreamed of the book.

Summer came and went, and I realized that the book was monstrous. What good did it do me to think that I, who looked upon the volume with my eyes, who held it in my hands, was any less monstrous? I felt that the book was a nightmarish object, an obscene thing that affronted and tainted reality itself.

I thought of fire, but I feared that the burning of an infinite book might likewise prove infinite and suffocate the planet with smoke. Somewhere I recalled reading that the best place to hide a leaf is in a forest. Before retirement, I worked on Mexico Street, at the Argentine National Library, which contains nine hundred thousand volumes. I knew that to the right of the entrance a curved staircase leads down into the basement, where books and maps and periodicals are kept. One day I went there and, slipping past a member of the staff and trying not to notice at what height or distance from the door, I lost the Book of Sand on one of the basement's musty shelves.

Words to Own

misanthropy (mis·an′thrə·pē) *n.:* hatred or mistrust of people.

contrivance (kən·trī′vəns) *n.:* artificial arrangement; invention, plan, or mechanical device.

Meet the Writer

Argentine Dreamer

At age six, **Jorge Luis Borges** (hôr′he lo͞o ēs′ bôr′hes) (1899–1986) knew that he wanted to be a writer, and by nine, he had translated a fairy tale by Oscar Wilde from English into Spanish. Borges learned English from his British grandmother, immersing himself in Edgar Allan Poe's stories and Robert Louis Stevenson's novels. In an autobiographical essay, Borges wrote,

“If I were asked to name the chief event of my life, I should say my father's library.”

Like many artists, Borges had a quirky upbringing. His parents were well educated and fairly well off, but they lived in a tough Buenos Aires suburb. Although Borges traveled to Europe with his family during his youth and to the United States and Japan as an adult, he once commented that he had seen little of the world. He suffered from poor eyesight, and after going through a series of grueling cataract operations in his twenties and thirties, he became totally blind in middle age.

Borges wrote like no one had before him—strange playful tales filled with puzzles, games, riddles, and paradoxes. In *The Garden of the Forking Paths* (1941) and *El Aleph* (1949), Borges wrote dreamlike stories that blur fantasy and reality, stories of transparent tigers, infinite houses, and mythical labyrinths.

“Writing is nothing more than a guided dream,” he wrote.

Making Meanings

First Thoughts

1. If you owned the Book of Sand, what would you do with it?

Shaping Interpretations

2. Why does the narrator come to feel that the book is "monstrous"?

3. A **paradox** is a seeming contradiction that nevertheless holds a truth. It can be hard to wrap your mind around a paradox, and that's what makes paradoxes so fascinating. For example, the illustrations in the Book of Sand are both there and not there. How would you explain this paradox or another one in the story?

> **Reading Check**
>
> You are the narrator of "The Book of Sand." Immediately after getting rid of the book, you run into an old friend. Tell him or her about your weird adventure, recounting all the **main events** from beginning to end.

Connecting with the Text

4. What dependable realities does Borges question in this story? Did the story make you think about how you take realities for granted? Explain. (Be sure to check your Quickwrite notes.)

5. How satisfied are you with the **resolution** of the story? Why? Looking back at the **predictions** you made while reading may help you decide how you feel about the resolution.

Choices: Building Your Portfolio

Writer's Notebook

1. Collecting Ideas for a Persuasive Essay

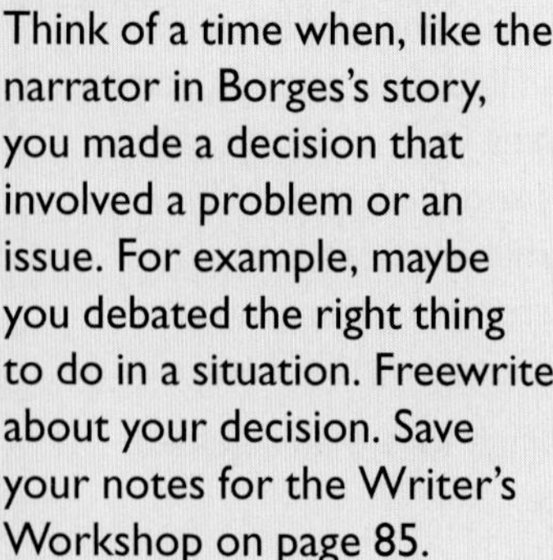

Making a decision. Think of a time when, like the narrator in Borges's story, you made a decision that involved a problem or an issue. For example, maybe you debated the right thing to do in a situation. Freewrite about your decision. Save your notes for the Writer's Workshop on page 85.

Creative Writing

2. A Never-Ending Story

With one or more partners, **predict** what happens next to the Book of Sand. Write a story about another adventure in the weird book's history. Introduce new **characters**, a new **setting**, and new **events**. When you place the book in its next resting place, pass your story on for another group to continue.

Writing an Explanation/ Mathematics

3. What's Infinity?

The concept of infinity is central to this story. Do you understand infinity well enough to teach it to someone else? Write an explanation of infinity that a fourth grader could understand. Consider adding **illustrations**, **examples**, or **analogies** (simple comparisons) to clarify the idea of infinity.

Grammar Link MINI-LESSON

Language Handbook HELP

See Using Pronouns, pages 1029–1031.

Technology HELP

See Language Workshop CD-ROM. *Key word entry: pronouns.*

Using Personal Pronouns—in the Right Places

The trouble with using **personal pronouns** is that you need to choose the right form to fit each sentence. Choose from these two forms, or **cases.**

Nominative Case: I, you, he, she, it, we, they
Objective Case: me, you, him, her, it, us, them

Use a **nominative case pronoun** if a pronoun functions as a subject or predicate nominative in a sentence.

She and *I* read the book. (subject)

The writer is *he.* (predicate nominative)

Use an **objective case pronoun** if the pronoun functions as a direct object, indirect object, or object of a preposition.

The book puzzled Wally and *me.* (direct object)

Please show Maria and *me* the book. (indirect object)

She read the story to Hans and *me.* (object of preposition)

Try It Out

Edit and rewrite the following paragraph, correcting the personal pronouns. Hint: Errors occur often when the pronoun is part of a compound structure—a compound subject, for example.

Julio told Carrie and I about his new episode for "The Book of Sand." Mara and him wrote a suspenseful episode with a lot of dialogue. Him and her took turns reading their story aloud to our teacher and us. In their story, a stranger gives he and I a page from the book.

Vocabulary HOW TO OWN A WORD

Word Bank

infinite
pedantically
bibliophile
misanthropy
contrivance

Prefixes, Suffixes, and Roots: Broken-Down Words

For each word in the Word Bank, consult its etymology in a dictionary to find the **root,** the part that carries the word's core meaning. Then, look for a **prefix** *before* the root or a **suffix** *after* it. Make a chart, like the one below, for the other words in the Word Bank. Remember that prefixes and suffixes are defined separately in the dictionary. Circle the word part that would help you guess the meanings of the related words.

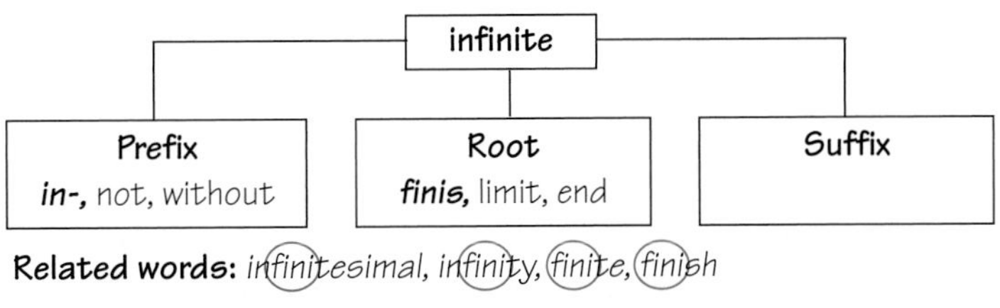

Elements of Literature

SETTING: Putting Us There *by* John Leggett

All Events Occur Somewhere

It is possible for an interesting story to have no **setting** at all—that is, no indication of when or where the action is set. If the characters and their situation are strong enough, they will hold our attention in empty space, just as a play presented on a bare stage can hold our interest.

But in life all events occur somewhere. Often a story's place and its **atmosphere**—its feeling of gloom or cheer, of beauty or ugliness—affect the characters and the way they lead their lives. Think of how crucial setting would be to a story about a prisoner, or to a story about castaways adrift on the Pacific, or to a story about a high-school graduation in a coal town.

It is this sense of place in fiction that gives us the chance for armchair travel.

Setting puts us there—it gives us a feeling of being *in* the situation with the characters. If we are in the square of a town in Honduras, we should feel hot, sweaty, and thirsty. We should see how the sun is baking the back of the little burro tethered at the side of the church. We should smell the *zozo,* the native delicacy of fish heads and banana skins, as it sizzles over the charcoal.

The setting tells us not only *where* we are, but also *when*—it can reveal a **time frame.** If the passing traffic is horse drawn, we can guess we have gone back in time. An inch of new-fallen snow on the porch rail tells us it's winter. If the sun is just up over the pine ridge or if the *Ledger* is being tossed onto the front steps, it is morning.

Setting can be a high school in Texas, the deck of a boat crossing the Atlantic, a winter evening in a New York brownstone. Setting can be a reservation in the American Southwest or a colony on Mars.

Setting can give the story a kind of truth or believability. We call this **verisimilitude** (ver′ə·si·mil′ə·to͞od′), which means "the appearance of being true to life."

It is this sense of place in fiction that gives us the chance for armchair travel—to visit faraway places without leaving home.

Setting and Our Emotions

A more important function of setting, however, is to contribute to a story's **emotional effect**. We all know that some settings can make us feel gloomy and others can make us feel cheerful. An autumnal setting can increase the sense of loss in a story about a doomed love. A spring setting can give a note of hope to a story of a girl's coming of age.

Here is a description of a rice paddy in Vietnam. How does it make you feel?

> . . . his boots sank into the thick paddy water, and he smelled it all around him. He would tell his mother how it smelled: mud and algae and cattle manure and chlorophyll; decay, breeding mosquitoes and leeches as big as mice; the fecund warmth of the paddy waters rising up to his cut knee.
>
> —Tim O'Brien, "Where Have You Gone, Charming Billy?" (page 198)

This Vietnam jungle setting is used in another part of the same story to contrast with

the young soldier's comforting memories of home in Iowa. The emotional effect of that contrast is shattering.

He was pretending he was a boy again, camping with his father in the midnight summer along the Des Moines River. In the dark, with his eyes pinched shut, he pretended. He pretended that when he opened his eyes, his father would be there by the campfire and they would talk softly about whatever came to mind and then roll into their sleeping bags. . . .

Setting and Characters

Setting also reveals character. We all affect our environment in one way or another, so a writer wishing to portray an untidy Alice will show us the mess in her bedroom—pajamas, hangers, sneakers in a snarl on the floor of her closet, CDs and magazines strewn beneath the unmade bed. We know something about Alice even before we see her.

Here is Jimmy's room with a set of weights in one corner; on the bedside table a copy of the *Guinness Book of World Records;* on the wall, school pennants, photographs of the basketball team, a set of antlers; and hanging from a hook on the closet door, a pair of boxing gloves. How much do we know about Jimmy before he even opens the door?

Here is a house, the home of a very old man whose life is almost over. What does the setting reveal about this character, even before he appears?

The house had only two rooms, but he owned it—the last scrap of the farm that he had sold off years ago. It stood in a hollow of dying trees beside a superhighway in Baltimore County. All it held was a few sticks of furniture, a change of clothes, a skillet, and a set of dishes.

— Anne Tyler, "With All Flags Flying" (pages 310–311)

HE DIDN'T KNOW HOW TO APPRECIATE NATURE.

Setting as a Character

Though we find that in some stories, setting hardly matters, in others the setting can have all the importance of a major character. We'd find this situation in a story where the main characters are pitted against the setting, such as a story about a polar expedition fighting against the harshness of the arctic tundra. We also find setting assuming the importance of a character in the story "The Cold Equations" (page 9), where the characters are in conflict with their environment—the cold, harsh realities of the space frontier.

In some stories, setting can have all the importance of a major character.

Before You Read

BOYS AND GIRLS

Make the Connection

Gender Issues

Do you think boys and girls have the same choices in life? Are boys and girls expected to feel and act in different ways? If so, are these expectations based on inborn differences, or are they the result of social customs that can change? Discuss these questions in a group. Note if the boys and girls respond differently from each other.

Quickwrite

In your notebook, record your thoughts about your group discussions on what is expected of boys and girls today. Use a chart like the one below.

Expectations	
Boys	
Girls	

Elements of Literature

The Moment of Truth

You can usually identify the **climax** in a story or movie because it is often marked by a significant action, even a moment of violence. In Shakespeare's *Romeo and Juliet,* for example, the horrifying climax comes right at the end, when Romeo and Juliet both kill themselves in the underground tomb. At the moment of climax, the conflict in the story is finally resolved.

The climax usually comes near the story's end. It might help to imagine the story as a movie and to listen in your mind for the dramatic crescendo of music at the climax.

The **climax** of a story is that emotional moment toward the end when something dramatic happens to determine the outcome of the conflict.

For more on Plot, see pages 32–33 and the Handbook of Literary Terms.

Reading Skills and Strategies

Making Generalizations

A **generalization** is a broad statement that can be applied to many situations. If you say, "Boys usually like adventure movies, while most girls prefer romances," you are making some generalizations. (Generalizations can be challenged—as those would be!) When you read, you make generalizations by combining what you learn from the text with what you already know. This story about an eleven-year-old girl and her younger brother suggests some generalizations about gender roles. Think about what they are as you read.

go.hrw.com
LEO 10-1

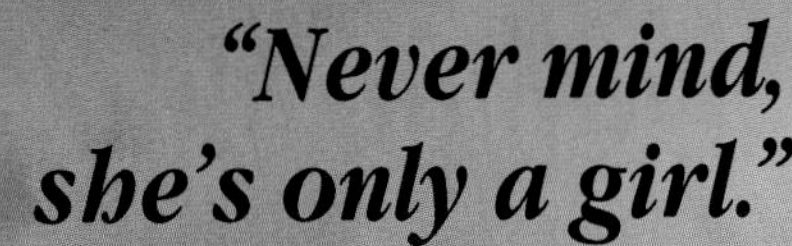
"Never mind,
she's only a girl."

Boys and Girls

Alice Munro

My father was a fox farmer. That is, he raised silver foxes, in pens; and in the fall and early winter, when their fur was prime, he killed them and skinned them and sold their pelts to the Hudson's Bay Company or the Montreal Fur Traders. These companies supplied us with heroic calendars to hang, one on each side of the kitchen door. Against a background of cold blue sky and black pine forests and treacherous northern rivers, plumed adventurers planted the flags of England or of France; magnificent savages bent their backs to the portage.[1]

For several weeks before Christmas, my father worked after supper in the cellar of our

1. **portage:** carrying of boats and supplies overland from one river or lake to another.

house. The cellar was whitewashed and lit by a hundred-watt bulb over the worktable. My brother Laird and I sat on the top step and watched. My father removed the pelt inside out from the body of the fox, which looked surprisingly small, mean, and ratlike deprived of its arrogant weight of fur. The naked, slippery bodies were collected in a sack and buried at the dump. One time the hired man, Henry Bailey, had taken a swipe at me with this sack, saying, "Christmas present!" My mother thought that was not funny. In fact she disliked the whole pelting operation—that was what the killing, skinning, and preparation of the furs was called—and wished it did not have to take place in the house. There was the smell. After the pelt had been stretched inside out on a long board, my father scraped away delicately, removing the little clotted webs of blood vessels, the bubbles of fat; the smell of blood and animal fat, with the strong primitive odor of the fox itself, penetrated all parts of the house. I found it reassuringly seasonal, like the smell of oranges and pine needles.

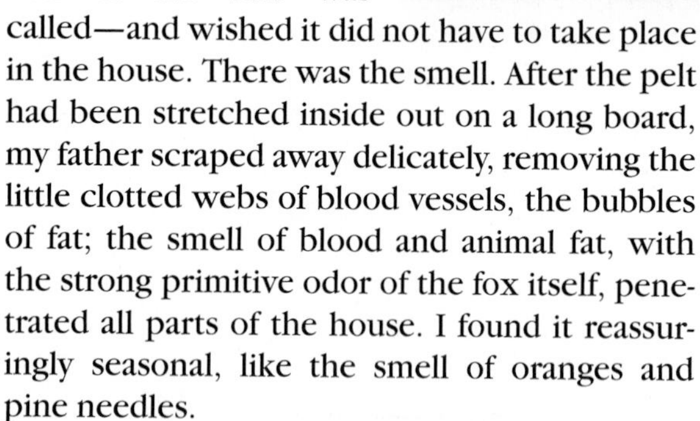

Henry Bailey suffered from bronchial[2] troubles. He would cough and cough until his narrow face turned scarlet and his light-blue, derisive eyes filled up with tears; then he took the lid off the stove and, standing well back, shot out a great clot of phlegm—hsss—straight into the heart of the flames. We admired him for this performance and for his ability to make his stomach growl at will, and for his laughter, which was full of high whistlings and gurglings and involved the whole faulty machinery of his chest. It was sometimes hard to tell what he was laughing at, and always possible that it might be us.

After we had been sent to bed, we could still smell fox and still hear Henry's laugh, but these things, reminders of the warm, safe, brightly lit downstairs world, seemed lost and diminished, floating on the stale, cold air upstairs. We were afraid at night in the winter. We were not afraid of *outside,* though this was the time of year when snowdrifts curled around our house like sleeping whales and the wind harassed us all night, coming up from the buried fields, the frozen swamp, with its old bugbear[3] chorus of threats and misery. We were afraid of *inside,* the room where we slept. At this time the upstairs of our house was not finished. A brick chimney went up one wall. In the middle of the floor was a square hole, with a wooden railing around it; that was where the stairs came up. On the other side of the stairwell were the things that nobody had any use for anymore—a soldiery roll of linoleum standing on end, a wicker baby carriage, a fern basket, china jugs and basins with cracks in them, a picture of the Battle of Balaclava, very sad to look at. I had told Laird, as soon as he was old enough to understand such things, that bats and skeletons lived over there; whenever a man escaped from the county jail, twenty miles away, I imagined that he had somehow let himself in the window and was hiding behind the linoleum. But we had rules to keep us safe. When the light was on, we were safe as long as we did not step off the square of worn carpet which defined our bedroom space; when the light was off, no place was safe but the beds themselves. I had to turn out the light kneeling on the end of my bed and stretching as far as I could to reach the cord.

In the dark we lay on our beds, our narrow

2. **bronchial** (bräŋ′kē·əl): relating to the major air passageways of the lungs.

3. **bugbear:** frightening. A bugbear is an imaginary creature used to scare children.

Words to Own

derisive (di·rī′siv) *adj.:* mocking.

life rafts, and fixed our eyes on the faint light coming up the stairwell and sang songs. Laird sang "Jingle Bells," which he would sing any-time, whether it was Christmas or not, and I sang "Danny Boy."[4] I loved the sound of my own voice, frail and supplicating, rising in the dark. We could make out the tall frosted shapes of the windows now, gloomy and white. When I came to the part *When I am dead, as dead I well may be*—a fit of shivering caused not by the cold sheets but by pleasurable emotion almost silenced me. *You'll kneel and say an Ave*[5] *there above me*—what was an Ave? Every day I forgot to find out.

Laird went straight from singing to sleep. I could hear his long, satisfied, bubbly breaths. Now, for the time that remained to me, the most perfectly private and perhaps the best time of the whole day, I arranged myself tightly under the covers and went on with one of the stories I was telling myself from night to night. These stories were about myself, when I had grown a little older; they took place in a world that was recognizably mine, yet one that presented opportunities for courage, boldness, and self-sacrifice, as mine never did. I rescued people from a bombed building (it discouraged me that the real war had gone on so far away from Jubilee). I shot two rabid wolves who were menacing the schoolyard (the teachers cowered terrified at my back). I rode a fine horse spiritedly down the main street of Jubilee, acknowledging the townspeople's gratitude for some yet-to-be-worked-out piece of heroism (nobody ever rode a horse there, except King Billy in the Orangemen's Day[6] parade). There was always riding and shooting in these stories, though I had only been on a horse twice—bareback because we did not own a saddle—and the second time I had slid right around and dropped under the horse's feet; it had stepped placidly over me. I really was learning to shoot, but I could not hit anything yet, not even tin cans on fence posts.

Alive, the foxes inhabited a world my father made for them. It was surrounded by a high guard fence, like a medieval town, with a gate that was padlocked at night. Along the streets of this town were ranged large, sturdy pens. Each of them had a real door that a man could go through, a wooden ramp along the wire for the foxes to run up and down on, and a kennel—something like a clothes chest with airholes—where they slept and stayed in winter and had their young. There were feeding and watering dishes attached to the wire in such a way that they could be emptied and cleaned from the outside. The dishes were made of old tin cans, and the ramps and kennels of odds and ends of old lumber. Everything was tidy and ingenious; my father was tirelessly inventive and his favorite book in the world was *Robinson Crusoe.*[7] He had fitted a tin drum on a wheelbarrow, for bringing water down to the pens. This was my job in summer, when the foxes had to have water twice a day. Between nine and ten o'clock in the morning, and again after supper, I filled the drum at the pump and trundled it down through the barnyard to the pens, where I parked it, and filled my watering can and went along the streets. Laird came too, with his little cream-and-green gardening can, filled too full and knocking against his legs and slopping water on his canvas shoes. I had the real watering can, my father's, though I could only carry it three-quarters full.

4. **"Danny Boy":** sad song in the words of an Irish mother whose son is going off to war.

5. **Ave** (ä′vā): prayer in Latin to the Virgin Mary, used in the Roman Catholic Church; it begins with the words "Ave, Maria," meaning "Hail, Mary."

6. **Orangemen's Day:** holiday celebrated by the Orangemen, an Irish Protestant society, on July 12. It marks the defeat in 1690 of the Catholic forces in Ireland by the Protestant English king known as William of Orange.

7. ***Robinson Crusoe:*** novel by Daniel Defoe that tells the story of a sailor stranded on an island for twenty-four years. Crusoe survives through skill, cleverness, and hard work.

Words to Own

supplicating (sup′lə·kāt′iŋ) *v.* used as *adj.:* appealing humbly and earnestly, as if in prayer.
placidly (plas′id·lē) *adv.:* calmly; in an undisturbed way.
ingenious (in·jēn′yəs) *adj.:* made or done in a clever or inventive way.

The foxes all had names, which were printed on a tin plate and hung beside their doors. They were named not when they were born but when they survived the first year's pelting and were added to the breeding stock. Those my father had named were called names like Prince, Bob, Wally, and Betty. Those I had named were called Star or Turk, or Maureen or Diana. Laird named one Maud after a hired girl we had when he was little, one Harold after a boy at school, and one Mexico, he did not say why.

Naming them did not make pets out of them or anything like it. Nobody but my father ever went into the pens, and he had twice had blood poisoning from bites. When I was bringing them their water, they prowled up and down on the paths they had made inside their pens, barking seldom—they saved that for nighttime, when they might get up a chorus of community frenzy—but always watching me, their eyes burning, clear gold, in their pointed, malevolent faces. They were beautiful for their delicate legs and heavy, aristocratic tails and the bright fur sprinkled on dark down their backs—which gave them their name—but especially for their faces, drawn exquisitely sharp in pure hostility, and their golden eyes.

Besides carrying water, I helped my father when he cut the long grass, and the lamb's-quarters and flowering money-musk, that grew between the pens. He cut with the scythe[8] and I raked into piles. Then he took a pitchfork and threw fresh-cut grass all over the top of the pens, to keep the foxes cooler and shade their coats, which were browned by too much sun. My father did not talk to me unless it was about the job we were doing. In this he was quite different from my mother, who, if she was feeling cheerful, would tell me all sorts of things—the name of a dog she had had when she was a little girl, the names of boys she had gone out with later on when she was grown up, and what certain dresses of hers had looked like—she could not imagine now what had become of them. Whatever thoughts and stories my father had were private, and I was shy of him and would never ask him questions. Nevertheless, I worked willingly under his eyes, and with a feeling of pride. One time a feed salesman came down into the pens to talk to him and my father said, "Like to have you meet my new hired man." I turned away and raked furiously, red in the face with pleasure.

"Could of fooled me," said the salesman. "I thought it was only a girl."

After the grass was cut, it seemed suddenly much later in the year. I walked on stubble in the earlier evening, aware of the reddening skies, the entering silences, of fall. When I wheeled the tank out of the gate and put the padlock on, it was almost dark. One night at this time I saw my mother and father standing talking on the little rise of ground we called the gangway, in front of the barn. My father had just come from the meathouse; he had his stiff bloody apron on and a pail of cut-up meat in his hand.

It was an odd thing to see my mother down at the barn. She did not often come out of the house unless it was to do something—hang out the wash or dig potatoes in the garden. She looked out of place, with her bare lumpy legs, not touched by the sun, her apron still on and damp across the stomach from the supper dishes. Her hair was tied up in a kerchief, wisps of it falling out. She would tie her hair up like this in the morning, saying she did not have time to do it properly, and it would stay tied up all day. It was true, too; she really did not have time. These days our back porch was piled with baskets of peaches and grapes and pears, bought in town, and onions and tomatoes and cucumbers grown at home, all waiting to be made into jelly and jam and preserves, pickles and chili sauce. In the kitchen there was a fire in the stove all day, jars clinked in boiling water, sometimes a cheesecloth bag was strung on a pole between two chairs, straining blue-black grape pulp for jelly. I was given jobs to do and I would sit at the table peeling peaches that had been soaked in the hot water, or cutting up onions, my eyes smarting and streaming. As soon as I was done, I ran out of the house, try-

8. **scythe** (sīth): tool with a long blade set at an angle on a long, curved handle.

ing to get out of earshot before my mother thought of what she wanted me to do next. I hated the hot, dark kitchen in summer, the green blinds and the flypapers, the same old oilcloth table and wavy mirror and bumpy linoleum. My mother was too tired and preoccupied to talk to me; she had no heart to tell about the Normal School Graduation Dance; sweat trickled over her face and she was always counting under her breath, pointing at jars, dumping cups of sugar. It seemed to me that work in the house was endless, dreary, and peculiarly depressing; work done out of doors, and in my father's service, was ritualistically[9] important.

I wheeled the tank up to the barn, where it was kept, and I heard my mother saying, "Wait till Laird gets a little bigger, then you'll have a real help."

What my father said I did not hear. I was pleased by the way he stood listening, politely as he would to a salesman or a stranger, but with an air of wanting to get on with his real work. I felt my mother had no business down here, and I wanted him to feel the same way. What did she mean about Laird? He was no help to anybody. Where was he now? Swinging himself sick on the swing, going around in circles, or trying to catch caterpillars. He never once stayed with me till I was finished.

"And then I can use her more in the house," I heard my mother say. She had a dead-quiet, regretful way of talking about me that always made me uneasy. "I just get my back turned and she runs off. It's not like I had a girl in the family at all."

I went and sat on a feed bag in the corner of the barn, not wanting to appear when this conversation was going on. My mother, I felt, was not to be trusted. She was kinder than my father and more easily fooled, but you could not depend on her, and the real reasons for the things she said and did were not to be known. She loved me, and she sat up late at night making a dress of the difficult style I wanted, for me to wear when school started, but she was also my enemy. She was always plotting. She was plotting now to get me to stay in the house more, although she knew I hated it (*because* she knew I hated it) and keep me from working for my father. It seemed to me she would do this simply

9. **ritualistically:** as if it were a rite, or ceremony.

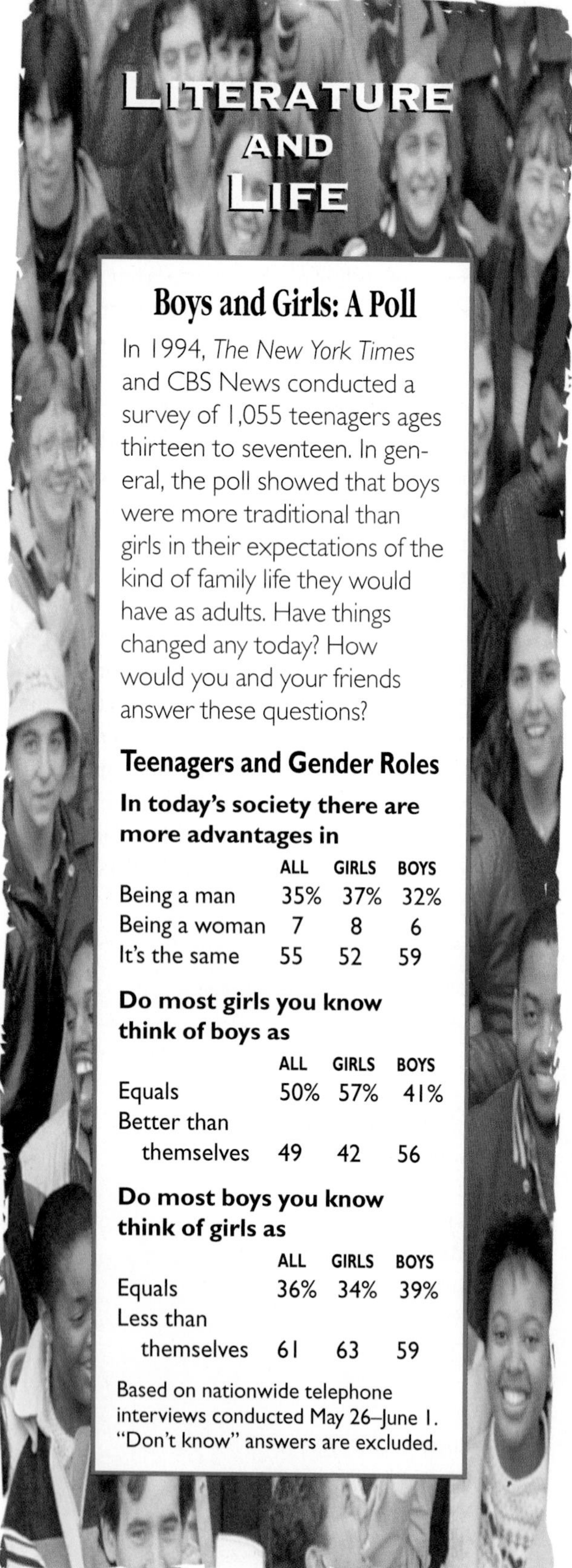

Boys and Girls: A Poll

In 1994, *The New York Times* and CBS News conducted a survey of 1,055 teenagers ages thirteen to seventeen. In general, the poll showed that boys were more traditional than girls in their expectations of the kind of family life they would have as adults. Have things changed any today? How would you and your friends answer these questions?

Teenagers and Gender Roles

In today's society there are more advantages in

	ALL	GIRLS	BOYS
Being a man	35%	37%	32%
Being a woman	7	8	6
It's the same	55	52	59

Do most girls you know think of boys as

	ALL	GIRLS	BOYS
Equals	50%	57%	41%
Better than themselves	49	42	56

Do most boys you know think of girls as

	ALL	GIRLS	BOYS
Equals	36%	34%	39%
Less than themselves	61	63	59

Based on nationwide telephone interviews conducted May 26–June 1. "Don't know" answers are excluded.

out of perversity and to try her power. It did not occur to me that she could be lonely, or jealous. No grown-up could be; they were too fortunate. I sat and kicked my heels monotonously against a feed bag, raising dust, and did not come out till she was gone.

At any rate, I did not expect my father to pay any attention to what she said. Who could imagine Laird doing my work—Laird remembering the padlock and cleaning out the watering dishes with a leaf on the end of the stick, or even wheeling the tank without its tumbling over? It showed how little my mother knew about the way things really were.

I have forgotten to say what the foxes were fed. My father's bloody apron reminded me. They were fed horsemeat. At this time most farmers still kept horses, and when a horse got too old to work, or broke a leg, or got down and would not get up, as they sometimes did, the owner would call my father, and he and Henry went out to the farm in the truck. Usually they shot and butchered the horse there, paying the farmer from five to twelve dollars. If they had already too much meat on hand, they would bring the horse back alive and keep it for a few days or weeks in our stable, until the meat was needed. After the war the farmers were buying tractors and gradually getting rid of horses altogether, so it sometimes happened that we got a good healthy horse that there was just no use for anymore. If this happened in the winter, we might keep the horse in our stable till spring, for we had plenty of hay, and if there was a lot of snow—and the plow did not always get our road cleared—it was convenient to be able to go to town with a horse and cutter.[10]

The winter I was eleven years old, we had two horses in the stable. We did not know what

10. **cutter:** small, light sleigh, usually drawn by one horse.

WORDS TO OWN

perversity (pər·vʉr′sə·tē) *n.:* stubborn opposition or contrariness.

names they had had before, so we called them Mack and Flora. Mack was an old black workhorse, sooty and indifferent. Flora was a sorrel mare,[11] a driver. We took them both out in the cutter. Mack was slow and easy to handle. Flora was given to fits of violent alarm, veering at cars and even at other horses, but we loved her speed and high stepping, her general air of gallantry and abandon. On Saturdays we went down to the stable, and as soon as we opened the door on its cozy, animal-smelling darkness, Flora threw up her head, rolled her eyes, whinnied despairingly, and pulled herself through a crisis of nerves on the spot. It was not safe to go into her stall; she would kick.

This winter also I began to hear a great deal more on the theme my mother had sounded when she had been talking in front of the barn. I no longer felt safe. It seemed that in the minds of the people around me there was a steady undercurrent of thought, not to be deflected, on this one subject. The word *girl* had formerly seemed to me innocent and unburdened, like the word *child;* now it appeared that it was no such thing. A girl was not, as I had supposed, simply what I was; it was what I had to become. It was a definition, always touched with emphasis, with reproach and disappointment. Also it was a joke on me. Once Laird and I were fighting, and for the first time ever I had to use all my strength against him; even so, he caught and pinned my arm for a moment, really hurting me. Henry saw this and laughed, saying, "Oh, that there Laird's gonna show you, one of these days!" Laird was getting a lot bigger. But I was getting bigger too.

My grandmother came to stay with us for a few weeks and I heard other things. "Girls don't slam doors like that." "Girls keep their knees together when they sit down." And worse still, when I asked some questions, "That's none of girls' business." I continued to slam the doors and sit as awkwardly as possible, thinking that by such measures I kept myself free.

When spring came, the horses were let out in the barnyard. Mack stood against the barn wall trying to scratch his neck and haunches, but Flora trotted up and down and reared at the fences, clattering her hooves against the rails. Snow drifts dwindled quickly, revealing the hard gray-and-brown earth, the familiar rise and fall of the ground, plain and bare after the fantastic landscape of winter. There was a great feeling of opening out, of release. We just wore rubbers now, over our shoes; our feet felt ridiculously light. One Saturday we went out to the stable and found all the doors open, letting in the unaccustomed sunlight and fresh air. Henry was there, just idling around looking at his collection of calendars, which were tacked up behind the stalls in a part of the stable my mother had probably never seen.

"Come to say goodbye to your old friend Mack?" Henry said. "Here, you give him a taste of oats." He poured some oats into Laird's cupped hands and Laird went to feed Mack. Mack's teeth were in bad shape. He ate very slowly, patiently shifting the oats around in his mouth, trying to find a stump of a molar to grind it on. "Poor old Mack," said Henry mournfully. "When a horse's teeth's gone, he's gone. That's about the way."

"Are you going to shoot him today?" I said. Mack and Flora had been in the stable so long I had almost forgotten they were going to be shot.

Henry didn't answer me. Instead he started to sing in a high, trembly, mocking-sorrowful voice, *Oh, there's no more work, for poor Uncle Ned, he's gone where the good folks go*. Mack's thick, blackish tongue worked diligently at Laird's hand. I went out before the song was ended and sat down on the gangway.

I had never seen them shoot a horse, but I knew where it was done. Last summer Laird and I had come upon a horse's entrails before they were buried. We had thought it was a big black

11. **sorrel mare:** reddish-brown female horse.

WORDS TO OWN

reproach (ri·prōch′) *n.:* blame; expression of disapproval.

diligently (dil′ə·jənt·lē) *adv.:* in a steady, careful, and hard-working manner.

snake, coiled up in the sun. That was around in the field that ran up beside the barn. I thought that if we went inside the barn and found a wide crack or a knothole to look through, we would be able to see them do it. It was not something I wanted to see; just the same, if a thing really happened, it was better to see it and know.

My father came down from the house, carrying the gun.

"What are you doing here?" he said.

"Nothing."

"Go on up and play around the house."

He sent Laird out of the stable. I said to Laird, "Do you want to see them shoot Mack?" and without waiting for an answer led him around to the front door of the barn, opened it carefully, and went in. "Be quiet or they'll hear us," I said. We could hear Henry and my father talking in the stable, then the heavy, shuffling steps of Mack being backed out of his stall.

In the loft it was cold and dark. Thin, crisscrossed beams of sunlight fell through the cracks. The hay was low. It was a rolling country, hills and hollows, slipping under our feet. About four feet up was a beam going around the walls. We piled hay up in one corner and I boosted Laird up and hoisted myself. The beam was not very wide; we crept along it with our hands flat on the barn walls. There were plenty of knotholes, and I found one that gave me the view I wanted—a corner of the barnyard, the gate, part of the field. Laird did not have a knothole and began to complain.

I showed him a widened crack between two boards. "Be quiet and wait. If they hear you, you'll get us in trouble."

My father came in sight carrying the gun. Henry was leading Mack by the halter. He dropped it and took out his cigarette papers and tobacco; he rolled cigarettes for my father and himself. While this was going on, Mack nosed around in the old, dead grass along the fence. Then my father opened the gate and they took Mack through. Henry led Mack away from the path to a patch of ground and they talked together, not loud enough for us to hear. Mack again began searching for a mouthful of fresh grass, which was not to be found. My father walked away in a straight line and stopped short at a distance which seemed to suit him. Henry was walking away from Mack too, but sideways, still negligently holding on to the halter. My father raised the gun and Mack looked up as if he had noticed something and my father shot him.

Mack did not collapse at once but swayed, lurched sideways, and fell, first on his side; then he rolled over on his back and, amazingly, kicked his legs for a few seconds in the air. At this Henry laughed, as if Mack had done a trick for him. Laird, who had drawn a long, groaning breath of surprise when the shot was fired, said out loud, "He's not dead." And it seemed to me it might be true. But his legs stopped; he rolled on his side again; his muscles quivered and sank. The two men walked over and looked at him in a businesslike way; they bent down and examined his forehead where the bullet had gone in and now I saw his blood on the brown grass.

"Now they just skin him and cut him up," I said. "Let's go." My legs were a little shaky and I jumped gratefully down into the hay. "Now you've seen how they shoot a horse," I said in a congratulatory way, as if I had seen it many times before. "Let's see if any barn cat's had kittens in the hay." Laird jumped. He seemed young and obedient again. Suddenly I remembered how, when he was little, I had brought him into the barn and told him to climb the ladder to the top beam. That was in the spring, too, when the hay was low. I had done it out of a need for excitement, a desire for something to happen so that I could tell about it. He was wearing a little bulky brown-and-white checked coat made down from one of mine. He went all the way up, just as I told him, and sat down on the top beam, with the hay far below him on one side and the barn floor and some machin-

WORDS TO OWN

negligently (neg′lə·jənt·lē) *adv.:* carelessly; in a neglectful or indifferent manner.

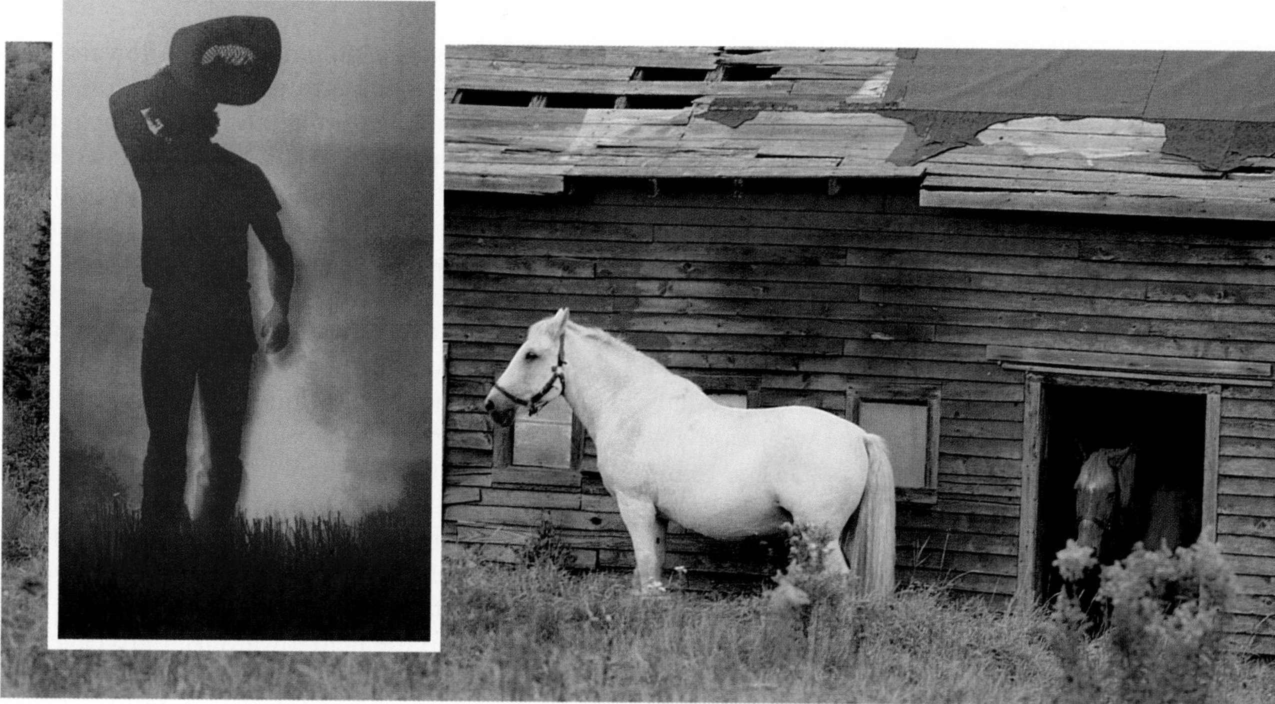

ery on the other. Then I ran screaming to my father, "Laird's up on the top beam!" My father came, my mother came; my father went up the ladder talking very quietly and brought Laird down under his arm, at which my mother leaned against the ladder and began to cry. They said to me, "Why weren't you watching him?" but nobody ever knew the truth. Laird did not know enough to tell. But whenever I saw the brown-and-white checked coat hanging in the closet, or at the bottom of the rag bag, which was where it ended up, I felt a weight in my stomach, the sadness of unexorcised[12] guilt.

I looked at Laird, who did not even remember this, and I did not like the look on his thin, winter-pale face. His expression was not frightened or upset, but remote, concentrating. "Listen," I said, in an unusually bright and friendly voice, "you aren't going to tell, are you?"

"No," he said absently.

"Promise."

"Promise," he said. I grabbed the hand behind his back to make sure he was not crossing his fingers. Even so, he might have a nightmare; it might come out that way. I decided I had better work hard to get all thoughts of what he had seen out of his mind—which, it seemed to me, could not hold very many things at a time. I got some money I had saved, and that afternoon we went into Jubilee and saw a show, with Judy Canova, at which we both laughed a great deal. After that I thought it would be all right.

Two weeks later I knew they were going to shoot Flora. I knew from the night before, when I heard my mother ask if the hay was holding out all right, and my father said, "Well, after tomorrow there'll just be the cow, and we should be able to put her out to grass in another week." So I knew it was Flora's turn in the morning.

This time I didn't think of watching it. That was something to see just one time. I had not thought about it very often since, but sometimes when I was busy, working at school, or standing in front of the mirror combing my hair and wondering if I would be pretty when I grew up, the whole scene would flash into my mind: I would see the easy, practiced way my father raised his gun and hear Henry laughing when

12. **unexorcised:** not driven out (said of something evil or distressing).

WORDS TO OWN

remote (ri·mōt′) *adj.:* distant.

Mack kicked his legs in the air. I did not have any great feeling of horror and opposition, such as a city child might have had; I was too used to seeing the death of animals as a necessity by which we lived. Yet I felt a little ashamed, and there was a new wariness, a sense of holding off, in my attitude to my father and his work.

It was a fine day, and we were going around the yard picking up tree branches that had been torn off in winter storms. This was something we had been told to do, and also we wanted to use them to make a teepee. We heard Flora whinny, and then my father's voice and Henry's shouting, and we ran down to the barnyard to see what was going on.

The stable door was open. Henry had just brought Flora out, and she had broken away from him. She was running free in the barnyard, from one end to the other. We climbed up on the fence. It was exciting to see her running, whinnying, going up on her hind legs, prancing and threatening like a horse in a Western movie, an unbroken ranch horse, though she was just an old driver, an old sorrel mare. My father and Henry ran after her and tried to grab the dangling halter. They tried to work her into a corner, and they had almost succeeded when she made a run between them, wild-eyed, and disappeared around the corner of the barn. We heard the rails clatter down as she got over the fence, and Henry yelled, "She's into the field now!"

That meant she was in the long L-shaped field that ran up by the house. If she got around the center, heading toward the lane, the gate was open; the truck had been driven into the field this morning. My father shouted to me, because I was on the other side of the fence, nearest the lane, "Go shut the gate!"

I could run very fast. I ran across the garden, past the tree where our swing was hung, and jumped across a ditch into the lane. There was the open gate. She had not got out; I could not see her up on the road; she must have run to the other end of the field. The gate was heavy. I lifted it out of the gravel and carried it across the roadway. I had it halfway across when she came in sight, galloping straight toward me. There was just time to get the chain on. Laird came scrambling through the ditch to help me.

Instead of shutting the gate, I opened it as wide as I could. I did not make any decision to do this; it was just what I did. Flora never slowed down; she galloped straight past me, and Laird jumped up and down, yelling, "Shut it, shut it!" even after it was too late. My father and Henry appeared in the field a moment too late to see what I had done. They only saw Flora heading for the township road. They would think I had not got there in time.

They did not waste any time asking about it. They went back to the barn and got the gun and the knives they used, and put these in the truck; then they turned the truck around and came bouncing up the field toward us. Laird called to them, "Let me go too, let me go too!" and Henry stopped the truck and they took him in. I shut the gate after they were all gone.

I supposed Laird would tell. I wondered what would happen to me. I had never disobeyed my father before, and I could not understand why I had done it. Flora would not really get away. They would catch up with her in the truck. Or if they did not catch her this morning, somebody would see her and telephone us this afternoon or tomorrow. There was no wild country here for her to run to, only farms. What was more, my father had paid for her, we needed the meat to feed the foxes, we needed the foxes to make our living. All I had done was make more work for my father, who worked hard enough already. And when my father found out about it, he was not going to trust me anymore; he would know that I was not entirely on his side. I was on Flora's side, and that made me no use to anybody, not even to her. Just the same, I did not regret it; when she came running at me and I held the gate open, that was the only thing I could do.

I went back to the house, and my mother said, "What's all the commotion?" I told her that Flora had kicked down the fence and got away. "Your poor father," she said, "now he'll have to go chasing over the countryside. Well, there

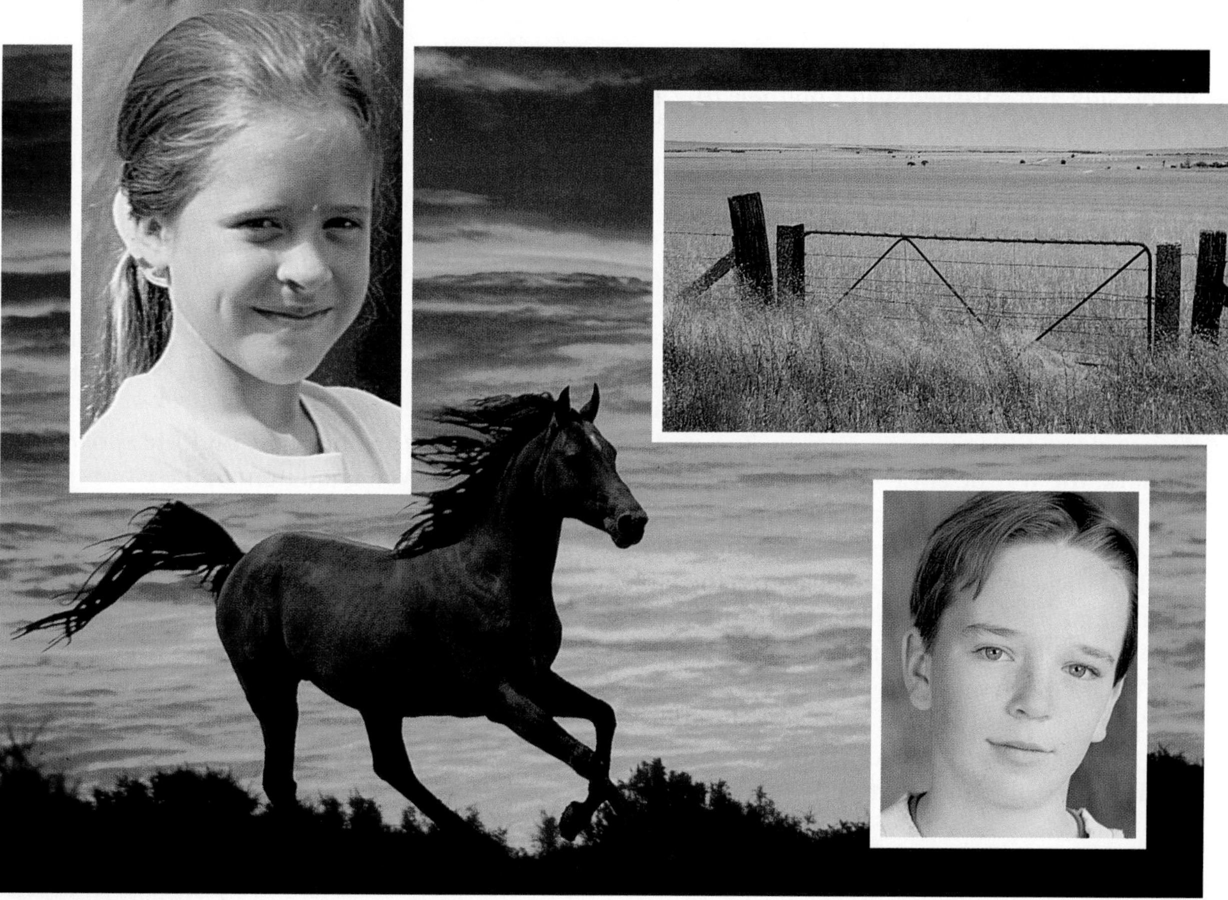

isn't any use planning dinner before one." She put up the ironing board. I wanted to tell her but thought better of it and went upstairs and sat on my bed.

Lately I had been trying to make my part of the room fancy, spreading the bed with old lace curtains and fixing myself a dressing table with some leftovers of cretonne[13] for a skirt. I planned to put up some kind of barricade between my bed and Laird's, to keep my section separate from his. In the sunlight, the lace curtains were just dusty rags. We did not sing at night anymore. One night when I was singing, Laird said, "You sound silly," and I went right on but the next night I did not start. There was not so much need to anyway; we were no longer afraid. We knew it was just old furniture over there, old jumble and confusion. We did not keep to the rules. I still stayed awake after Laird was asleep and told myself stories, but even in those stories something different was happening, mysterious alterations took place. A story might start off in the old way, with a spectacular danger, a fire or wild animals, and for a while I might rescue people; then things would change around, and instead, somebody would be rescuing me. It might be a boy from our class at school or even Mr. Campbell, our teacher, who tickled girls under the arms. And at this point the story concerned itself at great length with what I looked like—how long my hair was and what kind of dress I had on; by the time I had these details worked out, the real excitement of the story was lost.

It was later than one o'clock when the truck came back. The tarpaulin was over the back, which meant there was meat in it. My mother had to heat dinner up all over again. Henry and my father had changed from their bloody overalls into ordinary working overalls in the barn,

13. cretonne (krē·tän′): heavy printed cotton or linen cloth, named after Creton, a village in Normandy, France.

and they washed their arms and necks and faces at the sink and splashed water on their hair and combed it. Laird lifted his arm to show off a streak of blood. "We shot old Flora," he said, "and cut her up in fifty pieces."

"Well, I don't want to hear about it," my mother said. "And don't come to my table like that."

My father made him go and wash the blood off.

We sat down and my father said grace and Henry pasted his chewing gum on the end of his fork, the way he always did; when he took it off, he would have us admire the pattern. We began to pass the bowls of steaming, overcooked vegetables. Laird looked across the table at me and said proudly, distinctly, "Anyway, it was her fault Flora got away."

"What?" my father said.

"She could of shut the gate and she didn't. She just open' it up and Flora run out."

"Is that right?" my father said.

Everybody at the table was looking at me. I nodded, swallowing food with great difficulty. To my shame, tears flooded my eyes.

My father made a curt sound of disgust. "What did you do that for?"

I did not answer. I put down my fork and waited to be sent from the table, still not looking up.

But this did not happen. For some time nobody said anything; then Laird said matter-of-factly, "She's crying."

"Never mind," my father said. He spoke with resignation, even good humor, the words which absolved and dismissed me for good. "She's only a girl," he said.

I didn't protest that, even in my heart. Maybe it was true.

WORDS TO OWN

absolved (ab·zälvd′) *v.:* freed from guilt, blame, or responsibility.

MEET THE WRITER

Soul of a Story

For **Alice Munro** (1931–   ) a story is like a house. "I've got to make, I've got to build up, a house, a story to fit around the indescribable 'feeling' that is like the soul of a story." An important part of the "house" Munro builds is the details. "I'm very, very excited by what you might call the surface of life, and it must be that this seems to me meaningful in a way I can't analyze or describe."

The details of many of Munro's stories are drawn from her childhood in rural Ontario and British Columbia in Canada. She started writing when she was about fourteen or fifteen, and earlier than that she made up stories all the time. Her stories focus on ordinary lives. Her heroines are usually young girls or women who discover the uneasiness of adolescence, the tension that can exist within families, the impermanence of human relationships. "Boys and Girls" is from her first collection of stories, *Dance of the Happy Shades.* Asked why she writes only short stories, not novels, Munro said this:

"I never intended to be a short-story writer. I started writing them because I didn't have time to write anything else—I had three children. And then I got used to writing stories, so I saw my material that way, and now I don't think I'll ever write a novel. . . . There's a kind of tension that if I'm getting a story right I can feel right away, and I don't feel that when I try to write a novel. I kind of want a moment that's explosive, and I want everything gathered into that."

Connections | A Poem

Same Song

Pat Mora

While my sixteen-year-old son sleeps,
my twelve-year-old daughter
stumbles into the bathroom at six a.m.
plugs in the curling iron
squeezes into faded jeans
curls her hair carefully
strokes Aztec Blue shadow on her eyelids
smoothes Frosted Mauve blusher on her cheeks
outlines her mouth in Neon Pink
peers into the mirror, mirror on the wall
frowns at her face, her eyes, her skin,
not fair.

At night this daughter
stumbles off to bed at nine
eyes half-shut while my son
jogs a mile in the cold dark
then lifts weights in the garage
curls and bench presses
expanding biceps, triceps, pectorals,
one-handed push-ups, one hundred sit-ups
peers into that mirror, mirror and frowns too.

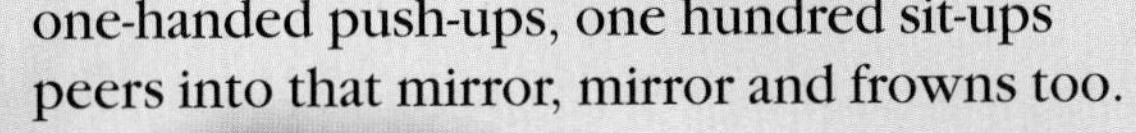

for Libby

MAKING MEANINGS

First Thoughts

1. Two important things happen at the end. How did you feel when the narrator's father dismissed her as "only a girl"? How did you feel about the girl's reaction?

Reading Check

Fill out a **story map** for "Boys and Girls" like the one that follows. Be sure to compare your map with those made by other readers.

Basic situation inc. **setting**	
Main **character**	
His/her **problem**	
Main events/ complications	
Climax	
Resolution	

Shaping Interpretations

2. One of the **conflicts** in the story takes place between the narrator and her mother. What does the mother expect of her daughter? Why does the narrator feel that her mother is her "enemy"?
3. Why does the girl find her father's work more interesting than her mother's?
4. After the girl watches her father shoot Mack, how does her attitude toward men's work change? How would you account for this change?
5. What other changes does the girl experience after the shooting incident? Try listing them on a chart like this one.

Girl's Attitude Toward	Before Mack Dies	After Mack Dies
her appearance her brother her daydreams boys her age her bedroom		

6. Another **conflict** in this story takes place in the girl's mind. What do you think the girl has decided when she says, "I was on Flora's side"?

Connecting with the Text

7. What **generalizations** about boys and girls could you make based on this story? What generalizations could you make based on the poll on page 58?

8. In your own experience, are the roles of girls and boys (or men and women) as distinct as they are in the rural Canada of this story? Refer to your own Quickwrite notes and to the poll results on page 58. Discuss your opinions with your group. Is there agreement or disagreement? You might also consider Barton's attitudes in "The Cold Equations" (page 9).

Challenging the Text

9. Do you like the way Alice Munro ended the story, or do you wish something else had happened? Explain.

CHOICES: Building Your Portfolio

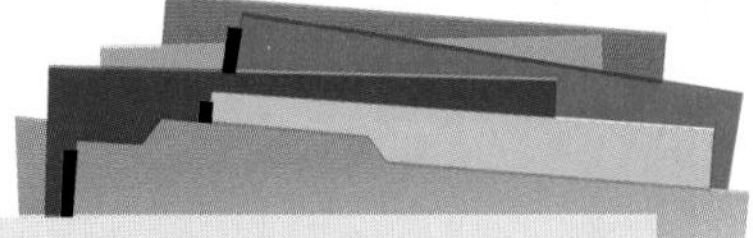

Writer's Notebook

1. Collecting Ideas for a Persuasive Essay

What's your view? Look at the poll on page 58. How would you answer these questions about men's and women's roles? (You might tally your classmates' answers and compare the results with the percentages given on page 58.) Look also at your Quickwrite notes. Then, in your notebook, freewrite about one or more experiences that helped shape your ideas about the roles of women and men. Keep your notes for the Writer's Workshop on page 85.

Issue: Stereotyped Roles
Incident: The time I signed up for a car repair class & I was the only girl—20 guys. They all laughed—thought girls can't do anything mechanical till I proved I could.

Critical Thinking/ Speaking

2. A Debate

Conduct a debate on this proposition: Boys' and girls' roles should be very distinct in our society. To prepare for the debate, divide the class into two teams, one to support and one to refute this proposition. Each side should first meet to assemble **evidence** and **arguments** and then engage the other side in a formal debate.

Creative Writing

3. Changing the Ending

Write a different ending, in which the narrator does protest her father's dismissal of her as just a girl. If she voices her protest, what does she say to her father? If she protests only in her heart, what does she think and feel? Read your new ending aloud to the class, and compare it with other revised endings.

Supporting an Opinion

4. Real Men Don't . . .

How have gender roles changed since Alice Munro wrote this story in the 1960s, and what do you think of the changes? What's it like for a man today? In a brief essay, express your views, using facts, examples, and anecdotes to support your opinions.

Creative Writing

5. Same Song?

Imagine that the narrator of "Boys and Girls" has read the poem "Same Song" (see *Connections* on page 65). How would she respond to that poem? (For that matter, how do *you* respond to it?) Would she agree with the portrayal of the son and daughter in the poem? Answer these questions in a creative medium of your choice. For example, the girl might write a diary entry or a letter to the daughter in the poem, or the girl might reply in a poem of her own.

Research/Viewing

6. The Way We Were

Look backward—sample the **media** (TV shows, movies, and magazines) of the 1940s and 1950s to see what they reveal about men's and women's roles in the "good old days." Watch some vintage TV (reruns of *I Love Lucy* are still shown), and rent some movie classics (such as *The Best Years of Our Lives*). Survey the advertisements in old copies of *Life, Saturday Evening Post,* and other magazines if you can find them in a library. Based on your research, what generalizations can you make about men's and women's roles in America during the 1940s and 1950s?

Language Link — MINI-LESSON

Connotations—How Words Can Make You Feel

Handbook of Literary Terms HELP

See Connotations.

The narrator in "Boys and Girls" discovers that a familiar word has shades of meaning she had not been aware of before:

> "The word *girl* had formerly seemed to me innocent and unburdened, like the word *child*; now it appeared that it was no such thing. A girl was not, as I had supposed, simply what I was; it was what I had to become. It was a definition, always touched with emphasis, with reproach and disappointment."

The narrator learns that the word *girl* suggests more than its strict literal dictionary meaning, or **denotation.** She learns that *girl* also carries a whole range of **connotations,** or emotional associations.

To help you choose the descriptive word with just the right shade of meaning, you may want to invent word chains like the ones that follow, which show a progression from negative to positive connotations.

miserly → cheap → thrifty
immature → childish → young

Try It Out

Think about the connotations of the underlined words in this passage from the story:

> My father removed the pelt inside out from the body of the fox, which looked surprisingly small, mean, and ratlike deprived of its arrogant weight of fur.

1. What are the connotations of *ratlike?*
2. How would you feel about the fox's being skinned if it had been described as *kittenlike?*
3. What are the connotations of *arrogant?*
4. How would you feel if the writer had used *proud* instead?

Vocabulary — HOW TO OWN A WORD

Word Bank

derisive
supplicating
placidly
ingenious
perversity
reproach
diligently
negligently
remote
absolved

Analogies: Matching Relationships

In an **analogy** two pairs of words have the same relationship. They may be antonyms or synonyms, for example, or they may share some other relationship. Work with a partner to complete each analogy with a word from the Word Bank. The first one has been done as an example.

1. *Darkness* is to *light* as *perversity* is to *compliance.*
2. *Slowly* is to *quickly* as__________ is to *nervously.*
3. *Relieved* is to *worry* as__________ is to *blame.*
4. *Powerful* is to *mighty* as__________ is to *distant.*
5. *Praise* is to *approval* as__________ is to *disapproval.*
6. *Strong* is to *weightlifter* as__________ is to *inventor.*
7. *Tired* is to *exhausted* as__________ is to *mocking.*
8. *Commanding* is to *ordering* as__________ is to *appealing.*
9. *Cautiously* is to *recklessly* as__________ is to *lazily.*
10. *Casually* is to *informally* as__________ is to *carelessly.*

Before You Read

Everyday Use

Make the Connection

Generation Clashes

To parents the new generation's choices often seem strange or wrong. To children the older generation often seems stuck in the past.

"Everyday Use" takes place in the rural South during the 1960s, when values and ways of life were changing rapidly. In this story, an African American mother is living an old-fashioned farm life with one of her daughters. When her other daughter visits, with new values and a new boyfriend, the mother must make a choice.

Quickwrite

Many families have traditions or heirlooms that are handed down to the younger generation. Do you have any in your family? Jot down your feelings about maintaining traditions and continuity in a family.

Elements of Literature

Conflict: Blocked Desires

It is the **conflict** in a story that stirs our emotions. If the conflict hooks our interest, it creates suspense and makes us want to read on.

Conflict often occurs when a character's desires are blocked in some way. Conflicts that stir our emotions can be big and dramatic, or they can be as quiet as the question of what to do with an old quilt.

> **Conflict** is a struggle that usually occurs when the main character's desires are blocked in some way.
>
> *For more on Conflict, see pages 32–33 and the Handbook of Literary Terms.*

Reading Skills and Strategies

Comparing and Contrasting Characters

Maggie and Dee are the two adult sisters in this story. Much of the conflict in the story arises because the sisters are separated by wide differences in appearance, education, values, and personalities. As you read, **compare and contrast** the sisters. Track any shifting feelings and sympathies you may have for one sister or the other.

"I can 'member
Grandma Dee
without the quilts."

His Grandmother's Quilt (1988) by Phoebe Beasley (1943–). Collage.

Courtesy of the artist.

Everyday Use

For Your Grandmama

Alice Walker

I will wait for her in the yard that Maggie and I made so clean and wavy yesterday afternoon. A yard like this is more comfortable than most people know. It is not just a yard. It is like an extended living room. When the hard clay is swept clean as a floor and the fine sand around the edges lined with tiny, irregular grooves, anyone can come and sit and look up into the elm tree and wait for the breezes that never come inside the house.

Maggie will be nervous until after her sister goes: She will stand hopelessly in corners, homely and ashamed of the burn scars down her arms and legs, eyeing her sister with a mixture of envy and awe.

She thinks her sister had held life always in the palm of one hand, that "no" is a word the world never learned to say to her.

You've no doubt seen those TV shows where the child who has "made it" is confronted, as a surprise, by her own mother and father, tottering in weakly from backstage. (A pleasant surprise, of course: What would they do if parent and child came on the show only to curse out and insult each other?) On TV mother and child embrace and smile into each other's faces. Sometimes the mother and father weep; the child wraps them in her arms and leans across the table to tell how she would not have made it without their help. I have seen these programs.

Sometimes I dream a dream in which Dee and I are suddenly brought together on a TV program of this sort. Out of a dark and soft-seated limousine I am ushered into a bright room filled with many people. There I meet a smiling, gray, sporty man like Johnny Carson who shakes my hand and tells me what a fine girl I have. Then we are on the stage, and Dee is embracing me with tears in her eyes. She pins on my dress a large orchid, even though she had told me once that she thinks orchids are tacky flowers.

In real life I am a large, big-boned woman with rough, man-working hands. In the winter I wear flannel nightgowns to bed and overalls during the day. I can kill and clean a hog as mercilessly as a man. My fat keeps me hot in zero weather. I can work outside all day, breaking ice to get water for washing; I can eat pork liver cooked over the open fire minutes after it comes steaming from the hog. One winter I knocked a bull calf straight in the brain between the eyes with a sledgehammer and had the meat hung up to chill before nightfall. But of course all this does not show on television. I am the way my daughter would want me to be: a hundred pounds lighter, my skin like an uncooked barley pancake. My hair glistens in the hot bright lights. Johnny Carson has much to do to keep up with my quick and witty tongue.

But that is a mistake. I know even before I wake up. Who ever knew a Johnson with a quick tongue? Who can even imagine me looking a strange white man in the eye? It seems to me I have talked to them always with one foot raised in flight, with my head turned in whichever way is farthest from them. Dee, though. She would always look anyone in the eye. Hesitation was no part of her nature.

"How do I look, Mama?" Maggie says, showing just enough of her thin body enveloped in pink skirt and red blouse for me to know she's there, almost hidden by the door.

"Come out into the yard," I say.

Have you ever seen a lame animal, perhaps a dog run over by some careless person rich enough to own a car, sidle up to someone who is ignorant enough to be kind to him? That is the way my Maggie walks. She has been like this, chin on chest, eyes on ground, feet in shuffle, ever since the fire that burned the other house to the ground.

Dee is lighter than Maggie, with nicer hair and a fuller figure. She's a woman now, though sometimes I forget. How long ago was it that the other house burned? Ten, twelve years? Sometimes I can still hear the flames and feel Maggie's arms sticking to me, her hair smoking and her dress falling off her in little black papery flakes. Her eyes seemed stretched open, blazed open by the flames reflected in them. And Dee. I see her standing off under the sweet gum tree she used to dig gum out of, a look of concentration on her face as she watched the last dingy gray board of the house fall in toward the red-hot brick chimney. Why don't you do a dance around the ashes? I'd wanted to ask her. She had hated the house that much.

I used to think she hated Maggie, too. But that was before we raised the money, the church and me, to send her to Augusta to

WORDS TO OWN

sidle (sīd′'l) *v.:* move sideways, especially in a shy or sneaky manner.

school. She used to read to us without pity, forcing words, lies, other folks' habits, whole lives upon us two, sitting trapped and ignorant underneath her voice. She washed us in a river of make-believe, burned us with a lot of knowledge we didn't necessarily need to know. Pressed us to her with the serious ways she read, to shove us away at just the moment, like dimwits, we seemed about to understand.

Dee wanted nice things. A yellow organdy dress to wear to her graduation from high school; black pumps to match a green suit she'd made from an old suit somebody gave me. She was determined to stare down any disaster in her efforts. Her eyelids would not flicker for minutes at a time. Often I fought off the temptation to shake her. At sixteen she had a style of her own: and knew what style was.

I never had an education myself. After second grade the school closed down. Don't ask me why: In 1927 colored asked fewer questions than they do now. Sometimes Maggie reads to me. She stumbles along good-naturedly but can't see well. She knows she is not bright. Like good looks and money, quickness passed her by. She will marry John Thomas (who has mossy teeth in an earnest face), and then I'll be free to sit here and I guess just sing church songs to myself. Although I never was a good singer. Never could carry a tune. I was always better at a man's job. I used to love to milk till I was hooked in the side in '49. Cows are soothing and slow and don't bother you, unless you try to milk them the wrong way.

I have deliberately turned my back on the house. It is three rooms, just like the one that burned, except the roof is tin; they don't make shingle roofs anymore. There are no real windows, just some holes cut in the sides, like the portholes in a ship, but not round and not square, with rawhide holding the shutters up on the outside. This house is in a pasture, too, like the other one. No doubt when Dee sees it she will want to tear it down. She wrote me once that no matter where we "choose" to live, she will manage to come see us. But she will never bring her friends. Maggie and I thought about this and Maggie asked me, "Mama, when did Dee ever *have* any friends?"

She had a few. Furtive boys in pink shirts hanging about on washday after school. Nervous girls who never laughed. Impressed with her, they worshiped the well-turned phrase, the cute shape, the scalding humor that erupted like bubbles in lye. She read to them.

When she was courting Jimmy T, she didn't have much time to pay to us but turned all her faultfinding power on him. He *flew* to marry a cheap city girl from a family of ignorant, flashy people. She hardly had time to recompose herself.

When she comes, I will meet—but there they are!

Maggie attempts to make a dash for the house, in her shuffling way, but I stay her with my hand. "Come back here," I say. And she stops and tries to dig a well in the sand with her toe.

It is hard to see them clearly through the strong sun. But even the first glimpse of leg out of the car tells me it is Dee. Her feet were always neat looking, as if God himself shaped them with a certain style. From the other side of the car comes a short, stocky man. Hair is all over his head a foot long and hanging from his chin like a kinky mule tail. I hear Maggie suck in her breath. "Uhnnnh" is what it sounds like. Like when you see the wriggling end of a snake just in front of your foot on the road. "Uhnnnh."

Dee next. A dress down to the ground, in this hot weather. A dress so loud it hurts my eyes. There are yellows and oranges enough to throw back the light of the sun. I feel my whole face warming from the heat waves it throws out. Earrings gold, too, and hanging down to her shoulders. Bracelets dangling and making noises when she moves her arm up to shake the folds

Words to Own

furtive (fur'tiv) *adj.:* acting as if trying not to be seen. *Furtive* also means "done secretly."

of the dress out of her armpits. The dress is loose and flows, and as she walks closer, I like it. I hear Maggie go "Uhnnnh" again. It is her sister's hair. It stands straight up like the wool on a sheep. It is black as night and around the edges are two long pigtails that rope about like small lizards disappearing behind her ears.

"Wa-su-zo-Tean-o!" she says, coming on in that gliding way the dress makes her move. The short, stocky fellow with the hair to his navel is all grinning, and he follows up with "Asalamalakim,[1] my mother and sister!" He moves to hug Maggie but she falls back, right up against the back of my chair. I feel her trembling there, and when I look up I see the perspiration falling off her chin.

"Don't get up," says Dee. Since I am stout, it takes something of a push. You can see me trying to move a second or two before I make it. She turns, showing white heels through her sandals, and goes back to the car. Out she peeks next with a Polaroid. She stoops down quickly and lines up picture after picture of me sitting there in front of the house with Maggie cowering behind me. She never takes a shot without making sure the house is included. When a cow comes nibbling around in the edge of the yard, she snaps it and me and Maggie *and* the house. Then she puts the Polaroid in the back seat of the car and comes up and kisses me on the forehead.

Meanwhile, Asalamalakim is going through motions with Maggie's hand. Maggie's hand is as limp as a fish, and probably as cold, despite the sweat, and she keeps trying to pull it back. It looks like Asalamalakim wants to shake hands but wants to do it fancy. Or maybe he don't know how people shake hands. Anyhow, he soon gives up on Maggie.

"Well," I say. "Dee."

"No, Mama," she says. "Not 'Dee,' Wangero Leewanika Kemanjo!"

"What happened to 'Dee'?" I wanted to know.

"She's dead," Wangero said. "I couldn't bear it any longer, being named after the people who oppress me."

"You know as well as me you was named after your aunt Dicie," I said. Dicie is my sister. She named Dee. We called her "Big Dee" after Dee was born.

"But who was *she* named after?" asked Wangero.

"I guess after Grandma Dee," I said.

"And who was she named after?" asked Wangero.

"Her mother," I said, and saw Wangero was getting tired. "That's about as far back as I can trace it," I said. Though, in fact, I probably could have carried it back beyond the Civil War through the branches.

"Well," said Asalamalakim, "there you are."

"Uhnnnh," I heard Maggie say.

"There I was not," I said, "before 'Dicie' cropped up in our family, so why should I try to trace it that far back?"

He just stood there grinning, looking down on me like somebody inspecting a Model A car. Every once in a while he and Wangero sent eye signals over my head.

"How do you pronounce this name?" I asked.

"You don't have to call me by it if you don't want to," said Wangero.

"Why shouldn't I?" I asked. "If that's what you want us to call you, we'll call you."

"I know it might sound awkward at first," said Wangero.

"I'll get used to it," I said. "Ream it out again."

Well, soon we got the name out of the way. Asalamalakim had a name twice as long and three times as hard. After I tripped over it two or three times, he told me to just call him Hakim-a-barber. I wanted to ask him was he a barber, but I didn't really think he was, so I didn't ask.

1. **Asalamalakim:** Asalaam aleikum (ä·sə·läm′ ä·lā′koom′), greeting used by Muslims meaning "peace to you."

Words to Own

cowering (kou′ər·iŋ) *v.* used as *adj.:* drawing back or huddling in fear.

"You must belong to those beef-cattle peoples down the road," I said. They said "Asalamalakim" when they met you, too, but they didn't shake hands. Always too busy: feeding the cattle, fixing the fences, putting up salt-lick shelters, throwing down hay. When the white folks poisoned some of the herd, the men stayed up all night with rifles in their hands. I walked a mile and a half just to see the sight.

Hakim-a-barber said, "I accept some of their doctrines, but farming and raising cattle is not my style." (They didn't tell me, and I didn't ask, whether Wangero—Dee—had really gone and married him.)

We sat down to eat and right away he said he didn't eat collards, and pork was unclean. Wangero, though, went on through the chitlins and corn bread, the greens, and everything else. She talked a blue streak over the sweet potatoes. Everything delighted her. Even the fact that we still used the benches her daddy made for the table when we couldn't afford to buy chairs.

"Oh, Mama!" she cried. Then turned to Hakim-a-barber. "I never knew how lovely these benches are. You can feel the rump prints," she said, running her hands underneath her and along the bench. Then she gave a sigh, and her hand closed over Grandma Dee's butter dish. "That's it!" she said. "I knew there was something I wanted to ask you if I could have." She jumped up from the table and went over in the corner where the churn stood, the milk in it clabber[2] by now. She looked at the churn and looked at it.

"This churn top is what I need," she said. "Didn't Uncle Buddy whittle it out of a tree you all used to have?"

"Yes," I said.

"Uh huh," she said happily. "And I want the dasher,[3] too."

"Uncle Buddy whittle that, too?" asked the barber.

Dee (Wangero) looked up at me.

"Aunt Dee's first husband whittled the dash," said Maggie so low you almost couldn't hear her. "His name was Henry, but they called him Stash."

"Maggie's brain is like an elephant's," Wangero said, laughing. "I can use the churn top as a centerpiece for the alcove table," she said, sliding a plate over the churn, "and I'll think of something artistic to do with the dasher."

When she finished wrapping the dasher, the handle stuck out. I took it for a moment in my hands. You didn't even have to look close to see where hands pushing the dasher up and down to make butter had left a kind of sink in the wood. In fact, there were a lot of small sinks; you could see where thumbs and fingers had sunk into the wood. It was beautiful light-yellow wood, from a tree that grew in the yard where Big Dee and Stash had lived.

After dinner Dee (Wangero) went to the trunk at the foot of my bed and started rifling through it. Maggie hung back in the kitchen over the dishpan. Out came Wangero with two quilts. They had been pieced by Grandma Dee, and then Big Dee and me had hung them on the quilt frames on the front porch and quilted them. One was in the Lone Star pattern. The other was Walk Around the Mountain. In both of them were scraps of dresses Grandma Dee had worn fifty and more years ago. Bits and pieces of Grandpa Jarrell's paisley shirts. And one teeny faded blue piece, about the size of a penny matchbox, that was from Great Grandpa Ezra's uniform that he wore in the Civil War.

"Mama," Wangero said sweet as a bird. "Can I have these old quilts?"

I heard something fall in the kitchen, and a minute later the kitchen door slammed.

"Why don't you take one or two of the others?" I asked. "These old things was just done by me and Big Dee from some tops your grandma pieced before she died."

"No," said Wangero. "I don't want those.

2. **clabber:** thickly curdled sour milk.
3. **dasher:** pole that stirs the milk in a churn.

Words to Own

doctrines (däk′trinz) *n.:* principles; teachings; beliefs.
rifling (rī′fliŋ) *v.* used as *n.:* searching thoroughly or in a rough manner.

They are stitched around the borders by machine."

"That'll make them last better," I said.

"That's not the point," said Wangero. "These are all pieces of dresses Grandma used to wear. She did all this stitching by hand. Imagine!" She held the quilts securely in her arms, stroking them.

"Some of the pieces, like those lavender ones, come from old clothes her mother handed down to her," I said, moving up to touch the quilts. Dee (Wangero) moved back just enough so that I couldn't reach the quilts. They already belonged to her.

"Imagine!" she breathed again, clutching them closely to her bosom.

"The truth is," I said, "I promised to give them quilts to Maggie, for when she marries John Thomas."

She gasped like a bee had stung her.

"Maggie can't appreciate these quilts!" she said. "She'd probably be backward enough to put them to everyday use."

"I reckon she would," I said. "God knows I been saving 'em for long enough with nobody using 'em. I hope she will!" I didn't want to bring up how I had offered Dee (Wangero) a quilt when she went away to college. Then she had told me they were old-fashioned, out of style.

"But they're *priceless*!" she was saying now, furiously; for she has a temper. "Maggie would put them on the bed and in five years they'd be in rags. Less than that!"

"She can always make some more," I said. "Maggie knows how to quilt."

Dee (Wangero) looked at me with hatred. "You just will not understand. The point is *these* quilts, these quilts!"

"Well," I said, stumped. "What would *you* do with them?"

"Hang them," she said. As if that was the only thing you *could* do with quilts.

Maggie by now was standing in the door. I could almost hear the sound her feet made as they scraped over each other.

"She can have them, Mama," she said, like somebody used to never winning anything or having anything reserved for her. "I can 'member Grandma Dee without the quilts."

I looked at her hard. She had filled her bottom lip with checkerberry snuff, and it gave her face a kind of dopey, hangdog look. It was Grandma Dee and Big Dee who taught her how to quilt herself. She stood there with her scarred hands hidden in the folds of her skirt. She looked at her sister with something like fear, but she wasn't mad at her. This was Maggie's portion. This was the way she knew God to work.

When I looked at her like that, something hit me in the top of my head and ran down to the soles of my feet. Just like when I'm in church and the spirit of God touches me and I get happy and shout. I did something I never had done before: hugged Maggie to me, then dragged her on into the room, snatched the quilts out of Miss Wangero's hands, and dumped them into Maggie's lap. Maggie just sat there on my bed with her mouth open.

"Take one or two of the others," I said to Dee.

But she turned without a word and went out to Hakim-a-barber.

"You just don't understand," she said, as Maggie and I came out to the car.

"What don't I understand?" I wanted to know.

"Your heritage," she said. And then she turned to Maggie, kissed her, and said, "You ought to try to make something of yourself, too, Maggie. It's really a new day for us. But from the way you and Mama still live, you'd never know it."

She put on some sunglasses that hid everything above the tip of her nose and her chin.

Maggie smiled, maybe at the sunglasses. But a real smile, not scared. After we watched the car dust settle, I asked Maggie to bring me a dip of snuff. And then the two of us sat there just enjoying, until it was time to go in the house and go to bed.

Alice Walker and her daughter, Rebecca.

MEET THE WRITER

Out of Eatonton

Alice Walker (1944–), shown above with her daughter, Rebecca, was born in the small town of Eatonton, Georgia, the youngest of eight children. Her father was a sharecropper, and her mother worked as a maid. When she was eight years old, Walker was blinded in one eye by a shot from a BB gun. The resulting scar tissue made her painfully shy and self-conscious, and she spent her free time alone outdoors, reading and writing stories. With the aid of a scholarship for handicapped students, she attended Spelman College, a college for African American women in Atlanta.

Women have always played an important role in Walker's life. She has said that she grew up believing there was absolutely nothing her mother couldn't do once she set her mind to it. So when the women's movement came along, she said that she was delighted because she felt they were trying to go where her mother was and where she had always assumed she would go.

Walker's third novel, *The Color Purple,* won the Pulitzer Prize for fiction in 1983 and was made into a popular movie. Walker has been a contributing editor of *Ms.* magazine and has been active in both the women's movement and the civil rights movement.

Walker has published short stories, poems, essays, and novels, so it comes as a surprise to learn that she never intended to be a writer.

“ I just kind of found myself doing it. I remember wanting to be a scientist, wanting to be a pianist, wanting to be a painter. But all the while I was wanting to be these other things, I was writing. We were really poor, and writing was about the cheapest thing to do. You know, I feel amazed that I have been able to do exactly what I wanted to do. ”

Connections A NEWS FEATURE

In Georgia's Swept Yards, a Dying Tradition

ANNE RAVER

ATHENS, Ga.—Mismatched pots of begonias and petunias hang from old porches that could use some work. Painted chicken feeders blossom with zinnias and red salvia. These yards have no grass—because they are swept clean with a broom made of dogwood branches gathered in the woods.

They don't look like much at first glance. But hidden in their unconscious design are traces of West Africa and the emergence of a hard-won independence.

Blacks here, descendants of slaves brought, mainly from West Africa, to work the cotton fields in Georgia's hard clay, are carrying on the traditions that their ancestors brought from the Gold Coast°—everything from cooking and washing outdoors to sharing the latest gossip under a shade tree. But these yards and the life they hold are fast disappearing, as the people who have long tended them grow old and their children move on.

The swept yard was the most important "room" of the household, the heart of the home. Slave quarters were cramped and hot. So you washed and cooked outside, and when the meal was over, everything could be swept into the fire.

Sixteen years ago, when Richard Westmacott, an Englishman, came to Athens to teach landscape architecture at the University of Georgia, he and his wife, Jean, moved into an abandoned pre–Civil War house in rural Oglethorpe County, about twenty miles east of town. In visiting the gardens of his neighbors, he realized that what the local people took for granted was the embodiment of a fast-disappearing culture.

"I have no doubt that the swept yard did come from Africa—and then was adopted by white folks," said Mr. Westmacott, whose book, *African-American Gardens and Yards in the Rural South,* was published last year by the University of Tennessee. "Almost everybody had swept yards, including the plantations, which were swept by slaves or servants."

Mr. Westmacott's book, which examines the traditions and folk art of these black gardeners, is the result of his travels through rural Georgia, Alabama, and South Carolina. His photographs capture a society that is fast disappearing, as children move to the cities for work and buy their vegetables at the supermarket. His book also includes photographs of villages in West Africa, taken at the turn of the century and preserved in British archives, that show striking similarities to the swept yards of the South.

Swept yards are so familiar to some that they have become invisible.

When Mr. Westmacott asked why they swept their yards, gardeners simply said that their mothers and grandmothers did it that way.

"It comes from way back," said Dell Appling, sitting on an old glider under some oak trees brought from the woods and "set out" years ago. "My mother—she was ninety when she passed—would sweep the yard with a brush broom we made out of dogwood."

—from *The New York Times,* August 8, 1993

° *The Gold Coast is a former British colony in western Africa, now an independent country called Ghana.*

Photo by Richard Westmacott.

Yard-sweeping near Lodge, South Carolina.

Making Meanings

First Thoughts

1. Which character did you side with in the conflict over the quilts, and why?

Shaping Interpretations

2. What do you think is the source of the **conflict** in this story? Consider:
   - Which **character** sets the action in motion?
   - Which of her desires are blocked?
   - Who or what is blocking them?
   - Is the battle **external** or **internal** or both?
3. Dee is referred to as the child who has "made it." What do you think that means, and what signs tell you that she has "made it"?

4. Use a diagram like the one on the right to **compare and contrast** Dee and Maggie. What is the most significant thing they have in common? What is their most compelling difference?

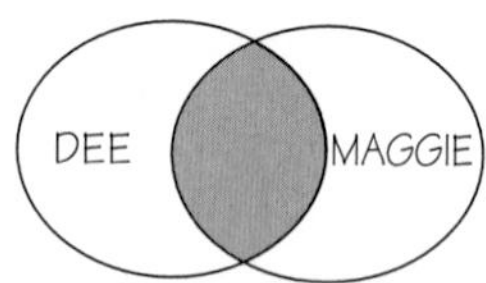

5. Near the end of the story, Dee accuses Mama of not understanding their African American heritage. Do you agree or disagree with Dee, and why?
6. Has any character changed by the end of the story? Go back to the text and find details to support your answer.
7. Why do you think Alice Walker dedicated her story "For Your Grandmama"?

Extending the Text

8. What do you think each of these three women will be doing ten years after the story ends?
9. This story takes place in a very particular **setting** and a very particular **culture.** Talk about whether or not the problems faced by this family could be experienced by any family, anywhere.

Challenging the Text

10. Do you think Alice Walker chose the right narrator for her story? How would the story differ if Dee or Maggie were telling it, instead of Mama? (What would we know that we don't know now?)

Reading Check

a. According to Mama, how is Dee different from her and from Maggie?

b. How would Maggie and Dee use the quilts differently?

c. When she was a child, something terrible happened to Maggie. What was it?

d. How did the mother choose to resolve the **conflict** over the quilts?

e. Find the passage in the text that explains the **title**.

Churn (1935–1942), rendering by Lelah Nelson. Watercolor, pen and ink, and graphite on paperboard ($18\frac{1}{16}'' \times 11\frac{3}{4}''$).

CHOICES: Building Your Portfolio

Writer's Notebook

1. Collecting Ideas for a Persuasive Essay

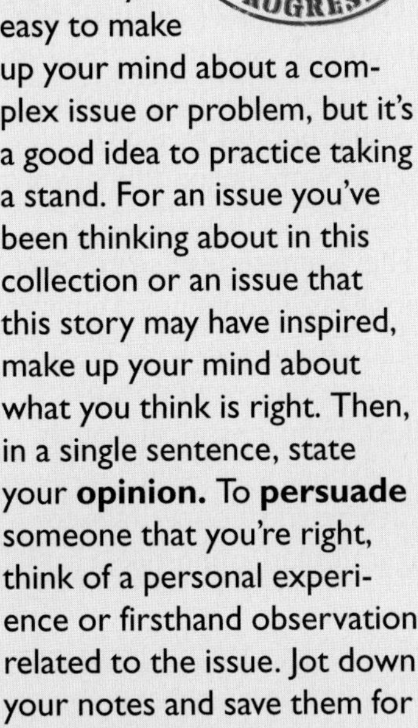

Taking a stand. It isn't always easy to make up your mind about a complex issue or problem, but it's a good idea to practice taking a stand. For an issue you've been thinking about in this collection or an issue that this story may have inspired, make up your mind about what you think is right. Then, in a single sentence, state your **opinion.** To **persuade** someone that you're right, think of a personal experience or firsthand observation related to the issue. Jot down your notes and save them for the Writer's Workshop on page 85.

Opinion: Communities should provide bikes for borrowing.
Support: Portland's experiment.
The time we refurbished 40 bikes & in a few weeks they were all gone.
Still a good idea, though.

Creative Writing

2. What Does Maggie Say?

Let Maggie narrate the climactic scene in her own voice. Start on page 74, at the moment Wangero/Dee says, "Can I have these old quilts?" Why does Maggie offer Dee the quilts? How does she feel when Mama dumps them on her lap? Why does she smile at the end?

Editorial Writing

3. Preserving Through Writing

Many newspapers today have opposite their main editorial page an op-ed page, which contains signed essays on topics of special interest. Write an **op-ed article** about something important in your family heritage. It might be a holiday, a recipe, a traditional style of clothing, or a way of fixing your yard (see *Connections* on page 77). Elaborate in your essay by adding a few vivid descriptive details. Share your op-ed article with classmates by reading it aloud.

Supporting an Opinion

4. Dear Author

Alice Walker once said that she gathers up the historical and psychological threads of the lives of her ancestors, and in writing about their lives, she feels the joy of continuity. Do you think all people find joy in continuity—in looking back at the lives of their ancestors? Write a **letter** to Walker agreeing or disagreeing with this idea.

Art/Culture

5. Design a Quilt

Quilts have been designed to commemorate bicentennials, historical events, family histories, and so on, as well as to honor people who have died from AIDS. Design a quilt that reflects an aspect or aspects of your **cultural heritage.** Write a brief explanation of why you chose the various elements of your design and how each reflects your cultural heritage.

The AIDS quilt in Washington, D.C.

LANGUAGE LINK — MINI-LESSON

Diction—Finding the Right Word

Handbook of Literary Terms HELP

See Diction.

Diction is **word choice.** Whether you say "diction" or "word choice" is a matter of diction—or word choice. Diction can be formal ("remove yourself") or informal ("get a move on"). Diction can be plain ("clothes") or fancy ("apparel").

Here are two sentences from "Everyday Use." Note the underlined words.

1. "In 1927 colored asked fewer questions than they do now."

   What does it suggest to you that Mama says "colored," not "African Americans" or "black people"?

2. "Hakim-a-barber said, 'I accept some of their doctrines, but farming and raising cattle is not my style.' "

   What impression of Hakim-a-barber do you get from his diction? How would he seem different if he'd said, "I hear that stuff they're saying, but I ain't no sodbuster"?

A Tip for Writers

In your own writing, especially in a personal narrative, you will probably use **dialogue.** To sound natural, the diction you use in dialogue must reflect how that person would really speak. Many people pronounce words carelessly and often speak in fragments. They sometimes use colorful expressions (as when Mama remarks "Ream it out again" instead of "Say it again"). Spoken language doesn't sound like a formal essay, although Hakim-a-barber's comes close. Always read your dialogue aloud. Practice rewriting it until it sounds like real speech.

VOCABULARY — HOW TO OWN A WORD

WORD BANK

sidle
furtive
cowering
doctrines
rifling

Diagraming Context

The diagram below shows how one reader figured out the meaning of *sidle* by using **context clues.** After noting this reader's strategies, locate the other words at the left as they appear in the story, and make a context diagram for each word.

"Have you ever seen a lame animal, perhaps a dog run over by some careless person rich enough to own a car, sidle up to someone who is ignorant enough to be kind to him?"

A lame dog might not walk straight.

Sidle might mean "move sideways." (It sounds like *side*.)

The dog wants someone to be nice to him, so *sidle* also probably means he's begging for attention, sort of pitifully.

EXTENDING *the theme*

TRAVEL WRITING

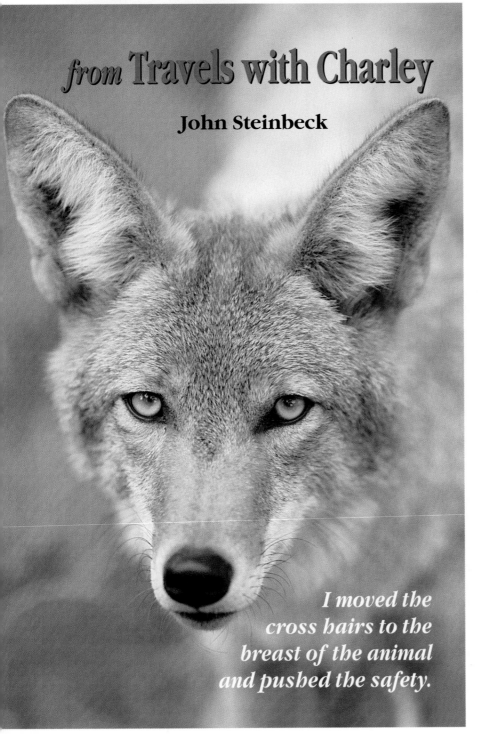

from Travels with Charley

John Steinbeck

I moved the cross hairs to the breast of the animal and pushed the safety.

Background

Every journey to a new place is also a journey toward oneself. In 1960, John Steinbeck took his aged poodle, Charley, and set out to "discover" America in a homemade camper he named Rocinante (after the run-down horse that carried the Spanish "knight" Don Quixote on his quests; see page 577). *Travels with Charley* is the book Steinbeck wrote about his travels. In this excerpt, a desert creature presents Steinbeck with a choice between public issues and private ones.

Reading Skills and Strategies

Dialogue with the Text

As you read this selection, be alert for sentences, phrases, or words that strike you, that make you stop and think or see something more clearly. Copy the passages in the left column of a two-column sheet. (If you'd rather not interrupt your reading, note the location of the passage so that you can return to it after you've finished.) Here is what this **double-entry journal** would look like:

Passages	My Comments

go.hrw.com

LEO 10-1

About fifty yards away two coyotes stood watching me, their tawny coats blending with sand and sun. I knew that with any quick or suspicious movement of mine they could drift into invisibility. With the most casual slowness I reached down my new rifle from its sling over my bed—the .222, with its bitter little high-speed, long-range stings. Very slowly I brought the rifle up. Perhaps in the shade of my house I was half hidden by the blinding light outside. The little rifle has a beautiful telescope sight with a wide field. The coyotes had not moved.

I got both of them in the field of my telescope, and the glass brought them very close. Their tongues lolled out so that they seemed to smile mockingly. They were favored animals, not starved but well furred, the golden hair tempered with black guard hairs. Their little lemon-yellow eyes were plainly visible in the glass. I moved the cross hairs to the breast of the right-hand animal and pushed the safety. My elbows on the table steadied the gun. The cross hairs lay unmoving on the brisket.[1] And then the coyote sat down like a dog and its right paw came up to scratch the right shoulder.

My finger was reluctant to touch the trigger. I must be getting very old and my ancient conditioning worn thin. Coyotes are vermin. They steal chickens. They thin the ranks of quail and all other game birds. They must be killed. They are the enemy. My first shot would drop the sitting beast, and the other would whirl to fade away. I might very well pull him down with a running shot because I am a good rifleman.

And I did not fire. My training said, "Shoot!" and my age replied, "There isn't a chicken within thirty miles, and if there are any, they aren't my chickens. And this waterless place is not quail country. No, these boys are keeping their figures with kangaroo rats and jack rabbits, and that's vermin eat vermin. Why should I interfere?"

"Kill them," my training said. "Everyone kills them. It's a public service." My finger moved to the trigger. The cross was steady on the breast just below the panting tongue. I could imagine the splash and jar of angry steel, the leap and struggle until the torn heart failed, and then, not too long later, the shadow of a buzzard, and another. By that time I would be long gone—out of the desert and across the Colorado River. And beside the sagebrush there would be a naked, eyeless skull, a few picked bones, a spot of black dried blood, and a few rags of golden fur.

I guess I'm too old and too lazy to be a good citizen. The second coyote stood sidewise to my rifle. I moved the cross hairs to his shoulder and held steady. There was no question of miss-

1. **brisket:** chest.

MEET THE WRITER

Laureate of Labor

John Steinbeck (1902–1968) came from much-traveled forebears: His mother was the daughter of an Irish immigrant to the United States, and his father had moved from Florida to California. As a young man Steinbeck worked at a wide variety of jobs and wrote books that were little noticed. In 1939, however, his novel *The Grapes of Wrath* won both the Pulitzer Prize and the National Book Award. The heroes of this novel are migrant laborers, Oklahoma farmers displaced by drought and by the Great Depression, who set off across the country for the promised land of California.

Steinbeck sought fame, but when it arrived, he tended to flee into anonymity—on the road or in Mexico. In 1962 he received the Nobel Prize, the highest award possible for a writer. Asked by a *Life* magazine reporter if he deserved it, Steinbeck said he was always afraid of the award because people never seemed to write anymore after they won it. "I wouldn't have accepted it," he said, "if I hadn't thought I could beat the rap." He didn't beat the rap. He died six years later, having published nothing more.

More by Steinbeck

Of Mice and Men (Viking Penguin)
The Red Pony (Viking Penguin)
The Pearl (Viking Penguin)

ing with that rifle at that range. I owned both animals. Their lives were mine. I put the safety on and laid the rifle on the table. Without the telescope they were not so intimately close. The hot blast of light tousled the air to shimmering.

Then I remembered something I heard long ago that I hope is true. It was unwritten law in China, so my informant told me, that when one man saved another's life, he became responsible for that life to the end of its existence. For, having interfered with a course of events, the savior could not escape his responsibility. And that has always made good sense to me.

Now I had a token responsibility for two live and healthy coyotes. In the delicate world of relationships, we are tied together for all time. I opened two cans of dog food and left them as a votive.[2]

2. **votive:** something offered to fulfill a vow or pledge or in thanks. In some churches, votive candles are lit in thanksgiving for answered prayers.

FINDING COMMON GROUND

Now that you've finished reading, go back to the passages you noted in your **double-entry journal.** Reflect for a few minutes, and then fill out the column labeled "My Comments." Do you agree or disagree with these passages? Did they make you see or feel something in a new way?

Form groups of three or four, and discuss the Steinbeck piece, using these approaches:

1. Discuss your journal entries. You might have each member read one passage and comment on it. Did other members of the group notice the same passage? Did you react similarly to it? Be sure each person has a chance to share at least one entry.
2. Move on to wider issues. Steinbeck doesn't directly comment on public issues, but he leaves plenty of room for them between the lines. In your groups talk about the public issues this desert narrative raises:
    - How do you think Steinbeck felt about nature, civilization, and progress?
    - How do you feel about the choices he made?
    - What range of views do you find in your group?
    - What impression did this selection give you of the man who wrote it?
3. Share your group's responses and conclusions with the entire class. Do you find agreement, or are some issues still controversial?

Burning Books

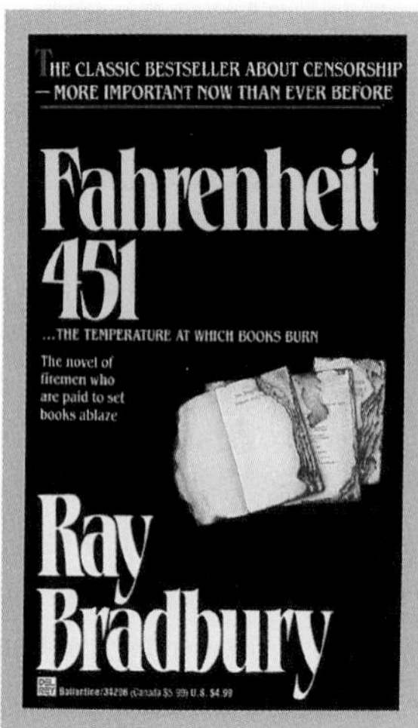

In Ray Bradbury's world of *Fahrenheit 451* (Ballantine), the censors have taken over. People can read only books that the state approves, and any unauthorized books are burned by "firemen." (Paper catches fire at 451 degrees Fahrenheit.) Then one fireman questions what he's doing. . . .

Questions of Identity

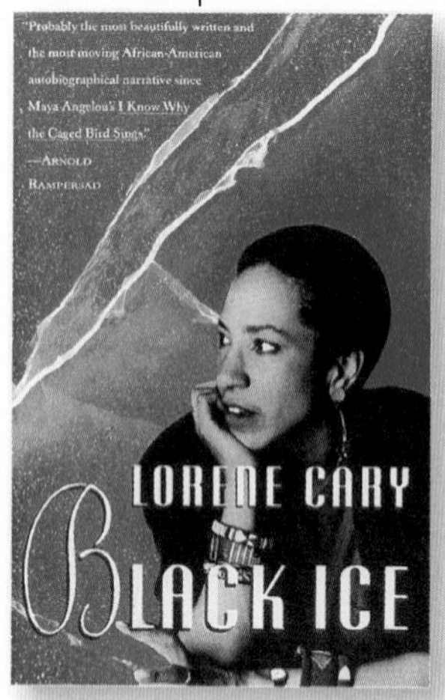

In her autobiography, *Black Ice* (Knopf), Lorene Cary tells of the choices she had to make when she moved from her African American neighborhood in Philadelphia to an elite prep school in New Hampshire. Cary learns a hard lesson—how difficult it is to succeed without seeming to reject her heritage.

Sand, Sand, Everywhere

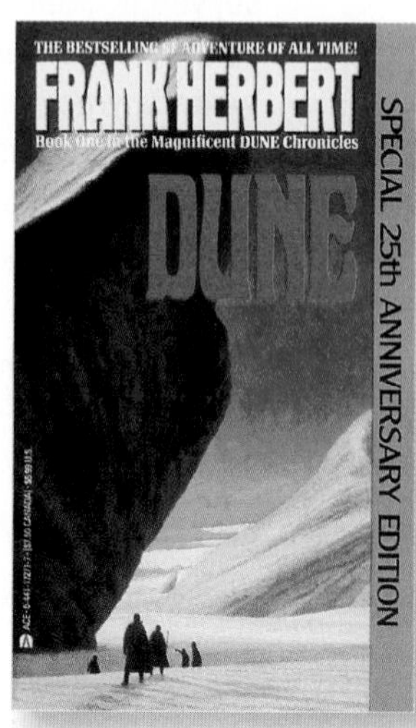

Frank Herbert's classic science fiction novel *Dune* (Berkley) takes place on a strange desert planet. There the colonizers must decide how to deal with unusual life forms called sandworms, which produce a substance that turns humans into bizarre creatures.

"It Is a Far, Far Better Thing . . ."

Charles Dickens's *A Tale of Two Cities* takes place during the French Revolution. Its sweeping action shifts between England and France. The novel contains everything—love, death, bloodshed, heroism, and villainy. The choice made by one character at the end is often quoted when people talk of heroic sacrifice. (This title is available in the HRW Library.)

Finding Their Own Way

In *The Chosen* by Chaim Potok (1929–   ), Danny Saunders and Reuven Malter, both Orthodox Jews, become friends after Danny's line drive to first base injures Reuven's eye. Danny's father expects his son to follow in his footsteps as a Hasidic rabbi, but Danny has other ideas. The boys' friendship survives obstacles as both struggle to find their own way in life. The 1981 movie version stars Rod Steiger and Robby Benson.

PERSUASIVE WRITING

PERSUADING THROUGH PERSONAL NARRATIVE

You often share with friends stories about hilarious, exciting, or upsetting things that happened in your life. Occasionally you might tell your real-life stories to **persuade** someone, as in the following examples:

- a college application essay designed to convince an admissions committee that you'd be a good student
- a job interview where you hope your story will convince an employer that you'd be the best person for the job
- a letter to the editor that expresses your opinion on an issue

In this Writer's Workshop you'll use a **personal narrative** in an essay to support your opinion on an issue. You'll be saying, in effect, "Here's what I think about this issue. I feel strongly about the issue because this is what happened to me."

Technology HELP

See Writer's Workshop 2 CD-ROM. *Assignments: Controversial Issue; Autobiographical Incident.*

ASSIGNMENT

Write an essay stating your opinion about a problem, a situation, or an issue. Support your opinion with a personal narrative.

AIM

To persuade.

AUDIENCE

Your teacher and classmates; readers of a school or local newspaper; a group with power to act on your ideas.

Topic Ideas
- *Is technology good or bad?*
- *Are there "correct" gender roles?*
- *What's the best way to handle sibling rivalry?*
- *What are children's obligations to elderly parents?*

Prewriting

1. Choose Your Issue

WORK IN PROGRESS

Check your Writer's Notebook entries for this collection. If you haven't settled on a topic yet, review the stories to see what ideas they suggest. (See the notepad on the right.) Do you still have no topic? Skim a newspaper or newsmagazine, or watch a TV news program. You might choose a problem or issue (something you think needs fixing) in your own community or school. Make sure you choose a topic with which you've had some personal experience.

2. State Your Opinion

The first—and sometimes the hardest—thing to do is to take a stand on an issue. So that you can base your opinion solidly on facts, you might read a little, ask questions, and talk to people who know something about the issue. For **background information** for your essay, do some research. Then, write an **opinion statement,** a single sentence that expresses your opinion clearly—for example, "Recent advances in technology have made our lives better."

My "Story"/Experience
Last summer worked with three friends painting and repairing dozens of bikes
Touch—beating sun, feel of sandpaper on rusty bikes
Sight—neon orange paint, splashes on clothes and driveway, grease on hands and arms
Sounds—Lots of laughter, boombox playing

3. Tell Your Story

Now, focus on the story part of your essay, the **personal narrative** that relates your experience to the issue. You might write about a one-time experience (helping to clean up a trash-filled vacant lot) or an experience that stretched over many weeks (a summer working in a nursing home). The Student Model on page 88 summarizes an experience that took place over several months.

When you tell a story, you generally use **chronological order,** relating events in the order in which they happened. List the main events of your story. You might try putting them on a time line to be sure they're in the correct order.

Then, make some notes about how you felt and what you thought about your experience. What did you learn from the experience that might interest others? How, exactly, does your experience relate to the issue?

4. Elaborate: Pile on the Details

Instead of writing about "a school on East Elm Street," help your readers see the school: "the crumbling red-brick school with the dirty windows and broken steps on East Elm Street." Try sitting patiently for a few minutes, perhaps with your eyes closed, and picturing where your experience took place. Remember everything that you can: Who was there? What did the place look like? Try to capture **sensory details:** the sights, sounds, smells, tastes, and touch sensations of your experience. These details will help make the experience come alive for your readers.

Dialogue is another sure-fire way to add interest to your narrative. Were important things said? Write them down just as the people said them. It's important to make dialogue as true to life as possible.

Try It Out

Elaborate each of the following statements by adding details that would create a vivid picture for readers.

1. A student sat with two senior citizens at a computer.
2. A woman and two children picked up litter.
3. I read to children at a day-care center.

5. Call to Action: What to Do?

You've stated an opinion and told your story. A good way to end a persuasive essay is with a **call to action,** a clear statement of what you want your audience to do. You might ask your readers to join an organization, write a letter, or contribute to a cause you support.

EXAMPLE

Make your voice heard, and send your views to your state representatives. Find their addresses on your state government's Web site.

Drafting

1. Organize!

You have two main choices for organizing your essay. Either one will work effectively. First, to intrigue your reader, you can tell your personal narrative at the start and save your opinion statement for the end, as in the Student Model on page 88. Second, you can start out with the issue and your opinion statement and end with your personal narrative, as in the brief **outline** at the right. (For more about outlining, see page 334.)

Decide how you'll tell your narrative, too. The most obvious way to tell a story—and it's a solid, traditional way—is to begin with the earliest event, go on to the second event, and proceed in **chronological order** to the last event. "What Happened During the Ice Storm" (page 4) is an example of a story that is narrated chronologically.

Another way to organize your narrative is to begin with an exciting moment right in the middle of the action—*in medias res* ("into the midst of things") is the Latin term. "The Cold Equations" (page 9), for instance, begins with that great sentence telling you that the space pilot is not alone; then the story **flashes back** to explain his mission.

EXAMPLES

Beginning at the beginning. First I checked out the project with the Scout Master, and then I began to check around to find out where I could get abandoned and decrepit bikes that could be repaired.

Beginning in the middle. With a great sense of accomplishment, I stepped back, splashed in orange, to admire the first freshly painted bike.

2. Use Your Own Voice

The experience happened to you, not to someone else, so write about it in your own words, the way you think about it or the way you would discuss it with a friend. Don't even try to write like Edgar Allan Poe or Alice Walker or another famous writer. Avoid difficult words and long, complicated sentences. Find your own voice, and express yourself clearly and directly (a good rule for every kind of writing).

EXAMPLES

Artificial voice. Bicycles of highly intense hues are logistically situated in vehicular retainers and at the shoulders of thoroughfares for all persons in the population to employ.

Authentic voice. Brightly colored bicycles are placed in bike racks and alongside streets for anyone to use.

Outline for a Persuasive Personal Narrative

I. Introduction
  A. Opinion statement
  B. Background information (if needed)
II. Personal narrative (elaborated with sensory details, maybe dialogue)
  A. What happened
    1. When and where
    2. Who
  B. Thoughts and feelings
III. Conclusion
  A. Call to action
  B. Restatement of opinion or summary of experience

Language/Grammar Link HELP

Subject-verb agreement: page 31. Imagery: page 42. Pronouns: page 49. Connotations: page 68. Diction: page 80.

Communications Handbook HELP

See Checking Your Comprehension.

Student Model

A Test of Honor

Are trustworthiness and the spirit of sharing still alive in our cities? Last June, as an Eagle Scout candidate with Troop 87 in Syracuse, I began a project that suggested some answers to that question.

Intriguing question as opener. Personal narrative begins.

I created a "community bicycle" program in our city, inspired by newspaper reports about such projects elsewhere. Attaining the Eagle Scout rank, the highest in Boy Scouting, requires a public service project, and I hoped I could create something that would have long-term success.

Community biking has existed in Europe for decades and has recently been transplanted to the United States. Brightly colored bicycles are placed in bike racks and alongside streets for anyone to use. The riders are asked to leave the bicycles for others when they are done.

Background information.

The benefits can be substantial. The bicycles provide an alternative to short-range trips by car, reducing automobile exhaust. And bicycling improves the fitness of the rider.

Persuasive argument: the benefits of bicycling.

Once I explained my idea, the local Kiwanis and Rotary Clubs donated fifty used, sometimes mangled bicycles. Volunteers from the Boy Scouts and Kiwanis put hundreds of hours into refurbishing as many of these bicycles as possible, painting them fluorescent orange and attaching tags explaining the concept. In the end, we had thirty-five working bicycles downtown and at Syracuse University.

Personal narrative resumes.

Descriptive details.

Three months later, there appear to be just seven or eight in use. As far as I can tell, the rest have been stolen.

I had hoped that the bright orange and the fact that the bicycles were almost worthless would deter theft, but apparently some people aren't too selective—in fact, the downtown bikes started disappearing within hours of being distributed.

Was my project a failure? Was I surprised, disappointed, angry?

Questions introduce writer's thoughts on experience.

I tell myself that the project was never intended to be anything more than an experiment, and that you can't call an experiment a failure simply because it did not produce the results you wanted. Still, I had hoped for better in a community that has always seemed warm, helpful, and generous. Syracuse has always shown the kind of good will that would make a bike project successful.

In fact, my esteem for our city has actually increased because of the cooperation and support I received from so many parts of the community. Yet the experience has made me acutely aware of the "bad apple" effect—it took only a few people

Persuasive argument: increase in writer's esteem for city.

Student Model (continued)

in a city of 300,000 to sink this project.

So how can community bicycle programs work? Some smaller towns, like Telluride, Colorado, have had success, but in larger cities the answer has often been no. In Portland, Oregon, and Boulder, Colorado, many community bikes have done a vanishing act, sometimes within weeks of their introduction. As a Portland police officer said, "It didn't take people long to figure out that a free bike is a free bike."

Topic sentence as question.

Factual information.

Quotation.

Perhaps we should adopt a more American version of the community bike program, with controlled sign-out and deposit points. The spirit wouldn't be the same, but maybe we've asked too much of the honor system.

Call to action.

—Owen Robinson
Corcoran High School
Syracuse, New York

Evaluating and Revising

1. Self-Evaluation

In a personal narrative, it's easy to fall into the trap of beginning too many sentences with *I*. ("I did this" and "I did that" and "I think" . . .) If you find more than two sentences in a row that begin with that pushy little word, rewrite at least one of the sentences. While you're revising, check to see that you've varied the length, beginnings, and structure of the sentences. Try reading your essay aloud, listening for awkward repetitions and sentences that sound like a thrumming, choppy march.

2. Peer Evaluation

Don't just give criticism: Point out passages that work for you, and tell why they impressed you. Is the essay clear? You should not have to question what issue is being discussed, what the writer thinks, and how the personal narrative relates to that issue. Is the narrative part of the essay deadly dull (so dull that it makes you wonder, "Who cares?"), or is it intriguing?

GRAMMAR INVADERS
"It's a new concept in teaching machines. You get 50 points for every grammatical error you blast away!"
GLASBERGEN

© Randy Glasbergen

■ *Evaluation Criteria*

A good persuasive personal narrative

1. *clearly states the writer's opinion on an issue*
2. *gives the readers background information, if needed*
3. *relates a personal narrative (a series of related events) that supports the writer's opinion*
4. *elaborates the personal narrative with specific sensory language*
5. *ends with a call to action or a restatement of the writer's views*

Sentence Workshop HELP

Sentence modeling: page 91.

Proofreading Tips

- If a word looks funny to you or you're not sure how to spell it, check the spelling in a dictionary (or with a spelling checker if you're using a computer).
- Keep a **proofreading log** (a special notebook or section of a notebook) in which you record all the grammar, usage, and spelling mistakes you've made. Review your log right before you start revising.

Communications Handbook HELP

See Proofreaders' Marks.

Revision Model

	Peer Comments
I created a "community bicycle" program in our city, ~~I got the idea~~ [inspired] by ~~reading~~ newspaper reports about ~~community bicycle~~ [such] projects ~~in other countries and in other cities. I hope~~ [elsewhere. Attaining the] ~~to become an~~ [rank, the highest in Boy Scouting, requires] Eagle Scout, ~~I need to do~~ a public service project, [and] I ~~sure~~ hoped I could create something ~~successful~~ that would ~~last a long time.~~ [have long-term success.]	*Too many sentences start with I.* *Can you avoid repetition?* *What's an Eagle Scout?* *Tighten wording and combine sentences?*

Publishing Tips

Share your essay with an audience; don't keep it to yourself.

- Send it as a letter to the editor of your school or local newspaper.
- Some local TV and radio stations give audiences a chance to air their views on important issues. Find out where and to whom you can send your essay.
- Post it on a Web site that publishes students' writing. Ask your librarian to help you find the relevant World Wide Web addresses.
- Convert your essay to a brief persuasive speech (or read it aloud). Ask for permission to present the speech to an appropriate body—perhaps the student council, school board, city government, or a local civic organization.

BUILDING YOUR PORTFOLIO

Sentence Workshop

SENTENCE MODELING: BUILDING FROM THE BASICS

The best way to learn to write well is to read widely. In this lesson, see how much you can learn about sentence building by modeling some sentences after the sentences of famous writers.

Although the sentences below sound varied, they all have the same basic structure: subject, verb, and complement. The writers have elaborated on these basic sentences with additional chunks of meaning. The basic sentence parts are underlined. Other chunks of meaning are set off by slashes.

1. "Back in the pilot's chair / he pressed the signal button / of the normal-space transmitter."

   —Tom Godwin, "The Cold Equations" (page 27)

2. "She held the quilts securely / in her arms, / stroking them."

   —Alice Walker, "Everyday Use" (page 75)

Here are sentences modeled after those above:

1. From the glider plane / I saw a patchwork quilt / of autumn colors.
2. He took the rudder quickly / with one turn, / regaining course.

Writer's Workshop Follow-up: Revision

The shaping and reshaping of sentences is done largely during revision. Look back at the essay you wrote for the Writer's Workshop (page 85). Have you built up your basic sentences in a variety of ways? Can you improve any of your sentences by elaborating on your basic structure the way the professionals do? Always read your work aloud (or try to hear it in your mind) to see if your sentences sound right.

Language Handbook HELP

See Sentence Structure, page 1038.

Try It Out

Underline the basic sentence in each of the following professional models, and set off the added chunks of meaning with slash marks.

1. "The boys slid their feet along slowly, trying not to break the ice that covered the snow."

   —Jim Heynen, "What Happened During the Ice Storm" (page 5)

2. "Instead of shutting the gate, I opened it as wide as I could."

   —Alice Munro, "Boys and Girls" (page 62)

3. "In real life I am a large, big-boned woman with rough, man-working hands."

   —Alice Walker, "Everyday Use" (page 71)

Now write three sentences of your own on any subject, imitating the pattern of elaboration in each of the preceding models. Exchange your work for a partner's, and use underscoring and slash marks to see if the sentences follow the models.

Reading for Life

Reading a Science Article

Situation

After reading "The Cold Equations," you want to research problems of space travel. Here are strategies to follow when you read scientific articles.

Strategies

Note the article's source.

- Does the author seem to be qualified in the field?
- Is the article dated or current?

Skim the entire article to get an overview.

- Read **headings** and notice words in **boldface** or *italic* type. Read the first sentence of each paragraph, which may give you the main ideas.

Read the article carefully.

- With a difficult text, read slowly; stop to **summarize** or **paraphrase** information.
- When you don't understand something, make a note of it in the form of a question. Then **reread** the sentence or paragraph. Your comprehension improves the more you reread.
- If you don't understand a sentence, break it down into its core parts—**subject** and **verb.**
- Look for **context clues** that can help you understand unfamiliar words.

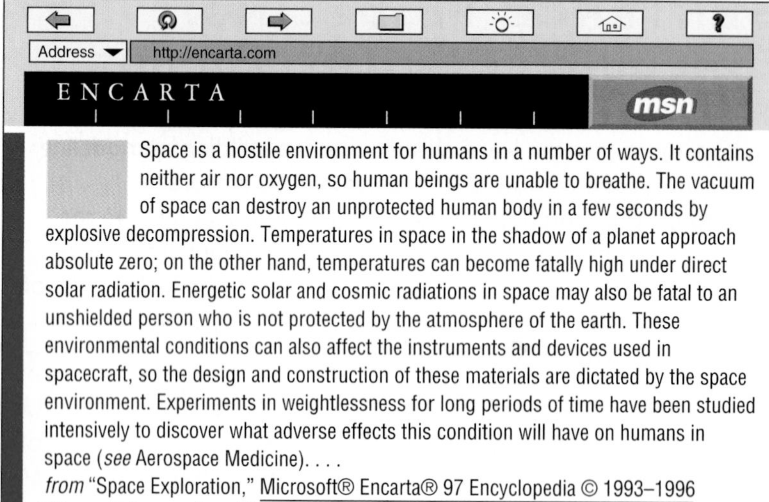

Address http://encarta.com

ENCARTA msn

Space is a hostile environment for humans in a number of ways. It contains neither air nor oxygen, so human beings are unable to breathe. The vacuum of space can destroy an unprotected human body in a few seconds by explosive decompression. Temperatures in space in the shadow of a planet approach absolute zero; on the other hand, temperatures can become fatally high under direct solar radiation. Energetic solar and cosmic radiations in space may also be fatal to an unshielded person who is not protected by the atmosphere of the earth. These environmental conditions can also affect the instruments and devices used in spacecraft, so the design and construction of these materials are dictated by the space environment. Experiments in weightlessness for long periods of time have been studied intensively to discover what adverse effects this condition will have on humans in space (*see* Aerospace Medicine). . . .

from "Space Exploration," Microsoft® Encarta® 97 Encyclopedia © 1993–1996 Microsoft Corporation. All rights reserved.

- Use a **dictionary** or **glossary** to look up words that remain unclear to you.
- Create a **graphic organizer,** such as an outline, word map, or chart, to help you understand the article.

Review the article.

- After carefully reading the article once, review its key points, using your notes and graphic organizer.
- Ask yourself: What is the main idea in this article?

Using the Strategies

1. Is an author cited for the above article? Where did the article come from? What is its date?
2. According to this paragraph, why would humans be unable to breathe in space?
3. What do you think the phrase "explosive decompression" means? How could you check the meaning?
4. Summarize, paraphrase, or outline this paragraph.
5. List any questions you have after reading the paragraph.
6. Do you think this information is reliable? Why or why not?

Extending the Strategies

Which of these strategies would be most useful and most important in reading science textbooks?

Collection 2

HEARTS THAT LOVE

WRITING FOCUS: Analyzing a Character

Love—we think about it, sing about it, dream about it, lose sleep worrying about it. When we don't have it, we search for it; when we discover it, we don't know what to do with it; when we have it, we fear losing it. It's a constant source of pleasure and pain, but we can't predict from one minute to the next which it's going to be today. It takes on many shapes and many disguises: We love our parents, our brothers and sisters, our boyfriends and girlfriends, our cats and dogs, our comfortable shoes, and our baseball gloves. Love—it's a short word, easy to spell, difficult to define, impossible to live without.

Where there is great love, there are always miracles.
—Willa Cather

Writer's Notebook

WORK IN PROGRESS

In the stories, novels, and plays that you've read over the past few years, which characters do you remember best? Were they involved in a search for love, or did they struggle to find something else? List the names of the fictional characters who stick in your memory—because you either liked them or thought them horrible. Save your notes. You may want to write about one of these characters in the Writer's Workshop on page 164.

La Verbena (1992) by Nick Quijano (1953–). Gouache on paper (30″ × 22″).

Collection of Dorothy and Phillip Zaro, New York

Before You Read

TWO KINDS

Make the Connection

Sometimes It Hurts to Love

Have you ever wondered why our biggest conflicts are often with the people we love the most? In this story about a Chinese immigrant mother and her American-born daughter, conflicts arise from differences in culture. They also arise from a more common source—the differing views of parent and child on how the child should live her life and what her goals should be.

Quickwrite

Write two or three sentences describing what you'd like to be doing in ten years and what you think other people would want you to be doing. You needn't show your writing to anyone.

Elements of Literature

Motivation

When actors get parts in a play, they ask themselves and the director, "Why do I do this?" and "Why do I say this?" What they're asking about is **motivation,** or the reasons for their character's behavior. Understanding motivation is important for anyone—actor or writer—who wants to create a convincing character.

> **Motivation** is a person's reasons for doing something or for feeling a certain way.
>
> *For more on Motivation, see page 111.*

Reading Skills and Strategies

Making Inferences About Character

To understand a character's motivation, you must make **inferences,** or intelligent guesses. You base your inferences on clues from the text—you think about the character's actions and words and you observe how others react to the character. Using these clues—and your own life experiences with people—think about what motivates both Jing-mei and her mother in this story.

go.hrw.com
LEO 10-2

Shadows at 687 (1988) by Flo Oy Wong (1938–). Graphite drawing on paper (20¼″ × 17½″).

Courtesy of Allison Kale Chop.

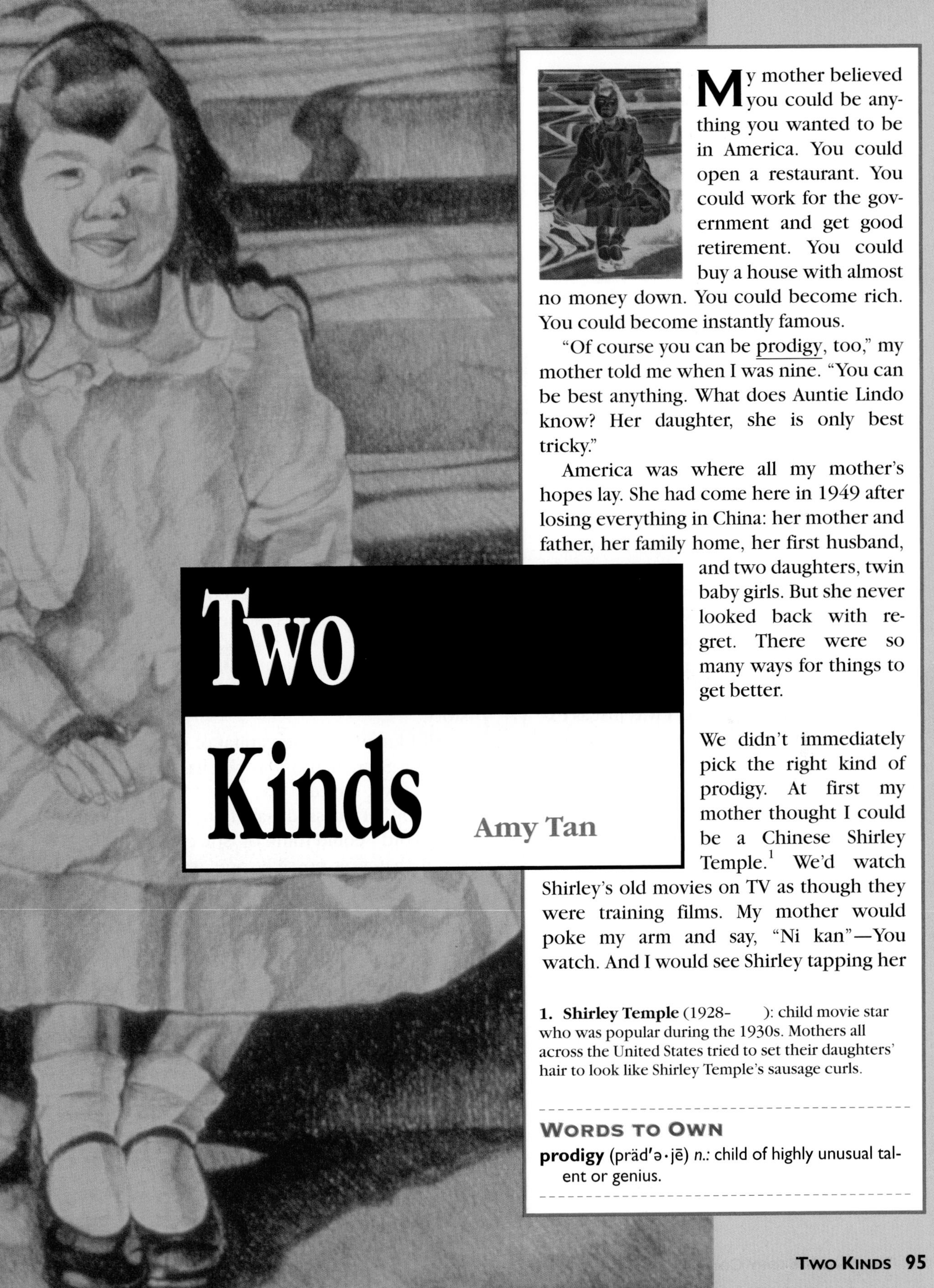

Two Kinds

Amy Tan

My mother believed you could be anything you wanted to be in America. You could open a restaurant. You could work for the government and get good retirement. You could buy a house with almost no money down. You could become rich. You could become instantly famous.

"Of course you can be prodigy, too," my mother told me when I was nine. "You can be best anything. What does Auntie Lindo know? Her daughter, she is only best tricky."

America was where all my mother's hopes lay. She had come here in 1949 after losing everything in China: her mother and father, her family home, her first husband, and two daughters, twin baby girls. But she never looked back with regret. There were so many ways for things to get better.

We didn't immediately pick the right kind of prodigy. At first my mother thought I could be a Chinese Shirley Temple.[1] We'd watch Shirley's old movies on TV as though they were training films. My mother would poke my arm and say, "Ni kan"—You watch. And I would see Shirley tapping her

1. **Shirley Temple** (1928–): child movie star who was popular during the 1930s. Mothers all across the United States tried to set their daughters' hair to look like Shirley Temple's sausage curls.

Words to Own

prodigy (präd′ə·jē) *n.:* child of highly unusual talent or genius.

feet, or singing a sailor song, or pursing her lips into a very round O while saying, "Oh my goodness."

"Ni kan," said my mother as Shirley's eyes flooded with tears. "You already know how. Don't need talent for crying!"

Soon after my mother got this idea about Shirley Temple, she took me to a beauty training school in the Mission district and put me in the hands of a student who could barely hold the scissors without shaking. Instead of getting big fat curls, I emerged with an uneven mass of crinkly black fuzz. My mother dragged me off to the bathroom and tried to wet down my hair.

"You look like Negro Chinese," she lamented, as if I had done this on purpose.

The instructor of the beauty training school had to lop off these soggy clumps to make my hair even again. "Peter Pan is very popular these days," the instructor assured my mother. I now had hair the length of a boy's, with straight-across bangs that hung at a slant two inches above my eyebrows. I liked the haircut and it made me actually look forward to my future fame.

In fact, in the beginning, I was just as excited as my mother, maybe even more so. I pictured this prodigy part of me as many different images, trying each one on for size. I was a dainty ballerina girl standing by the curtains, waiting to hear the right music that would send me floating on my tiptoes. I was like the Christ child lifted out of the straw manger, crying with holy indignity. I was Cinderella stepping from her pumpkin carriage with sparkly cartoon music filling the air.

In all of my imaginings, I was filled with a sense that I would soon become *perfect.* My mother and father would adore me. I would be beyond reproach. I would never feel the need to sulk for anything.

But sometimes the prodigy in me became impatient. "If you don't hurry up and get me out of here, I'm disappearing for good," it warned. "And then you'll always be nothing."

Every night after dinner, my mother and I would sit at the Formica kitchen table. She would present new tests, taking her examples from stories of amazing children she had read in *Ripley's Believe It or Not,* or *Good Housekeeping, Reader's Digest,* and a dozen other magazines she kept in a pile in our bathroom. My mother got these magazines from people whose houses she cleaned. And since she cleaned many houses each week, we had a great assortment. She would look through them all, searching for stories about remarkable children.

The first night she brought out a story about a three-year-old boy who knew the capitals of all the states and even most of the European countries. A teacher was quoted as saying the little boy could also pronounce the names of the foreign cities correctly.

"What's the capital of Finland?" my mother asked me, looking at the magazine story.

All I knew was the capital of California, because Sacramento was the name of the street we lived on in Chinatown. "Nairobi!"[2] I guessed, saying the most foreign word I could think of. She checked to see if that was possibly one way to pronounce "Helsinki" before showing me the answer.

The tests got harder—multiplying numbers in my head, finding the queen of hearts in a deck of cards, trying to stand on my head without using my hands, predicting the daily temperatures in Los Angeles, New York, and London.

One night I had to look at a page from the Bible for three minutes and then report

2. **Nairobi** (nī·rō′bē): capital of Kenya, a nation in Africa.

everything I could remember. "Now Jehoshaphat had riches and honor in abundance and . . . that's all I remember, Ma," I said.

And after seeing my mother's disappointed face once again, something inside of me began to die. I hated the tests, the raised hopes and failed expectations. Before going to bed that night, I looked in the mirror above the bathroom sink and when I saw only my face staring back—and that it would always be this ordinary face—I began to cry. Such a sad, ugly girl! I made high-pitched noises like a crazed animal, trying to scratch out the face in the mirror.

And then I saw what seemed to be the prodigy side of me—because I had never seen that face before. I looked at my reflection, blinking so I could see more clearly. The girl staring back at me was angry, powerful. This girl and I were the same. I had new thoughts, willful thoughts, or rather thoughts filled with lots of won'ts. I won't let her change me, I promised myself. I won't be what I'm not.

So now, on nights when my mother presented her tests, I performed listlessly, my head propped on one arm. I pretended to be bored. And I was. I got so bored I started counting the bellows of the foghorns out on the bay while my mother drilled me in other areas. The sound was comforting and reminded me of the cow jumping over the moon. And the next day, I played a game with myself, seeing if my mother would give up on me before eight bellows. After a while I usually counted only one, maybe two bellows at most. At last she was beginning to give up hope.

Two or three months had gone by without any mention of my being a prodigy again. And then one day my mother was watching *The Ed Sullivan Show* on TV. The TV was old and the sound kept shorting out. Every time my mother got halfway up from the sofa to adjust the set, the sound would go back on and Ed would be talking. As soon as she sat down, Ed would go silent again. She got up, the TV broke into loud piano music. She sat down. Silence. Up and down, back and forth, quiet and loud. It was like a stiff embraceless dance between her and the TV set. Finally she stood by the set with her hand on the sound dial.

She seemed entranced by the music, a little frenzied piano piece with this mesmerizing quality, sort of quick passages and then teasing, lilting ones before it returned to the quick, playful parts.

"Ni kan," my mother said, calling me over with hurried hand gestures. "Look here."

I could see why my mother was fascinated by the music. It was being pounded out by a little Chinese girl, about nine years old, with a Peter Pan haircut. The girl had the sauciness of a Shirley Temple. She was proudly modest like a proper Chinese child. And she also did this fancy sweep of a curtsy, so that the fluffy skirt of her white dress cascaded slowly to the floor like the petals of a large carnation.

In spite of these warning signs, I wasn't worried. Our family had no piano and we couldn't afford to buy one, let alone reams[3] of sheet music and piano lessons. So I could be generous in my comments when my mother bad-mouthed the little girl on TV.

"Play note right, but doesn't sound good! No singing sound," complained my mother.

3. **reams:** here, great amount. A ream of paper is about five hundred sheets.

Words to Own

listlessly (list′lis·lē) *adv.:* without energy or interest.

mesmerizing (mez′mər·īz′iŋ) *v.* used as *adj.:* spellbinding; hypnotic; fascinating.

"What are you picking on her for?" I said carelessly. "She's pretty good. Maybe she's not the best, but she's trying hard." I knew almost immediately I would be sorry I said that.

"Just like you," she said. "Not the best. Because you not trying." She gave a little huff as she let go of the sound dial and sat down on the sofa.

The little Chinese girl sat down also to play an encore of "Anitra's Dance" by Grieg.[4] I remember the song, because later on I had to learn how to play it.

Three days after watching *The Ed Sullivan Show,* my mother told me what my schedule would be for piano lessons and piano practice. She had talked to Mr. Chong, who lived on the first floor of our apartment building. Mr. Chong was a retired piano teacher, and my mother had traded housecleaning services for weekly lessons and a piano for me to practice on every day, two hours a day, from four until six.

When my mother told me this, I felt as though I had been sent to hell. I whined and then kicked my foot a little when I couldn't stand it anymore.

"Why don't you like me the way I am? I'm *not* a genius! I can't play the piano. And even if I could, I wouldn't go on TV if you paid me a million dollars!" I cried.

My mother slapped me. "Who ask you be genius?" she shouted. "Only ask you be your best. For you sake. You think I want you be genius? Hnnh! What for! Who ask you!"

"So ungrateful," I heard her mutter in Chinese. "If she had as much talent as she has temper, she would be famous now."

Mr. Chong, whom I secretly nicknamed Old Chong, was very strange, always tapping his fingers to the silent music of an invisible orchestra. He looked ancient in my eyes. He had lost most of the hair on top of his head and he wore thick glasses and had eyes that always looked tired and sleepy. But he must have been younger than I thought, since he lived with his mother and was not yet married.

I met Old Lady Chong once and that was enough. She had this peculiar smell like a baby that had done something in its pants. And her fingers felt like a dead person's, like an old peach I once found in the back of the refrigerator; the skin just slid off the meat when I picked it up.

I soon found out why Old Chong had retired from teaching piano. He was deaf. "Like Beethoven!" he shouted to me. "We're both listening only in our head!" And he would start to conduct his frantic silent sonatas.

Our lessons went like this. He would open the book and point to different things, explaining their purpose: "Key! Treble! Bass! No sharps or flats! So this is C major! Listen now and play after me!"

And then he would play the C scale a few times, a simple chord, and then, as if inspired by an old, unreachable itch, he gradually added more notes and running trills and a pounding bass until the music was really something quite grand.

I would play after him, the simple scale, the simple chord, and then I just played some nonsense that sounded like a cat running up and down on top of garbage cans. Old Chong smiled and applauded and then said, "Very good! But now you must learn to keep time!"

So that's how I discovered that Old Chong's eyes were too slow to keep up with the wrong notes I was playing. He went through the motions in half-time. To help me keep rhythm, he stood behind me,

4. **Grieg** (grēg): Edvard Grieg (1843–1907), Norwegian composer; "Anitra's Dance" is from his *Peer Gynt Suite.*

Wiping the Table (1985) by Flo Oy Wong (1938–). Graphite drawing on paper (17⅜″ × 20⅛″).

pushing down on my right shoulder for every beat. He balanced pennies on top of my wrists so I would keep them still as I slowly played scales and arpeggios.[5] He had me curve my hand around an apple and keep that shape when playing chords. He marched stiffly to show me how to make each finger dance up and down, staccato,[6] like an obedient little soldier.

He taught me all these things, and that was how I also learned I could be lazy and get away with mistakes, lots of mistakes. If I hit the wrong notes because I hadn't practiced enough, I never corrected myself. I just kept playing in rhythm. And Old Chong kept conducting his own private reverie.

So maybe I never really gave myself a fair chance. I did pick up the basics pretty quickly, and I might have become a good pianist at that young age. But I was so determined not to try, not to be anybody different, that I learned to play only the most earsplitting preludes, the most discordant hymns.

Over the next year, I practiced like this, dutifully in my own way. And then one day I heard my mother and her friend Lindo Jong both talking in a loud bragging tone of voice so others could hear. It was after church, and I was leaning against the brick wall, wearing a dress with stiff white petticoats. Auntie Lindo's daughter, Waverly, who was about my age, was standing farther down the wall, about five feet away. We had grown up together and shared all the closeness of two sisters squabbling over crayons and dolls. In other words, for the most part, we hated each other. I thought she was snotty. Waverly Jong had gained a certain amount of fame as "Chinatown's Littlest Chinese Chess Champion."

"She bring home too many trophy," lamented Auntie Lindo that Sunday. "All day she play chess. All day I have no time do nothing but dust off her winnings." She threw a scolding look at Waverly, who pretended not to see her.

"You lucky you don't have this problem," said Auntie Lindo with a sigh to my mother.

And my mother squared her shoulders

5. **arpeggios** (är·pej′ōz): chords whose notes are played quickly one after another, rather than at the same time.
6. **staccato** (stə·kät′ō): with clear-cut breaks between notes.

Words to Own

discordant (dis·kord′'nt) *adj.:* clashing; not in harmony.

lamented (lə·ment′id) *v.:* said with regret or sorrow. *Lamented* also means "mourned or grieved for" or "regretted deeply."

and bragged: "Our problem worser than yours. If we ask Jing-mei wash dish, she hear nothing but music. It's like you can't stop this natural talent."

And right then, I was determined to put a stop to her foolish pride.

A few weeks later, Old Chong and my mother conspired to have me play in a talent show which would be held in the church hall. By then, my parents had saved up enough to buy me a secondhand piano, a black Wurlitzer spinet with a scarred bench. It was the showpiece of our living room.

For the talent show, I was to play a piece called "Pleading Child" from Schumann's[7] *Scenes from Childhood.* It was a simple, moody piece that sounded more difficult than it was. I was supposed to memorize the whole thing, playing the repeat parts twice to make the piece sound longer. But I dawdled over it, playing a few bars and then cheating, looking up to see what notes followed. I never really listened to what I was playing. I daydreamed about being somewhere else, about being someone else.

The part I liked to practice best was the fancy curtsy: right foot out, touch the rose on the carpet with a pointed foot, sweep to the side, left leg bends, look up and smile.

My parents invited all the couples from the Joy Luck Club[8] to witness my debut. Auntie Lindo and Uncle Tin were there. Waverly and her two older brothers had also come. The first two rows were filled with children both younger and older than I was. The littlest ones got to go first. They recited simple nursery rhymes, squawked out tunes on miniature violins, twirled Hula-Hoops, pranced in pink ballet tutus, and when they bowed or curtsied, the audience would sigh in unison, "Awww," and then clap enthusiastically.

When my turn came, I was very confident. I remember my childish excitement. It was as if I knew, without a doubt, that the prodigy side of me really did exist. I had no fear whatsoever, no nervousness. I remember thinking to myself, This is it! This is it! I looked out over the audience, at my mother's blank face, my father's yawn, Auntie Lindo's stiff-lipped smile, Waverly's sulky expression. I had on a white dress layered with sheets of lace, and a pink bow in my Peter Pan haircut. As I sat down I envisioned people jumping to their feet and Ed Sullivan rushing up to introduce me to everyone on TV.

And I started to play. It was so beautiful. I was so caught up in how lovely I looked that at first I didn't worry how I would sound. So it was a surprise to me when I hit the first wrong note and I realized something didn't sound quite right. And then I hit another, and another followed that. A chill started at the top of my head and began to trickle down. Yet I couldn't stop playing, as though my hands were bewitched. I kept thinking my fingers would adjust themselves back, like a train switching to the right track. I played this strange jumble through two repeats, the sour notes staying with me all the way to the end.

When I stood up, I discovered my legs were shaking. Maybe I had just been nervous and the audience, like Old Chong, had seen me go through the right motions and had not heard anything wrong at all. I swept my right foot out, went down on my knee, looked up and smiled. The room was

7. **Schumann:** Robert Schumann (1810–1856), German composer.
8. **Joy Luck Club:** social club to which Jing-mei's mother and three other Chinese mothers belong.

WORDS TO OWN

dawdled (dôd''ld) *v.:* wasted time; lingered.

quiet, except for Old Chong, who was beaming and shouting, "Bravo! Bravo! Well done!" But then I saw my mother's face, her stricken face. The audience clapped weakly, and as I walked back to my chair, with my whole face quivering as I tried not to cry, I heard a little boy whisper loudly to his mother, "That was awful," and the mother whispered back, "Well, she certainly tried."

And now I realized how many people were in the audience, the whole world it seemed. I was aware of eyes burning into my back. I felt the shame of my mother and father as they sat stiffly throughout the rest of the show.

We could have escaped during intermission. Pride and some strange sense of honor must have anchored my parents to their chairs. And so we watched it all: the eighteen-year-old boy with a fake mustache who did a magic show and juggled flaming hoops while riding a unicycle. The breasted girl with white makeup who sang from *Madama Butterfly*[9] and got honorable mention. And the eleven-year-old boy who won first prize playing a tricky violin song that sounded like a busy bee.

After the show, the Hsus, the Jongs, and the St. Clairs from the Joy Luck Club came up to my mother and father.

"Lots of talented kids," Auntie Lindo said vaguely, smiling broadly.

"That was somethin' else," said my father, and I wondered if he was referring to me in a humorous way, or whether he even remembered what I had done.

Waverly looked at me and shrugged her shoulders. "You aren't a genius like me," she said matter-of-factly. And if I hadn't felt so bad, I would have pulled her braids and punched her stomach.

But my mother's expression was what devastated me: a quiet, blank look that said she had lost everything. I felt the same way, and it seemed as if everybody were now coming up, like gawkers at the scene of an accident, to see what parts were actually missing. When we got on the bus to go home, my father was humming the busy-bee tune and my mother was silent. I kept thinking she wanted to wait until we got home before shouting at me. But when my father unlocked the door to our apartment, my mother walked in and then went to the back, into the bedroom. No accusations. No blame. And in a way, I felt disappointed. I had been waiting for her to start shouting, so I could shout back and cry and blame her for all my misery.

I assumed my talent-show fiasco meant I never had to play the piano again. But two days later, after school, my mother came out of the kitchen and saw me watching TV.

"Four clock," she reminded me as if it were any other day. I was stunned, as though she were asking me to go through the talent-show torture again. I wedged myself more tightly in front of the TV.

"Turn off TV," she called from the kitchen five minutes later.

I didn't budge. And then I decided. I didn't have to do what my mother said anymore. I wasn't her slave. This wasn't China. I had listened to her before and look what happened. She was the stupid one.

She came out from the kitchen and stood in the arched entryway of the living room. "Four clock," she said once again, louder.

9. ***Madama Butterfly:*** opera by the Italian composer Giacomo Puccini.

Words to Own

stricken (strik′ən) *adj.:* heartbroken; affected by or suffering from something painful or distressing.

fiasco (fē·äs′kō) *n.:* complete failure.

"I'm not going to play anymore," I said nonchalantly. "Why should I? I'm not a genius."

She walked over and stood in front of the TV. I saw her chest was heaving up and down in an angry way.

"No!" I said, and I now felt stronger, as if my true self had finally emerged. So this was what had been inside me all along.

"No! I won't!" I screamed.

She yanked me by the arm, pulled me off the floor, snapped off the TV. She was frighteningly strong, half pulling, half carrying me toward the piano as I kicked the throw rugs under my feet. She lifted me up and onto the hard bench. I was sobbing by now, looking at her bitterly. Her chest was heaving even more and her mouth was open, smiling crazily, as if she were pleased I was crying.

"You want me to be someone that I'm not!" I sobbed. "I'll never be the kind of daughter you want me to be!"

"Only two kinds of daughters," she shouted in Chinese. "Those who are obedient and those who follow their own mind! Only one kind of daughter can live in this house. Obedient daughter!"

"Then I wish I wasn't your daughter. I wish you weren't my mother," I shouted. As I said these things, I got scared. It felt like worms and toads and slimy things crawling out of my chest, but it also felt good, as if this awful side of me had surfaced, at last.

"Too late change this," said my mother shrilly.

And I could sense her anger rising to its breaking point. I wanted to see it spill over. And that's when I remembered the babies she had lost in China, the ones we never talked about. "Then I wish I'd never been born!" I shouted. "I wish I were dead! Like them."

It was as if I had said the magic words. Alakazam!—and her face went blank, her mouth closed, her arms went slack, and she backed out of the room, stunned, as if she were blowing away like a small brown leaf, thin, brittle, lifeless.

***Mom, Pop, Me* (1984) by Flo Oy Wong (1938–). Graphite drawing on paper (19¼″ × 15½″).**

Courtesy of the Artist.

It was not the only disappointment my mother felt in me. In the years that followed, I failed her so many times, each time asserting my own will, my right to fall short of expectations. I didn't get straight A's. I didn't become class president. I didn't get into Stanford.[10] I dropped out of college.

For unlike my mother, I did not believe I

10. **Stanford:** high-ranking university in Stanford, California.

WORDS TO OWN

nonchalantly (nän′shə·länt′lē) *adv.:* without interest or concern; indifferently.

could be anything I wanted to be. I could only be me.

And for all those years, we never talked about the disaster at the recital or my terrible accusations afterward at the piano bench. All that remained unchecked, like a betrayal that was now unspeakable. So I never found a way to ask her why she had hoped for something so large that failure was inevitable.

And even worse, I never asked her what frightened me the most: Why had she given up hope?

For after our struggle at the piano, she never mentioned my playing again. The lessons stopped. The lid to the piano was closed, shutting out the dust, my misery, and her dreams.

So she surprised me. A few years ago, she offered to give me the piano, for my thirtieth birthday. I had not played in all those years. I saw the offer as a sign of forgiveness, a tremendous burden removed.

"Are you sure?" I asked shyly. "I mean, won't you and Dad miss it?"

"No, this your piano," she said firmly. "Always your piano. You only one can play."

"Well, I probably can't play anymore," I said. "It's been years."

"You pick up fast," said my mother, as if she knew this was certain. "You have natural talent. You could been genius if you want to."

"No, I couldn't."

"You just not trying," said my mother. And she was neither angry nor sad. She said it as if to announce a fact that could never be disproved. "Take it," she said.

But I didn't at first. It was enough that she had offered it to me. And after that, every time I saw it in my parents' living room, standing in front of the bay windows, it made me feel proud, as if it were a shiny trophy I had won back.

Last week I sent a tuner over to my parents' apartment and had the piano reconditioned, for purely sentimental reasons. My mother had died a few months before, and I had been getting things in order for my father, a little bit at a time. I put the jewelry in special silk pouches. The sweaters she had knitted in yellow, pink, bright orange—all the colors I hated—I put those in mothproof boxes. I found some old Chinese silk dresses, the kind with little slits up the sides. I rubbed the old silk against my skin, then wrapped them in tissue and decided to take them home with me.

After I had the piano tuned, I opened the lid and touched the keys. It sounded even richer than I remembered. Really, it was a very good piano. Inside the bench were the same exercise notes with handwritten scales, the same secondhand music books with their covers held together with yellow tape.

I opened up the Schumann book to the dark little piece I had played at the recital. It was on the left-hand side of the page, "Pleading Child." It looked more difficult than I remembered. I played a few bars, surprised at how easily the notes came back to me.

And for the first time, or so it seemed, I noticed the piece on the right-hand side. It was called "Perfectly Contented." I tried to play this one as well. It had a lighter melody but the same flowing rhythm and turned out to be quite easy. "Pleading Child" was shorter but slower; "Perfectly Contented" was longer but faster. And after I played them both a few times, I realized they were two halves of the same song.

Words to Own

betrayal (bē·trā′əl) *n.:* failure to fulfill another's hopes. *Betrayal* also means "act of disloyalty" or "deception."

Meet the Writer

Many Englishes

Amy Tan (1952–) says that she grew up with several Englishes. The Englishes were primarily American English and Chinese English. Tan was born in Oakland, California, two and a half years after her parents fled China's Communist revolution and settled in the United States. Although Tan's parents had wanted her to become a surgeon, with piano as a hobby, she got a master's degree in linguistics instead. Her first short story, written at a writers' workshop in 1985, was eventually published in *Seventeen.*

At the request of a literary agent, Tan next drafted a proposal for a novel based on the lives of four Chinese mothers and their American daughters. Then Tan left on a trip to China with her own mother, who had just recovered from a serious illness.

When she returned, Tan was amazed to find that her agent had obtained a sizable advance for a novel she hadn't even written yet. She immediately devoted herself full-time to writing *The Joy Luck Club*—a collection of related stories told from the points of view of four mothers and four daughters.

"When I wrote these stories, it was as much a discovery to me as to any reader reading them for the first time," Tan has said. "Things would surprise me. I would sit there laughing and I would say, 'Oh you're kidding!' It was like people telling me the stories, and I would write them down as fast as I could." Published in 1989 to rave reviews, *The Joy Luck Club* became an instant bestseller. In 1993, it was made into a movie.

Afraid of bombing after the huge success of *The Joy Luck Club,* Tan agonized over her second novel, *The Kitchen God's Wife* (1991). In writing that book, she says, she "had to fight for every single character, every image, every word." She needn't have worried. The novel, the story of a woman's harrowing life in pre-Communist China, was another blockbuster.

Here is what Tan says about being a writer who knows two cultures:

> "I am a writer. I am fascinated by language in daily life. I spend a great deal of my time thinking about the power of language—the way it can evoke an emotion, a visual image, a complex idea, or a simple truth. Language is the tool of my trade. And I use them all—all the Englishes I grew up with."

Connections | A NEWS FEATURE

Melting Pot Still Bubbles at IS 237

CHARISSE JONES

In parts of her India, it would not have been proper, this friendship between a young man and a young woman, says Nitu Singh. But here, in the United States, she believes it is necessary.

She is sixteen, and in less than two years has graduated quickly from one level to the next in the school's English-as-a-second-language program. He, Jatinder Singh, fifteen, has been here two months and speaks no English. Their bond is the Punjabi language and their shared understanding of what it is like to be new in a foreign country.

"He needs help, so I help him," she said. "I treat him like my brother."

The school that has brought Nitu and Jatinder together, Intermediate School 237, the Rachel L. Carson School, at a quiet intersection in Flushing, Queens, is a modern brick building that is among the most diverse schools in New York City. Its students fill the hallways with the accents of El Salvador, Taiwan, and Pakistan and go home to households where mothers scold and comfort them in Spanish, Mandarin, and Urdu.

To wander the halls of IS 237 is to see the baby steps and giant strides of young people wrestling with assimilation and ethnic pride, with change and acceptance.

"A lot of them are terrified," said Rosiland Tseng, who has been a guidance counselor at IS 237 for six years. "They're also very confused about the system, like changing the classrooms. They don't understand."

At the school, one approach has been a buddy system that pairs newcomers with immigrants who have been here longer.

The buddies are often in the same classes, their interdependence evolving into friendship.

Opening a Universe

Nitu helped Jatinder decipher the mystery of a combination lock on his locker, showing him as many as fifteen times how to unlock it until he got it right. She explained to him that here children are fed

(continued on next page)

Part of the diverse student population of IS 237.

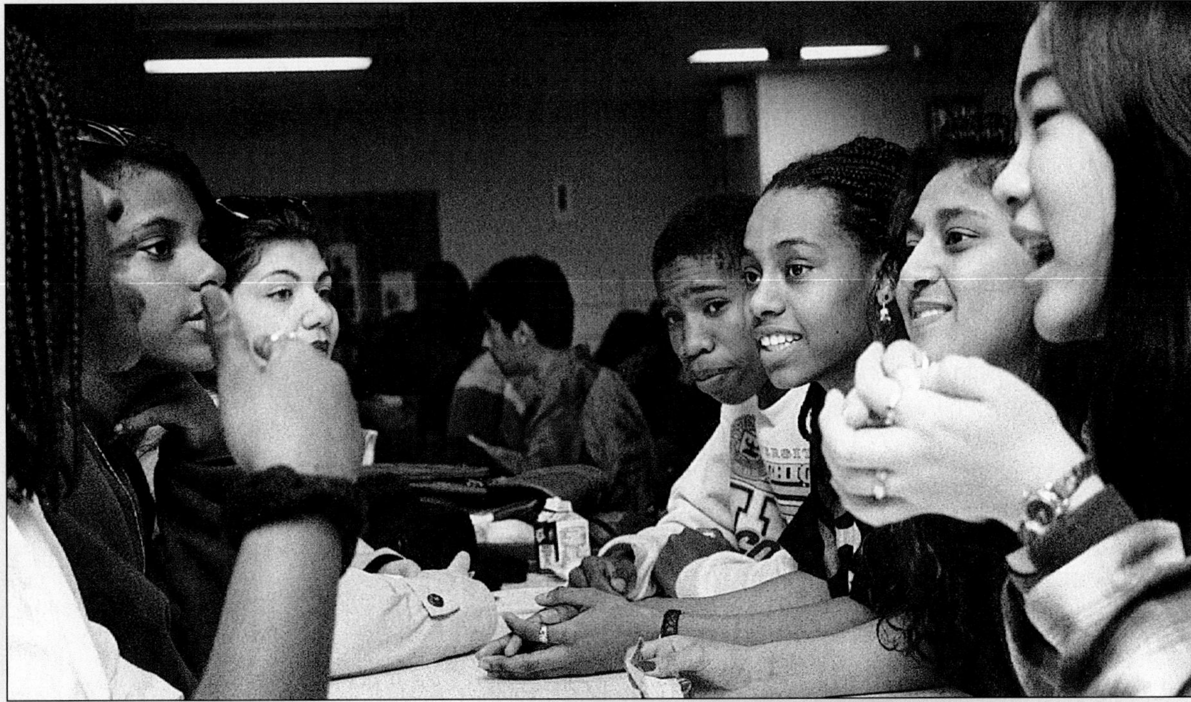

Melting Pot Still Bubbles at IS 237

Students working with a puzzle of the United States.

(continued from previous page)
in a cafeteria, instead of bringing their own food from home.

In a classroom recently, Nitu sat next to Jatinder quietly helping him piece together a puzzle of the United States. She smiled when he uttered the states' names correctly, and provided friendship when he felt different and alone.

The Start Is Bumpy

The first days are the hardest, the children say, filled with the noise of a language not understood, the strangeness of customs never before encountered.

"I felt excluded from the group," Lisa Hou, fourteen, remembered, "because you look different, because you don't dress the way they do. I wanted to be a part of them. Back home I never had this kind of problem."

That was nearly four years ago, when she first came from Taiwan. Now, she says, fitting in no longer matters. "I don't really care. I can't change the way I look."

But minutes earlier, as she tried to describe the taunts she had endured, her words got lost in tears.

Many immigrant children are initiated into the youthful mores° of American culture the painful way, compelled to get hip in a hurry to stop the insults that come from sporting no-name sneakers and speaking English with a heavy accent.

Cultural adaptation, and the pain that often comes with it, has always been part of the immigrant experience, said Dr. Stephan F. Brumberg, a historian and author. Another is conflict between children and parents.

"There are the problems that arise between generations," he said, "parents who come of age in one cultural, linguistic setting who are raising children in a different one. It's an unavoidable tension, and it's something that people who emigrate probably don't really foresee: that they're going to raise aliens."

Often it is the school's guidance counselors who must try to bridge the widening gulf between children and parents. Mrs. Tseng said that some immigrant children feel overwhelmed by the academic expectations their parents hold for them, as well as the clash of cultures. Parents may also be confused about how to deal with their children but feel it is improper to ask others for advice, especially school officials, whom they were often taught in their homelands to obey and fear.

Must Get Involved

"The parents often feel they're not supposed to be active in the schools because the school authorities know best," she said. "They don't understand that's part of the process, to get involved."

Programs are also in place for the children, who, once the newness has passed, still often face reminders that they are not originally from here.

The most vivid reminder is language. Luis Figueroa, fourteen, born in Peru, has lived in the United States for six years. He speaks English with ease and wears the teenage uniform: sweat shirt, bluejeans, and sneakers.

Still, there are moments he'll be sitting in class, and it will happen. "You read a book," he said, "and you always see a word that you don't know."

—from *The New York Times*

° **mores** (mōr′ēz′): here, customs and habits.

Making Meanings

First Thoughts

1. You may never have been forced to take piano lessons, but you've probably been expected to do *something* you didn't want to do. Did this story bring any experience like that back to your mind? When you talk about how the story connected with your own life, be sure to discuss whether or not it helped you see your experiences in a new light. Your Quickwrite notes might help you make this connection with the text.

Reading Check

a. What does Jing-mei's mother want for her daughter?

b. How does Jing-mei feel about her mother's plans for her?

c. What happens when Jing-mei plays the piano in front of an audience?

d. What does Jing-mei say to hurt her mother in their last struggle over the piano lessons?

e. What is the **resolution** to this mother-daughter **conflict**?

Shaping Interpretations

2. What do you think **motivates** the mother to push Jing-mei into being a prodigy? Consider:
   - the mother's life in China
   - her life in America

3. Why do you think Jing-mei's mother wants her to keep playing the piano, even after her disastrous performance? What kind of daughter does she really want Jing-mei to be?

4. How do you think other children might respond to the pressure to become a prodigy? What **inferences** can you make about Jing-mei's **character** from her response to her mother's pressure?

5. Near the end of the story, Jing-mei says, "In the years that followed, I failed her so many times. . . ." What do you think she means by that? Do you agree that Jing-mei failed her mother? Does Amy Tan think so? Give your reasons.

6. What do you think the **title** of the story means? Do you think Jing-mei's discovery about the two Schumann songs also relates to the story's title? Why, or why not?

7. This story is in a collection called "Hearts That Love." Are there "hearts that love" in Tan's story? Find details from the text to support your response.

Extending the Text

8. Do you think someone else's high expectations can make a person *want* to fail, or do you think failure results more often from *low* expectations? Explain your opinion, drawing examples when you can from your own experiences and those of people you know.

Choices: Building Your Portfolio

Writer's Notebook

1. Collecting Ideas for a Character Analysis

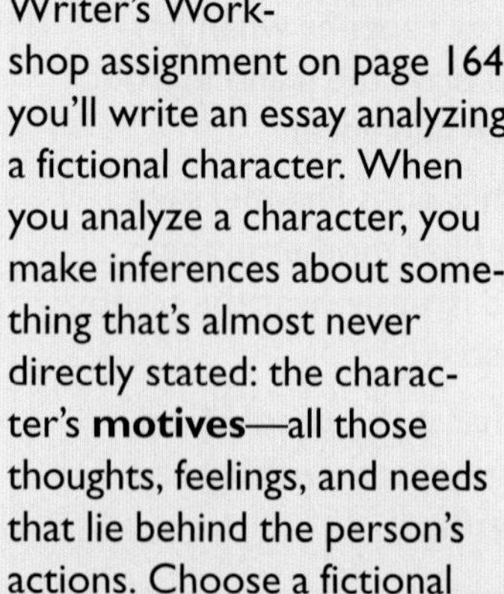

Why do they do that? For the Writer's Workshop assignment on page 164, you'll write an essay analyzing a fictional character. When you analyze a character, you make inferences about something that's almost never directly stated: the character's **motives**—all those thoughts, feelings, and needs that lie behind the person's actions. Choose a fictional character who interests you, and take notes on his or her motivation. (You might want to use a character from Tan's story or a character from the list you made at the start of this collection.) As you take notes, focus on motivation. What does the character do in the story? What causes this character to behave the way he or she does? Is the motivation simple? Or is it—as happens often in real life—very complicated and not easy to figure out?

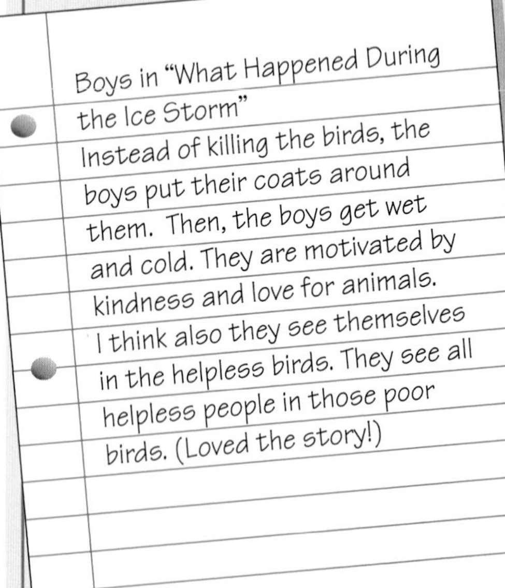

Boys in "What Happened During the Ice Storm"
Instead of killing the birds, the boys put their coats around them. Then, the boys get wet and cold. They are motivated by kindness and love for animals. I think also they see themselves in the helpless birds. They see all helpless people in those poor birds. (Loved the story!)

Describing a Character

2. My Unforgettable Character

Amy Tan's story is interesting in part because it lets us meet some unusual characters. Write a character sketch of your own about a person you know—preferably someone you can observe. You might find a subject by thinking about the characters in "Two Kinds." Does anyone in the story remind you of someone in your own life? Use specific descriptive details to tell what your character looks like, how he or she acts, what characteristic things he or she says, what he or she likes to do. How do you know this person? Open your sketch with a sentence that hooks your reader's interest.

Role-Playing

3. Meeting of the Moms

Imagine that Mama, the narrator of "Everyday Use" (page 70), and Jing-mei's mother have met and are discussing the joys and problems of raising daughters. What would the two mothers say to each other? With a partner, improvise a five-minute **conversation** between the two characters. Begin by imagining where they will meet: an airport? a bus tour? a graduation? When you've finished your improvisation, write a brief reflection on what it taught you about the mothers' characters and about yourself.

Supporting an Opinion/ Cultural Diversity

4. Dear Editor . . .

Write a **letter to the editor** of the newspaper that published the article about the "melting pot" (see *Connections* on page 105). Give your response to the article's main message about cultural diversity in the schools. If you wish, you can support your opinion with personal experience.

Language Link — Mini-Lesson

Technology HELP

See Language Workshop CD-ROM. *Key word entry: dialogue.*

Language Handbook HELP

See Quotation Marks, pages 1054–1056.

Dialogue—You Are What You Say

Using **dialogue,** or spoken words, is a powerful way to create characters. Good dialogue sounds like real speech and gives each character a distinct, individual style. Here is one of Amy Tan's characters talking:

- "Of course you can be prodigy, too," my mother told me when I was nine. "You can be best anything. What does Auntie Lindo know? Her daughter, she is only best tricky."
- "Who ask you be genius?" she shouted. "Only ask you be your best. For you sake."
- "Our problem worser than yours. If we ask Jing-mei wash dish, she hear nothing but music. It's like you can't stop this natural talent."

Amy Tan does something interesting with the mother's dialogue. When the mother is speaking English, as in the above examples, it is her own brand of English, not the more widely used standard form of spoken English. When she is speaking Chinese, however, her expression is quite correct, even elegant, as in the passage on page 98, "If she had as much talent as she has temper, she would be famous now."

Try It Out

With a partner, read aloud a scene from "Two Kinds" containing dialogue between mother and daughter. Experiment with **tones of voice, volume, pauses,** and **gestures** until you are satisfied with your interpretation. Does hearing the way they speak deepen your understanding of these complex characters?

A tip for writers: Dialogue works only if you develop an ear for the way real people talk, as Amy Tan has clearly done. You must be a listener: Professional writers are always jotting down things people say. Take your notebook to the cafeteria, or any place people gather, and try to write down some of the conversation you hear.

Vocabulary — How to Own a Word

Word Bank

prodigy
listlessly
mesmerizing
discordant
lamented
dawdled
stricken
fiasco
nonchalantly
betrayal

What's Wrong with This Picture?

Explain why the **context clues** are wrong in each sentence below.

1. The prodigy, as usual, played many wrong notes.
2. Her great energy enabled her to work listlessly.
3. The mesmerizing performance bored everyone.
4. Discordant music is so melodious and soothing.
5. Mei-Ling lamented her extraordinarily good grades.
6. Bolting his food, Tomás dawdled over lunch.
7. The success of the benefit left the club members stricken.
8. Allis recalled with pride the fiasco of her performance.
9. James spoke nonchalantly about his passion for tennis.
10. I thanked her for her betrayal of my loyalty.

Elements of Literature

CHARACTER: The Actors in a Story *by* John Leggett

Good fiction can tell us more about ourselves—about how human beings feel and behave in any imaginable situation—than just about any other form of art or science.

By entering a fictional world, we can experience how it feels to be a woman who has lived all her life on the prairie and never heard the sound of a piano. We can know how it feels to be a soldier lying wounded on the battlefield. We can understand how it feels to be a teenage boy disappointed by the person he trusted most.

The revelation fiction offers us lies largely in the element called **character**—that is, in the story's actors. When the characters in a story act in convincing ways—when we are persuaded that they are like actual people—not only do we believe in them but we also identify with them, admire them, envy them, even fear or love them, just as we do the real people we know. In fact, one of the pleasures of reading fiction is getting to know characters more intimately than we know people in real life.

Creating Characters: How Do They Do It?

The easiest way to reveal character is to use **direct characterization**—to describe directly the person's **traits,** or special qualities.

Esmeralda was the most serious person in school. She longed for fun, but she was afraid of disappointing her aunt, who was also very serious.

That's a quick, straightforward way for a writer to present a character, but most readers would rather make up their own minds.

Instead of telling us directly what Esmeralda is like, a more subtle writer will reveal her character through **indirect methods.** We may be told about her **appearance:**

Esmeralda always wore gray. In fact, she looked like a small gray mouse.

The writer may also show us Esmeralda's **actions** and let us hear what she **says:**

Esmeralda rarely smiled and could be found every afternoon in the library, taking notes on some worthwhile subject—but she sometimes looked dreamily out the window. Yesterday she lost her composure. "Can't you tell those squealing roller skaters to play somewhere else?" The librarian was shocked.

The writer may also take us into Esmeralda's mind to reveal her private **thoughts:**

Esmeralda wondered why she wasn't like other kids her age. Why did she sit poring over a book, while others were laughing and skating in the sun?

The writer could also show us **how other people respond** to Esmeralda:

Janet sneered, "I can't stand Esmeralda. She's such a snob."

Writers, then, can reveal characters and their **traits,** or special qualities, in these five indirect ways:

1. by appearance
2. by actions
3. by speech
4. by private thoughts
5. by the responses of other characters

Round vs. Flat

Critics often refer to flat or

round characters. A **flat character** is like a paper doll, with only one surface. Such a character has only one or two key personality traits and can be described in a single sentence. A **round character**, on the other hand, cannot be summed up so neatly. A round character is fleshed out. He or she is more complex—there are more sides to this character's personality, more dimensions.

In good fiction, flat characters are included for a reason: Too many round characters would be distracting. Most works of fiction, particularly short stories, require a certain number of flat characters to get the story told.

Stock Characters: Off the Shelf

The problem with second-rate fiction is that even the main characters are flat characters. These flat characters found in inferior fiction are often also stock characters. A **stock character** is a person who fits our preconceived notions about a type (a typical old man, a typical teenager, a typical detective, a typical politician). Stock characters have no individuality; there are dozens just like them on the shelf.

You know stock characters on sight (they exist on TV and in the movies, too): the mad scientist, the nerdy intellectual, the tough guy with the soft heart, the poor little rich girl.

It is their predictability that makes these stock characters so stale. We've met them all before in countless other stories, and we know that the writer has simply taken them off the shelf (or out of the "stockroom") and set them in motion by winding each character's key. We know that real people aren't like this—real people are endlessly complex and never wholly predictable. What fascinates and delights us in fiction is the portrayal of characters who somehow manage to confound our expectations yet still seem true to life.

What's the Motivation?

One of the ways a writer rounds out a character is to show us what **motivates**, or moves, that person to act as he or she does. Unless we understand why an otherwise dutiful daughter suddenly lashes out at her mother, her behavior will strike us as inconsistent and unbelievable. But once we recognize the need she is trying to satisfy (say, to punish someone—anyone she can get her hands on—for the way her boyfriend has neglected her), her behavior begins to make sense, and she is no longer the two-dimensional "dutiful daughter." She seems like a real person—someone who is usually kind but who is also capable (as all of us are) of cruelty.

Writers do not often state a character's motives directly. ("She screamed at her mother because Bill hadn't called in two weeks.") Instead, they imply what those motives are—maybe even scatter clues throughout the story—and trust their readers to make intelligent guesses about why their characters act as they do.

Trying to understand the motivation of characters in literature can be as puzzling and satisfying as it is in real life. While we may know that real people surprise us with their behavior, we also know that there are reasons for what they do. In real life we may never find out what those reasons are. In fiction we do.

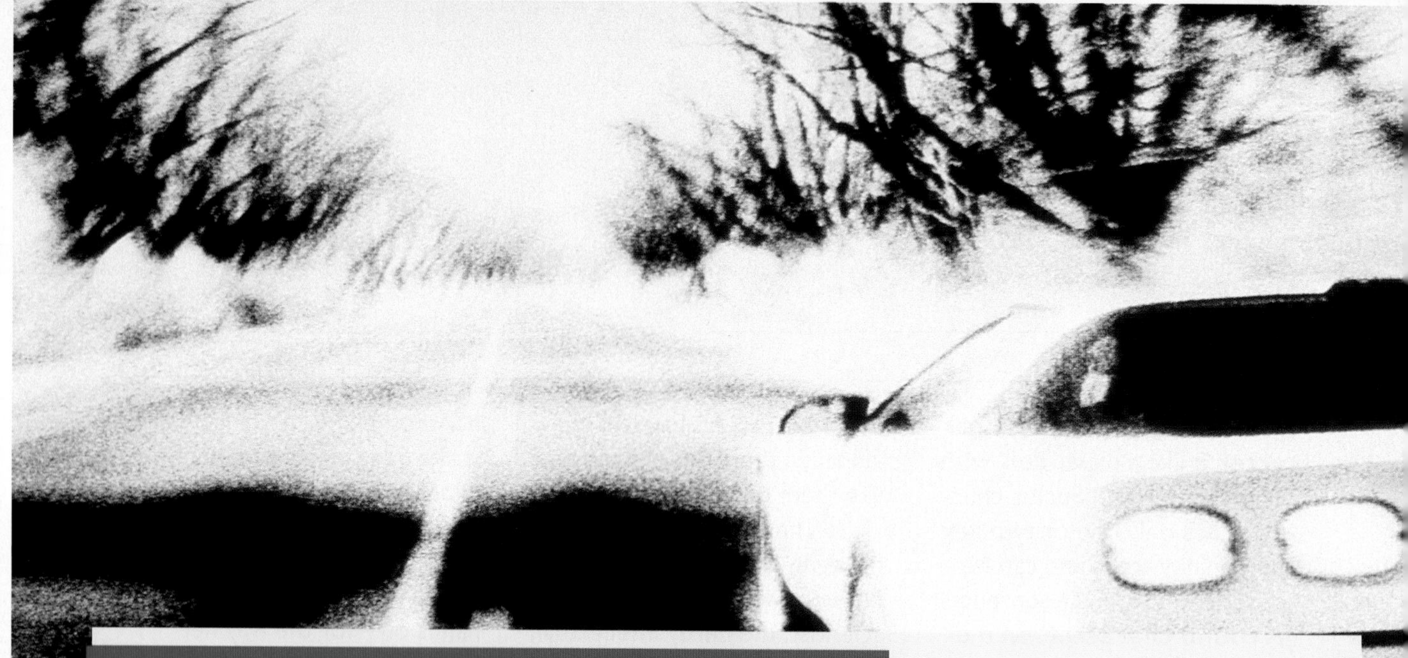

Before You Read

GERALDO NO LAST NAME

Make the Connection

We Are All One

There are billions of people on this planet, and each one is in some ways just like you and me, with a history and a need to love and share life. But unexpected things happen, and sometimes we lose a link to a person who might have become important to us.

Quickwrite

Make some notes about someone you met briefly whom you wish you could have known better. Jot down details about how you met the person and why you remember him or her.

go.hrw.com
LEO 10-2

Elements of Literature

Style: The Personal Stamp

Just as no two people in the world have the same fingerprints, so does everyone have a unique style. Your **style** is your own mode of expression. The way you dress is a style. So is the way you shape your sentences. Are they short and simple or long and complicated? When you read your writing aloud, does it have the rhythm of poetry, or does it sound plain and direct? Some writers' styles are so famous that people can read a single sentence and know they are reading, for example, Ernest Hemingway. A Cisneros story has that kind of distinctive style. Listen for it.

> **Style** is the particular way that writers use language to express themselves and their ideas.

Reading Skills and Strategies

Monitoring Your Reading: Questioning

Good readers ask **questions** as they read—perhaps about unfamiliar vocabulary, a confusing description, or a character's behavior. Good writers, like Cisneros, sometimes invite questions by purposely leaving some things unanswered.

Geraldo No Last Name

Sandra Cisneros

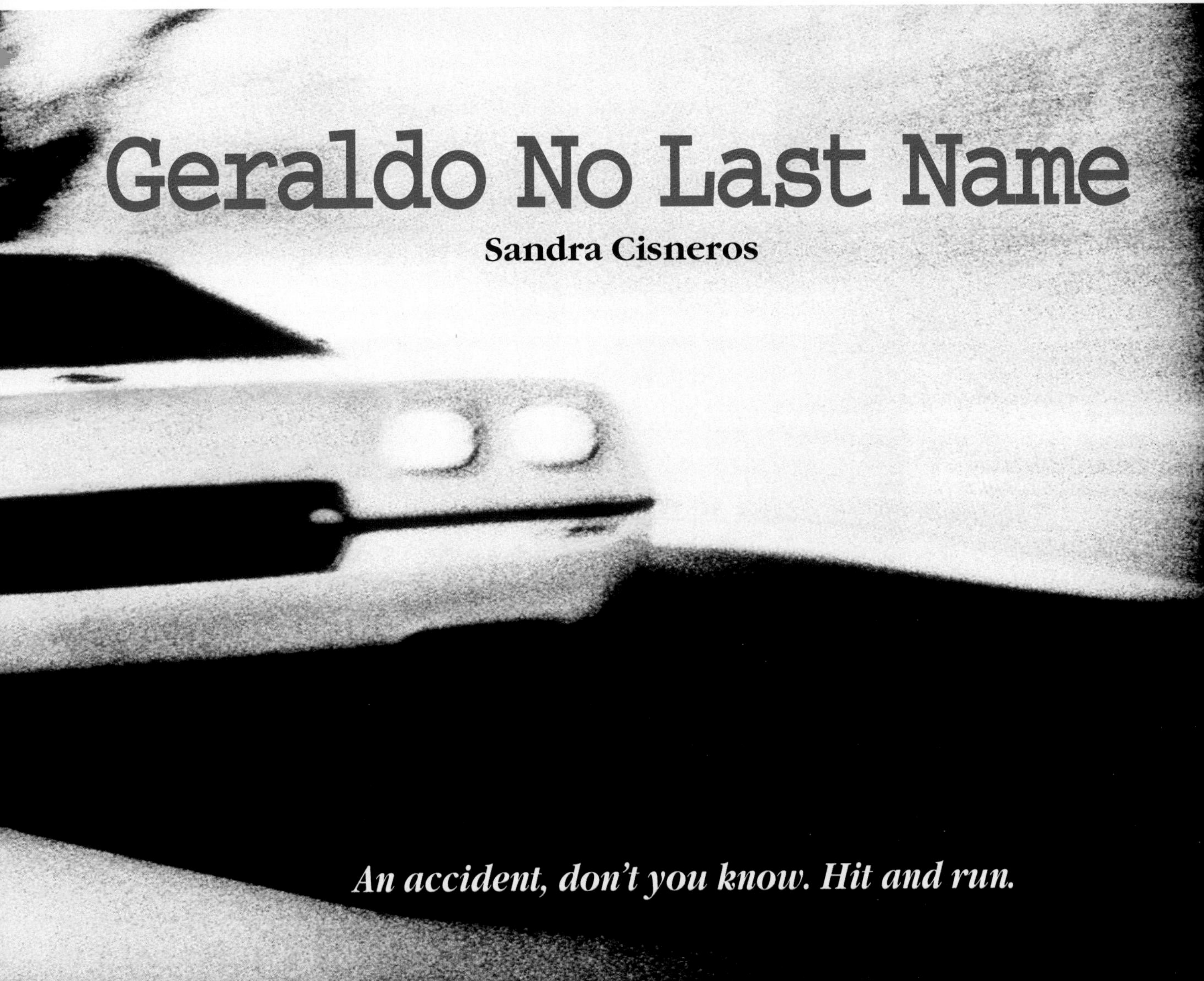

An accident, don't you know. Hit and run.

She met him at a dance. Pretty too, and young. Said he worked in a restaurant, but she can't remember which one. Geraldo. That's all. Green pants and Saturday shirt. Geraldo. That's what he told her.

And how was she to know she'd be the last one to see him alive. An accident, don't you know. Hit and run. Marin, she goes to all those dances. Uptown. Logan. Embassy. Palmer. Aragon. Fontana. The manor. She likes to dance. She knows how to do cumbias and salsas and rancheras even. And he was just someone she danced with. Somebody she met that night. That's right.

El Club (1990) by Nick Quijano (1953–). Gouache on paper (22″ × 30″).

Permanent Collection, Puerto Rico Tourism Museum, Old San Juan, Puerto Rico.

That's the story. That's what she said again and again. Once to the hospital people and twice to the police. No address. No name. Nothing in his pockets. Ain't it a shame.

Only Marin can't explain why it mattered, the hours and hours, for somebody she didn't even know. The hospital emergency room. Nobody but an intern working all alone. And maybe if the surgeon would've come, maybe if he hadn't lost so much blood, if the surgeon had only come, they would know who to notify and where.

But what difference does it make? He wasn't anything to her. He wasn't her boyfriend or anything like that. Just another brazer[1] who didn't speak English. Just another wetback.[2] You know the kind. The ones who always look ashamed. And what was she doing out at 3:00 A.M. anyway? Marin who was sent home with her coat and some aspirin. How does she explain?

She met him at a dance. Geraldo in his shiny shirt and green pants. Geraldo going to a dance.

What does it matter?

They never saw the kitchenettes. They never knew about the two-room flats[3] and sleeping rooms he rented, the weekly money orders sent home, the currency exchange. How could they?

His name was Geraldo. And his home is in another country. The ones he left behind are far away, will wonder, shrug, remember. Geraldo—he went north . . . we never heard from him again.

1. **brazer** (brā′zer): Americanization of the Spanish word *bracero,* used in the United States to refer to a Mexican laborer allowed into the United States temporarily to work.
2. **wetback:** offensive term for a Mexican laborer who illegally enters the United States, often by swimming or wading the Rio Grande.
3. **flats:** apartments.

Meet the Writer

Unforgettable as a First Kiss

Sandra Cisneros (1954–   ) spent her childhood moving back and forth between Chicago, where she was born, and Mexico, where her father was born. She currently lives in San Antonio, Texas.

Cisneros's first full-length work, *The House on Mango Street,* appeared in 1984. The narrator of this series of connected stories is a lively and thoughtful girl named Esperanza. (Her name means "hope" in Spanish.) Cisneros has also published collections of her poetry, including *My Wicked Wicked Ways* (1987), and another collection of stories, *Woman Hollering Creek* (1991). One critic has said that her stories "invite us into the souls of characters as unforgettable as a first kiss."

Cisneros did not find her unique voice as a writer until she attended the Writers' Workshop at the University of Iowa.

"Everyone seemed to have some communal knowledge which I did not have. It was not until [the] moment when I separated myself, when I considered myself truly distinct, that my writing acquired a voice. I knew I was a Mexican woman, but I didn't think it had anything to do with why I felt so much imbalance in my life, whereas it had everything to do with it! My race, my gender, my class! That's when I decided I would write about something my classmates couldn't write about."

Connections

A Letter Home

Ventura, CA
February 27, 1981

José Zarate and Family
Guadalajara, Mexico

Hello Papa, Mama, brothers and sisters,

I hope this finds you very well in spite of everything.

By now you will have found out I'm in the United States (California) and you will be asking yourselves what I'm doing here.

Before anything I want to ask you to have a lot of trust in me. I came with the desire to work here a few months in order to gather a little money.

I have great faith that it's going to go very well for me, and this is important. Here everything is different from Mexico, but I assure you I'm never going to forget anything I learned from you!!

I remember you a lot and this is going to be decisive in my behavior. I am not going to fail you! Of that I assure you!!

When I arrived in the U.S. Wednesday morning I had two addresses of people I could head for. One is of Panchi and his sisters. The other address is that of some married friends of mine, which was the one I opted for, and I'm sure that if you knew them you'd quit worrying. They're Mexican. They have two daughters, little ones. They work mornings. Someone takes care of the girls. Meanwhile I'm alone in the house until 4 P.M., when they return, and since it's different here, people don't go out into the street then. I've gone with them downtown and to look for work.

Papa, Mama, I consider it very important that you trust me. I know that with the way I did things you may distrust me, but I knew you were never going to let me do it. I'm going to behave myself very well! I'm going to go to my aunt Cuca and if she offers me her house I'll stay. I already spoke with her and she told me yes, to go to her house, I have her address and phone number. I also have the address of my uncle Felipe in case I need it.

I just want to work a few months and return to you to continue in school.

I want you to be calm. My being alone right now is going to help me a lot to start being responsible for myself.

I'm going to write constantly to tell you how it's going with me.

I hope you also write me, even if it is to box my ears. Until soon.

Loving you all,
Patricia Zarate

Just now we went to mass at a church called La Asunción de Maria. It was a bilingual mass with mariachi.

MAKING MEANINGS

First Thoughts

1. There's a lot we don't know when we finish reading Cisneros's sketch. Write down questions that you think are left unanswered. Be sure to share your questions, and some of their possible answers, with other readers.

Reading Check

Retell the events of this story to a classmate, as you imagine Marin told them to the police.

Shaping Interpretations

2. At the end of this little sketch, Cisneros says "they" never saw certain aspects of Geraldo's life. Who are "they"?
3. After Geraldo dies, Marin says she can't understand why their meeting mattered, why she spent so many hours in the hospital waiting room. Why do you think she keeps thinking about the meeting and wondering what it meant?
4. Exactly what do you know about the **character** of Geraldo? What **inferences,** or guesses, can you make about the kind of person he was?
5. Do you think this story is about love? Talk about your responses in class.

Connecting with the Text

6. Look back at your Quickwrite notes. Are there any similarities between the "brief encounter" you described and the one in the story? Explain.
7. Review the letter from a young woman who has immigrated to California from Mexico (see ***Connections*** on page 116). How does her letter home affect your responses to Geraldo's story?

Extending the Text

8. Geraldo has no identification papers and may be an illegal immigrant. In what other ways can people become lost in our society? How might that happen, and to whom?

Los Bailadores (1990) by Nick Quijano (1953–). Gouache on paper (6½″ × 6½″).

Collection Marc Briller, New York.

CHOICES: Building Your Portfolio

Writer's Notebook

1. Collecting Ideas for a Character Analysis

Finding the clues. Although we never meet Geraldo, we have an impression of the kind of person he was. How has Sandra Cisneros managed to create a character in less than two pages? (Does she use **direct** or **indirect characterization,** or some combination of both?) Look back at "Geraldo No Last Name" to find the clues that help you to know Geraldo. Then, fill in a cluster diagram like the one below. Save your notes for possible use in the Writer's Workshop on page 164.

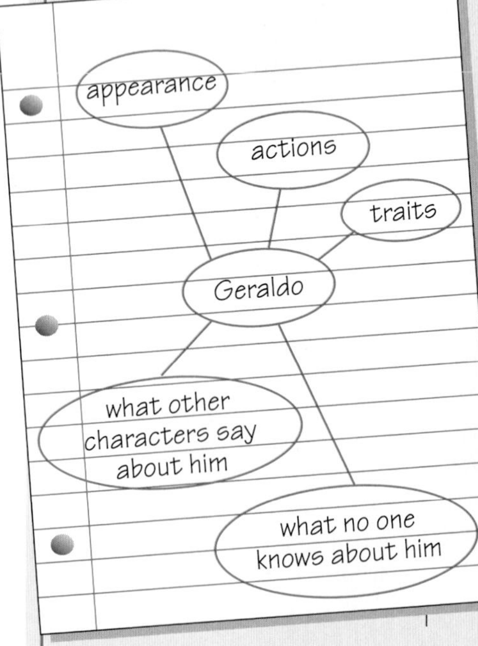

Opposite: *Miguel El Coreógrafo* (1991) by Margaret Garcia (1951–). Oil on wood (24″ × 24″).

Courtesy of Nancy Thomas and Kevin Goff.

Creative Writing

2. Healing Words

Imagine that you are Marin and you have just come home from the hospital on the night Geraldo died. Express your thoughts and feelings in a **poem** by finishing these lines:

I am ______________ .
I wonder ______________ .
I hear ______________ .
I see ______________ .
I wish ______________ .
I am ______________ .

Oral Interpretation

3. Hearing a Style

Present an **oral interpretation** of the story. Decide how you should use your voice to emphasize Cisneros's unusual **style.** Think of when you should pause, read slowly, read quickly, and raise or lower your voice. Ask your audience for feedback. (For help, see the Speaking and Listening Workshop on pages 750–751.)

Art

4. Creating a Portrait

Using details from the story, as well as your own imagination, draw a portrait of Geraldo, or create a **collage** of images and words that suggest his life or personality. When you share your artwork with your classmates, be prepared to explain why you presented Geraldo as you did.

Research/Social Studies

5. Database

Create a database containing statistical information about Mexican immigration to the United States. First, decide where you will find your data. The Internet would be a good source, particularly a U.S. government site. You might concentrate on numbers, quotas, areas where immigrants live, typical jobs, wages. Be sure to include some of your information in a graph or table.

Before You Read

THE FIRST SEVEN YEARS

Make the Connection

The Many Faces of Love

Love can blossom in the most unexpected places. People who seem totally unsuited sometimes fall in love, and those who appear well matched often leave each other cold. The seeming illogic of love is an age-old subject.

Quickwrite

How do you think most people feel when someone tries to arrange a date for them—or even find them a husband or wife? Jot down your feelings about this practice of matchmaking. You might want to use a pro and con chart.

Pros	Cons

Elements of Literature

The Protagonist: The Main Character

Most stories have a main character, called the **protagonist,** on whom our attention focuses. Usually, but not always, the protagonist is admirable and likable, the sort of person we identify with. It is also possible to have a protagonist who is not very nice at all. In a good story, the protagonist is a real, complicated human being, with just enough strengths, weaknesses, and contradictions to remind us of ourselves.

As a rule, the story's action begins when this main character wants something and sets out to get it. (The **antagonist** is the character or force that comes into conflict with the protagonist. Just as the protagonist is rarely all good, the antagonist is rarely all bad.)

The **protagonist** is the main character, usually the one who sets the action in motion.

For more on Protagonist, see the Handbook of Literary Terms.

Reading Skills and Strategies

Comparing and Contrasting Characters

Some stories are built around characters who present dramatic contrasts—in appearance, perhaps, or in values, or in actions or speech. Malamud has created two very different characters in this story. As you read (or in your rereading), track the characteristics of both Sobel and Max—do they also have qualities in common?

Background

In "The First Seven Years," love finds its way, almost unnoticed, into a poor shoemaker's shop in New York City in the 1950s. Feld, the old shoemaker, is a Jewish immigrant who came to America from Poland years before.

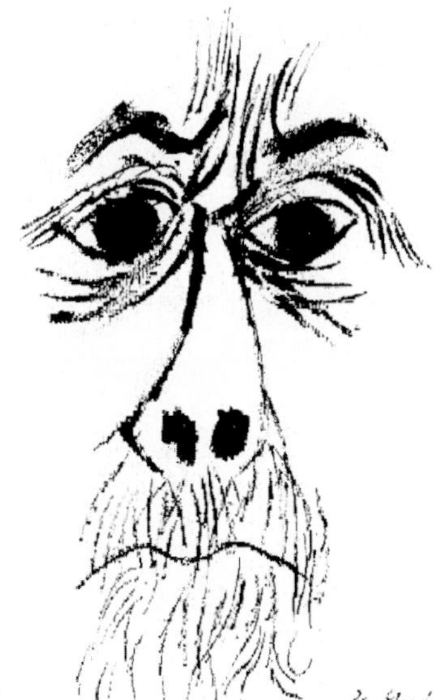

Facial Features from *The World of Sholom Aleichem* (1953) by Ben Shahn (1898–1969). Pen and ink ($8\frac{7}{8}'' \times 5\frac{7}{8}''$).

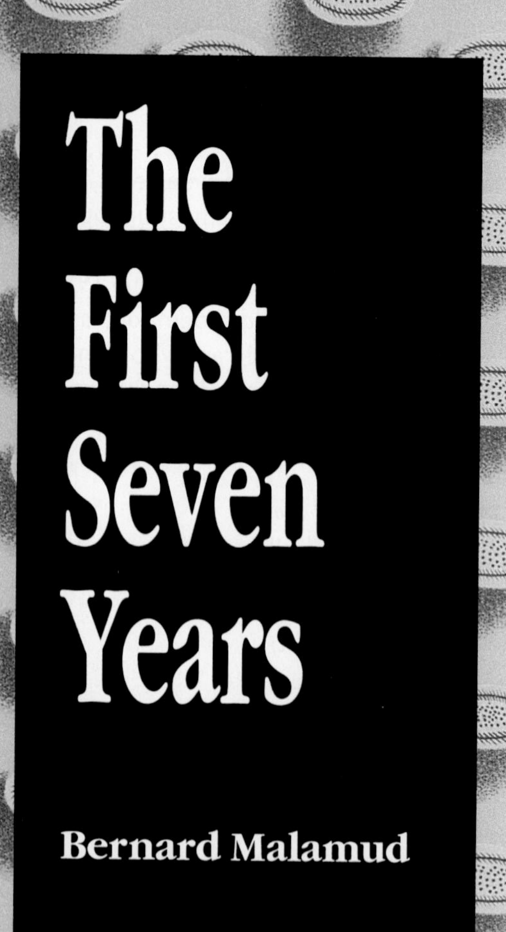

The First Seven Years

Bernard Malamud

"She will never marry a man so old and ugly like you."

Full Figure with Cane, Dressed in Long Coat and Large Brimmed Flat Hat from *The World of Sholom Aleichem* (1953) by Ben Shahn (1898–1969). Pen and ink (9″ × 5 15/16″).

Feld, the shoemaker, was annoyed that his helper, Sobel, was so insensitive to his reverie that he wouldn't for a minute cease his fanatic pounding at the other bench. He gave him a look, but Sobel's bald head was bent over the last[1] as he worked, and he didn't notice. The shoemaker shrugged and continued to peer through the partly frosted window at the nearsighted haze of falling February snow. Neither the shifting white blur outside nor the sudden deep remembrance of the snowy Polish village where he had wasted his youth could turn his thoughts from Max the college boy (a constant visitor in the mind since early that morning when Feld saw him trudging through the snowdrifts on his way to school), whom he so much respected because of the

1. **last:** wooden or metal model of a foot on which a shoemaker makes or repairs shoes.

WORDS TO OWN

reverie (rev′ər · ē) *n.:* daydreaming; state of being absorbed in thought.

sacrifices he had made throughout the years—in winter or direst heat—to further his education. An old wish returned to haunt the shoemaker: that he had had a son instead of a daughter; but this blew away in the snow, for Feld, if anything, was a practical man. Yet he could not help but contrast the diligence of the boy, who was a peddler's son, with Miriam's unconcern for an education. True, she was always with a book in her hand, yet when the opportunity arose for a college education, she had said no, she would rather find a job. He had begged her to go, pointing out how many fathers could not afford to send their children to college, but she said she wanted to be independent. As for education, what was it, she asked, but books, which Sobel, who diligently read the classics, would as usual advise her on. Her answer greatly grieved her father.

A figure emerged from the snow and the door opened. At the counter the man withdrew from a wet paper bag a pair of battered shoes for repair. Who he was, the shoemaker for a moment had no idea; then his heart trembled as he realized, before he had thoroughly discerned the face, that Max himself was standing there, embarrassedly explaining what he wanted done to his old shoes. Though Feld listened eagerly, he couldn't hear a word, for the opportunity that had burst upon him was deafening.

He couldn't exactly recall when the thought had occurred to him, because it was clear he had more than once considered suggesting to the boy that he go out with Miriam. But he had not dared speak, for if Max said no, how would he face him again? Or suppose Miriam, who harped so often on independence, blew up in anger and shouted at him for his meddling? Still, the chance was too good to let by: All it meant was an introduction. They might long ago have become friends had they happened to meet somewhere; therefore was it not his duty—an obligation—to bring them together, nothing more, a harmless connivance to replace an accidental encounter in the subway, let's say, or a mutual friend's introduction in the street? Just let him once see and talk to her and he would for sure be interested. As for Miriam, what possible harm for a working girl in an office, who met only loudmouthed salesmen and illiterate shipping clerks, to make the acquaintance of a fine scholarly boy? Maybe he would awaken in her a desire to go to college; if not—the shoemaker's mind at last came to grips with the truth—let her marry an educated man and live a better life.

When Max finished describing what he wanted done to his shoes, Feld marked them, both with enormous holes in the soles which he pretended not to notice, with large white-chalk X's, and the rubber heels, thinned to the nails, he marked with O's, though it troubled him he might have mixed up the letters. Max inquired the price, and the shoemaker cleared his throat and asked the boy, above Sobel's insistent hammering, would he please step through the side door there into the hall. Though surprised, Max did as the shoemaker requested, and Feld went in after him. For a minute they were both silent, because Sobel had stopped banging, and it seemed they understood neither was to say anything until the noise began again. When it did, loudly, the shoemaker quickly told Max why he had asked to talk to him.

"Ever since you went to high school," he said in the dimly lit hallway, "I watched you in the morning go to the subway to school, and I said always to myself, this is a fine boy that he wants so much an education."

"Thanks," Max said, nervously alert. He was tall and grotesquely thin, with sharply cut features, particularly a beaklike nose. He was wearing a loose, long, slushy overcoat that hung down to his ankles, looking like a rug draped over his bony shoulders, and a soggy old brown hat, as battered as the shoes he had brought in.

"I am a businessman," the shoemaker abruptly said to conceal his embarrassment, "so I will explain you right away why I talk to you. I have a girl, my daughter Miriam—she is nineteen—a very nice girl and also so pretty that everybody

WORDS TO OWN

discerned (di·zʉrnd′) *v.:* recognized; perceived.

illiterate (il·lit′ər·it) *adj.:* ignorant; uneducated; not knowing how to read or write.

looks on her when she passes by in the street. She is smart, always with a book, and I thought to myself that a boy like you, an educated boy—I thought maybe you will be interested sometime to meet a girl like this." He laughed a bit when he had finished and was tempted to say more but had the good sense not to.

Max stared down like a hawk. For an uncomfortable second he was silent; then he asked, "Did you say nineteen?"

"Yes."

"Would it be all right to inquire if you have a picture of her?"

"Just a minute." The shoemaker went into the store and hastily returned with a snapshot that Max held up to the light.

"She's all right," he said.

Feld waited.

"And is she sensible—not the flighty kind?"

"She is very sensible."

After another short pause, Max said it was OK with him if he met her.

"Here is my telephone," said the shoemaker, hurriedly handing him a slip of paper. "Call her up. She comes home from work six o'clock."

Max folded the paper and tucked it away into his worn leather wallet.

"About the shoes," he said. "How much did you say they will cost me?"

"Don't worry about the price."

"I just like to have an idea."

"A dollar—dollar fifty. A dollar fifty," the shoemaker said.

At once he felt bad, for he usually charged two twenty-five for this kind of job. Either he should have asked the regular price or done the work for nothing.

Later, as he entered the store, he was startled by a violent clanging and looked up to see Sobel pounding with all his might upon the naked last. It broke, the iron striking the floor and jumping with a thump against the wall, but before the enraged shoemaker could cry out, the assistant had torn his hat and coat from the hook and rushed out into the snow.

So Feld, who had looked forward to anticipating how it would go with his daughter and Max, instead had a great worry on his mind. Without his temperamental helper he was a lost man, especially since it was years now that he had carried the store alone. The shoemaker had for an age suffered from a heart condition that threatened collapse if he dared exert himself. Five years ago, after an attack, it had appeared as though he would have either to sacrifice his business upon the auction block and live on a pittance thereafter or put himself at the mercy of some unscrupulous employee who would in the end probably ruin him. But just at the moment of his darkest despair, this Polish refugee, Sobel, appeared one night from the street and begged for work. He was a stocky man, poorly dressed, with a bald head that had once been blond, a severely plain face, and soft blue eyes prone to tears over the sad books he read, a young man but old—no one would have guessed thirty. Though he confessed he knew nothing of shoemaking, he said he was apt and would work for a very little if Feld taught him the trade. Thinking that with, after all, a landsman,[2] he would have less to fear than from a complete stranger, Feld took him on, and within six weeks the refugee rebuilt as good a shoe as he and not long thereafter expertly ran the business for the thoroughly relieved shoemaker.

Feld could trust him with anything and did, frequently going home after an hour or two at the store, leaving all the money in the till, knowing Sobel would guard every cent of it. The amazing thing was that he demanded so little. His wants were few; in money he wasn't interested—in nothing but books, it seemed—which he one by one lent to Miriam, together with his profuse, queer written comments, manufactured during his lonely rooming house evenings, thick pads of commentary which the

2. **landsman** (länts′mən): fellow Jew originally from the same local area in Eastern Europe.

Words to Own

unscrupulous (un·skro͞o′pyə·ləs) *adj.:* not restrained by ideas of right and wrong.
profuse (prō·fyo͞os′) *adj.:* plentiful; given freely.

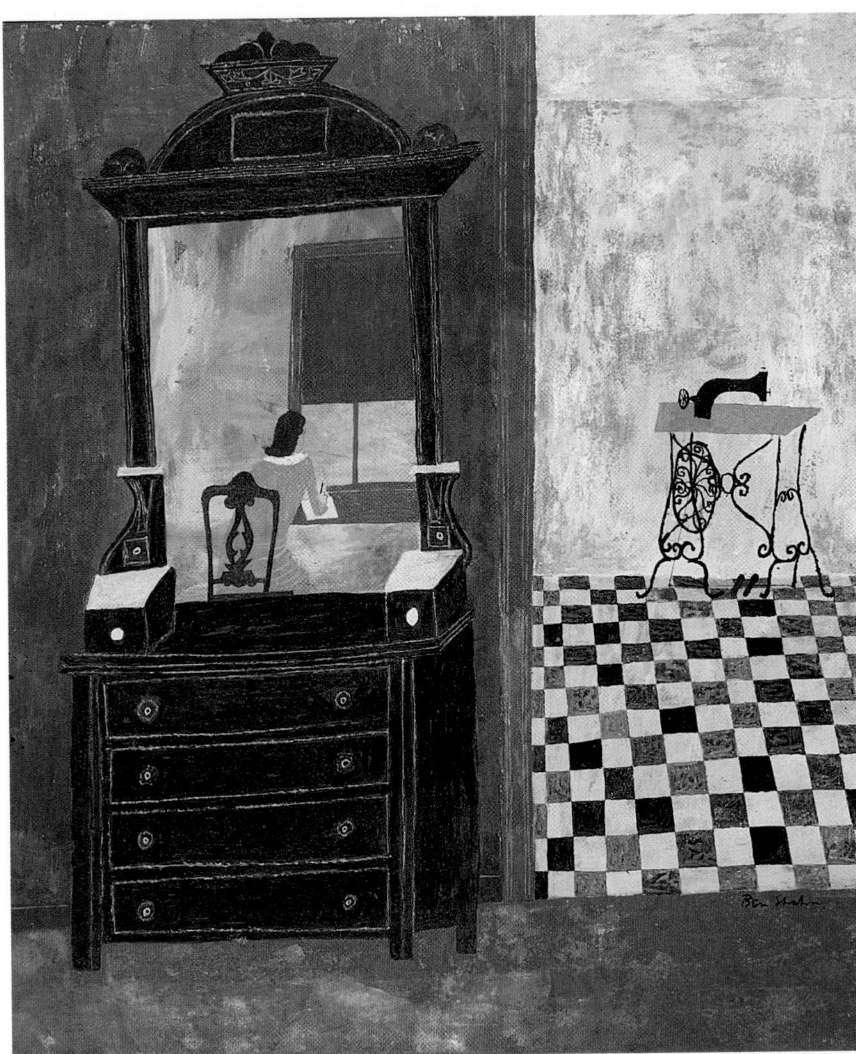

Inside Looking Out (1953) by Ben Shahn (1898–1969). Casein (17″ × 15″).

shoemaker peered at and twitched his shoulders over as his daughter, from her fourteenth year, read page by sanctified page, as if the word of God were inscribed on them. To protect Sobel, Feld himself had to see that he received more than he asked for. Yet his conscience bothered him for not insisting that the assistant accept a better wage than he was getting, though Feld had honestly told him he could earn a handsome salary if he worked elsewhere or maybe opened a place of his own. But the assistant answered, somewhat ungraciously, that he was not interested in going elsewhere, and though Feld frequently asked himself—what keeps him here? why does he stay?—he finally answered it that the man, no doubt because of his terrible experiences as a refugee, was afraid of the world.

After the incident with the broken last, angered by Sobel's behavior, the shoemaker decided to let him stew for a week in the rooming house, although his own strength was taxed dangerously and the business suffered. However, after several sharp, nagging warnings from both his wife and daughter, he went finally in search of Sobel, as he had once before, quite recently, when over some fancied slight—Feld had merely asked him not to give Miriam so

WORDS TO OWN

sanctified (saŋk′tə·fīd′) *adj.*: blessed; made holy.

many books to read, because her eyes were strained and red—the assistant had left the place in a huff, an incident which, as usual, came to nothing, for he had returned after the shoemaker had talked to him, and taken his seat at the bench. But this time, after Feld had plodded through the snow to Sobel's house—he had thought of sending Miriam but the idea became repugnant to him—the burly landlady at the door informed him in a nasal voice that Sobel was not at home, and though Feld knew this was a nasty lie, for where had the refugee to go? still, for some reason he was not completely sure of—it may have been the cold and his fatigue—he decided not to insist on seeing him. Instead he went home and hired a new helper.

Having settled the matter, though not entirely to his satisfaction, for he had much more to do than before and so, for example, could no longer lie late in bed mornings, because he had to get up to open the store for the new assistant, a speechless, dark man with an irritating rasp as he worked, whom he would not trust with the key, as he had Sobel. Furthermore, this one, though able to do a fair repair job, knew nothing of grades of leather or prices, so Feld had to make his own purchases; and every night at closing time it was necessary to count the money in the till and lock up. However, he was not dissatisfied, for he lived much in his thoughts of Max and Miriam. The college boy had called her, and they had arranged a meeting for this coming Friday night. The shoemaker would personally have preferred Saturday, which he felt would make it a date of the first magnitude, but he learned Friday was Miriam's choice, so he said nothing. The day of the week did not matter. What mattered was the aftermath. Would they like each other and want to be friends? He sighed at all the time that would have to go by before he knew for sure. Often he was tempted to talk to Miriam about the boy, to ask whether she thought she would like his type—he had told her only that he considered Max a nice boy and had suggested he call her—but the one time he tried she snapped at him—justly—how should she know?

At last Friday came. Feld was not feeling particularly well, so he stayed in bed, and Mrs. Feld thought it better to remain in the bedroom with him when Max called. Miriam received the boy, and her parents could hear their voices, his throaty one, as they talked. Just before leaving, Miriam brought Max to the bedroom door, and he stood there a minute, a tall, slightly hunched figure wearing a thick, droopy suit and apparently at ease as he greeted the shoemaker and his wife, which was surely a good sign. And Miriam, although she had worked all day, looked fresh and pretty. She was a large-framed girl with a well-shaped body, and she had a fine open face and soft hair. They made, Feld thought, a first-class couple.

Miriam returned after 11:30. Her mother was already asleep, but the shoemaker got out of bed and, after locating his bathrobe, went into the kitchen, where Miriam, to his surprise, sat at the table, reading.

"So, where did you go?" Feld asked pleasantly.

"For a walk," she said, not looking up.

"I advised him," Feld said, clearing his throat, "he shouldn't spend so much money."

"I didn't care."

The shoemaker boiled up some water for tea and sat down at the table with a cupful and a thick slice of lemon.

"So how," he sighed after a sip, "did you enjoy?"

"It was all right."

He was silent. She must have sensed his disappointment, for she added, "You can't really tell much the first time."

"You will see him again?"

Turning a page, she said that Max had asked for another date.

"For when?"

"Saturday."

"So what did you say?"

"What did I say?" she asked, delaying for a moment—"I said yes."

Afterward she inquired about Sobel, and

WORDS TO OWN

repugnant (ri·pug′nənt) *adj.:* distasteful; offensive.

Feld, without exactly knowing why, said the assistant had got another job. Miriam said nothing more and began to read. The shoemaker's conscience did not trouble him; he was satisfied with the Saturday date.

During the week, by placing here and there a deft question, he managed to get from Miriam some information about Max. It surprised him to learn that the boy was not studying to be either a doctor or lawyer but was taking a business course leading to a degree in accountancy. Feld was a little disappointed because he thought of accountants as bookkeepers and would have preferred a "higher profession." However, it was not long before he had investigated the subject and discovered that certified public accountants were highly respected people, so he was thoroughly content as Saturday approached. But because Saturday was a busy day, he was much in the store and therefore did not see Max when he came to call for Miriam. From his wife he learned there had been nothing especially revealing about their meeting. Max had rung the bell and Miriam had got her coat and left with him—nothing more. Feld did not probe, for his wife was not particularly observant. Instead, he waited up for Miriam with a newspaper on his lap, which he scarcely looked at, so lost was he in thinking of the future. He awoke to find her in the room with him, tiredly removing her hat. Greeting her, he was suddenly inexplicably afraid to ask anything about the evening. But since she volunteered nothing, he was at last forced to inquire how she had enjoyed herself. Miriam began something noncommittal but apparently changed her mind, for she said after a minute, "I was bored."

When Feld had sufficiently recovered from his anguished disappointment to ask why, she answered without hesitation, "Because he's nothing more than a materialist."

"What means this word?"

"He has no soul. He's only interested in things."

He considered her statement for a long time but then asked, "Will you see him again?"

"He didn't ask."

"Suppose he will ask you?"

"I won't see him."

He did not argue; however, as the days went by, he hoped increasingly she would change her mind. He wished the boy would telephone, because he was sure there was more to him than Miriam, with her inexperienced eye, could discern. But Max didn't call. As a matter of fact he took a different route to school, no longer passing the shoemaker's store, and Feld was deeply hurt.

Then one afternoon Max came in and asked for his shoes. The shoemaker took them down from the shelf where he had placed them, apart from the other pairs. He had done the work himself, and the soles and heels were well built and firm. The shoes had been highly polished and somehow looked better than new. Max's Adam's apple went up once when he saw them, and his eyes had little lights in them.

"How much?" he asked, without directly looking at the shoemaker.

"Like I told you before," Feld answered sadly. "One dollar fifty cents."

Max handed him two crumpled bills and received in return a newly minted silver half-dollar.

He left. Miriam had not been mentioned. That night the shoemaker discovered that his new assistant had been all the while stealing from him, and he suffered a heart attack.

Though the attack was very mild, he lay in bed for three weeks. Miriam spoke of going for Sobel, but sick as he was, Feld rose in wrath against the idea. Yet in his heart he knew there was no other way, and the first weary day back in the shop thoroughly convinced him, so that night after supper he dragged himself to Sobel's rooming house.

He toiled up the stairs, though he knew it was bad for him, and at the top knocked at the door. Sobel opened it and the shoemaker entered. The room was a small, poor one, with a single window facing the street. It contained a

Words to Own

deft *adj.:* skillful in a quick and sure way.

narrow cot, a low table, and several stacks of books piled haphazardly around on the floor along the wall, which made him think how queer Sobel was, to be uneducated and read so much. He had once asked him, Sobel, why you read so much? and the assistant could not answer him. Did you ever study in a college someplace? he had asked, but Sobel shook his head. He read, he said, to know. But to know what, the shoemaker demanded, and to know, why? Sobel never explained, which proved he read much because he was queer.

Feld sat down to recover his breath. The assistant was resting on his bed with his heavy back to the wall. His shirt and trousers were clean, and his stubby fingers, away from the shoemaker's bench, were strangely pallid. His face was thin and pale, as if he had been shut in this room since the day he had bolted from the store.

"So when you will come back to work?" Feld asked him.

To his surprise, Sobel burst out, "Never."

Jumping up, he strode over to the window that looked out upon the miserable street. "Why should I come back?" he cried.

"I will raise your wages."

"Who cares for your wages!"

The shoemaker, knowing he didn't care, was at a loss what else to say.

"What do you want from me, Sobel?"

"Nothing."

"I always treated you like you was my son."

Sobel vehemently denied it. "So why you look for strange boys in the street they should go out with Miriam? Why you don't think of me?"

The shoemaker's hands and feet turned freezing cold. His voice became so hoarse he couldn't speak. At last he cleared his throat and croaked, "So what has my daughter got to do with a shoemaker thirty-five years old who works for me?"

"Why do you think I worked so long for you?" Sobel cried out. "For the stingy wages I sacrificed five years of my life so you could have to eat and drink and where to sleep?"

"Then for what?" shouted the shoemaker.

"For Miriam," he blurted—"for her."

Meet the Writer

Redeemed by Love

Bernard Malamud (1914–1986), the son of Russian immigrants, grew up poor in New York City. His mother died when he was fourteen, and his father kept a small grocery store, working at the counter from dawn until late at night. Malamud's family's apartment had no books, no pictures, and no music except that of a neighbor's piano heard occasionally through the living-room window. He was an imaginative child, though, and "told stories for praise," as he recalled in a lecture at Bennington College in 1984.

Despite his gift for storytelling, Malamud began publishing fiction relatively late, after teaching English for many years in New York City schools. He soon made up for lost time, however. He won a National Book Award in 1959 for his first collection of short stories, *The Magic Barrel,* and the National Book Award and the Pulitzer Prize for his 1966 novel, *The Fixer.* Most of Malamud's stories are about characters who are redeemed by love.

The shoemaker, after a time, managed to say, "I pay wages in cash, Sobel," and lapsed into silence. Though he was seething with excitement, his mind was coldly clear, and he had to admit to himself he had sensed all along that Sobel felt this way. He had never so much as thought it consciously, but he had felt it and was afraid.

"Miriam knows?" he muttered hoarsely.

"She knows."

"You told her?"

"No."

"Then how does she know?"

Words to Own

pallid (pal′id) *adj.:* pale; lacking in color.

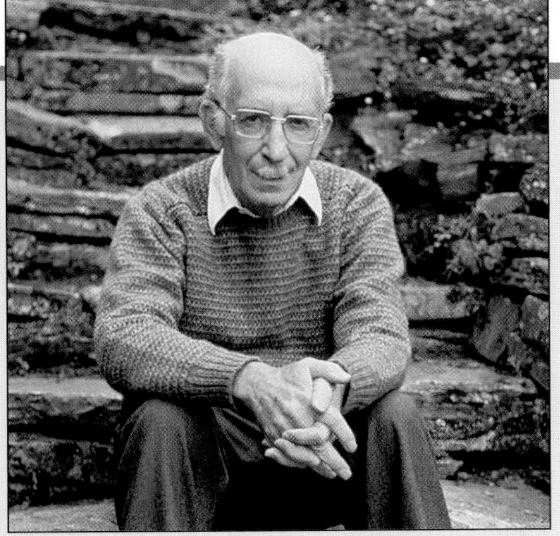

When he was once asked about writing, Malamud said this:

“You write by sitting down and writing. There's no particular time or place—you suit yourself, your nature. How one works, assuming he's disciplined, doesn't matter. If he or she is not disciplined, no sympathetic magic will help. The trick is to make time—not steal it—and produce the fiction. If the stories come, you get them written, you're on the right track. Eventually everyone learns his or her own best way. The real mystery to crack is you.”

"How does she know?" Sobel said. "Because she knows. She knows who I am and what is in my heart."

Feld had a sudden insight. In some devious way, with his books and commentary, Sobel had given Miriam to understand that he loved her. The shoemaker felt a terrible anger at him for his deceit.

"Sobel, you are crazy," he said bitterly. "She will never marry a man so old and ugly like you."

Sobel turned black with rage. He cursed the shoemaker, but then, though he trembled to hold it in, his eyes filled with tears and he broke into deep sobs. With his back to Feld, he stood at the window, fists clenched, and his shoulders shook with his choked sobbing.

Watching him, the shoemaker's anger diminished. His teeth were on edge with pity for the man, and his eyes grew moist. How strange and sad that a refugee, a grown man, bald and old with his miseries, who had by the skin of his teeth escaped Hitler's incinerators,[3] should fall in love, when he had got to America, with a girl less than half his age. Day after day, for five years he had sat at his bench, cutting and hammering away, waiting for the girl to become a woman, unable to ease his heart with speech, knowing no protest but desperation.

"Ugly I didn't mean," he said half aloud.

Then he realized that what he had called ugly was not Sobel but Miriam's life if she married him. He felt for his daughter a strange and gripping sorrow, as if she were already Sobel's bride, the wife, after all, of a shoemaker, and had in her life no more than her mother had had. And all his dreams for her—why he had slaved and destroyed his heart with anxiety and labor—all these dreams of a better life were dead.

The room was quiet. Sobel was standing by the window reading, and it was curious that when he read, he looked young.

"She is only nineteen," Feld said brokenly. "This is too young yet to get married. Don't ask her for two years more, till she is twenty-one; then you can talk to her."

Sobel didn't answer. Feld rose and left. He went slowly down the stairs, but once outside, though it was an icy night and the crisp falling snow whitened the street, he walked with a stronger stride.

But the next morning, when the shoemaker arrived, heavy-hearted, to open the store, he saw he needn't have come, for his assistant was already seated at the last, pounding leather for his love.

3. **Hitler's incinerators:** the furnaces in which the Nazis burned the bodies of Jews and other people whom they murdered in the death camps during World War II.

WORDS TO OWN

devious (dē′vē·əs) *adj.:* roundabout; indirect. *Devious* also means "deceitful."

Connections A BIBLICAL ALLUSION

Jacob and Rachel

The title of Malamud's story is an allusion to the Biblical story of Jacob and Rachel, which follows. As a young man, Jacob was sent by his father to his uncle Laban to marry one of Laban's daughters. Jacob stayed with Laban and worked for him for many years.

Laban said to Jacob, "Why should you work for me for nothing simply because you are my kinsman? Tell me what your wages ought to be." Now Laban had two daughters: The elder was called Leah, and the younger, Rachel. Leah was dull-eyed, but Rachel was graceful and beautiful. Jacob had fallen in love with Rachel, and he said, "I will work seven years for your younger daughter, Rachel." Laban replied, "It is better that I should give her to you than to anyone else. Stay with me."

So Jacob worked seven years for Rachel, and they seemed like a few days because he loved her. Then Jacob said to Laban, "I have served my time. Give me my wife so that we may sleep together."

So Laban gathered all the men of the place together and gave a feast. In the evening he took his daughter Leah and brought her to Jacob, and Jacob slept with her. . . . But when morning came, Jacob saw that it was Leah° and said to Laban, "What have you done to me? Did I not work for Rachel? Why have you deceived me?" Laban answered, "In our country it is not right to give the younger sister in marriage before the elder. Go through with the seven days' feast for the elder, and the younger shall be given you in return for a further seven years' work." Jacob agreed and completed the seven days for Leah.

Then Laban gave Jacob his daughter Rachel as wife; . . . [Jacob] loved her rather than Leah, and he worked for Laban for a further seven years.

—Genesis 29:15–30, New English Bible

° The deception was possible probably because Leah wore a veil.

Private Collection/Courtesy Superstock.

Jacob and Rachel (c. 1830) by William Dyce (1806–1864). Oil on canvas.

I Wish I Had Said . . .

I wish I had said . . .
Your beauty is like a light,
And I am drawn to it,
Fluttering by its flame.
I wish I had said . . .
Your body is to die for,
And I long to be martyred.
Yes, I wish I had said . . .
Your smile melts through
My heart, leaving only
Your warmth. Oh, how
I wish I had said . . .
Your translucent eyes
Send your soul to my heart,
Forcing it to beat again.
Yes, that is what I wish
I had said, but,
With confounded cowardice,
All I said was . . .
Hello, with a smile,
And I passed you by.

—Christian O'Connor
Gonzaga College High School
Washington, D.C.

Making Meanings

First Thoughts

1. Do you think Sobel will eventually marry Miriam? Why, or why not? Would Sobel identify with the speaker of the poem on page 128? Why, or why not?

Reading Check

Plot a **story map** to review the main elements of this story.

Setting	
Characters	
Their wants	
What blocks their wants	
Main events	
Climax	
Resolution	

Shaping Interpretations

2. At what point in the story did you realize that Sobel is in love with Miriam? What clues in the text do you think **foreshadow** Sobel's secret?

3. How would you describe Miriam's **character**, in view of what she says and does? Did any of Miriam's actions surprise you? Talk about your response to Miriam.

4. Use a circle diagram like the one at the right to **compare and contrast** the **characters** of Max and Sobel. List each man's individual qualities. In the shaded area, list the qualities they share. Which man do you think would make Miriam happier, and why? (On the other hand, do you feel that neither is a good match for Miriam?)

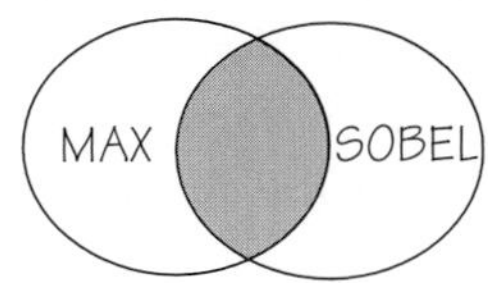

5. This story is about parental as well as romantic love. What do you think of the way Feld shows his love for his daughter? Despite the differences in culture, do you think Feld resembles the mother in "Two Kinds" (see page 95)? Why?

6. Suppose you were directing this story for a TV production. Whom would you focus on as the **protagonist,** and why? Who would be his or her **antagonist**? How would the production differ depending on who the protagonist was?

Connecting with the Text

7. How do you feel about arranged dates and about arranged marriages such as the one Feld wanted for his daughter? (Did this story affect the views you expressed in your Quickwrite notes?)

Extending the Text

8. This story is set in a specific **culture** that may be very different from yours. What can you learn about that culture from the text? Could these events take place in any other culture, including your own? Talk about your thoughts on this issue of culture and its influence on our lives.

9. Read the Biblical account of Jacob and Rachel (see ***Connections*** on page 128). What parallels and what important differences do you see between the Biblical story and Malamud's? Do you think the kind of love shown by Jacob and Sobel is believable? Why, or why not?

CHOICES: Building Your Portfolio

Writer's Notebook

1. Collecting Ideas for a Character Analysis

How do they change, and why? A good strategy to use for analyzing a character is to identify how the character changes—from your first glimpse of the person at the story's beginning to your last look at him or her at the end. Select a character from "The First Seven Years" or from another story, and take notes on how he or she changes in the course of the story. What does your character learn or discover by the story's end? How have the character's feelings changed? What has caused this change? Be sure you assess the change—is it believable? Save your notes for possible use in the Writer's Workshop on page 164.

WORK IN PROGRESS

Girl in "Boys and Girls"

Big change: First likes men's work and hates her mother's household work.

Discovery: that the men's work is brutal.

Cause: killing of beloved horse. Other causes??

Believable? Yes! Girl's feelings seem true to me from start to finish.

Creative Writing

2. What Does Miriam Think?

Rewrite any key event in this story from Miriam's **point of view.** Miriam might describe one of her dates with Max or report a conversation with Feld or describe her feelings for Sobel. Write as "I," as Miriam. You may want to write a **journal entry** or a **letter.** If you write a journal entry, be sure to make up a date. If you write a letter, make it clear whom Miriam is writing to. Read aloud your interpretations of Miriam's feelings, and respond to your classmates' interpretations. Are there differences of opinion?

Creative Writing

3. "When two years had passed . . ."

The ending of this love story is not entirely clear. Sobel appears to be willing to wait for two more years before asking Miriam to marry him. In two years, though, many things can change. In a paragraph, tell what you think might happen to Miriam and Sobel in the next two years.

Research/Social Studies

4. Reporting on an Immigrant Culture

Although Malamud does not locate this story specifically on the Lower East Side, his characters could have been among the millions of Eastern European Jewish immigrants who lived in this poor neighborhood in New York City in the early and middle years of the twentieth century. Using your library, the Internet, and electronic databases, prepare a brief **informal talk** on Jewish immigrant life in New York City. After you gather your data, you'll have to narrow your focus to a manageable topic. Be sure to tell what you learned from Malamud's text. Ask your audience for feedback. Was your presentation clear and focused?

Language Link MINI-LESSON

Dialect—How We Speak

Handbook of Literary Terms HELP

See Dialect.

A **dialect** is a form of a language spoken in a specific region (Maine, Appalachia, Brooklyn) or by a particular group of people. For example, if you pronounce *Mary, marry,* and *merry* exactly the same way, you are probably from the Midwest. If you are from the Northeast, you probably pronounce each word differently.

Besides differences in pronunciation, dialects are distinguished by differences in vocabulary and **syntax** (the way words are organized in a sentence). The dialect of a particular ethnic group usually contains traces of the syntax of the group's native language.

A Russian immigrant might omit the definite article *the* and the indefinite article *a* because in Russian those forms do not exist. ("He has big house in country.")

A French-speaking Haitian immigrant might add unnecessary articles because articles are used more often in French than in English. ("Do you know where is the Fifth Avenue?")

In "The First Seven Years," Feld and Sobel speak the English dialect of their ethnic group—Polish Jews whose native languages are Polish and Yiddish.

Try It Out

Find at least five examples in this story in which a character uses **syntax** that is not Standard English syntax. Rewrite these passages in Standard English. What does the use of Standard English change about the character?

A tip for writers: When you write dialogue, try to make it sound like your characters' real speech. When you reproduce dialect, you must try to make the speech sound authentic, but you must also avoid seeming to mock the characters. Malamud writes accurate dialect without ever seeming to belittle his characters.

Vocabulary HOW TO OWN A WORD

Word Bank

reverie
discerned
illiterate
unscrupulous
profuse
sanctified
repugnant
deft
pallid
devious

Word Charts: All You Need to Know

Work with a partner or small group to make a chart of basic information about each word in the Word Bank. You will have to use a **dictionary.** Hint: If you can't find a word's origin, try looking up the **root word** (*scruple* instead of *unscrupulous,* for example).

discerned
• **Meaning:** "recognized"; "perceived" • **Origin:** Latin *dis-,* "apart," and *cernere,* "to separate" • **Related words:** *discernible* and *discerning* (adj.); *discernibly* (adv.); *discernment* (n.) • **Examples (things that can be discerned):** light, colors, smells, tastes, cold, or heat; when a friend is upset; when someone is frightened

Before You Read

DISTILLATION

Make the Connection

The Power of Love

We all remember days from our childhood that made a special and lasting impression on us. The narrator of "Distillation" recalls one such day—a particular Saturday when he recognized suddenly the force of his father's love.

Distillation is a chemical process in which the essence of a substance is separated from impurities. Keep that definition in mind as you read the story, which is set in a poor Chicago neighborhood in the 1930s.

Quickwrite

Think back on your childhood, and remember a special day when you came to understand someone close to you. Write briefly about the day and your feelings.

Elements of Literature

Characters Who Change

Life changes people. We have victories and defeats and disappointments. Characters in stories change, too, or we wouldn't be much interested in their lives. Characters who change in significant ways are **dynamic characters.** By the end of the story, they have usually come to some new understanding, made some important decision, or taken a crucial action. Such a change often provides a clue to a story's meaning. **Static characters,** those who change less significantly, or not at all, are usually background figures.

Dynamic characters undergo change as a result of the story's action. **Static characters** do not change—they remain the same throughout the story.

For more on Character, see pages 110–111 and the Handbook of Literary Terms.

Reading Skills and Strategies

Establishing a Purpose for Reading

Maybe you're not consciously aware of it, but you usually have a **purpose** when you sit down to read. If you're reading fiction, you might simply want to **enjoy** getting caught up in a "good read" and appreciating a writer's style. You might read to **discover** another time and place and characters different from yourself. Sometimes, you might have a deeper purpose for reading—you might want to gain some insight into life and people. When you read for this purpose, you **interpret** a writer's message or a character's complex motivation. Often, when reading fiction, you combine all three purposes. Try it as you read "Distillation."

go.hrw.com
LEO 10-2

DISTILLATION

Hugo Martinez-Serros

One day alone remains--a day so different from the rest that I cannot forget it.

Fresh

He went on Saturdays because it was the best day. He did it for years and we, his sons, were his helpers. And yet one day alone remains, that single distant Saturday—a day so different from the rest that I cannot forget it:

Friday night I was in bed by nine. It would take us about an hour to get there, and we had to leave by eight the following morning to arrive just before the first tall trucks. All day the trucks would come and go, all day until five in the afternoon. My father wanted to get there before anyone else. He wanted to look it all over and then swoop down on the best places. There the spoils would go to the quickest hands, and we would work in swift thrusts, following his example, obeying the gestures and words he used to direct us.

That Saturday morning my father waited impatiently for us, his piercing whistles shrilling his annoyance at our delay. Anxious for us, my mother pushed us through the door as she grazed us with her lips. My father was flicking at his fingers with a rag and turned sharply to glower at us. I saw fresh grease on the hubs of the big iron wheels that supported the weight of his massive wagon, its great wooden bed and sides fixed on heavy steel axletrees.[1] He spoke harshly to us, for we had kept him waiting and he was angry: "What took you so long? ¡Vámonos!"[2]

He had already lowered the wagon's sides. Now, grasping us at the armpits, he picked us up and set us in beside the burlap sacks and a bag of food, starting with me, the youngest, and following the order of our ages—five, six and a half, eight, and eleven. He handed us a gallon jug of water and then pulled the guayín[3] through the door in the backyard fence, easing it out into the alley by the very long shaft that was its handle, like some vaguely familiar giant gently drawing a ship by its prow.

Yawning in the warmth of May, I leaned back, like my brothers, in anticipation of the joys of a crossing that would reach almost the full length of the longest line that could be drawn in the world as I knew it. That world, dense and more durable than a name, extended just beyond South Chicago. The day, a vast blue balloon stretched to its limits by a great flood of light, contained us and invited our blinking eyes to examine all that it enveloped.

The fastest route led us down alleys, away from pedestrians, cars, trucks, and wide horse-drawn wagons that plied the streets. The alleys, always familiar, seemed somehow new in the morning light that gleamed on piles of garbage and everywhere flashed slivers of rainbows in beads of moisture. Garbage men used shovels to clear away these piles. What garbage cans there were stood sheltered against walls and fences or lay fallen in heaps of refuse. Through the unpaved alleys we went, over black earth hard packed and inlaid with myriad fragments of glass that sparkled in the morning radiance. Ahead of us rats scattered, fleeing the noise and bulk that moved toward them. Stray dogs, poking their noses into piles, did not retreat at our approach. Sunlight and shadows mottled my vision as the wagon rolled past trees, poles, fences, garages, sheds. My father moved in and out of the light, in and out of the shadows. On clotheslines, threadbare garments waved and swelled. Without slowing down, my father navigated around potholes, and these sudden maneuvers shook loose squeals and laughter as our bodies swayed.

At 86th Street he had to leave the alleys to continue south. There the steel mills and train yards suddenly closed in on us. We rattled over the railroad crossing at Burley Avenue, a busy, noisy pass, and this made me stiffen and press my palms against my ears. For one block Burley

1. **axletrees:** bars connecting the opposite wheels of a wagon.
2. **Vâmonos** (vä′mô·nôs): Spanish for "Let's go."
3. **guayín** (gwä·yēn′): Spanish dialect term for a wagon that can be pulled by a person.

Words to Own

spoils *n.:* loot; goods gotten through special effort. Here, *spoils* can also be seen as a reference to spoiled food.
glower (glou′ər) *v.:* glare; stare angrily.
myriad (mir′ē·əd) *adj.:* countless or of a highly varied nature.

Avenue was a corridor—the only one for some distance around—that allowed movement north and south. At 89th Street my father followed a southwesterly course, going faster and faster, farther and farther from the steel mills, moving beyond the commercial area into a zone where the houses looked more and more expensive and the lawns grew thicker and greener. Already there were many flowers here, but no noise and few children, and there were no alleys. As my father rushed through these neighborhoods, we fell silent. I was baffled by the absence of garbage, and my eyes searched for an explanation that was to remain hidden from me for years.

At the end of a street that advanced between rows of brick bungalows stood the tunnel. We entered it and I tensed, at once exhilarated and alarmed by the wagon's din, frightened by the sudden darkness yet braving it because my father was there. A long time passed before we reached midpoint, where I feared everything would cave in on us. Then slowly my father's silhouette, pillarlike, filled the space ahead of me, growing larger and larger as we approached the light. Beyond the tunnel there were no houses, and we emerged into the radiance of 95th Street and Torrence Avenue.

There, stopping for the traffic that raced along 95th Street, my father quickly harnessed himself to the wagon with the double rope that was coiled around its prowlike handle. He was safe in this rude harness, for he could loosen it instantly and drop back alongside the great vehicle to brake it if the need arose. Now he pulled his wagon into Torrence Avenue, and his legs pumped, hard at first, and then they let up and soon he was running. Torrence Avenue, broad and well paved, shone like still water, and he ran smoothly, with long strides, at about three quarters of his top speed. We were smiling now, and we saw the smile on his face when he looked back over his shoulder. Breathing easily, he ran before us, and I watched his effortless movement forward. I felt a sudden keen desire to be just like him and for an instant found it difficult to breathe. To our right was a green expanse—trees, wildflowers, grasses, and a bountiful variety of weeds—like a green sea extending to the horizon. Torrence Avenue now curved gently to the left for a half block and farther ahead gradually straightened along a stretch of several blocks, flanked on the left by a high fence and a long dense row of poplars. As my father navigated out of the curve we urged him on.

"Faster, Pa, faster! ¡Más rápido!"

"Come on, Pa, you c'n go faster'n that!"

"Pa, as fast as you c'n go, Pa, as fast as you c'n go!"

"Like a car, Pa, like a car!"

The prow shot forward, chasing my father as he reached top speed, and the craft darted into the straight lane that would take us to 103rd Street. My heart unleashed and racing, I looked up into the row of trees at the shoreline, saw swift islets[4] of blue sky coursing brightly through the green current of foliage. Along the shoreline my father's pace gradually slowed until he seemed to be moving at half speed. Whenever he glanced backward, we saw sweat trickling down his forehead and following the line of his eyebrows to join the streamlets running from his temples. Beads of perspiration swelled at his hairline and slid down his neck into the blue denim shirt, which deepened to a dolphin color. Far beyond the fence, their smoking stacks thrust into the sky, the steel mills took on the appearance of enormous, dark, steam-driven vessels.

At 103rd Street my father veered due west. Ahead of us, at a distance of several blocks, loomed the 103rd Street Bridge. All his pacing had led to this, was a limbering up for this ascent. Many yards before the street rose, my father began to increase his speed with every stride. He did it gradually, never slackening, for the wagon was heavy and accelerated slowly. I placed the gallon jug of water between my legs and tightened them around it as he reached full speed just before storming the incline. He started up unfalteringly, tenaciously, with short, rapid steps and his body bent forward, his natural reaction to the exaggerated resistance sud-

4. **islets** (ī′lits): very small islands.

denly offered by the wagon. From a point high in the sky the pavement poured down on us. Immediately my father was drenched in sweat. His face, in profile now on the left, now on the right, became twisted with exertion while his broad back grew to twice its size under the strain. We held our breath, maintained a fragile silence, and did not move, our bodies taut from participation in his struggle. All the way up we lost speed by degrees. His breathing grew heavy, labored. His legs slowed, seeking now to recover with more powerful thrusts what they had lost with a diminished number of strokes. His jaw tightened, his head fell, sometimes he closed his eyes, and we could see his tortured face as his arms swung desperately at some invisible opponent, and still he went up, up, up.

When the pavement leveled off, he yielded for a moment, broke into a smile, and then, summoning reserves from the labyrinth of his will, lunged forward furiously, as if galvanized by his victory, and reached full speed at the moment the wagon began to descend. Miraculously, he freed himself from the harness, turned the shaft back into the wagon, and jumped on. Winking at us, he fell to his knees and leaned hard on the shaft. He was happy, wildly happy, and saw that we were too, and he laughed without restraint. "Miren, vean, look around you!" he shouted to us.

We were at the summit and the world fell away from us far into the horizon. To the east, steel mills, granaries, railroad yards, a profusion of industrial plants; to the north and south, prairies, trees, some houses; to the west, main arteries, more plants, the great smoking heaps of the city dump, and, farther still, houses and a green sweep of trees that extended as far as the eye saw. Years have changed this area in many ways, but that landscape, like a photo negative, glows in memory's light.

We had churned up the mountainous wave of the bridge, and now, as we coasted down ever faster, we screeched and I could feel my body pucker. Our excitement was different now. It came of expectancy, of the certain knowledge that we would soon be sailing. We were safe with our incomparable pilot, but we howled with nervous delight as we picked up speed. Down, down, straight down we fell, and then the guayín righted itself and my stomach shot forward, threatening for a fraction of a second to move beyond its body.

When the wagon finally came to a stop, my father got down. Again he harnessed himself to it and pulled us onward. He moved with haste but did not run. Looking into the immense blue dome above us, we knew our journey would soon end and we began to shift uneasily, anticipating our arrival. With cupped hands we covered our faces and grew silent while the wheels beneath us seemed to clack-clack louder and louder each time they passed over the pavement lines. At the divided highway my father turned south. We would be there in minutes.

The wagon stopped. We dropped our hands, exposing our faces, and climbed down. The full stink of decomposing garbage, fused to that of slow-burning trash, struck us. Before us was the city dump—a great raw sore on the landscape, a leprous[5] tract oozing flames and smoldering, hellish grounds columned in smoke and grown tumid across years. Fragments of glass, metal, wood, lay everywhere, some of them menacingly jagged where they had not been driven into the earth by the wheels of the ponderous trucks.

My father had learned that the dump yielded more and better on Saturdays. Truckloads of spoiled produce were dumped that day, truckloads from warehouses, markets, stores, truckloads of stale or damaged food. We would spend the entire day here, gathering, searching, sifting, digging, following the trucks' shifting centers of activity.

Along a network of roads that crisscrossed the dumping grounds, trucks lumbered to and fro, grinding forward over ruts, jerking back-

5. **leprous:** diseased; covered with sores, as in leprosy.

WORDS TO OWN

taut (tôt) *adj.:* tightly stretched; tense.
galvanized (gal′və · nīzd′) *v.:* stimulated; excited.

ward, all of them rocking from side to side. My father took some burlap sacks, scanned the area, and pointed to the site where we would work. He went toward it quickly, followed by my oldest brothers. Lázaro and I stationed the wagon beyond reach of the clumsy vehicles that were already dumping and then made our way to the site. We started to work on a huge pile of deteriorating fruit, picking only what a paring knife would later make edible.

After several trips to the wagon, my father and brothers moved on to other piles. My job was to stay and guard the wagon, neatly arranging all that went into it. When I remembered, I took the jug of water and buried it in the earth to keep it cool. Eager for their company, I waited for my brothers to return with their newest finds.

From where I stood guard, I could see my father and brothers hurrying toward a truck that had just arrived. It was rumbling toward a dump area just beyond me. The men on that high, wobbly truck were pointing, nodding, waving—gestures signaling my father and brothers to follow because they carried a rich load. Directed by a man who advanced slowly and seemed to walk on his knees, the truck waded into a heap of garbage, dumped its cargo to the whir of a hydraulic mechanism, and was pulling out as my father and brothers drew close enough to express their gratitude with a slight movement of their heads.

Now my father waved to me. It was a call to join them before others arrived. As I started toward them, my brother Lázaro foundered on a spongy mass, fell through it, and disappeared. I stopped in my tracks, stunned. "Buried," I whispered, "he's buried!" My father saw him fall, bolted to his side, and thundered a command, "Alzate, Lázaro, get up, get up!" and in seconds he had raised him. Unsteady on his feet, Lázaro shook himself off like a wet dog and then brushed away scabs of rotting stuff that clung to him. Suddenly the stench of decay, the idea of grabbing something that might crumble into muck, the thought of losing my footing in all that garbage, filled me with terror. On tentative feet I went forward cautiously, expecting the ground to give way beneath me. My steps were becoming steady when one of them set off a long, frenzied squeak. A rat sprang from under my foot and retreated grudgingly, black eyes unblinking, sharp teeth flashing beneath bristly whiskers, long tail stiffly trailing its fat body. I did not move until my father's shrill whistle roused me; then he called me in an angry voice and I moved on.

Working in silence, we gathered what we wanted from that mound. Now and again the sun's oppressive heat was dimmed by clouds that seemed to come from nowhere, bringing us relief.

By noon the sky was overcast. We pulled the wagon away from the dumping area and sat on the ground to eat what we had brought from home. By then the stench no longer bothered us. My father handed us bean and potato tacos that were still warm. Hunger made them exquisite, and I sat there chewing slowly, deliberately, making them last, too happy to say anything. We shared the jug of water, bits of damp earth clinging to our hands after we set it down.

Before us was the coming and going of trucks, the movement of men, rats scurrying everywhere, some dogs, and just beyond us, under a tentlike tarp, a big gas-powered pump that was used to drain water from that whole area, which flooded easily in a heavy rain. Behind us was a tiny shack, crudely assembled with cardboard, wood, and sheet metal, home of the dump's only dweller, Uñas. He was nowhere in sight, but my mind saw him—a monstrous dung beetle[6] rolling balls endlessly, determination on his pockmarked face, jaws in constant motion and his hands thrashing

6. **dung beetle:** beetle that lives in and feeds on animal waste, or dung. The dung beetle lays its egg in a large ball of dung, which it rolls along and finally buries in the ground.

Words to Own

tentative (ten′tə·tiv) *adj.:* uncertain; hesitant. *Tentative* also means "not definite or final."

nervously, searching the grounds with a frenzy unleashed by the appearance of intruders.

By 12:30 the sky's blue was completely eclipsed. Above us an ugly gray was pressing down the sky, flattening it by degrees. My father stood up and looked hard at the sky as he spun on his heel. The temperature dropped abruptly and a strong wind rose, blowing paper, cans, boxes, and other objects across the grounds in all directions. He issued orders rapidly: "¡Pronto! Block the wheels and cover the wagon with the lona! Tie it down!" Then he took a sack and hurried off to a heap he had been eyeing while we ate.

We leaped forward, the two youngest scurrying in search of something to anchor the wheels with, while the two eldest raised the wagon's sides and unfolded the tarp my father had designed for such an emergency. The wheels blocked, we turned to help our brothers. We had seen our father tie down the tarp many times. We pulled it taut over the wagon and carefully drew the ends down and under, tying securely the lengths of rope that hung from its edges.

Huddled around the wagon, we watched the day grow darker. Big black clouds, their outlines clearly visible, scudded across the sky. It was cold and we shivered in our shirt sleeves. Now the wind blew with such force that it lifted things and flung them into spasmodic flight. We moved in together and bent down to shield and anchor ourselves. Frightened, we held our silence and pressed in closer until one of us, pointing, gasped, "Look! No one's out there! No one! Jus' look! We're all alone!"

A bolt of lightning ripped the sky and a horrendous explosion followed. Terror gripped us and we began to wail. The clouds dumped their load of huge, cold drops. And suddenly my father appeared in the distance. He looked tiny as he ran, flailing his arms, unable to shout over the sound of wind and water. He was waving us into the shack and we obeyed at once. Inside, cowed by the roar outside and pressing together, we trembled as we waited for him. He had almost reached us when the wind sheared off the roof. Part of one side was blown away as the first small pebbles of ice began to fall. He was shouting as he ran, "Salgan, come out, come out!"

We tumbled out, arms extended as we groped toward him, clutched his legs when he reached us and pulled us away seconds before the wind leveled what remained of the shack. A knot of arms and legs, we stumbled to the wagon. There was no shelter for hundreds of yards around and we could not see more than several yards in front of us. The rain slashed down, diminished, and hail fell with increasing density as the size of the spheres grew. Now we cried out with pain as white marbles struck us. My father's head pitched furiously and he bellowed with authority, "¡Cállense! Be still! Don't move from here! I'll be right back, ahorita vuelvo!"

In seconds he was back, dragging behind him the huge tarp he had torn from the pump, moving unflinchingly under the cold jawbreakers[7] that were pummeling us. With a powerful jerk he pulled it up his back and over his head, held out his arms like wings, and we instinctively darted under. The growing force of the hailstorm crashed down on him. Thrashing desperately under the tarp, we found his legs and clung to them. I crawled between them. We could not stop bawling.

Once more he roared over the din. "There's nothing to fear! ¡Nada! You're safe with me, you know that, ya lo saben!" And then little by little he lowered his voice until he seemed to be whispering, "I would never let anything harm you, nunca, nunca. Ya, cállense, cállense ya. Cálmense, be still, you're safe, seguros, you're with me, with Papá. It's going to end now, very soon, very soon, it'll end, you'll see, ya verán, ya verán. Be still, be still, you're with me, with me. Ya, ya, cállense. . . ."

7. **jawbreakers:** round, very hard candies. The writer is comparing the hail to these candies.

Words to Own

eclipsed (i·klipst′) *v.:* covered over; darkened. *Eclipsed* also means "outshone" or "surpassed."

Bent forward, he held fast, undaunted, fixed to the ground, and we tried to cast off our terror. Huddled under the wings of that spreading giant, we saw the storm release its savagery, hurl spheres of ice like missiles shot from slings. They came straight down, so dense that we could see only a few feet beyond us. Gradually the storm abated, and we watched the spheres bounce with great elasticity from hard surfaces, carom when they collided, spring from the wagon's tarp like golf balls dropped on black-topped streets. When it stopped hailing, the ground lay hidden under a vast white beaded quilt. At a distance from us and down, the highway was a string of stationary vehicles with their lights on. Repeatedly, bright bolts of lightning tore the sky from zenith to horizon and set off detonations that seemed to come from deep in the earth. At last the rain let up. My father straightened himself, rose to his full height, and we emerged from the tarp as it slid from his shoulders. He ordered us with a movement of his head and eyes, and as he calmly flexed his arms, the four of us struggled to cover the damaged pump with his great canvas mantle.

His unexpected "¡Vámonos!" filled us with joy and we prepared to leave. Hail and water were cleared from the wagon's cover. My brothers and I dug through the ice to free the wheels, and when my father took up the handle and pulled, we pushed from behind with all our might, slipping, falling, rising, moving the wagon forward by inches, slowly gaining a little speed, and finally holding at a steady walk to keep from losing control. Where the road met the highway, we waded through more than a foot of water and threw our shoulders into the wagon to shove it over the last bump. Long columns of stalled cars lined the highway as drivers examined dents and shattered or broken windows and windshields. We went home in a dense silence, my father steering and pulling in front, we propelling from behind.

Entering the yard from the alley, we unloaded the wagon without delay. While

Words to Own

abated (ə·bāt′id) *v.:* let up; lessened; decreased.
zenith (zē′nith) *n.:* point directly overhead in the sky; highest point.

my father worked his wagon into the coal shed and locked the door, my brothers and I carried the sacks up to our second-floor flat. It was almost four when we finished emptying the sacks on newspapers spread on the kitchen floor. There we began to pare while my mother, scrubbing carefully, washed in the sink. We chattered furiously, my brothers and I, safe now from the danger outside.

Lázaro brought the knife down on the orange, the orange slipped from his hand, and the blade cut the tip of his thumb. He held his thumb in his fist and I got up to bring him gauze and tape from the bathroom. I knew my father would let me in even if he had already started to bathe.

Some object fallen between the bathroom door and its frame had kept it ajar, but he did not hear me approach. I froze. He was standing naked beside a heap of clothes, running his hands over his arms and shoulders, his fingertips pausing to examine more closely. His back and arms were a mass of ugly welts, livid flesh that had been flailed again and again until the veins beneath the skin had broken. His arms dropped to his sides and I thought I saw him shudder. Suddenly he seemed to grow, to swell, to fill the bathroom with his great mass. Then he threw his head back, shaking his black mane, smiled, stepped into the bathtub, and immersed himself in the water. Without knowing why, I waited a moment before timidly entering—even as I have paused all these years, and pause still, in full knowledge now, before entering that distant Saturday.

Words to Own

livid (liv′id) *adj.:* bruised; black-and-blue.

Meet the Writer

Celebrating Survival

Hugo Martinez-Serros (1930–   ) is a native of South Chicago where most of his stories take place. His characters, like his Mexican-born parents, are generally newcomers to a harsh urban environment that challenges their capacity to survive. Yet their stories are full of joy, and their ultimate triumph is reflected in the title of the book from which "Distillation" comes: *The Last Laugh and Other Stories* (1988).

Martinez-Serros became a professor of Spanish American literature at Lawrence University in Appleton, Wisconsin. He says that "Distillation" is fundamentally a true story and that he is the narrator.

“What I wanted to achieve in the story was the five-year-old's vision of a man who is both near and far. Near because he is his father, a familiar and intimate figure, with all that this implies; far because he is larger than life, heroic, a miracle worker . . . profoundly unlike the child. In a number of senses, 'Distillation' is the story of a journey—a journey into the past, to the 103rd Street bridge, to the city dump, into the father's character.”

Connections — A Short Story

Powder **Tobias Wolff**

Just before Christmas my father took me skiing at Mount Baker. He'd had to fight for the privilege of my company, because my mother was still angry with him for sneaking me into a nightclub during our last visit, to see Thelonious Monk.[1]

He wouldn't give up. He promised, hand on heart, to take good care of me and have me home for dinner on Christmas Eve, and she relented. But as we were checking out of the lodge that morning it began to snow, and in this snow he observed some quality that made it necessary for us to get in one last run. We got in several last runs. He was indifferent to my fretting. Snow whirled around us in bitter, blinding squalls, hissing like sand, and still we skied. As the lift bore us to the peak yet again, my father looked at his watch and said, "Criminey. This'll have to be a fast one."

By now I couldn't see the trail. There was no point in trying. I stuck to him like white on rice and did what he did and somehow made it to the bottom without sailing off a cliff. We returned our skis and my father put chains on the Austin-Healy while I swayed from foot to foot, clapping my mittens and wishing I were home. I could see everything. The green tablecloth, the plates with the holly pattern, the red candles waiting to be lit.

We passed a diner on our way out. "You want some soup?" my father asked. I shook my head. "Buck up," he said. "I'll get you there. Right, doctor?"

I was supposed to say, "Right, doctor," but I didn't say anything.

A state trooper waved us down outside the resort. A pair of sawhorses were blocking the road. The trooper came up to our car and bent down to my father's window. His face was bleached by the cold. Snowflakes clung to his eyebrows and to the fur trim of his jacket and cap.

"Don't tell me," my father said.

The trooper told him. The road was closed. It might get cleared, it might not. Storm took everyone by surprise. So much, so fast. Hard to get people moving. Christmas Eve. What can you do?

My father said, "Look. We're talking about four, five inches. I've taken this car through worse than that."

The trooper straightened up, boots creaking. His face was out of sight but I could hear him. "The road is closed."

My father sat with both hands on the wheel, rubbing the wood with his thumbs. He looked at the barricade for a long time. He seemed to be trying to master the idea of it. Then he thanked the trooper, and with a weird, old-maidy show of caution turned the car around. "Your mother will never forgive me for this," he said.

"We should have left before," I said. "Doctor."

He didn't speak to me again until we were both in a booth at the diner, waiting for our burgers. "She won't forgive me," he said. "Do you understand? Never."

"I guess," I said, but no guesswork was required; she wouldn't forgive him.

"I can't let that happen." He bent toward me. "I'll tell you what I want. I want us to be together again. Is that what you want?"

I wasn't sure, but I said, "Yes, sir."

He bumped my chin with his knuckles. "That's all I needed to hear."

When we finished eating he went to the pay phone in the back of the diner, then joined me in the booth again. I figured he'd called my mother, but he didn't give a report. He sipped at his coffee and stared out the window at the empty road. "Come on!" When the trooper's car went past, lights flashing, he got up and dropped some money on the check. "Okay. *Vámonos.*"[2]

1. **Thelonious Monk** (1920–1982): American jazz musician, famed as a pianist and composer; one of the creators of the "bop" style of jazz.

2. **Vámonos** (vä′mô·nôs): Spanish for "Let's go."

The wind had died. The snow was falling straight down, less of it now; lighter. We drove away from the resort, right up to the barricade. "Move it," my father told me. When I looked at him he said, "What are you waiting for?" I got out and dragged one of the sawhorses aside, then pushed it back after he drove through. When I got inside the car, he said, "Now you're an accomplice. We go down together." He put the car in gear and looked at me. "Joke, doctor."

"Funny, doctor."

Down the first long stretch I watched the road behind us, to see if the trooper was on our tail. The barricade vanished. Then there was nothing but snow: snow on the road, snow kicking up from the chains, snow on the trees, snow in the sky; and our trail in the snow. I faced around and had a shock. The lie of the road behind us had been marked by our own tracks, but there were no tracks ahead of us. My father was breaking virgin snow between a line of tall trees. He was humming "Stars Fell on Alabama." I felt snow brush along the floorboards under my feet. To keep my hands from shaking I clamped them between my knees.

My father grunted in a thoughtful way and said, "Don't ever try this yourself."

"I won't."

"That's what you say now, but someday you'll get your license and then you'll think you can do anything. Only you won't be able to do this. You need, I don't know—a certain instinct."

"Maybe I have it."

"You don't. You have your strong points, but not . . . you know. I only mention it because I don't want you to get the idea this is something just anybody can do. I'm a great driver. That's not a virtue, okay? It's just a fact, and one you should be aware of. Of course you have to give the old heap some credit, too—there aren't many cars I'd try this with. Listen!"

I listened. I heard the slap of the chains, the stiff, jerky rasp of the wipers, the purr of the engine. It really did purr. The car was almost new. My father couldn't afford it, and kept promising to sell it, but here it was.

I said, "Where do you think that policeman went to?"

"Are you warm enough?" He reached over and cranked up the blower. Then he turned off the wipers. We didn't need them. The clouds had brightened. A few sparse, feathery flakes drifted into our slipstream and were swept away. We left the trees and entered a broad field of snow that ran level for a while and then tilted sharply downward. Orange stakes had been planted at intervals in two parallel lines and my father ran a course between them, though they were far enough apart to leave considerable doubt in my mind as to where exactly the road lay. He was humming again, doing little scat riffs around the melody.

"Okay then. What are my strong points?"

"Don't get me started," he said. "It'd take all day."

"Oh, right. Name one."

"Easy. You always think ahead."

True. I always thought ahead. I was a boy who kept his clothes on numbered hangers to ensure proper rotation. I bothered my teachers for homework assignments far ahead of their due dates so I could make up schedules. I thought ahead, and that was why I knew that there would be other troopers waiting for us at the end of our ride, if we got there. What I did not know was that my father would wheedle and plead his way past them—he didn't sing "O Tannenbaum" but just about—and get me home for dinner, buying a little more time before my mother decided to make the split final. I knew we'd get caught; I was resigned to it. And maybe for this reason I stopped moping and began to enjoy myself.

Why not? This was one for the books. Like being in a speedboat, only better. You can't go downhill in a boat. And it was all ours. And it kept coming, the laden trees, the unbroken surface of snow, the sudden white vistas. Here and there I saw hints of the road, ditches, fences, stakes, but not so many that I could have found my way. But then I didn't have to. My father in his forty-eighth year, rumpled, kind, bankrupt of honor, flushed with certainty. He was a great driver. All persuasion, no coercion. Such subtlety at the wheel, such tactful pedalwork. I actually trusted him. And the best was yet to come—switchbacks and hairpins impossible to describe. Except maybe to say this: If you haven't driven fresh powder, you haven't driven.

Making Meanings

First Thoughts

1. How did your three **purposes—discover, interpret, enjoy**—come into play as you read "Distillation"? Which ended up being strongest for you? Why?

Shaping Interpretations

2. How did you feel about the father during the scene in the dump and the final scene in the bathroom? How do you think his sons felt about him?
3. The writer says on page 140 that he wanted to share his vision of a father who was "larger than life, heroic, a miracle worker." What details did he use to create this sense of the father? Do you think he succeeded? (Be sure to reread the part where the father saves Lázaro from being buried alive.)
4. The writer says that the landscape of the dump glows in his memory "like a photo negative." List all the **sensory details** that make that landscape vivid to you. What is the overall feeling you get for the dump?
5. Think about the character of the narrator. Is he a **dynamic** or **static** character—does he change or grow or discover anything in the course of the story? Go back to the text, and find passages to support your interpretation.
6. The word *distillation* is defined on page 132. How could this term apply to this story? What do you think of it as a **title**?
7. How is love displayed in this story? Consider:
   - the father's actions during the journey and at the dump
   - the father's words
   - the sons' feelings for their father

Reading Check

a. Which character in "Distillation" is the **protagonist**? (If you think there is more than one possibility, consider which character you focus on and which one sets the action in motion.)

b. Explain what the protagonist **wants.**

c. List the **actions** the protagonist takes to get what he or she wants.

d. What **obstacles** does the protagonist have to overcome to get what he wants?

e. Explain how the main **conflict** is finally resolved.

Connecting with the Text

8. Why do you suppose the narrator still pauses before thinking back upon that long-ago Saturday? Are his feelings at all like those you described in your Quickwrite notes? Explain.

Extending the Text

9. What connections can you find or feel between "Powder" (see ***Connections*** on pages 141–142) and this story?

CHOICES: Building Your Portfolio

Writer's Notebook

1. Collecting Ideas for a Character Analysis

Collecting evidence for elaboration. For the Writer's Workshop on page 164, you may want to analyze one of the characters in this story: the father, the son who tells the story, or the mother, who is largely behind the scenes. Pick one of these characters, and jot down all the **character traits,** or special personal qualities, you see in that character. Then, think about how you arrived at these traits. Skim the story, looking for passages that support the traits you've identified. Focus on the character's **words, actions,** and **thoughts.** Look also for **how other people respond** to the character. Use a chart like the one in column 1 to collect details that reveal certain character traits. Save your notes.

Character: Father in "Powder"

Traits	Evidence
Loving	Fights to see son

Creative Writing

2. "One day . . ."

We come to understand the father in "Distillation" by watching his actions and observing how they affect his sons. Tell your own story about a special day when you came to understand someone close to you. Refer to your Quickwrite notes, and describe

- who the person was
- what happened that day
- what you realized about the person
- how the day affected you

To make your story come alive, elaborate with sensory details and dialogue.

Reflective Essay

3. "Where there is great love . . ."

Look back at the quotation by Willa Cather on page 93. Write a reflection on how you think "Distillation" and "Powder" connect with Cather's statement about great love and miracles. Elaborate on your ideas with specific incidents from each story.

Drawing

4. Mapping the Journey

Create a **map** that traces the route the narrator and his family took to the garbage dump. Be sure to check the text closely so you can indicate all the streets and landmarks mentioned by the narrator. Illustrate the map with sights the family saw as they made their perilous journey.

Critical Thinking/ Speaking

5. A Modern Quest

The heroic quest is an age-old pattern in narrative fiction. Work with a partner to see if this modern story conforms to the quest pattern. To gather your information, complete a chart like the one below; it is filled in with details from Homer's great **epic** the *Odyssey*. When you've finished your chart, prepare a presentation of your findings to the class. You might even illustrate your talk with pictures of old and new quest stories (from the *Odyssey* to *Indiana Jones*).

The *Odyssey*	
Hero	warrior
Companions	fellow warriors
Journey	sea voyage
Perils	monsters, storms
Purpose	return home

GRAMMAR LINK MINI-LESSON

Language Handbook HELP

See Verbs, pages 1021 and 1026-1028.

MARTINEZ-SERROS'S VIVID VERBS

swoop
glower
dart
thrust
lunge
churn
bowl
fling
chatter
freeze

Verbs Make It Vivid

Notice how the **verbs** in the following sentence from "Distillation" give a clear picture of the mother's actions:

> "Anxious for us, my mother pushed us through the door as she grazed us with her lips."

The mother's actions would be less vivid if tamer verbs had been used:

> Anxious for us, my mother moved us through the door as she touched us with her lips.

Sometimes the use of a particular verb is significant. For example, on page 137, when little Lázaro is buried in the muck in the dump, the father thunders out "Alzate!" In Spanish, *alzar* means "to raise; to lift up." For many readers, this verb will bring to mind the raising from the dead of another Lazarus in the Gospels. (If the father had used the verb *subir*, the feeling would have been different. *Subir* means just "to get up.")

Try It Out

1. Look through "Distillation" for at least ten examples of lively verbs that describe precisely what characters are doing. (Find verbs different from those in the list at left.) Make a list of these words in your journal.
2. Here are five tame, overused verbs. Brainstorm a list of vivid, lively verbs that would make each action much more specific: *go, say, walk, look, move.*

➤ Take out a writing assignment you're working on—perhaps from this collection. Circle or highlight weak verbs that could be replaced with more vivid, precise verbs. You might keep a list of "verbs I like" in your notebook for reference and inspiration.

VOCABULARY HOW TO OWN A WORD

WORD BANK

spoils
glower
myriad
taut
galvanized
tentative
eclipsed
abated
zenith
livid

Which Word?

Work with a partner to choose the correct word.

1. Which word describes a suddenly energized person?
2. Which word names the highest point in the sky overhead?
3. Which word describes skin that is discolored and bruised?
4. Which word tells what a cloud did to a patch of sunlight?
5. Which word describes a hesitant or unsure movement?
6. Which word is another name for loot or booty?
7. Which word tells what a downpour did when it let up?
8. Which word tells what people do when they look at you angrily?
9. Which word applies to a rope that is tightly stretched?
10. Which word refers to a great variety of people or things?

Before You Read

Life Is Sweet at Kumansenu

Make the Connection

Love Is Sweet

The love between parent and child is one of the most powerful of all human bonds. In this story, the love of a mother and a son overcomes barriers that most people would say were insurmountable on this earth.

Quickwrite

Have you heard about the woman who lifted a car to save her child who was trapped underneath? Do you know of anyone who has done the "undoable" for love? Just how strong is the power of love? Freewrite for several minutes.

Elements of Literature

Foreshadowing: Finding the Clues

Sometimes a story's ending takes us completely by surprise. Sometimes we can predict a surprise ending (if we read carefully) because the writer has dropped clues into the text. These clues **foreshadow**, or hint at, future events. Part of our pleasure at the end of such a story is seeing how many clues we noticed—and how many details make sense to us only when the story is over.

Foreshadowing is the use of clues that hint at what is going to happen later in a story.

For more on Foreshadowing, see the Handbook of Literary Terms.

Reading Skills and Strategies

Comparing Cultures

Because this story is set in a culture very different from the one you live in, you may be puzzled by the way Bola and her West African family live and think. We quickly spot how people are different from us, but we may take for granted the characteristics that we all share. As you read "Life Is Sweet at Kumansenu," note details and questions you have about Bola and her family. Notice also feelings shared by families everywhere: love, grief, and hope.

Background

The story's characters—an old woman, Bola; her grown son, Meji; and his young daughter, Asi—are members of an extended Yoruba family. They live in a rural area in Nigeria, a West African country that was once a colony of Britain. Although many people in Bola's village have converted to Islam or Christianity, they have not abandoned their traditional African beliefs. (See Literature and Culture on page 150.) Almost every aspect of their everyday lives is affected by a strong belief in a spirit world.

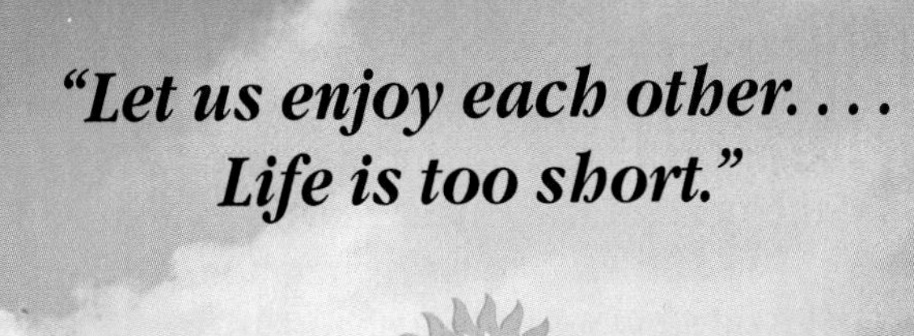

*"Let us enjoy each other. . . .
Life is too short."*

Life Is Sweet at Kumansenu

Abioseh Nicol

The sea and the wet sand to one side of it; green tropical forest on the other; above it, the slow, tumbling clouds. The clean, round, blinding disk of sun and the blue sky covered and surrounded the small African village, Kumansenu.

A few square mud houses with roofs like helmets were here thatched, and there covered with corrugated zinc,[1] where the prosperity of cocoa and trading had touched the head of the family.

The widow Bola stirred her palm-oil stew and thought of nothing in particular. She chewed a kola nut rhythmically with her strong toothless jaws, and soon unconsciously she was chewing in rhythm with the skipping of Asi, her granddaughter. She looked idly at Asi, as the seven-year-old brought the twisted palm-leaf rope smartly over her head and jumped over it, counting in English each time the rope struck the ground and churned up a little red dust. Bola herself did not understand English well, but she could easily count up to twenty in English, for market purposes. Asi shouted, "Six," and then said, "Nine, ten." Bola called out that after six came seven. "And I should know," she sighed. Although now she was old and her womb and breasts were withered, there was a time when she bore children regularly, every two years. Six times she had borne a boy child and six times they had died. Some had swollen up and with weak, plaintive cries had faded away. Others had shuddered in sudden convulsions, with burning skins, and had rolled up their eyes and died. They had all died; or rather he had died, Bola thought, because she knew it was one child all the time whose spirit had crept up restlessly into her womb to be born and mock her. The sixth time, Musa, the village magician whom time had now transformed into a respectable Muslim, had advised her and her husband to break the bones of the quiet little corpse and mangle it so that it could not come back to torment them alive again. But she had held on to the child and refused to let them mutilate it. Secretly, she had marked it with a sharp pointed stick at the left buttock before it was wrapped in a mat and taken away. When at the seventh time she had borne a son and the purification ceremonies had taken place, she had turned it surreptitiously to see whether the mark was there. It was. She showed it to the old woman who was the midwife[2] and asked her what it was, and she had forced herself to believe that it was an accidental scratch made while the child was being scrubbed with herbs to remove placental[3] blood. But this child had stayed. Meji, he had been called. And he was now thirty years of age and a second-class clerk in government offices in a town ninety miles away. Asi, his daughter, had been left with her to do the

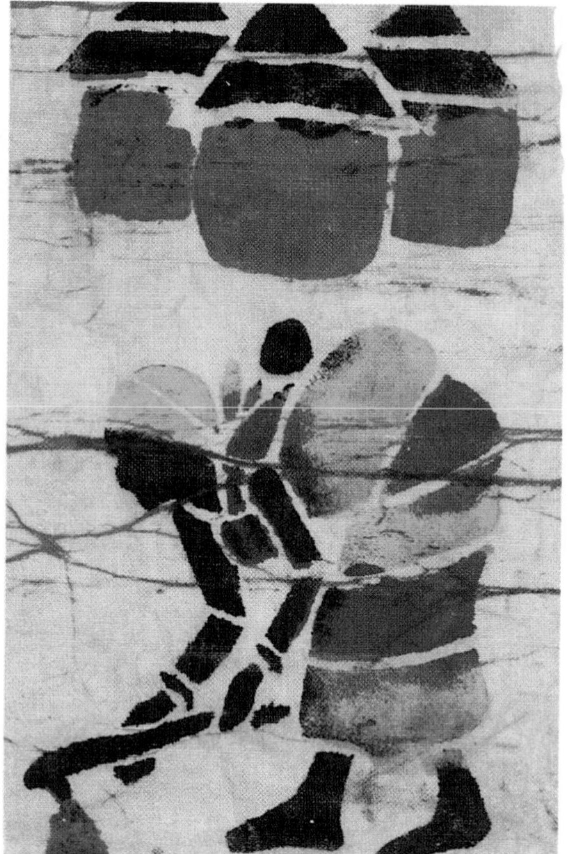

Batik by women of Burkina Faso, West Africa.

1. **corrugated zinc:** sheets made partially of zinc, a metal, that have been shaped into parallel ridges.

2. **midwife:** person who helps women in childbirth.
3. **placental:** from the placenta, the organ through which a fetus in its mother's uterus is nourished and its wastes are removed.

WORDS TO OWN
plaintive (plān′tiv) *adj.:* sad; expressing sorrow.

things an old woman wanted a small child for: to run and take messages to the neighbors, to fetch a cup of water from the earthenware pot in the kitchen, to sleep with her, and to be fondled.

She threw the washed and squeezed cassava leaves into the red, boiling stew, putting in a finger's pinch of salt, and then went indoors, carefully stepping over the threshold, to look for the dried red pepper. She found it and then dropped it, leaning against the wall with a little cry. He turned around from the window and looked at her with a twisted half smile of love and sadness. In his short-sleeved, open-necked white shirt and gray gabardine trousers, gold wristwatch, and brown suede shoes, he looked like the picture in African magazines of a handsome clerk who would get to the top because he ate the correct food or regularly took the correct laxative, which was being advertised. His skin was grayish brown and he had a large red handkerchief tied round his neck.

"Meji, God be praised," Bola cried. "You gave me quite a turn. My heart is weak and I can no longer take surprises. When did you come? How did you come? By truck, by fishing boat? And how did you come into the house? The front door was locked. There are so many thieves nowadays. I'm so glad to see you, so glad," she mumbled and wept, leaning against his breast.

Meji's voice was hoarse, and he said, "I'm glad to see you too, Mother," rubbing her back affectionately.

Asi ran in and cried, "Papa, Papa," and was rewarded with a lift and a hug.

"Never mind how I came, Mother," Meji said, laughing. "I'm here, and that's all that matters."

"We must make a feast, we must have a big feast. I must tell the neighbors at once. Asi, run this very minute to Mr. Addai, the catechist,[4] and tell him your papa is home. Then to Mami Gbera to ask her for extra provisions, and to Pa Babole for drummers and musicians . . ."

"Stop," said Meji, raising his hand. "This is all quite unnecessary. I don't want to see *anyone,* no one at all. I wish to rest quietly and completely. No one is to know I'm here."

Bola looked very crestfallen. She was so proud of Meji and wanted to show him off. The village would never forgive her for concealing such an important visitor. Meji must have sensed this because he held her shoulder comfortingly and said, "They will know soon enough. Let us enjoy each other, all three of us, this time. Life is too short."

Bola turned to Asi, picked up the packet of pepper, and told her to go and drop a little into the boiling pot outside, taking care not to go too near the fire or play with it. After the child had gone, Bola said to her son, "Are you in trouble? Is it the police?"

He shook his head. "No," he said, "it's just that I like returning to you. There will always be this bond of love and affection between us, and I don't wish to share it with others. It is our private affair and that is why I've left my daughter with you." He ended up irrelevantly, "Girls somehow seem to stay with relations longer."

4. **catechist** (kat′ə·kist′): person who teaches the principles of a religion through questions and answers.

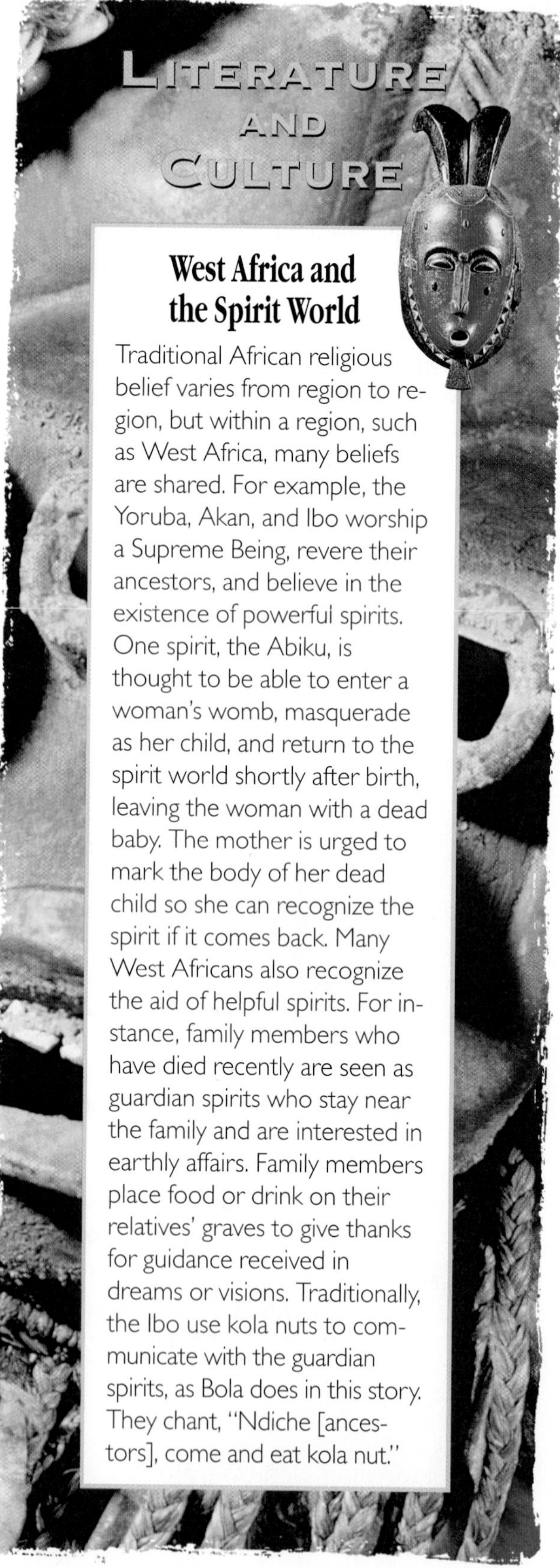

West Africa and the Spirit World

Traditional African religious belief varies from region to region, but within a region, such as West Africa, many beliefs are shared. For example, the Yoruba, Akan, and Ibo worship a Supreme Being, revere their ancestors, and believe in the existence of powerful spirits. One spirit, the Abiku, is thought to be able to enter a woman's womb, masquerade as her child, and return to the spirit world shortly after birth, leaving the woman with a dead baby. The mother is urged to mark the body of her dead child so she can recognize the spirit if it comes back. Many West Africans also recognize the aid of helpful spirits. For instance, family members who have died recently are seen as guardian spirits who stay near the family and are interested in earthly affairs. Family members place food or drink on their relatives' graves to give thanks for guidance received in dreams or visions. Traditionally, the Ibo use kola nuts to communicate with the guardian spirits, as Bola does in this story. They chant, "Ndiche [ancestors], come and eat kola nut."

"And don't I know it," said Bola. "But you look pale," she continued, "and you keep scraping your throat. Are you ill?" She laid her hand on his brow. "And you're cold, too."

"It's the cold, wet wind," he said, a little harshly. "I'll go and rest now if you can open and dust my room for me. I'm feeling very tired. Very tired indeed. I've traveled very far today, and it has not been an easy journey."

"Of course, my son, of course," Bola replied, bustling away hurriedly but happily.

Meji slept all afternoon till evening, and his mother brought his food to his room and, later, took the empty basins away. Then he slept again till morning.

The next day, Saturday, was a busy one, and after further promising Meji that she would tell no one he was about, Bola went off to market. Meji took Asi for a long walk through a deserted path and up into the hills. She was delighted. They climbed high until they could see the village below in front of them, and the sea in the distance, and the boats with their wide white sails. Soon the sun had passed its zenith and was halfway toward the west. Asi had eaten all the food, the dried fish and the flat tapioca pancakes and the oranges. Her father said he wasn't hungry, and this had made the day perfect for Asi, who had chattered, eaten, and then played with her father's fountain pen and other things from his pocket. They soon left for home because he had promised that they would be back before dark; he had carried her down some steep boulders and she had held on to his shoulders because he had said his neck hurt so and she must not touch it. She had said, "Papa, I can see behind you and you haven't got a shadow. Why?"

He had then turned her around facing the sun. Since she was getting drowsy, she had started asking questions, and her father had joked with her and humored her. "Papa, why has your watch stopped at twelve o'clock?" "Because the world ends at noon." Asi had chuckled at that. "Papa, why do you wear a scarf always around your neck?" "Because my head would fall off if I didn't." She had laughed out loud at that. But soon she had fallen asleep as he bore her homeward.

Just before nightfall, with his mother dressed in her best, they had all three, at her urgent request, gone to his father's grave, taking a secret route and avoiding the main village. It was a small cemetery, not more than twenty years or so old, started when the Rural Health Department had insisted that no more burials were to take place in the back yard of households. Bola took a bottle of wine and a glass and four split halves of kola, each a half sphere, two red and two white. They reached the graveside and she poured some wine into the glass. Then she spoke to her dead husband softly and caressingly. She had brought his son to see him, she said. This son whom God had given success, to the confusion and discomfiture of their enemies. Here he was, a man with a pensionable clerk's job and not a poor farmer, a fisherman, or a simple mechanic. All the years of their married life, people had said she was a witch because her children had died young. But this boy of theirs had shown that she was a good woman. Let her husband answer her now, to show that he was listening. She threw the four kola nuts up into the air and they fell onto the grave. Three fell with the flat face upward and one with its flat face downward. She picked them up again and conversed with him once more and threw the kola nuts up again. But still there was an odd one or sometimes two.

Batik by women of Burkina Faso, West Africa.

They did not fall with all four faces up, or with all four faces down, to show that he was listening and was pleased. She spoke endearingly, she cajoled, she spoke severely. But all to no avail. She then asked Meji to perform. He crouched by the graveside and whispered. Then he threw the kola nuts and they rolled a little, Bola following them eagerly with her sharp old eyes. They all ended up face downward. Meji emptied the glass of wine on the grave and then said that he felt nearer his father at that moment than he had ever done before in his life.

It was sundown, and they all three went back silently home in the short twilight. That night, going outside the house toward her son's window, she had found, to her sick disappointment, that he had been throwing all the cooked food away out there. She did not mention this when she went to say good night, but she did sniff and say that there was a smell of decay in the room. Meji said that he thought there was a dead rat up in the rafters, and he would clear it away after she had gone to bed.

That night it rained heavily, and sheet lightning turned the darkness into brief silver daylight for one or two seconds at a time. Then the darkness again and the rain. Bola woke soon after midnight and thought she could hear knocking. She went to Meji's room to ask him to open the door, but he wasn't there. She thought he had gone out for a while and had been locked out by mistake. She opened

WORDS TO OWN

cajoled (kə·jōld′) *v.:* coaxed with flattery, soothing words, or promises.

the door quickly, holding an oil lamp upward. He stood on the veranda, curiously unwet, and refused to come in.

"I have to go away," he said hoarsely, coughing.

"Do come in," she said.

"No," he said, "I have to go, but I wanted to thank you for giving me a chance."

"What nonsense is this?" she said. "Come in out of the rain."

"I did not think I should leave without thanking you."

The rain fell hard, the door creaked, and the wind whistled.

"Life is sweet, Mother dear, goodbye, and thank you."

He turned around and started running.

There was a sudden diffuse flash of silent lightning, and she saw that the yard was empty.

She went back heavily and fell into a restless sleep. Before she slept, she said to herself that she must see Mr. Addai next morning, Sunday, or better still, Monday, and tell him about all this, in case Meji was in trouble. She hoped Meji would not be annoyed. He was such a good son.

But it was Mr. Addai who came instead, on Sunday afternoon, quiet and grave, and met Bola sitting on an old stool in the veranda, dressing Asi's hair in tight, thin plaits.

Mr. Addai sat down and, looking away, he said, "The Lord giveth and the Lord taketh away." Soon half the village was sitting around the veranda and in the yard.

"But I tell you, he was here on Friday and left Sunday morning," Bola said. "He couldn't have died on Friday."

Bola had just recovered from a fainting fit after being told of her son's death in town. His wife, Asi's mother, had come with the news, bringing some of his property. She said Meji had died instantly at noon on Friday and had been buried on Saturday at sundown. They would have brought him to Kumansenu for burial. He had always wished that. But they could not do so in time, as bodies did not last more than a day in the hot season, and there were no trucks available for hire.

"He was here, he was here," Bola said, rubbing her forehead and weeping.

Asi sat by quietly. Mr. Addai said comfortingly, "Hush, hush, he couldn't have been, because no one in the village saw him."

"He said we were to tell no one," Bola said.

The crowd smiled above Bola's head and shook their heads. "Poor woman," someone said, "she is beside herself with grief."

"He died on Friday," Mrs. Meji repeated, crying. "He was in the office and he pulled up the window to look out and call the messenger. Then the sash broke. The window fell, broke his neck, and the sharp edge almost cut his head off; they say he died at once."

"My papa had a scarf around his neck," Asi shouted suddenly.

"Hush," said the crowd.

Mrs. Meji dipped her hand into her bosom and produced a small gold locket and put it around Asi's neck, to quiet her.

"Your papa had this made last week for your Christmas present. You may as well have it now."

Asi played with it and pulled it this way and that.

"Be careful, child," Mr. Addai said, "it is your father's last gift."

"I was trying to remember how he showed me yesterday to open it," Asi said.

"You have never seen it before," Mrs. Meji said sharply, trembling with fear mingled with anger.

She took the locket and tried to open it.

"Let me have it," said the village goldsmith, and he tried whispering magic words of incantation. Then he said, defeated, "It must be poor-quality gold; it has rusted. I need tools to open it."

"I remember now," Asi said in the flat, complacent voice of childhood.

The crowd gathered around quietly, and

WORDS TO OWN

diffuse (di·fyo͞os′) *adj.:* not focused; scattered.
complacent (kəm·plā′sənt) *adj.:* self-satisfied; smug.

the setting sun glinted on the soft red African gold of the dangling trinket. The goldsmith handed the locket over to Asi and asked in a loud whisper, "How did he open it?"

"Like so," Asi said and pressed a secret catch. It flew open and she spelled out gravely the word inside, "A-S-I."

The silence continued.

"His neck, poor boy," Bola said a little wildly. "That is why he could not eat the lovely meals I cooked for him."

Mr. Addai announced a service of intercession after vespers[5] that evening. The crowd began to leave quietly.

Musa, the magician, was one of the last to leave. He was now very old and bent. In times of grave calamity, it was known that even Mr. Addai did not raise objection to his being consulted.

He bent over further and whispered in Bola's ear, "You should have had his bones broken and mangled thirty-one years ago when he went for the sixth time, and then he would not have come back to mock you all these years by pretending to be alive. I told you so. But you women are naughty and stubborn."

Bola stood up, her black face held high, her eyes terrible with maternal rage and pride.

"I am glad I did not," she said, "and that is why he came back specially to thank me before he went for good."

She clutched Asi to her. "I am glad I gave him the opportunity to come back, for life is sweet. I do not expect you to understand why I did so. After all, you are only a man."

5. **service of intercession after vespers:** A service of intercession consists of prayers on behalf of someone. Vespers is an evening service.

Meet the Writer

The Real Africa

Abioseh Nicol (1924–1994) was born in Sierra Leone, a small country in western Africa. He was educated in Sierra Leone and Nigeria and later at Cambridge University in England, where he did research in biochemistry. When he returned to Africa in the 1960s, Nicol decided to write about his own people because "most of those who wrote about us seldom gave any nobility to their African characters." His poems and stories are usually set in rural villages, where he felt the true heart and spirit of Africa survive. In this story, the real Africa is found in the indomitable, life-affirming character of the old woman, Bola.

Making Meanings

First Thoughts

1. When did you begin to guess the truth about Meji?

Shaping Interpretations

2. Nicol uses **foreshadowing** to hint at what is going to happen later in the story. Go back and see how many clues you can find that foreshadow the truth about Meji. Make a chart like this one:

Clue	What It Foreshadows
1. The mark on Meji's body	1. He is the same child who has died six times.

Reading Check

a. How does Bola explain the death of her first six sons?

b. What does Musa tell Bola to do with the corpse of her sixth son?

c. What does she do instead?

d. What does Meji say is his reason for suddenly coming to visit his mother and daughter?

e. What shocking news reaches Bola near the end of the story?

3. Which passage in the story do you think best sums up its main **message**?

4. What do you make of Bola's final comment to Musa, the magician?

Connecting with the Text

5. This story takes place several years ago in a village in West Africa, where beliefs and visions of reality may be different from those of your culture. Despite those differences, how does the story suggest values that all people share? Talk over your responses with other readers.

Extending the Text

6. Think of other persons, from real life or literature, who, like Bola, have defied authority or the law (maybe even the laws of science) in order to save a loved one. (Refer to your Quickwrite notes.) What do these people and Bola have in common? How are they different?

7. Modern social pressures and changes are breaking down many of the old customs in Africa. What evidence of this do you find in Nicol's story? Do you think such changes are taking place today all over the world? Why, or why not?

8. **Compare** Bola with the father in "Distillation" (see page 133). How do both stories illustrate the power of love?

Challenging the Text

9. This story asks you to accept as a fact something that most people would probably find unreal. What is that "fact," and how did it affect your reading of the story?

CHOICES: Building Your Portfolio

Writer's Notebook

1. Collecting Ideas for a Character Analysis

Believable or not. When you analyze a character, you make judgments, or **evaluations.** Here are some questions to ask as you analyze a character:

- Is the character **credible** (believable)?
- Is the character **rounded** (complicated) or **flat** (one-dimensional, with only a single trait or two)?
- Is the character a **stereotype** (a **stock** character), or does the character seem unique?
- Does the character grow and change (**dynamic**) or stay the same (**static**)?

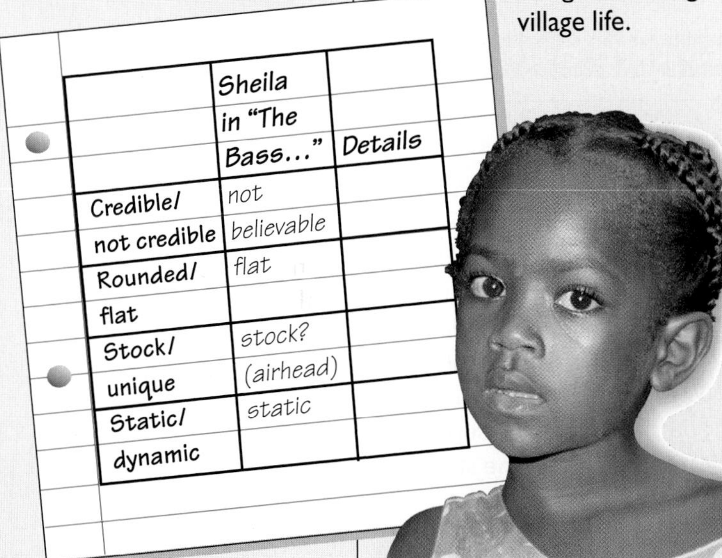

	Sheila in "The Bass..."	Details
Credible/ not credible	not believable	
Rounded/ flat	flat	
Stock/ unique	stock? (airhead)	
Static/ dynamic	static	

Using a chart like the one below, apply these criteria to a character from Nicol's story or from another story. Note details from the story that back up your evaluation. Save your notes for possible use in the Writer's Workshop on page 164.

Culture/Anthropology

2. Taking Field Notes

Suppose you are an anthropologist who is studying village life in Nigeria at the time this story takes place. Make notes, based on the story (and Literature and Culture on page 150), detailing what you have learned about West African village life. Focus on religious beliefs; attitudes toward the dead; social structures; food; male/female roles; family life; economics; changes affecting village life.

Comparing and Contrasting/Speaking

3. Connecting Cultures

Suppose (still as an anthropologist) you are now assigned to give an **informal speech** to a group of high school students comparing and contrasting your society and the village portrayed in the story. Focus on four of the categories cited in item two, Taking Field Notes. You might collect your data on index cards and use the cards as notes when you speak.

Economics	
Kumansenu	My society

Art

4. A Diorama of the Setting

What does Kumansenu look like? Create a diorama showing Bola's village. You will have to check the text to find specific descriptive details about physical geography, houses, and roads.

GRAMMAR LINK **MINI-LESSON**

Making Motion Pictures—Adverbs

Language Handbook HELP

See Adverbs, page 1031.

A modifier makes the meaning of another word more specific. An **adverb** modifies a verb, an adjective, or another adverb. Look at some specific meanings or shades of meaning adverbs can give to the verb *eats*.

In all these examples, the adverb specifies *how* the eating is done.

eats sloppily   eats constantly
eats neatly   eats daintily
eats fast   eats well

The adverbs in the following sentence from Nicol's story show *how* two actions are performed. Adverbs can also tell *where, when,* and *to what extent* (*how long, how much*).

"She looked idly at Asi, as the seven-year-old brought the twisted palm-leaf rope smartly over her head. . . ."

Try It Out

1. Delete the adverbs from Nicol's sentence at the left. What happens to your picture of the actions?
2. Substitute another adverb for each one in Nicol's sentence. How can adverbs change the meaning of the sentence?
3. Find five other adverbs in the story that show how an action is performed.

➤ Take out a piece of writing you are working on now or your notes about a character you might analyze for the Writer's Workshop on page 164. What adverbs could you add to help your readers visualize precisely how actions are performed?

VOCABULARY **HOW TO OWN A WORD**

WORD BANK

plaintive
cajoled
diffuse
complacent

Semantic Mapping

Working out a simple map or chart like the one here can help you own new or challenging words.

Make a **semantic map** like this for the other words from the Word Bank. Before you work out your maps, be sure to locate the word in the story to see how it is used.

plaintive

DEFINITION
"sad, expressing sorrow"

SYNONYMS
sad, mournful

EXAMPLES
the coo-coo cry of the dove
the wail of the blues singer

EXTENDING *the theme*

AN AUTOBIOGRAPHY

I had chosen to love a boy who was out of my reach.

Vistas from the Barrio (1985) by Pedro Villarini (1933–   ).
Oil on canvas (38″ × 36″).

Courtesy of the artist.

Lessons of Love

from **Silent Dancing**

Judith Ortiz Cofer

Background

First love—we yearn for it, but sometimes, when it finally comes, we can barely stand it. It's no surprise, then, that stories of first love are often mixtures of happiness, sadness, and foolishness.

This selection is from an autobiography about a young Puerto Rican girl whose family lives in the city of Paterson, New Jersey. The girl goes to a Catholic school.

Reading Skills and Strategies

Dialogue with the Text

Keep a **double-entry journal** as you read this true story. In the first column, note passages that you think are especially good (maybe they tap into your own experience), or passages that you disagree with. Write your response to each passage in the second column.

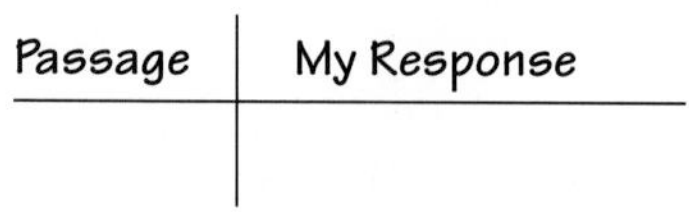

go.hrw.com
LEO 10-2

I fell in love, or my hormones awakened from their long slumber in my body, and suddenly the goal of my days was focused on one thing: to catch a glimpse of my secret love. And it had to remain secret, because I had, of course, in the great tradition of tragic romance, chosen to love a boy who was totally out of my reach. He was not Puerto Rican; he was Italian and rich. He was also an older man. He was a senior at the high school when I came in as a freshman. I first saw him in the hall, leaning casually on a wall that was the border line between girlside and boyside for underclassmen. He looked extraordinarily like a young Marlon Brando—down to the ironic little smile. The total of what I knew about the boy who starred in every one of my awkward fantasies was this: that he was the nephew of the man who owned the supermarket on my block; that he often had parties at his parents' beautiful home in the suburbs, which I would hear about; that this family had money (which came to our school in many ways); and that—this fact made my knees weak—he worked at the store near my apartment building on weekends and in the summer.

My mother could not understand why I became so eager to be the one sent out on her endless errands. I pounced on every opportunity from Friday to late Saturday afternoon to go after eggs, cigarettes, milk (I tried to drink as much of it as possible, although I hated the stuff)—the staple items that she would order from the "American" store.

Week after week I wandered up and down the aisles, taking furtive glances at the stock room in the back, breathlessly hoping to see my prince. Not that I had a plan. I felt like a pilgrim waiting for a glimpse of Mecca.[1] I did not expect him to notice me. It was sweet agony.

One day I did see him. Dressed in a white outfit, like a surgeon: white pants and shirt, white cap, and (gross sight, but not to my love-glazed eyes) blood-smeared butcher's apron. He was help-

1. **Mecca:** birthplace, in what is now Saudi Arabia, of Mohammed, the prophet who founded the Muslim religion. Mecca is a holy city for Muslims, who are strongly encouraged by their religion to make a pilgrimage there.

ing to drag a side of beef into the freezer storage area of the store. I must have stood there like an idiot, because I remember that he did see me; he even spoke to me! I could have died. I think he said, "Excuse me," and smiled vaguely in my direction.

After that, I *willed* occasions to go to the supermarket. I watched my mother's pack of cigarettes empty ever so slowly. I wanted her to smoke them fast. I drank milk and forced it on my brother (although a second glass for him had to be bought with my share of Fig Newton cookies, which we both liked, but we were restricted to one row each). I gave my cookies up for love, and watched my mother smoke her L&M's with so little enthusiasm that I thought that she might be cutting down on her smoking or maybe even giving up the habit. At this crucial time!

I thought I had kept my lonely romance a secret. Often I cried hot tears on my pillow for the things that kept us apart. In my mind there was no doubt that he would never notice me (and that is why I felt free to stare at him—I was invisible). He could not see me because I was a skinny Puerto Rican girl, a freshman who did not belong to any group he associated with.

At the end of the year I found out that I had not been invisible. I learned one little lesson about human nature—adulation[2] leaves a scent, one that we are all equipped to recognize, and no matter how insignificant the source, we seek it.

In June the nuns at our school would always arrange for some cultural extravaganza. In my freshman year it was a Roman banquet. We had been studying Greek drama (as a prelude to Church history—it was at a fast clip that we galloped through Sophocles and Euripides[3] toward the early Christian martyrs), and our young, energetic Sister Agnes was in the mood for spectacle. She ordered the entire student body (it was a small group of under three hundred students) to have our mothers make us togas[4] out of sheets. She handed out a pattern on mimeo pages fresh out of the machine. I remember the intense smell of the alcohol on the sheets of paper and how almost everyone in the auditorium brought theirs to their noses and inhaled deeply—mimeographed handouts were the school-day buzz that the new Xerox generation of kids is missing out on. Then, as the last couple of weeks of school dragged on, the city of Paterson becoming a concrete oven and us wilting in our uncomfortable uniforms, we labored like frantic Roman slaves to build a splendid banquet hall in our small auditorium. Sister Agnes wanted a raised dais where the host and hostess would be regally enthroned.

She had already chosen our Senator and Lady from among our ranks. The Lady was to be a beautiful new student named Sophia, a recent Polish immigrant, whose English was still practically unintelligible, but whose features, classically perfect without a trace of makeup, enthralled us. Everyone talked about her gold hair cascading past her waist, and her voice, which could carry a note right up to heaven in choir. The nuns wanted her for God. They kept saying that she had a vocation.[5] We just looked at her in awe, and the boys seemed afraid of her. She just smiled and did as she was told. I don't know what she thought of it all. The main privilege of beauty is that others will do almost everything for you, including thinking.

Her partner was to be our best basketball player, a tall, red-haired senior whose family sent its many offspring to our school. Together, Sophia and her Senator looked like the best combination of immigrant genes our community could produce. It did not occur to me to ask then whether anything but their physical beauty qualified them for the starring roles in our production. I had the highest average in the Church history class, but I was given the part of one of many "Roman citizens." I was to sit in front of the plastic fruit and recite a greeting in Latin along with the rest of the school when our hosts came into the hall and took their places on their throne.

2. **adulation** (a'jo͞o·lā'shən): intense admiration.
3. **Sophocles** (säf'ə·klēz') **and Euripides** (yo͞o·rip'ə·dēz'): Greek writers of tragic dramas in the fifth century B.C.
4. **togas** (tō'gəz): loose one-piece robes worn by citizens of ancient Rome.

5. **vocation:** divine call to enter the religious life (here, to be a nun).

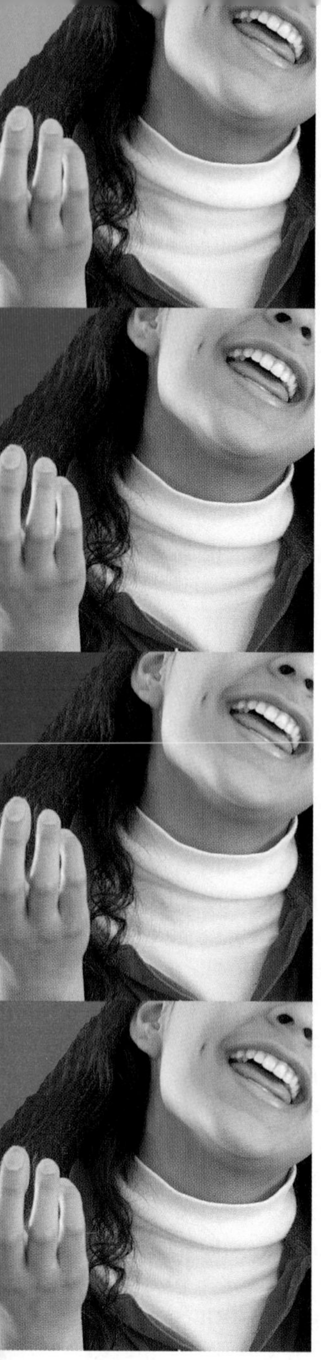

On the night of our banquet, my father escorted me in my toga to the door of our school. I felt foolish in my awkwardly draped sheet (blouse and skirt required underneath). My mother had no great skill as a seamstress. The best she could do was hem a skirt or a pair of pants. That night I would have traded her for a peasant woman with a golden needle. I saw other Roman ladies emerging from their parents' cars looking authentic in sheets of material that folded over their bodies like the garments on a statue by Michelangelo.[6] How did they do it? How was it that I always got it just slightly wrong, and worse, I believed that other people were just too polite to mention it. "The poor little Puerto Rican girl," I could hear them thinking. But in reality, I must have been my worst critic, self-conscious as I was.

Soon, we were all sitting at our circle of tables joined together around the dais. Sophia glittered like a golden statue. Her smile was beatific:[7] a perfect, silent Roman lady. Her Senator looked uncomfortable, glancing around at his buddies, perhaps waiting for the ridicule that he would surely get in the locker room later. The nuns in their black habits stood in the background watching us. What were they supposed to be, the Fates? Nubian slaves? The dancing girls did their modest little dance to tinny music from their finger cymbals; then the speeches were made. Then the grape juice "wine" was raised in a toast to the Roman Empire we all knew would fall within the week—before finals, anyway.

All during the program I had been in a state of controlled hysteria. My secret love sat across the room from me looking supremely bored. I watched his every move, taking him in gluttonously. I relished the shadow of his eyelashes on his ruddy cheeks, his pouty lips smirking sarcastically at the ridiculous sight of our little play. Once he slumped down on his chair, and our sergeant-at-arms nun came over and tapped him sharply on his shoulder. He drew himself up slowly, with disdain. I loved his rebellious spirit. I believed myself still invisible to him in my "nothing" status as I looked upon my beloved. But toward the end of the evening, as we stood chanting our farewells in Latin, he looked straight across the room and into my eyes! How did I survive the killing power of those dark pupils? I trembled in a new way. I was not cold—I was burning! Yet I shook from the inside out, feeling lightheaded, dizzy.

The room began to empty and I headed for the girls' lavatory. I wanted to relish the miracle in silence. I did not think for a minute that anything more would follow. I was satisfied with the enormous favor of a look from my beloved. I took my time, knowing that my father would be waiting outside for me, impatient, perhaps glowing in the dark in his phosphorescent[8] white Navy uniform. The others would ride home. I would walk home with my father, both of us in costume. I wanted as few witnesses as possible. When I could no longer hear the crowds in the hallway, I emerged from the bathroom, still under the spell of those mesmerizing eyes.

The lights had been turned off in the hallway, and all I could see was the lighted stairwell, at the bottom of which a nun would be stationed. My father would be waiting just outside. I nearly

6. **Michelangelo** (mī′kəl·an′jə·lō′) (1475–1564): Italian sculptor, painter, architect, and poet.

7. **beatific** (bē′ə·tif′ik): angelic; displaying delight or kindliness.

8. **phosphorescent** (fäs′fə·res′ənt): giving off light; glowing.

screamed when I felt someone grab me by the waist. But my mouth was quickly covered by someone else's mouth. I was being kissed. My first kiss and I could not even tell who it was. I pulled away to see that face not two inches away from mine. It was he. He smiled down at me. Did I have a silly expression on my face? My glasses felt crooked on my nose. I was unable to move or to speak. More gently, he lifted my chin and touched his lips to mine. This time I did not forget to enjoy it. Then, like the phantom lover that he was, he walked away into the darkened corridor and disappeared.

I don't know how long I stood there. My body was changing right there in the hallway of a Catholic school. My cells were tuning up like musicians in an orchestra, and my heart was a chorus. It was an opera I was composing, and I wanted to stand very still and just listen. But of course, I heard my father's voice talking to the nun. I was in trouble if he had had to ask about me. I hurried down the stairs, making up a story on the way about feeling sick. That would explain my flushed face and it would buy me a little privacy when I got home.

The next day Father announced at the breakfast table that he was leaving on a six-month tour of Europe with the Navy in a few weeks and that at the end of the school year my mother, my brother, and I would be sent to Puerto Rico to stay for half a year at Mamá's (my mother's mother) house. I was devastated. This was the usual routine for us. We had always gone to Mamá's to stay when Father was away for long periods. But this year it was different for me. I was in love, and . . . my heart knocked against my bony chest at this thought . . . he loved me too? I broke into sobs and left the table.

In the next week I discovered the inexorable truth about parents. They can actually carry on with their plans right through tears, threats, and the awful spectacle of a teenager's broken heart. My father left me to my mother, who impassively packed while I explained over and over that I was at a crucial time in my studies and that if I left my entire life would be ruined. All she would say was, "You are an intelligent girl, you'll catch up." Her head was filled with visions of casa[9] and family reunions, long gossip sessions with her mamá and sisters. What did she care that I was losing my one chance at true love?

In the meantime I tried desperately to see him. I thought he would look for me too. But the few times I saw him in the hallway, he was always rushing away. It would be long weeks of confusion and pain before I realized that the kiss was nothing but a little trophy for his ego. He had no interest in me other than as his adorer. He was flattered by my silent worship of him, and he had *bestowed* a kiss on me to please himself and to fan the flames. I learned a lesson about the battle of the sexes then that I have never forgotten: The object is not always to win, but most times simply to keep your opponent (synonymous at times with "the loved one") guessing.

But this is too cynical a view to sustain in the face of that overwhelming rush of emotion that is first love. And in thinking back about my own experience with it, I can be objective only to the point where I recall how sweet the anguish was, how caught up in the moment I felt, and how every nerve in my body was involved in this salute to life. Later, much later, after what seemed like an eternity of dragging the weight of unrequited love around with me, I learned to make myself visible and to relish the little battles required to win the greatest prize of all. And much later, I read and understood Camus's[10] statement about the subject that concerns both adolescent and philosopher alike: If love were easy, life would be too simple.

9. casa (kä′sä): Spanish for "house" or "home."
10. Camus (ka·mo͞o′): Albert Camus (1913–1960), French writer and philosopher.

Meet the Writer

Tracing Family Lives

Judith Ortiz Cofer (1952–) travels between two cultures. She was born in Puerto Rico and began her visits to the mainland when she was four. When her father, a career Navy man, was overseas, his family returned to Puerto Rico; when he sailed back to the States, his family rejoined him in Paterson, New Jersey. Judith Ortiz Cofer has said,

"My first language was Spanish. It was a challenge not only to learn English, but to master it enough to teach it and—the ultimate goal—to write poetry in it."

She has published poetry; a novel, *The Line of the Sun* (1989); a book of personal essays, *Silent Dancing* (1990); a collection of prose and poetry called *The Latin Deli* (1993); and *An Island like You: Stories of the Barrio* (1995).

"My family is one of the main topics of my poetry," she has said. "In tracing their lives, I discover more about mine."

Finding Common Ground

You are going to be working with a partner and talking about your responses to this story of first love and first rejection. Before you meet with your partner, make notes responding to these questions:

1. What did you see happening in the text? **Summarize** the main events of the story in your notes.
2. As you look back on your **double-entry journal,** decide what was the central focus for you. In other words, what was the most important image, event, or idea in the text? Why do you think so?
3. This is a true story. How believable do you find the girl's experiences with love? Are her feelings specific to her particular culture, or are they universal feelings?
4. Be sure to talk about the **title**. What lessons of love did the girl learn?

Now you are ready to share your notes with your partner. How do your responses differ? Does your understanding of the text change as you talk about it? What agreements can you reach about the text?

A Friendship like No Other

John and Lorraine, high school students, take turns telling "the truth and nothing but the truth" about Mr. Angelo Pignati, whom they nickname the Pigman. What starts as a telephone prank turns into a friendship that changes all their lives. *The Pigman* (HarperCollins), Paul Zindel's enormously popular novel, revolutionized young adult fiction when it appeared in 1968. (The book is available in the HRW Library.) The sequel, *The Pigman's Legacy,* continues John and Lorraine's story.

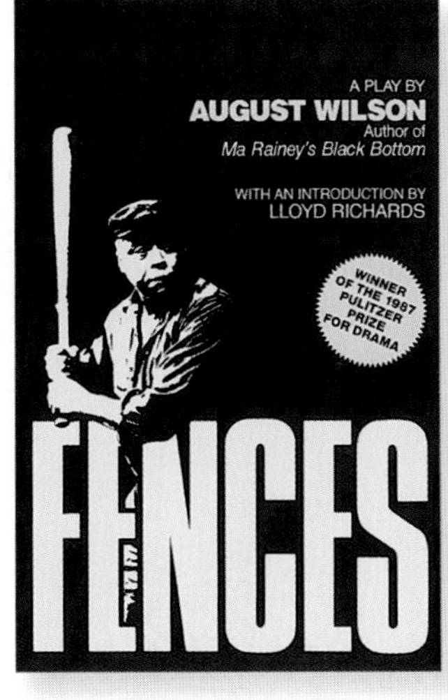

Father and Son

The father and son in August Wilson's 1987 Pulitzer Prize–winning play *Fences* (New American Library) have conflicting dreams for the boy's future. Excluded from the major leagues because of his race, the father finds it difficult to encourage his son's ball-playing ambitions.

Love Is the Glue

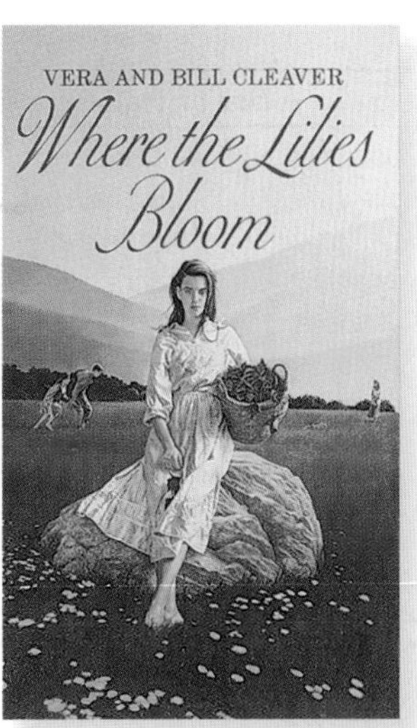

The teenage daughter of Appalachian sharecroppers, Mary Call Luther struggles to keep her brothers and sisters together after both parents die. You won't forget *Where the Lilies Bloom* (Lippincott) by Vera and Bill Cleaver.

Learning to Love Herself

Steven Spielberg's 1985 film of Alice Walker's Pulitzer Prize–winning novel, *The Color Purple* (Harcourt Brace), stars Whoopi Goldberg and Oprah Winfrey. The movie focuses on an African American woman who must overcome a tragic personal history and the legacy of slavery before she can take pride in who she is.

BUILDING YOUR PORTFOLIO

Writer's Workshop

ASSIGNMENT

Write an essay analyzing a fictional character in a short story, novel, movie, or TV show.

AIM

To use critical thinking skills; to give information.

AUDIENCE

Your teacher, classmates, or a friend.

A Box of Traits	
sociable	taciturn
playful	withdrawn
talkative	morose
stable	erratic
prudent	reckless
sensitive	insensitive
altruistic	self-centered
caring	manipulative
optimistic	pessimistic
hard-working	slothful

I don't have a very clear idea of who the characters are until they start talking.
—Joan Didion

EXPOSITORY WRITING

ANALYZING A CHARACTER

According to the writer W. Somerset Maugham, "You can never know enough about your characters." He was speaking as the *creator* of fictional characters—but the same can also be said for the reader. The more we know about the characters in a work of fiction, the more we understand its meaning.

In this workshop, you'll write an essay analyzing a fictional character. When you **analyze** something, you examine it closely to see how it works. You take it apart as if it were a puzzle or a machine, and try to discover how all its separate elements are put together and how each piece connects to the whole. When you analyze a fictional character, you do the same thing. You closely examine all the ways the writer reveals that character's nature or personality. Then, you put all these details back together again to create a portrait of what the character is like.

Prewriting

1. Choose a Character

WORK IN PROGRESS

Look back over the entries in your Writer's Notebook to see if you've already found a character you'd like to examine more closely. If you're having trouble deciding on one, consider the characters in novels, movies, or TV shows you've enjoyed. Try to find someone who seems particularly real or complex or mysterious to you. The stronger your feelings about the character, the better.

2. Gather Information

Once you've chosen a character, review the work, looking for details that reveal information about that character. As you take notes, think about these questions:

- **Does the writer show or tell?** What does the writer *tell* us directly about the character? What does the writer reveal indirectly by describing, or *showing,* the character's **appearance, speech, thoughts,** and **actions**? What can we infer by observing **how other characters respond** to that person?

The history
of the written
word is rich and
Page 1
Once upon a time

- **What's the personality?** From all the evidence you've noted, what would you say are the character's main **traits,** or personal qualities? Is he or she a **flat**—even a **stock**—character who exhibits only one or two personality traits? Is this a **round,** complex character with a many-sided personality?
- **Does the character change?** Is the character **static,** basically remaining the same throughout the story? Is he or she **dynamic,** changing in some significant way—by learning or realizing something, making an important decision, or taking some key action? If so, describe the change. Is it predictable, or did it surprise you in some way?
- **What motivates the character?** What are the reasons for the character's behavior? (If you're not sure, think about what the character wants or needs.) Do you find the motivation believable, or does it seem unrealistic or flimsy?
- **What's the character's role?** Is the character the **protagonist,** the person whose conflict sets the plot in motion?

Data Bank for Analyzing a Character
Appearance
Speech
Thoughts
Actions
Main traits
How others respond
Motivation
Change(s)?
Protagonist?

3. Develop a Thesis Statement

Narrow your focus to three or four key points, and write a **thesis statement** that sums up your **main idea** about this character. Consider the approaches on the next page.

Thesis Statement

In "Geraldo No Last Name," the sheer beauty of Sandra Cisneros's description of the character Marin is enthralling, while at the same time keeping Marin distant from us.

"O.K., so I dig a hole and put the bone in the hole. But what's my motivation for burying it?"

Language/Grammar Link
HELP

Dialogue: page 109.
Dialect: page 131.
Vivid verbs: page 145.
Adverbs: page 156.

Try It Out

When you **elaborate** on a **topic sentence** in a character analysis, you provide specific evidence from the story: dialogue, descriptive passages, interaction between characters, specific incidents.

1. How would you support the generalization that Feld in "The First Seven Years" is "a practical man"?
2. What evidence would you cite to show that Marin in "Geraldo No Last Name" is changed by the story's events?

Language Handbook
HELP

Using quotation marks: pages 1054–1056.

Sentence Workshop
HELP

Using adjectives and adverbs: page 169.

- Summarize the character's most important traits.
- Identify the character's change or discovery.
- Explain why the character is or is not the protagonist.

4. Organize Your Ideas

Think about the clearest order in which to present your three or four key points. (Each point will serve as the **topic sentence** for a paragraph in the body of your essay.) The Student Model, for example, arranges key points in this sequence: method of characterization, some character traits, the character's relationship with another character. Play around with several possibilities, and start an **outline** (see pages 334 and 450) showing your key points.

5. Elaborate: Back Up Your Ideas with Evidence

Now, fill in your outline with the strongest evidence to elaborate your topic sentences:

- **direct quotations** from the story
- references to **specific actions** and **dialogue**
- **specific adjectives** to describe the character's traits
- **comparisons** with other characters in the story or in other literary works

Drafting

You've already done a lot of planning, but there's still time to refocus your thesis or even discover new ideas during the writing process. You can either begin with your introduction or skip it for now and start with the body of your essay. Just get your thoughts down in writing—you can revise and polish later. Here are the three basic parts of your essay:

- **Introduction.** Your first paragraph should draw readers into your topic and present your **thesis statement.** Identify both the story (author and title) and the character you're analyzing.
- **Body.** You've already outlined the body of your essay and written a topic sentence for each paragraph. Now, turn your supporting details into complete sentences. Refer to specific events, descriptions, and dialogue to back up your generalizations about the character. Try to include direct quotations from the story. When you describe the character, choose specific and vivid adjectives that give the reader a clear picture.
- **Conclusion.** In your last paragraph, restate your thesis and add a final comment about the character or the meaning of the story as a whole. If possible, end with a dramatic clincher sentence, as in the Student Model.

Student Model

"Geraldo No Last Name"

Sandra Cisneros has a way with words that is unparalleled in her ability to grasp the essence of a character. In "Geraldo No Last Name," the sheer beauty of her description of the character Marin is enthralling, while at the same time keeping Marin distant from us.

Identifies author, title, and character

Thesis statement

Her description may seem meager at first glance (Cisneros says so little about her characters), but after reading the story, you discover that her description is bursting with insight. Marin is drawn as one might see her in one night. Cisneros lets you know that she is a stranger, not about to share dark secrets and wishes, a simple person.

Topic sentence: indirect characterization

Marin is just a girl who likes to have fun, twenty-something, vivacious and slightly materialistic while remaining innocent to life's tragedies. She doesn't realize that what exists can be gone in seconds, and reasons that were always so obvious cannot be explained. She went looking for a good time and was "sent home with her coat and some aspirin." She is not familiar with death, and the death of this stranger has left her confused.

Topic sentence: Marin's character traits (vivid adjectives)

How Marin changes—what she learns

Elaboration: quotation from the story

Geraldo is just as much a stranger to Marin as she is to the reader: "Just another brazer who didn't speak English. Just another wetback." Her relationship with him may seem cold at first, but as the experience unfolds, you find his hold on her is strong. She will not forget him. He has touched her, perhaps not in life, but most certainly in death, and this unexpected experience will change her outlook.

Topic sentence: Marin's relationship with Geraldo

By the conclusion of the story, Marin knows that Geraldo will forever remain a question unanswered. She knows then that she cannot change that; she cannot make it better; she can only accept its reality.

Clincher sentence

—Alicia Weaver
Communications Arts High School
San Antonio, Texas

Evaluating and Revising

1. Self-Evaluation

Read your essay aloud, looking for ways to eliminate wordiness, improve transitions, and sharpen your language. Consider adding words like *first, second, finally, because,* and *however* to clarify connections among ideas. Pay particular attention to replacing overused adjectives and adverbs with more vivid modifiers.

2. Peer Review

Try this experiment: Read your thesis statement aloud to a partner without identifying the character, story, or author. If your classmate can't guess the character, try making your thesis statement more specific. Then exchange drafts. Make comments about your partner's essay, focusing on the evaluation criteria at the left. Offer suggestions for how he or she might improve the essay, but also provide positive feedback about the paper's strengths.

Revision Model

	Peer Comments
Sandra Cisneros ~~The author~~ has a way with words that is unparalleled in her ability to grasp the essence of a character. In "Geraldo No Last Name," ~~her story~~ the sheer beauty of her	*Identify author and story.*
Marin description of the character is	*Who is the character?*
enthralling, while ~~distant~~ at the keeping Marin distant from us same time.	*This is confusing.*
Her description may seem meager at (Cisneros says so little about her characters) first glance, but after reading the	*What do you mean here?*
her description is story, you discover that ~~they are~~ bursting with insight.	*Who is "they"?*

■ ***Evaluation Criteria***

A good character analysis

1. *identifies the character, title, and author in the introduction*
2. *includes a thesis statement that sums up the main ideas*
3. *presents at least three main ideas about the character*
4. *supports each main idea with specific evidence from the story*
5. *ends by restating the thesis*

Proofreading Tip

A good way to catch mistakes is to slow yourself down by pointing to every word and punctuation mark with a pencil.

Communications Handbook HELP

See Proofreaders' Marks.

Publishing Tips

- If several students have analyzed the same character, collect your essays into a booklet: "All About . . ."
- If your school has a Web site, see if you can post your work on the student page.

Sentence Workshop

Expanding Sentences: Using Adjectives and Adverbs

Read the following sentences, which have been adapted from the stories in this collection.

1. He was wearing an overcoat that hung down to his ankles.
2. A rat sprang from under my feet and retreated.
3. The disk of sun and the sky covered and surrounded the village.

Now read the sentences as their writers wrote them. Notice how the underlined words help you to imagine more concretely and in greater detail the ideas, objects, and events described.

1. "He was wearing a loose, long, slushy overcoat that hung down to his ankles. . . ."

   —Bernard Malamud, "The First Seven Years" (page 121)

2. "A rat sprang from under my foot and retreated grudgingly. . . ."

   —Hugo Martinez-Serros, "Distillation" (page 137)

3. "The clean, round, blinding disk of sun and the blue sky covered and surrounded the small African village. . . ."

   —Abioseh Nicol, "Life Is Sweet at Kumansenu" (page 147)

In the first group, each sentence is a plain statement. In the second group, the underlined words are **adjectives** and **adverbs**, words that *modify* other words. Modifiers are used to elaborate—they limit or sharpen the meanings of other words.

Writer's Workshop Follow-up: Revision

Exchange drafts with a partner when you revise your work. Ask for reactions to your descriptions. If your partner calls for more specific details and sensory images, try expanding your sentences by using precise, vivid adjectives and adverbs. Remember that adjectives tell *What kind? Which one? How many?* Adverbs tell *How? How often? To what extent?*

Language Handbook HELP

See Using Modifiers, pages 1031–1033.

Technology HELP

See Language Workshop CD-ROM. *Key word entry: expanding sentences.*

Try It Out

1. Looking at How Modifiers Work

With a small group, look back at the stories in this collection. Copy at least five sentences that you think contain modifiers that give you vivid pictures of people and places—of their appearance and actions. Find at least two modifiers that establish a mood or emotional tone—words that make you feel positively or negatively about a character or place or thing.

2. Using Modifiers

Go back to the first three numbered sentences opposite. Use new modifiers to elaborate on the sentences to give them a different mood or tone. How many variations can you think of for each sentence? Be sure to compare your results in your group.

Reading for Life

Reading a Map

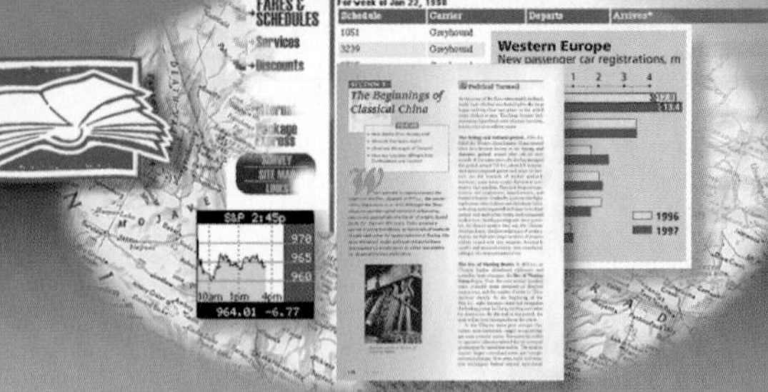

Situation

After reading "Distillation" (page 133), you want to see a map of the area in which the story takes place, South Chicago. To find the correct map and to read it, apply the strategies below.

Strategies

Understand the different types of maps.

- A **physical map** uses colors and shadings to show an area's natural landscape, including landforms and elevation.
- A **political map** shows political units, such as nations, states, capitals, and major cities.
- A **special purpose map** presents specific information. For example, a **road map** shows the system of roadways in an area, as well as campsites, parks, airports, and other places of special interest.

Learn to use map features.

- The **compass rose** indicates direction: north, south, east, and west. In most maps north is at the top.
- The **distance scale** relates distances on the map to actual distances.
- Many maps also have a **legend**, or **key**, that explains special symbols on the map.

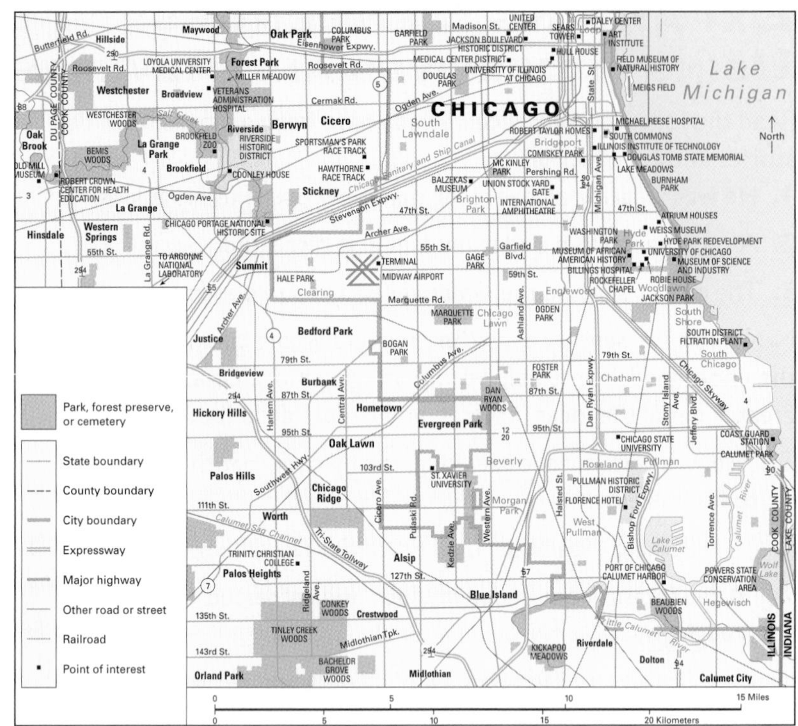

From *The World Book Encyclopedia* © 1998 World Book, Inc. By permission of the publisher.

- A map may also have a **locator map**, a secondary map that shows the relationship of the area in the main map to a larger area.

Using the Strategies

1. Using the map above, can you locate these places mentioned in the story: 86th Street, 95th Street, Torrence Avenue?
2. Which points of interest might you want to visit in Chicago?
3. If you were driving into Chicago from the south, what road could you take to get to the Sears Tower?
4. About how far, and in which direction, would you have to drive to get from Midway Airport to the Sears Tower?

Extending the Strategies

Locate a road map of your town, city, or state. List three of the area's major roads and the directions they take. Could you use the map if you wanted to take a camping trip?

Collection 3 EXILES, CASTAWAYS, AND STRANGERS

Writing Focus: Analyzing a Story

Where do I belong? What makes me feel at home? Writers have explored these questions by creating characters who have found their rightful homes or who are searching for answers to who they are and how they want to live. Perhaps you've felt a sense of peace with your life, or perhaps you've experienced uncertainty when you moved to a new neighborhood. If you've had experiences like these, you'll understand the characters in this collection. Like most of us at one time or another, they are trying to find their way to a place of peace, happiness, and freedom. They are searching for "home."

I been a wanderin'
Early and late,
New York City
To the Golden Gate,
An' it looks like
I'm never gonna cease
my wanderin'.

—American folk song

Writer's Notebook

WORK IN PROGRESS

You're backpacking alone for a week—high in the mountains or deep in a tropical forest. You won't have TV, e-mail, or a phone. What kinds of stories would you take along to read? List some of your favorite stories and some that you've disliked. Save your lists for possible use in the workshop on page 240.

Before You Read

THE PEDESTRIAN

Make the Connection

What's It All About?

Have you ever finished reading a story or sat through a whole movie and then asked, "What was that all about?" Some stories can leave us with more questions than answers. Yet often those stories can provide us with the most enjoyable kind of discussion—talking to others about what our questions are and what we think the answers might be.

Quickwrite

What questions do you have about what life will be like in the year 2053? Write them down and save your notes.

Elements of Literature

Setting and Atmosphere

Writers can use the setting of a story to create an atmosphere—a **mood** or very subtle emotional overtone that can strongly affect our feelings. Settings can be used to suggest freedom, community, and peace. Settings can also be used to suggest control, isolation, and anxiety. See what atmosphere you sense in Bradbury's very first paragraph.

The **setting** of a story establishes the time and place of the action. Setting can be used to establish a **mood,** or **atmosphere,** and to suggest the writer's particular worldview.

For more on Setting, see pages 50–51 and the Handbook of Literary Terms.

Reading Skills and Strategies

Does the Writer Have a Purpose?

Many fiction writers, poets, and dramatists have no **purpose** when they sit down to write other than to share a feeling or an experience, to re-create a whole world of their own making. Ray Bradbury, however, is the kind of fiction writer who often writes for another purpose. Like many nonfiction writers, Bradbury tries to persuade us to agree with his attitude, or viewpoint, on some issue. To discover a writer's attitude, you must read closely. Take notes as you read (or on a second reading). Look for **key passages** that directly express opinions. Watch for **loaded words.** Bradbury's comparison of the city to a graveyard in the second paragraph should immediately send off signals.

Background

In the early 1950s Ray Bradbury was a young man living in Southern California. He did not know how to drive, and he liked walking around his suburban neighborhood at night. Even back then, such behavior was so rare that one time the police stopped and questioned him. If an innocent walk could seem so suspicious in mid-twentieth-century America, Bradbury wondered how it might be viewed in a future society. Then he wrote this story.

A metallic voice called to him: "Stand still. Stay where you are!"

The Pedestrian

Ray Bradbury

Freeway Interchange (1982) by Wayne Thiebaud. Oil on canvas.

Courtesy of Allan Stone Gallery, New York City.

To enter out into that silence that was the city at eight o'clock of a misty evening in November, to put your feet upon that buckling concrete walk, to step over grassy seams and make your way, hands in pockets, through the silences, that was what Mr. Leonard Mead most dearly loved to do. He would stand upon the corner of an intersection and peer down long moonlit avenues of sidewalk in four directions, deciding which way to go, but it really made no difference; he was alone in this world of A.D. 2053, or as good as alone, and with a final decision made, a path selected, he would stride off, sending patterns of frosty air before him like the smoke of a cigar.

Sometimes he would walk for hours and miles and return only at midnight to his house. And on his way he would see the cottages and homes with their dark windows, and it was not unequal to walking through a graveyard where only the faintest glimmers of firefly light appeared in flickers behind the windows. Sudden gray phantoms seemed to manifest upon inner room walls where a curtain was still undrawn against the night, or there were whisperings and murmurs where a window in a tomblike building was still open.

Mr. Leonard Mead would pause, cock his head, listen, look, and march on, his feet making no noise on the lumpy walk. For long ago he had wisely changed to sneakers when strolling at night, because the dogs in intermittent squads would parallel his journey with barkings if he wore hard heels, and lights might click on and faces appear and an entire street be startled by the passing of a lone figure, himself, in the early November evening.

On this particular evening he began his journey in a westerly direction, toward the hidden sea. There was a good crystal frost in the air; it cut the nose and made the lungs blaze like a Christmas tree inside; you could feel the cold light going on and off, all the branches filled with invisible snow. He listened to the faint push of his soft shoes through autumn leaves with satisfaction and whistled a cold, quiet whistle between his teeth, occasionally picking up a leaf as he passed, examining its skeletal pattern in the infrequent lamplights as he went on, smelling its rusty smell.

"Hello, in there," he whispered to every house on every side as he moved. "What's up tonight on Channel 4, Channel 7, Channel 9? Where are the cowboys rushing, and do I see the United States Cavalry over the next hill to the rescue?"

The street was silent and long and empty, with only his shadow moving like the shadow of a hawk in midcountry. If he closed his eyes and stood very still, frozen, he could imagine himself upon the center of a plain, a wintry, windless Arizona desert with no house in a thousand miles, and only dry riverbeds, the streets, for company.

"What is it now?" he asked the houses, noticing his wristwatch. "Eight-thirty P.M.? Time for a dozen assorted murders? A quiz? A revue? A comedian falling off the stage?"

Was that a murmur of laughter from within a moon-white house? He hesitated but went on when nothing more happened. He stumbled over a particularly uneven section of sidewalk. The cement was vanishing under flowers and grass. In ten years of walking by night or day, for thousands of miles, he had never met another person walking, not one in all that time.

He came to a cloverleaf intersection which stood silent where two main highways crossed the town. During the day it was a thunderous surge of cars, the gas stations open, a great insect rustling, and a ceaseless jockeying for position as the scarab beetles,[1] a faint incense puttering from their exhausts, skimmed homeward to the far directions. But now these highways, too, were like streams in a dry season, all stone and bed and moon radiance.

He turned back on a side street, circling around toward his home. He was within a block of his destination when the lone car turned a corner quite suddenly and flashed a fierce white cone of light upon him. He stood entranced, not unlike a night moth, stunned by the illumination and then drawn toward it.

A metallic voice called to him:

"Stand still. Stay where you are! Don't move!"

He halted.

1. **scarab beetles:** stout-bodied, brilliantly colored beetles. Bradbury is using the term as a metaphor for automobiles.

WORDS TO OWN

manifest (man′ə·fest′) *v.:* appear; become evident. *Manifest* also means "show" or "reveal."

intermittent (in′tər·mit′′nt) *adj.:* appearing or occurring from time to time.

"Put up your hands!"

"But——" he said.

"Your hands up! Or we'll shoot!"

The police, of course, but what a rare, incredible thing; in a city of three million, there was only *one* police car left, wasn't that correct? Ever since a year ago, 2052, the election year, the force had been cut down from three cars to one. Crime was ebbing; there was no need now for the police, save for this one lone car wandering and wandering the empty streets.

"Your name?" said the police car in a metallic whisper. He couldn't see the men in it for the bright light in his eyes.

"Leonard Mead," he said.

"Speak up!"

"Leonard Mead!"

"Business or profession?"

"I guess you'd call me a writer."

"No profession," said the police car, as if talking to itself. The light held him fixed, like a museum specimen, needle thrust through chest.

"You might say that," said Mr. Mead. He hadn't written in years. Magazines and books didn't sell anymore. Everything went on in the tomblike houses at night now, he thought, continuing his fancy. The tombs, ill-lit by television light, where the people sat like the dead, the gray or multicolored lights touching their faces, but never really touching them.

"No profession," said the phonograph voice, hissing. "What are you doing out?"

"Walking," said Leonard Mead.

Words to Own

ebbing *v.:* lessening or weakening. The ebb is the flow of water away from the land as the tide falls.

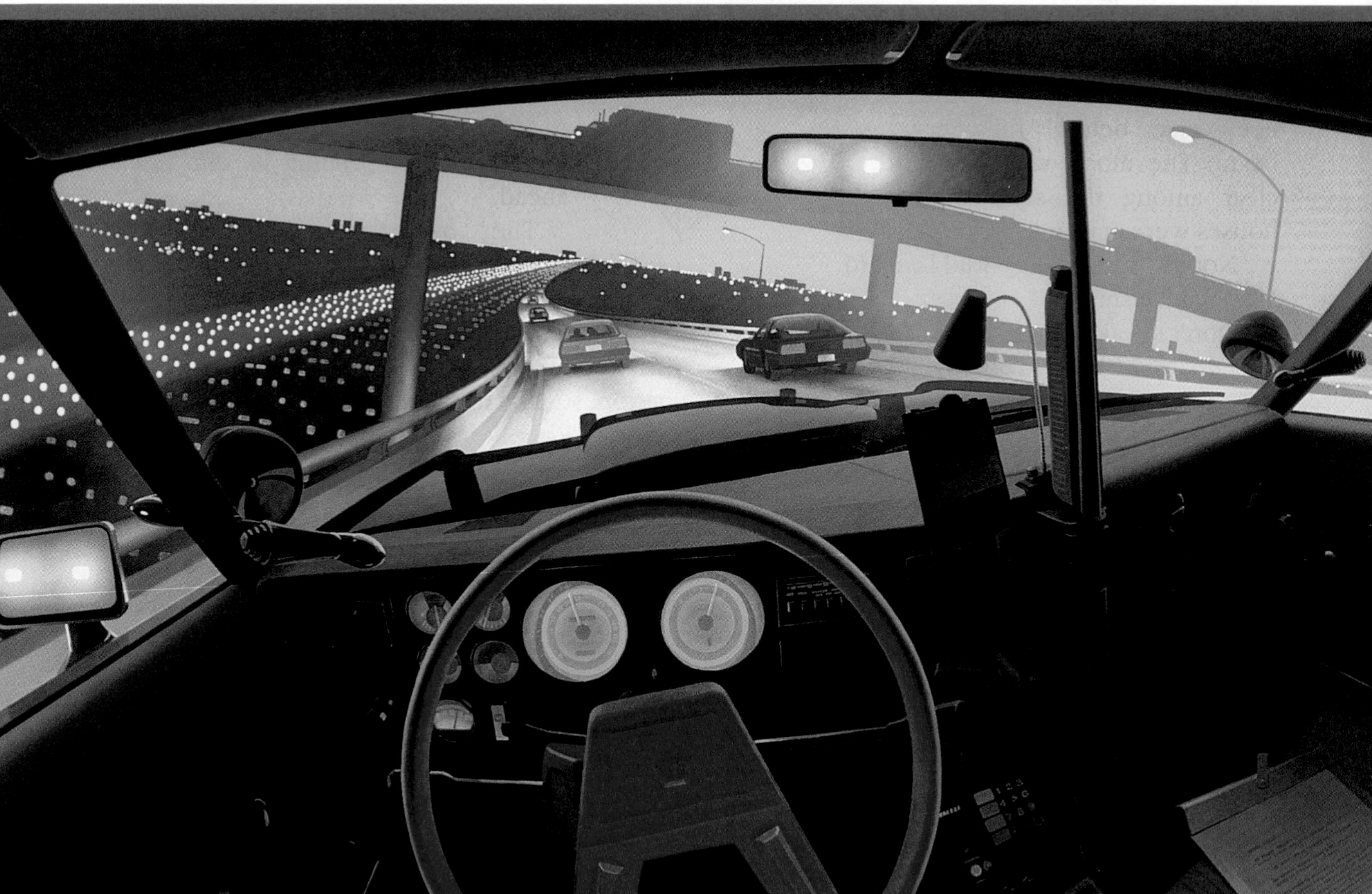

Highway Patrol (1986) by James Doolin. Oil on canvas.

Courtesy of Koplin Gallery, Los Angeles, California.

"Walking!"

"Just walking," he said simply, but his face felt cold.

"Walking, just walking, walking?"

"Yes, sir."

"Walking where? For what?"

"Walking for air. Walking to *see*."

"Your address!"

"Eleven South Saint James Street."

"And there is air *in* your house, you have an air *conditioner,* Mr. Mead?"

"Yes."

"And you have a viewing screen in your house to see with?"

"No."

"No?" There was a crackling quiet that in itself was an accusation.

"Are you married, Mr. Mead?"

"No."

"Not married," said the police voice behind the fiery beam. The moon was high and clear among the stars and the houses were gray and silent.

"Nobody wanted me," said Leonard Mead with a smile.

"Don't speak unless you're spoken to!"

Leonard Mead waited in the cold night.

"Just *walking,* Mr. Mead?"

"Yes."

"But you haven't explained for what purpose."

"I explained: for air, and to see, and just to walk."

"Have you done this often?"

"Every night for years."

The police car sat in the center of the street with its radio throat faintly humming.

"Well, Mr. Mead," it said.

"Is that all?" he asked politely.

"Yes," said the voice. "Here." There was a sigh, a pop. The back door of the police car sprang wide. "Get in."

"Wait a minute, I haven't done anything!"

"Get in."

"I protest!"

"Mr. Mead."

He walked like a man suddenly drunk. As he passed the front window of the car, he looked in. As he had expected, there was no one in the front seat, no one in the car at all.

"Get in."

He put his hand to the door and peered into the back seat, which was a little cell, a little black jail with bars. It smelled of riveted[2] steel. It smelled of harsh antiseptic; it smelled too clean and hard and metallic. There was nothing soft there.

"Now, if you had a wife to give you an alibi," said the iron voice. "But——"

"Where are you taking me?"

The car hesitated, or rather gave a faint, whirring click, as if information, somewhere, was dropping card by punch-slotted card under electric eyes. "To the Psychiatric Center for Research on Regressive Tendencies."

He got in. The door shut with a soft thud. The police car rolled through the night avenues, flashing its dim lights ahead.

They passed one house on one street a moment later, one house in an entire city of houses that were dark, but this one particular house had all of its electric lights brightly lit, every window a loud yellow illumination, square and warm in the cool darkness.

"That's *my* house," said Leonard Mead.

No one answered him.

The car moved down the empty riverbed streets and off away, leaving the empty streets with the empty sidewalks and no sound and no motion all the rest of the chill November night.

2. **riveted** (riv′it·id): held together by rivets (metal bolts or pins).

Words to Own

regressive (ri·gres′iv) *adj.:* moving backward or returning to an earlier or less advanced condition.

Meet the Writer

The Man with the Child Inside

Ray Bradbury (1920–) calls himself "that special freak—the man with the child inside who remembers all." Bradbury was born in Waukegan, Illinois, and began writing when he was seven.

Bradbury sees himself as a "magic realist" (see page 222) and as a disciple of Edgar Allan Poe (see page 302). He says that his lifelong hatred of thought control grows out of his sympathy for his ancestor Mary Bradbury, who was tried as a witch in seventeenth-century Salem, Massachusetts. Here is how his imagination grew:

“When I was three my mother snuck me in and out of movies two or three times a week. My first film was Lon Chaney in *The Hunchback of Notre Dame*. I suffered permanent curvature of the spine and of my imagination that day a long time ago in 1923. From that hour on, I knew a kindred and wonderfully grotesque compatriot of the dark when I saw one. . . .

I was in love, then, with monsters and skeletons and circuses and carnivals and dinosaurs and at last, the red planet, Mars.

From these primitive bricks I have built a life and a career. By my staying in love with all of these amazing things, all of the good things in my existence have come about.

In other words, I was *not* embarrassed at circuses. Some people are. Circuses are loud, vulgar, and smell in the sun. By the time many people are fourteen or fifteen, they have been divested of their loves, their ancient and intuitive tastes, one by one, until when they reach maturity there is no fun left, no zest, no gusto, no flavor. Others have criticized, and they have criticized themselves, into embarrassment. When the circus pulls in at five of a dark cold summer morn, and the calliope sounds, they do not rise and run, they turn in their sleep, and life passes by.

I did rise and run. . . .”

Books by Bradbury

The Martian Chronicles (Bantam), about early settlers on Mars.

Fahrenheit 451 (Ballantine), about a future society that burns books.

Dandelion Wine (Bantam), about a young boy with special mental powers.

Virtuality

Time passes, yet I am oblivious to it, forgetting that such a thing exists. Where I am, there is no time, no sense of minutes or hours. Days could be passing, but I do not care.

Where I am, there is beauty.

I stroll through a forest, a place that puts my mind at ease and comforts my soul. Massive trees tower above, their leaves creating a canopy that shields me from the bright sun. The forest is cool and crisp and damp; the smell of moist earth greets my nose. The wind whispers gently and rustles the trees, sounding like a calm ocean breaking on a shore. Serenity.

My stomach hungers and craves food. I ignore it, for I am now appreciating a tropical forest cleansed from an early morning rain, millions of droplets glittering like diamonds on the thick vegetation. There is a strong connection with the beginning of things here; I feel primal wonderment as humidity masks my face. I see a light haze hanging over the valleys and mountains of this prehistoric setting. The jungle is like a multifaceted gem, where myriad species mingle under the mysterious trees. The air, although hot, is clean.

My mouth thirsts for water; but it is a vague sensation now, and I do not pay much attention to it. Because where I am, there is nature and purity. I look up and think of rain and suddenly behold a thunderstorm. The sky darkens and heavy drops of rain shower the earth, like shards of a mirror falling from the heavens and reflecting the world about them. Fierce lightning shatters the dark sky, and I watch in childlike awe, staring in reverence at the electrified claw ripping the cosmos. The storm is not frightening; it cleanses this paradise.

I had a nightmare once about a world of steel and rust, of crowded buildings and slime-covered streets. It was a place where people dwell under a gray blanket of smog, where each intake of breath is like inhaling toxins, and the rain falling from the sky is greasy and oily and burns the skin. But here the world is fresh and clean, cool and crisp.

Where I am, there is such a thing as peace.

And it is all real; I can see the beauty and hear the sounds and feel what there is to be felt. In my nightmare, nature is dead. But I am awake, and here it is alive, and this is reality for me.

Then I stand on a grassy field where bright dandelions lie like flecks of sunlight, and I feel a cool breeze brushing by me, and . . .

There is an angry buzzing, an ugly mechanical sound, and my heart aches because I know where I really am and I fear being reminded. Bright white words flash across my field of vision: YOUR VIRTUAL WORLD MUST END NOW

No! It isn't virtual, it's real! No!

BATTERIES ARE OUT OF POWER

No! Please . . .

TIME TO RETURN TO REALITY

The visions of the nature-worlds fade and go black, and I take off the headset, trembling. My stomach aches for food, my mouth thirsts; days might have passed. The headset, called Virtuality Gear, provides computerized images which look real and perfect. The gear provides sensory stimuli: fantasy sight, sound, touch. I despair because I am out of the terribly expensive batteries which are the keys to my paradise. And I am reminded that I am just one of the growing number of cybertrippers, people who flee to the fantasy worlds Virtuality Gear gives them.

—Brian Trusiewicz
Sacred Heart High School
Waterbury, Connecticut

Making Meanings

First Thoughts

1. What question would you like to ask Bradbury?

Shaping Interpretations

2. What do you think Bradbury's **purpose** was in writing this story? Cite details from the story to support your opinion.

3. Bradbury doesn't tell us directly what has happened to cause the strange situation in this story. What do you guess has caused this severe limitation on individual freedom?

4. Which of today's problems seem to have been eliminated from Leonard Mead's society? What does Leonard miss that we still enjoy today?

5. How is technology used to control Leonard's world? What point about technology and its power do you think Bradbury is making? What key words or phrases or events in the story support your interpretation?

Reading Check

a. What ominous fact about this future society is **foreshadowed** at once by the "buckling concrete walk" in the first paragraph? As the story develops, what else are you told about the **setting** of "The Pedestrian"?

b. Find the sentences and phrases that at first suggest that Leonard Mead is the only person living in this setting in A.D. 2053. Find the passage that reveals that there are other living people in this setting.

c. Leonard Mead is the only human character in the story. Who, or what, appears to be in charge of this future world?

d. Explain Leonard Mead's "regressive tendencies."

e. Describe the police automaton's response when Mead says he is a writer.

Connecting with the Text

6. If you lived in the same time and place as Leonard, do you think you would go walking outside at night or stay inside as Leonard's neighbors do? Do you go walking on the streets at night where you live? Why or why not?

Extending the Text

7. In 1951, when "The Pedestrian" was published, it was read as a prediction of the future. Now that we are closer to 2053, **compare** Bradbury's vision of the future with today's reality. In what ways was he wrong or right?

Challenging the Text

8. Do you think Bradbury is too pessimistic about technology? Support your opinion with details from the text and from the real world.

CHOICES: Building Your Portfolio

Writer's Notebook

1. Collecting Ideas for Analyzing a Story

Finding a topic. In the Writer's Workshop on page 240, you'll analyze a short story. Your first task will be to find a topic—a story to focus on. Skim through the short-story collections in this book, and take a quick look at the stories you've read so far. Make a list of the stories you really liked and another of those you disliked. Be sure to include "The Pedestrian" on one of your lists. Now, freewrite for several minutes about one story and what you either liked or disliked about its plot, theme, characters, or language. Save your notes.

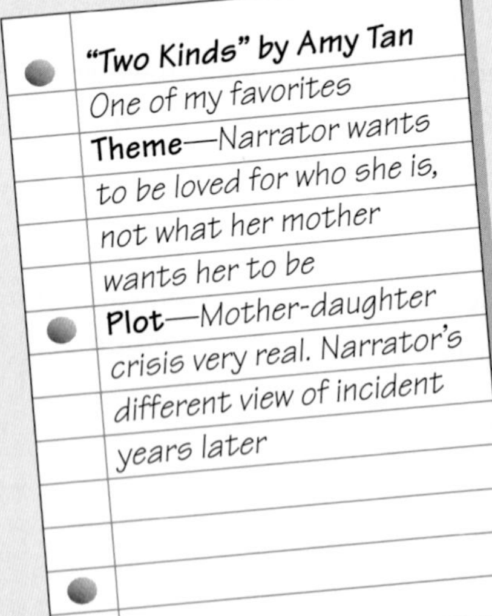

"Two Kinds" by Amy Tan
One of my favorites
Theme—Narrator wants to be loved for who she is, not what her mother wants her to be
Plot—Mother-daughter crisis very real. Narrator's different view of incident years later

Creative Writing / Performing

2. Continuing the Story

Imagine what happens when Leonard arrives at the Psychiatric Center for Research on Regressive Tendencies. Write a **dialogue** that he might have with the authorities there. Decide whether the researchers are humans or robots. How might Leonard try to explain his way of life? What might the authorities decide to do about him? With a group, act out the sequel to Leonard's story. If you like, wear costumes that suggest the **mood,** or **atmosphere,** of the story as you sense it.

Speaking and Listening

3. Debating the Future

Form a panel, and discuss what you think society will actually be like in the year 2053. Will technology isolate us from one another, as "The Pedestrian" suggests, or will technology be a force for good? Will the individual citizen be freer or less free? How do you think the technology described in "Virtuality" (page 178) might affect the future? As a class, be sure to check your Quickwrite notes for other questions. Before you start, assign a moderator and establish rules for the panel. At the end of the discussion, each person in the audience should prepare a **summary** of the panel's views and an **evaluation** of the participants' performances.

Drawing or Model Building

4. Creating a Stage Set

Ray Bradbury has dramatized many of his stories for the stage and television. Suppose you were the set designer for a TV adaptation of "The Pedestrian." Draw or build a model of a set for the play. Go back to the text, and use Bradbury's own descriptions of the **setting** as the basis for your design. Display your drawing or model to the class, and be prepared to explain the reasons for your design decisions.

Comparing and Contrasting Texts

5. Future Tech

Think about the use of technology in "The Pedestrian" and "The Cold Equations" (page 9). What similarities and differences can you find? Write a brief essay in which you **compare** and **contrast** the way the two stories view technology.

LANGUAGE LINK MINI-LESSON

The Power of Connotations

Handbook of Literary Terms HELP

See Connotations.

As you know, certain words have emotional overtones, or **connotations,** that go beyond their literal meanings, or **denotations.** Consider the difference between the two words in the following pairs:

unusual / odd
young / immature
proud / smug
assertive / pushy
frugal / stingy

In each pair, the first word has more positive connotations than the second word has. We might use the first word to describe ourselves but the second word to describe someone else. In fact, the British philosopher Bertrand Russell once gave a classic example of the different connotations of words: "I am firm. You are obstinate. He is a pigheaded fool."

Here are some passages from "The Pedestrian" that describe the **setting** by using words with powerful connotations.

1. "And on his way he would see the cottages and homes with their dark windows, and it was not unequal to walking through a graveyard. . . ."
2. "Sudden gray phantoms seemed to manifest upon inner room walls . . . , or there were whisperings and murmurs where a window in a tomblike building was still open."
3. "It [the inside of the car] smelled of harsh antiseptic; it smelled too clean and hard and metallic. There was nothing soft there."

Try It Out

➤ Write down what you think is the strongest word or phrase in each numbered passage below. Then, describe briefly what the word or phrase suggests to you or how it makes you feel.

➤ Rewrite each passage with words that have more positive connotations. The graveyard, for example, could become a sleepy village.

VOCABULARY HOW TO OWN A WORD

WORD BANK
manifest
intermittent
ebbing
regressive

Using Context Clues

Explain what each underlined word means, and point out the context clues that help you guess the meaning. Then, go back to Bradbury's story, and see if you can find context clues for the same underlined words. Write down any context clues that you find.

1. Passengers' anger is quick to manifest when flights are canceled.
2. Today's forecast is for cloudy weather and intermittent showers.
3. Pet ownership shows no signs of ebbing; the sale of pet foods and pet-related products continues to increase.
4. Temper tantrums and whining are regressive behaviors in adults.

Elements of Literature

THEME: The Story's Meaning and Roots

I once read a student's story that was full of action—a pair of mountain climbers were about to plunge down a ravine, a skier was schussing into peril, and a killer was waiting in the valley below. Despite all this action and intrigue, the story was boring to read because it was impossible to tell what the student writer meant by it. As it turned out, the student didn't know either. The story had no theme.

A story's characters and events take on significance only when we recognize what they mean to us. In other words, all the elements of a good story must add up to a **theme**—some idea or insight about human life and human nature that gives meaning to the story.

The Writer's Worldview

Theme can also reveal the writer's whole view of life, of how the world works—or fails to work.

Suppose, for example, that a writer has a heroine work diligently at her job in the fish cannery and be rewarded by a two-dollar-an-hour raise and a trip to Vancouver. We recognize this writer's world as demanding but fair, a place where human beings have some control over their destiny. Suppose another writer takes this same heroine and has her fired for her pains. As she leaves for home, she even finds that her bicycle has been stolen. We recognize in this story another kind of world—a barren world swept by cold and indifferent winds.

What Do We Mean by Theme?

The story's theme is really its roots. Theme is unseen and usually unstated, yet it is vital. It gives meaning to the story's characters and events, and at the same time it reveals the writer's own personal attitude toward the world, toward how people should behave and how they actually do behave. If we like the writer's view of the world, we may well come back for more; we may even adopt the writer's attitude as our own. But if that view of the world is one we don't accept as "true," we probably will stop reading that writer altogether.

We do not have to accept every theme, but we should not simply condemn or dismiss a story because we disagree with its theme. A writer's view of the world or of human nature may be different from our own, but it may be worthwhile to explore that viewpoint anyway. It is always interesting to learn how other people see the world.

Theme is unseen and usually unstated, yet it is vital.

Theme is neither the story's plot (what happens) nor the story's subject (which might be boxing or prospecting for gold). Rather, theme is an idea; it is what the writer means by everything he or she has set down. A story's theme may give us insight into some aspect of life that we have never really thought about before, or it may make us understand something we always knew but never realized we knew.

by John Leggett

Discovering a Story's Theme

Often a writer's theme cannot be stated easily or completely. (Remember that the writer has had to write the whole story to get that theme across to us.) After we have read a story, we may feel that we understand what it is about, and yet for some reason we cannot put our feeling into words. The story has struck us as true—it has touched our emotions on some profound, wordless level—but still we cannot state the truth it has revealed to us.

The attempt to put a story's theme into words can often help us understand the story more fully—it can reveal aspects of the story that we may have ignored. It is one thing to understand *what has happened* in a story, but it is quite another thing to understand *what those events mean.* Here are some general guidelines for discovering a story's theme:

1. A theme may be stated in a single sentence, or a full essay may be required to do it justice. But we must use at least one complete sentence to state a theme. In other words, a theme must be a statement about the subject of the story, rather than a phrase such as "the rewards of old age." (Sometimes you can reword this type of phrase to form a sentence: "Old age can be a time of great satisfaction.")

> It is one thing to understand *what has happened* in a story, but it is quite another thing to understand *what those events mean.*

2. A theme is not the same as a moral, which is a rule of conduct. A work of serious fiction is not a sermon intended to teach us how to live better or more successful lives. One critic has said that, in getting at a story's theme, we should ask ourselves "What does this story reveal?" rather than "What does this story teach?" Thus, it is usually a mistake to reduce a theme (at least a serious writer's theme) to a familiar saying or cliché, such as "Crime doesn't pay" or "The course of true love never did run smooth." A theme is usually a much more complex and original revelation about life.
3. One of the best ways to discover a story's theme is to ask how the protagonist has *changed* during the course of the story. Often, what this character has learned about life is the truth the writer also wants to reveal to the reader.
4. There is no one correct way to state the theme of a story. If there are twenty-five students in your English class, for instance, you will have twenty-five distinct ways of putting a story's central insight into words. You may also have several different ideas about what the story's major theme is.

> "To produce a mighty book, you must choose a mighty theme."
>
> —Herman Melville

Before You Read

LIBERTY

Make the Connection

Leaving It All Behind

Whether you love where you live or long to be somewhere different, moving is a jolt. Loading the last box, seeing the rooms bare, taking one last look at your neighborhood—memories flood in. If you've ever moved, you know how it feels to ache for the familiar. If you haven't, look around. What would break your heart to leave behind?

Quickwrite

Imagine that your family is leaving home because you're in great danger. You must leave *now*, and there's no chance of return. You can take with you only one special belonging. What will it be? List your top three choices. Then quickwrite about what you'd miss most about your home.

Elements of Literature

Tone: Revealing Attitude

"Don't take that tone with me!" When you speak, your voice reveals how you feel. Through their choice of words and details, writers also convey a **tone**—their attitude or feelings about a subject or character. When Alvarez describes two men in dark glasses "crouched" behind a hedge and behaving cruelly to a dog, we feel a sinister tone. The tone would be quite different if the men were friendly dog lovers. Tone is also influenced by the choice of narrator—an innocent, bewildered child conveys one tone; a worldly-wise adult would convey something very different.

> **Tone** is the attitude a writer takes toward a subject, a character, or the reader.
>
> *For more on Tone, see the Handbook of Literary Terms.*

Reading Skills and Strategies

Connecting Literature to Current Events

Journalists aren't the only writers who deal with what's happening in the real world. Today, many fiction writers base their stories on actual events. In "Liberty," Alvarez tells a story that could be in today's newspaper. Yet through the fiction writer's craft, Alvarez is able to pull us into these events in an intensely personal way.

When you read a story like "Liberty," you have to read between the lines to discover parallels between the story and actual events. Be on your toes as you read this story. The child narrator can tell us only what she sees and feels.

Background

In recent decades, many people have emigrated from the Dominican Republic (Julia Alvarez's childhood home) and other Caribbean and Latin American countries. They may have left their homelands because of political oppression, war, or harsh living conditions. Like immigrants throughout America's history, they've come to the United States for that precious gift of liberty.

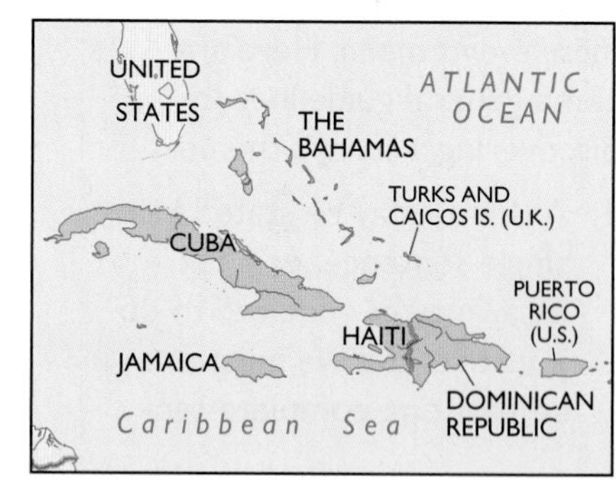

LIBERTY

Julia Alvarez

Papi came home with a dog whose kind we had never seen before. A black-and-white-speckled electric current of energy. It was a special breed with papers, like a person with a birth certificate. Mami just kept staring at the puppy with a cross look on her face. "It looks like a mess!" she said. "Take it back."

"Mami, it is a gift!" Papi shook his head. It would be an insult to Mister Victor, who had given us the dog. The American consul[1] wanted to thank us for all we'd done for him since he'd been assigned to our country.

"If he wanted to thank us, he'd give us our visas," Mami grumbled. For a while now, my parents had been talking about going to the United States so Papi could return to school. I couldn't understand why a grown-up who could do whatever he wanted would elect to go back to a place I so much wanted to get out of.

"We will call him Liberty. Life, liberty, and the pursuit of happiness."

1. **American consul:** person appointed by the United States government to represent American interests and provide assistance to Americans living in a foreign country.

WORDS TO OWN

elect (ē·lekt′): *v.:* choose.

On their faces when they talked of leaving there was a scared look I also couldn't understand.

"Those visas will come soon," Papi promised. But Mami just kept shaking her head about the dog. She had enough with four girls to take on puppies, too. Papi explained that the dog would stay at the end of the yard in a pen. He would not be allowed in the house. He would not be pooping in Mami's orchid garden. He would not be barking until late at night. "A well-behaved dog," Papi concluded. "An American dog."

The little black-and-white puppy yanked at Papi's trouser cuff with his mouth. "What shall we call you?" Papi asked him.

"Trouble," Mami suggested, kicking the puppy away. He had left Papi's trousers to come slobber on her leg.

"We will call him Liberty. Life, liberty, and the pursuit of happiness." Papi quoted the U.S.A Constitution. "Eh, Liberty, you are a lucky sign!"

Liberty barked his little toy barks and all us kids laughed. "Trouble." Mami kept shaking her head as she walked away. Liberty trotted behind her as if he agreed that that was the better name for him.

Mami was right, too—Liberty turned out to be trouble. He ate all of Mami's orchids, and that little hyperactive baton of a tail knocked things off the low coffee table whenever Liberty climbed on the couch to leave his footprints in among the flower prints. He tore up Mami's garden looking for buried treasure. Mami screamed at Liberty and stamped her foot. "Perro sin vergüenza!"[2] But Liberty just barked back at her.

"He doesn't understand Spanish," Papi said lamely. "Maybe if you correct him in English, he'll behave better!"

Mami turned on him, her slipper still in midair. Her face looked as if she'd light into him after she was done with Liberty. "Let him go be a pet in his own country if he wants instructions in English!" In recent weeks, Mami had changed her tune about going to the United States. She wanted to stay in her own country. She didn't want Mister Victor coming around our house and going off into the study with Papi to talk over important things in low, worried voices.

"All liberty involves sacrifice," Papi said in a careful voice. Liberty gave a few perky barks as if he agreed with that.

Mami glared at Papi. "I told you I don't want trouble—" She was going to say more, but her eye fell on me and she stopped herself. "Why aren't you with the others?" she scolded. It was as if I had been the one who had dug up her lily bulbs.

The truth was that after Liberty arrived, I never played with the others. It was as if I had found my double in another species. I had always been the tomboy, the live wire, the troublemaker, the one who was going to drive Mami to drink, the one she was going to give away to the Haitians. While the sisters dressed pretty and stayed clean in the playroom, I was out roaming the world looking for trouble. And now I had found someone to share my adventures.

"I'll take Liberty back to his pen," I offered. There was something I had figured out that Liberty had yet to learn: when to get out of Mami's way.

She didn't say yes and she didn't say no. She seemed distracted, as if something else was on her mind. As I led Liberty away by his collar, I could see her talking to Papi. Suddenly she started to cry, and Papi held her.

"It's okay," I consoled Liberty. "Mami doesn't mean it. She really does love you. She's just nervous." It was what my father always said when Mami scolded me harshly.

At the back of the property stood Liberty's pen—a chain-link fence around a dirt square at the center of which stood a doghouse. Papi had built it when Liberty first came, a cute little house, but then he painted it a putrid green that reminded me of all the vegetables I didn't like. It was always a job to get Liberty to go into that pen.

Sure enough, as soon as he saw where we were headed, he took off, barking, toward the

2. **"Perro sin vergüenza!"** (per′rō sēn ver·gwen′sä): Spanish for "shameless dog."

WORDS TO OWN

hyperactive (hī′pər·ak′tiv) *adj.:* abnormally active; very lively.

house, then swerved to the front yard to our favorite spot. It was a grassy knoll surrounded by a tall hibiscus hedge. At the center stood a tall, shady samán tree. From there, no one could see you up at the house. Whenever I did something wrong, this was where I hid out until the punishment winds blew over. That was where Liberty headed, and I was fast behind on his trail.

Inside the clearing I stopped short. Two strange men in dark glasses were crouched behind the hedge. The fat one had seized Liberty by the collar and was pulling so hard on it that poor Liberty was almost standing on his hind legs. When he saw me, Liberty began to bark, and the man holding him gave him a yank on the collar that made me sick to my stomach. I began to back away, but the other man grabbed my arm. "Not so fast," he said. Two little scared faces—my own—looked down at me from his glasses.

"I came for my dog," I said, on the verge of tears.

"Good thing you found him," the man said. "Give the young lady her dog," he ordered his friend, and then he turned to me. "You haven't seen us, you understand?"

I didn't understand. It was usually I who was the one lying and grown-ups telling me to tell the truth. But I nodded, relieved when the man released my arm and Liberty was back in my hands.

"It's okay, Liberty." I embraced him when I put him back in his pen. He was as sad as I was. We had both had a hard time with Mami, but this was the first time we'd come across mean and scary people. The fat man had almost broken Liberty's neck, and the other one had left his fingerprints on my arm. After I locked up the pen, I watched Liberty wander back slowly to his house and actually go inside, turn around, and stick his little head out the door. He'd always avoided that ugly doghouse before. I walked back to my own house, head down, to find my parents and tell them what I had seen.

Overnight, it seemed, Mister Victor moved in. He ate all his meals with us, stayed 'til late, and when he had to leave, someone from the embassy was left behind "to keep an eye on things." Now, when Papi and Mister Victor talked or when the *tíos*[3] came over, they all went down to the back of the property near Liberty's pen to talk. Mami had found some wires in the study, behind the portrait of Papi's great-grandmother fanning herself with a painted fan. The wires ran behind a screen and then out a window, where there was a little box with lots of other wires coming from different parts of the house.[4]

Mami explained that it was no longer safe to talk in the house about certain things. But the only way you knew what things those were was when Mami leveled her eyes on you as if she were pressing the off button on your mouth. She did this every time I asked her what was going on.

"Nothing," she said stiffly, and then she urged me to go outside and play. Forgotten were the admonitions to go study or I would flunk out of fifth grade. To go take a bath or the *microbios*[5] might kill me. To drink my milk or I would grow up stunted and with no teeth. Mami seemed absent and tense and always in tears. Papi was right—she was too nervous, poor thing.

I myself was enjoying a heyday of liberty. Several times I even got away with having one of Mister Victor's Coca-Colas for breakfast instead of my boiled milk with a beaten egg, which Liberty was able to enjoy instead.

"You love that dog, don't you?" Mister Victor asked me one day. He was standing by the pen with Papi waiting for the uncles. He had a funny accent that sounded like someone making fun of Spanish when he spoke it.

I ran Liberty through some of the little tricks I had taught him, and Mister Victor laughed. His face was full of freckles—so that it looked as if he and Liberty were kin. I had the impression that God had spilled a lot of his colors when he was making American things.

3. ***tíos*** (tē′ōs): Spanish for "uncles."
4. **little box . . . house:** probably refers to a device used to listen in secretly on conversations in the house.
5. ***microbios*** (mē·krō′bē·ōs): Spanish for "germs."

WORDS TO OWN

admonitions (ad′mə·nish′ənz) *n.:* scoldings; warnings.

Soon the uncles arrived and the men set to talking. I wandered into the pen and sat beside Liberty with my back to the house and listened. The men were speaking in English, and I had picked up enough of it at school and in my parents' conversations to make out most of what was being said. They were planning some hunting expedition for a goat with guns to be delivered by Mister Charlie. Papi was going to have to leave the goat to the others because his tennis shoes were missing. Though I understood the words—or thought I did—none of it made sense. I knew my father did not own a pair of tennis shoes, we didn't know a Mister Charlie, and who ever heard of hunting a goat?

As Liberty and I sat there with the sun baking the tops of our heads, I had this sense that the world as I knew it was about to end. The image of the two men in mirror glasses flashed through my head. So as not to think about them, I put my arm around Liberty and buried my face in his neck.

Late one morning Mami gave my sisters and me the news. Our visa had come. Mister Victor had arranged everything, and that very night we were going to the United States of America! Wasn't that wonderful! She flashed us a bright smile, as if someone were taking her picture.

We stood together watching her, alarmed at this performance of happiness when really she looked like she wanted to cry. All morning aunts had been stopping by and planting big kisses on our foreheads and holding our faces in their hands and asking us to promise we would be very good. Until now, we hadn't a clue why they were so worked up.

Mami kept smiling her company smile. She had a little job for each of us to do. There would not be room in our bags for everything. We were to pick the one toy we wanted to take with us to the United States.

I didn't even have to think twice about my choice. It had suddenly dawned on me we were leaving, and that meant leaving *everything* behind. "I want to take Liberty."

Mami started shaking her head no. We could not take a dog into the United States of America. That was not allowed.

"Please," I begged with all my might. "Please, please, Mami, please." Repetition sometimes worked—each time you said the word, it was like giving a little push to the yes that was having a hard time rolling out of her mouth.

"I said no!" The bright smile on Mami's face had grown dimmer and dimmer. *"N-O."* She spelled it out for me in case I was confusing no with another word like yes. "I said a toy, and I mean a toy."

I burst into tears. I was not going to the United States unless I could take Liberty! Mami shook me by the shoulders and asked me between clenched teeth if I didn't understand we had to go to the United States or else. But all I could understand was that a world without Liberty would break my heart. I was inconsolable. Mami began to cry.

Tía[6] Mimi took me aside. She had gone to school in the States and always had her nose in a book. In spite of her poor taste in how to spend her free time, I still loved her because she had smart things to say. Like telling Mami that punishment was not the way to make kids behave. "I'm going to tell you a little secret," she offered now. "You're going to find liberty when you get to the United States."

"Really?" I asked.

She hesitated a minute, and then she gave me a quick nod. "You'll see what I mean," she said. And then, giving me a pat on the butt, she added, "Come on, let's go pack. How about taking that wonderful book I got you on the Arabian Nights?"

Late in the night someone comes in and shakes us awake. "It's time!"

Half asleep, we put on our clothes, hands helping our arms to go into the right

6. **Tía** (tē′ä): Spanish for "aunt."

WORDS TO OWN

clenched (klench't) *v.:* tightly closed.
inconsolable (in′kən·sōl′ə·bəl) *adj.:* unable to be comforted; brokenhearted.

San Antonio de Oriente (1957) by José Antonio Velasquez. Oil on canvas (27″ x 37″).

sleeves, buttoning us up, running a comb through our hair.

We were put to sleep hours earlier because the plane had not come in.

But now it's time.

"Go sit by the door," we are ordered, as the hands, the many hands that now seem to be in control, finish with us. We file out of the bedroom, one by one, and go sit on the bench where packages are set down when Mami comes in from shopping. There is much rushing around. Mister Victor comes by and pats us on the head like dogs. "We'll have to wait a few more minutes," he says.

In that wait, one sister has to go to the bathroom. Another wants a drink of water. I am left sitting with my baby sister, who is dozing with her head on my shoulder. I lay her head down on the bench and slip out.

Through the dark patio down the path to the back of the yard I go. Every now and then a strange figure flashes by. I have said good-bye to Liberty a dozen times already, but there is something else I have left to do.

Sitting on the bench, I had an image again of those two men in mirror glasses. After we are gone, they come onto the property. They smash the picture of Papi's great-grandmother fanning herself. They knock over the things on the coffee table as if they don't know any better. They throw the flowered cushions on the floor. They smash the windows. And then they come to the back of the property and they find Liberty.

Quickly, because I hear calling from the big house, I slip open the door of the pen. Liberty is all over me, wagging his tail so it beats against my legs, jumping up and licking my face.

"Get away!" I order sharply, in a voice he is not used to hearing from me. I begin walking back to the house, not looking around so as not to encourage him. I want him to run away before the gangsters come.

He doesn't understand and keeps following me. Finally I have to resort to Mami's techniques. I kick him, softly at first, but then, when he keeps tagging behind me, I kick him hard. He whimpers and dashes away toward the front yard, disappearing in areas of darkness, then reappearing when he passes through lighted areas. At the front of the house, instead of turning toward our secret place, he keeps on going straight down the drive, through the big gates, to the world out there.

He will beat me to the United States is what I am thinking as I head back to the house. I will find Liberty there, like Tía Mimi says. But I already sense it is a different kind of liberty my aunt means. All I can do is hope that when we come back—as Mami has promised we will—my Liberty will be waiting for me here.

Meet the Writer

"Magic Happened in My Life"

When **Julia Alvarez** (1950–) says, "I write stories for different reasons," she means it. Like the girl in "Liberty," she knows political terror and exile firsthand, for her family fled from the Dominican Republic when she was ten. Alvarez says she "can't shut up" about important human events. One of her novels, *In the Time of the Butterflies* (1994), is based on the true story of the 1960 murders of the three Mirabal sisters, wives of political prisoners in her homeland.

Some of her fiction, she says, is "like cupping my hands around a moth" to save it, and some stories she writes to keep her heart from breaking.

"I think of myself at ten years old, newly arrived in this country, feeling out of place, feeling that I would never belong in this world. . . . And then, magic happened in my life. . . . An English teacher asked us to write little stories about ourselves. I began to put into words some of what my life had been like in the Dominican Republic. Stories about my gang of cousins and the smell of mangoes and the iridescent, vibrating green of hummingbirds. Since it was my own little world I was making with words, I could put what I wanted in it. . . . I could save what I didn't want to lose—memories and smells and sounds, things too precious to put anywhere else."

Julia Alvarez teaches English at Middlebury College in Vermont, yet having two cultures and two languages is still central to her world and writing. Two novels (*How the García Girls Lost Their Accents,* 1991, and *¡Yo!,* 1997) follow four sisters who grow up in America speaking "Spanglish," a mixture of Spanish and English.

"No matter what my motive is when I begin, I end up understanding myself and the world around me much better. I think that's why I like being a writer: with each revision, the world gets clearer and, ironically, though writing is so solitary, people get closer, more real."

Connections A FEATURE ARTICLE/ A JOURNAL

Written for a newspaper, this article is based on a journal the writer kept during a visit to Cuba, her childhood home.

HAVANA JOURNAL

A Sentimental Journey to la Casa of Childhood

MIRTA OJITO

HAVANA, Feb. 1—This is the moment when, in my dreams, I begin to cry. And yet, I'm strangely calm as I go up the stairs to the apartment of my childhood in Santos Suárez, the only place that, after all these years, I still refer to as la casa, home.

I am holding a pen and a reporter's notebook in my hand and, as I always do when I am working, I count the steps: 20. In my memory, there were only 16. The staircase seems narrower than I remember, the ceiling lower.

Perhaps I have grown taller, perhaps my whims have widened with age and pregnancy. I am buying mental time, distracting my mind from what I am certain will be a shock.

After 17 years and 8 months, I have returned to Cuba as a reporter. I am here to cover the visit of Pope John Paul II,° not to cry at the sight of a chipped, old tile on the floor.

The last time I went down these steps I was 16 years old and a police car was waiting for me and my family downstairs. They had come to tell us that my uncle, like thousands of other Cuban exiles who had returned to Cuba to claim their relatives, waited at the port of Mariel to take us to Miami in a leased shrimp boat.

It was May 7, 1980, the first days of what became known as the Mariel boat lift, the period from April to September 1980 when more than 125,000 Cubans left the island for the United States.

That day I left my house in a hurry. The police gave us 10 minutes to get ready and pack the few personal items we were allowed to take: an extra set of clothing, some pictures, toothbrushes. Everything else, from my books to my dolls and my parents' wedding china, remained behind. There were dishes in the sink and food in the refrigerator. My underwear in a drawer and my mother's sewing machine open for work.

Since then, I have often thought about this house, remembering every detail, every curve and tile and squeaky sound. The green walls of the living room, the view from the balcony, the feel of the cold tiles under my bare feet, the sound of my father's key in the keyhole and the muffled noise from the old refrigerator in the kitchen.

A stranger opens the door and I tell her who I am and what I want. "I used to live here," I say. "I'd like to take a look."

Surprisingly, she knows my name. She asks if I am the older or the younger child who used to live in the house. I say I am the older as I look over her head. Straight into my past. My home remains practically as we left it, seemingly frozen in time, like much of Cuba today. . . .

This is a strange feeling. I knew I would face my childhood by coming here, but I never expected to relive it as I am doing now. I go out to the balcony and then, as if on cue, I hear someone calling out my childhood nickname, "Mirtica! Mirtica!"

For a moment, I do not know who is calling or even if the call is real. It sounds like my mother calling me for dinner. But it is the neighbor from the corner who looked up from her terrace and somehow recognized me. I wave faintly. I want to stay in this apartment for a long time. I want to be left alone. But I cannot. It is no longer my home.

The Jiménez family now lives in the house. He is a truck driver, just as my father was. They have a 15-year-old son who sleeps on a sofa bed in the living room, just as my sister and I did. The Government gave them the apartment a few months after we left. Their own house, nearby, had been badly damaged in a hurricane. . . .

Had I stayed, would I have talked to a returning neighbor the way they talk to me? They tell me about the sadness of their lives, their husbands, their lovers, their misguided children, their ungrateful relatives, their never-ending litany of needs: bread, toilet paper, underwear, freedom. . . .

After a second visit to the apartment, I leave. And I leave exactly the way I left almost 18 years ago, profoundly sad, surrounded by friends and neighbors, people glad that I remembered them, unselfish people who are happy that I left and live better than they do.

Who says that Cubans are divided by politics or even by an ocean? In Enamorados Street, at the foot of a small hill called San Julio, my home and my people remain.

—from *The New York Times*
February 3, 1998

°***visit of Pope John Paul II:*** *John Paul II's visit to Cuba, from January 21 to 25, 1998, was the first by a pope to this island nation. It drew an unprecedented number of foreign reporters.*

Making Meanings

Reading Check

Sketch a map that shows the story's **setting.** Include the following: (a) the house, (b) the dog pen, (c) the grassy knoll and hedge, (d) the drive and big gates. Then make a map legend, identifying the important **events** that occur at each location.

First Thoughts

1. What is really happening in this story? Read between the lines (the hidden wires, the American consul's visits, etc.), and explain the family's situation.

Shaping Interpretations

2. The word *liberty* is central to this story—it's the title, the dog's name, and an important concept throughout. Explain how the story's **theme,** or insight about life, relates to liberty.
3. Does the narrator understand what is happening to her family? How does her attitude contribute to the **tone** of the story? Think of three words you could use to describe the tone.

Extending the Text

4. If you've ever had to leave a home, what do you miss most about it? Did you ever return to it, as Mirta Ojita did when she visited Havana (see ***Connections*** on page 191)? **Compare** your experiences with hers.
5. Check recent news reports about people immigrating to the United States today. What are their reasons for wanting to live in the United States?

Choices: Building Your Portfolio

Writer's Notebook

1. Collecting Ideas for Analyzing a Story

Focusing on plot. When you analyze a story, one of the main elements to consider is plot. Think about the plot of "Liberty" or of another story you've read, and jot down notes on your reactions to these questions: What is the cause of the **conflict,** and how is it resolved? What are the **main events?** Do they create suspense? When does the **climax** occur? Save your notes for the Writer's Workshop on page 240.

WORK IN PROGRESS

History/Research

2. Newcomers to America

With a small group, brainstorm questions you'd like to research about the history of American immigration. To answer the questions you've raised, explore various sources, including electronic databases and the Internet. You might, instead, trace your family's history, researching when and why relatives came to America and where they settled. Choose from a variety of media (maps, photos, oral or written reports) to present your information to classmates.

Creative Writing

3. Liberty's Tale

What happens to Liberty? Take up the little dog's story after he goes through the gate. You might want to tell the story from Liberty's point of view, using the pronoun "I." Tell what happens next and how you (Liberty) are feeling.

GRAMMAR LINK MINI-LESSON

Language Handbook HELP

Clear Pronoun Reference: page 1031.

Technology HELP

See Language Workshop CD-ROM. Key word entry: pronouns.

Who's Who? Making Pronouns Clear

Have you ever discovered, partway through a conversation, that you and a friend were talking about two different people? **Unclear pronoun reference,** a common mistake, causes misunderstandings. *You* always know whom you're referring to when you say *he, she,* or *they,* but your readers or listeners may have someone else in mind.

A **pronoun** should refer clearly to its **antecedent** (the noun or pronoun to which the pronoun refers). Avoid unclear, or **ambiguous,** pronoun references, which occur when a pronoun can refer to either of two antecedents. Usually, you can pin down your meaning by replacing the pronoun with the noun to which it refers.

UNCLEAR Papi and Mister Victor both talk to Liberty, but *he* speaks Spanish with an accent.

CLEAR Papi and Mister Victor both talk to Liberty, but Mister Victor speaks Spanish with an accent.

CLEAR Papi and Mister Victor, who speaks Spanish with an accent, both talk to Liberty.

Try It Out

➤ Reword the following sentences to correct the unclear pronoun references. You may reword the sentences any way you want.

1. Papi brought home a puppy, and he caused a lot of trouble.
2. When Liberty and the strange man with the sunglasses saw me, he looked frightened.
3. All morning aunts stopped by to kiss the sisters because they were leaving for America.
4. Tía Mimi said that Mami was upset, and she had a secret.

VOCABULARY HOW TO OWN A WORD

WORD BANK
elect
hyperactive
admonitions
clenched
inconsolable

Using a Thesaurus to Find Synonyms

A **synonym** is a word that has the same, or nearly the same, meaning as another word. To find synonyms, writers use a **thesaurus,** either in book or electronic form.

Most thesauruses list synonyms based on a word's different shades of meaning. You might want to look at all the synonyms and follow the cross-references given until you find the exact meaning you want to convey.

This chart shows how one student used a thesaurus to find synonyms for *admonitions.* Make a thesaurus chart for synonyms for the other four words in the Word Bank.

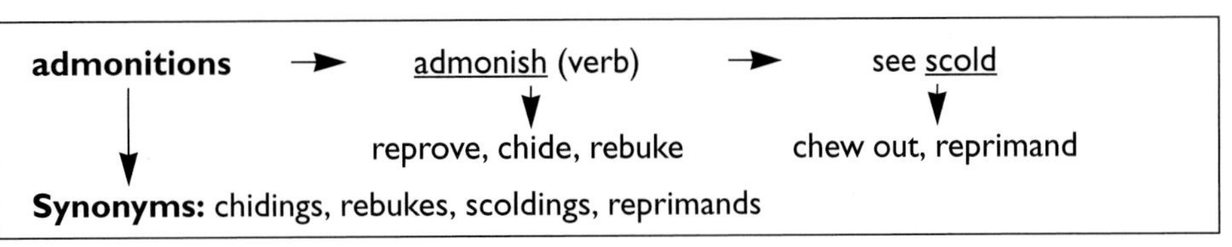

Elements of Literature

IRONY AND SATIRE: The Might of the Word

Three Types of Irony

Irony, in its original Greek sense, means acting ignorant in order to make fun of a person or to expose the truth about a situation. We see this very old kind of irony still at work today when a story or movie shows a shrewd farmer pretending to be dumb in order to make fun of a city slicker. But *irony* has also come to have far broader meanings.

We find three kinds of irony in stories, each of them involving some kind of contrast between expectation and reality. **Verbal irony**—the simplest kind—is being used when someone *says* one thing but *means* the opposite.

If we say "You sure can pick 'em" to the man whose team finished last, we are using verbal irony. A parent uses verbal irony when she looks up from the string of D's on Willie's report card and says "It is certainly gratifying to find you are getting so much out of your education."

If the speaker goes on to use words in a particularly harsh and cruel way, we see the use of **sarcasm**. Sarcasm is intended to wound, to bite in a hurtful way.

Someone looking at Willie's report card would be sarcastic if he said "I've seen shirts with higher IQs than yours."

Situational irony is much more important to the storyteller than other kinds of irony are: It describes an occurrence that is not just surprising; it is *contrary* to what we expected. In an ironic situation, what actually happens is so contrary to our expectations that it seems to mock human intentions and the confidence with which we plan our futures. The ironic possibility that this haughty rich man will come begging from us tomorrow or that this girl who is dreading tonight's party will meet her future husband there keeps our lives interesting. Of course, it does the same for our fiction.

An example of situational irony would be found in a story that told how, after years of searching and after many bloody quarrels over the treasure map, the characters discover the treasure chest and find that it is full of old bottle caps.

A classic example of situational irony is found in the myth of King Midas. This greedy king wishes for a golden touch, but when his wish is granted, something unexpected happens: Midas can no longer eat because even his food turns to gold when he touches it. The golden touch has brought him not only riches, but misery, even death, as well.

Dramatic irony is the kind of irony that occurs when *we* know what is in store for a character but the character does not know. This is called dramatic irony because it's so often used on stage.

Jean arranges a surprise party for Fred's birthday, and all his friends are hiding behind the curtains waiting for him to arrive home. When Fred, looking haggard, calls into an apparently empty hall "Hello? Jean? Anybody home? Boy, am I *tired*!" we recognize dramatic irony. Our sense that the exhausted Fred is soon going to be astonished by a happy-birthday chorus heightens our interest in Fred (we wonder if he'll just fall to the floor).

Dramatic irony adds to our enjoyment of a story because it mimics life, which is forever pulling surprises on us.

Irony of all kinds is somehow enormously satisfying,

by John Leggett

perhaps because we know instinctively that our carefully laid plans and ambitions and strivings often come to little, whereas good luck (or bad) often finds unlikely targets.

> Irony is enormously satisfying, perhaps because we know instinctively that our carefully laid plans and ambitions and strivings often come to little.

Satire: A Social Purpose

Satire is a close relative of irony and often uses irony to accomplish its purpose. **Satire** is any writing that uses ridicule with the intention of bringing about social reform. The satirist wants to expose and eliminate human stupidity and wickedness. Greed, injustice, cruelty, and deceit are all targets of the satirist.

Jonathan Swift's novel *Gulliver's Travels* is often read by children, but it is really one of the most stinging satires in the English language. The story mocks people in early eighteenth-century England who thought their nation was the most civilized on earth. George Orwell's novel *Animal Farm* is another famous satire, one that uses barnyard animals to mock the way people abuse political power.

Comedians on television use satire all the time, often to make fun of themselves. The long-running television show *M*A*S*H* used satire to make us laugh (and cry) at the insanity of war.

Ironic and satiric writing can be humorous. It can lay bare a weakness or a pretense, and it can also invite laughter at someone's expense. Irony and satire may sometimes sting. They may sometimes be cruel in purpose and in effect, but it would be a mistake to ignore them.

Whenever you hear the ancient claim that "the pen is mightier than the sword," think of irony and satire. A pen (or computer) that uses irony or satire can even become a sword, and it can be taken up in a good cause. Irony and satire can hold up to us the mirror of art and reveal our own faults and foolishnesses. They can make us aware of all the ways in which we humans persuade ourselves that we are righteous and right-minded—when, in fact, we just may be dead wrong.

Complete Peace

Before You Read

WHERE HAVE YOU GONE, CHARMING BILLY?

Make the Connection

What Does This All Mean?

The Vietnam War divided America with particular bitterness. Some of those who served in Vietnam have asked what it all meant. Although this war had a profound effect on our nation, few people have written fiction about Vietnam. Tim O'Brien, who served in Vietnam, is an exception. In the story that follows, he focuses on one soldier's feelings during his initiation into combat.

Quickwrite

Have you ever been in a frightening situation—an accident, a flood, a bad fight, maybe even war? What did you do to make yourself feel better? Write down a few notes about your experience. If you don't want to write about yourself, write about someone you know.

Elements of Literature

Theme and Character

The subject of this story is clearly war, but the story's **theme** is much more complex. One way of getting at the theme of any story is to look at how the main character changes in the course of the story, or at what he or she has learned by the story's end. Often, what this character has discovered about life is the truth the writer wants to reveal to us, too.

> What the main **character** learns in the course of a story often leads us to the story's **theme**.
>
> *For more on Theme, see pages 182–183 and the Handbook of Literary Terms.*

Reading Skills and Strategies

Understanding Historical Context

"Where Have You Gone, Charming Billy?" re-creates in harrowing detail a young soldier's fears on his first night in the field. To appreciate some of the details in the story, you need to understand its **historical context,** the war in Vietnam. There were no "front lines" in Vietnam, and fighting took the form of unexpected guerrilla skirmishes. From moment to moment, Paul doesn't know what to expect—from his strange surroundings or from his own heart. Nor do we.

Before you read, review with a partner some of the facts you know about the war in Vietnam. You might also want to read Tim O'Brien's note on the war on page 204.

He was pretending

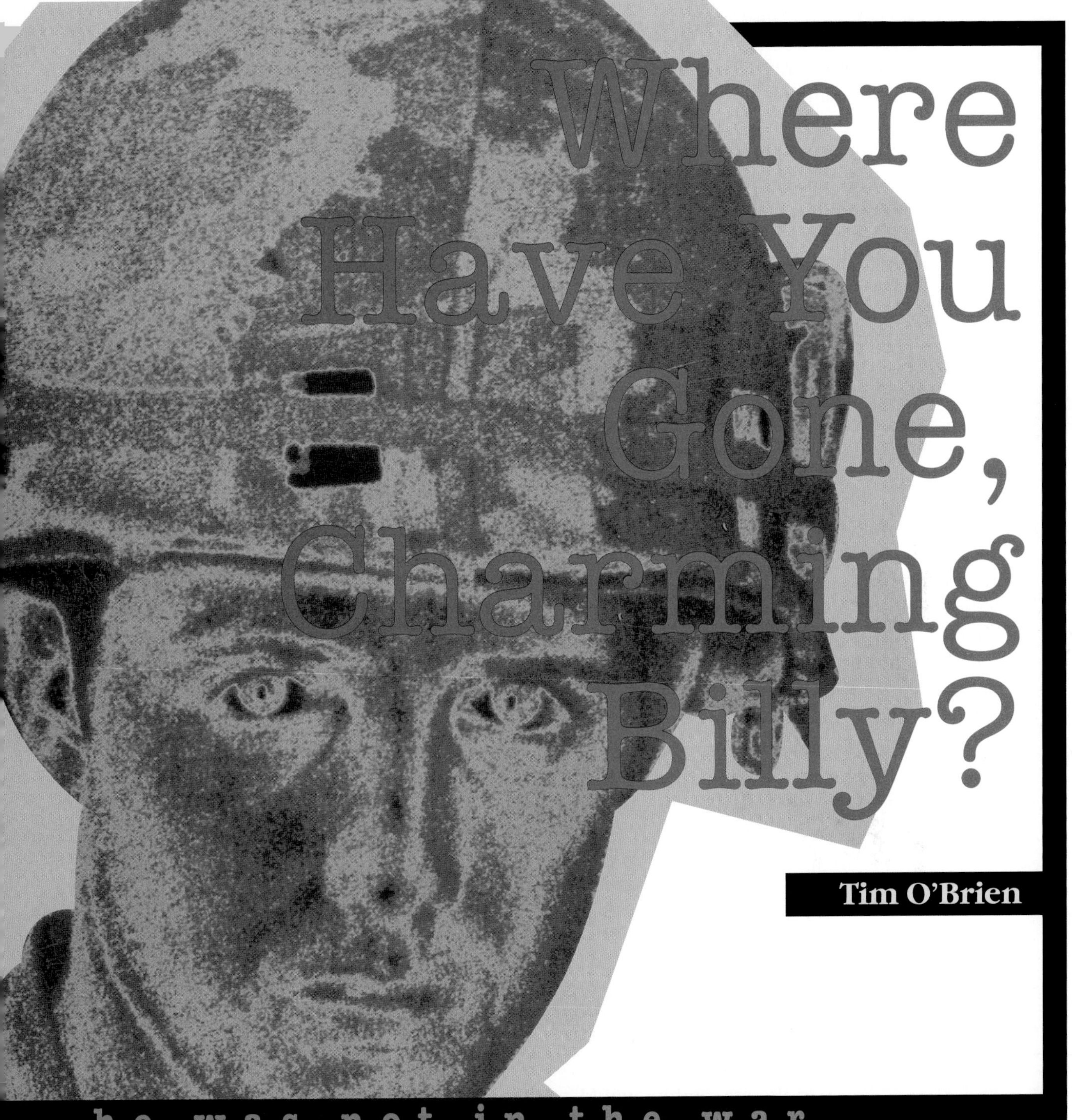

Where Have You Gone, Charming Billy?

Tim O'Brien

he was not in the war . . .

The platoon of twenty-six soldiers moved slowly in the dark, single file, not talking. One by one, like sheep in a dream, they passed through the hedgerow, crossed quietly over a meadow, and came down to the rice paddy. There they stopped. Their leader knelt down, motioning with his hand, and one by one the other soldiers squatted in the shadows, vanishing in the primitive stealth of warfare. For a long time they did not move. Except for the sounds of their breathing, the twenty-six men were very quiet: some of them excited by the adventure, some of them afraid, some of them exhausted from the long night march, some of them looking forward to reaching the sea, where they would be safe. At the rear of the column, Private First Class Paul Berlin lay quietly with his forehead resting on the black plastic stock of his rifle, his eyes closed. He was pretending he was not in the war, pretending he had not watched Billy Boy Watkins die of a heart attack that afternoon. He was pretending he was a boy again, camping with his father in the midnight summer along the Des Moines River. In the dark, with his eyes pinched shut, he pretended. He pretended that when he opened his eyes, his father would be there by the campfire and they would talk softly about whatever came to mind and then roll into their sleeping bags, and that later they'd wake up and it would be morning and there would not be a war, and that Billy Boy Watkins had not died of a heart attack that afternoon. He pretended he was not a soldier.

In the morning, when they

In the morning, when they reached the sea, it would be better. The hot afternoon would be over, he would bathe in the sea, and he would forget how frightened he had been on his first day at the war. The second day would not be so bad. He would learn.

There was a sound beside him, a movement, and then a breathed "Hey!"

He opened his eyes, shivering as if emerging from a deep nightmare.

"Hey!" a shadow whispered. "We're *moving*. Get up."

"Okay."

"You sleepin', or something?"

"No." He could not make out the soldier's face. With clumsy, concrete hands he clawed for his rifle, found it, found his helmet.

The soldier shadow grunted. "You got a lot to learn, buddy. I'd shoot you if I thought you was sleepin'. Let's go."

Private First Class Paul Berlin blinked.

Ahead of him, silhouetted against the sky, he saw the string of soldiers wading into the flat paddy, the black outline of their shoulders and packs and weapons. He was comfortable. He did not want to move. But he was afraid, for it was his first night at the war, so he hurried to catch up, stumbling once, scraping his knee, groping as though blind; his boots sank into the thick paddy water, and he smelled it all around him. He would tell his mother how it smelled: mud and algae and cattle manure and chlorophyll;[1] decay, breeding mosquitoes and leeches as big as mice; the fecund warmth of the paddy waters rising up to his cut knee. But he would not tell how frightened he had been.

Once they reached the sea, things would be better. They would have their rear guarded by three thousand miles of ocean, and they would swim and dive into the breakers and hunt crayfish and smell the salt, and they would be safe.

He followed the shadow of the man in front of him. It was a clear night. Already the Southern Cross[2] was out. And other stars he could not yet name—soon, he thought, he would learn their names. And puffy night clouds. There was not yet a moon. Wading through the paddy, his boots made sleepy, sloshing sounds, like a lull-

1. **chlorophyll** (klôr′ə·fil′): green substance found in plant cells.
2. **Southern Cross:** constellation, or group of stars, in the Southern Hemisphere.

WORDS TO OWN

fecund (fē′kənd) *adj.:* fertile; producing abundantly.

aby, and he tried not to think. Though he was afraid, he now knew that fear came in many degrees and types and peculiar categories, and he knew that his fear now was not so bad as it had been in the hot afternoon, when poor Billy Boy Watkins got killed by a heart attack. His fear now was diffuse and unformed: ghosts in the tree line, nighttime fears of a child, a boogeyman in the closet that his father would open to show empty, saying, "See? Nothing there, champ. Now you can sleep." In the afternoon it had been worse: The fear had been bundled and tight and he'd been on his hands and knees, crawling like an insect, an ant escaping a giant's footsteps, and thinking nothing, brain flopping like wet cement in a mixer, not thinking at all, watching while Billy Boy Watkins died.

reached the sea,

Now, as he stepped out of the paddy onto a narrow dirt path, now the fear was mostly the fear of being so terribly afraid again.

He tried not to think.

There were tricks he'd learned to keep from thinking. Counting: He counted his steps, concentrating on the numbers, pretending that the steps were dollar bills and that each step through the night made him richer and richer, so that soon he would become a wealthy man, and he kept counting and considered the ways he might spend the money after the war and what he would do. He would look his father in the eye and shrug and say, "It was pretty bad at first, but I learned a lot and I got used to it." Then he would tell his father the story of Billy Boy Watkins. But he would never let on how frightened he had been. "Not so bad," he would say instead, making his father feel proud.

it would be better.

Songs, another trick to stop from thinking: *Where have you gone, Billy Boy, Billy Boy, oh, where have you gone, charming Billy? I have gone to seek a wife, she's the joy of my life, but she's a young thing and cannot leave her mother,* and other songs that he sang in his thoughts as he walked toward the sea. And when he reached the sea, he would dig a deep hole in the sand and he would sleep like the high clouds and he would not be afraid anymore.

The moon came out. Pale and shrunken to the size of a dime.

The helmet was heavy on his head. In the morning he would adjust the leather binding. He would clean his rifle, too. Even though he had been frightened to shoot it during the hot afternoon, he would carefully clean the breech and the muzzle and the ammunition so that next time he would be ready and not so afraid. In the morning, when they reached the sea, he would begin to make friends with some of the other soldiers. He would learn their names and laugh at their jokes. Then when the war was over, he would have war buddies, and he would write to them once in a while and exchange memories.

Walking, sleeping in his walking, he felt better. He watched the moon come higher.

Once they skirted a sleeping village. The smells again—straw, cattle, mildew. The men were quiet. On the far side of the village, buried in the dark smells, a dog barked. The column stopped until the barking died away; then they marched fast away from the village, through a graveyard filled with conical-shaped burial mounds and tiny altars made of clay and stone. The graveyard had a perfumy smell. A nice place to spend the night, he thought. The mounds would make fine battlements, and the smell was nice and the place was quiet. But they went on, passing through a hedgerow and across another paddy and east toward the sea.

He walked carefully. He remembered what he'd been taught: Stay off the center of the path, for that was where the land mines and booby traps were planted, where stupid and lazy soldiers like to walk. Stay alert, he'd been taught.

WORDS TO OWN

skirted *v.:* passed around rather than through. *Skirted* also means "missed narrowly" or "avoided."

LITERATURE AND STATISTICS

Database: Vietnam

- Year first American military advisers were sent to Vietnam: **1954**
- Year first American combat troops were sent to Vietnam: **1965**
- Total number of Americans who served in Vietnam: **8.75 million**
- Number of women who served in noncombat positions: **7,500**
- Number of people who rallied for peace in Washington, D.C.: on April 17, 1965, **20,000;** on November 15, 1969, **300,000**
- Year cease-fire declared: **1973**
- Money spent by the U.S. government for direct costs: **$150 billion**
- Vietnamese deaths: **2 million**
- American deaths: **58,000**
- Americans wounded: **300,000**
- Americans missing and presumed dead: **2,300**
- Number of people who visit the Vietnam Memorial in Washington, D.C., every year: **2.5 million**

All statistics are estimates.

Better alert than inert. Ag-ile, mo-bile, hos-tile. He wished he'd paid better attention to the training. He could not remember what they'd said about how to stop being afraid; they hadn't given any lessons in courage—not that he could remember—and they hadn't mentioned how Billy Boy Watkins would die of a heart attack, his face turning pale and the veins popping out.

Better alert than inert.

Private First Class Paul Berlin walked carefully.

Stretching ahead of him like dark beads on an invisible chain, the string of shadow soldiers whose names he did not yet know moved with the silence and slow grace of smoke. Now and again moonlight was reflected off a machine gun or a wristwatch. But mostly the soldiers were quiet and hidden and faraway-seeming in a peaceful night, strangers on a long street, and he felt quite separate from them, as if trailing behind like the caboose on a night train, pulled along by inertia,[3] sleepwalking, an afterthought to the war.

So he walked carefully, counting his steps.

3. **inertia** (in·ur′shə): tendency to remain either at rest or in motion.

When he had counted to 3,485, the column stopped.

One by one the soldiers knelt or squatted down.

The grass along the path was wet. Private First Class Paul Berlin lay back and turned his head so that he could lick at the dew with his eyes closed, another trick to forget the war. He might have slept. "I *wasn't* afraid," he was screaming or dreaming, facing his father's stern eyes. "I wasn't afraid," he was saying. When he opened his eyes, a soldier was sitting beside him, quietly chewing a stick of Doublemint gum.

"You sleepin' again?" the soldier whispered.

"No," said Private First Class Paul Berlin. "Hell, no."

The soldier grunted, chewing his gum. Then he twisted the cap off his canteen, took a swallow, and handed it through the dark.

"Take some," he whispered.

"Thanks."

"You're the new guy?"

"Yes." He did not want to admit it, being new to the war.

The soldier grunted and handed him a stick of gum. "Chew it quiet—OK? Don't blow no bubbles or nothing."

"Thanks. I won't." He could not make out the man's face in the shadows.

They sat still and Private First Class Paul Berlin chewed the gum until all the sugars were gone; then the soldier said, "Bad day today, buddy."

Private First Class Paul Berlin nodded wisely, but he did not speak.

"Don't think it's always so bad," the soldier whispered. "I don't wanna scare you. You'll get used to it soon enough. . . . They been fighting wars a long time, and you get used to it."

"Yeah."

"You will."

They were quiet awhile. And the night was quiet, no crickets or birds, and it was hard to imagine it was truly a war. He searched for the soldier's face but could not find it. It did not matter much. Even if he saw the fellow's face, he would not know the name; and even if he knew the name, it would not matter much.

"Haven't got the time?" the soldier whispered.

"No."

"Rats. . . . Don't matter, really. Goes faster if you don't know the time, anyhow."

"Sure."

"What's your name, buddy?"

"Paul."

"Nice to meet ya," he said, and in the dark beside the path, they shook hands. "Mine's Toby. Everybody calls me Buffalo, though." The soldier's hand was strangely warm and soft. But it was a very big hand. "Sometimes they just call me Buff," he said.

And again they were quiet. They lay in the grass and waited. The moon was very high now and very bright, and they were waiting for cloud cover. The soldier suddenly snorted.

"What is it?"

"Nothin'," he said, but then he snorted again. "A bloody *heart attack*!" the soldier said. "Can't get over it—old Billy Boy croaking from a lousy heart attack. . . . A heart attack—can you believe it?"

The idea of it made Private First Class Paul Berlin smile. He couldn't help it.

"Ever hear of such a thing?"

"Not till now," said Private First Class Paul Berlin, still smiling.

"Me neither," said the soldier in the dark. "Gawd, dying of a heart attack. Didn't know him, did you."

"No."

"Tough as nails."

"Yeah."

"And what happens? A heart attack. Can you imagine it?"

"Yes," said Private First Class Paul Berlin. He wanted to laugh. "I can imagine it." And he imagined it clearly. He giggled—he couldn't help it. He imagined Billy's father opening the telegram: SORRY TO INFORM YOU THAT YOUR SON BILLY BOY WAS YESTERDAY SCARED TO DEATH IN AC-

Ag-ile, mo-bile, hos-tile.

TION IN THE REPUBLIC OF VIETNAM, VALIANTLY SUCCUMBING TO A HEART ATTACK SUFFERED WHILE UNDER ENORMOUS STRESS, AND IT IS WITH GREATEST SYMPATHY THAT . . . He giggled again. He rolled onto his belly and pressed his face into his arms. His body was shaking with giggles.

The big soldier hissed at him to shut up, but he could not stop giggling and remembering the hot afternoon, and poor Billy Boy, and how they'd been drinking Coca-Cola from bright-red aluminum cans, and how they'd started on the day's march, and how a little while later poor Billy Boy stepped on the mine, and how it made a tiny little sound—*poof*—and how Billy Boy stood there with his mouth wide open, looking down at where his foot had been blown off, and how finally Billy Boy sat down very casually, not saying a word, with his foot lying behind him, most of it still in the boot.

He giggled louder—he could not stop. He bit his arm, trying to stifle it, but remembering: "War's over, Billy," the men had said in consolation, but Billy Boy got scared and started crying and said he was about to die. "Nonsense," the medic said, Doc Peret, but Billy Boy kept bawling, tightening up, his face going pale and transparent and his veins popping out. Scared stiff. Even when Doc Peret stuck him with morphine, Billy Boy kept crying.

Where have you

"Shut up!" the big soldier hissed, but Private First Class Paul Berlin could not stop. Giggling and remembering, he covered his mouth. His eyes stung, remembering how it was when Billy Boy died of fright.

"Shut up!"

But he could not stop giggling, the same way Billy Boy could not stop bawling that afternoon.

Afterward Doc Peret had explained: "You see, Billy Boy really died of a heart attack. He was scared he was gonna die—so scared he had himself a heart attack—and that's what really killed him. I seen it before."

oh, where have you gone,

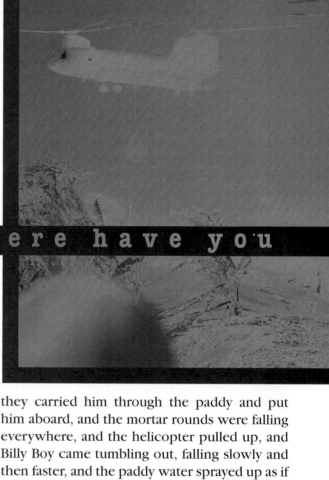

So they wrapped Billy in a plastic poncho, his eyes still wide open and scared stiff, and they carried him over the meadow to a rice paddy, and then when the Medevac helicopter arrived, they carried him through the paddy and put him aboard, and the mortar rounds were falling everywhere, and the helicopter pulled up, and Billy Boy came tumbling out, falling slowly and then faster, and the paddy water sprayed up as if Billy Boy had just executed a long and dangerous dive, as if trying to escape Graves Registration, where he would be tagged and sent home under a flag, dead of a heart attack.

"Shut up!" the soldier hissed, but Paul Berlin could not stop giggling, remembering: scared to death.

Later they waded in after him, probing for Billy Boy with their rifle butts, elegantly and del-

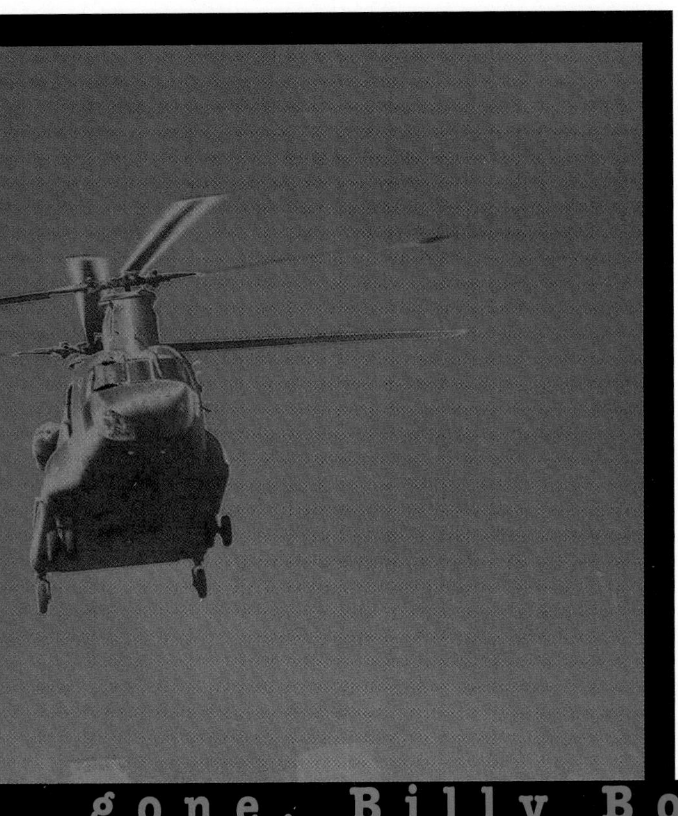

gone, Billy Boy, Billy Boy,

icately probing for Billy Boy in the stinking paddy, singing—some of them—*Where have you gone, Billy Boy, Billy Boy, oh, where have you gone, charming Billy?* Then they found him. Green and covered with algae, his eyes still wide open and scared stiff, dead of a heart attack suffered while——

charming Billy?

"Shut up!" the soldier said loudly, shaking him.

But Private First Class Paul Berlin could not stop. The giggles were caught in his throat, drowning him in his own laughter: scared to death like Billy Boy.

Giggling, lying on his back, he saw the moon move, or the clouds moving across the moon. Wounded in action, dead of fright. A fine war story. He would tell it to his father, how Billy Boy had been scared to death, never letting on . . . He could not stop.

The soldier smothered him. He tried to fight back, but he was weak from the giggles.

The moon was under the clouds and the column was moving. The soldier helped him up. "You OK now, buddy?"

"Sure."

"What was so bloody funny?"

"Nothing."

"You can get killed, laughing that way."

"I know. I know that."

"You got to stay calm, buddy." The soldier handed him his rifle. "Half the battle, just staying calm. You'll get better at it," he said. "Come on, now."

He turned away and Private First Class Paul Berlin hurried after him. He was still shivering.

He would do better once he reached the sea, he thought, still smiling a little. A funny war story that he would tell to his father, how Billy Boy Watkins was scared to death. A good joke. But even when he smelled salt and heard the sea, he could not stop being afraid.

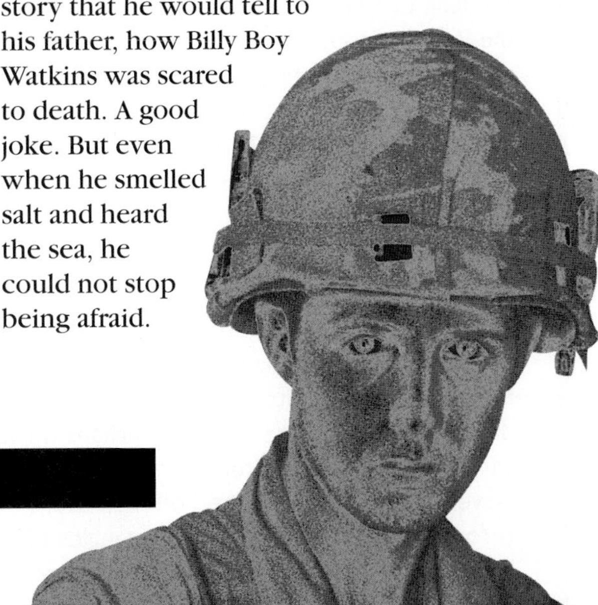

Meet the Writer

The Power of the Heart

It was the Vietnam War that made **Tim O'Brien** (1946–   ) a writer. He was drafted immediately after graduating from Macalester College in St. Paul, Minnesota, in 1968. He then spent two years as an infantryman in Vietnam.

When he returned from Vietnam, O'Brien used his imagination to cope with memories of the war. Many of his stories are told from the point of view of a young soldier named Paul Berlin. These stories eventually grew into a novel called *Going After Cacciato,* which won the National Book Award in 1979. "Where Have You Gone, Charming Billy?" was used, with some changes, as Chapter 31 of the novel.

In 1990, O'Brien published *The Things They Carried,* referring to the burdens, both material and emotional, carried by the American soldiers in Vietnam—the M-16 rifles, the comic books, the flak jackets, and the fear. In 1994, he published *In the Lake of the Woods,* another novel about his persistent theme—the lingering memory of Vietnam. The following account is from *If I Die in a Combat Zone, Box Me Up and Ship Me Home.* Mad Mark was the platoon leader.

" One of the most persistent and appalling thoughts which lumbers through your mind as you walk through Vietnam at night is the fear of getting lost, of becoming detached from the others, of spending the night alone in that frightening and haunted countryside. It was dark. We walked in a single file, perhaps three yards apart. Mad Mark took us along a crazy, wavering course. We veered off the road, through clumps of trees, through tangles of bamboo and grass, zigzagging through graveyards of dead Vietnamese who lay there under conical mounds of dirt and clay. The man to the front and the man to the rear were the only holds on security and sanity. We followed the man in front like a blind man after his dog, like Dante following Virgil through the Inferno, and we prayed that the man had not lost his way, that he hadn't lost contact with the man to his front. We tensed the muscles around our eyeballs and peered straight ahead. We hurt ourselves staring at the man's back. We strained. We dared not look away for fear the man might fade and dissipate and turn into absent shadow. Sometimes, when the jungle closed in, we reached out to him, touched his shirt.

The man to the front is civilization. He is the United States of America and every friend you have ever known; he is Erik and blond girls and a mother and a father. He is your life, and he is your altar and God combined. And, for the man stumbling along behind you, you alone are his torch. "

Connections

A POEM

For centuries, women have gone to war, but their contributions have rarely been acknowledged. Lily Lee Adams was one of the thousands of women who cared for wounded and dying soldiers in Vietnam. She served with the Army Nurse Corps at the Twelfth Evacuation Hospital in Cu Chi from 1969 to 1970.

The Friendship Only Lasted a Few Seconds

Lily Lee Adams

He said "Mom,"
And I responded
And became her.
I never lied
to him.
And I couldn't
Explain that to others.
I got all and more back.
But the friendship
Only lasted a few seconds.

And he called me Mary.
I wished she could
Be there for him.
I felt I was in
Second place,
But I did the
Best I could
And the friendship
Only lasted a few seconds.

And he told me,
"I don't believe this,
I'm dying for nothing."
Then he died.
Again, the friendship
Only lasted a few seconds.
How can the World
Understand any of this?
How can I keep the
World from forgetting?
After all the friendship
Only lasted a few seconds.

Vietnam Women's Memorial in Washington, D.C.

Making Meanings

First Thoughts

1. What was your reaction to Paul's uncontrolled giggling at the story's end?

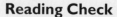

Reading Check

Tell the story of Billy Boy's death to a partner, as you imagine a war correspondent might report it on the nightly news. Tell **what** happened, **whom** it happened to, **where** it happened, **when** it happened, **why** it happened, and **how** it happened.

Shaping Interpretations

2. On page 199 the writer quotes a bit of the children's song that gives the story its title. (If you don't know the rest of this song, see if you can find someone who does.) What is **ironic** about the author's use of this particular song in a war story?
3. There is a central **irony** in warfare, which has to do with the fact that soldiers kill people they do not even know. What is ironic about how Billy Boy dies? about how his body is removed?
4. What do you think Paul has discovered about war and about himself on his first day of combat? What **theme,** or central idea, relating to war have you become aware of by sharing Paul's experiences?
5. In a sense, this is a story about a hero's journey, which often takes the form of a **quest**—a search for something of great value. What is it that Paul expects to find at the sea, the end point of his journey? Ironically, what does he find instead?
6. In what ways is Paul an exile and an outsider? What do you imagine Paul will be like a year after this story ends?

Connecting with the Text

7. How do you feel about the way this writer has treated the subject of war?
8.  Look back at the poem written by a nurse in Vietnam (see ***Connections*** on page 205). How does it affect your understanding of O'Brien's story and of the Vietnam War?

Extending the Text

9.  Think about the story's **historical context.** How does Paul's story resemble other war stories you have read or war movies you have seen? How is it different?

CHOICES: Building Your Portfolio

Writer's Notebook

1. Collecting Ideas for Analyzing a Story

Focusing on character. Now that you've met Paul Berlin, what can you say about him as a fictional character? In many stories, we come to know characters so well that we make **inferences** about why they behave the way they do and **predict** what they'll do next. Use a chart like the one below to gather details about Paul Berlin or a character in another story from Collections 1 to 3. Save your notes for the Writer's Workshop on page 240.

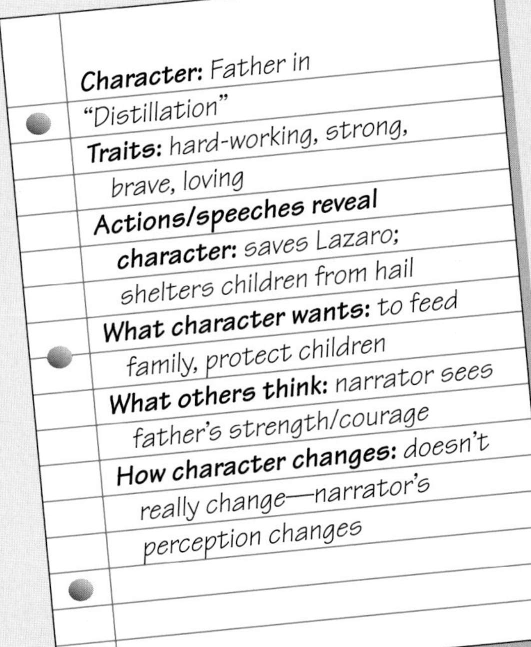

Character: Father in "Distillation"
Traits: hard-working, strong, brave, loving
Actions/speeches reveal character: saves Lazaro; shelters children from hail
What character wants: to feed family, protect children
What others think: narrator sees father's strength/courage
How character changes: doesn't really change—narrator's perception changes

Creative Writing

2. Happy Memories?

Paul Berlin pulls a happy childhood experience out of his memory to help him when he feels afraid. Recall an experience from your childhood that makes you feel happy or one that triggers other feelings. (Refer to your Quickwrite notes.) Write about that experience, recapturing its sights, sounds, and other sensory details. Include your thoughts about what the experience might reveal about life or even about the sources of joy or pain.

Supporting an Opinion

3. Why War?

War is a recurring subject in literature and film. Why do you think writers and moviemakers so often choose war as their subject? Write an essay proposing answers to this question. To support your opinion, give reasons why people *write* about war and its violence and why others *read* about it. At the end of your essay, explain how war stories like this one affect *you*.

History / Research

4. I Remember . . .

Suppose you are a historian who wants to collect firsthand data on the Vietnam era. Work with a partner to collect **oral histories** about the war years. Before you conduct an interview, be sure you make a list of the questions you want to ask your subject. You might want to record your interviews on audiotape, or even videotape the session. You'll have to decide on the final format you want your oral histories to take: Will you present them on audiotape, videotape, or in print?

Visual Literacy

5. Words into Graphics

Sometimes graphics communicate information more directly than words. Use the information in the database on page 200 to create one or more graphics. You might make a **time line** of events or a **bar graph** or **pie graph** of the numbers of casualties. What other kinds of graphics can you create using the information given?

LANGUAGE LINK MINI-LESSON

Imagery Puts Us There

Handbook of Literary Terms HELP

See Imagery.

Image comes from the Latin word *imago,* which means "copy." In a sense, an **image** is a copy of a sensory experience—a **sight,** a **sound,** a **smell,** a **taste,** or a **touch.**

For example, we read that Paul pretends he is a boy again, camping with his dad "in the midnight summer along the Des Moines River." He imagines "that when he opened his eyes, his father would be there by the campfire and they would talk softly about whatever came to mind and then roll into their sleeping bags." We can share Paul's remembered experience here because O'Brien gives us images of sight (a campfire in the darkness), of sound (talking quietly), and of touch (rolling into the softness of a sleeping bag on the hard ground).

To see how the right images can prompt your own imagination to supply all kinds of other details, describe to a partner exactly what *you* think that campsite was like. How different are your imagined pictures of Paul's memory?

Try It Out

➤Look back through the story, and write down at least five passages that use images that help you share the sights, smells, and sounds of Paul's journey. Identify the senses to which each image appeals.

➤Look carefully at your own descriptive passages. Ask: Have I made my people and settings real? Have I told how they looked, smelled, tasted, sounded, or felt?

VOCABULARY HOW TO OWN A WORD

WORD BANK

fecund
skirted

Meaning Maps

On page 200, Tim O'Brien uses the word *inertia* to describe a feeling of being pulled as if by a train. *Inertia* is a hard word to use. Many people think of it only as laziness or inactivity. The dictionary calls it the "tendency of an object in motion to keep moving in the same direction or of an object at rest to remain at rest, unless the object is affected by another force." Look at the meaning map one person made to understand this tough but important word.

inertia

How does a skier racing downhill show inertia?
→ The skier will keep racing downhill until she stops or some other force stops her.

How does a paperweight resting on a desk show inertia?
→ The paperweight will remain on the desk until someone moves it.

Make your own meaning maps for *skirted* and *fecund*. You will have to think of your own questions and answers.

Before You Read

THE BET

Make the Connection

The Search for Meaning

Would you give up all human company for years to win an amazing fortune? A character in this famous Russian story bets that he can do it, and his voluntary solitude raises some big questions—for him and for readers.

Quickwrite

Think about a time when you chose to be alone for a while. Maybe you needed to study to pass a test, or you may have wanted to be alone to think about an important decision. Jot down the details of your experience. What did you learn from your solitude?

Elements of Literature

Ambiguity: More Than One Meaning?

The **theme,** or overall meaning, of a story is almost never stated directly by the writer in any one place in the text. In fact, few writers want to reduce the meaning of their stories to *one* fixed and final statement. Instead, writers expect readers to make their own meaning after looking at the complex interplay of all the elements in the story. Because readers bring their own values and experiences to the reading of any text, individual interpretations are bound to differ. Some interpretations even go beyond what the writer consciously intended the story to mean. "The Bet" is a striking example of a story that raises more questions than it answers. Its theme is particularly **ambiguous,** or open to a variety of interpretations.

The **theme,** or overall meaning, of a story is **ambiguous** when the elements that make up the story are open to many interpretations. *For more on Theme, see pages 182–183 and the Handbook of Literary Terms.*

Reading Skills and Strategies

Making Inferences About Theme

How would you go about determining the theme of a story? You'll need to make **inferences,** or guesses based on clues in the story: You'll look at the title, at whether the characters change, and at what they learn. You'll look, too, for **key passages** that seem to hint at the author's message. In "The Bet," for example, the lawyer's letter certainly merits a careful look.

"The death penalty is more humane than imprisonment for life."

The Verandah at Liselund (detail) (1916) by Peter Ilsted. Oil on canvas.

Courtesy of Adelson Galleries, New York.

The Bet

Anton Chekhov
translated by Constance Garnett

1

It was a dark autumn night. The old banker was walking up and down his study and remembering how, fifteen years before, he had given a party one autumn evening. There had been many clever men there, and there had been interesting conversations. Among other things, they had talked of capital punishment. The majority of the guests, among whom were many journalists and intellectual men, disapproved of the death penalty. They considered that form of punishment out of date, immoral, and unsuitable for Christian states.[1] In the opinion of some of them, the death penalty ought to be replaced everywhere by imprisonment for life.

"I don't agree with you," said their host, the banker. "I have not tried either the death penalty or imprisonment for life, but if one may judge a priori,[2] the death penalty is more

Portrait of the Painter Konstantin Alekseevich Korovin (1891) by Valentin Serov. Oil on canvas. Tretiakov Gallery, Moscow, Russia.

Scala/Art Resource, New York.

1. **Christian states:** countries in which Christianity is the main religion.
2. **a priori** (ā′prī·ôr′ī): here, on the basis of theory rather than experience.

moral and more humane than imprisonment for life. Capital punishment kills a man at once, but lifelong imprisonment kills him slowly. Which executioner is the more humane, he who kills you in a few minutes or he who drags the life out of you in the course of many years?"

"Both are equally immoral," observed one of the guests, "for they both have the same object—to take away life. The state is not God. It has not the right to take away what it cannot restore when it wants to."

Among the guests was a young lawyer, a young man of five-and-twenty. When he was asked his opinion, he said: "The death sentence and the life sentence are equally immoral, but if I had to choose between the death penalty and imprisonment for life, I would certainly choose the second. To live anyhow is better than not at all."

A lively discussion arose. The banker, who was younger and more nervous in those days, was suddenly carried away by excitement; he struck the table with his fist and shouted at the young man: "It's not true! I'll bet you two million you wouldn't stay in solitary confinement for five years."

"If you mean that in earnest," said the young man, "I'll take the bet, but I would stay not five, but fifteen years."

"Fifteen? Done!" cried the banker. "Gentlemen, I stake two million!"

"Agreed! You stake your millions and I stake my freedom!" said the young man.

And this wild, senseless bet was carried out! The banker, spoiled and frivolous, with millions beyond his reckoning, was delighted at the bet. At supper he made fun of the young man and said: "Think better of it, young man, while there is still time. To me two million is a trifle, but you are losing three or four of the best years of your life. I say three or four, because you won't stay longer. Don't forget either, you unhappy man, that voluntary confinement is a great deal harder to bear than compulsory. The thought that you have the right to step out in liberty at any moment will poison your whole existence in prison. I am sorry for you."

And now the banker, walking to and fro, remembered all this and asked himself: "What was the object of that bet? What is the good of that man's losing fifteen years of his life and my throwing away two million? Can it prove that the death penalty is better or worse than imprisonment for life? No, no. It was all nonsensical and meaningless. On my part it was the caprice of a pampered man, and on his part simple greed for money. . . ."

Then he remembered what followed that evening. It was decided that the young man should spend the years of his captivity under the strictest supervision in one of the lodges in the banker's garden. It was agreed that for fifteen years he should not be free to cross the threshold of the lodge, to see human beings, to hear the human voice, or to receive letters and newspapers. He was allowed to have a musical instrument and books and was allowed to write letters, to drink wine, and to smoke. By the terms of the agreement, the only relations he could have with the outer world were by a little window made purposely for that object. He might have anything he wanted—books, music, wine, and so on—in any quantity he desired, by writing an order, but could receive them only through the window. The agreement provided for every detail and every trifle that would make his imprisonment strictly solitary, and bound the young man to stay there *exactly* fifteen years, beginning from twelve o'clock of November 14, 1870, and ending at twelve o'clock of November 14, 1885. The slightest attempt on his part to break the conditions, if only two minutes before the end, released the banker from the obligation to pay him two million.

For the first year of his confinement, as far as one could judge from his brief notes, the prisoner suffered severely from loneliness and depression. The sounds of the piano could be heard continually day and night from his lodge. He refused wine and tobacco. Wine, he wrote, excites the desires, and desires are the worst foes of the prisoner; and besides, nothing could

WORDS TO OWN

compulsory (kəm·pul′sə·rē) *adj.:* required; enforced.
caprice (kə·prēs′) *n.:* sudden notion or desire.

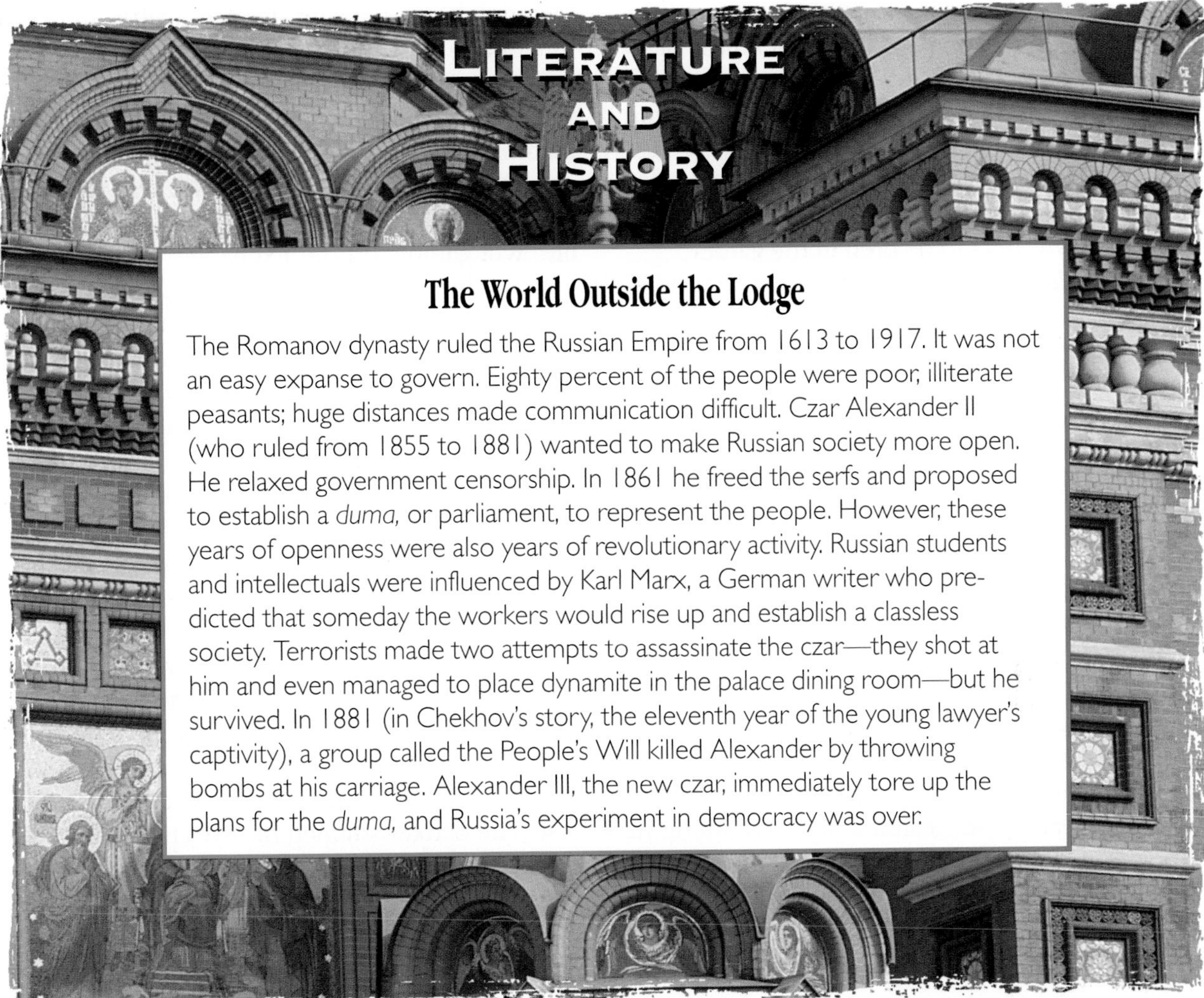

The World Outside the Lodge

The Romanov dynasty ruled the Russian Empire from 1613 to 1917. It was not an easy expanse to govern. Eighty percent of the people were poor, illiterate peasants; huge distances made communication difficult. Czar Alexander II (who ruled from 1855 to 1881) wanted to make Russian society more open. He relaxed government censorship. In 1861 he freed the serfs and proposed to establish a *duma,* or parliament, to represent the people. However, these years of openness were also years of revolutionary activity. Russian students and intellectuals were influenced by Karl Marx, a German writer who predicted that someday the workers would rise up and establish a classless society. Terrorists made two attempts to assassinate the czar—they shot at him and even managed to place dynamite in the palace dining room—but he survived. In 1881 (in Chekhov's story, the eleventh year of the young lawyer's captivity), a group called the People's Will killed Alexander by throwing bombs at his carriage. Alexander III, the new czar, immediately tore up the plans for the *duma,* and Russia's experiment in democracy was over.

be more dreary than drinking good wine and seeing no one. And tobacco spoiled the air of his room. In the first year the books he sent for were principally of a light character—novels with a complicated love plot, sensational and fantastic stories, and so on.

In the second year the piano was silent in the lodge, and the prisoner asked only for the classics. In the fifth year music was audible again, and the prisoner asked for wine. Those who watched him through the window said that all that year he spent doing nothing but eating and drinking and lying on his bed, frequently yawning and talking angrily to himself. He did not read books. Sometimes at night he would sit down to write; he would spend hours writing and in the morning tear up all that he had written. More than once he could be heard crying.

In the second half of the sixth year the prisoner began zealously studying languages, philosophy, and history. He threw himself eagerly into these studies—so much so that the banker had enough to do to get him the books he ordered. In the course of four years, some six hundred volumes were procured at his request. It was during this period that the banker received the following letter from his prisoner:

"My dear Jailer, I write you these lines in six languages. Show them to people who know the languages. Let them read them. If they find not one mistake, I implore you to fire a shot in the

WORDS TO OWN

audible (ô′də·bəl) *adj.:* capable of being heard.
zealously (zel′əs·lē) *adv.:* fervently; devotedly.

garden. That shot will show me that my efforts have not been thrown away. The geniuses of all ages and of all lands speak different languages, but the same flame burns in them all. Oh, if you only knew what unearthly happiness my soul feels now from being able to understand them!" The prisoner's desire was fulfilled. The banker ordered two shots to be fired in the garden.

Then, after the tenth year, the prisoner sat immovably at the table and read nothing but the Gospels. It seemed strange to the banker that a man who in four years had mastered six hundred learned volumes should waste nearly a year over one thin book easy of comprehension. Theology[3] and histories of religion followed the Gospels.

In the last two years of his confinement, the prisoner read an immense quantity of books quite indiscriminately. At one time he was busy with the natural sciences; then he would ask for Byron[4] or Shakespeare. There were notes in which he demanded at the same time books on chemistry, and a manual of medicine, and a novel, and some treatise on philosophy or theology. His reading suggested a man swimming in the sea among the wreckage of his ship and trying to save his life by greedily clutching first at one spar[5] and then at another.

2

The old banker remembered all this and thought: "Tomorrow at twelve o'clock he will regain his freedom. By our arrangement I ought to pay him two million. If I do pay him, it is all over with me: I shall be utterly ruined."

Fifteen years before, his millions had been beyond his reckoning; now he was afraid to ask himself which were greater, his debts or his assets. Desperate gambling on the Stock Exchange, wild speculation, and the excitability which he could not get over even in advancing years had by degrees led to the decline of his fortune, and the proud, fearless, self-confident millionaire had become a banker of middling rank, trembling at every rise and fall in his investments. "Cursed bet!" muttered the old man, clutching his head in despair. "Why didn't the man die? He is only forty now. He will take my last penny from me, he will marry, will enjoy life, will gamble on the Exchange, while I shall look at him with envy like a beggar and hear from him every day the same sentence: 'I am indebted to you for the happiness of my life; let me help you!' No, it is too much! The one means of being saved from bankruptcy and disgrace is the death of that man!"

It struck three o'clock. The banker listened; everyone was asleep in the house, and nothing could be heard outside but the rustling of the chilled trees. Trying to make no noise, he took from a fireproof safe the key of the door which had not been opened for fifteen years, put on his overcoat, and went out of the house.

It was dark and cold in the garden. Rain was falling. A damp, cutting wind was racing about the garden, howling and giving the trees no rest. The banker strained his eyes but could see neither the earth nor the white statues, nor the lodge, nor the trees. Going to the spot where the lodge stood, he twice called the watchman. No answer followed. Evidently the watchman had sought shelter from the weather and was now asleep somewhere either in the kitchen or in the greenhouse.

"If I had the pluck to carry out my intention," thought the old man, "suspicion would fall first upon the watchman."

He felt in the darkness for the steps and the door and went into the entry of the lodge. Then he groped his way into a little passage and lighted a match. There was not a soul there. There was a bedstead with no bedding on it, and in the corner there was a dark cast-iron stove. The seals on the door leading to the prisoner's rooms were intact.

3. **theology** (thē·äl′ə·jē): the study of religious teachings concerning God and God's relation to the world.
4. **Byron:** George Gordon Byron (1788–1824), known as Lord Byron, English Romantic poet.
5. **spar:** pole that supports or extends a ship's sail.

Words to Own

indiscriminately (in′di·skrim′i·nit·lē) *adv.:* without making careful choices or distinctions; randomly.

When the match went out, the old man, trembling with emotion, peeped through the little window. A candle was burning dimly in the prisoner's room. He was sitting at the table. Nothing could be seen but his back, the hair on his head, and his hands. Open books were lying on the table, on the two easy chairs, and on the carpet near the table.

Five minutes passed and the prisoner did not once stir. Fifteen years' imprisonment had taught him to sit still. The banker tapped at the window with his finger, and the prisoner made no movement whatever in response. Then the banker cautiously broke the seals off the door and put the key in the keyhole. The rusty lock gave a grating sound and the door creaked. The banker expected to hear at once footsteps and a cry of astonishment, but three minutes passed and it was as quiet as ever in the room. He made up his mind to go in.

At the table a man unlike ordinary people was sitting motionless. He was a skeleton with the skin drawn tight over his bones, with long curls like a woman's, and a shaggy beard. His face was yellow with an earthy tint in it, his cheeks were hollow, his back long and narrow, and the hand on which his shaggy head was propped was so thin and delicate that it was dreadful to look at it. His hair was already streaked with silver, and seeing his emaciated, aged-looking face, no one would have believed that he was only forty. He was asleep. . . . In front of his bowed head there lay on the table a sheet of paper, on which there was something written in fine handwriting.

"Poor creature!" thought the banker, "he is asleep and most likely dreaming of the millions. And I have only to take this half-dead man, throw him on the bed, stifle him a little with the pillow, and the most conscientious expert would find no sign of a violent death. But let us first read what he has written here. . . ."

The banker took the page from the table and read as follows:

"Tomorrow at twelve o'clock I regain my freedom and the right to associate with other men, but before I leave this room and see the sunshine, I think it necessary to say a few words to you. With a clear conscience I tell you, as before God, who beholds me, that I despise freedom and life and health and all that in your books is called the good things of the world.

"For fifteen years I have been intently studying earthly life. It is true I have not seen the earth or men, but in your books I have drunk fragrant wine, I have sung songs, I have hunted stags and wild boars in the forests, I have loved women. . . . Beauties as ethereal as clouds, created by the magic of your poets and geniuses, have visited me at night and have whispered in my ears wonderful tales that have set my brain in a whirl. In your books I have climbed to the peaks of Elburz and Mont Blanc,[6] and from there I have seen the sun rise and have watched it at evening flood the sky, the ocean, and the mountaintops with gold and crimson. I have watched from there the lightning flashing over my head and cleaving the storm clouds. I have seen green forests, fields, rivers, lakes, towns. I have heard the singing of the sirens,[7] and the strains of the shepherds' pipes; I have touched the wings of comely devils who flew down to converse with me of God. . . . In your books I have flung myself into the bottomless pit, performed miracles, slain, burned towns, preached new religions, conquered whole kingdoms. . . .

"Your books have given me wisdom. All that the unresting thought of man has created in the ages is compressed into a small compass in my brain. I know that I am wiser than all of you.

"And I despise your books, I despise wisdom and the blessings of this world. It is all worthless, fleeting, illusory, and deceptive, like a mirage. You may be proud, wise, and fine, but

6. **Elburz** (el·boorz′) **and Mont Blanc** (mōn blän′): Elburz is a mountain range in northern Iran; Mont Blanc, in France, is the highest mountain in the Alps.
7. **sirens:** in Greek mythology, partly human female creatures who lived on an island and lured sailors to their death with their beautiful singing.

WORDS TO OWN

ethereal (ē·thir′ē·əl) *adj.:* light and delicate; unearthly.
cleaving (klēv′iŋ) *v.* used as *adj.:* splitting.
illusory (i·lo͞o′sə·rē) *adj.:* not real; based on false ideas.

"You have lost your reason and taken the wrong path."

death will wipe you off the face of the earth as though you were no more than mice burrowing under the floor, and your posterity, your history, your immortal geniuses will burn or freeze together with the earthly globe.

"You have lost your reason and taken the wrong path. You have taken lies for truth and hideousness for beauty. You would marvel if, owing to strange events of some sort, frogs and lizards suddenly grew on apple and orange trees instead of fruit or if roses began to smell like a sweating horse; so I marvel at you who exchange heaven for earth. I don't want to understand you.

"To prove to you in action how I despise all that you live by, I renounce the two million of which I once dreamed as of paradise and which now I despise. To deprive myself of the right to the money, I shall go out from here five minutes before the time fixed and so break the compact. . . ."

When the banker had read this, he laid the page on the table, kissed the strange man on the head, and went out of the lodge, weeping. At no other time, even when he had lost heavily on the Stock Exchange, had he felt so great a contempt for himself. When he got home, he lay on his bed, but his tears and emotion kept him for hours from sleeping.

Next morning the watchmen ran in with pale faces and told him they had seen the man who lived in the lodge climb out of the window into the garden, go to the gate, and disappear. The banker went at once with the servants to the lodge and made sure of the flight of his prisoner. To avoid arousing unnecessary talk, he took from the table the writing in which the millions were renounced and, when he got home, locked it up in the fireproof safe.

WORDS TO OWN

posterity (päs·ter′ə·tē) *n.:* descendants or all future generations.

renounce (ri·nouns′) *v.:* give up, especially by formal statement; reject.

The Verandah at Liselund (1916) by Peter Ilsted. Oil on canvas.

Courtesy of Adelson Galleries, New York.

MEET THE WRITER

Master of Ironies

Anton Chekhov (1860–1904) was the grandson of a Russian serf—this means that his grandfather was a farm laborer who could be bought and sold with the land he worked. Eventually Chekhov's grandfather succeeded in purchasing his freedom and raising a family as a free man. Chekhov's father tried to move up the economic ladder by running a general store in a small town in southern Russia, but he did not prosper. The young Anton, trying in his turn to better himself, won a scholarship to medical school. While he was studying in Moscow, his father went bankrupt, and Chekhov had to support his parents, four brothers, and a sister. He managed to do this and stay in school by writing stories and sketches for humor magazines. These short, light pieces, published under an assumed name, earned Chekhov a popular following, a steady income, and an opportunity to develop as a writer. After receiving his medical degree, he practiced medicine for a short time only. He chose to continue writing instead. By the time he was in his thirties, Chekhov was recognized as a serious writer and was wealthy enough to purchase a country estate, an unexpected achievement for the grandson of a serf. In the last years of his short life, knowing he was dying from tuberculosis, Chekhov wrote five full-length plays, all dealing in some way with the theme of loss. Four of them are considered masterpieces of realistic drama: *The Sea Gull, Uncle Vanya, The Three Sisters,* and *The Cherry Orchard.* Chekhov died tragically young, when he was only forty-four years old. The critic V. S. Pritchett says that the stories are Chekhov's life, tunes that his Russia put into his head.

Anton Chekhov and Leo Tolstoy.

Anton Chekhov in Yalta at the beginning of the 1900s.

“ 'What is the meaning of life?' Olga [his wife] once asked in a letter . . . Chekhov replied: 'It is like asking what a carrot is. A carrot is a carrot and nothing more is known.' ”

Anton Chekhov reads his play *The Sea Gull* to the actors of the Art Theater.

Making Meanings

First Thoughts

1. Who do you think won the bet, and what did he win? Compare answers with your classmates.

Shaping Interpretations

2. Imagine you are a psychologist observing the lawyer periodically during his confinement. Write a year-by-year **summary** of how he spends his time and what his emotional state appears to be. Use a **time line.**

Year 1	Year 2
is lonely, depressed reads escapist fiction plays piano refuses wine, tobacco	stops playing piano

3. After making the bet, the banker tells himself that "greed for money" was the lawyer's **motivation** for betting. Do you agree or disagree? Look for evidence in the text to support your view.

4. For fifteen years, the lawyer lives in exile. How does this experience affect him? How do your Quickwrite responses compare with his experience?

5. Looking back, the banker believes he took the bet on "the caprice of a pampered man." How does he feel about himself at the end of the fifteen years? What do you think this reveals about Chekhov's view of what is important in life?

6. Identify what *you* think is the story's most important passage. How would *you* interpret the story's **theme**? Discuss your statement of theme with other readers. Are several thematic focuses possible?

Connecting with the Text

7. At the story's end, would you rather be the banker or the lawyer? Why?

Extending the Text

8. Russian history has been a long and troubled search for freedom. (See the article on page 213.) How do you think the political problems in the last years of the czar's reign might have influenced Chekhov's—and his characters'—ideas on freedom, materialism, and personal sacrifice?

9. Do you believe there is such a thing as "internal freedom"—the kind of freedom the lawyer comes to know in prison? Think of people imprisoned for their beliefs. Are they freer than their jailers? If so, how?

Reading Check

a. Explain the terms of the bet.

b. At the end of fifteen years, what has happened to the banker?

c. After the same period, what has happened to the lawyer?

d. Why does the banker go to the lodge on the last night of the lawyer's captivity?

e. What decision does the lawyer announce in a letter, and why?

CHOICES: Building Your Portfolio

Writer's Notebook

1. Collecting Ideas for Analyzing a Story

Focusing on theme. But what does it all *mean?* In a single sentence, try to express the **theme** of "The Bet" or of another story you've read in Collections 1 to 3. Use the chart below to help you. Remember:

- The theme expresses a general insight about human life or human nature.
- No single statement of theme is "correct."
- A story may have more than one theme.

Save your notes for the Writer's Workshop on page 240.

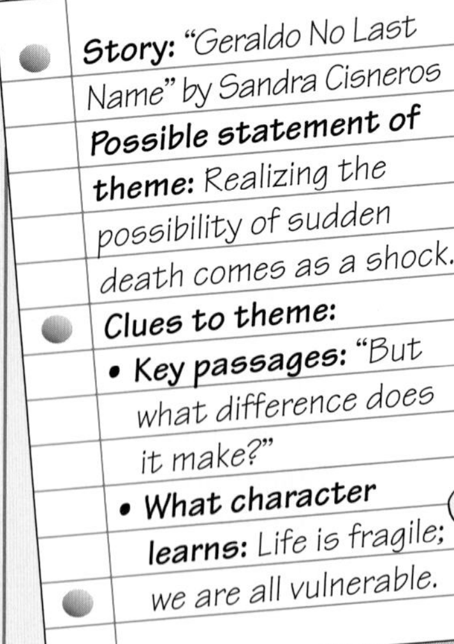

Story: "Geraldo No Last Name" by Sandra Cisneros
Possible statement of theme: Realizing the possibility of sudden death comes as a shock.
Clues to theme:
• **Key passages:** "But what difference does it make?"
• **What character learns:** Life is fragile; we are all vulnerable.

Creative Writing/ Dramatizing

2. Famous First Words

Suppose the fleeing lawyer finds himself at a village inn some distance from the lodge, among a group of strangers. He hasn't spoken to anyone in fifteen years, but he decides to confide his feelings to a stranger. Write a **dialogue** for the lawyer's first conversation as a "free" man. Work with a partner to develop the character of the confidant. How that person reacts to the lawyer will depend on his or her own background and values. Rehearse your **scene,** and present it to your class or group.

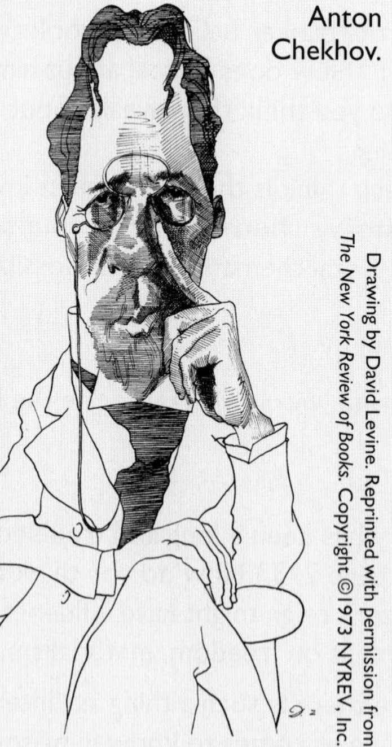
Anton Chekhov.

Reflective Essay

3. Home Alone

Imagine yourself in the lawyer's place: What would you do if you were confined alone for one year? The rules include no human contact, no exit, no TV or radio, no VCR, no phone, no computer. You can ask for books, hobby supplies, musical instruments, and exercise equipment. Write a brief essay, telling how you imagine you'd spend 365 days (the lawyer spent 15 times that) alone. It seems unimaginable, but think about it. How *would* you spend the time?

Speaking and Listening

4. Philosophy of Life

In Chekhov's story, the lawyer's letter to his "jailer" is quite specific about his philosophy of life—what he considers important and unimportant and what freedom means to him. In a small group, read the letter, and then hold a **round-table discussion** of the lawyer's views. Choose a discussion leader who will make sure that all who speak offer reasons and examples to support their views. At the close of the discussion, prepare a **summary** for the class of the group's responses to the lawyer's philosophy.

GRAMMAR LINK MINI-LESSON

Active or Passive? Pick the Right Voice

Language Handbook HELP

See Passive Voice, page 1028.

Technology HELP

See Language Workshop CD-ROM. *Key word entry: voice.*

Verbs that express action can be in the **active** or **passive voice.**

ACTIVE "At supper he made fun of the young man. . . ."
[The action is done *by* the subject, *he*.]

PASSIVE At supper the young man was made fun of.
[The action is done *to* the subject, *the young man*. The doer of the action is not even mentioned.]

In this story, Chekhov usually uses the active voice, but he moves to the passive voice more frequently after the lawyer becomes a prisoner. The passive voice emphasizes the lawyer's decreased ability to act for himself.

"He was allowed to have a musical instrument and books. . . ."

Try It Out

Find a paragraph in which Chekhov uses verbs in the passive voice. Make a list of the subjects and their passive verbs. How could you rephrase each sentence so that it uses an active verb?

A tip for writers: Writers and speakers often use the passive voice to conceal the person who performs the action. You might say "The machine was left on" instead of "Karl left the machine on" to save Karl's feelings or to hide the fact that Karl was responsible.

When you revise your own writing, circle your verbs, and notice the voice of each one. Be sure you use the passive voice only when you have a specific reason to downplay or conceal the doer of the action.

VOCABULARY HOW TO OWN A WORD

WORD BANK

compulsory
caprice
audible
zealously
indiscriminately
ethereal
cleaving
illusory
posterity
renounce

Yes or No?

Be sure that you justify your answers to these questions.

1. If attendance is compulsory, are you free to stay home?
2. Is a caprice something you think about for weeks?
3. Is a herd of elephants usually audible?
4. Are you likely to act zealously when you believe in a cause?
5. If you speak indiscriminately, might you regret it later?
6. Would you call the music that comes from a harp ethereal?
7. If lightning is cleaving the clouds, are the clouds being separated?
8. Can you rely on illusory promises?
9. Do you look to posterity for help with current problems?
10. If you renounce a bad habit, do you intend to stop it?

Before You Read

A Very Old Man with Enormous Wings

Make the Connection

The Strange Visits the Familiar

This story hangs on that intriguing hook of *What if?* What if one day an old man with huge, bug-infested wings dropped out of the sky into your backyard? How would people respond to this "miracle"? How would the "angel" himself feel?

Quickwrite

Brainstorm a list of characters from myth and legend who have wings. What happens to each of those characters? Then brainstorm a list of modern stories or movies in which an alien visits the ordinary world. What usually happens to those strangers visiting a strange land?

Elements of Literature

Magic Realism

Like many contemporary South American writers, García Márquez writes a kind of fiction called **magic realism**. This style of writing is characterized by elements of fantasy (often borrowed from mythology) that are casually inserted into the most earthy, realistic settings. The magic realists often suspend the usual laws of nature. In using this bizarre mixture of the commonplace and the outlandish, the magic realists can force us to think about our fixed notions of "reality" and "normality."

> **Magic realism** is a style of fiction associated with modern Latin American writers, in which fantasy and reality are casually combined, with humorous and thought-provoking results.

Reading Skills and Strategies

Appreciating a Writer's Craft

One of the great pleasures of reading is appreciating how talented writers work—creating captivating images, unforgettable characters, edge-of-your-seat suspense. As you read this story by García Márquez, notice the way he tosses together the offbeat, the homely, and the sublime into that strange mix known as **magic realism.** Notice, too, his startling combinations of images, and be aware of the things they help you to *see.* Try to decide why some of his images seem funny, some sad, and some—appropriately enough—magical.

The illustrations with this story were created by the artist Sergio Bustamante and the photographer Clint Clemens.

A flesh-and-blood angel was held captive in Pelayo's house.

A Very Old Man with Enormous WINGS

Gabriel García Márquez
translated by Gregory Rabassa

A Tale for Children

On the third day of rain they had killed so many crabs inside the house that Pelayo had to

cross his drenched courtyard and throw them into the sea, because the newborn child had a temperature all night and they thought it was due to the stench. The world had been sad since Tuesday. Sea and sky were a single ash-gray thing, and the sands of the beach, which on March nights glimmered like powdered light, had become a stew of mud and rotten shellfish. The light was so weak at noon that when Pelayo was coming back to the house after throwing away the crabs, it was hard for him to see what it was that was moving and groaning in the rear of the courtyard. He had to go very close to see that it was an old man, a very old man, lying face down in the mud, who, in spite of his tremendous efforts, couldn't get up, impeded by his enormous wings.

Frightened by that nightmare, Pelayo ran to get Elisenda, his wife, who was putting compresses on the sick child, and he took her to the rear of the courtyard. They both looked at the fallen body with mute stupor. He was dressed like a ragpicker. There were only a few faded hairs left on his bald skull and very few teeth in his mouth, and his pitiful condition of a drenched great-grandfather had taken away any sense of grandeur he might have had. His huge buzzard wings, dirty and half plucked, were forever entangled in the mud. They looked at him so long and so closely that Pelayo and Elisenda very soon overcame their surprise and in the end found him familiar. Then they dared speak to him, and he answered in an incomprehensible dialect with a strong sailor's voice. That was how they skipped over the inconvenience of the wings and quite intelligently concluded that he was a lonely castaway from some foreign ship wrecked by the storm. And yet, they called in a neighbor woman who knew everything about life and death to see him, and all she needed was one look to show them their mistake.

"He's an angel," she told them. "He must have been coming for the child, but the poor fellow is so old that the rain knocked him down."

On the following day everyone knew that a flesh-and-blood angel was held captive in Pelayo's house. Against the judgment of the wise neighbor woman, for whom angels in those times were the fugitive survivors of a celestial conspiracy,[1] they did not have the heart to club him to death. Pelayo watched over him all afternoon from the kitchen, armed with his bailiff's[2] club, and before going to bed, he dragged him out of the mud and locked him up with the hens in the wire chicken coop. In the middle of the night, when the rain stopped, Pelayo and Elisenda were still killing crabs. A short time afterward the child woke up without a fever and with a desire to eat. Then they felt magnanimous and decided to put the angel on a raft with fresh water and provisions for three days and leave him to his fate on the high seas. But when they went out into the courtyard with the first light of dawn, they found the whole neighborhood in front of the chicken coop having fun with the angel, without the slightest reverence, tossing him things to eat through the openings in the wire as if he weren't a supernatural creature but a circus animal.

Father Gonzaga arrived before seven o'clock, alarmed at the strange news. By that time onlookers less frivolous than those at dawn had already arrived and they were making all kinds of conjectures concerning the captive's future. The simplest among them thought that he should be named mayor of the world. Others of sterner mind felt that he should be promoted to the rank of five-star general in order to win all wars. Some visionaries hoped that he could be

1. **celestial conspiracy:** According to the Book of Revelation in the Bible (12:7–9), Satan originally was an angel who led a rebellion in Heaven. As a result, he and his followers, called the fallen angels, were cast out of Heaven.
2. **bailiff's:** A bailiff is a minor local official.

WORDS TO OWN

stench *n.:* offensive smell.
impeded (im·pēd′id) *v.* used as *adj.:* held back or blocked, as by an obstacle.
magnanimous (mag·nan′ə·məs) *adj.:* generous; noble.
reverence (rev′ər·əns) *n.:* attitude or display of deep respect.
frivolous (friv′ə·ləs) *adj.:* not properly serious; silly. *Frivolous* also means "of little value or importance."

put to stud in order to implant on earth a race of winged wise men who could take charge of the universe. But Father Gonzaga, before becoming a priest, had been a robust woodcutter. Standing by the wire, he reviewed his catechism[3] in an instant and asked them to open the door so that he could take a close look at that pitiful man who looked more like a huge decrepit hen among the fascinated chickens. He was lying in a corner drying his open wings in the sunlight among the fruit peels and breakfast leftovers that the early risers had thrown him. Alien to the impertinences of the world, he only lifted his antiquarian[4] eyes and murmured something in his dialect when Father Gonzaga went into the chicken coop and said good morning to him in Latin. The parish priest had his first suspicion of an impostor when he saw that he did not understand the language of God or know how to greet His ministers. Then he noticed that seen close up, he was much too human: He had an unbearable smell of the outdoors, the back side of his wings was strewn with parasites[5] and his main feathers had been mistreated by terrestrial winds, and nothing about him measured up to the proud dignity of angels. Then he came out of the chicken coop and in a brief sermon warned the curious against the risks of being ingenuous. He reminded them that the devil had the bad habit of making use of carnival tricks in order to confuse the unwary. He argued that if wings were not the essential element in determining the difference between a hawk and an airplane, they were even less so in the recognition of angels. Nevertheless, he promised to write a letter to his bishop so that the latter would write to his primate[6] so that the latter would write to the Supreme Pontiff[7] in order to get the final verdict from the highest courts.

His prudence fell on sterile hearts. The news of the captive angel spread with such rapidity that after a few hours the courtyard had the bustle of a marketplace, and they had to call in troops with fixed bayonets to disperse the mob that was about to knock the house down. Elisenda, her spine all twisted from sweeping up so much marketplace trash, then got the idea of fencing in the yard and charging five cents admission to see the angel.

The curious came from far away. A traveling carnival arrived with a flying acrobat, who buzzed over the crowd several times, but no one paid any attention to him because his wings

3. **catechism** (kat′ə·kiz′əm): book of religious principles consisting of a series of questions and answers.
4. **antiquarian** (an′ti·kwer′ē·ən): ancient.
5. **parasites:** plants or animals that live on or in other living things, on which they feed.
6. **primate** (prī′mit): archbishop or highest-ranking bishop in an area.
7. **Supreme Pontiff:** pope, head of the Roman Catholic Church.

Words to Own

impertinences (im·purt′'n·ən·siz) *n.:* insults; disrespectful acts or remarks.
ingenuous (in·jen′yo͞o·əs) *adj.:* trusting; innocent; tending to believe too readily.
prudence (pro͞od′'ns) *n.:* cautiousness; sound judgment.

were not those of an angel but, rather, those of a sidereal[8] bat. The most unfortunate invalids on earth came in search of health: a poor woman who since childhood had been counting her heartbeats and had run out of numbers; a Portuguese man who couldn't sleep because the noise of the stars disturbed him; a sleepwalker who got up at night to undo the things he had done while awake; and many others with less serious ailments. In the midst of that shipwreck disorder that made the earth tremble, Pelayo and Elisenda were happy with fatigue, for in less than a week they had crammed their rooms with money and the line of pilgrims waiting their turn to enter still reached beyond the horizon.

The angel was the only one who took no part in his own act. He spent his time trying to get comfortable in his borrowed nest, befuddled by the hellish heat of the oil lamps and sacramental candles that had been placed along the wire. At first they tried to make him eat some mothballs, which, according to the wisdom of the wise neighbor woman, were the food prescribed for angels. But he turned them down, just as he turned down the papal[9] lunches that the penitents brought him, and they never found out whether it was because he was an angel or because he was an old man that in the end he ate nothing but eggplant mush. His only supernatural virtue seemed to be patience. Especially during the first days, when the hens pecked at him, searching for stellar parasites that proliferated in his wings, and the cripples pulled out feathers to touch their defective parts with, and even the most merciful threw stones at him, trying to get him to rise so they could see him standing. The only time they succeeded in arousing him was when they burned his side with an iron for branding steers, for he had been motionless for so many hours that they thought he was dead. He awoke with a start, ranting in his hermetic[10] language and with tears in his eyes, and he flapped his wings a couple of times, which brought on a whirlwind of chicken dung and lunar dust and a gale of panic that did not seem to be of this world. Although many thought that his reaction had been one not of rage but of pain, from then on they were careful not to annoy him, because the majority understood that his passivity was not that of a hero taking his ease but that of a cataclysm in repose.

Father Gonzaga held back the crowd's frivolity with formulas of maidservant inspiration while awaiting the arrival of a final judgment on the nature of the captive. But the mail from Rome showed no sense of urgency. They spent their time finding out if the prisoner had a navel, if his dialect had any connection with Aramaic,[11] how many times he could fit on the head of a pin, or whether he wasn't just a Norwegian with wings. Those meager letters might have come and gone until the end of time if a providential event had not put an end to the priest's tribulations.

8. sidereal (sī·dir′ē·əl): of the stars.
9. papal (pā′pəl): here, fit for the pope.

10. hermetic: difficult to understand; mysterious.
11. Aramaic (ar′ə·mā′ik): ancient Middle Eastern language spoken by Jesus and his disciples.

Words to Own

cataclysm (kat′ə·kliz′əm) *n.:* disaster; sudden, violent event.
providential (präv′ə·den′shəl) *adj.:* fortunate; like something caused by a divine act.

It so happened that during those days, among so many other carnival attractions, there arrived in town the traveling show of the woman who had been changed into a spider for having disobeyed her parents. The admission to see her was not only less than the admission to see the angel, but people were permitted to ask her all manner of questions about her absurd state and to examine her up and down so that no one would ever doubt the truth of her horror. She was a frightful tarantula the size of a ram and with the head of a sad maiden. What was most heart-rending, however, was not her outlandish shape but the sincere affliction with which she recounted the details of her misfortune. While still practically a child, she had sneaked out of her parents' house to go to a dance, and while she was coming back through the woods after having danced all night without permission, a fearful thunderclap rent the sky in two and through the crack came the lightning bolt of brimstone[12] that changed her into a spider. Her only nourishment came from the meatballs that charitable souls chose to toss into her mouth. A spectacle like that, full of so much human truth and with such a fearful lesson, was bound to defeat without even trying that of a haughty angel who scarcely deigned to look at mortals. Besides, the few miracles attributed to the angel showed a certain mental disorder, like the blind man who didn't recover his sight but grew three new teeth, or the paralytic who didn't get to walk but almost won the lottery, or the leper whose sores sprouted sunflowers. Those consolation miracles, which were more like mocking fun, had already ruined the angel's reputation when the woman who had been changed into a spider finally crushed him completely. That was how Father Gonzaga was cured forever of his insomnia and Pelayo's courtyard went back to being as empty as during the time it had rained for three days and crabs walked through the bedrooms.

The owners of the house had no reason to lament. With the money they saved they built a two-story mansion with balconies and gardens and high netting so that crabs wouldn't get in during the winter, and with iron bars on the windows so that angels wouldn't get in. Pelayo also set up a rabbit warren close to town and gave up his job as bailiff for good, and Elisenda bought some satin pumps with high heels and many dresses of iridescent silk, the kind worn on Sunday by the most desirable women in those times. The chicken coop was the only thing that didn't receive any attention. If they washed it down with creolin and burned tears of myrrh[13] inside it every so often, it was not in

12. **brimstone:** sulfur, a pale-yellow element that burns with a blue flame and a suffocating odor.

13. **myrrh** (mʉr): sweet-smelling substance used in making perfume.

homage to the angel but to drive away the dungheap stench that still hung everywhere like a ghost and was turning the new house into an old one. At first, when the child learned to walk, they were careful that he not get too close to the chicken coop. But then they began to lose their fears and got used to the smell, and before the child got his second teeth, he'd gone inside the chicken coop to play, where the wires were falling apart. The angel was no less standoffish with him than with other mortals, but he tolerated the most ingenious infamies[14] with the patience of a dog who had no illusions. They both came down with chickenpox at the same time. The doctor who took care of the child couldn't resist the temptation to listen to the angel's heart, and he found so much whistling in the heart and so many sounds in his kidneys that it seemed impossible for him to be alive. What surprised him most, however, was the logic of his wings. They seemed so natural on that completely human organism that he couldn't understand why other men didn't have them too.

When the child began school, it had been some time since the sun and rain had caused the collapse of the chicken coop. The angel went dragging himself about here and there like a stray dying man. They would drive him out of the bedroom with a broom and a moment later find him in the kitchen. He seemed to be in so many places at the same time that they grew to think that he'd been duplicated, that he was reproducing himself all through the house, and the exasperated and unhinged Elisenda shouted that it was awful living in that hell full of angels. He could scarcely eat and his antiquarian eyes had also become so foggy that he went about bumping into posts. All he had left were the bare cannulae[15] of his last feathers. Pelayo threw a blanket over him and extended him the charity of letting him sleep in the shed, and only then did they notice that he had a temperature at night and was delirious with the tongue twisters of an old Norwegian. That was one of the few times they became alarmed, for they thought he was going to die and not even the wise neighbor woman had been able to tell them what to do with dead angels.

And yet he not only survived his worst winter but seemed improved with the first sunny days. He remained motionless for several days in the farthest corner of the courtyard,

14. **infamies:** here, disrespectful acts; insults.

15. **cannulae** (kan′yo͞o·lē′): tubes.

where no one would see him, and at the beginning of December some large, stiff feathers began to grow on his wings, the feathers of a scarecrow, which looked more like another misfortune of decrepitude. But he must have known the reason for those changes, for he was quite careful that no one should notice them, that no one should hear the sea chanteys[16] that he sometimes sang under the stars. One morning Elisenda was cutting some bunches of onions for lunch when a wind that seemed to come from the high seas blew into the kitchen. Then she went to the window and caught the angel in his first attempts at flight. They were so clumsy that his fingernails opened a furrow in the vegetable patch and he was on the point of knocking the shed down with the ungainly flapping that slipped on the light and couldn't get a grip on the air. But he did manage to gain altitude. Elisenda let out a sigh of relief, for herself and for him, when she saw him pass over the last houses, holding himself up in some way with the risky flapping of a senile vulture. She kept watching him even when she was through cutting the onions and she kept on watching until it was no longer possible for her to see him, because then he was no longer an annoyance in her life but an imaginary dot on the horizon of the sea.

16. **chanteys** (shan′tēz): songs sung by sailors to set a rhythm for their work.

Meet the Writer

Memory's Magician

Gabriel García Márquez (1928–   ) sets much of his fiction in the imaginary town of Macondo, which in many ways resembles the sleepy, decaying, backwater town of Aracataca, Colombia, where he was born. Because his parents were poor, young Gabriel was raised by his maternal grandparents, in a large old house crowded with relatives and relics of the family's past. His grandmother told him tales of ancestors, spirits, and ghosts; and his grandfather, a retired colonel (whom García Márquez has called "the most important figure of my life"), spoke continually of a past so vivid that it became as real to the young boy as the present.

After studying law and working abroad as a journalist for many years, García Márquez became an international celebrity with the publication of his novel *One Hundred Years of Solitude* (1967). This epic masterpiece tells the comic and tragic saga of seven generations of Macondo's founding family. The Chilean poet Pablo Neruda called the novel "the greatest revelation in the Spanish language since *Don Quixote*." García Márquez won the Nobel Prize for literature in 1982.

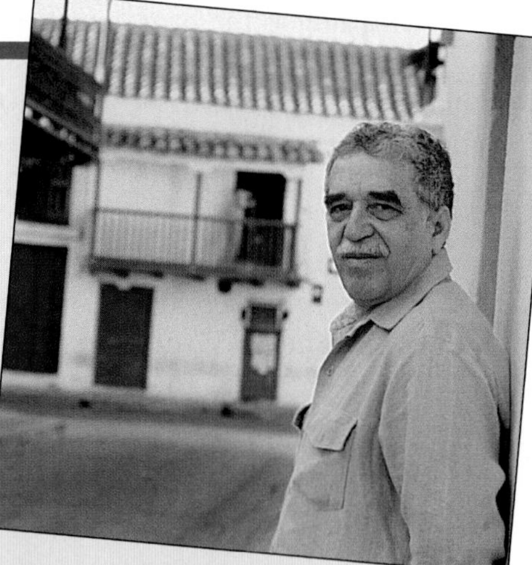

He says this about writing when you are young:

"When you are young, you write almost—well, every writer is different, I'm talking about myself—almost like writing a poem. You write on impulses and inspiration. You have so much inspiration that you are not concerned with technique. You just see what comes out, without worrying much about what you are going to say and how. On the other hand, later, you know exactly what you are going to say and what you want to say. And you have a lot to tell. Even if all of your life you continue to tell about your childhood, later you are better able to interpret it, or at least interpret it in a different way."

Connections A POEM

Like Gabriel García Márquez, Jack Agüeros transforms ordinary realities with a touch of fantasy. In this poem he presents a startling vision of the homeless people who use the subways of New York City for shelter. Agüeros roots his images in the everyday through realistic details—references to Calcutta, a city in India where hundreds of thousands live on the streets, and the Gowanus Canal, a polluted body of water in Brooklyn, New York. But he also includes an ***allusion*** *to Macondo, an imaginary village that is the setting for much of García Márquez's fiction.*

Sonnet for Heaven Below

Jack Agüeros

No, it wasn't Macondo, and it wasn't Calcutta in time past.
But subway magic turned the tunnels into Beautyrest mattresses
And plenty of God's children started sleeping there. Some
Were actually Angels fatigued from long hours and no pay.

This is an aside, but I have to alert you. Angels run
Around, don't shave or bathe; acid rain fractures their
Feathers, and french fries and coca cola corrupt
The color of their skin and make them sing hoarsely.
The gossamer shoes so perfect for kicking clouds
Stain and tear on the concrete and in the hard light
Of the city they start to look like abandoned barges
Foundering in the cancerous waters of the Gowanus Canal.

Shabby gossamer shoes always arouse the derision of smart New Yorkers.
Mercifully, Angels aren't tourists, so they are spared total disdain.

MAKING MEANINGS

Reading Check

a. The townspeople draw various conclusions about who, or rather what, the winged old man is. What do Pelayo and Elisenda think he is? What does their know-it-all neighbor think? and Father Gonzaga?

b. How does the old man change the lives of Pelayo and Elisenda?

c. What miracles are attributed to the old man?

d. What happens when a new novelty, the spider-woman, comes to town?

First Thoughts

1. What is the first question you'd like to ask García Márquez? What is your second question?

Shaping Interpretations

2. If an angel did come to Earth, what would you expect it to look like? How is this old man **ironically** unlike an angel?

3. What human shortcomings might García Márquez be **satirizing** in this story? Consider:

- How do Pelayo and Elisenda treat the old man?
- Why does Father Gonzaga suspect the old man is not an angel?
- How do people react to the "spectacles" of the angel and the spider-woman?

4. What details in this story are examples of **magic realism**? Which of García Márquez's **images** did you find most startling and memorable?

5. Do you think the old man is a divine figure or an evil one? Are there any other explanations for his identity? Did he fall into our world from the world of myth, or is he an alien from another universe that is full of winged persons? (Check your Quickwrite notes.)

6. Do you think this story is intended merely to amuse and astonish us, or does it mean something deeper? Consider:

- Does the old man **symbolize** the miracles we wish for but are unable to accept when they happen?
- Does the old man **symbolize** the artist, who is often mocked and misunderstood by other people and whose imagination longs to soar?

Connecting with the Text

7. Great literature, whether realistic or fantastic, connects to our hearts, imaginations, or minds. Did this story connect with you at all? Elaborate.

Extending the Text

8. How are the "angels" described in "Sonnet for Heaven Below" (see ***Connections*** on page 231) similar to the very old man with enormous wings? Do "smart New Yorkers" treat these angels the way the townspeople in the story treat the old man?

9. How do you suppose people in your community would act if an angel or another alien or being fell into someone's backyard?

CHOICES: Building Your Portfolio

Writer's Notebook

1. Collecting Ideas for Analyzing a Story

Focusing on setting. García Márquez writes fantasy, but he is also very earthy. Look back at the first paragraph, and list the details that help you see, touch, smell, and hear his rainy **setting.** Collect notes about the setting of Márquez's story or another story in this book. Comb through your story carefully to find all the details you can about setting. Is the setting crucial to the action—could the story happen anyplace else? Save your notes for the Writer's Workshop assignment on page 240.

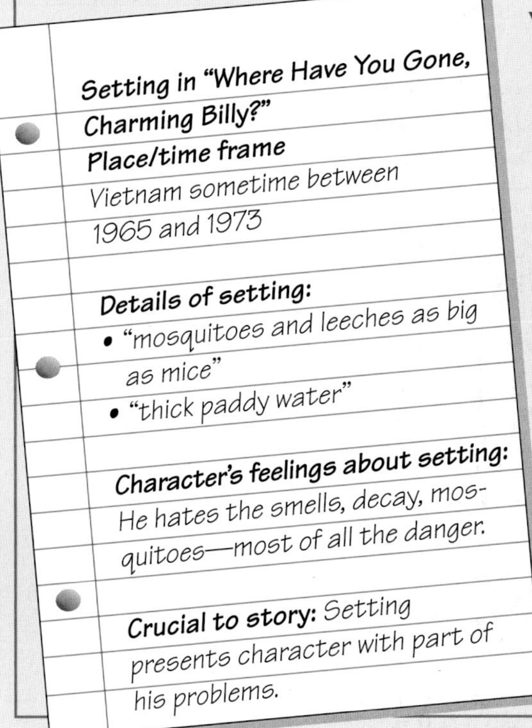

Setting in "Where Have You Gone, Charming Billy?"

Place/time frame

Vietnam sometime between 1965 and 1973

Details of setting:

- *"mosquitoes and leeches as big as mice"*
- *"thick paddy water"*

Character's feelings about setting: *He hates the smells, decay, mosquitoes—most of all the danger.*

Crucial to story: *Setting presents character with part of his problems.*

Creative Writing

2. The Angel Talks

The old man talks, but the townspeople do not understand his language. What do you imagine is going through the old man's mind as he patiently endures the indignities of the chicken coop? Write a **letter** to Pelayo and Elisenda that the old man might have written just before flying away. Include details about his true home, the reason he strayed into the yard, how human life looked from his perspective, and where he is heading now. Write in the first person, using *I.*

Viewing/ Critical Writing

3. What Do You See?

Look carefully at the illustrations that accompany this story. How appropriate do you think they are? What do you see happening in each illustration? Write a brief essay in which you describe these illustrations and evaluate their use for this story. How did you respond to them?

Creative Writing

4. Be a Magic Realist

Perhaps the old man in the story is Daedalus, the craftsman in Greek mythology who made himself wings to escape from prison. Write a **fantastic story** of your own about another person from folklore, mythology, or popular culture who falls into the actual world. You might consider these possibilities:

- Hercules, the strongest teenager in the world, enrolls at your school.
- A fairy godmother visits a poor girl in New York City.
- King Arthur is elected president.
- A dragon asks to be admitted to the zoo.

Art

5. A Different Angel

All kinds of angels have become popular lately, but García Márquez's angel is different. Make a **drawing** or **sculpture** or **collage** of this old man with enormous wings. Follow the description of his appearance in the story, but also feel free to add details of your own. Arrange a class display of your angel illustrations, perhaps using lines from the story as **captions.**

LANGUAGE LINK MINI-LESSON

Come to Your Senses: Images of a Magic Realist

Handbook of Literary Terms HELP

See Imagery.

Imagery is language that appeals directly to the senses and the imagination. Most images are visual—that is, they appeal to our sense of sight—but images may also appeal to our senses of sound, smell, touch, and taste. In addition to sensory appeal, García Márquez's imagery frequently has another interesting quality: It brings together experiences or details that are usually separate or in opposition.

1. ". . . the sands of the beach, which on March nights glimmered like powdered light, had become a stew of mud and rotten shellfish."
2. ". . . hens pecked at him, searching for stellar parasites that proliferated in his wings. . . ."
3. ". . . a whirlwind of chicken dung and lunar dust . . ."
4. ". . . the few miracles attributed to the angel showed a certain mental disorder, like the blind man who didn't recover his sight but grew three new teeth. . . ."
5. ". . . whose sores sprouted sunflowers."

Try It Out

Examine the passages quoted opposite and García Márquez's unusual images:

1. To which senses do the images appeal?
2. Where do you find opposing images or experiences?
3. Look back at the story, and find three other examples of García Márquez's imagery that you think are especially unusual or funny or unexpected.

A tip for writers: Be aware of the world around you. Add descriptive observations to your notebook from time to time so that you build up a kind of image bank.

VOCABULARY HOW TO OWN A WORD

WORD BANK

stench
impeded
magnanimous
reverence
frivolous
impertinences
ingenuous
prudence
cataclysm
providential

Roots and Relations

Using a dictionary, find the **root** and **part of speech** of each word in the Word Bank. Then, look for **related forms** and their parts of speech. (Some of the words have many related forms; one word has none.) Note that adding or changing a **suffix** often changes a word's part of speech. Summarize your findings in a graphic like the one below for the word *impeded.*

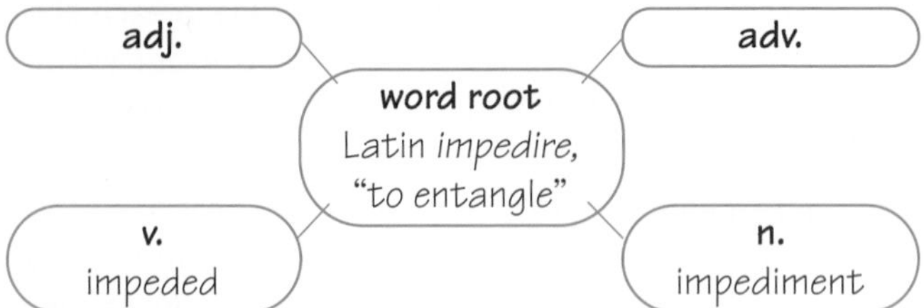

Quickwrite

Think of a time when you had to go through an experience that you feared, but you thought you absolutely had to avoid showing your fear. Write a few notes about how you felt about the experience later.

go.hrw.com
LEO 10-3

EXTENDING *the theme*

A PERSONAL ESSAY

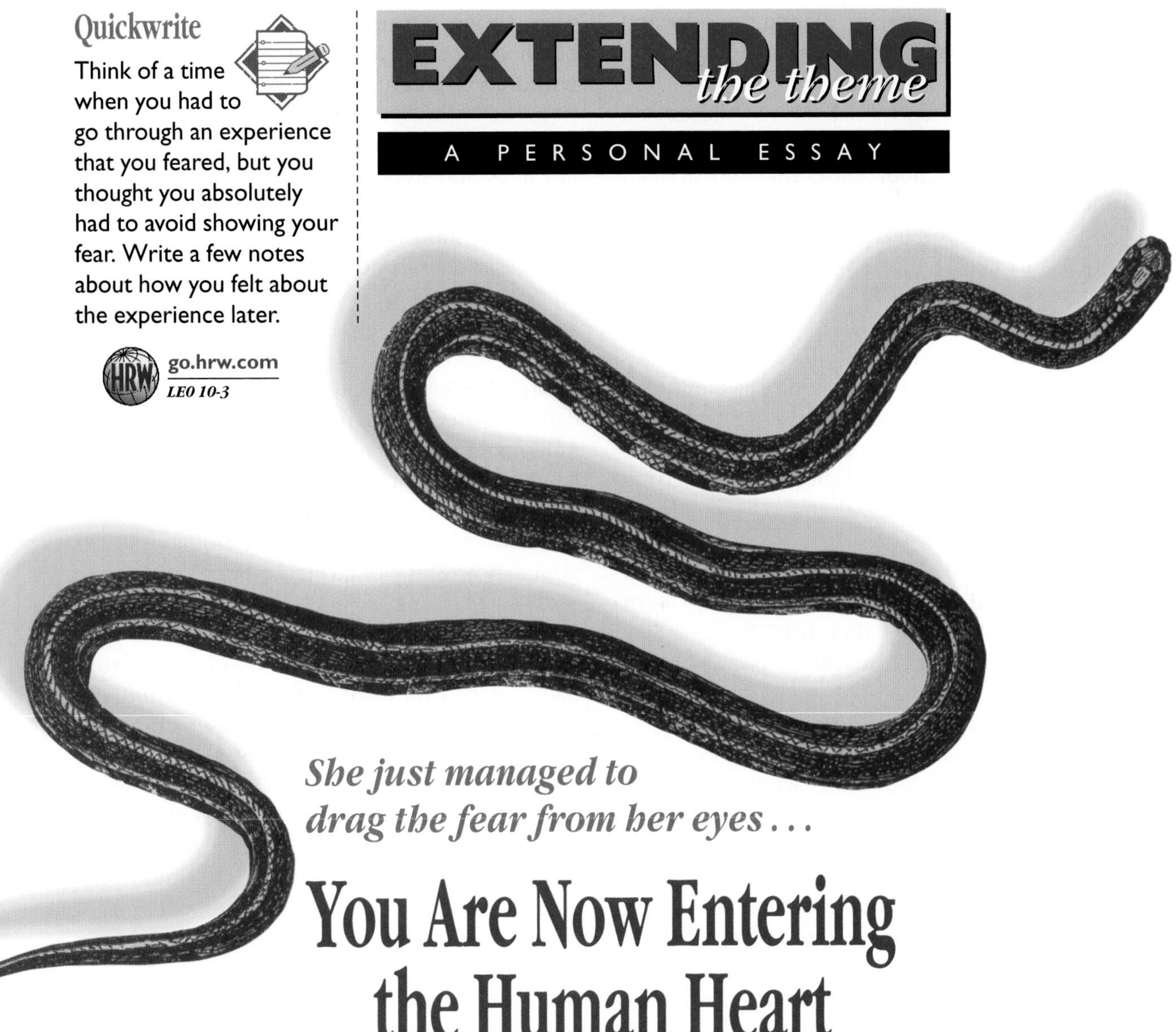

She just managed to drag the fear from her eyes . . .

You Are Now Entering the Human Heart

Janet Frame

I looked at the notice. I wondered if I had time before my train left Philadelphia for Baltimore in one hour. The heart, ceiling high, occupied one corner of the large exhibition hall, and from wherever you stood in the hall, you could hear it beating, *thum-thump-thum-thump*. It was a popular exhibit, and sometimes, when there were too many children about, the entrance had to be roped off, as the children loved to race up and down the blood vessels and match their cries to the heart's beating. I could see that the heart had already been punished for the day—the floor of the blood vessel was worn and dusty, the chamber walls were covered with marks, and the notice "You Are Now Taking the Path of a Blood Cell Through the Human Heart" hung askew. I wanted to see more of the Franklin Institute and the Natural Science Museum across the street, but a journey through the human heart would be fascinating. Did I have time?

Later. First, I would go across the street to

the Hall of North America, among the bear and the bison, and catch up on American flora and fauna.°

I made my way to the Hall. More children, sitting in rows on canvas chairs. An elementary class from a city school, under the control of an elderly teacher. A museum attendant holding a basket, and all eyes gazing at the basket.

"Oh," I said. "Is this a private lesson? Is it all right for me to be here?"

The attendant was brisk. "Surely. We're having a lesson in snake handling," he said. "It's something new. Get the children young and teach them that every snake they meet is not to be killed. People seem to think that every snake has to be knocked on the head. So we're getting them young and teaching them."

"May I watch?" I said.

"Surely. This is a common grass snake. No harm, no harm at all. Teach the children to learn the feel of them, to lose their fear."

He turned to the teacher. "Now, Miss—Mrs.——" he said.

"Miss Aitcheson."

He lowered his voice. "The best way to get through to the children is to start with teacher," he said to Miss Aitcheson. "If they see you're not afraid, then they won't be."

She must be near retiring age, I thought. A city woman. Never handled a snake in her life. Her face was pale. She just managed to drag the fear from her eyes to some place in their depths, where it lurked like a dark stain. Surely the attendant and the children noticed?

"It's harmless," the attendant said. He'd worked with snakes for years.

Miss Aitcheson, I thought again. A city woman born and bred. All snakes were creatures to kill, to be protected from, alike the rattler, the copperhead, king snake, grass snake—venom and victims. Were there not places in the South where you couldn't go into the streets for fear of the rattlesnakes?

Her eyes faced the lighted exit. I saw her fear. The exit light blinked, hooded. The children, none of whom had ever touched a live snake, were sitting hushed, waiting for the drama to begin; one or two looked afraid as the attendant withdrew a green snake about three feet long from the basket and with a swift movement, before the teacher could protest, draped it around her neck and stepped back, admiring and satisfied.

"There," he said to the class. "Your teacher has a snake around her neck and she's not afraid."

Miss Aitcheson stood rigid; she seemed to be holding her breath.

"Teacher's not afraid, are you?" the attendant persisted. He leaned forward, pronouncing judgment on her, while she suddenly jerked her head and lifted her hands in panic to get rid of the snake. Then, seeing the children watching her, she whispered, "No, I'm not afraid. Of course not." She looked around her.

"Of course not," she repeated sharply.

I could see her defeat and helplessness. The attendant seemed unaware, as if his perception had grown a reptilian covering. What did she care for the campaign for the preservation and welfare of copperheads and rattlers and common grass snakes? What did she care about someday walking through the woods or the desert and deciding between killing a snake and setting it free, as if there would be time to decide, when her journey to and from school in downtown Philadelphia held enough danger to occupy her? In two years or so, she'd retire and be in that apartment by herself and no doorman, and everyone knew what happened then, and how she'd be afraid to answer the door and to walk after dark and carry her pocketbook in the street. There was enough to think about without learning to handle and love the snakes, harmless and otherwise, by having them draped around her neck for everyone, including the children—most of all the children—to witness the outbreak of her fear.

"See, Miss Aitcheson's touching the snake. She's not afraid of it at all."

As everyone watched, she touched the snake. Her fingers recoiled. She touched it again.

"See, she's not afraid. Miss Aitcheson can

° **flora and fauna:** plants and animals.

stand there with a beautiful snake around her neck and touch it and stroke it and not be afraid."

The faces of the children were full of admiration for the teacher's bravery, and yet there was a cruelly persistent tension; they were waiting, waiting.

"We have to learn to love snakes," the attendant said. "Would someone like to come out and stroke teacher's snake?"

Silence.

One shamefaced boy came forward. He stood petrified in front of the teacher.

"Touch it," the attendant urged. "It's a friendly snake. Teacher's wearing it around her neck and she's not afraid."

The boy darted his hand forward, resting it lightly on the snake, and immediately withdrew his hand. Then he ran to his seat. The children shrieked with glee.

"He's afraid," someone said. "He's afraid of the snake."

The attendant soothed. "We have to get used to them, you know. Grown-ups are not afraid of them, but we can understand that when you're small, you might be afraid, and that's why we want you to learn to love them. Isn't that right, Miss Aitcheson? Isn't that right? Now, who else is going to be brave enough to touch teacher's snake?"

Two girls came out. They stood hand in hand side by side and stared at the snake and then at Miss Aitcheson.

I wondered when the torture would end. The two little girls did not touch the snake, but they smiled at it and spoke to it, and Miss Aitcheson smiled at them and whispered how brave they were.

"Just a minute," the attendant said. "There's really no need to be brave. It's not a question of bravery. The snake is absolutely *harmless*. Where's the bravery when the snake is harmless?"

Suddenly the snake moved around to face Miss Aitcheson and thrust its flat head toward her cheek. She gave a scream, flung up her hands, and tore the snake from her throat and threw it on the floor, and, rushing across the room, she collapsed into a chair beside the Bear Cabinet.

I didn't feel I should watch any longer. Some of the children began to laugh, some to cry. The attendant picked up the snake and nursed it. Miss Aitcheson, recovering, sat helplessly exposed by the small piece of useless torture. It was not her fault she was city bred, her eyes tried to tell us. She looked at the children, trying in some way to force their admiration and respect; they were shut against her. She was evicted from them and from herself and even from her own fear-infested tomorrow, because she could not promise to love and preserve what she feared. She had nowhere, at that moment, but the small canvas chair by the Bear Cabinet of the Natural Science Museum.

I looked at my watch. If I hurried, I would catch the train from Thirtieth Street. There would be no time to make the journey through the human heart. I hurried out of the museum. It was freezing cold. The icebreakers would be at work on the Delaware and the Susquehanna; the mist would have risen by the time I arrived home. Yes, I would just catch the train from Thirtieth Street. The journey through the human heart would have to wait until some other time.

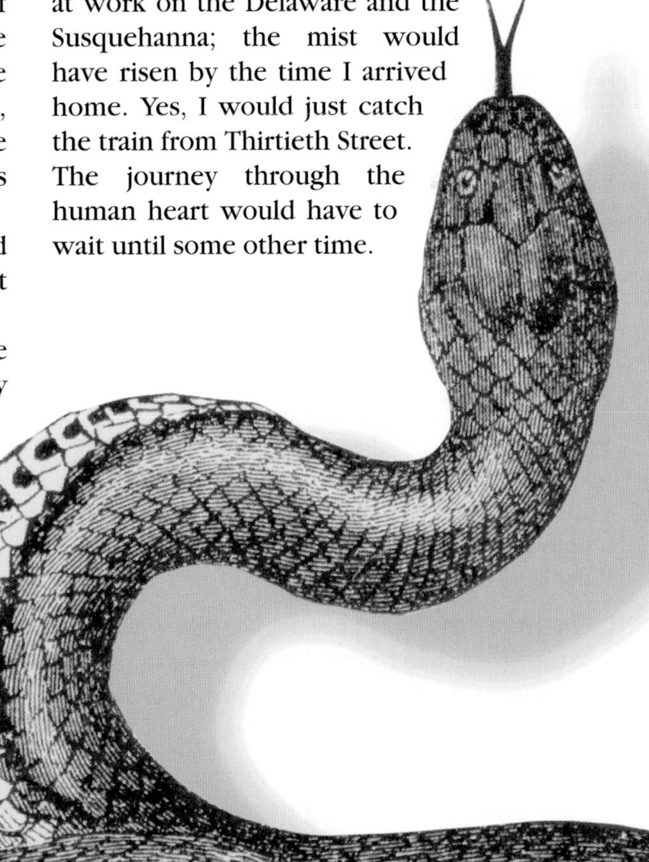

Meet the Writer

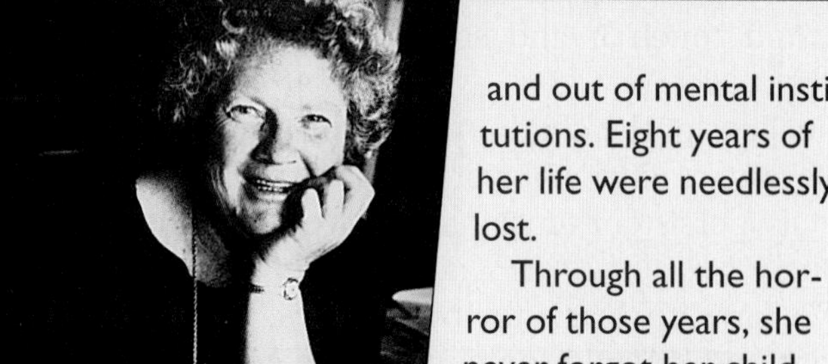

Shy

Janet Frame (1924–   ) was raised in the little town of Oamaru, New Zealand, and as a young woman she trained for a career as a teacher. Her life story, told in three volumes—*To the Island* (1982), *An Angel at My Table* (1984), and *The Envoy from Mirror City* (1985)—reads like a horror story. (Her autobiography was made into the movie *An Angel at My Table* in 1990.) Extremely shy as a child, Frame lived for a time with her aunt and her dying uncle in a cottage where there was not enough space, food, or heat. Her two beloved sisters accidentally drowned. Though she "delighted in the children at school and in teaching," Frame was so shy that she could not face the inspection needed to earn her teaching certificate.

When she sought help for her painful timidity, Frame became the victim of a devastating mistaken diagnosis. She was labeled "schizophrenic" and shipped off to a psychiatric ward. For the next eight years she was in and out of mental institutions. Eight years of her life were needlessly lost.

Through all the horror of those years, she never forgot her childhood dream to be recognized "as a true poet." When a New Zealand writer offered her an army hut in which to live and write, she accepted and began her first novel. Eventually, doctors concluded that Frame was not mentally ill; what's more, she never had been.

Though she still lives in New Zealand, Frame has traveled in America and worked at two famous writers' retreats, the Yaddo Foundation and the MacDowell Colony. "You Are Now Entering the Human Heart," an essay about an experience she had in Philadelphia, first appeared in *The New Yorker* magazine.

At last Janet Frame has realized her dream: The shy young woman who spent eight years cruelly shut away is now New Zealand's preeminent writer.

Finding Common Ground 

"You Are Now Entering the Human Heart" is an essay, a piece of personal writing in which the writer explores a subject and reflects on what it means. Essays can begin in many ways. Some writers get their ideas from questions: Why are people sometimes so cruel? What did the death of my little calf mean to me? What is friendship?

1. This essay explores how people deal with fear. If the writer had begun this essay with a question, what do you think that question would have been?
2. Write down the question, and then jot down your reasons for thinking that it could have been the starting point for the essay.
3. Check your Quickwrite notes. Do they raise other questions about how people deal with fear?
4. The writer, of course, didn't write her essay so that it could fit into this book in a collection called "Exiles, Castaways, and Strangers." Jot down your response to these questions: Does this essay fit here? Why, or why not?
5. In class, talk over all your questions, their answers, and your feelings about the essay's fit in this collection. After your discussion, think again about your own responses: Did the discussion add anything to your understanding of the essay?

The Other Side of the Mirror

Lewis Carroll's *Alice in Wonderland* presents *Alice's Adventures in Wonderland* and *Through the Looking-Glass.* Young Alice literally falls into another world and finds herself at times out of her depth with talking cats, flamingoes, and mad royalty. Available in many editions, these tales are presented with explanations in *The Annotated Alice* (Clarkson N. Potter), with an introduction and notes by Martin Gardner.

On a Desert Island with Uh-Oh . . .

Schoolboys find themselves on an island that has no grown-ups. Such freedom seems ideal . . . until the boys find that, even without the grown-ups who seem to cause so much trouble, they are perfectly capable of reinventing trouble—they don't even need models. William Golding's novel *Lord of the Flies* begins as an adventure story and explodes into a parable about the human conscience.

Don't Open That Door!

Charlotte Brontë's *Jane Eyre* has all the elements of a great adventure story—an orphan banished to a grim boarding school, a mysterious estate ruled by a more mysterious owner, a desperate cross-country journey, and a locked room that contains a dreadful secret. Try the book (available in the HRW Library) or the 1996 movie (starring William Hurt).

Troubled Teens in the '60s

The Outsiders, Francis Ford Coppola's 1983 movie version of S. E. Hinton's best-selling novel (1967), is set in Oklahoma during the 1960s. Hinton was only 16 when she began writing her novel about troubled teenagers. Howell, the narrator, likes poetry and *Gone with the Wind* but gets caught up in violence and gang rivalry. Tom Cruise, Matt Dillon, and Patrick Swayze star in the movie; S. E. Hinton, the author, appears briefly as a nurse.

Writer's Workshop

Technology HELP

See Writer's Workshop 2 CD-ROM. *Assignment: Interpretation.*

ASSIGNMENT

Write an essay analyzing one of the short stories in this book or another story of your choice.

AIM

To think critically; to inform.

AUDIENCE

Your teacher and your classmates.

EXPOSITORY WRITING

ANALYZING A STORY

You can often find out how a device like an old clock or a small motor works by taking it apart and seeing how it's put together. When you **analyze** a work of literature, you examine its literary elements and try to figure out how they interact to create meaning. In this workshop, you'll write an essay analyzing one of the stories you've read. You'll focus on three or four elements—such as **plot, character, setting, tone,** or **theme**—and discuss how they work together to create the story's meaning.

Prewriting

1. Choose a Story

WORK IN PROGRESS

Look through your Writer's Notebook for notes you've made on stories in this collection and in the first two collections. Choose a story that you feel strongly about —one you either love or hate. Is there one that stands out in your memory, maybe because it surprised you or touched your emotions or challenged your thinking?

2. Do a Close Reading

Reread your story two or three times, and take notes (perhaps in the form of a chart). You need to do two things: focus on the important literary elements and step back to look at the story as a whole. Think about these questions as you read:

- **Plot.** What **conflict** sets the plot in motion? Is it external or internal or both? Is the plot suspenseful? Does the writer use **foreshadowing** to hint at what will happen? What is the story's **climax**? Is the **resolution** satisfying? Is it **ambiguous** (open to more than one interpretation)?
- **Character.** Who are the story's main characters, and how does the writer reveal their natures? Who is the **protagonist**? What **motivates** these characters? Do they change, and if so, how? What do they learn during the story? Are their actions, motives, changes, and discoveries believable?

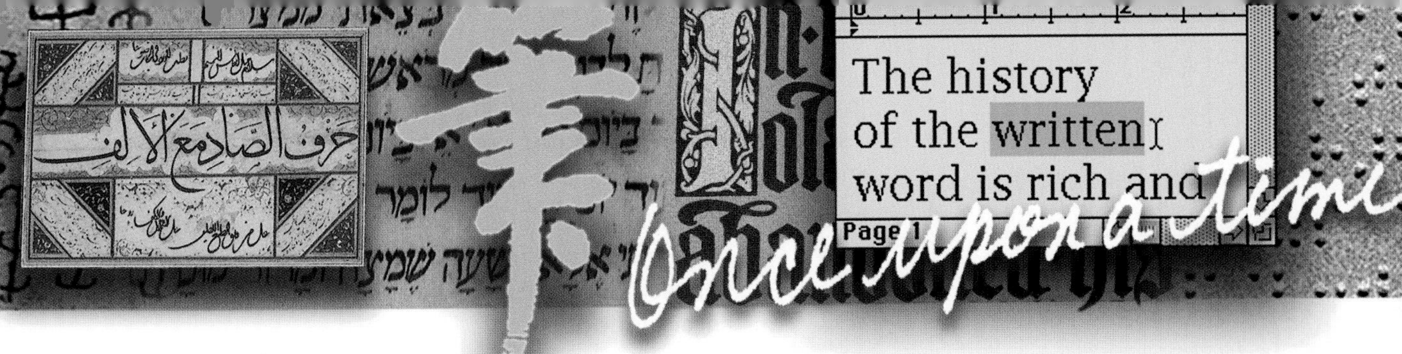
The history
of the written
word is rich and
Page 1
Once upon a time

- **Setting.** Where and when does the story take place? Does the setting reveal anything about the characters? Is it central to the conflict (as in "Trap of Gold," p. 249)? Does it evoke a **mood,** or **atmosphere**?
- **Tone.** How would you describe the writer's attitude, and how is it revealed? Does **irony** or **satire** play an important role in the story?
- **Theme.** What central insight into life or human nature does the story reveal? Is the theme stated **directly,** or do you have to piece together clues to find the story's meaning? What do you think of the theme? Do you agree with it? Is it important? overused? **ambiguous**?

"Two Kinds" by Amy Tan (page 95)		
Element	Examples	Importance in Story
Plot/ conflict	External conflict: mother wants Jing-mei to be a prodigy; Jing-mei fails, then rebels.	Crucial to story's theme.
Character	Jing-mei: strong-willed, angry; wants her mother's approval; sees her mother differently at the end.	Character of Jing-mei is well developed (we know her thoughts & feelings); so is that of her mother. Characters very memorable and believable.
Setting	Chinatown, somewhere in U.S.	Cultural conflict important to theme. But not Chinatown itself.
Theme	Universal: Love between mother and daughter goes beyond their differences and conflicts.	Most important.

Try It Out

With a partner, try filling in one or two rows of a chart of literary elements. Here are some ideas:

1. Make a character row for "Everyday Use" (page 70) or "Distillation" (page 133).
2. Make a theme row for "Boys and Girls" (page 53) or "Liberty" (page 185).

3. State Your Main Ideas

Look over your notes, and decide which elements play the biggest role in revealing the story's meaning. Try to state your

Language/Grammar Link HELP

Connotations: page 181.
Pronoun reference: page 193.
Imagery: pages 208 and 234.
Active and passive verbs: page 221.

Sentence Workshop HELP

Combining sentences: page 245.

Patterns of Organization

- In your essay as a whole (and in a paragraph about theme or character), you might organize your ideas in **order of importance** (from most to least important or vice versa).
- In a paragraph summarizing the plot, it makes more sense to use **chronological order** (the order in which events occur).
- In a paragraph about setting, you might use **spatial order** (in which objects are described from left to right, near to far, and so on).

main idea about each element in one or two sentences; you'll use these later to write **topic sentences**. Here is the Student Model writer's main idea about Jing-mei's **character:**

MAIN IDEA: Jing-mei is not a quiet, obedient daughter, but rather a strong-willed and frustrated child. She is caught between her mother's expectations and a growing anger inside herself.

Now, try drafting a **thesis statement** that sums up your ideas about your story. (You may need to make several drafts before you settle on a wording.) Here is the student writer's thesis statement:

THESIS STATEMENT: "Two Kinds" by Amy Tan gives insight into the relationship between a Chinese mother and her Chinese American daughter.

4. Elaborate: Back It Up

Don't worry if your analysis of a story differs from a classmate's; there is no one correct analysis of any story. Just be sure to back up your statements with specific details and examples from the story. Here are some types of supporting evidence you can use to **elaborate** on your topic sentences:

- references to specific events in the story
- descriptions of character traits with details to support them
- details describing the setting
- quotations from the story (not too many, though, so that your essay won't sound choppy)
- comparisons with other stories

Drafting

1. Start Writing

You've got notes, topic sentences, and a thesis statement—everything you need in order to begin writing. Now, start supporting each topic sentence with evidence. In your **introduction,** identify the title and author of your story and present your **thesis statement.** In the **body,** elaborate on three or four main ideas. In your **conclusion,** restate the thesis and perhaps add a final comment. You may want to begin by drafting your introduction, or you may prefer to begin with the body.

2. Don't Summarize—Analyze!

As you write, make sure you are truly *analyzing* the story. Don't just summarize the plot, string together quotations, and present your immediate reactions to the story. Your purpose is to reveal a level of meaning your readers may have missed. Assume that they've read the story—but not as closely as you have.

Student Model

"Two Kinds" by Amy Tan

"Two Kinds" by Amy Tan gives insight into the relationship between a Chinese mother and her Chinese American daughter. Jing-mei, the narrator and main character, now grown, is recalling childhood memories of her mother after her mother's death. As a child, Jing-mei is constantly pushed by her mother to be a prodigy. Tired of not being accepted for her true self, Jing-mei rebels by not even trying at anything anymore. The story's resounding theme is that the love between mother and daughter goes beyond their differences and problems.

Thesis statement.

Statement of the story's theme.

Because the story is told by Jing-mei, we know her thoughts and feelings. She is not a quiet, obedient daughter, but rather a strong-willed and frustrated child. She is caught between the pressure, on the one hand, of her mother's expectations and her own hopes of being something great and, on the other hand, a growing anger inside that multiplies with each new failure. One day, when looking in the mirror, Jing-mei discovers that "the girl staring back at me was angry, powerful. This girl and I were the same." That is when she decides never to let her mother change her, and she constantly attempts to fail. Thus begins the conflict between the two.

Topic sentence.

Character and motivation.

Quotation from the text.

Conflict.

Throughout the story, the mother finds new ways of testing Jing-mei through different talents she has discovered in magazines; and, of course, Jing-mei never succeeds. Finally, when her mother has almost given up all hope, she sees a young Chinese girl playing the piano on the Ed Sullivan Show. She works out a way for Jing-mei to get lessons, but the girl tries her best not to learn anything.

References to events in the story.

At the end of the story, Jing-mei is looking through her mother's things after her mother's death. She keeps the sweaters her mother made that she hated to wear and gets the piano tuned just for reminiscing. This shows how much she loved her mother, despite the fact that they could never see eye to eye. These actions all portray the story's theme of family ties: that the love between a mother and daughter cannot be spoiled by their differences.

Resolution reinforces theme.

I think this story teaches people not to take for granted those that they love. The relationship between Jing-mei and her mother is parallel to many mother-daughter relationships everywhere. The author's powerful writing and well-developed characters allow us to learn a lot from the events in the story.

Personal response to story and restatement of thesis.

—Elisabeth Kristof
Austin High School
Austin, Texas

Evaluating and Revising

1. Self-Evaluation

Reread your draft to make sure that questions and references to the story fit smoothly into your sentences. Pay particular attention to the flow of ideas. You may need to add transitional words or phrases (such as *first, second, finally, in addition, although,* or *as a result*) to signal where you're going and to show how your ideas are related. If your writing sounds choppy, consider combining sentences or paraphrasing some of your quotations.

2. Peer Review

Exchange drafts with a partner, and give him or her suggestions for revision. Focus on the evaluation criteria at the left, but also point out unnecessary or overused words, irrelevant or unconvincing evidence, and confusing or awkward transitions. Be sure to give your partner positive feedback as well.

■ ***Evaluation Criteria***

A good analysis of a story

1. *gives the story's title and author and presents a thesis statement in the introduction*
2. *discusses three or four literary elements*
3. *provides evidence (such as quotations and details from the text) to support main ideas*
4. *includes transitional expressions*
5. *concludes by restating the thesis*

Revision Model

	Peer Comments
At the end of the story, ^Jing-mei is looking through her	*When is this happening?*
mother's things^ [after her mother's death]. She keeps the	
sweaters her mother made that she	
hated to wear^ [and gets the piano tuned just for reminiscing]. This shows how much	*Mention other actions.*
she loved her mother, despite the	
fact that they could never see eye to	
eye. These actions all portray the	
story's theme of family ties: ^[that] the love	*You need to state the theme more fully.*
between a mother and daughter^ [cannot be spoiled by their differences].	

Proofreading Tip

If you're writing with a computer, use the spelling checker to check for words you often misspell.

Communications Handbook HELP

See Proofreaders' Marks.

Publishing Tip

Share your literary analysis by reading it aloud to your class or reading group or by posting it on your school's Web site.

BUILDING YOUR PORTFOLIO

Sentence Workshop

COMBINING SENTENCES: USING PHRASES

Read the following passage aloud. How does it sound?

> He turned back. He was on a side street. He was circling around. He circled toward his home.

To most readers, this series of short sentences, all beginning with "He," will sound choppy and monotonous. See how Ray Bradbury combined the short, choppy sentences into one smooth sentence by using **phrases**. The phrases are marked off by slash marks.

> "He turned back / on a side street, / circling around / toward his home."
>
> —Ray Bradbury, "The Pedestrian" (page 174)

Phrases are groups of words that do not have both subjects and verbs. Commonly used phrases include **prepositional phrases**, **verbal phrases**, and **appositive phrases**.

Here are two other sentences from the stories in this collection. The phrases are marked off by slash marks. How could each of these passages be written as two or more short sentences?

> "On the far side / of the village, / buried in the dark smells, / a dog barked."
>
> —Tim O'Brien, "Where Have You Gone, Charming Billy?" (page 199)

> "He was lying / in a corner / drying his open wings / in the sunlight / among the fruit peels and breakfast left-overs. . . ."
>
> —Gabriel García Márquez, "A Very Old Man with Enormous Wings" (page 225)

Writer's Workshop Follow-up: Revision

Do an oral reading of the essay you wrote for the Writer's Workshop on page 240. In the reading, listen for passages that sound choppy or awkward. Underline these passages, and see if you can improve them by combining sentences. Look for ideas that can be put into phrases that answer the questions *which one? what kind? where? when? how? why?*

Language Handbook HELP

See Phrases, pages 1034–1036.

Technology HELP

See Language Workshop CD-ROM. *Key word entry: combining sentences.*

Try It Out

Combining with phrases. Combine each of the following series of short, choppy sentences into a single, smooth sentence by using phrases. To test your revised sentences, look at the text on the page indicated in parentheses to see how the professional writer used phrases to combine the same series of ideas.

1. Private First Class Paul Berlin lay quietly. He was at the rear of the column. His forehead rested on his rifle. His rifle had a black plastic stock. He closed his eyes. (page 198)
2. He was a skeleton. The skin was drawn tight over his bones. His long curls were like a woman's. He had a shaggy beard. (page 215)

Reading for Life

Evaluating a Documentary

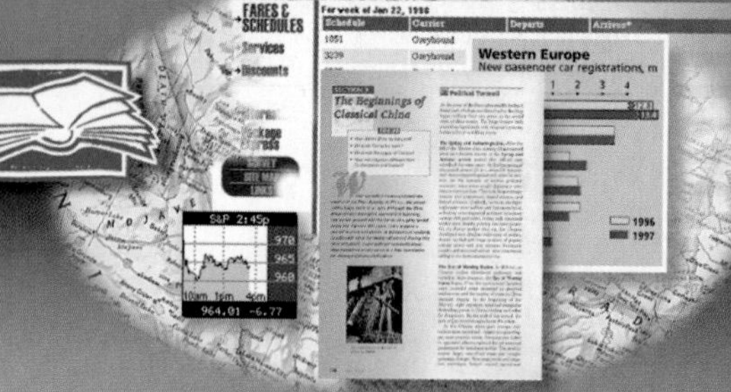

Situation

After reading Tim O'Brien's story on page 197, you want to know more about the war in Vietnam. At your local video store, you find a documentary film about this controversial war. Here are strategies you can use to evaluate any documentary.

Part of the film credits for the IMAX documentary *Everest* (1998). A MacGillivray Freeman Film. Greg MacGillivray, producer and director.

Strategies

Understand the purpose of a documentary.

- A documentary is now called a kind of "nonfiction." As such, a documentary is designed to present actual people and events in a factual way. You may not realize it, but a documentary, like print nonfiction, also presents a point of view. Indeed, two different documentaries may present dramatically opposing views of the same subject.

Assess its credibility.

- **Investigate the source of the documentary.** First, find out who directed and produced it. Ask yourself if the filmmakers have a special interest in presenting a particular point of view. Then, make sure that what you're watching is a true documentary, not a "docudrama." In a **docudrama,** for example, you're likely to see film of the Roman legions marching off to Carthage. In that case, of course, you would *know* you're not watching a documentary. But other docudramas are more subtle. You must be alert and read the credits carefully.
- **Who is narrating the documentary, and what are his or her qualifications?** Is the narrator associated with any particular political viewpoint?
- **Keep in mind what you already know.** A good documentary should add to your knowledge of the subject. It may even be persuasive enough to change your thinking about it. Use your prior knowledge to evaluate the depth and seriousness of the documentary's coverage.
- **Check the facts.** Use outside reference sources to check any new information you discover in the documentary, particularly any information that strikes you as questionable.
- **Be aware of how the filmmaker has used visual and sound techniques to convey a message, and perhaps to manipulate your emotions.** Documentaries are usually intended to persuade their audiences to accept a particular point of view. Film clips of actual events and people can be edited and sequenced to affect the audience in a certain way. Watch the way the filmmaker juxtaposes images. Listen carefully to the narrator's tone of voice and to music and other sound effects that accompany the film. Do they create a certain mood or effect?

Using the Strategies

Apply these strategies to a documentary currently on TV.

Collection 4

BREAKTHROUGHS

Writing Focus: Evaluating a Story or Movie

First you're a child, then you become an adolescent, then an adult. You may start out poor and become rich—or vice versa. You may start out foolish and become wise. Your life may be full of strife, but with effort or luck it becomes peaceful. You may be lonely and then find companionship. You may be sick and break through to health. You may be in a trap and suddenly find yourself free. All of us can probably think of breakthroughs we would like to make in our lives and of ones we've already made. In some respects, most fiction is about breakthroughs—maybe that's because we long so deeply for that lucky break, for those changes that will transform our lives.

I had been my whole life a bell, and never knew it until at that moment I was lifted and struck.

—Annie Dillard

Collection of Barry C. Scheck and Lawrence A. Vogelman.

Willie Mays (1978) (detail) by Ron Cohen. Acrylic and oil on canvas.

Writer's Notebook

WORK IN PROGRESS

What makes a story good? Write down all the factors that, for you, make a good story. (You may want to work with a partner.) Write freely now. You'll focus on these criteria for good storytelling and add to them as you read the stories in this collection. Save your notes for the Writer's Workshop on page 328.

Before You Read

TRAP OF GOLD

Make the Connection

Risky Business

In making decisions, we weigh the pros and cons: If I do this, what are the risks? What are the benefits?

Wetherton, the hero of this Western story, makes his own analysis of risks and benefits as he takes one chance after another—and moves us to the edge of our seats. How far will this prospector go to get rich?

Quickwrite

There's an old saying: Money makes the world go round. Is it true? Does money drive *your* actions? How much would you risk for a hundred dollars? a million? How much would tempt you to risk your life? Freewrite about the power of money and the risks people take to get it.

Elements of Literature

Setting as Antagonist

Louis L'Amour knew his West well. The **setting** he creates in this story is meticulously described, often in the specialized vocabulary of geology and mining. In this story, in fact, L'Amour has given the setting a major role. The mountain is Wetherton's **antagonist.** It is this mountain that the hero is struggling against. Try to visualize the setting so you can understand how, little by little, it is threatening to become Wetherton's tomb.

Setting is the time and place in which a story's action occurs. At times, setting can even assume the role of **antagonist** in a story.

For more on Setting, see pages 50–51 and the Handbook of Literary Terms.

Reading Skills and Strategies

Chronological Order

Most narratives, whether fiction or nonfiction, follow **chronological order**—that is, they show events unfolding in sequence over time. In "Trap of Gold," each moment might be the main character's last, so the use of chronological order is particularly effective in building **suspense.** As you look for words signaling the passage of time, notice too how the setting is very subtly changing as the minutes tick by.

go.hrw.com

LEO 10-4

Trap of Gold

Louis L'Amour

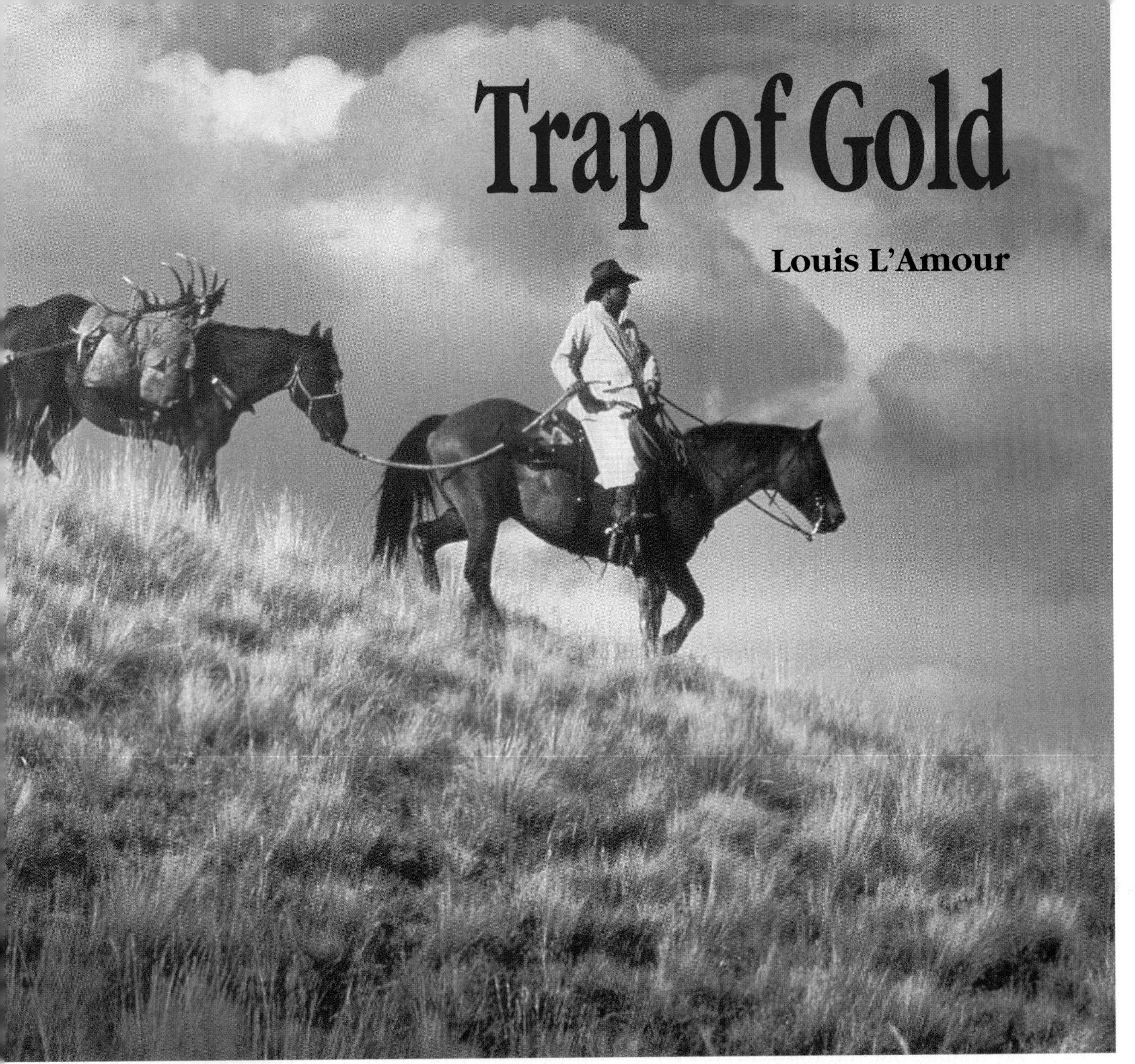

Enormous wealth was here for the taking.

Wetherton had been three months out of Horsehead before he found his first color.[1] At first it was a few scattered grains taken from the base of an alluvial fan[2] where millions of tons of sand and silt had washed down from a chain of rugged peaks; yet the gold was ragged under the magnifying glass.

1. **color:** here, trace of gold.
2. **alluvial fan:** fan-shaped deposit of soil or sand.

Gold that has carried any distance becomes worn and polished by the abrasive action of the accompanying rocks and sand, so this could not have been carried far. With caution born of harsh experience, he seated himself and lighted his pipe, yet excitement was strong within him.

A contemplative man by nature, experience had taught him how a man may be deluded by hope, yet all his instincts told him the source of the gold was somewhere on the mountain above. It could have come down the wash that skirted the base of the mountain, but the ragged condition of the gold made that impossible.

The base of the fan was a half-mile across and hundreds of feet thick, built of silt and sand washed down by centuries of erosion among the higher peaks. The point of the wide V of the fan lay between two towering upthrusts of granite, but from where Wetherton sat he could see that the actual source of the fan lay much higher.

Wetherton made camp near a tiny spring west of the fan, then picketed his burros and began his climb. When he was well over two thousand feet higher, he stopped, resting again, and while resting he dry-panned some of the silt. Surprisingly, there were more than a few grains of gold even in that first pan, so he continued his climb and passed at last between the towering portals of the granite columns.

Above this natural gate were three smaller alluvial fans that joined at the gate to pour into the greater fan below. Dry-panning two of these brought no results, but the third, even by the relatively poor method of dry-panning, showed a dozen colors, all of good size.

The head of this fan lay in a gigantic crack in a granitic[3] upthrust that resembled a fantastic ruin. Pausing to catch his breath, his gaze wandered along the base of this upthrust, and right before him the crumbling granite was slashed with a vein of quartz that was literally laced with gold!

Struggling nearer through the loose sand, his heart pounding more from excitement than from altitude and exertion, he came to an abrupt stop. The band of quartz was six feet wide, and that six feet was cobwebbed with gold.

It was unbelievable, but here it was.

Yet even in this moment of success, something about the beetling[4] cliff stopped him from going forward. His innate caution took hold, and he drew back to examine it at greater length. Wary of what he saw, he circled the batholith[5] and then climbed to the ridge behind it, from which he could look down upon the roof. What he saw from there left him dry-mouthed and jittery.

The granitic upthrust was obviously a part of a much older range, one that had weathered and worn, suffered from shock and twisting until finally this tower of granite had been violently upthrust, leaving it standing, a shaky ruin among younger and sturdier peaks. In the process the rock had been shattered and riven by mighty forces until it had become a miner's horror. Wetherton stared, fascinated by the prospect. With enormous wealth here for the taking, every ounce must be taken at the risk of life.

One stick of powder might bring the whole crumbling mass down in a heap, and it loomed all of three hundred feet above its base in the fan. The roof of the batholith was riven with gigantic cracks, literally seamed with breaks, like the wall of an ancient building that has remained standing after heavy bombing. Walking back to the base of the tower, Wetherton found he could actually break loose chunks of the quartz with his fingers.

3. **granitic** (grə·nit′ik): made of granite, a very hard rock.

4. **beetling:** projecting; jutting out.

5. **batholith** (bath′ō·lith′): large, deeply embedded mass of rock.

Words to Own

abrasive (ə·brā′siv) *adj.:* scraping; rubbing; wearing away. *Abrasive* also means "irritating" or "harsh."

contemplative (kən·tem′plə·tiv′) *adj.:* thoughtful.

deluded (di·lo͞od′id) *v.:* misled; fooled; deceived.

portals (pôrt′'lz) *n.:* doorways or gates, especially large, impressive ones.

The vein itself lay on the downhill side and at the very base. The outer wall of the upthrust was sharply tilted, so that a man working at the vein would be cutting his way into the very foundations of the tower, and any single blow of the pick might bring the whole mass down upon him. Furthermore, if the rock did fall, the vein would be hopelessly buried under thousands of tons of rock and lost without the expenditure of much more capital than he could command. And at this moment Wetherton's total of money in hand amounted to slightly less than forty dollars.

Thirty yards from the face he seated himself upon the sand and filled his pipe once more. A man might take tons out of there without trouble, and yet it might collapse at the first blow. Yet he knew he had no choice. He needed money, and it lay here before him. Even if he were at first successful, there were two things he must avoid. The first was tolerance of danger that might bring carelessness; the second, that urge to go back for that "little bit more" that could kill him.

It was well into the afternoon and he had not eaten, yet he was not hungry. He circled the batholith, studying it from every angle, only to reach the conclusion that his first estimate had been correct. The only way to get at the gold was to go into the very shadow of the leaning wall and attack it at its base, digging it out by main strength. From where he stood, it seemed ridiculous that a mere man with a pick could topple that mass of rock, yet he knew how delicate such a balance could be.

The tower was situated on what might be described as the military crest of the ridge, and the alluvial fan sloped steeply away from its lower side, steeper than a steep stairway. The top of the leaning wall overshadowed the top of the fan, and if it started to crumble and a man had warning, he might run to the north with a bare chance of escape. The soft sand in which he must run would be an impediment, but that could be alleviated by making a walk from flat rocks sunken into the sand.

It was dusk when he returned to his camp. Deliberately, he had not permitted himself to begin work, not by so much as a sample. He must be deliberate in all his actions, and never for a second should he forget the mass that towered above him. A split second of hesitation when the crash came—and he accepted it as inevitable—would mean burial under tons of crumbled rock.

The following morning he picketed his burros on a small meadow near the spring, cleaned the spring itself, and prepared a lunch. Then he

One stick of powder might bring the whole crumbling mass down in a heap . . .

Words to Own

impediment (im·ped′ə·mənt) *n.:* obstacle; something that slows or prevents movement or progress.
alleviated (ə·lē′vē·āt′id) *v.:* reduced; made easier to bear or deal with.
inevitable (in·ev′i·tə·bəl) *adj.:* certain to happen; unavoidable.

removed his shirt, drew on a pair of gloves, and walked to the face of the cliff. Yet even then he did not begin, knowing that upon this habit of care and deliberation might depend not only his success in the venture, but life itself. He gathered flat stones and began building his walk. "When you start moving," he told himself, "you'll have to be fast."

Finally, and with infinite care, he began tapping at the quartz, enlarging cracks with the pick, removing fragments, then prying loose whole chunks. He did not swing the pick, but used it as a lever. The quartz was rotten, and a man might obtain a considerable amount by this method of picking or even pulling with the hands. When he had a sack filled with the richest quartz, he carried it over his path to a safe place beyond the shadow of the tower. Returning, he tamped[6] a few more flat rocks into his path and began on the second sack. He worked with greater care than was, perhaps, essential. He was not and had never been a gambling man.

In the present operation he was taking a careful calculated risk in which every eventuality had been weighed and judged. He needed the money and he intended to have it; he had a good idea of his chances of success, but he knew that his gravest danger was to become too greedy, too much engrossed in his task.

Dragging the two sacks down the hill, he found a flat block of stone and with a single jack proceeded to break up the quartz. It was a slow and a hard job, but he had no better means of extracting the gold. After breaking or crushing the quartz, much of the gold could be separated by a knife blade, for it was amazingly concentrated. With water from the spring, Wetherton panned the remainder until it was too dark to see.

Out of his blankets by daybreak, he ate breakfast and completed the extraction of the gold. At a rough estimate, his first day's work would run to four hundred dollars. He made a cache for the gold sack and took the now empty ore sacks and climbed back to the tower.

6. **tamped:** packed down.

Shiprock (1994) by P. A. Nisbet. Oil on canvas.

Words to Own

cache (kash) *n.:* safe place for storing or hiding things. *Cache* may also refer to anything stored or hidden in such a place.

Courtesy of the artist.

The air was clear and fresh, the sun warm after the chill of night, and he liked the feel of the pick in his hands.

Laura and Tommy awaited him back in Horsehead, and if he was killed here, there was small chance they would ever know what had become of him. But he did not intend to be killed. The gold he was extracting from this rock was for them, and not for himself.

It would mean an easier life in a larger town,

a home of their own and the things to make the home a woman desires, and it meant an education for Tommy. For himself, all he needed was the thought of that home to return to, his wife and son—and the desert itself. And one was as necessary to him as the other.

The desert would be the death of him. He had been told that many times and did not need to be told, for few men knew the desert as he did. The desert was to him what an orchestra is to a fine conductor, what the human body is to a surgeon. It was his work, his life, and the thing he knew best. He always smiled when he looked first into the desert as he started a new trip. Would this be it?

The morning drew on, and he continued to work with an even-paced swing of the pick, a careful filling of the sack. The gold showed bright and beautiful in the crystalline quartz, which was so much more beautiful than the gold itself. From time to time as the morning drew on, he paused to rest and to breathe deeply of the fresh, clear air. Deliberately, he refused to hurry.

For nineteen days he worked tirelessly, eight hours a day at first, then lessening his hours to seven, and then to six. Wetherton did not explain to himself why he did this, but he realized it was becoming increasingly difficult to stay on the job. Again and again he would walk away from the rock face on one excuse or another, and each time he would begin to feel his scalp prickle, his steps grow quicker, and each time he returned more reluctantly.

Three times, beginning on the thirteenth, again on the seventeenth, and finally on the nineteenth day, he heard movement within the tower. Whether that whispering in the rock was normal he did not know. Such a natural movement might have been going on for centuries. He only knew that it happened now, and each time it happened, a cold chill went along his spine.

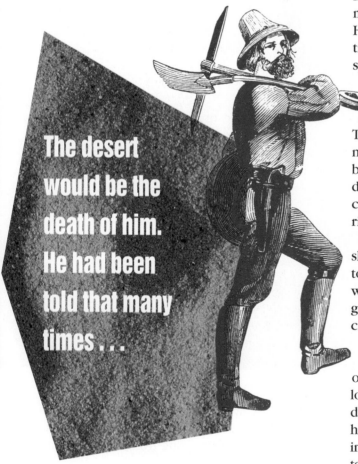

The desert would be the death of him. He had been told that many times . . .

His work had cut a deep notch at the base of the tower, such a notch as a man might make in felling a tree, but wider and deeper. The sacks of gold, too, were increasing. They now numbered seven, and their total would, he believed, amount to more than five thousand dollars—probably nearer to six thousand. As he cut deeper into the rock, the vein was growing richer.

He worked on his knees now. The vein had slanted downward as he cut into the base of the tower and he was all of nine feet into the rock with the great mass of it above him. If that rock gave way while he was working, he would be crushed in an instant with no chance of escape. Nevertheless, he continued.

The change in the rock tower was not the only change, for he had lost weight and he no longer slept well. On the night of the twentieth day he decided he had six thousand dollars and his goal would be ten thousand. And the following day the rock was the richest ever! As if to tantalize him into working on and on, the deeper he cut, the richer the ore became. By nightfall of that day he had taken out more than a thousand dollars.

Now the lust of the gold was getting into him, taking him by the throat. He was fascinated by the danger of the tower as well as the desire for the gold. Three more days to go—could he leave it then? He looked again at the tower and felt a peculiar sense of foreboding, a feeling that here he was to die, that he would never escape. Was it his imagination, or had the outer wall leaned a little more?

On the morning of the twenty-second day he climbed the fan over a path that use had built into a series of continuous steps. He had never counted those steps, but there must have been over a thousand of them. Dropping his canteen into a shaded hollow and pick in hand, he started for the tower.

The forward tilt *did* seem somewhat more than before. Or was it the light? The crack that ran behind the outer wall seemed to have widened, and when he examined it more closely, he found a small pile of freshly run silt near the bottom of the crack. So it had moved!

Wetherton hesitated, staring at the rock with wary attention. He was a fool to go back in there again. Seven thousand dollars was more than he had ever had in his life before, yet in the next few hours he could take out at least a thousand dollars more, and in the next three days he could easily have the ten thousand he had set for his goal.

He walked to the opening, dropped to his knees, and crawled into the narrowing, flat-roofed hole. No sooner was he inside than fear climbed up into his throat. He felt trapped, stifled, but he fought down the mounting panic and began to work. His first blows were so frightened and feeble that nothing came loose. Yet when he did get started, he began to work with a feverish intensity that was wholly unlike him.

When he slowed and then stopped to fill his sack, he was gasping for breath, but despite his hurry the sack was not quite full. Reluctantly, he lifted his pick again, but before he could strike a blow, the gigantic mass above him seemed to creak like something tired and old. A deep shudder went through the colossal pile and then a deep grinding that turned him sick with horror. All his plans for instant flight were frozen, and it was not until the groaning ceased that he realized he was lying on his back, breathless with fear and expectancy. Slowly, he edged his way into the air and walked, fighting the desire to run, away from the rock.

When he stopped near his canteen, he was wringing with cold sweat and trembling in every muscle. He sat down on the rock and fought for control. It was not until some twenty minutes had passed that he could trust himself to get to his feet.

Despite his experience, he knew that if he did not go back now, he would never go. He had out but one sack for the day and wanted another. Circling the batholith, he examined the widening crack, endeavoring again, for the third time, to find another means of access to the vein.

The tilt of the outer wall was obvious, and it could stand no more without toppling. It was possible that by cutting into the wall of the column and striking down, he might tap the vein at a safer point. Yet this added blow at the foundation would bring the tower nearer to collapse and render his other hole untenable. Even this new attempt would not be safe, although immeasurably more secure than the hole he had left. Hesitating, he looked back at the hole.

Once more? The ore was now fabulously rich, and the few pounds he needed to complete the sack he could get in just a little while. He stared at the black and undoubtedly narrower hole, then looked up at the leaning wall. He picked up his pick and, his mouth dry, started back, drawn by a fascination that was beyond all reason.

His heart pounding, he dropped to his knees at the tunnel face. The air seemed stifling and

---

WORDS TO OWN

foreboding (fôr·bōd′iŋ) *n.:* feeling that something bad is about to happen.

untenable (un·ten′ə·bəl) *adj.:* incapable of being defended, maintained, or occupied.

---

he could feel his scalp tingling, but once he started to crawl, it was better. The face where he now worked was at least sixteen feet from the tunnel mouth. Pick in hand, he began to wedge chunks from their seat. The going seemed harder now, and the chunks did not come loose so easily. Above him the tower made no sound. The crushing weight was now something tangible. He could almost feel it growing, increasing with every move of his. The mountain seemed resting on his shoulder, crushing the air from his lungs.

Suddenly he stopped. His sack almost full, he stopped and lay very still, staring up at the bulk of the rock above him.

No.

He would go no further. Now he would quit. Not another sackful. Not another pound. He would go out now. He would go down the mountain without a backward look, and he would keep going. His wife waiting at home, little Tommy, who would run gladly to meet him—these were too much to gamble.

With the decision came peace, came certainty. He sighed deeply, and relaxed, and then it seemed to him that every muscle in his body had been knotted with strain. He turned on his side and with great deliberation gathered his lantern, his sack, his hand-pick.

He had won. He had defeated the crumbling tower; he had defeated his own greed. He backed easily, without the caution that had marked his earlier movements in the cave. His blind, trusting foot found the projecting rock, a piece of quartz that stuck out from the roughhewn wall.

The blow was too weak, too feeble to have brought forth the reaction that followed. The rock seemed to quiver like the flesh of a beast when stabbed; a queer vibration went through that ancient rock, then a deep, gasping sigh.

He had waited too long!

Fear came swiftly in upon him, crowding him, while his body twisted, contracting into the smallest possible space. He tried to will his muscles to move beneath the growing sounds that vibrated through the passage. The whispers of the rock grew into a terrible groan, and there was a rattle of pebbles. Then silence.

The silence was more horrifying than the sound. Somehow he was crawling, even as he expected the avalanche of gold to bury him. Abruptly, his feet were in the open. He was out.

He ran without stopping, but behind him he heard a growing roar that he couldn't outrace. When he knew from the slope of the land that he must be safe from falling rock, he fell to his knees. He turned and looked back. The muted, roaring sound, like thunder beyond mountains, continued, but there was no visible change in the tower. Suddenly, as he watched, the whole rock formation seemed to shift and tip. The movement lasted only seconds, but before the tons of rock had found their new equilibrium, his tunnel and the area around it had utterly vanished from sight.

When he could finally stand, Wetherton gathered up his sack of ore and his canteen. The wind was cool upon his face as he walked away; and he did not look back again.

The rock
seemed to
quiver like
the flesh
of a beast
when
stabbed . . .

Meet the Writer

Best of the West

“I feel like a midwife to a thousand stories that have to be told and never would be unless I told . . . not the lives of generals and public men, but of all those buried in anonymous graves who suffered to build this country.”

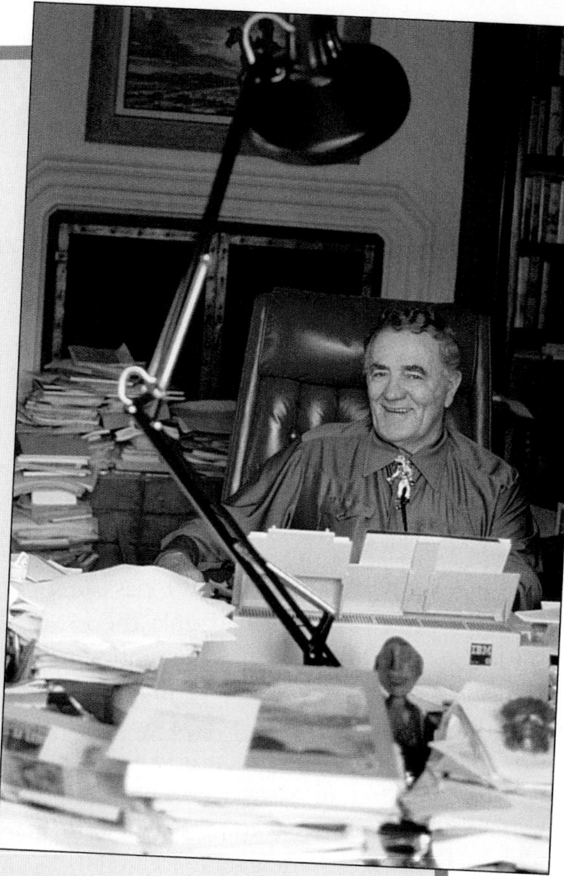

Louis L'Amour (1908–1988) may not have told a thousand stories in his lifetime, but since his death, the seventy novels and four hundred short stories that he did publish have continued to sell widely.

L'Amour, a fifteenth-generation American, was born in Jamestown, North Dakota. He was fascinated by stories about his pioneer ancestors, who included sod busters, trappers, cavalrymen, and cowboys.

After dropping out of school at fifteen, L'Amour traveled throughout the West, working as a fruit picker, lumberjack, miner, and elephant handler. Later he went to sea and spent time in the Far East. During World War II, he told Western tales to his fellow servicemen. Encouraged by their enthusiastic response, he began writing down some of his stories and publishing them.

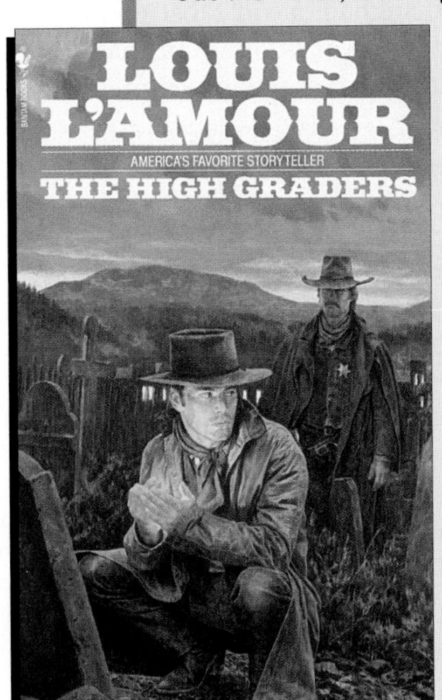

An avid reader and researcher on the history of the Old West, L'Amour took pride in the accuracy and realism of his stories. “I don't just tell you that a forty-niner panned for gold,” L'Amour asserted. “I tell you exactly how he panned for gold.”

This comment by writer Louise Erdrich might have been made about “Trap of Gold”: “The best parts of Mr. L'Amour's novels are the tight spots in which we find our hero—bushwhacked, surrounded, hanging over deep chasms, enslaved, defying no-good cowards who have somehow got him in their thrall.”

Connections
A DIARY

Gold has lured people to mountains, deserts, and even ancient tombs. For centuries, stories circulated about fabulous treasures buried in Egypt in the tombs of the pharaohs. In 1922, Howard Carter, a British Egyptologist working with Lord Carnarvon, uncovered the tomb of the young King Tutankhamen. In this excerpt from his diary, Carter describes his entry down into the tomb's antechamber.

"It Is Wonderful!"

Sunday, November 26, 1922

Feverishly we cleared away the remaining last scraps of rubbish on the floor of the passage before the doorway, until we had only the clean, sealed doorway before us, in which, after making preliminary notes, we made a tiny breach in the top left-hand corner to see what was beyond. . . . Candles were procured—the all-important telltale for foul gases when opening an ancient subterranean excavation. I widened the breach and by means of the candle looked in. . . .

As soon as one's eyes became accustomed to the glimmer of the light, the interior of the chamber gradually loomed before one, with its strange and wonderful medley of extraordinary and beautiful objects heaped upon one another.

There was naturally short suspense for those present who could not see. When Lord Carnarvon said to me "Can you see anything?" I replied to him, "Yes, it is wonderful!" I then with precaution made the hole sufficiently large for both of us to see. . . . Our sensations and astonishment are difficult to describe as the better light revealed to us the marvelous collection of treasures: two strange ebony-black effigies of a king, gold sandaled, bearing staff and mace, loomed out from the cloak of darkness; gilded couches in strange forms, lion-headed, Hathor-headed, and beast infernal; exquisitely painted, inlaid, and ornamental caskets; flowers, alabaster vases, some beautifully executed of lotus and papyrus device; strange black shrines with a gilded monster snake appearing from within; quite ordinary-looking white chests; finely carved chairs; a golden inlaid throne; a heap of large, curious white oviform boxes; beneath our very eyes, on the threshold, a lovely lotiform wishing cup in translucent alabaster; stools of all shapes and design, of both common and rare materials; and lastly a confusion of overturned parts of chariots glinting with gold, peering from amongst which was a manikin. The first impressions . . . suggested the property room of an opera of a vanished civilization.

Our sensations were bewildering and full of strange emotion. We questioned one another as to the meaning of it all. Was it a tomb or merely a cache? A sealed doorway between the two sentinel statues proved there was more beyond, and with the numerous cartouches bearing the name of Tutankhamen on most of the objects before us, there was little doubt that there, behind, was the grave of that pharaoh.

—from Howard Carter's diary of the discovery of the tomb of Tutankhamen

Tutankhamen's funerary mask. Gold, lapis, and carnelian (height 8⅞").

Making Meanings

First Thoughts

1. In "Trap of Gold," there's no dialogue, no confrontation between a hero and a villain. Does the story hold your attention anyway? Why?

Shaping Interpretations

2. Find the moments in the story when the writer makes you think Wetherton will fail in his quest. L'Amour said that writers, to heighten **suspense**, should refer to sights, sounds, and smells. What passages help you to *feel* Wetherton's physical responses to his ordeal?
3. Find at least three images that make the **setting** of the story—the tower of granite—seem like a human **antagonist.** Is the tower characterized as evil, as good, or as something else? Find details that support your answer.
4. Suppose Wetherton himself were telling the story. How would this change in **point of view** affect the impact of the story—particularly the element of suspense?
5. On one level, the **title** refers to a real rock formation. What else is the "trap of gold"?
6. What breakthroughs take place in this story?

Connecting with the Text

7. What do you find especially horrifying about Wetherton's situation? What deep-seated human fears do you think are aroused by this particular setting?

Extending the Text

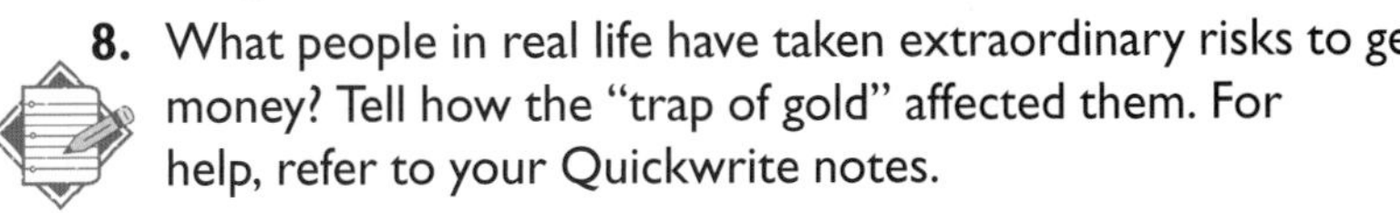

8. What people in real life have taken extraordinary risks to get money? Tell how the "trap of gold" affected them. For help, refer to your Quickwrite notes.

Challenging the Text

9. The story briefly mentions Wetherton's wife and son, Laura and Tommy. Would you have been less sympathetic if the writer had let you assume that Wetherton wanted the money just for himself? Or do you think that the information about Wetherton's family is corny and manipulative? Defend your opinion to another reader.

Reading Check

L'Amour builds **suspense** by gradually "paying out" information about Wetherton's progress toward his goal.

a. Make a numbered list in **chronological order** of all the actions Wetherton takes once he decides to mine the gold.

b. What is the purpose of each of these actions?

CHOICES: Building Your Portfolio

Writer's Notebook

1. Collecting Ideas for an Evaluation

Developing criteria. When you make a critical judgment about a story (as you will be doing in the Writer's Workshop on page 328), you need to know what your standards, or criteria, are. Work with a small group to develop a list of criteria for just one story element. For example, what makes a good **character** in fiction? an exciting **plot**? an interesting **setting**? Then apply your criteria to that one element in "Trap of Gold." You may want to evaluate the story element by rating it from 1 to 4, with 1 being least effective and 4 practically perfect.

Evaluation of Setting
"Trap of Gold"

Criteria	Ratings
Makes me feel I'm there.	4
Is part of the conflict.	4
Reveals character.	1
Could not be changed without greatly altering the story.	4
Creates an emotional effect or atmosphere.	4
Helps me learn something about a place.	2

Creative Writing

2. The Trap Wins

Rewrite the ending of "Trap of Gold," beginning with the line "He had waited too long!" on page 256. Suppose this line turned out to be literally true. What would happen to Wetherton? Write a **new ending** in which the trap of gold wins the struggle.

Creative Writing

3. Plotting the News

L'Amour said: "All stories fall into certain patterns of behavior which we call plots. Plots are nothing but a constantly recurring human situation, patterns of behavior. It's my belief that 90 percent of all fiction is based on just twelve to eighteen plots, and you can find them in any metropolitan newspaper in any given week."

Test this statement. Look in a major newspaper or in a national newsmagazine and see if you can find at least three news stories that could provide material for fiction. Write a report on your research in which you make a **story map** outlining a **plot** for each news story. Use an outline like this:

Basic Situation	
Characters	
Their problems	
Complications	
Resolution	
Setting	

Research/Oral Report

4. The Quest for Gold

Howard Carter's diary (see ***Connections*** on page 258) records his feelings at unearthing the long-buried treasure of Tutankhamen. The quest for treasure has captivated gold diggers throughout history. See what exciting facts you can discover, using print and Internet sources, about the topic below that most interests you. Present your findings in a brief oral report. Try to make your audience feel the thrill of "gold fever"!

- the gold rush of 1849
- Egyptian tomb caches
- sunken treasures

LANGUAGE LINK MINI-LESSON

Using Comparisons and Analogies to Clarify

Handbook of Literary Terms HELP

See Analogy, Metaphor, Simile.

To help us understand and visualize what's happening in "The Trap of Gold," L'Amour does something that good writers do instinctively: He takes a little time to make a **comparison** or an **analogy** between the new thing and something his readers are likely to recognize. (For a definition of analogy, see the Handbook of Literary Terms.) Most times the comparisons are explicit: L'Amour will say *how* one thing is like something else. Sometimes the comparison is made by a single word. In the sentences from "Trap of Gold" that follow, what comparisons and analogies help you understand the complex setting?

1. "The band of quartz was six feet wide, and that six feet was cobwebbed with gold."
2. "The roof of the batholith was riven with gigantic cracks, literally seamed with breaks, like the wall of an ancient building that has remained standing after heavy bombing."
3. ". . . the alluvial fan sloped steeply away from its lower side, steeper than a steep stairway."
4. ". . . the gigantic mass above him seemed to creak like something tired and old."

Try It Out

The best writers use **comparisons** and **analogies** (a type of comparison) to help readers understand complex ideas or structures. The discoverers of DNA, for example, described their discovery as a double helix (or spiral). A biology textbook helped students visualize DNA by comparing it to a twisted ladder. Think of something you know well and want to help someone else understand. It could be a car, a scientific experiment, even a hairstyle. Using a comparison, write a brief description so that someone totally unfamiliar with your subject can understand it.

VOCABULARY HOW TO OWN A WORD

WORD BANK

abrasive
contemplative
deluded
portals
impediment
alleviated
inevitable
cache
foreboding
untenable

Identifying Synonyms and Antonyms

In items 1–5, choose the *best* **synonym** (word that has the same, or a similar, meaning). In items 6–10, choose the *best* **antonym** (word that has an opposite meaning). This exercise format will give you practice for taking standardized tests.

1. IMPEDIMENT: (a) obstacle (b) aid (c) illness (d) law
2. DELUDED: (a) guided (b) bribed (c) lessened (d) misled
3. PORTALS: (a) harbors (b) cracks (c) doorways (d) tunnels
4. CACHE: (a) storage place (b) paper money (c) coins (d) sacks
5. FOREBODING: (a) luck (b) ending (c) beginning (d) prediction
6. INEVITABLE: (a) destined (b) avoidable (c) easy (d) careless
7. ABRASIVE: (a) harsh (b) irritating (c) soothing (d) angry
8. CONTEMPLATIVE: (a) unthinking (b) careful (c) alert (d) mad
9. UNTENABLE: (a) legible (b) defensible (c) empty (d) busy
10. ALLEVIATED: (a) cried (b) worsened (c) raised (d) improved

Elements of Literature

POINT OF VIEW: The Story's Voice *by* John Leggett

Point of view—the vantage point from which a writer tells a story—has a more powerful effect than you might imagine.

The Omniscient Point of View: Know It All

The traditional vantage point for storytelling, the one you are probably most familiar with, is the omniscient point of view.

Omniscient means "all-knowing." The **omniscient narrator** is a godlike observer who knows everything that is going on in the story and who can see into each character's heart and mind. This storyteller is outside the story's action altogether.

A newly married pair had boarded this coach at San Antonio. The man's face was reddened from many days in the wind and sun, and a direct result of his new black clothes was that his brick-colored hands were constantly performing in a most conscious fashion. From time to time he looked down respectfully at his attire. He sat with a hand on each knee, like a man waiting in a barber's shop. The glances he devoted to other passengers were furtive and shy.

The bride was not pretty, nor was she very young. She wore a dress of blue cashmere, with small reservations of velvet here and there, and with steel buttons abounding. She continually twisted her head to regard her puff sleeves, very stiff, straight, and high. They embarrassed her.

—Stephen Crane, "The Bride Comes to Yellow Sky"

The omniscient narrator can tell us as much—or as little—as the writer of the story permits. This narrator may tell us what all—or only some—of the characters are thinking, feeling, and observing. This narrator may comment on the meaning of the story or make asides about the story's characters or events.

The First-Person Point of View: "I" Speaks

At the opposite extreme from the omniscient point of view is the first-person point of view. In stories told in the **first person,** an "I" tells the story. This "I" also participates in the action (though possibly taking a very minor role). The omniscient point of view gives us the impression that we are standing nearby, watching and listening but with unusual insight into the events and the characters. The first-person point of view, on the other hand, lets us feel that we are being addressed directly by one of the characters or even that we have taken on the identity of one of the characters. Suppose Stephen Crane had let us hear the bride herself tell the story:

We boarded the Pullman car at San Antonio and sat stiffly in the plush seat, barely touching. First time on a train for me, but I was so nervous I didn't notice anything except that my new husband seemed ill at ease. Did he regret our marriage already? I felt myself falling in love with his shyness.

The first-person point of view presents only what the "I" character can see, hear, and know. This point of view also tells only what the "I" character chooses to tell. Consequently, we must always keep in mind that a first-person narrator may or may not be objective, reliable, honest—or even terribly perceptive about what's going on in the story. We must always ask ourselves how much the writer of the

story is allowing the narrator to know and understand—and how much the writer agrees with the narrator's perspective on life. In fact, the whole point of a story told from the first-person point of view may lie in the contrast between what the narrator tells us and what the writer allows us to understand in spite of the narrator.

> In choosing a point of view, the writer must consider how much information to tell the reader and how much to withhold.

The Third-Person Limited Point of View: Zooming In

Between the two extremes of the omniscient and first-person points of view lies the third-person limited point of view. Here the story is told by an outside observer speaking in the **third person** (like the godlike narrator of the omniscient point of view). But this narrator views the action only from the vantage point of a single character in the story. It is as if the narrator were standing alongside this one character and recording only his or her thoughts, perceptions, and feelings. Chances are that this narrator will tell us more than that character would be able to tell us (or might choose to tell us) if he or she were narrating the story. (This point of view is called third-person because the narrator never refers to himself or herself as "I." The third-person pronouns are used to refer to all characters.) Suppose Crane had decided to have a third-person limited narrator tell us the story of the bride. Now he might zoom in on the husband:

He was a working man—a sheriff—and dressed in a new suit for the first time in his life. His face was like a map—full of lines from exposure to the sun. He was terrified of what he'd done—married a woman he hardly knew—but pleased with himself. He was also pleased with his bride's quiet ways. He knew that what faced her in Yellow Sky would be anything but quiet.

In choosing a point of view, the writer must consider how much information to tell the reader and how much to withhold. And in reading a story, we might ask ourselves, "How would this story have been different if it had been told by someone else?"

What Is the Point of View?

Whenever you read a work of fiction, you should ask yourself five important questions about its point of view:

1. Who is telling the story?
2. How much does this narrator know and understand?
3. How much does this narrator want me to know?
4. How would the story be different if someone else were telling it?
5. Can I trust this narrator?

Before You Read

By the Waters of Babylon

Make the Connection

What Is This Place?

Part of the fun of reading a **fantasy** comes from imagining the invented setting and culture. In this fantasy story you'll accompany John, the narrator, as he tries to understand his world, his people's past, and their myths. Sharpen your detecting powers—you'll need them to solve the puzzle of this story.

Quickwrite

Think back thousands of years. Can whole civilizations disappear? Which ones have? Using what you know of world history, jot down some questions you have about a civilization so long gone that only faint traces of it remain.

Elements of Literature

First-Person Point of View

When a story is told from the **first-person point of view,** two important things happen. First, we share immediately in the narrator's experience and feelings. Second, we know *only* what the narrator knows. All we learn about the story's events and the other characters comes from the narrator's observations. Writers often choose the first-person point of view to create a sense of intimacy, as if the narrator is a friend talking directly to us. Benét uses this point of view to limit our knowledge—we know only what the narrator tells us as he makes his journey to the Place of the Gods.

A story written in the **first-person point of view** is told by a character who refers to himself or herself as "I."

For more on Point of View, see pages 262–263 and the Handbook of Literary Terms.

Reading Skills and Strategies

Drawing Conclusions: Detective Work

When you read mystery stories and other stories that present a puzzle, as "By the Waters of Babylon" does, you must act like a detective. You must look for clues and **draw conclusions** about what certain details in the story mean. As you read this story, be especially alert to clues about the setting. Read carefully the descriptions of objects and places. Think about what the narrator and writer may *not* be telling you. Then throw into the mix your own experience and knowledge as you try to solve the story's puzzles. Remember: like a detective, you'll have to keep monitoring and revising your conclusions as new clues surface.

Background

The title of this story is an **allusion** to Psalm 137 in the Bible. The psalm tells of the Israelites' great sorrow over the destruction of their Temple in Jerusalem (Zion) and their enslavement in the land of Babylon. The psalm begins:

> *By the waters of Babylon,*
> *there we sat down and wept,*
> *when we remembered Zion.*

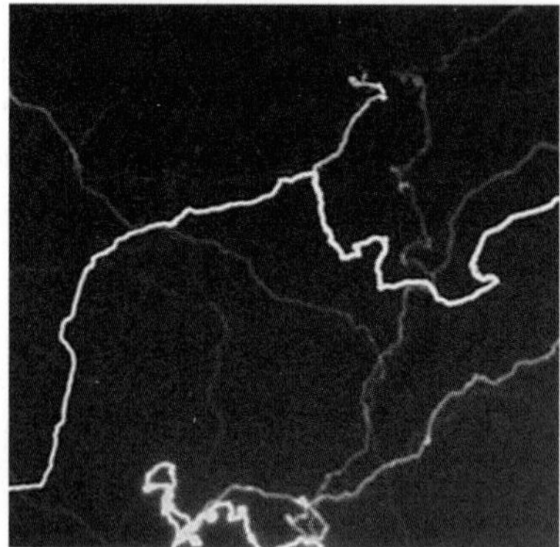

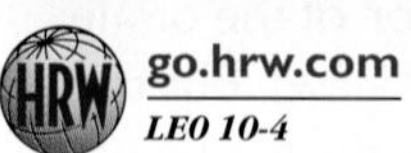

go.hrw.com

LEO 10-4

By the Waters of Babylon

Stephen Vincent Benét

At night, I would lie awake and listen to the wind—it seemed to me that it was the voice of the gods.

The north and the west and the south are good hunting ground, but it is forbidden to go east. It is forbidden to go to any of the Dead Places except to search for metal, and then he who touches the metal must be a priest or the son of a priest. Afterward, both the man and the metal must be purified. These are the rules and the laws; they are well made. It is forbidden to cross the great river and look upon the place that was the Place of the Gods—this is most strictly forbidden. We do not even say its name though we know its name. It is there that spirits live, and demons—it is there that there are the ashes of the Great Burning. These things are forbidden—they have been forbidden since the beginning of time.

My father is a priest; I am the son of a priest. I have been in the Dead Places near us, with my father—at first, I was afraid.

When my father went into the house to search for the metal, I stood by the door and my heart felt small and weak. It was a dead man's house, a spirit house. It did not have the smell of man, though there were old bones in a corner. But it is not fitting that a priest's son should show fear. I looked at the bones in the shadow and kept my voice still.

Then my father came out with the metal—a good, strong piece. He looked at me with both eyes but I had not run away. He gave me the metal to hold—I took it and did not die. So he knew that I was truly his son and would be a priest in my time. That was when I was very young—nevertheless, my brothers would not have done it, though they are good hunters. After that, they gave me the good piece of meat and the warm corner by the fire. My father watched over me—he was glad that I should be a priest. But when I boasted or wept without a reason, he punished me more strictly than my brothers. That was right.

After a time, I myself was allowed to go into the dead houses and search for metal. So I learned the ways of those houses—and if I saw bones, I was no longer afraid. The bones are light and old—sometimes they will fall into dust if you touch them. But that is a great sin.

I was taught the chants and the spells—I was taught how to stop blood from a wound and many secrets. A priest must know many secrets—that was what my father said. If the hunters think we do all things by chants and spells, they may believe so—it does not hurt them. I was taught how to read in the old books and how to make the old writings—that was hard and took a long time. My knowledge made me happy—it was like a fire in my heart. Most of all, I liked to hear of the Old Days and the stories of the gods. I asked myself many questions that I could not answer, but it was good to ask them. At night, I would lie awake and listen to the wind—it seemed to me that it was the voice of the gods as they flew through the air.

We are not ignorant like the Forest People—our women spin wool on the wheel, our priests wear a white robe. We do not eat grubs from the tree, we have not forgotten the old writings, although they are hard to understand. Nevertheless, my knowledge and my lack of knowledge burned in me—I wished to know more. When I was a man at last, I came to my father and said, "It is time for me to go on my journey. Give me your leave."

He looked at me for a long time, stroking his beard, then he said at last, "Yes. It is time." That night, in the house of the priesthood, I asked for and received purification. My body hurt but my spirit was a cool stone. It was my father himself who questioned me about my dreams.

He bade me look into the smoke of the fire and see—I saw and told what I saw. It was what I have always seen—a river, and, beyond it, a great Dead Place and in it the gods walking. I have always thought about that. His eyes were stern when I told him—he was no longer my father but a priest. He said, "This is a strong dream."

"It is mine," I said, while the smoke waved and my head felt light. They were singing the Star song in the outer chamber and it was like the buzzing of bees in my head.

He asked me how the gods were dressed and I told him how they were dressed. We know how they were dressed from the book, but I saw them as if they were before me. When I had finished, he threw the sticks three times and studied them as they fell.

"This is a very strong dream," he said. "It may eat you up."

"I am not afraid," I said and looked at him with both eyes. My voice sounded thin in my ears but that was because of the smoke.

He touched me on the breast and the forehead. He gave me the bow and the three arrows.

"Take them," he said. "It is forbidden to travel east. It is forbidden to cross the river. It is forbidden to go to the Place of the Gods. All these things are forbidden."

"All these things are forbidden," I said, but it was my voice that spoke and not my spirit. He looked at me again.

"My son," he said. "Once I had young dreams. If your dreams do not eat you up, you may be a great priest. If they eat you, you are still my son. Now go on your journey."

I went fasting, as is the law. My body hurt but not my heart. When the dawn came, I was out of sight of the village. I prayed and purified myself, waiting for a sign. The sign was an eagle. It flew east.

Sometimes signs are sent by bad spirits. I waited again on the flat rock, fasting, taking no food. I was very still—I could feel the sky above me and the earth beneath. I waited till the sun was beginning to sink. Then three deer passed in the valley, going east—they did not wind[1] me or see me. There was a white fawn with them—a very great sign.

I followed them, at a distance, waiting for what would happen. My heart was troubled about going east, yet I knew that I must go. My head hummed with my fasting—I did not even see the panther spring upon the white fawn. But, before I knew it, the bow was in my hand. I shouted and the panther lifted his head from the fawn. It is not easy to kill a panther with one arrow but the arrow went through his eye and into his brain. He died as he tried to spring—he rolled over, tearing at the ground. Then I knew I was meant to go east—I knew that was my journey. When the night came, I made my fire and roasted meat.

It is eight suns' journey to the east and a man passes by many Dead Places. The Forest People are afraid of them but I am not. Once I made my fire on the edge of a Dead Place at night and, next morning, in the dead house, I found a good knife, little rusted. That was small to what came afterward but it made my heart feel big. Always when I looked for game, it was in front of my arrow, and twice I passed hunting parties of the Forest People without their knowing. So I knew my magic was strong and my journey clean, in spite of the law.

Toward the setting of the eighth sun, I came to the banks of the great river. It was half a day's journey after I had left the god-road—we do not use the god-roads now, for they are falling apart into great blocks of stone, and the forest is safer going. A long way off, I had seen the water through trees but the trees were thick. At last, I came out upon an open place at the top of a cliff. There was the great river below, like a giant in the sun. It is very long, very wide. It could eat all the streams we know and still be thirsty. Its name is Ou-dis-sun, the Sacred, the Long. No man of my tribe had seen it, not even my father, the priest. It was magic and I prayed.

Then I raised my eyes and looked south. It was there, the Place of the Gods.

How can I tell what it was like—you do not know. It was there, in the red light, and they were too big to be houses. It was there with the red light upon it, mighty and ruined. I knew that in another moment the gods would see me. I covered my eyes with my hands and crept back into the forest.

Surely, that was enough to do, and live. Surely it was enough to spend the night upon the cliff. The Forest People themselves do not come near. Yet, all through the night, I knew that I should have to cross the river and walk in the places of the gods, although the gods ate me up. My magic did not help me at all and yet there was a fire in my bowels, a fire in my mind. When the sun rose, I thought, "My journey has been clean. Now I will go home from my journey." But, even as I thought so, I knew I could not. If I went to the Place of the Gods, I would surely die, but, if I did not go, I could never be at peace with my spirit again. It is better to lose one's life than one's spirit, if one is a priest and the son of a priest.

Nevertheless, as I made the raft, the tears ran out of my eyes. The Forest People could have killed me without fight, if they had come upon me then, but they did not come. When the raft was made, I said the sayings for the dead and painted myself for death. My heart was cold as a frog and my knees like water, but the burning in my mind would not let me have peace. As I pushed the raft from the shore, I began my death song—I had the right. It was a fine song.

1. **wind** (wind): detect the scent of.

"I am John, son of John," I sang. *"My people are the Hill People. They are the men.*
I go into the Dead Places but I am not slain.
I take the metal from the Dead Places but I am not blasted.
I travel upon the god-roads and am not afraid. E-yah! I have killed the panther, I have killed the fawn!
E-yah! I have come to the great river. No man has come there before.
It is forbidden to go east, but I have gone, forbidden to go on the great river, but I am there.
Open your hearts, you spirits, and hear my song. Now I go to the Place of the Gods, I shall not return.
My body is painted for death and my limbs weak, but my heart is big as I go to the Place of the Gods!"

All the same, when I came to the Place of the Gods, I was afraid, afraid. The current of the great river is very strong—it gripped my raft with its hands. That was magic, for the river itself is wide and calm. I could feel evil spirits about me, in the bright morning; I could feel their breath on my neck as I was swept down the stream. Never have I been so much alone—I tried to think of my knowledge, but it was a squirrel's heap of winter nuts. There was no strength in my knowledge anymore and I felt small and naked as a new-hatched bird—alone upon the great river, the servant of the gods.

Yet, after a while, my eyes were opened and I saw. I saw both banks of the river—I saw that once there had been god-roads across it, though now they were broken and fallen like broken vines. Very great they were, and wonderful and broken—broken in the time of the Great Burning when the fire fell out of the sky. And always the current took me nearer to the Place of the Gods, and the huge ruins rose before my eyes.

I do not know the customs of rivers—we are the People of the Hills. I tried to guide my raft with the pole but it spun around. I thought the river meant to take me past the Place of the Gods and out into the Bitter Water of the legends. I grew angry then—my heart felt strong. I said aloud, "I am a priest and the son of a priest!" The gods heard me—they showed me how to paddle with the pole on one side of the raft. The current changed itself—I drew near to the Place of the Gods.

When I was very near, my raft struck and turned over. I can swim in our lakes—I swam to the shore. There was a great spike of rusted metal sticking out into the river—I hauled myself up upon it and sat there, panting. I had saved my bow and two arrows and the knife I found in the Dead Place but that was all. My raft went whirling downstream toward the Bitter Water. I looked after it, and thought if it had trod me under, at least I would be safely dead. Nevertheless, when I had dried my bowstring and restrung it, I walked forward to the Place of the Gods.

It felt like ground underfoot; it did not burn me. It is not true what some of the tales say, that the ground there burns forever, for I have been there. Here and there were the marks and stains of the Great Burning, on the ruins, that is true. But they were old marks and old stains. It is not true either, what some of our priests say, that it is an island covered with fogs and enchantments. It is not. It is a great Dead Place—greater than any Dead Place we know. Everywhere in it there are god-roads, though most are cracked and broken. Everywhere there are the ruins of the high towers of the gods.

How shall I tell what I saw? I went carefully, my strung bow in my hand, my skin ready for danger. There should have been the wailings of spirits and the shrieks of demons, but there were not. It was very silent and sunny where I had landed—the wind and the rain and the birds that drop seeds had done their work—the grass grew in the cracks of the broken stone. It is a fair island—no wonder the gods built there. If I had come there, a god, I also would have built.

How shall I tell what I saw? The towers are not all broken—here and there one still stands, like a great tree in a forest, and the birds nest high. But the towers themselves look blind, for the gods are gone. I saw a fish-hawk, catching fish in the river. I saw a little dance of white butterflies over a great heap of broken stones and columns. I went there and looked about me—there was a carved stone with cut-letters, broken in half. I can read letters but I could not understand these. They said UBTREAS. There was also the shattered image of a man or a god. It had been made of white stone and he wore his hair tied back like a woman's. His name was ASHING, as I read on the cracked half of a stone. I thought it wise to pray to ASHING, though I do not know that god.

How shall I tell what I saw? There was no smell of man left, on stone or metal. Nor were there many trees in that wilderness of stone. There are many pigeons, nesting and dropping in the towers—the gods must have loved them, or, perhaps, they used them for sacrifices. There are wild cats that roam the god-roads, green-eyed, unafraid of man. At night they wail like demons but they are not demons. The wild dogs are more dangerous, for they hunt in a pack, but them I did not meet till later. Everywhere there are the carved stones, carved with magical numbers or words.

I went north—I did not try to hide myself. When a god or a demon saw me, then I would die, but meanwhile I was no longer afraid. My hunger for knowledge burned in me—there was so much that I could not understand. After a while, I knew that my belly was hungry. I could have hunted for my meat, but I did not hunt. It is known that the gods did not hunt as we do—they got their food from enchanted boxes and jars. Sometimes these are still found in the Dead Places—once, when I was a child and foolish, I opened such a jar and tasted it and found the food sweet. But my father found out and punished me for it strictly, for, often, that food is death. Now, though, I had long gone past what was forbidden, and I entered the likeliest towers, looking for the food of the gods.

I found it at last in the ruins of a great temple in the midcity. A mighty temple it must have been, for the roof was painted like the sky at night with its stars—that much I could see, though the colors were faint and dim. It went down into great caves and tunnels—perhaps they kept their slaves there. But when I started to climb down, I heard the squeaking of rats, so I did not go—rats are unclean, and there must have been many tribes of them, from the squeaking. But near there, I found food, in the heart of a ruin, behind a door that still opened. I ate only the fruits from the jars—they had a very sweet taste. There was drink, too, in bottles of glass—the drink of the gods was strong and made my head swim. After I had eaten and drunk, I slept on the top of a stone, my bow at my side.

When I woke, the sun was low. Looking down from where I lay, I saw a dog sitting on his haunches. His tongue was hanging out of his mouth; he looked as if he were laughing. He was a big dog, with a gray-brown coat, as big as a wolf. I sprang up and shouted at him but he did not move—he just sat there as if he were laughing. I did not like that. When I reached for a stone to throw, he moved swiftly out of the way of the stone. He was not afraid of me; he looked at me as if I were meat. No doubt I could have killed him with an arrow, but I did not know if there were others. Moreover, night was falling.

I looked about me—not far away there was a great, broken god-road, leading north. The towers were high enough, but not so high, and while many of the dead houses were wrecked, there were some that stood. I went toward this god-road, keeping to the heights of the ruins, while the dog followed. When I had reached the god-road, I saw that there were others behind him. If I had slept later, they would have come upon me asleep and torn out my throat. As it was, they were sure enough of me; they did not hurry. When I went into the dead house, they kept watch at the entrance—doubtless they thought they would have a fine hunt. But a dog cannot open a door and I knew, from the books, that the gods did not like to live on the ground but on high.

I had just found a door I could open when the dogs decided to rush. Ha! They were surprised when I shut the door in their faces—it was a good door, of strong metal. I could hear their foolish baying beyond it but I did not stop to answer them. I was in darkness—I found stairs and climbed. There were many stairs, turning around till my head was dizzy. At the top was another door—I found the knob and opened it. I was in a long small chamber—on one side of it was a bronze door that could not be opened, for it had no handle. Perhaps there was a magic word to open it but I did not have the word. I turned to the door in the opposite side of the wall. The lock of it was broken and I opened it and went in.

Within, there was a place of great riches. The god who lived there must have been a powerful god. The first room was a small anteroom—I waited there for some time, telling the spirits of the place that I came in peace and not as a robber. When it seemed to me that they had had time to hear me, I went on. Ah, what riches! Few, even, of the windows had been broken—it was all as it had been. The great windows that looked over the city had not been broken at all though they were dusty and streaked with many years. There were coverings on the floors, the colors not greatly faded, and the chairs were soft and deep. There were pictures upon the walls, very strange, very wonderful—I remember one of a bunch of flowers in a jar—if you came close to it, you could see nothing but bits of color, but if you stood away from it, the flowers might have been picked yesterday. It made my heart feel strange to look at this picture—and to look at the figure of a bird, in some hard clay, on a table and see it so like our birds. Everywhere there were books and writings, many in tongues that I could not read. The god who lived there must have been a wise god and full of knowledge. I felt I had right there, as I sought knowledge also.

Nevertheless, it was strange. There was a washing-place but no water—perhaps the gods washed in air. There was a cooking-place but no wood, and though there was a machine to cook food, there was no place to put fire in it. Nor were there candles or lamps—there were things that looked like lamps but they had neither oil nor wick. All these things were magic, but I touched them and lived—the magic had gone out of them. Let me tell one thing to show. In the washing-place, a thing said "Hot" but it was not hot to the touch—another thing said "Cold" but it was not cold. This must have been a strong magic but the magic was gone. I do not understand—they had ways—I wish that I knew.

It was close and dry and dusty in their house of the gods. I have said the magic was gone but that is not true—it had gone from the magic things but it had not gone from the place. I felt the spirits about me, weighing upon me. Nor had I ever slept in a Dead Place before—and yet, tonight, I must sleep there. When I thought of it, my tongue felt dry in my throat, in spite of my wish for knowledge. Almost I would have gone down again and faced the dogs, but I did not.

I had not gone through all the rooms when the darkness fell. When it fell, I went back to the big room looking over the city and made fire. There was a place to make fire and a box with wood in it, though I do not think they cooked there. I wrapped myself in a floor-covering and slept in front of the fire—I was very tired.

Now I tell what is very strong magic. I woke in the midst of the night. When I woke, the fire had gone out and I was cold. It seemed to me that all around me there were whisperings and voices. I closed my eyes to shut them out. Some will say that I slept again, but I do not think that I slept. I could feel the spirits drawing my spirit out of my body as a fish is drawn on a line.

Why should I lie about it? I am a priest and the son of a priest. If there are spirits, as they say, in the small Dead Places near us, what spirits must there not be in that great Place of the Gods? And would not they wish to speak? After such long years? I know that I felt myself drawn as a fish is drawn on a line. I had stepped out of my body—I could see my body asleep in front of the cold fire, but it was not I. I was drawn to look out upon the city of the gods.

It should have been dark, for it was night, but it was not dark. Everywhere there were lights—lines of light—circles and blurs of light—ten thousand torches would not have been the same. The sky itself was alight—you could barely see the stars for the glow in the sky. I thought to myself, "This is strong magic," and trembled. There was a roaring in my ears like the rushing of rivers. Then my eyes grew used to the light and my ears to the sound. I knew that I was seeing the city as it had been when the gods were alive.

That was a sight indeed—yes, that was a sight: I could not have seen it in the body—my body would have died. Everywhere went the gods, on foot and in chariots—there were gods beyond number and counting and their chariots blocked the streets. They had turned night to day for their pleasure—they did not sleep with the sun. The noise of their coming and going was the noise of many waters. It was magic what they could do—it was magic what they did.

I looked out of another window—the great vines of their bridges were mended and the god-roads went east and west. Restless, restless were the gods, and always in motion! They burrowed tunnels under rivers—they flew in the air. With unbelievable tools they did giant works—no part of the earth was safe from them, for, if they wished for a thing, they summoned it from the other side of the world. And always, as they labored and rested, as they feasted and made love, there was a drum in their ears—the pulse of the giant city, beating and beating like a man's heart.

Were they happy? What is happiness to the gods? They were great, they were mighty, they were wonderful and terrible. As I looked upon them and their magic, I felt like a child—but a little more, it seemed to me, and they would pull down the moon from the sky. I saw them with wisdom beyond wisdom and knowledge beyond knowledge. And yet not all they did was well done—even I could see that—and yet their wisdom could not but grow until all was peace.

Then I saw their fate come upon them and that was terrible past speech. It came upon them as they walked the streets of their city. I have been in the fights with the Forest People—I have seen men die. But this was not like that. When gods war with gods, they use weapons we do not know. It was fire falling out of the sky and a mist that poisoned. It was the time of the Great Burning and the Destruction. They ran about like ants in the streets of their city—poor gods, poor gods! Then the towers began to fall. A few escaped—yes, a few. The legends tell it. But, even after the city had become a Dead Place, for many years the poison was still in the ground. I saw it happen, I saw the last of them die. It was darkness over the broken city and I wept.

All this, I saw. I saw it as I have told it, though not in the body. When I woke in the morning, I was hungry, but I did not think first of my hunger, for my heart was perplexed and confused. I knew the reason for the Dead Places but I did not see why it had happened. It seemed to me it should not have happened, with all the magic they had. I went through the house looking for an answer. There was so much in the house I could not understand—and yet I am a priest and the son of a priest. It was like being on one side of the great river, at night, with no light to show the way.

Then I saw the dead god. He was sitting in his chair, by the window, in a room I had not entered before and, for the first moment, I thought that he was alive. Then I saw the skin on the back of his hand—it was like dry leather. The room was shut, hot and dry—no doubt that had kept him as he was. At first I was afraid to approach him—then the fear left me. He was sitting looking out over the city—he was dressed in the clothes of the gods. His age was neither young nor old—I could not tell his age. But there was wisdom in his face and great sadness. You could see that he would have not run away. He had sat at his window, watching his city die—then he himself had died. But it is better to lose one's life than one's spirit—and you could see from the face that his spirit had not been lost. I knew that, if I touched him, he would fall into dust—and yet, there was something unconquered in the face.

That is all of my story, for then I knew he was a man—I knew then that they had been men, neither gods nor demons. It is a great knowledge, hard to tell and believe. They were men—they went a dark road, but they were men. I had no fear after that—I had no fear going home, though twice I fought off the dogs and I was hunted for two days by the Forest People. When I saw my father again, I prayed and was purified. He touched my lips and my breast, he said, "You went away a boy. You come back a man and a priest." I said, "Father, they were men! I have been in the Place of the Gods and seen it! Now slay me, if it is the law—but still I know they were men."

He looked at me out of both eyes. He said, "The law is not always the same shape—you have done what you have done. I could not have done it my time, but you come after me. Tell!"

I told and he listened. After that, I wished to tell all the people but he showed me otherwise. He said, "Truth is a hard deer to hunt. If you eat too much truth at once, you may die of the truth. It was not idly that our fathers forbade the Dead Places." He was right—it is better the truth should come little by little. I have learned that, being a priest. Perhaps, in the old days, they ate knowledge too fast.

Nevertheless, we make a beginning. It is not for the metal alone we go to the Dead Places now—there are the books and the writings. They are hard to learn. And the magic tools are broken—but we can look at them and wonder. At least, we make a beginning. And, when I am chief priest we shall go beyond the great river. We shall go to the Place of the Gods—the place newyork—not one man but a company. We shall look for the images of the gods and find the god ASHING and the others—the gods Lincoln and Biltmore[2] and Moses.[3] But they were men who built the city, not gods or demons. They were men. I remember the dead man's face. They were men who were here before us. We must build again.

2. Biltmore: New York City hotel.
3. Moses: Robert Moses (1888–1981): New York City public official who oversaw many large construction projects, such as bridges and public buildings.

Meet the Writer

Mr. American History

Stephen Vincent Benét (1898–1943) found many of his subjects in American history, folklore, and legend. *John Brown's Body* (1928), a book-length narrative poem about the fiery abolitionist who led an attack on Harpers Ferry in 1859 and was hanged for treason, won him the Pulitzer Prize for poetry. According to one biographer, Benét "wrote short stories for money and poetry for love."

Despite his preference for poetry, some of Benét's stories have remained his best-known works. "The Devil and Daniel Webster," a fantasy about the great American orator, has been remade several times for the stage, radio, and television. "By the Waters of Babylon," another well-known fantasy, first appeared as "The Place of the Gods" in the *Saturday Evening Post* in July 1937. Benét later changed its title.

Emphasizing the importance of clear style, Benét advised one young writer: "Don't use four adjectives when one will do. Don't use five long words to say, 'We were happy.' 'It rained.' 'It was dark.' Write of the simple things simply."

MAKING MEANINGS

First Thoughts

1. Does John's story make you feel encouraged or discouraged about humanity? Why? Compare your responses with those of other classmates.

Reading Check

Imagine that you are John, the narrator, telling the Hill People about your journey to the Place of the Gods. Briefly **summarize** the **main events** of your journey, either orally or in writing. Explain why you went and what you learned.

Shaping Interpretations

2. At what point in the story did you first begin to guess what the Place of the Gods was?

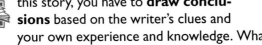

3. To understand what is really happening in this story, you have to **draw conclusions** based on the writer's clues and your own experience and knowledge. What do you think John is really seeing (and how are you able to tell) when he describes each of the items below? (You might want to work with a group to solve these puzzles.)

- the Great Burning
- Ou-dis-sun
- the statue of a man named ASHING
- the temple in mid-city with a roof painted like the sky at night
- the caves and tunnels where John thinks the gods kept their slaves

4. Find a place in the story where John achieves a breakthrough, and explain what he discovers. How does the **first-person point of view** help you appreciate his breakthrough?

5. The background on page 264 explains the Biblical **allusion** in the story's **title.** Now that you have read the story, explain how the words of the psalm connect with Benét's story.

Connecting with the Text

6. Near the end of the story, John says, "Perhaps in the old days, they ate knowledge too fast." What do you think he means? Are we "eating knowledge too fast" today? Explain.

Extending the Text

7. Benét wrote this story in 1937, before the first atom bomb was invented. World War II and the Cold War are over now. Do Benét's warnings about the complete destruction of a civilization still have relevance today? Why?

Challenging the Text

8. Do you think Benét made the secret of the Place of the Gods too easy to guess, or too hard, or were the clues just difficult enough? Explain.

CHOICES: Building Your Portfolio

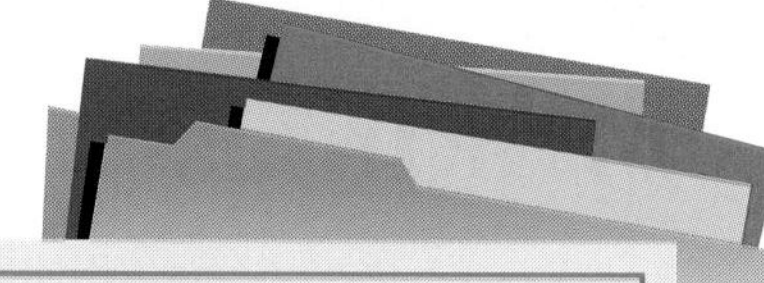

Writer's Notebook

1. Collecting Ideas for an Evaluation

Evaluating the author's craft. In your Writer's Notebook, freewrite your initial reactions to the way "By the Waters of Babylon" is written (or you might want to focus on the craft of another story in these collections). Did you find the plot and the ending believable? Is there anything in the story that doesn't make sense? Did the writer use description effectively, to help you feel you were "there"? In your Writer's Notebook, jot down your evaluation of the author's craft. Save your notes for possible use with the Writer's Workshop assignment on page 328.

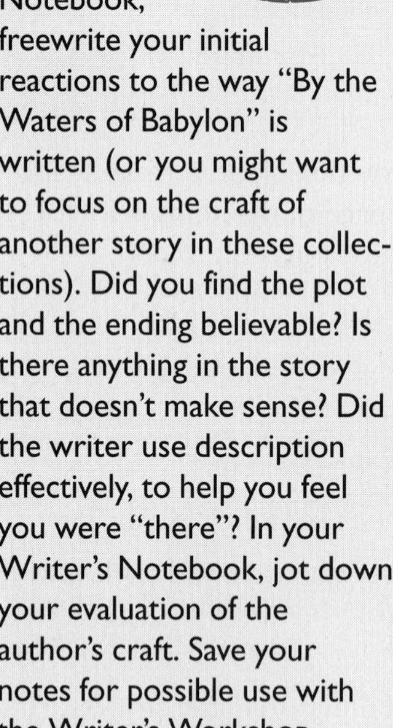

"The Pedestrian"
by Ray Bradbury
One of my favorite stories
because of its language.
Spooky setting. Great
descriptions (some
good comparisons).

Creative Writing

2. Babylon II?

What had happened to the city that John calls the Place of the Gods? Write a **prequel,** a story of the events that led up to "By the Waters of Babylon." You might write your story from the **first-person point of view** of the man John finds "sitting looking out over the city." Or you might write the story in the form of the man's last journal entries.

If you prefer, write a **sequel** to "By the Waters of Babylon," telling what happens after Benét's ending. Project the story several years into the future. What has become of John and his people?

Visual Literacy/ Comparing

3. The Apes Rule

Find and rent the science fiction movie classic *Planet of the Apes* (1968), starring Kim Hunter, Charlton Heston, and Roddy McDowall. How is the aftermath of nuclear war portrayed in the movie? Write a comparison of the movie and Benét's story. Consider **plot, characters, theme,** and how the **setting** is revealed.

Research/History

4. Into the Past

This story suggests several research projects. Benét wrote his story in 1937—long before the first nuclear weapons were tested and used. What was going on in world affairs at that time? When was the atom bomb first developed and first used?

You might want to focus on another long-gone civilization, such as those below:

- ancient Egypt
- the kingdom of Mali
- the kingdom of the Incas
- the people of Mesa Verde

First, brainstorm a list of questions you have about the period you'll focus on. Then, research your topic. Choose a presentation medium, such as a **time line, oral report,** or **photo essay,** and present your findings to your class.

Art

5. Designing the Place of the Gods

Suppose you are the **set designer** for a stage or screen adaptation of "By the Waters of Babylon." Sketch designs for at least two scenes, possibly including the Hill People's village, the forest, the view overlooking the Place of the Gods, and various parts of the ruined city.

GRAMMAR LINK MINI-LESSON

Inverted Order: Subjects Ahead

Language Handbook HELP

See Agreement of Subject and Verb: pages 1022–1024.

Technology HELP

See Language Workshop CD-ROM. *Key word entry: subject-verb agreement.*

As you know, singular subjects take singular verbs and plural subjects take plural verbs. The rule is easy, but finding the subject can be hard.

For example, some sentences or parts of sentences use **inverted order**—that is, the subject follows the verb. Inverted order is often used in questions and in sentences or clauses that begin with the word *here* or *there.* (Sometimes a sentence in inverted order will begin with a phrase or an adjective or adverb.) In the following examples from "By the Waters of Babylon," the subject is underscored once and the verb twice.

1. "Were they happy?"
2. "There was a white fawn with them—a very great sign."
3. "Restless, restless were the gods, and always in motion!"

Try It Out

➤ For each sentence, first find the subject and determine whether it is singular or plural. Then choose the verb that agrees with the subject. It will help to turn the inverted sentence into normal subject-verb-complement order. Thus, to decide whether to use was or were in the sentence "Was/were they happy?" you should turn the sentence around: "They were happy."

1. Here (lie, lies) our future.
2. Why (is, are) John on his journey?
3. There (was, were) coverings on the floor.
4. From hard journeys (come, comes) new breakthroughs.
5. Where (was, were) the dogs?

VOCABULARY HOW TO OWN A WORD

Clues to Word Meaning: Prefixes and Suffixes

Just a few letters tacked onto the beginning of a word (a **prefix**) or the end of a word (a **suffix**) change its meaning and often its part of speech. When you find an unfamiliar word, look for prefixes and suffixes that provide clues to how the **root,** the base meaning of the word, changes. Do a word chart like the one at right for each word from "By the Waters of Babylon" in the Word Bank below. If you need help with the meaning of a prefix or suffix, check a dictionary.

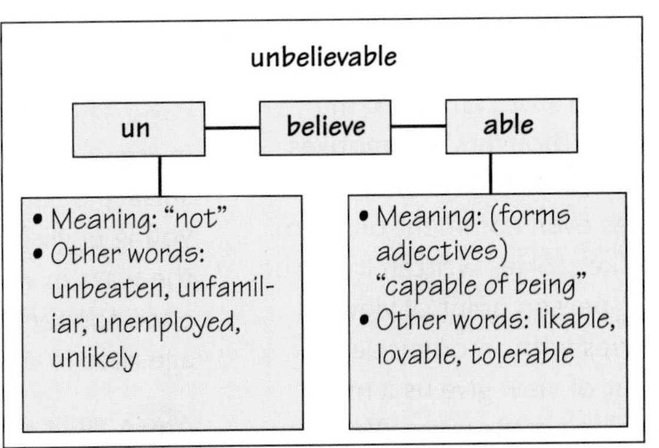

unbelievable
un
believe
able
• Meaning: "not"
• Other words: unbeaten, unfamiliar, unemployed, unlikely
• Meaning: (forms adjectives) "capable of being"
• Other words: likable, lovable, tolerable

WORD BANK

enchantments • destruction • forehead • restrung • anteroom

Before You Read

THROUGH THE TUNNEL

Make the Connection

A Need to Prove Yourself

Sometimes you need to prove yourself. Maybe you want so badly to play on the basketball team that you spend nights shooting baskets in the park. Maybe you practice alone for hours to learn a new dance. If what you want really matters to you, you'll endure tedium and possibly suffer physical pain to make the breakthrough—to accomplish your goal.

Quickwrite

Freewrite about a time you committed yourself to achieving something. What did you have to go through to get it? How did you feel at the end?

Elements of Literature

Knowing It All: Omniscient Point of View

An **omniscient**, or all-knowing, narrator can reveal the private thoughts and motives of all the characters and sometimes even comment on them. Unlike stories written from the first-person point of view, stories with an omniscient point of view give us a more reliable perspective. We know we are in the hands of an all-knowing narrator, and we trust that voice.

In a story told from the **omniscient point of view,** the narrator is an all-knowing observer who can reveal the thoughts and feelings of all the characters.

For more on Point of View, see pages 262–263 and the Handbook of Literary Terms.

Reading Skills and Strategies

Monitoring Your Reading: Using Resources

Many selections in this book have **resources** to enrich your reading. This story has the usual footnotes and photographs, but it also has a special feature called Literature and Anthropology (page 283), which provides information on initiation rites. This information should invite you to look beneath the surface of this story about a young English boy and consider the ways in which his experience connects with coming-of-age rites in other cultures.

go.hrw.com
LEO 10-4

Water surged into his mouth; he choked, sank, came up.

Through the Tunnel

Doris Lessing

Going to the shore on the first morning of the vacation, the young English boy stopped at a turning of the path and looked down at a wild and rocky bay and then over to the crowded beach he knew so well from other years. His mother walked on in front of him, carrying a bright striped bag in one hand. Her other arm, swinging loose, was very white in the sun. The boy watched that white naked arm and turned his eyes, which had a frown behind them, toward the bay and back again to his mother. When she felt he was not with her, she swung around. "Oh, there you are, Jerry!" she said. She looked impatient, then smiled. "Why, darling, would you rather not come with me? Would you rather——" She frowned, conscientiously worrying over what amusements he might secretly be longing for, which she had been too busy or too careless to imagine. He was very familiar with that anxious, apologetic smile. Contrition sent him running after her. And yet, as he ran, he looked back over his shoulder at the wild bay; and all morning, as he played on the safe beach, he was thinking of it.

Next morning, when it was time for the routine of swimming and sunbathing, his mother said, "Are you tired of the usual beach, Jerry? Would you like to go somewhere else?"

"Oh, no!" he said quickly, smiling at her out of that unfailing impulse of contrition—a sort of chivalry. Yet, walking down the path with her, he blurted out, "I'd like to go and have a look at those rocks down there."

She gave the idea her attention. It was a wild-looking place, and there was no one there, but she said, "Of course, Jerry. When you've had enough, come to the big beach. Or just go straight back to the villa, if you like." She walked away, that bare arm, now slightly reddened from yesterday's sun, swinging. And he almost ran after her again, feeling it unbearable that she should go by herself, but he did not.

She was thinking, Of course he's old enough to be safe without me. Have I been keeping him too close? He mustn't feel he ought to be with me. I must be careful.

He was an only child, eleven years old. She was a widow. She was determined to be neither possessive nor lacking in devotion. She went worrying off to her beach.

As for Jerry, once he saw that his mother had gained her beach, he began the steep descent to the bay. From where he was, high up among red-brown rocks, it was a scoop of moving bluish green fringed with white. As he went lower, he saw that it spread among small promontories and inlets of rough, sharp rock, and the crisping, lapping surface showed stains of purple and darker blue. Finally, as he ran sliding and scraping down the last few yards, he saw an edge of white surf and the shallow, luminous movement of water over white sand and, beyond that, a solid, heavy blue.

He ran straight into the water and began swimming. He was a good swimmer. He went out fast over the gleaming sand, over a middle region where rocks lay like discolored monsters under the surface, and then he was in the real sea—a warm sea where irregular cold currents from the deep water shocked his limbs.

When he was so far out that he could look back not only on the little bay but past the promontory that was between it and the big beach, he floated on the buoyant surface and looked for his mother. There she was, a speck of yellow under an umbrella that looked like a slice of orange peel. He swam back to shore, relieved at being sure she was there, but all at once very lonely.

On the edge of a small cape that marked the side of the bay away from the promontory was a loose scatter of rocks. Above them, some boys were stripping off their clothes. They came running, naked, down to the rocks. The English boy swam toward them but kept his distance at a stone's throw. They were of that coast; all of them were burned smooth dark brown and speaking a language he did not understand. To be with them, of them, was a craving that filled his whole body. He swam a little closer; they turned and watched him with narrowed, alert dark eyes. Then one smiled and waved. It was enough. In a minute, he had swum in and was on the rocks beside them, smiling with a desperate, nervous supplication. They shouted

Words to Own

contrition (kən·trish′ən) *n.:* regret or sense of guilt at having done wrong.

supplication (sup′lə·kā′shən) *n.:* humble appeal or request.

cheerful greetings at him; and then, as he preserved his nervous, uncomprehending smile, they understood that he was a foreigner strayed from his own beach, and they proceeded to forget him. But he was happy. He was with them.

They began diving again and again from a high point into a well of blue sea between rough, pointed rocks. After they had dived and come up, they swam around, hauled themselves up, and waited their turn to dive again. They were big boys—men, to Jerry. He dived, and they watched him; and when he swam around to take his place, they made way for him. He felt he was accepted and he dived again, carefully, proud of himself.

Soon the biggest of the boys poised himself, shot down into the water, and did not come up. The others stood about, watching. Jerry, after waiting for the sleek brown head to appear, let out a yell of warning; they looked at him idly and turned their eyes back toward the water. After a long time, the boy came up on the other side of a big dark rock, letting the air out of his lungs in a sputtering gasp and a shout of triumph. Immediately the rest of them dived in. One moment, the morning seemed full of chattering boys; the next, the air and the surface of the water were empty. But through the heavy blue, dark shapes could be seen moving and groping.

Jerry dived, shot past the school of underwater swimmers, saw a black wall of rock looming at him, touched it, and bobbed up at once to the surface, where the wall was a low barrier he could see across. There was no one visible; under him, in the water, the dim shapes of the swimmers had disappeared. Then one and then another of the boys came up on the far side of the barrier of rock, and he understood that they had swum through some gap or hole in it. He plunged down again. He could see nothing through the stinging salt water but the blank rock. When he came up, the boys were all on the diving rock, preparing to attempt the feat again. And now, in a panic of failure, he yelled up, in English, "Look at me! Look!" and he began splashing and kicking in the water like a foolish dog.

They looked down gravely, frowning. He knew the frown. At moments of failure, when he clowned to claim his mother's attention, it was with just this grave, embarrassed inspection that she rewarded him. Through his hot shame, feeling the pleading grin on his face like a scar that he could never remove, he looked up at the group of big brown boys on the rock and shouted, "Bonjour! Merci! Au revoir! Monsieur, monsieur!"[1] while he hooked his fingers round his ears and waggled them.

Water surged into his mouth; he choked, sank, came up. The rock, lately weighted with boys, seemed to rear up out of the water as their weight was removed. They were flying down

1. **Bonjour! Merci! Au revoir! Monsieur, monsieur!:** French for "Hello! Thank you! Goodbye! Mr., Mr.!"—probably the only French words Jerry knows.

past him now, into the water; the air was full of falling bodies. Then the rock was empty in the hot sunlight. He counted one, two, three . . .

At fifty, he was terrified. They must all be drowning beneath him, in the watery caves of the rock! At a hundred, he stared around him at the empty hillside, wondering if he should yell for help. He counted faster, faster, to hurry them up, to bring them to the surface quickly, to drown them quickly—anything rather than the terror of counting on and on into the blue emptiness of the morning. And then, at a hundred and sixty, the water beyond the rock was full of boys blowing like brown whales. They swam back to the shore without a look at him.

He climbed back to the diving rock and sat down, feeling the hot roughness of it under his thighs. The boys were gathering up their bits of clothing and running off along the shore to another promontory. They were leaving to get away from him. He cried openly, fists in his eyes. There was no one to see him, and he cried himself out.

It seemed to him that a long time had passed, and he swam out to where he could see his mother. Yes, she was still there, a yellow spot under an orange umbrella. He swam back to the big rock, climbed up, and dived into the blue pool among the fanged and angry boulders. Down he went, until he touched the wall of rock again. But the salt was so painful in his eyes that he could not see.

He came to the surface, swam to shore, and went back to the villa to wait for his mother. Soon she walked slowly up the path, swinging her striped bag, the flushed, naked arm dangling beside her. "I want some swimming goggles," he panted, defiant and beseeching.

She gave him a patient, inquisitive look as she said casually, "Well, of course, darling."

But now, now, now! He must have them this minute, and no other time. He nagged and pestered until she went with him to a shop. As soon as she had bought the goggles, he grabbed them from her hand as if she were going to claim them for herself, and was off, running down the steep path to the bay.

Jerry swam out to the big barrier rock, adjusted the goggles, and dived. The impact of the water broke the rubber-enclosed vacuum, and the goggles came loose. He understood that he must swim down to the base of the rock from the surface of the water. He fixed the goggles tight and firm, filled his lungs, and floated, face down, on the water. Now he could see. It was as if he had eyes of a different kind—fish eyes that showed everything clear and delicate and wavering in the bright water.

Under him, six or seven feet down, was a floor of perfectly clean, shining white sand, rippled firm and hard by the tides. Two grayish shapes steered there, like long, rounded pieces of wood or slate. They were fish. He saw them nose toward each other, poise motionless, make a dart forward, swerve off, and come around again. It was like a water dance. A few inches above them the water sparkled as if sequins were dropping through it. Fish again—myriads of minute fish, the length of his fingernail—were drifting through the water, and in a moment he could feel the innumerable tiny touches of them against his limbs. It was like swimming in flaked silver. The great rock the big boys had swum through rose sheer out of the white sand—black, tufted lightly with greenish weed. He could see no gap in it. He swam down to its base.

Again and again he rose, took a big chestful of air, and went down. Again and again he groped over the surface of the rock, feeling it, almost hugging it in the desperate need to find the entrance. And then, once, while he was clinging to the black wall, his knees came up and he shot his feet out forward and they met no obstacle. He had found the hole.

He gained the surface, clambered about the stones that littered the barrier rock until he found a big one, and with this in his arms, let himself down over the side of the rock. He dropped, with the weight, straight to the sandy floor. Clinging tight to the anchor of stone, he

Words to Own

inquisitive (in·kwiz′ə·tiv) *adj.:* questioning; curious.
minute (mī·no͞ot′) *adj.:* small; tiny.

lay on his side and looked in under the dark shelf at the place where his feet had gone. He could see the hole. It was an irregular, dark gap; but he could not see deep into it. He let go of his anchor, clung with his hands to the edges of the hole, and tried to push himself in.

He got his head in, found his shoulders jammed, moved them in sidewise, and was inside as far as his wrist. He could see nothing ahead. Something soft and clammy touched his mouth; he saw a dark frond moving against the grayish rock, and panic filled him. He thought of octopuses, of clinging weed. He pushed himself out backward and caught a glimpse, as he retreated, of a harmless tentacle of seaweed drifting in the mouth of the tunnel. But it was enough. He reached the sunlight, swam to shore, and lay on the diving rock. He looked down into the blue well of water. He knew he must find his way through that cave, or hole, or tunnel, and out the other side.

First, he thought, he must learn to control his breathing. He let himself down into the water with another big stone in his arms, so that he could lie effortlessly on the bottom of the sea. He counted. One, two, three. He counted steadily. He could hear the movement of blood in his chest. Fifty-one, fifty-two. . . . His chest was hurting. He let go of the rock and went up into the air. He saw that the sun was low. He rushed to the villa and found his mother at her supper. She said only, "Did you enjoy yourself?" and he said, "Yes."

All night the boy dreamed of the water-filled cave in the rock, and as soon as breakfast was over, he went to the bay.

That night, his nose bled badly. For hours he had been underwater, learning to hold his breath, and now he felt weak and dizzy. His mother said, "I shouldn't overdo things, darling, if I were you."

That day and the next, Jerry exercised his lungs as if everything, the whole of his life, all that he would become, depended upon it. Again his nose bled at night, and his mother insisted on his coming with her the next day. It was a torment to him to waste a day of his careful self-training, but he stayed with her on that other beach, which now seemed a place for small children, a place where his mother might lie safe in the sun. It was not his beach.

He did not ask for permission, on the following day, to go to his beach. He went, before his mother could consider the complicated rights and wrongs of the matter. A day's rest, he discovered, had improved his count by ten. The big boys had made the passage while he counted a hundred and sixty. He had been counting fast, in his fright. Probably now, if he tried, he could get through that long tunnel, but he was not going to try yet. A curious, most unchildlike persistence, a controlled impatience, made him wait. In the meantime, he lay underwater on the white sand, littered now by stones he had brought down from the upper air, and studied the entrance to the tunnel. He knew every jut and corner of it, as far as it was possible to see. It was as if he already felt its sharpness about his shoulders.

He sat by the clock in the villa, when his mother was not near, and checked his time. He was incredulous and then proud to find he could hold his breath without strain for two minutes. The words "two minutes," authorized by the clock, brought close the adventure that was so necessary to him.

In another four days, his mother said casually one morning, they must go home. On the day before they left, he would do it. He would do it if it killed him, he said defiantly to himself. But two days before they were to leave—a day of triumph when he increased his count by fifteen—his nose bled so badly that he turned dizzy and had to lie limply over the big rock like a bit of seaweed, watching the thick red blood flow onto the rock and trickle slowly down to the sea. He was frightened. Supposing he turned dizzy in the tunnel? Supposing he died there, trapped? Supposing—his head went around, in the hot sun, and he almost gave up. He thought he would return to the house and lie down, and

---

WORDS TO OWN

incredulous (in·krej′o͞o·ləs) *adj.:* disbelieving; skeptical.

---

next summer, perhaps, when he had another year's growth in him—then he would go through the hole.

But even after he had made the decision, or thought he had, he found himself sitting up on the rock and looking down into the water; and he knew that now, this moment, when his nose had only just stopped bleeding, when his head was still sore and throbbing—this was the moment when he would try. If he did not do it now, he never would. He was trembling with fear that he would not go; and he was trembling with horror at the long, long tunnel under the rock, under the sea. Even in the open sunlight, the barrier rock seemed very wide and very heavy; tons of rock pressed down on where he would go. If he died there, he would lie until one day—perhaps not before next year—those big boys would swim into it and find it blocked.

He put on his goggles, fitted them tight, tested the vacuum. His hands were shaking. Then he chose the biggest stone he could carry and slipped over the edge of the rock until half of him was in the cool enclosing water and half in the hot sun. He looked up once at the empty sky, filled his lungs once, twice, and then sank fast to the bottom with the stone. He let it go and began to count. He took the edges of the hole in his hands and drew himself into it, wriggling his shoulders in sidewise as he remembered he must, kicking himself along with his feet.

Soon he was clear inside. He was in a small rock-bound hole filled with yellowish-gray water. The water was pushing him up against the roof. The roof was sharp and pained his back. He pulled himself along with his hands—fast, fast—and used his legs as levers. His head knocked against something; a sharp pain dizzied him. Fifty, fifty-one, fifty-two . . . He was without light, and the water seemed to press upon him with the weight of rock. Seventy-one, seventy-two . . . There was no strain on his lungs. He felt like an inflated balloon, his lungs were so light and easy, but his head was pulsing.

He was being continually pressed against the sharp roof, which felt slimy as well as sharp. Again he thought of octopuses, and wondered if the tunnel might be filled with weed that could tangle him. He gave himself a panicky, convulsive kick forward, ducked his head, and swam. His feet and hands moved freely, as if in open water. The hole must have widened out. He thought he must be swimming fast, and he was frightened of banging his head if the tunnel narrowed.

A hundred, a hundred and one . . . The water paled. Victory filled him. His lungs were beginning to hurt. A few more strokes and he would be out. He was counting wildly; he said a hundred and fifteen and then, a long time later, a hundred and fifteen again. The water was a clear jewel-green all around him. Then he saw, above his head, a crack running up through the rock. Sunlight was falling through it, showing the clean, dark rock of the tunnel, a single mussel[2] shell, and darkness ahead.

He was at the end of what he could do. He looked up at the crack as if it were filled with air and not water, as if he could put his mouth to it to draw in air. A hundred and fifteen, he heard himself say inside his head—but he had said that long ago. He must go on into the blackness ahead, or he would drown. His head was swelling, his lungs cracking. A hundred and fifteen, a hundred and fifteen, pounded through his head, and he feebly clutched at rocks in the dark, pulling himself forward, leaving the brief space of sunlit water behind. He felt he was dying. He was no longer quite conscious. He struggled on in the darkness between lapses into unconsciousness. An immense, swelling pain filled his head, and then the darkness cracked with an explosion of green light. His hands, groping forward, met nothing; and his feet, kicking back, propelled him out into the open sea.

He drifted to the surface, his face turned up to the air. He was gasping like a fish. He felt he would sink now and drown; he could not swim the few feet back to the rock. Then he was clutching it and pulling himself up onto it. He lay face down, gasping. He could see nothing

2. mussel: shellfish, similar to a clam or an oyster, that attaches itself to rocks.

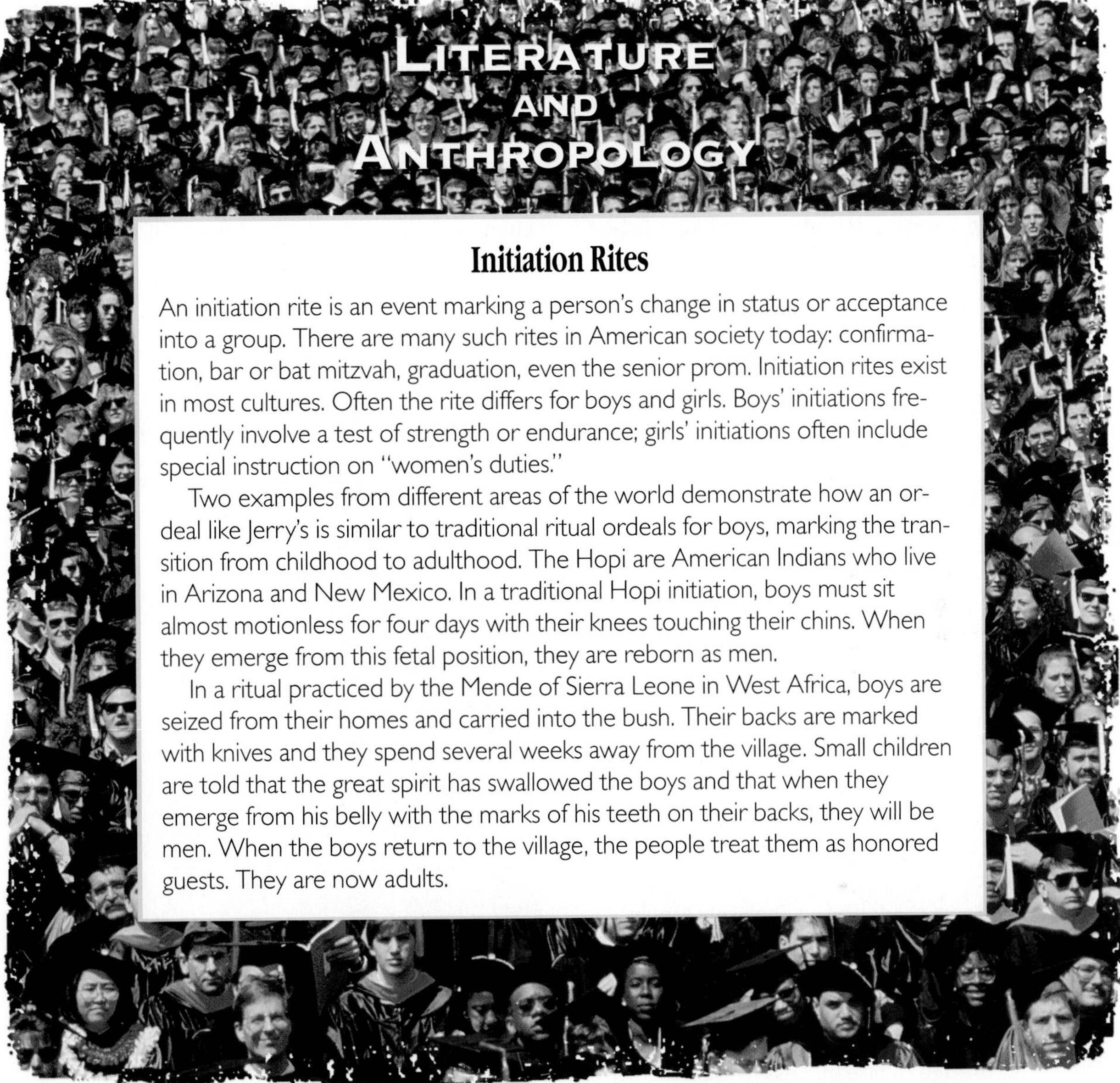

Initiation Rites

An initiation rite is an event marking a person's change in status or acceptance into a group. There are many such rites in American society today: confirmation, bar or bat mitzvah, graduation, even the senior prom. Initiation rites exist in most cultures. Often the rite differs for boys and girls. Boys' initiations frequently involve a test of strength or endurance; girls' initiations often include special instruction on "women's duties."

Two examples from different areas of the world demonstrate how an ordeal like Jerry's is similar to traditional ritual ordeals for boys, marking the transition from childhood to adulthood. The Hopi are American Indians who live in Arizona and New Mexico. In a traditional Hopi initiation, boys must sit almost motionless for four days with their knees touching their chins. When they emerge from this fetal position, they are reborn as men.

In a ritual practiced by the Mende of Sierra Leone in West Africa, boys are seized from their homes and carried into the bush. Their backs are marked with knives and they spend several weeks away from the village. Small children are told that the great spirit has swallowed the boys and that when they emerge from his belly with the marks of his teeth on their backs, they will be men. When the boys return to the village, the people treat them as honored guests. They are now adults.

but a red-veined, clotted dark. His eyes must have burst, he thought; they were full of blood. He tore off his goggles and a gout[3] of blood went into the sea. His nose was bleeding, and the blood had filled the goggles.

He scooped up handfuls of water from the cool, salty sea, to splash on his face, and did not know whether it was blood or salt water he tasted. After a time, his heart quieted, his eyes cleared, and he sat up. He could see the local boys diving and playing half a mile away. He did not want them. He wanted nothing but to get back home and lie down.

In a short while, Jerry swam to shore and climbed slowly up the path to the villa. He flung himself on his bed and slept, waking at the sound of feet on the path outside. His mother was coming back. He rushed to the bathroom, thinking she must not see his face with bloodstains, or tearstains, on it. He came out of the bathroom and met her as she walked into the villa, smiling, her eyes lighting up.

"Have a nice morning?" she asked, laying her hand on his warm brown shoulder a moment.

3. **gout:** large glob.

"Oh, yes, thank you," he said.

"You look a bit pale." And then, sharp and anxious, "How did you bang your head?"

"Oh, just banged it," he told her.

She looked at him closely. He was strained; his eyes were glazed-looking. She was worried. And then she said to herself, Oh, don't fuss! Nothing can happen. He can swim like a fish.

They sat down to lunch together.

"Mummy," he said, "I can stay underwater for two minutes—three minutes, at least." It came bursting out of him.

"Can you, darling?" she said. "Well, I shouldn't overdo it. I don't think you ought to swim anymore today."

She was ready for a battle of wills, but he gave in at once. It was no longer of the least importance to go to the bay.

Meet the Writer

Out of Africa

Doris Lessing (1919–) was born in Persia (now Iran), where her British father was in charge of a bank. When she was five, her father, growing tired of the corruption around him and longing for a freer life, moved the family to a three-thousand-acre farm in Southern Rhodesia (now Zimbabwe). Life was extremely hard there. The farm's thirty to fifty African laborers lived in mud huts with no sanitation. Lessing's mother was homesick for England and often ill; her impulsive father was increasingly unpredictable. The nearest neighbor was miles away. Lessing has described this childhood as "hellishly lonely." She has also acknowledged the advantage of such a childhood: Lacking company, she enriched her mind by reading classic European and American literature.

At the age of fifteen, Lessing quit school and went to work in Salisbury, the capital of Rhodesia, first as a nursemaid and then as a stenographer and telephone operator. Salisbury had a white population of about ten thousand and a larger black population that Lessing discovered "didn't count." During this period of her life, she became involved in radical politics, and she was twice married and twice divorced. In 1949, with her two-year-old son and the manuscript of her first novel, *The Grass Is Singing,* she fulfilled a lifelong wish by immigrating to England. The novel, about the complex relationship between a white farm wife and her African servant, was published in 1950, one of the earliest treatments in fiction of Africa's racial problems. From then on, Lessing supported herself by her writing. Her powerful stories and novels are among the most admired writings of our day.

Lessing admits she writes to be "an instrument of change."

"It is not merely a question of preventing evil, but of strengthening a vision of good which may defeat the evil."

Making Meanings

First Thoughts

1. Is Jerry crazy to risk his life, or does he get something important out of his ordeal? Talk about your responses.

Reading Check

Retell the **main events** of this story as Jerry might tell them to his best friend back home when he returns from vacation or later in life to his own son.

Shaping Interpretations

2. Why do you think it is so important to Jerry to be with the boys on the wild beach?

3. What physical and mental "tortures" does Jerry go through, first as he prepares for his ordeal and then as he swims through the tunnel?

4. A ticking clock is usually good for creating **suspense**. How does this story use a "ticking clock" to increase our anxiety?

5. What breakthroughs has Jerry achieved by the story's end? Consider:

- his conquest of the tunnel
- his feelings about himself
- his dependence on his mother

6. What do you think is the main focus of this story—in other words, what would you say is its **theme**? Consider:

- what the swim through the tunnel means to Jerry
- why Jerry no longer feels he has to go to the bay

7. Read carefully the information provided in Literature and Anthropology on page 283. Do you think Jerry's experience can be viewed as an initiation rite? What similarities and differences can you find between his experience and the coming-of-age rites in other cultures?

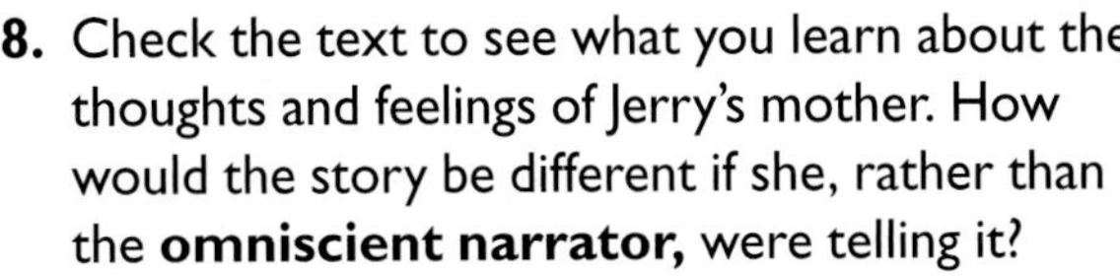

8. Check the text to see what you learn about the thoughts and feelings of Jerry's mother. How would the story be different if she, rather than the **omniscient narrator,** were telling it?

Connecting with the Text

9. What details about Jerry's swim through the tunnel were most vivid and terrifying to you?

Challenging the Text

10. Have you ever taken great risks to prove yourself? (Check your Quickwrite notes.) Do you find it convincing that Jerry takes such a risk and survives? Explain.

CHOICES: Building Your Portfolio

Writer's Notebook

1. Collecting Ideas for an Evaluation

WORK IN PROGRESS

Gathering evidence. Although your evaluation of a story begins with your reactions to it, you need to look closely at the aspects of the text that evoked those responses. Make an evaluation of just one story element in "Through the Tunnel." Look for evidence in the text to support your judgment. You may want to record your evidence in a chart like the one here.

Story Element: Plot	
Evaluation	Evidence
Very suspenseful; made me really think Jerry would drown.	"He felt he was dying. He was no longer quite conscious. He struggled on in the dark-ness. . . ." (page 282) Blood. (page 283)

Analyzing Setting

2. Settings and Deep Meanings

Write a brief essay analyzing the significance of three settings in the story: the wild bay, the safe beach, and the tunnel. Tell what you think each setting represents to Jerry. Also consider this question: Could the passage through the tunnel be seen as either a birth or a death? Support your analysis and elaborate with direct references to details in the story.

Art

3. A Collage of the Wild Bay

A collage is an arrangement of images (photographs, magazine art, drawings), words, and other objects (sand, shells, stones, and so forth) glued to a surface. Make a collage called "The Wild Bay." Find words from the text that can go with your images. What mood do you want to convey in your collage?

Speaking and Listening

4. Stories "To Go"

National Public Radio often features short stories read aloud by writers or by actors. Many people like to listen to these stories as they travel by car—it's a good way to learn something new and to get where you are going at the same time. Record "Through the Tunnel" as if for National Public Radio. Use no sound effects—only your own voice. You'll have to practice reading aloud before you do your taping. (For help, see the Speaking and Listening Workshop on **oral interpretation,** pages 750–751.) Be sure to begin by giving the title of the story and its author. Present your tape to someone who enjoys listening to stories while driving.

GRAMMAR LINK MINI-LESSON

Powerful Participles

Language Handbook HELP

See Participles, pages 1034–1035.

Technology HELP

See Language Workshop CD-ROM. *Key word entry: participles.*

Participles are verb forms that can be used as adjectives to modify nouns and pronouns: hanging head, spotted foot, running water. Present participles always end in *-ing*, and most past participles end in *-ed* or *-d*. Because they combine the action of verbs and the descriptive power of adjectives, participles can create vivid pictures in just a few words. Look at how Doris Lessing uses participles in the following items:

1. "He could see nothing through the stinging salt water but the blank rock."
2. "It was like swimming in flaked silver."

Participial phrases are participles with all their complements and modifiers.

1. "Her other arm, swinging loose, was very white in the sun."
2. "He was in a small rock-bound hole filled with yellowish-gray water."

An introductory participial phrase is followed by a comma to prevent confusion.

Swinging loose her other arm was very white in the sun. [confusing]

Swinging loose, her other arm was very white in the sun. [clear]

Try It Out

Write five sentences about "Through the Tunnel," using one of the following participles in each sentence. Be sure you use the participle as an adjective.

lapping	rippled
diving	glittered
clinging	

Now, write five more sentences, using the same participles in phrases. Compare your sentences with a partner's.

Tips for writers: You can tighten your writing with participles. Whenever you have long, cumbersome sentences, see if there's a clause that can be reduced to a participle or participial phrase.

VOCABULARY HOW TO OWN A WORD

WORD BANK

contrition
supplication
inquisitive
minute
incredulous

Analogies: Make It Complete

In an **analogy** the words in one pair relate to each other in the same way as the words in a second pair. For example, a pair of words could be synonyms or antonyms, or one word could describe a characteristic of the other or be a part of the other. Work with a partner to fill in each blank below with the word from the Word Bank that completes the analogy. Here, analogies are written out. Sometimes they are written like this: *huge : elephant :: ____________ : gnat*

1. *Huge* is to *elephant* as ____________ is to *gnat.*
2. *Sadness* is to *mourning* as ____________ is to *regretting.*
3. *Secure* is to *safe* as ____________ is to *curious.*
4. *Needy* is to *beggar* as ____________ is to *skeptic.*
5. *Whisper* is to *shout* as ____________ is to *demand.*

Before You Read

THE PIT AND THE PENDULUM

Make the Connection

Our Deepest Fears

Here is Poe's horrifying story of confinement in a prison cell during the Spanish Inquisition. Poe's story uses a grotesque form of torture that stirs our deepest fears.

Quickwrite

What things arouse your fears? Freewrite for a few minutes about some of your fears and the feelings and images you associate with them.

Reading Skills and Strategies

Summarizing

When you read long stories, it helps to stop at key points and sum up what is happening. Try this strategy with Poe's horror story. You'll find the symbol at certain points in the story. Stop at these points, and **summarize** what has just happened. Focus on the main events or on the narrator's last crisis. If you need to, go back and reread certain sections to be sure you have understood what has happened.

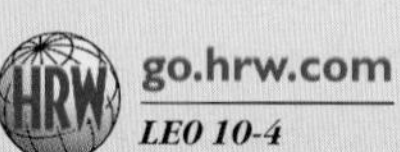

go.hrw.com
LEO 10-4

Elements of Literature

Symbolic Meaning: More Than a Scare

When we read, we often sense that a story means more than what happens on the surface. For instance, if a young woman in a story is in serious conflict with her parents over her earrings, we should suspect that those earrings represent something more important to her—perhaps freedom or maturity. One of the pleasures of reading lies in thinking about symbols.

What elements in Poe's story could be symbolically significant? What might they mean?

> The **symbolic meaning** of a story emerges from an overall interpretation of the story's individual symbols.
>
> *For more on Symbol, see pages 306–307 and the Handbook of Literary Terms.*

Background

The purpose of the Spanish Inquisition was to punish people who were suspected of not being true believers in the Christian faith.

Poe may have gotten his idea for this story from a book by Juan Antonio Llorente. Poe read a review of this book, which contains the following passage:

". . . the Inquisition was thrown open, in 1820, by the orders of the Cortes of Madrid. Twenty-one prisoners were found in it . . . . Some had been confined three years, some a longer period, and not one knew perfectly the nature of the crime of which he was accused. One of these prisoners had been condemned and was to have suffered on the following day. His punishment was to be death by the Pendulum. The method of thus destroying the victim is as follows: The condemned is fastened in a groove, upon a table, on his back; suspended above him is a Pendulum, the edge of which is sharp, and it is so constructed as to become longer with every movement. The wretch sees this implement of destruction swinging to and fro above him, and every moment the keen edge approaching nearer and nearer."

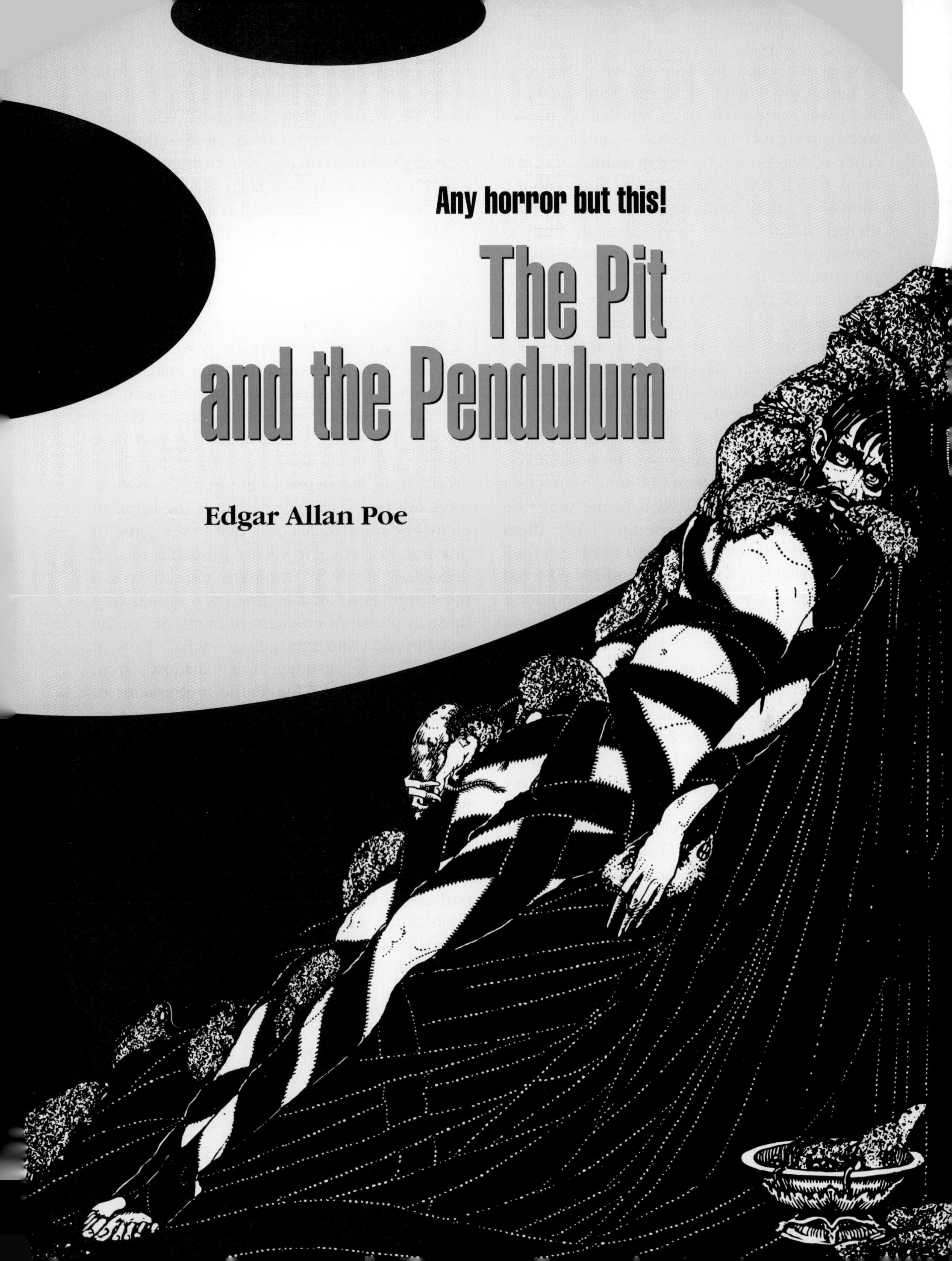

Any horror but this!

The Pit and the Pendulum

Edgar Allan Poe

I was sick—sick unto death with that long agony; and when they at length unbound me, and I was permitted to sit, I felt that my senses were leaving me. The sentence—the dread sentence of death—was the last of distinct accentuation which reached my ears. After that, the sound of the Inquisitorial voices seemed merged in one dreamy, indeterminate hum. It conveyed to my soul the idea of *revolution*[1]—perhaps from its association in fancy[2] with the burr of a mill wheel. This only for a brief period, for presently I heard no more. Yet for a while, I saw—but with how terrible an exaggeration! I saw the lips of the black-robed judges. They appeared to me white—whiter than the sheet upon which I trace these words—and thin even to grotesqueness; thin with the intensity of their expression of firmness—of immovable resolution—of stern contempt of human torture. I saw that the decrees of what to me was Fate were still issuing from those lips. I saw them writhe with a deadly locution.[3] I saw them fashion the syllables of my name; and I shuddered because no sound succeeded.[4] I saw, too, for a few moments of delirious horror, the soft and nearly imperceptible waving of the sable draperies which enwrapped the walls of the apartment. And then my vision fell upon the seven tall candles upon the table. At first they wore the aspect of charity and seemed white, slender angels who would save me; but then, all at once, there came a most deadly nausea over my spirit, and I felt every fiber in my frame thrill as if I had touched the wire of a galvanic battery, while the angel forms became meaningless specters, with heads of flame, and I saw that from them there would be no help. And then there stole into my fancy, like a rich musical note, the thought of what sweet rest there must be in the grave. The thought came gently and stealthily, and it seemed long before it attained full appreciation; but just as my spirit came at length properly to feel and entertain it, the figures of the judges vanished, as if magically, from before me; the tall candles sank into nothingness! Their flames went out utterly; the blackness of darkness supervened; all sensations appeared swallowed up in a mad rushing descent, as of the soul into Hades. Then silence, and stillness, and night were the universe.

I had swooned;[5] but still will not say that all of consciousness was lost. What of it there remained I will not attempt to define, or even to describe; yet all was not lost. In the deepest slumber—no! In delirium—no! In a swoon—no! In death—no! Even in the grave all *is not* lost. Else there is no immortality for man. Arousing from the most profound of slumbers, we break the gossamer web of *some* dream. Yet in a second afterward (so frail may that web have been), we remember not that we have dreamed. In the return to life from the swoon, there are two stages: first, that of the sense of mental or spiritual; second, that of the sense of physical existence. It seems probable that if, upon reaching the second stage, we could recall the impressions of the first, we should find these impressions eloquent in memories of the gulf beyond. And that gulf is—what? How at least shall we distinguish its shadows from those of the tomb? But if the impressions of what I have termed the first stage are not, at will, recalled, yet, after long interval, do they not come unbidden, while we marvel whence they come? He who has never swooned is not he who finds strange palaces and wildly familiar faces in coals that glow; is not he who beholds floating in midair the sad visions that the many may not view; is not he who ponders over the perfume of some novel flower; is not he whose brain grows bewildered with the meaning of some musical cadence which has never before arrested his attention.

1. **revolution:** here, rotation; turning motion.
2. **fancy:** here, imagination.
3. **locution** (lō·kyo͞o′shən): utterance; statement.
4. **succeeded:** here, followed.

5. **swooned:** fainted.

WORDS TO OWN

imperceptible (im′pər·sep′tə·bəl) *adj.:* not clear or obvious to the senses or the mind; too slight or gradual to be noticeable.

ponders (pän′dərz) *v.:* thinks deeply.

Literature and History

The Inquisition: Power, Greed, and Suffering

King Ferdinand and Queen Isabella of Spain had political as well as religious motives for establishing the Spanish Inquisition in 1478. The Catholic monarchs wished to regain control over a fragmented country that had been ruled for centuries by the Moors (Muslims from North Africa) and that had a large population of influential Jews, many of whom had converted to Christianity. By finding Spanish Jews and Muslims guilty of converting to Christianity not out of true religious conviction but from a desire to keep their lands and property, the monarchy used the Inquisition to seize the converts' wealth and destroy their influence. The methods of the Inquisition included imprisonment, torture, confiscation of property, and public execution. At its height, from 1483 to 1498, a Dominican priest, Tomás de Torquemada, presided over thousands of trials and about two thousand burnings at the stake. These burnings were preceded by a public religious ceremony, called an auto-da-fé (act of faith), in which the accused was marched in procession into a church, a Mass was held, and the death sentence was read. Then the convicted person was handed over to the state authorities for execution.

The Inquisition was temporarily halted in 1808 when Napoleon's army invaded and defeated Spain. General Lasalle commanded the French troops who seized the city of Toledo. Napoleon proclaimed his older brother king of Spain, but in 1813, he was ousted by the Spanish with British aid. The Spanish monarchy was restored and with it the Inquisition, which persisted in a limited form in Spain and Latin America until 1834.

Amid frequent and thoughtful endeavors to remember, amid earnest struggles to regather some token of the state of seeming nothingness into which my soul had lapsed, there have been moments when I have dreamed of success; there have been brief, very brief, periods when I have conjured up remembrances which the lucid reason of a later epoch assures me could have had reference only to that condition of

Words to Own

lucid (lo͞o′sid) *adj.:* clearheaded; not confused. *Lucid* also means "understandable" or "bright and shining."

View of Toledo (1608) by El Greco. Oil on canvas.

The Metropolitan Museum of Art, H. O. Havemeyer Collection, Bequest of Mrs. H. O. Havemeyer, 1929 (29.100.6)

seeming unconsciousness. These shadows of memory tell, indistinctly, of tall figures that lifted and bore me in silence down—down—still down—till a hideous dizziness oppressed me at the mere idea of the interminableness of the descent. They tell also of a vague horror at my heart, on account of that heart's unnatural stillness. Then comes a sense of sudden motionlessness throughout all things; as if those who bore me (a ghastly train!) had outrun, in their descent, the limits of the limitless, and paused from the wearisomeness of their toil. After this I call to mind flatness and dampness; and then all is *madness*—the madness of a memory which busies itself among forbidden things.

Very suddenly there came back to my soul motion and sound—the tumultuous motion of the heart and, in my ears, the sound of its beating. Then a pause in which all is blank. Then again sound, and motion, and touch—a tingling sensation pervading my frame. Then the mere consciousness of existence, without thought—a condition which lasted long. Then, very suddenly, *thought*, and shuddering terror, and earnest endeavor to comprehend my true state. Then a strong desire to lapse into insensibility. Then a rushing revival of soul and a successful effort to move. And now a full memory of the trial, of the judges, of the sable draperies, of the sentence, of the sickness, of the swoon. Then entire forgetfulness of all that followed; of all that a later day and much earnestness of endeavor have enabled me vaguely to recall.

So far, I had not opened my eyes. I felt that I lay upon my back, unbound. I reached out my hand, and it fell heavily upon something damp and hard. There I suffered[6] it to remain for many minutes, while I strove to imagine where and *what* I could be. I longed, yet dared not, to employ my vision. I dreaded the first glance at objects around me. It was not that I feared to look upon things horrible, but that I grew aghast lest there should be *nothing* to see. At length, with a wild desperation at heart, I quickly unclosed my eyes. My worst thoughts, then, were confirmed. The blackness of eternal night encompassed me. I struggled for breath. The intensity of the darkness seemed to oppress and stifle me. The atmosphere was intolerably close. I still lay quietly, and made effort to exercise my reason. I brought to mind the Inquisitorial proceedings and attempted from that point to deduce my real condition. The sentence had passed; and it appeared to me that a very long interval of time had since elapsed. Yet not for a moment did I suppose myself actually dead. Such a supposition, notwithstanding what we read in fiction, is altogether inconsistent with real existence—but where and in what state was I? The condemned to death, I knew, perished usually at the autos-da-fé, and one of these had been held on the very night of the day of my trial. Had I been remanded to my dungeon, to await the next sacrifice, which would not take place for many months? This I at once saw could not be. Victims had been in immediate demand. Moreover, my dungeon, as well as all the condemned cells at Toledo, had stone floors, and light was not altogether excluded.

A fearful idea now suddenly drove the blood in torrents upon my heart, and for a brief period I once more relapsed into insensibility. Upon recovering, I at once started to my feet, trembling convulsively in every fiber. I thrust my arms wildly above and around me in all directions. I felt nothing; yet dreaded to move a step, lest I should be impeded by the walls of a *tomb*. Perspiration burst from every pore and stood in cold, big beads upon my forehead. The agony of suspense grew at length intolerable, and I cautiously moved forward, with my arms extended and my eyes straining from their sockets in the hope of catching some faint ray of light. I proceeded for many paces; but still all was blackness and vacancy. I breathed more freely. It seemed evident that mine was not, at least, the most hideous of fates.

And now, as I still continued to step cautiously onward, there came thronging upon my recollection a thousand vague rumors of the horrors of Toledo. Of the dungeons there had been strange things narrated—fables I had always deemed them—but yet strange, and too ghastly to repeat, save in a whisper. Was I left to perish of starvation in the subterranean world of darkness; or what fate, perhaps even more

6. **suffered:** here, allowed; tolerated.

Words to Own

tumultuous (to͞o·mul′cho͞o·əs) *adj.:* violent; greatly agitated or disturbed. *Tumultuous* also means "wild, noisy, and confused."

fearful, awaited me? That the result would be death, and a death of more than customary bitterness, I knew too well the character of my judges to doubt. The mode and the hour were all that occupied or distracted me.

In the confusion attending my fall, I did not immediately apprehend a somewhat startling circumstance . . .

My outstretched hands at length encountered some solid obstruction. It was a wall, seemingly of stone masonry—very smooth, slimy, and cold. I followed it up, stepping with all the careful distrust with which certain antique narratives had inspired me. This process, however, afforded me no means of ascertaining the dimensions of my dungeon, as I might make its circuit and return to the point whence I set out without being aware of the fact, so perfectly uniform seemed the wall. I therefore sought the knife which had been in my pocket when led into the Inquisitorial chamber, but it was gone; my clothes had been exchanged for a wrapper of coarse serge. I had thought of forcing the blade in some minute crevice of the masonry, so as to identify my point of departure. The difficulty, nevertheless, was but trivial; although, in the disorder of my fancy, it seemed at first insuperable. I tore a part of the hem from the robe and placed the fragment at full length and at right angles to the wall. In groping my way around the prison, I could not fail to encounter this rag upon completing the circuit. So, at least, I thought; but I had not counted upon the extent of the dungeon, or upon my own weakness. The ground was moist and slippery. I staggered onward for some time, when I stumbled and fell. My excessive fatigue induced me to remain prostrate; and sleep soon overtook me as I lay.

Upon awaking and stretching forth an arm, I found beside me a loaf and a pitcher with water. I was too much exhausted to reflect upon this circumstance, but ate and drank with avidity.[7] Shortly afterward, I resumed my tour around the prison and, with much toil, came at last upon the fragment of the serge. Up to the period when I fell, I had counted fifty-two paces, and upon resuming my walk, I had counted forty-eight more—when I arrived at the rag. There were in all, then, a hundred paces; and, admitting two paces to the yard, I presumed the dungeon to be fifty yards in circuit. I had met, however, with many angles in the wall, and thus I could form no guess at the shape of the vault, for vault I could not help supposing it to be.

I had little object—certainly no hope—in these researches; but a vague curiosity prompted me to continue them. Quitting the wall, I resolved to cross the area of the enclosure. At first, I proceeded with extreme caution, for the floor, although seemingly of solid material, was treacherous with slime. At length, however, I took courage and did not hesitate to step firmly—endeavoring to cross in as direct a line as possible. I had advanced some ten or twelve paces in this manner when the remnant of the torn hem of my robe became entangled between my legs. I stepped on it and fell violently on my face.

In the confusion attending my fall, I did not immediately apprehend a somewhat startling circumstance, which yet, in a few seconds afterward and while I still lay prostrate, arrested my attention. It was this—my chin rested upon the floor of the prison, but my lips and the upper portion of my head, although seemingly at a less elevation than the chin, touched nothing. At the same time, my forehead seemed bathed in a clammy vapor, and the peculiar smell of decayed fungus arose to my nostrils. I put forward my arm, and shuddered to find that I had fallen

7. **avidity** (ə·vid′ə·tē): great eagerness.

Words to Own

insuperable (in·sōō′pər·ə·bəl) *adj.*: incapable of being overcome or passed over.

prostrate (präs′trāt′) *adj.*: lying flat. *Prostrate* also means "helpless; overcome" or "lying with the face downward to show devotion or submission."

at the very brink of a circular pit, whose extent, of course, I had no means of ascertaining at the moment. Groping about the masonry just below the margin, I succeeded in dislodging a small fragment and let it fall into the abyss. For many seconds I hearkened to its reverberations as it dashed against the sides of the chasm in its descent; at length, there was a sullen plunge into water, succeeded by loud echoes. At the same moment, there came a sound resembling the quick opening and as rapid closing of a door overhead, while a faint gleam of light flashed suddenly through the gloom and as suddenly faded away.

I saw clearly the doom which had been prepared for me, and congratulated myself upon the timely accident by which I had escaped. Another step before my fall, and the world had seen me no more. And the death just avoided was of that very character which I had regarded as fabulous and frivolous in the tales respecting the Inquisition. To the victims of its tyranny, there was the choice of death with its direst physical agonies or death with its most hideous moral horrors. I had been reserved for the latter. By long suffering, my nerves had been unstrung, until I trembled at the sound of my own voice and had become in every respect a fitting subject for the species of torture which awaited me.

Shaking in every limb, I groped my way back to the wall; resolving there to perish rather than risk the terrors of the wells, of which my imagination now pictured many in various positions about the dungeon. In other conditions of mind, I might have had courage to end my misery at once, by a plunge into one of these abysses; but now I was the veriest[8] of cowards. Neither could I forget what I had read of these pits—that the *sudden* extinction of life formed no part of their most horrible plan.

Agitation of spirit kept me awake for many long hours, but at length I again slumbered. Upon arousing, I found by my side, as before, a loaf and a pitcher of water. A burning thirst consumed me, and I emptied the vessel at a draft. It must have been drugged; for scarcely had I drunk before I became irresistibly drowsy. A deep sleep fell upon me—a sleep like that of death. How long it lasted of course I know not; but when, once again, I unclosed my eyes, the objects around me were visible. By a wild, sulfurous luster,[9] the origin of which I could not at first determine, I was enabled to see the extent and aspect of the prison.

In its size I had been greatly mistaken. The whole circuit of its walls did not exceed twenty-five yards. For some minutes this fact occasioned me a world of vain trouble; vain indeed, for what could be of less importance, under the terrible circumstances which environed me, than the mere dimensions of my dungeon? But

A scene from "The Pit and the Pendulum," illustrated by Arthur Rackham.

8. **veriest** (ver′ē·ist): greatest.

9. **sulfurous** (sul′fər·əs) **luster:** glow like that of burning sulfur, which produces a blue flame. The word *sulfurous* is also used to mean "suggesting the fires of hell."

my soul took a wild interest in trifles, and I busied myself in endeavors to account for the error I had committed in my measurement. The truth at length flashed upon me. In my first attempt at exploration I had counted fifty-two paces, up to the period when I fell; I must then have been within a pace or two of the fragment of serge; in fact, I had nearly performed the circuit of the vault. I then slept, and upon awaking, I must have returned upon my steps—thus supposing the circuit nearly double what it actually was. My confusion of mind prevented me from observing that I began my tour with the wall to the left and ended it with the wall to the right.

I had been deceived, too, in respect to the shape of the enclosure. In feeling my way I had found many angles and thus deduced an idea of great irregularity; so potent is the effect of total darkness upon one arousing from lethargy or sleep! The angles were simply those of a few slight depressions, or niches, at odd intervals. The general shape of the prison was square. What I had taken for masonry seemed now to be iron, or some other metal, in huge plates, whose sutures or joints occasioned the depression. The entire surface of this metallic enclosure was rudely daubed[10] in all the hideous and repulsive devices to which the charnel[11] superstition of the monks has given rise. The figures of fiends in aspects of menace, with skeleton forms, and other, more really fearful images, overspread and disfigured the walls. I observed that the outlines of these monstrosities were sufficiently distinct, but that the colors seemed faded and blurred, as if from the effects of a damp atmosphere. I now noticed the floor, too, which was of stone. In the center yawned the circular pit from whose jaws I had escaped; but it was the only one in the dungeon.

All this I saw indistinctly and by much effort: for my personal condition had been greatly changed during slumber. I now lay upon my back, and at full length, on a species of low framework of wood. To this I was securely bound by a long strap resembling a surcingle.[12] It passed in many convolutions about my limbs and body, leaving at liberty only my head, and my left arm to such extent that I could, by dint of much exertion, supply myself with food from an earthen dish which lay by my side on the floor. I saw, to my horror, that the pitcher had been removed. I say to my horror, for I was consumed with intolerable thirst. This thirst it appeared to be the design of my persecutors to stimulate—for the food in the dish was meat pungently seasoned.

In the center yawned the circular pit from whose jaws I had escaped . . .

Looking upward, I surveyed the ceiling of my prison. It was some thirty or forty feet overhead and constructed much as the side walls. In one of its panels a very singular figure riveted my whole attention. It was the painted figure of Time as he is commonly represented, save[13] that, in lieu of[14] a scythe, he held what, at a casual glance, I supposed to be the pictured image of a huge pendulum, such as we see on antique clocks. There was something, however, in the appearance of this machine which caused me to regard it more attentively. While I gazed directly upward at it (for its position was immediately over my own), I fancied that I saw it in motion. In an instant afterward the fancy was confirmed. Its sweep was brief and of course slow. I watched it for some minutes somewhat

10. **daubed:** painted crudely or unskillfully.
11. **charnel:** suggestive of death. A charnel house is a building or place where bones or bodies are deposited.

12. **surcingle** (sur′siŋ′gəl): strap passed around a horse's body to bind on a saddle or a pack.
13. **save:** here, except.
14. **in lieu** (lo͞o) **of:** instead of.

WORDS TO OWN

potent (pōt′'nt) *adj.:* powerful or effective.
lethargy (leth′ər · jē) *n.:* abnormal drowsiness. *Lethargy* also means "great lack of energy; dull or indifferent state."

in fear, but more in wonder. Wearied at length with observing its dull movement, I turned my eyes upon the other objects in the cell.

A slight noise attracted my notice, and looking to the floor, I saw several enormous rats traversing it. They had issued from the well which lay just within view to my right. Even then, while I gazed, they came up in troops, hurriedly, with ravenous eyes, allured by the scent of the meat. From this it required much effort and attention to scare them away.

It might have been half an hour, perhaps even an hour (for I could take but imperfect note of time), before I again cast my eyes upward. What I then saw confounded and amazed me. The sweep of the pendulum had increased in extent by nearly a yard. As a natural consequence its velocity was also much greater. But what mainly disturbed me was the idea that it had perceptibly *descended.* I now observed—with what horror it is needless to say—that its nether extremity[15] was formed of a crescent of glittering steel, about a foot in length from horn to horn; the horns upward, and the under edge evidently as keen as that of a razor. Like a razor also, it seemed massy and heavy, tapering from the edge into a solid and broad structure above. It was appended to a weighty rod of brass, and the whole *hissed* as it swung through the air.

I could no longer doubt the doom prepared for me by monkish ingenuity in torture. My cognizance[16] of the pit had become known to the Inquisitorial agents—*the pit,* whose horrors had been destined for so bold a recusant[17] as myself—*the pit,* typical of hell and regarded by rumor as the ultima Thule[18] of all their punishments. The plunge into this pit I had avoided by the merest of accidents, and I knew that surprise, or entrapment into torment, formed an important portion of all the grotesquerie of these dungeon deaths. Having failed to fall, it was no part of the demon plan to hurl me into the abyss, and thus (there being no alternative) a different and a milder destruction awaited me. Milder! I half smiled in my agony as I thought of such application of such a term.

What boots it[19] to tell of the long, long hours of horror more than mortal, during which I counted the rushing vibrations of the steel! Inch by inch—line by line—with a descent only appreciable at intervals that seemed ages—down and still down it came! Days passed—it might have been that many days passed—ere it swept so closely over me as to fan me with its acrid breath. The odor of the sharp steel forced itself into my nostrils. I prayed—I wearied heaven with my prayer for its more speedy descent. I grew frantically mad and struggled to force myself upward against the sweep of the fearful scimitar.[20] And then I fell suddenly calm and lay smiling at the glittering death, as a child at some rare bauble.

There was another interval of utter insensibility; it was brief; for, upon again lapsing into life, there had been no perceptible descent in the pendulum. But it might have been long—for I knew there were demons who took note of my swoon and who could have arrested the vibration at pleasure. Upon my recovery, too, I felt very—oh! inexpressibly—sick and weak, as if through long inanition.[21] Even amid the agonies of that period, the human nature craved food. With painful effort I outstretched my left arm as far as my bonds permitted and took possession of the small remnant which had been spared me by the rats. As I put a portion of it within my lips, there rushed to my mind a half-formed thought of joy—of hope. Yet what business had *I* with hope? It was, as I say, a half-formed thought—man has many such, which are never completed. I felt that it was of joy—of hope; but I felt also that it had perished in its formation. In vain I struggled to perfect—to regain it. Long suffering had nearly annihilated all my ordinary powers of mind. I was an imbecile—an idiot.

15. **nether** (ne*th*′ər) **extremity:** lower end.
16. **cognizance** (käg′nə·zəns): awareness.
17. **recusant** (rek′yoo·zənt): person who refuses to obey an established authority.
18. **ultima Thule** (ul′ti·mə thōō′lē): most extreme. The term is Latin for "northernmost region of the world."
19. **what boots it:** of what use is it.
20. **scimitar** (sim′ə·tər): sword with a curved blade, used mainly by Arabs and Turks.
21. **inanition** (in′ə·nish′ən): weakness from lack of food.

The vibration of the pendulum was at right angles to my length. I saw that the crescent was designed to cross the region of the heart. It would fray the serge of my robe—it would return and repeat its operations—again—and again. Notwithstanding its terrifically wide sweep (some thirty feet or more) and the hissing vigor of its descent, sufficient to sunder these very walls of iron, still the fraying of my robe would be all that, for several minutes, it would accomplish. And at this thought I paused. I dared not go further than this reflection. I dwelt upon it with a pertinacity[22] of attention—as if, in so dwelling, I could arrest[23] *here* the descent of the steel. I forced myself to ponder upon the sound of the crescent as it should pass across the garment—upon the peculiar thrilling sensation which the friction of cloth produces on the nerves. I pondered upon all this frivolity until my teeth were on edge.

Down—steadily down it crept. I took a frenzied pleasure in contrasting its downward with its lateral velocity. To the right—to the left—far and wide—with the shriek of a damned spirit! to my heart, with the stealthy pace of the tiger! I alternately laughed and howled, as the one or the other idea grew predominant.

Down—certainly, relentlessly down! It vibrated within three inches of my bosom! I struggled violently—furiously—to free my left arm. This was free only from the elbow to the hand. I could reach the latter, from the platter beside me, to my mouth, with great effort, but no farther. Could I have broken the fastenings above the elbow, I would have seized and attempted to arrest the pendulum. I might as well have attempted to arrest an avalanche!

Down—still unceasingly—still inevitably down! I gasped and struggled at each vibration. I shrunk convulsively at its every sweep. My eyes followed its outward or upward whorls with the eagerness of the most unmeaning despair; they closed themselves spasmodically at the descent, although death would have been a relief, oh, how unspeakable! Still I quivered in every nerve to think how slight a sinking of the machinery would precipitate that keen, glistening ax upon my bosom. It was *hope* that prompted the nerve to quiver—the frame to shrink. It was *hope*—the hope that triumphs on the rack—that whispers to the death-condemned even in the dungeons of the Inquisition.

I saw that some ten or twelve vibrations would bring the steel in actual contact with my robe, and with this observation there suddenly came over my spirit all the keen, collected calmness of despair. For the first time during many hours—or perhaps days—I *thought.* It now occurred to me that the bandage, or surcingle, which enveloped me, was *unique.* I was tied by no separate cord. The first stroke of the razorlike crescent athwart any portion of the band would so detach it that it might be unwound from my person by means of my left hand. But how fearful, in that case, the proximity of the steel! The result of the slightest struggle, how deadly! Was it likely, moreover, that the minions[24] of the torturer had not foreseen and provided for this possibility? Was it probable that the bandage crossed my bosom in the track of the pendulum? Dreading to find my faint and, as it seemed, my last hope frustrated, I so far elevated my head as to obtain a distinct view of my breast. The surcingle enveloped my limbs and body close in all directions—*save in the path of the destroying crescent.*

Scarcely had I dropped my head back into its original position when there flashed upon my mind what I cannot better describe than as the unformed half of that idea of deliverance to which I had previously alluded, and of which a moiety[25] only floated indeterminately through my brain when I raised food to my burning lips. The whole thought was now present—feeble, scarcely sane, scarcely definite—but still entire. I proceeded at once, with the nervous energy of despair, to attempt its execution.

22. **pertinacity** (pʉr'tə·nas'ə·tē): stubborn persistence.
23. **arrest:** here, stop.

24. **minions:** servants; followers.
25. **moiety** (moi'ə·tē): part.

WORDS TO OWN

proximity (präks·im'ə·tē) *n.:* nearness.

A scene from "The Pit and the Pendulum," illustrated by John Byam Shaw.

For many hours the immediate vicinity of the low framework upon which I lay had been literally swarming with rats. They were wild, bold, ravenous—their red eyes glaring upon me as if they waited but for motionlessness on my part to make me their prey. "To what food," I thought, "have they been accustomed in the well?"

I knew that in more than one place it must be already severed. With a more than human resolution I lay *still.*

They had devoured, in spite of all my efforts to prevent them, all but a small remnant of the contents of the dish. I had fallen into a habitual seesaw or wave of the hand about the platter; and, at length, the unconscious uniformity of the movement deprived it of effect. In their voracity, the vermin frequently fastened their sharp fangs in my fingers. With the particles of the oily and spicy viand which now remained, I thoroughly rubbed the bandage wherever I could reach it; then, raising my hand from the floor, I lay breathlessly still.

At first, the ravenous animals were startled and terrified at the change—at the cessation of movement. They shrank alarmedly back; many sought the well. But this was only for a moment. I had not counted in vain upon their voracity. Observing that I remained without motion, one or two of the boldest leaped upon the framework and smelled at the surcingle. This seemed the signal for a general rush. Forth from the well they hurried in fresh troops. They clung to the wood—they overran it and leaped in hundreds upon my person. The measured movement of the pendulum disturbed them not at all. Avoiding its strokes, they busied themselves with the anointed bandage. They pressed—they swarmed upon me in ever accumulating heaps. They writhed upon my throat; their cold lips sought my own; I was half stifled by their thronging pressure; disgust for which the world has no name swelled my bosom and chilled, with a heavy clamminess, my heart. Yet one minute, and I felt that the struggle would be over. Plainly I perceived the loosening of the bandage. I knew that in more than one place it must be already severed. With a more than human resolution I lay *still.*

Nor had I erred in my calculations—nor had I endured in vain. I at length felt that I was *free.* The surcingle hung in ribbons from my body. But the stroke of the pendulum already pressed upon my bosom. It had divided the serge of the robe. It had cut through the linen beneath. Twice again it swung, and a sharp sense of pain shot through every nerve. But the moment of escape had arrived. At a wave of my hand my deliverers hurried tumultuously away. With a steady movement—cautious, sidelong, shrinking, and slow—I slid from the embrace of the bandage and beyond the reach of the scimitar. For the moment, at least, *I was free.*

Free!—and in the grasp of the Inquisition! I had scarcely stepped from my wooden bed of horror upon the stone floor of the prison when the motion of the hellish machine ceased, and I beheld it drawn up, by some invisible force, through the ceiling. This was a lesson which I took desperately to heart. My every motion was undoubtedly watched. Free!—I had but escaped death in one form of agony to be delivered unto worse than death in some other. With that thought I rolled my eyes nervously around on the barriers of iron that hemmed me in. Something unusual—some change which at first I could not appreciate distinctly—it was obvious, had taken place in the apartment. For many minutes of a dreamy and trembling abstraction, I busied myself in vain, unconnected conjecture. During this period, I became aware, for the first time, of the origin of the sulfurous light which illumined the cell. It proceeded from a fissure, about half an inch in width, extending entirely around the prison at the base of the walls, which thus appeared, and were, completely separated from the floor. I endeavored, but of course in vain, to look through the aperture.

As I arose from the attempt, the mystery of the alteration in the chamber broke at once upon my understanding. I had observed that, although the outlines of the figures upon the walls were sufficiently distinct, yet the colors seemed blurred and indefinite. These colors had now assumed and were momentarily assuming, a startling and most intense brilliance that gave to the spectral and fiendish portraitures an aspect that might have thrilled even firmer nerves than my own. Demon eyes, of a wild and ghastly vivacity, glared upon me in a thousand directions where none had been visible before, and gleamed with the lurid luster of a fire that I could not force my imagination to regard as unreal.

Unreal!—even while I breathed, there came to my nostrils the breath of the vapor of heated iron! A suffocating odor pervaded the prison! A deeper glow settled each moment in the eyes that glared at my agonies! A richer tint of crimson diffused itself over the pictured horrors of blood. I panted! I gasped for breath! There could be no doubt of the design of my tormenters—oh! most unrelenting! oh! most demoniac of men! I shrank from the glowing metal to the center of the cell. Amid the thought of the fiery destruction that impended, the idea of the coolness of the well came over my soul like balm. I rushed to its deadly brink. I threw my straining vision below. The glare from the enkindled roof illumined its inmost recesses. Yet for a wild moment did my spirit refuse to comprehend the meaning of what I saw. At length it forced—it wrestled its way into my soul—it burned itself in upon my shuddering reason.—Oh! for a voice to speak!—oh! horror!—oh! any horror but this! With a shriek, I rushed from the margin and buried my face in my hands—weeping bitterly.

The heat rapidly increased, and once again I looked up, shuddering as with a fit of the ague.[26] There had been a second change in the cell—and now the change was obviously in the *form.* As before, it was in vain that I at first endeavored to appreciate or understand what was taking place. But not long was I left in doubt. The Inquisitorial vengeance had been hurried by my twofold escape, and there was to be no more dallying with the King of Terrors. The room had been square. I saw that two of its iron angles were now acute[27]—two, consequently, obtuse.[28] The fearful difference quickly increased with a low rumbling or moaning sound. In an instant the apartment had shifted its form into that of a lozenge.[29] But the alteration stopped not here—I neither hoped nor desired it to stop. I could have clasped the red walls to my bosom as a garment of eternal peace. "Death," I said, "any death but that of the pit!" Fool! Might I not have known that *into the pit* it was the object of the burning iron to urge me? Could I resist its glow? Or if even that, could I withstand its pressure? And now, flatter and flatter grew the lozenge, with a rapidity that left me no time for contemplation. Its center, and of course its greatest width, came just over the yawning gulf. I shrank back—but the closing walls pressed me resistlessly onward. At length, for my seared and writhing body, there was no longer an inch of foothold on the firm floor of the prison. I struggled no more, but the agony of my soul found vent in one loud, long, and final scream of despair. I felt that I tottered upon the brink—I averted my eyes——

There was a discordant hum of human voices! There was a loud blast as of many trumpets! There was a harsh grating as of a thousand thunders! The fiery walls rushed back! An outstretched arm caught my own as I fell, fainting, into the abyss. It was that of General Lasalle. The French army had entered Toledo. The Inquisition was in the hands of its enemies.

26. **ague** (ā′gyo͞o′): chills.

27. **acute** (ə·kyo͞ot′): of less than 90 degrees.
28. **obtuse** (äb·to͞os′): of more than 90 degrees and less than 180 degrees.
29. **lozenge** (läz′ənj): diamond shape.

Words to Own

averted (ə·vurt′id) *v.:* turned away. *Averted* also means "prevented."

Meet the Writer

Nightmare Worlds

Edgar Allan Poe (1809–1849) was a moody, sensitive person whose stories and poems dwell on the supernatural and on crime, torture, premature burial, and death. His writing, which brought him little comfort or security, reflects the dark, nightmare side of the imagination.

Poe's stormy personal history began when his father deserted his mother, a popular young actress, who died in 1811 in a theatrical rooming house in Richmond, Virginia, just before Edgar was three years old.

A wealthy, childless couple, the Allans of Richmond, took him in and gave him a good education, expecting him to take over John Allan's business eventually. Edgar wanted to be a writer, though, not a businessman. This disagreement and John Allan's persistent refusal to adopt Edgar legally led to frequent fights. By the time he was twenty-one, Poe and John Allan had severed all connections, and Poe had entered upon a hectic, full-time literary career, working for a number of periodicals in Baltimore and New York.

In 1836, Poe married his thirteen-year-old cousin, Virginia Clemm. Although a drinking problem often led him into destructive fights with other writers and critics, Poe managed somehow to keep his household together. In 1845, he sold his poem "The Raven" to a newspaper for about fifteen dollars. "The Raven" was soon on everyone's lips, as popular as a top-ten song hit is today.

Poe was to know no peace, however. Virginia had already fallen victim to that plague of nineteenth-century life, tuberculosis. In 1847, she died, and Poe's loneliness and drinking increased. On October 3, 1849, when he was only forty years old, Poe was found, disoriented and suffering from exposure, at a tavern in rainy, windswept Baltimore. He died in a Baltimore hospital, from unspecified causes, three days later.

Poe, a meticulous writer who was devoted to his craft, invented two genres: the mystery story and the horror story. Both forms have flourished ever since.

More Murder and Mayhem by Poe

"The Murders in the Rue Morgue"

"The Gold-Bug"

"The Masque of the Red Death"

"Hop-Frog"

Making Meanings

First Thoughts

1. What **image** in this horror story do you think you will remember longest? Why?

Shaping Interpretations

2. Probably the scariest aspect of this story is its **setting**. List all its horrible details. Did any of these horrors connect with your own fears? (Check your Quickwrite notes.)

3. On one level, this is the story of a man tortured by the Inquisition. However, some critics read it on another level, as the story of a man who dies, almost loses his soul to Hell, and is rescued at the end by God. See if the story "works" if it is read **symbolically** with this interpretation. Consider:

- The man, above all, fears falling into the pit. What could the pit symbolize?
- What does a pendulum suggest to you, and what does an old man with a scythe represent? What connection might there be between these symbols and the scythe on the pendulum in this story?
- Rats are often used as symbols of death, decay, and the lower world. How does the prisoner's response to these rats—especially when they crawl all over him—suggest that he might see them in this way?
- What sounds are usually associated with Judgment Day at the end of the world? Do you hear these sounds at the story's end?

Do you think this symbolic reading makes sense, or is it stretching the meaning of a "simple" horror story? Explain.

Challenging the Text

4. Did General Lasalle's arrival seem an exceptionally lucky coincidence to you? If so, did the last-minute rescue lessen the story's credibility or your enjoyment of it? Explain your responses.

Reading Check

Refer back to the **summaries** you made while reading the story. They should help you answer the following questions:

a. Find the details at the start that suggest that the prisoner's experience might be part of a dream or a lapse into madness.

b. When the narrator first regains consciousness, what "most hideous of fates" does he think the Inquisition has planned for him? How does he discover the truth?

c. When he wakens from a drugged sleep, the narrator discovers that he is in a second and even worse crisis. What new torture does he face? How does he escape?

d. What third crisis does he face when he has scarcely stepped from his "bed of horror"?

e. What sensational breakthrough occurs at the end?

CHOICES: Building Your Portfolio

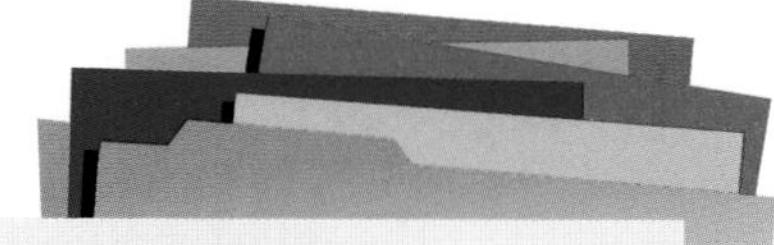

Writer's Notebook

1. Collecting Ideas for an Evaluation

Stating your opinion. Evaluations (you'll write one for the Writer's Workshop on page 328) usually begin by identifying the subject of the evaluation and stating the writer's opinion. The evaluation then goes on to offer reasons for the opinion. Write a one-sentence evaluation statement in which you state your opinion of Poe's story or another story in this book. You may want to focus on a single element of the story: plot, setting, point of view, theme.

WORK IN PROGRESS

Edgar Allan Poe creates an atmosphere of terror in his story "The Pit and the Pendulum" by creating a setting that brings out our worst fears—of being eaten alive by rats or being entombed alive.

Creative Writing

2. Updating the Story

"The Pit and the Pendulum" is a famous psychological horror story. Do you think the story has relevance to events that could take place today? In a paragraph or two, tell how you would update the story but maintain its basic plot. Filling out the following chart might help you organize your ideas.

	Poe Story	Updated Story
Setting (when and where?)		
Protagonist (what is his or her crime?)		
Punishment		
Opponents or jailers		
Rescuers		

Research/Report

3. Digging Deeper

For a brief **oral report,** tell how you'd research one of the three topics below, using both print and Internet sources. List questions you have about the topic, and cite the sources that should help you unearth the answers. Be sure to tell how you evaluated the reliability of your sources, especially if they are from the Internet.

- the Spanish Inquisition
- the Moors in Spain during the Middle Ages
- El Greco (artist, see page 292)

Art and Symbolism

4. Looking into the Pit

On page 301, the narrator rushes to the pit's brink. You are never told what he sees there. Draw or paint the images that you imagine meet his eye. As you visualize the pit, recall what you think it symbolizes.

Creative Writing

5. Poems for Poe

Respond to Poe's story in a poem. Your poem could be any one of a number of types. It might express your reactions and feelings after reading "The Pit and the Pendulum." It might be about one of your own personal fears. You might even address your poem directly to Poe. If you want a real challenge, either alone or with a small group, try rewriting "The Pit and the Pendulum" in the form of a story-poem. Read a few of Poe's famous poems like "The Raven" before you begin. For the ultimate challenge, make your poem imitate Poe's haunting rhythm and rhymes.

LANGUAGE LINK MINI-LESSON

The Effect of Rhythm and Repetition

Handbook of Literary Terms HELP

See Alliteration and Rhythm.

Poe paid as much attention to the sound of his words as he did to their sense. Skillful use of **rhythm, repetition,** and other **sound effects** reinforces the emotional effect of his story. In the following passage, note how the repetition of words and consonants and the slow, steady rhythm of the long sentences reflect the relentless, downward movement of the blade.

> "Inch by inch—line by line—with a descent only appreciable at intervals that seemed ages—down and still down it came! Days passed—it might have been that many days passed—ere it swept so closely over me as to fan me with its acrid breath."

Try It Out

Working with a group, select passages from the story for oral reading. Look for passages that contain especially good sound effects and rhythmical qualities. An excellent passage begins on page 298 with "The vibration of the pendulum" and ends on page 298 with "dungeons of the Inquisition."

The repetition of consonant sounds, usually at the beginnings of words, is called **alliteration**. Poe uses alliteration for sound effects. Notice in the sentence below how the swishing, hissing s sounds reproduce the hissing sound of the blade as it swings over the prisoner.

> "With a steady movement—cautious, sidelong, shrinking, and slow—I slid from the embrace of the bandage and beyond the reach of the scimitar."

VOCABULARY HOW TO OWN A WORD

WORD BANK

imperceptible
ponders
lucid
tumultuous
insuperable
prostrate
potent
lethargy
proximity
averted

Using Context Clues

Justify your response to each numbered item below. Then, indicate the **context clues** in each sentence that gave you hints to the meaning of each underlined word. After you've done that, go back to Poe's story and see if you can find context clues for each of the same underlined words. Write down any context clues that you find in the story.

1. Why would simple, lucid instructions help someone who ponders over how to operate a videocassette recorder?
2. A mystery movie's sound track begins faintly with an almost imperceptible noise quickly followed by tumultuous sounds. Suggest examples for each type of sound.
3. Explain why a woman averted her eyes for protection in the proximity of a blinding flash of light.
4. Why might desperate people facing an insuperable enemy prostrate themselves on the ground?
5. Name three potent smells that would rouse you from a couch potato's lethargy.

Elements of Literature

SYMBOLS: Signs of Something More

Our everyday lives are heaped with symbols. The ring on your finger, though actually a piece of metal with a stone in it, may also be a symbol of something less concrete. For you it may symbolize love, calling to mind the special person who saved for months to buy it for you.

> The ring on your finger, though actually a piece of metal with a stone in it, may also be a symbol of something less concrete.

There are many symbols in our culture that we know and recognize at once. We automatically make the associations suggested by a cross, a six-pointed star, a crown, a skull and crossbones, a clenched fist, the Stars and Stripes, and a dove with an olive branch. These commonly accepted symbols are **public symbols**.

Symbols in Literature: Making Associations

Writers of fiction, poetry, and drama create new, personal symbols in their work. Some literary symbols, like the great white whale in *Moby-Dick* and like that stubborn spot of blood on Lady Macbeth's hand, become so widely known that eventually they too become a part of our public stockpile of symbols.

In literature, a **symbol** is an object, a setting, an event, an animal, or even a person that functions in a story the way you'd expect it to but, more important, also stands for something more than itself, usually for something abstract. The white whale in *Moby-Dick* is a very real white whale in the novel, and Captain Ahab spends the whole book chasing it. But certain passages in that novel make clear to us that this whale is also associated with the mystery of evil in the world. That is how symbols work—by association. Most people associate the color green with new life, and therefore with hope. In some cultures, the color white is associated with innocence and purity; in others, white is a color of death. We usually associate gardens with joy and wastelands with futility and despair. We associate winter with sterility and spring with fertility. We associate cooing doves with peace and pecking ravens with death, but these are associations, not equations.

A symbol isn't just a sign with one specific meaning. The picture of a cigarette in a circle with a line drawn diagonally through it is a sign meaning, precisely and specifically, "No Smoking." The white whale, on the other hand, doesn't mean, precisely and specifically, "the mystery of evil." Instead, the associations suggested by the writer, made by the characters in the story, and ultimately made by the reader evoke images of evil (and perhaps other elements), suggest aspects of the darker side of life, and hint at possible ways of seeing and thinking about the events portrayed.

> That is how symbols work—by association.

Symbols invite the reader to participate in making sense of the text by building on the associations and connections that the symbols suggest.

by John Leggett

Is It a Symbol?

However, you must be careful not to start looking for symbols in everything you read: They won't be there. Here are some guidelines to follow when you sense that a story is operating on a symbolic level:

1. Symbols are often visual.
2. When some event or object or setting is used as a symbol in a story, you will usually find that the writer has given it a great deal of emphasis. Often it reappears throughout the story. In a story called "The Scarlet Ibis" by James Hurst, a rare bird dies because it has strayed out of its natural tropical setting. The scarlet ibis, which symbolizes the special delicacy and beauty of the narrator's younger brother, is mentioned many times in the story and even is used as the title.
3. A symbol in literature is a form of **figurative language**. Like a metaphor, a symbol is something that is identified with something else that is *very different* from it but that shares some quality. When you are thinking about whether something is used symbolically, ask yourself this: Does this item also stand for something essentially different from itself? Think of "The Scarlet Ibis" again. The beautiful, fragile ibis functions as a real bird in the story (it actually falls into the family's yard), but it also functions as a symbol of the frail, little boy and his unusual nature.
4. A symbol usually has something to do with a story's **theme**. When we think about the ibis, we realize that the death of the exotic bird points to the fact that the little brother also died because he could not survive in a world in which he was an outsider.

"I don't know. What do you think it is?"

Reprinted from The Saturday Evening Post.

Why Use Symbols?

Why do writers use symbols? Why don't they just come out and tell us directly what they want to say?

One answer is that people are born symbol makers. It seems to be part of our nature. Even in the earliest paintings and writings, we find symbols. Think of all those mysterious markings on the walls of caves. Think of the owl used in ancient Greek art to symbolize the great goddess of wisdom, Athena. Think of our language itself, which uses sounds to symbolize certain abstract and concrete things in the world.

In some sense, we never fully exhaust the significance of the great symbols. For example, critics have written whole books to explain *Moby-Dick,* yet probably no one is certain that the meaning of that white whale has been fully explored.

You may not be able to articulate fully what a symbol means. But you will find that the symbol, if it is powerful and well chosen, will speak forcefully to your emotions and to your imagination. You may also find that you will remember and think about the symbol long after you have forgotten other parts of the story's plot.

Before You Read

WITH ALL FLAGS FLYING

Make the Connection

I Did It My Way

Old age is different from what it used to be. Years ago older people tended to stay with their adult children. Below are some generalizations about old age. Talk about them with a partner. Do you share these opinions?

- Older people have lost their interest in adventure.
- Most older people prefer to live with their families.
- The worst thing about old age is failing health.
- Older people do not want someone else to make decisions for them.

Quickwrite

Take notes on your talk with your partner, and record your thoughts on this subject of old age.

go.hrw.com
LEO 10-4

Elements of Literature

Third-Person Limited Point of View

Like the omniscient narrator, the narrator of a story written from the **third-person limited point of view** stands outside the action and refers to all the characters by name or as "he" or "she." Unlike the omniscient narrator, however, this narrator zooms in on the thoughts, actions, and feelings of only *one* character. We almost never know what the other people are thinking. This point of view is popular with modern writers because it combines the possibilities of the omniscient point of view with the intense, personal focus of first-person narration.

A story told from the **third-person limited point of view** focuses on the experiences and thoughts of one character.

For more on Point of View, see pages 262–263 and the Handbook of Literary Terms.

Reading Skills and Strategies

Comparing and Contrasting Themes

The **theme** is the central idea or insight in a literary work. When you read works about similar subjects, you can **compare and contrast** their themes by looking for similarities and differences in the views of life they present. Each of the following two selections—the story, "With All Flags Flying," and the ***Connections*** poem, "Señora X No More"—presents a view of independence. Consider what these views have in common and how they differ.

Frank Murphy and His Family (1980) by Catherine Murphy. Oil on canvas.

He had chosen long ago what kind of old age he would have . . .

With All Flags Flying

Anne Tyler

Gary's Chopper (1972) by Tom Blackwell. Oil on canvas.
Courtesy Louis K. Meisel Gallery, New York.

Weakness was what got him in the end. He had been expecting something more definite—chest pains, a stroke, arthritis—but it was only weakness that put a finish to his living alone. A numbness in his head, an airy feeling when he walked. A wateriness in his bones that made it an effort to pick up his coffee cup in the morning. He waited some days for it to go away, but it never did. And meanwhile the dust piled up in corners; the refrigerator wheezed and creaked for want of defrosting. Weeds grew around his rosebushes.

He was awake and dressed at six o'clock on a Saturday morning, with the patchwork quilt pulled up neatly over the mattress. From the kitchen cabinet he took a hunk of bread and two Fig Newtons, which he dropped into a paper bag. He was wearing a brown suit that he had bought on sale in 1944, a white T-shirt, and copper-toed work boots. Those and his other set of underwear, which he put in the paper bag along with a razor, were all the clothes he took with him. Then he rolled down the top of the bag and stuck it under his arm, and stood in the middle of the kitchen, staring around him for a moment.

The house had only two rooms, but he owned it—the last scrap of the farm that he had sold off years ago. It stood in a hollow of dying trees beside a superhighway in Baltimore County. All it held was a few sticks of furniture, a change of clothes, a skillet, and a set of dishes. Also odds and ends, which disturbed him. If his inventory was complete, he would have to include six clothespins, a salt and a pepper shaker, a broken-toothed comb, a cheap ballpoint pen—oh, on and on, past logical numbers. Why should he be so cluttered? He was eighty-two years old. He had grown from an infant owning nothing to a family man with a wife, five children, everyday and Sunday china, and a thousand appurtenances,° down at last to solitary old age and the bare essentials again, but not bare enough to suit him. Only what he needed surrounded him. Was it possible he needed so much?

Now he had the brown paper bag; that was all. It was the one satisfaction in a day he had been dreading for years.

He left the house without another glance, heading up the steep bank toward the superhighway. The bank was covered with small, crawling weeds planted especially by young men with scientific training in how to prevent soil erosion. Twice his knees buckled. He had to sit and rest, bracing himself against the slope of the bank. The scientific weeds, seen from close up, looked straggly and gnarled. He sifted dry earth through his fingers without thinking, concentrating only on steadying his breath and calming the twitching muscles in his legs.

Once on the superhighway, which was fairly level, he could walk for longer stretches of time. He kept his head down and his fingers clenched tight upon the paper bag, which was growing limp and damp now. Sweat rolled down the back of his neck, fell in drops from his temples. When he had been walking maybe half an hour, he had to sit down again for a rest. A black motorcycle buzzed up from behind and stopped a few feet away from him. The driver was young and shabby, with hair so long that it drizzled out beneath the back of his helmet.

°**appurtenances:** items that go with other things but are not strictly necessary.

"Give you a lift, if you like," he said. "You going somewhere?"

"Just into Baltimore."

"Hop on."

He shifted the paper bag to the space beneath his arm, put on the white helmet he was handed, and climbed on behind the driver. For safety he took a clutch of the boy's shirt, tightly at first, and then more loosely when he saw there was no danger. Except for the helmet, he was perfectly comfortable. He felt his face cooling and stiffening in the wind, his body learning to lean gracefully with the tilt of the motorcycle as it swooped from lane to lane. It was a fine way to spend his last free day.

Half an hour later they were on the outskirts of Baltimore, stopped at the first traffic light. The boy turned his head and shouted, "Whereabouts did you plan on going?"

"I'm visiting my daughter, on Belvedere near Charles Street."

"I'll drop you off, then," the boy said. "I'm passing right by there."

The light changed, the motor roared. Now that they were in traffic, he felt more conspicuous, but not in a bad way. People in their automobiles seemed sealed in, overprotected; men in large trucks must envy the way the motorcycle looped in and out, hornetlike, stripped to the bare essentials of a motor and two wheels. By tugs at the boy's shirt and single words shouted into the wind, he directed him to his daughter's house, but he was sorry to have the ride over so quickly.

His daughter had married a salesman and lived in a plain, square stone house that the old man approved of. There were sneakers and a football in the front yard, signs of a large, happy family. A bicycle lay in the driveway. The motorcycle stopped just inches from it. "Here we are," the boy said.

"Well, I surely do thank you."

He climbed off, fearing for one second that his legs would give way beneath him and spoil everything that had gone before. But no, they held steady. He took off the helmet and handed it to the boy, who waved and roared off. It was a really magnificent roar, ear-dazzling. He turned toward the house, beaming in spite of himself, with his head feeling cool and light now that the helmet was gone. And there was his daughter on the front porch, laughing. "Daddy, what on *earth*?" she said. "Have you turned into a teeny-bopper?" Whatever that was. She came rushing down the steps to hug him—a plump, happy-looking woman in an apron. She was getting on toward fifty now. Her hands were like her mother's, swollen and veined. Gray had started dusting her hair.

"You never *told* us," she said. "Did you ride all this way on a motorcycle? Oh, why didn't you find a telephone and call? I would have come. How long can you stay for?"

"Now . . ." he said, starting toward the house. He was thinking of the best way to put it. "I came to a decision. I won't be living alone anymore. I want to go to an old folks' home. That's what I *want,*" he said, stopping on the grass so she would be sure to get it clear. "I don't want to live with you—I want an old folks' home." Then he was afraid he had worded it too strongly. "It's nice *visiting* you, of course," he said.

"Why, Daddy, you know we always asked you to come and live with us."

"I know that, but I decided on an old folks' home."

"We couldn't do that. We won't even talk about it."

"Clara, my mind is made up."

Then in the doorway a new thought hit her, and she suddenly turned around. "Are you sick?" she said. "You always said you would live alone as long as health allowed."

"I'm not up to that anymore," he said.

"What is it? Are you having some kind of pain?"

"I just decided, that's all," he said. "What I *will* rely on you for is the arrangements with the home. I know it's a trouble."

"We'll talk about that later," Clara said. And she firmed the corners of her mouth exactly the way her mother used to do when she hadn't won an argument but wasn't planning to lose it yet either.

In the kitchen he had a glass of milk, good and cold, and the hunk of bread and the two Fig Newtons from his paper bag. Clara wanted to make him a big breakfast, but there was no sense wasting what he had brought. He munched on the dry bread and washed it down with milk, meanwhile staring at the Fig Newtons, which lay on the smoothed-out bag. They were the worse for their ride—squashed and pathetic looking, the edges worn down and crumbling. They seemed to have come from somewhere long ago and far away. "Here, now, we've got cookies I baked only yesterday," Clara said; but he said, "No, no," and ate the Fig Newtons, whose warmth on his tongue filled him with a vague, sad feeling deeper than homesickness. "In my house," he said, "I left things a little messy. I hate to ask it of you, but I didn't manage to straighten up any."

"Don't even think about it," Clara said. "I'll take out a suitcase tomorrow and clean everything up. I'll bring it all back."

"I don't want it. Take it to the poor people."

"Don't want any of it? But, Daddy——"

He didn't try explaining it to her. He finished his lunch in silence and then let her lead him upstairs to the guest room.

Clara had five boys and a girl, the oldest twenty. During the morning as they passed one by one through the house on their way to other places, they heard of his arrival and trooped up to see him. They were fine children, all of them, but it was the girl he enjoyed the most. Francie. She was only thirteen, too young yet to know how to hide what she felt. And what she felt was always about love, it seemed: whom she just loved, who she hoped loved her back. Who was just a darling. Had thirteen-year-olds been so aware of love in the old days? He didn't know and didn't care; all he had to do with Francie was sit smiling in an armchair and listen. There was a new boy in the neighborhood who walked his English sheep dog past her yard every morning, looking toward her house. Was it because of her, or did the dog just like to go that way? When he telephoned her brother Donnie, was he hoping for her to answer? And when she did answer, did he want her to talk a minute or to hand the receiver straight to Donnie? But what would she say to him, anyway? Oh, all her questions had to do with where she might find love, and everything she said made the old man wince and love her more. She left in the middle of a sentence, knocking against a doorknob as she flew from the room, an unlovable-looking tangle of blond hair and braces and scrapes and Band-Aids. After she was gone, the room seemed too empty, as if she had accidentally torn part of it away in her flight.

Getting into an old folks' home was hard. Not only because of lack of good homes, high expenses, waiting lists; it was harder yet to talk his family into letting him go. His son-in-law argued with him every evening, his round, kind face anxious and questioning across the supper table. "Is it that you think you're not welcome here? You are, you know. You were one of the reasons we bought this big house." His grandchildren, when they talked to him, had a kind of urgency in their voices, as if they were trying to impress him with their acceptance of him. His other daughters called long-distance from all across the country and begged him to come to them if he wouldn't stay with Clara. They had room, or they would make room; he had no idea what homes for the aged were like these days. To all of them he gave the same answer: "I've made my decision." He was proud of them for asking, though. All his children had turned out so well, every last one of them. They were good, strong women with happy families, and they had never given him a moment's worry. He was luckier than he had a right to be. He had felt lucky all his life, dangerously lucky, cursed by luck; it had seemed some disaster must be waiting to even things up. But the luck had held. When his wife died, it was at a late age, sparing her the pain she would have had to face, and his life had continued in its steady, reasonable pattern with no more sorrow than any other man's. His final lot was to weaken, to crumble, and to die—only a secret disaster, not the one he had been expecting.

He walked two blocks daily, fighting off the weakness. He shelled peas for Clara and mended little household articles, which gave him an excuse to sit. Nobody noticed how he arranged to climb the stairs only once a day, at bedtime. When he had empty time, he chose a chair without rockers, one that would not be a symbol of age and weariness and lack of work. He rose every morning at six and stayed in his room a full hour, giving his legs enough warning to face the day ahead. Never once did he disgrace himself by falling down in front of people. He dropped nothing more important than a spoon or a fork.

Meanwhile the wheels were turning; his name was on a waiting list. Not that that meant anything, Clara said. "When it comes right down to driving you out there, I just won't let you go," she told him. "But I'm hoping you won't carry things that far. Daddy, won't you put a stop to this foolishness?"

He hardly listened. He had chosen long ago what kind of old age he would have; everyone does. Most, he thought, were weak and chose to be loved at any cost. He had seen women turn soft and sad, anxious to please, and had watched with pity and impatience their losing battles. And he had once known a schoolteacher, no weakling at all, who said straight out that when she grew old, she would finally eat all she wanted and grow fat without worry. He admired that—a simple plan, dependent upon no one. "I'll sit in an armchair," she had said, "with a ladies' magazine in my lap and a box of homemade fudge on the lamp stand. I'll get as fat as I like and nobody will give a hang." The schoolteacher was thin and pale, with a kind of stooped, sloping figure that was popular at the time. He had lost track of her long ago, but he liked to think that she had kept her word. He imagined her fifty years later, cozy and fat in a puffy chair, with one hand moving constantly between her mouth and the candy plate. If she had died young or changed her mind or put off her eating till another decade, he didn't want to hear about it.

He had chosen independence. Nothing else had even occurred to him. He had lived to himself, existed on less money than his family would ever guess, raised his own vegetables, and refused all gifts but an occasional tin of coffee. And now he would sign himself into the old folks' home and enter on his own two feet, relying on the impersonal care of nurses and cleaning women. He could have chosen to die alone of neglect, but for his daughters that would have been a burden too—a different kind of burden, much worse. He was sensible enough to see that.

Meanwhile, all he had to do was to look as busy as possible in a chair without rockers and hold fast against his family. Oh, they gave him no peace. Some of their attacks were obvious—the arguments with his son-in-law over the supper table—and some were subtle; you had to be on your guard every minute for those. Francie, for instance, asking him questions about what she called the "olden days." Inviting him to sink unnoticing into doddering reminiscence. "Did I see Granny ever? I don't remember her. Did she like me? What kind of person was she?" He stood his ground, gave monosyllabic answers. It was easier than he had expected. For him, middle age tempted up more memories. Nowadays events had telescoped. The separate agonies and worries—the long, hard births of each of his children, the youngest daughter's chronic childhood earaches, his wife's last illness—were smoothed now into a single, summing-up sentence: He was a widowed farmer with five daughters, all married, twenty grandchildren, and three great-grandchildren. "Your grandmother was a fine woman," he told Francie; "just fine." Then he shut up.

Francie, not knowing that she had been spared, sulked and peeled a strip of sunburned skin from her nose.

Clara cried all the way to the home. She was the one who was driving; it made him nervous. One of her hands on the steering wheel held a balled-up tissue, which she had stopped using. She let tears run unchecked down her face and drove jerkily, with a great deal of brake slamming and gear gnashing.

"Clara, I wish you wouldn't take on so," he told her. "There's no need to be sad over *me*."

"I'm not sad so much as mad," Clara said. "I feel like this is something you're doing *to* me, just throwing away what I give. Oh, why do you have to be so stubborn? It's still not too late to change your mind."

The old man kept silent. On his right sat Francie, chewing a thumbnail and scowling out the window, her usual self except for the unexplainable presence of her other hand in his, tight as wire. Periodically she muttered a number; she was counting red convertibles and had been for days. When she reached a hundred, the next boy she saw would be her true love.

He figured that was probably the reason she had come on this trip—a greater exposure to red convertibles.

Whatever happened to DeSotos? Didn't there used to be a car called a roadster?

They parked in the U-shaped driveway in front of the home, under the shade of a poplar tree. If he had had his way, he would have arrived by motorcycle, but he made the best of it—picked up his underwear sack from between his feet, climbed the front steps ramrod straight. They were met by a smiling woman in blue who had to check his name on a file and ask more questions. He made sure to give all the answers himself, overriding Clara when necessary. Meanwhile Francie spun on one squeaky sneaker heel and examined the hall, a cavernous, polished square with old-fashioned parlors on either side of it. A few old people were on the plush couches, and a nurse sat idle beside a lady in a wheelchair.

They went up a creaking elevator to the second floor and down a long, dark corridor deadened by carpeting. The lady in blue, still carry-

Words to Own

telescoped (tel′ə·skōpt′) *v.:* slid or collapsed into one another, like the sections of a collapsible telescope.

chronic (krän′ik) *adj.:* constant; lasting a long time or recurring often.

ing a sheaf of files, knocked at number 213. Then she flung the door open on a narrow green room flooded with sunlight.

"Mr. Pond," she said, "this is Mr. Carpenter. I hope you'll get on well together."

Mr. Pond was one of those men who run to fat and baldness in old age. He sat in a rocking chair with a gilt-edged Bible on his knees.

"How-do," he said. "Mighty nice to meet you."

They shook hands cautiously, with the women ringing them like mothers asking their children to play nicely with each other. "Ordinarily I sleep in the bed by the window," said Mr. Pond, "but I don't hold it in much importance. You can take your pick."

"Anything will do," the old man said.

Clara was dry-eyed now. She looked frightened.

"You'd best be getting on back now," he told her. "Don't you worry about me. I'll let you know," he said, suddenly generous now that he had won, "if there is anything I need."

Clara nodded and kissed his cheek. Francie kept her face turned away, but she hugged him tightly, and then she looked up at him as she stepped back. Her eyebrows were tilted as if she were about to ask him one of her questions. Was it her the boy with the sheep dog came for? Did he care when she answered the telephone?

They left, shutting the door with a gentle click. The old man made a great business out of settling his underwear and razor in a bureau drawer, smoothing out the paper bag and folding it, placing it in the next drawer down.

"Didn't bring much," said Mr. Pond, one thumb marking his page in the Bible.

"I don't need much."

"Go on—take the bed by the window. You'll feel better after a while."

"I *wanted* to come," the old man said.

"That there window is a front one. If you look out, you can see your folks leave."

He slid between the bed and the window and looked out. No reason not to. Clara and Francie were just climbing into the car, the sun lacquering the tops of their heads. Clara was blowing her nose with a dot of tissue.

"*Now* they cry," said Mr. Pond, although he had not risen to look out himself. "Later they'll buy themselves a milkshake to celebrate."

"I wanted to come. I made them bring me."

"And so they did. *I* didn't want to come. My son wanted to put me here—his wife was expecting. And so he did. It all works out the same in the end."

"Well, I could have stayed with one of my daughters," the old man said, "but I'm not like some I have known. Hanging around making burdens of themselves, hoping to be loved. Not me."

"If you don't care about being loved," said Mr. Pond, "how come it would bother you to be a burden?"

Then he opened the Bible again, at the place where his thumb had been all the time, and went back to reading.

The old man sat on the edge of the bed, watching the tail of Clara's car flash as sharp and hard as a jewel around the bend of the road. Then, with nobody to watch that mattered, he let his shoulders slump and eased himself out of his suit coat, which he folded over the foot of the bed. He slid his suspenders down and let them dangle at his waist. He took off his copper-toed work boots and set them on the floor neatly side by side. And although it was only noon, he lay down full-length on top of the bedspread. Whiskery lines ran across the plaster of the ceiling high above him. There was a crackling sound in the mattress when he moved; it must be covered with something waterproof.

The tiredness in his head was as vague and restless as anger; the weakness in his knees made him feel as if he had just finished some exhausting exercise. He lay watching the plaster cracks settle themselves into pictures, listening to the silent, neuter voice in his mind form the words he had grown accustomed to hearing now: Let me not give in at the end. Let me continue gracefully till the moment of my defeat. Let Lollie Simpson be alive somewhere even as I lie on my bed; let her be eating homemade fudge in an overstuffed armchair and growing fatter and fatter and fatter.

Meet the Writer

Still Just Writing

One time a friend made the mistake of asking **Anne Tyler** (1941–), "Have you found work yet? Or are you still just writing?"

Anne Tyler was born in a Quaker community in Minneapolis, Minnesota, and grew up in Raleigh, North Carolina. She graduated from high school at sixteen and from Duke University at nineteen. Her first novel, written when she was twenty-two, has been followed by a steady stream of other novels and stories.

Anne Tyler's perceptions about the lives of ordinary people have won her widespread praise. One critic sees a kind of innocence in her view of life, a sense of wonder at all the crazy things in the world, and an abiding affection for her own flaky characters.

Some of Tyler's popular novels include *Dinner at the Homesick Restaurant* (1982); *The Accidental Tourist* (1985), which was made into a movie; *Breathing Lessons* (1988), which won a Pulitzer Prize; *Saint Maybe* (1991); and *A Patchwork Planet* (1998).

Here is an excerpt from an essay by Anne Tyler, written in response to that friend's question about her writing. Titled "Still Just Writing," the essay examines her life as a writer:

"I think I was born with the impression that what happened in books was much more reasonable, and interesting, and *real,* in some ways, than what happened in life. I hated childhood and spent it sitting behind a book waiting for adulthood to arrive. When I ran out of books, I made up my own. At night, when I couldn't sleep, I made up stories in the dark. Most of my plots involved girls going west in covered wagons. I was truly furious that I'd been born too late to go west in a covered wagon. . . .

I spent my adolescence planning to be an artist, not a writer. After all, books had to be about major events, and none had ever happened to me. All I knew were tobacco workers stringing the leaves I handed them and talking up a storm. Then I found a book of Eudora Welty's short stories in the high school library. She was writing about Edna Earle, who was so slow-witted she could sit all day just pondering how the tail of the *C* got through the loop of the *L* on the Coca-Cola sign. Why, I knew Edna Earle. You mean you could *write* about such people? I have always meant to send Eudora Welty a thank-you note, but I imagine she would find it a little strange. . . ."

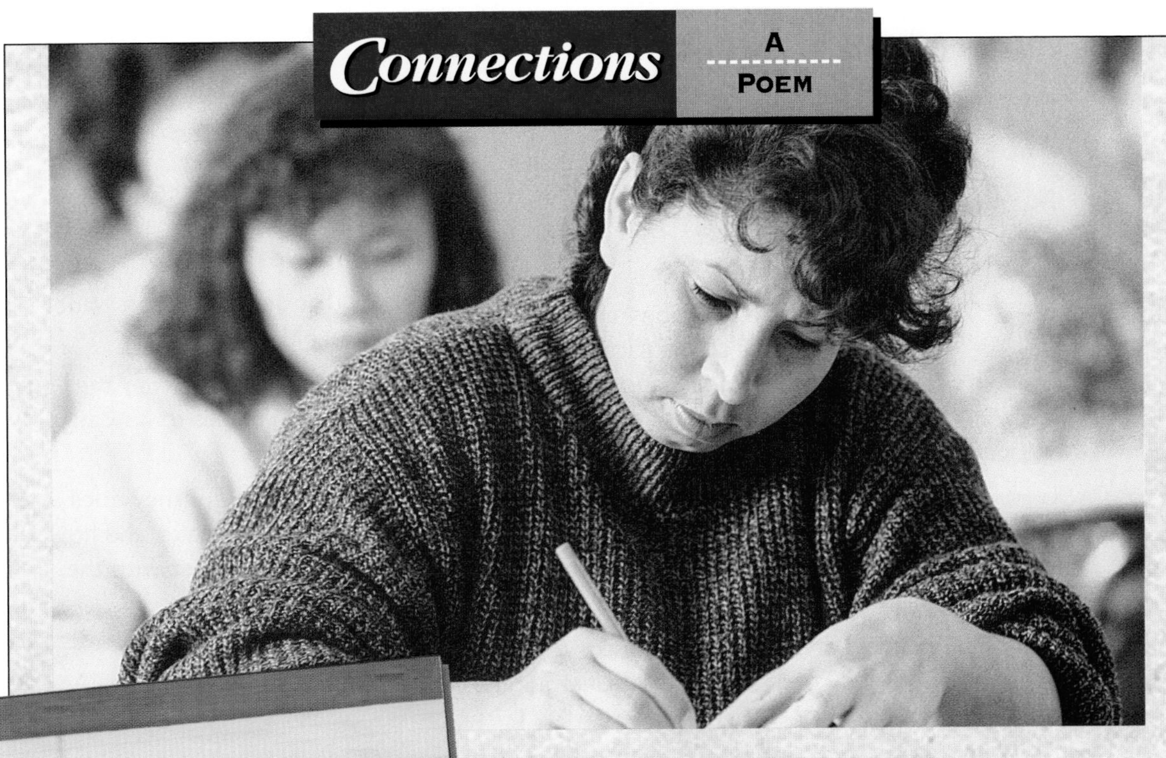

Señora X No More

Pat Mora

Straight as a nun I sit.
My fingers foolish before paper and pen
hide in my palms. I hear the slow, accented echo
How are yu? I ahm fine. How are yu?
of the other women who clutch notebooks
and blush at their stiff lips resisting
sounds that float gracefully as
bubbles from their children's mouths.
My teacher bends over me, gently squeezes
my shoulders, the squeeze I give my sons,
hands louder than words.
She slides her arms around me:
a warm shawl, lifts my left arm
onto the cold, lined paper.
"*Señora,* don't let it slip away," she says
and opens the ugly, soap-wrinkled fingers
of my right hand with a pen like I pry open
the lips of a stubborn grandchild.
My hand cramps around the thin hardness.
"Let it breathe," says this woman who knows
my hand and tongue knot, but she guides
and I dig the tip of my pen into that white.
I carve my crooked name, and again at night
until my hand and arm are sore,
I carve my crooked name,
my name.

MAKING MEANINGS

First Thoughts

1. How did you feel about the old man's decision in "With All Flags Flying"?

Reading Check

a. Why has the old man made this decision—what are his **motives**?

b. What do his children want the old man to do?

c. Describe the journey the old man makes to his daughter's home.

d. What other journey does the old man make, and how does it **contrast** with the first one?

Shaping Interpretations

2. This story's **title** describes a ship proudly displaying all the flags and pennants that proclaim its national identity. How does the title relate to the old man and what he wants?
3. Why do you think the writer put the **character** Francie in the story? What does she bring out in the old man?
4. Why do you think the writer put the **character** Mr. Pond in the story? What does Mr. Pond help to make clear about the old man?
5. At the end of the story, the old man is thinking of Lollie Simpson eating fudge. What does Lollie represent to the old man? How does she relate to the story's **title**?
6. Do you see the story's outcome as a victorious breakthrough for the old man or as something less triumphant and clear-cut? Explain.

Connecting with the Text

7. Refer to the discussion about old age that you had with a partner before beginning this story. Did the story affect any of your feelings about old age? Review your opinions (see your Quickwrite notes), and see how you feel now.

Extending the Text

8. "With All Flags Flying" and "Señora X No More" (see *Connections* on page 317) express different attitudes about independence. **Compare and contrast** the **themes,** or the views about independence, in these two works.

Challenging the Text

9. Do you think this is an upbeat story, or did it leave you with other feelings? How do you think the writer wants you to feel at the story's end?

CHOICES: Building Your Portfolio

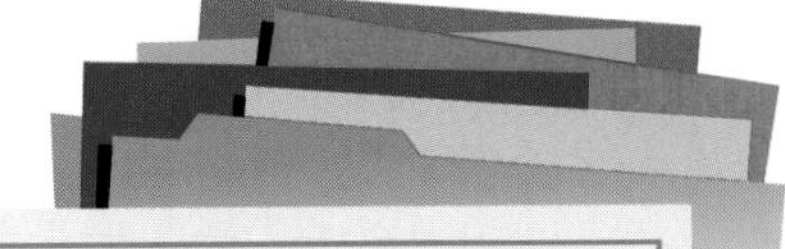

Writer's Notebook

1. Collecting Ideas for an Evaluation

Comparing works. Many reviewers, in evaluating a literary work, compare that work with another work that has a similar theme or similar characters or a similar plot. In the evaluation you'll write for the Writer's Workshop on page 328, you might want to compare the work you're writing about to some other work. The notebook page below shows notes for a comparison of the old man in Tyler's story with the father in Anderson's play *I Never Sang for My Father* (page 636).

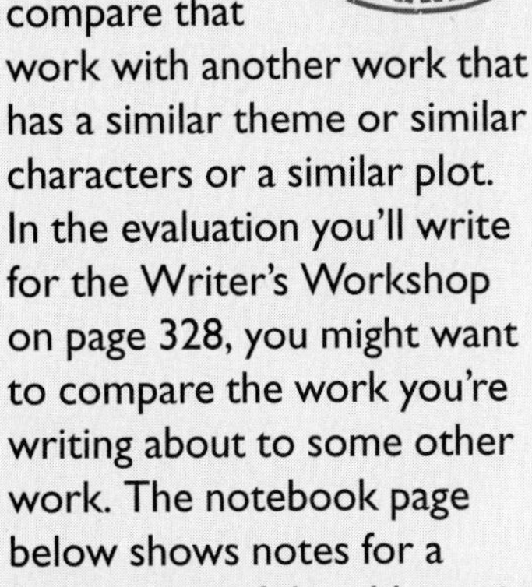

Look back at the stories you've read, and choose one that you think has elements you can compare with elements of "With All Flags Flying." List all the similarities and differences you can think of. Then, state your evaluation.

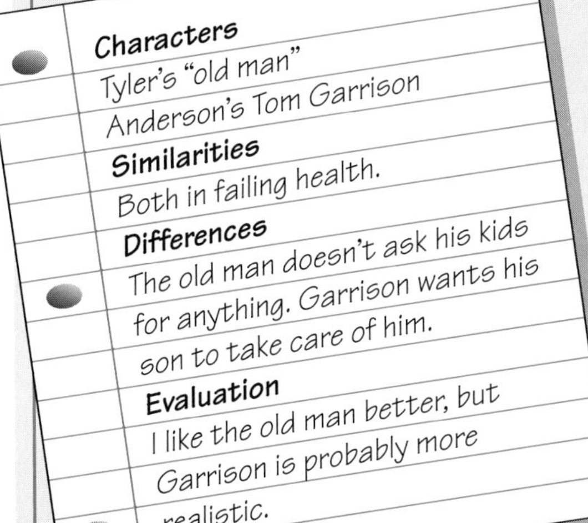

Characters
Tyler's "old man"
Anderson's Tom Garrison
Similarities
Both in failing health.
Differences
The old man doesn't ask his kids
for anything. Garrison wants his
son to take care of him.
Evaluation
I like the old man better, but
Garrison is probably more
realistic.

Writing or Drawing

2. Setting Can Reveal Character

On page 310, Tyler reveals something about the old man's character simply by describing his house: "The house had only two rooms, but he owned it. . . ." Reread her description, and then characterize an older person you know by describing his or her surroundings. You can use words or pictures. Be sure to include specific objects that suggest their owner's personality and way of life—as Tyler mentions six clothespins, a broken-toothed comb, and a cheap ballpoint pen.

Supporting an Opinion

3. Doing the Right Thing?

How do you feel about the old man in this story? Do you consider him heroic for wanting to end his life "with all flags flying," or do you think he has made a serious mistake in hurting his children? In a paragraph, give your opinion of the old man's actions, and elaborate with reasons *why* you feel as you do. Does he do the right thing—and for whom?

Creative Writing

4. What Are They Feeling?

When Clara drives her father to the nursing home, she says to him, "I'm not sad so much as mad . . . I feel like this is something you're doing *to* me, just throwing away what I give." Because the story is told from the **third-person limited point of view** of the old man, we know what Clara says, but we never know her thoughts. What do you imagine Clara is thinking and feeling on the way home? Would she share her feelings with Francie? For that matter, what are Francie's thoughts and feelings? Write the going-home scene. Use either the **first-person point of view,** with Clara as the narrator, or the **omniscient point of view,** and analyze what is going on with both Clara and Francie.

GRAMMAR LINK MINI-LESSON

Verbs Add Vigor

Tyler's Vivid Verbs

creak
buckle
loop
munch
tear
sulk
peel
spin
flash
slump

How can you make your writing strong and vivid and inventive? One of the most influential books ever written about the art of composition gives this advice:

> Write with nouns and verbs, not with adjectives and adverbs. The adjective hasn't been built that can pull a weak or inaccurate noun out of a tight place. This is not to disparage adjectives and adverbs; they are indispensable parts of speech. . . . In general, however, it is nouns and verbs, not their assistants, that give good writing its toughness and color.
>
> —William Strunk, Jr., and E. B. White, *The Elements of Style*

Anne Tyler makes good use of verbs. For example, in the first paragraph of the story, she says, ". . . the refrigerator wheezed and creaked for want of defrosting." Consider how diluted her description would have been if she had merely said, ". . . the refrigerator made noises for want of defrosting." In the following sentences, Tyler's tough and colorful verbs are underscored.

1. "A black motorcycle buzzed up from behind and stopped a few feet away from him."
2. "The driver was young and shabby, with hair so long that it drizzled out beneath the back of his helmet."

Try It Out

➤ Rewrite each numbered sentence so that it has a similar meaning but a different tough, colorful verb.

➤ When you revise your own writing, check your verbs. If you are continually repeating verbs like *do, say,* or *go,* replace them with more specific, vivid verbs.

A tip for writers: Using too many tough, vivid verbs will result in what is called overwriting. The key is balance, and that's a skill you learn by wide reading and by practice.

VOCABULARY HOW TO OWN A WORD

Word Bank

telescoped
chronic

Word Mapping: What Do You Know About a Word?

When you read a new or unfamiliar word, find out how much you know about the word. Look at the **word map** for *wheeze.* (On page 310, a refrigerator wheezed.) Make word maps for the two words in the Word Bank. You'll need to create your own questions and answers.

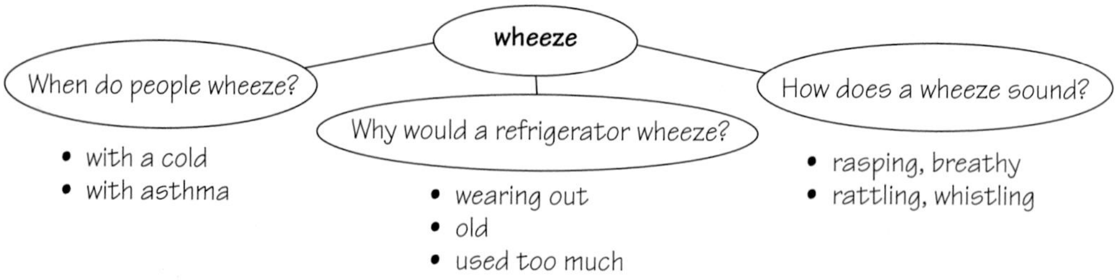

wheeze

When do people wheeze?
- with a cold
- with asthma

Why would a refrigerator wheeze?
- wearing out
- old
- used too much

How does a wheeze sound?
- rasping, breathy
- rattling, whistling

EXTENDING *the theme*

AN AUTOBIOGRAPHY

Quickwrite

How important is a person's name? Suppose that someone suddenly took your name away, and from then on you were referred to only by a seven-digit number: 5831680. How would that affect you? Quickwrite your response in two or three sentences.

Background

At the time this account takes place, educated natives of India were expected to learn English in addition to their own native languages. (Hindi, Urdu, and Gujarati are just a few of the many languages spoken in India.) The headmistress of the type of school in the essay was white and British. Many of the students were also white and British, from families of British civil servants sent to India as colonial rulers.

The title of the essay is from William Shakespeare's *Romeo and Juliet.* Juliet is wishing that her beloved Romeo's surname, Montague, were some other name because the Montagues are sworn enemies of her family. "What's in a name?" she asks. "That which we call a rose/By any other name would smell as sweet."

By Any Other Name

Santha Rama Rau

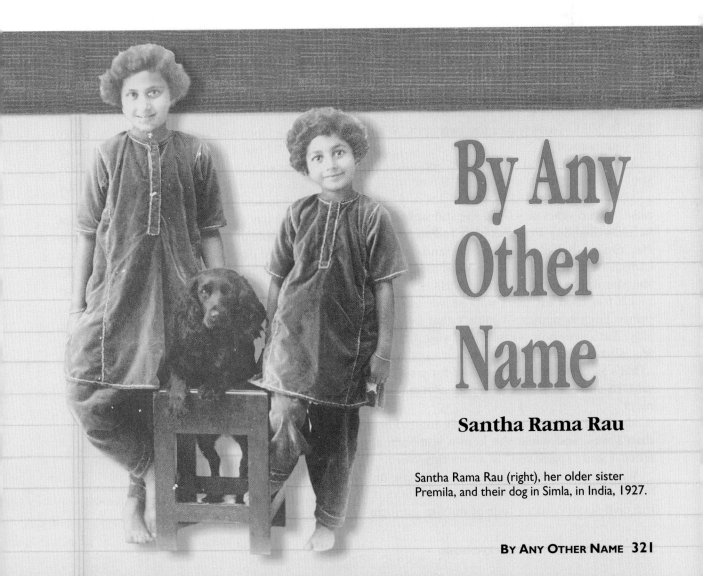

Santha Rama Rau (right), her older sister Premila, and their dog in Simla, in India, 1927.

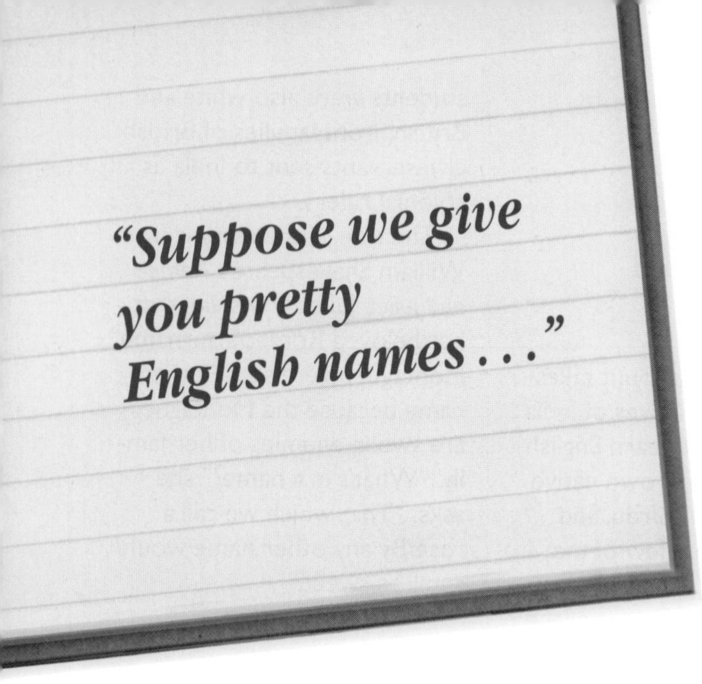
"Suppose we give you pretty English names . . ."

At the Anglo-Indian day school in Zorinabad to which my sister and I were sent when she was eight and I was five and a half, they changed our names. On the first day of school, a hot, windless morning of a north Indian September, we stood in the headmistress's study, and she said, "Now you're the *new* girls. What are your names?"

My sister answered for us. "I am Premila, and she"—nodding in my direction—"is Santha."

The headmistress had been in India, I suppose, fifteen years or so, but she still smiled her helpless inability to cope with Indian names. Her rimless half-glasses glittered, and the precarious bun on the top of her head trembled as she shook her head. "Oh, my dears, those are much too hard for me. Suppose we give you pretty English names. Wouldn't that be more jolly? Let's see, now—Pamela for you, I think." She shrugged in a baffled way at my sister. "That's as close as I can get. And for *you,*" she said to me, "how about Cynthia? Isn't that nice?"

My sister was always less easily intimidated than I was, and while she kept a stubborn silence, I said "Thank you," in a very tiny voice.

We had been sent to that school because my father, among his responsibilities as an officer of the civil service, had a tour of duty to perform in the villages around that steamy little provincial town, where he had his headquarters at that time. He used to make his shorter inspection tours on horseback, and a week before, in the stale heat of a typically postmonsoon[1] day, we had waved goodbye to him and a little procession—an assistant, a secretary, two bearers, and the man to look after the bedding rolls and luggage. They rode away through our large garden, still bright green from the rains, and we turned back into the twilight of the house and the sound of fans whispering in every room.

Up to then, my mother had refused to send Premila to school in the British-run establishments of that time, because, she used to say, "You can bury a dog's tail for seven years and it still comes out curly, and you can take a Britisher away from his home for a lifetime and he still remains insular." The examinations and degrees from entirely Indian schools were not, in those days, considered valid. In my case, the question had never come up and probably never would have come up if Mother's extraordinary good health had not broken down. For the first time in my life, she was not able to continue the lessons she had been giving us every morning. So our Hindi[2] books were put away, the stories of the Lord Krishna[3] as a little boy were left in midair, and we were sent to the Anglo-Indian school.

That first day at school is still, when I think of it, a remarkable one. At that age, if one's name is changed, one develops a curious form of dual personality. I remember having a certain detached and disbelieving concern in the actions of "Cynthia," but certainly no responsibility. Accordingly, I followed the thin, erect back of the headmistress down the veranda to my classroom, feeling, at most, a passing interest in what was going to happen to me in this strange, new atmosphere of School.

1. **postmonsoon:** after the monsoon, or seasonal heavy rains.

2. **Hindi:** official language of India.

3. **Lord Krishna:** in the Hindu religion, human form taken by the god Vishnu. Many Hindu stories recount episodes in the life of Krishna.

The building was Indian in design, with wide verandas opening onto a central courtyard, but Indian verandas are usually whitewashed, with stone floors. These, in the tradition of British schools, were painted dark brown and had matting on the floors. It gave a feeling of extra intensity to the heat.

I suppose there were about a dozen Indian children in the school—which contained perhaps forty children in all—and four of them were in my class. They were all sitting at the back of the room, and I went to join them. I sat next to a small, solemn girl, who didn't smile at me. She had long, glossy black braids and wore a cotton dress, but she still kept on her Indian jewelry—a gold chain around her neck, thin gold bracelets, and tiny ruby studs in her ears. Like most Indian children, she had a rim of black kohl[4] around her eyes. The cotton dress should have looked strange, but all I could think of was that I should ask my mother if I couldn't wear a dress to school, too, instead of my Indian clothes.

I can't remember too much about the proceedings in class that day, except for the beginning. The teacher pointed to me and asked me to stand up. "Now, dear, tell the class your name."

I said nothing.

"Come along," she said, frowning slightly. "What's your name, dear?"

"I don't know," I said, finally.

The English children in the front of the class—there were about eight or ten of them—giggled and twisted around in their chairs to look at me. I sat down quickly and opened my eyes very wide, hoping in that way to dry them off. The little girl with the braids put out her hand and very lightly touched my arm. She still didn't smile.

Most of that morning I was rather bored. I looked briefly at the children's drawings pinned to the wall, and then concentrated on a lizard clinging to the ledge of the high, barred window behind the teacher's head. Occasionally it would shoot out its long yellow tongue for a fly, and then it would rest, with its eyes closed and its belly palpitating, as though it were swallowing several times quickly. The lessons were mostly concerned with reading and writing and simple numbers—things that my mother had already taught me—and I paid very little attention. The teacher wrote on the easel-blackboard words like "bat" and "cat," which seemed babyish to me; only "apple" was new and incomprehensible.

When it was time for the lunch recess, I followed the girl with braids out onto the veranda. There the children from the other classes were assembled. I saw Premila at once and ran over to her, as she had charge of our lunchbox. The children were all opening packages and sitting down to eat sandwiches. Premila and I were the only ones who had Indian food—thin wheat chapatis,[5] some vegetable curry, and a bottle of buttermilk. Premila thrust half of it into my hand and whispered fiercely that I should go and sit with my class, because that was what the others seemed to be doing.

The enormous black eyes of the little Indian girl from my class looked at my food longingly, so I offered her some. But she only shook her head and plowed her way solemnly through her sandwiches.

I was very sleepy after lunch, because at home we always took a siesta. It was usually a pleasant time of day, with the bedroom darkened against the harsh afternoon sun, the drifting off into sleep with the sound of Mother's voice reading a story in one's mind, and, finally, the shrill, fussy voice of the ayah[6] waking one for tea.

At school, we rested for a short time on low, folding cots on the veranda, and then we were expected to play games. During the hot part of the afternoon we played indoors, and after the shadows had begun to lengthen and the slight breeze of the evening had come up, we moved outside to the wide courtyard.

I had never really grasped the system of competitive games. At home, whenever we played

4. **kohl** (kōl): dark powder used as eye makeup.

5. **chapatis** (chə·pät′ēz): thin, flat bread.

6. **ayah** (ä′yə): Indian term for "nanny" or "maid."

tag or guessing games, I was always allowed to "win"—"because," Mother used to tell Premila, "she is the youngest, and we have to allow for that." I had often heard her say it, and it seemed quite reasonable to me, but the result was that I had no clear idea of what "winning" meant.

When we played twos-and-threes[7] that afternoon at school, in accordance with my training I let one of the small English boys catch me but was naturally rather puzzled when the other children did not return the courtesy. I ran about for what seemed like hours without ever catching anyone, until it was time for school to close. Much later I learned that my attitude was called "not being a good sport," and I stopped allowing myself to be caught, but it was not for years that I really learned the spirit of the thing.

When I saw our car come up to the school gate, I broke away from my classmates and rushed toward it yelling, "Ayah! Ayah!" It seemed like an eternity since I had seen her that morning—a wizened, affectionate figure in her white cotton sari,[8] giving me dozens of urgent and useless instructions on how to be a good girl at school. Premila followed more sedately, and she told me on the way home never to do that again in front of the other children.

When we got home, we went straight to Mother's high, white room to have tea with her, and I immediately climbed onto the bed and bounced gently up and down on the springs. Mother asked how we had liked our first day in

7. **twos-and-threes:** game similar to tag.

8. **sari** (sä′rē): long piece of cloth wrapped around the body. One end forms a skirt. The other end goes across the chest and over one shoulder.

school. I was so pleased to be home and to have left that peculiar Cynthia behind that I had nothing whatever to say about school, except to ask what "apple" meant. But Premila told Mother about the classes, and added that in her class they had weekly tests to see if they had learned their lessons well.

I asked, "What's a test?"

Premila said, "You're too small to have them. You won't have them in your class for donkey's years."[9] She had learned the expression that day and was using it for the first time. We all laughed enormously at her wit. She also told Mother, in an aside, that we should take sandwiches to school the next day. Not, she said, that *she* minded. But they would be simpler for me to handle.

That whole lovely evening I didn't think about school at all. I sprinted barefoot across the lawns with my favorite playmate, the cook's son, to the stream at the end of the garden. We quarreled in our usual way, waded in the tepid water under the lime trees, and waited for the night to bring out the smell of the jasmine.[10] I listened with fascination to his stories of ghosts and demons, until I was too frightened to cross the garden alone in the semidarkness. The ayah found me, shouted at the cook's son, scolded me, hurried me in to supper—it was an entirely usual, wonderful evening.

It was a week later, the day of Premila's first test, that our lives changed rather abruptly. I was sitting at the back of my class, in my usual inattentive way, only half listening to the teacher. I had started a rather guarded friendship with the girl with the braids, whose name turned out to be Nalini (Nancy in school). The three other Indian children were already fast friends. Even at that age, it was apparent to all of us that friendship with the English or Anglo-Indian children was out of the question. Occasionally, during the class, my new friend and I would draw pictures and show them to each other secretly.

The door opened sharply and Premila marched in. At first, the teacher smiled at her in a kindly and encouraging way and said, "Now, you're little Cynthia's sister?"

Premila didn't even look at her. She stood with her feet planted firmly apart and her shoulders rigid and addressed herself directly to me. "Get up," she said. "We're going home."

I didn't know what had happened, but I was aware that it was a crisis of some sort. I rose obediently and started to walk toward my sister.

"Bring your pencils and your notebook," she said.

I went back for them, and together we left the room. The teacher started to say something just as Premila closed the door, but we didn't wait to hear what it was.

In complete silence we left the school grounds and started to walk home. Then I asked Premila what the matter was. All she would say was, "We're going home for good."

It was a very tiring walk for a child of five and a half, and I dragged along behind Premila with my pencils growing sticky in my hand. I can still remember looking at the dusty hedges and the tangles of thorns in the ditches by the side of the road, smelling the faint fragrance from the eucalyptus trees, and wondering whether we would ever reach home. Occasionally a horse-drawn tonga[11] passed us, and the women, in their pink or green silks, stared at Premila and me trudging along on the side of the road. A few coolies[12] and a line of women carrying baskets of vegetables on their heads smiled at us. But it was nearing the hottest time of day, and the road was almost deserted. I walked more and more slowly, and shouted to Premila, from time to time, "Wait for me!" with increasing peevishness. She spoke to me only once, and that was to tell me to carry my notebook on my head, because of the sun.

9. **donkey's years:** expression meaning "a very long time."

10. **jasmine:** (jaz′min): tropical plant with fragrant flowers.

11. **tonga:** two-wheeled carriage.

12. **coolies:** unskilled laborers.

When we got to our house, the ayah was just taking a tray of lunch into Mother's room. She immediately started a long, worried questioning about what are you children doing back here at this hour of the day.

Mother looked very startled and very concerned and asked Premila what had happened.

Premila said, "We had our test today, and She made me and the other Indians sit at the back of the room, with a desk between each one."

Mother said, "Why was that, darling?"

"She said it was because Indians cheat," Premila added. "So I don't think we should go back to that school."

Mother looked very distant and was silent a long time. At last she said, "Of course not, darling." She sounded displeased.

We all shared the curry she was having for lunch, and afterward I was sent off to the beautifully familiar bedroom for my siesta. I could hear Mother and Premila talking through the open door.

Mother said, "Do you suppose she understood all that?"

Premila said, "I shouldn't think so. She's a baby."

Mother said, "Well, I hope it won't bother her."

Of course, they were both wrong. I understood it perfectly, and I remember it all very clearly. But I put it happily away, because it had all happened to a girl called Cynthia, and I never was really particularly interested in her.

Meet the Writer

A Stranger in Her Own Land

Santha Rama Rau (1923–) was born into one of India's most influential families but has spent most of her life in other lands. Her father was a knighted diplomat, her mother a social reformer. Santha Rama Rau made her first trip to England at the age of six and returned for a much longer stay when she was eleven. In 1939, as war was breaking out in Europe, Lady Rama Rau took her two daughters back to India for safety. Feeling somewhat like an outsider, Santha made a conscious effort to reorient herself to her homeland and her extended family. In 1947, she witnessed the turmoil of India's independence from Britain. Five years later, she married an American and settled in New York City.

Finding Common Ground

With a small group of classmates, compare the notes you made for your Quickwrite, and talk about the importance of getting a person's name right. Use your notes to come up with ideas for a group discussion of Santha Rama Rau's experiences. If you need more questions to stimulate discussion, you might try these:

1. Describe the breakthroughs in this selection. Who do you think made them, and why are the breakthroughs important?
2. What would you have done if you had been in Premila's situation? What would you have done as her parent?
3. What does this autobiographical excerpt say about the nature of prejudice? Do you think events like the ones Rau described are happening in other settings today? Explain.

A Country Divided

Cry, the Beloved Country by Alan Paton (Scribner) is one of the great novels of this century, a touching story of two fathers and their sons, one father a Zulu pastor and the other a white planter. The story takes place in South Africa before that tragic country granted equality to all its people. The 1995 movie, filmed in South Africa, stars James Earl Jones and Richard Harris.

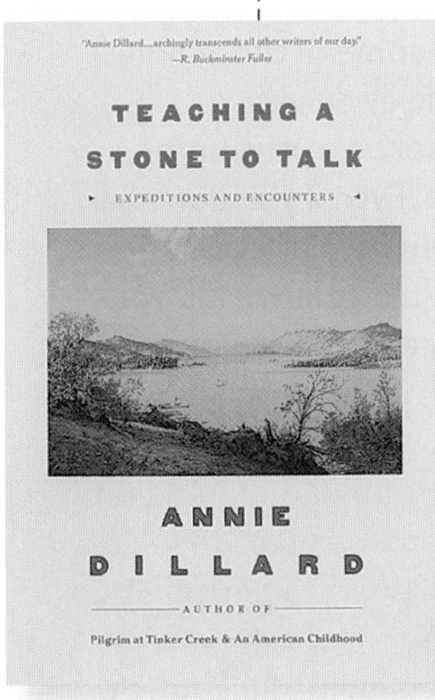

So Near and Yet So Far

In *Teaching a Stone to Talk* (Harper Colophon), Annie Dillard once again takes a journey through different places and cultures, recording the shock and amazement of her meetings with people and creatures, plants and landscapes. From Ecuador to the Galápagos Islands to Tinker Creek, Dillard shares her discoveries about life and living on our planet.

Tiny? Yes . . . Dangerous? Yes!

For a true story that even Stephen King said was one of the most horrifying things he'd ever read, get *The Hot Zone* by Richard Preston (Random House). This nonfiction chiller focuses on a deadly new virus that nearly escaped from a laboratory in Reston, Virginia.

Hidden Memories

Incidents in the Life of a Slave Girl by Harriet A. Jacobs (Harvard) is a moving firsthand account of slavery told by a woman who became a fugitive in 1835 and hid for nearly seven years in a tiny crawl space above a storehouse in her grandmother's home in Edenton, North Carolina.

Writer's Workshop

Technology HELP

See Writer's Workshop 2 CD-ROM. *Assignment: Evaluation.*

ASSIGNMENT

Write an evaluation of a story or movie.

AIM

To persuade; to inform.

AUDIENCE

Your teacher, classmates, friends, or family; readers of a school newspaper. (You choose.)

PERSUASIVE WRITING

EVALUATING A STORY OR MOVIE

When you **evaluate** something, you give your opinion or judgment about its value. If a friend asked you what you thought of a movie, you might say, "Well, the acting was great, but the plot had a lot of holes in it." That's an evaluation. If you then pointed out some of those holes, you'd be supporting your evaluation with specific evidence.

Some people get paid to make precisely this sort of evaluation—and to convince others to accept their judgment. Even if you don't become a movie critic or book reviewer, you'll often have to evaluate something: a college you might attend, a car you might buy, a job you might take, a politician you might vote for. Be sure your evaluation is based on solid evidence and specific standards.

Prewriting

1. Review Your Writer's Notebook

WORK IN PROGRESS

In your notebook entries for this collection, you've explored several techniques for evaluating a short story. You may already have decided on a subject from working through these exercises.

2. Choose a Work to Evaluate

One way to find a topic is to quickwrite a list of stories or movies that you remember well. Circle the works that seem to create the strongest feeling or the most vivid images for you—it doesn't matter if those feelings and images are positive or negative. You may sometimes write best about something you dislike. The important thing is to write about a work that you respond to strongly.

3. Decide What's Important

Because you won't have the time or space to discuss every aspect of the work you are evaluating, you'll need to select a few key elements and focus on those. If you're evaluating one of the short stories in this collection, look back at your notebook for help.

The history
of the written
word is rich and
Page 1
Once upon a time

4. Think About Your Standards

To make a judgment on the worth of something, you must have **criteria,** or standards, to measure it by. The more specific your standards, the easier it is to make an evaluation and to give good reasons for your judgment. When you develop your criteria, ask yourself questions like these:

- What makes a mystery story a good mystery?
- What makes a novel hard to put down?
- What's the best fantasy movie I've ever seen? the worst?

5. Review the Work

If possible, read the story or see the movie again, jotting down notes on aspects that seem particularly praiseworthy or problematic. Consider making a **double-entry journal** like the one below. In the left column, make notes on passages or elements from the work; in the right column, record your responses.

Notes for "The Pit and the Pendulum"

Passage	My Response
Setting: "For many hours the immediate vicinity of the low framework upon which I lay had been literally swarming with rats. They were wild, bold, ravenous—their red eyes glaring upon me. . . ."	Great description. I can really see this. Visual details good and weird. "Ravenous" suggests they're going to nibble at the prisoner.

Evaluation Statements

Despite its clichéd characters and corny dialogue, James Cameron's Titanic is a masterpiece that's worth every penny of the $200 million it cost to produce.

The short story "Trap of Gold" by Louis L'Amour is more than an exciting Western; it's a heart-stopping psychological struggle.

6. Develop Your Evaluation Statement

Try writing an **evaluation statement** that expresses your overall opinion of the work. Go back over your notes and the work itself, and decide on the **main idea** that you'd like readers to get from your evaluation. Write it down in one sentence. You may need to write several versions of this statement until you come up with the best possible wording. Since an evaluation is an opinion, be prepared to back it up with evidence from the work.

Try It Out

For the story or movie you're evaluating—

1. List the three or four key elements you'll focus on in your essay.
2. Then, to elaborate, list at least one example that supports your evaluation of each element. *Be specific.*

Sentence Workshop HELP

Combining sentences: page 333.

Language / Grammar Link HELP

Comparisons and analogies to clarify: page 261. Subject-verb agreement: page 275. Participles: page 287. Rhythm and repetition: page 305. Verbs: page 320.

Drafting

1. Introductory Paragraphs

Start with an attention grabber: a funny comment, an intriguing quotation, or a personal anecdote (as in the Student Model below). Include your thesis statement in the introduction as well as some basic information about the work. (For a story, identify the title and author; for a movie, give the title and names of the director and major actors.) Then tell just enough of the plot to get your readers interested, without spoiling any surprises.

2. Elaborate: Be Specific and Concrete

It's a good idea to focus your evaluation on three or four key elements of the work. Be direct and honest. If you really think something is excellent or awful, say so—as long as you can back up your statement. Support your opinions with detailed, concrete **examples,** such as this one from the Student Model: ". . . the mechanical contraptions of rubber and steel seem more lifelike than their flesh and blood adversaries." **Comparisons** provide another kind of specific support. If you say the hero in a thriller is unbelievable, compare him to a stronger, more credible hero in another thriller.

3. Wrap It Up

End your evaluation by summing up or restating your main ideas and overall opinion of the work. You might choose to add a final thought or response that brings your evaluation to a definite close.

Student Model

JURASSIC PARK

Remember when your parents would take you to the Natural History Museum as a kid? I'd always rush past the other animal exhibits and go straight to my favorite section: the dinosaurs. Even though they had been reduced to mere skeletons, the extinct beasts still captivated me.

Writer draws readers in with a personal anecdote and expression of feeling.

In *Jurassic Park,* Steven Spielberg has taken those dusty bone formations and, with a lot of imagination and a little computer technology, transformed them into the majestic creatures of yesteryear.

Gives title and director and states his view of the film's major achievement.

In the movie, genetic engineering is the magic wand that makes dinosaurs walk the earth again. Based on the novel by

Student Model (continued)

Michael Crichton (who also wrote the screenplay), *Jurassic Park* creates a world that is only a short step from the present. An idealistic, Santa-like billionaire (Richard Attenborough) discovers a way to create dinosaurs by obtaining DNA from the blood of prehistoric mosquitoes preserved in amber. The dino DNA is then used to create a good number and variety of dinosaurs.

Summarizes the plot without giving away surprises and identifies the major characters and actors.

The full-grown reptiles are then placed in a kind of island zoo called Jurassic Park. The park needs scientific approval before it can open, so the owner invites a paleontologist (Sam Neill), a biologist (Laura Dern), and a sarcastic mathematician (Jeff Goldblum) to check things out. He also brings along his two grandchildren so they can see the fun. As luck would have it, though, the dinosaurs escape their enclosure and begin to wreak havoc on the island.

Like Jurassic Park's proprietor, Steven Spielberg spared no expense on his pets. Over sixty million dollars and two years of preproduction supposedly went into the project. Unfortunately, Spielberg was having such great fun with his lizard pals that he all but forgot about the film's human characters. As a result, the mechanical contraptions of rubber and steel seem more lifelike than their flesh and blood adversaries.

Evaluates the work: weighs weaknesses against strengths.

The character development in *Jurassic Park* is give-and-take—Crichton gives us a little character insight, and Spielberg takes it away to make room for the dinos. Neill and Dern supposedly have a romantic interest, but their time together on screen is less than that of the opening credits. Dern delivers some token feminist lines, but she never gets to build on them. Attenborough does well as the whimsical, disillusioned billionaire, but the best lines he gets are about a flea circus.

Gives specific examples of the film's poor character development.

Children, be warned—*Barney* this ain't. *Jurassic Park* is very intense and suspenseful at times. There are no friendly, singing lizards or frolicking youngsters here. In fact, it is the children who go through the most suffering in this movie; getting electrocuted, crushed, chased, sneezed on, and kicked are only a few of their misfortunes.

Uses a comparison. A good technique in a critical evaluation.

No bones about it, *Jurassic Park* is a monster thriller to rival *Jaws*. Although character development is virtually extinct and the ending is left wide open, Spielberg is finally back doing what he does best—making great films that charge to the edges of the imagination.

Restates evaluation: essentially favorable.

—Matthew Harry
Westlake High School
Westlake, Ohio

First appeared in *Merlyn's Pen: The National Magazines of Student Writing.*

Evaluating and Revising

1. Self-Evaluation

Go over your draft to make sure you haven't used overworked and empty adjectives such as *great, unique, terrific,* and *terrible.* Also be on the lookout for short, choppy sentences that could be combined for a smoother flow.

2. Peer Review

If possible, give your evaluation to at least one classmate who is familiar with your subject and one who is not. Ask your readers to consider these questions:

- If you're familiar with the subject, does the summary in the review match your memory of the work?
- Does the evaluation make you think about the work in a new way or challenge your previous opinions?
- If you're unfamiliar with the subject, does the evaluation give you a clear idea of what the work is about?
- Does the evaluation help you decide if you would like to read (or see) the work?
- Does the evaluation present evidence to convince you to accept the writer's opinions?

Revision Model

	Peer Comments
Based on the novel by Michael Crichton (who also wrote the screenplay), *Jurassic Park* creates ~~an almost familiar world. A~~ a world that is only a short step from the present. An idealistic, Santa-like billionaire	*How is the film's world almost familiar? Be more specific.*
(Richard Attenborough) discovers a way to create dinosaurs by obtaining	*This character sounds interesting. Add more descriptive details.*
DNA from the blood of prehistoric mosquitoes preserved in amber.	*Where did he get the prehistoric mosquitoes?*

■ ***Evaluation Criteria***

A good evaluation

1. *identifies and summarizes the work*
2. *makes its evaluation statement clear*
3. *offers specific supporting evidence*
4. *sums up or restates its evaluation in the conclusion*

Proofreading Tip

Double-check all titles and names for correct capitalization, punctuation, and spelling.

Communications Handbook HELP

See Proofreaders' Marks.

Publishing Tip

Submit your evaluation to your school or local newspaper. Send or e-mail it to a magazine of student writing, such as *Merlyn's Pen.*

BUILDING YOUR PORTFOLIO

Sentence Workshop

Combining Sentences: Using Coordination

Read the following passage aloud.

CHOPPY Clara nodded and kissed his cheek. Francie kept her face turned away. She hugged him tightly. Then she looked up at him as she stepped back.

To most readers, these sentences sound childish—choppy and repetitive. Look at how a professional writer combined these sentences. Read this passage aloud to see if it sounds smoother.

REVISED Clara nodded and kissed his cheek. Francie kept her face turned away, *but* she hugged him tightly, *and* then she looked up at him as she stepped back.

—Anne Tyler, "With All Flags Flying" (page 315)

The **coordinating conjunctions** (*and, or, but, for, nor, so, yet*) can help you avoid a monotonous series of simple sentences that repeat the same subject or the same verb. They can also help you create **compound sentences** by connecting one or more simple sentences.

There are many ways that sentences can be combined using coordination. Can you think of another way of revising the choppy passage above?

Language Handbook HELP

See Coordinating Conjunctions: page 1021; Compound Sentences: page 1040.

Technology HELP

See Language Workshop CD-ROM. *Key word entry: combining sentences.*

Writer's Workshop Follow-up: Revision

When you are revising the draft of your evaluation for the Writer's Workshop on page 328, read your sentences aloud to hear the way they sound. Underline your subjects once and your verbs twice. Have you unnecessarily repeated subjects or verbs in strings of short sentences? Can you combine any of these short sentences into one sentence?

Pay attention to your peer reviewer's comments. Often another pair of eyes can spot problems that the writer doesn't notice.

Try It Out

Act as an editor, and use coordinating conjunctions to make the following passages smoother and more varied. Look for places where you can create compound subjects or verbs or compound sentences.

1. Wetherton made camp near a tiny spring west of the fan. Then he picketed his burros. He began his climb.
2. The impact of the water broke the rubber-enclosed vacuum. The goggles came loose.
3. He took off his copper-toed work boots. He set them on the floor neatly, side by side.
4. Jerry ran after his mother. He looked back over his shoulder at the bay. He thought about it all morning.

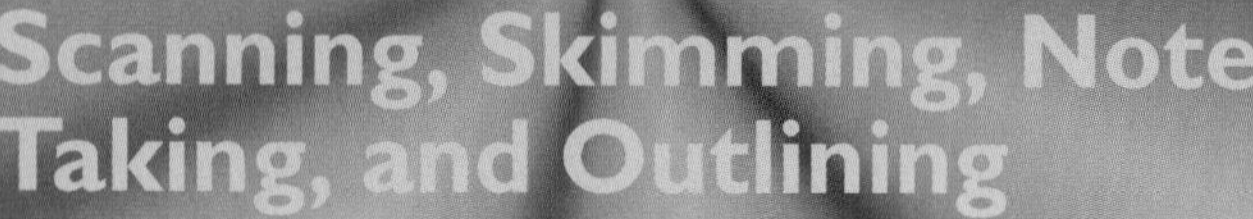

Reading for Life

Scanning, Skimming, Note Taking, and Outlining

Situation

You and a friend have just read "Trap of Gold" (see page 249). You think that the treacherous gold-filled rock has symbolic meaning, and your teacher has asked you to present your viewpoint to the class. To help clarify your thinking, you decide to reread and outline the Elements of Literature essay on symbols (see pages 306–307).

Symbols: Signs of Something More

I. Symbols in everyday life
  A. Personal symbols
  B. Public symbols
    1. Examples: flag, cross, doves, clenched fist
    2. Images with commonly accepted associations
II. Symbols in literature
  A. Function on a concrete level but also mean something more
  B. Are created by associations
    1. Colors have associations
    2. Seasons have associations
  C. Have multiple meanings

Strategies

Preview the material.

- Notice any headings, boxed information, or boldfaced terms. These will help you concentrate on the most important points.

Pace yourself.

- Whenever you read, you should adjust your reading rate to serve your purpose.
- **Scanning** is rapidly searching for key words and then checking the context to make sure you've found what you were looking for.
- **Skimming** is reading quickly to identify main ideas.
- **Close reading** is reading slowly and carefully enough to understand the words and think about their implications.

Take notes in an outline.

- An outline reveals the basic organization of a text: The entries list the ideas in order, and the indentations show the relative importance of the ideas.

Use formal outline structure.

- Use Roman numerals for main topics.
- Use letters and numbers for the subtopics, in the order shown in the sample. (The sample also shows how to capitalize and indent entries.)
- Never use just one subtopic; use either two (or more) or none at all.
- Use parallel grammatical forms for parallel entries. For example, if the first item in a group is a verb, make the others verbs as well.

Using the Strategies

1. Refer to the essay on pages 306–307. What are the three main parts of the essay?
2. Scan the first column of the essay to find examples of symbols in our culture.
3. Scan the essay to find the definition of symbol. (What signals you that this definition is found in column 2?)
4. Complete the topic outline shown here for this essay.

Extending the Strategies

Use the strategies here to read and outline another Elements of Literature essay in this book, or use an outline to review a selection in Collection 6.

Learning for Life

Conflict Resolution

Problem

Stories derive their power from **conflict,** opposing forces that create tension and cause action. Conflict may be necessary in stories, but it can cause serious problems in real life. The ability to defuse conflicts and to arrive at fair and reasonable solutions is one of the most valuable social skills that you can learn.

Project

Identify a series of steps that can be used to resolve conflicts fairly.

Preparation

1. With a group of classmates, decide on a first step to take in resolving a conflict. This normally includes identifying the parties involved in the conflict and their opposing positions.
2. Continue listing all of the steps needed to resolve a conflict. Another important one might be to get both sides to agree to discuss their dispute before a peer mediator. Note that a **mediator** (a person who listens objectively to both sides of the disagreement) can often help two opposing sides reach a peaceful settlement.
3. Choose a familiar conflict, and test each step you've listed.
4. With your group, evaluate how well your steps work to resolve a conflict.

Procedure

1. Draw up a list of common conflicts that students face in daily life. For example, one student complains that another student is spreading rumors about him.
2. Adapt the list of steps you drew up to fit each specific conflict.

Presentation

Use one of the following formats (or another that your teacher approves):

1. Role-Play

Role-play the resolution of one of the conflicts you listed. Invite comments from the audience, and discuss the issues raised. If possible, have members of the audience take turns trying out some of the conflict-resolution steps on their own. Discuss how well the steps seem to work.

2. Poster Campaign

Create a poster campaign about conflict resolution for your school. List each step in a shortened form. For example:

- Listen without interrupting.
- No name-calling.

Illustrate the steps or create logos or symbols for conflict resolution.

3. Radio Broadcasts

Using your school's public-address system or in-school TV channel, plan and air a series of short programs that illustrate conflict resolution. For each program, write a script that shows conflict-resolution in action. Be sure to include two opposing sides and a mediator. As part of your broadcasts, tell students how they can find out more about conflict resolution.

Processing

What did you learn from this project about the process of managing and resolving conflicts? How important is the idea of **compromise** (each side giving in a little to reach an agreement) in the resolution of a conflict? Write a brief reflection for your portfolio.

Telephone Booths (1967) by Richard Estes. Acrylic on masonite (122 x 175.3 cm).

Museo Thyssen-Bornemisza, Madrid./ ©Richard Estes/
Licensed by VAGA, New York, NY.

The Nonfiction Collections

If you want to write what the world is about, you have to write details . . . real life is in the dishes. Real life is pushing strollers up the street, folding T-shirts, the alarm clock going off early and you dropping into bed exhausted every night. That's real life.

—Anna Quindlen

A WRITER ON NONFICTION

A CONVERSATION WITH BARRY LOPEZ

As you read through this unit, you'll sample the variety, the range, and the power of nonfiction. Listen as Barry Lopez talks about the nonfiction writer's role and responsibility to readers. (You'll read Lopez's report "A Presentation of Whales" on page 434.)

Barry Lopez: I'm conscious of trying to clarify, to make the language work beautifully, and of the reader's needs—how easy is it going to be for the reader to follow, or how can the reader be brought into the scene without violating the scene or violating the reader. By violating the reader I mean making the reader feel like an outsider, choosing a kind of vocabulary or a tone of voice that makes the reader feel uncomfortable or unwelcome. I always mean for a reader to feel welcome in a place. . . .

Q: It's interesting that you think of yourself as an intermediary because in so much of the writing, you seem to disappear, you remove even yourself from being a possible obstacle between the reader and the setting.

Lopez: I try. It's a curious thing to do, in a way. When the reader comes to a writer's work, he or she should sense, very quickly I think, the presence of a distinct personality. Someone with a certain ethical, moral, and artistic dimension. And insofar as that writer is a worthy illuminator of the world for the reader, he or she continues to read the writer's work. Writing is really an extraordinary act of self-assertion. You put down on paper the way you understand the world. But for me there must be a point where the reader loses sight of the writer, where he gains another understanding, a vision of what lies before the writer; so that by the time the reader finishes a book or an essay, he's really thinking about his own thoughts with regard to that subject, or that place, or that set of events and not so much about the writer's. . . .

Q: In a *Publishers Weekly* interview, you said that the Alaskan landscape pulls you "up and out of yourself, and you feel yourself extending into the landscape." Is that feeling of being in harmony with the universe possible to maintain when you come back into the normal routines of life?

Lopez: It's a bit like being in love. When you're in the presence of the beloved, you can't imagine any other moment. But then day-to-day life impinges, the person you love recedes, and you find yourself concentrating on something utterly different. But there is still this very strong attachment in the heart which has to do with memory and longing. I don't think a sense of awe or respect for a particular place diminishes as much as it becomes an isolated memory. Part of the function of literature for me is to rekindle memory and make it part of the present, to compress time. There is a certain amount of ordinary chaos in the human spirit, inside the human mind. I think literature helps to clear that chaos.

Reading Skills and Strategies

READING NONFICTION

When you read nonfiction, you interact with the text in some of the same ways you interact with a story or a poem. You may also have a specific purpose in mind—perhaps you are looking for information, or you want to think about a point of view the text offers on an issue that concerns you.

Here are some of the ways we interact with a nonfiction text:

1. **We connect with the text.** We might think, "This is just like Tonya's mother's childhood in Russia," or "I felt this way when I saw the Vietnam Veterans Memorial in Washington."
2. **We ask about the writer.** Careful readers don't believe everything that's printed. We need to evaluate the writer's qualifications and credibility. We need to know the writer's motivation and purpose for writing.
3. **We try to determine if the piece is based on factual evidence or subjective responses.** We evaluate as we read, separating facts from opinions. "Why should I believe you?" is a good question to ask when the writer hands you an opinion.
4. **We interpret.** We figure out the messages the writer is sending us.
5. **We extend the text.** We take the information we're looking for and use it; or we go in search of more information; or we decide that we agree with an argument and take sides accordingly, perhaps even taking action on the issue.
6. **We challenge the text.** We decide how we feel about the writer's main idea. We may find evidence inadequate, an argument faulty, or the writer biased.

HOW TO OWN A WORD

Word Mapping: Pinning Down Meanings

Sometimes you can figure out the meaning of a word from its **context.** Sometimes you can't. Consider this sentence from "R.M.S. Titanic" (page 396):

> "An officer's fist flies out; three shots are fired in the air, and the panic is *quelled.* . . . "

Do things get worse, or better? In this case, you have to refer to a dictionary. Here's how one reader went on to make a **word map** to pin down the precise meaning of *quelled.*

> *Quelled* means "calmed," "quieted," or "subdued."

quelled

What kinds of things can be quelled?
- riots
- rumors
- panic

Describe a situation that needs quelling.
- audience screaming at rock concert
- people rioting over an arrest
- spreading of nasty rumor

What might you say to quell a rumor?
- "That's totally, absolutely not true!"
- "Did you see it yourself?"

What's the opposite of quelled?
- incited
- intensified
- stirred up

Apply the strategy on the next page.

Reading Skills and Strategies

I suddenly realized life was getting shorter . . .

The Wrestlers

Gary Soto

> **Dialogue with the Text**
>
> Don't look yet! Before you begin reading "The Wrestlers," cover the student's responses in the side column with a piece of paper. As you read, jot down your own responses. Then, when you're done, compare your responses to the story with this reader's responses.
>
> Who is telling this story?
>
> Why wasn't the coach upset?
>
> Who is "I"?

It hurt to be pinned in twelve seconds in a nonleague wrestling match, especially at the end of the 1960s when, except for a few dads and moms and the three regulars with faces like punched-in paper bags, the bleachers were empty of spectators. It hurt to stand under the shower looking at fingerprints still pressed in my arm where my opponent, whose name was Bloodworth, gripped, yanked, and with a grin on his face threw me on my back. The guy next to me had fingerprints around his wrists and arm. Another guy was red around his chest. His eyes were also red. We lost by plenty that night, but coach wasn't too mad. He beat his clipboard against his khaki thigh and joked, "You were a bunch of fishes," by which he meant that we were an easy catch. He pretended to be upset, but we knew that it was the beginning of the season and there was still hope.

I showered and dressed. My best friend Scott was waiting in his Ford Galaxy. He was throwing corn nuts into his mouth, churning beautifully on the taste of salt and roasted nuts. I told him that corn nuts were not good for him, and he asked how that could be, because they tasted good. That night we drove around for a while before he dropped me off at my house and asked me for a quarter. "Gas don't come free," he said. "It costs money when you lose before you get started."

I wrestled that year and needed to be driven around because I could manage only three feeble wins against nine losses. Driving around Fresno was therapy. We took the corners sharply and felt the give of Pep-Boy shocks,[1] which for me was the most exciting discovery since our biology teacher made a pretty girl kiss a petri dish[2] and three days later, fungus climbed over the sides. We cornered so that the tires squealed and the inertia[3] pulled our saliva from one side of our mouths to the other. I liked that feeling, liked how Scott would be talking about an episode of *Bonanza* or *Gunsmoke* and suddenly brake hard so that we had to brace ourselves against the dash. Sometimes it hurt, and sometimes it felt just wonderful to lift from the seat and almost smash into the glass.

I had taken driver's ed from my coach, and on the second day of class he said, "Don't be scared but you're gonna see some punks getting killed." The film was called something like *Red Asphalt* or *Blood on the Pavement,* but I remember a narrator with a crew cut and a neck as thick as a canned ham. When he spoke while holding up a tennis shoe, the muscles in his neck jumped around. He said, "The boy who wore this sneaker is dead." He held it up, and the camera moved in close on the high-top, then flashed to a freeway accident as dramatic music started along with the title credits.

It could have been my sneaker because, like the dead kid, I liked high-tops. It could have been Scott's or any other boy's. The film was meant to scare us, but most of the boys enjoyed it. The girls looked away when the film showed six seconds of a car wreck from different angles. The sound of metal and glass breaking made us listen up. It stopped us from chewing our gum or slipping a corn nut into the inside of our cheeks. Then all was quiet. A bird pumped his tail and chirped on a chain-link fence. The narrator came back on. He was stand-

1. **Pep-Boy shocks:** shock absorbers from Pep-Boys, a national chain of automobile-parts stores.
2. **petri** (pē′trē) **dish:** shallow glass dish in which microorganisms are grown.
3. **inertia** (in·ʉr′shə): in physics, the tendency of something that is at rest to remain at rest and something that is in motion to remain in motion.

Dialogue with the Text

Why did Scott and "I" drive around before going home?

Why did the girl have to kiss the petri dish?

Why were the boys driving in this manner?

I feel this film will help teach students the dangers of driving.

Were these students actually getting an understanding of the real moral of this film?

Dialogue with the Text

What does all of this have to do with wrestling?

How was this wrestler comparing the film with wrestling?

Chicano Lowrider (1993) by Frank Romero. Oil on paper (30" × 40").

Courtesy Frank Romero.

I feel this story is about different struggles adolescents go through during high school. It lets others know that when the going gets tough, the tough get tougher. People should never give up.

Sara Hunter

— Sara Hunter
Southeast High School
Bradenton, Florida

ing on the shoulder of a freeway, his tie whipping in the wind of traffic. He warned us that during a head-on collision, your clothes rip off: shirts, skirts, shoes, the whole works—naked as you were born, only you were dead.

I recalled Bloodworth pinning me in twelve seconds and suddenly realized life was getting shorter: A car wreck could kill you in six seconds. It was tough luck—only half the time for the kids in the film. I watched the film, then watched coach laugh along with the boys and turn on the overhead lights, jumble the dimes and quarters in his deep pockets, and slap his clipboard against his thigh. His neck was thick like the narrator's. His hair was a little longer and shiny as the black industrial shoes on his feet. Right in driver's ed, among the idiot boys smelling of sunflower seeds and corn nuts, I realized that wrestlers went on to do more than slam people into mats.

I was a junior that year. During my senior year I was so lonely that I needed to drive around Fresno. Scott was at the wheel, more lonely than me, more desperate because a girl said no, then yes, then finally no again to a Halloween date. It was no for both of us. We had no choice but to drive around corners, the centrifugal force[4] pulling us one way, then another. We had no choice but to throw bottles from the car and sneer at old drivers in long cars.

We often parked at the levee[5] and looked at the water. I said things like, "Scott, I think I've lived before," or, "Scotty, do you ever feel that someone is gripping your shoulder and when you turn around, no one is there? It's spooky." I could still feel Bloodworth's grip on my arm, and would feel it for years.

I didn't like high school. Coach knew only so many words. The dean's hand trembled when he touched doorknobs. Our teacher kept repeating that a noun was a person, place, or thing. She stood at the blackboard, lipstick overrunning her mouth, and said for the thousandth time: Elvis is a noun. Fresno is a noun. Elvis's guitar is also a noun.

The water in the canal was quick as a windblown cloud. The 1960s were coming to an end, and the first of the great rock stars were beginning to die. We were dying to leave home, by car, thumb, or on water, racing west to where the sun went down.

4. **centrifugal** (sen·trif′yo͞o·gəl) **force:** force that tends to pull something outward when it is rotating rapidly.
5. **levee** (lev′ē)**:** artificial river bank, built to prevent flooding.

Collection 5

BECOMING MYSELF

WRITING FOCUS: Autobiographical Incident

Something in me strives to connect with the past. Not my past, but another's past. An ancestral past. And so, after all, it is my past.

—Karen Cooper

If someone asked "Who are you?" how would you answer? Maybe you'd give your name, age, where you live, a description of your family. That's hardly the whole story, though. So much goes into making up "who you are"—the complete, total story of your life till now.

The three writers in this collection have looked at their lives and found they had stories to tell. From a hairy experience in Boston to a Japanese American internment camp in the desert to a fever hospital in Ireland—these writers have looked at their experiences and tried to get in touch with "who they were." As you read these autobiographies (literally, "self-life-writings"), see what they say to you about that interesting process of becoming yourself.

Writer's Notebook

WORK IN PROGRESS

In your Writer's Notebook, freewrite about the first experience that comes to your mind when you think: What has helped make me the person I am right now? Your writing is yours to share with others or to keep for your eyes alone.

Before You Read

HAIR

Make the Connection

Everyone Does It

Maybe it's baggy shorts, a baseball cap worn backward, and one earring. The way we choose to look is one way we express who we are. The problem is that sometimes we conform to what is in fashion, instead of daring to be ourselves.

Quickwrite

Brainstorm in class to make a list of some of the fashions in hair, clothing, music, and dancing that are "in" at your school and some that are "out." In your notebook, jot down very quickly how you yourself feel about pressures to conform to what's "in" and to reject what's "out."

Elements of Literature

"Hearing" Tones

"I like your hair." Say this sentence aloud three times so that it communicates three attitudes: "I really do like your hair." "I know I'm supposed to say something nice about your hair, so I'm saying it." "I can't stand your hair, and I want you to feel foolish about it." The person with the hair can infer your meaning from listening to the tone of your voice.

Tone is the writer's attitude toward the audience, the subject, or a character.

For more on Tone, see the Handbook of Literary Terms.

Reading Skills and Strategies

Making Inferences about Tone

When you read, you can't hear the tone of the speaker's or narrator's voice. Writers have to rely on word choice and details to communicate their **tone,** or attitude toward their subjects. Readers must then piece together these clues to **infer,** or make an intelligent guess about, the writer's feelings. What tones do you hear in "Hair"?

Background

For many young African American men in the 1940s, a zoot suit and conked hair were cool. A zoot suit was a big, baggy suit with wide, padded shoulders, an extra-long jacket, and pants that narrowed at the ankle. Conked hair was straightened with congolene—a mixture of harsh lye, potatoes, eggs, and soap. In this excerpt from his autobiography, Malcolm X writes about his first conk and how it made him feel. At this point, Malcolm was living in the Roxbury section of Boston.

Malcolm X, then Malcolm Little (top row, third from right), as a fourth-grader in Lansing, Michigan.

THEN MY HEAD CAUGHT FIRE.

HAIR

from **The Autobiography of Malcolm X**

Malcolm X with Alex Haley

Shorty soon decided that my hair was finally long enough to be conked. He had promised to school me in how to beat the barbershops' three- and four-dollar price by making up congolene and then conking ourselves.

The teenage Malcolm, whose reddish hair gave him his nickname, "Big Red."

Barber Shop (1946) by Jacob Lawrence (1917–2000). Gouache on paper (21⅛″ × 29⅜″). (1975.15)

The Toledo Museum of Art, Toledo, Ohio. Purchased with funds from the Libbey Endowment. Gift of Edward Drummond Libbey. Courtesy of the artist and Francine Seders Gallery, Seattle, Washington.

I took the little list of ingredients he had printed out for me and went to a grocery store, where I got a can of Red Devil lye, two eggs, and two medium-sized white potatoes. Then at a drugstore near the poolroom, I asked for a large jar of Vaseline, a large bar of soap, a large-toothed comb and a fine-toothed comb, one of those rubber hoses with a metal sprayhead, a rubber apron, and a pair of gloves.

"Going to lay on that first conk?" the drugstore man asked me. I proudly told him, grinning, "Right!"

Shorty paid six dollars a week for a room in his cousin's shabby apartment. His cousin wasn't at home. "It's like the pad's mine, he spends so much time with his woman," Shorty said. "Now, you watch me—"

He peeled the potatoes and thin-sliced them into a quart-sized Mason fruit jar, then started stirring them with a wooden spoon as he gradually poured in a little over half the can of lye. "Never use a metal spoon; the lye will turn it black," he told me.

A jellylike, starchy-looking glop resulted from

the lye and potatoes, and Shorty broke in the two eggs, stirring real fast—his own conk and dark face bent down close. The congolene turned pale yellowish. "Feel the jar," Shorty said. I cupped my hand against the outside and snatched it away. "Damn right, it's hot, that's the lye," he said. "So you know it's going to burn when I comb it in—it burns *bad*. But the longer you can stand it, the straighter the hair."

He made me sit down, and he tied the string of the new rubber apron tightly around my neck and combed up my bush of hair. Then, from the big Vaseline jar, he took a handful and massaged it hard all through my hair and into the scalp. He also thickly Vaselined my neck, ears, and forehead. "When I get to washing out your head, be sure to tell me anywhere you feel any little stinging," Shorty warned me, washing his hands, then pulling on the rubber gloves and tying on his own rubber apron. "You always got to remember that any congolene left in burns a sore into your head."

The congolene just felt warm when Shorty started combing it in. But then my head caught fire.

I gritted my teeth and tried to pull the sides of the kitchen table together. The comb felt as if it was raking my skin off.

My eyes watered, my nose was running. I couldn't stand it any longer; I bolted to the washbasin. I was cursing Shorty with every name I could think of when he got the spray going and started soap-lathering my head.

He lathered and spray-rinsed, lathered and spray-rinsed, maybe ten or twelve times, each time gradually closing the hot-water faucet, until the rinse was cold, and that helped some.

"You feel any stinging spots?"

"No," I managed to say. My knees were trembling.

"Sit back down, then. I think we got it all out OK."

The flame came back as Shorty, with a thick towel, started drying my head, rubbing hard. *"Easy, man, easy!"* I kept shouting.

"The first time's always worst. You get used to it better before long. You took it real good, homeboy. You got a good conk."

When Shorty let me stand up and see in the mirror, my hair hung down in limp, damp strings. My scalp still flamed, but not as badly; I could bear it. He draped the towel around my shoulders, over my rubber apron, and began again Vaselining my hair.

I could feel him combing, straight back, first the big comb, then the fine-toothed one.

Then he was using a razor, very delicately, on the back of my neck. Then, finally, shaping the sideburns.

My first view in the mirror blotted out the hurting. I'd seen some pretty conks, but when it's the first time, on your *own* head, the transformation, after the lifetime of kinks, is staggering.

The mirror reflected Shorty behind me. We both were grinning and sweating. And on top of my head was this thick, smooth sheen of shining red hair—real red—as straight as any white man's.

How ridiculous I was! Stupid enough to stand there simply lost in admiration of my hair now looking "white," reflected in the mirror in Shorty's room. I vowed that I'd never again be without a conk, and I never was for many years.

This was my first really big step toward self-degradation: when I endured all of that pain, literally burning my flesh to have it look like a white man's hair. I had joined that multitude of Negro men and women in America who are brainwashed into believing that the black people are "inferior"—and white people "superior"—that they will even violate and mutilate their God-created bodies to try to look "pretty" by white standards.

Words to Own

self-degradation (self′deg′rə·dā′shən) *n.:* act of destroying or weakening one's moral character and self-respect.
multitude (mul′tə·to͞od′) *n.:* large number.
violate (vī′ə·lāt′) *v.:* fail to show proper respect for.
mutilate (myo͞ot′'l·āt′) *v.:* damage; injure.

Meet the Writer

A Charismatic Leader

Malcolm X (1925–1965) changed his life and then lost it. One of the most influential African American leaders of the twentieth century, Malcolm wrote an autobiography that has become a modern classic.

Malcolm's father, a Baptist minister active in Marcus Garvey's Universal Negro Improvement Association, died when Malcolm was six, reportedly pushed under a streetcar by white racists. His mother suffered an emotional breakdown and spent twenty-six years in a mental hospital.

At sixteen, Malcolm moved to Boston to live with his half-sister. A life of hustling and burglary landed him in prison from 1946 to 1952, and there he changed his life. He read hundreds of books, starting with the letter *A* in a dictionary ("People don't realize how a man's whole life can be changed by one book," he said), and joined the weekly prison debates.

“Standing up and speaking before an audience was a thing that throughout my previous life never would have crossed my mind. But I will tell you that, right there, in the prison, debating, speaking to a crowd, was as exhilarating to me as the discovery of knowledge through reading had been. Standing up there, the faces looking up at me, things in my head coming out of my mouth, while my brain searched for the next best thing to follow what I was saying, and if I could sway them to my side by handling it right, then I had won the debate—once my feet got wet, I was gone on debating.”

Malcolm had converted to the Muslim faith in prison and after his release became the most popular, charismatic preacher in the Nation of Islam movement. He abandoned his "slave name" and took the surname "X," a letter that in algebra stands for the unknown.

Award-winning oil painting of Malcolm X (1993) by Victor Zavala, a student at California State University at Fullerton, California.

In 1963, after openly challenging the movement's leader, Elijah Muhammad, Malcolm was suspended from the Black Muslim ministry. On February 21, 1965, just as he was about to speak in the Audubon Ballroom in New York City, he was shot and killed.

Barber shop sign (oil on board) in Burkina Faso, a West African country.

A "Piercing" Issue

"C'mon, Jen," they leered, an outstretched hand clutching onto a gleaming needle poised to plunge into my skin at any minute. "Everybody's doin' it."

"NO," I shouted vehemently, shaking my head and glaring at the so-called friends surrounding me. "I won't do it. I'm not giving in to you guys or to all this peer pressure."

My best friend finally collapsed onto a nearby couch, holding her hands up in exasperation and staring at me as if I were some lunatic.

"For Pete's sake, Jenny," she cried. "We're not asking you to do drugs or anything! All we want to do is to pierce your stupid ears!"

All right, so maybe I am acting a bit paranoid about pierced ears. Maybe my friends are right when they say that a high school female has to have her ears pierced; that it is some sort of unofficial tradition spreading throughout both genders of our society even as we speak. Maybe men really are attracted to dangling objects hanging from lobes of the skin and that when I become an old maid with no man, I will finally give in to the peer pressure and have my ears punched through. Maybe, maybe, maybe . . .

In a world where insecurity is the norm and where "Maybe" is the obsolete answer for so many questions, it is reassuring to know that I have made a decision based on what I know is right for me. Rather than allowing the conforming roles of society to dominate my entire life, I have stood up for myself and won.

Won? How could something so obscure as unblemished earlobes be considered a victory when the world is filled with issues that concern our lives more intensely, such as abortion, politics, and drugs? Have I nothing better to do than stand in front of a mirror and say to myself, "Boy, Jenny, you sure are brave not to have your ears pierced"?

The fact of the matter is, there are very serious issues that we as intelligent people must face every day. With each issue, we must make some sort of decision that will change our lives some way or another. When making such life-altering decisions, how will we know that we have made the correct choice for ourselves, without having someone else cloud our opinions?

For me, all I have to do is glance at the mirror and see my plain, boring earlobes. That glance will always tell me that since I was able to make one decision based on my personal beliefs, I can make a thousand more and know that each and every one was made by me, not by a conforming society.

Maybe I'm just trying to be a pseudo-intellectual nonconformist. Maybe I'm writing this just to impress you with my essay-writing abilities. Maybe it's time to look in the mirror again.

—Jennifer Yu
Warren Township High School
Gurnee, Illinois

Making Meanings

First Thoughts

1. What do you think is the most important—or powerful—word or phrase in Malcolm's story? Why?

Reading Check

Write a brief **summary** of what happens when Malcolm conks his hair. Then, in one sentence, summarize what Malcolm says about his efforts to look like a white man.

Shaping Interpretations

2. Why do you think Malcolm feels that conking his hair is a step toward self-degradation?

3. What would you **infer** about Malcolm's **tone** at the end of this selection? (List words or passages that help establish the tone.)

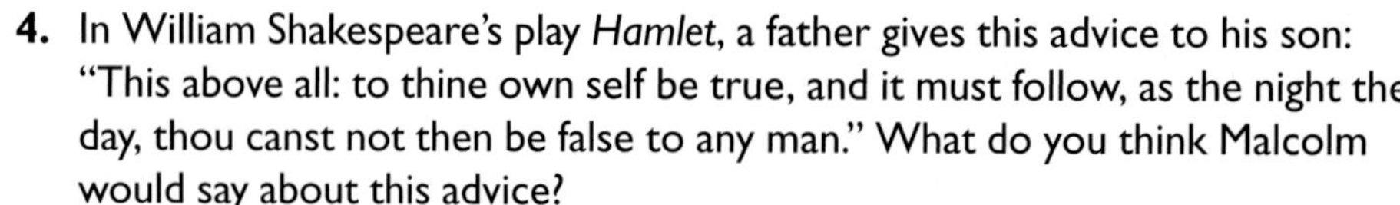

4. In William Shakespeare's play *Hamlet*, a father gives this advice to his son: "This above all: to thine own self be true, and it must follow, as the night the day, thou canst not then be false to any man." What do you think Malcolm would say about this advice?

Connecting with the Text

5. Get together with a small group to talk about the pressures to conform—to be like everyone else—that young people face today. What could happen as a result of these pressures? Be sure to check your Quickwrite notes and refer to the student essay "A Piercing Issue" on page 349.

Extending the Text

6. Malcolm talks about behavior that leads toward self-degradation. What, on the other hand, do you think gives people a sense of self-respect or self-esteem?

Shorty (played by Spike Lee) and Malcolm X (Denzel Washington) wearing zoot suits in a scene from Spike Lee's movie *Malcolm X* (1992).

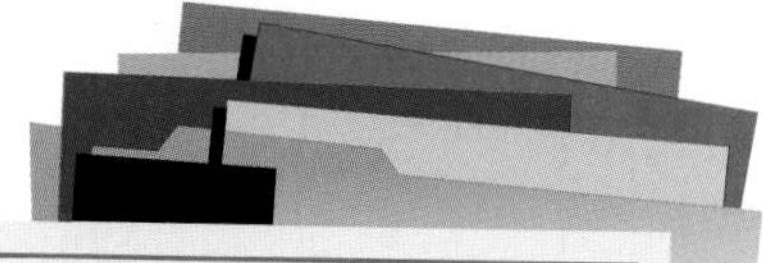

CHOICES: Building Your Portfolio

Writer's Notebook

1. Collecting Ideas for an Autobiographical Incident

Finding an experience. Think of an experience you remember vividly, one that had a mighty impact on you and that you're willing to share with others. Maybe you'll want to talk about your experiences with pressures to conform to the "in" fashions you listed in the Quickwrite before you started reading "Hair." Maybe you'll want to start by making lists (Five Incidents I'd Rather Forget; Three Triumphs). Take notes about your experience to see if it will give you enough material to develop into an autobiographical incident (see the Writer's Workshop on page 380). Check the experience that interests you most.

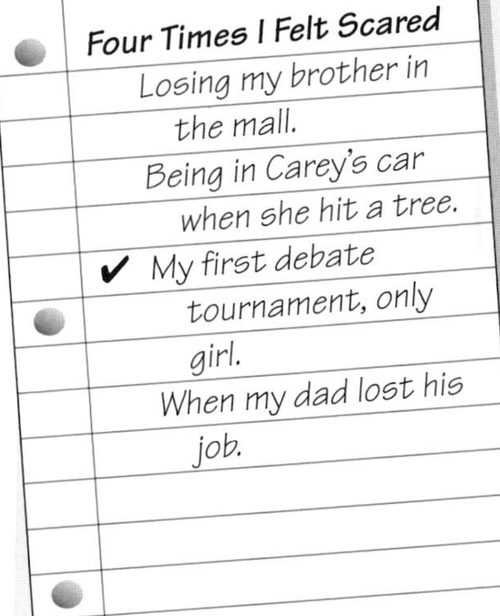

Four Times I Felt Scared
Losing my brother in the mall.
Being in Carey's car when she hit a tree.
✔ My first debate tournament, only girl.
When my dad lost his job.

Research/Art History

2. Creative Giants

During the 1940s, the African American communities in Harlem, Chicago, and Los Angeles were wellsprings of artistic creativity. Research the life and work of one of the following artists (or others you discover):

Music: Duke Ellington, Count Basie, Charlie Parker, Dizzy Gillespie

Dance: Katherine Dunham

Painting: Romare Bearden, Jacob Lawrence

Literature: Gwendolyn Brooks, Langston Hughes, Richard Wright

Share with your class the results of your research as well as samples (recordings, writing, reproductions) of the artist's work.

Language Study

3. Where *Hip* Was Invented

Many words that later entered mainstream English slang were used by African Americans during the era when "Hair" takes place. Report on the **origins** of *hip, cool, dig, cat, jive, pad,* and *homeboy.* You'll find these words in a dictionary of American slang.

Drawing/Research

4. Hair Through the Ages

Look up pictures of hairstyles throughout the course of history. Draw four or five of them, and write an informative caption for each. Some possible examples: conked hair; the pageboy; the Afro; cornrows; long hippie hair; punk hair; the crewcut, ponytail, and ducktail; powdered wigs; the squash-blossom hairstyle of the Hopis.

Young, unmarried Hopi women once signaled their eligibility by wearing their hair in maiden's (also called squash-blossom) whorls. Now this traditional hairstyle is worn only on special occasions.

LANGUAGE LINK MINI-LESSON

Watch Your Tone

Handbook of Literary Terms HELP

See Connotations.

In written communication, **tone** is conveyed by word choice, or **diction.** See how a change in a single word can change the tone of each of Malcolm's sentences below:

1. "How ridiculous I was!" [Change the word *ridiculous* to *humorous.* What happens to the tone?]
2. "I had joined that multitude of Negro men and women in America who are brainwashed into believing that the black people are 'inferior.' . . ." [Change *brainwashed* to *persuaded.* What happens to the tone?]
3. "A jellylike, starchy-looking glop resulted from the lye and potatoes, . . ." [Change *glop* to *mixture.* What happens to the tone?]

Try It Out

First read each of the following sentences aloud to a partner. Then, find a word from the list below that describes its tone. Finally, reword each sentence to create a different tone. Express basically the same idea, but say it differently. Compare your rewritten sentences.

1. It was quiet on the street—deathly, eerily quiet.
2. That's the kind of answer I'd expect from the likes of her.
3. We met on a wild, wonderful night that shaped my life.

A BOX OF TONES

angry	comic	humorous	mocking	romantic
awed	critical	ironic	mournful	sarcastic
bitter	cynical	loving	ominous	sympathetic

VOCABULARY HOW TO OWN A WORD

WORD BANK

self-degradation
multitude
violate
mutilate

Mapping a Word's Roots

Every word has a **root,** the part of the word that carries its core meaning. You can discover each word's root by checking its **etymology,** or **origin,** in a dictionary. (Since etymologies trace a word's history backward in time, the oldest known root is the one mentioned last.) Create a word map like the one below for each of the other words in the Word Bank.

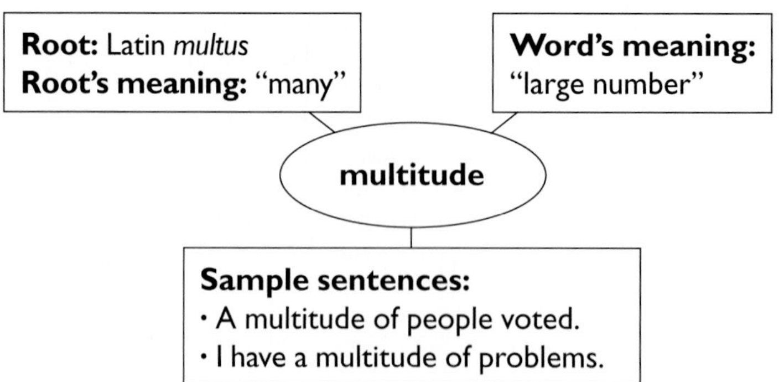

Root: Latin *multus*
Root's meaning: "many"
Word's meaning: "large number"
multitude
Sample sentences:
• A multitude of people voted.
• I have a multitude of problems.

Elements of Literature

AUTOBIOGRAPHY: Written Memory *by* Janet Burroway

"It is not true that we have only one life to live," said the linguist S. I. Hayakawa. "If we can read, we can live as many more lives and as many kinds as we wish."

One way we can "live more lives" is by reading **biographies**—stories of people's lives that are written by other people. The best biographies are well researched and objective.

Another way we can enter a person's life is by reading an **autobiography**—someone's personal account of his or her own life.

Many biographies and autobiographies read just like novels—they contain suspense, characters, settings, even plot (the events of the person's life).

If a biography or autobiography is well told, we may even experience "the shock of recognition" as we find something of ourselves in a stranger's life story.

Often, the most interesting autobiographies are the most honest. The writers of these works don't seek to glorify or glamorize or justify themselves; nor do they flinch from reporting that they are less than perfect. They try to tell the truth.

Honesty is difficult. Some writers would never attempt autobiography. "It does no good to write autobiographical fiction," warns fiction writer Toni Cade Bambara, "cause the minute this book hits the stand here comes your mama screamin how could you. . . ."

What We Remember: "Facts" and "Truth"

Writer Harry Crews has said: "What has been most significant in my life had all taken place by the time I was six years old." Crews is stating his strong personal sense of something that most scientists acknowledge as a fact: The preschool years are the "formative" years, and most traits of our character are in place before we reach the age of five.

What an autobiographer remembers about those years is likely to be faulty from the standpoint of absolute fact. What most of us remember most accurately is the significance things had for us, which is something that only *we* can know and judge. Memory has this in common with autobiography (which is, after all, simply written memory): that the facts may be distorted or misremembered, but the significance of these facts is what we make of them.

Living Like a Writer

Here is how writer Ray Bradbury (see his story on page 173) uses images from his past to help him write:

> . . . I was gathering images all of my life, storing them away, and forgetting them. Somehow I had to send myself back, with words as catalysts, to open the memories and see what they had to offer.
>
> So, from the age of twenty-four to thirty-six hardly a day passed when I didn't stroll myself across a recollection of my grandparents' northern Illinois grass, hoping to come across some old half-burnt firecracker, a rusted toy, or a fragment of letter written to myself in some young year, hoping to contact the older person I became, to remind him of his past, his life, his people, his joys, and his drenching sorrows.

Your own life will provide rich background for the Writer's Workshop on page 380.

Before You Read

It Can't Be Helped

Make the Connection

Insiders and Outsiders

In what groups do you feel like an "insider"—safe, comfortable, free to be yourself? If you're like most people, in other groups you probably feel like an "outsider"—uncomfortable and ill at ease. That's because groups tend to set up invisible boundaries to keep insiders in and outsiders out. Sometimes these boundaries are actual walls or fences.

Quickwrite

Meet with a partner and share your knowledge and feelings about Japanese American internment camps in the United States during World War II. (See the Background on this page.) Then, as a class, exchange your ideas. Take notes on what you've learned from the quick-sharing.

go.hrw.com

LEO 10-5

Elements of Literature

Anecdotes: Mini-Stories

> An **anecdote** is a very brief story, often one that makes a special point.

Real life doesn't have a clear plot. We go from day to day, incident to incident, sometimes feeling that our experiences are only casually connected. That's why **biographies** and **autobiographies** are often sprinkled with **anecdotes**—very brief stories about their subjects that make some point, told in capsule form.

Anecdotes can provide a welcome change of pace. They can also reveal something important about the real-life characters or events. "Hair" (page 345) could be called an anecdote. Look for anecdotes as you read "It Can't Be Helped."

Reading Skills and Strategies

Chronological Order

Events in **chronological order** follow a time sequence: this happened, then this, then this. When you read something structured in chronological order, look for transitions that signal when time is moving forward. Watch also for other important changes as time passes. For example, note the changes in setting in "It Can't Be Helped" as Jeanne's family moves several times within a few months.

Background

In this autobiographical excerpt, a woman remembers what it was like to be a Japanese American on the coast of California during World War II. Executive Order 9066, signed by President Roosevelt in February 1942, ordered all Japanese Americans to leave coastal areas and go to relocation camps inland because many government officials worried that people of Japanese ancestry would cooperate with the Japanese government if there were an invasion. Manzanar was one of ten such camps. It opened in 1942 in a desert near California's eastern Sierras.

We went because the government ordered us to.

It Can't Be Helped

from **Farewell to Manzanar**

Jeanne Wakatsuki Houston and James Houston

In December of 1941 Papa's disappearance didn't bother me nearly so much as the world I soon found myself in.

He had been a jack-of-all-trades. When I was born, he was farming near Inglewood. Later, when he started fishing, we moved to Ocean Park, near Santa Monica, and until they picked him up, that's where we lived, in a big frame house with a brick fireplace, a block back from the beach. We were the only Japanese family in the neighborhood. Papa liked it that way. He didn't want to be labeled or grouped by anyone. But with him gone and no way of knowing what to expect, my mother moved all of us down to Terminal Island. Woody already lived there, and one of my older sisters had married a Terminal Island boy. Mama's first concern now was to keep the family together; and once the war began, she felt safer there than isolated racially in Ocean Park. But for me, at age seven, the island was a country as foreign as India or Arabia would have been. It was the first time I had lived among other Japanese, or gone to school with them, and I was terrified all the time.

This was partly Papa's fault. One of his threats to keep us younger kids in line was "I'm going to sell you to the Chinaman." When I had entered kindergarten two years earlier, I was the only Oriental in the class. They sat me next to a Caucasian girl who happened to have very slanted eyes. I looked at her and began to scream, certain Papa had sold me out at last. My fear of her ran so deep I could not speak of it, even to Mama, couldn't explain why I was screaming. For two weeks I had nightmares about this girl, until the teachers finally moved me to the other side of the room. And it was still with me, this fear of Oriental faces, when we moved to Terminal Island.

In those days it was a company town, a ghetto owned and controlled by the canneries. The men went after fish, and whenever the boats came back—day or night—the women would be called to process the catch while it was fresh. One in the afternoon or four in the morning, it made no difference. My mother had to go to work right after we moved there. I can still hear the whistle—two toots for French's, three for Van Camp's—and she and Chizu would be out of bed in the middle of the night, heading for the cannery.

The house we lived in was nothing more than a shack, a barracks with single plank walls and rough wooden floors, like the cheapest kind of migrant workers' housing. The people around us were hard-working, boisterous, a little proud of their nickname, *yo-go-re,* which meant literally uncouth one, or roughneck, or dead-end kid. They not only spoke Japanese exclusively, they spoke a dialect peculiar to Kyushu, where their families had come from in Japan, a rough, fisherman's language, full of oaths and insults. Instead of saying *ba-ka-ta-re,* a common insult meaning stupid, Terminal Islanders would say *ba-ka-ya-ro,* a coarser and exclusively masculine use of the word, which implies gross stupidity. They would swagger and pick on outsiders and persecute anyone who didn't speak as they did. That was what made my own time there so hateful. I had never spoken anything but English, and the other kids in the second grade despised me for it. They were tough and mean, like ghetto kids anywhere. Each day after school I dreaded their ambush. My brother Kiyo, three years older, would wait for me at the door, where we would decide whether to run straight home together, or split up, or try a new and unexpected route.

None of these kids ever actually attacked. It was the threat that frightened us, their fearful looks, and the noises they would make, like miniature samurai,[1] in a language we couldn't understand.

At the time it seemed we had been living under this reign of fear for years. In fact, we lived there about two months. Late in February the navy decided to clear Terminal Island completely. Even though most of us were American-born, it was dangerous having that many Orientals so close to the Long Beach Naval Station, on the opposite end of the island. We had known something like this was coming. But, like Papa's

1. **samurai** (sam′ə·rī′): soldiers who worked for noblemen in Japan between the twelfth and nineteenth centuries.

arrest, not much could be done ahead of time. There were four of us kids still young enough to be living with Mama, plus Granny, her mother, sixty-five then, speaking no English, and nearly blind. Mama didn't know where else she could get work, and we had nowhere else to move *to*. On February 25 the choice was made for us. We were given forty-eight hours to clear out.

The secondhand dealers had been prowling around for weeks, like wolves, offering humiliating prices for goods and furniture they knew many of us would have to sell sooner or later. Mama had left all but her most valuable possessions in Ocean Park, simply because she had nowhere to put them. She had brought along her pottery, her silver, heirlooms like the kimonos[2] Granny had brought from Japan, tea sets, lacquered tables, and one fine old set of china, blue and white porcelain, almost translucent. On the day we were leaving, Woody's car was so crammed with boxes and luggage and kids we had just run out of room. Mama had to sell this china.

One of the dealers offered her fifteen dollars for it. She said it was a full setting for twelve and worth at least two hundred. He said fifteen was his top price. Mama started to quiver. Her eyes blazed up at him. She had been packing all night and trying to calm down Granny, who didn't understand why we were moving again and what all the rush was about. Mama's nerves were shot, and now navy jeeps were patrolling the streets. She didn't say another word. She just glared at this man, all the rage and frustration channeled at him through her eyes.

He watched her for a moment and said he was sure he couldn't pay more than seventeen fifty for that china. She reached into the red velvet case, took out a dinner plate, and hurled it at the floor right in front of his feet.

The man leaped back shouting, "Hey! Hey, don't do that! Those are valuable dishes!"

Mama took out another dinner plate and hurled it at the floor, then another and another, never moving, never opening her mouth, just quivering and glaring at the retreating dealer, with tears streaming down her cheeks. He finally turned and scuttled out the door, heading for the next house. When he was gone, she stood there smashing cups and bowls and platters until the whole set lay in scattered blue and white fragments across the wooden floor.

The American Friends Service[3] helped us find a small house in Boyle Heights, another minority ghetto, in downtown Los Angeles, now inhabited briefly by a few hundred Terminal Island refugees. Executive Order 9066 had been signed by President Roosevelt, giving the War Department authority to define military areas in the western states and to exclude from them anyone who might threaten the war effort. There was a lot of talk about internment, or moving inland, or something like that in store for all Japanese Americans. I remember my brothers sitting around the table talking very intently about what we were going to do, how we would keep the family together. They had seen how quickly Papa was removed, and they knew now that he would not be back for quite a while. Just before leaving Terminal Island Mama had received her first letter, from Bismarck, North Dakota. He had been imprisoned at Fort Lincoln, in an all-male camp for enemy aliens.

Papa had been the patriarch. He had always decided everything in the family. With him gone, my brothers, like councilors in the absence of a chief, worried about what should be done. The ironic thing is, there wasn't much left to decide. These were mainly days of quiet, desperate waiting for what seemed at the time to be inevitable. There is a phrase the Japanese use

2. **kimonos** (kə·mō′nəz): traditional Japanese robes with wide sleeves and a sash.

3. **American Friends Service:** American Friends Service Committee, a Quaker organization formed in 1917 to aid victims of war.

Words to Own

translucent (trans·lo͞o′sənt) *adj.:* partially transparent.

ironic (ī·rän′ik) *adj.:* opposite of what is expected.

inevitable (in·ev′i·tə·bəl) *adj.:* unavoidable; certain to happen.

in such situations, when something difficult must be endured. You would hear the older heads, the issei,[4] telling others very quietly, *"Shikata ga nai"* (It cannot be helped). *"Shikata ga nai"* (It must be done).

Mama and Woody went to work packing celery for a Japanese produce dealer. Kiyo and my sister May and I enrolled in the local school, and what sticks in my memory from those few weeks is the teacher—not her looks, her remoteness. In Ocean Park my teacher had been a kind, grandmotherly woman who used to sail with us in Papa's boat from time to time and who wept the day we had to leave. In Boyle Heights the teacher felt cold and distant. I was confused by all the moving and was having trouble with the classwork, but she would never help me out. She would have nothing to do with me.

This was the first time I had felt outright hostility from a Caucasian. Looking back, it is easy enough to explain. Public attitudes toward the Japanese in California were shifting rapidly. In the first few months of the Pacific war, America was on the run. Tolerance had turned to distrust and irrational fear. The hundred-year-old tradition of anti-Orientalism on the West Coast soon resurfaced, more vicious than ever. Its result became clear about a month later, when we were told to make our third and final move.

The name Manzanar meant nothing to us when we left Boyle Heights. We didn't know where it was or what it was. We went because the government ordered us to. And, in the case of my older brothers and sisters, we went with a certain amount of relief. They had all heard stories of Japanese homes being attacked, of beatings in the streets of California towns. They were as frightened of the Caucasians as Caucasians were of us. Moving, under what appeared to be government protection, to an area less directly threatened by the war seemed not such a bad idea at all. For some it actually sounded like a fine adventure.

Our pickup point was a Buddhist church in Los Angeles. It was very early, and misty, when we got there with our luggage. Mama had bought heavy coats for all of us. She grew up in eastern Washington and knew that anywhere inland in early April would be cold. I was proud of my new coat, and I remember sitting on a duffel bag trying to be friendly with the Greyhound driver. I smiled at him. He didn't smile back. He was befriending no one. Someone tied a numbered tag to my collar and to the duffel bag (each family was given a number, and that became our official designation until the camps were closed), someone else passed out box lunches for the trip, and we climbed aboard.

I had never been outside Los Angeles County, never traveled more than ten miles from the coast, had never even ridden on a bus. I was full of excitement, the way any kid would be, and wanted to look out the window. But for the first few hours the shades were drawn. Around me other people played cards, read magazines, dozed, waiting. I settled back, waiting too, and finally fell asleep. The bus felt very secure to me. Almost half its passengers were immediate relatives. Mama and my older brothers had succeeded in keeping most of us together, on the same bus, headed for the same camp. I didn't realize until much later what a job that was. The strategy had been, first, to have everyone living in the same district when the evacuation began, and then to get all of us included under the same family number, even though names had been changed by marriage. Many families weren't as lucky as ours and suffered months of anguish while trying to arrange transfers from one camp to another.

We rode all day. By the time we reached our destination, the shades were up. It was late afternoon. The first thing I saw was a yellow swirl across a blurred, reddish setting sun. The bus was being pelted by what sounded like splattering rain. It wasn't rain. This was my first look at something I would soon know very well, a billowing flurry of dust and sand churned up by the wind through Owens Valley.

We drove past a barbed-wire fence, through a gate, and into an open space where trunks and

4. issei (ē′sā′): Japanese for "first generation," referring to Japanese who immigrated to the United States after 1907 but were not allowed to become citizens until 1952.

sacks and packages had been dumped from the baggage trucks that drove out ahead of us. I could see a few tents set up, the first rows of black barracks, and beyond them, blurred by sand, rows of barracks that seemed to spread for miles across this plain. People were sitting on cartons or milling around, with their backs to the wind, waiting to see which friends or relatives might be on this bus. As we approached, they turned or stood up, and some moved toward us expectantly. But inside the bus no one stirred. No one waved or spoke. They just stared out the windows, ominously silent. I didn't understand this. Hadn't we finally arrived, our whole family intact? I opened a window, leaned out, and yelled happily. "Hey! This whole bus is full of Wakatsukis!"

Outside, the greeters smiled. Inside there was an explosion of laughter, hysterical, tension-breaking laughter that left my brothers choking and whacking each other across the shoulders.

WORDS TO OWN

ominously (äm'ə·nəs·lē) *adv.:* in a way that suggests something bad is going to happen.

intact (in·takt') *adj.:* kept together; not broken up.

MEET THE WRITERS

An Innocent Victim

Jeanne Wakatsuki Houston (1934–) kept her feelings about her World War II internment largely bottled up until the age of thirty-seven, when she and her husband, **James D. Houston** (1933–), wrote *Farewell to Manzanar* (1974). Until then, she said in an interview, she had felt "sullied" by the experience, even though she had been an innocent victim. "You feel you must have *done* something. You feel you are part of the act."

Writing about Manzanar, she explained, was a way of "coming to terms" with the impact of the experience on her whole life:

"We began with a tape recorder and an old 1944 yearbook put together at Manzanar High School. It documented the entire camp scene—the graduating seniors, the guard towers, the Judo pavilion, the creeks I used to wade in, my family's barracks. As the photos brought that world back, I began to dredge up feelings that had lain submerged since the forties. I began to make connections I had previously been afraid to see. . . . But this is not political history. It is a story, or a web of stories—my own, my father's, my family's—tracing a few paths, out of the multitude of paths that led up to and away from the experience of the internment."

Connections — A Poem

The speaker in this poem is a nisei, *a second-generation Japanese American. Her mother came to the United States because a marriage had been arranged for her with* "Ito-San," *or Mr. Ito, a man she had never met.*

Nisei Daughter: The Second Generation

Rose Furuya Hawkins

When people ask
About my mother
I look away and say,
"Oh, she's been gone
A long time now.
I hardly knew her
Anyway."

But I know she was
A renegade.° Why else
Was she standing on some foreign shore,
Uncomfortable in high-heeled shoes
And black dress with bust darts,
Her cherry-blossom kimono
Left far behind?

How else did she consent
To trade her rice-paper walls
For corrugated tin
And to love, honor, and obey
This crude stranger, *Ito-San*,
Who sipped Coca-Cola
Through a straw?

Woman Reading a Letter by Kitagawa Utamaro (1753?–1806). Color woodblock print.

Scala/Art Resource, NY.

9. renegade: one who departs from custom or tradition.

Yes, my mother was a renegade.
She braved the future
By swallowing her pride,
Her delicate fingers
Shaping paper swans
After a long day
Of picking cotton
In the Imperial Valley.

Midnight, the Hour of the Rat: Mother and Sleepy Child from the series *The Clock of Beauty's Daily Round* (c.1790) by Kitagawa Utamaro (1753?–1806). Woodcut ($14\frac{3}{8}'' \times 9\frac{5}{8}''$).

The Metropolitan Museum of Art. Rogers Fund, 1922 (JP 1278). Photograph ©1979 The Metropolitan Museum of Art.

She sewed dresses
For my doll
Long after her feet
Were too tired to work the treadle
Of her prized Singer.°
She taught me words:
Mi-mi, ha-na, ku-chi,
Pointing to my ear,
My nose, my mouth.
She fed me full
Of fat rice balls
And pickled radishes,
Afraid I might ask
For bologna sandwiches.

Mama, forgive me.
I guess I knew you well.
I was your miracle child,
Your second generation
Nisei daughter,
Born to you
When you were already too old,
Already too torn
By barbed-wire fences
And mixed loyalty.

Oh, where have you gone
Little moon-faced child,
Who once chased fireflies
For paper lanterns
In old Japan?

34. Singer: brand name of a sewing machine.

Making Meanings

First Thoughts

1. Which of Jeanne Wakatsuki Houston's experiences surprised you? What other feelings did you have about her story?

Shaping Interpretations

2. How did this firsthand account add to what you knew about this period of American history? (Check your Quick-write notes.) Be sure to share responses with your classmates.
3. The writers have tried to recapture a child's **point of view** of the events. What part of "the big picture" didn't Jeanne understand as a child? Does this autobiography strike you as being honest, even though it might have been painful to write? Explain.
4. What can we **infer** from the **anecdote** on page 357, when Jeanne's mother smashes the good china?
5. What do you think is the **tone** of the **title** "It Can't Be Helped"? Find details that suggest how the writers feel about these events.

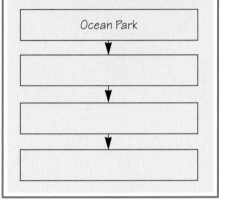

Reading Check

This text is structured in **chronological order.** Complete the flow chart below to show the three moves that the family made. Add details that describe each new **setting.**

Ocean Park
↓
↓
↓

Connecting with the Text

6. How do you think you would have felt if you had been in the Wakatsuki family and had been sent to an internment camp? What do you think would have helped you get through?

Extending the Text

7. Which do you think is better: living in a community of people like yourself—people of the same ethnic, racial, or religious background—or living among people of all kinds mixed together? Talk in a small group about how you feel.
8. Another point of view about being a first-generation American is expressed in "Nisei Daughter" (see *Connections* on page 360). What feelings does this speaker express about her mother and herself? Could these feelings be extended to other national groups?

Japanese Americans in Seattle, Washington, on their way to a relocation camp during World War II.

CHOICES: Building Your Portfolio

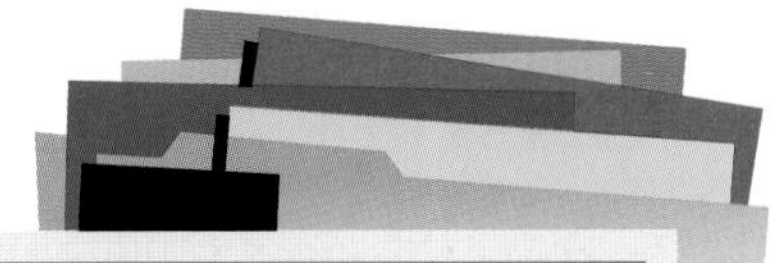

Writer's Notebook

1. Collecting Ideas for an Autobiographical Incident

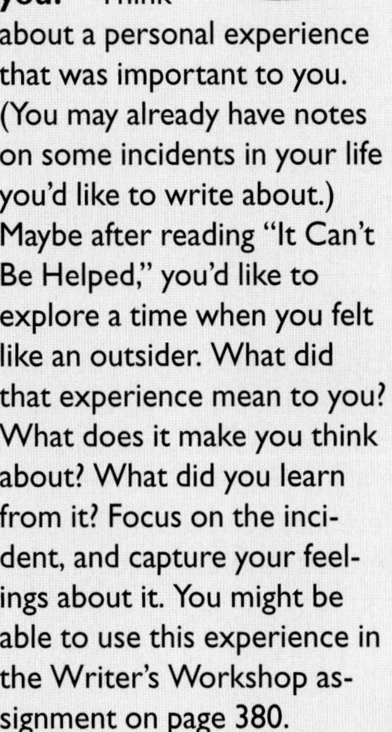

What does it mean to you? Think about a personal experience that was important to you. (You may already have notes on some incidents in your life you'd like to write about.) Maybe after reading "It Can't Be Helped," you'd like to explore a time when you felt like an outsider. What did that experience mean to you? What does it make you think about? What did you learn from it? Focus on the incident, and capture your feelings about it. You might be able to use this experience in the Writer's Workshop assignment on page 380.

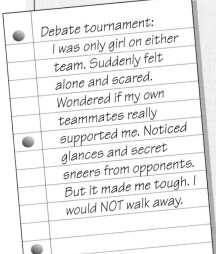

Debate tournament:
I was only girl on either team. Suddenly felt alone and scared. Wondered if my own teammates really supported me. Noticed glances and secret sneers from opponents. But it made me tough. I would NOT walk away.

Critical Thinking/ Speaking

2. Resolved: Solve the Crisis!

How should a country treat the naturalized citizens and the resident aliens from an enemy country during wartime? Make this crisis the focus of a **debate.** Your first task is to form teams of people with similar opinions. Then each team must write a proposition—a solution to the problem they will have to defend. In order to win a debate, you have to assemble evidence. In this case, a great deal of your evidence must come from historical sources.

Speaking and Listening

3. Shared Reading, Shared Feelings

Find sections of "It Can't Be Helped" and "Nisei Daughter" (see ***Connections*** on page 360) that made an impact on you— scenes, paragraphs, or single sentences or words. In a circle of students, read your choices aloud, one passage per student per turn. More than one person may read the same passage aloud. (Does a different reader produce a difference in **tone**?) Afterward, discuss your responses to these passages—both as a reader and as a listener.

Critical Writing/ Research

4. The Ten Camps

Look up the history of the internment of Japanese Americans during World War II, and prepare a brief written **report.** If you use the Internet, what key words will you use for your search? Where else will you look for information? Start by using the map below to list the names and states of the ten camps.

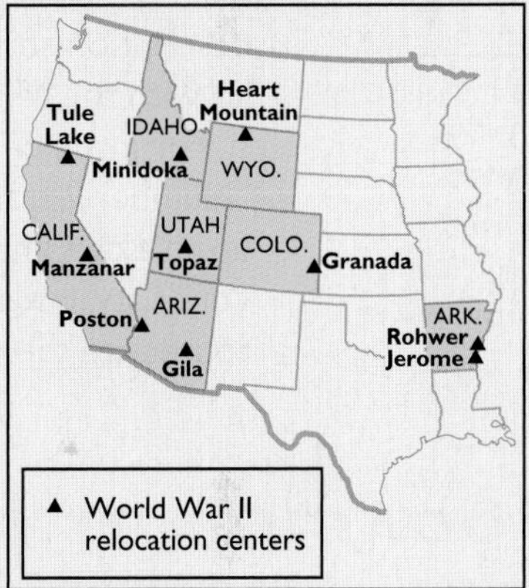

Research/Culture

5. Kimonos and Tea Sets

These selections mention many aspects of Japanese culture (for example, kimonos, lacquer, china, paper lanterns). For a brief **oral report,** research Japanese color woodblocks (see pages 360–361) or another aspect of traditional Japanese art or culture. If possible, use visuals with your report.

GRAMMAR LINK **MINI-LESSON**

Specific and Proper Nouns

Language Handbook HELP

See Capitalizing Proper Nouns, page 1047.

Nouns can be classified as specific or general, proper or common. You can always tell a **proper noun**—it's capitalized and names a particular person, place, or thing.

General	Specific	Proper
building	factory	French's
place	relocation camp	Manzanar
relative	sister	May

There are pluses and minuses to using proper nouns and very specific nouns in writing. A plus is that a proper noun can make your description more specific. A minus is that a proper noun can make a description so specific that readers unfamiliar with the reference can't identify it.

For instance, the very specific description "Number 2 train to 241st Street" conjures up an exact image for residents of New York City, but a reader elsewhere might appreciate the general term "subway train."

Technology HELP

See Language Workshop CD-ROM. *Key word entry: nouns.*

Try It Out

Replace the underscored nouns and phrases with specific or proper nouns, and compare the two versions. Which creates a clearer picture for the reader?

1. The boy in the car blasted a song as he drove along.
2. For the holiday, a lot of relatives get together at my relative's house in the city.
3. The soccer team trounced another team in the tournament.

A tip for writers: In deciding when to use proper nouns and specific nouns, ask yourself: "Will my readers understand this reference?" Overuse of proper nouns can confuse readers.

VOCABULARY **HOW TO OWN A WORD**

WORD BANK

translucent
ironic
inevitable
ominously
intact

Beginnings and Endings: Prefixes and Suffixes

Some **prefixes** (word parts added before a root) and **suffixes** (word parts added after a root) have several meanings. Using the chart below, decide which meaning is used in each Word Bank word. (Check a dictionary's **etymology** for help.) Then, with a partner, list other words containing these prefixes and suffixes.

Prefixes	Suffixes
trans- across, over, above and beyond, through **in-** in, within, not, no	**-ly** *(forms adverbs or adjectives):* in a manner or direction, like, characteristic of **-ic** *(forms adjectives or nouns):* dealing with, having the quality of; person or thing showing

Before You Read

TYPHOID FEVER

Make the Connection

Remembering Myself

Think about it: you have years of stories in your life already. What do you remember from your early life that is important or unusual or funny? It might be a memory of a visit someplace. It might be a memory of a house you lived in. It might even be a memory of a time when you were sick.

Quickwrite

Take some notes on a childhood memory. Try to remember the event from a child's point of view. Ideas might come to you if you begin something like this: "I am seven years old . . . " or "I'm in a playground . . . ." Save your notes.

Elements of Literature

Comic Relief: Horror and Hilarity

Cracking a joke when everyone is tense can provide a terrific relief. That's exactly what **comic relief** does in literature: it eases emotional tension. A humorous character, scene, or bit of dialogue adds variety and keeps tragedy from being overwhelming. Mixing comedy with sadness is lifelike, too, because in the cycles of our life experiences, laughter and joy often give way to sadness, which in turn gives way once again to laughter and joy. As you read "Typhoid Fever," look for examples where a comic remark makes a sad situation easier to bear—at least for a moment.

A humorous incident or speech in a serious literary work provides **comic relief.**

Reading Skills and Strategies

Evaluating Credibility: Testing/Trusting Memory

"People are always asking, how does he remember so much," McCourt told an interviewer, "and how much is an Irish storyteller's embroidery?"

Credibility means "believability." How can you judge the credibility of an autobiography? (Some people are now calling this kind of writing "faction"—suggesting that it's a combination of "fact" and "fiction.") Can adults remember exact conversations and events that took place when they were ten years old? Is factual accuracy important, or is it the significance of an event that's of greater interest? Keep all these questions in mind as you read "Typhoid Fever." Does it ring true to you? Could any of the story's facts be checked out?

Background

Angela's Ashes is Frank McCourt's gritty, moving memoir of growing up poor in Limerick, Ireland, in the 1930s and '40s. Frank's family lived in a filthy, overcrowded slum. Bacterial diseases such as typhoid fever and diphtheria were common everywhere, but especially in poor neighborhoods.

Typhoid fever, caused by contaminated food or water, wastes the whole body. Diphtheria, spread by contact with others, starts as a sore throat and can end in suffocation. Because both infections spread easily, sick people are quarantined. In Ireland they were isolated in "fever hospitals." Most of these hospitals were run by the Catholic Church and staffed by nuns. Frank McCourt caught typhoid fever at the age of ten, on the day of his Confirmation. He was sent to a fever hospital.

go.hrw.com

LEO 10-5

Typhoid Fever

from **Angela's Ashes**

Frank McCourt

Yoo hoo, are you there, typhoid boy?

The room next to me is empty till one morning a girl's voice says, Yoo hoo, who's there?

I'm not sure if she's talking to me or someone in the room beyond.

Yoo hoo, boy with the typhoid, are you awake?

I am.

Are you better?

I am.

Well, why are you here?

I don't know. I'm still in the bed. They stick needles in me and give me medicine.

What do you look like?

I wonder, What kind of a question is that? I don't know what to tell her.

Yoo hoo, are you there, typhoid boy?

I am.

What's your name?

Frank.

That's a good name. My name is Patricia Madigan. How old are you?

Ten.

Oh. She sounds disappointed.

But I'll be eleven in August, next month.

Well, that's better than ten. I'll be fourteen in September. Do you want to know why I'm in the Fever Hospital?

I do.

I have diphtheria and something else.

What's something else?

They don't know. They think I have a disease from foreign parts because my father used to be in Africa. I nearly died. Are you going to tell me what you look like?

I have black hair.

You and millions.

I have brown eyes with bits of green that's called hazel.

You and thousands.

I have stitches on the back of my right hand and my two feet where they put in the soldier's blood.

Oh, did they?

They did.

You won't be able to stop marching and saluting.

There's a swish of habit and click of beads and then Sister Rita's voice. Now, now, what's this? There's to be no talking between two rooms especially when it's a boy and a girl. Do you hear me, Patricia?

I do, Sister.

Do you hear me, Francis?

I do, Sister.

You could be giving thanks for your two remarkable recoveries. You could be saying the rosary.[1] You could be reading *The Little Messenger of the Sacred Heart*[2] that's beside your beds. Don't let me come back and find you talking.

She comes into my room and wags her finger at me. Especially you, Francis, after thousands of boys prayed for you at the Confraternity.[3] Give thanks, Francis, give thanks.

She leaves and there's silence for awhile. Then Patricia whispers, Give thanks, Francis, give thanks, and say your rosary, Francis, and I laugh so hard a nurse runs in to see if I'm all right. She's a very stern nurse from the County Kerry and she frightens me. What's this, Francis? Laughing? What is there to laugh about? Are you and that Madigan girl talking? I'll report you to Sister Rita. There's to be no laughing for you could be doing serious damage to your internal apparatus.

She plods out and Patricia whispers again in a heavy Kerry accent, No laughing, Francis, you could be doin' serious damage to your internal apparatus. Say your rosary, Francis, and pray for your internal apparatus.

Mam visits me on Thursdays. I'd like to see my father, too, but I'm out of danger, crisis time is over, and I'm allowed only one visitor. Besides, she says, he's back at work at Rank's Flour Mills and please God this job will last a while with the war on and the English desperate for flour. She brings me a chocolate bar and that proves Dad is working. She could never afford it on the dole.[4] He sends me notes. He tells me my brothers are all praying for me, that I should be a good boy, obey the doctors, the nuns, the nurses, and don't forget to say my prayers. He's sure St. Jude pulled me through the crisis because he's the patron saint of desperate cases and I was indeed a desperate case.

Patricia says she has two books by her bed. One is a poetry book and that's the one she loves. The other is a short history of England and do I want it? She gives it to Seamus, the man who mops the floors every day, and he brings it to me. He says, I'm not supposed to be bringing anything from a dipteria room to a typhoid room with all the germs flying around and hiding between the pages and if you ever catch dipteria on top of the typhoid they'll know and I'll lose my good job and be out on the street singing patriotic songs with a tin cup in my hand, which I could easily do because there isn't a song ever written about Ireland's sufferings I don't know and a few songs about the joy of whiskey too.

Oh, yes, he knows Roddy McCorley. He'll sing it for me right enough but he's barely into the first verse when the Kerry nurse rushes in. What's this, Seamus? Singing? Of all the people in this hospital you should know the rules against singing. I have a good mind to report you to Sister Rita.

Ah, don't do that, nurse.

Very well, Seamus. I'll let it go this one time. You know the singing could lead to a relapse in these patients.

When she leaves he whispers he'll teach me a few songs because singing is good for passing the time when you're by yourself in a

1. **rosary:** group of prayers that Roman Catholics recite while holding a string of beads.
2. ***The Little Messenger of the Sacred Heart*:** religious publication for children.
3. **Confraternity:** here, a religious organization made up of nonclergy, or lay people.
4. **dole:** government payment to the unemployed; also, money or food given to those in need.

typhoid room. He says Patricia is a lovely girl the way she often gives him sweets from the parcel her mother sends every fortnight. He stops mopping the floor and calls to Patricia in the next room, I was telling Frankie you're a lovely girl, Patricia, and she says, You're a lovely man, Seamus. He smiles because he's an old man of forty and he never had children but the ones he can talk to here in the Fever Hospital. He says, Here's the book, Frankie. Isn't it a great pity you have to be reading all about England after all they did to us, that there isn't a history of Ireland to be had in this hospital.

The book tells me all about King Alfred and William the Conqueror and all the kings and queens down to Edward, who had to wait forever for his mother, Victoria, to die before he could be king. The book has the first bit of Shakespeare I ever read.

I do believe, induced by potent
circumstances,
That thou art mine enemy.

The history writer says this is what Catherine, who is a wife of Henry the Eighth, says to Cardinal Wolsey, who is trying to have her head cut off. I don't know what it means and I don't care because it's Shakespeare and it's like having jewels in my mouth when I say the words. If I had a whole book of Shakespeare they could keep me in the hospital for a year.

Patricia says she doesn't know what induced means or potent circumstances and she doesn't care about Shakespeare, she has her poetry book and she reads to me from beyond the wall a poem about an owl and a pussycat that went to sea in a green boat with honey and money and it makes no sense and when I say that Patricia gets huffy and says that's the last poem she'll ever read to me. She says I'm always reciting the lines from Shakespeare and they make no sense either. Seamus stops mopping again and tells us we shouldn't be fighting over poetry because we'll have enough to fight about when we grow up and get married. Patricia says she's sorry and I'm sorry too so she reads me part of another poem[5] which I have to remember so I can say it back to her early in the morning or late at night when there are no nuns or nurses about,

The wind was a torrent of darkness among
the gusty trees,
The moon was a ghostly galleon tossed
upon cloudy seas,
The road was a ribbon of moonlight over
the purple moor,
And the highwayman came riding—
Riding—riding—
The highwayman came riding, up to the
old inn door.

He'd a French cocked-hat on his forehead, a
bunch of lace at his chin,
A coat of the claret velvet, and breeches of
brown doeskin,
They fitted with never a wrinkle. His boots
were up to the thigh.
And he rode with a jeweled twinkle,
His pistol butts a-twinkle,
His rapier hilt a-twinkle, under the jeweled
sky.

Every day I can't wait for the doctors and nurses to leave me alone so I can learn a new verse from Patricia and find out what's happening to the highwayman and the landlord's red-lipped daughter. I love the poem because it's exciting and almost as good as my two lines of Shakespeare. The redcoats are after the highwayman because they know he told her, I'll come to thee by moonlight, though hell should bar the way.

5. **part . . . poem:** reference is to the poem "The Highwayman" by British poet Alfred Noyes (1880–1958). The poem is based on a true story about a highwayman who falls in love with an innkeeper's daughter in 18th-century England. Highwaymen, who robbed rich stagecoaches, were at that time popular, romantic figures.

Words to Own

induced (in·do͞ost′) *v.:* persuaded; led on.
potent (pōt′'nt) *adj.:* powerful; convincing.
torrent (tôr′ənt) *n.:* violent, forceful rush.

I'd love to do that myself, come by moonlight for Patricia in the next room not giving a hoot though hell should bar the way. She's ready to read the last few verses when in comes the nurse from Kerry shouting at her, shouting at me, I told ye there was to be no talking between rooms. Dipthteria is never allowed to talk to typhoid and visa versa. I warned ye. And she calls out, Seamus, take this one. Take the by. Sister Rita said one more word out of him and upstairs with him. We gave ye a warning to stop the blathering but ye wouldn't. Take the by, Seamus, take him.

Ah, now, nurse, sure isn't he harmless. 'Tis only a bit o' poetry.

Take that by, Seamus, take him at once.

He bends over me and whispers, Ah, I'm sorry, Frankie. Here's your English history book. He slips the book under my shirt and lifts me from the bed. He whispers that I'm a feather. I try to see Patricia when we pass through her room but all I can make out is a blur of dark head on a pillow.

Sister Rita stops us in the hall to tell me I'm a great disappointment to her, that she expected me to be a good boy after what God had done for me, after all the prayers said by hundreds of boys at the Confraternity, after all the care from the nuns and nurses of the Fever Hospital, after the way they let my mother and father in to see me, a thing rarely allowed, and this is how I repaid them lying in the bed reciting silly poetry back and forth with Patricia Madigan knowing very well there was a ban on all talk between typhoid and diphtheria. She says I'll have plenty of time to reflect on my sins in the big ward upstairs and I should beg God's forgiveness for my disobedience reciting a pagan English poem about a thief on a horse and a maiden with red lips who commits a terrible sin when I could have been praying or reading the life of a saint. She made it her business to read that poem so she did and I'd be well advised to tell the priest in confession.

The Kerry nurse follows us upstairs gasping and holding on to the banister. She tells me I better not get the notion she'll be running up to this part of the world every time I have a little pain or a twinge.

There are twenty beds in the ward, all white, all empty. The nurse tells Seamus put me at the far end of the ward against the wall to make sure I don't talk to anyone who might be passing the door, which is very unlikely since there isn't another soul on this whole floor. She tells Seamus this was the fever ward during the Great Famine[6] long ago and only God knows how many died here brought in too late for anything but a wash before they were buried and there are stories of cries and moans in the far reaches of the night. She says 'twould break your heart to think of what the English did to us, that if they didn't put the blight on the potato they didn't do much to take it off. No pity. No feeling at all for the people that died in this very ward, children suffering and dying here while the English feasted on roast beef and guzzled the best of wine in their big houses, little children with their mouths all green from trying to eat the grass in the fields beyond, God bless us and save us and guard us from future famines.

Seamus says 'twas a terrible thing indeed and he wouldn't want to be walking these halls in the dark with all the little green mouths gaping at him. The nurse takes my temperature, 'Tis up a bit, have a good sleep for yourself now that you're away from the chatter with Patricia Madigan below who will never know a gray hair.

She shakes her head at Seamus and he gives her a sad shake back.

Nurses and nuns never think you know what they're talking about. If you're ten going on eleven you're supposed to be simple like my uncle Pat Sheehan who was dropped on his head. You can't ask questions. You can't show you understand what the nurse said about Patricia Madigan, that she's going to die, and you can't show you want to cry over this girl who taught you a lovely poem which the nun says is bad.

6. **Great Famine:** refers to the great famine in Ireland in 1845–1847, when failed potato crops resulted in the starvation and death of about one million people.

The nurse tells Seamus she has to go and he's to sweep the lint from under my bed and mop up a bit around the ward. Seamus tells me she's a right oul' witch for running to Sister Rita and complaining about the poem going between the two rooms, that you can't catch a disease from a poem unless it's love ha ha and that's not bloody likely when you're what? ten going on eleven? He never heard the likes of it, a little fella shifted upstairs for saying a poem and he has a good mind to go to the *Limerick Leader* and tell them print the whole thing except he has this job and he'd lose it if ever Sister Rita found out. Anyway, Frankie, you'll be outa here one of these fine days and you can read all the poetry you want though I don't know about Patricia below, I don't know about Patricia, God help us.

He knows about Patricia in two days because she got out of the bed to go to the lavatory when she was supposed to use a bedpan and collapsed and died in the lavatory. Seamus is mopping the floor and there are tears on his cheeks and he's saying, 'Tis a dirty rotten thing to die in a lavatory when you're lovely in yourself. She told me she was sorry she had you reciting that poem and getting you shifted from the room, Frankie. She said 'twas all her fault.

It wasn't, Seamus.

I know and didn't I tell her that.

Patricia is gone and I'll never know what happened to the highwayman and Bess, the landlord's daughter. I ask Seamus but he doesn't know any poetry at all especially English poetry. He knew an Irish poem once but it was about fairies and had no sign of a highwayman in it. Still he'll ask the men in his local pub where there's always someone reciting something and he'll bring it back to me. Won't I be busy meanwhile reading my short history of England and finding out all about their perfidy.[7] That's what Seamus says, perfidy, and I don't know what it means and he doesn't know what it means but if it's something the English do it must be terrible.

He comes three times a week to mop the floor and the nurse is there every morning to take my temperature and pulse. The doctor listens to my chest with the thing hanging from his neck. They all say, And how's our little soldier today? A girl with a blue dress brings meals three times a day and never talks to me. Seamus says she's not right in the head so don't say a word to her.

The July days are long and I fear the dark. There are only two ceiling lights in the ward and they're switched off when the tea tray is taken away and the nurse gives me pills. The nurse tells me go to sleep but I can't because I see people in the nineteen beds in the ward all dying and green around their mouths where they tried to eat grass and moaning for soup Protestant soup any soup and I cover my face with the pillow hoping they won't come and stand around the bed clawing at me and howling for bits of the chocolate bar my mother brought last week.

No, she didn't bring it. She had to send it in because I can't have any more visitors. Sister Rita tells me a visit to the Fever Hospital is a privilege and after my bad behavior with Patricia Madigan and that poem I can't have the privilege anymore. She says I'll be going home in a few weeks and my job is to concentrate on getting better and learn to walk again after being in bed for six weeks and I can get out of bed tomorrow after breakfast. I don't know why she says I have to learn how to walk when I've been walking since I was a baby but when the nurse stands me by the side of the bed I fall to the floor and the nurse laughs, See, you're a baby again.

I practice walking from bed to bed back and forth back and forth. I don't want to be a baby. I don't want to be in this empty ward with no Patricia and no highwayman and no red-lipped landlord's daughter. I don't want the ghosts of

7. **perfidy** (pur′fə·dē): treachery; betrayal.

children with green mouths pointing bony fingers at me and clamoring for bits of my chocolate bar.

Seamus says a man in his pub knew all the verses of the highwayman poem and it has a very sad end. Would I like him to say it because he never learned how to read and he had to carry the poem in his head? He stands in the middle of the ward leaning on his mop and recites,

Tlot-tlot, *in the frosty silence!* Tlot-tlot *in the echoing night!*
Nearer he came and nearer! Her face was like a light!
Her eyes grew wide for a moment; she drew one last deep breath,
Then her fingers moved in the moonlight,
Her musket shattered the moonlight,
Shattered her breast in the moonlight and warned him—with her death.

He hears the shot and escapes but when he learns at dawn how Bess died he goes into a rage and returns for revenge only to be shot down by the redcoats.

Blood-red were his spurs in the golden noon; wine-red was his velvet coat,
When they shot him down on the highway,
Down like a dog on the highway,
And he lay in his blood on the highway, with a bunch of lace at his throat.

Seamus wipes his sleeve across his face and sniffles. He says, There was no call at all to shift you up here away from Patricia when you didn't even know what happened to the highwayman and Bess. 'Tis a very sad story and when I said it to my wife she wouldn't stop crying the whole night till we went to bed. She said there was no call for them redcoats to shoot that highwayman, they are responsible for half the troubles of the world and they never had any pity on the Irish, either. Now if you want to know any more poems, Frankie, tell me and I'll get them from the pub and bring 'em back in my head.

WORDS TO OWN
clamoring (klam′ər·iŋ) *v.:* crying out; asking.

MEET THE WRITER
"We Were Street Kids"

Frank McCourt (1930–   ), who regards himself as more a New Yorker than an Irishman, was born in Brooklyn, New York, the first child of Irish immigrants. When Frank was four, the McCourts made a bad decision and moved back to Ireland, where they lived in worse conditions than the ones they had fled in Brooklyn. Eventually, Frank's father abandoned his wife, Angela, and their three surviving children.

Frank McCourt moved back to New York City at age nineteen. Ten years later he began teaching writing to high school students. Encouraged by his students to write about his own experiences (see *Connections* on page 372), McCourt finally published his first book, *Angela's Ashes,* when he was sixty-six. The book dominated best-seller lists and won a 1997 Pulitzer Prize.

When he was asked how he found such humor in his poverty-stricken childhood, McCourt replied: "When you have nothing—no TV, no radio, no music—you have only the language. So you use it. We were street kids—we saw the absurdity and laughed at it. And we were fools; we were always dreaming. Bacon and eggs—we dreamed of that."

Connections — A BIOGRAPHICAL ARTICLE

The Education of Frank McCourt

Barbara Sande Dimmitt

"Yo, Teach!" a voice boomed. Frank McCourt scanned the adolescents in his classroom. It was the fall of 1970 and his first week of teaching at Seward Park High School, which sat in the midst of dilapidated tenement buildings on Manhattan's Lower East Side. McCourt located the speaker and nodded. "You talk funny," the student said. "Where ya from?"

"Ireland," McCourt replied. With more than ten years of teaching experience under his belt, this kind of interrogation no longer surprised him. But one question in particular still made him squirm: "Where'd you go to high school?" someone else asked.

If I tell them the truth, they'll feel superior to me, McCourt thought. *They'll throw it in my face.* Most of all, he feared an accusation he'd heard before—from himself: *You come from nothing, so you are nothing.*

But McCourt's heart whispered another possibility: maybe these kids are yearning for a way of figuring out this new teacher. *Am I willing to risk being humiliated in the classroom to find out?*

"Come on, tell us! Where'd you go to high school?"

"I never did," McCourt replied.

"Did you get thrown out?"

I was right, the teacher thought. *They're curious.* McCourt explained he'd left school after the eighth grade to take a job.

"How'd you get to be a teacher, then?" they asked.

"When I came to America," he began, "I dreamed bigger dreams. I loved reading and writing, and teaching was the most exalted profession I could imagine. I was unloading sides of beef down on the docks when I decided enough was enough. By then I'd done a lot of reading on my own, so I persuaded New York University to enroll me."

McCourt wasn't surprised that this story fascinated his students. Theirs wasn't the kind of poverty McCourt had known; they had electricity and food. But he recognized the telltale signs of need in some of his students' threadbare clothes, and sensed the bitter shame and hopelessness he knew all too well. If recounting his own experiences would jolt these kids out of their defeatism so he could teach them something, that's what he would do.

A born storyteller, McCourt drew from a repertoire of accounts about his youth. His students would listen, spellbound by the gritty details, drawn by something more powerful than curiosity. He'd look from face to face, recognizing a bit of himself in each sober gaze.

Since humor had been the McCourts' weapon against life's miseries in Limerick, he used it to describe those days. "Dinner usually was bread and tea," he told the students. "Mam used to say, 'We've got our balanced diet: a solid and a liquid. What more could we want?'"

The students roared with laughter. . . .

One day McCourt lugged a tape recorder to class. "We're going to work on writing. Each of you will tell a story into this," he announced. McCourt then transcribed the stories. One boy described the time he was climbing down a fire escape past an open window when an awful smell hit him. "There was a body in the bed," McCourt typed. "The corpse was all juicy and swollen."

McCourt handed back the essay the next day. "See? You're a writer!"

"I was just talking," the boy protested. "I didn't write this."

"Yes, you did. These words came out of your head. They helped me understand something that was important to you. That's what writing's about. Now, learn to do it on paper." The boy's shoulders squared with pride.

The incident reminded McCourt of something that had happened at college. A creative-writing professor had asked him to describe an object from his childhood. McCourt chose the decrepit bed he and his brothers had shared. He wrote of their being scratched by the stiff stuffing protruding from the mattress and of ending up jumbled together in the sagging center with fleas leaping all over their bodies. The professor gave McCourt an A, and asked him to read the essay to the class.

"No!" McCourt said, recoiling at the thought. But for the first time, he began to see his sordid childhood, with all the miseries, betrayals, and longings that tormented him still, as a worthy topic. *Maybe that's what I was born to put on the page,* he thought.

While teaching, McCourt wrote occasional articles for newspapers and magazines. But his major effort, a memoir of 150 pages that he churned out in 1966, remained unfinished. Now he leafed through his students' transcribed essays. They lacked polish, but somehow they worked in a way his writing didn't. *I'm trying to teach these kids to write,* he thought, *yet I haven't found the secret myself.*

The bell rang in the faculty lounge at Stuyvesant High School in Manhattan. When McCourt began teaching at the prestigious public high school in 1972, he joked that he'd finally made it to paradise. . . .

The bits and pieces that bubbled into his consciousness enlivened the stories he told in class. "Everyone has a story to tell," he said. "Write about what you know with conviction, from the heart. Dig deep," he urged. "Find your own voice and dance your own dance!"

On Fridays the students read their compositions aloud. To draw them out, McCourt would read excerpts from his duffel bag full of notebooks. "You had such an interesting childhood, Mr. McCourt," they said. "Why don't you write a book?" They threw his own words back at him: "It sounds like there's more to that story; dig deeper. . . ."

McCourt was past fifty and painfully aware of the passage of time. But despite his growing frustration at his unfinished book, he never tired of his students' work.

Over the years some talented writers passed through McCourt's popular classes. Laurie Gwen Shapiro, whose first novel will be published in the spring, was one of them. He decided she was coasting along on her technical skills. "You're capable of much more," McCourt told her. "Try writing something that's meaningful to you for a change."

Near the end of the semester, McCourt laid an essay—graded 100—on Laurie's desk. "If Laurie is willing to read her essay," he announced to the class, "I think we'll all benefit."

Laurie began to read a portrait of love clouded by anger and shame. She told of her father, partially paralyzed, and of resenting his inability to play with her or help her ride a bicycle. The paper shook in her trembling hands, and McCourt understood all too well what it cost her to continue. She also admitted she was embarrassed by her father's limp. The words, McCourt knew, were torn straight from her soul.

When Laurie finished, with tears streaming down her face, the students broke into applause. McCourt looked around the room, his own vision blurred.

These young people have been giving you lessons in courage, he thought. *When will you dare as mightily as they?*

It was October 1994. Frank McCourt, now retired, sat down and read his book's new opening, which he had written a few days before and still found satisfying. But many blank pages lay before him. *What if I never get it right?* he wondered grimly.

He stared at the logs glowing in the fireplace and could almost hear students' voices from years past, some angry, some defeated, others confused and seeking guidance. "It's no good, Mr. McCourt. I don't have what it takes."

Then Frank McCourt, author, heard the steadying tones of Frank McCourt, teacher: *Of course you do. Dig deeper. Find your own voice and dance your own dance.*

He scribbled a few lines. "I'm in a playground on Classon Avenue in Brooklyn with my brother Malachy. He's two, I'm three. We're on the seesaw." In the innocent voice of an unprotected child who could neither comprehend nor control the world around him, Frank McCourt told his tale of poverty and abandonment.

—from *Reader's Digest,* November 1997

MAKING MEANINGS

First Thoughts

1. In your opinion, what was the saddest or most shocking episode in Frankie's story?

Shaping Interpretations

2. The Kerry nurse asks sharply, "What is there to laugh about?" Find two examples of **comic relief** in McCourt's memoir. How do you feel about the use of comedy in such a sad story?
3. What do you think young Frankie discovered about himself in the hospital? Be sure to consider the role that language, and especially poetry, plays in this story.

Challenging the Text

4. McCourt's mother called one of his stories "a pack of lies," but one reviewer says *Angela's Ashes* is "a truth-teller's work." Using examples from "Typhoid Fever," discuss the writer's **credibility**. Do you think parts of the story sound as if they were made-up?

Reading Check

Briefly **summarize** the **main events** in McCourt's story by answering the questions in the **cause-and-effect** chart below:

Why are the children in the hospital?
↓
Why is Frankie moved to another floor?
↓
What happens to each child?

CHOICES: Building Your Portfolio

Writer's Notebook

1. Collecting Ideas for an Autobiographical Incident

WORK IN PROGRESS

Putting us there. Frank McCourt puts us right inside a young boy's head, right in his Fever Hospital bed, right in the midst of a pack of colorful characters. Whatever past event you use for the Writer's Workshop on page 380, make it "come alive." Choose an incident—perhaps from your Quickwrite notes or your Writer's Notebook. Jot down notes answering these questions: Who was there? What did people say? How did you feel? Did anything comical happen? Help the reader enter your scene.

Creative Response

2. My Reading Experience

"The Highwayman" played an important role in Frankie's young life. What novel, poem, or story do you remember from your childhood? Why did it mean so much to you? Write a brief personal essay about your reading memory.

Oral Interpretation

3. Live from Limerick!

"Typhoid Fever" is full of voices: Frankie, Patricia, Sister Rita, the Kerry nurse, Seamus, even Seamus's wife. It has singing and poetry recitations. With a group, plan, practice, and present an oral interpretation of part of "Typhoid Fever." Try to include some of the parts with "The Highwayman." (For help, see the Speaking and Listening Workshop on pages 750–751.)

LANGUAGE LINK MINI-LESSON

Language Handbook HELP

See Run-on Sentences, page 1042.

Technology HELP

See Language Workshop CD-ROM. *Key word entry: run-on sentences.*

Voice—A Bit o' Poetry

Frank McCourt repeatedly told his students, "Find your own voice" (see ***Connections*** on page 372). When McCourt found *his* voice, his memoirs took off. The voice he found was that of an innocent child, talking in a stream-of-consciousness style with a child's personal quirks and dialect. McCourt decided not to use standard punctuation and quotation marks because he wanted us to sense that we are overhearing someone's thoughts. To appreciate the effect, read these passages aloud.

1. "Patricia says she doesn't know what induced means or potent circumstances and she doesn't care about Shakespeare, she has her poetry book and she reads to me from beyond the wall a poem about an owl and a pussycat that went to sea in a green boat with honey and money and it makes no sense and when I say that Patricia gets huffy and says that's the last poem she'll ever read to me."
2. "We gave ye a warning to stop the blathering but ye wouldn't. Take the by, Seamus, take him.

   Ah, now, nurse, sure isn't he harmless. 'Tis only a bit o' poetry."

Try It Out

➤ **Cleaning Up the Style.** Suppose you are a very diligent editor in the publishing house that has accepted McCourt's manuscript. Your job is to "clean up" his style, to make it conform to accepted formal usage. Correct the passages opposite. Correct spellings and punctuate sentences for clarity and correctness. Compare your edited manuscripts in class. What has happened to Frankie's voice?

VOCABULARY HOW TO OWN A WORD

WORD BANK
induced
potent
torrent
clamoring

Antonyms: Just the Opposite

An **antonym** is a word that has the opposite, or nearly opposite, meaning of another word. Choose the best antonym for each word in capital letters. This exercise format will give you practice for taking standardized tests. Remember, you're looking for the best antonym—not **synonym** (word with the same meaning).

1. INDUCED: (a) persuaded (b) attempted (c) increased (d) discouraged
2. POTENT: (a) impossible (b) weak (c) strong (d) safe
3. TORRENT: (a) trickle (b) flood (c) law (d) tornado
4. CLAMORING: (a) creating (b) whispering (c) opening (d) studying

A POEM

Background

The speaker in this poem is an African American student at Columbia University in New York City—the college on the hill above Harlem. Hughes was a student there for a year. As you read, think about how well—or badly—the poem fulfills the instructor's assignment.

Quickwrite

If you were given the same assignment ("Go home and write a page tonight. And let that page come out of you. . . ."), what would you say? Quickwrite whatever comes to your mind in response. You don't have to write a whole paper or a poem!

go.hrw.com
LEO 10-5

Theme for English B

Langston Hughes

The instructor said,

Go home and write
a page tonight.
And let that page come out of you—
then, it will be true.

I wonder if it's that simple?
I am twenty-two, colored, born in Winston-Salem.
I went to school there, then Durham, then here
to this college on the hill above Harlem.
I am the only colored student in my class.
The steps from the hill lead down into Harlem,
through a park, then I cross St. Nicholas,
Eighth Avenue, Seventh, and I come to the Y,
the Harlem Branch Y, where I take the elevator
up to my room, sit down, and write this page:

It's not easy to know what is true for you or me
at twenty-two, my age. But I guess I'm what
I feel and see and hear. Harlem, I hear you:
hear you, hear me—we two—you, me, talk on this page.
(I hear New York, too.) Me—who?

Well, I like to eat, sleep, drink, and be in love.
I like to work, read, learn, and understand life.
I like a pipe for a Christmas present,
or records—Bessie,° bop, or Bach.

I guess being colored doesn't make me *not* like
the same things other folks like who are other races.
So will my page be colored that I write?
Being me, it will not be white.
But it will be

24. Bessie: Bessie Smith (1898–1937), a jazz and blues singer.

Rooftops (No. 1, This Is Harlem) (1942–1943) by Jacob Lawrence. Gouache on paper ($14\frac{3}{8}'' \times 21\frac{7}{8}''$).

Hirshhorn Museum and Sculpture Garden/Smithsonian Institution. Gift of Joseph H. Hirshhorn, 1966. Photographer Lee Stalsworth. (66.2921).
Courtesy of the artist and the Francine Seders Gallery, Seattle, Washington.

a part of you, instructor.
You are white—
yet a part of me, as I am a part of you.
That's American.
Sometimes perhaps you don't want to be a part of me.
Nor do I often want to be a part of you.
But we are, that's true!
As I learn from you,
I guess you learn from me—
although you're older—and white—
and somewhat more free.

This is my page for English B.

Meet the Writer

Discovery

Langston Hughes (1902–1967) was a struggling young writer, working as a busboy in an expensive Washington, D.C., hotel restaurant. One day Hughes heard that Vachel Lindsay, a famous American poet, was going to dine in the hotel that night and then give a reading of his poems. In his autobiography, Hughes describes what happened:

“I wanted very much to hear him read his poems, but I knew they did not admit colored people to the auditorium. That afternoon, I wrote out three of my poems, ‘Jazzonia,’ ‘Negro Dancers,’ and ‘The Weary Blues,’ on some pieces of paper and put them in the pocket of my white busboy’s coat. In the evening when Mr. Lindsay came down to dinner, quickly I laid them beside his plate and went away, afraid to say anything to so famous a poet. . . . I looked back once and saw Mr. Lindsay reading the poems as I picked up a tray of dirty dishes from a side table and started for the dumbwaiter. The next morning on my way to work, as usual I bought a paper—and there I read that Vachel Lindsay had discovered a Negro busboy poet! At the hotel the reporters were already waiting for me.”

Langston Hughes (c. 1925) by Winold Reiss (1886–1953). Pastel on artist board ($30\frac{1}{16}'' \times 21\frac{5}{8}''$).

National Portrait Gallery, Smithsonian Institution / Art Resource, NY.

For more about Hughes’s life and poetry, see page 510.

Finding Common Ground

Meet with a small group of classmates and decide on your agenda: Which questions and responses to the poem do you want to discuss? What issues has the poem raised in your group? Be sure to cover two topics: (1) How does your own Quickwrite compare with the poem? and (2) What is the **tone** of the poem?

When all groups have finished talking about the poem, each group should assign a spokesperson to summarize for the whole class what that group discovered about the poem. Do you find any consensus?

A Hero?

"Whether I shall turn out to be the hero of my own life, or whether that station will be held by anybody else, these pages must show." Thus opens *David Copperfield* by Charles Dickens (available in several paperback editions). Of all his wonderful novels, this story of Davy's coming of age, beginning with the cruelty he endured as a child, is the one that Dickens loved the best.

Growing Up Despite It All

Gary Soto's *A Summer Life* (University Press of New England) tells what it was like growing up Chicano in Fresno, California. In a series of funny and touching essays, Soto focuses on topics like "The Shirt," "The Haircut," "The Drive-In Movies," and "The Computer Date."

In *The Pigman & Me* (Bantam), writer Paul Zindel describes the funny-sad teenage year he spent in Staten Island, New York. In Zindel's autobiography, you'll meet Nonno Frankie, the real-life neighbor and friend who inspired Zindel's prize-winning first novel *The Pigman.* You'll also discover the secret of life, according to the pigman.

Beautiful, Haunting Africa

The extraordinary adventures of a childhood in Kenya are recounted in Elspeth Huxley's *The Flame Trees of Thika* (Penguin). A version of the story, with its haunting images of Africa, was serialized on television.

Writer's Workshop

Technology
HELP

See Writer's Workshop 2 CD-ROM. *Assignment: Autobiographical Incident.*

ASSIGNMENT

Write about an autobiographical incident you remember vividly.

AIM

To express yourself; to reflect on the significance of an experience.

AUDIENCE

Your teacher and classmates; a relative or friend.

NARRATIVE WRITING

AUTOBIOGRAPHICAL INCIDENT

I'M WRITING A BOOK ABOUT MY LIFE.
IT'S CALLED, "CALVIN: THE SHOCKING TRUE STORY OF THE BOY WHOSE EXPLOITS PANICKED A NATION."
INTERESTING TITLE.
THANKS.
SPECIFICALLY WHAT EXPLOITS ARE YOU REFERRING TO?
THAT'S THE PROBLEM. CAN YOU HELP ME THINK OF SOME I COULD DO?

CALVIN AND HOBBES © 1989 Watterson. Reprinted with permission of UNIVERSAL PRESS SYNDICATE.

If Calvin wrote an account of one of his exploits, he'd be writing a special kind of narrative—an **autobiographical incident,** a true story about a particular incident in the writer's life. In this workshop, you'll face the same challenges and solve the same problems that Malcolm X, Jeanne Wakatsuki Houston, and Frank McCourt did: how to express your feelings about something that happened to you and how to make that story interest your readers.

Prewriting

1. Tell a Single Story

WORK IN PROGRESS

In your Writer's Notebook, you've made some notes about one or more autobiographical incidents that are important to you. Continue with one of those incidents or brainstorm to find a new incident.

Try to choose something that happened in a few hours or in a single day. A time-limited incident (as in Malcolm X's "Hair," which happened in one afternoon) has more intensity than one that extends over a long period.

If you're stuck on finding a topic, preview some possibilities with your writing group—using a sentence or two for each incident—and ask which one they'd most like to read about. You might try thinking about these possibilities: a triumph, a failure, a challenge, friends, bullies, a family story, love, loss, standing up for a cause.

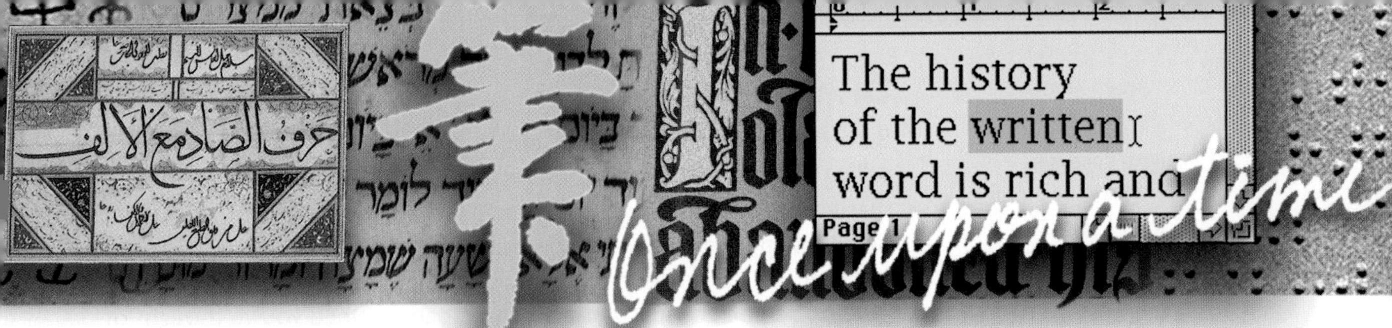
The history
of the written
word is rich and
Page 1
Once upon a time

2. Elaborate: Dig for Details

Imagine yourself reliving the incident, and take notes on these essentials. A cluster diagram will help you gather ideas.

- **Context (setting):** Where and when did the incident happen? How old were you? Who was there besides you?
- **Events:** List your main events in chronological order (the order in which they happened). Do you need to add a flashback to explain something that happened in the past?
- **Sensory details:** Help your readers see the characters and places in your story. Record details of sights, smells, sounds, tastes, touch, and movement.
- **Dialogue/Monologue:** What did people say? What did you say to yourself?

Start Here: The Raw Material of Autobiography

Your own memories: What do you recall immediately (the bare bones)? What details do you recall as you dig deeper?

Other people's memories: What do others who were present tell you about the same incident? (What do you suppose Shorty would have written about Malcolm X's first conk?)

Photographs, home movies, videotapes: These "frozen moments" may jog your memory.

Journals, letters, souvenirs: Explore these sources for additional details.

A visit to the place where your story happened—even in memory (see Bradbury's experience on page 353).

3. Tell What the Incident Means to You

What did you learn from the incident? What do you think and feel about it now, and what did you think and feel when it happened? (Look back at page 347 for Malcolm X's powerful reflection on the significance of his first conk.) Plan to conclude your autobiographical incident as Malcolm X does, with a paragraph or two on the significance of your incident. Try a quickwrite (like the sample on the right) or a cluster diagram to discover how you feel about the incident and what you learned from it.

Try It Out

Elaborate by adding descriptive details of sight, sound, smell, taste, or touch (texture, temperature) to each statement. Add as many sentences to each statement as you wish.

1. We lived in a small town.
2. I saw my dog run into the street.
3. They were talking in the next room.

I learned how much I enjoy working with young children. Admire their tremendous energy & eagerness to learn. They're curious about everything. What happens to them later? Tutoring was fun. Felt important. Made me think I might want to be a teacher—la profesora—especially of young kids.

Language/Grammar Link HELP

Tone: page 352. Specific and proper nouns: page 364. Voice: page 375.

Drafting

Before you start writing, think about the **tone** you'll use. Are you telling a humorous incident? an ironic one? Choose words and details that let the reader know—or guess—how you felt about the incident when it happened and how you feel about it now.

Draft your autobiographical incident in a single sitting. It doesn't have to be perfect; just get it down on paper. Once you've thought of an attention-grabbing beginning (dialogue, a startling statement, a description of the setting), dive right into the action. Elaborate with sensory details, comparisons, and dialogue—everything that makes a narrative interesting to read.

A well-known writer got collared by a university student, who asked, "Do you think I could be a writer?"

"Well," the writer said, "I don't know. . . . Do you like sentences?"

The writer could see the student's amazement. Sentences? Do I like sentences? I am twenty years old and do I like sentences? If he had liked sentences, of course, he could begin, like a joyful painter I knew. I asked him how he came to be a painter. He said, "I liked the smell of paint."

—Annie Dillard

Student Model

La Profesora

I was to spend an hour each Tuesday afternoon with five second-graders and have the chance to be the kind of teacher I always wanted to have. I was relatively calm that first day when I met those five smiling, little angels; I figured, how hard could it be? They quietly and obediently followed me down the long hall to our new classroom, and I thought to myself, "No problem!" But the instant I opened the door, I knew I was wrong. They nearly knocked me over in a mad rush to get to one of the two teacher's chairs in the room. They did not emerge from their shells gradually but broke out of them the way the Incredible Hulk bursts out of his clothes. Well, only fifty-eight minutes and twenty-two seconds left.

That second week I knew I would have to face the ultimate test. I had no choice; I had to address and effectively deal with the age-old elementary school problem: running in the halls. If I did not, I could not be a successful teacher. They knew where the room was, and they knew that whoever got there first would get the big chair in which all little

This is Spanish for "The Teacher." The title creates interest, makes us wonder why the Spanish.

Sets up the context of the incident.

The writer reveals her thoughts.

A hint at what the problem/conflict will be.

Good comparison—the writer uses humor well.

Time-limited incident begins here. She is very specific here about the conflict.

Student Model (continued)

children dream of sitting. We met in the cafeteria, and when all five were there, I took a deep breath and began to speak those fateful words. "I think it's time . . . "—the sprinters lined up and prepared for the race of their lives—" . . . to go."

Uses dialogue.

Then they were off! I knew at once that the usual "Don't run!" was futile, and so I resorted to Plan B: "¡Caminen Uds.! ¡Más despacio!"

Spanish: "Walk! More slowly!"

Their miniature Nikes came to a screeching halt. They turned around, panting, and Matthew, the spokesperson, asked, "What does that mean?" I breathed a sigh of relief.

Sensory details: sound.

"I'll only tell you if you wait for me." They waited. Luckily for me their curiosity had gotten the best of them. Those five little children had so much energy and such an eagerness to learn; all I had to do was channel it in the right direction. Although it can be quite a challenge sometimes and I am always exhausted when I leave, I cherish every moment I spend with them. At four o'clock every week when little Calvin wraps himself around my legs and asks hopefully, "Can we come back tomorrow?" I see the excitement dancing in their eyes and I wonder where the time has gone.

Tells how the problem was resolved.

Significance—her thoughts and feelings about the incident.

I wish we could, Calvin.

A powerful ending.

—Melissa Wafer
Half Hollow Hills High School
Dix Hills, New York

"There's someone here to see you, Howard. He said to mention a pet goldfish you flushed down the toilet when you were six years old."

Reprinted from *The Saturday Evening Post.*

Sentence Workshop HELP

Using subordination: page 385.

Some Autobiographical Incidents

Each of these essays focuses on an autobiograpical incident. Do the titles give you any ideas for your own essay topic?

- "The Night the Bed Fell" by James Thurber
- "Looking for Work" by Gary Soto
- "Only Daughter" by Sandra Cisneros
- "In the Kitchen" by Henry Louis Gates

■ ***Evaluation Criteria***

A good autobiographical incident

1. *narrates a time-limited incident*
2. *has an attention-grabbing beginning, sensory details, and dialogue*
3. *has an easy-to-follow sequence of events (usually in chronological order)*
4. *explains the incident's significance to the writer*

Evaluating and Revising

1. Self-evaluation

To give your autobiographical incident the appeal of a good story, try the following:

- **Add** more specific details and dialogue.
- **Subtract** (cut) details that wander off the subject.
- **Replace** vague or overused words with more precise or more original ones.

2. Peer Review

Once you've done some early-round revision on your own, share your draft with your writing group. Ask them if the sequence of events is clear.

Revision Model

	Peer Comments
Then they were off! ~~They ran down the hall again,~~ I knew at once that the usual "Don't run!" was futile, and so I resorted to Plan B: "¡Caminen Uds.! ¡Más despacio!" ~~another solution and yelled at them in Spanish.~~	*Can you make this a little livelier? Fix run-on sentence.* *What exactly did you say to them?*
Their miniature Nikes came to a screeching halt. ~~They stopped running.~~ They turned around, panting, and Matthew, the spokesperson, ~~one of the boys I was tutoring,~~ asked, "What does that mean?" ~~me what I meant.~~ I breathed a sigh of relief.	*Add some sensory details?* *Choppy—combine some sentences here.* *Use dialogue.*

Proofreading Tip

As you proofread, slow your reading down by pointing to every word and punctuation mark.

Communications Handbook HELP

See Proofreaders' Marks.

Publishing Tip

Illustrate your essay, put it in a binder or folder, and give it to a friend or relative who experienced the incident with you.

BUILDING YOUR PORTFOLIO

Sentence Workshop

Language Handbook HELP

See Subordinate Clause, page 1037.

Technology HELP

See Language Workshop CD-ROM. *Key word entry: combining sentences.*

COMBINING SENTENCES: USING SUBORDINATION

When you combine sentences using **subordinating conjunctions** (see the list below), the ideas aren't equal. A **subordinate clause** adds to the meaning of the main clause. In the sentences that follow, the subordinate clauses (underscored) tell *when* or *why* the action in the main clause takes place:

CHOPPY Shorty started combing the congolene in. It just felt warm.

COMBINED "The congolene just felt warm <u>when Shorty started combing it in.</u>"

—Malcolm X, "Hair" (page 347)

CHOPPY He was farming near Inglewood. I was born at that time.

COMBINED "<u>When I was born</u>, he was farming near Inglewood."

— Jeanne Wakatsuki Houston and James Houston, "It Can't Be Helped" (page 356)

CHOPPY They think I have a disease from foreign parts. My father used to be in Africa.

COMBINED "They think I have a disease from foreign parts <u>because my father used to be in Africa.</u>"

— Frank McCourt, "Typhoid Fever" (page 366)

Try It Out

Combine the following sentences by turning one of the sentences into a subordinate clause. You might experiment with different subordinating conjunctions to see how the emphasis of your sentence can change. You might also experiment with placing your subordinate clause in different positions in the sentence.

1. I was cursing Shorty with every name I could think of. He got the spray going and started soap-lathering my head.
2. Shorty let me stand up and see in the mirror. My hair hung down in limp, damp strings.
3. I love the poem. It's exciting and almost as good as my two lines of Shakespeare.
4. It was very early, and misty. We got there with our luggage.

A Box of Subordinating Conjunctions

after	because	so that	whenever
although	before	unless	where
as	if	until	wherever
as if	since	when	while

Writer's Workshop Follow-up: Revising

Read aloud your autobiographical incident or, better, have someone read it aloud to you. Listen for choppy sentences. See if your writing sounds smoother when the choppy sentences are combined using a subordinate clause. You should also notice that your meaning is more specific.

Reading for Life

Reading a Textbook

Situation

After reading a firsthand account of Japanese internment camps in "It Can't Be Helped," you want to see how the subject is treated in an American history textbook. Try these strategies to help you read a textbook.

Strategies

Identify the text organizers and other helpful features.

- Review the **table of contents** to see what is covered in the book and how the text is organized.
- Note **special features,** such as primary sources. You should find these listed in the table of contents.
- Does the book supply chapter **overviews** and **reviews**?
- Look for important terms in **boldfaced** type.
- Note **charts** and other **graphic organizers,** such as time lines, maps, and graphs.
- Review photographs and illustrations and their captions.
- At the back of the book, look for an **index**. If you are researching a particular subject, check the index to see how well the topic is covered.

Chapter Outline

1 American Isolationism and the European War
2 Rallying Round the Flag
3 Internment of Japanese Americans: Patriotism's Dark Side

TIME LINE

September 1939	June 1940	December 1941	February 1942
War begins in Europe	France falls; Aerial Battle of Britain begins	Japanese attack Pearl Harbor naval base	Roosevelt orders internment of Japanese Americans

Chapter Overview

In the late 1930s, the **isolationist movement** drew support from many Americans, who believed that the war looming in Europe was none of their country's concern. However, with the fall of France and the Battle of Britain, more and more Americans began to feel that U.S. entry into the war was only a matter of time. The Japanese attack on Pearl Harbor propelled the country into a war many had come to see as inevitable.

The sacrifices demanded by the war effort were made in a spirit of patriotism. However, one group of Americans was required to sacrifice more than any others: Japanese Americans living on the West Coast were ordered to report to **relocation camps** for fear they would cooperate with the Japanese government.

Study the material.

- Scan chapter headings and subheadings. Then, **skim** the content to get an overview.
- Make a list of questions you want answered.
- Next, **read slowly** to note important information and to find the answers to your questions.

Using the Strategies

1. How many subsections are in the chapter shown here, and what are they?
2. When did President Roosevelt order the internment of Japanese Americans and why? Where did you find these pieces of information?
3. List two questions about the internment of Japanese Americans you expect the textbook to answer.

Extending the Strategies

If you wanted to compare the treatment of Japanese American internment in different textbooks, how would you go about it?

Collection 6

BEING THERE!

WRITING FOCUS: Research Paper

Right now you have access to more information about the past and present than people have ever had. In print, on television, by computer, you can witness history being made and find out almost anything you want to know about the past.

The writers represented in this collection make you an eyewitness to events aboard the *Titanic* one icy night in 1912 and to the horrors of Auschwitz in 1944. A reporter's story of his involvement in a tragic climbing expedition on Mt. Everest gives literal meaning to the term *cliffhanger,* and a report about beached whales puts you on a stench-filled, windswept beach in Oregon.

The reports in this collection are examples of nonfiction at its best—they capture our imagination and, like other kinds of literature, help us share experiences we would otherwise never have.

> *My ambition was to embrace those general qualities that Ernest Hemingway, a former newspaperman, once said should be present in all good books: "the good and the bad, the ecstasy, the remorse and sorrow, the people and the places and how the weather was."*
>
> *—Pete Hamill*

Writer's Notebook

WORK IN PROGRESS

Think of some famous people you'd like to interview or an event you wish you could have witnessed. In your Writer's Notebook, list five or six people or events that you'd like to know more about. Then, rank your choices. Keep your list. Reviewing it may help you choose a topic for the research paper you'll write for the Writer's Workshop on page 448.

Before You Read

R.M.S. TITANIC

Make the Connection

Facing Disaster

This account of the sinking of the *Titanic* will remind you of other disaster stories. Reporters present such catastrophes in several ways. The worst writers aim for sensational effects to such an extent that their accounts wind up becoming not only sentimental but also inaccurate. Other writers strive for a more objective rendition of the facts. Still others fictionalize the event, presenting made-up details. What stance does Baldwin strike immediately in his first paragraph?

Quickwrite

Choose any kind of disaster—a sinking ship, a raging tornado, a flood, an avalanche. Put yourself there. Write briefly about how you'd feel and what you'd do. Save your notes.

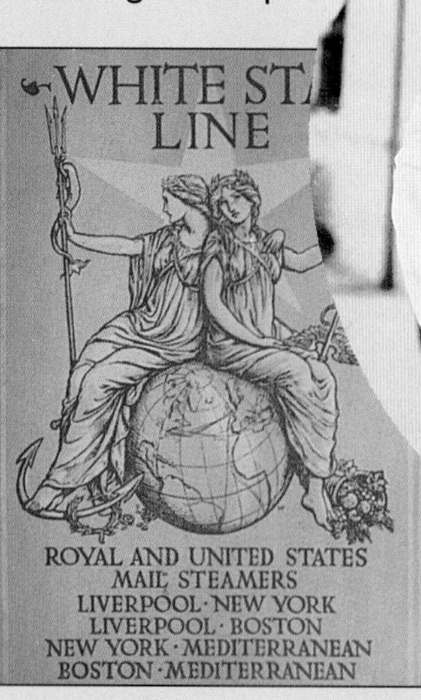

WHITE STA
LINE
ROYAL AND UNITED STATES
MAIL STEAMERS
LIVERPOOL · NEW YORK
LIVERPOOL · BOSTON
NEW YORK · MEDITERRANEAN
BOSTON · MEDITERRANEAN

The *Titanic*'s captain, E. C. Smith.

Elements of Literature

Expect the Unexpected

Irony shows us what we all know—that we can't control everything that happens in our lives, much as we may want to or try.

The passengers on the *Titanic,* including the great ship's builders and its financial backers, believed that they were on an unsinkable ship. In that confidence or arrogance lies one of the great ironies of twentieth-century technology.

In **dramatic irony**, the reader knows something important that the characters don't know. In **situational irony**, what happens is the opposite of what is expected to happen or should have happened.

For more on Irony, see pages 194–195 and the Handbook of Literary Terms.

The Titans were ancient Greek gods depicted as possessing enormous size and incredible strength. For eons they reigned supreme in the universe, according to Greek mythology. Perhaps those who named the ship *Titanic* did not know that even the legendary Titans did not rule forever.

Out of the darkness she came, a vast, dim, white, monstrous shape . . .

Reading Skills and Strategies

Using Text Organizers

If you have seen the film *Titanic,* you know that this great tragedy involved a complex series of actions occurring within a few hours. In writing this account of the disaster, Hanson Baldwin used the **headings** I–V as **text organizers** to divide that complicated rush of events. Each numbered part covers a different stage in the tragedy. Other, less obvious organizers are notations of the minutes ticking by in part II. These reminders build up suspense and help you keep stark track of the unfolding disaster.

The *Titanic,* underwater 375 miles southeast of Newfoundland, in summer 1991.

R.M.S. Titanic

Hanson W. Baldwin

I

The White Star liner *Titanic,* largest ship the world had ever known, sailed from Southampton on her maiden voyage to New York on April 10, 1912. The paint on her strakes[1] was fair and bright; she was fresh from Harland and Wolff's Belfast yards, strong in the strength of her forty-six thousand tons of steel, bent, hammered, shaped, and riveted through the three years of her slow birth.

1. **strakes:** single lines of metal plating extending the whole length of a ship.

There was little fuss and fanfare at her sailing; her sister ship, the *Olympic*—slightly smaller than the *Titanic*—had been in service for some months and to her had gone the thunder of the cheers.

But the *Titanic* needed no whistling steamers or shouting crowds to call attention to her superlative qualities. Her bulk dwarfed the ships near her as longshoremen singled up her mooring lines and cast off the turns of heavy rope from the dock bollards.[2] She was not only the largest ship afloat, but was believed to be the safest. Carlisle, her builder, had given her double bottoms and had divided her hull into sixteen watertight compartments, which made her, men thought, unsinkable. She had been built to be and had been described as a gigantic lifeboat. Her designers' dreams of a triple-screw[3] giant, a luxurious, floating hotel, which could speed to New York at twenty-three knots, had been carefully translated from blueprints and mold loft lines at the Belfast yards into a living reality.

The *Titanic*'s sailing from Southampton, though quiet, was not wholly uneventful. As the liner moved slowly toward the end of her dock that April day, the surge of her passing sucked away from the quay[4] the steamer *New York,* moored just to seaward of the *Titanic*'s berth. There were sharp cracks as the manila mooring lines of the *New York* parted under the strain. The frayed ropes writhed and whistled through the air and snapped down among the waving crowd on the pier; the *New York* swung toward the *Titanic*'s bow, was checked and dragged back to the dock barely in time to avert a collision. Seamen muttered, thought it an ominous start.

Past Spithead and the Isle of Wight the *Titanic* steamed. She called at Cherbourg at dusk and then laid her course for Queenstown. At 1:30 P.M. on Thursday, April 11, she stood out of Queenstown harbor, screaming gulls soaring in her wake, with 2,201 persons—men, women, and children—aboard.

Occupying the Empire bedrooms and Georgian suites of the first-class accommodations were many well-known men and women—Colonel John Jacob Astor and his young bride; Major Archibald Butt, military aide to President Taft, and his friend Frank D. Millet, the painter; John B. Thayer, vice president of the Pennsylvania Railroad, and Charles M. Hays, president of the Grand Trunk Railway of Canada; W. T. Stead, the English journalist; Jacques Futrelle, French novelist; H. B. Harris, theatrical manager, and Mrs. Harris; Mr. and Mrs. Isidor Straus; and J. Bruce Ismay, chairman and managing director of the White Star Line.

Down in the plain wooden cabins of the steerage class were 706 immigrants to the land of promise, and trimly stowed in the great holds was a cargo valued at $420,000: oak beams, sponges, wine, calabashes,[5] and an odd miscellany of the common and the rare.

The *Titanic* took her departure on Fastnet Light[6] and, heading into the night, laid her course for New York. She was due at quarantine[7] the following Wednesday morning.

Sunday dawned fair and clear. The *Titanic* steamed smoothly toward the west, faint streamers of brownish smoke trailing from her funnels. The purser held services in the saloon in the morning; on the steerage deck aft[8] the immigrants were playing games and a Scotsman was puffing "The Campbells Are Coming" on his bagpipes in the midst of the uproar.

2. **bollards** (bäl′ərdz): strong posts on a pier or wharf for holding a ship's mooring ropes.
3. **triple-screw:** three-propellered.
4. **quay** (kē): dock.

5. **calabashes** (kal′ə·bash′əz): large smoking pipes made from the necks of gourds.
6. **Fastnet Light:** lighthouse at the southwestern tip of Ireland. After the Fastnet Light, there is only open sea until the coast of North America.
7. **quarantine** (kwôr′ən·tēn): place where a ship is held in port after arrival to determine that its passengers and cargo are free of communicable diseases. *Quarantine* can also be used for the length of time a ship is held.
8. **aft:** in the rear of a ship.

Words to Own

superlative (sə·pur′lə·tiv) *adj.:* supreme; better than all others.

Message from the *Caronia*, warning of icebergs and tracts of floating ice.

Second Operator Harold Bride.

At 9:00 A.M. a message from the steamer *Caronia* sputtered into the wireless shack:

> Captain, *Titanic*—Westbound steamers report bergs growlers and field ice 42 degrees N. from 49 degrees to 51 degrees W. 12th April.
>
> Compliments—Barr.

It was cold in the afternoon; the sun was brilliant, but the *Titanic,* her screws turning over at seventy-five revolutions per minute, was approaching the Banks.[9]

In the Marconi cabin[10] Second Operator Harold Bride, earphones clamped on his head, was figuring accounts; he did not stop to answer when he heard *MWL,* Continental Morse for the nearby Leyland liner, *Californian,* calling the *Titanic.* The *Californian* had some message about three icebergs; he didn't bother then to take it down. About 1:42 P.M. the rasping spark of those days spoke again across the water. It was the *Baltic,* calling the *Titanic,* warning her of ice on the steamer track. Bride took the message down and sent it up to the bridge.[11] The officer-of-the-deck glanced at it; sent it to the bearded master of the *Titanic,* Captain E. C. Smith, a veteran of the White Star service. It was lunchtime then; the captain, walking along the promenade deck, saw Mr. Ismay, stopped, and handed him the message without comment. Ismay read it, stuffed it in his pocket, told two ladies about the icebergs, and resumed his walk. Later, about 7:15 P.M., the captain requested the return of the message in order to post it in the chart room for the information of officers.

Dinner that night in the Jacobean dining room was gay. It was bitter on deck, but the night was calm and fine; the sky was moonless but studded with stars twinkling coldly in the clear air.

After dinner some of the second-class passengers gathered in the saloon, where the Reverend Mr. Carter conducted a "hymn singsong." It was almost ten o'clock and the stewards were waiting with biscuits and coffee as the group sang:

> O, hear us when we cry to Thee
> For those in peril on the sea.

On the bridge Second Officer Lightoller—short, stocky, efficient—was relieved at ten o'clock by First Officer Murdoch. Lightoller had talked with other officers about the proximity of ice; at least five wireless ice warnings had reached the ship; lookouts had been cautioned to be alert; captains and officers expected to reach the field at any time after 9:30 P.M. At twenty-two knots, its speed unslackened, the *Titanic* plowed on through the night.

Lightoller left the darkened bridge to his relief and turned in. Captain Smith went to his cabin. The steerage was long since quiet; in the first and second cabins lights were going out; voices were growing still; people were asleep. Murdoch paced back and forth on the bridge,

9. Banks: Grand Banks, shallow waters near the southeast coast of Newfoundland.

10. Marconi cabin: room where messages were received and sent by radio.

11. bridge: raised structure on a ship. The ship is controlled from the bridge.

peering out over the dark water, glancing now and then at the compass in front of Quartermaster Hichens at the wheel.

In the crow's-nest, lookout Frederick Fleet and his partner, Leigh, gazed down at the water, still and unruffled in the dim, starlit darkness. Behind and below them the ship, a white shadow with here and there a last winking light; ahead of them a dark and silent and cold ocean.

There was a sudden clang. "Dong-dong. Dong-dong. Dong-dong. Dong!" The metal clapper of the great ship's bell struck out 11:30. Mindful of the warnings, Fleet strained his eyes, searching the darkness for the dreaded ice. But there were only the stars and the sea.

In the wireless room, where Phillips, first operator, had relieved Bride, the buzz of the *Californian*'s set again crackled into the earphones:

Californian: "Say, old man, we are stuck here, surrounded by ice."

Titanic: "Shut up, shut up; keep out. I am talking to Cape Race; you are jamming my signals."

Then, a few minutes later—about 11:40 . . .

Lookout Frederick Fleet.

First Operator Jack Phillips.

II

Out of the dark she came, a vast, dim, white, monstrous shape, directly in the *Titanic*'s path. For a moment Fleet doubted his eyes. But she was a deadly reality, this ghastly *thing.* Frantically, Fleet struck three bells—*something dead ahead.* He snatched the telephone and called the bridge:

"Iceberg! Right ahead!"

The first officer heard but did not stop to acknowledge the message.

"Hard-a-starboard!"

Hichens strained at the wheel; the bow swung slowly to port. The monster was almost upon them now.

Murdoch leaped to the engine-room telegraph. Bells clanged. Far below in the engine room those bells struck the first warning. Danger! The indicators on the dial faces swung round to "Stop!" Then "Full speed astern!" Frantically the engineers turned great valve wheels; answered the bridge bells . . .

There was a slight shock, a brief scraping, a small list to port. Shell ice—slabs and chunks of it—fell on the foredeck. Slowly the *Titanic* stopped.

Captain Smith hurried out of his cabin.

"What has the ship struck?"

Murdoch answered, "An iceberg, sir. I hard-a-starboarded and reversed the engines, and I was going to hard-a-port around it, but she was too close. I could not do any more. I have closed the watertight doors."

Fourth Officer Boxhall, other officers, the carpenter, came to the bridge. The captain sent Boxhall and the carpenter below to ascertain the damage.

A few lights switched on in the first and second cabins; sleepy passengers peered through porthole glass; some casually asked the stewards:

"Why have we stopped?"

"I don't know, sir, but I don't suppose it is anything much."

In the smoking room a quorum[12] of gamblers and their prey were still sitting round a poker table; the usual crowd of kibitzers[13] looked on. They had felt the slight jar of the collision and had seen an eighty-foot ice mountain glide by the smoking-room windows, but the night was calm and clear, the *Titanic* was "unsinkable"; they hadn't bothered to go on deck.

But far below, in the warren of passages on the starboard side forward, in the forward holds and boiler rooms, men could see that the *Titanic*'s hurt was mortal. In No. 6 boiler room, where the red glow from the furnaces lighted up the naked, sweaty chests of coal-blackened firemen, water was pouring through a great gash about two feet above the floor plates. This was no slow leak; the ship was open to the sea; in ten minutes there were eight feet of water in No. 6. Long before then the stokers had raked the flaming fires out of the furnaces and had scrambled through the watertight doors in No. 5 or had climbed up the long steel ladders to safety. When Boxhall looked at the mailroom in No. 3 hold, twenty-four feet above the keel, the mailbags were already floating about in the slushing water. In No. 5 boiler room a stream of water spurted into an empty bunker. All six compartments forward of No. 4 were open to the sea; in ten seconds the iceberg's jagged claw had ripped a three-hundred-foot slash in the bottom of the great *Titanic.*

12. **quorum** (kwôr′əm): the number of people required for a particular activity—in this case, for a game.

13. **kibitzers** (kib′its·ərz): talkative onlookers who often give unwanted advice.

Reports came to the bridge; Ismay in dressing gown ran out on deck in the cold, still, starlit night, climbed up the bridge ladder.

"What has happened?"

Captain Smith: "We have struck ice."

"Do you think she is seriously damaged?"

Captain Smith: "I'm afraid she is."

Ismay went below and passed Chief Engineer William Bell, fresh from an inspection of the damaged compartments. Bell corroborated the captain's statement; hurried back down the glistening steel ladders to his duty. Man after man followed him—Thomas Andrews, one of the ship's designers, Archie Frost, the builder's chief engineer, and his twenty assistants—men who had no posts of duty in the engine room but whose traditions called them there.

On deck, in corridor and stateroom, life flowed again. Men, women, and children awoke and questioned; orders were given to uncover the lifeboats; water rose into the firemen's quarters; half-dressed stokers streamed up on deck. But the passengers—most of them—did not know that the *Titanic* was sinking. The shock of the collision had been so slight that some were not awakened by it; the *Titanic* was so huge that she must be unsinkable; the night was too calm, too beautiful, to think of death at sea.

Captain Smith half ran to the door of the radio shack. Bride, partly dressed, eyes dulled with sleep, was standing behind Phillips, waiting.

"Send the call for assistance."

The blue spark danced: "CQD—CQD—CQD—CQ——"[14]

Miles away Marconi men heard. Cape Race heard it, and the steamships *La Provence* and *Mt. Temple.*

14. **CQD:** call by radio operators, inviting others to communicate with them.

Words to Own

ascertain (as′ər tān′) *v.:* find out with certainty; determine.

corroborated (kə·räb′ə·rāt′id) *v.:* supported; upheld the truth of.

The sea was surging into the *Titanic*'s hold. At 12:20 the water burst into the seamen's quarters through a collapsed fore-and-aft wooden bulkhead. Pumps strained in the engine rooms—men and machinery making a futile fight against the sea. Steadily the water rose.

The boats were swung out—slowly, for the deckhands were late in reaching their stations; there had been no boat drill, and many of the crew did not know to what boats they were assigned. Orders were shouted; the safety valves had lifted, and steam was blowing off in a great rushing roar. In the chart house Fourth Officer Boxhall bent above a chart, working rapidly with pencil and dividers.

12:25 A.M. Boxhall's position is sent out to a fleet of vessels: "Come at once; we have struck a berg."

To the Cunarder *Carpathia* (Arthur Henry Rostron, Master, New York to Liverpool, fifty-eight miles away): "It's a CQD, old man. Position 41-46N.; 50-14 W."

The blue spark dancing: "Sinking; cannot hear for noise of steam."

12:30 A.M. The word is passed: "Women and children in the boats." Stewards finish waking their passengers below; life preservers are tied on; some men smile at the precaution. "The *Titanic* is unsinkable." The *Mt. Temple* starts for the *Titanic;* the *Carpathia,* with a double watch in her stokeholds, radios, "Coming hard." The CQD changes the course of many ships—but not of one; the operator of the *Californian,* nearby, has just put down his earphones and turned in.

The CQD flashes over land and sea from Cape Race to New York; newspaper city rooms leap to life and presses whir.

On the *Titanic,* water creeps over the bulkhead between Nos. 5 and 6 firerooms. She is going down by the head; the engineers—fighting a losing battle—are forced back foot by foot by the rising water. Down the promenade deck, Happy Jock Hume, the bandsman, runs with his instrument.

12:45 A.M. Murdoch, in charge on the starboard side, eyes tragic, but calm and cool, orders boat No. 7 lowered. The women hang back; they want no boat ride on an ice-strewn sea; the *Titanic* is unsinkable. The men encourage them, explain that this is just a precautionary measure: "We'll see you again at breakfast." There is little confusion; passengers stream slowly to the boat deck. In the steerage the immigrants chatter excitedly.

A sudden sharp hiss—a streaked flare against the night; Boxhall sends a rocket toward the sky. It explodes, and a parachute of white stars lights up the icy sea. "God! Rockets!" The band plays ragtime.

No. 8 is lowered, and No. 5. Ismay, still in dressing gown, calls for women and children, handles lines, stumbles in the way of an officer, is told to "get the hell out of here." Third Officer Pitman takes charge of No. 5; as he swings into the boat, Murdoch grasps his hand. "Goodbye and good luck, old man."

No. 6 goes over the side. There are only twenty-eight people in a lifeboat with a capacity of sixty-five.

A light stabs from the bridge; Boxhall is calling in Morse flashes, again and again, to a strange ship stopped in the ice jam five to ten miles away. Another rocket drops its shower of sparks above the ice-strewn sea and the dying ship.

1:00 A.M. Slowly the water creeps higher; the fore ports of the *Titanic* are dipping into the sea. Rope squeaks through blocks; lifeboats drop jerkily seaward. Through the shouting on the decks comes the sound of the band playing ragtime.

The "Millionaires' Special" leaves the ship—boat No. 1, with a capacity of forty people, carries only Sir Cosmo and Lady Duff Gordon and ten others. Aft, the frightened immigrants mill and jostle and rush for a boat. An officer's fist flies out; three shots are fired in the air, and the panic is quelled. . . . Four Chinese sneak unseen into a boat and hide in the bottom.

1:20 A.M. Water is coming into No. 4 boiler room. Stokers slice and shovel as water laps

WORDS TO OWN

quelled (kweld) *v.:* quieted; subdued.

Molly Brown (nicknamed "unsinkable" by the Associated Press) helped row a lifeboat and nurse survivors.

Colonel John Jacob Astor, wealthy hotel owner, went down with the *Titanic.*

about their ankles—steam for the dynamos, steam for the dancing spark! As the water rises, great ash hoes rake the flaming coals from the furnaces. Safety valves pop; the stokers retreat aft, and the watertight doors clang shut behind them.

The rockets fling their splendor toward the stars. The boats are more heavily loaded now, for the passengers know the *Titanic* is sinking. Women cling and sob. The great screws aft are rising clear of the sea. Half-filled boats are ordered to come alongside the cargo ports and take on more passengers, but the ports are never opened—and the boats are never filled. Others pull for the steamer's light miles away but never reach it; the lights disappear; the unknown ship steams off.

The water rises and the band plays ragtime.

1:30 A.M. Lightoller is getting the port boats off; Murdoch, the starboard. As one boat is lowered into the sea, a boat officer fires his gun along the ship's side to stop a rush from the lower decks. A woman tries to take her Great Dane into a boat with her; she is refused and steps out of the boat to die with her dog. Millet's "little smile which played on his lips all through the voyage" plays no more; his lips are grim, but he waves goodbye and brings wraps for the women.

Benjamin Guggenheim, in evening clothes, smiles and says, "We've dressed up in our best and are prepared to go down like gentlemen."

1:40 A.M. Boat 14 is clear, and then 13, 16, 15, and C. The lights still shine, but the *Baltic* hears the blue spark say, "Engine room getting flooded."

The *Olympia* signals, "Am lighting up all possible boilers as fast as can."

Major Butt helps women into the last boats and waves goodbye to them. Mrs. Straus puts her foot on the gunwale of a lifeboat; then she draws back and goes to her husband: "We have been together many years; where you go, I will go." Colonel John Jacob Astor puts his young wife in a lifeboat, steps back, taps cigarette on fingernail: "Goodbye, dearie; I'll join you later."

1:45 A.M. The foredeck is under water; the fo'c'sle[15] head almost awash; the great stern is lifted high toward the bright stars; and still the band plays. Mr. and Mrs. Harris approach a lifeboat arm in arm.

Officer: "Ladies first, please."

Harris bows, smiles, steps back: "Of course, certainly; ladies first."

Boxhall fires the last rocket, then leaves in charge of boat No. 2.

2:00 A.M. She is dying now; her bow goes deeper, her stern higher. But there must be steam. Below in the stokeholds the sweaty firemen keep steam up for the flaring lights and the dancing spark. The glowing coals slide and tumble over the slanted grate bars; the sea pounds behind that yielding bulkhead. But the spark dances on.

15. **fo'c'sle** (fōk′s'l): forecastle, front upper deck of a ship.

The *Asian* hears Phillips try the new signal—SOS.

Boat No. 4 has left now; boat D leaves ten minutes later. Jacques Futrelle clasps his wife: "For God's sake, go! It's your last chance; go!" Madame Futrelle is half forced into the boat. It clears the side.

There are about 660 people in the boats and 1,500 still on the sinking *Titanic.*

On top of the officers' quarters, men work frantically to get the two collapsibles stowed there over the side. Water is over the forward part of A deck now; it surges up the companionways toward the boat deck. In the radio shack, Bride has slipped a coat and life jacket about Phillips as the first operator sits hunched over his key, sending—still sending—"41-46 N.; 50-14 W. CQD—CQD—SOS—SOS——"

The captain's tired white face appears at the radio-room door. "Men, you have done your full duty. You can do no more. Now, it's every man for himself." The captain disappears—back to his sinking bridge, where Painter, his personal steward, stands quietly waiting for orders. The spark dances on. Bride turns his back and goes into the inner cabin. As he does so, a stoker, grimed with coal, mad with fear, steals into the shack and reaches for the life jacket on Phillips's back. Bride wheels about and brains him with a wrench.

2:10 A.M. Below decks the steam is still holding, though the pressure is falling—rapidly. In the gymnasium on the boat deck, the athletic instructor watches quietly as two gentlemen ride the bicycles and another swings casually at the punching bag. Mail clerks stagger up the boat-deck stairways, dragging soaked mail sacks. The spark still dances. The band still plays—but not ragtime:

> Nearer my God to Thee.
> Nearer to Thee . . .

A few men take up the refrain; others kneel on the slanting decks to pray. Many run and scramble aft, where hundreds are clinging above the silent screws on the great uptilted stern. The spark still dances and the lights still flare; the engineers are on the job. The hymn comes to its close. Bandmaster Hartley, Yorkshireman violinist, taps his bow against a bulkhead, calls for "Autumn" as the water curls about his feet, and the eight musicians brace themselves against the ship's slant. People are leaping from the decks into the nearby water—the icy water. A woman cries, "Oh, save me, save me!" A man answers, "Good lady, save yourself. Only God can save you now." The band plays "Autumn":

> God of Mercy and Compassion!
> Look with pity on my pain . . .

The water creeps over the bridge where the *Titanic*'s master stands; heavily he steps out to meet it.

2:17 A.M. "CQ——" The *Virginian* hears a ragged, blurred CQ, then an abrupt stop. The blue spark dances no more. The lights flicker out; the engineers have lost their battle.

2:18 A.M. Men run about blackened decks; leap into the night; are swept into the sea by the curling wave that licks up the *Titanic*'s length. Lightoller does not leave the ship; the ship leaves him; there are hundreds like him, but only a few who live to tell of it. The funnels still swim above the water, but the ship is climbing to the perpendicular; the bridge is under and most of the foremast; the great stern rises like a squat leviathan.[16] Men swim away from the sinking ship; others drop from the stern.

The band plays in the darkness, the water lapping upward:

> Hold me up in mighty waters,
> Keep my eyes on things above,
> Righteousness, divine atonement,
> Peace and everlas . . .

16. **leviathan** (lə·vī′ə·thən): Biblical sea monster, perhaps a whale.

The forward funnel snaps and crashes into the sea; its steel tons hammer out of existence swimmers struggling in the freezing water. Streams of sparks, of smoke and steam, burst from the after funnels. The ship upends to 50—to 60 degrees.

Down in the black abyss of the stokeholds, of the engine rooms, where the dynamos have whirred at long last to a stop, the stokers and the engineers are reeling against the hot metal, the rising water clutching at their knees. The boilers, the engine cylinders, rip from their bed plates; crash through bulkheads; rumble—steel against steel.

The *Titanic* stands on end, poised briefly for the plunge. Slowly she slides to her grave—slowly at first, and then more quickly—quickly—quickly.

2:20 A.M. The greatest ship in the world has sunk. From the calm, dark waters, where the floating lifeboats move, there goes up, in the white wake of her passing, "one long continuous moan."

III

The boats that the *Titanic* had launched pulled safely away from the slight suction of the sinking ship, pulled away from the screams that came from the lips of the freezing men and women in the water. The boats were poorly manned and badly equipped, and they had been unevenly loaded. Some carried so few seamen that women bent to the oars. Mrs. Astor tugged at an oar handle; the Countess of Rothes took a tiller. Shivering stokers in sweaty, coal-blackened singlets and light trousers steered in some boats; stewards in white coats rowed in others. Ismay was in the last boat that left the ship from the starboard side; with Mr. Carter of Philadelphia and two seamen he tugged at the oars. In one of the lifeboats an Italian with a bro-

Words to Own

poised (poizd) *v.* used as *adj.:* balanced; in position.

ken wrist—disguised in a woman's shawl and hat—huddled on the floorboards, ashamed now that fear had left him. In another rode the only baggage saved from the *Titanic*—the carryall of Samuel L. Goldenberg, one of the rescued passengers.

There were only a few boats that were heavily loaded; most of those that were half empty made but perfunctory efforts to pick up the moaning swimmers, their officers and crew fearing they would endanger the living if they pulled back into the midst of the dying. Some boats beat off the freezing victims; fear-crazed men and women struck with oars at the heads of swimmers. One woman drove her fist into the face of a half-dead man as he tried feebly to climb over the gunwale. Two other women helped him in and staunched the flow of blood from the ring cuts on his face.

One of the collapsible boats, which had floated off the top of the officers' quarters when the *Titanic* sank, was an icy haven for thirty or forty men. The boat had capsized as the ship sank; men swam to it, clung to it, climbed upon its slippery bottom, stood knee-deep in water in the freezing air. Chunks of ice swirled about their legs; their soaked clothing clutched their bodies in icy folds. Colonel Archibald Gracie was cast up there, Gracie who had leaped from the stern as the *Titanic* sank; young Thayer who had seen his father die; Lightoller who had twice been sucked down with the ship and twice blown to the surface by a belch of air; Bride, the second operator, and Phillips, the first. There were many stokers, half naked; it was a shivering company. They stood there in the icy sea, under the far stars, and sang and prayed—the Lord's Prayer. After a while a lifeboat came and picked them off, but Phillips was dead then or died soon afterward in the boat.

Only a few of the boats had lights; only one—No. 2—had a light that was of any use to the *Carpathia,* twisting through the ice field to the rescue. Other ships were "coming hard" too; one, the *Californian,* was still dead to opportunity.

The blue sparks still danced, but not the *Titanic*'s. *La Provence* to *Celtic:* "Nobody has heard the *Titanic* for about two hours."

It was 2:40 when the *Carpathia* first sighted the green light from No. 2 boat; it was 4:10 when she picked up the first boat and learned that the *Titanic* had foundered.[17] The last of the moaning cries had just died away then.

Captain Rostron took the survivors aboard, boatload by boatload. He was ready for them, but only a small minority of them required much medical attention. Bride's feet were twisted and frozen; others were suffering from exposure; one died, and seven were dead when taken from the boats, and were buried at sea.

It was then that the fleet of racing ships learned they were too late; the *Parisian* heard the weak signals of *MPA,* the *Carpathia,* report the death of the *Titanic.* It was then—or soon afterward, when her radio operator put on his earphones—that the *Californian,* the ship that had been within sight as the *Titanic* was sinking, first learned of the disaster.

And it was then, in all its white-green majesty, that the *Titanic*'s survivors saw the iceberg, tinted with the sunrise, floating idly, pack ice jammed about its base, other bergs heaving slowly nearby on the blue breast of the sea.

IV

But it was not until later that the world knew, for wireless then was not what wireless is today, and garbled messages had nourished a hope that all of the *Titanic*'s company were safe. Not until Monday evening, when P.A.S. Franklin, vice president of the International Mercantile Marine Company, received relayed messages in New York that left little hope, did the full extent of

17. **foundered:** filled with water, so that it sank; generally, collapsed or failed.

WORDS TO OWN

perfunctory (pər·fuŋk'tə·rē) *adj.:* not exerting much effort; unconcerned.

garbled *v.* used as *adj.:* confused; mixed up.

the disaster begin to be known. Partial and garbled lists of the survivors; rumors of heroism and cowardice; stories spun out of newspaper imagination, based on a few bare facts and many false reports, misled the world, terrified and frightened it. It was not until Thursday night, when the *Carpathia* steamed into the North River, that the full truth was pieced together.

Flashlights flared on the black river when the *Carpathia* stood up to her dock. Tugs nosed about her, shunted her toward Pier 54. Thirty thousand people jammed the streets; ambulances and stretchers stood on the pier; coroners and physicians waited.

In midstream the Cunarder dropped over the *Titanic*'s lifeboats; then she headed toward the dock. Beneath the customs letters on the pier stood relatives of the 711 survivors, relatives of the missing—hoping against hope. The *Carpathia* cast her lines ashore; stevedores[18] looped them over bollards. The dense throngs stood quiet as the first survivor stepped down the gangway. The woman half staggered—led by customs guards—beneath her letter. A "low wailing" moan came from the crowd; fell, grew in volume, and dropped again.

Thus ended the maiden voyage of the *Titanic.* The lifeboats brought to New York by the *Carpathia,* a few deck chairs and gratings awash in the ice field off the Grand Bank eight hundred miles from shore, were all that was left of the world's greatest ship.

V

The aftermath of weeping and regret, of recriminations and investigations, dragged on for weeks. Charges and countercharges were hurled about; the White Star Line was bitterly criticized; Ismay was denounced on the floor of the Senate as a coward but was defended by those who had been with him on the sinking *Titanic* and by the Board of Trade investigation in England.

18. **stevedores** (stē′və·dôrz′): persons who load and unload ships.

It was not until weeks later, when the hastily convened Senate investigation in the United States and the Board of Trade report in England had been completed, that the whole story was told. The Senate investigating committee, under the chairmanship of Senator Smith, who was attacked in both the American and the British press as a "backwoods politician," brought out numerous pertinent facts, though its proceedings verged at times on the farcical.[19] Senator Smith was ridiculed for his lack of knowledge of the sea when he asked witnesses, "Of what is an iceberg composed?" and "Did any of the passengers take refuge in the watertight compartments?" The senator seemed particularly interested in the marital status of Fleet, the lookout, who was saved. Fleet, puzzled, growled aside, "Wot questions they're arskin' me!"

The report of Lord Mersey, wreck commissioner in the British Board of Trade's investigation, was tersely damning.

The *Titanic* had carried boats enough for 1,178 persons, only one third of her capacity. Her sixteen boats and four collapsibles had saved but 711 persons; 400 people had needlessly lost their lives. The boats had been but partly loaded; officers in charge of launching them had been afraid the falls[20] would break or the boats buckle under their rated loads; boat crews had been slow in reaching their stations; launching arrangements were confused because no boat drill had been held; passengers were loaded into the boats haphazardly because no boat assignments had been made.

But that was not all. Lord Mersey found that sufficient warnings of ice on the steamer track had reached the *Titanic,* that her speed of twenty-two knots was "excessive under the

19. **farcical** (fär′si·kəl): absurd; ridiculous; like a farce (an exaggerated comedy).
20. **falls:** chains used for hoisting.

WORDS TO OWN

recriminations (ri·krim′ə·nā′shənz) *n.:* accusations against an accuser; countercharges.
pertinent (pur′tə·nənt) *adj.:* having some connection with the subject.

circumstances," that "in view of the high speed at which the vessel was running it is not considered that the lookout was sufficient," and that her master made "a very grievous mistake"—but should not be blamed for negligence. Captain Rostron of the *Carpathia* was highly praised. "He did the very best that could be done." The *Californian* was damned. The testimony of her master, officers, and crew showed that she was not, at the most, more than nineteen miles away from the sinking *Titanic* and probably no more than five to ten miles distant. She had seen the *Titanic*'s lights; she had seen the rockets; she had not received the CQD calls because her radio operator was asleep. She had attempted to get in communication with the ship she had sighted by flashing a light, but vainly.

"The night was clear," reported Lord Mersey, "and the sea was smooth. When she first saw the rockets, the *Californian* could have pushed through the ice to the open water without any serious risk and so have come to the assistance of the *Titanic.* Had she done so she might have saved many if not all of the lives that were lost.

"She made no attempt."

WORDS TO OWN

vainly *adv.:* without success; fruitlessly.

MEET THE WRITER

Journalist and Seaman

Hanson Weightman Baldwin (1903–1991) was one of America's great journalists. He graduated with an ensign's commission from the U.S. Naval Academy at Annapolis. After only three years of service aboard battleships, Baldwin resigned from the Navy and launched a career as a military correspondent and editor. His longest hitch was with *The New York Times*.

During World War II Baldwin covered battles in North Africa and the D-day invasion of Normandy. His series of articles on the war in the South Pacific won him a Pulitzer Prize in 1943. After the war, he reported on the second atomic bomb test at Bikini Island, on guided-missile and rocket-firing installations, and on the organization of U.S. military forces in the nuclear age.

Relatively early in his writing career (1934), Baldwin wrote an article for *Harper's* magazine about the sinking of the *Titanic,* which had occurred twenty-two years earlier. His research was thorough: He pieced together information from ship logs, from interviews with survivors, and from written reports detailing the ship's design and launching. The subject of the *Titanic* was by no means new for Baldwin's readers. The sinking of the "unsinkable" ship had been fictionalized, sensationalized, and sentimentalized many times before 1934. Nevertheless, Baldwin's article became a textbook example of excellent reporting. His fast-paced account, with its mixture of factual details and irony, makes the disaster and all the human foibles associated with it seem tragically real again.

Connections | EYEWITNESS ACCOUNTS

The lifeboats of the "unsinkable" Titanic *carried fewer than one third of the approximately 2,200 people aboard. A U.S. Senate investigating committee in 1912 found that a total of 1,517 lives were lost—a high proportion of them poor passengers who were far below decks in steerage.*

J. Bruce Ismay, director of the White Star Line.

A Fireman's Story

Harry Senior

I was in my bunk when I felt a bump. One man said, "Hello. She has been struck." I went on deck and saw a great pile of ice on the well deck before the forecastle, but we all thought the ship would last some time, and we went back to our bunks. Then one of the firemen came running down and yelled, "All muster for the lifeboats." I ran on deck, and the captain said, "All firemen keep down on the well deck. If a man comes up, I'll shoot him."

Mrs. J. Bruce Ismay.

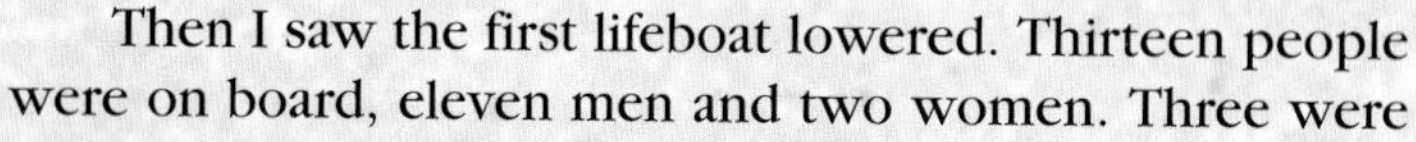

Then I saw the first lifeboat lowered. Thirteen people were on board, eleven men and two women. Three were millionaires, and one was Ismay [J. Bruce Ismay, managing director of the White Star Line; a survivor].

Then I ran up onto the hurricane deck and helped to throw one of the collapsible boats onto the lower deck. I saw an Italian woman holding two babies. I took one of them and made the woman jump overboard with the baby, while I did the same with the other. When I came to the surface, the baby in my arms was dead. I saw the woman strike out in good style, but a boiler burst on the *Titanic* and started a big wave. When the woman saw that wave, she gave up. Then, as the child was dead, I let it sink too.

I swam around for about half an hour, and was swimming on my back when the *Titanic* went down. I tried to get aboard a boat, but some chap hit me over the head with an oar. There were too many in her. I got around to the other side of the boat and climbed in.

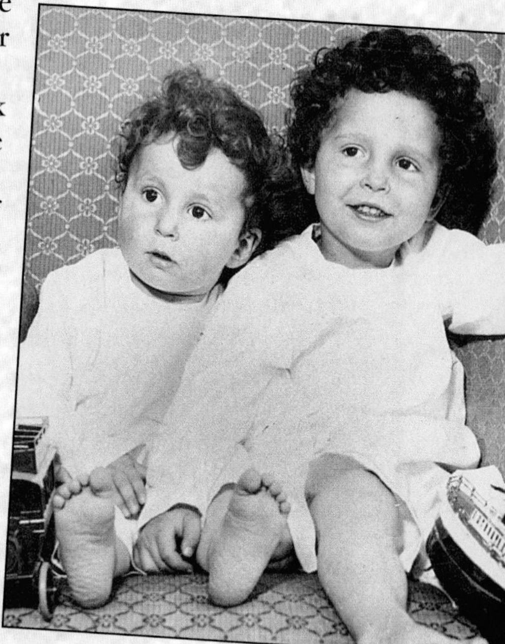

"The *Titanic* orphans"—Edmond (age 2) and Michel (age 3) Navratil.

From a Lifeboat

Mrs. D. H. Bishop

We did not begin to understand the situation till we were perhaps a mile or more away from the *Titanic*. Then we could see the rows of lights along the decks begin to slant gradually upward from the bow. Very slowly, the lines of light began to point downward at a greater and greater angle. The sinking was so slow that you could not perceive the lights of the deck changing their position. The slant seemed to be greater about every quarter of an hour. That was the only difference.

Ruth Becker and her brother Richard survived in separate lifeboats.

In a couple of hours, though, she began to go down more rapidly. Then the fearful sight began. The people in the ship were just beginning to realize how great their danger was. When the forward part of the ship dropped suddenly at a faster rate, so that the upward slope became marked, there was a sudden rush of passengers on all the decks toward the stern. It was like a wave. We could see the great black mass of people in the steerage sweeping to the rear part of the boat and breaking through into the upper decks. At the distance of about a mile, we could distinguish everything through the night, which was perfectly clear. We could make out the increasing excitement on board the boat as the people, rushing to and fro, caused the deck lights to disappear and reappear as they passed in front of them.

This panic went on, it seemed, for an hour. Then suddenly the ship seemed to shoot up out of the water and stand there perpendicularly. It seemed to us that it stood upright in the water for four full minutes.

Then it began to slide gently downward. Its speed increased as it went down headfirst, so that the stern shot down with a rush.

The lights continued to burn till it sank. We could see the people packed densely in the stern till it was gone. . . .

As the ship sank, we could hear the screaming a mile away. Gradually it became fainter and fainter and died away. Some of the lifeboats that had room for more might have gone to their rescue, but it would have meant that those who were in the water would have swarmed aboard and sunk them.

Marion Wright from Somerset, England, married her fiancé when she arrived in New York City.

MAKING MEANINGS

First Thoughts

1. The *Titanic* sank a long time ago, and most of its survivors have since died. How did you feel about all the people involved in the disaster?

Reading Check

a. What caused the *Titanic* to sink?

b. Why didn't the closest ship rush to the rescue?

c. Why weren't the lifeboats full?

d. Cite two heroic acts and two cowardly acts that took place aboard the *Titanic*.

Shaping Interpretations

2. Baldwin uses numbers as **headings** to organize his text. Briefly summarize what is covered in each numbered part. Why are these divisions logical?

3. Find as many examples of **irony**—both **dramatic** and **situational**—in the story of the *Titanic* as you can. Which instance of irony do you think is the most incredible?

4. Baldwin spent hundreds of hours sifting through reports of the sinking, the records of other ships, eyewitness accounts (see ***Connections*** on pages 404–405), and court proceedings. How **objective** (strictly factual) or **subjective** (based on opinions, feelings, and biases) do you think his report is? Explain.

5. Baldwin returns many times to the music played by the ship's band. What **moods** are suggested by the music? What other examples of **repetition** can you find, and how do these repeated details affect your feelings?

Connecting with the Text

6. What more recent events remind you of this old tragedy at sea? Did any survivors of those events behave heroically or selfishly? What were the causes of those disasters?

7. After reading about the events on board ship, how do you think (or hope) you would have acted if you'd been a passenger? a crew member? Look back at your Quickwrite to see whether you've changed your mind about how you'd behave in a catastrophe.

Extending the Text

8. What, if any, truths about human nature can you **infer** from this story and from the survivors' eyewitness accounts (see ***Connections*** on pages 404–405)?

Scene from the movie *Titanic* (1997), starring Leonardo DiCaprio and Kate Winslet.

CHOICES: Building Your Portfolio

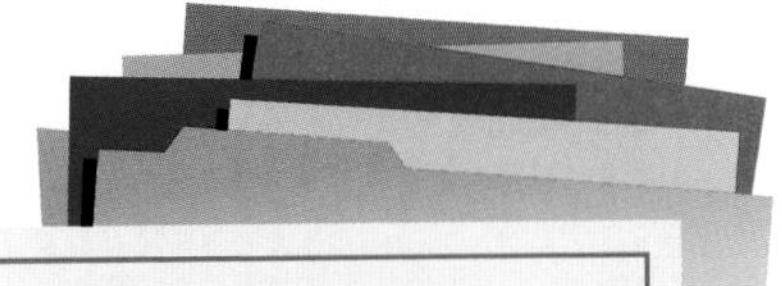

Writer's Notebook

1. Collecting Ideas for a Research Paper

WORK IN PROGRESS

Listing questions. The *Titanic* never seems to go out of the news. You might be interested enough in the disaster to do further research. Start by skimming back over Baldwin's article, which was written in 1934. Jot down all the questions you have about the disaster and about details in the report. For example, have there been any new findings on the sunken ship: Are any of Baldwin's details now dated? One writer's first question is cited on the notepad below. (Be sure to save your notes.)

Questions to research
- Is the "big slash" theory for the ship's sinking still accurate?
- Have any new theories been proposed?

Writing a Summary

2. Just the Facts, Please

Write a one-page **summary** of "R.M.S. *Titanic*," including the most significant facts and Baldwin's most important conclusions. Before you write your summary, first **outline** the article, showing what Baldwin covers in each of the five numbered sections. (See page 334 for a model of an outline.) Include in your summary a **time line** showing the major events in the disaster.

Art

3. Disaster: An Artist's View

The illustration on pages 398–399 shows how one artist imagined the sinking *Titanic*. Create your own visual representation of the disaster (the impact of the iceberg, the ship's sinking, the unfilled lifeboats) in any medium you wish. If you prefer, illustrate a different disaster—the explosion of the *Challenger*, the San Francisco earthquake and fire, tornadoes—you choose.

Role-Play

4. A Senate Investigation

With a group, role-play an improvised sketch depicting a Senate hearing on the *Titanic* disaster. You'll need a table and chairs, several volunteers to play senators, including the chairperson, and witnesses. Senator Smith is a plum role. Other characters that you may want to include in your sketch are the crewman Fleet, the *Carpathia* captain Rostron, the radio operator Bride, and the shipping company chairman Ismay. Review the information about these characters in Baldwin's report. Then, use your imagination to further develop each role.

Comparing Responses to a Review

5. Why the Lineup?

Here's what one critic wrote about James Cameron's movie *Titanic* (1997):

> There's not a single superhero, alien, or bloodthirsty slasher in the three-hour tear-jerker. The story is crammed with ancient history, and everyone already knows that the ship sinks in the end.
>
> So, why are teens lining up for more?
>
> —Su Avasthi, *New York Post*

If you have seen the movie, compare your response to *Titanic* with the critic's. Then, try to explain the movie's enormous popularity. Be sure to cite details from the movie to support your responses.

Language Link MINI-LESSON

Combining Narration and Exposition

Handbook of Literary Terms HELP

See Exposition and Narration.

In his long article about the *Titanic,* Baldwin combines a **chronological** account (a **narrative,** or story) with **factual** information (**exposition**). (On page 392 alone, see how many facts you can locate.) Facts enhance the narrative because they give information that allows us to feel like experts. The narrative techniques (**characterization,** use of **dialogue,** and **suspense**) make the article as compelling as a fast-paced adventure novel. In fact, Baldwin uses an old narrative device based on the ticking clock. A similar narrative device is used in the tense science fiction story "The Cold Equations" (page 9).

Try It Out

➤Go back to the text as you look for these examples of Baldwin's narrative techniques.

1. Baldwin introduces us to some of the people involved in the disaster, and we learn more than their names. How does he "show, not tell," us about these **characters**?
2. Find places where Baldwin uses **dialogue** or **quotations.** Try reading those passages without the dialogue—what happens to the story? How do you suppose Baldwin discovered what these people said, or do you think he made up the dialogue?
3. Most readers know that the *Titanic* sank. What techniques does Baldwin use to create **suspense** in a story whose outcome is known?

A tip for writers: Whenever you write an informative essay, look for places where you might use narrative devices (characterization, use of dialogue, and suspense) to make your information more interesting to your readers.

Vocabulary HOW TO OWN A WORD

Word Bank

superlative
ascertain
corroborated
quelled
poised
perfunctory
garbled
recriminations
pertinent
vainly

Does It Apply? The Right Word

Would you use the word *superlative* to describe a person? How about *supreme*? When is a word appropriate, and when isn't it? The question isn't always easy to answer. Work with a partner or group to make **semantic features charts** like the one below. At the left, list one word in the Word Bank and a synonym. Along the top, list features (ideas, things, feelings, situations) to which the word might apply. Write a plus sign (+) if the word usually can be applied to that feature; write a minus sign (–) if it can't.

	Bomb	Riot	Objections	Disturbance
quell	–	+	+	+
subdue	–	+	–	+

Before You Read

No News from Auschwitz

Make the Connection

Remembering History

In 1958, when A. M. Rosenthal was *The New York Times*'s correspondent in Warsaw, Poland, he visited the concentration camp at Auschwitz. About fourteen years had passed since the camps had been liberated, and virtually no mention of them had appeared in American newspapers for several years. There was "no news" to report from those sites, and Americans seemed all too willing to put the ugly memories behind them. Rosenthal's piece for *The Times* was a powerful reminder of the dangers that could befall people who forgot what had happened there.

Quickwrite

In a few sentences, write what you know about the Holocaust. (Perhaps you've read *The Diary of Anne Frank* or the speech from the Nuremberg trials on page 885. Save your notes.)

Reading Skills and Strategies

Dialogue with the Text

In your notebook, describe your feelings as you read this essay. Note the passages that you find most moving and your reactions to them.

A. M. Rosenthal saw these photos of concentration camp prisoners when he visited the museum at Auschwitz in 1958.

Elements of Literature

Objective and Subjective Writing

At the moment, you are reading this book. That's a fact. You are somewhere. It is some hour of the day, some day of the week. All of these statements refer to **objective** facts, which means that they can be proved true.

You may also be interested or bored or worried about a test next period. These are **subjective,** or personal, feelings and judgments.

Two writers may start out with the same facts and yet report an event in vastly different ways. An encyclopedia article about the Holocaust, for example, that contains only facts and gives no clue to the writer's thoughts and feelings is **objective** writing. In revealing their own thoughts, judgments, feelings, and attitudes, writers are writing **subjectively**. As you read A. M. Rosenthal's report from Auschwitz, consider which type of writing—objective or subjective—is more important in his essay.

> **Objective** writing reports only the facts; the writer is invisible. In **subjective** writing, the writer adds his or her opinions, judgments, or feelings.

go.hrw.com
LEO 10-6

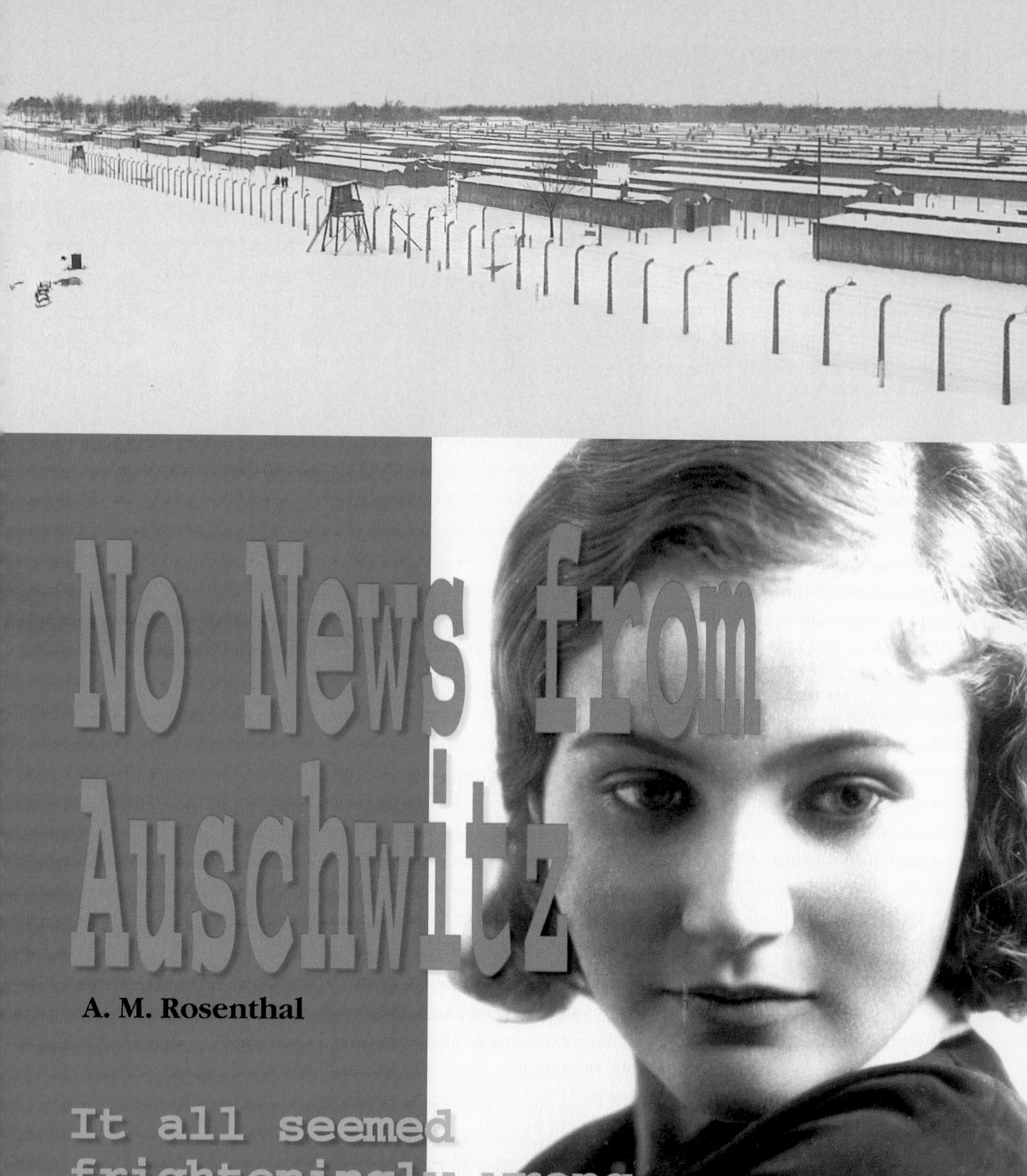

No News from Auschwitz

A. M. Rosenthal

It all seemed frighteningly wrong . . .

(Above) The abandoned Auschwitz II, or Birkenau, outside the town of Brzezinka, Poland, in February 1945. As the Soviet army advanced, Nazis moved prisoners to Dachau and other German concentration camps. (Left) Zdenka Gruenwald, age 15, who died in the Holocaust.

Brzezinka, Poland—The most terrible thing of all, somehow, was that at Brzezinka the sun was bright and warm, the rows of graceful poplars were lovely to look upon, and on the grass near the gates children played.

It all seemed frighteningly wrong, as in a nightmare, that at Brzezinka the sun should ever shine or that there should be light and greenness and the sound of young laughter. It would be fitting if at Brzezinka the sun never shone and the grass withered, because this is a place of unutterable terror.

And yet every day, from all over the world, people come to Brzezinka, quite possibly the most grisly tourist center on earth. They come for a variety of reasons—to see if it could really have been true, to remind themselves not to forget, to pay homage to the dead by the simple act of looking upon their place of suffering.

Brzezinka is a couple of miles from the better-known southern Polish town of Oświęcim.° Oświęcim has about 12,000 inhabitants, is situated about 171 miles from Warsaw, and lies in a damp, marshy area at the eastern end of the pass called the Moravian Gate. Brzezinka and Oświęcim together formed part of that minutely organized factory of torture and death that the Nazis called Konzentrationslager Auschwitz.

By now, fourteen years after the last batch of prisoners was herded naked into the gas chambers by dogs and guards, the story of Auschwitz has been told a great many times. Some of the inmates have written of those memories of which sane men cannot conceive. Rudolf Franz Ferdinand Hoess, the superintendent of the camp, before he was executed wrote his detailed memoirs of mass exterminations and the experiments on living bodies. Four million people died here, the Poles say.

°**Oświęcim** (ôsh · vyan′tsim): Polish name for Auschwitz.

Entrance to one of the gas chambers at Auschwitz.

And so there is no news to report about Auschwitz. There is merely the compulsion to write something about it, a compulsion that grows out of a restless feeling that to have visited Auschwitz and then turned away without having said or written anything would somehow be a most grievous act of discourtesy to those who died here.

Brzezinka and Oświęcim are very quiet places now; the screams can no longer be heard. The tourist walks silently, quickly at first to get it over with and then, as his mind peoples the barracks and the chambers and the dungeons and flogging posts, he walks draggingly. The guide does not say much either, because there is nothing much for him to say after he has pointed.

For every visitor there is one particular bit of horror that he knows he will never forget. For some it is seeing the rebuilt gas chamber at Oświęcim and being told that this is the "small one."

For others it is the fact that at Brzezinka, in the ruins of the gas chambers and the crematoria the Germans blew up when they retreated, there are daisies growing.

There are visitors who gaze blankly at the gas chambers and the furnaces because their minds simply cannot encompass them, but stand shivering before the great mounds of human hair behind the plate-glass window or the piles of babies' shoes or the brick cells where men sentenced to death by suffocation were walled up.

One visitor opened his mouth in a silent scream simply at the sight of boxes—great stretches of three-tiered wooden boxes in the women's barracks. They were about six feet wide, about three feet high, and into them from five to ten prisoners were shoved for the night. The guide walks quickly through the barracks. Nothing more to see here.

A brick building where sterilization experiments were carried out on women prisoners. The guide tries the door—it's locked. The visitor is grateful that he does not have to go in, and then flushes with shame.

A long corridor where rows of faces stare from the walls. Thousands of pictures, the photographs of prisoners. They are all dead now, the men and women who stood before the cameras, and they all knew they were to die.

They all stare blank-faced, but one picture, in the middle of a row, seizes the eye and wrenches the mind. A girl, twenty-two years old, plumply pretty, blond. She is smiling gently, as at a sweet, treasured thought. What was the thought that passed through her young mind and is now her memorial on the wall of the dead at Auschwitz?

Into the suffocation dungeons the visitor is taken for a moment and feels himself strangling. Another visitor goes in, stumbles out, and crosses herself. There is no place to pray in Auschwitz.

The visitors look pleadingly at each other and say to the guide, "Enough."

There is nothing new to report about Auschwitz. It was a sunny day and the trees were green and at the gates the children played.

Meet the Writer

Journalist of Distinction

Abraham Michael Rosenthal (1922–) was born in Ontario, Canada, but moved with his family to New York City when he was four. For many years he served as the executive editor of *The New York Times.* When he "retired," he began to write a column for *The Times* called "On My Mind," in which he often takes a moral and ethical stand on events in the news.

In November 1959, after Rosenthal had written "No News from Auschwitz," the Polish government expelled him for his probing reporting. He won a Pulitzer Prize in May 1960 for the same reports. Rosenthal is also the author of *Thirty-Eight Witnesses* (1964), an account of a murder in a quiet New York City neighborhood. The title refers to the thirty-eight people who witnessed a young woman's murder but did nothing to help the victim.

When asked if he thought that reporters' opinions are slipping into news stories more often today than they did in the past, Rosenthal replied:

“Yes, I do. But we don't try for objectivity, because there is no such thing as pristine objectivity. There is an approach to doing a fair job, . . . but if you start thinking the most important thing to do is present your opinion, by stealth or not, to change your readers' minds, then you can't do your job the same way. There are plenty of places in the paper to do that. . . .

The editorial writer gets paid to do it; if you don't like your job, become an editorial writer. Or stick around, be a reporter for thirty years, then become the executive editor, and then become a columnist.”

Connections

A POEM

The Nazis used the Czech town of Terezín as a concentration camp between 1941 and 1945. From 1942 to 1944, a total of 15,000 children passed through the camp. Only about 100 of them survived. Pavel Friedmann, the writer of this poem, was one of the young people imprisoned in the camp. He died in Auschwitz in September 1944.

(Right) *Terezín Barracks* (detail) by Sonja Valdstein. (Below) *Flower and Butterfly* (detail) by Marika Friedman.

From *I never saw another butterfly* (Schocken Books, 1993). Courtesy U.S. Holocaust Memorial Museum, Washington, D.C.

The Butterfly

Pavel Friedmann

The last, the very last,
So richly, brightly, dazzlingly yellow.
Perhaps if the sun's tears would sing
against a white stone . . .

Such, such a yellow
Is carried lightly 'way up high.
It went away I'm sure because it wished to
kiss the world goodbye.

For seven weeks I've lived in here,
Penned up inside this ghetto
But I have found my people here.
The dandelions call to me
And the white chestnut candles in the court.
Only I never saw another butterfly.

That butterfly was the last one.
Butterflies don't live in here,
in the ghetto.

Making Meanings

First Thoughts

1. If you had a chance to visit Auschwitz, would you go? Why or why not?

Shaping Interpretations

2. Explain why the title of the essay is **ironic**. What "news" does Rosenthal want his readers to know?
3. What **purpose,** or aim, do you think Rosenthal had in writing this essay?

Extending the Text

4. What relationship do you see between Rosenthal's essay and the poem "The Butterfly" (see ***Connections*** on page 414)?

Reading Check

Write a paragraph telling what this essay is about. Include the items below. Then, write a few sentences explaining what you learned about the Holocaust from the essay (refer to your Quickwrite notes).

Situation:________________

Setting: ________________

What happens:________________

The writer's main idea:________________

____

Choices: Building Your Portfolio

Writer's Notebook

1. Collecting Ideas for a Research Paper

WORK IN PROGRESS

Exploring sources. For a topic you're considering researching, think about where you will find information. List and then explore some specific sources. Consider both **print sources** (books, magazines, encyclopedias) and **nonprint sources** (the Internet, on-line databases, TV documentaries, interviews). Before you finalize your topic, check to see if you can find enough information.

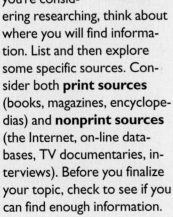

Visual Arts/History

2. Memorial

Maya Ying Lin was a 21-year-old architecture student when she submitted the winning design for the Vietnam Veterans Memorial in Washington, D.C.: two long black granite walls inscribed with the names of those who died in the war. With a partner, choose an important historic event that you want to portray. Then, create a poster, collage, exhibit, model, or drawing to memorialize the event. Display your work in a classroom mini-museum.

Supporting an Opinion

3. Objective? Subjective? Both?

Does Rosenthal carefully maintain the stance of an objective reporter, or do we know what his feelings are? Does he make judgments, or does he stick to reporting just the facts and his own observations? In a brief essay, tell whether you think Rosenthal's essay is an example of **objective** or **subjective** reporting—or some combination of both. Cite specific words, phrases, and sentences from the essay to support your view.

Elements of Literature

ESSAYS AND HISTORY: Thoughts and Reports

Though they dealt with real-life events, A. M. Rosenthal and Hanson W. Baldwin wrote two different kinds of nonfiction: "No News from Auschwitz" is an essay, and "R.M.S. *Titanic*" is a history.

Essays: Thinking on Paper

The personal **essay** is a younger genre (literary form) than history, biography, drama, or poetry. The personal essay was "born" in 1572, when a well-to-do Frenchman named Michel de Montaigne (män•tān′) retired from the practice of law, moved to his family's castle, and spent his time reading, thinking, writing, and enjoying himself. (Of course, a person who owns a family castle rarely has to worry about earning a living.)

Montaigne wrote short prose pieces on many different topics. He called them *essais* (French for "attempts" or "tries") because they were attempts to test his ideas and judgments on subjects that interested him.

Montaigne's essays were chatty, casual, and opinionated. They were also filled with digressions. The essays were written in the first person, but they weren't autobiographies because they weren't about Montaigne's life. They were about his thoughts—in fact, they *were* his thoughts.

Montaigne's success—and readers loved his three collections of *essais*—made the essay a popular form. In England, Francis Bacon took up the essayist's pen in 1597. Since then it's been used constantly.

Essays Today: From the Cosmos to Lost Socks

The subject matter of today's **personal** (or **informal**) **essays** is as wide as human experience—from the mysteries of the cosmos to the clothes dryer's habit of stealing and eating socks. The tone can range from somber, as in Rosenthal's essay on Auschwitz, to comic, as in essays by James Thurber, Dave Barry, and Erma Bombeck.

The Essayist's Art

Essayists take a particular subject—any subject—and examine it from different perspectives. It's like looking at an onion (or any other object) through a telescope, a microscope, and a kaleidoscope.

In "No News from Auschwitz" (page 410), for example, A. M. Rosenthal begins with what he sees at the gates: children playing, sun, grass, and trees. Then he moves deeper into Auschwitz and shows us the horrors visitors see and tells us how they feel. Though he doesn't state his insight directly, we know what he's telling us: We must not forget what happened there.

> "Every man has within himself the entire human condition."

Essays are thought journeys. "Every man has within himself the entire human condition," Montaigne once wrote. Essayists, writing about their own thoughts and feelings, touch us because they are writing about all of us.

History and Journalism: Reporting Information

Hanson W. Baldwin (page 390) isn't expressing his thoughts, his feelings, or his experiences. Baldwin is conveying information about events that he

by Richard Cohen

hasn't experienced directly.

Part of the job of historians and reporters is to distinguish facts from opinions. A **fact** is something that can be proved true; an **opinion** is a belief that can't be proved. It is a fact that the *Titanic* struck an iceberg on the night of April 14, 1912; it is an opinion that the tragedy was avoidable.

Seeking "the Truth"

Writing **history** and **informative articles** is a formidable task. Suppose you're updating a U.S. history textbook, and your assignment is to write about the 1990s in ten pages. How would you choose which events to include? How would you know what to say about them? Where would you begin?

Before historians and reporters begin to write, they must seek "the truth" in a wilderness of facts and opinions. Generally there are too few facts or too many opinions. William Shakespeare, for example, left us the world's greatest poetry and drama, yet he provided amazingly few facts about his life.

The opposite problem—too many facts—can confuse the researcher and make evaluation difficult. Who was to blame for the lives lost when the *Titanic* sank? Baldwin carefully provides us with facts so that we can answer this complex question for ourselves.

Luring the Reader

After spending countless hours in research—interviewing, reading, sorting, discarding, arranging, comparing, and summarizing—historians and reporters must evaluate and analyze the material they've collected. Is it true? Is it useful? How will it illuminate the story I'm telling?

Then they face the equally difficult job of selecting and presenting their material. More than two thousand people were on board the sinking *Titanic*. Baldwin had to decide which stories to tell, which details to include, and how to present them to give the reader a complete and realistic picture of the tragedy.

Nonfiction writers use all their skills, including storytelling techniques, to lure and hook readers who might otherwise be watching television, playing soccer, or talking on the telephone. The best nonfiction writers make us eyewitnesses to events that really happened.

"Truth," the old saying goes, "is stranger than fiction." The writers in this collection present true stories that are just as exciting and entertaining as the world's best novels, short stories, and plays.

What Readers Demand: One Writer's Opinion

Those of us who are trying to write well about the world we live in, or to teach students to write well about the world they live in, are caught in a time warp, where literature by definition consists of forms that were certified as "literary" in the 19th century: novels and short stories and poems. But in fact these have become quite rarefied forms in American life. The great preponderance of what writers now write and sell, what book and magazine publishers publish, and what readers demand is nonfiction.

—William Zinsser

Before You Read

INTO THIN AIR

Make the Connection

Hot Story, Cold Mountain

You're standing on the 29,028-foot top of the world. The temperature is bone-numbing. Your oxygen is almost gone. The climb up Everest was grueling, and now you face the dangerous trek down. Can you imagine that experience? Jon Krakauer, the writer of this magazine article, lived through it.

Quickwrite

Why do you think some people are drawn to climb mountains? Would you like to? Briefly jot down why or why not.

Elements of Literature

Imagery: What It Looks and Feels Like

Jon Krakauer takes us up Mt. Everest with him, shivering in icy winds, feeling numb fear in a blinding snow squall. It is **sensory images** that help us—safe in our chairs—feel that "we are there" in temperatures low enough to freeze flesh in minutes.

Sensory **details** are specific images that appeal to our senses of sight, hearing, smell, taste, and touch. Sensory details are especially important in descriptive writing.

Reading Skills and Strategies

Understanding Cause and Effect

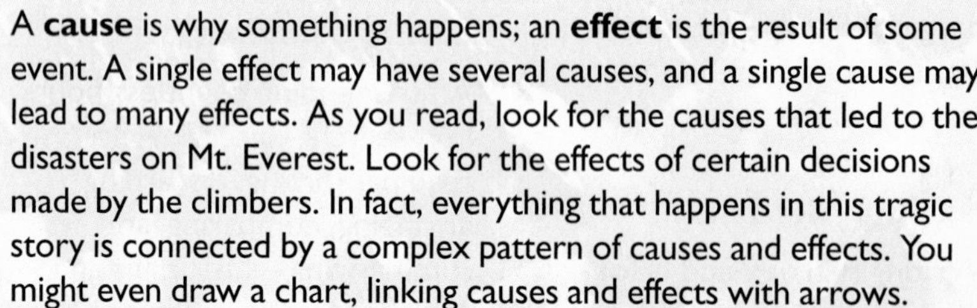

A **cause** is why something happens; an **effect** is the result of some event. A single effect may have several causes, and a single cause may lead to many effects. As you read, look for the causes that led to the disasters on Mt. Everest. Look for the effects of certain decisions made by the climbers. In fact, everything that happens in this tragic story is connected by a complex pattern of causes and effects. You might even draw a chart, linking causes and effects with arrows.

Background

The Top of the World

The man who said he wanted to climb Mt. Everest "because it's there," George Leigh Mallory, disappeared in a mist near the summit in 1924. The first recorded conquest of the 29,028-foot peak was achieved by Edmund Hillary of New Zealand and Tenzing Norgay of Nepal in 1953. Since then more than 600 climbers have reached the summit, but 150 have lost their lives to the mountain.

The journalist who wrote this true story barely escaped with his. In 1996, *Outside* magazine financed Jon Krakauer as a client on an Everest expedition. The day he reached the summit, eight other climbers (including Krakauer's tour leader) died on the mountain. (This is the riskiest form of **participatory journalism,** in which a reporter actually takes part in the events.)

Since the May 1996 tragedy, more and more people have caught Everest fever, some paying $70,000 for a guided climb. Although many of these climbers are experts, some are inexperienced—a problem that creates grave dangers.

Making a Climb

Everest expeditions ascend the mountain in stages. From Base Camp at 17,600 feet, they make short trips up and down to acclimatize, or get used to higher elevations. This process may last several weeks before the final climb to the top, which is also done in stages. Krakauer's group made camp at 19,500 feet, 21,300 feet, 24,000 feet, and 26,000 feet. The area above 25,000 feet is known as the Death Zone. Here, the air is so poor in oxygen it's almost impossible to make rational decisions. Yet even at Base Camp, symptoms of altitude sickness can occur, including headaches, dizziness, and inability to eat or sleep. Note: No helicopter rescue has ever been made above 19,860 feet.

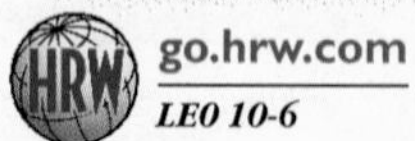

go.hrw.com
LEO 10-6

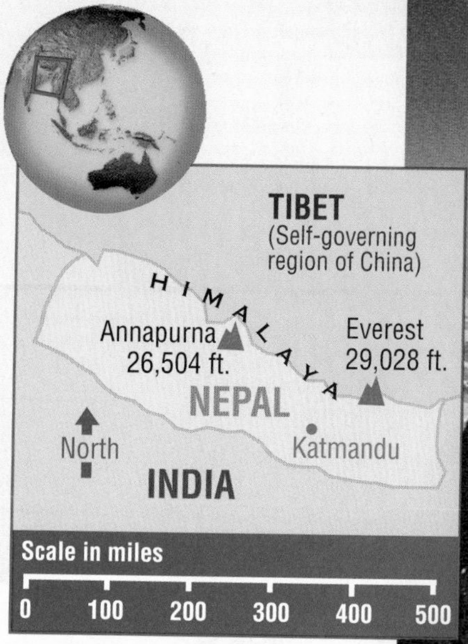

TIBET
(Self-governing region of China)
HIMALAYA
Annapurna 26,504 ft.
Everest 29,028 ft.
NEPAL
Katmandu
North
INDIA
Scale in miles
0 100 200 300 400 500

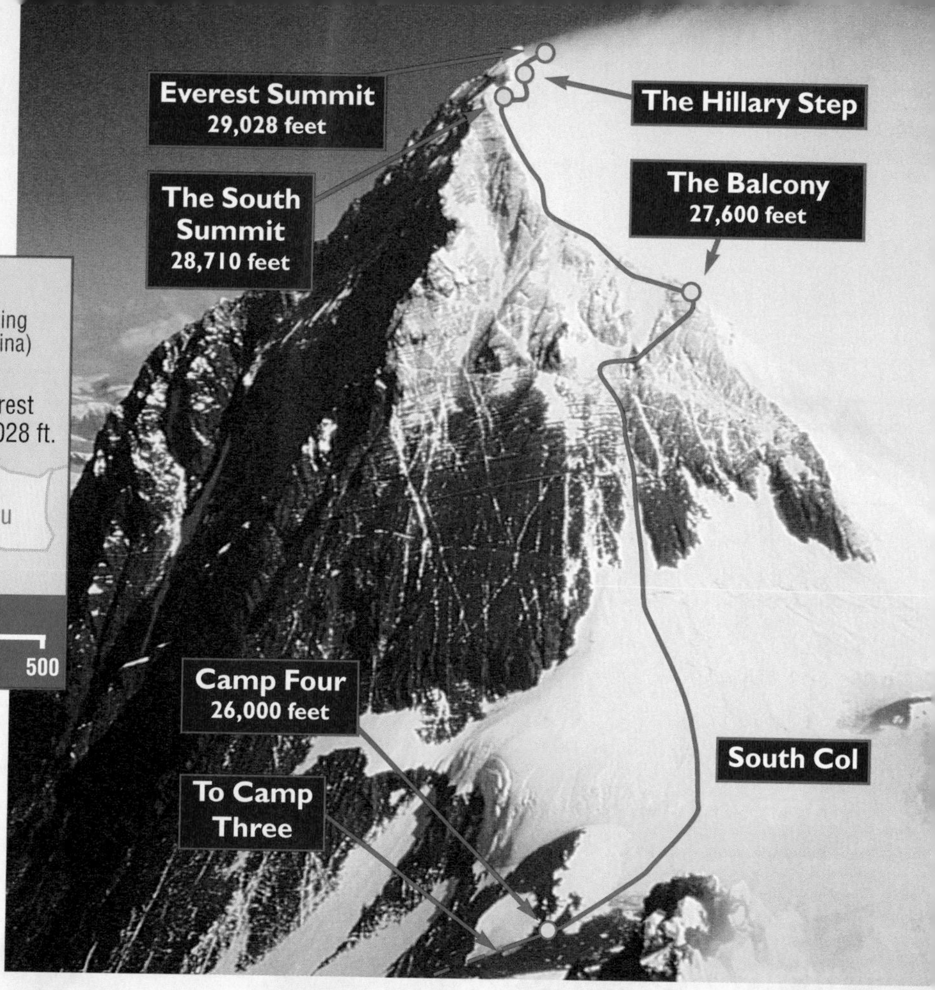

Everest Summit 29,028 feet
The Hillary Step
The South Summit 28,710 feet
The Balcony 27,600 feet
Camp Four 26,000 feet
South Col
To Camp Three

SOME OF THE CLIMBERS INVOLVED IN THE TRAGEDY

New Zealand-Based Team

① Rob Hall, *leader, head guide*
② Mike Groom, *guide*
③ Andy "Harold" Harris, *guide*
④ Doug Hansen, *client*
⑤ Jon Krakauer, *client, journalist*
⑥ Yasuko Namba, *client*
⑦ Beck Weathers, *client*
Lhakpa Chhiri Sherpa, *climbing Sherpa*

American-Based Team

Scott Fischer, *leader, head guide*
Anatoli Boukreev, *guide*

Taiwan Team

"Makalu" Gau Ming-Ho, *leader*

IMAX Film Crew

David Breashears, *leader, film director*
Ed Viesturs, *climber, film talent*

Members of Jon Krakauer's expedition team, led by Rob Hall. The numbers identify team members in the list of expedition members above.

from **Into**

Everest deals with trespassers harshly: The dead vanish beneath the snows, while the living struggle to explain what happened, and why. A survivor of the mountain's worst disaster examines the business of Mount Everest and the steep price of ambition.

Into Thin Air

Jon Krakauer

Straddling the top of the world, one foot in Tibet and the other in Nepal, I cleared the ice from my oxygen mask, hunched a shoulder against the wind, and stared absently at the vast sweep of earth below. I understood on some dim, detached level that it was a spectacular sight. I'd been fantasizing about this moment, and the release of emotion that would accompany it, for many months. But now that I was finally here, standing on the summit of Mount Everest, I just couldn't summon the energy to care.

It was the afternoon of May 10. I hadn't slept in 57 hours. The only food I'd been able to force down over the preceding three days was a bowl of Ramen soup and a handful of peanut M&M's. Weeks of violent coughing had left me with two separated ribs, making it excruciatingly painful to breathe. Twenty-nine thousand twenty-eight feet up in the troposphere, there was so little oxygen reaching my brain that my mental capacity was that of a slow child. Under the circumstances, I was incapable of feeling much of anything except cold and tired.

I'd arrived on the summit a few minutes after Anatoli Boukreev,[1] a Russian guide with an American expedition, and just ahead of Andy Harris, a guide with the New Zealand–based commercial team that I was a part of and someone with whom I'd grown to be friends during the last six weeks. I snapped four quick photos of Harris and Boukreev striking summit poses, and then turned and started down. My watch read 1:17 P.M. All told, I'd spent less than five minutes on the roof of the world.

After a few steps, I paused to take another photo, this one looking down the Southeast Ridge, the route we had ascended. Training my lens on a pair of climbers approaching the summit, I saw something that until that moment had escaped my attention. To the south, where the sky had been perfectly clear just an hour earlier, a blanket of clouds now hid Pumori, Ama Dablam, and the other lesser peaks surrounding Everest.

1. **Anatoli Boukreev:** Boukreev (pictured at left on Mt. Everest) was killed about a year and a half later, on December 26, 1997. He was trapped in an avalanche while climbing Annapurna, a mountain peak in the Himalayas.

Days later—after six bodies had been found, after a search for two others had been abandoned, after surgeons had amputated the gangrenous right hand of my teammate Beck Weathers—people would ask why, if the weather had begun to deteriorate, had climbers on the upper mountain not heeded the signs? Why did veteran Himalayan guides keep moving upward, leading a gaggle of amateurs, each of whom had paid as much as $65,000 to be ushered safely up Everest, into an apparent death trap?

Nobody can speak for the leaders of the two guided groups involved, for both men are now dead. But I can attest that nothing I saw early on the afternoon of May 10 suggested that a murderous storm was about to bear down on us. To my oxygen-depleted mind, the clouds drifting up the grand valley of ice known as the Western Cwm looked innocuous, wispy, insubstantial. Gleaming in the brilliant midday sun, they appeared no different from the harmless puffs of convection condensation that rose from the valley almost daily. As I began my descent, I was indeed anxious, but my concern had little to do with the weather. A check of the gauge on my oxygen tank had revealed that it was almost empty. I needed to get down, fast.

The uppermost shank of the Southeast Ridge is a slender, heavily corniced fin of rock and wind-scoured snow that snakes for a quarter-mile toward a secondary pinnacle known as the South Summit. Negotiating the serrated ridge presents few great technical hurdles, but the route is dreadfully exposed. After 15 minutes of cautious shuffling over a 7,000-foot abyss, I arrived at the notorious Hillary Step, a pronounced notch in the ridge named after Sir Edmund Hillary, the first Westerner to climb the mountain, and a spot that does require a fair amount of technical maneuvering. As I clipped into a fixed rope and prepared to rappel[2] over the lip, I was greeted by an alarming sight.

2. **rappel** (ra·pel′): descend a mountain by means of a double rope arranged around the climber's body so that he or she can control the slide downward.

Thirty feet below, some 20 people were queued up[3] at the base of the Step, and three climbers were hauling themselves up the rope that I was attempting to descend. I had no choice but to unclip from the line and step aside.

The traffic jam comprised climbers from three separate expeditions: the team I belonged to, a group of paying clients under the leadership of the celebrated New Zealand guide Rob Hall; another guided party headed by American Scott Fischer; and a nonguided team from Taiwan. Moving at the snail's pace that is the norm above 8,000 meters, the throng labored up the Hillary Step one by one, while I nervously bided my time.

Harris, who left the summit shortly after I did, soon pulled up behind me. Wanting to conserve whatever oxygen remained in my tank, I asked him to reach inside my backpack and turn off the valve on my regulator, which he did. For the next ten minutes I felt surprisingly good. My head cleared. I actually seemed less tired than with the gas turned on. Then, abruptly, I felt like I was suffocating. My vision dimmed and my head began to spin. I was on the brink of losing consciousness.

Instead of turning my oxygen off, Harris, in his hypoxically[4] impaired state, had mistakenly cranked the valve open to full flow, draining the tank. I'd just squandered the last of my gas going nowhere. There was another tank waiting for me at the South Summit, 250 feet below, but to get there I would have to descend the most exposed terrain on the entire route without benefit of supplemental oxygen.

But first I had to wait for the crowd to thin. I removed my now useless mask, planted my

3. **queued** (kyo͞od) **up:** lined up.
4. **hypoxically:** characterized by hypoxia, a condition resulting from a decrease in the oxygen reaching body tissues. Hypoxia is a common condition at very high altitudes.

Words to Own

deteriorate (dē·tir′ē·ə·rāt) *v.:* worsen.
innocuous (in·näk′yo͞o·əs) *adj.:* harmless.
notorious (nō·tôr′ē·əs) *adj.:* famous, usually in an unfavorable sense.

ice ax into the mountain's frozen hide, and hunkered on the ridge crest. As I exchanged banal congratulations with the climbers filing past, inwardly I was frantic: "Hurry it up, hurry it up!" I silently pleaded. "While you guys are messing around here, I'm losing brain cells by the millions!"

Most of the passing crowd belonged to Fischer's group, but near the back of the parade two of my teammates eventually appeared: Hall and Yasuko Namba. Girlish and reserved, the 47-year-old Namba was 40 minutes away from becoming the oldest woman to climb Everest and the second Japanese woman to reach the highest point on each continent, the so-called Seven Summits.

Later still, Doug Hansen—another member of our expedition, a postal worker from Seattle who had become my closest friend on the mountain—arrived atop the Step. "It's in the bag!" I yelled over the wind, trying to sound more upbeat than I felt. Plainly exhausted, Doug mumbled something from behind his oxygen mask that I didn't catch, shook my hand weakly, and continued plodding upward.

The last climber up the rope was Fischer, whom I knew casually from Seattle, where we both lived. His strength and drive were legendary—in 1994 he'd climbed Everest without using bottled oxygen—so I was surprised at how slowly he was moving and how hammered he looked when he pulled his mask aside to say hello. "Bruuuuuuce!" he wheezed with forced cheer, employing his trademark, fratboyish greeting. When I asked how he was doing, Fischer insisted he was feeling fine: "Just dragging a little today for some reason. No big deal." With the Hillary Step finally clear, I clipped into the strand of orange rope, swung quickly around Fischer as he slumped over his ice ax, and rappelled over the edge.

It was after 2:30 when I made it down to the South Summit. By now tendrils of mist were wrapping across the top of 27,890-foot Lhotse and lapping at Everest's summit pyramid. No longer did the weather look so benign. I grabbed a fresh oxygen cylinder, jammed it onto my regulator, and hurried down into the gathering cloud.

Four hundred vertical feet above, where the summit was still washed in bright sunlight under an immaculate cobalt sky, my compadres were dallying, memorializing their arrival at the apex of the planet with photos and high-fives—and using up precious ticks of the clock. None of them imagined that a horrible ordeal was drawing nigh. None of them suspected that by the end of that long day, every minute would matter. . . .

By the end of that long day, every minute would matter.

At 3 P.M., within minutes of leaving the South Summit, I descended into clouds ahead of the others. Snow started to fall. In the flat, diminishing light, it became hard to tell where the mountain ended and where the sky began. It would have been very easy to blunder off the edge of the ridge and never be heard from again. The lower I went, the worse the weather became.

When I reached the Balcony again, about 4 P.M., I encountered Beck Weathers standing alone, shivering violently. Years earlier, Weathers had undergone radial keratotomy to correct his vision. A side effect, which he discovered on Everest and consequently hid from Hall, was that in the low barometric pressure at high altitude, his eyesight failed. Nearly blind when he'd left Camp Four in the middle of the night but hopeful that his vision would improve at daybreak, he stuck close to the person in front of him and kept climbing.

Upon reaching the Southeast Ridge shortly after sunrise, Weathers had confessed to Hall that he was having trouble seeing, at which point Hall declared, "Sorry, pal, you're going

---

WORDS TO OWN

benign (bi·nīn′) *adj.:* here, favorable or harmless.
apex (ā′peks′) *n.:* highest point; top.

---

down. I'll send one of the Sherpas[5] with you." Weathers countered that his vision was likely to improve as soon as the sun crept higher in the sky; Hall said he'd give Weathers 30 minutes to find out—after that, he'd have to wait there at 27,500 feet for Hall and the rest of the group to come back down. Hall didn't want Weathers descending alone. "I'm dead serious about this," Hall admonished his client. "Promise me that you'll sit right here until I return."

"I crossed my heart and hoped to die," Weathers recalls now, "and promised I wouldn't go anywhere." Shortly after noon, Hutchison, Taske, and Kasischke[6] passed by with their Sherpa escorts, but Weathers elected not to accompany them. "The weather was still good," he explains, "and I saw no reason to break my promise to Rob."

By the time I encountered Weathers, however, conditions were turning ugly. "Come down with me," I implored, "I'll get you down, no problem." He was nearly convinced, until I made the mistake of mentioning that Groom was on his way down, too. In a day of many mistakes, this would turn out to be a crucial one. "Thanks anyway," Weathers said. "I'll just wait for Mike. He's got a rope; he'll be able to short-rope[7] me." Secretly relieved, I hurried toward the South Col, 1,500 feet below.

These lower slopes proved to be the most difficult part of the descent. Six inches of powder snow blanketed outcroppings of loose shale. Climbing down them demanded unceasing concentration, an all but impossible feat in my current state. By 5:30, however, I was finally within 200 vertical feet of Camp Four, and only one obstacle stood between me and safety: a steep bulge of rock-hard ice that I'd have to descend without a rope. But the weather had deteriorated into a full-scale blizzard. Snow pellets born on 70-mph winds stung my face; any exposed skin was instantly frozen. The tents, no more than 200 horizontal yards away, were only intermittently visible through the whiteout. There was zero margin for error. Worried about making a critical blunder, I sat down to marshal my energy.

Suddenly, Harris[8] appeared out of the gloom and sat beside me. At this point there was no mistaking that he was in appalling shape. His cheeks were coated with an armor of frost, one

5. **Sherpas:** A Tibetan people living on the southern slopes of the Himalayas. As experienced mountain climbers, the Sherpas are hired by expeditions to haul loads and set up camps and ropes.
6. Stuart Hutchison, Dr. John Taske, and Lou Kasischke were three clients on Rob Hall's team.

7. **short-rope:** assist a weak or injured climber by hauling him or her.
8. After writing this article, Krakauer discovered through conversations with Martin Adams (a client from Scott Fischer's team) that the person he thought was Harris was, in fact, Martin Adams.

Words to Own

crucial (krōō'shəl) *adj.:* extremely important; decisive.

Doug Hansen approaching the summit.

eye was frozen shut, and his speech was slurred. He was frantic to reach the tents. After briefly discussing the best way to negotiate the ice, Harris started scooting down on his butt, facing forward. "Andy," I yelled after him, "it's crazy to try it like that!" He yelled something back, but the words were carried off by the screaming wind. A second later he lost his purchase[9] and was rocketing down on his back.

Two hundred feet below, I could make out Harris's motionless form. I was sure he'd broken at least a leg, maybe his neck. But then he stood up, waved that he was OK, and started stumbling toward camp, which was for the moment in plain sight, 150 yards beyond.

I could see three or four people shining lights outside the tents. I watched Harris walk across the flats to the edge of camp, a distance he covered in less than ten minutes. When the clouds closed in a moment later, cutting off my view, he was within 30 yards of the tents. I didn't see him again after that, but I was certain that he'd reached the security of camp, where Sherpas would be waiting with hot tea. Sitting out in the storm, with the ice bulge still standing between me and the tents, I felt a pang of envy. I was angry that my guide hadn't waited for me.

Twenty minutes later I was in camp. I fell into my tent with my crampons still on, zipped the door tight, and sprawled across the frost-covered floor. I was drained, more exhausted than I'd ever been in my life. But I was safe. Andy was safe. The others would be coming into camp soon. We'd done it. We'd climbed Mount Everest.

It would be many hours before I learned that everyone had in fact not made it back to camp—that one teammate was already dead and that 23 other men and women were caught in a desperate struggle for their lives. . . .

Meanwhile, Hall and Hansen were still on the frightfully exposed summit ridge, engaged in a grim struggle of their own. The 46-year-old Hansen, whom Hall had turned back just below this spot exactly a year ago, had been determined to bag the summit this time around. "I want to get this thing done and out of my life," he'd told me a couple of days earlier. "I don't want to have to come back here."

Indeed Hansen had reached the top this time, though not until after 3 P.M., well after Hall's predetermined turnaround time. Given Hall's conservative, systematic nature, many people wonder why he didn't turn Hansen around when it became obvious that he was running late. It's not far-fetched to speculate that because Hall had talked Hansen into coming back to Everest this year, it would have been especially hard for him to deny Hansen the summit a second time—especially when all of Fischer's clients were still marching blithely toward the top.

"It's very difficult to turn someone around high on the mountain," cautions Guy Cotter, a New Zealand guide who summited Everest with Hall in 1992 and was guiding the peak for him in 1995 when Hansen made his first attempt. "If a client sees that the summit is close and they're dead set on getting there, they're going to laugh in your face and keep going up."

In any case, for whatever reason, Hall did not turn Hansen around. Instead, after reaching the summit at 2:10 P.M., Hall waited for more than an hour for Hansen to arrive and then headed down with him. Soon after they began their descent, just below the top, Hansen apparently ran out of oxygen and collapsed. "Pretty much the same thing happened to Doug in '95," says Ed Viesturs, an American who guided the peak for Hall that year. "He was fine during the ascent, but as soon as he started down he lost it mentally and physically. He turned into a real zombie, like he'd used everything up."

At 4:31 P.M., Hall radioed Base Camp to say that he and Hansen were above the Hillary Step and urgently needed oxygen. Two full bottles were waiting for them at the South Summit; if Hall had known this he could have retrieved the gas fairly quickly and then climbed back up to give Hansen a fresh tank. But Harris, in the throes of his

9. **purchase:** firm hold.

WORDS TO OWN

speculate (spek′yo͞o·lāt′) *v.:* think; guess.

oxygen-starved dementia,[10] overheard the 4:31 radio call while descending the Southeast Ridge and broke in to tell Hall that all the bottles at the South Summit were empty. So Hall stayed with Hansen and tried to bring the helpless client down without oxygen, but could get him no farther than the top of the Hillary Step.

Cotter, a very close friend of both Hall and Harris, happened to be a few miles from Everest Base Camp at the time, guiding an expedition on Pumori. Overhearing the radio conversations between Hall and Base Camp, he called Hall at 5:36 and again at 5:57, urging his mate to leave Hansen and come down alone. . . . Hall, however, wouldn't consider going down without Hansen.

There was no further word from Hall until the middle of the night. At 2:46 A.M. on May 11, Cotter woke up to hear a long, broken transmission, probably unintended: Hall was wearing a remote microphone clipped to the shoulder strap of his backpack, which was occasionally keyed on by mistake. In this instance, says Cotter, "I suspect Rob didn't even know he was transmitting. I could hear someone yelling—it might have been Rob, but I couldn't be sure because the wind was so loud in the background. He was saying something like 'Keep moving! Keep going!' presumably to Doug, urging him on."

If that was indeed the case, it meant that in the wee hours of the morning Hall and Hansen were still struggling from the Hillary Step toward the South Summit, taking more than 12 hours to traverse a stretch of ridge typically covered by descending climbers in half an hour.

Hall's next call to Base Camp was at 4:43 A.M. He'd finally reached the South Summit but was unable to descend farther, and in a series of transmissions over the next two hours he sounded confused and irrational. "Harold[11] was with me last night," Hall insisted, when in fact Harris had reached the South Col at sunset. "But he doesn't seem to be with me now. He was very weak."

Mackenzie[12] asked him how Hansen was doing. "Doug," Hall replied, "is gone." That was all he said, and it was the last mention he ever made of Hansen.

On May 23, when Breashears and Viesturs, of the IMAX team,[13] reached the summit, they found no sign of Hansen's body but they did find an ice ax planted about 50 feet below the Hillary Step, along a highly exposed section of ridge where the fixed ropes came to an end. It is quite possible that Hall managed to get Hansen down the ropes to this point, only to have him lose his footing and fall 7,000 feet down the sheer Southwest Face, leaving his ice ax jammed into the ridge crest where he slipped.

During the radio calls to Base Camp early on May 11, Hall revealed that something was wrong with his legs, that he was no longer able to walk and was shaking uncontrollably. This was very disturbing news to the people down below, but it was amazing that Hall was even alive after spending a night without shelter or oxygen at 28,700 feet in hurricane-force wind and minus-100-degree windchill.

At 5 A.M., Base Camp patched through a call on the satellite telephone to Jan Arnold, Hall's wife, seven months pregnant with their first child in Christchurch, New Zealand. Arnold, a respected physician, had summited Everest with Hall in 1993 and entertained no illusions about the gravity of her husband's predicament. "My heart really sank when I heard his voice," she recalls. "He was slurring his words markedly. He sounded like Major Tom[14] or something, like he was just floating away. I'd been up there; I knew what it could be like in bad weather. Rob and I had talked about the

10. **dementia** (di·men′shə): mental impairment; madness.

11. **Harold:** Andy Harris's nickname.

12. **Mackenzie:** Dr. Caroline Mackenzie was Base Camp doctor for Rob Hall's team.

13. **IMAX team:** Another team of climbers, who were shooting a $5.5 million giant-screen movie about Mt. Everest. The movie was released in 1998.

14. **Major Tom:** refers to the song "Space Oddity" by David Bowie about an astronaut, Major Tom, who is lost and floating in space.

WORDS TO OWN

traverse (trə·vurs′) *v.:* cross.

impossibility of being rescued from the summit ridge. As he himself had put it, 'You might as well be on the moon.' "

By that time, Hall had located two full oxygen bottles, and after struggling for four hours trying to de-ice his mask, around 8:30 A.M. he finally started breathing the life-sustaining gas. Several times he announced that he was preparing to descend, only to change his mind and remain at the South Summit. The day had started out sunny and clear, but the wind remained fierce, and by late morning the upper mountain was wrapped with thick clouds. Climbers at Camp Two reported that the wind over the summit sounded like a squadron of 747s, even from 8,000 feet below. . . .

Throughout that day, Hall's friends begged him to make an effort to descend from the South Summit under his own power. At 3:20 P.M., after one such transmission from Cotter, Hall began to sound annoyed. "Look," he said, "if I thought I could manage the knots on the fixed ropes with me frostbitten hands, I would have gone down six hours ago, pal. Just send a couple of the boys up with a big thermos of something hot—then I'll be fine."

At 6:20 P.M., Hall was patched through a second time to Arnold in Christchurch. "Hi, my sweetheart," he said in a slow, painfully distorted voice. "I hope you're tucked up in a nice warm bed. How are you doing?"

"I can't tell you how much I'm thinking about you!" Arnold replied. "You sound so much better than I expected. . . . Are you warm, my darling?"

"In the context of the altitude, the setting, I'm reasonably comfortable," Hall answered, doing his best not to alarm her.

"How are your feet?"

"I haven't taken me boots off to check, but I think I may have a bit of frostbite."

Guide Rob Hall.

"I'm looking forward to making you completely better when you come home," said Arnold. "I just know you're going to be rescued. Don't feel that you're alone. I'm sending all my positive energy your way!" Before signing off, Hall told his wife, "I love you. Sleep well, my sweetheart. Please don't worry too much."

These would be the last words anyone would hear him utter. Attempts to make radio contact with Hall later that night and the next day went unanswered. Twelve days later, when Breashears and Viesturs climbed over the South Summit on their way to the top, they found Hall lying on his right side in a shallow ice-hollow, his upper body buried beneath a drift of snow.

Early on the morning of May 11, when I returned to Camp Four, Hutchison, standing in for Groom, who was unconscious in his tent, organized a team of four Sherpas to locate the bodies of our teammates Weathers and Namba. The Sherpa search party, headed by Lhakpa Chhiri, departed ahead of Hutchison, who was so exhausted and befuddled that he forgot to put his boots on and left camp in his light, smooth-soled liners. Only when Lhakpa Chhiri pointed out the blunder did Hutchison return for his boots. Following Boukreev's directions, the Sherpas had no trouble locating the two bodies at the edge of the Kangshung Face.

The first body turned out to be Namba, but Hutchison couldn't tell who it was until he knelt in the howling wind and chipped a three-inch-thick carapace of ice from her face. To his shock, he discovered that she was still breathing. Both her gloves were gone, and her bare hands appeared to be frozen solid. Her eyes were dilated. The skin on her face was the color of porcelain. "It was terrible," Hutchison recalls. "I was overwhelmed. She was very near death. I didn't know what to do."

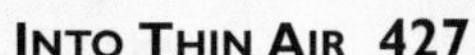

He turned his attention to Weathers, who lay 20 feet away. His face was also caked with a thick armor of frost. Balls of ice the size of grapes were matted to his hair and eyelids. After cleaning the frozen detritus from his face, Hutchison discovered that he, too, was still alive: "Beck was mumbling something, I think, but I couldn't tell what he was trying to say. His right glove was missing and he had terrible frostbite. He was as close to death as a person can be and still be breathing."

Badly shaken, Hutchison went over to the Sherpas and asked Lhakpa Chhiri's advice. Lhakpa Chhiri, an Everest veteran respected by Sherpas and sahibs[15] alike for his mountain savvy, urged Hutchison to leave Weathers and Namba where they lay. Even if they survived long enough to be dragged back to Camp Four, they would certainly die before they could be carried down to Base Camp, and attempting a rescue would needlessly jeopardize the lives of the other climbers on the Col, most of whom were going to have enough trouble getting themselves down safely.

He was as close to death as a person can be and still be breathing.

Hutchison decided that Chhiri was right. There was only one choice, however difficult: Let nature take its inevitable course with Weathers and Namba, and save the group's resources for those who could actually be helped. It was a classic act of triage.[16] When Hutchison returned to camp at 8:30 A.M. and told the rest of us of his decision, nobody doubted that it was the correct thing to do.

Later that day a rescue team headed by two of Everest's most experienced guides, Pete Athans and Todd Burleson, who were on the mountain with their own clients, arrived at Camp Four. Burleson was standing outside the tents about 4:30 P.M. when he noticed someone lurching slowly toward camp. The person's bare right hand, naked to the wind and horribly frostbitten, was outstretched in a weird, frozen salute. Whoever it was reminded Athans of a mummy in a low-budget horror film. The mummy turned out to be none other than Beck Weathers, somehow risen from the dead.

A couple of hours earlier, a light must have gone on in the reptilian core of Weathers' comatose brain, and he regained consciousness. "Initially I thought I was in a dream," he recalls. "Then I saw how badly frozen my right hand was, and that helped bring me around to reality. Finally I woke up enough to recognize that the cavalry wasn't coming so I better do something about it myself."

Although Weathers was blind in his right eye and able to focus his left eye within a radius of only three or four feet, he started walking into the teeth of the wind, deducing correctly that camp lay in that direction. If he'd been wrong he would have stumbled immediately down the Kangshung Face, the edge of which was a few yards in the opposite direction. Ninety minutes later he encountered "some unnaturally smooth, bluish-looking rocks," which turned out to be the tents of Camp Four.

The next morning, May 12, Athans, Burleson, and climbers from the IMAX team short-roped Weathers down to Camp Two. On the morning of May 13, in a hazardous helicopter rescue, Weathers and Gau[17] were evacuated from the top of the icefall by Lieutenant Colonel Madan Khatri Chhetri of the Nepalese army. A month later, a team of Dallas surgeons would amputate Weather's dead right hand just below the wrist and use skin grafts to reconstruct his left hand.

After helping to load Weathers and Gau into the rescue chopper, I sat in the snow for a long while, staring at my boots, trying to get some

15. **sahibs** (sä′ibz′): term used by Sherpas to refer to the paying members of the expeditions.
16. **triage** (trē·äzh′): assigning of priorities of medical care based on chances for survival.

17. **Gau:** "Makalu" Gau Ming-Ho, leader of the Taiwanese National Expedition, another team climbing on Everest.

WORDS TO OWN

jeopardize (jep′ər·dīz′) *v.:* endanger.

grip, however tenuous, on what had happened over the preceding 72 hours. Then, nervous as a cat, I headed down into the icefall for one last trip through the maze of decaying seracs.[18]

I'd always known, in the abstract, that climbing mountains was a dangerous pursuit. But until I climbed in the Himalayas this spring, I'd never actually seen death at close range. And there was so much of it: Including three members of an Indo-Tibetan team who died on the north side just below the summit in the same May 10 storm and an Austrian killed some days later, 11 men and women lost their lives on Everest in May 1996, a tie with 1982 for the worst single-season death toll in the peak's history. . . .[19]

18. seracs: pointed masses of ice.
19. It actually was the worst death toll on record. After Krakauer wrote this article, a twelfth death was discovered.

Climbing mountains will never be a safe, predictable, rule-bound enterprise. It is an activity that idealizes risk-taking; its most celebrated figures have always been those who stuck their necks out the farthest and managed to get away with it. Climbers, as a species, are simply not distinguished by an excess of common sense. And that holds especially true for Everest climbers: When presented with a chance to reach the planet's highest summit, people are surprisingly quick to abandon prudence altogether. "Eventually," warns Tom Hornbein, 33 years after his ascent of the West Ridge, "what happened on Everest this season is certain to happen again."

WORDS TO OWN
tenuous (ten′yo͞o·əs) *adj.:* weak, slight.

MEET THE WRITER

Journalist Climber

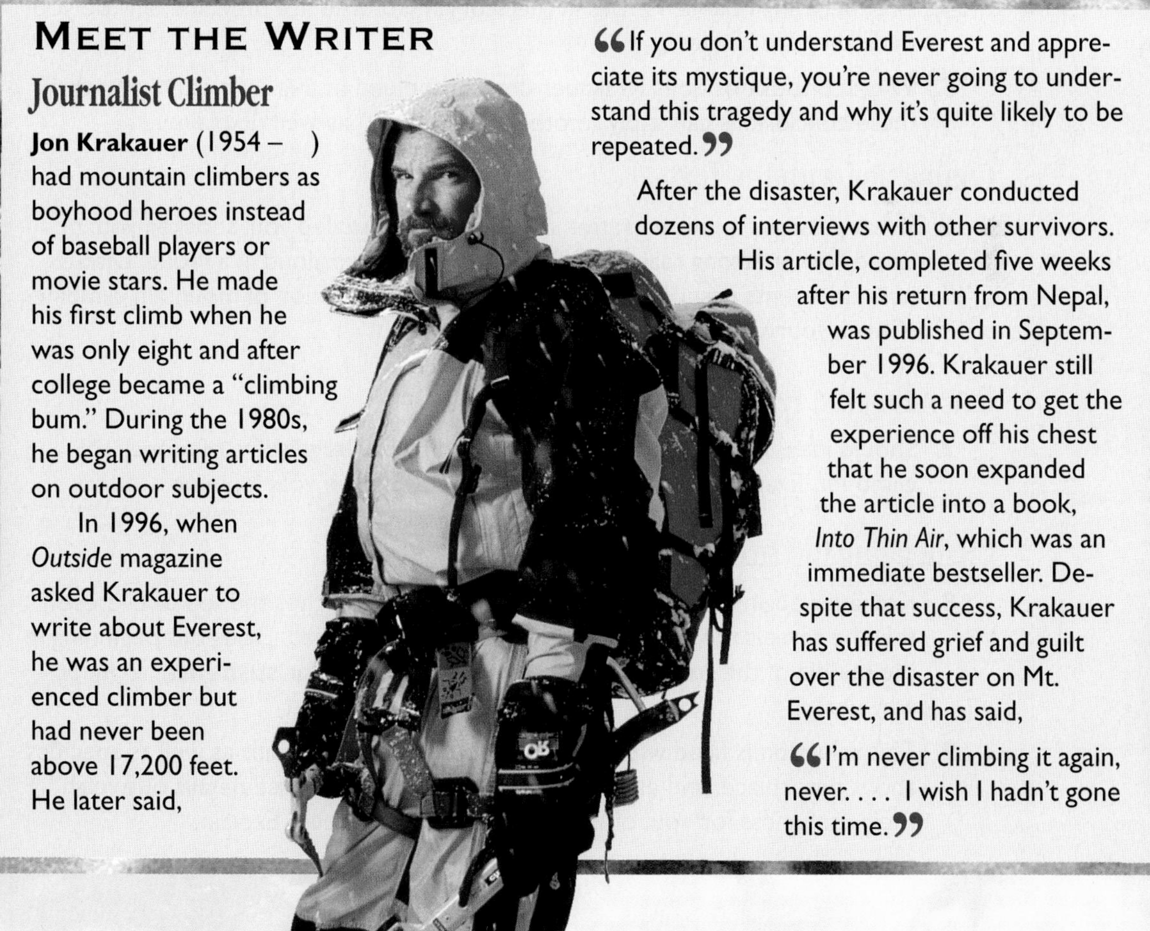

Jon Krakauer (1954–) had mountain climbers as boyhood heroes instead of baseball players or movie stars. He made his first climb when he was only eight and after college became a "climbing bum." During the 1980s, he began writing articles on outdoor subjects.

In 1996, when *Outside* magazine asked Krakauer to write about Everest, he was an experienced climber but had never been above 17,200 feet. He later said,

“If you don't understand Everest and appreciate its mystique, you're never going to understand this tragedy and why it's quite likely to be repeated.”

After the disaster, Krakauer conducted dozens of interviews with other survivors. His article, completed five weeks after his return from Nepal, was published in September 1996. Krakauer still felt such a need to get the experience off his chest that he soon expanded the article into a book, *Into Thin Air*, which was an immediate bestseller. Despite that success, Krakauer has suffered grief and guilt over the disaster on Mt. Everest, and has said,

“I'm never climbing it again, never. . . . I wish I hadn't gone this time.”

Making Meanings

First Thoughts

1. Which person in this true story did you sympathize with most? Why?

Reading Check

Make a list of the **main events** in this Everest story. Then, circle the events in which Krakauer or other climbers were in grave danger. Tell the outcome of each circled event.

Shaping Interpretations

2. Which **sensory details** in Krakauer's descriptions have remained most vivid in your memory after reading the article? Why?

3. Choose one tragedy that happened on the mountain—for example, the death of Rob Hall or Doug Hansen or the loss of Beck Weathers's right hand. Draw a **cause-and-effect diagram** similar to the one below to show the complex causes that led to the tragedy.

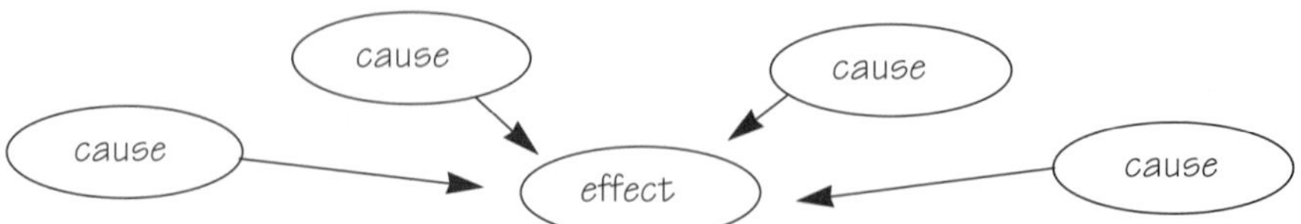

4. Are there any real-life heroes in this story? If so, who are they, and why do you think they are heroes?

5. What conclusions does Krakauer draw at the end of this article? Do you think these conclusions can apply to other "risk takers" as well? Explain.

Connecting with the Text

6. What passages in this narrative impressed you, puzzled you, shocked you, or caused other strong reactions? Read those passages aloud in a group. Discuss how the events described affected your previous opinion of mountain climbing. (Check your Quickwrite notes.)

Extending the Text

7. Should inexperienced climbers be allowed to pay large sums of money to climb Mt. Everest, or should they be barred? Explain your opinion.

Challenging the Text

8. Krakauer begins his article at the point when he reaches the top of Everest; then he reveals the nature of the tragedy that occurred. Does this beginning in the middle of the story spoil the element of surprise or **suspense**? Why or why not?

9. This selection is filled with technical mountaineering details as well as specifics about time, place, and elevation. Did the difficulty of these details outweigh their usefulness for you, or did they enhance the piece? Explain.

CHOICES: Building Your Portfolio

Writer's Notebook

1. Collecting Ideas for a Research Paper

Taking notes. In the midst of his ordeal while he was fighting to save his life, Krakauer continued to take notes in his spiral notebooks. (It was too cold for a tape recorder.) As you collect information on the topic you've chosen for your research paper (for the Writer's Workshop on page 448), take notes in a notebook or on cards. Be sure to record direct quotations exactly and to cite the sources of all facts, statistics, quotes, and paraphrases.

WORK IN PROGRESS

K. hadn't slept in 57 hrs., had only eaten bowl of soup & handful of peanut M & M's ("Into Thin Air," p. 421).

29,028 feet reduces 'mental capacity" to "that of a slow child" ("Air," same page).

Debate

2. To Climb or Not?

With a small group of classmates, debate one of these questions: (a) *Is mountain climbing a foolhardy risk of life and limb, or a worthwhile adventure?* (b) *Should people pursuing dangerous sports or hobbies have to pass a test or be licensed?* Base your views on evidence as well as on personal feelings. If you focus on mountain climbing, you might want to read more of the book *Into Thin Air.*

Research/ Oral Presentation

3. Inquiring Minds

Had you ever heard of the Seven Summits before? or hypoxia? What do you know about Nepal and Tibet? What gear do you need to go mountain climbing? These are only a few of the many topics suggested by Krakauer's article that curious minds might want to investigate. Pick a topic that interests you and one or two partners. Draw up a list of research questions, and begin your investigation. Check the library, the Internet and databases, and experts, if you can. Report your findings to the class in an **oral presentation** using visuals or props or even demonstrations.

Descriptive Essay

4. What "Pulls" You?

About his decision to climb Everest, Krakauer said, "I'd had this secret desire to climb Everest that never left me from the time I was nine." Do you have something that "pulls" you, that you are passionate about? Maybe it's a sport, or music, or a hobby. In a brief essay, describe your "passion" in a way that communicates your love for your topic. Elaborate with specific **sensory details** that paint a clear "you are there" picture for readers.

Creative Writing/Media

5. Camera! Action!

Krakauer's story would make a good movie and, indeed, a film of his book was made for television. Pick a section from this selection, and work with a small group to write a movie script for the scene. Pick up dialogue that's there. You might even add some dialogue (be sure it sounds realistic) if you feel the scene needs expansion. Include camera and stage directions and notes about the setting (visual and sound effects) and characters (including costumes). Note: You'll find an example of a movie script on page 683.

LANGUAGE LINK MINI-LESSON

Technical Vocabulary—Widgets, Whatsits, Thingamajigs

If you are a football fan, you know the meaning of *touchdown*, *off-tackle*, and *scrimmage*. Before reading "Into Thin Air," did you know the meaning of *rappel* and *short-rope?*

"As I clipped into a fixed rope and prepared to rappel over the lip, . . ." (page 422)

"He's got a rope; he'll be able to short-rope me." (page 424)

Almost every kind of work or play has its own special **technical vocabulary**, or **jargon**. When writers cover a technical subject for a general audience, they must use technical terms in a way that readers will understand. Usually that means including **context clues** that will help the reader guess the meaning. Writers may also provide footnotes. (In fact, check the context clues and footnotes for *rappel* and *short-rope*. Could you explain the words to a friend?)

Try It Out

1. Find at least three technical terms in "Into Thin Air" that are not defined in footnotes. (They may be mountain climbing, scientific, or medical terms.) With a partner, use context clues to guess the meaning of each term. Check your guesses in a dictionary.
2. Write a list of technical terms for any field that you know well. Choose the most obscure term, and write a sentence using context clues that would enable a reader to understand the term.

➤ As you write your research paper (page 448), make sure that you include context clues for any technical terms you use.

VOCABULARY HOW TO OWN A WORD

WORD BANK

deteriorate
innocuous
notorious
benign
apex
crucial
speculate
traverse
jeopardize
tenuous

Analogies

In an **analogy** the words in one pair relate to each other in the same way as the words in a second pair. Fill in each blank below with the word from the Word Bank that best completes the analogy. (Two words on the list are synonyms; they may be used interchangeably.) Analogies are sometimes written like this: *base: bottom:: ________: top*

1. *Base* is to *bottom* as __________ is to *top*.
2. *Safe* is to *dangerous* as __________ is to *harmful*.
3. *Mislead* is to *deceive* as __________ is to *endanger*.
4. *Trivial* is to *minor* as __________ is to *important*.
5. *Try* is to *attempt* as __________ is to *guess*.
6. *Minor* is to *major* as __________ is to *malignant*.
7. *Famous* is to *star* as __________ is to *criminal*.
8. *Weaken* is to *strengthen* as __________ is to *improve*.
9. *Climb* is to *stairs* as __________ is to *bridge*.
10. *Strong* is to *powerful* as __________ is to *weak*.

Before You Read

A Presentation of Whales

Make the Connection

To the Rescue!

Suppose you are walking on a beach on a gray, windy day. You climb over a rocky ledge, and suddenly you are part of the scene in the photo below. How would you react?

Some people rise to such an occasion; some shrink from it; some just keep shooting videotape. Being on the scene of a disaster can bring out unexpected qualities in people. This report about rescuing whales is a sad story without a clear or simple moral. What would you have done if you'd been there?

Reading Skills and Strategies

Dialogue with the Text

Use a **KWL chart** to organize information about this report. KWL means "what I *know,* what I *want to know,* what I've *learned.*" In the K (for *know*) column, write what you know about whales, especially beached whales. In the W column, write a few things you'd like to learn about whales. You'll fill in the L column after you read the report.

K	W	L

Elements of Literature

Ordering Information

You don't usually skip through a text. You start at the beginning and (unless you jump ahead—risking the loss of important information) follow the sequence in which the writer has chosen to present information. In this report, Barry Lopez uses the familiar order of narrative writing: **chronological order,** the sequence in which events occur. "A Presentation of Whales" starts on a Saturday and ends the following Wednesday. See if you can find places where Lopez interrupts the chronological order, and try to figure out why he does so.

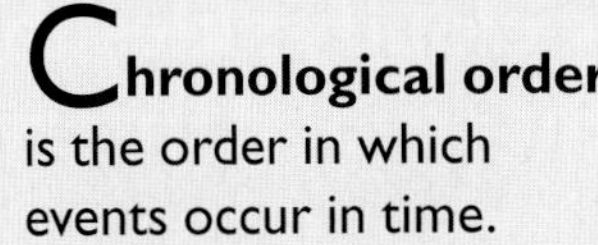

Chronological order is the order in which events occur in time.

Why did they come ashore?

go.hrw.com

LEO 10-6

A Presentation of Whales

Barry Lopez

On that section of the central Oregon coast on the evening of June 16, 1979, gentle winds were blowing onshore from the southwest. It was fifty-eight degrees. Under partly cloudy skies the sea was running with four-foot swells at eight-second intervals. Moderately rough. State police cadets Jim Clark and Steve Bennett stood at the precipitous edge of a foredune a few miles south of the town of Florence, peering skeptically into the dimness over a flat, gently sloping beach. Near the water's edge they could make out a line of dark shapes, and what they had taken for a practical joke, the

---

Words to Own

precipitous (prē·sip′ə·təs) *adj.:* steep.

Near the water's edge they could make out a line of dark shapes . . .

exaggeration a few moments before of a man and a woman in a brown Dodge van with a broken headlight, now sank in for the truth.

Clark made a hasty, inaccurate count and plunged with Bennett down the back of the dune to their four-wheel-drive. Minutes before, they had heard the voice of Corporal Terry Crawford over the radio; they knew he was patrolling in Florence. Rather than call him, they drove the six miles into town and parked across the street from where he was issuing a citation to someone for excessive noise. When Crawford had finished, Clark went over and told him what they had seen. Crawford drove straight to the Florence State Police office and phoned his superiors in Newport, forty-eight miles up the coast. At that point the news went out over police radios: thirty-six large whales, stranded and apparently still alive, were on the beach a mile south of the mouth of the Siuslaw River.

There were, in fact, forty-one whales—twenty-eight females and thirteen males, at least one of them dying or already dead. There had never been a stranding quite like it. It was first assumed that they were gray whales, common along the coast, but they were sperm whales: *Physeter catodon.* Deep-ocean dwellers. They ranged in age from ten to fifty-six and in length from thirty to thirty-eight feet. They were apparently headed north when they beached around 7:30 P.M. on an ebbing high tide.

The information shot inland by phone, crossing the Coast Range to radio and television stations in the more populous interior of Oregon, in a highly charged form: giant whales stranded on a public beach accessible by paved road on a Saturday night, still alive. Radio announcers urged listeners to head for the coast to "save the whales." In Eugene and Portland, Greenpeace volunteers, already alerted by the police, were busy throwing sheets and blankets into their cars. They would soak them in the ocean, to cool the whales.

The news moved as quickly through private homes and taverns on the central Oregon coast, passed by people monitoring the police bands. In addition to phoning Greenpeace—an international organization with a special interest in protecting marine mammals—the police contacted the Oregon State University Marine Science Center in South Beach near Newport, and the Oregon Institute of Marine Biology in Charleston, fifty-eight miles south of Florence. Bruce Mate, a marine mammalogist at the OSU Center, phoned members of the Northwest Regional [Stranding] Alert Network and people in Washington, D.C.

By midnight, the curious and the awed were crowded on the beach, cutting the night with flashlights. Drunks, ignoring the whales' sudden thrashing, were trying to walk up and down on their backs. A collie barked incessantly; flash cubes burst at the huge, dark forms. Two men inquired about reserving some of the teeth, for scrimshaw.[1] A federal agent asked police to move people back, and the first mention of disease was in the air. Scientists arrived with specimen bags and rubber gloves and fishing knives. Greenpeace members, one dressed in a bright orange flight suit, came with a large banner. A man burdened with a television camera labored over the foredune after them. They wished to tie a rope to one whale's flukes,[2] to drag it back into the ocean. The police began to congregate with the scientists, looking for a rationale to control the incident.

In the intensifying confusion, as troopers motioned onlookers back (to "restrain the common herd of unqualified mankind," wrote one man later in an angry letter-to-the-editor), the thinking was that, somehow, the whales might be saved. Neal Langbehn, a federal protection officer with the National Marine Fisheries Service, denied permission to one scientist to begin removing teeth and taking blood samples. In his report later he would write: "It was my feeling that the whales should be given their best chance to survive."

This hope was soon deemed futile, as it had appeared to most of the scientists from the beginning—the animals were hemorrhaging[3] under the crushing weight of their own flesh

1. **scrimshaw:** intricate decoration and carving, usually done on whales' teeth and bones.
2. **flukes:** lobes of a whale's tail.
3. **hemorrhaging** (hem′ər·ij·iŋ′): bleeding heavily.

and were beginning to suffer irreversible damage from heat exhaustion. The scientific task became one of securing as much data as possible.

As dawn bloomed along the eastern sky, people who had driven recreational vehicles illegally over the dunes and onto the beach were issued citations and turned back. Troopers continued to warn people over bullhorns to please stand away from the whales. The Oregon Parks Department, whose responsibility the beach was, wanted no part of the growing confusion. The U.S. Forest Service, with jurisdiction over land in the Oregon Dunes National Recreation Area down to the foredune, was willing to help, but among all the agencies there was concern over limited budgets; there were questions, gently essayed,[4] about the conflict of state and federal enforcement powers over the body parts of an endangered species. A belligerent few in the crowd shouted objections as the first syringes appeared, and yelled to scientists to produce permits that allowed them to interfere in the death of an endangered species.

Amid this chaos, the whales, sealed in their slick black neoprene[5] skins, mewed and clicked. They slammed glistening flukes on the beach, jarring the muscles of human thighs like Jell-O at a distance of a hundred yards. They rolled their dark, purple-brown eyes at the scene and blinked.

They lay on the western shore of North America like forty-one derailed boxcars at dawn on a Sunday morning, and in the days that followed, the worst and the best of human behavior were shown among them.

The sperm whale, for many, is the most awesome creature of the open seas. Imagine a forty-five-year-old male fifty feet long, a slim, shiny black animal with a white jaw and marbled belly cutting the surface of green ocean water at twenty knots. Its flat forehead protects a sealed chamber of exceedingly fine oil; sunlight sparkles in rivulets running off folds in its corrugated back. At fifty tons it is the largest carnivore on earth. Its massive head, a third of its body length, is scarred with the beak, sucker, and claw marks of giant squid, snatched out of subterranean canyons a mile below, in a region without light, and brought writhing to the surface. Imagine a four-hundred-pound heart the size of a chest of drawers driving five gallons of blood at a stroke through its aorta: a meal of forty salmon moving slowly down twelve hundred feet of intestine; the blinding, acrid fragrance of a two-hundred-pound wad of gray ambergris[6] lodged somewhere along the way; producing sounds more shrill than we can hear—like children shouting on a distant playground—and able to sort a cacophony of noise: electric crackling of shrimp, groaning of undersea quakes, roar of upwellings, whining of porpoise, hum of oceanic cables. With skin as sensitive as the inside of your wrist.

What makes them awesome is not so much these things, which are discoverable, but the mysteries that shroud them. They live at a remarkable distance from us and we have no *Pioneer II* to penetrate their world. Virtually all we know of sperm whales we have learned on the slaughter decks of oceangoing whalers and on the ways at shore stations. We do not even know how many there are; in December 1978, the Scientific Committee of the International Whaling Commission said it could not set a quota for a worldwide sperm whale kill—so little was known that any number written down would be ridiculous.[7]

4. **essayed** (e·sād′): tried out.
5. **neoprene** (nē′ō·prēn′): rubberlike. *Neoprene* is generally used to mean "a kind of synthetic rubber."

6. **ambergris** (am′bər·grēs′): substance from the intestines of sperm whales, used in some perfumes to make the scent last.
7. A quota of 5,000 was nevertheless set. In June 1979, within days of the Florence stranding but apparently unrelated to it, the IWC dropped the 1980 world sperm whale quota to 2,203 and set aside the Indian Ocean as a sanctuary. (By 1987 the quota was 0, though special exemptions permit some 200 sperm whales per year still to be taken worldwide.)—Author's note.

Words to Own

belligerent (bə·lij′ər·ənt) *adj.:* quarrelsome; ready to fight.
acrid (ak′rid) *adj.:* sharp or bitter smelling. *Acrid* is also used to describe tastes.

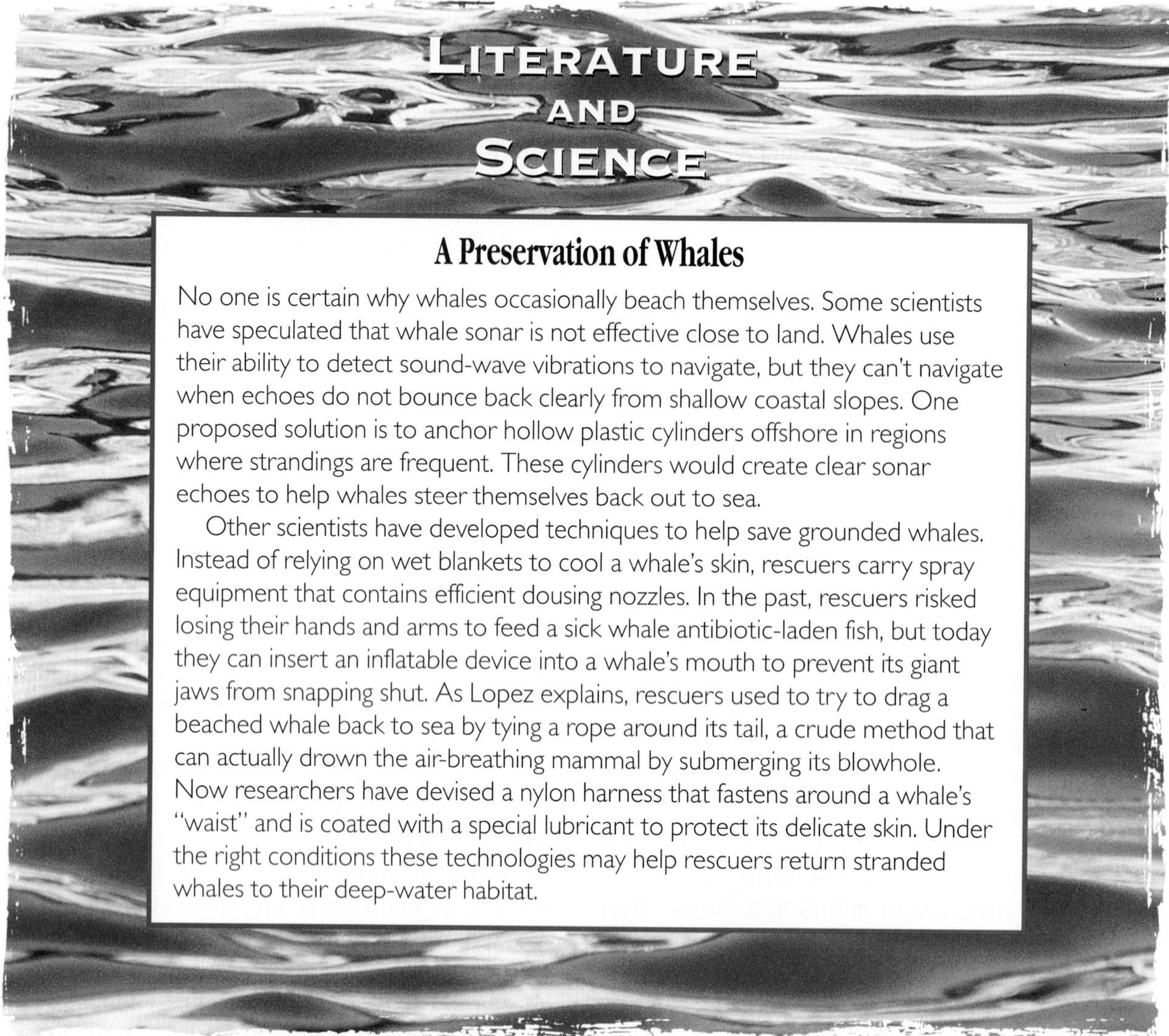

A Preservation of Whales

No one is certain why whales occasionally beach themselves. Some scientists have speculated that whale sonar is not effective close to land. Whales use their ability to detect sound-wave vibrations to navigate, but they can't navigate when echoes do not bounce back clearly from shallow coastal slopes. One proposed solution is to anchor hollow plastic cylinders offshore in regions where strandings are frequent. These cylinders would create clear sonar echoes to help whales steer themselves back out to sea.

Other scientists have developed techniques to help save grounded whales. Instead of relying on wet blankets to cool a whale's skin, rescuers carry spray equipment that contains efficient dousing nozzles. In the past, rescuers risked losing their hands and arms to feed a sick whale antibiotic-laden fish, but today they can insert an inflatable device into a whale's mouth to prevent its giant jaws from snapping shut. As Lopez explains, rescuers used to try to drag a beached whale back to sea by tying a rope around its tail, a crude method that can actually drown the air-breathing mammal by submerging its blowhole. Now researchers have devised a nylon harness that fastens around a whale's "waist" and is coated with a special lubricant to protect its delicate skin. Under the right conditions these technologies may help rescuers return stranded whales to their deep-water habitat.

The sperm whale, in all its range of behaviors—from the enraged white bull called Mocha Dick that stove[8] whaling ships off the coast of Peru in 1810, to a nameless female giving birth to a fourteen-foot, one-ton calf in equatorial waters in the Pacific—remains distant. The general mystery is enhanced by specific mysteries: The sperm whale's brain is larger than the brain of any other creature that ever lived. Beyond the storage of incomprehensible amounts of information, we do not know what purpose such size serves. And we do not know what to make of its most distinctive anatomical feature, the spermaceti organ. An article in *Scientific American,* published several months before the stranding, suggests that the whale can control the density of its spermaceti oil, thereby altering its specific gravity[9] to assist it in diving. It is argued also that the huge organ, located in the head, serves as a means of generating and focusing sound, but there is not yet any agreement on these speculations.

Of the many sperm whale strandings in recorded history, only three have been larger than the one in Oregon. The most recent was of

8. **stove:** punctured or smashed; broke up.

9. **specific gravity:** ratio of the weight of one object (in this case, a whale) to the weight of something else that takes up the same amount of space (in this case, water).

fifty-six on the eastern Baja coast near Playa San Rafael on January 6, 1979. But the Florence stranding is perhaps the most remarkable. Trained scientists arrived almost immediately; the site was easily accessible, with even an airstrip close by. It was within an hour's drive of two major West Coast marine-science centers. And the stranding seemed to be of a whole social unit. That the animals were still alive meant live blood specimens could be taken. And by an uncanny coincidence, a convention of the American Society of Mammalogists was scheduled to convene June 18 at Oregon State University in Corvallis, less than a two-hour drive away. Marine experts from all over the country would be there. (As it turned out, some of them would not bother to come over; others would secure access to the beach only to take photographs; still others would show up in sports clothes—all they had—and plunge into the gore that by the afternoon of June 18 littered the beach.)

The state police calls to Greenpeace on the night of June 16 were attempts to reach informed people to direct a rescue. Michael Piper of Greenpeace, in Eugene, was the first to arrive with a small group at about 1:30 A.M., just after a low tide at 12:59 A.M.

"I ran right out of my shoes," Piper says. The thought that they would still be alive—clicking and murmuring, their eyes tracking human movement, lifting their flukes, whooshing warm air from their blowholes—had not penetrated. But as he ran into the surf to fill a bucket to splash water over their heads, the proportions of the stranding and the impending tragedy overwhelmed him.

"I knew, almost from the beginning, that we were not going to get them out of there, and that even if we did, their chances of survival were a million to one," Piper said.

Just before dawn, a second contingent of Greenpeace volunteers arrived from Portland. A Canadian, Michael Bailey, took charge and announced there was a chance with the incoming tide that one of the smaller animals could be floated off the beach and towed to sea (weights ranged from an estimated three and a half to twenty-five tons). Bruce Mate, who would become both scientific and press coordinator on the beach (the latter to his regret), phoned the Port of Coos Bay to see if an oceangoing tug or fishing vessel would be available to anchor offshore and help—Bailey's crew would ferry lines through the surf with a Zodiac boat. No one in Coos Bay was interested. A commercial helicopter service with a Skycrane capable of lifting nine tons also begged off. A call to the Coast Guard produced a helicopter, but people there pronounced any attempt to sky-tow a whale too dangerous.

The refusal of help combined with the apparent futility of the effort precipitated a genuinely compassionate gesture: Bailey strode resolutely into the freezing water and, with twenty-five or thirty others, amid flailing flukes, got a rope around the tail of an animal that weighed perhaps three or four tons. The waves knocked them down and the whale yanked them over, but they came up sputtering, to pull again. With the buoyancy provided by the incoming tide they moved the animal about thirty feet. The effort was heroic and ludicrous. As the rope began to cut into the whale's flesh, as television cameramen and press photographers crowded in, Michael Piper gave up his place on the rope in frustration and waded ashore. Later he would remark that, for some, the whale was only the means to a political end—a dramatization of the plight of whales as a species. The distinction between the suffering individual, its internal organs hemorrhaging, its flukes sliced by the rope, and the larger issue, to save the species, confounded Piper.

A photograph of the Greenpeace volunteers pulling the whale showed up nationally in newspapers the next day. A week later, a marine mammalogist wondered if any more damaging picture could have been circulated. It would convince people something could have been done, when in fact, he said, the whales were doomed as soon as they came ashore.

For many, transfixed on the beach by their own helplessness, the value of the gesture transcended the fact.

By midmorning Piper was so disturbed, so

embarrassed by the drunks and by people wrangling to get up on the whales or in front of photographers, that he left. As he drove off through the crowds (arriving now by the hundreds, many in campers and motor homes), gray whales were seen offshore, with several circling sperm whales. "The best thing we could have done," Piper said, alluding to this, "was offer our presence, to be with them while they were alive, to show some compassion."

Irritated by a callous (to him) press that seemed to have only one question—Why did they come ashore?—Piper had blurted out that the whales might have come ashore "because they were tired of running" from commercial whalers. Scientists scoffed at the remark, but Piper, recalling it a week later, would not take it back. He said it was as logical as any other explanation offered in those first few hours.

Uneasy philosophical disagreement divided people on the beach from the beginning. Those for whom the stranding was a numinous event were estranged by the clowning of those who regarded it as principally entertainment. A few scientists irritated everyone with their preemptive, self-important air. When they put chain saws to the lower jaws of dead sperm whales lying only a few feet from whales not yet dead, there were angry shouts of condemnation. When townspeople kept at bay—"This is history, dammit," one man screamed at a state trooper, "and I want my kids to see it!"—saw twenty reporters, each claiming an affiliation with the same weekly newspaper, gain the closeness to the whales denied them, there were shouts of cynical derision.

"The effect of all this," said Michael Gannon, director of a national group called Oregonians Cooperating to Protect Whales, of the undercurrent of elitism and outrage, "was that it interfered with the spiritual and emotional ability of people to deal with the phenomenon. It was like being at a funeral where you are not allowed to mourn."

The least understood and perhaps most disruptive incident on the beach on that first day was the attempt of veterinarians to kill the whales, first by injecting M-99, a morphine-based drug, then by ramming pipes into their pleural cavities[10] to collapse their lungs, and finally by severing major arteries and letting them bleed to death. The techniques were crude, but no one knew enough sperm whale anatomy or physiology to make a clean job of it, and no one wanted to try some of the alternatives—from curare[11] to dynamite—that would have made the job quicker. The ineptitude of the veterinarians caused them a private embarrassment to which they gave little public expression. Their frustration at their own inability to do anything to "help" the whales was exacerbated by nonscientists demanding from the sidelines that the animals be "put out of their misery." (The reasons for attempting euthanasia[12] were poorly understood, philosophically and medically, and the issue nagged people long after the beach bore not a trace of the incident itself.)

As events unfolded on the beach, the first whale died shortly after the stranding, the last almost thirty-six hours later; suffocation and overheating were the primary causes. By waiting as long as they did to try to kill some of the animals and by allowing others to die in their own time, pathologists, toxicologists, parasitologists, geneticists,[13] and others got tissues of

10. **pleural** (ploor′əl) **cavities:** spaces that contain the lungs.
11. **curare** (kyo͞o·rä′rē): poison that causes paralysis.
12. **euthanasia** (yo͞o′thə·nā′zhə): deliberately causing death in order to bring an end to suffering.
13. **Pathologists** study the nature of disease. **Toxicologists** study poisons and their effects. **Parasitologists** study diseases caused by parasites. **Geneticists** study heredity.

Words to Own

callous (kal′əs) *adj.:* hardened; unfeeling; pitiless.
numinous (no͞o′mə·nəs) *adj.:* deeply spiritual or mystical.
elitism (ā·lēt′iz′əm) *n.:* belief that one belongs to a group that is better than others.
ineptitude (in·ep′tə·to͞od′) *n.:* clumsiness; inefficiency.
exacerbated (eg·zas′ər·bāt′id) *v.:* increased; aggravated.

poor quality to work with. The disappointment was all the deeper because never had so many scientists been in a position to gather so much information. (Even with this loss and an initial lack of suitable equipment—chemicals to preserve tissues, blood-analysis kits, bone saws, flensing knives[14]—the small core of twenty or so scientists "increased human knowledge about sperm whales several hundred percent," according to Mate.)

The fact that almost anything learned was likely to be valuable was meager consolation to scientists hurt by charges that they were cold and brutal people, irreverently jerking fetuses from the dead. Among these scientists were people who sat alone in silence, who departed in anger, and who broke down and cried.

Beginning Sunday morning, scientists had their first chance to draw blood from live, unwounded sperm whales (they used comparatively tiny one-and-a-half-inch, 18-gauge hypodermic needles stuck in vessels near the surface of the skin on the flukes). With the help of a blue organic tracer, they estimated blood volume at five hundred gallons. In subsequent stages, blubber, eyes, teeth, testicles, ovaries, stomach contents, and specific tissues were removed—the teeth for aging, the eyes for corneal cells to discover genetic relationships within the group. Post-mortems[15] were performed on ten females; three near-term fetuses were removed. An attempt was made to photograph the animals systematically.

The atmosphere on the beach shifted perceptibly over the next six days. On Sunday, a cool, cloudy day during which it rained, as many as three thousand people may have been on the beach. Police finally closed the access road to the area to discourage more from coming. Attempts to euthanize the animals continued, the jaws of the dead were being sawed off, and in the words of one observer, "there was a television crew with a backdrop of stranded whales every twenty feet on the foredune."

By Monday the crowds were larger, but, in the estimation of a Forest Service employee, "of a higher quality. The type of people who show up at an automobile accident were gone; these were people who really wanted to see the whales. It was a four-and-a-half-mile walk in from the highway, and I talked with a woman who was seven months pregnant who made it and a man in a business suit and dress shoes who drove all the way down from Seattle."

Monday afternoon the crowds thinned. The beach had become a scene of post-mortem gore sufficient to turn most people away. The outgoing tide had carried off gallons of blood and offal, drawing spiny dogfish sharks and smoothhound sharks into the breakers. As the animals died, scientists cut into them to relieve gaseous pressure—the resultant explosions could be heard half a mile away. A forty-pound chunk of liver whizzed by someone's back-turned shoulders; sixty feet of pearly-gray intestine unfurled with a snap against the sky. By evening the

"It was like being at a funeral where you are not allowed to mourn."

14. **flensing knives:** knives designed to cut blubber and skin from a dead whale or seal.
15. **post-mortems** (pōst′môr′təmz): autopsies; detailed examinations of dead bodies to determine the causes of death.

beach was covered with more than a hundred tons of intestines. Having to open the abdominal cavities so precipitately precluded, to the scientists' dismay, any chance of an uncontaminated examination.

By Tuesday the beach was closed to the public. The whale carcasses were being prepared for burning and burial, a task that would take four days, and reporters had given up asking why the stranding had happened, to comment on the stench.

On Wednesday afternoon the whales were ignited in pits at the foot of the foredune. As they burned they were rendered,[16] and when their oil caught fire they began to boil in it. The seething roar was muffled by a steady onshore breeze; the oily black smoke drifted southeast over the dunes, over English beach grass and pearly everlasting, sand verbena, and the purple flowers of beach pea, green leaves of sweet clover, and the bright yellow blooms of the monkey flower. It thinned until it disappeared against a weak-blue sky.

While fire cracked the blubber of one-eyed, jawless carcasses, a bulldozer the size of a two-car garage grunted in a trench being dug to the north for the last of them. These were still sprawled at the water's edge. Up close, the black, blistered skin, bearing scars of knives and gouging fingernails, looked like the shriveled surface of a pond evaporated beneath a summer sun. Their gray-blue innards lay about on the sand like bags of discarded laundry. Their purple tongues were wedged in retreat in their throats. Spermaceti oil dripped from holes in their heads, solidifying in the wind to stand in translucent stalagmites twenty inches high. Around them were tidal pools opaque with coagulated blood and, beyond, a pink surf.

16. **rendered:** melted down, releasing oil or fat.

As far as I know, no novelist, no historian, no moral philosopher, no scholar of Melville, no rabbi, no painter, no theologian had been on the beach. No one had thought to call them or to fly them in. At the end they would not have been allowed past the barricades.

The whales made a sound, someone had said, like the sound a big fir makes breaking off the stump just as the saw is pulled away. A thin screech.

Words to Own

precipitately (prē·sip′ə·tit·lē) *adv.:* hurriedly; unexpectedly.

precluded (prē·klo͞od′id) *v.:* prevented; made impossible.

Meet the Writer

Nature Is His Subject

Barry Lopez (1945–) is a writer who can't wait to get up in the morning. That is how another "nature writer," Edward Hoagland, described the author of *Arctic Dreams* (1986), a book that celebrates the northern landscape and the people and animals who live there. Lopez always combines observations of nature with insights into human life.

In a recent interview, Lopez identified two issues that matter most to him and the kind of writing he likes to do best:

"A writer has a certain handful of questions. Mine seem to be the issues of tolerance and dignity. You can't sit down and write directly about those things, but if they are on your mind and if you're a writer, they're going to come out in one form or another. The form I feel most comfortable with, where I do a lot of reading and aimless thinking, is natural history."

Lopez also retold the Native American myths about the great trickster Coyote in a book subtitled *Coyote Builds North America* (1977). Lopez and his family live close to nature, beside the McKenzie River in western Oregon.

Making Meanings

First Thoughts

1. What details in "A Presentation of Whales" were disturbing to you? Are you glad or sorry that you read it? Why?

Reading Check

Make a **time line** showing the main events in this report in **chronological order.**

Shaping Interpretations

2. What does Lopez think about the tragic events he describes? Does he state his **opinions** directly, or does he suggest them? Find passages that reveal his views on the whales and on the people at the beach.
3. Has Lopez written this report so that the story has heroes and villains? Support your answer with specific details from the text.
4. Reread Lopez's next to last paragraph. Why do you think he wrote it?
5. Take out the **KWL** chart you began before you read this report. What can you now add to the L column? Skim the report again to be sure you have enough information to complete the column.

Choices: Building Your Portfolio

Writer's Notebook

1. Collecting Ideas for a Research Paper

WORK IN PROGRESS

Organizing information. To write this report, Barry Lopez had to transform his notes into a coherent form. You'll face the same task in the Writer's Workshop on page 448. Find some notes you've made for a research paper, perhaps from another Writer's Notebook assignment in this collection. Try organizing your facts and details in **outline** form. (If you need help with outlining, see page 334).

Writing an Analogy

2. Science Is Like Art?

Go back to the text and find at least three passages in which Lopez uses **analogies,** or comparisons, to help us understand something about the whales. Scientist Polly Matzinger also uses analogies to explain something complex in this interview excerpt:

> **Q.** I'm told you dislike the way science and technology have become hyphenated terms—why?
> **A.** Because they are very different. Science is more like art and true scientists are more like artists. . . . Technology is about vaccines and plastics and drugs and things that work in the world. Science is about describing nature, and so is art: We are painting nature.
> **Q.** Do you think the scientific world is too solemn?
> **A.** Oh, no. Not true science. It's art. Actually, it's a sandbox and scientists get to play all our lives.

Write your own analogy to explain some field or topic or activity that interests you—a sport, music, reading, cooking, running, etc. Elaborate on your analogy as Matzinger does.

LANGUAGE LINK MINI-LESSON

Topic Sentences

A **topic sentence,** which states the **main idea** of a paragraph, helps keep both writers and readers on track. A topic sentence helps the writer organize the paragraph, keeping out any unrelated, stray ideas. For the reader a topic sentence works as a signal, announcing the paragraph's main idea.

Not every kind of writing has topic sentences, but informative writing often does. Here are some examples from the beginning of "A Presentation of Whales." Look at the rest of the paragraph in which each appears to see how the topic sentence actually controls what is presented in the paragraph.

1. "The sperm whale, for many, is the most awesome creature of the open seas." (page 437)
2. "By Monday the crowds were larger, but, in the estimation of a Forest Service employee, 'of a higher quality.' " (page 441)

With a partner, find three more topic sentences in Lopez's article. They're usually at the beginning of a paragraph but sometimes appear at the end (to sum up the main idea) or in the middle.

Try It Out

Write a **topic sentence** for the following paragraph, and state where you'd insert it. Be sure to compare your sentences in class.

> As part of their classes, kindergarten children are learning conflict resolution skills. In junior and senior high schools, peer mediators are being trained to help settle students' disputes without teachers or administrators. Mediators, who remain neutral in a dispute, help students focus on the problem and listen to one another respectfully.

➤ Select an essay or report from your writing portfolio, and check it for topic sentences. Did you use them? Are they effective? Do all the sentences in the paragraph stick to the main idea? If you haven't used topic sentences, try inserting some for clarity.

VOCABULARY HOW TO OWN A WORD

WORD BANK

precipitous
belligerent
acrid
callous
numinous
elitism
ineptitude
exacerbated
precipitately
precluded

Synonyms and Antonyms

A **synonym** means the same (more or less) as another word. An **antonym** means the opposite.

1. What word means the opposite of *sweet-smelling?*
2. What word means the same as *prevented?*
3. What word refers to a belief that's the opposite of *equality?*
4. What word means the same as *worsened?*
5. What word means the opposite of *peace-loving?*
6. What word means the same as *steep?*
7. What word means the opposite of *sensitive?*
8. What word means the same as *hastily?*
9. What word means the opposite of *competence?*
10. What word means the same as *mystical* or *spiritual?*

EXTENDING *the theme*

A PROSE POEM

Celestial Combat by Nikolai Roerich (1874–1947).

Russian State Museum, St. Petersburg.

Quickwrite

Nature can remind us of how fragile we are—consider Jon Krakauer's harrowing experience on Mt. Everest (page 420). Can you think of a time when nature gave you a wake-up call? You might recall a bad storm, blizzard, hurricane, tornado, earthquake, flood, or forest fire. Quickly jot down as many details as you can remember about "being there."

Where I was	
What happened	
Sensory details	
What I thought/felt	

go.hrw.com

LEO 10-6

A Storm in the Mountains

Aleksandr Solzhenitsyn ***translated by Michael Glenny***

It caught us one pitch-black night at the foot of the pass. We crawled out of our tents and ran for shelter as it came towards us over the ridge.

Everything was black—no peaks, no valleys, no horizon to be seen, only the searing flashes of lightning separating darkness from light, and the gigantic peaks of Belaya-Kaya and Djuguturlyuchat[1] looming up out of the night. The huge black pine trees around us seemed as high as the mountains themselves. For a split second we felt ourselves on terra firma;[2] then once more everything would be plunged into darkness and chaos.

The lightning moved on, brilliant light alternating with pitch blackness, flashing white, then pink, then violet, the mountains and pines always springing back in the same place, their hugeness

1. **Belaya-Kaya** (bye·lī´ ə kī´ ə) **and Djuguturlyuchat** (djo͞o·go͞o·to͞or·lyo͞o´chət): two mountains in Russia.
2. **terra firma** (ter´ ə fur´mə): Latin expression meaning "solid ground."

filling us with awe; yet when they disappeared we could not believe that they had ever existed.

The voice of the thunder filled the gorge, drowning the ceaseless roar of the rivers. Like the arrows of Sabaoth,[3] the lightning flashes rained down on the peaks, then split up into serpentine streams as though bursting into spray against the rock face, or striking and then shattering like a living thing.

As for us, we forgot to be afraid of the lightning, the thunder, and the downpour, just as a droplet in the ocean has no fear of a hurricane. Insignificant yet grateful, we became part of this world—a primal world in creation before our eyes.

3. **Sabaoth** (sab´ā·äth´): biblical term meaning "armies."

Meet the Writer

Russia's Nobel Laureate

Aleksandr Solzhenitsyn (sōl´zhə·nēt´sin) (1918–) spent many years in Soviet prisons. Solzhenitsyn catapulted to fame with the publication of his first novel, *One Day in the Life of Ivan Denisovich* (1962), which details the daily life of a political prisoner. Solzhenitsyn wrote from firsthand knowledge, for in 1945 he was arrested for criticizing Soviet leader Joseph Stalin and sentenced to eight years in prison and labor camps, plus three years in exile.

After his release, he taught mathematics and physics and continued writing. After the publication of *The Gulag Archipelago* (1974), he was exiled from Russia. In 1976 Solzhenitsyn and his wife settled quietly in Vermont, where he continued to write and publish novels about Soviet life under the Communist regime.

In his acceptance speech for the 1970 Nobel Prize for Literature, Solzhenitsyn commented on the relationship between life and literature:

"The sole substitute for an experience which we have not ourselves lived through is art and literature."

In 1994, with the Cold War over, and Russia's Communist regime out of power, Solzhenitsyn and his wife returned at last to their homeland.

Finding Common Ground

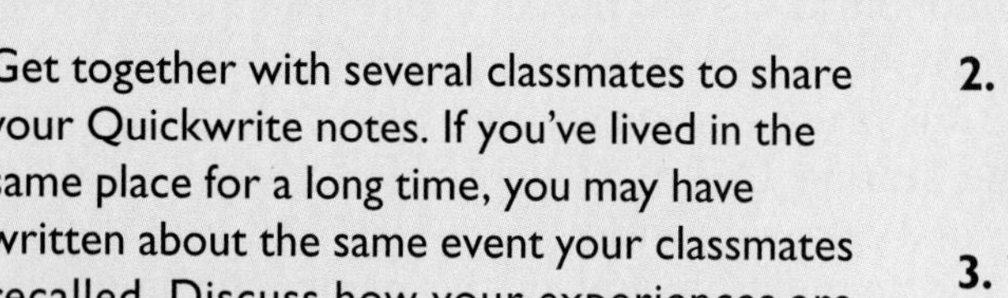

Get together with several classmates to share your Quickwrite notes. If you've lived in the same place for a long time, you may have written about the same event your classmates recalled. Discuss how your experiences are alike and different.

Then, **compare and contrast** your own experiences with Solzhenitsyn's. Let your group decide what you'd like to discuss, but if you need some help in setting your agenda, consider the following questions:

1. How does Solzhenitsyn manage to make his experience seem real, as if you are standing at his side?
2. What makes this description a **prose poem** (see page 605) rather than a news report—or some other kind of writing?

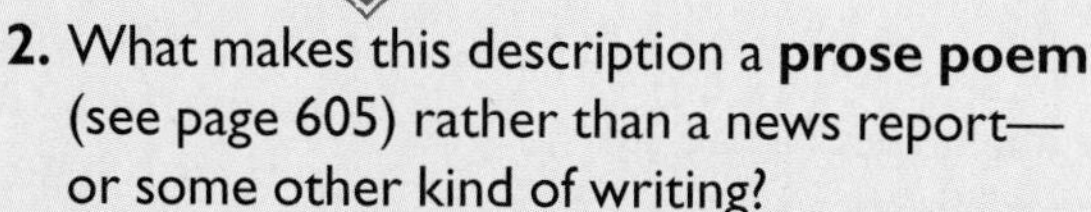

3. What does Solzhenitsyn conclude from his experience? If everyone shared this thought, how might people behave differently?

After your group finishes discussing Solzhenitsyn's prose poem, turn back to your Quickwrite notes. Write about your experience of "being there" in any form you choose: a journal entry, an eyewitness report, a poem or prose poem, or a letter. Try, as Solzhenitsyn does, to find a lesson or meaning in your experience.

Nuclear Fallout

Hiroshima by John Hersey (Vintage) tells what happened on August 6, 1945, when the United States dropped the first atomic bomb on Hiroshima, Japan. Hersey's detailed, compelling narrative focuses on two women and four men, five Japanese and one German, who survived that day.

Witnessing the Civil Rights Movement

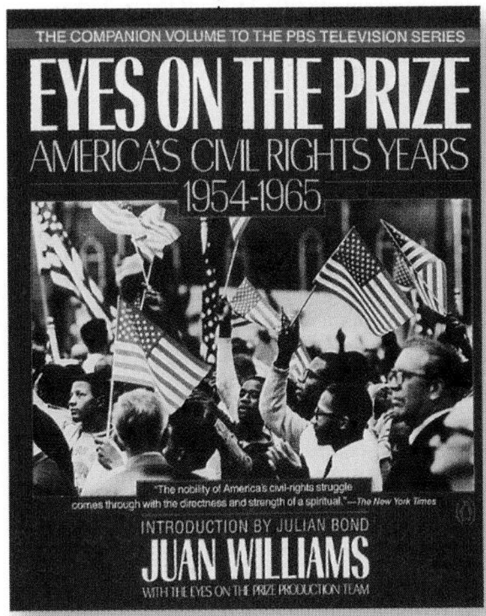

Eyes on the Prize by Juan Williams (Viking Penguin) documents eleven years (1954–1965) of the civil rights movement with text, photos, and oral histories that make you an eyewitness to the Montgomery bus boycott, the marches and freedom rides, and landmark desegregation cases.

What Happened in Salem

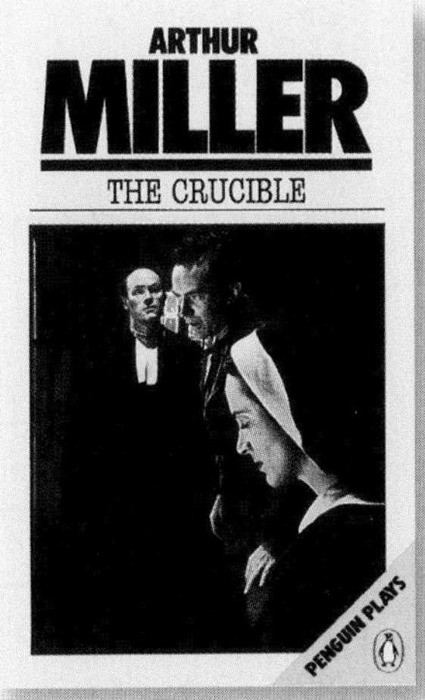

Arthur Miller's great play *The Crucible* (Viking Penguin) puts a historical event onstage. The play takes place in Salem, Massachusetts, in 1692, when anyone could "cry witch" against a neighbor and twenty people were executed as witches. The McCarthy hearings (1952–1954), investigating suspected Communists in the United States, have been compared to these hysterical witch hunts in old Salem. Daniel Day-Lewis and Winona Ryder starred in the 1996 movie version, whose screenplay was written by Arthur Miller.

How They Lived

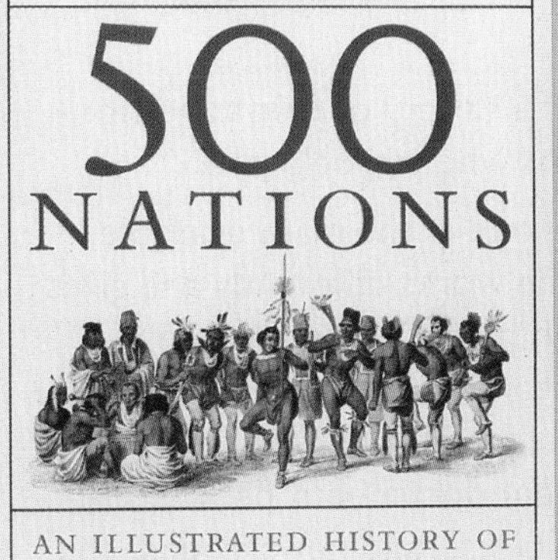

Alvin M. Josephy's lavishly illustrated *500 Nations: An Illustrated History of North American Indians* (Knopf) begins with origin stories, Mexican empires, and the way of life of the Indian nations before Columbus arrived. The text, photographs, and interviews with contemporary American Indians show the clashes with European settlers and the destruction of the old way of life.

BUILDING YOUR PORTFOLIO

Writer's Workshop

Technology HELP

See Writer's Workshop 2 CD-ROM. *Assignment: Informative Report.*

ASSIGNMENT

Write a research paper, using information gathered from several sources.

AIM

To inform.

AUDIENCE

Your teacher and classmates.

Broad topic: whales

↓

Narrower topic: dangers to whales

↓

Still narrower topic: recent theories about whale strandings

go.hrw.com

LE0 Research Paper

EXPOSITORY WRITING

RESEARCH PAPER

You'll be asked to write **research papers** throughout your school years—and possibly beyond. Researching is a two-part job. First you search for the most accurate, reliable information available, just as a scientist does. Then, like a reporter, you assemble those facts into an informative, accurate, and well-documented report.

Prewriting

WORK IN PROGRESS

1. Explore Topic Ideas

Review the entries in your Writer's Notebook to find a topic that interests you and that you think will interest your readers. If you can't find one there, try skimming magazines and newspapers or browsing the Internet. Cross out any topics on your list that seem too broad (the history of mountain climbing), too complex (how an ocean liner is built), or too hard to find information about. Keep in mind that you'll need to consult several sources.

2. Track Down Reliable Sources

As you gather information, you'll probably use both **secondary sources** (such as magazine and encyclopedia articles, textbooks, biographies, history books, and book reviews) and **primary sources** (such as interviews, journals, speeches, and literary works). Here's where to look:

- **Check out the library.** You'll find a variety of **print** and **nonprint sources**—as well as librarians who can help you.
- **Log on.** Explore the Internet using one of the many available **search engines.** Each search engine works differently and gives varied results. Learn to use the search engines on your computer. (For more help with online searches, see Using the Internet in the Communications Handbook.) Through the Internet you can access databases, government documents, periodicals, professional Web sites, scholarly projects, and newsgroups. You can also **e-mail** experts and organizations to ask questions or request information.

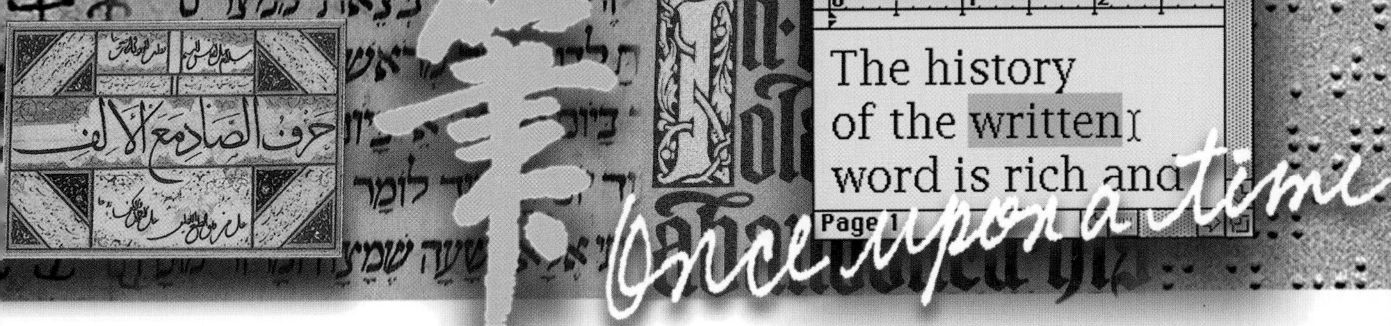

• **Explore your community.** Visit a museum, contact a private organization or government agency, interview an expert, or conduct your own opinion poll or survey.

Before you use a source, be sure to **evaluate** its reliability; some sources are biased, inaccurate, outdated, or just plain silly. Be particularly careful with sources on the Internet, where anyone can post anything. Web sites with addresses ending in *gov* (government source) are the most reliable. (See pages 454 and 758 and the Communications Handbook for more on evaluating sources.)

3. Take Notes

As you research, take notes on any information you think you may want to use in your paper. Make a **source card** for each work, assigning it a number and recording the publication data; use a separate **note card** or page in a computer document for every fact or idea you record from that source. Avoid **plagiarism** (copying someone else's words or ideas without giving credit to the source) by putting information in your own words, enclosing quoted material in quotation marks, and giving credit to writers when you mention their ideas.

4. Document Your Sources

In your notes, be sure to record the source of every piece of information so that you can **document** it. The style set by the Modern Language Association (MLA), the style preferred by most English teachers, requires two types of documentation. You'll need both **parenthetical citations** (names of authors and page numbers enclosed in parentheses) within the paper and a **works**

Communications Handbook HELP

See Research Strategies (Using a Media Center or Library, Using the Internet, Evaluating the Credibility of Web Sources).

Research Tip

To focus a Web search, familiarize yourself with each search engine's options for entering **key words** and **exact phrases.** They vary.

Try It Out

Choose a brief passage from one of the selections in this collection. Prepare three note cards:

1. Summarize the **main idea** of the passage, using your own words.

2. Paraphrase the entire passage (restate every sentence in your own words).

3. Directly quote the most important idea in the passage. Be sure to enclose the quoted words in quotation marks.

Language/Grammar Link HELP

Combining Narration and Exposition: page 408. Technical Vocabulary: page 432. Topic Sentences: page 444.

Communications Handbook HELP

See Taking Notes and Documenting Sources.

Thesis statement: Scientists have learned a lot about whales, but they still don't know why whales become stranded.

I. Recent theories
   A. Sickness or injury
      1. Natural causes
         a. Ear infections
         b. Parasites
      2. Human causes
         a. Injuries resulting from swallowing plastic
         b. Injuries caused by fishing gear
         c. Injuries caused by boats
         d. Sickness caused by exposure to toxins
   B. Damage to echolocation (whale's sonar navigation)
      1. etc.

cited list (an alphabetical list of your sources with publication information) at the end. The box below shows some sample entries from a works cited list. (See the Communications Handbook for detailed guidelines and more examples of citations in the MLA style.)

- **Book with two authors:**

  Mallory, Kenneth, and Andrea Conley. Rescue of the Stranded Whales. New York: Simon and Schuster, 1989.

- **Magazine article:**

  Frantzis, A. "Does Acoustic Testing Strand Whales?" Nature 5 Mar. 1998: 29.

- **On-line professional site:**

  National Aquarium, Marine Animal Rescue Program. Baltimore. 23 Oct. 1999. <http://www.aqua.org/animals/environments/rescue.html>.

- **E-mail:**

  Morin, David (staff scientist, Cetacean Research Unit, Gloucester, Massachusetts). "Whale Strandings." E-mail to Pamela Ozaroff. 31 Oct. 1999.

5. Write a Thesis Statement

Before you start writing, draft a **thesis statement** that presents your paper's **main idea.** You may need to write several drafts before you come up with one that works.

EXAMPLE Scientists still know very little about why whales become stranded, or beached.

6. Organize Your Information

The advantage of taking notes on separate index cards or computer pages is that you can sort them into piles, discarding any that seem weak or irrelevant. Arrange your note cards into "topic piles," and rearrange them as necessary until you find the topics and organization that make the most sense for your paper.

When you have a basic structure in place, **outline** the body of your paper. Begin with your thesis statement; then, list every main idea and its supporting details. (Outlining will help you organize your thoughts as well as your information.) You can make either a **topic outline,** like the one at the left, with words and phrases as headings, or a **sentence outline,** with complete sentences as headings. If you put subheadings under a heading, you'll need at least two.

Drafting

1. Elaborate on Your Thesis

Many writers draft the body of a paper first, leaving the introduction for later. Start by turning your notes into complete sentences; then, link the sentences to form paragraphs, with **topic sentences** based on your outline headings. Elaborate on each topic sentence with relevant **facts, descriptions, comparisons, quotations,** and other **supporting details.** Don't be afraid to depart from your outline or to drop information that no longer seems useful.

2. Begin and End

Begin your **introduction** by drawing your readers into your topic with an intriguing quotation, question, statistic, or description of the issue. Then, provide any necessary **background information,** and present your **thesis statement.**

In your **conclusion,** sum up by restating your thesis and perhaps adding a final comment on the topic. At the end of your paper, include your works cited list, giving complete publication information for every source referred to in your paper.

■ *Evaluation Criteria*

A good research report

1. *begins with a strong opener and a thesis statement*
2. *is organized logically*
3. *is based on a variety of reliable sources*
4. *elaborates on its main ideas with facts, quotations, examples, and other evidence*
5. *identifies quoted material and doesn't plagiarize*
6. *documents its sources in MLA or another approved style*
7. *ends with a restatement of the thesis statement*

Model

FROM WHALE STRANDINGS: CURRENT THEORIES

[*Introduction*]

Nearly two decades have passed since the mass stranding of sperm whales that Barry Lopez describes in his essay "A Presentation of Whales." Since that 1979 incident, we have made much progress in our ability to rescue and rehabilitate stranded whales and other marine mammals. They are no longer simply left to die, with scientists and anguished observers "transfixed on the beach by their own helplessness" (439). Yet we still know very little about why these complex animals become stranded in the first place.

Opening paragraph refers to specific essay.

Essay already cited; only page number is needed.

Thesis statement.

[*From the body*]

Scientists have proposed several theories to explain these mass strandings. Some involve human factors; others do not. One theory is that a sick or injured animal in a pod, or herd, becomes disoriented and heads toward shore. The rest of the pod follows (Morin), possibly in response to distress calls (Fulton). Whales become sick or injured for various reasons, some of which are related to human activity. Stranded animals have occasionally been found to have ear infections or parasites (Charles). Others

Topic sentence. Categorizes theories.

Cites electronic sources with no page numbers.

(continued on next page)

Model (continued)

have swallowed plastic debris (National Aquarium), become entangled in fishing gear, or been struck by boats (National Marine Fisheries Service 10). Almost all stranded animals are contaminated by toxins (Geraci).

Cites examples of human-related injury.

[Conclusion]

The ancient Romans believed that stranded whales were being punished by the sea god Neptune. Today scientists have proposed many theories to explain whale strandings, but they are still simply "educated guesses" (Mallory and Conley 10). We have learned so much in the last twenty years about how to rescue and release stranded whales. Now we must learn how to prevent at least some of these tragedies from occurring in the first place.

Restates thesis.

Quotes phrase.

Ends with challenge for the future.

Proofreading Tip

Make sure that a source is given for every quotation and reference to another writer's ideas. Then, make sure that the works cited list is complete and correctly punctuated.

Sentence Workshop HELP

Correcting run-on sentences: page 453.

Communications Handbook HELP

See Proofreaders' Marks.

Evaluating and Revising

Ask a partner for suggestions for improving your report, using the evaluation criteria on page 451. Think about your partner's comments, and use this feedback to decide what changes to make. Don't be afraid to cut sentences or paragraphs, add new material, or rearrange ideas.

Revision Model

	Peer Comments
Scientists have proposed ~~There actually are~~ several theories	Use a stronger verb.
to explain these mass strandings. ~~about this~~. Some theories involve	Explain "this." Be more specific.
human factors; others do not. One theory is that ~~A~~ a	Is this one of the theories? Clarify.
sick or injured animal in a pod, or herd, be-	Define "pod"?
comes disoriented and heads toward shore. ~~confused~~, the rest of the pod	Fix run-on.
follows (Morin), ~~the sick or injured whale,~~	Repetitious.
possibly in response to distress calls (Fulton). ~~order to help.~~	Cite your source or sources.

BUILDING YOUR PORTFOLIO

Sentence Workshop

Correcting Run-on Sentences

Like a car running a red light or stop sign, a **run-on sentence** (like this one) doesn't stop when it's supposed to, it just keeps on going. A run-on sentence is made up of two or more sentences separated by a comma (like the preceding sentence) or with no punctuation. Here are three strategies you can use to correct run-on sentences:

1. Separate the run-on sentence into two sentences.

   RUN-ON Forty-one whales were stranded on the beach all of them died.

   CORRECT Forty-one whales were stranded on the beach**. A**ll of them died.

2. Change the run-on sentence to a compound sentence. You can use either a comma and a coordinating conjunction (such as *and, but, or,* or *so*) or a semicolon.

   RUN-ON Volunteers tried to help, they failed.

   CORRECT Volunteers tried to help**, but** they failed.

   CORRECT Volunteers tried to help**;** they failed.

3. Make one of the sentences a subordinate clause.

   RUN-ON Scientists arrived on the scene they could not save the whales.

   CORRECT Scientists **who arrived on the scene** could not save the whales.

Notice that each of these run-on sentences could have been corrected in other ways:

EXAMPLE Volunteers **who tried to help** failed.

Writer's Workshop Follow-up: Proofreading

Reread the research paper that you wrote for the Writer's Workshop (page 448). As you read, focus on sentence structure. Do you see any run-on sentences? If so, correct them. Be sure to think carefully about which strategy you want to use to correct your run-ons.

Language Handbook HELP

See Run-on Sentences, page 1042.

Technology HELP

See Language Workshop CD-ROM. *Key word entry: run-on sentences.*

Try It Out

Act as an editor, and correct each run-on sentence two ways. Then, check the page cited to see how the professional writer wrote it.

1. A collie barked incessantly flash cubes burst at the huge, dark forms. (page 436)
2. I began my descent, I was indeed anxious, my concern had little to do with the weather. (page 422)
3. A woman tries to take her Great Dane into a boat with her she is refused and steps out of the boat to die with her dog. (page 397)
4. It was a sunny day the trees were green, at the gates the children played. (page 413)
5. They all stare blank-faced, one picture, in the middle of a row, seizes the eye and wrenches the mind. (page 413)

Reading for Life

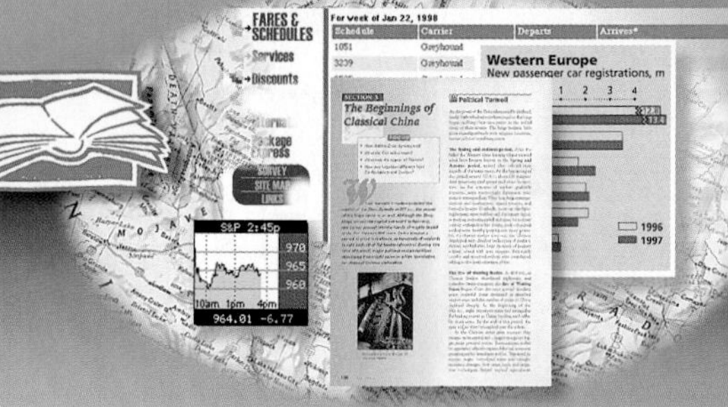

Evaluating the Credibility of Sources: Print and Nonprint

Situation

You and a friend have just seen the movie *Titanic,* and you disagree about the accuracy of the movie. To settle the argument, you decide to find out more about efforts to salvage artifacts from the R.M.S. *Titanic.* You've identified several sources (in the box at the right), but you want to focus only on those that will be the most accurate and reliable.

List of Possible Sources of Information

- *Titanic* (videorecording) starring Leonardo DiCaprio and Kate Winslet; directed by James Cameron. Paramount/20th Century Fox, 1997
- "Descent to the *Titanic*" by P. Skinner. *il Petersen's Photographic Magazine,* Mar. 1989
- "How We Found *Titanic*" by Dr. Robert D. Ballard (Woods Hole Oceanographic Institution). *National Geographic,* Dec. 1985
- "Epilogue for the *Titanic*" by R. D. Ballard. *National Geographic,* Oct. 1987
- Dave's *Titanic* Home Page (Web site)
- Ocean Planet: How Deep Can They Go? RMS *Titanic's Final Resting Place. http://seawifs.gsfc.nasa.gov/titanic.html* (Web site)

Strategies

Evaluate the source's credentials.

- If a writer is cited in the source, check to see if he or she is qualified to speak on the subject. For example, does the writer have an advanced degree in the field? Has the writer written other books or articles on this topic?
- Does the writer or producer have any biases toward the topic that you can detect, or any vested interest in a particular viewpoint?
- Is the writer or producer associated with a recognized institution?

Evaluate the medium.

- If the source is in a print medium, is it from a reputable publisher rather than a special interest group?
- If the source is a videotape, is it a documentary?
- If the source is electronic, does the name of the Web site sound serious? Look for the abbreviations *.edu* (for educational) or *.gov* (for government) in the Internet address. Government sources and pages posted by a university are usually reliable. Someone's home page is not reliable.

Evaluate the source's timeliness.

- Check publication dates. Recent information may be more useful and accurate, but older information may provide important historical details.

Using the Strategies

1. For a formal research report, which sources cited in the box above would you definitely *not* use? Why?
2. For an article for a general interest magazine, which sources would you want to examine?
3. For a multimedia presentation, which sources might provide good visuals?
4. Of all the sources, which would be most reliable for checking your facts?

Extending the Strategies

Do research in a library or on the Internet to investigate sources available on another topic featured in this collection, such as the Holocaust or Mt. Everest expeditions.

Collection 7

MAKING A POINT

WRITING FOCUS: Persuasive Essay

In many ways writing is the act of saying I,

of imposing oneself upon other people, of saying

listen to me, see it my way, change your mind.

—Joan Didion

"I'M RIGHT." "YOU'RE WRONG." "NO, I'M *RIGHT!*" "NO, YOU'RE *WRONG!*"

Insisting on your view doesn't get you anywhere (unless, of course, you're a parent dealing with a small child or a supervisor overruling a worker). You're more likely to influence others if you use the strategies of persuasion. Persuasion relies on logic or emotion or both; it can be used fairly with skill, or it can be abused. As a citizen and a consumer exposed to persuasive writing and speaking, you must be able to think critically about persuasion, to distinguish between what's fair and reasonable and what's manipulative.

Writer's Notebook

WORK IN PROGRESS

When you're watching a commercial or a political speech, notice what techniques are used to convince you that the product is worth buying or that the candidate is worth voting for. Write a brief reflection on the kinds of persuasive language you see on TV or in magazines and how you respond to them. Save your notes.

Before You Read

THE LOWEST ANIMAL

Make the Connection

Speaking Out—What's Wrong?

A utopia is a perfect world that exists only in the imagination. Utopian writers paint a picture of the way they think things should be—an ideal world in which everyone is happy and all needs are satisfied.

So what's wrong with the real world as you see it? And what can you do to fix it? In the essay you're about to read, Mark Twain directs his comic, stinging barbs against some of the things he thinks are wrong.

Quickwrite

In your notebook, list some things in life that you think should be changed to make the world better. Freewrite for several minutes.

go.hrw.com
LEO 10-7

Elements of Literature

Satire: The Weapon of Laughter

Mark Twain wrote that we have only "one really effective weapon—laughter. Power, money, persuasion, supplication—these can lift a colossal humbug—push it a little—weaken it a little, century by century; but only laughter can blow it to rags and atoms at a blast."

Satire uses humor to criticize all human beings or a particular person or institution. One of the favorite techniques of the satirist is **exaggeration**—overstating something to make it look absurd or worse than it is. Another favorite technique is **irony**—stating the opposite of what's really meant. Like many great satires, this famous essay is clearly outrageous. Twain doesn't really mean much of what he says. But sometimes the most exaggerated and maddening pieces of writing force us to think critically. You may disagree with a lot of what Twain says, but see if he also helps sharpen some of your own opinions about the world and what is wrong—or right—with it.

Satire is the use of language to ridicule human weaknesses, vices, or stupidity, with the hope of bringing about social reform.

For more on Satire, see the Handbook of Literary Terms.

Reading Skills and Strategies

What's the Writer's Purpose? What's the Point of View?

You should ask yourself two important questions when you read nonfiction: What is the writer's purpose? What is the writer's point of view? A writer's **purpose** may be to entertain, to share an experience, to inform, or to persuade. The **point of view,** or **perspective,** is the writer's position, thoughts, or feelings on a particular subject. A writer's purpose and point of view may be expressed directly—"This is what I think about X, and you should think so too because . . ." But most writers are not so direct. To determine a writer's purpose and point of view, follow these steps:

- Decide why this particular subject is important to the writer.
- Decide what the writer wants you to think about the subject.

Man is the only animal that blushes —

or has occasion to.

The Lowest Animal

Mark Twain

I have been studying the traits and dispositions of the "lower animals" (so-called) and contrasting them with the traits and dispositions of man. I find the result humiliating to me. For it obliges me to renounce my allegiance to the Darwinian theory of the Ascent of Man from the Lower Animals, since it now seems plain to me that that theory ought to be vacated in favor of a new and truer one, this new and truer one to be named the *De*scent of Man from the Higher Animals.

In proceeding toward this unpleasant conclusion, I have not guessed or speculated or conjectured, but have used what is commonly called the scientific method. That is to say, I have subjected every postulate[1] that presented itself to the crucial test of actual experiment and have adopted it or rejected it according to the result. Thus, I verified and established each step of my course in its turn before advancing to the next. These experiments were made in the London Zoological Gardens and covered many months of painstaking and fatiguing work.

Before particularizing any of the experiments, I wish to state one or two things which seem to more properly belong in this place than further along. This in the interest of clearness. The massed experiments established to my satisfaction certain generalizations, to wit:

1. That the human race is of one distinct species. It exhibits slight variations—in color, stature, mental caliber, and so on—due to climate, environment, and so forth; but it is a species by itself and not to be confounded with any other.

2. That the quadrupeds[2] are a distinct family, also. This family exhibits variations—in color, size, food preferences, and so on; but it is a family by itself.

3. That the other families—the birds, the fishes, the insects, the reptiles, etc.—are more or less distinct, also. They are in the procession. They are links in the chain which stretches down from the higher animals to man at the bottom.

Some of my experiments were quite curious. In the course of my reading, I had come across a case where, many years ago, some hunters on our Great Plains organized a buffalo hunt for the entertainment of an English earl—that, and to provide some fresh meat for his larder.[3] They had charming sport. They killed seventy-two of those great animals and

1. **postulate** (päs′tyo͞o·lit): basic principle.
2. **quadrupeds** (kwä′dro͞o·pedz′): four-footed animals.
3. **larder:** supply of food or place where food supplies are kept.

WORDS TO OWN

dispositions (dis′pə·zish′ənz) *n.:* natures; temperaments.
allegiance (ə·lē′jəns) *n.:* loyalty or devotion.
caliber (kal′ə·bər) *n.:* quality or ability; worth.

ate part of one of them and left the seventy-one to rot. In order to determine the difference between an anaconda[4] and an earl—if any—I caused seven young calves to be turned into the anaconda's cage. The grateful reptile immediately crushed one of them and swallowed it, then lay back satisfied. It showed no further interest in the calves and no disposition to harm them. I tried this experiment with other anacondas, always with the same result. The fact stood proven that the difference between an earl and an anaconda is that the earl is cruel and the anaconda isn't; and that the earl wantonly destroys what he has no use for, but the anaconda doesn't. This seemed to suggest that the anaconda was not descended from the earl. It also seemed to suggest that the earl was descended from the anaconda, and had lost a good deal in the transition.

I was aware that many men who have accumulated more millions of money than they can ever use have shown a rabid hunger for more, and have not scrupled to cheat the ignorant and the helpless out of their poor servings in order to partially appease that appetite. I furnished a hundred different kinds of wild and tame animals the opportunity to accumulate vast stores of food, but none of them would do it. The squirrels and bees and certain birds made accumulations, but stopped when they had gathered a winter's supply and could not be persuaded to add to it either honestly or by chicane.[5] In order to bolster up a tottering reputation, the ant pretended to store up supplies, but I was not deceived. I know the ant. These experiments convinced me that there is this difference between man and the higher animals: He is avaricious and miserly, they are not.

In the course of my experiments, I convinced myself that among the animals man is the only one that harbors insults and injuries, broods over them, waits till a chance offers, then takes revenge. The passion of revenge is unknown to the higher animals.

Roosters keep harems, but it is by consent of their concubines;[6] therefore no wrong is done. Men keep harems, but it is by brute force, privileged by atrocious laws which the other sex was allowed no hand in making. In this matter man occupies a far lower place than the rooster.

4. **anaconda** (an′ə·kän′də): long, heavy snake that crushes its prey.
5. **chicane** (shi·kān′): clever deception; trickery. (*Chicanery* is the more common form.)
6. **concubines** (kän′kyo͞o·bīnz′): secondary wives.

Words to Own

wantonly (wän′tən·lē) *adv.:* carelessly, often with deliberate malice.
transition (tran·zish′ən) *n.:* passing from one condition, form, or stage to another.
scrupled (skro͞o′pəld) *v.:* hesitated because of feelings of guilt.
appease (ə·pēz′) *v.:* satisfy; pacify.
avaricious (av′ə·rish′əs) *adj.:* greedy.
atrocious (ə·trō′shəs) *adj.:* evil; brutal; very bad.

Cats are loose in their morals, but not consciously so. Man, in his descent from the cat, has brought the cat's looseness with him but has left the unconsciousness behind—the saving grace which excuses the cat. The cat is innocent, man is not.

Indecency, vulgarity, obscenity—these are strictly confined to man; he invented them. Among the higher animals there is no trace of them. They hide nothing; they are not ashamed. Man, with his soiled mind, covers himself. He will not even enter a drawing room with his breast and back naked, so alive are he and his mates to indecent suggestion. Man is the Animal that Laughs. But so does the monkey, as Mr. Darwin pointed out, and so does the Australian bird that is called the laughing jackass. No—Man is the Animal that Blushes. He is the only one that does it—or has occasion to.

At the head of this article[7] we see how "three monks were burnt to death" a few days ago and a prior was "put to death with atrocious cruelty." Do we inquire into the details? No; or we should find out that the prior was subjected to unprintable mutilations. Man—when he is a North American Indian—gouges out his prisoner's eyes; when he is King John, with a nephew to render untroublesome, he uses a red-hot iron; when he is a religious zealot dealing with heretics in the Middle Ages, he skins his captive alive and scatters salt on his back; in the first Richard's[8] time, he shuts up a multitude of Jewish families in a tower and sets fire to it; in Columbus's time he captures a family of Spanish Jews and—but *that* is not printable; in our day in England, a man is fined ten shillings for beating his mother nearly to death with a chair, and another man is fined forty shillings for having four pheasant eggs in his possession without being able to satisfactorily explain how he got them. Of all the animals, man is the only one that is cruel. He is the only one that inflicts pain for the pleasure of doing it. It is a trait that is not known to the higher animals. The cat plays with the frightened mouse; but she has this excuse, that she does not know that the mouse is suffering. The cat is moderate—unhumanly moderate: She only scares the mouse, she does not hurt it; she doesn't dig out its eyes, or tear off its skin, or drive splinters under its nails—man fashion; when she is done playing with it she makes a sudden meal of it and puts it out of its trouble. Man is the Cruel Animal. He is alone in that distinction.

The higher animals engage in individual fights, but never in organized masses. Man is the only animal that deals in that atrocity of atrocities, war. He is the only one that gathers his brethren about him and goes forth in

7. Twain is referring to 1897 newspaper reports of religious persecution in Crete.

8. **Richard I** ("the Lion-Hearted"), king of England from 1189 to 1199.

cold blood and with calm pulse to exterminate his kind. He is the only animal that for sordid wages will march out, as the Hessians[9] did in our Revolution, and as the boyish Prince Napoleon did in the Zulu war,[10] and help to slaughter strangers of his own species who have done him no harm and with whom he has no quarrel.

Man is the only animal that robs his helpless fellow of his country—takes possession of it and drives him out of it or destroys him. Man has done this in all the ages. There is not an acre of ground on the globe that is in possession of its rightful owner, or that has not been taken away from owner after owner, cycle after cycle, by force and bloodshed.

Man is the only Slave. And he is the only animal who enslaves. He has always been a slave in one form or another, and has always held other slaves in bondage under him in one way or another. In our day he is always some man's slave for wages and does that man's work; and this slave has other slaves under him for minor wages, and they do *his* work. The higher animals are the only ones who exclusively do their own work and provide their own living.

Man is the only Patriot. He sets himself apart in his own country, under his own flag, and sneers at the other nations, and keeps multitudinous uniformed assassins on hand at heavy expense to grab slices of other people's countries and keep *them* from grabbing slices of *his*. And in the intervals between campaigns, he washes the blood off his hands and works for "the universal brotherhood of man"—with his mouth.

Man is the Religious Animal. He is the only Religious Animal. He is the only animal that has the True Religion—several of them. He is the only animal that loves his neighbor as himself, and cuts his throat if his theology isn't straight. He has made a graveyard of the globe in trying his honest best to smooth his brother's path to happiness and heaven. He was at it in the time of the Caesars, he was at it in Mahomet's[11] time, he was at it in the time of the Inquisition, he was at it in France a couple of centuries, he was at it in England in Mary's day, he has been at it ever since he first saw the light, he is at it today in Crete—he will be at it somewhere else tomorrow. The higher animals have no religion. And we are told that they are going to be left out, in the hereafter. I wonder why. It seems questionable taste.

Man is the Reasoning Animal. Such is the claim. I think it is open to dispute. Indeed, my experiments have proven to me that he is the Unreasoning Animal. Note his history, as sketched above. It seems plain to me

9. **Hessians** (hesh′ənz): German soldiers who served for pay in the British Army during the American Revolution.
10. **Prince Napoleon . . . Zulu war:** In search of adventure, Prince Napoleon, son of Napoleon III, joined the British campaign against Zululand (part of South Africa) in 1879.
11. **Mahomet:** Mohammed (c. A.D. 570–632), Arab prophet and founder of Islam.

WORDS TO OWN

sordid (sôr′did) *adj.:* dirty; cheap; shameful; tainted.

that whatever he is, he is *not* a reasoning animal. His record is the fantastic record of a maniac. I consider that the strongest count against his intelligence is the fact that with that record back of him, he blandly sets himself up as the head animal of the lot; whereas by his own standards, he is the bottom one.

In truth, man is incurably foolish. Simple things which the other animals easily learn he is incapable of learning. Among my experiments was this. In an hour I taught a cat and a dog to be friends. I put them in a cage. In another hour I taught them to be friends with a rabbit. In the course of two days I was able to add a fox, a goose, a squirrel, and some doves. Finally a monkey. They lived together in peace, even affectionately.

Next, in another cage I confined an Irish Catholic from Tipperary, and as soon as he seemed tame I added a Scottish Presbyterian from Aberdeen. Next a Turk from Constantinople, a Greek Christian from Crete, an Armenian, a Methodist from the wilds of Arkansas, a Buddhist from China, a Brahman from Benares. Finally, a Salvation Army colonel from Wapping. Then I stayed away two whole days. When I came back to note results, the cage of Higher Animals was all right, but in the other there was but a chaos of gory odds and ends of turbans and fezzes and plaids and bones and flesh—not a specimen left alive. These Reasoning Animals had disagreed on a theological detail and carried the matter to a higher court.

Meet the Writer

The Voice of America

One of the many legends about **Mark Twain** (1835–1910) is that he was born on the day that Halley's comet appeared and died on the day of its return, seventy-five years later. Twain (who said that both he and the comet were "two unaccountable frauds") shifted from job to job when he was young, making and squandering fortunes. He was a great humorist who had a prickly disposition, a natural actor who lived a series of poses and disguises and believed in all of them—believed, along with his Connecticut Yankee, Hank Morgan, that "you can't throw too much style into a miracle."

Mark Twain was born Samuel Clemens in Florida, Missouri. He moved with his family to Hannibal, on the banks of the Mississippi, when he was four years old. (He later began to sign newspaper reports with the boatman's call "Mark Twain," which means "mark two fathoms [12 feet]," a safe depth for boats.) Twain seemed to have inherited the wit and vivacity of his beautiful mother and the extravagant temperament of his father. When the boy was eleven, his father died, almost bankrupt. Three of Twain's six brothers and sisters died in infancy, and a fourth, Henry, was killed in a steamboat accident at the age of twenty.

After his father's death, Twain left school to become a printer's apprentice, the first of a dozen jobs that failed to satisfy him during the next fifteen years. He tried soldiering, newspaper reporting, piloting a steamboat, prospecting, lecturing, and publishing. Through his various professions and lifestyles, however, two began to emerge as constants: that of a writer and that of a family man.

In 1869, Twain bought an interest in a Buffalo newspaper, believing that journalism

Mark Twain by "Spy," the pseudonym of English caricaturist Sir Leslie Ward (1851–1922). This illustration first appeared in *Vanity Fair* magazine.

would be his career. Then, almost immediately his fictionalized account of his European adventures, *Innocents Abroad,* was published and became a best-seller.

In 1870, he married the elegant and delicate Olivia Langdon of Elmira, New York, who would eventually inherit a quarter of a million dollars from her father. Twain sold his interest in the newspaper (at a loss) and moved to Hartford, Connecticut, where his first daughter, Susy, was born. The publication of *Roughing It* confirmed Twain's success as a writer, and he and his beloved "Livy" built a house that was a monument to domesticity. (This elaborate three-storied turreted mansion is still a Hartford landmark.) Two more daughters, Clara and Jean, were born. The Clemenses lived in an atmosphere of intense familiarity, scarcely leaving one another's company except when Twain had to go on whirlwind lecture tours to pay for the cost of his extravagant establishment. The girls were educated at home. When Susy left home to attend college at Bryn Mawr, she was so homesick that she withdrew in the first year. When Clara went to Europe to study music, the whole family followed and set up housekeeping near her.

In the meantime, Twain wrote *The Adventures of Tom Sawyer* (1876) and *Adventures of Huckleberry Finn* (1884). *Huckleberry Finn* is generally considered a masterpiece of American fiction, yet in his own lifetime, Twain was thought of as a mere humorist and popular writer, seldom taken seriously by critics.

In an echo of his father's extravagance, Twain invested and lost more than $200,000 in an impractical typesetting machine. He was saved from bankruptcy by a Standard Oil executive, whom he insisted on paying back mainly with money earned from lecture tours that strained his health and robbed him of time to write.

Twain's last years were marked by a series of embittering misfortunes. Between 1902 and 1909, his wife and two of his treasured daughters died: Susy died of spinal meningitis, and Jean died during an epileptic seizure. Twain himself developed heart disease, and his energy declined as he struggled to complete novels and stories. There is no way he could have realized that within half a century he would stand as a literary giant, the one writer above all others who captured the American voice—vernacular, exuberant, ironic, and strong.

Connections

A POEM

Royal Tern (1832) by John J. Audubon. Watercolor and graphite.

Gracious Goodness

Marge Piercy

On the beach where we had been idly
telling the shell coins
cat's paw, crossbarred Venus, china cockle,
we both saw at once
the sea bird fall to the sand
and flap grotesquely.
He had taken a great barbed hook
out through the cheek and fixed
in the big wing.
He was pinned to himself to die,
a royal tern with a black crest blown back
as if he flew in his own private wind.
He felt good in my hands, not fragile
but muscular and glossy and strong,
the beak that could have split my hand
opening only to cry
as we yanked on the barbs.
We borrowed a clippers, cut and drew out the hook.
Then the royal tern took off, wavering,
lurched twice,
then acrobat returned to his element, dipped,
zoomed, and sailed out to dive for a fish.
Virtue: what a sunrise in the belly.
Why is there nothing
I have ever done with anybody
that seems to me so obviously right?

MAKING MEANINGS

First Thoughts

1. What is your first response to Twain's essay?

Shaping Interpretations

2. What is Twain's **purpose** in this essay? What is his **point of view**, or perspective—that is, what does he want you to think about humanity?

3. What are the targets of Twain's **satire**, and where does he use **exaggeration** and **irony** to hit his targets? Does his satire work, or does he overdo it?

Extending the Text

4. If Twain were alive today, what people, events, and institutions do you think he would satirize? How do Twain's targets compare with your Quickwrite list?

Reading Check

a. What three **generalizations** does Twain make as a result of his experiments at the London Zoo?

b. What animals does Twain compare to human beings?

c. Why does he think that each animal is superior to humans?

d. Twain repeats the following phrase several times: "Man is the only animal that . . ." List as many of these assertions as you can find.

Challenging the Text

5. Explain why you think "The Lowest Animal" is or isn't (a) convincing and (b) funny.

6. A **generalization** is a statement that is meant to apply to every individual in a class. A valid generalization is true. (These examples are valid generalizations: Pigs have curly tails. All insects have six legs. These are *not* valid: Pigs are stupid. Insects carry disease.) Twain uses many often very funny generalizations. If you were debating with Twain, how would you attack his arguments?

7. What aspects of humanity does Twain leave out? How is Piercy's poem (see ***Connections*** on page 464) an answer of sorts to Twain's arguments?

8. **Contrast** Twain's view of humanity with the view expressed by Roger Rosenblatt in his essay "The Man in the Water" (see page 471). Whose view comes closer to your own? Explain.

CHOICES: Building Your Portfolio

Writer's Notebook

1. Collecting Ideas for a Persuasive Essay

Brainstorming a topic. A topic for a persuasive essay, such as the one you'll write for the Writer's Workshop on page 492, should be

- debatable (Reasonable people have different opinions about it.)
- important (You should feel that it matters.)
- current (You should be able to gather information easily.)

For now jot down as many issues as you can think of. (Your Quickwrite list may give you ideas.) Then phrase your issues as questions. The issues can be local, national, or global. Maybe Twain's essay made you so angry that you'll find your topic there. Check the two issues you'd most like to write about.

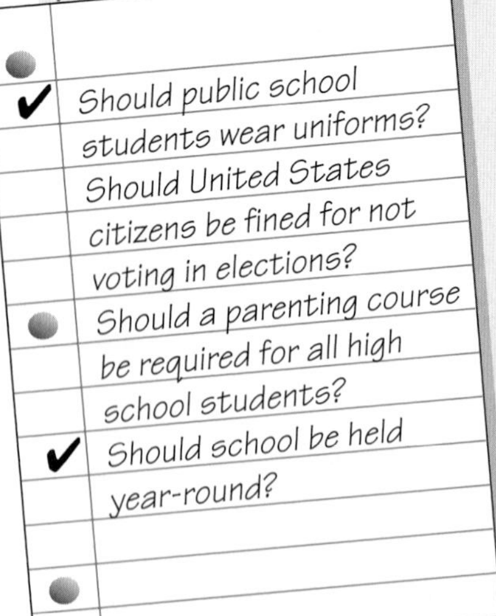

✔ Should public school students wear uniforms?
Should United States citizens be fined for not voting in elections?
Should a parenting course be required for all high school students?
✔ Should school be held year-round?

—Rob Noyes, from *Voices of Youth*

Writing a Rebuttal

2. Dear Mr. Twain

Write a rebuttal of Twain's essay. Your rebuttal may be in any form you like: a letter to Mark Twain, a parody of Twain's essay, a serious essay, a dramatic sketch, a poem, an anecdote, a TV or newspaper editorial, or something else. Try to elaborate with specific examples, just as Twain does.

Creative Writing

3. That's a Tall Tale!

Twain, America's most celebrated humorist, was known for writing tall tales such as "The Celebrated Jumping Frog of Calaveras County." A **tall tale** is an exaggerated, far-fetched story that is obviously untrue but is told as though it should be believed. Stories about Paul Bunyan and Pecos Bill are popular American tall tales.

Parts of this essay read almost like a tall tale—for example, Twain's "anecdote" about leaving several people alone in a cage and the mayhem that results. Obviously, this didn't really happen. Take a section of this essay, such as the one just mentioned, and rewrite it as a tall tale. Remember, your story must be exaggerated and untrue, but tell it with "a straight face."

Drawing

4. A Cartoon Satire

Draw a cartoon that satirizes an event or a situation that you think needs fixing. Rob Noyes, a high school student in Amherst, Massachusetts, won third place for the cartoon at the top of this page in a contest sponsored by a literary magazine. The cartoon probably would have delighted Mark Twain.

LANGUAGE LINK MINI-LESSON

Handbook of Literary Terms HELP

See Connotations.

Connotations Give Loaded Words Their Punch

What do *patriotism, honesty,* and *truth* have in common with *terrorism, lazy, sneaky,* and *lies?* They're all **loaded words**, heavy with emotional associations, or **connotations**. The connotations of a word carry meaning beyond the word's literal meaning, or **denotation**. The first group above have positive connotations that make us feel good; the second group arouse negative feelings.

Skillful persuaders use loaded words to influence our feelings. "The lowest animal," for example, is a negatively loaded term. If Twain had called humans "a species that exhibits many contradictions," he would have been using neutral, unemotional terms. However, Twain wasn't interested in being unemotional; he was presenting a view he deeply believed in.

It's important to know when loaded words are being used to persuade you, often to get your vote or your money. Although loaded words are not necessarily bad, they're no substitute for reason and evidence. They are, however, very effective in arousing feelings.

Try It Out

➤ With a partner, reread a portion of Twain's essay, listing every loaded word or phrase you find. Substitute a neutral (unloaded) word for each loaded term. Which is more persuasive?

➤ Images can be loaded, too. Advertisers know that athletes, babies, young animals, and gardens have positive connotations. Find and share examples of positive and negative images in ads.

➤ If you've started to work on a persuasive essay, pull out your notes now and circle any loaded words you find. Do you see other places where you could use loaded words effectively?

VOCABULARY HOW TO OWN A WORD

WORD BANK

dispositions
allegiance
caliber
wantonly
transition
scrupled
appease
avaricious
atrocious
sordid

What's in a Noun? Suffixes That Form Nouns

A **suffix** is a word part added to the end of a word or to a **root** to create a new word. Certain suffixes change words into nouns—for example, *sordid* + *-ness* = *sordidness.* Study the following noun-forming suffixes and their meanings.

–ition *meaning:* action, result, state
–ance *meaning:* act, condition, quality
–ment *meaning:* means, result, action
–ness *meaning:* quality, state

Now, write down the words in the Word Bank, and indicate whether each is a noun. If it is a noun and it contains one of the noun-forming suffixes listed above, circle the suffix. If the word is *not* a noun, turn it into a noun by adding one of the suffixes above. (Note: For one of the words, you will have to remove a suffix before you add the noun-forming suffix. For another word, you need only remove its suffix to form a noun.) Finally, look up the meanings of the new words in a dictionary.

Elements of Literature

PERSUASION: See It My Way

BIG BROTHER (*trying to persuade* LITTLE BROTHER *to stop using the TV screen for a video game so that he can watch a football game on TV*): If we watch the game together, you'll learn how to improve your game. I'll even give you some of the tips Coach Jackson taught us. If my team wins, I'll play "Demon Warrior" with you for an hour right after the game's over, and I'll wash the dishes for you tonight when it's really your turn.

If you were Little Brother, would you be persuaded?

Writers who have a **persuasive aim** are trying to lead you to think or act in a certain way—to agree with their opinions, buy their products, vote for their candidates, support their causes. In "The Lowest Animal," Mark Twain is trying to persuade you *not* to behave in certain ways—all the ways he ridicules.

Skillful persuaders have a whole trunkful of no-holds-barred techniques—just short of twisting your arm—designed to get you to see things their way. Learning these techniques will make your writing and speaking more forceful and convincing. It will also make you aware of the ways in which others try to persuade you.

Aim for the Brain: Logical Appeals

Logic is the science of correct reasoning that's been slowly built into your brain by your experiences in the world. It deals with things like "If this is true, then that must be true" and "This must be true because . . ." and "Yes, that makes sense to me." A logical **persuasive argument,** such as the one you'll present for the Writer's Workshop on page 492, is built on an **opinion** supported by reasons and evidence.

- **Reasons** tell *why* everyone should accept an opinion as **valid** (true).

Suppose you are in favor of all public school students' wearing uniforms. Two reasons to support your opinion might be that uniforms eliminate expensive competition over clothes and lessen classroom distractions.

Reasons can't stand alone; they need to be backed up by sufficient **evidence.**

- **Facts and statistics (number facts)** give strong support to your reasons because nobody can argue with them. A fact is, by definition, true (see page 479).

A recent survey shows that 61% of all students in this school and 86% of all their parents and guardians favor uniforms.

- **Expert testimony.** Statements made by an expert in the field are always convincing.

"Since we adopted uniforms two years ago," said Kate Applegate, Shaw's principal for the past twenty years, "school morale has definitely improved."

Beware of Faulty Reasoning: Fallacies

Some statements sound logical and factual, but they're not. Whenever someone tries to persuade you, ask yourself, "*How* is this person trying to convince me?" Be alert to these common kinds of faulty reasoning, or **logical fallacies,** and watch for them in your own writing and speaking.

- **Hasty generalization**—coming to a conclusion on the basis of insufficient evidence

All my friends prefer uniforms;

by Richard Cohen

most tenth-graders would rather wear uniforms than faddish clothing.

- **Name calling**—attacking the person who holds the view rather than the view itself

Loren has been campaigning for school uniforms, but everyone knows what bad judgment he's shown in the past.

- **Either/or**—describing a situation as if there were only two choices when in fact there may be several

Either the school board requires that students wear uniforms, or we face increased disruptions in the classrooms and in the halls.

- **False cause and effect**—asserting that because Event B followed Event A, A caused B

Since he began to wear a uniform, Jed's been getting better grades on English tests.

Zeroing In on Feelings: Emotional Appeals

In the persuasive writing that you do for school, you'll be expected to rely mainly on logical appeals. But a little feeling never hurts. Think of emotional appeals as an extra nudge that moves the audience in your direction. The key point is that emotional appeals should reinforce logical arguments, not replace them.

- **Loaded words.** You've studied the power of loaded words on page 467. How many can you spot in this statement?

Neat, attractive school uniforms promote feelings of mutual respect and equality among students, who are judged by how they act rather than by the cost of their designer running shoes.

- **Glittering generalities**. A type of loaded words, they are so strongly positive that they "glitter" and make you feel good. Slogans are often glittering generalities.

School uniforms—they're all-American.

- **Bandwagon appeal.** This is the "Don't miss out" or "Don't be the last person to have one" appeal often used by advertisers.

In this district, all but two schools have voted to require uniforms for students.

- **Testimonials.** When a basketball star endorses a candidate for the Senate or a brand of cereal, he's making an emotional appeal to fans. Famous people who endorse products unrelated to their field of expertise are persuading by means of their talent, glamour, and fame.

Leila Lovelace, glamorous movie star, and Tyrone Washington, MVP quarterback, agree that they owe their success in life to wearing school uniforms as teenagers.

Check It Out

So there you have it. Effective persuasion is always built on logical appeals and sometimes on emotional appeals. It avoids all fallacies. Look for these characteristics of good persuasion in

- a commercial
- an editorial, a column, or a letter to the editor
- a political or campaign speech
- a persuasive argument made by a friend
- a persuasive argument you make

Before You Read

THE MAN IN THE WATER

Make the Connection

Who's a Hero?

Have you ever seen a real-life hero? We see so many inflated heroes in movies and on TV that the real thing is sometimes hard to recognize.

This essay is about a person who was unmistakably a hero, an ordinary man who didn't ask for the opportunity to display his courage. The disaster described in the essay occurred on the Potomac River, near Washington National Airport in Washington, D.C., in the winter of 1982.

Quickwrite

In your notebook, define *hero* and *heroism* in a sentence or two. Then list some people, past or present, famous or ordinary, whom you regard as heroes. Briefly tell why you think each person is a hero. Save your notes.

Elements of Literature

The Main Idea

When Rosenblatt sat down to write his feature article about the man in the water, he probably had his **main idea** in mind—some insight or message he wished to communicate about the tragedy. He was not writing a news article in which he'd have to report the facts of the event. That article had already been written. Rosenblatt wanted to do something else. He wanted to talk about something important that he saw in the incident. He had an idea to share.

> A **main idea** is an opinion, a message, an insight, or a lesson that is the focus of a piece of writing. Some essayists directly state their main idea. Others let us infer the idea for ourselves.

Reading Skills and Strategies

Summarizing the Main Idea

When you **summarize** an essay such as Rosenblatt's, you state its most important idea in your own words. You should also cite some of the essay's key **supporting details**. To find the **main idea** of Rosenblatt's—or any—essay, look for key statements that express the writer's opinion. You might want to organize your thoughts by filling out a chart like this:

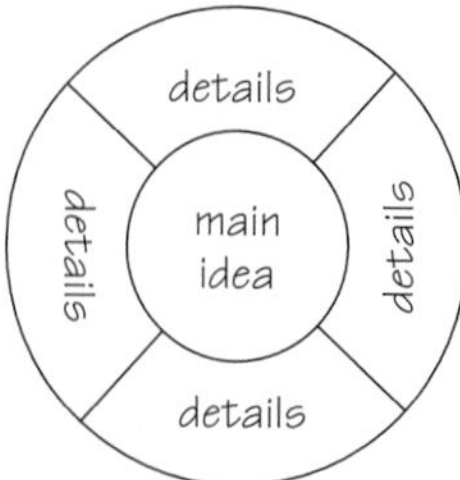

Like every other person on that flight, he was desperate to live.

The Man in the Water

Roger Rosenblatt

As disasters go, this one was terrible but not unique, certainly not among the worst on the roster of U.S. air crashes. There was the unusual element of the bridge, of course, and the fact that the plane clipped it at a moment of high traffic, one routine thus intersecting another and disrupting both. Then, too, there was the location of the event. Washington, the city of form and regulations, turned chaotic, deregulated, by a blast of real winter and a single slap of metal on metal. The jets from Washington National Airport that normally swoop around the presidential monuments like famished gulls were, for the moment, emblemized[1] by the one that fell; so there was that detail. And there was the aesthetic clash[2] as well—blue-and-green Air Florida, the name a flying garden, sunk down among gray chunks in a black river. All that was worth noticing, to be sure. Still, there was nothing very special in any of it, except death, which, while always special, does not necessarily bring millions to tears or to attention. Why, then, the shock here?

Perhaps because the nation saw in this disaster something more than a mechanical failure. Perhaps because people saw in it no failure at all, but rather something successful about their makeup. Here, after all, were two forms of nature in collision: the elements and human character. Last Wednesday, the elements, indifferent as ever, brought down Flight 90. And on that same afternoon, human nature—groping and flailing in mysteries of its own—rose to the occasion.

Of the four acknowledged heroes of the event, three are able to account for their behavior. Donald Usher and Eugene Windsor, a park-police helicopter team, risked their lives every time they dipped the skids[3] into the water to pick up survivors. On television, side by side in

1. **emblemized** (em′bləm·īzd′): represented; symbolized.
2. **aesthetic** (es·thet′ik) **clash:** unpleasant visual contrast.
3. **skids:** long, narrow pieces used in place of wheels for aircraft landing gear.

Words to Own

flailing (flāl′iŋ) *v.:* waving wildly.

Literature and the News

The Last Conversation: A Database

Roger Rosenblatt's essay focuses on one aspect of a news event. Here are other facts:

Date: Wednesday, January 20, 1982; late afternoon.
Weather: Wet snow flurries.
Location: Plane hit 14th Street Bridge, crushing five cars and one truck, crashed into Potomac River, Washington, D.C.
Death toll: seventy-eight, including four motorists. Of the seventy-nine people aboard the plane, only five survived (four passengers, one flight attendant).
Probable cause of crash: ice on wings.

[Black box retrieved from wreckage of Air Florida Flight 90.]

COPILOT: It's been a while since we've been de-iced.
PILOT: Think I'll go home and . . .
COPILOT: Boy . . . this is a losing battle here on trying to de-ice those things . . . a false sense of security, that's all that does.
PILOT: That, ah, satisfies the Feds. Right there is where the icing truck, they oughta have two . . .
COPILOT: Yeah, and you taxi through kinda like a carwash or something.
PILOT: Hit that thing with about eight billion gallons of glycol . . .
COPILOT: Slushy runway. Do you want me to do anything special for this or just go for it?

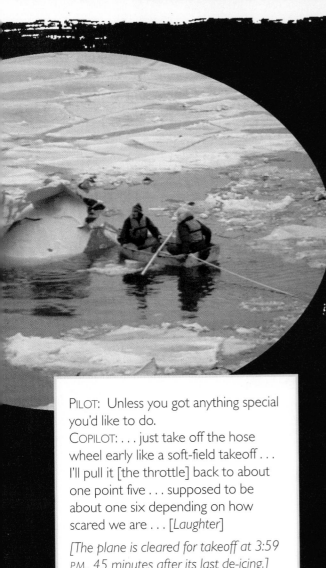

PILOT: Unless you got anything special you'd like to do.
COPILOT: . . . just take off the hose wheel early like a soft-field takeoff . . . I'll pull it [the throttle] back to about one point five . . . supposed to be about one six depending on how scared we are . . . [*Laughter*]

[The plane is cleared for takeoff at 3:59 P.M., 45 minutes after its last de-icing.]

COPILOT: God, look at that thing.
COPILOT: That don't seem right, does it?
COPILOT: Ah, that's not right.
PILOT: Yes, it is, there's eighty.
COPILOT: Naw, I don't think that's right.
COPILOT: Ah, maybe it is.
PILOT: Hundred and twenty.
COPILOT: I don't know. . . .
PILOT: Come on, forward. . . .
PILOT: Just barely climb.
SPEAKER UNDETERMINED: Stalling, we're [falling].
COPILOT: Larry, we're going down, Larry.
PILOT: I know it. [*Sound of impact*]

bright blue jumpsuits, they described their courage as all in the line of duty. Lenny Skutnik, a 28-year-old employee of the Congressional Budget Office, said: "It's something I never thought I would do"—referring to his jumping into the water to drag an injured woman to shore. Skutnik added that "somebody had to go in the water," delivering every hero's line that is no less admirable for its repetitions. In fact, nobody had to go into the water. That somebody actually did so is part of the reason this particular tragedy sticks in the mind.

But the person most responsible for the emotional impact of the disaster is the one known at first simply as "the man in the water." (Balding, probably in his 50s, an extravagant moustache.) He was seen clinging with five other survivors to the tail section of the airplane. This man was described by Usher and Windsor as appearing alert and in control. Every time they lowered a lifeline and flotation ring to him, he passed it on to another of the passengers. "In a mass casualty, you'll find people like him," said Windsor. "But I've never seen one with that commitment." When the helicopter came back for him, the man had gone under. His selflessness was one reason the story held national attention; his anonymity another. The fact that he went unidentified invested him with a universal character. For a while he was Everyman, and thus proof (as if one needed it) that no man is ordinary.

Still, he could never have imagined such a capacity in himself. Only minutes before his character was tested, he was sitting in the ordinary plane among the ordinary passengers, dutifully listening to the stewardess telling him to fasten his seat belt and saying something about the "No Smoking" sign. So our man relaxed with the others, some of whom would owe their lives to him. Perhaps he started to read, or to doze, or to regret some harsh remark made in the office that morning. Then suddenly he knew that the trip would not be ordinary. Like every other person on that flight, he was desperate to live, which makes his final act so stunning.

For at some moment in the water he must have realized that he would not live if he contin-

A park-police helicopter team airlifts one of the five survivors of Air Florida Flight 90 from the Potomac River's icy waters on January 20, 1982.

ued to hand over the rope and ring to others. He *had* to know it, no matter how gradual the effect of the cold. In his judgment he had no choice. When the helicopter took off with what was to be the last survivor, he watched everything in the world move away from him, and he deliberately let it happen.

Yet there was something else about our man that kept our thoughts on him, and which keeps our thoughts on him still. He was *there,* in the essential, classic circumstance. Man in nature. The man in the water. For its part, nature cared nothing about the five passengers. Our man, on the other hand, cared totally. So the timeless battle commenced in the Potomac. For as long as that man could last, they went at each other, nature and man; the one making no distinctions of good and evil, acting on no principles, offering no lifelines; the other acting wholly on distinctions, principles, and, one supposes, on faith.

Since it was he who lost the fight, we ought to come again to the conclusion that people are powerless in the world. In reality, we believe the reverse, and it takes the act of the man in the water to remind us of our true feelings in this matter. It is not to say that everyone would have acted as he did, or as Usher, Windsor, and Skutnik. Yet whatever moved these men to challenge death on behalf of their fellows is not peculiar to them. Everyone feels the possibility in himself. That is the abiding wonder of the story. That is why we would not let go of it. If the man in the water gave a lifeline to the people gasping for survival, he was likewise giving a lifeline to those who observed him.

The odd thing is that we do not even really believe that the man in the water lost his fight. "Everything in Nature contains all the powers of Nature," said Emerson. Exactly. So the man in the water had his own natural powers. He could not make ice storms, or freeze the water until it froze the blood. But he could hand life over to a stranger, and that is a power of nature too. The man in the water pitted himself against an implacable, impersonal enemy; he fought it with charity; and he held it to a standoff. He was the best we can do.

Words to Own

abiding *adj.:* continuing; lasting.
pitted *v.:* placed in competition.
implacable (im·plā′kə·bəl) *adj.:* relentless; not affected by attempts at change.

Meet the Writer

Searching for the Good

Roger Rosenblatt (1940–) has had a career's worth of practice in writing short opinion essays, first as the author of a weekly column for *The New Republic*, then as an editorial writer and columnist for *The Washington Post*, then as a commentator on Public Television's *MacNeil/Lehrer Newshour.*

After receiving a bachelor's degree from New York University and master's and doctoral degrees from Harvard, Rosenblatt taught literature for several years before turning to journalism. His 1983 book, *Children of War*, covers his journey through five war-torn countries—Ireland, Israel, Lebanon, Cambodia, and Vietnam. In each he interviewed children who had experienced war as a way of life.

Two years later, he followed that publication with *Witness: The World Since Hiroshima.* Both books, like "The Man in the Water," show Rosenblatt's search for the redeeming aspects of human existence.

Rosenblatt says that an expression of mystery characterizes his best essays and stories.

"Often I will wait to write till the last possible minute before deadline, hoping not to solve a particular mystery, but to feel it more deeply. 'The Man in the Water' . . . was written in forty-five minutes, but I brooded about it for many days. . . . Three full days that air crash led the evening news. I came to believe that the man in the water was the reason, yet no one had said so because he had done something people could not understand.

In too many ways the piece shows that it was written in forty-five minutes, but it resonated with readers at the time because it dwelt on the mystery of an act that people did not understand, or want to understand. Certain stories people do not want to understand. The mystery makes them feel closer to one another than would any solution."

Making Meanings

First Thoughts

1. As you read the essay, what did you think or feel about the man in the water? First, describe each response in a phrase; then elaborate.

Shaping Interpretations

2. According to Rosenblatt, the man in the water symbolizes an "essential, classic circumstance": the conflict between human beings and nature. How does Rosenblatt characterize nature? How does nature differ from the man in the water?

3. **Summarize** Rosenblatt's most important points, and state his **main idea**. Which passages support this idea most effectively? Does Rosenblatt ever state the idea directly? (Be sure to check the chart you made while reading.)

4. Rosenblatt says that the man in the water is proof that "no man is ordinary." What do you think he means by this? What other people have proved that we are "not ordinary"?

5. The final two paragraphs of the essay make specific points about human nature. Tell how you feel about the opinions Rosenblatt expresses there.

Reading Check

a. Briefly describe the disaster.

b. What does Rosenblatt think the nation saw in this disaster?

c. Besides the man in the water, Rosenblatt mentions three other heroes. Who are they, and what did they do?

d. Describe what the man in the water looked like and what he did.

e. What ultimately happened to him?

Connecting with the Text

6. How would you react in a situation in which you might save a stranger's life but risk losing your own life? Would your behavior change if the person in danger was someone you loved? Talk about your responses to what the four heroes did.

Extending the Text

7. Twain satirizes the bad in human nature (see page 457), and Rosenblatt praises the good. In what specific ways does Rosenblatt provide answers to Twain?

Challenging the Text

8. What do you think of the details the writer tells you—and doesn't tell you—about the man in the water? (What questions would you like to ask Rosenblatt?)

Choices: Building Your Portfolio

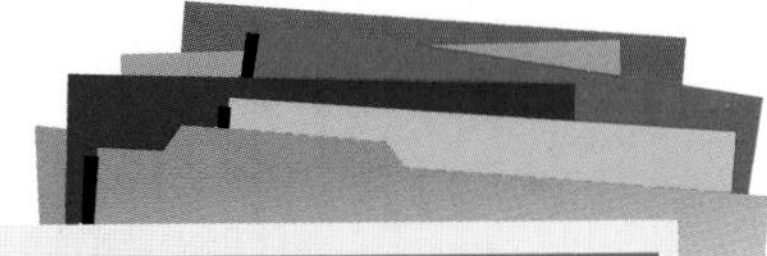

Writer's Notebook

1. Collecting Ideas for a Persuasive Essay

Looking in the news. Did Rosenblatt's essay give you any ideas about where you might find topics for a persuasive essay of your own? (See the Writer's Workshop assignment on page 492.) Look through the papers (or watch TV) and find some news or sports stories that could contain some revelation about life. Make a cluster diagram for each news story to see if you can find enough material for a persuasive essay.

WORK IN PROGRESS

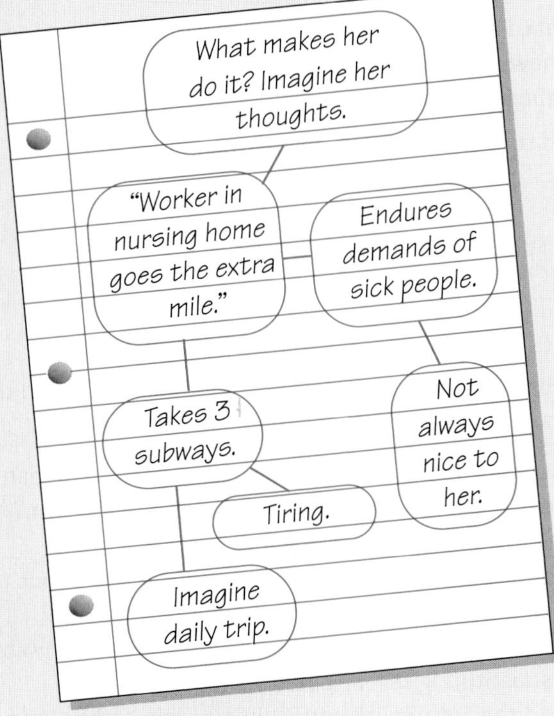
What makes her do it? Imagine her thoughts.
"Worker in nursing home goes the extra mile."
Endures demands of sick people.
Takes 3 subways.
Not always nice to her.
Tiring.
Imagine daily trip.

Creative Writing

2. A Biography of the Man in the Water

Give the man in the water a life. Imagine who he was, where he came from, where he was going, what his work and family were like. Then imagine his thoughts and feelings during and after the crash. Write an imaginary **biographical sketch** that elaborates on all these details. Read it aloud if you wish.

Writing/Drawing

3. A Gallery of Heroes

Create a poster or portrait of one of the heroes you listed in your Quickwrite notes. Show your hero in his or her surroundings. In a caption, tell a little about the person's life and why he or she is a hero. You might include quotations by and about your hero. You can work with other classmates to create a gallery of heroes for young readers or a bulletin-board display for your classroom. Remember that your hero can be ordinary. (He or she can be an "unsung" hero—someone anonymous, unlike the heroes made famous in poetry, songs, and books.)

Speaking/Performance

4. Life Is with People

With a group, prepare materials for a **performance** that presents your ideas on what people are capable of. You might organize your performance around human traits like courage, generosity, and kindness. You will have to decide what materials to present: Will you limit your performance to **readings** from poems, stories, and nonfiction pieces in this book? Will you include pieces from outside sources, like newspapers or even student publications? Will you include **music, art,** and photography? What title will you use? Who will your audience be?

Language Link MINI-LESSON

Streamlining Your Prose

Technology HELP

See Language Workshop CD-ROM. *Key word entry: wordiness.*

Compare these two sentences:

1. Every time, hoping to rescue him, they lowered a lifeline and flotation ring to him and hoped he would allow himself to be rescued out of the water, but he conveyed the rescue device to yet another one of the passengers who were in the plane with him, waiting in the water to be rescued after the crash.
2. *Rosenblatt*: "Every time they lowered a lifeline and flotation ring to him, he passed it on to another of the passengers."

Roger Rosenblatt's sentence is not only much better than the first sentence; it's also harder to write. That's because it's easier to be wordy than to write concisely. Rosenblatt states everything simply and in few words. When you are writing an informative essay, be concise. Avoid repetition. If you can say something in two words, don't use ten. If you can use a short, familiar word, don't use a long, difficult one.

WORDY Those who heard about the airline disaster from reading the paper or watching the news expressed a desire to be enlightened with additional details about the life and identity of the passenger in the water.

IMPROVED People wanted to know more about the man in the water.

Try It Out

Pick another short passage from "The Man in the Water" and inflate it, as shown in the first example. (By rewriting good, spare prose, you'll appreciate what makes it good.) Then ask a partner to pare your inflated passage to its essentials. Compare the "edited" version with Rosenblatt's. Did your partner come close to finding the original amid the wordiness?

➤ If you're like most writers, you probably could improve any page of prose you've written by cutting some words. Take a piece of prose you're working on or a piece from your writer's portfolio. See if you can do some pruning.

Vocabulary HOW TO OWN A WORD

Word Bank

flailing
abiding
pitted
implacable

In Other Words: Synonyms and Connotations

From a number of **synonyms,** Rosenblatt chose the word that had the **connotations** he wanted. Examine his word choices.

1. Rosenblatt says that in the aftermath of the crash, human nature found itself "groping and flailing in mysteries of its own." Why wouldn't *waving* have the same effect as *flailing?*
2. What does abiding add to the author's conclusion about the "wonder of the story" that *lingering* wouldn't convey?
3. The man in the water "pitted" himself against nature. Why wouldn't substituting *set* for *pitted* work as well?
4. Why would the author call nature implacable rather than firm?

Before You Read

. . . That's Scary!

Make the Connection

Too Horrible for Kids

Horror and violence on television—do they harm kids? How to regulate what children watch on TV is an issue that concerns many parents, including Stephen King, who has become rich and famous by writing horror novels that have been turned into movies. Can you guess his position on the controversial issue of censoring scary TV shows?

Quickwrite

What do you remember about watching—or not being allowed to watch—scary movies and TV shows when you were little? In your notebook, write an anecdote or example.

Elements of Literature

Fact vs. Opinion

In this 1981 essay, King writes, "Three of my books have been made into films, and at this writing, two of them have been shown on TV." These are facts. A **fact** can be verified by consulting a reliable source or by personal observation.

About films of violent fairy tales, King writes, "All these films would certainly get G ratings if they were produced today." That's an **opinion**—a belief or conclusion that can't be proved. Although King may be confident that the films would get G ratings, there's no way to verify that conclusion.

A **fact** is a statement that can be proved. An **opinion** is a statement of belief that can't be proved. It can only be supported.

For more on Facts and Opinions, see pages 468–469.

Reading Skills and Strategies

Evaluating Motivation and Credibility

King wants to persuade you to accept his opinion, so he uses facts, examples, and arguments to support that opinion. As a critical reader, you need to weigh his **motivation**—why is this issue especially important to him? You also need to evaluate the **credibility** of his information. Are his arguments convincing? Can they be substantiated or proved? Read carefully.

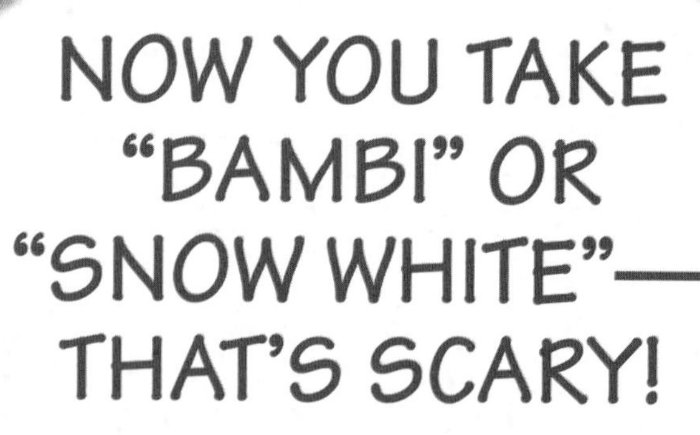

NOW YOU TAKE "BAMBI" OR "SNOW WHITE"—THAT'S SCARY!

Stephen King

Read the story synopsis below and ask yourself if it would make the sort of film you'd want your kids watching on the Friday- or Saturday-night movie:

A good but rather weak man discovers that, because of inflation, recession, and his second wife's fondness for overusing his credit cards, the family is tottering on the brink of financial ruin. In fact, they can expect to see the repossession men coming for the car, the almost

SHOULD CHILDREN WATCH VIOLENT OR HORRIFYING PROGRAMS?

new recreational vehicle, and the two color TVs any day; and a pink warning-of-foreclosure[1] notice has already arrived from the bank that holds the mortgage on their house.

The wife's solution is simple but chilling: Kill the two children, make it look like an accident, and collect the insurance. She browbeats her husband into going along with this homicidal scheme. A wilderness trip is arranged, and while wifey stays in camp, the father leads his two children deep into the Great Smoky wilderness. In the end, he finds he cannot kill them in cold blood; he simply leaves them to wander around until, presumably, they die of hunger and exposure.

The two children spend a horrifying three days and two nights in the wilderness. Near the end of their endurance, they stumble upon a back-country cabin and go to it, hoping for rescue. The woman who lives alone there turns out to be a cannibal. She cages the two children and prepares to roast them in her oven as she has roasted and eaten other wanderers before them. The boy manages to get free. He creeps up behind the woman as she stokes her oven and pushes her in, where she burns to death in her own fire.

You're probably shaking your head no, even if you have already recognized the origin of this bloody little tale (and if you didn't, ask your kids: they probably will) as "Hansel and Gretel," a so-called fairy tale that most kids are exposed to even before they start kindergarten. In addition to this story, with its grim and terrifying images of child abandonment, children lost in the woods and imprisoned by an evil woman, cannibalism, and justifiable homicide, small children are routinely exposed to tales of mass murder and mutilation ("Bluebeard"), the eating of a loved one by a monster ("Little Red Riding-Hood"), treachery and deceit ("Snow White"), and even the specter of a little boy who must face a black-hooded, ax-wielding headsman[2] ("The 500 Hats of Bartholomew Cubbins," by Dr. Seuss).

I'm sometimes asked what I allow my kids to watch on the tube, for two reasons: First, my three children, at ten, eight, and four, are still young enough to be in the age group that opponents of TV violence and horror consider to be particularly impressionable and at risk; and sec-

1. **foreclosure** (fôr·klō′zhər): forced sale of a property to recover money lent for its purchase.

2. **headsman:** executioner who cuts off the head of a person condemned to die.

WORDS TO OWN

specter (spek′tər) *n.:* frightening figure; ghost.

ond, my seven novels have been popularly classified as "horror stories." People tend to think those two facts contradictory. But . . . I'm not sure that they are.

Three of my books have been made into films, and at this writing,[3] two of them have been shown on TV. In the case of *Salem's Lot,* a made-for-TV movie, there was never a question of allowing my kids to watch it on its first run on CBS; it began at nine o'clock in our time zone, and all three children go to bed earlier than that. Even on a weekend, and even for the oldest, an eleven o'clock bedtime is just not negotiable. A previous *TV Guide* article about children and frightening programs mentioned a three-year-old who watched *Lot* and consequently suffered night terrors. I have no wish to question any responsible parent's judgment—all parents raise their children in different ways—but it did strike me as passingly odd that a three-year-old should have been allowed to stay up that late to get scared.

But in my case, the hours of the telecast were not really a factor, because we have one of those neat little time machines, a videocassette recorder. I taped the program and, after viewing it myself, decided my children could watch it if they wanted to. My daughter had no interest; she's more involved with stories of brave dogs and loyal horses these days. My two sons, Joe,

3. King wrote this article in 1981.

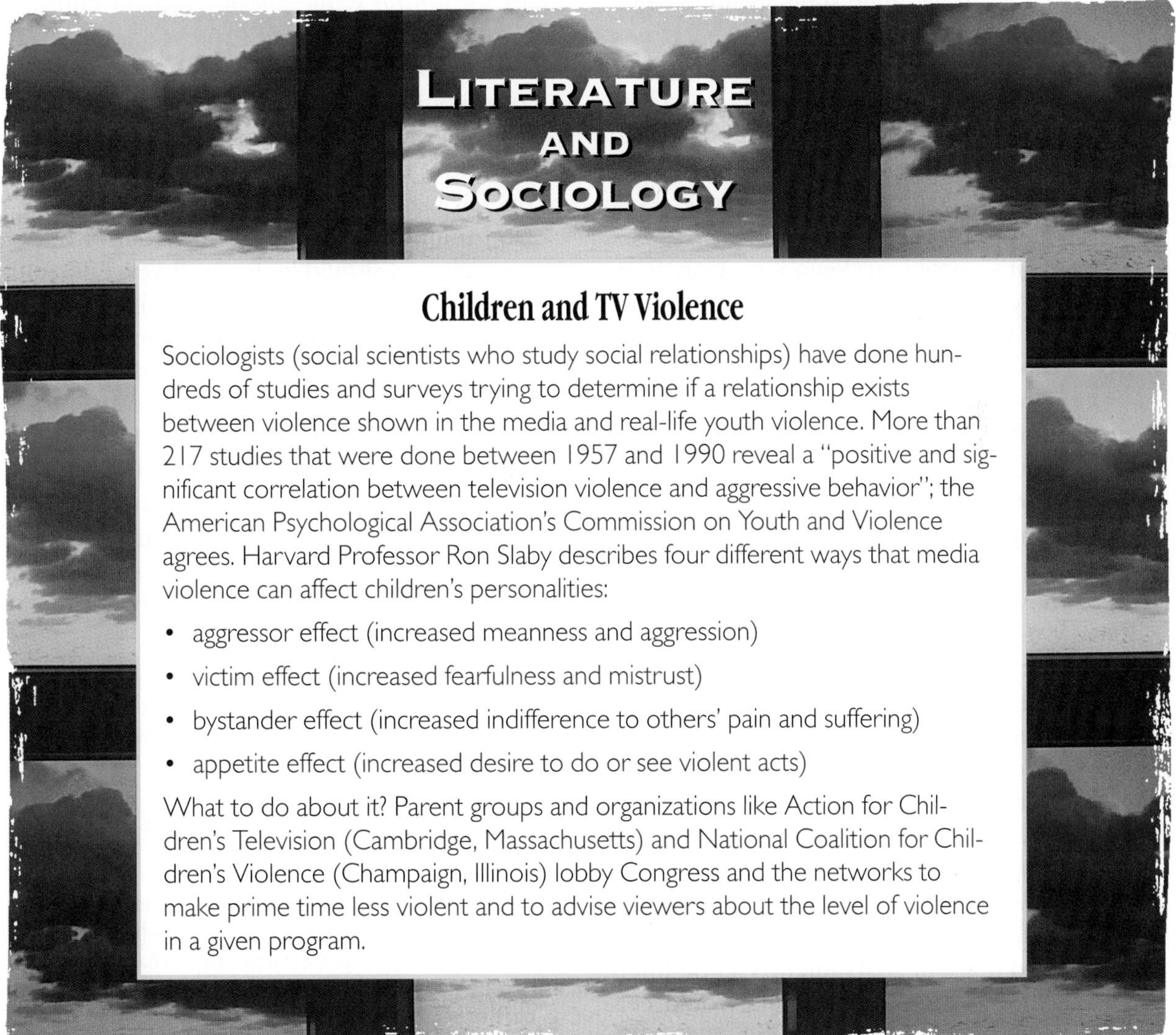

Literature and Sociology

Children and TV Violence

Sociologists (social scientists who study social relationships) have done hundreds of studies and surveys trying to determine if a relationship exists between violence shown in the media and real-life youth violence. More than 217 studies that were done between 1957 and 1990 reveal a "positive and significant correlation between television violence and aggressive behavior"; the American Psychological Association's Commission on Youth and Violence agrees. Harvard Professor Ron Slaby describes four different ways that media violence can affect children's personalities:

- aggressor effect (increased meanness and aggression)
- victim effect (increased fearfulness and mistrust)
- bystander effect (increased indifference to others' pain and suffering)
- appetite effect (increased desire to do or see violent acts)

What to do about it? Parent groups and organizations like Action for Children's Television (Cambridge, Massachusetts) and National Coalition for Children's Violence (Champaign, Illinois) lobby Congress and the networks to make prime time less violent and to advise viewers about the level of violence in a given program.

eight, and Owen, then three, did watch. Neither of them seemed to have any problems, either while watching it or in the middle of the night—when those problems most likely turn up.

I also have a tape of *Carrie,* a theatrical film first shown on TV about two and a half years ago. I elected to keep this one on what my kids call "the high shelf" (where I put the tapes that are forbidden to them), because I felt that its depiction of children turning against other children, the lead character's horrifying embarrassment at a school dance, and her later act of homicide would upset them. *Lot,* on the contrary, is a story that the children accepted as a fairy tale in modern dress.

Other tapes on my "high shelf" include *Night of the Living Dead* (cannibalism), *The Brood* (David Cronenberg's film of intergenerational breakdown and homicidal "children of rage" who are set free to murder and rampage), and *The Exorcist.* They are all up there for the same reason: They contain elements that I think might freak the kids out.

Not that it's possible to keep kids away from everything on TV (or in the movies, for that matter) that will freak them out; the movies that terrorized my own nights most thoroughly as a kid were not those through which Frankenstein's monster or the Wolfman lurched and growled, but the Disney cartoons. I watched Bambi's mother shot and Bambi running frantically to escape being burned up in a forest fire. I watched, appalled, dismayed, and sweaty with fear, as Snow White bit into the poisoned apple while the old crone giggled in evil ecstasy. I was similarly terrified by the walking brooms in *Fantasia* and the big, bad wolf who chased the fleeing pigs from house to house with such grim and homicidal intensity. More recently, Owen, who just turned four, crawled into bed with my wife and me. "Cruella DeVille is in my room," he said. Cruella DeVille is, of course, the villainess of *101 Dalmatians,* and I suppose Owen had decided that a woman who would want to turn puppies into dogskin coats might also be interested in little boys. All these films would certainly get G ratings if they were produced today, and frightening excerpts of them have been shown on TV during "the children's hour."

Do I believe that all violent or horrifying programming should be banned from network TV? No, I do not. Do I believe it should be telecast only in the later evening hours, TV's version of the "high shelf"? Yes, I do. Do I believe that children should be forbidden all violent or horrifying programs? No, I do not. Like their elders, children have a right to experience the entire spectrum of drama, from such warm and mostly unthreatening programs as *Little House on the Prairie* and *The Waltons* to scarier fare. It's been suggested again and again that such entertainment offers us a catharsis[4]—a chance to enter for a little while a scary and yet controllable world, where we can express our fears, aggressions, and possibly even hostilities. Surely no one would suggest that children do not have their own fears and hostilities to face and overcome; those dark feelings are the basis of many of the fairy tales children love best.

Do I think a child's intake of violent or horrifying programs should be limited? Yes, I do, and that's why I have a high shelf. But the pressure groups who want to see all horror (and anything smacking of sex, for that matter) arbitrarily removed from television make me both uneasy and angry. The element of Big Brotherism[5] inherent in such an idea causes the unease; the idea of a bunch of people I don't even know presuming to dictate what is best for my children causes the anger. I feel that deciding such things myself is my right—and my responsibility.

4. **catharsis** (kə·thär′sis): release of emotional tension, often by some form of art.

5. **Big Brotherism:** invasion of people's privacy by the government, as in George Orwell's novel *1984.* This novel refers to the government as "Big Brother."

WORDS TO OWN

appalled (ə·pôld′) *v.* used as *adj.:* horrified.

arbitrarily (är′bə·trer′ə·lē) *adv.:* on the basis of whim or personal preference rather than reason.

inherent (in·hir′ənt) *adj.:* existing as a basic, essential part of something.

Meet the Writer

Mr. Scary

Stephen King (1947–) is by far the best-known contemporary writer of horror fiction. His novels have sold more than a hundred million copies. Five of them have been on *The New York Times* best-seller list at the same time, and his name has remained on the list for more than ten years.

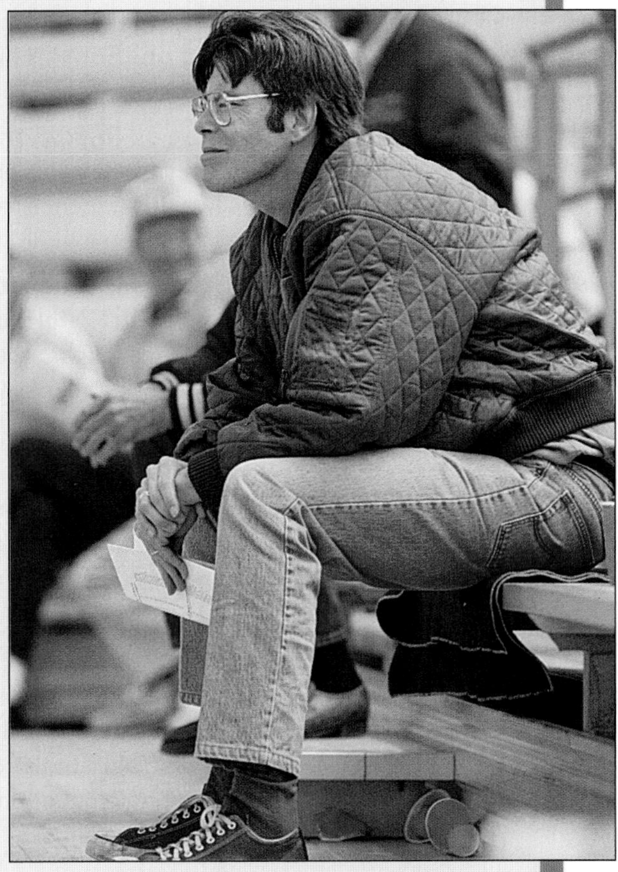

Born in Portland, Maine, King grew up in relative poverty after his father, a merchant sailor, deserted the family when King was two. King recalls that in his childhood he was subject to "very ordinary fears," such as fear of the dark. His love of horror movies and radio shows, he admits, contributed to scaring him. "I had friends and all that," King recalls, "but I often felt unhappy and different, estranged from other kids my age."

King is no longer estranged from the world: He is extraordinarily popular and has a happy family life in Bangor, Maine. In fact, people meeting him for the first time are often disappointed to find that he's so normal.

King sticks to a rigid writing schedule. After a brisk morning walk, he writes six pages every day ("and that's like engraved in stone," he says), revising in the afternoon. One odd aspect of his writing process is that he does his research *after* he writes his first draft, almost as if he's gathering facts to support a position he's already expressed.

Making Meanings

First Thoughts

1. How convincing did you find King's essay? Did he fail to change your mind, or were you already on his side? Talk about some of your reactions.

Shaping Interpretations

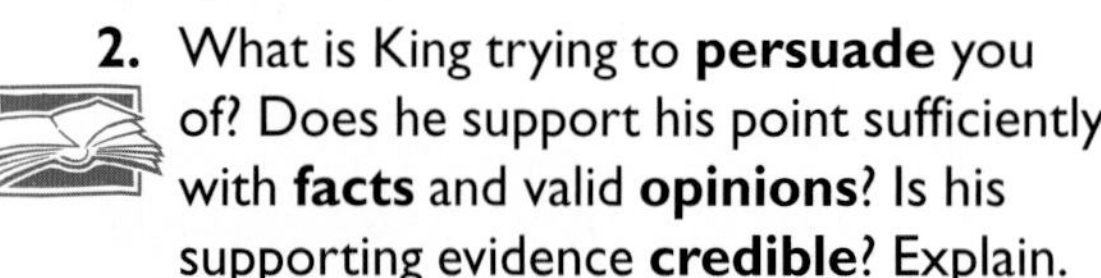

2. What is King trying to **persuade** you of? Does he support his point sufficiently with **facts** and valid **opinions**? Is his supporting evidence **credible**? Explain.
3. Does King rely more on **logical** or **emotional appeals** to make his point? Support your view with evidence from the text.

Reading Check

a. What point does King make in his retelling of "Hansel and Gretel" and his summary of other fairy tales?

b. What does King put on his "high shelf"?

c. Name some movies that frightened King when he was a child.

d. What is King's position on banning all horror material from TV?

4. Many people are concerned about the effects of television violence on viewers. Read "Children and TV Violence" on page 483, and see what **generalizations,** if any, you can make from the data given. Do the studies and surveys support or contradict King? Explain.

Connecting with the Text

5. In your Quickwrite notes, you wrote about scary movies and TV programs you watched as a child. **Compare and contrast** your experiences with King's descriptions of his own and his children's experiences.

Extending the Text

6. Imagine that twenty years from now social pressures result in entertainment that contains no horror, violence, or sex. What might that entertainment contain? Brainstorm inventive possibilities.

Challenging the Text

7. Respond to this comment: "Stephen King cannot possibly be objective on the issue of horror and violence. He is **motivated** by the fact that he makes money from his violent movies."
8. How would you respond to this essay if you were a parent? a child? a writer? a broadcaster? a movie director? a psychologist?

Robot on a Swing (1993) by Nam June Paik.

Courtesy Carl Solway Gallery, Cincinnati, Ohio.

Choices: Building Your Portfolio

Writer's Notebook

1. Collecting Ideas for a Persuasive Essay

Pros and cons. King weighs the pros and cons of violence on TV. Choose a specific solution to some issue that you're interested in, and make a Pro and Con chart. At the top, write the proposed solution, stated in the form of a question. Under it, list the Pros (reasons to support that proposal) in one column and the Cons (reasons to oppose that proposal) in a second column. When you write your persuasive essay for the Writer's Workshop on page 492, listing pros and cons may help you support your position and anticipate opposing arguments.

WORK IN PROGRESS

Issue: *Should horror movies be banned from TV?*

Pro *[Yes, they should.]*	**Con** *[No, they shouldn't.]*
1. They overexcite young children.	*1. They're exciting.*
2. They're not harmless—lead to nightmares and violence.	*2. They're a safe way to express fears and aggression.*
3. Very young children think they're real.	*3. Everyone knows they're not real.*
4. People should be protected from bad influences.	*4. Censorship is wrong.*

Creative Writing

2. Updating a Fairy Tale

To make a point, King updates the old fairy tale about Hansel and Gretel. Bring to class one of the stories from *The Stinky Cheese Man and Other Fairly Stupid Tales* by Jon Scieszka (Viking) or a fable from *Fables for Our Time* by James Thurber (Harper). Using one of those **parodies** as a model, write an updated version of a fairy tale or fable. Focus on the **plot, characters, setting, resolution,** and **moral.**

Persuasive Letter

3. What's Your Opinion?

Write a response to Stephen King's essay, stating your views on the subject of whether children should be allowed to watch horror movies and if so, how much and which ones. Put your response in the form of a letter to Stephen King or a letter to the editor of your local newspaper.

Critical Thinking and Listening

4. Evaluating the Media

Read, watch, or listen to one example of each of the following kinds of communication:

- newspaper editorial
- letter to the editor
- radio or television commercial
- magazine advertisement

What does each one try to **persuade** you to believe or do? Make some notes on **facts** and **opinions** (or their absence) and how they're used. Does each communication appeal to your **reason** or to your **emotions**? Does it contain **logical fallacies**? Write a brief essay evaluating all the communications. (You might want to review pages 468–469 for help.)

GRAMMAR LINK — MINI-LESSON

Setting Off Parenthetical Information

Language Handbook HELP

See Commas, page 1052; Dashes, page 1057; Parentheses, page 1058.

Technology HELP

See Language Workshop CD-ROM. *Key word entry: parenthetical expressions.*

Parenthetical expressions are asides, remarks that are made almost as afterthoughts to a sentence. When you come to a parenthetical expression as you are reading aloud, you pause to set it off from the rest of the sentence.

1. ". . . even if you have already recognized the origin of this bloody little tale (and if you didn't, ask your kids: they probably will) as 'Hansel and Gretel' . . . " [parenthetical aside set off with parentheses]
2. "I have no wish to question any responsible parent's judgment—all parents raise their children in different ways—but it did strike me as passingly odd that a three-year-old should have been allowed to stay up that late to get scared." [parenthetical aside set off with dashes]
3. "*Lot,* on the contrary, is a story that the children accepted as a fairy tale in modern dress." [parenthetical expression set off with commas]

Try It Out

1. In King's essay, look for more sentences that contain parentheses and dashes. Check to see where each parenthetical remark begins and ends. Why wouldn't commas do in each situation?
2. Sometimes the use of punctuation is a judgment call. Could you use dashes or parentheses to set off the underscored words below?
   - **a.** "Even on a weekend, and even for the oldest, an eleven o'clock bedtime is just not negotiable."
   - **b.** "My two sons, Joe, eight, and Owen, then three, did watch."

VOCABULARY — HOW TO OWN A WORD

WORD BANK

specter
appalled
arbitrarily
inherent

Overlapping Synonyms: Venn Diagrams

Using a dictionary or the definitions provided in the text, find a **synonym** for each word in the Word Bank. You can explore the similarities and differences between the two synonyms by making a Venn diagram like the one below for the word *appalled.* In the overlapping area, write the meanings that apply to both words.

Appalled	Both	Horrified
• stunned • suggests disgust and dismay at situation	shocked	• filled with intense fear or loathing or terror

Quickwrite

What is the most courageous thing you have done? Write a brief account of your action, explaining what you did and why, if it was difficult, and how you felt during and after the experience. Was anything accomplished by your action?

A FEATURE ARTICLE

The Unknown Rebel

Pico Iyer

Almost nobody knew his name. Nobody outside his immediate neighborhood had read his words or heard him speak. Nobody knows what happened to him even one hour after his moment in the world's living rooms. But the man who stood before a column of tanks near Tiananmen Square—June 5, 1989—may have impressed his image on the global memory more vividly, more intimately than even Sun Yat-sen[1] did. Almost certainly he was seen in his moment of self-transcendence by more people than ever laid eyes on Winston Churchill, Albert Einstein, and James Joyce combined.

The meaning of his moment—it was no more than that—was instantly decipherable in any tongue, to any age: even the billions who cannot read and those who have never heard of Mao Tse-tung[2] could follow what the "tank man" did. A small, unexceptional figure in slacks and white shirt, carrying what looks to be his shopping, posts himself before an approaching tank, with a line of seventeen more tanks behind it. The tank swerves right; he, to block it, moves left. The tank swerves left; he moves right. Then this anonymous bystander clambers up onto the vehicle of war and says something to its driver, which comes down to us as: "Why are you here? My city is in chaos because of you." One lone Everyman standing up to machinery, to force, to all the massed weight of the People's Republic—the largest nation

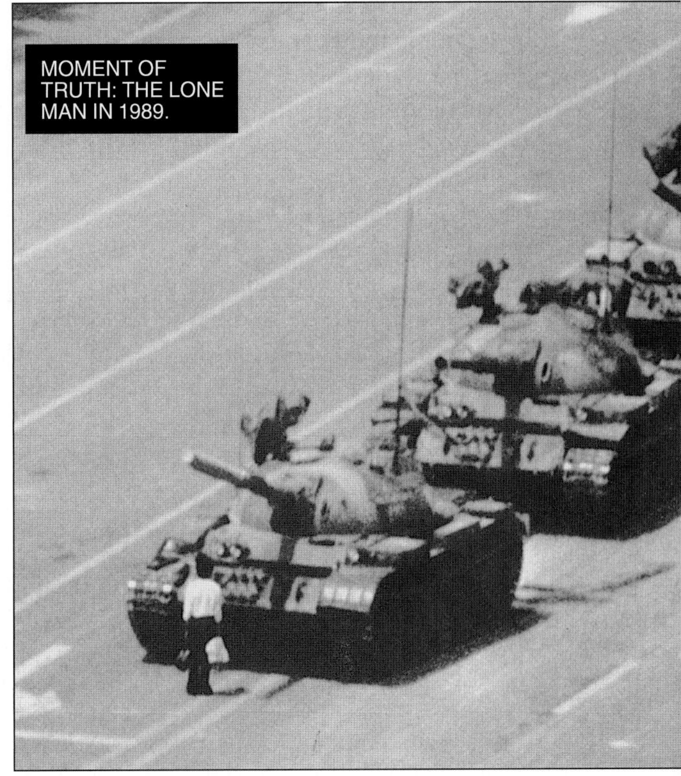

MOMENT OF TRUTH: THE LONE MAN IN 1989.

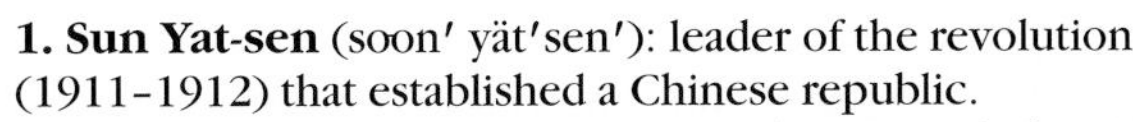

1. **Sun Yat-sen** (soon′ yät′sen′): leader of the revolution (1911–1912) that established a Chinese republic.
2. **Mao Tse-tung** (mou′ dzu′do͞oŋ′): chairman of China's Communist Party from 1949 to 1976.

go.hrw.com
LEO 10-7

in the world, comprising more than 1 billion people—while its all-powerful leaders remain, as ever, in hiding somewhere within the bowels of the Great Hall of the People.

Occasionally, unexpectedly, history consents to disguise itself as allegory, and China, which traffics in grand impersonals, has often led the world in mass-producing symbols in block capitals. The man who defied the tank was standing, as it happens, on the Avenue of Eternal Peace, just a minute away from the Gate of Heavenly Peace, which leads into the Forbidden City. Nearby Tiananmen Square—the very heart of the Middle Kingdom, where students had demonstrated in 1919; where Mao had proclaimed a "People's Republic" in 1949 on behalf of the Chinese people who had "stood up"; and where leaders customarily inspect their People's Liberation Army troops—is a virtual monument to People Power in the abstract. Its western edge is taken up by the Great Hall of the People. Its eastern side is dominated by the Museum of Chinese Revolution. The Mao Tsetung mausoleum swallows up its southern face.

For seven weeks, though, in the late spring of 1989—the modern year of revolutions—the Chinese people took back the square, first a few workers and students and teachers and soldiers, then more and more, until more than 1 million had assembled there. They set up, in the heart of the ancient nation, their own world within the world, complete with a daily newspaper, a broadcasting tent, even a 30-ft. plaster-covered statue they called the "Goddess of Democracy." Their "conference hall" was a Kentucky Fried Chicken parlor on the southwest corner of the square, and their spokesmen were 3,000 hunger strikers who spilled all over the central Monument to the People's Heroes. The unofficials even took over, and reversed, the formal symbolism of the government's ritual pageantry: when Mikhail Gorbachev[3] came to the Great Hall of the People for a grand state banquet during the demonstrations—the first visit by a Soviet leader in 30 years—he had to steal in by the back door.

Then, in the dark early hours of June 4, the government struck back, sending tanks from all directions toward Tiananmen Square and killing hundreds of workers and students and doctors and children, many later found shot in the back. In the unnatural quiet after the massacre, with the six-lane streets eerily empty and a burned-out bus along the road, it fell to the tank man to serve as the last great defender of the peace, an Unknown Soldier in the struggle for human rights.

As soon as the man had descended from the tank, anxious onlookers pulled him to safety, and the waters of anonymity closed around him once more. Some people said he was called Wang Weilin, was 19 years old and a student; others said not even that much could be confirmed. Some said he was a factory worker's son, others that he looked like a provincial just arrived in the capital by train. When American newsmen asked Chinese leader Jiang Zemin a year later what had happened to the symbol of Chinese freedom—caught by foreign cameramen and broadcast around the world—he replied, not very ringingly, "I think never killed."

—from *Time*, April 13, 1998

3. **Mikhail Gorbachev** (gôr′bə·chôf′): leader of the Soviet Union's Communist Party from 1985 to 1991.

Finding Common Ground

Get together with two or three classmates to discuss the point this essay makes.

1. Summarize your Quickwrite notes, and listen to your classmates' summaries of their experiences. Compare the circumstances surrounding the courageous acts and the results of the actions.
2. Use your experiences as a basis for understanding the unknown rebel's action near Tiananmen Square. You might discuss these questions:
   - Why do you think he risked his life?
   - What point did his action make to the watching world?
   - When is a grand gesture like this worth risking a life—or do you think it never is?

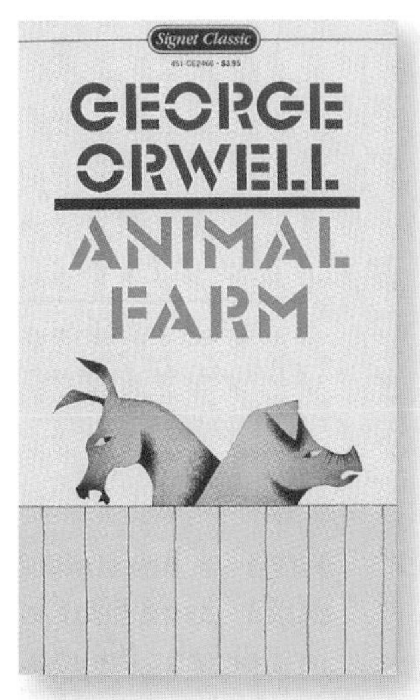

Beware of Pigs Who Act Like People

Mr. Jones is such a cruel farmer that the animals at Manor Farm revolt, renaming their farm Animal Farm. Things are cool for a while, as the animals run the farm themselves, but then a group of sly pigs proclaim, "Some animals are more equal than others." George Orwell's *Animal Farm* is a short, easy-to-read classic—a fable and a satire on totalitarian governments. (This title is available in the HRW library.)

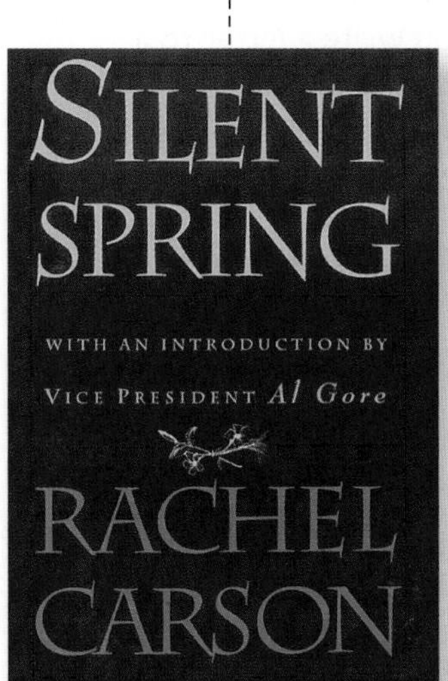

Why No Songbirds Sing

Why are the birds dying, and what's happened to the butterflies? In 1962, Rachel Carson's award-winning *Silent Spring* (Fawcett) exposed the horrors of the pesticide DDT, which was in widespread use then, and set off the environmental movement.

Our Country's Future

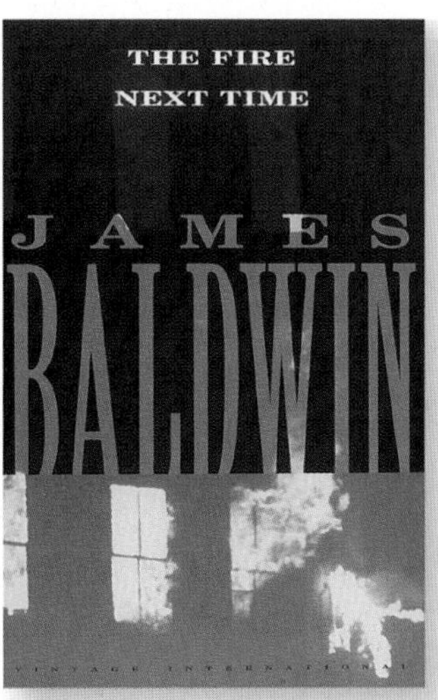

The Fire Next Time by James Baldwin (Dell) contains two essays—a letter to Baldwin's fourteen-year-old nephew James and an essay about Baldwin's experiences as an African American growing up in New York's Harlem. Baldwin, one of the first to proclaim that "black is beautiful," calls for an end to America's "racial nightmare." Written in 1963, the book remains a searing statement by one of America's finest novelists and essayists. (It is available in the HRW library.)

Remember Kindergarten?

So what did *you* learn there? Robert Fulghum claims *All I Really Need to Know I Learned in Kindergarten* (Ballantine). In his best-selling collection of short essays, Fulghum discovers wisdom and humor in everyday events and people.

#1 BESTSELLER
ALL I REALLY NEED TO KNOW I LEARNED IN KINDERGARTEN
Uncommon Thoughts on Common Things
ROBERT FULGHUM

Writer's Workshop

Technology HELP

See Writer's Workshop 2 CD-ROM. *Assignment: Controversial Issue.*

ASSIGNMENT

Write a persuasive essay on an issue that is important to you.

AIM

To persuade.

AUDIENCE

Your teacher, classmates, readers of a newspaper, a group or organization concerned about your topic. (You choose.)

PERSUASIVE WRITING

PERSUASIVE ESSAY

Whenever you try to persuade, you appeal to your readers or listeners to open their minds to the validity of your opinions and ideas. At the same time, you need to keep your own mind open so you can understand, anticipate, and refute the arguments of those who disagree with you. You use persuasion when you write a letter to a newspaper editor or review a book or a movie. You'll need to understand the techniques of persuasion to evaluate advertising claims and political speeches.

When you write persuasively, your goal is to express yourself convincingly so that readers understand the topic and your position. To do this, you provide reasons and support for your position.

Prewriting

1. Choose a Topic

WORK IN PROGRESS

In your Writer's Notebook, you've already jotted down ideas for a persuasive essay. If you haven't yet decided on a topic, check current news stories for topic ideas, such as the one in the model below. Reviewing the selections in this collection might also suggest a topic idea.

Professional Model

Appearances Are Destructive

As public schools reopen for the new year, strategies to curb school violence will once again be hotly debated. Installing metal detectors and hiring security guards will help, but the experience of my two sisters makes a compelling case for greater use of dress codes as a way to protect students and promote learning.

Introduction.

Opinion statement.

Shortly after my sisters arrived here from South Africa, I enrolled them at the local public school. I had great expectations for their educational experience. Compared with black schools under apartheid, American schools are Shangri-Las, with modern textbooks, school buses, computers, libraries, lunch programs, and dedicated teachers.

Reason 1 is a personal anecdote.

Despite these benefits, which students in many parts of the world

The history
of the written
word is rich and
Page 1
Once upon a time

Professional Model (continued)

only dream about, my sisters' efforts at learning were almost derailed. They were constantly taunted for their homely outfits. A couple of times they came home in tears. In South Africa students were required to wear uniforms, so my sisters had never been preoccupied with clothes and jewelry.

Loaded words: taunted, homely.

They became so distraught that they insisted on transferring to different schools, despite my reassurances that there was nothing wrong with them because of what they wore. . . .

Teachers shared their frustrations with me at being unable to teach those students willing to learn because classes are frequently disrupted by other students ogling themselves in mirrors, painting their fingernails, combing their hair, shining their gigantic shoes, or comparing designer labels on jackets, caps, and jewelry. . . .

Reason 2 deals with teachers' complaints. This is a generalization. How many teachers?

The argument by civil libertarians that dress codes infringe on freedom of expression is misleading. We observe dress codes in nearly every aspect of our lives without any diminution of our freedoms—as demonstrated by flight attendants, bus drivers, postal employees, high school bands, military personnel, sports teams, Girl and Boy Scouts, and employees of fast-food chains, restaurants, and hotels.

Here he deals with counterarguments — infringing on freedom.

In many countries where students outperform their American counterparts academically, school dress codes are observed as part of creating the proper learning environment. Their students tend to be neater, less disruptive in class, and more disciplined, mainly because their minds are focused more on learning and less on materialism.

Reason 3 is based on other countries' experiences with uniforms and learning.

It's time Americans realized that the benefits of safe and effective schools far outweigh any perceived curtailment of freedom of expression brought on by dress codes.

Conclusion sums up: pros outweigh cons.

—Mark Mathabane

2. Take a Stand: Formulate a Position

What is your initial reaction to your topic? Consider all sides of the issue, including the **pros** and **cons** (the arguments for and against). Then, write a clear one-sentence **opinion statement** expressing your position. Use this statement to focus

Communications Handbook HELP

See Using the Internet.

your thinking as you collect supporting data and organize your argument. If you change your position as you find more information, you can revise your opinion statement.

3. Gather Support

You'll need convincing **reasons** to support your position, and you'll need to use **evidence** to develop your reasons. Since your goal is to persuade others to see things your way, review the persuasive strategies on pages 468–469. Rely on logical appeals and watch out for faulty reasoning. Although emotional appeals may help persuade some audiences, use them sparingly. They're no substitute for strong reasons and evidence.

State two or three convincing reasons in support of your position, and then search for evidence to elaborate each reason. Look for recent facts and statistics in print sources (books, newspapers, magazines) and nonprint sources (the Internet, videotapes, TV shows, databases). An expert's opinion can add strong support to your argument. You might conduct an interview (in person or by phone, mail, or e-mail).

4. Organize Your Argument

After coming up with reasons and evidence in support of your position, you need to figure out the best order in which to present them. You might use the **order of importance,** saving your strongest reason and evidence for last. The pattern of organization shown at the left presents a well-ordered, logical argument.

5. Target Your Audience

Identify your audience and shape your argument to fit. What are they likely to know about the topic, and what will you need to explain? What concerns do you and your audience share? What arguments might your readers make against your position (these are called **counterarguments**), and how can you refute them? While you were formulating your own opinion, you considered the pros and cons of the issue. Now, shape your argument to anticipate the possible objections of your targeted audience.

Drafting

1. Set Your Tone

Aim for a confident, direct tone that comes from knowing your subject and believing in the effectiveness of your research. As you write, avoid wordiness and such terms as "in my opinion" and "I think." Using waffling qualifiers like *might, maybe, probably, perhaps* will weaken your argument. Appeal to your readers with strong statements such as "the facts show."

Strategies for Support and Elaboration

1. To develop your reasons, choose from the following kinds of evidence:
   - facts and statistics
   - examples
   - analogies (comparisons)
   - anecdotes (brief stories)
   - quotes by experts
   - quotes from TV news shows, documentaries, talk shows
   - surveys (questionnaires)
   - interviews
2. Rely mainly on logical appeals.
3. Use emotional appeals sparingly.

Model for a Persuasive Essay	
Paragraph 1	Introduction (includes opinion statement)
Paragraph 2	Reason #1 and Support Evidence 1 Evidence 2
Paragraph 3	Reason #2 and Support Evidence 1 Evidence 2
Paragraph 4	Reason #3 and Support Evidence 1 Evidence 2
Paragraph 5	Conclusion

2. All Three Basic Parts

- **Introduction.** For a strong opening that intrigues or even startles your reader, try one of these: anecdote, description, question, dialogue, surprising fact, quotation. Your introduction should include a clearly worded opinion statement.
- **Body.** The body is made up of supporting reasons, each in a separate paragraph. A bare-bones argument has two strong reasons; three are more convincing. State each reason clearly, and elaborate with evidence that will sway your audience.
- **Conclusion.** Drive your point home by refuting at least one counterargument and strongly restating your position.

■ Evaluation Criteria

A good persuasive essay

1. *has an attention-grabbing introduction and a clear opinion statement*
2. *uses logical appeals, providing at least two strong reasons supported by evidence*
3. *may also contain emotional appeals*
4. *states counterarguments (opposition's reasons) and refutes them*
5. *presents an effective conclusion that restates the writer's position*

Student Model

Dear School Board:

One of the major issues facing our education system today is the dress code that many schools are imposing upon their students. In schools all over the country, students are required to wear uniforms. As a plan to help students learn better, uniforms fail to solve the problem. A dress code would be unfair and must not be forced upon students.

The opening sentence states the topic.

Opinion statement.

Many students identify each other by the clothes that they wear. They can look at each other and recognize common interests. For example, if two students are wearing basketball shirts, they immediately know that they have something in common. My best friend and I met because I was wearing a brightly colored sailing shirt, and it turned out that we both enjoyed sailing. If I did not have the freedom to wear that shirt, I might not have ever met her.

Reason 1 is supported by a personal anecdote.

Some students are only comfortable in a particular type of clothing. For example, my sister can only wear cotton. Other materials scratch her skin and sometimes cause a rash. Some students simply would not be comfortable in uniforms because of the materials used and the way they are designed to fit. How can students be expected to learn when they are uncomfortable?

Reason 2 is supported by an example from personal experience.

(Continued)

Student Model (continued)

For some students, clothing is a form of expression. They express different tastes, ideas, and interests according to what they wear. My friend decorates all his T-shirts with designs and pictures. If the school board enforced a dress code, he would lose his right to express himself through his art. A dress code would inhibit students from expressing themselves, which is one of the most important parts of maturing.

Reason 3 uses details and opinions as support.

Although a dress code might eliminate some of the conditions that interfere with students' learning, it would cause more problems for them. Freedom of expression is what makes everyone unique, and taking it away strips students of their right to be individuals. Clearly, a dress code is not the best answer to school problems.

Conclusion anticipates a counterargument and refutes it with a strong restatement of the writer's opinion.

—Kimberly Phillips
Communications Arts High School
San Antonio, Texas

Language / Grammar Link HELP

Loaded words: page 467. Streamlining prose: page 478. Parenthetical information: page 488.

Sentence Workshop HELP

Varying sentences: page 497.

Communications Handbook HELP

See Proofreaders' Marks.

Evaluating and Revising

Work with a partner, slowly reading each other's essays aloud. Ask your partner to point out confusing passages, wordiness, faulty reasoning (see pages 468–469), and lack of convincing support.

Revision Model

	Peer Comments
In ~~many~~ schools ^all over the country^, students are required to wear uniforms.	*Where are these schools?*
^As a plan to help^ ~~They say that~~ students learn better, ~~but~~ uniforms fail to	*Who is "they"?*
solve the problem. ^A dress code would be unfair and must not be forced upon students.^ ~~I think uniforms are unfair.~~	*Use a stronger opinion statement.*

BUILDING YOUR PORTFOLIO

Sentence Workshop

VARYING SENTENCE STRUCTURE AND LENGTH

Experienced writers use a variety of sentence structures and sentence lengths so that their paragraphs don't have the singsong sound of beginning readers' books.

1. A **simple sentence** has one independent clause and no subordinate clauses. Its subject or verb or both subject and verb may be compound.

   "Singhā, the lion, stands for courage and strength."

   —Pria Devi and Richard Kurin, *Aditi, the Living Arts of India*

2. A **compound sentence** has two or more independent clauses but no subordinate clause.

   "So we all went to bed, but none of us could get to sleep."

   —Anne Frank, *The Diary of a Young Girl*

3. A **complex sentence** has one independent clause and at least one subordinate clause. (Notice in the example below that the writer begins with the subordinate clause. In what other way could she have structured this sentence?)

   "Because it was the largest, most finely wrapped of all the boxes, she had noticed it for days."

   —Lorraine Hansberry, *To Be Young, Gifted and Black*

4. A **compound-complex** sentence has two or more independent clauses and at least one subordinate clause. (In what other ways could Dickens have begun the sentence below?)

   "The hours went on as he walked to and fro, and the clocks struck the numbers he would never hear again."

   —Charles Dickens, *A Tale of Two Cities*

Writer's Workshop Follow-up: Revising

Read your persuasive essay aloud, listening to the way the sentences flow together. If you find awkward, singsong passages, experiment with varying sentence structure and length.

Language Handbook HELP

See Classifying Sentences by Structure, pages 1040–1041.

Technology HELP

See Language Workshop CD-ROM. *Key word entry: sentence structure.*

Try It Out

Edit these choppy sentences by combining them into compound, complex, or compound-complex sentences. Check page 459 to see how Twain wrote them.

> I caused seven young calves to be turned into the anaconda's cage. The grateful reptile immediately crushed one of them. It swallowed the calf. It then lay back satisfied. It showed no further interest in the calves. It showed no disposition to harm them. . . . The fact stood proven. The difference between an earl and an anaconda is that the earl is cruel. The anaconda isn't.

Reading for Life

Reading to Take Action

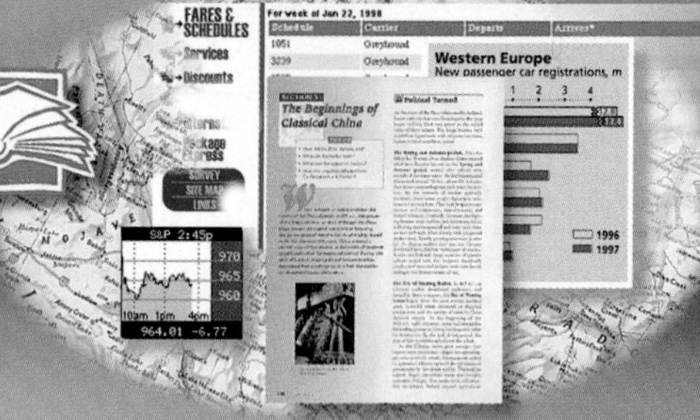

Situation

When you read or hear persuasive texts, such as editorials, political speeches, or petitions, you may feel moved to act on some issue. How do you decide whether or not to take action? The following strategies can help.

Strategies

Check the facts.

- Have the facts been reported accurately?
- Have important facts been omitted?
- Are reputable experts quoted? Are the experts unbiased?

Test the logic.

- Look for logical **fallacies** such as hasty generalizations, name-calling, either/or reasoning, and false cause and effect. (For more on these uses of persuasion, see pages 468–469.)

Be wary of emotional appeals.

- Notice loaded words, bandwagon appeals, and testimonials (see pages 468–469), and be aware of their effect on you.
- Remember that persuasive writing can touch your emotions, but it should also hold up under cooler, reasoned consideration.

(Clean) Up The Creek!

San Jacinto Creek has become a public disgrace in the past few years. It used to be a pleasant spot for family picnics. Now it's an eyesore—or worse, a potentially dangerous place, filled with litter, occupied by derelicts, and occasionally invaded by gangs. The city has done little to remedy the situation. So we are calling on our readers and other members of the San Jacinto community to take the following steps. First, sign the petition circulating around the city this week in support of a measure to clean up the creek and increase the police presence there. Second, appear at the next City Council meeting (7 P.M., Monday, September 14) to urge the Council to vote for this measure. Third, join the members of Up the Creek, a local organization formed to clean up the litter from San Jacinto Creek and patrol it, until the police are authorized by the city to do so.

Spending time at San Jacinto Creek used to be one of the greatest pleasures of living in this city. It could be again. So, instead of being up the creek, let's take our creek back.

Evaluate the objective.

- What are you being urged to do, and why?
- Who is urging the action?
- Does the objective seem well thought out, reasonable, and worthwhile?
- Is the objective personally meaningful to you?

Using the Strategies

1. What objective is urged in the editorial on this page?
2. Summarize the logic that runs through the editorial. Can you find any fallacies? Explain.
3. How has the writer appealed to your emotions?
4. Are the proposed actions likely to produce the desired result? Why or why not?
5. What, if any, actions would you take in response to the editorial, and why?

Extending the Strategies

Find an editorial in your local paper that urges some community action. With a group, examine the editorial using these strategies.

Learning for Life

Using Ads to Make Your Point

Problem

Suppose you have an important message you want to get across to a group of your peers. How can you sell an idea, an action, or a cause to a group of teenagers?

Project

Work with a small group to produce an ad campaign designed to get a teenage audience to do something your group agrees is important.

Preparation

1. You'll want to investigate the kinds of appeals that speak to teenagers. Discuss in class any ads you think are particularly successful with teenage audiences. The ads can be from print media (newspapers or magazines), TV, radio, or billboards. Identify the images (pictures), words, music, story line, and **persuasive techniques** used in these ads. Summarize your findings.
2. Brainstorm to gather a list of **"messages"** or **issues** your classmates consider important (for example, fight racism; stay in school; don't drink). Join the creative team working on the issue or message that interests you most.

Procedure

1. With your group, brainstorm to find ideas about how to sell your message. What **facts** do you want to get across? What **advertising techniques** can you use?
2. Choose your **media**: print ads, radio spots, TV ads, billboards, or some combination of these. You might plan a walkathon or think of some unusual way to sell your message.
3. Plan your campaign, using some of the persuasive techniques you discovered in the ads you analyzed earlier.
4. Work with your creative team to produce a draft of your message or a detailed plan for your campaign. If you're using art, try out alternative layouts and create a storyboard like the ones ad agencies produce. (Your **storyboard** can be a large poster board with a series of rough sketches outlining the ad or video from beginning to end.)
5. Try out your draft with a focus group, a small sampling of your target audience. Ask members of the group what they like and dislike about the draft and what specific suggestions they have for improving it.

Presentation

Choose one of the following formats (or another your teacher approves):

1. Print Media

Create a series of newspaper or magazine ads, and tell where you'd place them to reach your audience. (If you have a school newspaper, that's one market for your campaign.) Think of other ways you might use print ads: on T-shirts? posters? billboards? flyers?

2. On the Air

Write a script or series of spot announcements for your school's radio or public address system. Get permission to broadcast your messages.

3. A Wider Audience

Contact local radio and TV stations to see what their requirements are for airing public-service messages. If you create a TV message, videotape it and submit it to the stations.

Processing

What did you learn about advertising techniques from doing this project? Do you think your attitudes and responses to advertisements have changed? If so, how?

The Poetry Collections

A poem . . . begins as a lump in the throat, a sense of wrong, a homesickness, a lovesickness. It is never a thought to begin with. It is at its best when it is a tantalizing vagueness.

—Robert Frost

The Large Blue Horses (1911) by Franz Marc.

Collection Walker Art Center, Minneapolis.
Gift of the T. B. Walker Foundation, Gilbert M. Walker Fund, 1942.

A Writer on Poetry
A Conversation with Alice Walker

Alice Walker writes poems as well as nonfiction and fiction. (Her short story "Everyday Use" begins on page 70.)

Q: **How young were you when you began to write?**

Alice Walker: My mother says that when I was crawling, she would look for me and I would have crawled to the back of the house, having snatched the Sears Roebuck catalog. I would quietly sit scribbling in the catalog with a twig. That either meant that I came into this lifetime already writing and thinking about things that I had written before I got here, or that in some ways I was a neglected child because my parents always had to work, so I had to make my own diversions. I think I must have gone about it in a very contained way, because I didn't want to be underfoot. My parents were sharecroppers. Our housing was very shabby and small, and there were ten in the family. We lived in awful little shacks that leaked, and we couldn't get them warm in winter or cool in summer. But my mother planted flowers all around. I couldn't move anywhere without my eye hitting flowers. . . .

Q: **Are there certain situations in which your creative juices are most likely to flow?**

Walker: I have learned that I can't force poems. But if I spend a long time in silence, which I really love, that's very good for my writing. The main thing is just to live intensely and to feel. If there's the slightest little bubble from the spring coming up, I try to go with the bubble until it gets to the top of the water and then try to be there for it so that I can begin to understand what is happening down in the depths.

I can recall one morning in which I wrote five poems. I had gone to New York from California and was living with a friend. She put me in her guest room, and the bed was very short and lumpy. It didn't have good covers, and I was cold so I couldn't sleep. The surface of my brain was really busy with what it meant for someone to invite you to her house and to put you in a cold room with insufficient covers. I was thinking about that, and then, at about five o'clock in the morning, poetry just announced itself. It more or less said, "Well, it's time to write, so why don't you just put on something warm and get up?" And I did.

Sometimes writing poems is like falling in love. If you haven't done it for a long time, you can barely remember how wonderful it was, and you think that it probably won't happen again. That's why you resist. But that morning I gave in and liked every one of the poems that I wrote.

Reading Skills and Strategies

Reading a Poem

In some ways, reading a poem is just like reading a story or nonfiction. You respond to it with your experiences and feelings; you make meanings from the text. Yet reading poetry is also very different from reading prose. It requires strategies all its own.

1. **Read on—until there's a punctuation mark.** A poem's line breaks indicate thought groupings, but don't *brake* at the end of each line.
2. **If you're baffled, find the subject and verb.** Sometimes, when passages are difficult to understand, you can clarify the meaning by finding the subject, verb, and complement of each sentence. (For help, see pages 1038–1040 of the Language Handbook.) Try to **paraphrase**—say in your own words—a complicated passage.
3. **Look for figures of speech—and think about them. Figurative language** is part of what makes poetry poetry.
4. **Listen to the sounds.** Always read a poem aloud to yourself. Poets choose evocative words for their sound as well as their meaning.
5. **One reading isn't enough.** Respond to a poem on first meeting it, and then talk about the poem with other readers before you read it carefully again. On your second reading, you'll notice new details and develop new insights; and when you read it for the third time, the poem will feel comfortably "yours."
6. **Perform the poem.** When you give a poem a dramatic reading for an audience, you can emphasize the mood and feelings the words and images evoke. Then the poem really comes alive.

How to Own a Word

Multiple Meanings—Specific Meanings

When a word has **multiple meanings**—and many words do—you have to choose the **specific meaning** that fits the context.

Take *back,* for instance. In the poem on the next page, the speaker describes a Bible as having a "broken back." Do you know what that phrase means? According to one dictionary, the word *back* used as a noun has ten meanings. Can you think of five more meanings to add to this cluster? Which meaning applies to the poem?

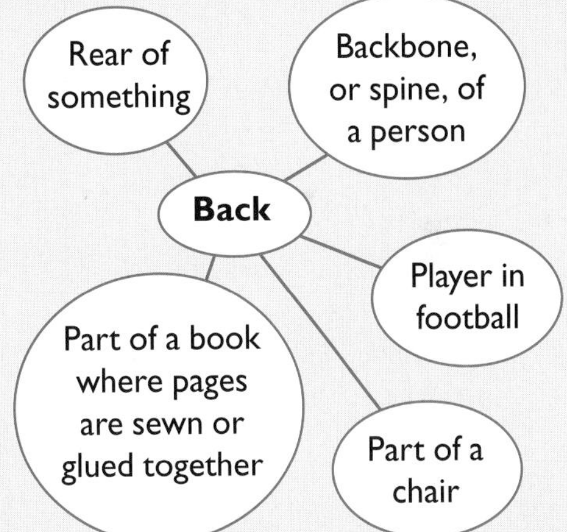

Now think of what the poet might have wanted to suggest by describing the Bible as having a *broken* back. Does he just want to suggest that someone read the Bible a lot? Does the phrase suggest violence instead—was the back broken deliberately?

Part of the pleasure of poetry is its suggestiveness. The answer to why the Bible's back is broken is up to *you.*

Apply the strategy on the next page.

Dialogue with the Text

The following notes were made by a student reading "Abandoned Farmhouse" for the first time. Cover her notes with a piece of paper, and jot down your own responses and questions. When you finish your first reading, **compare your responses** with Paula's.

I like the way they use the size of the shoes to show he was a big man—neat reference.

Good detail—I like the way it forms a picture in my mind.

This part reminds me of my house because we have the same sort of sandbox, and money was a problem for our family. My mom canned tomato juice and made different types of jelly.

The gravel road gives a lonely, sad feeling to the poem, like you're out in the middle of nowhere with no neighbors for miles.

What happened? Why did they have to leave? What was the hurry?

If his dad wasn't a farmer, why did the child have a toy tractor and plow?

Paula Stoller

—Paula Stoller
Eureka High School, Eureka, Illinois

Abandoned (1994) by Robert Klein. Oil on canvas.

Courtesy Robert Klein.

Abandoned Farmhouse

Ted Kooser

He was a big man, says the size of his shoes
on a pile of broken dishes by the house;
a tall man too, says the length of the bed
in an upstairs room; and a good, God-fearing man,
says the Bible with a broken back
on the floor below the window, dusty with sun;
but not a man for farming, say the fields
cluttered with boulders and the leaky barn.

A woman lived with him, says the bedroom wall
papered with lilacs and the kitchen shelves
covered with oilcloth, and they had a child
says the sandbox made from a tractor tire.
Money was scarce, say the jars of plum preserves
and canned tomatoes sealed in the cellar-hole,
and the winters cold, say the rags in the window
frames.
It was lonely here, says the narrow gravel road.

Something went wrong, says the empty house
in the weed-choked yard. Stones in the fields
say he was not a farmer; the still-sealed jars
in the cellar say she left in a nervous haste.
And the child? Its toys are strewn in the yard
like branches after a storm—a rubber cow,
a rusty tractor with a broken plow,
a doll in overalls. Something went wrong, they say.

Collection 8

HOW TO LIVE

Writing Focus: Poetry

When we want to know the values, the character, and the particular genius of any country—ancient or modern—we turn to its poets. From them we learn what statistics and charts and economic surveys cannot tell us. We learn what common experiences unite their people. We learn what they cherish from the past and what they aspire to in the future.

Poets express the values we live by. Though it would be difficult to put this conviction to any practical test, history provides much evidence to show that the minds of poets have functioned like antennae. Poets express beliefs, hopes, and ambitions that are shared by everyone.

Americans who want to *know* the facts of their own history may turn to the huge volumes of the *Congressional Record.* Americans who want to *understand* their history can do no better than to turn to their poets.

Poetry has a way of teaching one what one needs to know . . . if one is honest.

—May Sarton

Writer's Notebook

Try an experiment. Write down your first thoughts on these questions: "What is poetry? What does poetry have to do with everyday life?" Save your notes.

Elements of Literature

FIGURATIVE LANGUAGE: Language of the Imagination

Long before people began to communicate through writing, they uttered combinations of words having the sound of poetry. Yet after thousands of years, no one has produced a single definition of poetry that takes into account all the ways in which poetry makes itself heard. Though you can find enough definitions to fill a book, you won't be able to point to any one of them and say, "That's it!"

Recognizing Poetry When We Hear It

Yet we all know poetry when we hear it—whether it's a passage from the Bible, the chorus of a song, or some striking phrase overheard on a city street. Poetry is different from the plain prose we speak and from the flat language of the committee report we read. Poetry has a beat or a **rhythm**, a melody, and a texture. It's full of expressions that please us, surprise us, and make us laugh or cry. Our instincts alone tell us that when words are put together in a certain way, they are poetry. In the long run, our instinct for poetry may be more useful than a thousand definitions.

Speaking Figuratively

One of the elements that make poetry poetry is **figurative language**—language based on some sort of **comparison** that is not literally true. Such language is so natural to us that we use it every day. Let's say you read this in the newspaper:

The Budget Committee hammered at the Treasury secretary for three hours.

You don't ask in horror, "Will they be charged with murder?" You understand immediately from the context that the writer is speaking figuratively. A **figure of speech** is language shaped by the play of the imagination in which one thing (here, the continual questioning) is compared to something that seems to be entirely different (repeated blows with a hammer). A figure of speech is never literally true, but a good one always suggests a powerful truth to our imaginations.

Stated Likenesses: Similes

A **simile** is a figure of speech that uses the word *like, as, than,* or *resembles* to compare things that seem to have little or nothing in common. In a literal comparison, we might say,

"Remorse sits in my stomach like a piece of stale bread. How does that *sound?"*

Drawing by Booth: © 1991 The New Yorker Magazine, Inc.

"His face was as red as his father's." But when we use a simile, the comparison becomes more striking and imaginative: "His face was as red as a ripe tomato," or "His face was like a stoplight."

Similes are part of every poet's equipment. In a good simile, the comparison is unexpected but entirely reasonable. The nineteenth-century English poet William Wordsworth opened a poem with this now-famous simile:

I wandered lonely as a cloud

This simile helps us see at once that the wandering speaker has

by John Malcolm Brinnin

no more sense of purpose or direction than a cloud driven by the wind. Wordsworth's simile was drawn from nature. Today a poet might make different connections, even ones taken from science or technology, as Marge Piercy does in describing city streets in a poem called "Some Collisions Bring Luck":

The streets shimmered
like laboratory beakers.

Making Identifications: Metaphors

A **metaphor** is another kind of comparison between unlike things in which some reasonable connection is instantly revealed. A metaphor is a more forceful version of a simile because the connective *like, as, resembles,* or *than* is not used. A **direct metaphor** says that something *is* something else: not "I wandered lonely as a cloud" but "I was a lonely cloud."

Metaphors, in fact, are basic to everyday conversation because they allow us to speak in a kind of imaginative shorthand. Suppose a man enters a diner and asks for two scrambled eggs on an English muffin. The waiter might call to the kitchen "two wrecks on a raft!" The waiter is using an **implied metaphor**.

Many of the metaphors we use in conversation are implied: "the long arm of the law," "this neck of the woods," "the foot of the mountain." All these metaphors suggest comparisons between parts of the body and things quite different from the body.

Even single words can contain implied metaphors: "She *barked* her command" compares human speech to the sound a dog makes. Metaphors like these are now so familiar that we forget that once upon a time, they represented brand-new ways of seeing the world.

Metaphors in poetry can be startling. Here is how the American poet Robert Lowell uses metaphor to describe a construction site in Boston in a poem called "For the Union Dead":

. . . Behind their cage,
yellow dinosaur steamshovels
were grunting
as they cropped up tons of
mush and grass
to gouge their underworld
garage.

Extending the Comparison

Metaphors are often **extended** over several lines of a poem and taken as far as they can logically go. Langston Hughes finds many points of comparison between a hard life and an old, torn-up stairway in the poem you'll read on page 508.

Humanizing the World: Personification

When we attribute human qualities to a nonhuman thing or to an abstract idea, we are using **personification**. We call computers "user-friendly," for example, or say that "misery loves company" or that "the future beckons." Personification is widely used by cartoonists, especially political cartoonists. You've probably seen justice personified as a blindfolded woman carrying scales and love personified as a chubby infant with a bow and arrow.

In poetry, figurative language is the most important means of imaginative expression. It is a tool that poets have used through the centuries to translate the experiences of their times into personal statements.

Before You Read

MOTHER TO SON

Make the Connection

Powerful Words

Sometimes words have the power to help a person through hard times. What effect do you think the words of the mother in this poem have on her son?

Quickwrite

If you were talking to a younger person about life and its struggles, what would you **compare** life to? Make a list of concrete "things" you might compare your life to. *(Keep your notes for use on page 511.)*

Elements of Literature

Extending the Metaphor

Starting in line 2 of this poem and continuing to the end, the mother makes many comparisons between her life and a particular kind of staircase. She is **extending** the **metaphor** stated in line 2 as far as she can logically take it.

An **extended metaphor** is a metaphor that develops its comparison over several lines of a poem or even throughout a whole poem.

For more on Metaphor, see pages 506–507 and the Handbook of Literary Terms.

Mother to Son

Langston Hughes

Well, son, I'll tell you:
Life for me ain't been no crystal stair.
It's had tacks in it,
And splinters,
And boards torn up,
And places with no carpet on the floor—
Bare.
But all the time
I'se been a-climbin' on,
And reachin' landin's,
And turnin' corners,
And sometimes goin' in the dark
Where there ain't been no light.
So boy, don't you turn back.
Don't you set down on the steps
'Cause you finds it's kinder hard.
Don't you fall now—
For I'se still goin', honey,
I'se still climbin',
And life for me ain't been no crystal stair.

Proletarian (1934)
by Gordon Samstag.
Oil on canvas ($48\frac{5}{16}'' \times 42''$).
The Toledo Museum of Art, Toledo, Ohio. Museum Purchase Fund. (1935.34)

MEET THE WRITER

In Harlem's Heart

Langston Hughes (1902–1967) was born in Joplin, Missouri, but is primarily identified with New York City's Harlem. A man of many talents, Hughes wrote plays, novels, screenplays, and prose sketches for newspapers. His work, he said, was an attempt to "explain and illuminate the Negro condition in America." Hughes made his most lasting contribution as a lyric poet, introducing to American poetry the rhythms of jazz and blues music and of black urban dialect.

Another poem by Hughes appears on page 376.

Connections A BIOGRAPHICAL SKETCH

Crystal is a tenth-grader who has been in trouble with the law and is now living in a group home while trying to finish high school.

The Power of a Poem

Susan Sheehan

Crystal had continued to do poorly at Flushing High. She didn't do her homework, but once, when she was assigned by an English teacher to read a play of Shakespeare's ("That language was too much of a drag; there was too many complications," she says), she went to a movie theater to see *Macbeth* instead. "I remember witches, and a witch killed a man or a man killed a witch," she says. "It was OK, but it was corny. It was nothing like as good as *The Wizard of Oz*." Crystal is unfamiliar with the names of most renowned poets—Keats, Emily Dickinson, and Countee Cullen, for example—but "one day at Flushing when I decided to play student out of the many days I cut," she was exposed to a Langston Hughes poem she admired and still half remembers: "Something about an old lady looking back and telling a little boy never to give up on hisself. She said something like, 'Life for me ain't been no crystal stairs; it had many boards torn up.' Because her life was not laid out on a red carpet, it made her want to do more, to get more better. It was saying to the boy even if he have to live in an apartment with no electricity, only candles, don't give up; you can always find something good at the end. I understood that poem."

—from "A Lost Childhood," *The New Yorker*

Dark Symphony

Reading Old Langston whose
Mulatto words stretched my mind to
edge of knowing—
Good Langston made me proud to be
the same color as black America's
Renaissance, brown as the dirt
Momma plant those greens in.
Shoot, Europe has their Golden Age,
we Black America got ours.
As I read of Simple° I quickly realize
I love his forgotten prose as much
as his poetry.

Reciting Old Langston,
My mother yells with a burst of
strength—
"Life for me ain't been no
crystal stair,
You know who wrote that"
with a sinful giggle she says
I say "yeah, Good Langston
wrote that"
My mother then smiles
and swallows me up in her love.
I'm older now, still reading.
His stuff has set my mind free.

—David Askia-Forbes
Gonzaga College High School
Washington, D.C.

6. **Simple:** the apparently simple but deeply wise hero of a popular series of sketches that Langston Hughes wrote in the 1940s.

Making Meanings

Mother to Son

First Thoughts

1. "Don't, don't," says the mother in Hughes's poem. What is she really telling her son to *do*?

Shaping Interpretations

2. What kinds of experiences do you think the mother is talking about in lines 3–7? What kinds of responses to these experiences is she describing in lines 8–13?

3. What do you think might have motivated this mother's "speech" to her son?

Choices: Building Your Portfolio

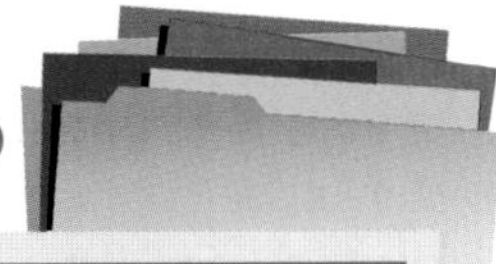

Writer's Notebook

1. Collecting Ideas for a Poem

Extending a metaphor. Look back in your Quickwrite notes at the list of things you compared life to. Try extending one of these comparisons. Here, for example, are three ways life is like a tennis match: We try to "win points," it's hard work, it takes a lot of practice.

Supporting an Opinion

2. The Power of a Poem

Read the ***Connections*** on page 510 and the student poem on this page. Then, think about how Hughes's poem "Mother to Son" could help young people who are having trouble. Write a **memo** to your principal telling why this poem should be displayed on a school bulletin board.

Before You Read

Courage

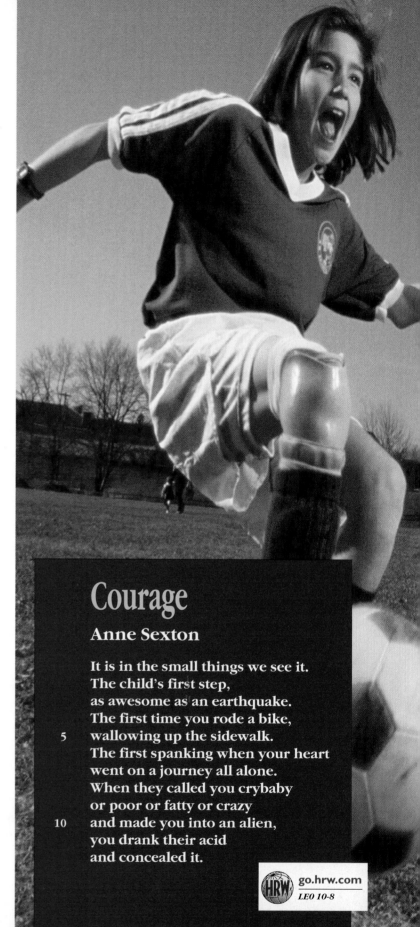

Make the Connection

What It Takes

It takes courage to face life's difficulties, but not everyone views the same people or actions as courageous. In this poem, the speaker finds courage "in the small things." See if you agree.

Reading Skills and Strategies

Dialogue with the Text

List some examples from your own experience that illustrate your view of courage. As you read the poem, list the actions in each stanza that the speaker thinks are courageous. Do you agree that courage lies in acts like these? *(Keep your notes for use on page 514.)*

Elements of Literature

Figurative Language

Anne Sexton uses daring **figures of speech—similes** and **metaphors—** as "shock tactics" to grab our attention. Jot down responses to her unusual comparisons. If you're puzzled, see if the context helps you understand them.

Figures of speech make unusual comparisons between two things that are basically unlike. Figures of speech are not meant to be taken literally.

For more on Figure of Speech, see pages 506–507 and the Handbook of Literary Terms.

Courage

Anne Sexton

It is in the small things we see it.
The child's first step,
as awesome as an earthquake.
The first time you rode a bike,
wallowing up the sidewalk.
The first spanking when your heart
went on a journey all alone.
When they called you crybaby
or poor or fatty or crazy
and made you into an alien,
you drank their acid
and concealed it.

go.hrw.com
LEO 10-8

Later,
if you faced the death of bombs and bullets
you did not do it with a banner,
you did it with only a hat to
cover your heart.
You did not fondle the weakness inside you
though it was there.
Your courage was a small coal
that you kept swallowing.
If your buddy saved you
and died himself in so doing,
then his courage was not courage,
it was love; love as simple as shaving soap.

Later,
if you have endured a great despair,
then you did it alone,
getting a transfusion from the fire,
picking the scabs off your heart,
then wringing it out like a sock.
Next, my kinsman, you powdered your sorrow,
you gave it a back rub
and then you covered it with a blanket
and after it had slept a while
it woke to the wings of the roses
and was transformed.

Later,
when you face old age and its natural conclusion
your courage will still be shown in the little ways,
each spring will be a sword you'll sharpen,
those you love will live in a fever of love,
and you'll bargain with the calendar
and at the last moment
when death opens the back door
you'll put on your carpet slippers
and stride out.

Meet the Writer

Poet of Pain

Anne Sexton (1928–1974) was twenty-eight years old and a suburban homemaker in Newton, Massachusetts, when she began to study poetry. She made up for her late start with a stream of poems that were received enthusiastically both by general readers and by her fellow poets. In 1966, she won the Pulitzer Prize for poetry. Sexton was associated with a group of poets called "confessional" because they wrote openly about intimate and often painful details of their lives. Sexton believed that poetry should be a "shock to the senses," that "it should almost hurt."

" . . . everyone said, 'You can't write this way. It's too personal; it's confessional; you can't write this, Anne,' and everyone was discouraging me. "

Although much of Sexton's work is intensely personal, she also wrote about wider social issues, especially about the problems of women. One critic described her poetry as turning "wounds to words," and another said that it "delights even as it disturbs."

MAKING MEANINGS
COURAGE

First Thoughts

1. Do you agree that it's in small things that people show the most courage? Why?

Shaping Interpretations

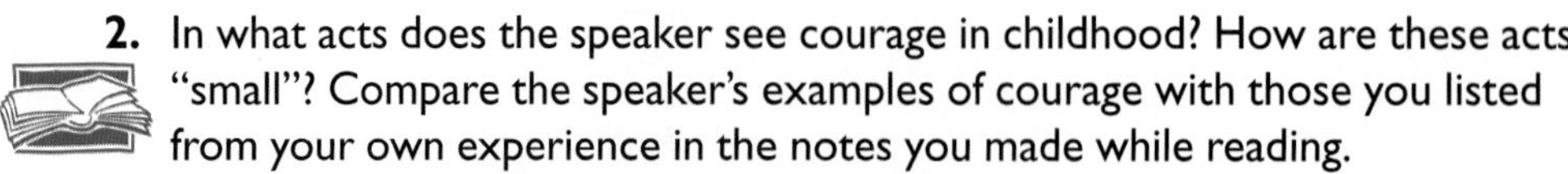

2. In what acts does the speaker see courage in childhood? How are these acts "small"? Compare the speaker's examples of courage with those you listed from your own experience in the notes you made while reading.
3. List the **figures of speech** (**similes** and **implied metaphors**) in the first stanza. Which comparisons make these small acts seem large and heroic?
4. What other unusual **comparisons** can you find in lines 20, 30, and 31? Do you think they all "work"? Why or why not?
5. The last three stanzas begin with the word *later.* What progression does each stanza represent? What acts of courage does the speaker praise in each?
6. How does the speaker **personify** sorrow in lines 32–37? What seems to transform sorrow in the poem? Do you think this is true to life?

Extending the Text

7. Can you see any connections between this poem and the story "With All Flags Flying," which begins on page 309? Talk over your responses.

CHOICES: Building Your Portfolio

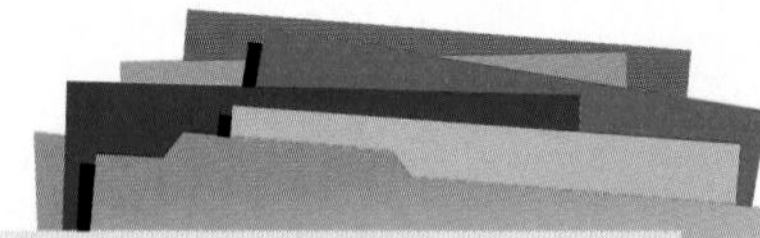

Writer's Notebook

WORK IN PROGRESS

1. Collecting Ideas for a Poem

Finding a feeling. Poetry starts with feelings. Sexton's poem may have reminded you of a person you know who has shown courage—someone whose actions, large or small, touched your feelings. Try to **describe** the person with **sensory details**, especially ones that might "shock the senses."

Creative Writing

2. What Is Love?

Sexton's poem says: Love is "as simple as shaving soap." Create a list of **similes** about love: Love is as complicated as ____. Love is as sweet as ____. Love is as simple as ____.

Then, with a partner or group, list some "small things" that show love. Arrange your examples and similes into a poem about love that begins: "It is in the small things we see it."

Comparing and Contrasting Poems

3. A Conversation

Imagine that Langston Hughes and Anne Sexton met to talk about "Mother to Son" (page 508) and "Courage" (page 512). What similarities would they find in these two poems? what differences? Write a dialogue that Hughes and Sexton might have in which they discuss the poems' **themes**, **characters**, and **figurative language**.

Elements of Literature

SYMBOLS *by* John Malcolm Brinnin

What Symbols Stand For

A **symbol** is often an ordinary object, event, person, or animal to which we have attached extraordinary meaning and significance. We use a rectangle of dyed cloth to symbolize a country. We use a skull and crossbones to stand for poison or danger. We send red roses as a symbol of love.

Where Do Symbols Come From?

Symbols can be inherited or invented. The most familiar symbols have been inherited—that is, they have been handed down over time. For example, no one knows exactly who first thought of using the lion to symbolize power, courage, and domination. But once these qualities were associated with the animal, images of lions appeared on flags, banners, coats of arms, and castle walls, and the lion became a **public symbol** that shows up in art and literature even today.

People throughout history have endowed simple objects with meanings far beyond their simple functions: A crown symbolizes royalty, a dove symbolizes peace, a bull and bear symbolize the stock market, five linked rings symbolize the Olympics.

Symbols can also be invented. You probably have a symbol for your school. Writers often take a new object, character, or event and make it the embodiment of some human concern. Some invented symbols in literature have become so widely known that they have gained the status of public symbols. Peter Pan as the symbol of eternal childhood is an example.

Why Create Symbols?

You may ask why poets don't just come right out and say what they mean. Symbols, like all **figures of speech**, allow the poet to suggest layers and layers of meanings—possibilities that a simple, literal statement could never convey. A symbol is like a pebble cast into a pond: It sends off ever-widening ripples of meaning.

Some symbols are so rich in meanings that their significance has never been fully understood. Herman Melville's great white whale called Moby-Dick, for example, has traditionally been interpreted as a symbol of the mystery of evil. Yet for more than a hundred years, this whale has provided research topics for students and scholars who still find new ways to look at Melville's famous monster.

A symbol is like a pebble cast into a pond: It sends off ever-widening ripples of meaning.

Here is a very, very small poem that makes a big point about life by using two symbols from nature: dust and a rainbow. What do you think they stand for?

Oh, God of dust and rainbows,
  help us see
That without dust the rainbow
  would not be.

—Langston Hughes

Before You Read

STOPPING BY WOODS ON A SNOWY EVENING

Make the Connection

More Than a Winter's Ride

This famous poem seems at first to be a simple account of a man who stops briefly to watch snow falling in the woods at night. Yet there's much more to this poem than a literal journey.

Reading Skills and Strategies

Monitoring Your Reading: Rereading

Read the poem several times. On your second reading, jot down what you see in the poem. On your third reading, jot down all the things you think are going through the *traveler's* mind as he gazes at the woods. *(Keep your notes for use on page 519.)*

Elements of Literature

Symbolic Meaning

Literally, snow is snow, a horse is a horse, and woods are woods. In the hands of a poet, however, ordinary things can become **symbols,** suggesting deep layers of meaning. As you read this poem, you must make those unspoken connections that only the imagination can make.

> **Symbolic meaning** is the deeper layer of meaning suggested by a work's literal, or surface, meaning.
>
> *For more on Symbol, see pages 306–307 and 515 and the Handbook of Literary Terms.*

Stopping by Woods on a Snowy Evening

Robert Frost

Whose woods these are I think I know.
His house is in the village, though;
He will not see me stopping here
To watch his woods fill up with snow.

My little horse must think it queer
To stop without a farmhouse near
Between the woods and frozen lake
The darkest evening of the year.

He gives his harness bells a shake
To ask if there is some mistake.
The only other sound's the sweep
Of easy wind and downy flake.

The woods are lovely, dark, and deep,
But I have promises to keep,
And miles to go before I sleep,
And miles to go before I sleep.

Brooding Silence (detail) by John Fabian Carlson.

National Museum of American Art, Smithsonian Institution, Washington, D.C.

MEET THE WRITER

Only Seemingly Simple

Robert Frost at President John F. Kennedy's inauguration.

Robert Frost (1874–1963), whom most Americans consider the voice of rural New England, was actually born in San Francisco and lived as a child in the industrial city of Lawrence, Massachusetts. He attended Dartmouth College for a few months but left to write poetry and work in a cotton mill. Years later, after he had become a husband and father, Frost returned to college but left after two years, again to write seriously.

In 1912, Frost moved his young family to England. During the three years he spent there, he wrote and published two books of poems—*A Boy's Will* (1913) and *North of Boston* (1914)—that were immediate successes on both sides of the Atlantic.

Frost went home to New England in 1915, finally able to make his living as a poet. During his long career, he won four Pulitzer Prizes and often gave public readings and lectures. One of his last public appearances was at the 1961 inauguration of President John F. Kennedy, where he recited his poem "The Gift Outright."

Like the independent New England farmers he frequently wrote about, Frost went his own way. He refused to join his contemporaries in their experimental search for new poetic forms, finding all the freedom he needed within the bounds of traditional verse. Despite their apparently homespun subjects and traditional form, Frost's poems are only seemingly simple. Beneath their surface is a complex and often dark view of human life and personality. Frost said:

"Like a piece of ice on a hot stove, the poem must ride on its own melting. . . . Read it a hundred times; it will forever keep its freshness as a metal keeps its fragrance. It can never lose its sense of a meaning that once unfolded by surprise as it went."

You'll find another poem by Frost on page 526.

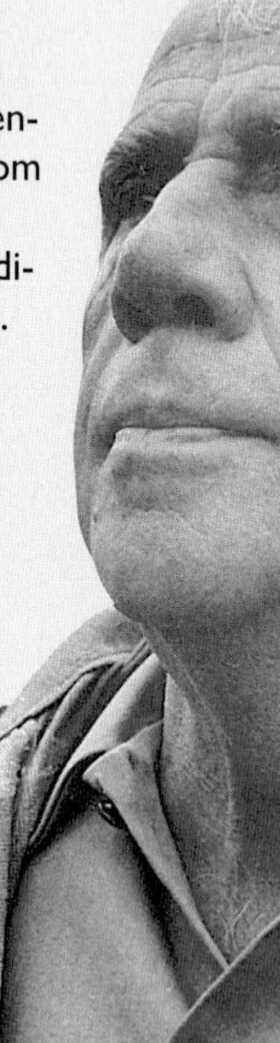

Making Meanings
Stopping by Woods on a Snowy Evening

First Thoughts

1. What did you see happening in the poem? Check your rereading notes.

Shaping Interpretations

2. On the literal level, the speaker decides to keep going because he has promises to keep. What do you suppose his promises are?
3. When the speaker first says he has miles to go before he can sleep, what is he probably thinking of? What other **metaphorical** sleep might he be referring to when he repeats the line?
4. The big question set up by the poem is what those lovely, dark, and deep woods **symbolize** to the traveler. What do you think? What has the speaker said no to in passing them by?
5. Whatever the woods stand for, what has the speaker said yes to in deciding to go on? In other words, how has he resolved his **conflict**?

Connecting with the Text

6. Do you think this poem is about a feeling that we all might have at one time or another in our lives? Explain.

Choices: Building Your Portfolio

Writer's Notebook

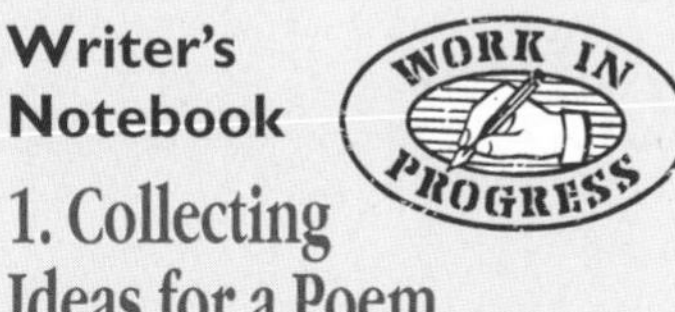

1. Collecting Ideas for a Poem

Finding a topic. Maybe the sight of the deep, dark woods on a winter night gave Frost the idea for this poem. Suppose you are passing a beautiful spot, a place you know well. You stop, stare, and start to think. What are you looking at? What time is it? Where are you heading? What are you thinking? Take notes describing your impressions and images. Your poem might open with Frost's line: "Whose _____ these are [this is] I think I know." (You may want to use these notes for the Writer's Workshop assignment on page 541.)

Describing a Character

2. Imagining the Speaker

Who is this traveler? Try to elaborate. Is it a man or a woman? Do you think the speaker is married or single? old or young? Is the speaker happy? sad? Write a brief **character sketch** of Frost's traveler.

Speaking

3. A Performance

Prepare to perform an **oral interpretation** of Frost's poem. You'll have to make these decisions: Will you use a single voice or several? Will you use a chorus? When will you slow down? speed up? pause for effect? You might even set the poem to music. Decide on your audience—for example, classmates, adults, or young children. What style of music would suit them best—ballad? hymn? rock? rap?

Before You Read

LOVELIEST OF TREES

Make the Connection

Capturing Time

A poem, like a snapshot, can capture a moment in words. What you might remember best about this poem is the image of the cherry tree. But look closely at those blossoms.

Quickwrite

Shut your eyes for a minute and think of your favorite place. It could be a place in nature, a city, or someplace indoors. Write down all that you see, smell, taste, feel, and hear. *(Keep your notes for use on page 525.)*

Elements of Literature

Connotations

If it weren't for **connotations** (associations and emotions that become attached to a word), poets would be out of business. Why, for example, do you think Housman uses the word *snow* in his last line?

> **Connotations** are all the associations and emotions attached to a word.
>
> *For more on Connotations, see the Handbook of Literary Terms.*

Loveliest of Trees

A. E. Housman

Loveliest of trees, the cherry now
Is hung with bloom along the bough,
And stands about the woodland ride°
Wearing white for Eastertide.

Now, of my threescore years and ten,
Twenty will not come again,
And take from seventy springs a score,
It only leaves me fifty more.

And since to look at things in bloom
Fifty springs are little room,
About the woodlands I will go
To see the cherry hung with snow.

3. **ride:** path for horseback riding.

go.hrw.com
LEO 10-8

Meet the Writer

Poems as Clear as Water

A. E. Housman (1859–1936) spent the early years of his life near a part of western England called Shropshire. He wrote about its people, towns, and countryside in poems as clear as water from a brook. Housman is one of those rare poets whose whole career is associated with one book. In his case, that book is called *A Shropshire Lad.* Housman's themes are universal: the sad beauty of nature as it reminds us of our mortality, the brevity of youth, and regret for what has passed.

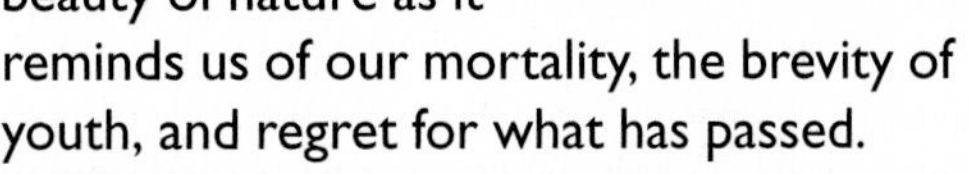

"Poetry is not the thing said but a way of saying it," Housman once said.

“Experience has taught me, when I am shaving of a morning, to keep watch over my thoughts, because if a line of poetry strays into my memory, my skin bristles so that the razor ceases to act. This particular symptom is accompanied by a shiver down the spine; there is another which consists in a constriction of the throat and a precipitation of water to the eyes. . . . ”

Spring—Fruit Trees in Blossom (1873) by Claude Monet (1840–1926). Oil on canvas (24½″ × 39⅝″).

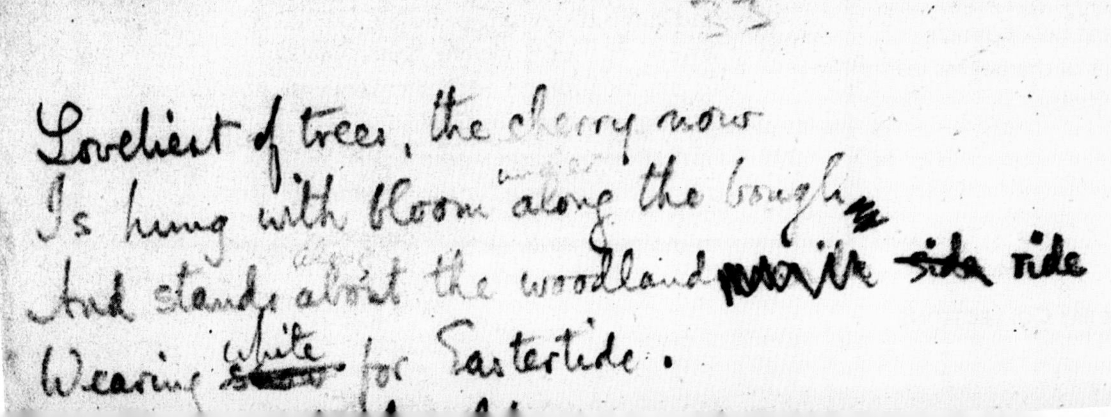

33

Loveliest of trees, the cherry now
Is hung with bloom along the bough
And stands about the woodland ride
Wearing white for Eastertide.

Before You Read

George Gray

Make the Connection

Looking Back at Life

Spoon River Anthology, from which this poem is taken, is one of the most famous books in American literature. Each poem in *Spoon River Anthology* is spoken by someone who once lived in Spoon River, Illinois. Each speaker now "sleeps" on the hill of Spoon River Cemetery. Here, George Gray comes forward to comment on the symbol chiseled on his tombstone. Read the poem aloud to hear the speaker's tone of voice.

Quickwrite

Someone asks you for advice: "What are the most important things in life?" Quickwrite your answer. (*Keep your notes for use on page 525.*)

Elements of Literature

The Poem's Speaker

All poems have speakers, and it's a mistake to think the writer and speaker are always the same. The **speaker** of a poem may be a fictional character, as George Gray is, or even an animal or object. Masters uses a whole graveyard full of people as the speakers of the poems in *Spoon River Anthology*.

The **speaker** is the voice that talks directly to us in a poem; the speaker is not always the poet.

For more on Speaker, see the Handbook of Literary Terms.

Background

What has made *Spoon River Anthology* so appealing to millions of readers is its combination of down-to-earth realism and poetic imagination. The realism comes from Edgar Lee Masters' close observation of life in a small Illinois town. The poetic imagination comes from the lawyer-poet's grasp of psychology. These gifts enable Masters to reveal the deeper and darker meanings of what, on the surface, looks like ordinary lives being lived by ordinary people. Underneath are lives full of drama and secret desires.

George Gray **Edgar Lee Masters**

I have studied many times
The marble which was chiseled for me—
A boat with a furled sail at rest in a harbor.
In truth it pictures not my destination
But my life.
For love was offered me and I shrank from its
  disillusionment;
Sorrow knocked at my door, but I was afraid;
Ambition called to me, but I dreaded the chances.
Yet all the while I hungered for meaning in my life.
And now I know that we must lift the sail
And catch the winds of destiny
Wherever they drive the boat.
To put meaning in one's life may end in madness,
But life without meaning is the torture
Of restlessness and vague desire—
It is a boat longing for the sea and yet afraid.

Chelsea Wharf: Gray and Silver (c. 1875) by James A. McNeill Whistler (1834–1903). Oil on canvas ($24\frac{1}{4}'' \times 18\frac{1}{8}''$).

MEET THE WRITER

Portraits in a Small Town

Edgar Lee Masters (1868–1950) was born in Garnett, Kansas, and grew up in Lewistown, Illinois. Though Masters became a lawyer, like his father, he abandoned law for writing. His reputation today rests solely on one book, *Spoon River Anthology*. In this collection of 244 poems, the dead of Spoon River speak, revealing uncomfortable truths about their lives. Masters struck a new note in American literature when he looked beneath the surface of small-town life. Much of what he observed did not conform to widely held beliefs in the harmony between rich and poor and the even hand of justice.

Spoon River's free verse aroused both praise and criticism. In London, American poet Ezra Pound proclaimed, "AT LAST! . . . America has discovered a poet," but novelist William Dean Howells dismissed Masters' poems as "shredded prose."

Masters remembers that the idea for his Spoon River poems occurred to him after he talked with his mother about the towns where he'd grown up:

> "Finally on the morning she was leaving for Springfield, we had a last and rather sobering talk. It was Sunday, too, and after putting her on the train at 53rd Street, I walked back home full of strange pensiveness. The little church bell was ringing, but spring was in the air. I went to my room and immediately wrote 'The Hill' [the introductory poem] and two or three of the portraits of *Spoon River Anthology*."

MAKING MEANINGS

LOVELIEST OF TREES
GEORGE GRAY

First Thoughts

1. Do you think "Loveliest of Trees" and "George Gray" have basically the same message or different messages? What line or phrase in each poem do you think is the most important?

Shaping Interpretations

2. **Compare** these poems by filling out a chart like the one below:

	Housman	Masters
What is the poem's central **symbol**?		
What does it symbolize?		
What feelings does the **speaker** express?		
What does the speaker discover?		

3. In "Loveliest of Trees," what does the speaker tell us about the kind of life he wants to lead? What meaning does the poem have for you?

4. Write the **denotations**, or literal meanings, of the words *snow* and *gray*. Then, list all the **connotations**, good and bad, that you associate with these words. Why do you think Housman put snow on that cherry bough in "Loveliest of Trees"? Why is Gray an appropriate last name for the speaker in Masters' poem?

Connecting with the Text

5. These two speakers have discovered what's important in life. How do their ideas compare with the ones you described in your Quickwrite notes for "George Gray"? **Compare** your ideas with those of your classmates. What "important things" appear on everyone's list? What other things appear?

CHOICES: Building Your Portfolio

Writer's Notebook

1. Collecting Ideas for a Poem

Sensory details. Think of a place where you'd like to be right now. List what you see, smell, hear, touch. Who is with you? Be sure to check your Quickwrite notes for "Loveliest of Trees." Save your list.

Place: kitchen in our old apartment
Characters: my mother, myself
Sights: dim overhead light; mother reading magazine; small TV; spider-shaped crack in ceiling; dark red linoleum; wooden kitchen table & chairs painted blue; pink geraniums on windowsill

Creative Writing

2. Reverse the Metaphor

The speaker of "George Gray" says that "life without meaning . . . is a boat longing for the sea and yet afraid." Create four metaphors that suggest the quality of a life *with* meaning. Model your metaphors after the one George Gray uses: "Life with meaning is . . ."

Creative Writing

3. Bumper-Sticker Philosophy

Write slogans for bumper stickers that sum up the philosophy, or **main idea** about life, expressed by the speaker of each poem in this collection. Write the slogans on bumper-sized strips of paper, and see if other students can match slogans with speakers.

Comparing and Contrasting Poems

4. Are They Similar?

Compare and contrast A. E. Housman's "Loveliest of Trees" (page 520) with Robert Frost's "Stopping by Woods on a Snowy Evening" (page 516). Before you write, fill in a chart like the one below to help you organize your thoughts.

	Housman	Frost
What happens to the **speaker**?		
What does nature remind the speaker of?		
What is the poem's main **image**?		
What is the speaker's **main idea** about life?		

Before You Read

MENDING WALL

Make the Connection

Frost vs. Walls

People who live in cold climates know that water freezing in the soil can dislocate stone walls, crack sidewalks, and push underground boulders onto the landscape. Frost's wall is made of boulders that are balanced one on another. Although low, this wall can effectively keep the neighbors at a distance.

Quickwrite

List all the different kinds of walls and boundaries you can think of. What's good about boundaries—and what's bad about them? (*Keep your notes for use on page 529.*)

Elements of Literature

A Matter of Interpretation

This is one of Frost's most controversial poems. The poem is **ambiguous**—that is, it allows for opposing interpretations. There are two mind-sets presented in the poem. The question is, which mind-set does the poet seem to favor: the neighbor's view that walls are good, or the speaker's view that walls should be torn down? There are other ambiguities: If the speaker dislikes walls, why does he initiate the wall mending each spring?

When a work of literature allows for opposing interpretations, it is called **ambiguous**.

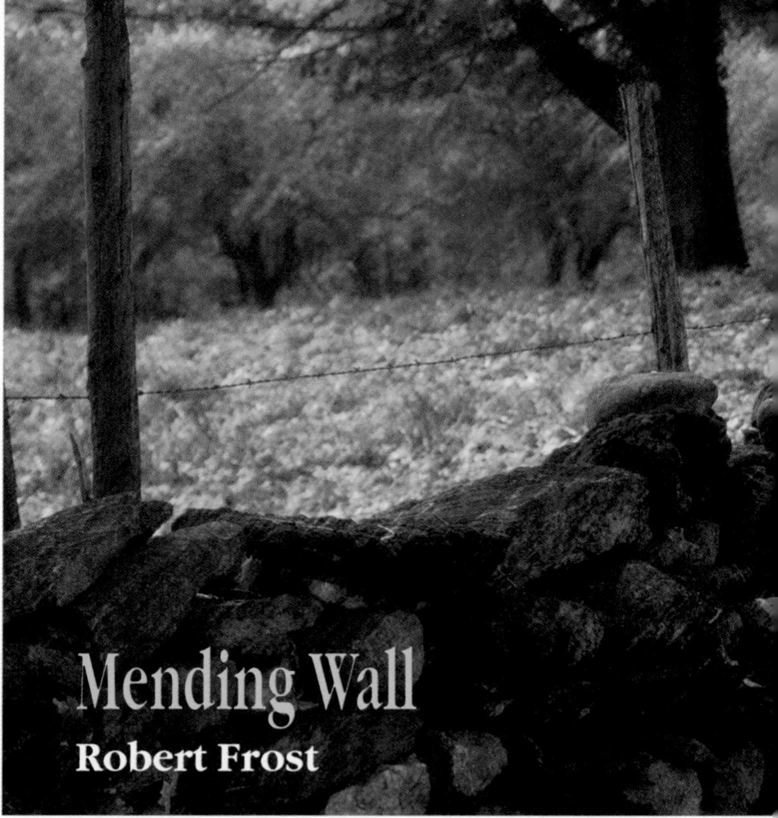

Mending Wall

Robert Frost

Something there is that doesn't love a wall,
That sends the frozen-ground-swell under it
And spills the upper boulders in the sun,
And makes gaps even two can pass abreast.
The work of hunters is another thing:
I have come after them and made repair
Where they have left not one stone on a stone,
But they would have the rabbit out of hiding,
To please the yelping dogs. The gaps I mean,
No one has seen them made or heard them made,
But at spring mending-time we find them there.
I let my neighbor know beyond the hill;
And on a day we meet to walk the line
And set the wall between us once again.
We keep the wall between us as we go.
To each the boulders that have fallen to each.
And some are loaves and some so nearly balls
We have to use a spell to make them balance:
"Stay where you are until our backs are turned!"
We wear our fingers rough with handling them.
Oh, just another kind of outdoor game,
One on a side. It comes to little more:
There where it is we do not need the wall:

go.hrw.com
LEO 10-8

He is all pine and I am apple orchard.
My apple trees will never get across
And eat the cones under his pines, I tell him.
He only says, "Good fences make good neighbors."
Spring is the mischief in me, and I wonder
If I could put a notion in his head:
"*Why* do they make good neighbors? Isn't it
Where there are cows? But here there are no cows.
Before I built a wall I'd ask to know
What I was walling in or walling out,
And to whom I was like to give offense.
Something there is that doesn't love a wall,
That wants it down." I could say "Elves" to him,
But it's not elves exactly, and I'd rather
He said it for himself. I see him there,
Bringing a stone grasped firmly by the top
In each hand, like an old-stone savage armed.
He moves in darkness as it seems to me,
Not of woods only and the shade of trees.
He will not go behind his father's saying,
And he likes having thought of it so well
He says again, "Good fences make good neighbors."

Connections

A PARODY

This poem was written by a teacher in Lakeside, California.

Mending Test

(Apologies to Robert Frost)

Penelope Bryant Turk

Something there is that doesn't love a test,
That sends the frozen mind-set under it
And spills the grade objectives in the room,
And makes gaps students often fall between.
No one has seen them made or heard them made
But at spring testing time we find them here.
I let my classes know within my room
And on a day we meet to take the test
And set the norms between us once again.
We wear our minds quite rough with handling them.
Oh, just another kind of indoor game,
One on a side. It comes to little more.
There where it is, we do not need the test.
The teachers can assess their goals, I tell him,
The district's high inquisitor, once more.
He only says, "Good tests will make good students."
Spring is the mischief in me, and I wonder
If I could put a notion in his head.
"Why do they make good students?" I inquire.
"Before I gave a test, I'd ask to know
What I was testing in or testing out.
And to whom I was like to do some good.
Something there is that doesn't love a test,
That wants it done." I could say this to him
But it's not politic, and then I'd rather
He said it for himself. I see him there
Bringing a test grasped firmly in each hand,
With pencils like an old-time pedant° armed.
He moves in darkness as it seems to me,
Not of woods only and the shade of trees.
He will not go behind the state's command,
And he likes having thought of it so well,
He says again, "Good tests will make good students."

28. pedant (ped′ 'nt): fussy, narrow-minded teacher.

A LETTER

In a 1995 opinion written for the Supreme Court, Justice Antonin Scalia justified a "high wall" separating the levels of government by quoting the neighbor in Frost's poem. The New York Times *published an editorial reminding Justice Scalia that Frost did* not *think good fences made good neighbors. Here is one letter about the controversy.*

To the Editor:

Robert Frost's "Mending Wall" has been subjected to many conflicting interpretations, but your April 22 editorial gives the correct one. The "pro-wall" speaker was Frost's French Canadian neighbor, Napoleon Guay. In the opening lines,

Something there is that doesn't love a wall,
That sends the frozen-ground-swell under it

the "something," a natural force that breaks down the wall and indicates the poet's point of view, is frost. Frost liked to pun on his name, calling his satire "frostbite."

When this poem was translated into Russian and printed in the newspapers for Frost's official visit to the Soviet Union in 1962, many writers and intellectuals saw a negative reference to the Berlin Wall put up by East Germany in 1961. So the Soviet translators jump-started the poem with line two.

—Jeffrey Meyers
Kensington, California
April 22, 1995

MAKING MEANINGS
MENDING WALL

First Thoughts

1. Do you agree or disagree that "good fences make good neighbors"? Why?

Shaping Interpretations

2. Frost creates two **characters** in this poem, and we come to know them by what they say and do and think. How would you describe each character?
3. What do you think the word *darkness* means in line 41? What could the **simile** in line 40 have to do with the darkness?
4. What might the wall in the poem **symbolize**?
5. The poem is **ambiguous** and presents opposing views about the wall. Do you think Frost favors the view of the speaker or the neighbor? Which details lead you to this interpretation? Check the ***Connections*** on page 528.

Extending the Text

6. What other famous walls or boundaries have separated neighbors? (Be sure to check your Quickwrite notes.) Which speaker (maybe both?) would think these walls serve or served a useful purpose? What do you think?

CHOICES: Building Your Portfolio

Writer's Notebook

WORK IN PROGRESS

1. Collecting Ideas for a Poem

A poem about a poem. If you have feelings about walls and boundaries, **describe** an experience you've had with them. Frost writes his poem as a little story—a series of connected events that lead to a discovery. Think of a story to tell about your experience. Elaborate with descriptive details that might make the story more interesting. Also, notice how Frost's poem sounds like an informal conversation but is actually written in strict **meter**. (For more on meter, see pages 543–544 and 558–559.) You might start with Frost's first line and try to imitate his **rhythm**. Save your notes for the Writer's Workshop on page 541.

Creative Writing

2. Let's Hear It from the Neighbor

Using the **first-person point of view** (with "I" as the neighbor), write a letter or journal entry. Tell what you think about your neighbor (the speaker in "Mending Wall"), of the need to mend walls each spring, and of the way you've been portrayed in this poem. Make up details about your life.

Creative Writing/Music

3. Parody, Anyone?

A **parody** is a work that makes fun of another work by imitating some aspect of the writer's style. Penelope Bryant Turk's parody (see ***Connections*** on page 528), meaning no disrespect to Frost, offers her apologies at the outset. Work with a partner or group to parody the **style** or **format** of a poem or a song lyric.

Before You Read

THE LEGEND

Make the Connection

Imagination's Eye

One night, Garrett Hongo saw a TV news story about an Asian man killed in an act of street violence. Much later, Hongo claims, the poem "just appeared." Which details do you think Hongo imagined?

Quickwrite

Look up, and focus on a person or a scene that you can observe closely. Note what you see and what you *imagine*. *(Keep your notes for use on page 537.)*

See	Imagine

Elements of Literature

Tone: An Attitude

A poet's attitude, or **tone,** can be inferred from words and details in the text. Read "The Legend" more than once to get the speaker's tone.

Tone is the attitude of the writer or the speaker toward the subject of the poem or toward the audience.

For more on Tone, see the Handbook of Literary Terms.

The Hermitage Museum, Saint Petersburg, Russia. Courtesy Scala/Art Resource, NY.

Portrait of an Old Man in Red (c. 1652–1654) by Rembrandt. Oil on canvas (108 cm × 86 cm).

The Legend

Garrett Hongo

In Chicago, it is snowing softly
and a man has just done his wash for the week.
He steps into the twilight of early evening,
carrying a wrinkled shopping bag
full of neatly folded clothes,
and, for a moment, enjoys
the feel of warm laundry and crinkled paper,
flannellike against his gloveless hands.
There's a Rembrandt° glow on his face,

9. Rembrandt: Dutch painter (1606–1669), famous for his dramatic use of color and of light and shadow.

a triangle of orange in the hollow of his cheek
as a last flash of sunset
blazes the storefronts and lit windows of the street.

He is Asian, Thai or Vietnamese,
and very skinny, dressed as one of the poor
in rumpled suit pants and a plaid mackinaw,
dingy and too large.
He negotiates the slick of ice
on the sidewalk by his car,
opens the Fairlane's back door,
leans to place the laundry in,
and turns, for an instant,
toward the flurry of footsteps
and cries of pedestrians
as a boy—that's all he was—
backs from the corner package store
shooting a pistol, firing it,
once, at the dumbfounded man
who falls forward,
grabbing at his chest.

A few sounds escape from his mouth,
a babbling no one understands
as people surround him
bewildered at his speech.
The noises he makes are nothing to them.
The boy has gone, lost
in the light array of foot traffic
dappling the snow with fresh prints.
Tonight, I read about Descartes'
grand courage to doubt everything
except his own miraculous existence°
and I feel so distinct
from the wounded man lying on the concrete
I am ashamed.

Let the night sky cover him as he dies.
Let the weaver girl cross the bridge of heaven
and take up his cold hands.

IN MEMORY OF JAY KASHIWAMURA

38–40. Descartes' . . . existence: René Descartes (1596–1650), French philosopher and mathematician, attempted to explain the universe by reason alone. In his search for truth, he discarded all traditional ideas and doubted everything. The one thing he could not doubt was the fact that he was doubting, which led him to conclude, "I think; therefore I am" (in Latin, *Cogito, ergo sum*).

Connections A REFLECTION

When he was asked about "The Legend," here is what Hongo answered:

What I wanted, the city could not give me. I wanted *mercy*. I wanted the universe to bend down and kiss its own creation, like a parent does to a child just after it's born, as if a tenderness were the pure expression of the world for itself. I wanted to believe that what was not given could be given, that were a man or a woman to cry out for solace, that the world, for all of its steel plants and tire factories, for all of its liquor stores and razor wire, for all of its buses that belched carcinogenic poisons and people who passed you by on the freeway who cursed you with their eyes—for all of that, it would still lay its soft wings of blessing upon you if you cried out in need.

From time to time, I'd recollect a story I'd heard during childhood, probably in Hawaii, a legend about the creation of the universe. From an aunt baking *pan dulce*[1] or a cousin flinging stones with me into waves along Hau'ula Beach, into abandoned canefields or at the headboards of the Japanese graves on the promontory at the Kahuku plantation, I'd heard that, in order for the stars to turn and remain where they were, it took two creatures and their sacrifice. It took a Weaver Maid to make the stars—Being—and a Herd Boy to make sure they all stayed together or apart as they should. The Weaver Maid and the Herd Boy lived on opposite sides of the Milky Way, that band of stars that is our galaxy and which Asians see as a mighty river of stars. They call it The River of Heaven. The Herd Boy and Weaver Maid are stars on its opposite banks, the one in a cluster around Antares,[2] the

1. ***pan dulce*** (pän′ do͞ol′sā): sweet bread.
2. **Antares** (an·ter′ēz′): brightest star in the constellation Scorpius; its name derives from the Greek for "rival of Ares" (Mars).

other far away and down along the flow, in a spot near Aldebaran.[3] They labor, dutifully fabricating the web and warp of Being, herding the star bands in an eternal solitude, celibate, without love or companionship. Yet, for one night of the year, on an evening when the star sky is said to be clearest, the universe is supposed to succumb to an overwhelming pity for the two lovers, living out lives in exile from each other, lives in deprivation of passion, without emotional compass or root in material certainties. In the form of a flock of compassionate starlings or swallows in the Japanese or Chinese versions, in the folded and gigantic wing of Crow in the Tlingit and Haida versions of the North Coast Pacific Indians, the universe, *one turning,* responds by making a footbridge across the River of Heaven out of its own interlocking bodies, out of its own need to create mercy and requital in a night of love for the effortful sacrifices of two of its children.

It is a vision of the afterlife, in a sense, a promise that the world will provide for us a reward and a reason for our struggles. It is a parable[4] about mercy and fulfillment, the response of the universe to needs of the human heart. The poem is the story of the Weaver Girl and the Herd Boy, told in inner-city, contemporary terms. It is about my own needs for mercy, for a fulfillment to a broad, urban, and contemporary story that baffled me.

Meet the Writer

Looking for Mercy

Garrett Hongo (1951–) was born in Volcano, Hawaii, and grew up in Hawaii and Los Angeles. After graduating with honors from Pomona College, he toured Japan for a year and then returned to the United States to write and teach poetry. Hongo says he writes

“for my father in a very personal way. He was a great example to me of a man who refused to hate or, being different himself, to be afraid of difference. . . . I want my poems to be equal to his heart.”

3. **Aldebaran** (al·deb′ə·rən): brightest star in the constellation Taurus.
4. **parable** (par′ə·b′l): brief story that teaches a moral or religious lesson.

Before You Read

MISS ROSIE

Make the Connection

Portrait of a Woman

No one can say that Clifton's portrait of Miss Rosie is very pretty. Yet beauty—and what can happen to it—is the subject of the poem. Notice how figures of speech help you see contrasting pictures, past and present, of Miss Rosie.

Quickwrite

How do you feel when you see a homeless person or someone on the street asking for money? Write a few sentences in your notebook. *(Keep your notes for use on page 536.)*

Elements of Literature

Idioms: Not Literally True

An **idiom** is an expression that is peculiar to a certain language and that cannot be understood by a mere literal definition of its individual words. For example, the literal meaning of the expression "to fall in love" would be absurd. Like many idioms, this one implies a comparison. The experience of love can be so overwhelming that it feels like losing your footing or like falling into a trap, although not necessarily an unpleasant one.

One of the problems in translating a work from one language to another is the difficulty in translating the idioms.

If an idiom is unfamiliar to you—as the idiom "I stand up" in this poem may be—the context might help you understand it.

Mirage (1993) by Catherine Howe. Oil on canvas.
Collection Alan P. Power (Venice, California).

> An **idiom** is an expression peculiar to a particular language. An idiom means something different from the literal meaning of each word.

Miss Rosie

Lucille Clifton

When I watch you
wrapped up like garbage
sitting, surrounded by the smell
of too old potato peels
or
when I watch you
in your old man's shoes
with the little toe cut out
sitting, waiting for your mind
like next week's grocery
I say
when I watch you
you wet brown bag of a woman
who used to be the best looking gal in Georgia
used to be called the Georgia Rose
I stand up
through your destruction
I stand up

Meet the Writer

Celebrating Survival

Lucille Clifton (1936–) writes both fiction and poetry and has published many books for children. One of Clifton's best-known works is *Generations* (1976), a poetic memoir composed of portraits of five generations of her family. It begins with her great-great-grandmother, who was brought from Africa to New Orleans and sold into slavery. Like all of Clifton's work, *Generations* is honest but rarely bitter. As one critic observed, her purpose is perpetuation and celebration, not judgment.

Clifton says that family stories are part of the ingredients that make us who we are. She remembers hearing her own family's stories when she was growing up.

“My father told those stories to me over and over. That made them seem important. He told the stories to whoever was present, but I was the only person who listened. I think there is a matter of preserving the past for the future's sake. I think if we see our lives as an ongoing story, it's important to include all the ingredients of it and not have it in little compartments. I like to think of it as not just that was then, this is now, but that they all connect. For some reason, I've always been a person who found more interesting the stories between the stories. I've always wondered the hows and the whys to things. Why is this like this? What has gone into making us who we are? Is it good or not so good? What is destroying us? What will keep us warm?”

Making Meanings
The Legend
Miss Rosie

First Thoughts

1. In "The Legend" and "Miss Rosie," we meet two figures seen briefly on city streets. How do you feel about each of these people?

Shaping Interpretations

2. In "The Legend," an ordinary street scene is suddenly transformed by a tragic event. How would you describe the poem's **tone**? In other words, what is the poet's attitude toward the event he's made into a poem? List some of the words, phrases, and details that you think create the tone.
3. Read Hongo's explanation of how he came to write "The Legend" (see ***Connections*** on page 532). Do you think the poem expresses what he wants it to? Talk about Hongo's comment about needing mercy.
4. Which **figure of speech** in "Miss Rosie" do you think is most powerful? What picture of Miss Rosie does it create for you?
5. The **idiom** "I stand up," used twice, gives the most important clue to how the writer wants us to feel about Miss Rosie. What does standing up in the face of Miss Rosie's destruction mean? (What does it make you see?) Why do you think the speaker is moved to "stand up" for Miss Rosie?
6. In a way, Miss Rosie seems to represent something more than herself, something never named. What do you think she might **symbolize**?

Extending the Text

7. What contemporary urban problems come alive in these poems by Hongo and Clifton? Do most people feel the way these poets felt about these problems? Talk about the ways in which people like Miss Rosie and events like the one in "The Legend" are regarded by society. (You may want to refer to your Quickwrite notes for "Miss Rosie.")

The Shoemaker (1945) by Jacob Lawrence.
Tempera on hardboard (30″ × 40″).

The Metropolitan Museum of Art, George A. Hearn Fund, 1946. (46.73.2) Courtesy of the artist and Francine Seders Gallery, Seattle, Washington. Photograph ©1985 The Metropolitan Museum of Art.

CHOICES: Building Your Portfolio

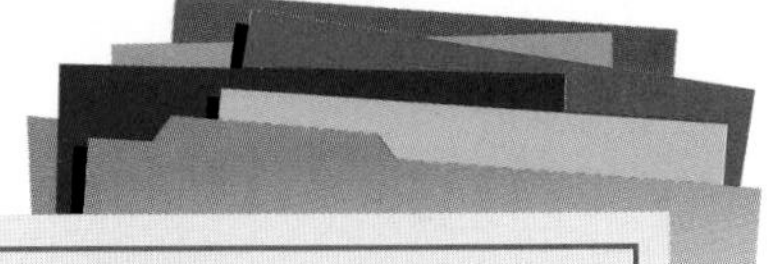

Writer's Notebook

1. Collecting Ideas for a Poem

Finding figures of speech. Try to write figures of speech that tell what some person or scene reminds you of. Remember to think in **descriptive** images. Let your imagination free-associate; **comparisons** should come quickly to you. Write them all down, even those you might not totally understand. You might want to focus on the person or scene from your Quickwrite notes for "The Legend."

Old Mr. Dan in the garden.

Like an oak tree,
a flagpole with all flags
flying.

A loaf of homemade
bread.

A prayer, a song, a
soldier.

Creative Writing

2. Changing the Tone

Write at least three new lines to end "The Legend" and "Miss Rosie." Let your lines reveal a **tone**, or attitude toward the characters (the Asian man, Miss Rosie), that's different from the present tone of the poems. Use **figures of speech** and **sensory details** in your lines.

Visual Arts/Oral History

3. Portraits of a Neighborhood

In photographs, drawings, or paintings, show your neighborhood and the people who live there. **Interview** one person if you can, and add his or her words to your portrait. Try to elaborate with **images** that reveal the way you feel about this place.

Creative Writing

4. News Stories Are True Poems

"The true poem is the daily paper," wrote Walt Whitman in 1852. Write a poem that is based on a newspaper story or a television report. Follow Hongo's pattern in "The Legend": Begin with a close observation of the scene; focus on one or more unnamed characters; and then tell what happens, using present-tense verbs. End with a comment on your own feelings and thoughts about the event. Use your imagination to elaborate with **sensory details**.

Critical Thinking/ Speaking and Listening

5. The Poems as Clues

Imagine that extraterrestrials visit America in the year 4000 and the only bits of writing they discover are these two poems. No other books or writings have survived. What might the newcomers **infer** about American life from these poems? Would their **conclusions** be valid? Discuss this scenario in a small group, and then report to the class.

Research/Survey

6. Idioms, Anyone?

With a small group, survey students in your school or your family or neighbors. Challenge them to think of as many idioms as they can, in English or in other languages. Read a few idioms to get them started—for example, "big shot," "go in one ear and out the other," and "He jumped out of his skin." Afterward, prepare a chart listing the idioms in one column, their literal meanings in the second column, and their real meanings in the third column. Do you have any favorites?

EXTENDING *the theme*

AN ESSAY

Quickwrite

Divide a page of your notebook into two columns. In one column, list all the jobs you think you'd like to have—if you could make a living doing them. In the other column, list (and don't be modest) your talents, the things you do well, and the things you really enjoy doing. Save your lists.

Is There Really Such a Thing as Talent?

Annie Dillard

The very thought of hard work makes me queasy.

It's hard work, doing something with your life. The very thought of hard work makes me queasy. I'd rather die in peace. Here we are, all equal and alike and none of us much to write home about—and some people choose to make themselves into physicists or thinkers or major-league pitchers, knowing perfectly well that it will be nothing but hard work. But I want to tell you that it's not as bad as it sounds. Doing something does not require discipline; it creates its own discipline—with a little help from caffeine.

People often ask me if I discipline myself to write, if I work a certain number of hours a day on a schedule. They ask this question with envy in their voices and awe on their faces and a sense of alienation all over them, as if they were addressing an armored tank or a talking giraffe or Niagara Falls. We want to believe that other people are natural wonders; it gets us off the hook.

Now, it happens that when I wrote my first book of prose, I worked an hour or two a day for a while, and then in the last two months, I got excited and worked very hard, for many hours a day. People can lift cars when they want to. People can recite the Koran,[1] too, and run in marathons. These things aren't ways of life; they are merely possibilities for everyone on certain occasions of life. You don't lift cars around the clock or write books every year. But when you do, it's not so hard. It's not superhuman. It's very human. You do it for love. You do it for love and respect for your own life; you do it for love and respect for the world; and you do it for love and respect for the task itself.

If I had a little baby, it would be hard for me to rise up and feed that little baby in the middle of the night. It would be hard but certainly wouldn't be a discipline. It wouldn't be a regimen I imposed on myself out of masochism,[2] nor would it be the flowering of some extraordinary internal impulse. I would do it, grumbling, for love and because it has to be done.

Something has to be done with your life too: something specific, something human.

Of course it has to be done. And something has to be done with your life too: something specific, something human. But don't wait around to be hit by love. Don't wait for anything. Learn something first. Then, when you are getting to know it, you will get to love it, and that love will direct you in what to do. So many times when I was in college, I used to say of a course like seventeenth-century poetry or European history, "I didn't like it at first, but now I like it." All of life is like that—a sort of dreary course which gradually gets interesting if you work at it.

I used to live in perpetual dread that I would one day read all the books that I would ever be interested in and have nothing more to read. I always figured that when that time came I would force myself to learn wildflowers, just to keep awake. I dreaded it, because I was not very interested in wildflowers but thought I should be. But things kept cropping up and one book has led to another and I haven't had to learn wildflowers yet. I don't think there's much danger of coming to the end of the line. The line is endless. I urge you to get in it, to get in line. It's a long line—but it's the only show in town.

1. **Koran** (kə·ran′): sacred book of Islam.
2. **masochism** (mas′ə·kiz′əm): getting pleasure from pain.

Meet the Writer

Rockhound, Naturalist, and Writer

When **Annie Dillard** (1945–) was twelve, her grandparents' paperboy handed her three shopping bags full of large rocks from an elderly neighbor. With the help of books, she identified each of the 340 rocks; she became a "rockhound," a rock collector. Later, looking out a car window at miles of dull gray rock, she realized:

> "But now I knew that even rock was interesting. . . . Even I could tap some shale just right, rain or shine, and open the rock to bones of fossil fish. There might be trilobites on the hilltops, star sapphires. . . . If even rock was interesting, if even this ugliness was worth whole shelves at the library, required sophisticated tools to study, and inspired grown men to crack mountains and saw crystals—then what wasn't?"

Dillard's continuing interest in nature resulted in her Pulitzer Prize–winning first book, *Pilgrim at Tinker Creek* (1974). In it she chronicles a year's worth of observations of the beauties and terrors along a Virginia creek. Dillard's other works include an autobiography, *An American Childhood* (1987); essays on writing, *The Writing Life* (1989); and a novel, *The Living* (1992).

To aspiring writers Dillard gives this advice:

> "You have enough experience by the time you're five years old. What you need is the library. What you have to learn is the best of what is being thought and said. If you had a choice between spending a summer in Nepal and spending a summer in the library, go to the library."

Finding Common Ground

Get together in small groups to discuss this essay. First, vote yes or no on the question in the title and explain your vote. Here is what you could focus on in your group discussions, though you can also set agendas of your own. Your purpose is to explore your responses to the text and **compare** them with the responses of other readers.

1. If Dillard visited your class, what questions would you ask? What would you tell her?
2. Share your Quickwrite notes about jobs you'd love to have. Is anyone else in your group interested in the same kinds of jobs? How could you get any of these jobs?
3. How did the essay make you feel about your future? What do you think of Dillard's advice about how to discover something you'll be happy doing?

BUILDING YOUR PORTFOLIO

Writer's Workshop

ASSIGNMENT

Write a poem or a group of poems that describe something or someone.

AIM

To express yourself; to create literature.

AUDIENCE

Your classmates, your family, or readers of a magazine of student writing. (You choose.)

I thought poetry was just something about dried roses and violets until I discovered that it could be about my shoestrings, about the neighborhood, about the sky, about my mother, about being a basketball player or a musician.

—Quincy Troupe

DESCRIPTIVE WRITING

POETRY

To write a poem is to give inner feelings outward expression. The process begins with finding the first word that will start the magic that translates what you feel into what you say.

In this workshop you will write a poem using **descriptive details**—sensory details that help the reader see, hear, smell, taste, even touch your subject.

Prewriting

1. Review Your Notebooks and Journals

WORK IN PROGRESS

When you are assigned to write a poem, your first reaction is likely to be, "What am I going to write about?" As you worked through the poems in this collection, you took notes on various subjects. You also experimented with **descriptive writing,** especially with figures of speech. Review your notes to find ideas for a poem.

2. Imagine You're a Camera

Here's a technique for finding a subject: Imagine that you've just been given a new camera and three rolls of film. You have nothing to do all day but wander wherever you'd like and snap anything you see. At first, you'll probably take shots of any object in range just because it's there. But as your supply of film gets lower and lower, you'll be more apt to snap things that have particular meaning for you. Make a list of subjects you might photograph.

- a corner of the schoolyard where you used to play in fourth grade
- your shoes
- the "For Sale" sign on your house
- your best friends
- a bird in flight
- your mom, the traffic officer
- rooftops silhouetted against the sky
- your dog, Gus, sleeping
- your father's chair
- your school cafeteria
- your favorite place

A Box of Descriptive Words

Can you add to the list?
Sight: radiant, flickering, lopsided, hazy, golden
Sound: roaring, raspy, tinkling, beeping, hissing
Smell: reeking, woodsy, fragrant, fresh-baked, rotting, flowery
Touch: icy, silken, yielding, prickly, gooey
Taste: spicy, buttery, salty, mouthwatering, tart, sweet

Handbook of Literary Terms HELP

See Imagery, Description, Connotations, Figure of Speech.

Strategies for Elaboration

Team up with a partner to practice using your **descriptive skills.** Observe a place together. Without comparing impressions, jot down several details that appeal to your senses. Then, compare your perceptions. Did you and your partner notice the same things? Here are some settings you might observe:

- the school cafeteria
- an empty classroom
- a city street at 5:00 P.M.
- a back yard
- a storage room

Once you stop taking pictures of everything in sight, you'll begin to choose your subjects. Your choices are likely to be subjects that remind you of something else—an event, a person, a place—or that evoke a particular feeling you'd like to express.

3. Elaborating: Finding Descriptive Details

Once you've chosen your subject, the big question will be: "How can I make this thing and what I feel about it come alive for someone besides me?" The answer is *describe, describe, describe.* What you feel will be made apparent by the details you emphasize. So, as your next step, make another list.

a. Write down the details you want to emphasize.

b. Write down the colors, shapes, and textures of what you see.

c. Describe any sounds, tastes, smells, or movements you notice.

d. Be aware of the **connotations,** or suggestive powers, of the words and **figures of speech** you choose. Is that motorcycle leaning against the wall shining like a new toy, or does it look like a sinister war machine? Does the rain on that window look like tears or like a spray of diamonds? Does the wind in the trees sound like a moan or like a song? Try out some imaginative **comparisons** using the details you've listed.

At this point, jot down whatever comes into your mind. Later, you can select the descriptive details you will use. As you look over your list, you will also decide on your focus. Think of yourself again as a photographer: Will your picture be a wide-sweeping panorama, or will it be a tight close-up?

"Write about dogs."

Drafting

1. Finding a Form

If you want to be informal or conversational about your chosen subject, write your poem in **free verse.** (See page 559.) If you want to be more structured, try using **meter** and **rhyme.** (See pages 558–559 and 588–589.)

2. Using Free Verse

a. If you choose free verse, be as economical as possible with words, phrases, and sentences. Don't "string out" what you mean in the casual language of a personal letter or the outpourings of school gossip. Pack your meaning into the smallest parcel that will contain it.

b. Free verse can be free-flowing and hypnotic, but it can also be as clipped and terse as something measured off with a ruler. In either case, free verse is free only to this extent: It allows natural **conversational rhythms** to do the work of meter, and it allows hard, precise images to carry the emotional weight of the poem. Find the proper images and your poem will almost write itself. Note the opening images in this poem describing a New England town.

> I must be mad, or very tired,
> When the curve of a blue bay beyond a railroad track
> Is shrill and sweet to me like the sudden springing of a tune,
> And the sight of a white church above thin trees in a city square
> Amazes my eyes as though it were the Parthenon.
>
> —Amy Lowell, from "Meeting-House Hill"

c. Try to open with a line that captures your reader's attention.

d. Pay special attention to where you end your lines. In writing free verse, poets may break a line to indicate a pause for breath or to show a natural break in thought.

e. Though free verse does not usually use end rhymes, it does often include **alliteration, onomatopoeia, internal rhyme,** and **approximate rhyme.**

3. Using Meter and Rhyme

a. If you are writing in a metric form, you will have to experiment until you find a pattern that suits your purpose. (You'll find the common meters under Meter in the Handbook of Literary Terms.) Try writing lines of three or four iambs. (An **iamb** is a pair of syllables made up of an unstressed syllable followed by a stressed syllable: daDAH daDAH daDAH daDAH.)

Poetry is a conversation with the world; poetry is a conversation with the words on the page in which you allow those words to speak back to you; and poetry is a conversation with yourself. Many times I meet students and see a little look of wariness in their faces—"I'm not sure I want *to do this or I'm not sure I* can *do this"—I like to say, "Wait a minute. How nervous are you about the conversation you're going to have at lunch today with your friends?" And they say, "Oh, we're not nervous at all about* that. *We do* that *every day." Then I tell them they can come to feel the same way about writing. Writing doesn't have to be an exotic or stressful experience. You can just sit down with a piece of paper and begin talking and see what speaks back.*

—Naomi Shihab Nye

Handbook of Literary Terms HELP

See Meter, Rhyme, Couplet, Stanza.

b. For the most part, try to maintain your beat exactly, but allow for some variation so that your verse doesn't sound mechanical and forced. If you use a three-foot line, for example, you might occasionally vary the meter by beginning with a **trochee:** DAHda daDAH daDAH.

c. A simple form of rhyme is the **couplet**—two successive lines that rhyme. Another popular form of rhyme is the **quatrain**—four successive lines of verse that have a certain rhyme pattern.

4. Finding Your Own Style

A poem in meter and rhyme will amount to little unless you can overcome the mechanical sounds of the metrical form and let your own voice be heard. Think of meter and rhyme as a dress or suit hanging on a rack. Nobody can change its basic shape or cut; but anyone who tries it on will find a way to wear it that is just a little different from everyone else's way. That difference is called **style.**

Whether you write your poem in meter or in free verse (like the Student Model below), try out sounds and phrasings that sound like *you.* Read your poem aloud to yourself: Does it sound like your individual voice? Once you've found your voice, the resulting style will be all yours, and so will the poem.

Inside a Poem

It doesn't always have to
rhyme,
but there's the repeat of a
beat, somewhere
an inner chime that makes
you want to
tap your feet or swerve in
a curve;
a lilt, a leap, a lightning-
split:—
thunderstruck the
consonants jut,
while the vowels open
wide as waves in the
noon-blue sea.

You hear with your heels,
your eyes feel
what they never touched
before:
fins on a bird, feathers on
a deer;
taste all colors, inhale
memory and tomorrow
and always the tang is
today.

—Eve Merriam

Student Model

OCEAN BEACH CHILDHOOD

I liked the little slab of gray porch
bordered by marigolds in black cauldrons.
I kicked the pebbles of the driveway
and over me squawked the gulls—
the same cry that woke me.
I sat on a rocky stool at the kitchen counter,
plum juice running down my chin,
spinning and spinning,
until the cool, dark rooms swirled, too.
Barefoot on the beach at sunset,
warm, white sand between my toes,
the ocean breeze flapped my clothing
and lurched trim white boats on the horizon
as it carried my laughter into the sky.

—Ann Marie Hoppel
Bishop George Ahr High School
Edison, New Jersey

First appeared in *Merlyn's Pen: The National Magazines of Student Writing*

Revising

See how many different words and lines E. E. Cummings tried out when he was revising "one wintry afternoon" (below). Tinker with words, phrases, images until you're satisfied that the poem says what you want it to say. Don't rush: The "right" word or image may take some time to appear—or it could pop into your brain immediately. Be sure to read the poem aloud as you revise it to hear its sound effects.

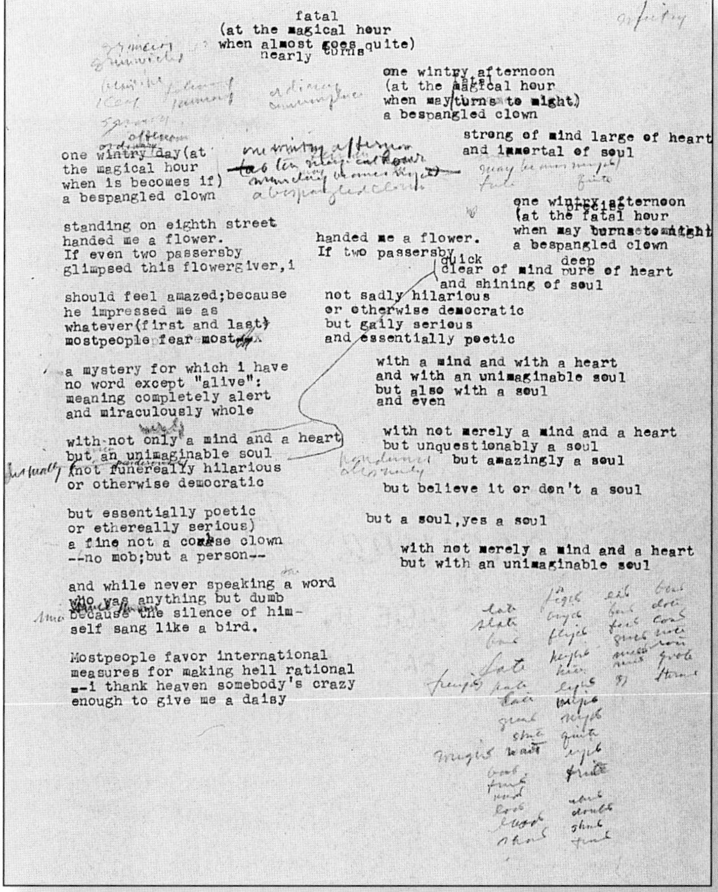

fatal
(at the magical hour
when almost goes quite)
nearly turns

one wintry afternoon
(at the magical hour
when may turns to might)
a bespangled clown

strong of mind large of heart
and immortal of soul

one wintry day(at
the magical hour
when is becomes if)
a bespangled clown

one wintry afternoon
(at the fatal hour
when may turns to might
a bespangled clown

standing on eighth street
handed me a flower.
If even two passersby
glimpsed this flowergiver,i

handed me a flower.
If two passersby

quick deep
clear of mind pure of heart
and shining of soul

should feel amazed;because
he impressed me as
whatever(first and last)
mostpeople fear most

not sadly hilarious
or otherwise democratic
but gaily serious
and essentially poetic

a mystery for which i have
no word except "alive":
meaning completely alert
and miraculously whole

with a mind and with a heart
and with an unimaginable soul
but also with a soul
and even

with not only a mind and a heart
but an unimaginable soul
(not funereally hilarious
or otherwise democratic

with not merely a mind and a heart
but unquestionably a soul
but amazingly a soul

but believe it or don't a soul

but essentially poetic
or ethereally serious)
a fine not a coarse clown
--no mob;but a person--

but a soul,yes a soul

with not merely a mind and a heart
but with an unimaginable soul

and while never speaking a word
who was anything but dumb
because the silence of himself sang like a bird.

Mostpeople favor international
measures for making hell rational
--i thank heaven somebody's crazy
enough to give me a daisy

> *I wouldn't even know whether a poem was finished or not unless my ear told me.*
>
> —Paul Blackburn

Proofreading Tips

- Double-check your spelling.
- Read the poem aloud, checking to see that line breaks, punctuation, and indents indicate natural pauses or breaks in thought.

Communications Handbook HELP

See Proofreaders' Marks.

Publishing Tips

- Publish your favorite poem as a broadsheet (a poem published on a single page of good paper with an artistic design or illustration).
- Compile a classroom anthology, bulletin-board display, or audiotape of each student reading his or her favorite poem.
- Submit your poem to a magazine that publishes student writing.

Reading for Life

Reading Memos and E-Mail

Situation

It's your first week at your dream job: helping to create film ideas for young adult audiences. You've just received an e-mail memo about an idea for a film. The following strategies will guide you in handling workplace memos and e-mail.

For e-mail

Date: 99-11-01 09:14:38 EST
From: CYNBAD@rbi.com
To: MGONZALEZ@rbi.com
CC: MREILLY@rbi.com, KNAKA@aol.com
Subj: "Weaver Maid"

MEMORANDUM

Date: November 1, 1999
To: Manuel Gonzalez, Research Associate, RightBrain, Inc.
From: Cynthia Baddington, Director, RightBrain, Inc.
cc: Michael Reilly, Art Director, RightBrain, Inc.
Kay Nakagama
Subject: "Weaver Maid"

Kay Nakagama called this morning—she's been developing a treatment for a live-action film based on the Weaver Maid figure in Asian folklore. We'll meet with her next Thursday (the 11th) at 10 to discuss her ideas. (She'll try to get an outline to us Tuesday.) Please give me whatever relevant information, including visuals, you can find about the Weaver Maid. Actually, whatever you can find in the way of similar figures in Japanese/Hawaiian folklore would help. Could I have the material sometime on the day before our meeting? And please plan on coming to the meeting to take notes and to add anything relevant your research turns up.

Thanks!

Strategies

Understand the function of memos and e-mail.

- A **memo** (short for "memorandum") is a type of print or electronic communication.
- In offices today, memos are increasingly sent in the form of **e-mail,** which arrives over an electronic computer network. E-mail can also be sent between people anywhere.

Be aware of the form of a memo.

- A memo begins with a heading that includes the date, the name of the person who wrote the memo, the person(s) to whom it is sent, and a brief description of the subject (look for the abbreviation *Re,* meaning "regarding"). The remainder of the memo deals with the subject.
- Learn to read an e-mail address, which includes some form of the person's name (or a chosen nickname) as well as the name of the e-mail server (the company providing the e-mail service).

Read the specific content.

- Note the date and subject. Timeliness is crucial.
- Does the memo require you to take any action?
- Notice who, besides you, was sent the memo. (The abbreviation "cc" stands for "courtesy copy," which is sent to someone only for information.)
- Is the memo important enough to be filed for reference?

Using the Strategies

1. What is the purpose of the memo above?

2. What is Manuel Gonzalez required to deliver to his supervisor, and by when?

3. What else is Gonzalez asked to do?

4. What is Kay Nakagama's e-mail address?

Extending the Strategies

Apart from the workplace, what other uses can you see for e-mail?

CAN THIS BE LOVE?

WRITING FOCUS: Comparison/Contrast Essay

What can you say about the joy of love except that it's wonderful and about the pain of love except that it hurts? What can you say that hasn't been said a million times before? What's amazing is that poets still manage to say anything new about love at all. But they do, as you'll see from the poems in this collection. From tenth-century Japan to the modern world, has love stayed the same—or is love always different?

Tête à tête am Wolkenkratzer 968 étage. Color lithograph by Moriz Jung (1885–1915). Postcard published by Wiener Werkstätte, Vienna.

The Metropolitan Museum of Art, New York, Museum Accession, 1943. (WW340) Photograph © 1981 The Metropolitan Museum of Art.

All you need is love.
—The Beatles

What's love got to do with it?
—Tina Turner

Writer's Notebook

WORK IN PROGRESS

Think of two popular songs about love. Are they alike in feeling, or are they different? Are their messages the same or different? Are their styles the same or different? Make some notes and save them for the Writer's Workshop (page 580).

Elements of Literature

IMAGERY: Seeing with Our Minds

An **image** is a representation of anything we can see, hear, taste, touch, or smell. A realistic painter or sculptor can create an image of an apple so true to life that we'd like to eat it or feel its weight and roundness in our hands. A poet, using only words, can make us see and feel, taste and smell an apple by describing it as "rosy," "shiny," "heavy," "mushy," "sweet."

We can even distinguish poets on the basis of the imagery they use. Poets who live in the country, as Robert Frost did (pages 516 and 526), usually draw their images from nature. Poets who live in cities, as Langston Hughes did (page 508), usually draw their images from the sights, smells, and sounds of city life.

Two Poets, One Moon

To see how imagery works, look at two poems about the moon on the opposite page. The first poem, by John Haines, introduces many variations on the image of the moon. Can you find the image that tells us the poem was written sometime after 1969, when humans first disturbed the dust of the moon and left their debris on its surface? The

second poem, by Emily Dickinson, was written more than a hundred years earlier than Haines's poem, long before the romantic "moon of the poet" had been soiled and scratched by scientific instruments. More important, Dickinson also wrote long before two terrible world wars changed the ways poets looked at the world.

Imagery and Feelings

These two moon poems show us something else that imagery

> Images are not made just for the eye.

can do. The poets, through their evocative imagery, tell us how they *feel* about the moon. Haines's images of the "moon of the poet" are ironic and violent. As we see this moon in our minds, we share his sadness and even anger over the human capacity for destruction.

Dickinson, on the other hand, uses romantic images

by John Malcolm Brinnin

Moons

There are moons like continents,
diminishing to a white stone
softly smoking
in a fog-bound ocean.

Equinoctial° moons,
immense rainbarrels spilling
their yellow water.

Moons like eyes turned inward,
hard and bulging
on the blue cheek of eternity.

And moons half-broken,
eaten by eagle shadows . . .

But the moon of the poet
is soiled and scratched, its seas
are flowing with dust.

And other moons are rising,
swollen like boils—

in their bloodshot depths
the warfare of planets
silently drips and festers.

—John Haines

5. **equinoctial** (ē′kwi·näk′shəl): of the spring and fall equinoxes, when day and night are of equal length.

The Moon was but a Chin of Gold

The Moon was but a Chin of Gold
A Night or two ago—
And now she turns Her perfect Face
Upon the World below—

Her Forehead is of Amplest Blonde—
Her Cheek—a Beryl° hewn—
Her Eye unto the Summer Dew
The likest I have known—

Her Lips of Amber never part—
But what must be the smile
Upon Her Friend she could confer
Were such Her Silver Will—

And what a privilege to be
But the remotest Star—
For Certainty She takes Her Way
Beside Your Palace Door—

Her Bonnet is the Firmament°—
The Universe—Her Shoe—
The Stars—the Trinkets at Her Belt—
Her Dimities°—of Blue—

—Emily Dickinson

6. **beryl:** mineral that usually occurs in crystals of blue, green, pink, or yellow.
17. **firmament:** sky.
20. **dimities:** dresses made of dimity, a sheer, cool, cotton material.

that help us see another moon and share other feelings. Her moon is personified as a beautiful woman, even a queen, dressed in all the beauties of the night sky. Images of gold, beryl, dew, amber, silver, trinkets, and dimities help us share her feelings of wonder, admiration, and perhaps playfulness.

Thus, images are not made just for the eye. When we read poetry, we must arrive at that point where we can say to the poet not only "I see the picture you are creating," but also "I see what you are feeling. I see what you mean."

Before You Read

I Am Offering This Poem

Make the Connection

The Gift of Love

Suppose someone said to you, "I have nothing to give you—except love." How would you feel? Think about whether love is a small gift or a great one.

Reading Skills and Strategies

Dialogue with the Text

Make a double-entry journal to track this poem's images and your responses to them. *(Keep your notes for use on pages 556–557.)*

Image	My Feeling/Response

Elements of Literature

Singing Your Feelings

Lyric poetry owes its name to the ancient Greeks, who used the word *lyrikos* to refer to brief poems they sang to the accompaniment of the lyre, a stringed instrument. Today most lyrics are still short and still musical. Lyrics use evocative words to suggest (rather than state directly) a single, strong emotion. Most of the poems in this collection are lyrics.

> A **lyric** is a short poem that expresses strong feelings. Unlike a narrative poem, a lyric does not tell a story.
>
> *For more about Lyric Poetry, see the Handbook of Literary Terms.*

I Am Offering This Poem

Jimmy Santiago Baca

I am offering this poem to you,
since I have nothing else to give.
Keep it like a warm coat
when winter comes to cover you,
or like a pair of thick socks
the cold cannot bite through,

I love you,

I have nothing else to give you,
so it is a pot full of yellow corn
to warm your belly in winter,
it is a scarf for your head, to wear
over your hair, to tie up around your face,

I love you,

Keep it, treasure this as you would
if you were lost, needing direction,
in the wilderness life becomes when mature;
and in the corner of your drawer,
tucked away like a cabin or hogan
in dense trees, come knocking,
and I will answer, give you directions,
and let you warm yourself by this fire,
rest by this fire, and make you feel safe,

I love you,

It's all I have to give,
and all anyone needs to live,
and to go on living inside,
when the world outside
no longer cares if you live or die;
remember,

I love you.

Meet the Writer

To Prove That He Exists

Jimmy Santiago Baca (1952–) says he began to write so the world would know he existed. Born in New Mexico of Mexican American and Apache ancestry, he was abandoned by his parents when he was two. His grandmother took care of him until he was sent to an orphanage at five. At eleven, he ran away, living on the streets until he landed in prison at eighteen for possessing drugs. In prison, he felt sure he was going to die:

> " And I had to tell somebody that I was here. . . . It's unthinkable to come to a universe, to live as a human being, and then to die and not have anyone ever know you were there. "

Baca taught himself to read and write in prison. He also began to keep a journal and eventually attended a poetry workshop. Then he "took a wild chance." He sent some poems to a magazine, and the magazine published them. Five books of poetry followed, along with essays, a screenplay, and a novel. Today Baca, his wife, and sons live in an old adobe house south of Albuquerque.

Before You Read

SINCE FEELING IS FIRST

Make the Connection

Feeling Your Way

At first sight, this poem looks difficult. Its lines break at unusual places, there's little capitalization, the punctuation isn't standard, and words are used in odd ways. But if you read the poem silently a couple of times and then read it aloud, you'll quickly "own" it—you'll be able to say "I see what you mean!"

Quickwrite

This poet is sending a message to all of us. After you've read the poem twice, write what you think that message is. To get the message, you have to know English grammar. *(Keep your notes for use on pages 556–557.)*

Elements of Literature

Metaphors: Grammar and Love

Lovers cannot bear to think of their love ending or of death separating them. Here, the poet sings of love and puts down death in two metaphors that only a writer would think of.

> A **metaphor** is a surprising comparison between two dissimilar things.
>
> *For more on Metaphor, see page 507 and the Handbook of Literary Terms.*

since feeling is first

E. E. Cummings

since feeling is first
who pays any attention
to the syntax° of things
will never wholly kiss you;

wholly to be a fool
while Spring is in the world

my blood approves,
and kisses are a better fate
than wisdom
lady i swear by all flowers.   Don't cry
—the best gesture of my brain is less than
your eyelids' flutter which says

we are for each other:then
laugh,leaning back in my arms
for life's not a paragraph

And death i think is no parenthesis

3. **syntax** (sin′taks′): the arrangement of words, phrases, and clauses in sentences; here, a systematic, orderly arrangement.

The Lovers (1954–1955) by Marc Chagall (1887–1985). Watercolor, gouache, and ink on paper.
Collection Israel Museum, Jerusalem.

Marc Chagall

Meet the Writer

"Nobody Else Can Be Alive for You"

E. E. (Edward Estlin) **Cummings** (1894–1962) was born in Cambridge, Massachusetts. This son of a Unitarian minister grew up "only a butterfly's glide" from Harvard and "attended four Cambridge schools: the first, private—where everybody was extraordinarily kind; and where (in addition to learning nothing) I burst into tears and nosebleeds—the other three, public; where I flourished like the wicked and learned what the wicked learn, and where almost nobody cared about somebody else."

After graduating from Harvard, Cummings joined a volunteer American ambulance corps in France. (The United States had not yet entered World War I.) A French censor decided that one of Cummings's odd-looking letters home was suspicious. So Cummings was arrested as a spy and held for three months in a prison camp, an experience he wrote about in a novel he called *The Enormous Room* (1922).

In his poetry, Cummings liked to use lowercase letters, space his words oddly across the page, and punctuate in his own style, although those oddities are only typographical. His themes are familiar: the joy, wonder, and mystery of life and the miracle of individual identity. He once advised young poets to be themselves:

> " . . . remember one thing only: that it's you—nobody else—who determines your destiny and decides your fate. Nobody else can be alive for you; nor can you be alive for anybody else. "

E. E. Cummings in 1933. "Since feeling is first" was published in 1926 in his fourth book of poems, which he titled *is 5*.

Just Another Love Poem

Maybe that's why I need you.
You, and
standing in the middle
of a
dark, raging thunderstorm
(the power making me tremble),
Riding in a
fast, sleek convertible
(30 over the limit),
Absorbing the
sensation of the
largest roller coaster
(seat belt discarded)
and
a 180-foot parachute free fall
all
somehow
give me the
unexplainable
thrill
of delighting in
something so
terribly,
wonderfully,
out of control.

—Erika Banick
Warren Township High School
Gurnee, Illinois

Making Meanings

I Am Offering This Poem

since feeling is first

First Thoughts

1. Which of these love poems (Baca's poem or Cummings's) would you like to receive? Which one do you wish you had written? Try to find reasons for your choices.

Shaping Interpretations

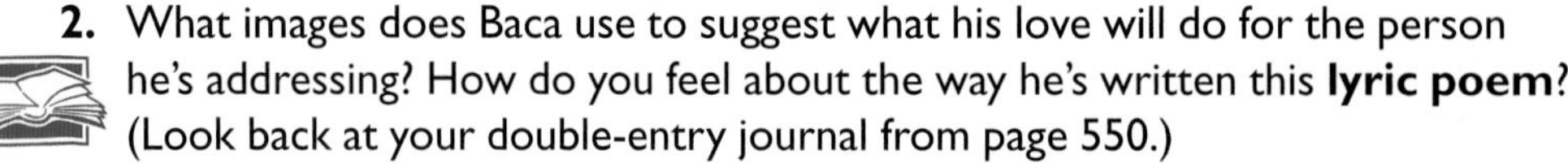

2. What images does Baca use to suggest what his love will do for the person he's addressing? How do you feel about the way he's written this **lyric poem**? (Look back at your double-entry journal from page 550.)

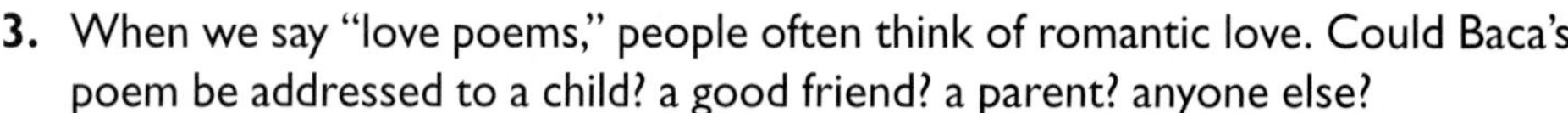

3. When we say "love poems," people often think of romantic love. Could Baca's poem be addressed to a child? a good friend? a parent? anyone else?

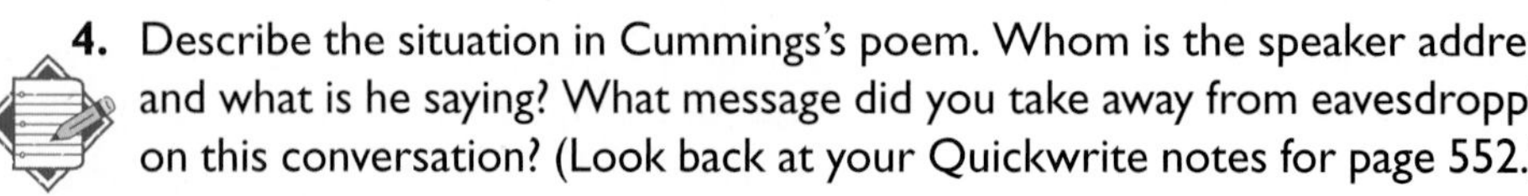

4. Describe the situation in Cummings's poem. Whom is the speaker addressing, and what is he saying? What message did you take away from eavesdropping on this conversation? (Look back at your Quickwrite notes for page 552.)
5. What **metaphors** does Cummings use to express his feelings about love and even its power over death? How do you like his metaphors?
6. Notice the opposites Cummings uses in "since feeling is first." A person who pays attention "to the syntax of things" (lines 2–3) is **contrasted** with someone who is "wholly . . . a fool" (line 5). What opposites does he pose to wisdom (line 9), the brain (line 11), and life (line 15)? In each case, which of the opposites does the speaker choose?
7. It's not easy to be original in a love poem—so many have been written over the ages. What exaggerated **comparisons** does Erika Banick use to express the wonder of love in her poem on page 555?

Extending the Texts

8. For any one of these poems, think of more **images** or **comparisons** that the poet could have used if he or she had wanted to write another ten lines or so about love.

Portrait of a Man and Woman at a Casement by Fra Filippo Lippi (c. 1406–1469). Tempera on wood (25¼″ × 16½″).

The Metropolitan Museum of Art, New York. Gift of Henry G. Marquand, 1889. Marquand Collection. (89.15.19)

CHOICES: Building Your Portfolio

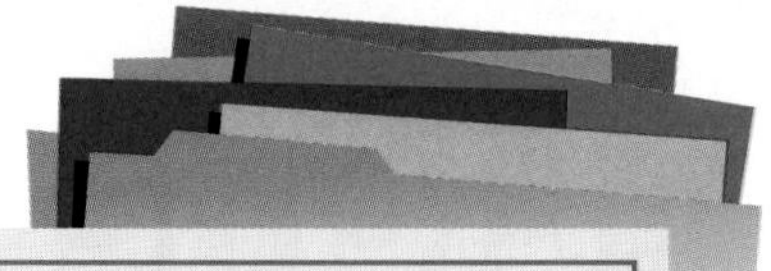

Writer's Notebook

1. Collecting Ideas for a Comparison/Contrast Essay

WORK IN PROGRESS

Noting similarities. When poems are grouped under a theme, you should be able to find some points of comparison or contrast between them. Look again at the poems by Baca and Cummings. Take notes on what each poet is saying about love. Try to put their messages in your own words. Then, take notes on this question: Are the poets' feelings the same in any way? (Be sure to check your double-entry journal and your Quickwrite.) Save your notes for the Writer's Workshop on page 580. The notebook below shows notes on two stories in the collection "Hearts That Love."

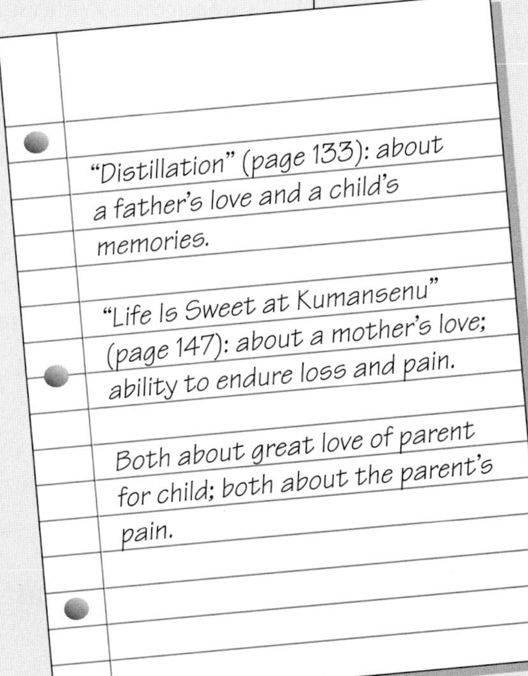
"Distillation" (page 133): about a father's love and a child's memories.

"Life Is Sweet at Kumansenu" (page 147): about a mother's love; ability to endure loss and pain.

Both about great love of parent for child; both about the parent's pain.

Creative Writing

2. What Do You Say?

"I Am Offering This Poem" and "since feeling is first" were both written by men. But could the **speakers** also be women? Suppose you were the person being addressed in Baca's or Cummings's poem. Write your answer to the speaker in a prose paragraph or in verse. Do you like what the speaker says to you or about you, or are your feelings something else? Who *is* the speaker, in your imagination? What **title** will you give your answer?

Speaking/ Critical Thinking

3. What Love Is

Imagine that a poetry-loving scientist sends Baca's and Cummings's poems in an interstellar probe to deep space. Eventually, they are found and translated by aliens in a world without the concept of love. On the basis of these two poems alone, what might the aliens conclude about the nature of human love? Get together with a small group to discuss this question. Point to specific passages that you think would especially interest the curious aliens.

Visual Arts

4. Imagining Images

Suppose that you have been commissioned to illustrate either "I Am Offering This Poem" or "since feeling is first." Using whatever medium you prefer—pencil, paint, or collage—present the images suggested by the poem. Give your images a title, perhaps a line from the poem. Try to use colors that will capture the tone and the mood of the poem.

Elements of Literature

THE SOUNDS OF POETRY: Rhythm and Meter

Rhythm: Music in Speech

Poetry is a musical kind of speech. Like music, poetry is based on **rhythm**—that is, on the alternation of stressed and unstressed sounds that makes the voice rise and fall. Here's a little prayer that many children memorize and say at bedtime. Say it out loud, and you'll feel the regular rise and fall of its rhythm:

Now I lay me down to sleep.
I pray the Lord my soul to keep.
If I should die before I wake,
I pray the Lord my soul to take.

If you listen closely, you'll hear exactly four stressed syllables repeated in each line. This repetition of stressed syllables balanced by unstressed syllables creates the rhythm in the poem.

Poets have a choice in the kind of rhythm they can use. They can use **meter**—a strict rhythmic pattern of stressed and unstressed syllables in each line (as in "Now I lay me down to sleep"), or they can write in **free verse**—a loose kind of rhythm in which the sounds of long phrases are balanced against the sounds of short phrases. A poem written in free verse sounds more like natural speech than like formal poetry.

Meter: Patterns of Sounds

The emphasis given to a word or a syllable is called a **stress** or an accent. In **metrical poetry** (poetry that has a meter), stressed and unstressed syllables are arranged in a regular pattern.

Here's a famous stanza from a long poem called *The Rime of the Ancient Mariner* by Samuel Taylor Coleridge. Years ago schoolchildren could recite this poem from memory. The meter helped:

He prayeth best, who loveth best
All things both great and small;
For the dear God who loveth us,
He made and loveth all.

The mark ´ indicates a stressed syllable. The mark ˘ indicates an unstressed syllable. Indicating the stresses this way is called **scanning** the poem.

Welcome Variations

You'll notice how these four lines sound alike and are about the same length. Coleridge sets up his pattern in the first two lines and then sticks to it with only one variation. Read aloud the third line and hear how the first three syllables break the pattern.

In metrical poetry, variation is important. Without any variation at all, meter becomes mechanical and monotonous, like the steady ticktock ticktock of a clock or like a verse on a birthday card. An occasional change in rhythm, as in the third line of the stanza from *The Rime of the Ancient Mariner,* also allows the poet

There was a young man from Japan
Whose verses never would scan.
When they said this was so,
He said, "Yes, I know,
But I always try to get as many words in the last line as I possibly can."

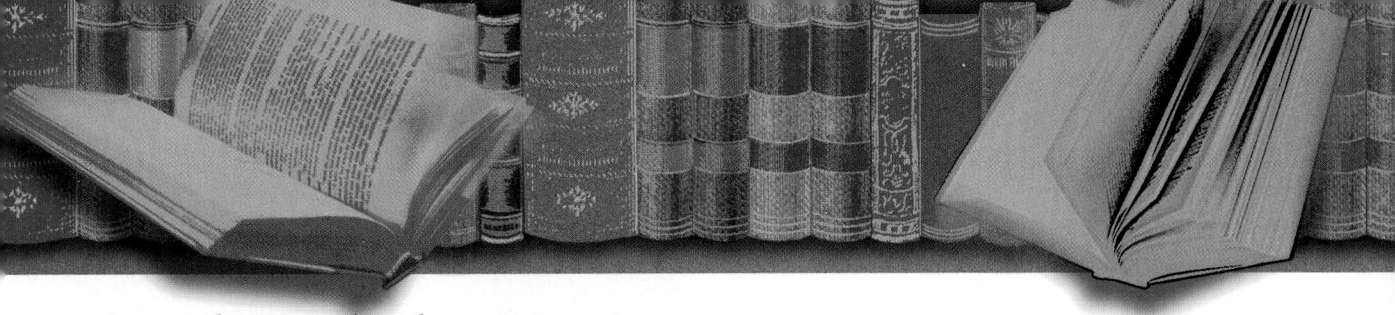

by John Malcolm Brinnin

to draw attention to key words in the poem.

Five Kinds of Feet

A line of metrical poetry is made up of metrical units called feet. A **foot** is a unit consisting of at least one stressed syllable and usually one or more unstressed syllables. There are five common types of feet used by poets writing in English, and their names come from Greek. Here are their names, with an example of a single word that matches the pattern of stressed and unstressed syllables in each foot:

iamb (insist)

trochee (double)

anapest (understand)

dactyl (excellent)

spondee (football).

(For more about these feet, see Meter in the Handbook of Literary Terms.)

Free Verse: Freedom from Rules

Early in this century, some American and English poets decided that they would rid poetry of its prettiness, sentimentality, and artificiality by concentrating on a new kind of poetry. Calling themselves **Imagists,** they declared that imagery alone—without any elaborate metrics or stanza patterns—could carry the full emotional message of a poem. They called their poetry **free verse** because it is free from the old metric rules.

Robert Frost, who disliked free verse, said that writing without the metric rules was "like playing tennis with the net down." What he meant was that the net on the tennis court is like meter in poetry—the essential part of the game that players must both respect and overcome. But in the twentieth century, more and more poets have accepted free verse as a challenge. Instead of conforming to meter, they write in cadences that follow "curves of thought" or "shapes of speech." They trust their own sense of balance and measure to lead to poems as well composed as any written in meter.

A Trochee (left) encountering a Spondee.

Addressed to the Ear

As in ancient days, when poetry was not written down but only spoken or sung, poetry today is still addressed to the ear. You can't really say that you "know" a poem until you've heard it read aloud. Poets at work are not likely to be silent; they test what they're writing by reading it aloud to *hear* what it sounds like.

When you've heard the voices of many poets, chances are you'll have a favorite. And you'll probably find that you've chosen your favorite poet not only for what his or her poems *say* but also for the way they *sound.*

Before You Read

SHALL I COMPARE THEE . . .

Make the Connection

Love in Fourteen Lines

In Shakespeare's day, every gentleman was expected to write sonnets in praise of his loved one. Writing a sonnet was a challenge, a kind of game. The speaker of this sonnet expresses passionate feelings within very strict rules—not an easy task.

Quickwrite

Before you read this poem, write your response to this question: Why would someone want to compare the person he loves to a summer's day? *(Keep your notes for use on pages 562–563.)*

Elements of Literature

The Sonnet: Strict Structure

The sonnet form favored (but not invented) by Shakespeare is the **Shakespearean**, or **English, sonnet**. Its fourteen lines are divided into three quatrains (rhyming groups of four lines) and a concluding **couplet** (pair of rhyming lines). Each quatrain makes a point or gives an example. The couplet sums it all up.

A **sonnet** is a fourteen-line lyric poem written within very strict rules.

For more on the Sonnet, see the Handbook of Literary Terms.

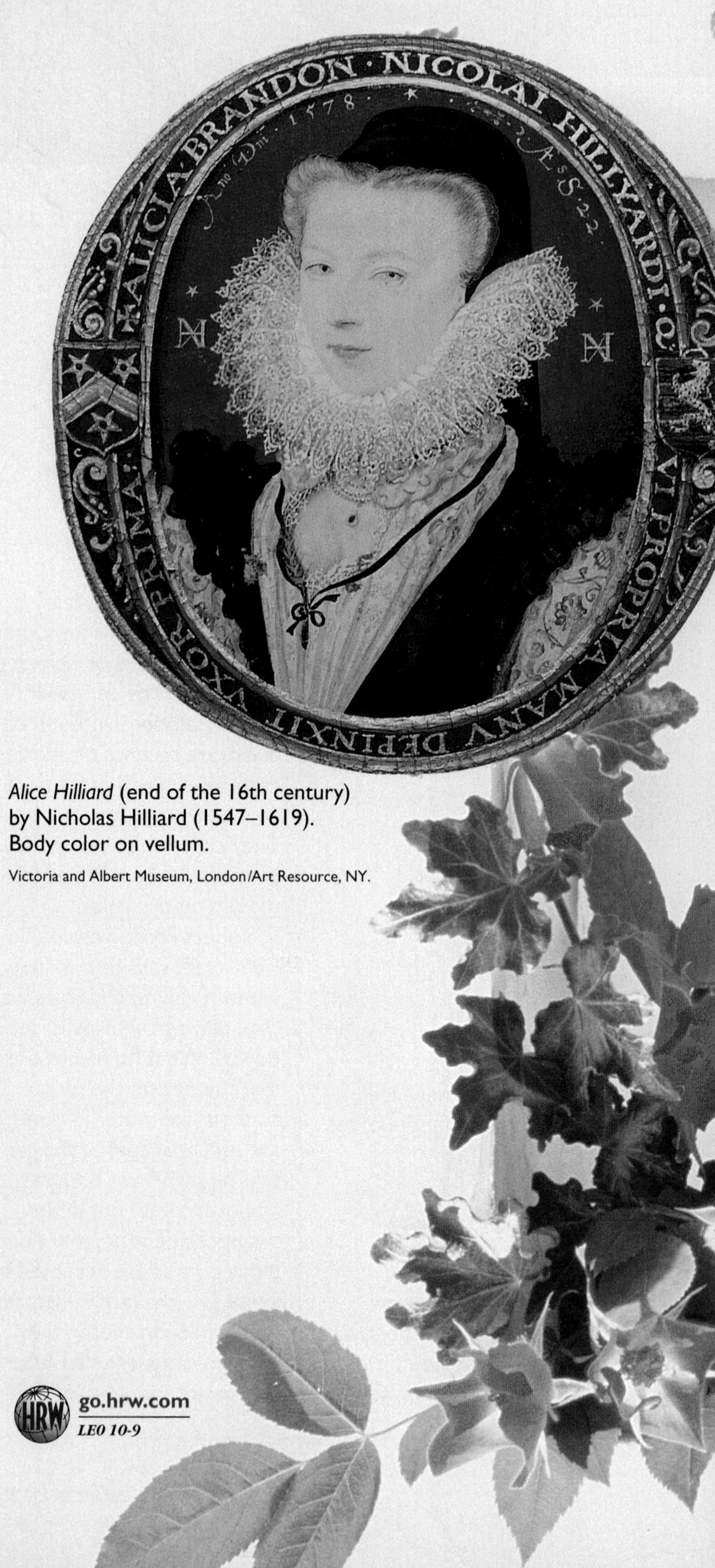

Alice Hilliard (end of the 16th century) by Nicholas Hilliard (1547–1619). Body color on vellum.

Victoria and Albert Museum, London/Art Resource, NY.

go.hrw.com
LEO 10-9

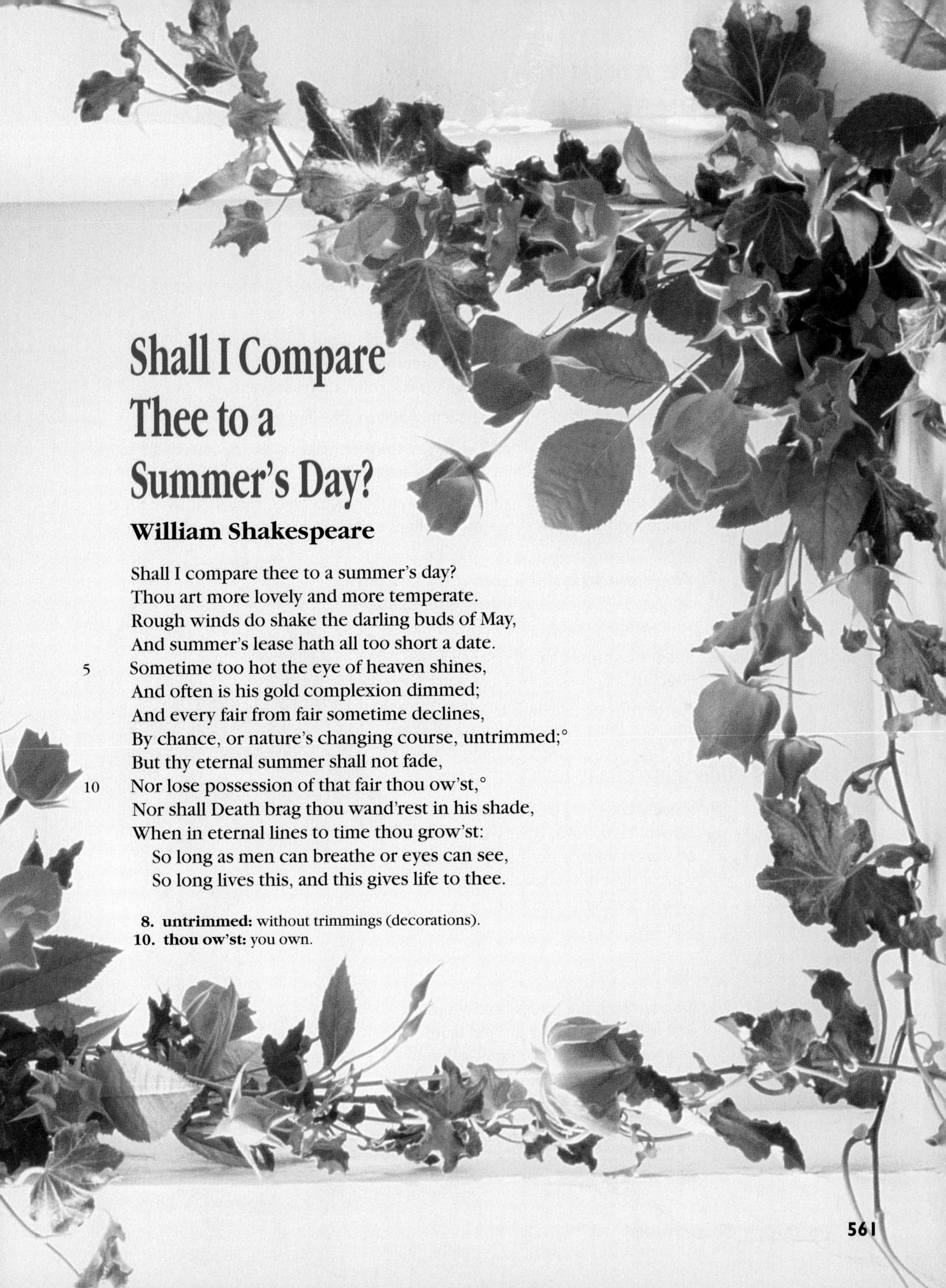

Shall I Compare Thee to a Summer's Day?

William Shakespeare

Shall I compare thee to a summer's day?
Thou art more lovely and more temperate.
Rough winds do shake the darling buds of May,
And summer's lease hath all too short a date.
Sometime too hot the eye of heaven shines,
And often is his gold complexion dimmed;
And every fair from fair sometime declines,
By chance, or nature's changing course, untrimmed;°
But thy eternal summer shall not fade,
Nor lose possession of that fair thou ow'st,°
Nor shall Death brag thou wand'rest in his shade,
When in eternal lines to time thou grow'st:
  So long as men can breathe or eyes can see,
  So long lives this, and this gives life to thee.

8. **untrimmed:** without trimmings (decorations).
10. **thou ow'st:** you own.

Making Meanings
Shall I Compare Thee to a Summer's Day?

First Thoughts

1. The speaker opens the sonnet by wondering if he should compare his lover to a summer's day. How does he answer his own question?

Shaping Interpretations

2. In line 2, what two general reasons does the speaker give for rejecting his comparison?

3. In lines 3–8, the speaker continues to think about his comparison. What **image** does he use to show that summer weather is unpredictable? What is the "eye of heaven," and why isn't it constant, or trustworthy?

4. According to lines 7–8, what can happen to any kind of beauty?

5. In the third quatrain (lines 9–12), the speaker makes a daring statement to his lover. What does he claim will never happen?

6. What does the speaker mean by "eternal lines to time" (line 12)? What is the connection between those eternal lines and the prediction he makes in lines 9–11?

7. Would you say that this sonnet is a love poem, or is it really about something else? Explain your interpretation.

8. Read the **sonnet** aloud to analyze its **rhythm**. Mark down the pattern of stressed and unstressed syllables you hear in each line. Are there variations in the **meter**?

Connecting with the Text

9. If you were going to describe someone you love, what would you **compare** him or her to? (See what you thought of the speaker's suggested comparison in your Quickwrite.)

Extending the Text

10. Do you think the poet's bold assertion in his couplet has proved true? In what ways can other kinds of art immortalize someone?

For a biography of William Shakespeare, see page 762.

William Shakespeare. Drawing by David Levine.

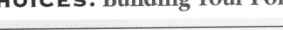

CHOICES: Building Your Portfolio

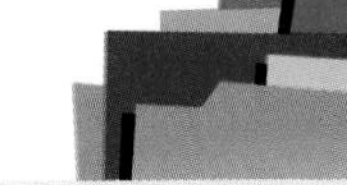

Writer's Notebook

1. Collecting Ideas for a Comparison/Contrast Essay

Finding subjects. You can compare and contrast two of anything (poems, stories, plays, essays, movies) as long as they have at least one thing in common. In your notebook, list several pairs of works (from this book or other things you've read), and note at least one thing each pair has in common. Save your list for the Writer's Workshop on page 580.

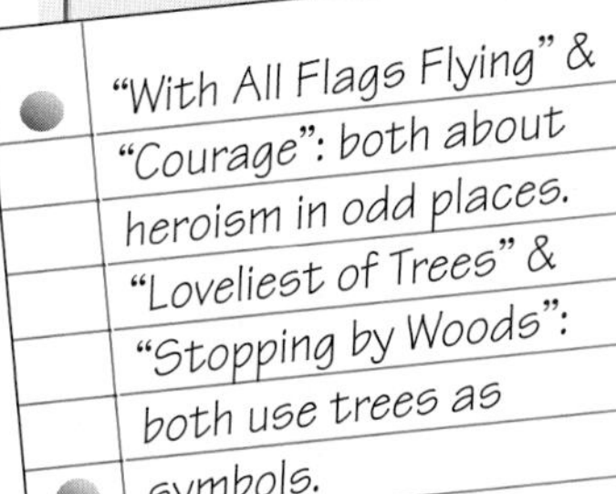

"With All Flags Flying" &
"Courage": both about
heroism in odd places.
"Loveliest of Trees" &
"Stopping by Woods":
both use trees as
symbols.

Creative Writing

2. A Stab at a Sonnet

Accept the challenge: Write a poem imitating the **structure** of a Shakespearean sonnet. You might imitate "Shall I Compare Thee . . ." for a start. In the first four lines, state your question and a quick answer. In the next eight lines, elaborate on your answer. In the last two lines, sum up your main point. You may even use Shakespeare's opener: "Shall I compare thee to . . . ?" You might try using Shakespeare's meter, too.

Speaking/Listening

3. An Answer

Suppose you are the person addressed in Shakespeare's sonnet. Prepare an oral response. What do you think of his rejection of the summer-day comparison? What do you think of the speaker's saying you'll never get old or die because of his poem? Decide what **tone** you'll take: flattered, irritated, sarcastic, confused? Meet with a classmate to present your responses.

GRAMMAR LINK MINI-LESSON

Language Handbook HELP

See Subject and Predicate and Complements, pages 1038–1040.

Handbook of Literary Terms HELP

See Inversion.

Inverted Sentences—Variety and Challenge

Syntax refers to the structure of a sentence, to the ways words, phrases, and clauses are arranged to show their relationships. In his poem on page 552, E. E. Cummings lightly mocks people who worry about syntax. Without rules of syntax, however, our language would be unintelligible.

Most English sentences begin with the subject, followed by the verb and, if there is one, a complement. Modifiers are usually placed near the words they modify. Some writers choose to wrench this syntax out of its usual order. Shakespeare, for example, to keep his rhymes and meter going, uses what we call **inverted sentences**: sentences in which the order is not subject-verb-complement and in which modifiers sometimes appear in unexpected places.

Try It Out

Answer these questions about the sonnet on page 561.

1. What other word order could you use within lines 5 and 6?
2. In line 7, where would the prepositional phrase "from fair" ordinarily be placed?
3. What other word order could you propose for line 12?

Before You Read

BONNY BARBARA ALLAN

Make the Connection

Love and Death

As you read this ballad, think about whether this love story is timely or out of date. Could it happen today?

Quickwrite

Write down the titles of some love songs popular today. Then take notes on these questions: Are the songs happy or tragic? Are any about betrayal? What are their refrains? *(Keep your notes for use on page 567.)*

Elements of Literature

The Ballad

"Bonny Barbara Allan" is a **ballad,** a story-poem meant to be sung. Most ballads use simple language and two of the oldest elements of poetry: a strong **meter** and a **refrain** (whole lines or stanzas repeated at regular intervals). **Folk ballads** such as this one, which have been passed down orally from generation to generation, often tell tales of love or violence. Folk ballads often use certain formulas—phrases such as "white as milk," "red, red lips," "red-roan steed," and "true, true love." The images of plants that grow on lovers' graves also are formulas. All of these formulas are part of the ballad singer's repertoire; whenever the singer needed to describe a woman's skin, for example, a formula was available.

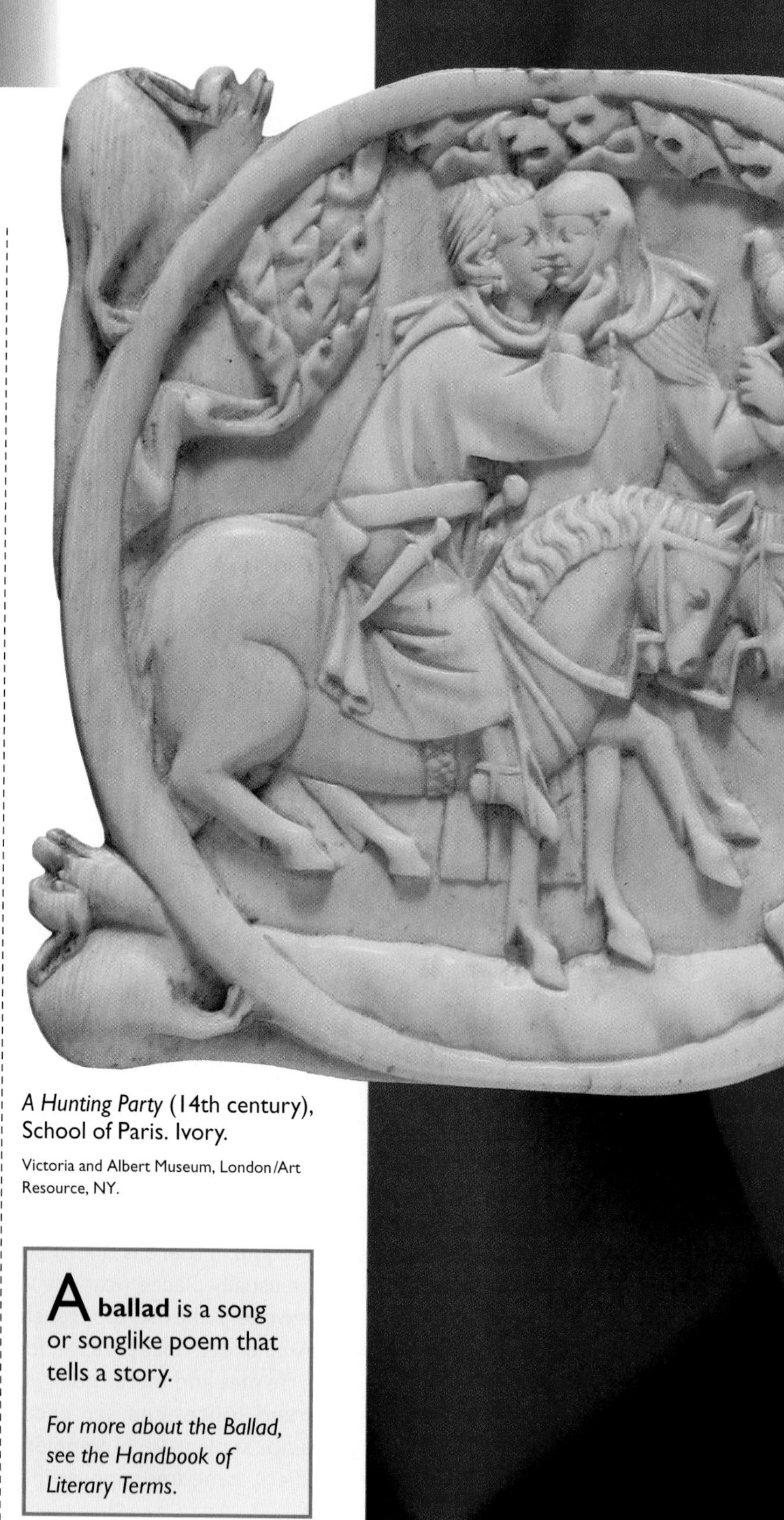

A Hunting Party (14th century), School of Paris. Ivory.

Victoria and Albert Museum, London/Art Resource, NY.

A **ballad** is a song or songlike poem that tells a story.

For more about the Ballad, see the Handbook of Literary Terms.

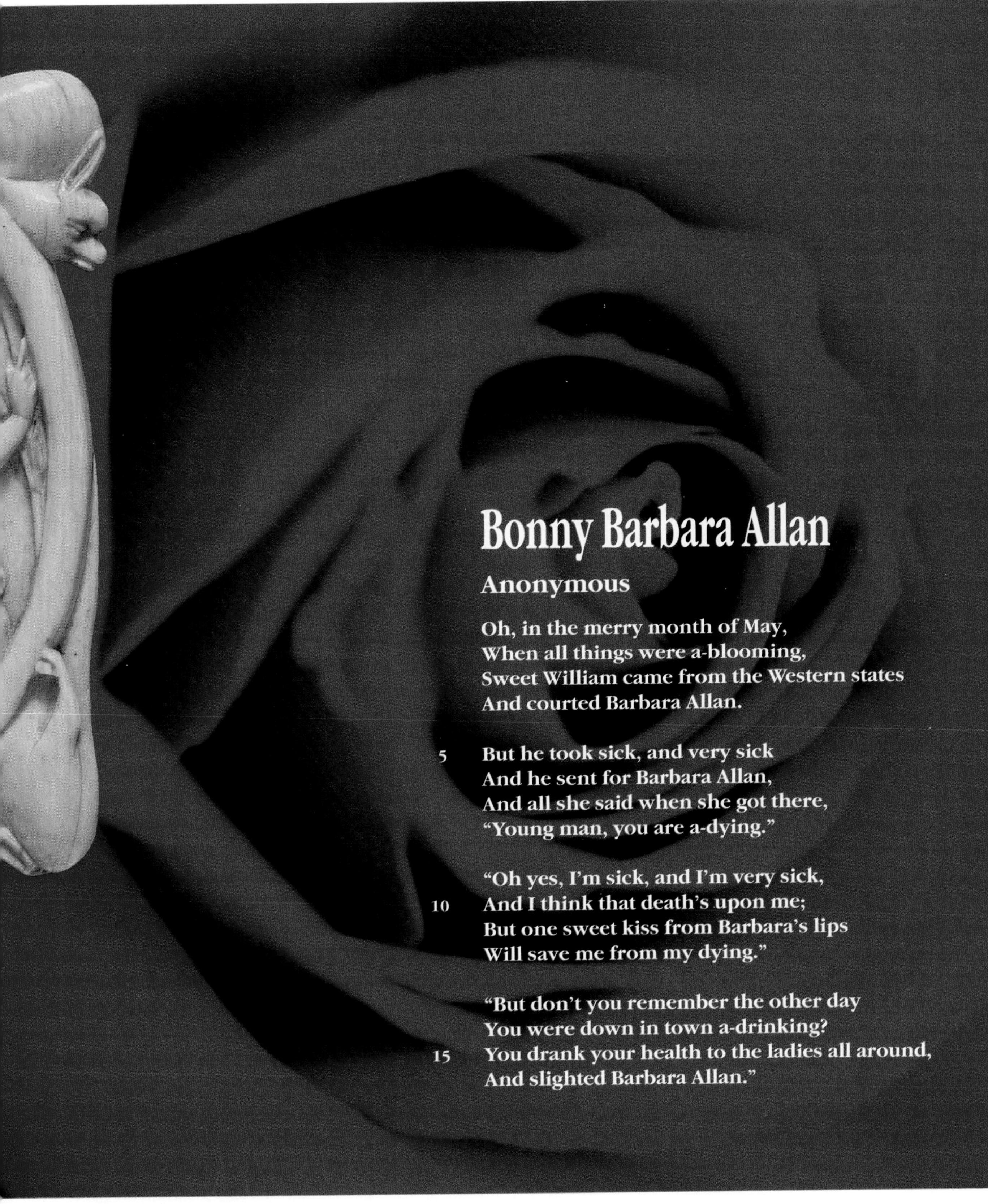

Bonny Barbara Allan

Anonymous

Oh, in the merry month of May,
When all things were a-blooming,
Sweet William came from the Western states
And courted Barbara Allan.

But he took sick, and very sick
And he sent for Barbara Allan,
And all she said when she got there,
"Young man, you are a-dying."

"Oh yes, I'm sick, and I'm very sick,
And I think that death's upon me;
But one sweet kiss from Barbara's lips
Will save me from my dying."

"But don't you remember the other day
You were down in town a-drinking?
You drank your health to the ladies all around,
And slighted Barbara Allan."

"Oh yes, I remember the other day
I was down in town a-drinking;
I drank my health to the ladies all 'round,
But my love to Barbara Allan."

He turned his face to the wall;
She turned her back upon him;
The very last word she heard him say,
"Hardhearted Barbara Allan."

As she passed on through London Town,
She heard some bells a-ringing,
And every bell, it seemed to say,
"Hardhearted Barbara Allan."

She then passed on to the country road,
And heard some birds a-singing;
And every bird it seemed to say,
"Hardhearted Barbara Allan."

She hadn't got more than a mile from town
When she saw his corpse a-coming;
"O bring him here, and ease him down,
And let me look upon him.

"Oh, take him away! Oh, take him away!
For I am sick and dying!
His death-cold features say to me,
'Hardhearted Barbara Allan.'

"O Father, O Father, go dig my grave,
And dig it long and narrow;
Sweet William died for me today;
I'll die for him tomorrow."

They buried them both in the old graveyard,
All side and side each other.
A red, red rose grew out of his grave,
And a green briar out of hers.

They grew and grew so very high
That they could grow no higher;
They lapped, they tied in a truelove knot—
The rose ran 'round the briar.

A Choral Reading: The Balladeers

As far as we know, ballads were sung by individuals. Even so, here are some ideas for a choral reading of a ballad—no instruments required!

- First, examine the ballad: How many people are speaking? Which lines could be recited by a chorus? (Refrains are often a good choice for several speakers.)
- Next, think of how the speakers are feeling. (Usually in a ballad, feelings run pretty strong.) How can you express those feelings, using volume, pitch, and tone of voice? Where do feelings change?
- Will you use gestures? props? How will you dress?
- Finally, mark up a copy of your choral reading to use as a script. Watch the punctuation, and let it guide you in deciding where to pause and when to speed up. Indicate words to emphasize.
- Practice. Evaluate and adjust your performance before you present it to an audience. Have you and your fellow balladeers caught the texture of this sad story of love and betrayal?

Making Meanings
Bonny Barbara Allan

First Thoughts

1. How did you feel about Barbara Allan and William as you began to read this poem? Did your feelings change by the end?

Shaping Interpretations

2. **Ballads** never tell the whole story. What details are left out of this one?
3. What evidence shows that Barbara Allan is indeed "hardhearted"? Does anything indicate that she is *not* hardhearted? Explain.
4. We'd expect the aggressive vines of a briar to grow around any nearby plant. Which plant entwines the other in this story? Which character and which emotion have triumphed?
5. Read the ballad aloud. Then write it out on a separate piece of paper and **scan** it. Where does the singer vary the strict **meter** of the song?

Extending the Text

6. Are popular songs today at all like this old ballad? Check your Quickwrite notes.

Choices: Building Your Portfolio

Writer's Notebook

1. Collecting Ideas for a Comparison/Contrast Essay

WORK IN PROGRESS

Finding points of comparison. So you've chosen two works to compare. How do you begin? A good start is to list all the elements usually found in that type of writing. If you're comparing poems, you might start with **figurative language**. In your notebook, list all the other elements of poetry you can think of. Save your notes for the Writer's Workshop on page 580.

Speaking/Listening

2. Deaths Raise Doubts

Ballads often took their subjects from stories of domestic tragedy that would today be featured on the evening news. Prepare your own interpretation of the ballad as if it's tomorrow's **news story**. Remember that a good reporter answers *Who? What? When? Where? Why? How?* You might want to record your newscast presentation on videotape or audiotape.

Music

3. Love Set to Music

With a partner (or alone, if you prefer), try writing a melody for one poem you've read so far. Before you start, study your poem's **tone,** or mood. What type of music will best suit it? Folk? Rock? Country western? Rap?

Before You Read

HEART! WE WILL FORGET HIM!

Make the Connection

Trying to Forget

In this poem, Emily Dickinson tells the old, sad story of unrequited love—of love that is not returned. The poem is about conflict: between will and emotion, between the thinking mind and the feeling heart.

Quickwrite

Which do you think is more powerful—the mind or the heart? Does one control the other, or are they completely independent systems? Think about your own experiences, and freewrite your response. *(Keep your notes for use on page 573.)*

Elements of Literature

Personification

In this poem the speaker addresses her heart as if it were a person who could listen, act, and feel. She's using **personification**, giving human qualities to something nonhuman.

Personification is a kind of metaphor in which a nonhuman thing or quality is talked about as if it were human.

For more on Personification, see page 507 and the Handbook of Literary Terms.

go.hrw.com

LEO 10-9

Heart! We will forget him!

Emily Dickinson

Heart! We will forget him!
You and I— tonight!
You may forget the warmth he gave—
I will forget the light!

When you have done, pray tell me
That I may straight begin!
Haste! lest while you're lagging
I remember him!

Emily Dickinson (1848). Oil over a photograph.

The Granger Collection, New York.

Meet the Writer

Shy Woman in White

Emily Dickinson (1830–1886) rarely left Amherst, Massachusetts, her birthplace. There she lived unknown as a poet except to her family and a few friends, and there she produced almost eighteen hundred exquisite short poems that are now regarded as one of the great expressions of American genius.

She was the bright daughter of a well-to-do religious family; her father was a lawyer. As a girl at boarding school, she seemed high-spirited and happy. But something happened when she was a young woman (a love that was not, could not be requited, biographers speculate), and at thirty-one, she simply withdrew from the world. She dressed all in white, refused to leave her home or meet strangers, and devoted her life to her family—and to writing poetry. Of her own poetry, she wrote, "This is my letter to the World / That never wrote to Me. . . ."

She wrote her poems on little pieces of paper, tied them in neat packets, and occasionally gave them to relatives as valentine or birthday greetings or attached them to gifts of cookies or pies. In 1862, she sent four poems to the editor of *Atlantic Monthly*. Only seven of her poems were published (anonymously) during her lifetime. When she died at fifty-six, she had no notion that one day she would be honored as one of America's greatest poets.

Before You Read

THREE JAPANESE TANKAS

Make the Connection

Love's Obstacles

A loves B more than B loves A; B used to love A but feared rejection and has decided to snub A. If you think you hear a lot of that kind of gossip in your cafeteria, take a look at love in Japan more than a thousand years ago.

Quickwrite

In your notebook, finish these sentence starters with images or figures of speech:

Love is . . . Life is . . .

(Keep your notes for use on page 573.)

Elements of Literature

Tanka Structure

Japanese tankas, which date to the seventh century, are written within the strictest rules. Tankas have five unrhymed lines and a total of thirty-one syllables. Lines 1 and 3 have five syllables each. Lines 2, 4, and 5 have seven each. (The English translations don't always follow this strict syllable count.)

Tanka poems, a Japanese **poetic form,** have five unrhymed lines and a total of thirty-one syllables. A tanka evokes a strong feeling with a single image.

Three Japanese Tankas

Ono Komachi

translated by Jane Hirshfield with Mariko Aratani

1

Sent anonymously to a man who had passed in front of the screens of my room

Should the world of love
end in darkness,
without our glimpsing
that cloud-gap
where the moon's light fills the sky?

2

Sent to a man who seemed to have changed his mind

Since my heart placed me
on board your drifting ship,
not one day has passed
that I haven't been drenched
in cold waves.

3

Sent in a letter attached to a rice stalk with an empty seed husk

How sad that I hope
to see you even now,
after my life has emptied itself
like this stalk of grain
into the autumn wind.

The Poetess Ono Komachi (c. 1820) by Hokkei. Surimono print (20 cm × 17 cm).

Spencer Museum of Art/University of Kansas. The William Bridges Thayer Memorial.

MEET THE WRITER

A Leading Lady and Poet

Ono Komachi (834–?) may have been the daughter of a ninth-century Japanese lord and may have served at the imperial court. Though little is known about her life, she is believed to have had at least one child and one grandchild. She was supposed to have been one of the most beautiful women of her time but is said to have died in poverty—aged and forgotten but still writing poetry.

Whatever the facts of her life, it is indisputable that Komachi was one of the great figures in an age when women dominated Japanese society and literature. In her hundred or so short poems that survive, she illuminated the subject of love through her understanding of Buddhist ideas about the fleeting nature of existence.

LITERATURE AND HISTORY

Poetry in the Golden Age of Japan

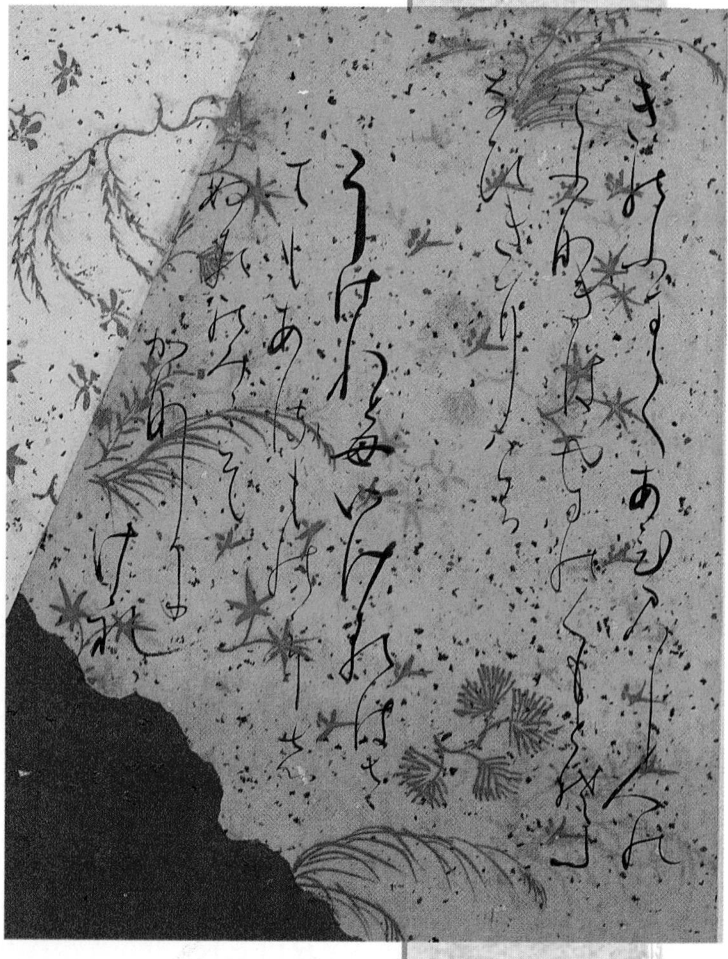

Page from *Ishiyama-gire: Poems of Ki no Tsurayuki* (872?–c. 946). Calligraphy on ornamented paper.

Courtesy of the Freer Gallery of Art/Smithsonian Institution, Washington, D.C. (69.4)

In the imperial court of Heian-era Japan (794–1185), poetry had both private and public functions. In private, poetry was the accepted language of love. A gentleman showed his interest in a lady of the court by sending her an admiring five-line poem (a tanka). If the poem she wrote in reply was encouraging, he paid her a visit. Their exchange of poems continued throughout their relationship, and each new message had to be original and intriguing. Lovers also valued skillful calligraphy, exquisite paper, and a tasteful presentation. To match the mood of their poems, they covered tinted bamboo paper with scattered designs and tiny flecks of gold and silver foil. The final creation, carefully sealed with a twig or spray of flowers, was often lovely enough to decorate a folding screen.

Public poetry could be as romantic and beautiful as private poems, but it was presented and evaluated very differently. At popular poetry contests (*uta-awase*), competitors grouped themselves into two teams, Right and Left. A judge gave the teams a topic, such as "spring" or "names of things," and awarded a point to the side that created and recited the more pleasing composition. The team that had the most points after several rounds won. The government Office of Poetry preserved exceptional spoken poems in written anthologies.

Making Meanings

Heart! We will forget him!/Three Japanese Tankas

First Thoughts

1. Do the three tankas leave you with the same feeling you get from Emily Dickinson's poem, or do they make you feel something different? Explain.

Shaping Interpretations

2. Dickinson **personifies** her heart by telling it to do things that only a person can do. What does she tell Heart? How would you paraphrase what she means by "warmth" and "light" (lines 3–4)?
3. Refer to the Quickwrite on page 568. Which do you think is more powerful: the mind or the heart? How does Dickinson feel?
4. Look back at the **images** in the tankas. What feelings do they suggest?

Extending the Text

5. These poems were written many years ago—the tankas are centuries old. Are they dated? Could they still apply to people's feelings and experiences today?

Choices: Building Your Portfolio

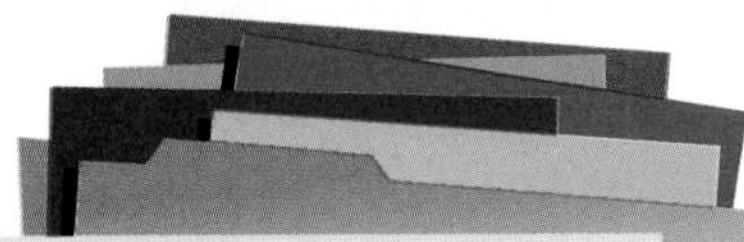

Writer's Notebook

1. Collecting Ideas for a Comparison/Contrast Essay

WORK IN PROGRESS

Finding details. Work out a chart like the following, in which you compare and contrast one of the tankas and Dickinson's poem according to the various elements of poetry you've looked at in these collections. Keep your notes for possible use in the Writer's Workshop on page 580.

Elements	*Dickinson*	*Tanka*
Subject		
Mood/Feeling		
Images		
Figures of Speech		
Message		

Creative Writing

2. The Hidden Characters

These four poems contain hidden, unidentified characters—the men in Komachi's poems and the lost love in Dickinson's poem. Write a letter or journal entry in the voice of one of these hidden characters, responding to the way the poet/speaker has written about you and about your love.

Creative Writing

3. Try a Tanka

Review the information about Japanese poetry on page 572 and the **tanka form** on page 570. Then, in tanka style, write a series of poems that trace a relationship. Try to use the images or figures of speech that you created for the Quickwrite on page 570. Describe a symbolic object you might send with the tanka.

Before You Read

HANGING FIRE

Make the Connection

What the Title Tells

The expression *to hang fire* refers to shooting a gun. It means "to delay firing or to fail to fire." *Hang fire* has a general meaning too: "to be delayed."

Quickwrite

You're about to meet a speaker who has a lot of questions and worries. Right after you read the poem, jot down your impressions of the speaker. What does she seem to be waiting for? What's being delayed in her life? *(Keep your notes for use on page 576.)*

Elements of Literature

The Speaker

Every poem in this collection except "Bonny Barbara Allan" has a speaker who speaks as "I." When you come across poems like these, which speak in the first person, be sure you can identify the voice. Speakers are sometimes, but not always, the poet. In Langston Hughes's "Mother to Son" (page 508), the speaker is a woman addressing a young son. (The poet, of course, is a man.) In "George Gray" (page 522), the speaker is someone buried in Spoon River Cemetery, not the poet.

> The **speaker** in a poem is the voice talking to us. A speaker can be the poet, but he or she (or it) can also be almost anyone (or anything) else—even something nonhuman that can't speak at all.

Hanging Fire

Audre Lorde

I am fourteen
and my skin has betrayed me
the boy I cannot live without
still sucks his thumb
in secret
how come my knees are
always so ashy
what if I die
before morning
and momma's in the bedroom
with the door closed.

I have to learn how to dance
in time for the next party
my room is too small for me
suppose I die before graduation
they will sing sad melodies
but finally
tell the truth about me
There is nothing I want to do
and too much
that has to be done
and momma's in the bedroom
with the door closed.

Nobody even stops to think
about my side of it
I should have been on Math Team
my marks were better than his
why do I have to be
the one
wearing braces
I have nothing to wear tomorrow
will I live long enough
to grow up
and momma's in the bedroom
with the door closed.

Meet the Writer

"I Am Black, Woman, and Poet"

Audre Lorde's (1934–1992) first published poem was rejected by her high school literary magazine as "much too romantic." Undaunted, she sent it to *Seventeen* magazine, which published it. She remembers how she started to write poems:

> "I used to speak in poetry. I would read poems, and I would memorize them. People would say, well, what do you think, Audre? What happened to you yesterday? And I would recite a poem, and somewhere in that poem would be a line or a feeling I would be sharing. In other words, I literally communicated through poetry. And when I couldn't find the poems to express the things I was feeling, that's what started me writing poetry, and that was when I was twelve or thirteen."

Lorde worked as a librarian and a teacher while her poetry began to accumulate honors and awards. Her poems deal with racial and feminist issues, love relationships (there is a recurring image of a mother who withholds her love, as in "Hanging Fire"), urban and nature images. Her language is unadorned, sometimes laced with fury.

"I am Black, Woman, and Poet," she once told an interviewer.

Making Meanings
Hanging Fire

First Thoughts

1. What questions would you like to ask about this poem? How would you answer your own questions?

Shaping Interpretations

2. Who is the "I" in this poem? What are some words you'd use to describe this **speaker**?
3. In what ways is this speaker "hanging fire"—waiting for things to happen? What do you think of this as the poem's **title**? (Review your Quickwrite notes.)
4. What meanings and feelings does the poem's **refrain** suggest to you? How does this refrain help create the poem's mood?

Connecting with the Text

5. What does this poem have to do with love? Could the question posed in the collection title be a question this speaker would ask? Talk over the poem's connection to love.

Choices: Building Your Portfolio

Writer's Notebook

1. Collecting Ideas for a Comparison/Contrast Essay

WORK IN PROGRESS

Finding details. Here's another chance to find details in two poems that will help you compare and contrast them. Fill in this chart with details from "I Am Offering This Poem" by Jimmy Santiago Baca (page 551) and "Hanging Fire" by Audre Lorde (page 574). Keep your notes for possible use in the Writer's Workshop on page 580.

Elements	Baca	Lorde
Topic/Subject		
Message		
Feeling		
Refrain		
Images		
Figures of Speech		
Speaker		

Speaking/Listening

2. Choral Interpretation

In a group of four students, present a choral reading of "Hanging Fire." To prepare, read the poem carefully several times, and consider the speaker's **tone,** or **mood.** Think about the **structure of the poem**: Few lines have end punctuation, so where will you pause in your reading? Decide which lines will be read by each speaker. Experiment with **pitch, tone of voice,** and **facial expressions.** You may want the entire group to read the refrain. Present your choral interpretation to the class, and ask for their responses.

Quickwrite

What do you think people mean when they say that someone has fallen in love with the idea of love? Can love inspire even the frailest, least likely person to acts of heroism? Take notes on your responses.

Background

One of the world's most famous books is a satiric Spanish novel about the power of love and idealism. Titled *The History of That Ingenious Gentleman Don Quijote de la Mancha*,[1] it is popularly known simply as *Don Quijote* (dän´ kē·hōt′ē). Its hero is a faded old gentleman living in a backward village in the province of La Mancha, Spain, during the early 1600s. The old man has read so many **romances** (popular books about knights and their heroic deeds) that he has lost touch with reality. He now imagines himself a knight about to set off in quest of adventures, ready to rescue beautiful damsels and right the world's wrongs.

One day he goes into action: He takes his great-grandfather's suit of rusty armor out of a closet, attaches a cardboard visor to an old headpiece, and hits the road. He calls himself Don Quijote and names his skinny old horse Rocinante (rō·sē·nän′tā), roughly "worn-out old horse."

1. The English spelling is *Don Quixote*; in Spanish, the title is *El ingenioso hidalgo Don Quijote de la Mancha*.

go.hrw.com
LEO 10-9

EXTENDING *the theme*

A NOVEL EXCERPT

from Don Quijote

Miguel de Cervantes
translated by Burton Raffel

"A knight errant without love entanglements would be like a tree without leaves or fruit."

Well, with his armor scrubbed clean, and his helmet ready, and then his horse christened and himself confirmed, he realized that all he needed and had to hunt for was a lady to be in love with, since a knight errant without love entanglements would be like a tree without leaves or fruit, or a body without a soul. So he said to himself:

"Now, if for my sins, or by good fortune, I happen to find a giant right here in this neighborhood, which after all is something that usually happens to knights errant, and we have a go at it and I overthrow him, or maybe split him right down the middle, or, however it happens, conquer and utterly defeat him, wouldn't it be a good idea to have someone to whom I could send him, so he could go and kneel down in front of my sweet lady and say, his voice humble and submissive, 'I, my lady, am the giant Caraculiambro, lord of the island of Malindrania, defeated in man-to-man combat by that knight who can never be too much praised, Don Quijote de la Mancha, who has sent me here to offer myself at your pleasure, to be dealt with however your Grace may happen to think best'?"

Oh, how our good knight relished the delivery of this speech, especially once he'd decided who was going to be his lady love! It turns out, according to some people, that not too far from where he lived there was a very pretty peasant girl, with whom he was supposed, once upon a time, to have been in love,

Musée d'Art et d'Histoire, St. Denis, France.

Don Quixote (1955) by Pablo Picasso.

although (as the story goes) she never knew it nor did he ever say a word to her. Her name was Aldonza Lorenzo, and he thought it a fine idea to bestow on her the title of Mistress of his Thoughts. Hunting for a name as good as the one he'd given himself, a name that would be appropriate for that princess and noble lady, he decided to call her *Dulcinea del Toboso*, since Toboso was where she came from. To him it seemed a singularly musical name, rare, full of meaning, like all the others he'd assigned to himself and everything that belonged to him.

Having taken care of these arrangements, he had no desire to postpone his plan for even a moment longer, propelled by the thought of how badly the world might suffer if he delayed, for he intended to undo endless wrongs, set right endless injustices, correct endless errors, fix endless abuses, and atone for endless sins. One morning before dawn, on a steaming July day, without telling anyone what he was up to or being seen by a single soul, he put on all his armor, climbed onto Rocinante, settled his flimsy helmet into place, grasped his shield, picked up his spear and, riding through the back gate, set out for the open fields, wonderfully well content at how easily his noble desire had been set in motion.

Meet the Writer

"Like a Madman Lived"

Miguel de Cervantes (1547–1616) wrote a best-selling novel—the first European novel, critics say—but he never received royalties. The publisher of *Don Quijote* (1605) and pirated editions pocketed all the profits from Cervantes' long, leisurely, episodic novel.

Cervantes' life was a tale of poverty, woe, and imprisonment. A poor young man from a town near Madrid, Spain, he enlisted in the army and was so gravely wounded in a famous naval battle that he lost permanent use of his left hand. Next, pirates captured him and held him as a slave in Algiers for years. Ransomed by his family, Cervantes worked as a playwright and tax collector before being thrown into debtors' prison. There he probably conceived the idea for *Don Quijote*, a **parody** (humorous imitation) of the wildly popular romances about knightly adventures.

In the preface to his great work, Cervantes wrote:

"So what could my sterile, half-educated wit give birth to except the history of a whimpering child, withered, whining, its head stuffed with all kinds of thoughts no one else would even think of, like a man bred in a jail cell, where everything grates on your nerves and every new sound makes you still sadder."

Cervantes, who died within days of William Shakespeare, wrote his own epitaph:

"For if he like a madman lived,
At least he like a wise one died."

Finding Common Ground 

Get together in groups of three or four to talk about the *Don Quijote* excerpt.

1. You might start by reading aloud your Quickwrite notes. Then **compare and contrast** Don Quijote's quest for love with everyone's quest for someone to love and dedicate themselves to. How do people today seek and find love?
2. Does the prospect of love—having it, finding as well as searching for it—make us better people? Explain your response.
3. Don Quijote was inspired by the popular **romances** he read, stories like the heroic King Arthur tales (see pages 950–971), in which every morning brought a new chance for glory for the knights of the Round Table. What elements of Don Quijote's story here are parodies of the old romances?
4. What stories do we read today? Do they inspire us to heroic deeds, to make the world a better place—or do they have different effects?

Share your group's conclusions in a whole-class discussion. Does everyone agree, or are there strongly different opinions? See if you can reach a consensus on some points.

BUILDING YOUR PORTFOLIO

Writer's Workshop

ASSIGNMENT

Write an essay comparing and contrasting two texts. The texts can be poems, stories, or essays or a combination of those forms.

AIM

To inform.

AUDIENCE

Your teacher, classmates, other English classes, readers of a magazine of student writing. (You choose.)

Relevant Features
Stories: subject, theme, plot, conflict, characters, point of view, setting, tone, style
Essays: subject, main idea or theme, purpose, subjective/objective details, tone, diction
Poems: subject, theme, imagery, figures of speech, speaker, tone, rhyme, rhythm and meter, other sound effects

EXPOSITORY WRITING

COMPARISON/CONTRAST ESSAY

You use the skills of **comparing** (finding similarities) and **contrasting** (finding differences) all the time—to see how your sneakers are different from your friend's, to decide which TV show to watch next, to see how the war in Vietnam was different from World War II. These thinking skills—comparing and contrasting—are especially useful in talking and writing about literature. In this workshop, you'll write a **comparison/contrast essay,** which is one kind of **expository writing**—writing that explains or gives information.

Prewriting

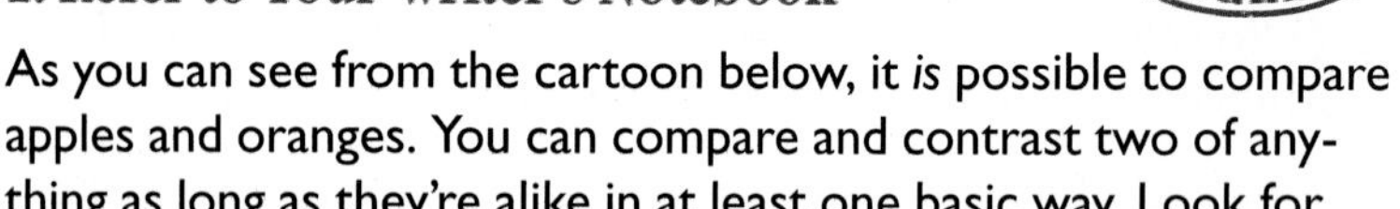

1. Refer to Your Writer's Notebook

As you can see from the cartoon below, it *is* possible to compare apples and oranges. You can compare and contrast two of anything as long as they're alike in at least one basic way. Look for two works that are alike enough to give you something interesting to say about them. If you're not happy with the subjects you've been working on in your Writer's Notebook, choose two new ones now.

2. Find Relevant Features to Focus On

If you were judging a photography contest, the **features** you'd use to compare the photos might be lighting, color, composition, subject matter, and emotional effects. When you write about literature, finding the features is easy. You'll recognize them as the **elements of literature** you've been studying.

The history
of the written
word is rich and
Page 1
Once upon a time

3. Gather Information

Using a chart, take notes about how your works are alike and different, element by element. (The chart below shows the beginning of a comparison of two stories from the short-story collections in this book.)

Element	The Cold Equations (page 9)	The Pedestrian (page 173)
Subject	Power of technology to control our lives	Same
Message/Theme	Technology allows no room for human emotions.	Technology can limit our freedoms.
Tone	Sad, tragic	Bitter, satirical

4. Plan the Essay

You have two choices for organizing your information, and either one is fine. (See the chart on the right.)

- **Block Method**
  With this organization, you discuss the *works,* one at a time. First, you write about the elements of one work; then, you discuss the same elements in the same order for the second work.
- **Point-by-Point Method**
  With this method, you discuss the *elements,* one at a time. You might discuss the theme in work 1 and then the theme in work 2. In the next paragraph, you might talk about conflict in work 1 and then conflict in work 2. The Student Model on pages 582–583 uses the point-by-point method.

Block Method
Work 1: "The Cold Equations" Element 1: its subject Element 2: its theme Element 3: its tone
Work 2: "The Pedestrian" Element 1: its subject Element 2: its theme Element 3: its tone
Point-by-Point Method
Element 1: subject in "The Cold Equations" in "The Pedestrian"
Element 2: theme in "The Cold Equations" in "The Pedestrian"
Element 3: tone in "The Cold Equations" in "The Pedestrian"

Drafting

1. Three Basic Parts

Like most essays, comparison/contrast essays have three parts:

- The **introduction**, usually a single paragraph, provides meat-and-potatoes information: titles and authors and necessary background. It also includes your **thesis statement**, in which you say briefly how the works are alike and different.

- The **body** of your essay is where you put the information you've gathered in your chart. Using either the block or the point-by-point method, discuss how at least two (preferably three) elements of the works are alike and different.
- In the **conclusion**, sum up your major points, add a new thought, and include your personal responses to both works. Here are some strategies to help you discover your responses:
  - **a.** In one minute, tell a partner how you feel about the works.
  - **b.** Write a **blurb** for each work—a short, forceful comment that could be used on a book jacket or as the headline of a book review.
  - **c.** Close your eyes and remember both works in as much detail as you can. What feelings accompany your memories?

2. Elaborate: Get Down to Specifics

You should elaborate on every general statement you make, using details, facts, examples, or quotations from the works. For example, look at the second paragraph of the Student Model below. The writer mentions two similarities and cites specific details from each story to support each similarity.

Sentence Workshop HELP

Varying sentence beginnings: page 585.

3. Keep It Crisp

Your essay should be formal, not chatty. Use a logical method of organization and clear transitions. In the Student Model, notice the key words and phrases ("both," "one difference," "another difference") that guide the reader from one point to the next. For a smooth flow, vary your sentence lengths and beginnings. Avoid padding your ideas with unnecessary words.

Language/Grammar Link HELP

Inverted sentences: page 563.

Student Model

In both "The Cold Equations" by Tom Godwin and "The Pedestrian" by Ray Bradbury, the goals of the main characters are ultimately denied them, and the punishment does not fit the crime.

Thesis statement identifies works and main idea.

Neither character gets what he or she wants more than anything. Marilyn doesn't get to see her brother before she dies, and Mr. Mead is locked up so that he can't walk anymore. Both characters learn that the world isn't fair. Marilyn has to die for her igno-

Similarity 1.

Similarity 2.

Student Model (continued)

rance of "foreign" laws, and Mr. Mead's independence results in his imprisonment.

One difference between "The Cold Equations" and "The Pedestrian" is that Marilyn commits her violation without thinking about it, while Mr. Mead is willfully different. Marilyn only thinks about how much she wants to see her brother. Mr. Mead is well aware of what he is doing. Another difference is that "The Pedestrian" opens with the second-person point of view in the first paragraph, which gave me a feeling of understanding Mr. Mead's situation.

Contrast 1.

Contrast 2 and personal response.

In both of these stories, the main characters' actions bring about severe consequences, even though one character acts out of ignorance and the other in full awareness. Both stories made me feel anger at the end. "The Pedestrian" made me feel anger toward the society Mr. Mead lived in, but with "The Cold Equations" the anger was directed toward the unfairness of life.

Conclusion gives summary and writer's personal responses.

Writer's style is extremely clear; good variety in sentence length, structure.

— Christina Meller
North High School
Bakersfield, California

Evaluating and Revising

1. Peer Review

Exchange papers with a few classmates, preferably some who have written about the same works as you have and some who haven't. As you read one another's essays, refer to the evaluation guidelines at the right, and consider these questions as well:

- If I hadn't read the works, would this essay get me interested in them and give me a good idea of what they're about?
- What do I learn about the writer's views?
- What does the essay leave me wishing I knew more about?

Words and Phrases That Signal Similarities
also, similarly, both, just as, in the same way, like, too, and, in addition, another

Words and Phrases That Signal Differences
on the other hand, by contrast, however, unlike, one difference

Evaluation Criteria

A good comparison/contrast essay

1. *has an introduction that identifies the works being compared, gives background information (if needed), and contains a thesis statement*
2. *compares and contrasts at least two elements in the body of the essay*
3. *clearly expresses the writer's ideas using a logical method of organization (block or point-by-point)*
4. *supports general statements with details, examples, and quotations*
5. *has a conclusion that summarizes the main points, adds a new thought, or states the writer's response*

Proofreading Tips

- Use the grammar and spelling checkers on your computer.
- Exchange papers with a classmate, and proofread your classmate's paper carefully.
- Record spelling, punctuation, and usage errors in a proofreading log. Check your log to avoid repeating these mistakes.
- Be sure you have used quotation marks correctly.

Communications Handbook HELP

See Proofreaders' Marks.

Language Handbook HELP

See Quotation Marks, pages 1054–1056.

Publishing

Exchange papers with classmates; discuss what you learned about the works from writing this essay.

Revision Model

Neither characters gets what he or she wants more than anything. ~~Both characters are frustrated in their attempts and desires to achieve the goals they are seeking above all other goals~~. Marilyn ~~sure~~ doesn't get to see her brother ~~again—or anyone else either, for that matter~~ before she dies, and ~~steps out of the ship and passes away.~~ Mr. Mead ~~gets thrown in the loony bin, which prevents him from his habit of being a pedestrian, walking alone at night, because he~~ is locked up so that he can't walk anymore. ~~and can't get out.~~

Peer Comments

You've given good examples to support your topic sentence, but I'm having trouble following your ideas. Can you make your sentences less wordy?

I'd avoid slang.

Why not drop "pedestrian" and keep the idea of walking alone?

2. Self-Evaluation

Use these same questions and guidelines to revise your own essay. At this point, you might ask yourself, "Do I understand these two works as fully as I'd like to?" It's still not too late to explore other ideas and issues (afterthoughts are often the most interesting thoughts). If you feel you've reached the limits of your understanding, however, decide how closely you'll follow your peer editors' suggestions, and polish your prose. Remember that your goal is to express your ideas in the clearest possible way.

BUILDING YOUR PORTFOLIO

Sentence Workshop

Varying Sentence Beginnings

On page 497, you practiced some ways to vary your sentences' structures and lengths. There's another way you can add variety to your sentences—by varying their beginnings. Here is a text that begins every sentence the same way—with the subject and verb:

> The alarm went off. It rang shrilly in the pitch-black room. Karen opened her eyes reluctantly. She couldn't see anything. She knew it was still dark outside. The clocks had been set ahead the night before. She thought that daylight saving time was horrible. She lost an hour last night. She wouldn't regain that hour for six months.

Here are some strategies an editor uses to vary a monotonous series of sentences that have the same structure. The examples that follow are by professional writers.

1. **Begin with a single-word modifier:** "Drearily I wound my way downstairs: I knew what I had to do, and I did it mechanically."

   —Charlotte Brontë, *Jane Eyre*

2. **Begin with a prepositional phrase:** "After lunch I felt at loose ends and roamed about the little flat."

   —Albert Camus, *The Stranger*

3. **Begin with a participial phrase:** "Overjoyed at this discovery, he hastened to the house. . . ."

   —Mary Shelley, *Frankenstein*

4. **Begin with a subordinate clause:** "When he had stood, for a minute or two, by the side of Defarge, the shoemaker looked up."

   —Charles Dickens, *A Tale of Two Cities*

Writer's Workshop Follow-up: Revising

Try reading aloud your comparison/contrast essay a paragraph at a time. If every sentence in a paragraph starts the same way, add variety by beginning some sentences with an adverb, a phrase, or a subordinate clause.

Technology HELP

See Language Workshop CD-ROM. *Key word entry: sentences.*

Try It Out

1. Edit and revise the paragraph about Karen so that it's smoother, more readable. Combine some sentences, and vary the sentences' beginnings and structures. Be sure to compare your edited paragraphs in class.
2. Write an original sentence imitating the structure of each professional sentence at the left, especially its beginning. Exchange sentences with a partner to check that you've modeled your sentences correctly. Here is a sample modeling of Brontë's sentence:
   Tiredly I trekked over the sand dunes: I knew what I had to say, and I said it immediately.
3. Here is a challenge. Remember that poetry is often written in sentences. Look at two poems from this collection, and find where at least five of their sentences begin and end. Write these sentences as if they were ordinary prose. Then, write your own sentences, modeling them on the sentences from the poems. (Do poets vary the beginnings of *their* sentences too?)

Reading for Life

Analyzing and Appreciating Art

Situation

You've probably noticed the fine art used in this book. Here are strategies you can use to learn more about how "to read" works of art.

Strategies

Describe the content.

- Describe *everything* you see in the painting.
- Tell what you think is happening. Do you see a "story" in the painting?

Try to pinpoint how the painting makes you feel.

- Art conveys emotions. What mood does the painting create?

Notice the composition of the painting.

- Artists take great care to draw viewers' eyes to the most important parts of the painting. This is composition: the arrangement of lines, shapes, and color.
- What do you first see in the painting—what is its *focus*? (Is it a face, a piece of light, a shape?)

Describe the main elements of the painting: colors, lines, shapes, and textures.

- **Color** helps create meaning by suggesting moods and associations. What color or colors dominate? Are certain colors repeated? What mood does the color create for you?
- What **lines** and **shapes** dominate the painting or catch your eye? Do you see curves, circles, angles? Do you see soft edges or hard edges? What **textures** do you see? What mood do these elements create?

Check the title.

- Titles of works of art are often merely descriptive (Picasso's *Three Musicians,* for example), but at times titles, such as Salvador Dali's *The Persistence of Memory,* might be revealing.

Picture Fund. Courtesy, Museum of Fine Arts, Boston.

Dance at Bougival (1883) by Pierre Auguste Renoir. Oil on canvas (71⅝″ × 38⅝″).

Using the Strategies

Apply each strategy to the Renoir painting above.

Extending the Strategies

Use these strategies to analyze another piece of fine art in this book. Be sure to discuss your "reading" of the art with other viewers.

DREAMS—LOST AND FOUND

WRITING FOCUS: Supporting an Interpretation

Dreams are necessary to life.

—Anaïs Nin

Dreams *can* come true, but sometimes reality falls short of the dream. A family might dream of operating a farm and might work as hard as they can, but the realities of soil and weather might force them to find a new dream. Even successful dreams rarely turn out to be exactly as we imagined them. You may dream of becoming a movie star and make your dream come true—but you may also find that the life of a celebrity brings problems. The poems in this collection are about the imperfect fit between dream and reality—and the need to keep dreaming despite the imperfections.

Writer's Notebook

WORK IN PROGRESS

A dream sought by every generation in the United States is called the American Dream. What does this phrase mean to you? Jot down *your* interpretation of the phrase "American Dream." (You will have to use this kind of interpretive skill for the Writer's Workshop assignment on page 618.)

Elements of Literature

SOUND EFFECTS: Rhyme, Alliteration, Onomatopoeia

Rhyme: Chiming Sounds

Rhyme works along with rhythm to create the special music of a poem. **Rhyme** is the repetition of the accented vowel sound and all subsequent sounds in a word (*time/dime, history/mystery, lobster/mobster*). Rhyme sets up the expectation that the pattern of chiming sounds we hear in the opening lines will continue throughout the poem. Chiming sounds that punctuate the rhythm of a poem also give the poem structure and make it easy to remember. (In the cartoon, Edgar Allan Poe searches for words to rhyme with the refrain "Nevermore" in his poem "The Raven.")

Rhyme is the most familiar aspect of sound in poetry, and not long ago, it was part of every poet's craft. Today rhyme has fallen out of favor with some serious poets, though many poets still continue to explore its musical possibilities.

In poetry, rhymes may occur at the ends of lines—**end rhyme**—or within a line—**internal rhyme.** A perfect rhyme, like *cat/mat*

> Today rhyme has fallen out of favor with some serious poets.

or *verging/merging,* is called an **exact rhyme.** When sounds are similar but not exact, as in *fellow/follow* or *mystery/mastery,* the rhyme is called **approximate rhyme**. Approximate rhymes are also called half rhymes or slant rhymes, or imperfect rhymes by readers who don't like them. The following verse from "Father William," a comic poem by Lewis Carroll, contains exact rhymes:

"You are old, Father William,"
    the young man said,
"And your hair has become
    very white;
And yet you incessantly stand
    on your head—
Do you think, at your age, it is
    right?"

In the next poem, the rhymes are both approximate rhymes (*washes/rushes, bales/orioles*) and exact (*sea/mystery*):

This is the land the Sunset washes

This is the land the Sunset
    washes—
These are the banks of the
    Yellow Sea—
Where it rose—or whither it
    rushes—
These are the Western
    Mystery!

Night after night her purple
    traffic
Strews the landing with Opal
    Bales—
Merchantmen poise upon
    horizons—
Dip—and vanish like Orioles!

—Emily Dickinson

This is the original wording of Dickinson's poem. Editors who prepared the poem for publication after her death disliked

by John Malcolm Brinnin

approximate rhymes. They changed the words *like orioles* to *with fairy sails.*

Alliteration: Tongue Twisters and Poetry

The tongue twister "Peter Piper picked a peck of pickled peppers" uses alliteration, and so does "She sells seashells by the seashore." **Alliteration** is the repetition of consonant sounds in words that appear close together; strictly speaking, alliteration occurs at the beginning of words or on accented syllables. Tongue twisters make exaggerated use of alliteration just for the fun of it. But alliteration used with restraint can result in lines as memorable as this one from Percy Bysshe Shelley's "Ode to the West Wind":

O wild west wind, thou breath
of autumn's being

Or this one from John Masefield's "Sea Fever"(page 591):

To the gull's way and the
whale's way where the
wind's like a whetted knife

Or this one from Robert Frost's "Acquainted with the Night":

I have stood still and stopped
the sound of feet

Onomatopoeia: Sounds into Words

Beyond rhyme and rhythm, the most important aspect of sound in poetry is onomatopoeia. **Onomatopoeia** (än′ō·mat′ō·pē′ə) is the use of words that sound like what they mean (*snap, crackle, pop*). *Onomatopoeia* (Greek, literally, for "the making of words") has come to mean "the making of words by imitating or suggesting sounds." For the poet, onomatopoeia is a way of conveying meaning through evocative words that also provide musical accompaniment—the way background music in a movie can affect the mood of a scene.

In its most basic form, onomatopoeia is a single word (*gurgle, bang, rattle, boom, hiss, buzz, sputter, honk, thud, sizzle, fizzle, twitter, clunk, whine*) that echoes a natural or mechanical sound.

In the next two lines from Isabella Gardner's poem "Summer Remembered," alliteration creates onomatopoeia—the sounds of *p*'s and *k*'s imitate the sound of ice in a glass:

The pizzicato plinkle of ice
in an auburn
uncle's amber glass

Here, from the same poem, the sounds of *s*'s and *p*'s imitate the sound of waves breaking against the side of a sloop (a sailboat):

The slap and slop of waves on
little sloops

The use of onomatopoeia can be so obvious that it seems deliberately or accidentally comic. But, as in this famous example from Tennyson's *The Princess*, onomatopoeia can be used with such exactness that the sounds of the poem voice a particular feeling that words alone could only approximate:

The moan of doves in
immemorial elms
And murmuring of
innumerable bees

Before You Read

SEA FEVER

Make the Connection

A Sea Dream

Although supertankers and cruise ships are much taller than any sailing ship, the term *tall ship* still denotes a sailing vessel with high masts.

For millions of landlubbers, the image of a tall ship triggers dreams of romance, freedom, and adventure, just as it did for Masefield.

"The wheel's kick" in line 3 is a reference to what can happen when a sudden shift in the wind or the tide causes a ship's steering wheel to "kick over"—to spin out of control until the helmsman can grab it and put the ship back on course. "Trick" (line 12) is a sailing term for a round-trip voyage. Years ago, a "long trick" might have involved a voyage from England to China and back, a trip that could last for more than a year.

Quickwrite

Write down your initial interpretation of this poem's title. Does the title remind you of any other uses of the word *fever*? *(Keep your notes for use on pages 596–597.)*

Elements of Literature

Rhythms of the Sea

Read this famous poem aloud to hear how the poet's use of meter suggests the motion of a ship on the high seas. Where do you hear and feel the rolling rhythm of the sea swells? Where do you hear and feel the slap of waves against the ship?

> **Meter** is a pattern of stressed and unstressed syllables in poetry.
>
> *For more on Meter, see pages 558–559 and the Handbook of Literary Terms.*

go.hrw.com
LEO 10-10

Sea Fever

John Masefield

I must go down to the seas again, to the lonely sea and the sky,
And all I ask is a tall ship and a star to steer her by;
And the wheel's kick and the wind's song and the white sail's shaking,
And a gray mist on the sea's face and a gray dawn breaking.

I must go down to the seas again, for the call of the running tide
Is a wild call and a clear call that may not be denied;
And all I ask is a windy day with the white clouds flying,
And the flung spray and the blown spume, and the sea gulls crying.

I must go down to the seas again, to the vagrant gypsy life,
To the gull's way and the whale's way where the wind's like a whetted
knife;
And all I ask is a merry yarn from a laughing fellow-rover.
And quiet sleep and a sweet dream when the long trick's over.

Meet the Writer

Sailor-Poet

John Masefield (1878–1967), born in England, was orphaned by the time he was thirteen years old. At once, as boys could do in those days, he joined the merchant navy and shipped around the world for several years. On a trip to New York, he jumped ship and lived for a time in the city as what we'd call today a homeless person. He began to write poetry after coming across a collection of Chaucer's *Canterbury Tales* in a New York bookstore.

Masefield is best remembered today for poems inspired by the years he spent as a seaman, first on windjammers in the last days of the sailing ships and then on tramp steamers and ocean liners. No one has better evoked for the landlubber the sense of freedom and adventure, the taste of salt and spray associated with sailing "before the mast," or the pride that marked the crews of even the rustiest and dingiest of freighters.

For more than thirty years, Masefield served as Britain's poet laureate. Of his passion for sailing ships, the poet said:

"They were the only youth I had, and the only beauty I knew in my youth, and now that I am old, not many greater beauties seem to be in the world."

Before You Read

EX-BASKETBALL PLAYER

Make the Connection

Stuck in a Past Dream

Sometimes people get stuck in dreams of their past. They keep looking backward instead of forward. Every school has a sports hero, someone who is a "natural" at the game. But like the glittering stars whose brilliance fades overnight, some of these bright heroes seem to dim after graduation. Do you recognize Flick Webb in this poem?

Quickwrite

How important are school athletics to you? Do you think they prepare young people for life? Why? Jot down a brief response. *(Keep your notes for use on pages 596–597.)*

Elements of Literature

Sound Effects

Even though Updike's poem sounds free and conversational, it's really written within a tight **structure.** The basic beat is **iambic pentameter**—five iambs (˘ ´) to a line. This meter is closest to the rhythm of everyday English speech, and its use gives the poem an informal, conversational sound. You'll find the same meter providing the beat in a poem written centuries before Updike's—Shakespeare's sonnet on page 561. Updike uses other sound devices: **Internal rhymes** and **alliteration** lend his unrhymed poem verbal music. Read it aloud.

Iambic pentameter is a line of poetry made up of five iambs. An **iamb** contains one unstressed syllable followed by a stressed syllable.

For more on Meter, see pages 558–559 and the Handbook of Literary Terms.

Ex-Basketball Player

John Updike

Pearl Avenue runs past the high-school lot,
Bends with the trolley tracks, and stops, cut off
Before it has a chance to go two blocks,
At Colonel McComsky Plaza. Berth's Garage
Is on the corner facing west, and there,
Most days, you'll find Flick Webb, who helps Berth out.

Flick stands tall among the idiot pumps—
Five on a side, the old bubble-head style,
Their rubber elbows hanging loose and low.
One's nostrils are two S's, and his eyes
An E and O. And one is squat, without
A head at all—more of a football type.

Once Flick played for the high-school team, the Wizards.
He was good: in fact, the best. In '46

Gas (1940) by Edward Hopper.
Oil on canvas (26¼″ × 40¼″).

The Museum of Modern Art, New York.
Mrs. Simon Guggenheim Fund. Photograph ©2000
The Museum of Modern Art, New York.

He bucketed three hundred ninety points,
A county record still. The ball loved Flick.
I saw him rack up thirty-eight or forty
In one home game. His hands were like wild birds.

He never learned a trade, he just sells gas,
Checks oil, and changes flats. Once in a while,
As a gag, he dribbles an inner tube,
But most of us remember anyway.
His hands are fine and nervous on the lug wrench.
It makes no difference to the lug wrench, though.

Off work, he hangs around Mae's luncheonette.
Grease-gray and kind of coiled, he plays pinball,
Smokes thin cigars, and nurses lemon phosphates.
Flick seldom says a word to Mae, just nods
Beyond her face toward bright applauding tiers
Of Necco Wafers, Nibs, and Juju Beads.

Meet the Writer

Observer of American Life

John Updike (1932–   ) was born in the small town of Shillington, Pennsylvania. A year after he graduated from Harvard University, he got a job on the staff of *The New Yorker* magazine, which has published much of his writing ever since.

Though he has won fame for his novels and short stories, Updike is also a poet of great wit and craft. He is particularly drawn to occasional poetry—pieces inspired by odd or funny incidents reported in the newspapers or observed in the American suburban landscape of housing developments, service stations, and supermarkets. Despite his humorous approach, Updike is a sharp social observer and a serious moralist.

Among the most successful of Updike's novels are the Rabbit tales (the last two won Pulitzer Prizes): *Rabbit, Run* (1960), *Rabbit Redux* (1971), *Rabbit Is Rich* (1981), and *Rabbit at Rest* (1991). These novels chronicle the life of Harry "Rabbit" Angstrom, an ex-basketball player. Rabbit lives an outwardly conventional life in a small Pennsylvania town, but his hidden yearnings and disappointing relationships reveal the uncertainties of contemporary American life.

In accepting the American Book Award in 1982, Updike spoke to young writers:

“Have faith. May you surround yourselves with parents, editors, mates, and children as supportive as mine have been. But the essential support and encouragement of course comes from within, arising out of the mad notion that your society needs to know what only you can tell it.”

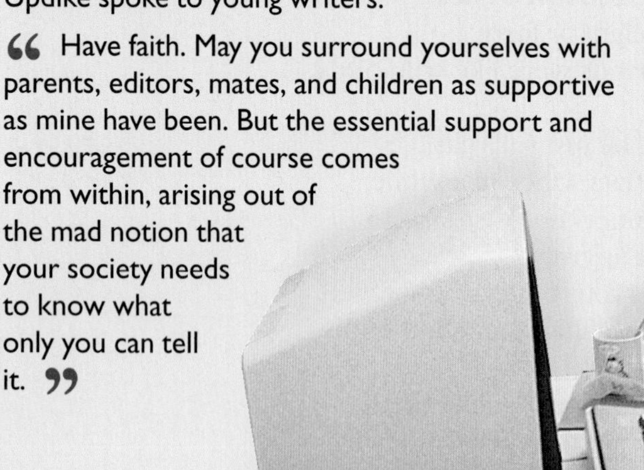

I Want to Be Somebody

Let me take you back to when I was just a child
with big wants and dreams,
but no one to encourage me on how to reach them.

I wanted to be a doctor
I wanted to be a teacher
I wanted to be the president
I wanted to be noticed
I wanted to be noticed

"You little Black child,
You ain't neva gonna be nobody.
You have big dreams.
Do you hear what I'm saying?
You ain't gonna be nobody."

I wanted to be a doctor
I wanted to be a teacher
I wanted to be the president
I wanted to be noticed
I wanted to be noticed

"You think you something!
You ain't no betta than nobody else.
You think you too good to get your hands dirty?
Black child, all you doing is dreamin'.
You ain't gonna be nobody."

I wanted to be the president
I wanted to be a millionaire
I wanted to be famous
I wanted to be noticed

"Yeah, I knew her when she was just a little sweet thang.
I knew she was gonna be somebody.
I even remember tellin' her
she was gonna be somebody."

I'm 4th in the nation
I'm 2nd in the nation as a forward
I'm 1st in the West Coast
I'm Angel Bagley #44
the best female basketball player in the West

I wanted to be the president
I wanted to be a millionaire
I wanted to be famous
I wanted to be noticed

All I wanted was to be somebody
I wanted to be somebody
I wanna be somebody
I'm somebody
I'm somebody

—Angel Bagley
Thomas Jefferson High School
Portland, Oregon

Making Meanings
Sea Fever
Ex-Basketball Player

First Thoughts

1. What picture did you see as you read each poem?

Shaping Interpretations

2. In what ways is the **speaker** of Masefield's poem in the grip of a "fever"? (Check your Quickwrite interpretation of the title.) Can you think of other "fevers"—like mountain fever or spring fever?
3. Given the intensity of his feelings, what do you think the life of the speaker of "Sea Fever" is like?
4. In the final line of "Sea Fever," what **metaphor** describes life in terms of a sea voyage? What sort of afterlife does this speaker dream of?
5. In "Ex-Basketball Player," look back at the opening description of Pearl Avenue. How can this street be seen as a **metaphor** for Flick's life?
6. In stanza 2 of Updike's poem, find words that **personify** the gas pumps. Do you think Flick is similar to the pumps—why or why not?
7. In the last stanza of "Ex-Basketball Player," what is the candy **compared** to, and who sees it that way? What do you think this suggests about Flick's fantasies—or dreams?

Connecting with the Text

8. If Flick Webb were a friend of yours, what advice would you give him? Be sure to check your Quickwrite notes.

Extending the Text

9. How does Flick **compare** with the speaker in "I Want to Be Somebody" (page 595)?

CHOICES: Building Your Portfolio

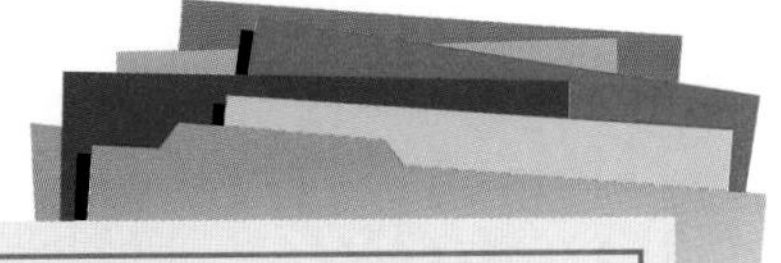

Writer's Notebook

1. Collecting Ideas for an Interpretation

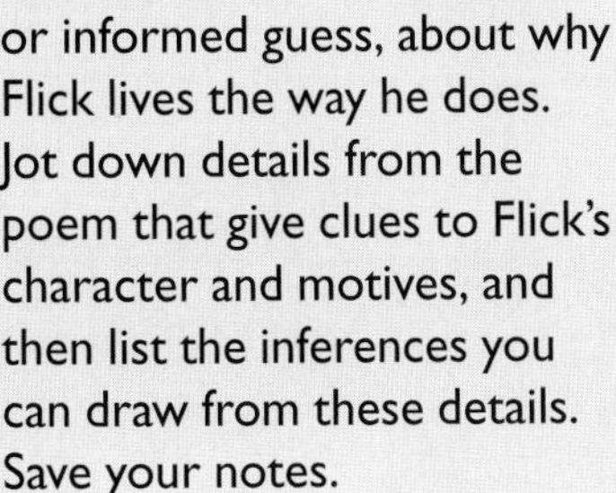

Using details. Make an **inference,** or informed guess, about why Flick lives the way he does. Jot down details from the poem that give clues to Flick's character and motives, and then list the inferences you can draw from these details. Save your notes.

Critical Thinking

2. What Makes It Tick?

Write a brief essay in which you discuss the **sound effects** of one of these poems—"Sea Fever" or "Ex-Basketball Player." First, on a separate piece of paper, type the poem you are examining (be sure to leave extra space between the lines). Then, scan the poem to see if you can determine its **meter.** (Reading aloud will help.) Next, circle all the **rhymes** and examples of **alliteration.** Is there a **refrain**? In your essay, describe how the poem's sound effects "work" and what they contribute to the poem as a whole.

Creative Writing

3. Flick's Poem

Imitate the structure of the student poem on page 595, and let Flick speak. You could keep the title "I Want to Be Somebody" and the first line if you think they work.

VOCABULARY

HOW TO OWN A WORD

Context Clues

When you come across unfamiliar **technical words,** look for **clues** in the words' **context** that will help you make an educated guess about meaning. For example, suppose you know nothing about basketball. What clues in Updike's poem would help you figure out what his basketball jargon means?

Remember: Always check your guesses in a dictionary. Sometimes context delivers no clues at all.

Jargon: Technical Vocabulary on the Job

Jargon is the specialized words, or **technical vocabulary,** used by people in particular jobs or groups. Doctors have jargon, as do athletes, actors, computer users, and sailors. Jargon often uses language in playful, imaginative ways—for example, "dunking" a basketball (as you might a doughnut) or, better yet, "slam-dunking" it.

Look at the sample chart below for the word *dunk.* Set up a chart similar to the one for *dunk* to study each of the basketball terms Updike uses in his poem. If you're hooked on sports jargon, do the same for other sports terms.

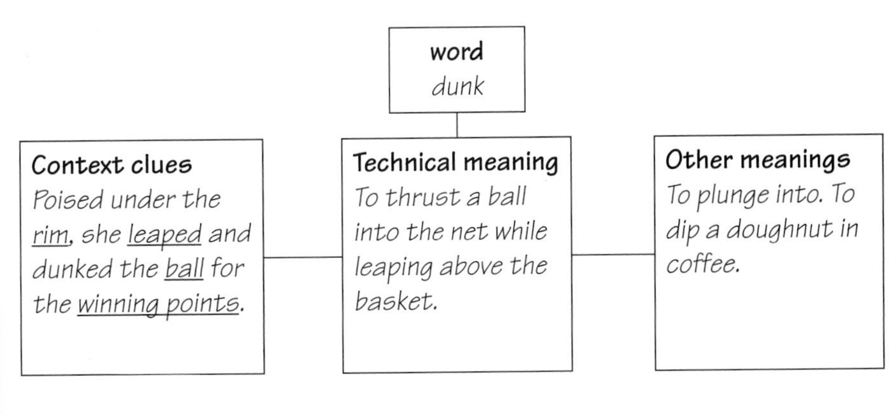

Before You Read

The Bean Eaters
We Real Cool

Make the Connection

Slices of Life

Old people eating beans off chipped plates; young people playing pool. The old people spend their time remembering; the pool players spend their time acting cool. What happened to their dreams?

Quickwrite

Read the poems aloud several times, and imagine how the old couple and the young people look, dress, and move. Jot down what you visualize. *(Keep your notes for use on page 601.)*

Elements of Literature

Rhyme

Read both poems aloud to hear Brooks's use of **rhyme**. Is there a regular pattern of rhymes in each poem?

> **Rhyme** is the repetition of accented vowel sounds and all sounds following them in words that are close together in a poem.
>
> *For more on Rhyme, see pages 588–589 and the Handbook of Literary Terms.*

go.hrw.com

LEO 10-10

Waiting Room (1984) by Phoebe Beasley. Collage (36″ × 36″).

The Bean Eaters

Gwendolyn Brooks

They eat beans mostly, this old yellow pair.
Dinner is a casual affair.
Plain chipware on a plain and creaking wood,
Tin flatware.

Two who are Mostly Good.
Two who have lived their day,
But keep on putting on their clothes
And putting things away.

And remembering . . .
Remembering, with twinklings and twinges,
As they lean over the beans in their rented back room that
is full of beads and receipts and dolls and cloths, tobacco
crumbs, vases and fringes.

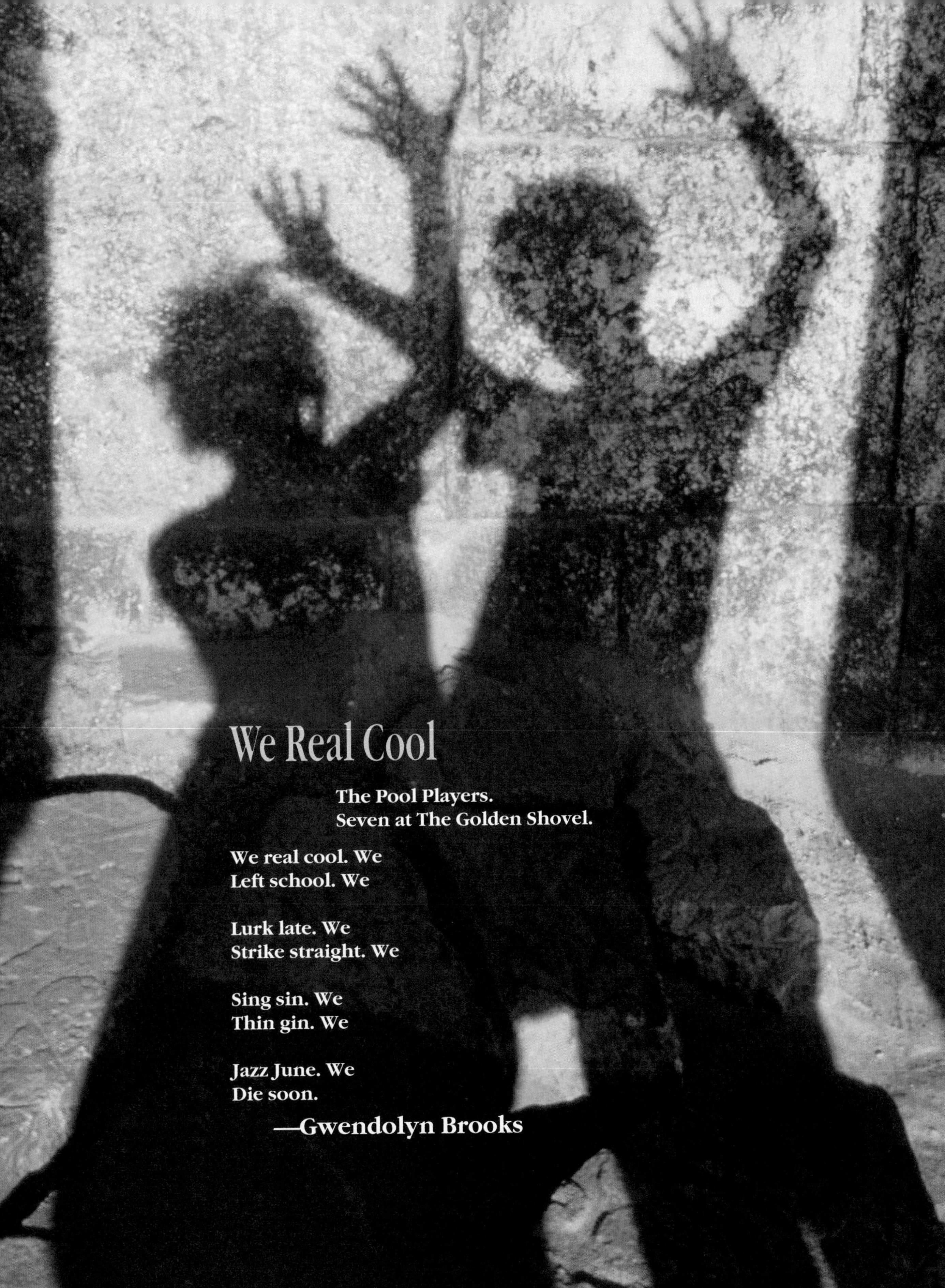

We Real Cool

The Pool Players.
Seven at The Golden Shovel.

We real cool. We
Left school. We

Lurk late. We
Strike straight. We

Sing sin. We
Thin gin. We

Jazz June. We
Die soon.

—Gwendolyn Brooks

Meet the Writer

Chicago's Voice

Gwendolyn Brooks (1917–2000) was born in Topeka, Kansas, but for most of her life she was associated with Chicago, especially with its large African American population. Skilled in many different kinds of poetry, Brooks wrote with both formal elegance and an ear for the natural speech rhythms of the people of Chicago's South Side. In an interview, Brooks answered questions about her work:

Q. Why do you write poetry?

A. I like the concentration, the crush; I like working with language, as others like working with paints and clay or notes.

Q. Has much of your poetry a racial element?

A. Yes. It is organic, not imposed. It is my privilege to state "Negroes" not as curios but as people.

Q. What is your poet's premise (basic principle)?

A. "Vivify the contemporary fact," said Whitman. I like to vivify the *universal* fact, when it occurs to me. But the universal wears contemporary clothing very well.

Book by Brooks

Brooks's novel *Maud Martha* (1953) is made up of a series of episodes that follow a young black girl as she grows up and finds her dream.

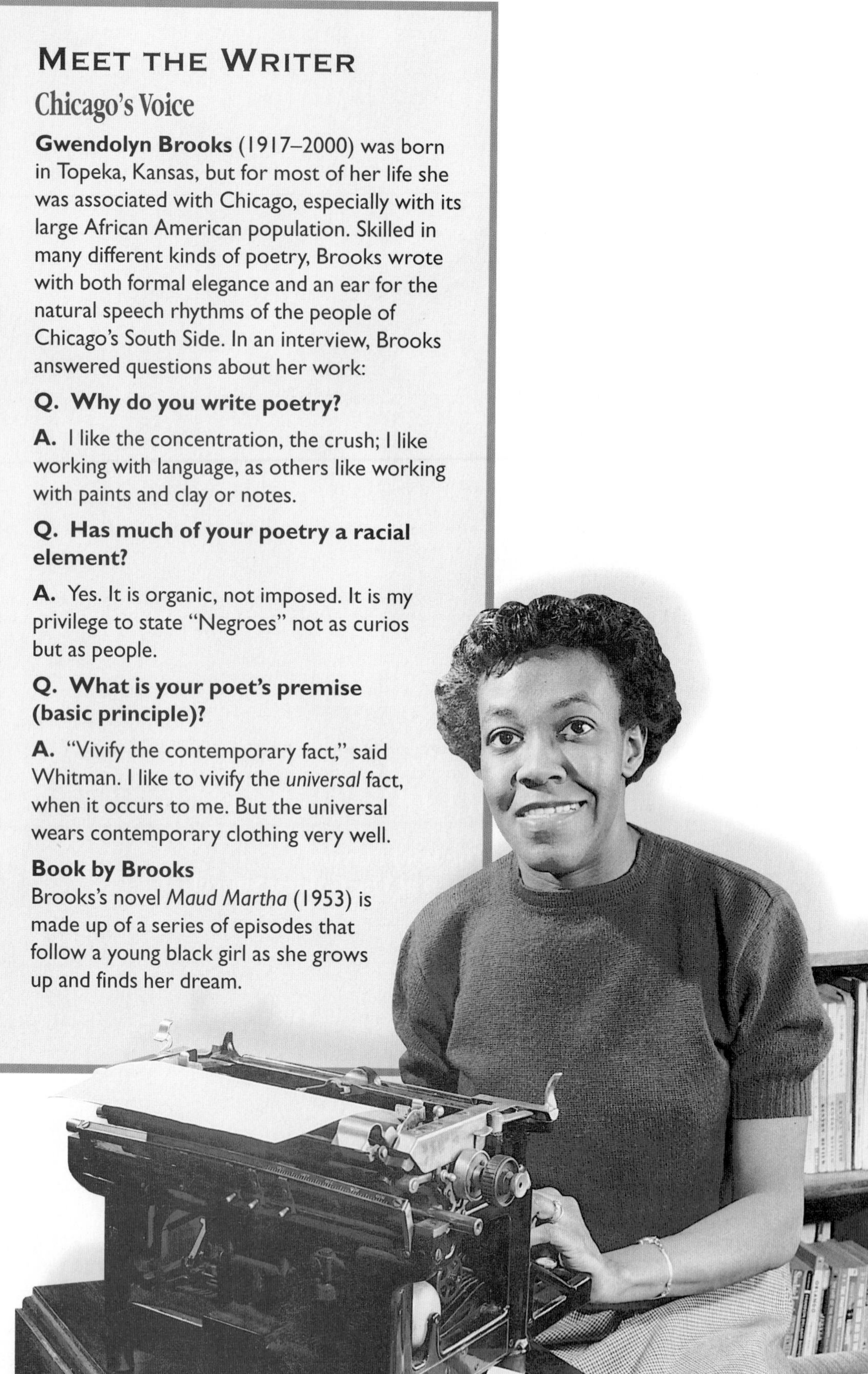

Making Meanings
The Bean Eaters
We Real Cool

First Thoughts

1. What were the first things you thought about after reading each poem? Try reading each poem a second time. Do your thoughts change?

Shaping Interpretations

2. What do you think is the most important word or phrase in each poem?
3. Are the bean eaters and the pool players alike at all? Explain. (Refer to your Quickwrite notes.)
4. **Irony** is a discrepancy between expectations and reality. Do you think the poet believes the pool players are really "cool"? Why?
5. Were you surprised at the last thing the pool players say? Why do you think they believe they'll "die soon"?
6. How does Brooks use **rhyme** in each poem?

Extending the Text

7. Are people like the bean eaters and the pool players found in our world today? Explain your response.

Choices: Building Your Portfolio

Writer's Notebook

1. Collecting Ideas for an Interpretation

Interpreting messages. What messages or social commentary do you find in these two poems? Take notes on the messages you find in each poem and on how they connect with life today. Save your notes for possible use in the workshop on page 618.

Creative Writing

2. Strike It Up in Spondees

"We Real Cool" may be the only poem in English written entirely in **spondees**. A spondee is two strongly accented syllables. Read the poem aloud. Are there any unaccented syllables? Try to write your own poem in imitation of "We Real Cool." You could open with Brooks's title. Who will your speakers be?

Speaking and Listening

3. A Reading

With a group, prepare and present these two poems in class. You'll have to decide if you'll use a single voice or several voices or even a chorus. You'll also have to decide if you'll use music as background. Be sure to prepare scripts indicating where your speakers will pause and how they'll vary their volume. Ask the audience to evaluate the class performances.

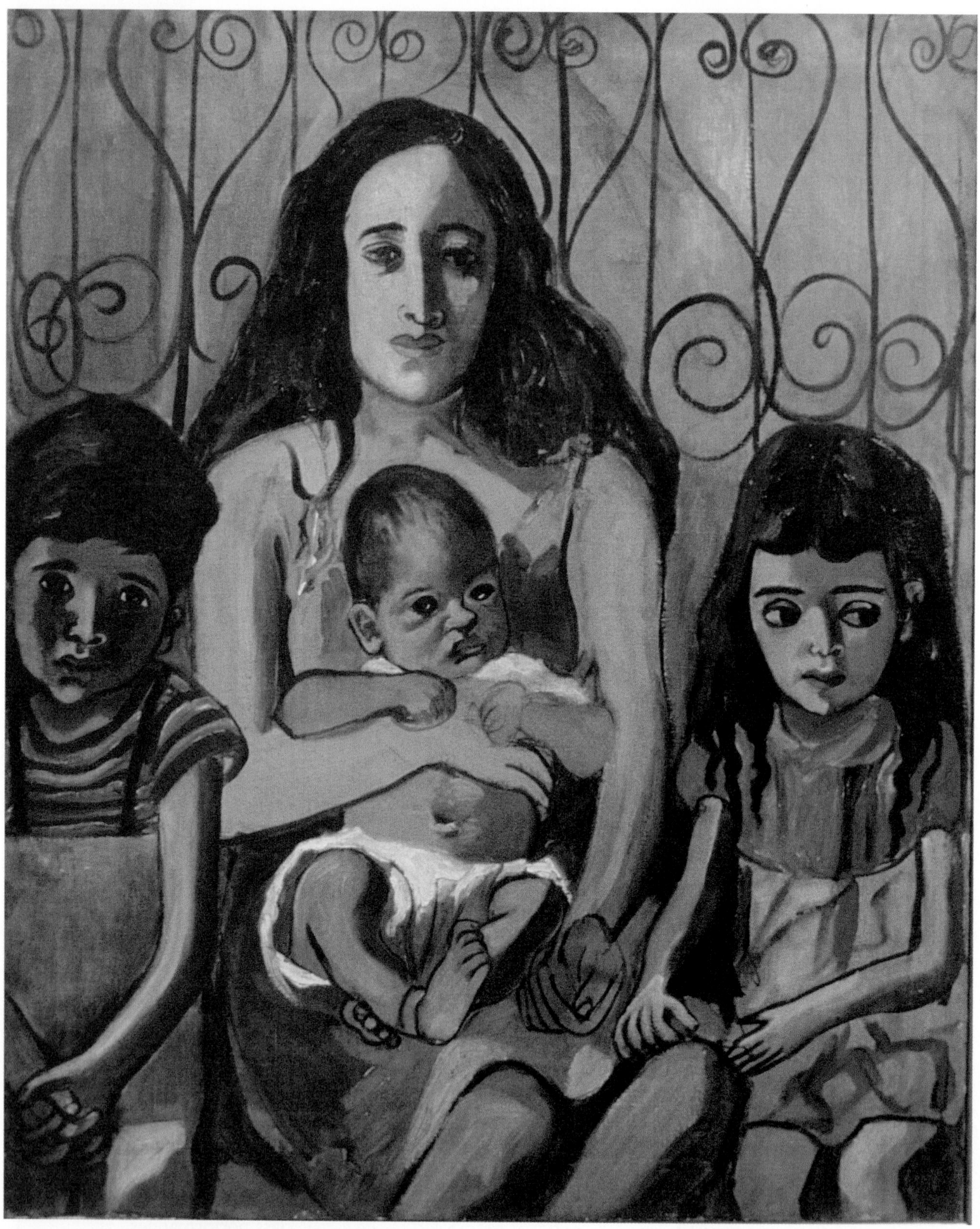

The Spanish Family (1943) by Alice Neel. Oil on canvas (34″ × 28″).

Before You Read

A Voice

Make the Connection

"This Is America, Mom"

Dreams take work. Sometimes that work requires courage. Perhaps it's the courage to move to a new country. Perhaps it's the courage to learn a new language. Pat Mora sees courage in something her mother did as a child. (Mora's mother grew up in El Paso, Texas. At home, the family spoke Spanish.)

Quickwrite

Write the name of someone who has fulfilled a dream. State what you admire about this person. *(Keep your notes for use on page 611.)*

Elements of Literature

Tone: What's the Attitude?

People reveal attitudes in the **tones** of their voices. They may sound humorous or sarcastic, cheerful or angry, sharp or sweet, bitter or sad. Read "A Voice" aloud. Do you hear more than one tone?

> **Tone** is the attitude a writer takes toward the reader, a subject, or a character. In writing, tone is revealed by word choice.
>
> *For more on Tone, see the Handbook of Literary Terms.*

go.hrw.com
LEO 10-10

A Voice

Pat Mora

Even the lights on the stage unrelenting
as the desert sun couldn't hide the other
students, their eyes also unrelenting,
students who spoke English every night

as they ate their meat, potatoes, gravy.
Not you. In your house that smelled like
rose powder, you spoke Spanish formal
as your father, the judge without a courtroom

in the country he floated to in the dark
on a flatbed truck. He walked slow
as a hot river down the narrow hall
of your house. You never dared to race past him

to say, "Please move," in the language
you learned effortlessly, as you learned to run,
the language forbidden at home, though your mother
said you learned it to fight with the neighbors.

You liked winning with words. You liked
writing speeches about patriotism and democracy.
You liked all the faces looking at you, all those eyes.
"How did I do it?" you ask me now. "How did I do it

when my parents didn't understand?"
The family story says your voice is the voice
of an aunt in Mexico, spunky as a peacock.
Family stories sing of what lives in the blood.

You told me only once about the time you went
to the state capitol, your family proud as if
you'd been named governor. But when you looked
around, the only Mexican in the auditorium,

you wanted to hide from those strange faces.
Their eyes were pinpricks, and you faked
hoarseness. You, who are never at a loss
for words, felt your breath stick in your throat

like an ice cube. "I can't," you whispered.
"I can't." Yet you did. Not that day but years later.
You taught the four of us to speak up.
This is America, Mom. The undoable is done

in the next generation. Your breath moves
through the family like the wind
moves through the trees.

Meet the Writer

A Force of Words

Pat Mora (1942–) was born in El Paso, Texas, and received a master's degree from the University of Texas in El Paso. She has taught in public schools and college while writing a body of poetry that has been collected in several volumes, including *Chants* (1985) and *Borders* (1993). (You can find another one of her poems on page 65.) Mora offers these thoughts on "A Voice":

" This poem brings together two different experiences: hearing a story from my mother and hearing the sound of wind in the trees, the sound of an invisible force. My maternal grandparents came to El Paso, Texas, from Mexico. They did not speak English. My mother, though, knew English and Spanish when she started school. She was an excellent student and always liked participating in speech contests. One aspect of the poem is about her breath, her force, in our family. "

Before You Read

AUNT FANNIE FIXES BISON BOURGUIGNON

Make the Connection

Mixing Cultures

Bison, or buffalo, once roamed the American plains, supplying American Indians with food and the raw materials for clothing and shelter. Beef bourguignon (bo͞or′gēn·yōn′) is a French stew made of beef cooked in red wine. Why has the poet put bison in this French stew?

Quickwrite

How important to you is your specific ethnicity, religion, or culture? Rate its importance on a scale of 1 to 5, with 1 meaning "not important" and 5 meaning "very important." Freewrite for a few minutes, explaining your response. *(Keep your notes for use on page 611.)*

Elements of Literature

A Prose Poem

Although this little piece is written in ordinary paragraph form, it uses the elements of poetry—especially very powerful **images** that make the speaker's world easy to see and feel. Also, like most poetry, its message is elusive—its point is never directly stated. Like other poems, this **prose poem** by Diane Glancy allows us to enter the speaker's world and make our own meaning of it. After you've read Glancy's work once, read it aloud. Does it *sound* like a poem to you?

Granddaughter, I Am Teaching You (1993) by Joanna Osburn-Bigfeather (Western Band Cherokee). Clay with raku glaze (24″ × 17″).

Photograph by Neil McGreevy. Courtesy Joanna Osburn-Bigfeather.

A **prose poem** is a short piece that is written in the form of prose but uses the elements of poetry.

Aunt Fannie Fixes Bison Bourguignon

Diane Glancy

My father was Cherokee. My mother English & German. My father decided he would live in this world and migrated north to the stockyards in Kansas City. My mother also came north, from a small farm in Kansas. They married, struggled through the Depression, and bought a small house by the time I was born. I was integrated into my mother's white family. I went to a white grade school. In the winter our faces lined the window. Once my tongue stuck to the frost on the glass. I was just a little darker than the others, a little quieter. I walked home over the field, breaking thin plates of ice like locust wings. There was always a sense of puzzlement & loss. Something undefined wasn't there. The smell of old campfires? The green corn dance? I had the feeling I was always at the window, my tongue forever on the cold glass.

Meet the Writer

Reinventing Ceremony

Diane Glancy (1941–) was born in Kansas City, Missouri, graduated from the University of Missouri, and earned a master's degree in creative writing from the University of Iowa. She has explored her American Indian heritage in poetry and prose, including a series of reflections called *Claiming Breath*, which won the first North American Indian Prose Award in 1990. Presently Glancy is teaching writing and Native American literature at Macalester College in St. Paul, Minnesota. In her dedication to *Iron Woman* (1990), a book of poems, Glancy writes:

> "I keep thinking why bother with my Native American heritage. What does it matter? Let it go. How does it relate to my life in this 'world that is' anyway? But I pass the Noguchi sculpture on my way to class at Macalester and I see 'Iron Woman.' I hear old footsteps of the ancestors in the leaves in autumn. In winter I feel a sense of loss that blows in the cold wind between the buildings. So I dedicate this book to the 'visage,' if that's the right word, the 'remains' of a heritage I feel every day."

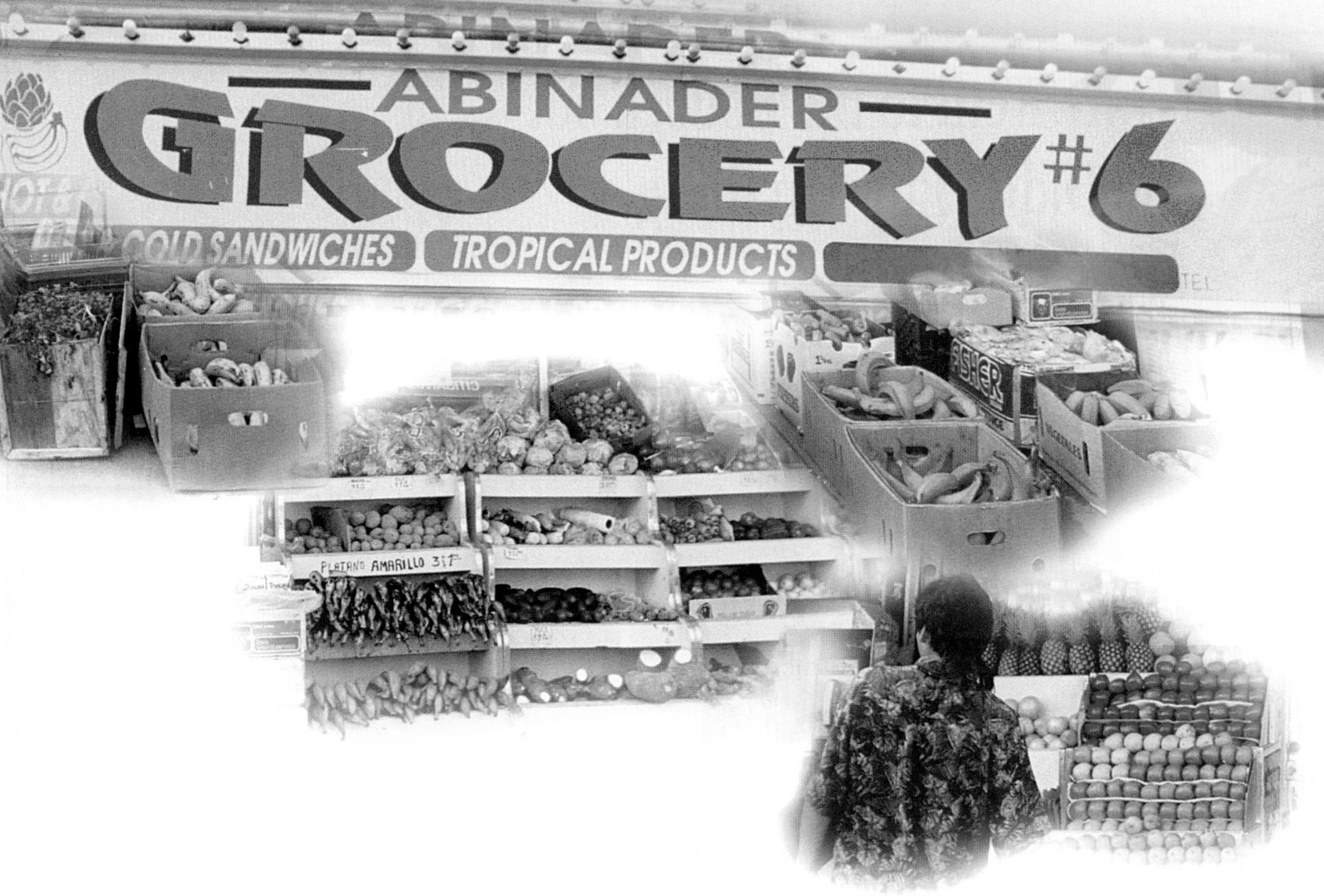

Before You Read

Tony Went to the Bodega but He Didn't Buy Anything

Make the Connection

A Rice and Beans Story

The course of a successful life is not always a straight line from where we are to where we want to be. Sometimes we move in unexpected directions, as Tony does in this "rice and beans success story."

Quickwrite

When you're an adult, how do you think you'll decide if you've succeeded or not? Write your thoughts on this question.

Elements of Literature

Free Verse

Like many contemporary poets, Martín Espada writes in **free verse**, using no regular meter or rhyme scheme. But the poem has a distinct rhythm, created by the use of long and short sentences and by the use of many run-on lines, lines that do not end with any mark of punctuation. To get their sense, you have to keep on reading, without pausing, to the next line. Read the poem aloud and listen to the rhythms. How would you describe what you hear? Does the sound remind you of any particular type of music?

Free verse is poetry that has no regular meter or rhyme scheme. Free verse often creates its rhythm by alternating long and short sentences and by using run-on lines.

For more on Free Verse, see page 559 and the Handbook of Literary Terms.

Tony Went to the Bodega but He Didn't Buy Anything

para Angel Guadalupe

Martín Espada

Tony's father left the family
and the Long Island City projects,
leaving a mongrel-skinny puertorriqueño° boy
nine years old
who had to find work.

Makengo the Cuban
let him work at the bodega.°
In grocery aisles
he learned the steps of the dry-mop mambo,
banging the cash register
like piano percussion
in the spotlight of Machito's orchestra,
polite with the abuelas° who bought on credit,
practicing the grin on customers
he'd seen Makengo grin
with his bad yellow teeth.

Tony left the projects too,
with a scholarship for law school.
But he cursed the cold primavera°
in Boston;
the cooking of his neighbors
left no smell in the hallway,
and no one spoke Spanish
(not even the radio).

So Tony walked without a map
through the city,
a landscape of hostile condominiums
and the darkness of white faces,
sidewalk-searcher lost
till he discovered the projects.

Tony went to the bodega
but he didn't buy anything:
he sat by the doorway satisfied
to watch la gente° (people
island-brown as him)

3. **puertorriqueño** (pwer′tō·rē·kā′nyō): Spanish for "Puerto Rican."

7. **bodega** (bō·dā′gä): small grocery shop in a Hispanic neighborhood.

13. **abuelas** (ä·bwā′läs): Spanish for "grandmothers."

19. **primavera** (prē′mä·ver′ä): Spanish for "spring."

34. **la gente** (lä hen′tā): Spanish for "the people."

crowd in and out,
hablando español,°
thought: this is beautiful,
and grinned
his bodega grin.

This is a rice and beans
success story:
today Tony lives on Tremont Street,
above the bodega.

37. hablando español (ä·blän′dō es·pä·nyōl′): Spanish for "speaking Spanish."

Meet the Writer

Home Boy

Martín Espada (1957–) was born in Brooklyn, New York, and moved to Boston to study law. Like Tony's trip through life, Espada's life journey has been varied and complex. It has taken him as far away as Nicaragua (where he worked as a radio journalist) and back to Boston (where he provides legal services for tenants and poor people). Along the way, Espada has worked as a hotel clerk, a bouncer, an attendant in a primate nursery, a groundskeeper in a minor league ballpark, a welfare-rights activist, and an advocate for mental patients. At the heart of his poetry are his experiences in the Latino communities of New York City and Boston. Espada now teaches English at the University of Massachusetts at Amherst.

Martín Espada and his son Clemente.

Connections

A NEWS ARTICLE

The Streets of the Barrio

LUIS RODRIGUEZ

Here in the barrios we can open up, be ourselves, and be funny in a Chicano sort of way. We can use both Spanish and English to twist around the obvious. And we can be sad and cry in a way that does not make us feel weak.

In the barrios I can walk down these streets and know that always somebody will call out my name. The postman is a family friend, and the owner of the corner store will give me credit because he knows I am not going to skip town. Summer nights are the times when all the neighborhood doors are open and the barrio is especially alive. People are on their porches, music blares from open windows, and circles of brown children slurp snow cones and play games. So much is happening, so many people are friendly, there is so much to experience and learn.

True, there is death and violence here, but there is much more life. . . . Drugs and gang warfare are a part of life in the barrios, but they are not at its heart.

—from "Over There in East L.A.," *L.A. Weekly*

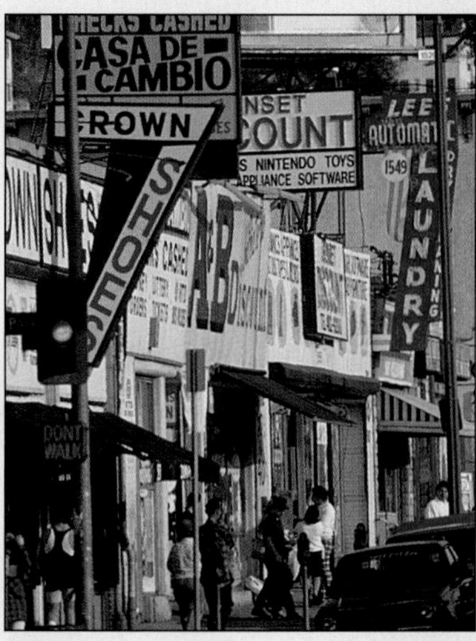

Echo Park, Los Angeles, a Mexican American neighborhood.

Making Meanings

A Voice
Aunt Fannie Fixes Bison Bourguignon
Tony Went to the Bodega . . .

First Thoughts

1. Describe the **speaker** in each of these poems with the first words that come to your mind.

Shaping Interpretations

2. Who is speaking in "A Voice"? To whom is she speaking?
3. What lines tell what the speaker in "A Voice" learned from her mother? What **tones** do you hear in this speaker's voice?
4. How does the speaker in Diane Glancy's poem feel about her heritage? What do you think she means by saying that her tongue is forever on the cold glass?
5. Summarize the main events of Tony's life journey as presented in Martín Espada's poem. Do you consider his life a success story? Why or why not?
6. These three poems *sound* like ordinary conversation, not like poetry. Two are written in **free verse**, and the **prose poem** is written as a paragraph. If someone said "But these aren't poetry," what would you say?

CHOICES: Building Your Portfolio

Writer's Notebook

1. Collecting Ideas for an Interpretation

Interpreting titles. When you interpret a poem (as you will in the Writer's Workshop on page 618), you begin with an interpretive claim and then back it up with evidence from the poem. One element of the poem you might want to interpret is its **title**. Choose one of the poems in this collection, and take notes as you think about how you would interpret the significance of the title. If you think the title is confusing, or not very good, say so!

WORK IN PROGRESS

"Aunt Fannie Fixes Bison Bourguignon" is a very odd title. The poem is about clashes of cultures. Aunt Fannie might be American Indian, and maybe she's showing off by fixing a French dish. But she's mixing cultures by using bison, not beef. BUT she's not in the poem at all! Why?

Creative Writing

2. Share Your Dream

Write a **prose poem** or a poem in **free verse** that expresses a dream about the future. You may want to focus on personal dreams or on the dreams of a group. Before you start, think about how you feel about the dream. Are you hopeful about it, disillusioned about it, or determined to win it? The Writer's Notebook activity you did on page 587 and the Quickwrite you did on page 607 might give you some ideas.

Speaking and Listening

3. Speaking for the Poets

Imagine that the **speakers** in these three poems are holding a round-table discussion on "Redefining the American Dream." Brainstorm to come up with some questions and problems they might discuss. Then, have volunteers play the roles of the speakers in the poems and one student serve as the moderator. You can expand the round-table discussion to include speakers from other poems you've read, such as "Mother to Son" (page 508), "George Gray" (page 522), and "I Am Offering This Poem" (page 551).

Creative Writing

4. Dream Chasers

Write about a person you know who's had the courage to fulfill a dream. Your subject could be an ordinary person, even someone in your family. Check the Quickwrite notes you took before reading "A Voice." You may want to try writing a poem.

Creative Writing

5. A Collection of Cultures

How important to you are your community and your ethnic background? Look back at the Quickwrite you did before reading "Aunt Fannie . . . ," and reread Rodriguez's comment (see ***Connections*** on page 610). Then, with a partner or alone, brainstorm words and images for a poem about your community or ethnic heritage. Collect your finished poems in an anthology.

Visual Literacy

6. Mapping Tony's Journey

Draw a map of Tony's life journey. Indicate Tony's age at his various stops, and illustrate the important places in his odyssey. Give the map an appropriate title.

EXTENDING *the theme*

AN ORAL HISTORY

Background

In 1890, the Miniconjou Sioux of South Dakota were made desperate by hunger, disease, and the loss of their land. Many of them found hope in a new ceremony, the Ghost Dance, that had been taught to them by a Paiute religious leader called Wovoka. In November 1890, alarmed by the frequent dances, and not understanding what they were, the Bureau of Indian Affairs' agent at Pine Ridge Reservation in South Dakota called for troops: 5,000 soldiers, led by General Nelson A. Miles, responded. Soldiers and Sioux alike wanted a nonviolent confrontation, but on December 15, 1890, soldiers killed the great leader Sitting Bull while trying to arrest him. Tensions mounted. On December 28, the Seventh Cavalry rounded up about 350 Sioux, led by Big Foot, who had been trying to reach safety at the Pine Ridge Reservation. The Sioux were placed in a camp on Wounded Knee Creek.

The next morning, 500 cavalrymen attempted to disarm Big Foot's people. Though neither side expected it, firing broke out—and when it was over, 153 Sioux, including Big Foot, were dead, and 44 were wounded—about half of them women and children (25 soldiers were killed and 39 wounded). The Sioux survivors were tracked down and killed.

Here is an oral history of the tragedy. It was told by a man who heard the story from his uncle, an eyewitness to the events.

Reading Skills and Strategies

Dialogue with the Text

Before you read, write in one column all you know or think you know about Wounded Knee and the Ghost Dance. In a second column, write some things you'd like to know. After you finish the oral history, fill in what you learned in a third column.

Know	Want to Know	Learned

The Ghost Dance at Wounded Knee

The dance leader told them not to be afraid of white men . . .

Chief Sitting Bull Copyrighted

told by **Dick Fool Bull**
recorded by Richard Erdoes

This is a true story; I wish it weren't. When it happened, I was a small boy, only about six or seven. To tell the truth, I'm not sure how old I am. I was born before the census takers[1] came in, so there's no record.

When I was a young boy, I liked to stick around my old uncle, because he always had stories to tell. Once he said, "There's something new coming, traveling on the wind. A new dance. A new prayer." He was talking about wanagi-wachipi, the ghost dance. "Short Bull and Kicking Bear traveled far," my uncle told me. "They went to see a holy man of another tribe far in the south, the Paiute tribe. They had heard that this holy man could bring dead people to life again, and that he could bring the buffalo back."

My uncle said it was very important and I must listen closely. Old Unc said:

> This holy man let Short Bull and Kicking Bear look into his hat. There they saw their dead relatives walking about. The holy man told them, "I'll give you something to eat that will kill you, but don't be afraid. I'll bring you back to life again." They believed him. They ate something and died, then found themselves walking in a new, beautiful land. They spoke with their parents and grandparents and with friends that the white soldiers had killed. Their friends were well, and this new world was like the old one, the one the white man had destroyed. It was full of game, full of antelope and buffalo. The grass was green and high, and though long-dead people from other tribes also lived in this new land, there was peace. All the Indian nations formed one tribe and could understand each other. Kicking Bear and Short Bull walked around and saw everything, and they were happy. Then the holy man of the Paiutes brought them back to life again.
>
> "You have seen it," he told them, "the new land I'm bringing. The earth will roll up like a blanket with all that bad white man's stuff, the fences and railroads and mines and telegraph poles; and underneath will be our old-young Indian earth with all our relatives come to life again."
>
> Then the holy man taught them a new dance, a new song, a new prayer. He gave them sacred red paint. He even made the sun die: It was all covered with black and disappeared. Then he brought the sun to life again.
>
> Short Bull and Kicking Bear came back bringing us the good news. Now everywhere we are dancing this new dance to roll up the earth, to bring back the dead. A new world is coming.

This Old Unc told me.

Then I saw it myself: the dancing. People were holding each other by the hand, singing, whirling around, looking at the sun. They had a little spruce tree in the middle of the dance circle. They wore special shirts painted with the sun, the moon, the stars, and magpies.[2] They whirled around; they didn't stop dancing.

Some of the dancers fell down in a swoon, as if they were dead. The medicine men fanned them with sweet-smelling cedar smoke and they came to life again. They told the people, "We were dead. We went to the moon and the morning star. We found our dead fathers and mothers there, and we talked to them." When they woke up, these people held in their hands star rocks, moon rocks, different kinds of rocks from those we have on this earth. They clutched strange meats from star and moon animals. The dance leader told them not to be afraid of white men who forbade them to dance this wanagi-wachipi. They told them that the ghost shirts they wore would not let any white man's bullets through. So they danced; I saw it.

The earth never rolled up. The buffalo never came back, and the dead relatives never came to life again. It was the soldier who came; why, nobody knew. The dance was a peaceful one,

1. census (sen′səs) **takers:** official recorders of a population's size and its makeup in terms of income, age, gender, and other categories.

2. magpies (mag′pīz′): black-and-white birds with long, tapering tails and a habit of noisy chattering. The magpie was one of several sacred birds of the Ghost Dance.

harming nobody, but I guess the white people thought it was a war dance.

Many people were afraid of what the soldiers would do. We had no guns anymore and hardly had any horses left. We depended on the white man for everything, yet the whites were afraid of us, just as we were afraid of them.

Then when the news spread that Sitting Bull had been killed at Standing Rock for being with the ghost dancers, the people were really scared. Some of the old people said: "Let's go to Pine Ridge and give ourselves up, because the soldiers won't shoot us if we do. Old Red Cloud will protect us. Also, they're handing out rations up there."

So my father and mother and Old Unc got the buggy and their old horse and drove with us children toward Pine Ridge. It was cold and snowing. It wasn't a happy ride; all the grown-ups were worried. Then the soldiers stopped us. They had big fur coats on, bear coats. They were warm and we were freezing, and I remember wishing I had such a coat. They told us to go no further, to stop and make a camp right there. They told the same thing to everybody who came, by foot, or horse, or buggy. So there was a camp but little to eat and little firewood, and the soldiers made a ring around us and let nobody leave.

Then suddenly there was a strange noise, maybe four, five miles away, like the tearing of a big blanket, the biggest blanket in the world. As soon as he heard it, Old Unc burst into tears. My old ma started to keen[3] as for the dead, and people were running around, weeping, acting crazy.

I asked Old Unc, "Why is everybody crying?"

He said, "They are killing them; they are killing our people over there!"

My father said, "That noise—that's not the ordinary soldier guns. These are the big wagon guns which tear people to bits—into little pieces!" I could not understand it, but everybody was weeping, and I wept too. Then a day later—or was it two? No, I think it was the next day, we passed by there. Old Unc said:

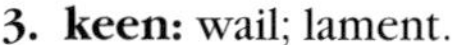

3. **keen:** wail; lament.

Arapaho Ghost Dance shirt (c. 1890). Tanned elk hide, eagle feather, pigment (40″× 24½″).

Buffalo Bill Historical Center, Cody, Wyoming. Chandler-Pohrt Collection, Gift of The Searle Family Trust and The Paul Stock Foundation.

"You children might as well see it; look and remember."

There were dead people all over, mostly women and children, in a ravine near a stream called Chankpe-opi Wakpala, Wounded Knee Creek. The people were frozen, lying there in all kinds of postures, their motion frozen too. The soldiers, who were stacking up bodies like firewood, did not like us passing by. They told us to leave there, double-quick or else. Old Unc said: "We'd better do what they say right now, or we'll lie there too."

So we went on toward Pine Ridge, but I had seen. I had seen a dead mother with a dead baby sucking at her breast. The little baby had on a tiny beaded cap with the design of the American flag.

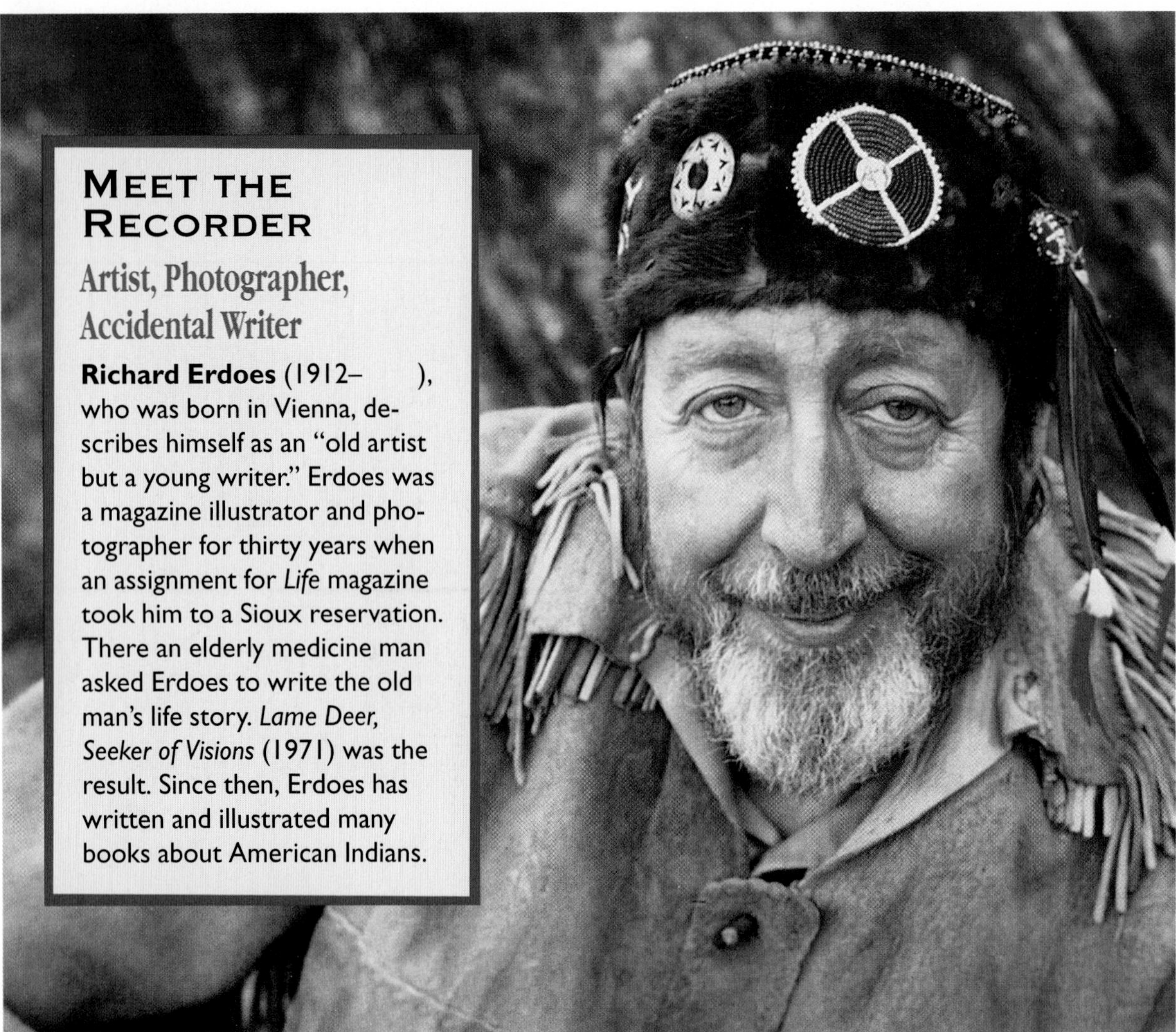

Meet the Recorder

Artist, Photographer, Accidental Writer

Richard Erdoes (1912–   ), who was born in Vienna, describes himself as an "old artist but a young writer." Erdoes was a magazine illustrator and photographer for thirty years when an assignment for *Life* magazine took him to a Sioux reservation. There an elderly medicine man asked Erdoes to write the old man's life story. *Lame Deer, Seeker of Visions* (1971) was the result. Since then, Erdoes has written and illustrated many books about American Indians.

Finding Common Ground

1. Get together with three or four classmates to compare your responses to this oral history. Be sure to refer to the notes you made before and immediately after your reading. Do you and other readers have the same kinds of questions and comments, or are they quite different?
2. After comparing your responses, draw up some questions your group would like to discuss about Wounded Knee and about this oral history in particular.
3. After you discuss those questions with your group, open up the discussion to the whole class.
4. Try to find points of view and details you agree on. At the end of your talks, what points of discussion are you, as a class, ready to agree and disagree on?
5. Be sure to include in your discussions your feelings about including this piece in a collection on dreams—lost and found.

Cats, the Poems

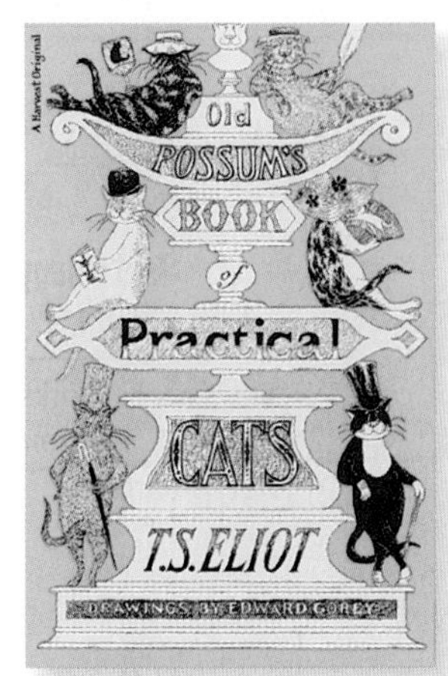

If you liked Andrew Lloyd Webber's musical *Cats*, don't miss *Old Possum's Book of Practical Cats* by T. S. Eliot (Harcourt Brace), the poems that inspired the musical. Meet Macavity the Mystery Cat and his fellow felines—Rum Tum Tugger, the Jellicles, Mr. Mistoffelees, and many other big-deal cats—in this little volume illustrated by Edward Gorey. Or listen to the audio cassette of Sir John Gielgud and Irene Worth reading these poems aloud (HarperCollins).

The World Outside and Within

Here is a collection of some favorite poems by Emily Dickinson carefully selected by Thomas H. Johnson, the Dickinson expert. In *Final Harvest* (Little, Brown), you'll hear the voice of a careful observer, a writer aware of the world around her and of the world within.

Celebrating Earth, Sea, and Sky

Poetry for the Earth, edited by Sara Dunn and Alan Scholefield (Fawcett Columbine), contains a wide selection of nature poems from around the world. From haiku and tribal riddles to blank verse and free verse, poets past and present express delight in nature and concern for our environment.

Now Hear This

You may think of poetry as a quiet pursuit, but *Poetry Out Loud*, edited by Robert Alden Rubin (Algonquin Books), reminds us that poems are meant to be heard as well as seen. You'll find more than a hundred poems to read aloud in this "Burst of Verses"—from Shakespeare's songs to "Casey at the Bat," from "Jabberwocky" to the haunting ballad "The Unquiet Grave."

Put Your Headphones On

Find out the favorite poems of actors such as Patrick Stewart and James Earl Jones. On *The Silver Lining* (BMP Audio) you will hear twenty-three actors read their favorites, by poets including Emily Dickinson and E.E. Cummings. This recording has been critically acclaimed in *USA Today, Poet's Corner,* and *Billboard.*

BUILDING YOUR PORTFOLIO

Writer's Workshop

Technology HELP

See Writer's Workshop 2 CD-ROM. *Assignment: Interpretation.*

ASSIGNMENT

Write an essay that presents your interpretation of a poem, a play, a story, a novel, or an essay. Support your interpretation with evidence from the work.

AIM

To inform; to persuade.

AUDIENCE

Your teacher, your classmates, or readers of a school literary magazine. (You choose.)

EXPOSITORY WRITING

SUPPORTING AN INTERPRETATION

In this workshop, you'll interpret a text and support your interpretation with detailed evidence. This activity may also help you master test taking. You've probably taken tests in which you've been asked to show your comprehension of literary passages. The essay you'll write for this Writer's Workshop will be similar to an essay you might write for such a test—a college entrance exam, for instance.

Prewriting

1. Choose a Text to Interpret

WORK IN PROGRESS

What have you read recently that moved you? Which literary work (in the poetry collections or somewhere else in this book) struck you as the most beautifully written? Which made you think the most? Which would you recommend to a friend? Did any make you angry? You can choose to interpret any text, but you'll do your best work if you write about one that you have very strong feelings about. Be sure to check your Writer's Notebook entries for this collection. You might find your topic there.

2. Record Your Responses to Your Text

Once you've chosen your text, reread it. Write your responses to specific passages in a two-column format (see the chart opposite). Comment on passages that seem important to the work or ones that puzzle you or please you. Record any emotional reactions or personal experiences that the text brings up for you. You don't have to make judgments; just respond. Jot down feelings, thoughts, memories, questions.

You will want to read the text several times. After each reading, you might **freewrite** for five or ten minutes. Compare your comments after each reading. What new insights have you added? What passages still puzzle you?

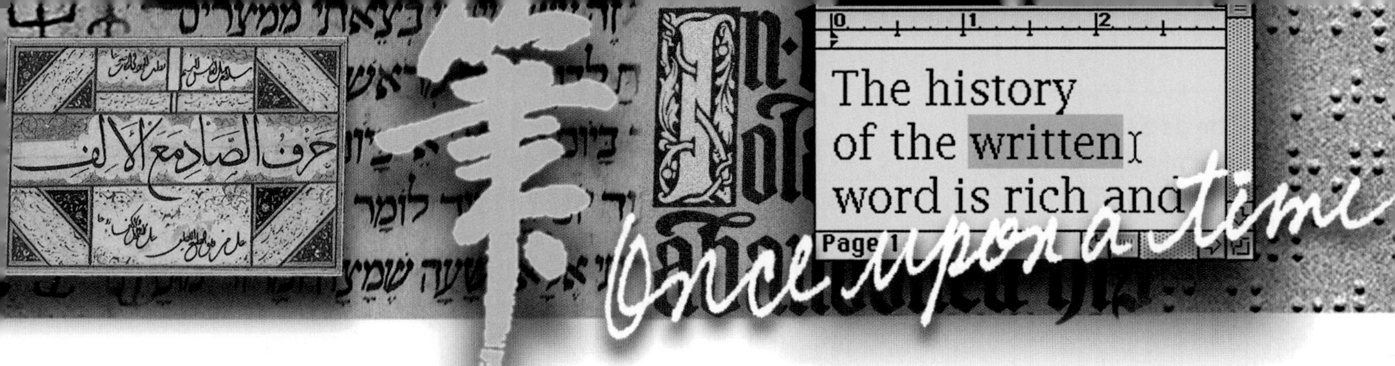
The history
of the written
word is rich and
Once upon a time
Page 1

Text: "We Real Cool" (page 599)	
Passage	**My Response**
1. Subtitle: "The Pool Players./Seven at The Golden Shovel."	Reveals who the "we" of the poem are. I would have preferred imagining their identity. Why The Golden Shovel?
2. "We/Strike straight."	Strike could mean "hit" the pool ball or "use force" in general.
3. "Sing sin."	They glamorize something they shouldn't do.
4. "Die soon."	Key line; shocks me.

3. Focus on a Main Idea

What have you discovered that interests you most about the text? What suggests itself to you as a **main idea**? Jot down some possible statements about your interpretation of the text. Focus on one. This will be your **interpretive claim**, the main idea that binds your work together as a unified whole. This is the claim you'll need to support with evidence.

4. Collect Supporting Evidence

In order to make your interpretation of the text convincing, you need to do more than state your main idea or interpretive claim. You have to back up your interpretation by showing exactly where and how you found evidence for your idea in the text itself. Look over the text again to be sure that no parts contradict your interpretation. Jot down direct quotations (in poetry, exact words and images) that support each claim you'll make. You may also support your interpretation by recalling your own experience.

Try It Out

You might want to **paraphrase,** or restate in your own words, the text you are focusing on, especially any key passages and important figures of speech. How would you paraphrase these lines of poetry? (Go back and read them in the context of the entire poem.)

1. "Flick stands tall among the idiot pumps" (line 7, page 592)
2. "Family stories sing of what lives in the blood." (line 24, page 603)

Now choose three to five complex lines or passages from the text you want to write about. Paraphrase these lines as you just did for the lines in "Ex-Basketball Player" and "A Voice." What does this paraphrasing add to your understanding of the text?

Drafting

1. Introduce Your Subject and Orient Your Readers

Your introduction should identify the text (title and author) and give any background information your audience needs to understand the work as a whole or the particular aspect of it you'll be focusing on. Write a **thesis statement** in which you present your main idea. Then, try to incorporate it into your opening statement or paragraph.

2. Elaborate: Present Your Evidence

Devote the bulk of your essay to supporting your interpretive claim with details from the text (quotes, paraphrases) and reasoned argument. Elaborate further by describing your own experiences or the experiences of others as evidence. (For instance, the personal experience related by Luis Rodriguez in "The Streets of the Barrio" (page 610) could support an interpretation of Espada's poem as a celebration of the poet's ethnic roots.)

3. Be Orderly

Organize and present your evidence in a logical order. You could move through the text chronologically, or you could work from your strongest argument to your weakest, or vice versa. Transitional words and expressions (like *first* and *most important*) will help your readers follow the logic of your presentation.

4. Make Your Conclusion Count

In your concluding paragraph, don't simply repeat your claim. Give your audience some sense of what is important about the text and what new insights you've gained. The Student Model that follows is an interpretation of David Wagoner's poem "Tumbleweed" (see the side columns at left and on page 621).

Student Model

On the surface, "Tumbleweed" by David Wagoner is about a tumbleweed. The underlying subject of the poem is a certain kind of person.

Gives title and author and makes interpretive claim.

In the first stanza, the speaker is watching tumbleweeds wobble, bounce, and spring aimlessly along the ground. Nature's own tumbleweed seems to carry with it some human characteristics, reminding you of a drifter or an unstable

Paraphrases first stanza and supports claim with personal experience.

Thesis Statements (Interpretive Claims)

Examples

- In "Ex-Basketball Player" by John Updike, Pearl Avenue, which comes to a dead end (lines 1–3), embodies the poem's central meaning: Flick is on a dead-end path in life.
- "Aunt Fannie Fixes Bison Bourguignon" by Diane Glancy is a very ironically (maybe satirically) titled poem about loss.

Tumbleweed

Here comes another,
bumping over the
sage
Among the grease-
wood, wobbling
diagonally
Downhill, then
skimming a mo-
ment on its edge,
Tilting lopsided,
bounding end over
end
And springing from
the puffs of its own
dust
To catch at the barbed
wire
And hang there,
shaking, like a
riddled prisoner.

Half the sharp seeds
have fallen from
this tumbler,

(continued)

Student Model (continued)

person who is just going through life doing this or that. Such people are, in a sense, tumbleweeds.

A tumbleweed wasn't always a tumbler. It used to be a plant rooted in the earth. Since these roots were shallow, when a strong wind or storm came along, they were ripped right out of the ground. Now the plant merely tumbles along, pushed by the wind, because it has been detached from its source of life. Many people are just like the tumbleweed. Once happily rooted in a job, family, or religion, when an overpowering circumstance came along, they were torn apart. They are now lost without their daily job and comfortable lifestyle and are pushed along to nowhere by society.

Logically develops parallels between image of tumbleweed and image of persons who drift.

In the second stanza, the speaker states that half of the seeds have been knocked out of the tumbleweed. Then, when the tumbleweed is stopped by a fence, the speaker carries it to freedom. It jerks wildly, as if to get away from the helping hands. In the same way, many people who have lost things important to them become dull from the experience and come to a stopping point. When they have the chance of freedom, they lash out and yaw away as soon as they are let go.

Proceeds chronologically through the poem, citing supporting words and images.

This poem reveals a comparison between tumbleweeds and people. I thought it was humorous in many ways. You can see tumbleweeds along the side of a road. You will also meet many of them.

Concludes with a restatement of her interpretation and gives strong response to the poem.

—Denise Vibe
North High School
Bakersfield, California

Tumbleweed *(continued)*

Knocked out for good
by head-stands and
pratfalls
Between here and
wherever it grew up.
I carry it in the wind
across the road
To the other fence.
It jerks in my
hands,
Butts backwards,
corkscrews, lunges
and swivels,
Then yaws away as
soon as it's let go,
Hopping the scrub
uphill like a kicked
maverick.
The air goes hard and
straight through
the wires and
weeds.
Here comes another,
flopping among
the sage.

—David Wagoner

Evaluation Criteria

A good interpretive essay

1. *identifies the subject*
2. *makes a clear interpretive claim*
3. *supports the claim with sufficient evidence, details, and quotations*
4. *argues logically and consistently*
5. *concludes with a compelling response*

Sentence Workshop HELP

Streamlining wordy sentences: page 623.

Proofreading Tips

- Check punctuation (quotation marks or underlining) of titles.
- Check quotations for accuracy against your sources, and be sure you have used quotation marks correctly with other marks of punctuation.

Communications Handbook HELP

See Proofreaders' Marks.

Language Handbook HELP

See Italics (underlining), pages 1053–1054, and Quotation Marks, 1054–1056.

Publishing Tip

Read your essay aloud to classmates familiar with your text, and lead a group discussion of your interpretation.

Evaluating and Revising

1. Peer Review

Exchange papers with students who have read the same texts. As you read a classmate's work, ask yourself questions like those below and offer specific suggestions for improvement:

- Does the interpretation make sense to me? Is it an issue worth considering, or does it seem too obvious to argue?
- Is evidence presented to support every aspect of the claim? Is there enough evidence from the text?

Revision Model

	Peer Comments
In the first stanza, the speaker ~~in this poem~~ is ~~standing somewhere and~~ watching ~~the kinds of plant called~~	*First sentence is wordy. Try to tighten.*
tumbleweeds ~~move~~ ^wobble, bounce, and spring^ aimlessly ~~without a clear direction~~ along the ground.	*Replace "move" with a specific verb?*
Nature's own tumbleweed seems to carry with it some human characteristics, reminding you of a ^drifter or an unstable^ person who is just ^going through life^ doing this or that.	*Can you elaborate here?*

2. Self-Evaluation

Evaluate your peers' responses carefully. How successful have you been in convincing them of your interpretation? If your readers seem unconvinced, include additional evidence. Decide which of your thoughts and your peers' advice you want to follow. Rework your draft.

BUILDING YOUR PORTFOLIO

Sentence Workshop

Streamlining Wordy Sentences

When you are writing fiction or essays, use varied and interesting sentences that say what you want to say in the fewest number of words. Unnecessary words are distracting and make it more difficult for your reader to get your basic message. Compare the following sentences:

WORDY Back in my childhood when I was a young boy, I had a desire to stick close around an old relative, who was my uncle, because he always had stories to tell that interested me greatly.

REVISED "When I was a young boy, I liked to stick around my old uncle, because he always had stories to tell."

—Dick Fool Bull, "The Ghost Dance at Wounded Knee" (page 614)

Notice that a wordy sentence like the one above often repeats the same idea in different words. The unnecessary words in the phrases below are in brackets.

[Back in my childhood] when I was a young boy, I had a desire to stick [close] around [an old relative, who was] my uncle . . .

Writers of wordy sentences often use two or three words to say what could be said in one word:

liked
~~had a desire~~ to stick

Writer's Workshop Follow-up: Revising

As you revise your essay for the Writer's Workshop (page 618), read your sentences aloud or ask a classmate to read them to you. Circle any sentences that seem to go on too long or are hard to follow. Cross out repeated or unnecessary words and phrases, and tighten your ideas by trying to express the same thought in fewer words.

Language Handbook HELP

See Revising Wordy Sentences, page 1045.

Try It Out

Streamline the following wordy sentences. Since there is more than one effective way to convey a message, compare your revisions with those of other students and with the original sentences.

1. The man who delivers the mail is in the position of being a family friend, and the owner of the store that is on the corner will let me buy from him without paying cash because he knows that I am not going to skip out of town without paying him what I owe him. (page 610)
2. People are on their porches, sitting and standing; loud music blares from windows that are open in the buildings; and round circles of brown children noisily slurp ice-cold snow cones and engage in playing games. (page 610)
3. When the news spread far and wide that Sitting Bull had been murdered and killed at the place called Standing Rock for the reason of his being with the ghost dancers, the people were really overtaken with fear and anxiety. (page 615)

Reading for Life

Interpreting Graphs

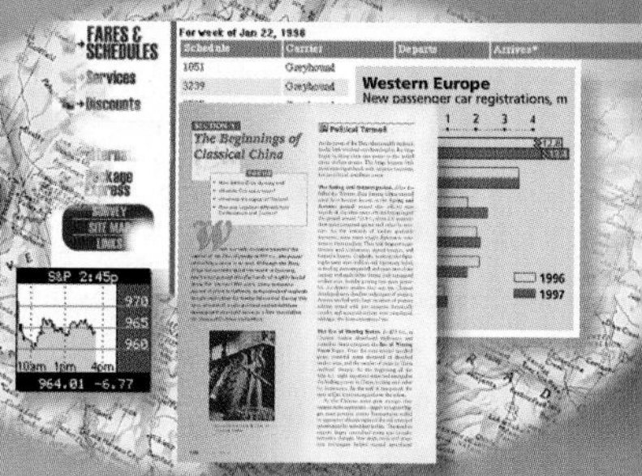

Situation

After reading "The Ghost Dance at Wounded Knee," you and a friend have become interested in the American Indian population in the United States. You find information on the Internet displayed in graphic form, and you want to interpret it correctly.

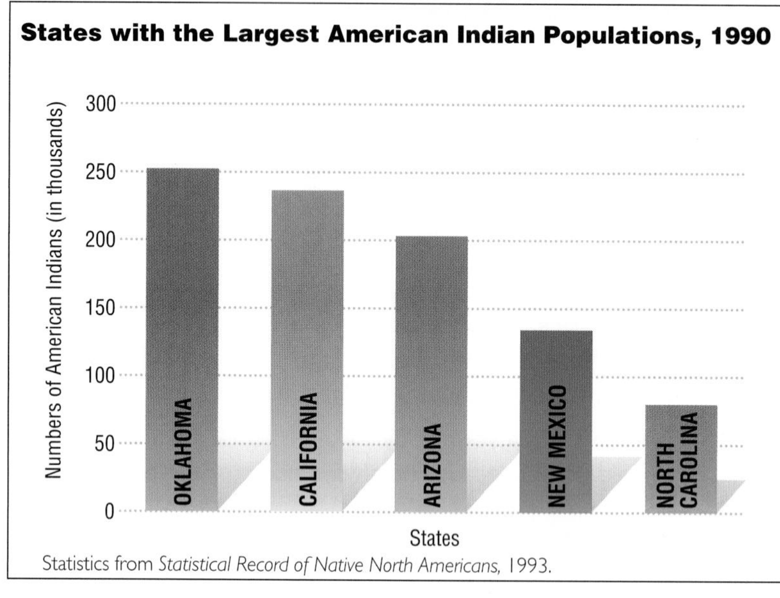

Statistics from *Statistical Record of Native North Americans,* 1993.

Strategies

Understand graphic forms.

- There are several kinds of graphic forms. A **bar graph** (shown at right) compares quantities within categories. A **line graph** usually shows changes in quantities over time. A **pie graph**, or **circle graph**, shows percentages of a whole. A **time line** shows the order of events in time. For more information about these types of graphs, see Reading Maps, Charts, and Graphs in the Communications Handbook.

Interpret the information.

- Read the **title** carefully to identify the subject and purpose of the graph.
- Read all **headings** and **labels**. Make sure you understand the categories of information being depicted.
- Note how the data are organized. For example, do numbers increase or decrease? What relationships exist between groups of data? Is there an order of events? Are there trends?
- For a bar graph (like the one above), note the units of measurement used on the vertical axis. Look for a key indicating the amounts represented by the numbers: a "5," for example, might mean "5 thousand." (If the units are very large, the graph might indicate estimates rather than specific numbers.)

Using the Strategies

Apply these strategies in order to analyze the bar graph in the box above.

1. How are American Indian populations categorized? What does each bar represent?
2. How many people are represented between increments on the vertical axis? How can you tell?
3. Which state on the graph has the largest American Indian population? the smallest?
4. According to the graph, what is the American Indian population in Arizona? Is this number exact or an approximation?

Extending the Strategies

Find a graph in a magazine on a topic that interests you. Analyze the information and share your findings.

Learning for Life

Presenting an Arts Festival

Problem

Imaginations need to be nourished, or they will shrink. Young children confidently draw and paint and make up stories and songs. Later, however, most insist they "can't draw" and "can't write." How can you encourage and celebrate creativity?

Project

Form committees to plan a festival celebrating the arts (literature, painting, drawing, photography, music, dance, drama). Choose the art form that interests you most.

Preparation

Each committee will decide these questions:

1. What kind of festival? Brainstorm to gather ideas: perhaps a series of poetry readings to which you'll invite the whole community; perhaps a month-long student art and photography exhibit and contest. You might search the Internet for sites that offer information on other festivals, exhibits, and arts presentations. Choose a format that seems both exciting *and* workable for your school or community.
2. Where and when will you hold the festival?
3. Who is your target audience? (The students in your school? a special audience of elementary school students or senior citizens?)
4. List all the steps needed to turn your idea into an event. What problems do you foresee? Who can help?
5. How much will the festival cost? Where will the money come from?

Procedure

1. Write a clear proposal and present it to whoever needs to give permission. Persuade that person or group that the festival is a good idea and that your class can do it.
2. Publicize the festival: first, to invite participation; later, to round up an audience.
3. Encourage everyone to submit a work or to perform. If a student's work is not selected, encourage him or her to submit other entries.

Presentation

Suppose, for example, you're planning a poetry festival. You might try one of these formats:

1. A Single Performance

In an assembly or evening event, students might recite poems they've written, interpret poems they especially like by other poets, or perform original songs and raps. Students might also comment briefly on their works. You might consider videotaping the performance.

2. Poetry Week

Every day for a week (maybe during lunch or after school), students might perform original poems or interpret their favorite ones. You might display manuscripts of students' poems and class anthologies, too.

3. Festival Documentary

Plan a Poetry Day and invite family and friends. You might have all-day performances in the library, an exhibit, a contest, and a Meet-the-Poets talk show. Keep a written record or videotape a documentary of your planning, preparation, and presentation. Put a copy of the written record or videotape in your school's media center so that students in other classes can appreciate the festival and use your experience as a resource.

Processing

What did you learn about working in groups to accomplish a major project? What did you learn about getting people to participate in events? What would you do differently next time?

The Drama Collection

A scene from Thornton Wilder's *Our Town,* as produced at the Long Wharf Theater, New Haven, Connecticut, December 1987.

Drama began as the act of a whole community. Ideally, there would be no spectators. In practice, every member of the audience should feel like an understudy.

—W. H. Auden

A Writer on Playwriting

A Conversation with Robert Anderson

Playwrights may have a special approach to their writing because they deal with the quicksilver of the spoken word. Without the luxury of detailed physical descriptions or long passages of exposition, the playwright must cut to the chase and give the characters life through their speeches and actions. Before you read Robert Anderson's* I Never Sang for My Father, *which begins on page 638, think about what Anderson has to say about writing plays.

Q: Where do you get ideas for plays? Are they autobiographical?

Anderson: Arthur Miller has said that he is in every play he writes. This does not mean he is a character in the play; it means that the play is in some way an expression of his response to his world, to his experience. Tennessee Williams said that he wrote about what bugged him. Each of us is "bugged," or disturbed, by something different. Each of us has a kind of built-in Geiger counter which responds to different things, is sensitive to different areas of life, is moved by different experiences. This leads each of us to speak and to write with passion and intensity in different voices.

When I am asked "Is the story autobiographical?" I answer, "If I told you it was all made up, you'd feel cheated. If I told you it was all real, you'd be embarrassed." But I would not have written the play if I had not been moved to write it by something meaningful to me.

As to where I get the ideas for my plays: I keep journals and notebooks mostly of my own thoughts, things that "bug" me, meaningful moments I want to record.

So when I want to write a play, I will often go back to these notebooks and journals and see what has "bugged" me.

Q: Have you ever had a time when you couldn't think of anything to write about?

Anderson: You go through bad periods. Shortly after my wife died, I was really stuck. I took John Steinbeck out to breakfast and asked, "What do you do when you're stuck?" He said he wrote poetry to find out what he felt strongly about, because poetry cannot be written without emotion. There has to be passion—something that reaches out. The plays we treasure are the ones that move us to laughter or excitement or tears.

Q: How would you describe your process as a writer?

Anderson: Everybody has a different process. Neil Simon tells me he just sits down

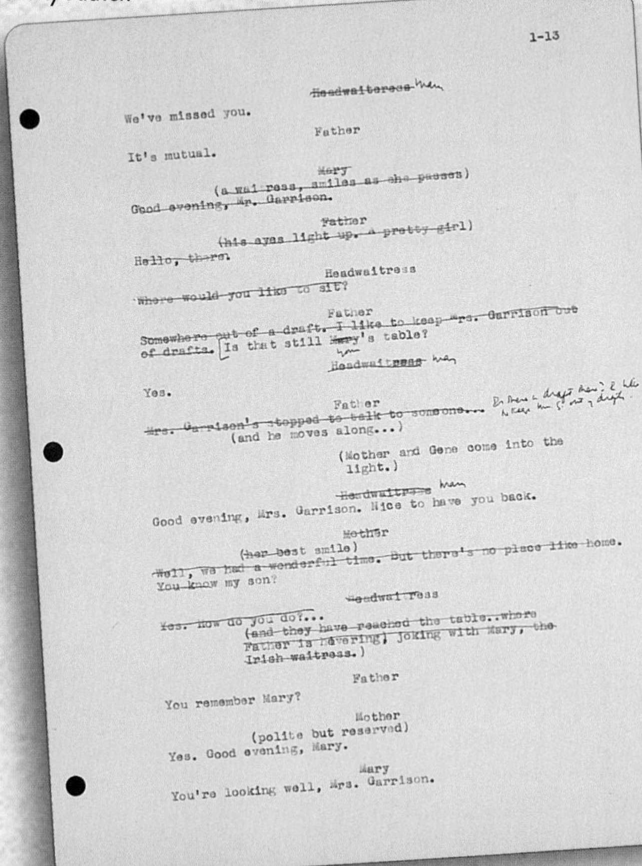
1-13

~~Headwaiteress~~ man

We've missed you.

Father

It's mutual.

~~Mary~~

~~(a waitress, smiles as she passes)~~

~~Good evening, Mr. Garrison.~~

~~Father~~

~~(his eyes light up. A pretty girl)~~

~~Hello, there.~~

Headwaitress

~~Where would you like to sit?~~

Father

~~Somewhere out of a draft. I like to keep Mrs. Garrison out of drafts.~~ Is that still ~~Mary~~'s table?

~~Headwaitress~~ man

Yes.

Father

~~Mrs. Garrison's stopped to talk to someone...~~

(and he moves along...)

(Mother and Gene come into the light.)

~~Headwaitress~~ man

Good evening, Mrs. Garrison. Nice to have you back.

~~Mother~~

(~~her best~~ smile)

~~Well, we had a wonderful time. But there's no place like home.~~

~~You know~~ my son?

~~Headwaitress~~

~~Yes. How do you do?...~~

~~(and they have reached the table..where Father is hovering) joking with Mary, the Irish waitress.~~)

Father

You remember Mary?

Mother

(polite but reserved)

Yes. Good evening, Mary.

Mary

You're looking well, Mrs. Garrison.

Manuscript page from *I Never Sang for My Father.*

with an idea and starts to write the scenes and the dialogue. If his writing doesn't go anyplace, he throws it away. I can't do that. After I have found something in my journals or notebook that "wriggles," that seems promising and that engages me, I go "fishing." Each day for many weeks I cast my hook, baited with the idea that interested me . . . I don't try for any shape or form at this point: I just write down thoughts and ideas spun off from the original notebook idea.

Q: When do you get to writing the dialogue?

Anderson: After I have worked out where I am going to begin the story and where I am going to end it. It's like knowing I'm going from Boston to New York, but I'm not sure which towns I'll go through. As I write, I may change the route, but I usually don't change the ending, because the resolution of the story is what I have been building up to.

Q: What do you do when you revise?

Anderson: I don't revise as I go along. The most important thing is to get the scene "off the floor." To keep the emotional intensity between the characters and to get it rising, I don't want to stop and rewrite. A first draft is a "white-hot" experience for me. It is in a sense an unconscious act based on conscious preparation. Writing dialogue is a joy. If you know the characters, they just speak.

After the first draft, I put the play away for a short while, and then I read it as though someone else had written it. It is in some way still fresh for me. If I had revised as I went along, I would have lost this effect of a "first reading." Then, still working in longhand, I make notes for revisions in the margins.

Q: Do you ever think as you're writing that no one will be interested in your work?

Anderson: Yes. I often push away from a good day's writing and say to myself, "Nobody is going to be interested in this. It's too personal." And, of course, that is exactly what they *are* interested in. They hear the lines, and they say, "You, too?"

I don't talk about my work or show it to anyone while I'm working on it. It's as though I had a secret or a gift, and I'm not going to show it to anybody until I'm finished. And then, of course, everyone will love it!

Q: Why do you refer to English courses as Life 101?

Anderson: It's the only course you take in which you talk about people and families. That's what stories are about.

Drama: Taking Action

by Robert Anderson

Drama is probably the oldest form of storytelling. The earliest dramatists, in order to get and hold the attention of their audiences, probably used the same principles that great playwrights followed much later.

Imagine a Stone Age hunter coming in from the hunt with his companions. He is eager to tell the people in his village what happened, and he starts his story: "We came upon this bear and we followed him and then he turned on us and we killed him." As he gets to the exciting part, one of the other hunters might jump up and act the bear. Then another might join in to show what part he played in the hunt by jabbing at the bear with his spear.

A week later someone might say, "Tell us again how you killed that bear." And in repeating the performance, the tribesmen are no longer reporting; they are acting out a drama.

© Paul Davis

The "Bare Bones" of Drama

The first time they reported the kill, the tribesmen might simply have told what happened: They went out hunting, found a bear, and killed it. But the second time they act out the story, they want to make the hunt more exciting, so they include a **foreshadowing,** or hint, of danger. Perhaps they create **suspense** by indicating that there had been rumors of a marauding bear in the vicinity.

Now the hunter-actor-playwrights have created the story of a **desperate situation:** The people in the "drama" must do something to save themselves from the bear, who might return and destroy the village. A great deal is at stake. After some discussion they decide to take action: They will hunt the bear.

THE GLASS MENAGERIE
THE PLAYBILL
FOR · THE · PLAYHOUSE

Since plays and stories are usually not about groups, let's imagine that the story now becomes personalized and focused as the chief tells his young son that he must come along. Suppose further that the playwrights decide to make it the young son's first hunt and that he is afraid.

Now we have two matters at stake: the safety of the village and the testing of the son. We also have two different types of **conflict:** the **external** threat posed by the bear and the son's **internal** struggle to overcome his fear.

In reenacting their drama, the hunter-actors now meet the bear and throw their spears, but they either miss or only wound the bear. Now what? The action mounts to a new crisis: Enraged, the bear charges and kills the chief. Seeing his father dead, the youth overcomes his fear, recovers one of the spears, rushes wildly at the bear, and kills it. Now the play is over.

In this story of the bear hunt, we have most of the basic elements of drama. That is, we have the **bare bones,** or the framework, on which any drama is built.

1. **Characters** the audience cares about are placed in a more or less desperate situation with a great deal at stake.
2. The characters have a **conflict,** or problem, that engages them in a struggle—they want something (to save themselves), and they take action against a formidable opponent (the bear) to get it.
3. The story mounts in tension because **suspense** is created. Questions come to the audience's minds. (Will the hunters kill the bear? Will the boy measure up?)
4. The story progresses to its **climax,** or the moment of greatest emotional intensity, just before the outcome of the conflict is revealed. (The boy takes up his father's spear in fury.)
5. The main character undergoes a **change** (from fear to courage) under the pressure of the action. (He kills the bear.)

The Importance of Conflict and Action

Because conflict is central to any story, almost all plays involve action. But most plays do not involve physical action like hunting bears. (The movies can do this kind of thing better, though of course in some of Shakespeare's plays, there are duels and street fights and battles.) Plays are usually concerned with more subtle conflicts between characters, which must be worked out not in physical action but rather through speech.

Most plays do not involve physical action like hunting bears. Plays are usually concerned with more subtle conflicts between characters, which must be worked out not in physical action but rather through speech.

Speech is itself a kind of action. When we open our mouths to speak, we do so with some kind of intention: We want to convey some information, to argue, to communicate with someone. In fact, we can fight and struggle and wound and try to achieve our "wants" and overcome obstacles with words. In a courtroom, two lawyers can use words to argue, to develop evidence, to drag out admissions from unwilling witnesses, and even to destroy a witness on the stand. A person trying to persuade a friend not to give up hope is engaged in an action as serious and as tense as a police officer chasing a thief through the streets of San Francisco. A man, desperately in love, trying to convince a skeptical woman that he is in love with her, is struggling in an action as important as two people dueling. He, too, is dueling—but with words.

In each of these cases, the conflict is the result not of opposing physical forces but of opposing attitudes and wants. The actions taken to work out the conflicts are not physical; they are expressions of ideas and attitudes—that is, they are *words.*

The important thing in any conflict is the meaning of the struggle to the man or woman involved.

The important thing in any conflict is the meaning of the struggle to the man or woman involved: At stake might be life, self-respect, belief, security, happiness. No conflict in and of itself is very interesting for long unless the dramatist makes us care about the person, unless we become involved with the psychological complexity arising from the situation, and unless we know how desperately important the outcome is to the character.

The same is true of life itself. If we suddenly come upon a baseball game being played by teams we know nothing about, we may take a mild interest in the skill of both sides. But obviously mere skill is not what makes fans jump up and down and scream. They care fervently about one side or the other. They know the various problems of the team and the players. Will the rookie pitcher be demoted to the bullpen because of his fight last night with the manager? Will he be able to pitch, knowing his son is in the hospital?

The merely skillful use of the "bare bones" of playwriting does not make plays good. Good plays are made by the mind and sensitivity of the playwrights, their depth of feeling, their powers of observation and imagination, as well as their understanding of the complexities of human nature.

Scene from the movie *Death of a Salesman* by Arthur Miller, starring Dustin Hoffman (center).

One of the pleasures of the theater is watching the *process* through which things happen. A novelist telling the story of *I Never Sang for My Father,* for example, might tell you, "Alice and Gene discussed their feelings about their mother." In the theater that is not enough. In fact, it is not *anything,* because we want to see *how* it happened. *What* did they say to each other? Show us! Let us live through the experience. Play it! Sometimes a playwright may write an outline of a scene between two people but then, on trying to write the scene itself, finds "it won't play." In other words, the outline might say, "Alice and Gene talk about how they feel about their mother." But when the playwright comes to write the scene, for some reason Alice and Gene just won't say anything.

When I have written movies based on novels, I have frequently been faced with the difference between the *telling* done by the novelist and the *showing* demanded of the dramatic writer. Let us say that at the end of a chapter, the novelist has a boy fall down a well. At the opening of the next chapter, the novelist might say, "After his friends had helped him out of the well, the boy went home." If I had to rewrite this as a drama,where the audience delights in *seeing* and demands to see *process,* I would have to invent the whole scene of getting the boy out of the well.

Thus drama is a medium in which *process* is important—we care about *how* a scene develops, not just *what* a scene accomplishes. This is why we can go back so many times to see plays and movies when we already know the outcome. We want to see again that funny scene where . . . or that sad scene when. . . .

The Playwright's Collaborators

A novel or a short story exists in its final form on the page. Readers, in a sense, "perform" the story in their own minds. But a play is meant to be presented on a stage, so the **actors, directors, stage designers, lighting designers, costumers,** and even musicians become the playwright's collaborators.

It is this collaboration that can make playwriting the most rewarding kind of writing—and the most difficult. In addition to having a story to tell and the ability to conceive it in a basically dramatic form, playwrights must know *how* to write for the theater. They must know how to evoke a response from an audience, not by using words alone but by creating a "theater poetry"—by using all the talents of their collaborators, all the elements of the theater available to them.

We care about *how* a scene develops, not just *what* a scene accomplishes. This is why we can go back so many times to see plays and movies when we already know the outcome.

For example, suppose a beautiful actress, who creates by her personal magnetism a kind of magic, slowly moves across a dimly lit stage to a man sitting despondently in a chair. She hesitates, then touches his shoulder. He turns, surprised, pleased. She lowers her head toward his. The lights dim slowly, finally leaving the man and woman in a faintly glowing spot of light. Then the spot fades away. Do we still see them, or don't we see them? And the curtain is finally down.

The stage direction for a scene like this might look very ordinary on the page. "She crosses slowly to him and touches his shoulder. He looks up, surprised. She lowers her head toward him, and they kiss." This stage direction was not written to be read as literature. It was written with the knowledge of what a fine actress, working with a skilled director and an expert lighting designer, could do to help communicate this wordless moment. If it is done well, the audience will remember the moment forever. In the theater we tend to remember what we *see* even more than what we *hear*. That scene between the man and the woman is no less the playwright's scene because there is no dialogue. It is the playwright who devised the situation, created the characters, and organized the story so that this wordless scene is possible.

> In the theater we tend to remember what we *see* even more than what we *hear.*

The Playwright and the Audience: We Are Not Alone

The playwright's final collaborator is the audience. The play exists somewhere between the stage and the spectator. In a sense, we get out of a play only what we bring to it. Out of some deep feeling of joy or sadness or excitement, a playwright writes a story, sounds a note, hoping to evoke a responsive chord from the audience. This response is what might be called the "Oh, yes!" reaction. Playwrights write about particular experiences or observations. Enhancing these particulars with their imagination, they hope to reach something universal, something in everyone's experience. If they succeed, then members of the audience might ask, "How did you know what my family is like?" The playwright, of course, did not know about the audience's families, but he knew his own, and in some ways all families are the same.

> One of the special qualities of the theater is that when we respond, we respond as a group. This mass response of laughter or tears or excitement gives us a reassuring feeling that we are not alone.

One of the special qualities of the theater is that when we respond, we respond as a group. This mass response of laughter or tears or excitement gives us a reassuring feeling that we are not alone, that we are one with the people sitting around us, with everyone in the theater, and in a sense, with our community and the world.

Collection 11

DOING THE RIGHT THING

WRITING FOCUS: Cause-and-Effect Essay

Some people believe that fate determines their destiny. Some believe that they alone control their lives. Others believe that childhood influences dictate what they will become. Still others believe that it is all just a matter of luck. But no matter what we believe, life offers us choices and forces us to live with the consequences of our decisions. Writers have recognized that for centuries. Here, for example, are two plays, separated by roughly twenty-five centuries, in which parents and children struggle to deal with choices they have made—and their consequences.

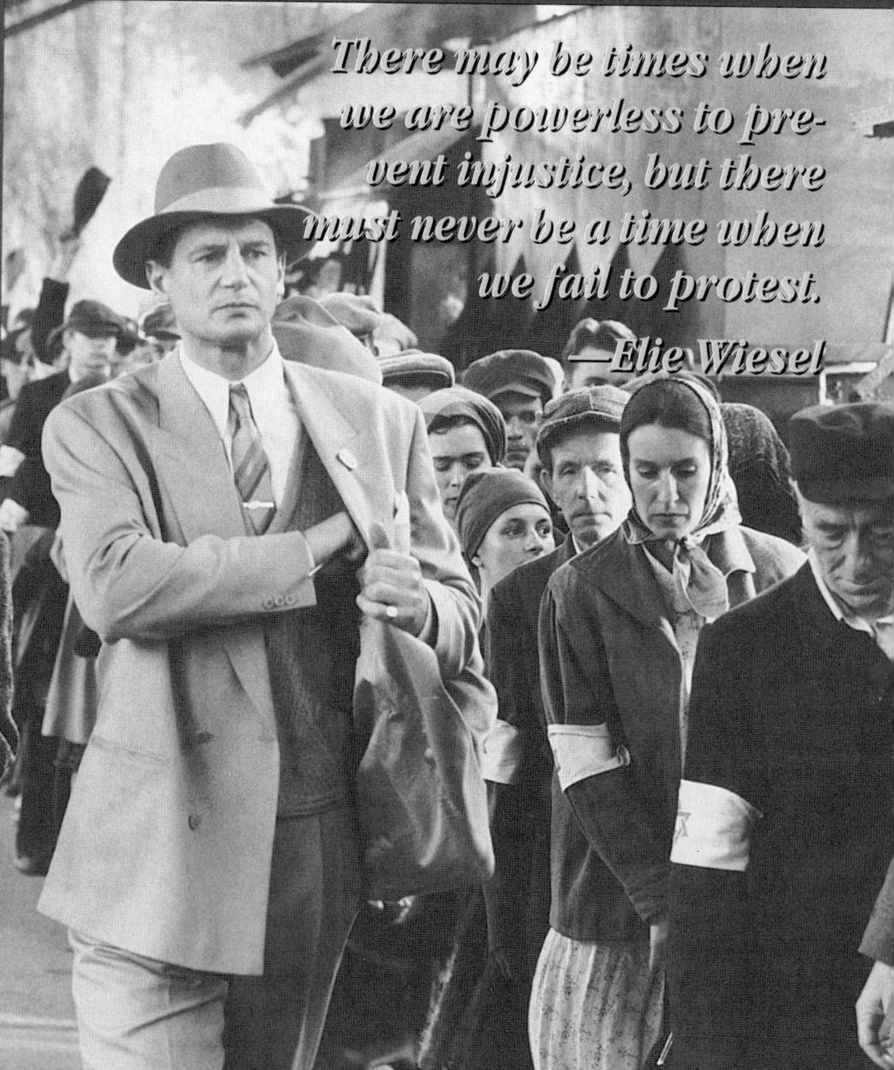

There may be times when we are powerless to prevent injustice, but there must never be a time when we fail to protest.
—Elie Wiesel

Scene from the movie *Schindler's List.*

Writer's Notebook

WORK IN PROGRESS

Both of the plays in this collection are about families and issues involving choices and conscience. In one play, a brother and sister must make decisions about the care of an elderly parent. In the other play, characters must choose between following their consciences and obeying the laws of the state. Come up with some topics you care about that involve families, choices, or conscience. Jot them down, and save your notes.

Before You Read

I Never Sang for My Father

Make the Connection

My Way or Yours?

Is this situation familiar? Someone close to you wants you to do something, but you want desperately to do something else. Maybe you have to attend a family party that conflicts with a game that's important to you. When two "wants" collide, conflict exists, and conflict makes drama.

The narrator in this play is on a collision course with his father—the two characters seem to agree about almost nothing.

Reading Skills and Strategies

Monitoring Your Reading: Questioning

As you read *I Never Sang for My Father,* pay special attention to questions that come up about the text, and jot them down in your notes. For example, you may wonder why a character behaves in a certain way or what will happen next. You may want to note a quotation you especially like. Even though the play's characters are older than you, you'll probably discover places where you find yourself saying "Oh, yes, I know what that feels like," or "But that's happened to me," or "My dad has that feeling about my grandmother." Be sure to note when you have that "shock of recognition."

Death ends a life, but it does not end a relationship . . .

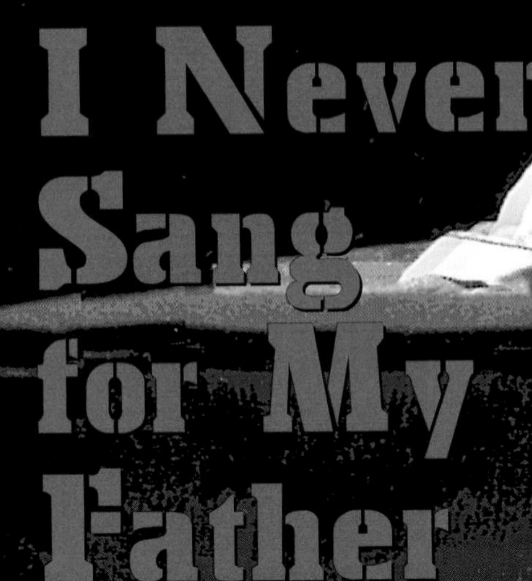

I Never Sang for My Father

Robert Anderson

The performance photographs illustrating this play are of the original Broadway production.

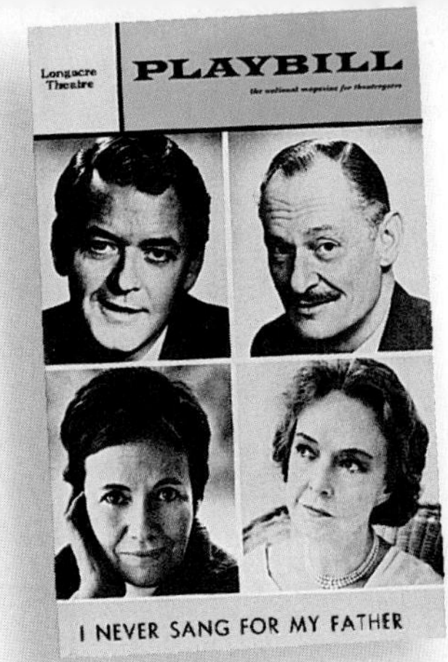

I Never Sang for My Father was first presented on January 25, 1968, by Gilbert Cates in association with Doris Vidor at the Longacre Theatre, New York, with the following cast:

Characters

(in order of appearance)

Gene Garrison
Hal Holbrook
Porter
Earl Sydnor
Tom Garrison
Alan Webb
Margaret Garrison
Lillian Gish
Mary
Sloane Shelton
Nurse
Laurinda Barrett
Reverend Pell
Allan Frank
Marvin Scott
Matt Crowley
Waiter
James A. Spearman
Dr. Mayberry
Daniel Keyes
Alice
Teresa Wright

Directed by: Alan Schneider
Scenery and Lighting by: Jo Mielziner
Costumes by: Theoni V. Aldredge

Synopsis of Scenes: The time is the present and the past. The places are New York City and a town in Westchester County.

Act One

There are no sets. Lighting is the chief means for setting the stage.

A man comes from the shadows in the rear. He is GENE GARRISON, *age forty. He checks his watch. A* PORTER *passes through with a baggage cart.*

Gene. I wonder if you could help me. *(The* PORTER *stops.)* My father and mother are coming in on the Seaboard Express from Florida. I'd like a wheelchair for my mother if I could get one.
Porter. You have the car number?
Gene. Yes. *(He checks a slip of paper.)* One-oh-seven.
Porter. Due in at three-ten. I'll meet you on the platform.
Gene. Thank you. *(The* PORTER *moves away and off. Gene comes down and addresses the audience.)* Death ends a life, but it does not end a relationship, which struggles on in the survivor's mind toward some final resolution, some clear meaning, which it perhaps never finds. *(He changes the mood.)* Pennsylvania Station, New York, a few years ago. My mother and father were returning from Florida. They were both bored in Florida, but they had been going each winter for a number of years. If they didn't go, my father came down with pneumonia and my mother's joints stiffened cruelly with arthritis. My mother read a great deal, liked to play bridge and chatter and laugh gaily with "the girls," . . . make her eyes sparkle in a way she had, and pretend that she had not had two operations for cancer, three heart attacks, and painful arthritis. . . . She used to say, "Old age takes courage." She had it. My father, though he had never been in the service, had the air of a retired brigadier general. He read the newspapers, all editions, presumably to help him make decisions about his investments. He watched westerns on television and told anyone who would listen the story of his life. I loved my mother. . . . I wanted to love my father. . . .

[*The lights come up on another area of the*

stage, where the PORTER *is already standing with the wheelchair and baggage cart.* TOM GARRISON *is standing amid the suitcases which have been piled up on the platform. He is a handsome man, almost eighty, erect in his bearing, neat in his dress. He speaks distinctly, and when he is irritated, his voice takes on a hard, harsh edge. At the moment he is irritated, slightly bewildered, on the brink of exasperation.*]

Tom. We had four bags. I don't see any of them. We had one in the compartment with us. That can't have been lost.

[*He fumes for a moment. As* GENE *watches his father for a moment, we can see in his face something of his feelings of tension. On the surface he shows great kindness and consideration for the old man. Underneath there is usually considerable strain.*]

Gene. Hello, Dad.

Tom *(beaming).* Well, Gene, as I live and breathe. This *is* a surprise.

Gene. I wrote you I'd be here.

Tom. Did you? Well, my mind is like a sieve.

WORDS TO OWN

exasperation (eg·zas′pər·ā′shən) *n.:* great irritation or annoyance.

fumes (fyo͞omz) *v.:* shows anger or annoyance.

(They have shaken hands and kissed each other on the cheek.) Am I glad to see you! They've lost all our bags.

Gene. I'm sure they're somewhere, Dad.

Tom *(firmly).* No. I've looked. It's damnable!

Gene. Well, let's just take it easy. I'll handle it. *(He looks around at the luggage piled on the platform.)*

Tom. I'm confident we had four bags.

Gene *(quietly showing the redcap).* There's one. . . . They'll show up. Where's Mother?

Tom. What? . . . Oh, she's still on the train. Wait a minute. Are you sure that's ours? *(He looks around for bags, fussing and fuming. He shakes his head in exasperation with the world.)*

Gene. Yes, Dad. You just relax now.

[TOM *is seized with a fit of coughing.*]

Tom *(is exasperated at the cough).* Damnable cough. You know the wind never stops blowing down there.

Gene. Don't worry about anything now, Dad. We've got a porter, and everything's under control. (TOM *snorts at this idea. The redcap proceeds in a quiet, efficient, and amused way to work the luggage.)* I brought a wheelchair for Mother.

Tom. Oh. That's very considerate of you.

Gene. I'll go get her.

Tom. I didn't hear you.

Gene *(raising his voice).* I said I'll go get Mother.

Tom. Yes, you do that. I've got to get these bags straightened out. *(His rage and confusion are rising.)*

Gene *(to the* PORTER*).* There's one. The gray one.

Tom. That's not ours.

Gene *(patient but irritated).* Yes, it is, Dad.

Tom. No. Now wait. We don't want to get the wrong bags. Mine is brown.

Gene. The old one was brown, Dad. I got you a new one this year for the trip.

Tom *(smiling reasonably).* Now. Gene. I've had the bag in Florida all winter. I should know.

Gene. Dad. Please. . . . Please let me handle this.

Tom *(barks out an order to his son without looking at him).* You go get your mother. I'll take care of the bags.

[GENE'S *mouth thins to a line of annoyance. He points out another bag to the* PORTER, *who is amused.* GENE *moves with the wheelchair to another area of the stage, where his mother,* MARGARET GARRISON, *is sitting.* MARGARET *is waiting patiently. She is seventy-eight, still a pretty woman. She has great spirit and a smile that lights up her whole face. She is a good sport about her problems. When she is put out, she says "darn." She is devoted to her son, but she is not the possessive and smothering mother. She is wearing a white orchid on her mink stole.*]

Gene. Hello, Mother.

Margaret *(Her face lights up).* Well, Gene. *(She opens her arms but remains seated. They embrace.)* Oh, my, it's good to see you. *(This with real feeling as she holds her son close to her)*

Gene *(when he draws away).* You look wonderful.

Margaret. What?

Gene *(Raises his voice slightly. His mother wears a hearing aid).* You look wonderful.

Margaret *(little-girl coy).* Oh . . . a little rouge. . . . This is your Easter orchid. I had them keep it in the icebox in the hotel. This is the fourth time I've worn it.

Gene. You sure get mileage out of those things.

Margaret *(raising her voice slightly).* I say it's the fourth time I've worn it. . . . Some of the other ladies had orchids for Easter, but mine was the only white one. *(She knows she is being snobbishly proud and smiles as she pokes at the bow.)* I was hoping it would last so you could see it.

Gene. How do you feel?

Margaret *(serious, pouting).* I'm all right, but your father . . . did you see him out there?

Gene. Yes.

Margaret. He's sick and he won't do anything about it.

WORDS TO OWN

coy *adj.:* pretending innocence or shyness.

Gene. I heard his cough.

Margaret. It makes me so darned mad. I couldn't get him to see a doctor.

Gene. Why not?

Margaret. Oh, he's afraid they'd send him a big bill. He says he'll see Mayberry tomorrow. . . . But I can't tell you what it's been like. You tell him. Tell him he's got to see a doctor. He's got me sick with worry. *(She starts to cry.)*

Gene *(comforts her).* I'll get him to a doctor, Mother. Don't you worry.

Margaret. He makes me so mad. He coughs all night and keeps us both awake. Poor man, he's skin and bone. . . . And he's getting so forgetful. This morning he woke up here on the train and he asked me where we were going.

Gene. Well, Mother, he's almost eighty.

Margaret. Oh, I know. And he's a remarkable man. Stands so straight. Everyone down there always comments on how handsome your father is. . . . But I've given up. You get him to a doctor.

Gene. I've got a wheelchair for you, Mother. Save you the long walk up the ramp.

Margaret. Oh, my precious. What would we ever do without you?

Gene *(He is always embarrassed by these expressions of love and gratitude).* Oh, you manage pretty well.

[*He helps her up from the chair, and she gives him a big hug as she stands . . . and looks at him.*]

Margaret. Oh, you're a sight for sore eyes.

Gene *(embarrassed by the intensity).* It's good to see you.

Margaret *(She sits in the wheelchair).* You know, much as we appreciate your coming to meet us . . . I say, much as we appreciate your coming like this, the last thing in the world I'd want to do is take you away from your work.

Gene. You're not, Mother.

[*Father coughs his hacking cough.*]

Margaret. Do you hear that? I'm so worried and so darned mad.

[*They arrive at the platform area.*]

Tom. Oh, Gene, this is damnable. They've lost a suitcase. We had four suitcases.

Gene. Let's see, Dad. There are four there.

Tom. Where?

Gene. Under the others. See?

Tom. That's not ours.

Gene. Yes. Your new one.

Tom. Well, I'm certainly glad you're here. My mind's like a sieve. *(Low, to* GENE*)* It's the confusion and worrying about your mother.

Gene. Well, everything's under control now, Dad, so let's go. We'll take a cab to my apartment, where I've got the car parked, and then I'll drive you out home.

Tom. Your mother can't climb the stairs to your apartment.

Gene. She won't have to. We'll just change from the cab to my car.

Tom. But she might have to use the facilities.

Margaret. No. No. I'm all right.

Tom *(with a twinkle in his eye . . . the operator).* You know, if you handle it right, you can get away with parking right out there in front of the station. When I used to come to meet the Senator . . .

Gene. I know, but I'd prefer to do it this way. I'm not very good at that sort of thing.

Tom. Well, all right. You're the boss. It's just that you can get right on the West Side Drive.

Gene. It's easier for me to go up the Major Deegan.

Tom. Rather than the Cross County?

Gene. Yes.

Tom. I don't like to question you, old man, but I'm sure if you clocked it, you'd find it shorter to go up the West Side Drive and——

Margaret *(annoyed with him).* Father, now come on. Gene is handling this.

Tom. All right. All right. Just a suggestion.

Gene. Come on, Dad.

Tom. You go along with your mother. I'll keep an eye on this luggage.

Gene *(trying to be patient).* It will be all right.

Tom *(clenching his teeth and jutting out his jaw, sarcastic).* You don't mind if I want to keep an eye on my luggage, do you? I've traveled a good deal more than you have in my day, old man, and I know what these guys will do if you let them out of your sight. *(*GENE *is embarrassed. The* PORTER *smiles and starts moving off.)* Hey, not so fast there.

[*And he strides after the* PORTER *and the bags.* GENE *moves to the front of the stage again, as the lights dim on the retreating wheelchair and luggage, and on* TOM *and* MARGARET.]

Gene. My father's house was in a suburb of New York City, up in Westchester County. It had been a quiet town with elms and chestnut trees, lawns, and old sprawling houses with a certain nondescript elegance. My father had been mayor of this town a long time ago. . . . Most of the elms and chestnut trees had gone, and the only elegance left was in the pretentious names of the developments and ugly apartment houses . . . Parkview Meadows Estates . . . only there was no meadow, and no park, and no view except of the neon signs of the chain stores. Some old houses remained, like slightly frowzy dowagers.[1] The lawns were not well kept, and the houses were not painted as often as they should have been, but they remained. My father's house was one of these.

[TOM *and* MARGARET *have now started coming in from the back.*]

Tom. Just look at this town.
Margaret. What, dear?
Tom *(raises his voice in irritation).* Do you have that thing turned on?
Margaret. Yes.
Tom. I said just look at this town.
Margaret. I know, dear, but time marches on.
Tom. Junky, ugly mess. When we came here . . .
Margaret. Don't get started on that. You can't play the show over again.
Tom. I can make a comment, can't I?
Margaret. But you always dwell on the gloomy side. Look at the good things.
Tom. Like what? . . . I'll bet you Murphy didn't bring the battery back for the Buick. I wrote him we'd be home today. *(He heads for the garage.)*

1. **frowzy dowagers** (frou′zē dou′ə·jərz): elderly women of wealth and dignity who are untidy and not well groomed.

Margaret *(to* GENE*).* I don't know what we're going to do about that car. Your father shouldn't be driving anymore. But they just keep renewing his license by mail. *(She moves stiffly, looking at her garden and trees and lawn.)* I must say, there's no place like home. *Mmmmm.* Just smell the grass.
Gene *(taking his mother's arm).* You all right?
Margaret. It's just my mean old joints getting adjusted. I want to look at my garden. I think I see some crocuses. *(And she moves into the shadows to see her garden.)*
Tom *(coming back).* Well, he did bring it back.
Gene. Good.
Tom. Can't count on anyone these days. Where's your mother?
Gene. She's walking around her garden.
Tom. What?
Gene. She's walking around her garden.
Tom. You know, Gene, I don't mean to criticize, but I notice you're mumbling a great deal. It's getting very difficult to understand you.
Gene *(friendly, his hand on his father's shoulder).* I think you need a hearing aid, Dad.
Tom. I can hear perfectly well if people would only enunciate. "Mr. Garrison, if you would only *E-NUN-CI-ATE.*" Professor Aurelio, night school. Didn't you ever have to take any public speaking?
Gene. No, Dad.
Tom. All your education. Well . . . Where did you say your mother was?
Gene. Walking around her garden.
Tom *(Intense. He has been waiting for someone to say this to).* I tell you, the strain has been awful.
Gene. She looks well.
Tom. I know. But you never know when she might get another of those damnable seizures. *(He looks at the ground and shakes his head at the problem of it all.)*

Words to Own

nondescript (nän′di·skript′) *adj.:* uninteresting; lacking in recognizable qualities.
enunciate (ē·nun′sē·āt′) *v.:* pronounce words clearly and distinctly.

Gene *(pats his father's shoulder).* It's rough. I know.

Tom. Well, we'll manage. She's a good soldier. But you know, she eats too fast. The doctor said she must slow down. But not your mother. Incidentally, don't forget she has a birthday coming up.

Gene *(who knows his mother's birthday and hates being reminded of it each year).* Yes, I know.

Tom. Before you go, I want to give you some money. Go get something nice for me to give her. Handkerchiefs. You know what she likes.

Gene *(who has done this every Christmas and birthday for years . . . smiles).* All right. *(*TOM *coughs, deep and thick.)* We're going to have to get that cough looked into.

Tom. I fully intend to, now I'm home. But I wasn't going to let them get their hands on me down there. If you're a tourist, they just soak you.

Gene. With the problems you've had with pneumonia . . .

Tom. I can take care of myself. Don't worry about me.

Gene. Let's go see if Dr. Mayberry can see you.

Tom. First thing tomorrow.

Gene. Why not make the appointment today?

Tom *(irked).* Now, look, I'm perfectly able to take care of myself.

Gene. Mother would feel better if——

Tom *(that smile again).* Now, Gene, don't you think I have the sense to take care of myself?

Gene *(smiling, but a little angry).* Sometimes, no.

Tom *(considers this, but is mollified by the smile).* Well, I appreciate your solicitude, old man. Why don't you stay for supper?

Gene. I was planning to take you to Schrafft's.

Tom. Hooray for our side! *(*GENE *starts out toward the garden.)* Oh, Gene. I want to talk to you a minute. We received your four letters from California. . . .

Gene. I'm sorry I didn't write more often.

Tom. Well, we *do* look forward to your letters. But this girl, this woman you mentioned several times . . .

Gene. Yes?

Tom. You seemed to see a lot of her.

Gene. Yes. I did.

Tom. Carol's been dead now, what is it . . . ?

Gene. About a year.

Tom. And there's no reason why you shouldn't go out with other women. *(*GENE *just waits.)* I was in California with the Senator, and before that. It's a perfectly beautiful place. I can understand your enthusiasm for it. Gorgeous place.

Gene. Yes. I like it a lot.

Tom. But listen, Gene . . . *(He bites his upper lip, and his voice is heavy with emotion.)* If you were to go out there, I mean, to live, it would kill your mother. *(He looks at his son with piercing eyes, tears starting. This has been in the nature of a plea and an order.* GENE *says nothing. He is angry at this order, that his father would say such a thing.)* You know you're her whole life. *(*GENE *is further embarrassed and troubled by this statement of what he knows to be the truth from his father.)* Yes, you are! Oh, she likes your sister. But you . . . are . . . her . . . life!

Gene. Dad, we've always been fond of each other, but——

Tom. Just remember what I said.

[MARGARET *can now be heard reciting to herself, very emotionally.*]

Margaret. "Loveliest of trees, the cherry now / Is hung with bloom along the bough, / And stands about the woodland ride, / Wearing white for Eastertide."[2] *(She opens her eyes.)* Oh, Gene, I've just been looking at your garden. Give me a real hug. You haven't given me a real hug yet. *(*GENE *hugs her, uncomfortable, but loving and dutiful. It is, after all, a small thing.* MARGARET *looks at him, then kisses him on the lips.) Mmmmmmm. (She smiles, making a playful thing of it.)* Oh, you're a sight for sore eyes.

2. **"Loveliest . . . Eastertide":** lines from the poem "Loveliest of Trees" by A. E. Housman. (See page 520.)

WORDS TO OWN

mollified (mäl′ə·fīd′) *v.:* soothed; pacified.

solicitude (sə·lis′ə·to͞od′) *n.:* care or concern for other people.

[TOM *has watched this and looks significantly at* GENE.]

Tom *(moving off).* Gene is staying for dinner. We're going to Schrafft's.
Margaret. Oh. Can you give us all that time?
Tom. He said he would. Now come along. You shouldn't be standing so long. You've had a long trip. *(He exits.)*
Margaret. He worries so about me. I suppose it is a strain, but he makes me nervous reminding me I should be sitting or lying down. . . . Oh, well . . . *(She takes* GENE*'s arm.)* How are you, my precious?
Gene. Fine.
Margaret. We haven't talked about your trip to California.
Gene. No.
Margaret *(raising her voice).* I say, we haven't talked about your trip.
Gene. We will.
Margaret *(low).* Did you speak to your father about seeing a doctor?
Gene. He promised me tomorrow.
Margaret. I'll believe it when I see it. He's so darned stubborn. Alice takes after him.
Gene. Oh, I got a piece of it too.
Margaret *(her tinkling laugh).* You? You don't have a stubborn bone in your body.

[*We fade, as they move up and into the shadows. Immediately the lights come up on another part of the stage—Schrafft's.*]

Mary *(A pretty Irish waitress, she is just finishing setting up her table as* TOM *enters).* Well, good evening, Mr. Garrison. Welcome back.
Tom *(the charmer).* Greetings and salutations.
Mary. We've missed you.
Tom. It's mutual. Is this your table?
Mary. Yes.
Tom. Is there a draft here? I like to keep Mrs. Garrison out of drafts.

[*He looks around for windows.* MARGARET *and* GENE *come into the area. He is helping her, as she moves slowly and deliberately*.]

Mary. Good evening, Mrs. Garrison. Nice to have you back.
Tom. You remember Mary?
Margaret *(polite but reserved).* Yes. Good evening, Mary.
Mary. You're looking well, Mrs. Garrison.
Margaret *(as* TOM *holds the chair for her).* But look at him. *(She nods at* TOM.*)*
Mary. We'll fatten him up.
Tom *(smiling, flirtatiously).* Will you do that now? Oh, we've missed you. We've had a girl down there in Florida, no sense of humor. Couldn't get a smile out of her.
Mary. Well, we'll have some jokes. Dry martini?
Tom *(a roguish twinkle).* You twist my arm. Six to one. *(He says this as though he were being quite a man to drink his martini so dry.* GENE *finds all this byplay harmless but uncomfortable.)* You remember my son, Gene.
Mary *(smiles).* Yes.

[GENE *smiles back.*]

Tom. What's your pleasure, Gene . . . Dubonnet?
Gene. I'll have a martini too, please.
Tom. But not six to one.
Gene. Yes. The same.
Tom. Well!
Gene. Mother?
Margaret. No, nothing. My joints would be stiff as a board.
Tom *(with a twinkle in his eye).* You said you'd be stiff?
Margaret. What?
Tom *(raising his voice).* You said you'd be stiff?
Margaret. My joints. My joints.
Tom. Oh, wouldn't want you stiff. *(He thinks he's being very funny and tries to share his laugh with* GENE*, who smiles reluctantly.* MARY *exits. To* GENE*)* Have I ever shown you this ring?
Margaret. Oh, Tom, you've shown it to him a hundred times.
Tom *(ignoring her reminder).* I never thought I'd wear a diamond ring, but when the Senator died, I wanted something of his. Last time I had it appraised, they told me it was worth four thousand.

WORDS TO OWN
appraised (ə·prāzd′) *v.:* examined with the aim of estimating the value.

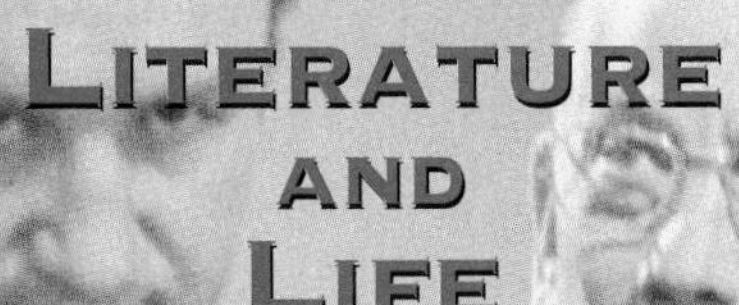

Literature and Life

"Is It True?"

by Robert Anderson

Like many other plays, *I Never Sang for My Father* has been called autobiographical. Most authors are uncomfortable when their work is called autobiographical. While they know there is some truth in their stories, writers also know how much they have invented, changed, and heightened during the creative process. Playwrights in particular know how often they have recollected an actual situation and then let themselves think, "What would have happened if . . . ?" The great artist Pablo Picasso said, "Art is a lie that makes us realize the truth." A biography should tell the facts, but a play is a work of art that *uses* the facts, builds on them, and takes them beyond where they really went in actual life.

Two examples from *I Never Sang for My Father* show that much of the play is imagination. First: I do not have a sister, and Alice in the play is not like my brother. Alice is an imagined character. She is, in a sense, Gene's alter ego, his "other self," so that the arguments Gene has with Alice are really arguments with himself.

Second: When we went into rehearsal, the play did not end the way it does now. Gene still left his father, but under different circumstances, which in fact were fairly close to the actual facts in life. The director and the producer kept urging me to invent different circumstances and end the play another way, but in the theater the playwright has the right to say no. Finally, at a run-through just before we were starting our pre-Broadway tour, I saw what the producer and director meant. I went home that night and sat at my desk and said to my father (long dead), "All right, Dad, let's have the scene we never had." Then I wrote the scene that saved the play. I changed the plot, but not the story. The son still leaves the father, but the event that makes him leave is different. This anecdote raises two important points. One, I went beyond the real experiences to find the "truth." Two, a story is not always right "because it happened that way." Even though the facts in a play or novel may not be strictly autobiographical, what we call "the voice" often is. In fact, the works of many contemporary playwrights are very personal expressions. *I Never Sang for My Father* is obviously written about what Gene describes in the play's opening scene as ". . . a relationship, which struggles on in the survivor's mind toward some final resolution, some clear meaning, which it perhaps never finds."

The background photograph is of Gene Hackman and Melvyn Douglas in the 1970 movie of *I Never Sang for My Father.*

Margaret. It's his favorite occupation, getting that ring appraised.

Tom *(again ignoring her).* Don't let anyone ever tell you it's a yellow diamond. It's a golden diamond. Of course, when I go to see a doctor, I turn it around.

[*He gives a sly smile. The others look embarrassed.*]

Margaret *(looking at the menu).* What are you going to have?

Tom *(taking out his glasses).* Now, this is my dinner, understand?

Gene. No. I invited you.

Tom. Uh-uh. You had all the expenses of coming to get us.

Gene. No, it's mine. And order what you want. Don't go reading down the prices first.

Tom *(smiles at the idea, though he knows he does it).* What do you mean?

Gene. Whenever I take you out to dinner, you always read down the prices first.

Margaret. Oh, he does that anyway.

Tom. I do not. But I think it's ridiculous to pay, look, three seventy-five for curried shrimp.

Gene. You like shrimp. Take the shrimp.

Tom. If you'll let me pay for it.

Gene *(getting annoyed).* No! Now, come on.

Tom. Look, I appreciate it, Gene, but on what you make . . .

Gene. I can afford it. Now let's not argue.

Margaret. Tell me, lovey, do you get paid your full salary on your sabbatical?[3]

Gene. No. Fifty percent.

Tom. Well, then, look . . .

Margaret. Now, Father, he wants to pay. Let him pay. *(They consult their menus.)* Incidentally, Tom, you should go over and say hello to Bert Edwards. Gene and I stopped on our way in.

Tom. Why?

Margaret. While we were gone, he lost his wife.

Tom. Where'd he lose her?

Margaret. Tom!

Tom. Just trying to get a rise.

Margaret. And Mrs. Bernard. She looks terrible.

Tom. Always did.

Margaret. She lost her husband six months ago. She told me, just before we left for Florida, "I hope I go soon."

Tom. Why are you so morbid tonight?

Margaret. I'm not morbid. They're just there. We really should see them, have them in.

Tom. Phooey! Who needs them?

Margaret. Oh, Tom! I can't have anyone in. Your father won't play bridge or do anything. He just wants to watch westerns or tell the story of his life.

Tom. Now, wait a minute.

Margaret. I can't invite people to come over to watch westerns or to listen to you go on and on. You embarrass me so. You insist on going into the most gruesome details of your life.

Tom. People seem to be interested.

Margaret. What?

Tom. Have you got that turned up?

Margaret. Yes. *(She adjusts the volume.)*

Tom. I said they seem to be interested. *(He tries to take* GENE *in on an exasperated shaking of the head, but* GENE *looks the other way.)*

Margaret. I admit it's a remarkable story, your life. But there are other things to talk about. People want to talk about art or music or books.

Tom. Well, let them.

Margaret. He keeps going over and over the old times. Other people have had miserable childhoods, and they don't keep going over and over them. . . . That story of your mother's funeral. And you say I'm morbid.

Gene. What was that? I don't remember that.

Margaret. Oh, don't get him started.

Tom. Your mother wants me to play cards with a lot of women who just want to gossip and chatter about styles. That's why I won't play.

Margaret. You won't play because you can't follow the play of the cards anymore.

Tom. I beg to disagree.

Gene. Please! Don't fight . . . don't fight. *(He's said this in a mock-serious singsong.)*

Margaret. He kept telling everyone how he wouldn't allow his father to come to his mother's funeral.

3. **sabbatical** (sə·bat′i·kəl): leave of absence given to college teachers.

Tom *(defensively angry).* Are you implying that I should have let him?

Margaret. I'm not saying——

Tom. He'd run out on us when we were kids, and I told him——

Margaret. I'm not saying you were wrong. You're so defensive about it. I'm saying you're wrong to keep bringing it up.

Tom. You brought it up this time.

Margaret. Well, I'm sorry. Imagine going around telling everyone he shoved his father off the funeral coach. *(She is consulting the menu.)*

Tom. And I'd do it again. I was only ten, but I'd do it again. We hadn't seen him in over a year, living, the four of us, in a miserable two-room tenement, and suddenly he shows up weeping and begging, and drunk, as usual. And I shoved him off! *(He almost relives it.)* I never saw him again till some years later when he was dying in Bellevue . . . of drink. *(The hatred and anger are held in, but barely.)*

Margaret *(She has been studying the menu).* What looks good to you?

Tom *(a hard, sharp edge to his voice).* I have not finished! I went down to see him, to ask him if he wanted anything. He said he wanted an orange. I sent him in a half-dozen oranges. I would have sent more, except I knew he was dying, and there was no point in just giving a lot of oranges to the nurses. The next morning he died.

[*There is a silence for a moment, while* GENE *and* MARGARET *look at the menu, and* TOM *grips and ungrips his hand in memory of his hatred for his father.*]

Margaret *(gently).* Look at your menu now, Father. What are you going to eat?

Tom. I don't feel like anything. I have no appetite. *(He lights a cigarette.)*

Margaret *(to* GENE*).* This is the way it's been.

Gene. He'll see a doctor tomorrow. Don't get upset.

[MARY *arrives with the martinis.*]

Tom. Ah, here we are.

Mary. Six to one. *(She puts the martini in front of him.)*

Tom. Oh . . . ! *(He shakes his head in exasperation and fishes out the lemon peel.)*

Mary. But you always ask for lemon peel.

Tom *(demonstrating).* Twisted over it, not dumped in it. It's all right. It's all right. *(With an Irish accent)* Well, to your smilin' Irish eyes.

Mary. He hasn't changed, has he?

Tom. What county are you from, did you say?

Mary. Armagh.

Tom. I knew there was something I liked about you. That's where my people came from. To County Armagh. *(He drinks.)* Do you have any burnt ice cream tonight?

Mary. Ah, you.

Tom *(smiling).* No, I mean it. *(To* GENE*)* They have burnt ice cream here.

Mary. I'll be back.

[*And she exits.* MARGARET *sits embarrassed and piqued by this kind of flirtation, which has gone on all their lives.*]

Tom *(the sport, to* GENE*).* I like to get a rise out of them. If they kid with me, I give them a good tip. If they don't, a straight ten percent. *(He draws a line on the tablecloth to emphasize this. He looks at* MARGARET.*)* What's the matter?

Margaret. If you want to make a fool of yourself, go right ahead.

[TOM *is angry, hurt, and exasperated. He looks at her, and then tries to include* GENE, *to make him share his anger. But* GENE *looks away and to the menu.* TOM *stares at his glass, and his jaw muscles start to work. The scene dims in the Schrafft's area, and* GENE *moves from the table to another side of the stage.*]

Gene. We hurried through the last part of our dinner. My father ate only his dessert, burnt almond ice cream. We hurried through to rush home to one of my father's rituals, the television western. He would sit in front of them hour after hour, falling asleep in one and waking up in the middle of the next one, never knowing the difference. When my father fell in love with

WORDS TO OWN

piqued (pēkt) *v.* used as *adj.:* resentful; displeased because of being treated inconsiderately.

I don't feel like anything.
I have no appetite.

a program, it was forever. All during my childhood we ate our dinner to the accompaniment of Lowell Thomas and Amos and Andy.[4] If anyone dared to talk, Father would storm away from the table and have his dinner served at the radio. . . . I say, we rushed away from Schrafft's. Actually, my father rushed. We just lived down the street. I walked my mother home very slowly, stopping every fifty yards or so.

[MARGARET *has joined* GENE *and taken his arm.*]

Margaret. I don't know how he can sit through hour after hour of those westerns.

Gene. I think he always wished he'd been a cowboy. "Take 'em out and shoot 'em!"

Margaret. He won't listen to the things I want to hear. Down in Florida there's only one TV in the lounge, and he rode herd on it. And then he'd fall asleep in three minutes. . . . Still, he's a remarkable man.

4. **Lowell Thomas and Amos and Andy:** a reporter (Thomas) and a comedy team (Amos and Andy) popular on radio in the 1930s and 1940s.

Gene. Good old Mom.

Margaret. Well, he is. Not many boys have fathers they could be as proud of.

Gene. I know that, Mom. I'm very . . . proud of him.

Margaret. *(She catches his tone).* Everything he's done, he's done for his family. *(*GENE *just looks at her, smiling.)* So he didn't dance with me at parties. *(She smiles at* GENE.*)* You took care of that.

Gene. You were just a great dancer, Mother.

Margaret. I was a terrible dancer. You just couldn't stand seeing me sitting alone at a table at the club while your father was . . . *(She stops, realizing she's about to make* GENE*'s point.)*

Gene. . . . off dancing with various other people, table-hopping, or playing poker with the boys in the locker room.

Margaret. What a shame that children can't see their parents when they're young and courting, and in love. All they see them being is tolerant, sympathetic, forbearing, and devoted. All the qualities that are so unimportant to passionate young people.

[TOM *appears.*]

Tom. Gene . . . Gene . . . Come watch this one. This is a real shoot-'em-up.
Gene. In a minute, Dad.
Margaret. Gene, I want to talk to you.
Gene. You should be in bed. You've had a big day.

[*They move to another part of the stage.*]

Margaret. I took another nitro.[5] And I've had something on my mind for a long time now. You remember you gave me that heart-shaped pillow when I was in the hospital once, when you were a boy? *(She sits on the chaise longue.)*
Gene. Yes.
Margaret. Fidget used to curl up here. *(She indicates the crook in her leg.)* And you'd sit over there, and we'd listen to the Metropolitan Opera broadcasts.

[GENE *is made uncomfortable by this attempt to evoke another time, another kind of relationship, but he doesn't show it.*]

Gene. Yes. I remember.
Margaret. You'd dress up in costumes and act in front of that mirror. I remember you were marvelous as d'Artagnan in *The Three Musketeers. (For the fun of it, a forty-year-old man, he assumes the dueling stance and thrusts at his image in an imaginary mirror.* GENE *sits on a footstool and watches her adjust herself in her chaise. After a moment)* Tell me about California.
Gene *(A little taken by surprise. Here is the subject).* I loved it.
Margaret. And the girl, the woman with the children? The doctor? *(*GENE *doesn't say anything. He frowns, wondering what to say.)* You love her too, don't you?
Gene. I think so.
Margaret. I know when Carol died, you said you'd never marry again. But I hoped you would. I know it's hard, but I think Carol would have wanted you to.

5. nitro (nī'trō): nitroglycerin, medicine taken to relieve chest pain.

Gene. I don't know.
Margaret. Gene, your sabbatical is over soon, isn't it?
Gene. A few more months.
Margaret. I think you want to move to California and get a job teaching there and marry this woman.
Gene *(after a moment).* Yes. I think I do. I wasn't sure while I was there. I suddenly felt I should get away and think. But when I walked into my old apartment, with all Carol's things there . . .
Margaret. I think it would be the best thing in the world for you to get away, to marry this girl.
Gene *(touched . . . very simply).* Thanks.
Margaret. A new place, a new wife, a new life. I would feel just terrible if you didn't go because of me. There are still planes, trains, and telephones, and Alice comes from Chicago once or twice a year and brings the children.
Gene. Thanks, Mother. You've always made things very easy. I think you'll like Peggy.
Margaret. I'm sure I will. You have good taste in women. And they have good taste when they like you.
Gene. I'm not so sure. I never really knew if I made Carol happy. . . . If I did make her happy, I wish she'd let me know it.
Margaret. I guess a lot of us forget to say thank you until it's too late. *(She takes his hand and smiles at him.)* Thank you. . . . You have such nice hands. I've always loved your hands. . . . You've been so good to me, Gene, so considerate. Perhaps I've let you be too considerate. But it was your nature, and your father just withdrew behind his paper and his investments and his golf. And our interests seem to go together. You liked to sing, and I played the piano, oh, miserably, but I played. *(She strokes his hand.)* I tried not to be one of those possessive mothers, Gene. If I did things wrong, I just did the best I knew how.
Gene. You did everything just fine. *(He pats his mother's hand before he draws his own away.)*
Margaret. And your father has done the best he knew how.
Gene *(with no conviction).* Yes. *(This is her old song. She knows that* GENE *knows it's prob-*

ably true, but he gets no satisfaction from the knowledge.)

Margaret. Of course you know your father will object to your going away.

Gene. He already has. He said it would kill you.

Margaret. How sad. Why can't he say it would kill him? He doesn't think it would hold you or mean anything to you. *(She shakes her head.)* He dotes on your letters down there. Reads them and re-reads them. Tells everyone what a fine relationship he has with you. "My door is always open. . . . Anything he wants, he can have. . . . We have always had each other's confidence. . . ." (GENE *smiles at this and sadly shakes his head.)* Well, you go to California. Your father and I can take care of each other. I'll remember where he put his checkbook, and he'll make the beds, which is the only thing I'm really not supposed to do. And, for your information, I have my old-lady's home all picked out. That's what I want, so I won't be a burden to any of you.

Gene. You a burden!

Margaret *(wisely).* Oh, yes! Now don't mention this business to your father tonight. He's not well, and it's been such a nice day. In the next few days I'll talk to him, tell him it's important for you to——

Gene. No, I'll do it. *(He kisses her on the cheek.)*

Margaret. Good night, my precious.

Gene. Where would you like to celebrate your birthday?

Margaret. Oh, lovey, you've already given me so much time. Just call me on the phone.

Gene. No. . . . We can at least have dinner. . . . I'll make some plans.

Margaret. Gene, if your father gives you money to buy his present for me, please, no more handkerchiefs.

Gene. He always says handkerchiefs.

Margaret. I know, but I've got dozens and dozens from my past birthdays and Christmases.

Gene. What would you like?

Margaret. Get me some perfume. You choose the kind, except I don't like lily of the valley or gardenia.

Gene. You're a hard woman to please. . . . Good night. . . . You look great.

Margaret. Oh, a little rouge and lipstick. Thanks for coming to meet us. Tell your father I've gone to bed, and don't let him keep you there to all hours watching television. *(Calling after him)* I don't like carnation either.

[GENE *waves back affectionately and moves away, as the lights dim on* MARGARET*'s area.* GENE *moves, then stands and looks at the back of his father's chair as the TV sounds come up, and lights come on in that area.* GENE *moves to his father's chair and gently touches his arm while turning the knob of the TV volume.*]

Tom *(stirring).* What? . . . What? *(He comes to slowly, shakes his head, and looks at* GENE*, bewildered.)*

Gene *(gently).* I'm going now, Dad.

Tom. Oh, so soon?

Gene *(Controls his irritation. This has always been his father's response, no matter how long he has been with him).* Yes. I have to go.

Tom. Where's your mother?

Gene. She's upstairs. She's fine. *(*TOM *starts to cough.)* You see about that in the morning, Dad.

Tom *(getting up, steadying himself).* I fully intend to. I would have done it down there, but I wasn't going to be charged outrageous prices. *(He glances at the TV screen.)* Oh, this is a good one. Why don't you just stay for this show?

Gene *(the anger building).* No, Dad. I've got to run along.

Tom. Well, all right. We see so little of you.

Gene. I'm up at least once a week, Dad.

Tom. Oh, I'm not complaining. *(But he is.)* There just doesn't seem to be any time. And when you are here, your mother's doing all the talking. The way she interrupts. She just doesn't listen. And I say, "Margaret, please." . . . But she goes right on. . . . Well, "all's lost, all's spent, when we our desires get without content . . . 'tis better to be that which we destroy, than by destruction dwell with doubtful joy."[6]

6. **"all's lost . . . doubtful joy":** refers to lines spoken by Lady Macbeth in Shakespeare's *Macbeth,* Act III, Scene 2.

Gene *(He is always puzzled by his father's frequent use of this quotation. It never is immediately appropriate, but it indicates such unhappiness that it is sad and touching to him).* We'll get a chance to talk, Dad. *(He moves toward the porch.)*
Tom. I can't tell you what a comfort it is knowing you are just down in the city. Don't know what we'd do without you. No hat or coat?
Gene. No.
Tom. It's still chilly. You should be careful.
Gene *(kissing his father on the cheek).* Good night, Dad. I'll call you tomorrow to see if you've gone to the doctor's.
Tom. Well, I may and I may not. I've looked after myself pretty well for almost eighty years. I guess I can judge if I need to see the doctor or not.
Gene *(angry).* Look, Dad . . .
Tom. Seventy years ago when I was a snot-nosed kid up in Harlem, a doctor looked at me and said if I were careful, I'd live to be twenty. That's what I think about doctors. Ten dollars to look at your tongue. Phooey! Out! Who needs them?
Gene. Look, Dad, you're worrying Mother to death with that cough.
Tom. All right, all right. I'll go. I'll be a good soldier. . . . You're coming up for your mother's birthday, aren't you?
Gene. Yes.
Tom. And don't forget, Mother's Day is coming up.
Gene. Well . . .
Tom. Why don't we make reservations at that restaurant in Connecticut where you took us last Mother's Day?
Gene. We'll see.
Tom. It will be my party. And, Gene, remember what I said about California!
Gene *(straining to get away from all the encirclements).* Good night, Dad. *(He moves off.)*
Tom. Drive carefully. I noticed you were inclined to push it up there a little. *(GENE burns.)* Make a full stop going out the driveway, then turn right.
Gene *(angry, moves further down).* Yes, Dad.
Tom *(calling after him).* Traffic is terrible out there now. Used to be a quiet little street. Take your first left, and your second right.
Gene *(He has driven this route for many years).* Yes.
Tom. Then left under the bridge. It's a little tricky down there. *(When he gets no response, he calls.)* Gene?
Gene *(in a sudden outburst).* I've driven this road for twenty years! *(He is immediately sorry and turns away from his father's direction.)*
Tom. Just trying to be helpful.

[*The lights fade on* TOM *as he goes back into the house.* GENE *is now downstage.*]

Gene. Take your first left and your second right. Then turn left under the bridge. But do not go as far as California, because it would kill your mother. . . . I hated him for that, for sending up warning flares that if I left, it would not be with his blessing, but with a curse . . . as he had banished my sister Alice years ago for marrying someone he didn't approve of . . . and the scene so terrified me at fourteen, I was sick. . . . He knew his man . . . that part of me at least . . . a gentleman who gave way at intersections. . . . And yet, when I looked at those two old people, almost totally dependent on me for their happiness . . . This is the way the world ends, all right. . . .[7]

[*A phone rings. A light picks out* TOM *holding the phone.*]

Tom. I was downstairs in the kitchen, and suddenly I heard your mother scream. . . . "Tom! Tom" . . . I ran up the stairs . . . *(He is seized with a fit of coughing.)* I ran up the stairs, and there she was stretched out on the floor of the bedroom, . . . "Nitro" . . . "nitro." . . . That's all she could say. You know we have nitroglycerin all over the house.

[*A nurse comes to* TOM *as the lights come up; she leads him into a hospital waiting-room area.* GENE *joins them.*]

7. Reference to T. S. Eliot's poem "The Hollow Men," which ends with the lines: "This is the way the world ends / Not with a bang but a whimper."

Gene. Dad. *(He shakes his hand and kisses him on the cheek.)*

Tom. Am I glad to see you! Have you seen your mother?

Gene. Yes. She's sleeping. *(*TOM *starts to cough.)* That doesn't sound any better.

Tom. Well, I've had a shot. After your mother got settled over here, the doctor took me to his office and gave me a shot. I *would* have gone down there in Florida, you know, but . . . well . . . *(shakes his head)* I just don't know. I was in the kitchen getting breakfast. . . . You know I've been getting the breakfasts, when suddenly I heard her scream, "Tom. Tom." I went running up the stairs, and there she was stretched out on the floor. She'd had an attack. "Nitro," she whispered. We've got it all over the house, you know. She'd had attacks before, but I knew at once that this was something more. I gave her the pills and called the doctor, . . . "This is an emergency. Come quick." . . . The doctor came, gave her a shot . . . and called the ambulance . . . and here we are. *(He shakes his head, partly in sorrow, but also partly in exasperation that such a thing could happen.)* She had a good time in Florida. I don't understand it. She ate too fast, you know. And the doctor had said she should do everything more slowly.

Suddenly I heard her scream, "Tom. Tom."

Gene. There's no explaining these things, Dad.

Tom. I suppose I could have seen more of her down there. But she just wanted to play bridge, and I didn't play, because the ladies just chattered all the time about styles and shops. . . . And I met some very interesting people. Oh, some of them were bores and just wanted to tell you the story of their life. But there were others. You know, I met a man from Waterbury, Connecticut, used to know Helen Moffett. . . . I've told you about Helen Moffett, haven't I? When I was a kid, when the clouds were low and dark, my grandfather'd take me up there sometimes on Sundays . . . a city slum kid in that lovely country . . . And Helen and I . . . oh . . . it never amounted to much. We'd go to church, and then we'd take a walk and sit in a hammock or under an apple tree. I think she liked that. But I didn't have any money, and I couldn't go up there often. Her mother didn't like me. . . . "That young man will end up the same way as his father." . . . And that scared her off. . . . This man in Florida, I've got his name somewhere. . . . *(He fishes out a notebook and starts to go through it.)* He said Helen had never married. . . . Said she'd been in love as a kid . . . and had never married. *(Tears come to his eyes.)* Well, I can't find it. No matter. *(*GENE *doesn't know what to say. He is touched by this naked and unconscious revelation of an early and deeply meaningful love. But it seems so incongruous under the circumstances.)* Some day we might drive out there and look him up. . . . Helen's dead now, but it's nice country. I was a kid with nothing . . . living with my grandfather. . . . Maybe if she hadn't been so far away. . . . Well, that's water over the dam.

Gene *(After a long pause, he touches his father).* Yes.

Tom *(just sits for a few moments, then seems to come back to the present and takes out his watch).* You know, I'd like to make a suggestion.

Gene. What, Dad?

Tom. If we move right along, we might be able to make the Rotary Club for dinner. *(*GENE *frowns in bewilderment.)* I've been away for three months. They don't like that very much if you're absent too often. They drop you or fine you. How about it? *(He asks this with a cocked head and a twinkle in his eye.)*

Gene. I thought we might eat something around here in the hospital.

Tom. I had lunch in the coffee shop downstairs, and it's terrible. It will only take a little longer. We won't stay for the speeches, though

WORDS TO OWN

incongruous (in·käŋ′gro͞o·əs) *adj.:* not suitable; not what would reasonably be expected.

sometimes they're very good, very funny. We'll just say hello to the fellows and get back. . . . Your mother's sleeping now. That's what they want her to do.

Gene *(bewildered by this, but doesn't want to get into an argument).* Let's drop by and see Mother first.

Tom. They want her to rest. We'd only disturb her.

Gene. All right.

Tom *(As they turn to go, he puts his arm around* GENE*'s shoulder).* I don't know what I'd do without you, old man.

[*As the lights shift, and* TOM *and* GENE *head away, we move to the Rotary gathering, held in the grill room of one of the local country clubs. A piano is heard offstage, playing old-fashioned singing-type songs (badly). A tinkle of glasses . . . a hum of men talking and laughing. This area is presumably an anteroom with two comfortable leather chairs. A man enters, wearing a large name button and carrying a glass. This is the minister,* REVEREND PELL, *a straightforward, middle-aged man.*]

Reverend Pell. Hello, Tom, good to see you back.

Tom *(His face lights up in a special "greeting the fellows" type grin).* Hello, Sam.

Reverend Pell. Did you have a good trip?

Tom. All except for the damned wind down there. *Oooops.* Excuse my French, Sam. . . . You know my son, Gene. Reverend Pell.

Reverend Pell. Yes, of course. Hello, Gene. *(They shake hands.)*

Tom. Gene was a Marine. *(*GENE *frowns.)* You were a Marine, weren't you, Sam?

Reverend Pell. No. Navy.

Tom. Well, same thing.

Reverend Pell. Don't say that to a Marine.

[GENE *and* REVEREND PELL *smile.*]

Tom. Gene saw the flag go up on Iwo.[8]

Gene *(embarrassed by all this inappropriate line).* Let's order a drink, Dad.

Tom. Sam, I've been wanting to talk to you. Now is not the appropriate time, but some bozo has been crowding into our pew at church. You know Margaret and I sit up close because she doesn't hear very well. Well, this guy has been there in our pew. I've given him a pretty sharp look several times, but it doesn't seem to faze him. Now, I don't want to seem unreasonable, but there is a whole church for him to sit in.

Reverend Pell. Well, we'll see what we can do, Tom.

Tom *(calling to a bartender).* A martini, George. Six to one. *(To* GENE*)* Dubonnet?

Gene. A martini.

Tom. Six to one?

Gene. Yes. Only make mine vodka.

Tom. Vodka? Out! Phooey!

Reverend Pell. What have you got against vodka, Tom?

Tom. It's Russian, isn't it? However, I don't want to influence you. Make his vodka. Six to one, now! These fellows like to charge you extra for a six to one, and then they don't give you all the gin you've got coming to you.

Reverend Pell. I hope you don't drink many of those, Tom, six to one.

Tom. My grandmother used to give me, every morning before I went to school, when I was knee-high to a grasshopper . . . she used to give me a jigger of gin with a piece of garlic in it, to keep away colds. I wonder what the teacher thought. Phew. I must have stunk to high heaven. . . . She used to put a camphor ball in my necktie too. That was for colds, too, I think. . . . But they were good people. They just didn't know any better. That's my grandfather and my grandmother. I lived with them for a while when I was a little shaver, because my father . . . well, that's another story . . . but my grandfather——

Reverend Pell *(He puts his hand on* TOM*'s arm).* I don't mean to run out on you, Tom, but I was on my way to the little-boys' room. I'll catch up with you later.

Tom. Go ahead. We don't want an accident.

Reverend Pell *(as he is going, to* GENE*).* You got a great dad there. *(And he disappears.)*

Tom. I don't really know these fellows any-

8. Iwo (ē'wō): Iwo Jima, Pacific island, the site of fierce battles in World War II and the subject of a famous photograph of Marines raising a U.S. flag after capturing the island.

more. *(Indicating people offstage)* All new faces. Most of them are bores. All they want to do is tell you the story of their lives. But sometimes you hear some good jokes. . . . Now, here's someone I know. Hello, Marvin.

[MARVIN SCOTT, *a man about sixty-five, enters.*]

Marvin Scott. Hello, Tom. Good to see you back.
Tom. You remember my son, Gene.
Marvin Scott. Yes. Hello.
Gene. Hello, Mr. Scott.
Marvin Scott *(to* TOM*).* Well, young feller, you're looking great!
Tom. Am I? Well, thank you.
Marvin Scott. How's Margaret?

[TOM *goes very dramatic, pauses for a moment, and bites his lip.* MARVIN *looks at* GENE.]

Gene. Mother's . . .
Tom. Margaret's in an oxygen tent in the hospital.
Marvin Scott *(Surprised that* TOM *is here, he looks at* GENE*, then at* TOM*).* I'm terribly sorry to hear that, Tom.
Tom. Heart. *(He shakes his head and starts to get emotional.)*
Gene *(embarrassed).* We're just going to grab a bite and get back. Mother's sleeping, and if we were there, she'd want to talk.
Marvin Scott. I'm sorry to hear that, Tom. When did it happen?
Tom *(Striving for control. His emotion is as much anger that it could happen, and self-pity, as anything else).* This morning . . . I was in the kitchen, getting something for Margaret, when suddenly I heard her scream, . . . "Tom . . . Tom. . ." and I ran upstairs . . . and there she was stretched out on the bedroom floor. . . . "Nitro . . . nitro," . . . she said. . . . We have nitroglycerin all over the house, you know . . . since her last two attacks. . . . So, I get her the nitro and call the doctor . . . and now she's in an oxygen tent in the hospital. . . .

[*The bell starts to ring to call them to dinner.*]

Marvin Scott. Well, I hope everything's all right, Tom.
Gene. Thank you.
Tom. What happened to those martinis? We've got to go into dinner and we haven't gotten them yet.
Gene. We can take them to the table with us.
Tom. I have to drink mine before I eat anything. It brings up the gas. Where are they? *(And he heads off.)*
Marvin Scott *(to* GENE*).* He's quite a fella.

[*And they move off as Rotarians start singing to the tune of "Auld Lang Syne," "We're awfully glad you're here," etc.*
As the lights fade on this group, they come up on the hospital bed and MARGARET. *The* NURSE *is sitting there, reading a movie magazine. The oxygen tent has been moved away.*
TOM *and* GENE *enter quietly, cautiously. The* NURSE *gets up.* GENE *approaches the bed.*]

Gene *(whispers to the* NURSE*).* Anything?
Nurse. The doctor was just here. He said things looked much better.
Tom *(too loud).* Hooray for our side.
Margaret *(stirs). Hm* . . . What? *(She looks around.)*
Gene. Hello, Mother.
Margaret. Oh, Gene. *(She reaches as though to touch him.)* Look where I ended up.
Gene. The doctor says you're better tonight.
Margaret *(her eyes flashing).* You know how this happened, don't you? Why it happened? *(She nods her head in the direction of* TOM, *who is at the foot of the bed chatting with the* NURSE.*)*
Gene *(quieting).* Now, Mother. Take it easy. He's seen the doctor. He's had his shot.
Margaret. Well!
Gene. You should be sleeping.
Margaret. That's all I've been doing. *(She takes his hand.)* It makes me so mad. I was feeling so well. All the ladies down in Florida said I've never looked so well.
Gene. You've had these before, Mother. Easy does it.
Margaret. He's seen the doctor for himself?
Gene. Yes. Just a bad cold. He's had a shot.
Margaret. Why wouldn't he have that down there?

Gene. Mother, we'll have to go if you talk like this, because you should be resting.
Tom *(leaving the* NURSE, *cheerful).* Well, how goes it?
Margaret. How do I know?
Tom *(takes her hand and smiles).* You look better.
Margaret. You know I came without anything. I've still got my stockings on.
Tom *(kidding, very gentle).* Well, it all happened pretty quick, my darling.
Margaret. I'll need some things.
Tom. Your wish is our command.
Gene. I'll write it down. But don't talk too much.
Margaret. Toothbrush . . . some night clothes. I'm still in my slip . . . a hairbrush.
Tom. We'll collect some things.
Margaret *(joshing).* Oh, you. You wouldn't know what to bring. Gene, you look around.
Gene. Yes. Now, take it easy.
Margaret. I hate being seen this way.
Tom. We think you look beautiful.
Gene. Mother, we're just going to sit here now, because you're talking too much. You're being a bad girl. *(*MARGARET *makes a childlike face at him, puckering her lips and wrinkling her nose. She reaches out for his hand.)* Those are lovely flowers Alice sent. She knows your favorites. I called her. I'll keep in touch with her. She said she'd come on, but I said I didn't think she had to.
Margaret. Did you have any dinner?
Tom. We went to Rotary. Everyone asked for you.
Margaret. That's nice.

[DR. MAYBERRY *comes into the room, in the shadows of the entrance.* GENE *spots him and goes to him.*]

Dr. Mayberry. Hello, Gene. How are you?
Gene *(trying to catch him before he enters the room entirely).* I'd like to——
Dr. Mayberry *(pleasant and hearty).* We can talk right here. She seems to be coming along very well.
Gene. Good.
Tom. That's wonderful news.
Dr. Mayberry *(kidding her).* She's tough. *(*MARGARET *smiles and makes a face at him.)* We won't know the extent of it until we're able to take a cardiogram tomorrow. It was nothing to toss off lightly, but it looks good now.
Gene. Well . . . thank you. *(*TOM *coughs.)* What about that?
Dr. Mayberry. He'll be all right. Just a deep cough. He'll get another shot tomorrow.
Gene *(low).* You don't think we should . . . stay around?
Dr. Mayberry. I wouldn't say so. And she should rest.
Gene. Thanks, Doctor. *(They shake hands.)*
Dr. Mayberry. Do I have your number in New York? I'll keep in touch with you. Your dad's a little vague about things. *(*GENE *jots the number on a slip of paper.)* Good night, Mrs. Garrison. I'm going to kick your family out now so that you can get some rest.
Margaret *(smiles and makes a small wave of the fingers).* Take care of Tom.
Dr. Mayberry. He's going to be fine. *(To* TOM*)* Drop into the office for another shot tomorrow.
Tom *(kidding).* Will you ask that girl of yours to be a little more considerate next time?
Dr. Mayberry. Oh, you can take it.
Tom. Oh, I'm a good soldier. But, wow! *(He indicates a sore rump.)*
Dr. Mayberry. Good night. *(He waves his hand and disappears.)*
Gene. We'll run along now, Mother. *(She reaches her hand out.)*
Margaret. My precious.
Gene *(leans down and kisses her hand).* Good night. Sleep well.
Tom. Well, my dearest, remember what we used to say to the children. "When you wake up, may your cheeks be as red as roses and your eyes as bright as diamonds."
Margaret *(pouts, half kidding).* Just you take care of yourself. And get the laundry ready for Annie tomorrow.
Tom *(with a flourish).* Your wish is my command.
Margaret. I put your dirty shirts from Florida in the hamper in the guest bathroom, and my things are——

Gene *(trying to stop her talking).* We'll find them.
Margaret *(to* GENE*).* Thanks for coming. Don't bother to come tomorrow. Father will keep in touch with you.
Gene. We'll see. Good night.

[*He stops at the door for a little wave. She wiggles her fingers in a small motion. The lights dim on the hospital scene as* TOM *and* GENE *move away.*]

Tom. Well, that's good news.
Gene. Yes.
Tom. She looks a lot better than when they brought her in here this morning, I can tell you that.
Gene. She looked pretty good.
Tom. She's a good soldier. Do you remember what she asked us to bring her? My mind is like a sieve.
Gene. I'll come along and get the bag ready and round up the laundry.
Tom. We should get the laundry ready tonight because Annie arrives at eight sharp, and she starts getting paid the minute she enters the door. But we could leave the bag till morning.
Gene *(uneasy).* I've got an early appointment at college tomorrow, Dad. I'll have to run along after we have a nightcap.
Tom. Oh, I thought you might spend the night.
Gene. I . . . uh . . . I've got an early appointment at college tomorrow.
Tom. I thought you were on your sabbatical.
Gene. I am. . . . But I arranged a meeting with someone there, Dad.
Tom. You could stay and still make it.
Gene. It's very early, Dad.
Tom. We've got an alarm. Alarm clocks all over the house.
Gene. I want to change before the appointment. . . . Shirt . . .
Tom. I've got plenty of shirts . . . underwear . . . socks . . .
Gene *(more uncomfortable).* I don't wear your sizes, Dad.
Tom. I could get you up earlier, then. I don't sleep beyond five these days.

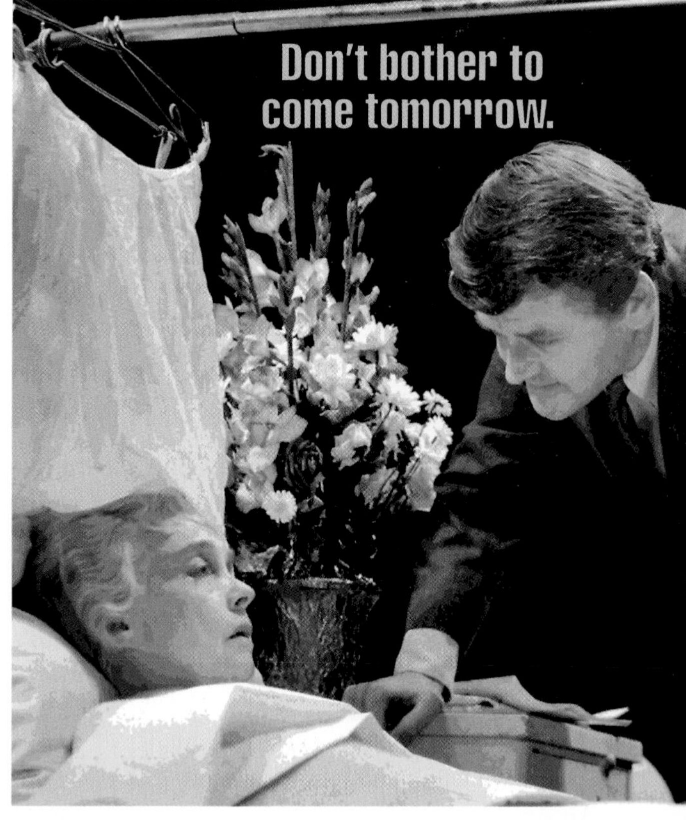
Don't bother to come tomorrow.

Gene *(tense).* No, Dad . . . I just . . . No. I'll come by and——
Tom. There may be something good on television . . . Wednesday night. I think there is. . . .
Gene. . . . We'll watch a little television, Dad . . . and have some drinks. . . . But then I'll have to go.
Tom *(after a moment).* All right, old man.

[GENE *instinctively reaches out to touch his father's arm, to soften the rejection. They look at each other a moment; then* TOM *drifts off into the dark, as* GENE *moves directly downstage.*]

Gene. I sat with my father much longer than I meant to. . . . Because I knew I should stay the night. But . . . I couldn't. . . . We watched television. He slept on and off . . . and I went home. . . . The next morning, around nine-thirty, my mother died. . . . (GENE *turns and walks upstage, as the lights dim.)*

Curtain

Making Meanings
Act One

First Thoughts

1. Even loving family members sometimes disagree strongly. What do you think of the way Gene and his father talk and behave when they are with each other?

Reading Check

Make a **flow chart** like the one below for the scenes in this act. Tell what happens in each scene to dramatize Gene's problems with his mother and father.

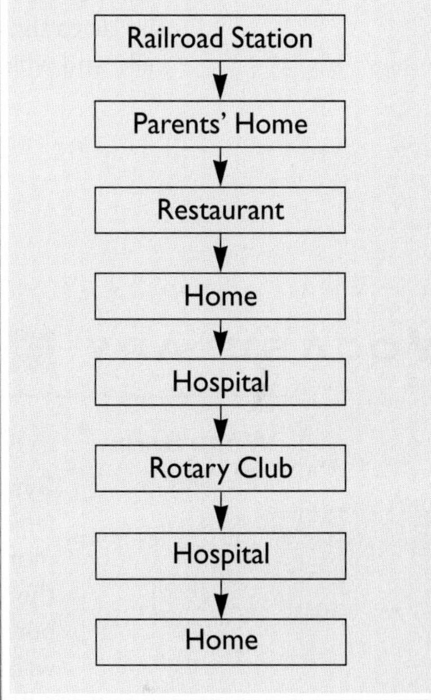

Shaping Interpretations

2. What do Tom and Margaret want for themselves? What does each of them want from Gene? Make a **character web** to identify the "wants" that drive the play. Begin with Gene, his mother, and his father. Keep your web, and add other characters as you meet them.

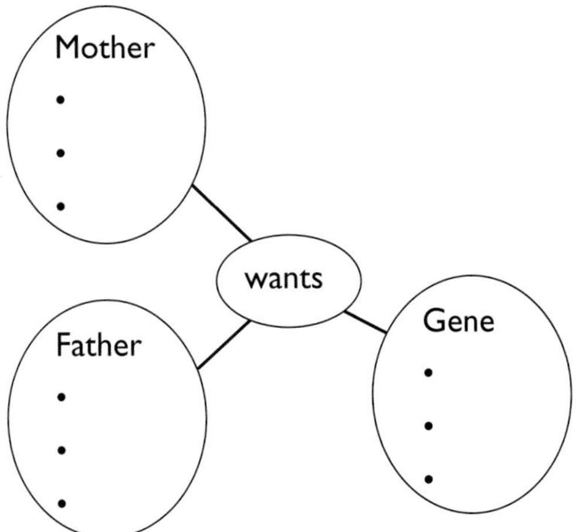

3. How does the information about the father's early life help you to understand his **character**? Does this information make you sympathize with Gene's father? Why, or why not?
4. Gene and his mother are very close. Is Gene entirely happy with this closeness? What incidents give you the answer? Explain what you think of Gene's mother and why you find her sympathetic, unsympathetic, or both.
5. In Gene's last speech in this act, he expresses an **internal conflict**. Why do you think he tells his father he cannot stay the night?
6. What **conflicts** do you **predict** will arise in Act Two? What are some ways the play could end?

Connecting with the Text

7. Margaret tells Gene, "I guess a lot of us forget to say thank you until it's too late." In your experience, is Margaret's remark true?

8. One of the pleasures of seeing or reading a play is feeling the "shock of recognition," the "Oh, yes!" reaction. Did you feel a shock of recognition anywhere in the play so far? Explain. (Be sure to refer to your reading notes.)

Extending the Text

9. Do you agree with Margaret when she says that to "passionate young people," tolerance, sympathy, forbearance, and devotion are unimportant? How important do you think these qualities are in a relationship?

10. Think of movies or television programs that reflect relationships or conflicts similar to those in this play. Which conflicts do you think are handled realistically, and which are not?

VOCABULARY HOW TO OWN A WORD

WORD BANK

exasperation
fumes
coy
nondescript
enunciate
mollified
solicitude
appraised
piqued
incongruous

Synonyms and Antonyms

Synonyms are words that mean more or less the same thing: *warm/tepid, legal/permissible, happy/contented.* **Antonyms** are words with more or less opposite meanings: *warm/cool, legal/illegal, happy/sad.* In the English language there are few perfect synonyms or antonyms, but many words are broadly synonymous or antonymous. A good writer is careful with word choice and is aware of the similarities and the differences between words.

Make a synonym map or an antonym map like the one below for each word at the left (the first one has been done for you). For the next four words, make *antonym* maps: Write an antonym for each word and a sentence about the play or your responses to it, using the antonym. For the last five words, make *synonym* maps. Feel free to use a **thesaurus** for help.

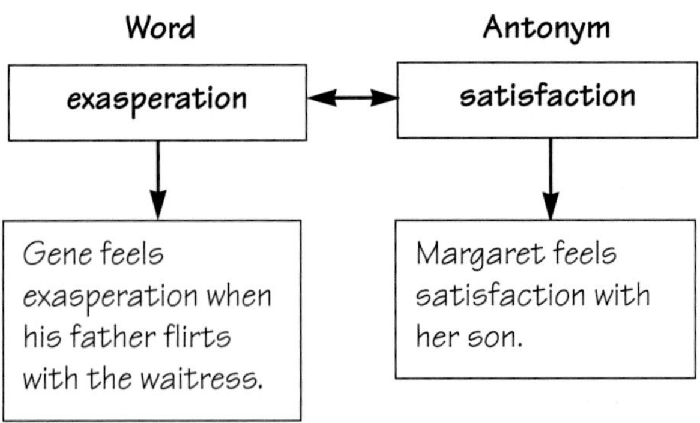
Word
Antonym
exasperation
satisfaction
Gene feels exasperation when his father flirts with the waitress.
Margaret feels satisfaction with her son.

Act Two

GENE *and* DR. MAYBERRY *enter from the rear.* GENE *is carrying a small overnight case containing his mother's things.*

Gene. Thank you for all you've done for her over the years. It's been a great comfort to her, to us all.
Dr. Mayberry. I was very fond of her.
Gene. She was terribly worried about my father's health. Yesterday she said to me, "You know what put me here."
Dr. Mayberry. Well, Gene, I think that's a little too harsh. She's been living on borrowed time for quite a while, you know.
Gene. Yes. . . . Where's Dad?
Dr. Mayberry. He's gone along to the undertaker's. He wanted to wait for you, but since we couldn't reach you this morning, he went along. We sent your mother's nurse to be with him till you arrived.
Gene. Thank you.
Dr. Mayberry. He's all right. You know, Gene, old people live with death. He's been prepared for this for years. It may in some way be a relief. He's taken wonderful care of her.
Gene. Yes, he has.
Dr. Mayberry. Alice will be coming on, I suppose.
Gene. I've called her.
Dr. Mayberry. He shouldn't be staying in that house alone. *(*GENE *nods.)* Now, you have the suitcase and the envelope with your mother's things.
Gene. Yes. I think she should have her wedding ring.
Dr. Mayberry. Maybe you ought to check with your father. . . .
Gene. No. . . . Will you? . . .

[*He hands the ring to* DR. MAYBERRY *and moves away. The lights come up on the undertaker's office.* TOM *and the* NURSE *are there.*]

Tom. I find the constant wind down there very annoying. Every year I think it's going to be different, but it isn't. You get a little overheated in the sun, and when you walk out from behind some shelter, it knifes into you.
Gene *(He has stood looking at his father for a moment. He now comes to him with tenderness, to share the experience).* Dad.
Tom *(looks up in the middle of his story).* Oh, Gene.

[*He gets up shakily. They embrace.* GENE *pats him on the back.* TOM *steps away and shakes his head. His mouth contorts, showing emotion and anger that this should have happened. He looks at the floor in moments like this.*]

Nurse. We've given him a little sedative.[1]
Tom *(looks up).* What?
Nurse. I said we'd given you a little sedative.
Tom *(at once the charmer).* Oh, yes. This lovely lady has taken wonderful care of me.
Gene *(to the* NURSE*).* Thank you.
Tom. It turns out she's been to Florida, very near to where we go.
Gene *(a little surprised at this casual conversation, but playing along).* Oh, really?
Tom. I was telling her it was too bad we didn't have the pleasure of meeting her down there. But she goes in the summer. Isn't it terribly hot down there in the summer?
Nurse. The trade winds are always blowing.
Tom. Oh, yes those damnable winds. We wanted this young man to come join us there, but he went to California instead. *(To* GENE*)* You'll have to come down to Florida sometime. See what lovely girls you'd meet there!
Gene *(baffled and annoyed by this chatter, but passes it off).* I will.
Tom. What was your name again? My mind's like a sieve.
Nurse. Halsey.
Tom *(courtly).* Miss Halsey . . . My son, Gene.
Gene. How do you do?

1. **sedative** (sed′ə·tiv): medication that soothes and calms.

Words to Own
contorts (kən·tôrts′) *v.:* twists out of shape.

Tom. Miss Halsey and I are on rather intimate terms. She . . . uh . . . gave me my shot.
Gene. Good.
Tom *(to the* NURSE*).* I had this terrible cough down there. The winds. But I'll be all right. Don't worry about me. If I can get some regular exercise, get over to the club.

[*For a moment they all just sit there. Obviously there is to be no sharing of the experience of the mother's death.*]

Gene. I called Alice.
Tom. Oh. Thank you. *(To the* NURSE*)* Alice was my daughter. She . . . uh . . . lives in Chicago.
Nurse *(shaking his hand, kindly).* Goodbye, Mr. Garrison.
Tom. Oh, are you going?
Nurse. Yes. Take good care of yourself.
Tom. Oh, well. Thank you very much, my dear. You've been very kind.
Gene. Thank you.

[*The* NURSE *exits.*]

Marvin Scott *(entering with some forms and papers).* Now, Tom, all we have to do is—— *(He looks up from papers and sees* GENE.*)* Oh, hello, Gene.
Gene. Mr. Scott.
Marvin Scott. I'm terribly sorry.
Gene. Thank you.
Marvin Scott. Now, the burial is to be where, Tom? *(Throughout he is simple, considerate, and decent.)*
Tom. The upper burial ground. I've got the deed at home in my file cabinet, if I can ever find it. For years I've meant to clean out that file cabinet. But I'll find it.
Marvin Scott *(to* GENE*).* Will you see that I get it? At least the number of the plot?
Gene. It's 542.
Marvin Scott. You're sure of that?
Gene. My wife was buried there last year.
Tom *(suddenly remembering).* That's right.

[*He reaches out and puts his hand on* GENE*'s arm, implying that they have something to share.* GENE *doesn't really want to share his father's kind of emotionalism.*]

Marvin Scott *(He has been making notes).* We'll need some clothes . . . uh . . .
Gene *(quickly).* Yes, all right. I'll take care of that.
Marvin Scott. Do you want the casket open or closed while she's resting here?

[*There is a pause.*]

Gene. Dad?
Tom. What was that?
Gene. Do you want the casket open or closed?
Tom. Oh . . . open, I think.

[GENE *would have preferred it closed.*]

Marvin Scott. Now, an obituary. Perhaps you would like to prepare something, Tom.
Tom. Yes. Well, . . . Gene? Gene was very close to his mother.

[MARVIN SCOTT *looks at* GENE.]

Gene. Yes, I'll work something up.
Marvin Scott. If you could come by this afternoon, so that it would catch the——
Tom. She was my inspiration. When I met her, the clouds hung low and dark. I was going to night school, studying shorthand and typing and *elocution*[2] . . . and working in a lumberyard in the daytime . . . wearing a cutaway coat, if you please, someone at the church had given me. . . . I was making a home for my brother and sister. . . . My mother had died, and my father had deserted us. . . . *(He has gone hard on his father . . . and stops a moment.)* "He did not know the meaning of the word 'quit.'" They said that some years ago when the Schoolboys of Old Harlem gave me an award. You were there, Gene.
Gene. Yes.
Tom. "Obstructions, yes. But go through them or over them, but never around them." Teddy Roosevelt said that. I took it down in shorthand for practice. . . . Early in life I developed a will of iron. . . . *(You can feel the iron in the way he says it.)* Any young man in this country who has a sound mind and a sound body, who will set himself an objective, can achieve anything he

2. **elocution** (el'ə·kyo͞o'shən): art of public speaking.

wants, within reason. *(He has said all this firmly, as though lecturing or giving a speech. He now looks at his cigarette.)* Ugh. . . . Filthy habit. Twenty years ago a doctor told me to give these things up, and I did. But when things pile up . . . Well, . . . All's lost, all's spent, when we our desires get without content. . . . *(He looks around. There is a pause.)*

Gene. I'll write something.

Tom. About what?

Gene. Mother. For an obituary.

Tom. Oh, yes, you do that. He's the lit'ry member of the family. You'll use the church, won't you? Not the chapel. I imagine there'll be hundreds of people there . . . Garden Club . . . Woman's Club . . . Mother's Club.

Marvin Scott. I'm sure that Reverend Pell will use whichever you want. *(He shuffles some papers.)* Now, Tom, the only thing that's left is the most difficult. We have to choose a coffin.

Tom. Do we have to do that now?

Marvin Scott. It's easier now, Tom. To get it over with.

Tom *(to* GENE, *who is standing back).* Well, we'll have your car, so we shouldn't need another. Anybody else wants to come, let them drive their own car. *(Looks back at the caskets)* Oh, dear . . . Gene! (GENE *comes alongside. He is tender and considerate to the part of his father that is going through a difficult time, though irritated by the part that has always angered him. They walk silently among the caskets for a few moments.* TOM *lifts a price tag and looks at it.)* Two thousand! *(He taps an imaginary casket.)* What are these made of?

Marvin Scott *(coming forward).* They vary, Tom. . . . Steel, bronze, . . . wood.

Tom. What accounts for the variation in prices?

Marvin Scott. Material . . . workmanship . . . the finish inside. You see, this is all silk.

Tom. I suppose the metal stands up best.

Marvin Scott. Well, yes. (TOM *shakes his head, confused.)* Of course the casket does not go directly into the ground. We first sink a concrete outer vault.

Tom. Oh?

She was my inspiration. When I met her, the clouds hung low and dark.

Tom *(firm).* I want the best. That's one thing. I want the best!

Marvin Scott *(moves across the stage with* TOM *and* GENE*).* There are many kinds.

Tom *(As he takes a few steps, he takes* GENE'S *arm).* I don't know what I'd do without this young fellow. *(This kind of word bribery disturbs* GENE. *In the coffin area, overhead lights suddenly come on. Shafts of light in the darkness indicate the coffins.* TOM *claps his hand to his forehead.)* Do I have to look at all these?

Marvin Scott *(gently).* It's the only way, Tom. The best way is to just let you wander around alone and look at them. The prices are all marked on the cards inside the caskets. *(He lifts an imaginary card.)*

Tom *(puts on his glasses to look).* Nine hundred? For the casket?

Marvin Scott. That includes everything, Tom. All our services, and one car for the mourners. Other cars are extra.

Marvin Scott. That prevents seepage, et cetera.

Tom. That's included in the price?

Marvin Scott. Yes.

[TOM *walks on.* GENE *stays in the shadows.*]

Tom. How long do any of these stand up?

[GENE *closes his eyes.*]

Marvin Scott. It's hard to say, Tom. It depends on the location. Trees, roots, and so on.

Tom. I suppose these metal ones are all welded at the seams?

Marvin Scott. Oh, yes.

Tom. Our plot up there is on a small slope. I suppose that's not so good for wear. I didn't think of that when I bought it. . . . And the trees looked so lovely. . . . I never thought.

Marvin Scott *(gently).* I don't think it makes that much difference, Tom.

Tom *(moves along, stops).* For a child?

Marvin Scott. Yes.

Tom. *(shakes his head, moved).* My mother would have fit in that. She was a little bit of a thing. . . . Died when I was ten. *(Tears come to his eyes.)* I don't remember much about her funeral except my father. . . . He'd run out on us, but he came back when she died . . . and I wouldn't let him come to the cemetery. *(He gets angry all over again . . . then:)* Oh, well, . . . water over the dam. But this made me think of her . . . a little bit of a thing. *(GENE is touched by his father's memory of his own mother but still upset at this supermarket type of shopping.)* Five hundred. What do you think of this one, Gene? *(GENE comes up.)* I like the color of the silk. Did you say that was silk or satin?
Marvin Scott. Silk.
Gene. I don't think it makes much difference, Dad. Whatever you think.
Tom. I mean, they all go into this concrete business. *(He senses some disapproval on GENE's part and moves on, then adjusts his glasses.)* This one is eight hundred. I don't see the difference. Marvin, what's the difference?
Marvin Scott. It's mostly finish and workmanship. They're both steel.
Tom. I don't like the browns or blacks. Gray seems less somber. Don't you agree, Gene?
Gene. Yes, I do.
Tom. Eight hundred. Is there a tax, Marvin?

[GENE *turns away.*]

Marvin Scott. That includes the tax, Tom.
Tom. All right. Let's settle for that, then, and get out of here. *(He shivers.)*
Marvin Scott. Fine. *(To GENE)* And you'll send some clothes over?
Gene. Yes. *(GENE bobs his head up and down, annoyed with the details, though MARVIN has been considerate and discreet.)*
Marvin Scott. I'd estimate that Mrs. Garrison should be . . . that is, if people want to come to pay their respects, about noon tomorrow.
Gene. All right.
Marvin Scott. Would you like to see where Mrs. Garrison will be resting?
Gene *(definite).* No, thank you. I think we'll be moving along.
Marvin Scott. I assume your sister Alice will be coming on?
Gene. She arrives this evening. *(He looks around for his father and sees him standing in front of the child's coffin, staring at it. He goes over to his father and takes him gently by the arm.)* Shall we go, Dad?
Tom *(nods his head, far away).* She was just a little bit of a thing.

[*And they start moving out of the room, as the lights dim out.*
As the lights come up again on another part of the stage, ALICE, GENE*'s older sister, is coming on. She is in her early forties, attractive, brisk, realistic, unsentimental.*]

Alice. Shouldn't we be getting home to Dad?
Gene *(Carrying two highballs. He is blowing off steam).* I suppose so, but I'm not ready to go home yet. . . . Let's sit over here, where we can get away from the noise at the bar.
Alice. You've had quite a day.
Gene. I'm sorry for blowing off, but damn it, Alice, our mother died this morning, and I've wanted to talk about her, but she hasn't been mentioned except as "my inspiration," which is his cue to start the story of his life.
Alice. I'm sorry you've had to take it all alone.
Gene. Well, I'm glad you're here, and I'm glad of the chance to get out of the house to come to meet you. . . . I'm so tired of hearing about "when the clouds hung low and dark." . . . I'm so tired of people coming up to me and saying, "Your dad's a remarkable man." Nobody talks about Mother. Just, "He's a remarkable man." You'd think he died! . . . I want to say to them, "My mother was a remarkable woman. . . . You don't know my father. You only know the man in the newspapers. He's a selfish man who's lived on the edge of exasperation all his life. You don't know the bite of his sarcasm. The night he banished my sister for marrying someone he didn't approve of did not get into the papers."
Alice. *Shhh* . . .
Gene. What a night that was! Mother running from the room sobbing. You shouting at him and storming out, and the two of us, father and

But you were so good to her.
You made her life.

son, left to finish dinner, in silence. Afterward I threw up.

Alice. I shouted and you threw up. That was pretty much the pattern.

Gene. I know I'm being unfair. But I'm in the mood to be unfair. I've wanted to turn to him all day and say, "Will you for once shut up about your miserable childhood and say something about Mother?" *(A little ashamed of his outburst)* But I can't say that. He's an old man and my father, and his wife has died, and he may be experiencing something, somewhere, I know nothing about. *(He shakes his head for going on like this.)* I'm sorry.

Alice. It's all right.

Gene. No. *(He touches her arm, smiles.)* Mother loved your flowers.

Alice. I've felt guilty about Mother all the way coming here. I should have seen her more, invited her more often, brought the kids more often. Instead I sent flowers.

Gene. I guess that's an inevitable feeling when a person dies. I feel the same way.

Alice. But you were so good to her. You made her life.

Gene *(He has always hated that phrase. Slowly, quietly).* A son is not supposed to make his mother's life. . . . Oh, I loved Mother. You know that. But to be depended on to make her life . . . Dad says, he boasts, he never knew the meaning of the word "quit." Well, he quit on her all right. And I . . . I was just there. *(*ALICE *looks at this sudden revelation of his feelings, his resentment that he was left to save his mother from loneliness and unhappiness.)* Still, wait till you see him. There's something that comes through . . . the old Tiger. Something that reaches you and makes you want to cry. . . . He'll probably be asleep when we get home, in front of the television. And you'll see. The Old Man . . . the Father. But then he wakes up and becomes Tom Garrison, and I'm in trouble. . . . Last night he asked me to stay with him, and I didn't. . . . I couldn't. I'm ashamed of that now.

Alice *(Touched by the complexity of* GENE*'s feelings, she looks at him a long moment, then).* Have you called California?

Gene *(Frowns. A problem).* No. *(He takes a drink, wanting to avoid the subject.)*

Alice. I suppose we have enough problems for the next few days, but . . .

Gene. After?

Alice. Yes. We'll have to start thinking about Dad, about what we're going to do.

Gene *(nods his head).* I don't know. *(They look at each other a moment, then)* Well, let's go home. *(He rises.)* Thanks for listening to all this, Alice. You had to pay good money to get someone to listen to you. I appreciate it. *(He smiles.)* I thought I wanted to talk to you about Mother, but all I've done is talk about him, just like the others.

Alice. We'll talk. There'll be time.

[*And they leave. The lights dim out on the bar area and come up on the home area.* TOM *is asleep, his head forward, his glasses on, some legal papers in his lap. Quiet like this, he is a touching picture of old age. The strong face . . . the good but gnarled hands. He is the symbol of Father. The television is on. As* GENE *and* ALICE *come in, they pause and look. They are impressed by the sad dignity. Finally* GENE *approaches and gently puts his hand on his father's arm, then turns down the television.*]

Gene. Dad?

Tom *(barely stirs).* Hm?

Gene. Dad?

Tom. Mm? Margaret? *(Coming to a little more and looking up at* GENE*)* . . . Oh, Gene . . . I must have dozed off.

Gene. Alice is here.

Tom. Alice? . . . What for? *(He is genuinely confused.)*

Alice *(comes from the shadows).* Hello, Dad.

Tom *(Looks around, a bit panicky, confused. Then he remembers).* Oh. . . . Oh, yes.

[*He bites his upper lip and with his gnarled hands grips theirs for a moment of affection and family strength.* ALICE *kisses him on the cheek. They help him from the chair and start putting on his coat. As the lights dim on the home area, they come up on a graveyard area.* TOM, GENE, *and* ALICE, *and all the people we have met are gathering as* REVEREND PELL *starts his eulogy.*]

Reverend Pell. Margaret Garrison was a loving wife and a kind and generous mother, and a public-spirited member of the community. The many people who were touched by her goodness can attest to the pleasure and joy she brought them through her love of life and her power to communicate this love to others. The many children, now grown . . .

Gene *(turns from the family group).* Only a dozen or so people were at my mother's funeral. Most of her friends were dead or had moved to other cities or just couldn't make it. Fifteen years earlier the church would have been filled. There were a few men sent from Rotary, a few women from the Garden Club, the Mother's Club, the Woman's Club, and a few of the members of her bridge club were there. . . . The hundreds of children who had listened to her tell stories year after year on Christmas Eve were all gone, or had forgotten. . . . Perhaps some of them who were still in the neighborhood looked up from their evening papers to say, "I see Mrs. Garrison died. She was nice. . . . Well, she was an old lady." *(He turns to rejoin the family group.)*

Reverend Pell. Earth to earth . . . ashes to ashes . . . dust to dust. . . . The Lord giveth and the Lord taketh away. . . . Blessed be the name of the Lord. . . . Amen.

[TOM *comes to shake hands with* REVEREND PELL.

Words to Own

eulogy (yo͞o′lə·jē) *n.:* formal speech praising a person who has recently died.

Margaret Garrison was
a loving wife . . .

The others drift about, exchanging nods, and gradually leave during the following.]

Tom. Well, it's a nice place up here.
Gene *(who has wandered over to look at another grave).* Yes.
Tom. Your mother and I bought it soon after we were married. She thought it a strange thing to do, but we bought it. *(He looks at the grave* GENE *is looking at.)* Now, let's see, that's . . .
Gene. Carol.
Tom. Who?
Gene. Carol. My wife.
Tom. Oh, yes. *(He reaches out a sympathetic hand toward* GENE, *then moves away.)* There's room for three more burials up here, as I remember. There . . . there . . . and there. I'm to go there, when the time comes. *(He looks around for a moment.)* This plot is in terrible shape. . . . I paid three hundred dollars some years ago for perpetual care, and now look at it. Just disgraceful . . . I'm going to talk to that superintendent.

[*And he strides off. The lights change.* ALICE *and* GENE *move into another area, what might be a garden with a bench. For a moment neither says anything.* GENE *lights a cigarette and sits on the grass.*]

Alice. I don't know how you feel, but I'd like to figure out some kind of memorial for Mother. . . . Use some of the money she left.
Gene. Yes, definitely.
Alice. Maybe some shelves of books for the children's library. Christmas books with the stories she liked to tell.
Gene. That's a good idea.

WORDS TO OWN
perpetual (pər·pech′o͞o·əl) *adj.:* continual; constant.

[*There is a long and awkward pause.*]

Alice. Well, Gene, what are we going to do?

Gene *(frowns).* Mother always said to put her in an old-people's home. She had one all picked out.

Alice. Sidney's mother and father saw it coming and arranged to be in one of those cottage colonies for old people.

Gene. Mother and Dad didn't.

Alice. I think you should go ahead and get married and move to California. . . . But . . . I might as well get this off my chest, it would be murder if he came to live with us. In the first place, he wouldn't do it, feeling as he does about Sid, and the kids can't stand how he tells them how to do everything.

Gene. I think you're right. That would never work. *(There is a pause.* GENE *looks out at the garden.)* I can't tell you what it does to me as a man . . . to see someone like that . . . a man who was distinguished, remarkable . . . just become a nuisance.

Alice *(She is disturbed at what her brother may be thinking).* I know I sound hard, but he's had his life . . . and as long as we can be assured that he's taken care of . . . Oh, I'll feel some guilt, and you, maybe more. But my responsibility is to my husband and my children.

Gene. Yes. That's *your* responsibility.

Alice. And your responsibility is to yourself . . . to get married again, to get away from memories of Carol and her whole world. Have you called California?

Gene *(frowns).* No.

Alice. If I were the girl you were planning to marry, and you didn't call me to tell me your mother had died . . .

Gene *(gets up, disturbed).* I just haven't wanted to go into it all with her.

Alice *(understanding, but worried).* Gene, my friend . . . my brother . . . Get out of here!

Gene. Look, Alice, your situation is quite different. Mine is very complex. You fortunately see things very clearly, but it's not so easy for me. *(*ALICE *looks at* GENE*, troubled by what his thinking seems to be leading to. After a moment . . . reflective)* We always remember the terrible things about Dad. I've been trying to remember some of the others. . . . How much he *did* do for us.

Alice. I'm doing a lot for my kids. I don't expect them to pay me back at the other end. *(*GENE *wanders around, thinking, scuffing the grass.)* I'm sure we could find a full-time housekeeper. He can afford it.

Gene. He'd never agree.

Alice. It's that or finding a home. *(*GENE *frowns.)* Sidney's folks like where they are. Also, we might as well face it, his mind's going. Sooner or later, we'll have to think about powers of attorney, perhaps committing him to an institution.

Gene. It's all so ugly.

Alice *(smiling).* Yes, my gentle Gene, a lot of life is.

Gene. Now, look, don't go trying to make me out some softhearted . . . *(He can't find the word.)* I know life is ugly.

Alice. Yes, I think you know it. You've lived through a great deal of ugliness. But you work like a Trojan to deny it, to make it not so. *(After a moment, not arguing)* He kicked me out. He said he never wanted to see me again. He broke Mother's heart over that for years. He was mean, unloving. He beat you when you were a kid. . . . You've hated and feared him all your adult life. . . .

Gene *(cutting in).* Still he's my father, and a man. And what's happening to him appalls me as a man.

Alice. We have a practical problem here.

Gene. It's not as simple as all that.

Alice. To me it is. I don't understand this mystical haze you're casting over it. I'm going to talk to him tomorrow, after the session with the lawyer, about a housekeeper. *(*GENE *reacts, but says nothing.)* Just let me handle it. He can visit us, and we can take turns coming to visit him. Now, I'll do the dirty work. Only when he turns to you, don't give in.

Gene. I can't tell you how ashamed I feel . . . not to say with open arms, "Poppa, come live with me . . . I love you, Poppa, and I want to take care of you." . . . I need to love him. I've always wanted to love him.

[*He drops his arms and wanders off.* ALICE *watches her brother drift off into the garden as the lights go down in that area. The lights come up in the living room area.* TOM *is seated in his chair, writing.* ALICE *comes into the room. Small packing boxes are grouped around.*]

Alice. How are you coming?
Tom. Oh, Alice, I've written out receipts for you to sign for the jewelry your mother left you. And if you'll sign for the things she left the children.
Alice. All right.

[*Signs.* GENE *comes into the room carrying a box full of his mother's things. He exchanges a look with* ALICE, *knowing the time has come for the discussion.*]

Tom. It may not be necessary, but as executor, I'll be held responsible for these things.
Alice. Dad, I'd like to talk a little . . . with you . . . about——
Tom. Yes, all right. But first I'd like to read you this letter I've written to Harry Hall. . . . He and I used to play golf out in New Jersey. . . . He wrote a very nice letter to me about your mother . . . and I've written him as follows, . . . it will only take a minute, . . . if I can read my own shorthand . . . *(He adjusts his glasses.)* "Dear Harry, . . . How thoughtful of you to write me on the occasion of Margaret's death. It was quite a blow. As you know, she was my inspiration, and had been ever since that day fifty-five years ago when I met her, . . . when the clouds hung low and dark for me. At that time I was supporting my younger brother and my sister and my aged grandfather in a two-room flat . . . going to work every day in a lumber mill. Providence, which has always guided me, prompted me to take a night course in shorthand and typing, and also prompted me to go to the Underwood Typewriting Company seeking a position as stenographer. They sent me, God be praised, to the office of T. J. Parks . . . and a job that started at five dollars a week ended in 1929 when I retired at fifty thousand a year. . . ." That's as far as I've gotten at the moment. *(He looks up for approval.)*
Gene. Dad, I don't think financial matters are particularly appropriate in answering a letter of condolence.
Tom. Oh? *(He looks at the letter.)* But it's true. You see, it follows. I'm saying she was my inspiration . . . and it seems entirely appropriate to explain that.
Gene. Well, it's your letter, Dad.
Tom *(looks it over).* Well . . .
Alice. Dad, I'm leaving tomorrow . . . and . . .
Tom *(looking up).* What?
Alice. I'm going home tomorrow.
Tom *(formal).* Well, Alice, I'm grateful you came. I know it was difficult for you, leaving home. Your mother would have appreciated it. She was very fond of you, Alice.
Alice. I think we ought to talk over, maybe, what your plans are.
Tom. My plans? I have many letters to answer, and a whole mess in my files and accounts. If the income tax people ever asked me to produce my books . . .
Gene. They're not likely to, Dad. Your income is no longer of that size.
Tom *(with a twinkle in his eye).* Don't be too sure.
Alice. I didn't mean exactly that kind of plan. I meant . . . Well, you haven't been well.
Tom *(belligerent).* Who said so?
Alice. Mother was worried to death about—— *(She stops.)*
Tom. I was under a strain. Your mother's health . . . never knowing when it might happen. Trying to get her to take care of herself, to take it easy. You know, the doctor said if she didn't eat more slowly, this might happen.
Alice. You plan to keep the house?
Tom. Oh, yes. All my things are here. . . . It's a . . . It's a . . . I'll be back on my feet, and my . . . *(points to his head)* . . . will clear up. Now this strain is over, I'm confident I'll be in shape any day now.

Words to Own

executor (eg·zek′·yo͞o·tər) *n.:* person who carries out the provisions of a will.

Alice. I worry, leaving you in this house . . . alone, Dad.

Tom *(looks around, very alert, defensively).* I'm perfectly all right. Now don't worry about me . . . either of you. Why, for the last year, since your mother's first attack, I've been getting the breakfast, making the beds, using a dust rag. . . . *(He makes quite a performance of this. It is a gallant struggle.)* And the laundress comes in once a week and cleans up for me. . . . And Gene here . . . if Gene will keep an eye on me, drop in once or twice a week . . .

Alice. That's the point.

Gene *(low).* Alice!

Alice. We think you should have a full-time housekeeper, Dad. To live here.

Tom *(trying to kid it off, but angry).* Alone here with me? That wouldn't be very proper, would it?

Alice *(smiling).* Nevertheless . . .

Tom. No. Now that's final!

Alice. Dad, Gene and I would feel a lot better about it if——

Tom. Look, you don't have to worry about me.

Alice. Dad, you're forgetting things more and more.

Tom. Who says so?

Alice. Mother wrote me, and——

Tom. I was under a strain. I just finished telling you. Look, Alice, you can go, leave with a clear mind. I'm all right. *(*GENE *is touched and moved by his father's effort, his desperate effort to maintain his dignity, his standing as a functioning man.)* Of course, I will appreciate Gene's dropping in. But I'm all right.

Alice. We still would like to get a full-time housekeeper.

Tom *(bristling).* What do you mean, you would get? I've hired and fired thousands of people in my day. I don't need anyone *getting* someone for me.

Alice. Will you do it yourself, then?

Tom. No, I told you. No! *(He gets very angry. His voice sharpens and hardens.)* Since I was eight years old, I've taken care of myself. What do you two know about it? You were given everything on a platter. At an age when you two were swinging on that tree out there, breaking the branches, I was selling newspapers five hours a day, and at night dancing a jig in saloons for pennies. . . . And you're trying to tell me I can't take care of myself. . . . If I want a housekeeper, and I don't, I'll hire one. . . . I've hired and fired thousands of people in my time. When I was vice president of Colonial Brass at fifty thousand a year . . . two thousand people. And you tell me I'm incompetent . . . to hire a housekeeper. And how many people have you hired? *(To* GENE*)* You teach. . . . Well, all right. That's your business, if that's what you want to do. But don't talk to me about hiring and firing.

I took care of myself at eight.

[*The children are saddened and perhaps a little* cowed *by this naked outburst, the defense of a man who knows that he is slipping, and an angry outburst of hatred and jealousy for his own children. Everyone is quiet for a moment . . . then:*]

Alice. Dad, you might fall down.

Tom. Why fall down? There's nothing wrong with my balance.

[GENE *is sick at this gradual attempt to bring to a man's consciousness the awareness that he is finished.*]

Alice. Sometimes, when you get up, you're dizzy.

Tom. Nonsense. *(He gets up abruptly. He makes great effort and stands for a moment, then one foot moves slightly to steady his balance . . . and the children both look away.)* Now I appreciate your concern. . . . *(Very fatherly)* But I'm perfectly able to carry on by myself. As I said, with Gene's help from time to

WORDS TO OWN

cowed (koud) *v.* used as *adj.:* made timid and submissive; unwilling to argue.

time. I imagine we could have dinner every once in a while, couldn't we, Gene . . . once a week or so? Take you up to Rotary. Some of the speakers are quite amusing.

[ALICE *looks at* GENE *to see if he is going to speak up.*]

Gene. Sure, Dad.
Tom. Give us some time together at last. Get to know each other.
Alice *(quietly but firmly).* Gene wants to get married.
Gene. Alice!
Tom. What?
Alice. Gene wants to move to California and get married.
Tom. I have long gotten the impression that my only function in this family is to supply the money to——
Gene *(anguished).* Dad!
Tom. ——to supply the funds for your education, for your——
Gene. Dad, stop it!

[TOM *staggers a little, dizzy.* GENE *goes to his side to steady him.* TOM *breathes heavily in and out in rage. The rage of this man is a terrible thing to see, old as he is. He finally gets some control of himself.*]

Tom. As far as I am concerned, this conversation is ended. Alice, we've gotten along very well for some years now without your attention.

I can take care of myself at eighty.

Gene. Alice, shut up.
Alice *(almost in tears).* I can't help it. You've never faced up to him. You'd let him ruin your life.
Gene *(angry).* I can take care of my own life.
Alice. You can't!
Tom *(loud).* Children! . . . Children! *(They stop arguing and turn to their father at his command.* TOM *speaks with a note of sarcasm.)* I have no desire to interfere with either of your lives. I took care of myself at eight. I can take care of myself at eighty. I have never wanted to be a burden to my children.
Gene. I'm going to hang around, Dad.
Gene *(protesting, but hating the fight).* Dad!
Alice. You sent me away. Don't forget that.
Tom. You chose to lead your own life. Well, we won't keep you now.
Gene. Dad . . .
Tom *(rage again).* I was competent to go into the city year after year to earn money for your clothes, your food, the roof over your head. Am I now incompetent? Is that what you're trying to tell me? *(He looks at* ALICE *with a terrible look. He breathes heavily for a moment or two; then, shaking his head, he turns away from both of them and leaves, disappearing into the shadows.)*

I have never wanted to be a burden to my children.

Tom. There's no need to.
Gene. I'll move in here at least till you're feeling better.

[ALICE *turns away, angry and despairing.*]

Tom *(sarcastically).* I don't want to ruin your life.
Gene *(angry now at his father).* I didn't say that.
Gene *(angry, troubled).* Alice!
Alice. I'm only trying to get a practical matter accomplished.
Gene. You don't have to destroy him in the process.
Alice. I wasn't discussing his competence. Although that will be a matter for discussion soon.
Gene. Look, Alice, just leave it now, the way it is. Don't say any more.

Alice. With you staying on.

Gene. Yes. You can go with a clear conscience.

Alice. My conscience is clear.

Gene. I am doing this because I want to.

Alice. You're doing it because you can't help yourself.

Gene. Look, when I want to be analyzed, I'll pay for it.

Alice *(pleading).* But I saw you. Didn't you see yourself there, when he started to rage? Didn't you feel yourself pull in? You shrank.

Gene. I shrank at the ugliness of what was happening.

Alice. You're staying because you can't stand his wrath the day you say, "Dad, I'm leaving." You've never been able to stand up to his anger. He's cowed you.

Gene. Look, Alice . . .

Alice. He'll call you ungrateful, and you'll believe him. He'll lash out at you with his sarcasm, and that will kill this lovely, necessary image you have of yourself as the good son. Can't you see that?

Gene *(lashing out).* What do you want us to do? Shall we get out a white paper?[3] Let it be known that we, Alice and Gene, have done all that we can to make this old man happy in his old age, without inconveniencing ourselves, of course. And he has refused our help. So, if he falls and hits his head and lies there until he rots, it is not our fault. Is that it?

Alice. You insist on——

Gene *(running on).* Haven't you learned on the couch[4] that people do *not* always do what you want them to do? It is sometimes *we* who have to make the adjustments?

Alice. The difference between us is that I accept the inevitable sadness of this world without an acute sense of personal guilt. You don't. I don't think anyone expects either of us to ruin our lives for an unreasonable old man.

Gene. It's not going to ruin my life.

Alice. It is.

Gene. A few weeks, a month.

Alice. Forever!

3. **white paper:** official report.
4. **on the couch:** reference to the couch on which patients in a psychiatrist's office often lie down.

Gene. Alice, let's not go on discussing it. I know what I am going to do. Maybe I can't explain my reasons to you. I just know I can't do anything else. Maybe there isn't the same thing between a mother and a daughter, but the "old man" in me feels something very deep, wants to extend some kind of mercy to that old man. I never had a father. I ran away from him. He ran away from me. Maybe he's right. Maybe it is time we found each other.

Alice. Excuse me for saying so, but I find that sentimental slop! I think this is all rationalization to make tolerable a compulsion you have to stay here. You hate the compulsion, so you've dressed it up to look nice.

Gene. How do you know what you're saying isn't a rationalization to cover up a callousness, a selfishness, a coldness in yourself? To make *it* smell nice?

Alice. What do you think you'll find?

Gene. I don't know.

Alice. You hope to find love. Couldn't you tell from what he just said what you're going to find? Don't you understand he's got to hate you? He may not think it in his head or feel it in his heart, but you are his enemy! From the moment you were born a boy, you were a threat to this man and his enemy.

Gene. That sounds like the textbooks, Alice.

Alice. He wants your guts . . . and he's had them! *(GENE stands, starts to leave the room.)* I'm sorry. I want to shock you. When has he ever regarded you as a man, an equal, a male? When you were a Marine. And that you did for him. Because even back there you were looking for his love. You didn't want to be a Marine. "Now, Poppa, will you love me?" And he did. No, not love. But he was proud and grateful because you gave him an extension of himself he could boast about, with his phony set of values.

Words to Own

compulsion (kəm·pul′shən) *n.:* strong urge to do something even if there is no sensible reason for doing it.

callousness (kal′əs·nis) *n.:* hardheartedness; lack of feeling for other people.

When was he ever proud about the things *you* do? The things *you* value? When did he ever mention your teaching or your books, except in scorn?

Gene. You don't seem to have felt the absence of a father. But I feel incomplete, deprived. I just do not want to let my father die a stranger to me.

Alice. You're looking for something that isn't there, Gene. You're looking for a mother's love in a father. Mothers are soft and yielding. Fathers are hard and rough, to teach us the way of the world, which is rough, which is mean, which is selfish and prejudiced.

Gene. All right. That's your definition. And because of what he did to you, you're entitled to it.

Alice. I've always been grateful to him for what he did. He taught me a marvelous lesson and has made me able to face a lot. And there has been a lot to face, and I'm grateful to him. Because if I couldn't get the understanding and compassion from a father, who could I expect it from in the world? Who in the world, if not from a father? So I learned and didn't expect it, and I've found very little, and so I'm grateful to him. I'm grateful to him. *(The growing intensity ends in tears, and she turns her head.)*

Gene *(Looks in pity at the involuntary revelation of her true feeling. He moves to her and touches her)*. I'll stay, Alice . . . for a while, at least . . . for whatever reasons. Let's not argue anymore.

Alice. And Peggy?

Gene. She'll be coming in a week or two, we'll see.

Alice. Don't lose her, Gene. Maybe I'm still fouled up on myself, but I think I've spoken near the truth about you.

Gene. I keep wondering why I haven't called her, or wanted to call her. Why I seem so much closer to Carol at the moment.

Alice *(gently, tentatively).* The image . . . of the eternally bereaved husband . . . forgive me . . . the dutiful son . . . they're very appealing and seductive. . . . But they're not living. *(GENE just stands, looking at her, thinking about what she has said. ALICE kisses him on the cheek.)* Good night, Gene.

Gene *(his hands on her shoulders).* Good night.

Alice *(She suddenly puts her head tight against his shoulder and holds him).* Suddenly, I miss Mother so.

[*She sobs. He just holds her and strokes her back.*]

Gene. Yes. *(And he holds her, comforting her, as the lights dim.)*

[*After a few moments of darkness the lights come up on* TOM *in his bedroom in pajamas and bathrobe, kneeling by his bed, praying. On his bed is a small top drawer of a bureau, filled with mementos.* GENE *comes in. He stands in the shadows and watches his father at his prayers.* GENE *does not pray anymore, and he has always been touched by the sight of his father praying.* TOM *gets up and starts to untie his bathrobe.*]

Gene. You ready to be tucked in?

Tom *(smiling).* Yes. *(Loosening his robe)* Look at the weight I've lost.

Gene *(Troubled at the emaciated body, which is pathetic. The face is ruddy and strong, the body that of an old man).* Since when?

Tom. Oh, I don't know.

Gene *(tapping his father's stomach).* Well, you had quite a little pot there, Dad.

Tom *(smiling).* Did I?

Gene. Yes.

Tom. But look, all through here, through my chest.

Gene. Well, we'll put some back on you. You've been eating pretty well this last week.

Tom *(looking at his own chest).* You know, I never had hair on my chest. I don't understand it. You have hair on your chest. I just didn't have any. Well, I'm confident if I could get some exer-

WORDS TO OWN

bereaved (bē·rēvd') *adj.:* sad or lonely because of the death of a loved one.

emaciated (ē·mā'shē·āt'id) *adj.:* abnormally thin, usually because of disease or starvation.

cise, . . . Do you remember when I used to get you up in the morning, and we'd go down and do calisthenics to the radio?

Gene *(smiling).* Yes.

Tom *(stands very straight, swings his arms).* One-two-three-four . . . One-two-three-four . . .

Gene. Hey, take it easy.

Tom. I used to swing the Indian clubs every day at lunchtime. I gave you a set once, didn't I?

Gene. I think so.

Tom. We'll have to dig them out. *(Starts bending exercises)* One-two-three-four . . . one-two-three-four.

Gene. Why don't you wait till morning for that?

Tom. Remember when we used to put on the gloves and spar down on the side porch? . . . I don't think you ever liked it very much. *(He crouches in boxing position.)* The manly art of self-defense . . . Gentleman Jim Corbett . . . Now it's something else again. . . . Oh, well, things to worry about. But I intend to get over to the club, play some golf, sit around and swap stories with the boys. Too bad you never took up golf. Alice could have played a good game of golf. But she had a temper. Inherited it from your mother's father. *(He fishes in the bureau drawer on the bed.)* I was looking through my bureau drawer . . . I don't know, just going over things . . . Did you ever see this? *(He takes out a small revolver.)*

Gene. Yes.

Tom. Never had occasion to use it. Oh, I took it out west one winter when we went to Arizona instead of Florida. Shot at rattlesnakes in a rock pile. *(Takes potshots)* I don't have a permit for this anymore. *(Starts putting it back in its box)* I suppose they wouldn't give me one. I don't know anyone up there anymore. When I was mayor, cops on every corner would wave, . . . "Hello, Mr. Garrison. . . . 'Morning, Mr. Garrison." Now, one of the young whippersnappers gave me a ticket, just before we left for Florida. Said I'd passed a full-stop sign. That's what *he* said. First ticket I had in forty or more years of driving, so keep this quiet. *(He takes out a packet of photographs wrapped in tissue paper.)* Pictures . . . I think you've seen most of them. . . . The family.

Gene *(very tentatively).* You know, Dad, I've never seen a picture of your father. *(*TOM *looks at him a long time. Then finally, with his hatred showing on his face, he unwraps another tissue and hands over a small picture.* GENE *looks at it a long moment.)* He's just a boy.

Tom. That was taken about the time he was married.

Gene. I'd always thought of him as . . . the way

Your mother used to talk of you children as her jewels.

you talked about him . . . as . . . *(*GENE *is obviously touched by the picture.)*

Tom. Oh, he was a fine-looking man before he started to drink. Big, square, high color. But he became my mortal enemy. . . . Did I ever show you that? *(He takes out a small piece of paper.)* Careful. . . . When I set up a home for my brother and sister, one day we were all out, and he came around and ripped up all my sister's clothes and shoes. Drunk, of course. A few days later he came around to apologize and ask for some money, and I threw him out. . . . The next day he left this note, . . . "You are welcome to your burden."

Gene. And you kept it?

Tom. Yes. I never saw him again until many years later he was dying, in Bellevue, and someone got word to me, and I went down and asked him if he wanted anything. He said he'd like some fruit. So I sent him a few oranges. He died the next day.

Gene. There must have been something there to love, to understand.

Tom. In my father? *(Shakes his head "no." Then he shows* GENE *another card.)* Do you remember this? *(He reads.)* "To the best dad in the world on Father's Day." That was in . . . *(Turns over and reads the notation)* 1946. . . . Yes. *(Emotional)* I appreciate that, Gene. That's a lovely tribute. I think I have all your Father's Day cards here. You know, your mother used to talk of you children as her jewels. Maybe because my interests were different, I've always said you were my dividends. . . . You know, I didn't want children, coming from the background I did . . . and we didn't have Alice for a long time. But your mother finally persuaded me. She said they would be a comfort in our old age. And you are, Gene.

Gene *(touched, but embarrassed and uncomfortable).* Well . . .

Tom *(fishes in the drawer and brings out a sheet of paper).* A program of yours from college . . . some glee club concert . . . I've got everything but the kitchen stove in here. *(Looks over the program)* Do you still sing?

Gene *(smiling).* Not in years.

Tom. That's too bad. You had a good voice. But we can't do everything. . . . I remember your mother would sit at the piano, hour after hour, and I'd be up here at my desk and I'd hear you singing.

Gene. You always asked me to sing "When I Grow Too Old to Dream."

Tom. Did I? . . . I don't remember your ever singing that. . . . You always seemed to be just finishing when I came into the room. . . . *(Looks at* GENE*)* Did you used to sing that for me?

Gene *(not a joke anymore).* No. . . . But you always asked me to sing it for you.

Tom. Oh . . . *(puts the program away).* Well, I enjoyed sitting up here and listening. *(He pokes around in his box and takes something out . . . in tissue paper. He unwraps a picture carefully.)* And that's my mother.

Gene *(gently).* Yes. I've seen that, Dad. It's lovely.

Tom. She was twenty-five when that was taken. She died the next year. . . . I carried it in my wallet for years. . . . And then I felt I was wearing it out. So I put it away. . . . Just a little bit of a thing . . . *(He starts to cry, and the deep, deep sobs finally come, and his emaciated body is wracked by them. It is a terrible, almost soundless sobbing.* GENE *comes to his father and puts his arms around him and holds him. After moments)* I didn't think it would be this way. . . . I always thought I'd go first. *(He sobs again, gasping for air.* GENE *continues to hold him, inevitably moved and touched by this genuine suffering. Finally,* TOM *gets a stern grip on himself.)* I'm sorry. . . . *(Tries to shake it off)* It just comes over me. . . . It'll pass. . . . I'll get a hold of myself.

Gene. Don't try, Dad. . . . Believe me, it's best.

Tom *(angry with himself).* No. . . . It's just that . . . I'll be all right. *(He turns and blows his nose.)*

I've always said you were my dividends.

Gene. It's rough, Dad. . . . It's bound to be rough.

Tom *(shakes his head to snap out of it).* It'll pass . . . it'll pass. . . . *(Starts to wrap up the picture of his mother)*

Gene. Can I help you put these things away, Dad?

Tom. No . . . No . . . I can . . . *(He seems to be looking for something he can't find.)* Well, if you would. *(*GENE *helps him wrap the pictures.)* I don't know what we'd do without you. . . .

[*And together they put the things back in the box. As they do so,* GENE *is deeply moved with feelings of tenderness for his father. After a few moments he starts, with great consideration.*]

Gene. Dad?

Tom. Yes?

Gene *(carefully).* You remember . . . I wrote you about California . . . and Peggy?

Tom. What?

Gene. The girl . . . in California.

Tom *(on guard).* Oh, yes.

Gene *(putting it carefully, and slowly).* I'm thinking very seriously, Dad . . . of going out there . . . to marry . . . and to live. *(*TOM *straightens up a little.)* Now, I know this is your home, where you're used to . . . but I'd like you to come out there with me, Dad. . . . It's lovely out there, as you said, and we could find an apartment for you near us. *(This is the most loving gesture* GENE *has made to his father in his life.)*

Tom *(thinks for a moment, then looks at* GENE *with a smile).* You know, I'd like to make a suggestion. . . . Why don't you all come live here?

Gene *(explaining calmly).* Peggy has a practice out there.

Tom. A what?

Gene. She's a doctor. I told you. And children with schools and friends.

Tom. We have a big house here. You always liked this house. It's wonderful for children. You used to play baseball out back, and there's that basketball thing.

Gene. Dad, I'd like to get away from this part of the country for a while. It's been rough here ever since Carol died. It would be good for you too, getting away.

Tom. Your mother would be very happy to have the house full of children again. I won't be around long, and then it would be all yours.

Gene. That's very kind of you, Dad. But I don't think that would work. Besides her work and the children, all Peggy's family is out there.

Tom. Your family is here.

Gene. Yes, I know.

Tom. Just me, of course.

Gene. You see, the children's father is out there, and they're very fond of him and see him a lot.

Tom. Divorced?

Gene. Yes.

Tom. You know, Gene, I'm only saying this for your own good, but you went out there very soon after Carol's death, and you were exhausted from her long illness, and well, naturally, very susceptible. . . . I was wondering if you've really waited long enough to know your own mind.

Gene. I know my own mind.

Tom. I mean, taking on another man's children. You know, children are far from the blessing they're supposed to be. . . . And then there's the whole matter of discipline, of keeping them in line. You may rule them with a rod of iron, but if this father——

Gene *(cutting in).* I happen to love Peggy.

Tom *(looks at* GENE *a long moment).* Did you mention this business of California to your mother?

Gene *(gets the point, but keeps level).* She mentioned it to me and told me to go ahead, with her blessings.

Tom. She would say that, of course. . . . But I warned you.

Gene *(turns away).* For God's sake——

Tom *(giving up, angry).* All right, go ahead. I can manage. . . . *(His sarcasm)* Send me a Christmas card, . . . if you remember.

Gene *(enraged).* Dad!

Tom. What?

Gene. I've asked you to come with me!

Tom. And I've told you I'm not going.

Gene. I understand that, but not this "send me a Christmas card, if you remember."

Tom. I'm very sorry if I offended you. Your mother always said I mustn't raise my voice to you. *(Suddenly hard and vicious)* Did you want me to make it easy for you the way your mother did? Well, I won't. If you want to go, go!

Gene. Dad!

Tom *(running on).* I've always known it would come to this when your mother was gone. I was tolerated around this house because I paid the bills and——

Gene. Shut up!

Tom *(coming at him).* Don't you——

Gene *(shouting).* Shut up! I asked you to come with me. What do you want? For God's sake, what do you want? If I lived here the rest of my life, it wouldn't be enough for you. I've tried, I've tried to be the dutiful son, to maintain the image of the good son. . . . Commanded into your presence on every conceivable occasion . . . Easter, Christmas, birthdays, Thanksgiving . . . Even that Thanksgiving when Carol was dying, and I was staying with her in the hospital. "We miss you so. Our day is nothing without you. Couldn't you come up for an hour or two after you leave Carol?" You had no regard for what was really going on. . . . My wife was dying!

Words to Own

susceptible (sə·sep′tə·bəl) *adj.:* easily affected emotionally; easily influenced.

Tom. Is it so terrible to want to see your own son?

Gene. It is terrible to want to possess him . . . entirely and completely!

Tom *(coldly . . . after a moment).* There will be some papers to sign for your mother's estate. Be sure you leave an address with my lawyer . . .

Gene *(cutting in).* Dad!

Tom *(cutting, with no self-pity).* From tonight on, you can consider me dead. *(Turns on him in a rage of resentment)* I gave you everything. Since I was a snot-nosed kid I've worked my fingers to the bone. You've had everything and I had nothing. I put a roof over your head, clothes on your back——

Gene. Food on the table.

Tom. ——things I never had.

Gene. I know!

Tom. You ungrateful . . . !

Gene *(seizes him, almost as though he would hit him).* What do you want for gratitude? Nothing, nothing would be enough. You have resented everything you ever gave me. The orphan boy in you has resented everything. I'm sorry about your miserable childhood. When I was a kid, and you told me those stories, I used to go up to my room at night and cry. But there is nothing I can do about it . . . and it does not excuse everything. . . . I *am* grateful to you. I also admire you and respect you and stand in awe of what you have done with your life. I will never be able to touch it. *(*TOM *looks at him with contempt.)* But it does not make me love you. And I wanted to love you. *(*TOM *snorts his disbelief.)* You hated your father. I saw what it did to you. I did not want to hate you.

Tom. I don't care what you feel about me.

Gene. I do! *(He moves away from his father.)* I came so close to loving you tonight. . . . I'd never felt so open to you. You don't know what it cost me to ask you to come with me . . . when I have never been able to sit in a room alone with you. . . . Did you really think your door was always open to me?

Tom. It was not my fault if you never came in.

Gene *(starts to move out).* Goodbye, Dad. I'll arrange for someone to come in.

Tom *(shouting).* I don't want anyone to come in! I can take care of myself! I have always had to take care of myself. Who needs you? Get out!

[*This last, wildly at* GENE. *The lights dim out quickly, except for a lingering light on* GENE.]

Gene *(after a few moments).* That night I left my father's house forever. . . . I took the first right and the second left . . . and this time I went as far as California. . . . Peggy and I visited him once or twice . . . and then he came to California to visit us and had a fever and swollen ankles, and we put him in a hospital, and he never left. . . . The reason we gave, and which he could accept, for not leaving, . . . the swollen ankles. But the real reason . . . the arteries were hardening, and he gradually over several years slipped into complete and speechless senility . . . with all his life centered in his burning eyes. *(A* NURSE *wheels in* TOM, *dressed in a heavy, warm bathrobe and wearing a white linen golf cap to protect his head from drafts. The* NURSE *withdraws into the shadows.)* When I would visit him, and we would sit and look at each other, his eyes would mist over and his nostrils would pinch with emotion. . . . But I never could learn what the emotion was . . . anger . . . or love . . . or regret. . . . One day, sitting in his wheelchair and staring without comprehension at television . . . he died . . . alone . . . without even an orange in his hand. *(The light fades on* TOM.*)* Death ends a life, . . . but it does not end a relationship, which struggles on in the survivor's mind . . . toward some resolution, which it never finds. Alice said I would not accept the sadness of the world. . . . What did it matter if I never loved him, or if he never loved me? . . . Perhaps she was right. . . . But, still, when I hear the word "father" . . . *(He cannot express it . . . there is still the longing, the emotion. He looks around . . . out . . . as though he would finally be able to express it, but he can only say . . .)* It matters. *(He turns and walks slowly away, into the shadows . . . as the lights dim.)*

Curtain

Meet the Writer

"I Intend to Keep On Writing"

Three months after I was born in 1917 in New York City, my family moved to a suburb, New Rochelle, where I lived until I went away to school, first to Phillips Exeter Academy and then to Harvard. I stayed on at Harvard, studying for graduate degrees, with the idea that I would teach and write on the side.

While I was with the Pacific Fleet in World War II, I wrote a play that was judged the best play written by a serviceman overseas. This play contest changed my life.

Shortly after my return from the war, while I was living on a Rockefeller Play-Writing Grant, I was fortunate to get work writing for the radio. This began my routine of writing stage plays in the morning, radio (and later television) plays in the afternoon, and teaching play-writing four nights a week. In 1953 the production of my first Broadway play, *Tea and Sympathy,* ended this routine, though I have continued writing occasionally for movies and television because, as I have often said, "You can make a killing in the theater but not a living."

With the production of *Tea and Sympathy,* I became a member of The Playwrights Producing Company (with dramatists Robert Sherwood, Maxwell Anderson, and Elmer Rice). My later plays include *I Never Sang for My Father; Silent Night, Lonely Night;* and *You Know I Can't Hear You When the Water's Running.*

In spite of the desperate situation that faces playwrights today, I intend to keep on writing till "The End." On his deathbed, my good friend Marc Connelly (he wrote the classic *The Green Pastures*) came out of a coma briefly to say, "They've raised the money. We go into rehearsal tomorrow." May those also be my final words.

—Robert Anderson

Connections | A Movie Review

Her Heart Belongs to "Father"

MARYA MANNES

On this gray afternoon, the line at the box office for *I Never Sang for My Father* was predominantly of older women, in pairs or single, although once inside a crowded house you saw a sprinkling of men and some young girls with flowing hair.

Word had clearly got around since the movie opened that this was a film about people over thirty, dominated by that splendid and durable actor, Melvyn Douglas; and the words sentiment, heartwarming, and touching doubtless drew many adults who had ceased being regular moviegoers because what they saw at their local cinemas had either bludgeoned or bewildered them into absence. And not just little old ladies shocked by sex . . . or middle-aged squares yearning for the traditional American values. These, I suspect, are only a part of the adult population looking for some identification with the people they see on the screen, some recognitive stirring of the heart or mind.

Instead they are confronted with films, some of them brilliant, in which the word has no meaning, emotion no stature, and the mind no place. They see the nonhero, the bum, the drifter, even the killer, as the central focus, sex as a standard

Melvyn Douglas in the movie *I Never Sang for My Father.*

exercise, violence as an obligatory "comment," and obscenity as "truth." They see superb photography, beautiful bodies, and breathtaking juxtapositions. They hear a pounding or plaintive score. They are told that "this is reality, this is now, this is where it's at," and if they don't dig it, they're dead. They listen to young audiences cackling at private jokes and signs, at sexual fumbles and small crudities, and they leave the theater feeling not only disoriented but in a very real sense disenfranchised.

At *I Never Sang for My Father,* they are at home. Not everybody, fortunately, has a father like Tom Garrison, nor, unfortunately, a mother like Margaret Garrison. But they know them to be true, as the Garrison son and daughter are true. Playwright Robert Anderson and producer Gilbert Cates have created a real family in a real house filled with real agonies in a film that is solely concerned with the human condition. Not headlines, not slogans, not movements, not cinematic or psychedelic tricks. Just people, individuals, breathing, choking, loving, hating, trying to love, dying.

Certainly the picture is about older people, middle-aged or verging on senescence. If what they think and feel and suffer is irrelevant, then half the population of this country is irrelevant.

But they are not. Old Garrison, so magnificently played by Melvyn Douglas, is far more relevant to our present condition than even an appreciative audience (and unappreciative critics) might think. For he is the precursor and embodiment of almost everything wrong with this country and its people today.

Here is the American folk hero who came up the hard way and made it. Child of a hated drunken father and a mother who died when he was ten, Tom Garrison spent the rest of his life making money and taking power. Business leader, president of the Board of Education, and finally mayor of his town, he is now in his eighties, living in his past, his mighty ego subsisting on Rotarian pats on the back, smiles from a waitress, and the love of a frail wife who endures his endless recitals and pomposities with heroic sweetness. She loves him for the way he was, and for the way he walks. . . .

Old Tom also feeds on his forty-year-old son, Gene (played by Gene Hackman), who has tried, but has never been able to love him. Gene has seen Tom crush the life out of his wife, banish his daughter, . . . and load Gene himself with a terrible guilt that turns the natural filial instinct into fury and frustration.

Old Tom is, in fact, the prototype of the successful American man whose obsessive need for material security has stripped him of the capacity for love and pity—except for himself. Charming as he can be (the old gallant, the old quipster), he weeps only for himself. Women are dependents, children are possessions, and possessions are life.

. . . No power on earth could make his son want to be like him or think as he did. It took Gene a long time to spring his trap, but he finally did. What's more, he married a free woman (Elizabeth Hubbard), a doctor, whose love and need for him is no less real than the demands of her profession.

The fact that he chooses to move across a continent to where her practice is may be a hopeful indication of a new breed of men who find such accommodations neither demeaning nor unnatural. For that matter, the women in *I Never Sang for My Father* share a distinction absent in the majority of films, however "now." They are three-dimensional human beings. The mother, superbly evoked by Dorothy Stickney, reveals capacities of mind and heart far beyond the "little woman" image imposed by her marriage. . . . And Gene's sister, Alice (Estelle Parsons), is a wife and mother compact with integrity and intelligence, a sturdy soul.

Young people who choose to expose themselves to this film might find their compassion engaged by one more oppressed minority. When they see, as Gene does, the doom of the rejected and discarded old of this society, rotting in institutions and fearful exile, they might discover, as he does, that the parental bond transcends time, discord, even hate. Whether we like them or not, fathers and mothers are part of us and with us forever. And therefore relevant.

—from *The New York Times,* November 15, 1970

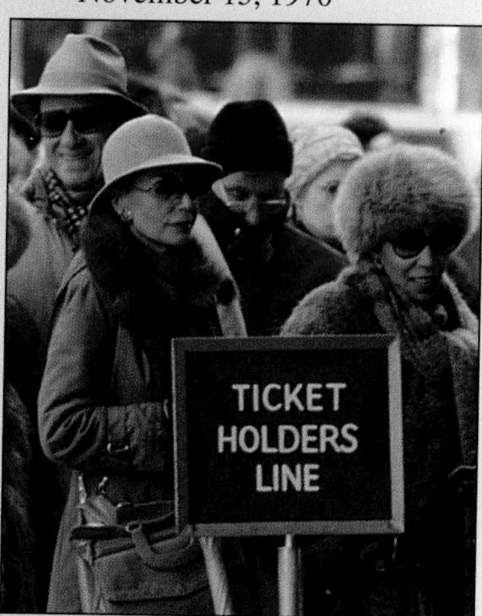

Connections A POEM

Those Winter Sundays

Robert Hayden

Sundays too my father got up early
and put his clothes on in the blueblack cold,
then with cracked hands that ached
from labor in the weekday weather made
banked fires blaze. No one ever thanked him.

I'd wake and hear the cold splintering, breaking.
When the rooms were warm, he'd call,
and slowly I would rise and dress,
fearing the chronic angers of that house,

Speaking indifferently to him,
who had driven out the cold
and polished my good shoes as well.
What did I know, what did I know
of love's austere and lonely offices?°

14. offices: services; duties.

Daddy, Where Are You? by Dannielle B. Hayes. Photo on rag paper (22" x 30").

Connections A PERSONAL ESSAY

Daddy Doll Under the Bed

Erma Bombeck

When I was a little kid, a father was like the light in the refrigerator. Every house had one, but no one really knew what either of them did once the door was shut.

My dad left the house every morning and always seemed glad to see everyone at night.

He opened the jar of pickles when no one else could.

He was the only one in the house who wasn't afraid to go in the basement by himself.

He cut himself shaving, but no one kissed it or got excited about it. It was understood whenever it rained, he got the car and brought it around to the door. When anyone was sick, he went out to get the prescription filled.

He kept busy enough. He set mousetraps. He cut back the roses so the thorns wouldn't clip you when you came to the front door. He oiled my skates, and they went faster. When I got my bike, he ran alongside me for at least a thousand miles until I got the hang of it.

He signed all my report cards. He put me to bed early. He took a lot of pictures but was never in them. He tightened up Mother's sagging clothesline every week or so.

I was afraid of everyone else's father, but not my own. Once I made him tea. It was only sugar water, but he sat on a small chair and said it was delicious. He looked very uncomfortable.

Once I went fishing with him in a rowboat. I threw huge rocks in the water, and he threatened to throw me overboard. I wasn't sure he wouldn't, so I looked him in the eye. I finally decided he was bluffing and threw in one more. He was a bad poker player.

Whenever I played house, the mother doll had a lot to do. I never knew what to do with the daddy doll, so I had him say "I'm going off to work now" and threw him under the bed.

When I was nine years old, my father didn't get up one morning and go to work. He went to the hospital and died the next day.

There were a lot of people in the house who brought all kinds of good food and cakes. We never had so much company before.

I went to my room and felt under the bed for the father doll. When I found him, I dusted him off and put him on my bed.

He never did anything. I didn't know his leaving would hurt so much.

I still don't know why.

Making Meanings
Act Two

First Thoughts

1. How did you respond to Gene's last speech, in which he tells how he feels when he hears the word *father*?

Shaping Interpretations

2. The events of Tom Garrison's early life are mentioned in Act One, and more details are revealed in Act Two. How does Tom's difficult childhood affect the way you feel about him? Explain how Tom's relationship with *his* father is like Gene's relationship with Tom.
3. What has Gene gained and lost at the end of the play? How do you think he feels about his gains and his losses?
4. Alice is a key figure in Act Two. Describe the **conflicts** that are forced into the open in her scene with Gene and in her scene with Gene and their father. How do you think she is helpful to Gene? How is she not helpful?
5. Toward the end of the play, Tom says to Gene, "It was not my fault if you never came in." When Hal Holbrook, the actor playing Gene, encountered this line during rehearsals, he was upset. He asked, "Do I hear that line? If I did, I wouldn't leave." The director told him, "It's the kind of line you hear ten years after it is spoken." What do you think the director meant? Why do you think Gene did not go through his father's open door?
6. The playwright says on page 645 that in a way, Alice and Gene represent two sides of the same person. What do you think this means? **Compare and contrast** Alice's and Gene's **conflicts** with their father.
7. What is the significance of the play's **title**?
8. Shortly after this play opened in New York, a good friend of the playwright's father wrote a note with a single line: "You have sung for your father." What do you think the friend meant? Do you think she was right?
9. Explain what Gene means when he says his father died "without even an orange in his hand." What is Gene feeling when he says this line?
10. Change is a key element in drama. Remember that the most interesting change is internal. An **internal change** can be a change of heart, the reversal of a belief, or a new awareness. Do any of the characters change under the pressure of the action in this play? Which character does not seem to change, and how do you feel about this character as the play ends?

Reading Check

a. What painful memories does Margaret's death bring up for Gene and his father?

b. What is Alice's plan for the care of her father?

c. Why does Gene object to Alice's plan? What does he propose instead?

d. What steps does Gene take to carry out his plan?

e. How does Tom want to spend the rest of his life? How successful is he in getting what he wants?

Connecting with the Text

11. This play is about characters older than you—perhaps they are the ages of your parents and grandparents. Did any problems in the play sound familiar to you? Did any of these characters mirror people in your own life—maybe even yourself? As you share responses, check the notes you took while reading the play (see page 636).

12. "Mothers are soft and yielding," Alice tells Gene. "Fathers are hard and rough, to teach us the way of the world, which is rough. . . ." If you could talk with Alice, how would you respond to her opinion?

Extending the Text

13. The father thinks of his children as dividends. The mother sees them as her jewels. How would you explain these two ways that some people think about their children? Are these common ways of thinking about children?

Challenging the Text

14. Refer to the notes you took while you were reading this play. Did you have trouble with any aspect of the play—with language? characters? time frame? With a group, discuss your experiences reading the play.

VOCABULARY — HOW TO OWN A WORD

WORD BANK

contorts
eulogy
perpetual
executor
cowed
compulsion
callousness
bereaved
emaciated
susceptible

Etymology: Word Origins

An **etymology** traces a **word's origin**. The word *invent,* for example, comes from two Latin roots: *in-,* which means "in" or "on"; and *venire,* which means "to come." An inventor literally "comes upon" ideas for new tools, devices, or creations. Related words include *invention, inventive,* and even *inventory.*

You can find information about the etymologies of words in most dictionaries. Use your **dictionary** to make an etymology map for each of the words in the Word Bank. Then, use each word (or a word closely related to it) in a sentence. The first one is done for you.

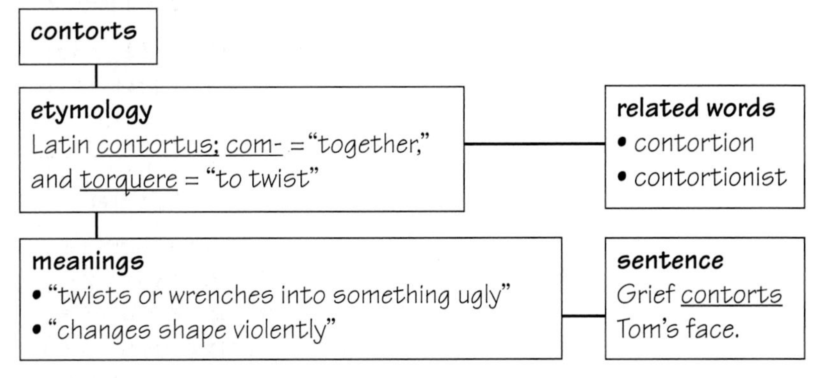

CHOICES: Building Your Portfolio

Writer's Notebook

WORK IN PROGRESS

1. Collecting Ideas for a Cause-and-Effect Essay

Finding a topic. For the Writer's Workshop on page 752, you'll write an essay explaining the causes or effects of something. You might find some ideas for your essay in this play. For example, you might focus on the *causes* of the characters' problems, explaining *why* they behave or feel the way they do. You might focus instead on the *effects* of their experiences or of the various decisions they make. Review the play and the notes you took while reading to find a topic that you want to explore in this intensely human play.

Causes of problems
Gene: problem with his dad.
Cause: Tom wants Gene to live with him.
Tom: problem showing he loves Gene.
Cause: Tom's sad childhood and bad relationship with his dad.

Speaking and Listening

2. Act It Out

With a group of classmates, prepare a scene from this play for **performance** in front of the rest of the class. To prepare for your performance, you'll have to select a scene and make a **script** for your **actors**. You'll have to choose players for the parts, rehearse the scene, and decide on **costumes** and **sets**. After your presentation, ask your audience for feedback. (For help, consult the Speaking and Listening Workshops on pages 683–684 and 890–891.)

Writing About Theme

3. What It Means

In a brief essay, explain what you think is the theme of this play. Remember that **theme** is the central idea about human life that is revealed through the play's action. A theme is usually something that can be expressed in more than one sentence—some themes are so complex it would take a book to explain them. Do not express the theme in terms of this play only. For example, instead of "Gene learns in this play that . . . ," say, "This play reveals that . . .". Find at least two quotations from the play to support your statement of the theme.

Analyzing a Character

4. Father Knows Best?

Although Gene controls the play and is the only character allowed to speak to the audience directly, Tom often dominates the action. In an essay, analyze the character of Tom. In your concluding paragraph, describe your own responses to his character.

Comparing and Contrasting

5. Fathers All

There are as many father-child relationships as there are fathers and children. Reread the works by Hayden and Bombeck (see ***Connections*** on pages 678–679). In an essay, **compare and contrast** the father-child relationships depicted in those works with Gene and Tom's relationship. Support your points by elaborating with quotations from the works.

Supporting an Opinion

6. Evaluating a Critic

In her movie review of *I Never Sang for My Father* (see ***Connections*** on pages 676–677), Mannes presents a particular view of the film. How do you feel about the way she evaluates the movie's characters and emotional relevance? Present your opinions in a **letter to the editor.**

Speaking and Listening Workshop

ASSIGNMENT

Interpret stage directions, using voice and body language.

STAGECRAFT: USING STAGE DIRECTIONS

When playwrights prepare the written texts of their plays, they provide **stage directions,** information about how the actors are to move on the stage and what emotions they are to communicate to the audience. Stage directions can also include descriptions of **scenery, costumes, lighting,** and **props** (or *properties*). In a **script** for a stage play, stage directions appear in parentheses or brackets.

In movie and TV scripts, stage directions become **camera directions,** which are often more extensive than the dialogue. In movie and TV scripts, camera directions are set off the way they are in the following little scene from a famous screenplay. (*Int.* means "interior"—an indoor shot.)

HELEN. Come—

Int. Helen's Front Room—as Kane enters, looks around, sees no one, waits.

Int. Helen's Bedroom. She stops, puzzled, then goes to the front room.

Int. Helen's Front Room. Helen enters the room, stops short as she sees Kane. Their eyes meet and hold. The silent tension grows, seeming to fill the room as with an explosive gas. It is Helen who breaks the silence.

HELEN (*quietly*). What are you looking at? You think I've changed?

—Carl Foreman, *High Noon*

Here are five extracts from the play script of *I Never Sang for My Father*. The stage directions are in italics.

1. **Tom** (*considers this, but is mollified by the smile*). Well, I appreciate your solicitude, old man. Why don't you stay for supper?
2. **Gene** (*straining to get away from all the encirclements*). Good night, Dad.
3. **Alice.** I didn't mean exactly that kind of plan. I meant . . . Well, you haven't been well.

   Tom (*belligerent*). Who said so?

Act It Out

When actors read stage directions, they look for key words. Act like an actor. First, practice reading aloud each numbered speech at bottom right, shaping your reading according to the stage direction. Use your **voice** and **body language,** including **facial expressions.** Then, change the key word in each stage direction. For example, in the first passage, change the word *mollified* to the word *irritated.* Now, try reading that speech again, still using your voice and body language, to show annoyance instead of calmness.

Try several replacements for the key word in each stage direction. When you are satisfied with your interpretations, read the lines aloud to a group and get their feedback. Remember that an audience can't *read* the stage directions. They have to see feelings communicated by skilled actors. See if your audience can identify how you are *feeling* or *responding* as you play Tom, Gene, and Alice.

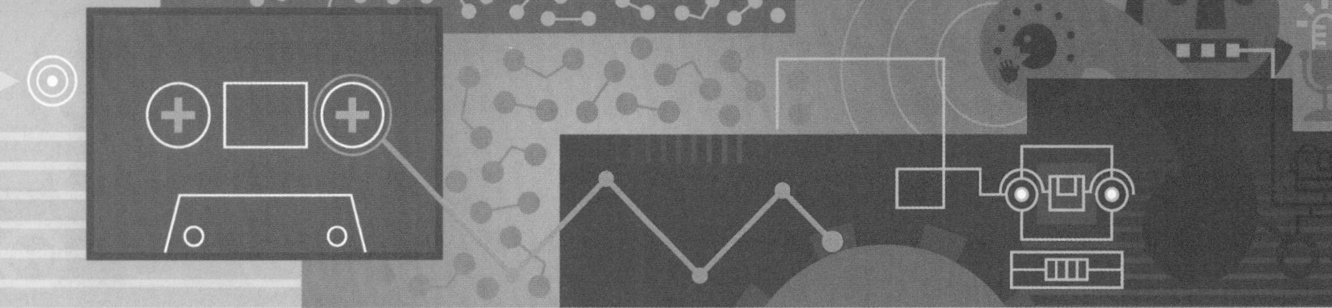

4. Alice. I worry, leaving you in this house . . . alone, Dad.

Tom (*looks around, very alert, defensively*). I'm perfectly all right. Now don't worry about me . . . either of you. Why, for the last year, since your mother's first attack, I've been getting the breakfast, making the beds, using a dust rag. . . .

5. Tom. I have long gotten the impression that my only function in this family is to supply the money to——

Gene (*anguished*). Dad!

Using Emotional Memory

Actors sometimes find stage directions they disagree with or don't understand. (See Hal Holbrook's question to his director about a line from *I Never Sang for My Father,* which appears in question 5 on page 680.) Sometimes the playwright (or the director) will change a stage direction. In most cases, when actors have problems, they must dig into themselves to find a way to communicate the emotion or attitude. This technique is called **emotional memory** or **emotional recall**.

The use of emotional memory was promoted by the famous Russian actor and director Konstantin Stanislavsky (1863–1938) in a realistic acting style called the Method. Experimental use of the Method began in the United States in the 1920s. Many people misinterpreted the Method, thinking that it required you to "become" the character you played. For example, if you were playing a butcher, you would have to find work, at least for a time, as a butcher. Although some actors did try to follow this approach, most Method actors try to become the character imaginatively rather than actually. They try to remember personal experiences and emotions that will build a close identification with the character, so that their acting will become more natural and realistic.

Here is how the technique works: An actor remembers a time when he or she actually experienced the emotion called for in the stage direction. The actor recalls the sensation of having that emotion and the ways it affected his or her body and behavior. Then the actor applies those memories to the dialogue, in effect overlaying a new situation with a remembered feeling.

"Actually, I don't know how to act my age. I've never been my age before."

Reprinted from *The Saturday Evening Post.*

Act It Out

Try this technique of using emotional memory in reading aloud the numbered passages beginning on page 683. In each case, think of an emotion or attitude you felt that was like the one noted in the stage direction. The situation in which you felt the emotion can be entirely different from the one in the play. This memory is for you alone. You don't need to tell anyone about it. You just express it as you read the lines.

Museo Archeologico Nazionale, Naples. Erich Lessing/Art Resource, NY.

Theatrical mask in a wall painting from Pompeii (first century A.D.).

Greek Drama: Out of Ritual

by David Adams Leeming

You probably never thought of religious services as being forms of drama, but in ancient Greece they were. Greek drama grew out of religious rituals honoring Dionysos (dī′ə·nī′səs), the god of wine and fertility. During these old celebrations, worshipers would dance around the altar of the god of wine and ecstasy, singing hymns to the wild, passionate accompaniment of the flute.

At some point during the sixth century B.C., these Dionysian celebrations became an annual festival held in Athens at a large outdoor amphitheater. Eventually, the dancing choruses of worshipers began competing for prizes (a bull or a goat). Tradition has it that a man named Thespis transformed these hymns into songs that still honored Dionysos but also told the story of a famous hero or even another god. Then Thespis added another innovation: One chorus member would step away from the others to play the part of that hero or god. This actor wore a mask and entered into a dialogue with the chorus. Drama as we know it was born when the playwright Aeschylus (es′ki·ləs) added a second individual actor to the performance, creating the possibility of conflict. (Thespis is immortalized in our word *thespian,* which refers to an actor or actress.)

By the end of the fifth century B.C., this annual festival, called the Dionysia, had become a four-day extravaganza. Public business was suspended; prisoners were released on bail. As many as fourteen thousand spectators gathered in the open-air Theater of Dionysos to watch as playwrights chosen by the city magistrates competed for prizes in tragedy and comedy. After an opening day of traditional choral hymns, three dramatists in each category presented their plays over the next three days. Each morning, one of the playwrights presented three tragedies and a satyr (sat′ər) play, and that afternoon, another playwright presented a comedy. The **tragedies,** which had heroic characters and unhappy endings, were serious treatments of religious and mythic questions. The **satyr plays** were comic and even lewd treatments of the same themes. The **comedies** differed from the tragedies in having ordinary people as characters and happy endings.

The Theater of Dionysos: Like a Football Stadium

The Theater of Dionysos looked like a semicircular football stadium. The seats were carved out of stone on a hillside; at the bottom was a performance area divided into two parts. In the front was a rounded place called the orchestra, a fairly large space where the chorus sang and danced around the remnant of an altar. Behind the orchestra was a platform where the actors spoke their lines from behind huge masks. These masks had exaggerated mouthpieces that amplified the actors' voices—an ancient solution to the problem resolved today by microphones. Many masks were stylized into familiar character types that were easily recognized by the audience. All the actors were men, and the choruses were well-trained boys. By switching masks, each actor could play several roles.

Greek Dionysian mask (early first century A.D.).

The Metropolitan Museum of Art, New York. Gift of Mrs. Gérard van der Kemp, 1958. (58.140) Photograph © 1985 The Metropolitan Museum of Art.

A few days before the festival of Dionysos began, that year's competing

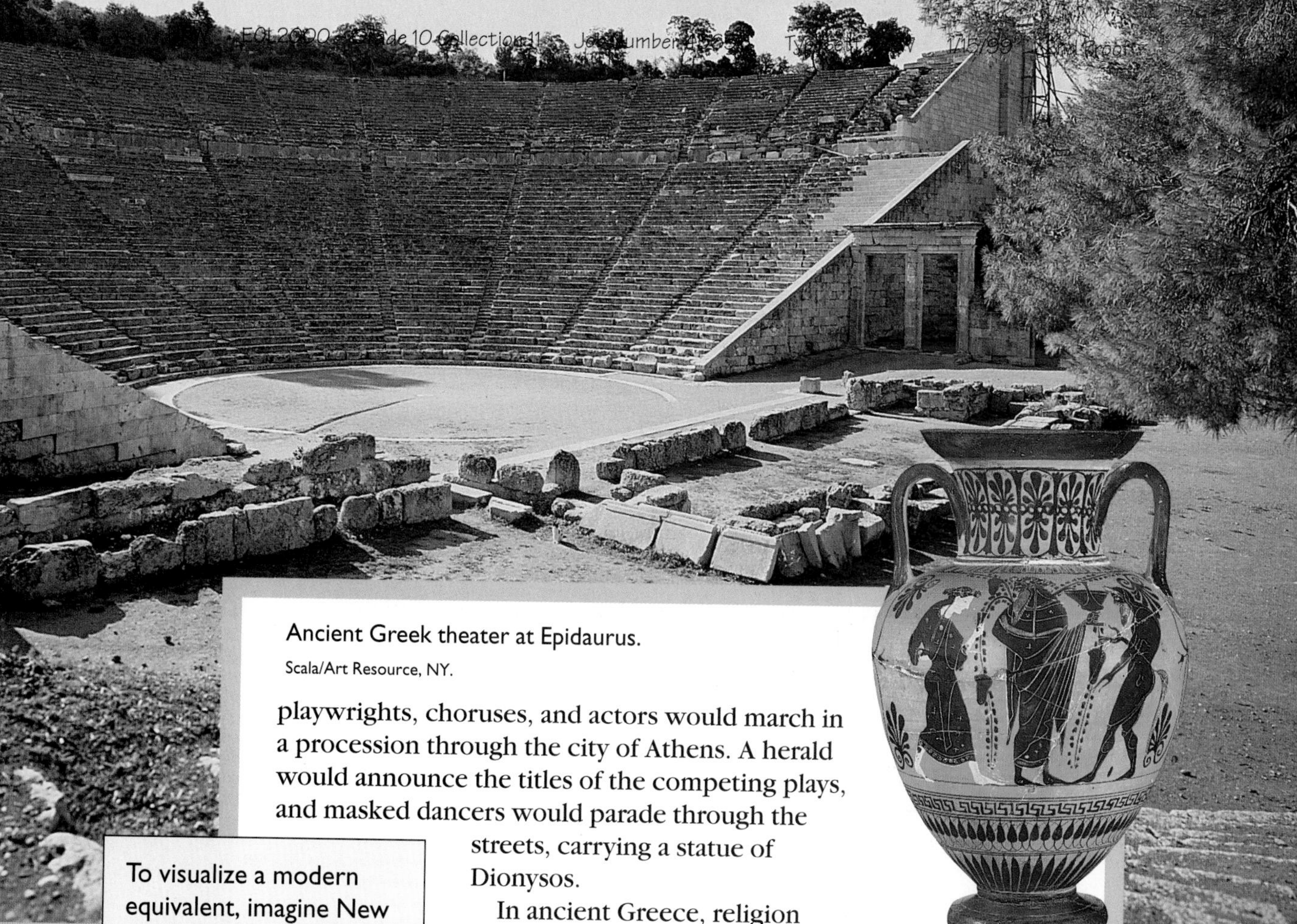

Ancient Greek theater at Epidaurus.

Scala/Art Resource, NY.

playwrights, choruses, and actors would march in a procession through the city of Athens. A herald would announce the titles of the competing plays, and masked dancers would parade through the streets, carrying a statue of Dionysos.

In ancient Greece, religion and dramatic "entertainment" were closely related. To visualize a modern equivalent, imagine New York City's Broadway theaters as the center of a four-day religious festival in which everyone in the city took part.

To visualize a modern equivalent, imagine New York City's Broadway theaters as the center of a four-day religious festival in which everyone in the city took part.

Greek vase (late sixth century B.C.) showing Dionysos standing between a maenad and a satyr.

The Metropolitan Museum of Art, New York. Rogers Fund, 1906. (06.1021.85) Photograph © 1979 The Metropolitan Museum of Art.

A Tragic Myth: The House of Thebes

The basic plot of *Antigone* is part of a long myth that was as familiar to Athenian audiences as stories about the Pilgrims are to Americans today. A **myth** is an old story, rooted in a particular society, that explains a belief, a ritual, or some mysterious aspect of nature. Many myths also try to explain human suffering. In many cases, the myths explain our sufferings in terms of the workings of the gods—of fates that cannot be avoided, of curses that haunt generation after generation.

The following story is the myth the Athenians knew and the one that we must also know if we are to understand *Antigone.*

The Myth of Oedipus

"He will kill his father and marry his mother . . ."

King Laios (lī′əs) and Queen Jocasta of Thebes learned from an oracle that their newborn son would kill his father and marry his mother. Horrified by this prediction, they gave their baby to a shepherd with orders to leave the infant to die on a lonely mountainside with his ankles pinned together. The shepherd, however, took pity on the baby. Instead of abandoning him, he gave him to a Corinthian shepherd, who in turn gave the baby to the childless king and queen of Corinth. They named him Oedipus (ed′i·pəs), which means "swollen foot" or "club foot," and raised him as their son.

When Oedipus was a young man, he learned of the oracle's prophecy. Believing the king and queen of Corinth to be his real parents, he ran away from home in horror. In the course of his lonely wanderings, he encountered an arrogant old man who tried to run him off the road with his chariot. Because honor was at stake, the two men fought, and Oedipus killed the stranger. Thinking no more of the incident—such occurrences were probably common on the roads in those days—Oedipus continued on his journey to the city of Thebes.

Meeting the Monster Sphinx

At the outskirts of the city, he encountered the Sphinx, a terrible monster with the wings of an eagle, the body of a lion, and the breasts and face of a woman. This Sphinx had been menacing Thebes by ambushing travelers going to the city and challenging them to answer a riddle. If they could answer it correctly—which no one had done—they could proceed; if not, the Sphinx devoured them. The city was in a state of siege: No one wanted to enter it for fear of the monster. Famine was near at hand. The Sphinx's riddle went like this: "What creature goes on four legs in the morning, two legs in the afternoon, and three legs in the evening?"

Oedipus immediately guessed that the answer to the riddle was "man," who crawls on all fours as an infant, walks on two legs as an adult, and leans on a cane in old age. Upon hearing Oedipus's answer, the defeated Sphinx leaped off a high rock. Thebes was saved.

A Hero's Welcome in Thebes

When Oedipus arrived in Thebes, the city where (unknown to him) he had been born, the people welcomed him as their savior. Since Laios, their king, had recently been killed, the Thebans offered Oedipus their throne and the widowed queen, Jocasta, as his bride. So Oedipus became king of Thebes, married Jocasta, and had four children with her: two sons, Polyneices (päl′i·nī′sēz′) and Eteocles (ē·tē′ə·klēz); and two daughters, Antigone (an·tig′ə·nē′) and Ismene (is·men′ē).

All went well for many years until a plague struck Thebes. People, crops, and animals were dying. Desperate to learn the cause, Oedipus sent Jocasta's brother, Creon, to consult the great oracle at Delphi.

A Horrible Discovery

The oracle warned that the plague would not end until Thebes had punished the murderer of King Laios, who lived among them undetected. Oedipus vowed to save Thebes once again by finding this murderer. After questioning several people, including the blind prophet Teiresias (tī·rē′sē·əs), he discovered that the man he had killed on the road years before was none other than King Laios. Furthermore, he learned that he was not the son of the king and queen of Corinth, but rather the son of Laios and Jocasta. Thus Oedipus had in fact fulfilled the oracle's prophecy—he had killed his father and married his mother. When Oedipus and Jocasta discovered this horrible truth, she killed herself and he gouged out his eyes to punish himself for having been blind to the truth.

After these disasters, Creon took over as regent (acting ruler) of Thebes, and after several years he decided to exile Oedipus. Accompanied only by his daughter Antigone (in some versions of the myth, also by Ismene), Oedipus wandered the countryside as a beggar until he reached the sanctuary of Colonus, where he died.

Oedipus and the Sphinx. Detail from a cup (c. 470–430 B.C.).

Vatican Museum. Courtesy Scala/Art Resource, NY.

God's Laws or Man's?

Antigone returned to Thebes, where her two brothers had agreed to rule in alternate years. Eteocles' turn came first, but when it ended, he refused to give up his throne to Polyneices. Polyneices fled to the city of Argos, where he raised an army; he then returned with his men and attacked the seven gates of Thebes. The Thebans repulsed each assault, but in the course of battle, Eteocles and Polyneices killed each other.

Creon then became king of Thebes and gave Eteocles, his ally, a hero's burial. Creon considered Polyneices a traitor, so he decreed that his body be left unburied, to rot in the sun outside the city gates. To the Greeks, this was a terrible punishment: Their holiest laws demanded that certain burial rites be performed, or else the soul of the dead person would be condemned to eternal unrest. This is the basis of Creon's conflict with the strong-willed Antigone. As you will see, she believes that God's laws must be obeyed, whatever the consequences.

Before You Read

ANTIGONE

Make the Connection

Conscience vs. Authority

The conflict in *Antigone*—individual conscience at odds with established authority—is eternally relevant. When we know that those in power are morally wrong, do we break their laws, or do we collaborate with them by obeying? This was a crucial question for some Europeans during World War II. It was against the law in some countries, for instance, to help Jews escape the Nazis. Despite the official censorship that existed in occupied France during World War II, the French playwright Jean Anouilh (zhän a·no͞o′y′) presented his own version of *Antigone*. His characters wore modern military uniforms and carried guns instead of swords. Anouilh's play was an outcry against the French who were collaborating with the Nazis. In writing this play, Anouilh himself was a kind of Antigone figure—a person of conscience speaking out against moral wrongs at the risk of his own life. Perhaps both Sophocles and Anouilh are asking us whether we would be so brave if put to the test.

Reading Skills and Strategies

Monitoring Your Reading: Using Resources

You'll find many resources in this text to help you as you read *Antigone*. For example, the preceding essays provide background on Greek drama and the myth of Oedipus. The side notes, or glosses, alongside the play explain allusions, or references, to characters in Greek mythology, and they define important terms in Greek drama, such as *parados* and *antistrophe*. Other features, such as Literature and Religion and Connections, provide further insights. As you read, jot down in your notes how these resources affect your understanding of the play. If you have questions that are still unanswered, write them down.

The performance photographs that illustrate this play are of the 1971 production of *Antigone* at Lincoln Center, New York.

Antigone

Sophocles

translated by Dudley Fitts and Robert Fitzgerald

How dreadful it is when the right judge judges wrong!

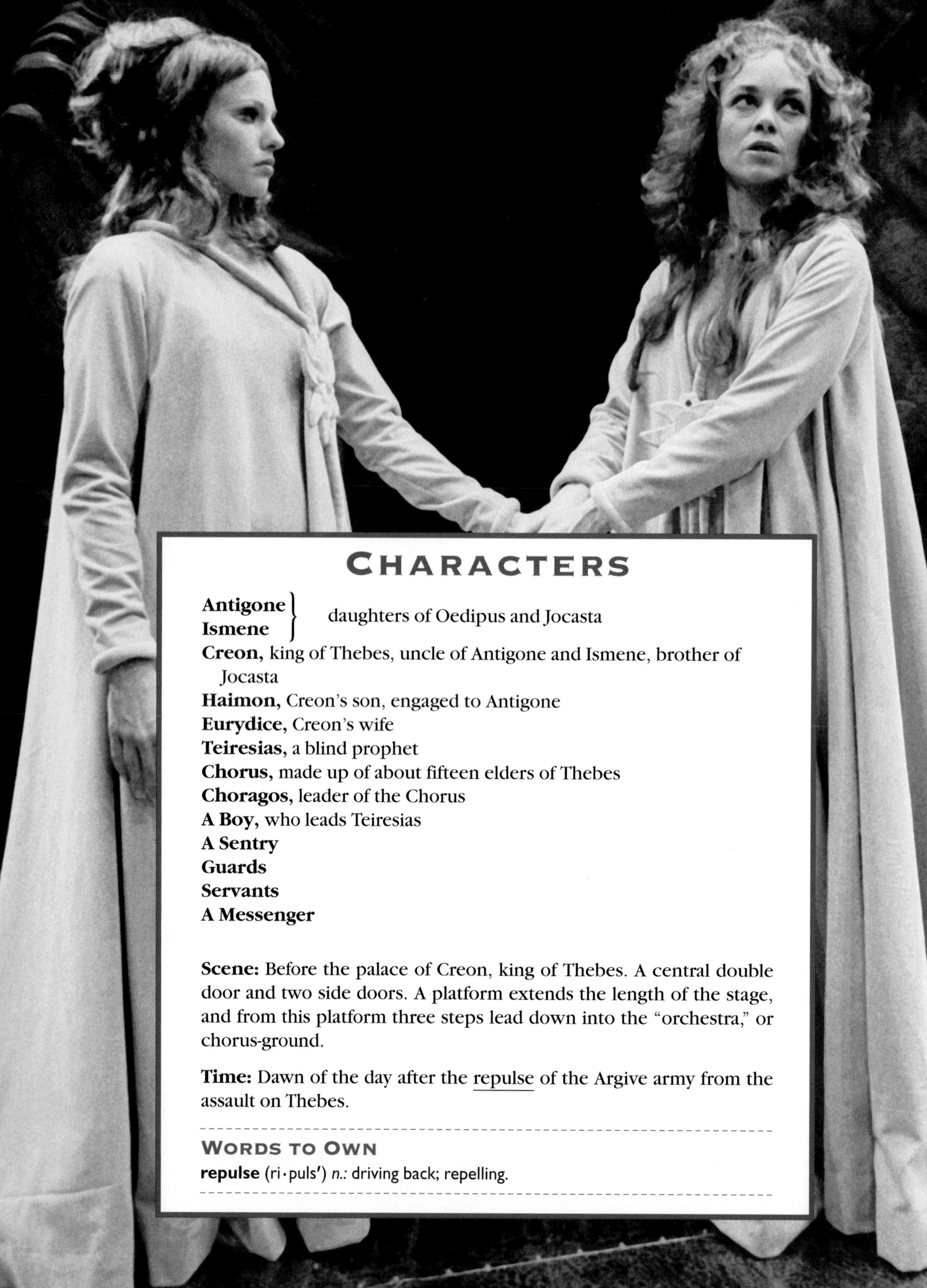

CHARACTERS

Antigone } daughters of Oedipus and Jocasta
Ismene }

Creon, king of Thebes, uncle of Antigone and Ismene, brother of Jocasta

Haimon, Creon's son, engaged to Antigone

Eurydice, Creon's wife

Teiresias, a blind prophet

Chorus, made up of about fifteen elders of Thebes

Choragos, leader of the Chorus

A Boy, who leads Teiresias

A Sentry

Guards

Servants

A Messenger

Scene: Before the palace of Creon, king of Thebes. A central double door and two side doors. A platform extends the length of the stage, and from this platform three steps lead down into the "orchestra," or chorus-ground.

Time: Dawn of the day after the repulse of the Argive army from the assault on Thebes.

WORDS TO OWN

repulse (ri·puls′) *n.:* driving back; repelling.

Prologue

ANTIGONE and ISMENE enter from the central door of the palace.

Antigone.
Ismene, dear sister,
You would think that we had already suffered enough
For the curse on Oedipus.
I cannot imagine any grief
That you and I have not gone through. And now—
Have they told you of the new decree of our King
Creon?

Ismene.
I have heard nothing: I know
That two sisters lost two brothers, a double death
In a single hour; and I know that the Argive army
Fled in the night; but beyond this, nothing.

Antigone.
I thought so. And that is why I wanted you
To come out here with me. There is something we
must do.

Ismene.
Why do you speak so strangely?

Antigone.
Listen, Ismene:
Creon buried our brother Eteocles
With military honors, gave him a soldier's funeral,
And it was right that he should; but Polyneices,
Who fought as bravely and died as miserably—
They say that Creon has sworn
No one shall bury him, no one mourn for him,
But his body must lie in the fields, a sweet treasure
For carrion birds to find as they search for food.
That is what they say, and our good Creon is coming
here
To announce it publicly; and the penalty—
Stoning to death in the public square!
There it is,
And now you can prove what you are:
A true sister, or a traitor to your family.

Ismene.
Antigone, you are mad! What could I possibly do?

Antigone.
You must decide whether you will help me or not.

Ismene.
I do not understand you. Help you in what?

Antigone.
Ismene, I am going to bury him. Will you come?

"... the penalty—
Stoning to death
in the public
square!"

Ismene.
Bury him! You have just said the new law forbids it.
Antigone.
He is my brother. And he is your brother, too.
Ismene.
But think of the danger! Think what Creon will do!
Antigone.
Creon is not strong enough to stand in my way.
Ismene.
Ah sister!
Oedipus died, everyone hating him
For what his own search brought to light, his eyes
Ripped out by his own hand; and Jocasta died,
His mother and wife at once: she twisted the cords
That strangled her life; and our two brothers died,
Each killed by the other's sword. And we are left:
But oh, Antigone,
Think how much more terrible than these
Our own death would be if we should go against Creon
And do what he has forbidden! We are only women,
We cannot fight with men, Antigone!
The law is strong, we must give in to the law
In this thing, and in worse. I beg the Dead
To forgive me, but I am helpless: I must yield
To those in authority. And I think it is dangerous business
To be always meddling.
Antigone. If that is what you think,
I should not want you, even if you asked to come.
You have made your choice, you can be what you want to be.
But I will bury him; and if I must die,
I say that this crime is holy: I shall lie down
With him in death, and I shall be as dear
To him as he to me.
It is the dead,
Not the living, who make the longest demands:
We die forever . . .
You may do as you like,
Since apparently the laws of the gods mean nothing to you.
Ismene.
They mean a great deal to me; but I have no strength
To break laws that were made for the public good.
Antigone.
That must be your excuse, I suppose. But as for me,
I will bury the brother I love.

Ismene. Antigone,
I am so afraid for you!
Antigone. You need not be:
You have yourself to consider, after all.
Ismene.
But no one must hear of this, you must tell no one!
I will keep it a secret, I promise!
Antigone. Oh tell it! Tell everyone!
Think how they'll hate you when it all comes out
If they learn that you knew about it all the time!
Ismene.
So fiery! You should be cold with fear.
Antigone.
Perhaps. But I am doing only what I must.
Ismene.
But can you do it? I say that you cannot.
Antigone.
Very well: when my strength gives out, I shall do no more.
Ismene.
Impossible things should not be tried at all.
Antigone.
Go away, Ismene:
I shall be hating you soon, and the dead will too,
For your words are hateful. Leave me my foolish plan:
I am not afraid of the danger; if it means death,
It will not be the worst of deaths—death without honor.
Ismene.
Go then, if you feel that you must.
You are unwise,
But a loyal friend indeed to those who love you.
[*Exit into the palace.* ANTIGONE *goes off left.*]

[*Enter the* CHORUS.]

Literature and Religion

Ancient Greek Burial Practices

Creon says that Eteocles is to be buried "with all the ceremony that is usual when the greatest heroes die." What might such a burial have been like? In ancient Greece the rituals honoring the dead were performed with immense care, as the Greeks feared that the gods would punish those who neglected even the smallest detail. After death, the family closed the dead person's eyes and mouth and began to prepare the body for the *próthesis,* the wake. The women of the house washed the body and dressed it in white or in wedding clothes. Then they placed the body on a bier, a portable framework, making sure that the feet pointed toward the door, and sprinkled it with wild marjoram and other herbs, which were believed to keep evil spirits away. At the próthesis, while the women waited near the body, the men entered in a formal procession, their right arms raised high in the air. When the closest relative reached out and held the dead person's head with both hands, the other mourners began to beat their faces and tear their hair. They also wailed and sang, accompanied by the *aulós,* the reed pipe. (Antigone knows she will die alone, entombed in rock, and have "no song, but silence.") These lamentations continued at the *ekphorá,* the burial, which usually took place several days after the *próthesis.* Offerings at the tomb, consisting mainly of wine, milk, honey, and an animal sacrifice, were made on the third, ninth, and thirtieth days after death, then again after one year, and on certain festivals. Because heroes supposedly brought luck to the area where they were buried, special annual festivals were held to remember their deeds and mourn their passing.

(Background) Funeral of Patroclus (detail from a Greek vase).

Museo Archeologico Nazionale, Naples. Alinari/Art Resource, NY.

Parodos°

Parodos (par′ə·däs): first ode, or choral song, in a Greek tragedy, chanted by the chorus as it enters the area in front of the stage.

Strophe° 1

Strophe (strō′fē): part of the ode that the chorus chants as it moves from right to left across the stage.

Chorus.

Now the long blade of the sun, lying
Level east to west, touches with glory
Thebes of the Seven Gates. Open, unlidded
Eye of golden day! O marching light
Across the eddy and rush of Dirce's stream,°
Striking the white shields of the enemy
Thrown headlong backward from the blaze of
 morning!

5. Dirce's stream: stream near Thebes. Dirce (dur′sē), an early queen of Thebes, was murdered and her body was thrown into the stream.

Choragos.

Polyneices their commander
Roused them with windy phrases,
He the wild eagle screaming
Insults above our land,
His wings their shields of snow,
His crest their marshaled helms.

Antistrophe° 1

Antistrophe (an·tis′trə·fē): part of the ode chanted as the chorus moves back across the stage from left to right.

Chorus.

Against our seven gates in a yawning ring
The famished spears came onward in the night;
But before his jaws were sated with our blood,
Or pine fire took the garland of our towers,
He was thrown back; and as he turned, great Thebes—
No tender victim for his noisy power—
Rose like a dragon behind him, shouting war.

Choragos.

For God hates utterly
The bray of bragging tongues;
And when he beheld their smiling,
Their swagger of golden helms,
The frown of his thunder blasted
Their first man from our walls.°

21–26. For God . . . walls: Zeus, who sided with the Thebans, struck the first Argive attacker with a thunderbolt.

Strophe 2

Chorus.

We heard his shout of triumph high in the air
Turn to a scream; far out in a flaming arc

Words to Own

sated (sāt′əd) *v.:* filled; satisfied.
swagger *n.:* bold, arrogant strut.

He fell with his windy torch, and the earth struck him.
And others storming in fury no less than his
Found shock of death in the dusty joy of battle.

Choragos.

Seven captains at seven gates
Yielded their clanging arms to the god
That bends the battle line and breaks it.
These two only, brothers in blood,
Face to face in matchless rage,
Mirroring each the other's death,
Clashed in long combat.

Antistrophe 2

Chorus.

But now in the beautiful morning of victory
Let Thebes of the many chariots sing for joy!
With hearts for dancing we'll take leave of war:
Our temples shall be sweet with hymns of praise,
And the long night shall echo with our chorus.

Funeral of Patroclus (detail from a Greek vase). Patroclus was a friend of Achilles and was killed in the Trojan War. He was given a huge funeral.

Making Meanings
Prologue and Parodos

First Thoughts

1. How do you feel about Antigone's attitude toward her brothers and toward her sister, Ismene?

Shaping Interpretations

2. In their first scenes together, Antigone and Ismene are **foils,** characters who have contrasting or opposite qualities. How would you characterize each sister? Does Sophocles seem to side with one sister over the other? Do you? Explain.
3. The feature on page 696 describes ancient Greek burial practices. What did you learn there that helps explain the importance to Antigone of a proper burial for Polyneices? (Check the notes you took while reading.)
4. We haven't met Creon yet. What reasons do you think he would have given for leaving Polyneices' body unburied?
5. In **verbal irony,** what is said is the opposite of what is meant. Where does Antigone use verbal irony in her scenes with Ismene? How does this make you feel about Antigone?
6. At the end of the Parodos, what hopes for the future does the Chorus express? Do you think these expectations will be fulfilled? Why, or why not?

Reading Check

Make a **conflict** web to show the problems in this play. Use Antigone as the center of the web, and attach the names of other **characters** you've learned about so far. Describe briefly what each character wants that puts him or her in conflict with Antigone.

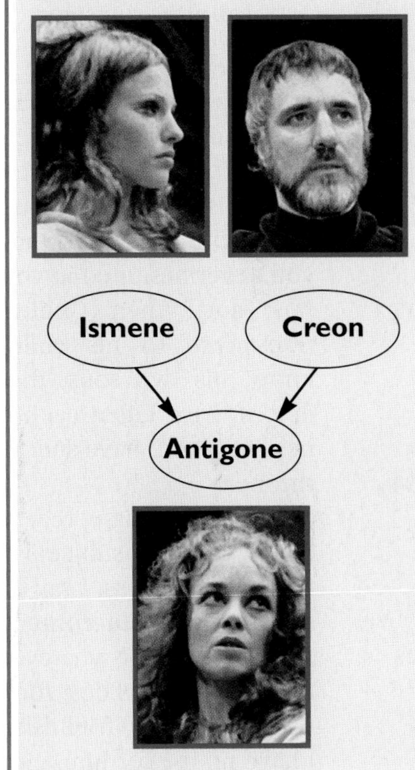

Connecting with the Text

7. In line 54, Antigone says to Ismene, "You have made your choice, you can be what you want to be." How would you respond to this statement about our ability to control our lives?

Extending the Text

8. In lines 46–47, Ismene says, ". . . We are only women, / We cannot fight with men, Antigone!" What do you think of this argument? Is it an argument that people still use today? Explain.
9. What **motivates** Antigone to break Creon's law? What motivates Ismene to respect it? Do people today have similar attitudes toward the law? Explain.

SCENE 1

Choragos.
But now at last our new king is coming:
Creon of Thebes, Menoikeus'° son.
In this auspicious dawn of his reign
What are the new complexities
That shifting Fate has woven for him?
What is his counsel? Why has he summoned
The old men to hear him?

[*Enter* CREON *from the palace, center. He addresses the* CHORUS *from the top step.*]

Creon. Gentlemen: I have the honor to inform you that our Ship of State, which recent storms have threatened to destroy, has come safely to harbor at last, guided by the merciful wisdom of Heaven. I have summoned you here this morning because I know that I can depend upon you: your devotion to King Laios was absolute; you never hesitated in your duty to our late ruler Oedipus; and when Oedipus died, your loyalty was transferred to his children. Unfortunately, as you know, his two sons, the princes Eteocles and Polyneices, have killed each other in battle; and I, as the next in blood, have succeeded to the full power of the throne.

I am aware, of course, that no ruler can expect complete loyalty from his subjects until he has been tested in office. Nevertheless, I say to you at the very outset that I have nothing but contempt for the kind of governor who is afraid, for whatever reason, to follow the course that he knows is best for the State; and as for the man who sets private friendship above the public welfare— I have no use for him, either. I call God to witness that if I saw my country headed for ruin, I should not be afraid to speak out plainly; and I need hardly remind you that I would never have any dealings with an enemy of the people. No one values friendship more highly than I; but we must remember that friends made at the risk of wrecking our Ship are not real friends at all.

These are my principles, at any rate, and that is why I have made the following decision concerning the sons of Oedipus: Eteocles, who died as a man should die, fighting for his country, is to be buried with full military honors, with all the ceremony that is usual when the greatest heroes die; but his brother Polyneices, who broke his exile to come back with fire and sword

2. **Menoikeus** (me·noi'kē·əs): an early hero, the father of Creon and Jocasta.

North Wind Picture Archives.

against his native city and the shrines of his fathers' gods, whose one idea was to spill the blood of his blood and sell his own people into slavery—Polyneices, I say, is to have no burial: no man is to touch him or say the least prayer for him; he shall lie on the plain, unburied; and the birds and the scavenging dogs can do with him whatever they like.

This is my command, and you can see the wisdom behind it. As long as I am king, no traitor is going to be honored with the loyal man. But whoever shows by word and deed that he is on the side of the State—he shall have my respect while he is living, and my reverence when he is dead.

Choragos.
If that is your will, Creon son of Menoikeus,
You have the right to enforce it: we are yours.

Creon.
That is my will. Take care that you do your part.

Choragos.
We are old men: let the younger ones carry it out.

Creon.
I do not mean that: the sentries have been appointed.

Choragos.
Then what is it that you would have us do?

Creon.
You will give no support to whoever breaks this law.

Choragos.
Only a crazy man is in love with death!

Creon.
And death it is; yet money talks, and the wisest
Have sometimes been known to count a few coins too
many.

"Only a crazy man is in love with death!"

[*Enter* SENTRY *from left.*]

Sentry. I'll not say that I'm out of breath from running, King, because every time I stopped to think about what I have to tell you, I felt like going back. And all the time a voice kept saying, "You fool, don't you know you're walking straight into trouble?"; and then another voice: "Yes, but if you let somebody else get the news to Creon first, it will be even worse than that for you!" But good sense won out, at least I hope it was good sense, and here I am with a story that makes no sense at all; but I'll tell it anyhow, because, as they say, what's going to happen's going to happen, and——

Creon.
Come to the point. What have you to say?

Sentry.

I did not do it. I did not see who did it. You must not punish me for what someone else has done.

Creon.

A comprehensive defense! More effective, perhaps,
If I knew its purpose. Come: what is it?

Sentry.

A dreadful thing . . . I don't know how to put it——

Creon.

Out with it!

Sentry. Well, then;
The dead man—
Polyneices—

[*Pause. The* SENTRY *is overcome, fumbles for words.* CREON *waits impassively.*]

out there—
someone—
New dust on the slimy flesh!

[*Pause. No sign from* CREON.]

Someone has given it burial that way, and
Gone . . .

[*Long pause.* CREON *finally speaks with deadly control.*]

Creon.

And the man who dared do this?

Sentry. I swear I
Do not know! You must believe me!
Listen:
The ground was dry, not a sign of digging, no,
Not a wheel track in the dust, no trace of anyone.
It was when they relieved us this morning: and one of them,
The corporal, pointed to it.
There it was,
The strangest—
Look:
The body, just mounded over with light dust: you see?
Not buried really, but as if they'd covered it
Just enough for the ghost's peace. And no sign
Of dogs or any wild animal that had been there.
And then what a scene there was! Every man of us

"New dust on the slimy flesh!"

Words to Own

comprehensive (käm′prē·hen′siv) *adj.:* including all of the relevant details.

Accusing the other: we all proved the other man did it,
We all had proof that we could not have done it.
We were ready to take hot iron in our hands,
Walk through fire, swear by all the gods,
It was not I!
I do not know who it was, but it was not I!

[CREON'S *rage has been mounting steadily, but the* SENTRY *is too intent upon his story to notice it.*]

And then, when this came to nothing, someone said
A thing that silenced us and made us stare
Down at the ground: you had to be told the news,
And one of us had to do it! We threw the dice,
And the bad luck fell to me. So here I am,
No happier to be here than you are to have me:
Nobody likes the man who brings bad news.

Choragos.

I have been wondering, King: can it be that the gods have done this?

Creon.

(Furiously) Stop!
Must you doddering wrecks
Go out of your heads entirely? "The gods!"
Intolerable!
The gods favor this corpse? Why? How had he served them?
Tried to loot their temples, burn their images,
Yes, and the whole State, and its laws with it!
Is it your senile opinion that the gods love to honor bad men?
A pious thought!
No, from the very beginning
There have been those who have whispered together,
Stiff-necked anarchists,° putting their heads together,
Scheming against me in alleys. These are the men,
And they have bribed my own guard to do this thing.
(Sententiously) Money!
There's nothing in the world so demoralizing as money,
Down go your cities,

"There's nothing in the world so demoralizing as money . . ."

124. anarchists (an′ər·kists′): people opposed to any kind of law or organized form of government.

WORDS TO OWN

senile (sē′nīl′) *adj.*: mentally impaired. *Senile* is often used to describe the mental deterioration that may accompany old age.
sententiously (sen·ten′shəs·lē) *adv.*: in a trite and moralizing way.

Homes gone, men gone, honest hearts corrupted,
Crookedness of all kinds, and all for money!

(To SENTRY*)* But you—!
I swear by God and by the throne of God,
The man who has done this thing shall pay for it!
Find that man, bring him here to me, or your death
Will be the least of your problems: I'll string you up
Alive, and there will be certain ways to make you
Discover your employer before you die;
And the process may teach you a lesson you seem to have missed:
The dearest profit is sometimes all too dear:
That depends on the source. Do you understand me?
A fortune won is often misfortune.

Sentry.
King, may I speak?

Creon. Your very voice distresses me.

Sentry.
Are you sure that it is my voice, and not your conscience?

Creon.
By God, he wants to analyze me now!

Sentry.
It is not what I say, but what has been done, that hurts you.

Creon.
You talk too much.

Sentry. Maybe; but I've done nothing.

Creon.
Sold your soul for some silver: that's all you've done.

Sentry.
How dreadful it is when the right judge judges wrong!

Creon.
Your figures of speech
May entertain you now; but unless you bring me the man,
You will get little profit from them in the end.

[*Exit* CREON *into the palace.*]

Sentry.
"Bring me the man"—!
I'd like nothing better than bringing him the man!
But bring him or not, you have seen the last of me here.
At any rate, I am safe! [*Exit* SENTRY.]

"A fortune won is often misfortune."

ODE° 1

Ode: Each scene is followed by an ode. These odes served both to separate one scene from the next, since there were no curtains, and also to provide the chorus's response to the preceding scene.

Strophe 1

Chorus.

Numberless are the world's wonders, but none
More wonderful than man; the storm-gray sea
Yields to his prows, the huge crests bear him high;
Earth, holy and inexhaustible, is graven
With shining furrows where his plows have gone
Year after year, the timeless labor of stallions.

Antistrophe 1

The light-boned birds and beasts that cling to cover,
The lithe fish lighting their reaches of dim water,
All are taken, tamed in the net of his mind;
The lion on the hill, the wild horse windy-maned,
Resign to him; and his blunt yoke has broken
The sultry shoulders of the mountain bull.

Strophe 2

Words also, and thought as rapid as air,
He fashions to his good use; statecraft is his,
And his the skill that deflects the arrows of snow,
The spears of winter rain: from every wind
He has made himself secure—from all but one:
In the late wind of death he cannot stand.

Antistrophe 2

O clear intelligence, force beyond all measure!
O fate of man, working both good and evil!
When the laws are kept, how proudly his city stands!
When the laws are broken, what of his city then?
Never may the anarchic man find rest at my hearth,
Never be it said that my thoughts are his thoughts.

Mosaic from Pompeii (first century A.D.).

Erich Lessing/Art Resource, NY.

WORDS TO OWN

lithe (līth) *adj.:* flexible and graceful.

Making Meanings
Scene 1 and Ode 1

First Thoughts

1. Does Creon remind you of any contemporary politicians? Does he appear to be concerned with the common good, or do you think he is simply a clever politician scheming to maintain his power?

Reading Check

a. What reasons does Creon give for not allowing Polyneices to be buried?

b. How does the Choragos react to Creon's decision?

c. In lines 83–87, what news is the Sentry reluctant to deliver to Creon?

d. What attitude toward human beings does the Chorus express in Ode 1? What one fact tempers their attitude?

Shaping Interpretations

2. Why do you think the Choragos does not oppose Creon's decree? What **motive** does Creon assign to those who might oppose him?
3. In line 113, the Choragos asks Creon, ". . . can it be that the gods have done this?" Why does this suggestion enrage Creon? What does the suggestion imply?
4. **Dramatic irony** is a situation in which the audience knows something that a character does not. What dramatic irony do you sense each time Creon refers to the "man" who has buried Polyneices?
5. On the basis of Scene 1, how would you **characterize** Creon's strengths and weaknesses as a leader? Is he a believable character? Why, or why not?
6. What law does Creon champion in this scene, and who supports his view here? What other view has been expressed in the play so far, and who expresses it?
7. What do you **predict** will happen when Creon discovers the truth about the burial of Polyneices? How might he and Antigone resolve their conflicting values?

Extending the Text

8. Reread Creon's first speech. How is it like the speeches of contemporary heads of state and political officeholders? What response do you think Creon wanted to get from his audience?
9. If a person like Creon were to run for president of the United States today, do you think he would have a chance of being elected? What "spin" might his political advisers put on his beliefs to enhance his appeal to the public?
10. In Ode 1, what opinion does the Chorus express about the importance of law in society? Is that opinion pertinent to our attitude toward law today? Explain.

Scene 2

Reenter SENTRY *leading* ANTIGONE.

Choragos.
What does this mean? Surely this captive woman
Is the princess Antigone. Why should she be taken?

Sentry.
Here is the one who did it! We caught her
In the very act of burying him. Where is Creon?

Choragos.
Just coming from the house.

North Wind Picture Archives.

[*Enter* CREON, *center.*]

Creon. What has happened?
Why have you come back so soon?

Sentry *(expansively).* O King,
A man should never be too sure of anything:
I would have sworn
That you'd not see me here again: your anger
Frightened me so, and the things you threatened me with;
But how could I tell then
That I'd be able to solve the case so soon?

No dice-throwing this time: I was only too glad to come!

Here is this woman. She is the guilty one:
We found her trying to bury him.
Take her, then; question her; judge her as you will.
I am through with the whole thing now, and glad of it.

Creon.
But this is Antigone! Why have you brought her here?

Sentry.
She was burying him, I tell you!

Creon *(severely).* Is this the truth?

Sentry.
I saw her with my own eyes. Can I say more?

Creon.
The details: come, tell me quickly!

Sentry. It was like this:
After those terrible threats of yours, King,
We went back and brushed the dust away from the body.
The flesh was soft by now, and stinking,
So we sat on a hill to windward and kept guard.
No napping this time! We kept each other awake.
But nothing happened until the white round sun

Whirled in the center of the round sky over us:
Then, suddenly,
A storm of dust roared up from the earth, and the sky
Went out, the plain vanished with all its trees
In the stinging dark. We closed our eyes and endured it.
The whirlwind lasted a long time, but it passed;
And then we looked, and there was Antigone!
I have seen
A mother bird come back to a stripped nest, heard
Her crying bitterly a broken note or two
For the young ones stolen. Just so, when this girl
Found the bare corpse, and all her love's work wasted,
She wept, and cried on heaven to damn the hands
That had done this thing.
And then she brought more dust
And sprinkled wine three times for her brother's ghost.

We ran and took her at once. She was not afraid,
Not even when we charged her with what she had done.
She denied nothing.
And this was a comfort to me,
And some uneasiness: for it is a good thing
To escape from death, but it is no great pleasure
To bring death to a friend.
Yet I always say
There is nothing so comfortable as your own safe skin!

Creon.
(Slowly, dangerously) And you, Antigone,
You with your head hanging, do you confess this thing?

Antigone.
I do. I deny nothing.

Creon *(to* SENTRY*).* You may go. [*Exit* SENTRY.]
(To ANTIGONE*)* Tell me, tell me briefly:
Had you heard my proclamation touching this matter?

Antigone.
It was public. Could I help hearing it?

Creon.
And yet you dared defy the law.

Antigone. I dared.
It was not God's proclamation. That final Justice
That rules the world below makes no such laws.
Your edict, King, was strong,
But all your strength is weakness itself against
The immortal unrecorded laws of God.

> "... all your strength is weakness itself against The immortal unrecorded laws of God."

They are not merely now: they were, and shall be,
Operative forever, beyond man utterly.

I knew I must die, even without your decree:
I am only mortal. And if I must die
Now, before it is my time to die,
Surely this is no hardship: can anyone
Living, as I live, with evil all about me,
Think Death less than a friend? This death of mine
Is of no importance; but if I had left my brother
Lying in death unburied, I should have suffered.
Now I do not.
You smile at me. Ah Creon,
Think me a fool, if you like; but it may well be
That a fool convicts me of folly.

Choragos.
Like father, like daughter: both headstrong, deaf to reason!
She has never learned to yield.

Creon.
She has much to learn.
The inflexible heart breaks first, the toughest iron
Cracks first, and the wildest horses bend their necks
At the pull of the smallest curb.
Pride? In a slave?
This girl is guilty of a double insolence,
Breaking the given laws and boasting of it.
Who is the man here,
She or I, if this crime goes unpunished?
Sister's child, or more than sister's child,
Or closer yet in blood—she and her sister
Win bitter death for this!
(To SERVANTS*)* Go, some of you,
Arrest Ismene. I accuse her equally.
Bring her: you will find her sniffling in the house there.

Her mind's a traitor: crimes kept in the dark
Cry for light, and the guardian brain shudders;
But how much worse than this
Is brazen boasting of barefaced anarchy!

Antigone.
Creon, what more do you want than my death?

Creon.
Nothing.
That gives me everything.

Antigone.
Then I beg you: kill me.
This talking is a great weariness: your words

WORDS TO OWN

insolence (in'sə·ləns) *n.:* bold disrespect.

Are distasteful to me, and I am sure that mine
Seem so to you. And yet they should not seem so:
I should have praise and honor for what I have done.
All these men here would praise me
Were their lips not frozen shut with fear of you.
(Bitterly) Ah the good fortune of kings,
Licensed to say and do whatever they please!

Creon.
You are alone here in that opinion.

Antigone.
No, they are with me. But they keep their tongues in leash.

Creon.
Maybe. But you are guilty, and they are not.

Antigone.
There is no guilt in reverence for the dead.

Creon.
But Eteocles—was he not your brother too?

Antigone.
My brother too.

Creon. And you insult his memory?

Antigone.
(Softly) The dead man would not say that I insult it.

Creon.
He would: for you honor a traitor as much as him.

Antigone.
His own brother, traitor or not, and equal in blood.

Creon.
He made war on his country. Eteocles defended it.

Antigone.
Nevertheless, there are honors due all the dead.

Creon.
But not the same for the wicked as for the just.

Antigone.
Ah Creon, Creon,
Which of us can say what the gods hold wicked?

Creon.
An enemy is an enemy, even dead.

Antigone.
It is my nature to join in love, not hate.

Creon.
(Finally losing patience) Go join them, then; if you must have your love,
Find it in hell!

Chorágos.
But see, Ismene comes:

[*Enter* ISMENE, *guarded.*]

Those tears are sisterly, the cloud

"It is my nature
to join in love,
not hate."

That shadows her eyes rains down gentle sorrow.

Creon.

You too, Ismene,
Snake in my ordered house, sucking my blood
Stealthily—and all the time I never knew
That these two sisters were aiming at my throne!
Ismene,
Do you confess your share in this crime, or deny it?
Answer me.

Ismene.

Yes, if she will let me say so. I am guilty.

Antigone.

(Coldly) No, Ismene. You have no right to say so.
You would not help me, and I will not have you help me.

Ismene.

But now I know what you meant; and I am here
To join you, to take my share of punishment.

Antigone.

The dead man and the gods who rule the dead
Know whose act this was. Words are not friends.

Ismene.

Do you refuse me, Antigone? I want to die with you:
I too have a duty that I must discharge to the dead.

Antigone.

You shall not lessen my death by sharing it.

Ismene.

What do I care for life when you are dead?

Antigone.

Ask Creon. You're always hanging on his opinions.

Ismene.

You are laughing at me. Why, Antigone?

Antigone.

It's a joyless laughter, Ismene.

Ismene. But can I do nothing?

Antigone.

Yes. Save yourself, I shall not envy you.
There are those who will praise you; I shall have honor, too.

Ismene.

But we are equally guilty!

Antigone. No more, Ismene.

You are alive, but I belong to Death.

Creon.

(To the CHORUS*)* Gentlemen, I beg you to observe these girls:
One has just now lost her mind; the other,
It seems, has never had a mind at all.

North Wind Picture Archives.

Ismene.
Grief teaches the steadiest minds to waver, King.
Creon.
Yours certainly did, when you assumed guilt with the guilty!
Ismene.
But how could I go on living without her?
Creon. You are.
She is already dead.
Ismene. But your own son's bride!
Creon.
There are places enough for him to push his plow.
I want no wicked women for my sons!
Ismene.
O dearest Haimon, how your father wrongs you!
Creon.
I've had enough of your childish talk of marriage!
Choragos.
Do you really intend to steal this girl from your son?
Creon.
No; Death will do that for me.
Choragos. Then she must die?
Creon.
(Ironically) You dazzle me.
—But enough of this talk!
(To GUARDS*)* You, there, take them away and guard them well:
For they are but women, and even brave men run
When they see Death coming.
[*Exeunt* ISMENE, ANTIGONE, *and* GUARDS.]

WORDS TO OWN
waver *v.*: show doubt or uncertainty about what to do.

Ode 2

Strophe 1

Chorus.

Fortunate is the man who has never tasted God's vengeance!
Where once the anger of heaven has struck, that house is shaken
Forever: damnation rises behind each child
Like a wave cresting out of the black Northeast,
When the long darkness under sea roars up
And bursts drumming death upon the wind-whipped sand.

Antistrophe 1

I have seen this gathering sorrow from time long past
Loom upon Oedipus' children: generation from generation
Takes the compulsive rage of the enemy god.
So lately this last flower of Oedipus' line
Drank the sunlight! but now a passionate word
And a handful of dust have closed up all its beauty.

Strophe 2

What mortal arrogance
Transcends the wrath of Zeus?
Sleep cannot lull him, nor the effortless long months
Of the timeless gods: but he is young forever,
And his house is the shining day of high Olympus.
All that is and shall be,
And all the past, is his.
No pride on earth is free of the curse of heaven.

Antistrophe 2

The straying dreams of men
May bring them ghosts of joy:
But as they drowse, the waking embers burn them;
Or they walk with fixed eyes, as blind men walk.
But the ancient wisdom speaks for our own time:
Fate works most for woe
With Folly's fairest show.
Man's little pleasure is the spring of sorrow.

Silver coin of Athens, showing Athena's symbol, the owl.

Kunsthistorisches Museum, Muenzkabinett, Vienna. Erich Lessing/Art Resource, NY.

Words to Own

transcends (tran·sendz′) *v.:* goes beyond the limits of.

Making Meanings
Scene 2 and Ode 2

First Thoughts

1. What would you say is the greatest force motivating Antigone in this scene—pride, love, or principle? Explain your response.

Reading Check

Make a Character Score Card. List each **character,** and give him or her a plus or a minus score for behavior up to this point. Briefly explain your reason for each score.

Shaping Interpretations

2. Since there is usually only one stage setting in a Greek drama, important actions often take place offstage. In Scene 2, the Sentry describes a crucial event that we do not witness. What does he compare Antigone to when she discovers that Polyneices' corpse has been unburied? How does this **simile** make you feel about Antigone?
3. In lines 75–76, the Choragos accuses Antigone of being "headstrong, deaf to reason," and unyielding. Later, Creon calls her behavior "barefaced anarchy." Could either accusation apply to Creon himself? Would you support Antigone's view of herself or Creon's view of Antigone? Why?
4. Why do you think Ismene changes her mind about her brother's burial? Do you think Antigone is justified in rejecting Ismene's support, or is she being too hard on her sister? Explain.
5. In Ode 2, the Chorus makes an **allusion,** or reference, to the Oedipus **myth** that you read about on pages 688–689. Look back at those pages. Why does "God's vengeance" loom over the House of Oedipus? What human fault does the Chorus say is responsible for this "curse of heaven"?

Extending the Text

6. In line 49 of Scene 2, the Sentry says, "There is nothing so comfortable as your own safe skin!" Where do you hear similar sentiments in the world today—about saving your own skin first?
7. Antigone tells Creon she is obeying the laws of God, not the law imposed by the king. Do such conflicts still happen today? In a democracy, how are such conflicts resolved?
8. Antigone says the citizens of Thebes are afraid to speak out against Creon, even though they disagree with him (lines 99–100). What historical and contemporary examples can you give of citizens who failed to protest immoral actions by their leaders? What motives besides fear might cause citizens to remain silent in such cases?

Gold earrings (c. 380 B.C.).

Historical District Museum, Vraca, Bulgaria. Erich Lessing/Art Resource, NY.

VOCABULARY HOW TO OWN A WORD

WORD BANK

repulse
sated
swagger
comprehensive
senile
sententiously
lithe
insolence
waver
transcends

Word Origins: Latin and Greek Roots

Many English words have interesting **word origins**—they may have been borrowed from the French, who borrowed them from the Romans (Latin), who in turn borrowed from the Greeks. Learning a word's **roots** can deepen your understanding of the meaning of the word and can help you to figure out the meanings of other words derived from the same or similar roots. Make a root chart like the one below for each of the words in the Word Bank. In this case, all but two of the words have Latin roots (and none have Greek roots). Use a dictionary, and include any related words you find.

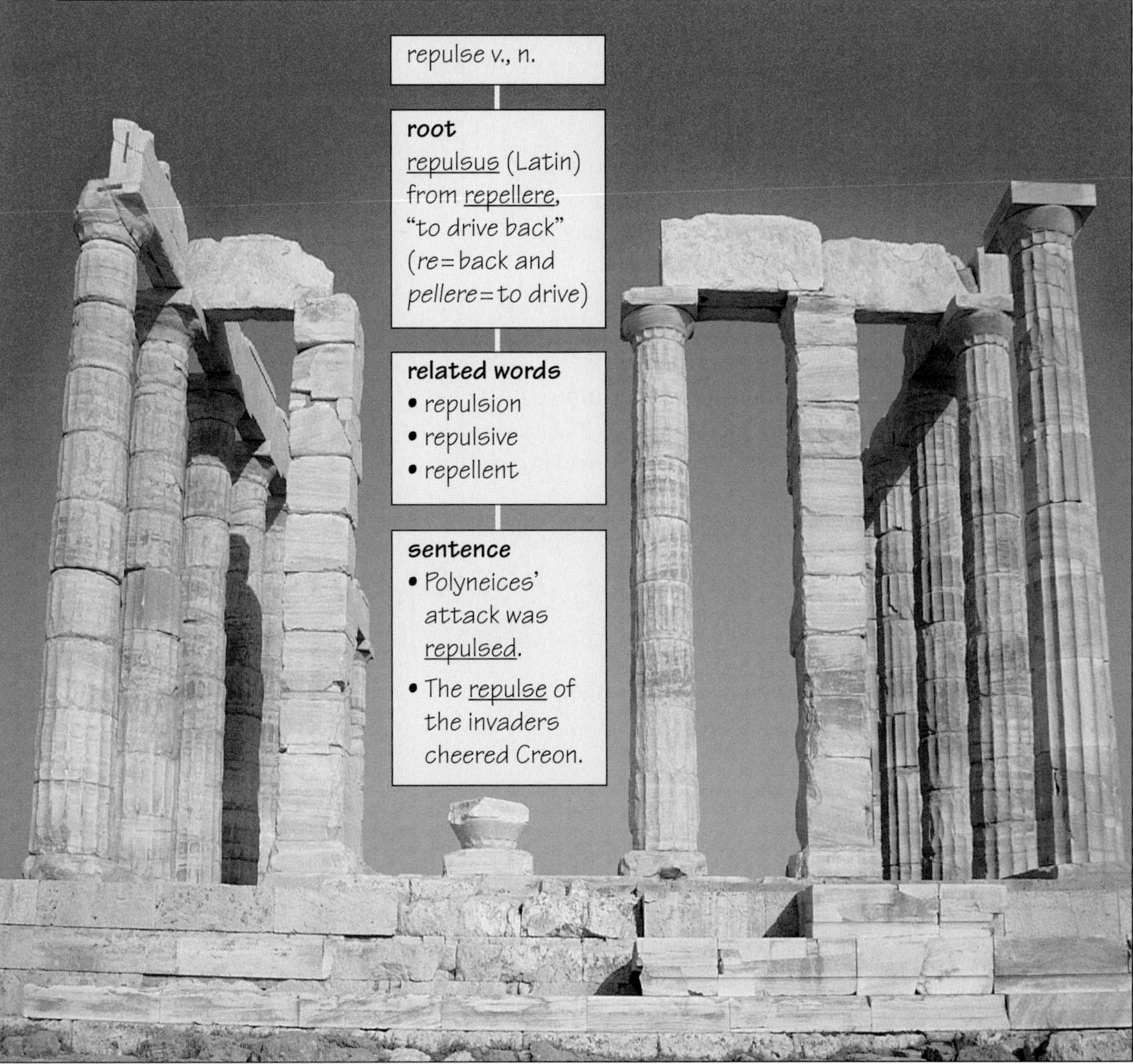

repulse v., n.

root
repulsus (Latin) from repellere, "to drive back" (*re*=back and *pellere*=to drive)

related words
- repulsion
- repulsive
- repellent

sentence
- Polyneices' attack was repulsed.
- The repulse of the invaders cheered Creon.

Scene 3

Choragos.
But here is Haimon, King, the last of all your sons.
Is it grief for Antigone that brings him here,
And bitterness at being robbed of his bride?

[*Enter* HAIMON.]

Creon.
We shall soon see, and no need of diviners.°
—Son,
You have heard my final judgment on that girl:
Have you come here hating me, or have you come
With deference and with love, whatever I do?

Haimon.
I am your son, Father. You are my guide.
You make things clear for me, and I obey you.
No marriage means more to me than your continuing
wisdom.

Creon.
Good. That is the way to behave: subordinate
Everything else, my son, to your father's will.
This is what a man prays for, that he may get
Sons attentive and dutiful in his house,
Each one hating his father's enemies,
Honoring his father's friends. But if his sons
Fail him, if they turn out unprofitably,
What has he fathered but trouble for himself
And amusement for the malicious?
So you are right
Not to lose your head over this woman.
Your pleasure with her would soon grow cold,
Haimon,
And then you'd have a hellcat in bed and elsewhere.
Let her find her husband in hell!
Of all the people in this city, only she
Has had contempt for my law and broken it.
Do you want me to show myself weak before the
people?
Or to break my sworn word? No, and I will not.
The woman dies.
I suppose she'll plead "family ties." Well, let her.
If I permit my own family to rebel,

4. diviners: people who claim to foretell the future by interpreting certain signs or events.

North Wind Picture Archives.

Words to Own

deference (def′ər·əns) *n.:* courteous respect.
malicious (mə·lish′əs) *adj.* used as *n.:* mean-spirited, spiteful people.

How shall I earn the world's obedience?
Show me the man who keeps his house in hand,
He's fit for public authority.
I'll have no dealings
With lawbreakers, critics of the government:
Whoever is chosen to govern should be obeyed—
Must be obeyed, in all things, great and small,
Just and unjust! O Haimon,
The man who knows how to obey, and that man only,
Knows how to give commands when the time comes.
You can depend on him, no matter how fast
The spears come: he's a good soldier, he'll stick it out.

Anarchy, anarchy! Show me a greater evil!
This is why cities tumble and the great houses rain down,
This is what scatters armies!

No, no: good lives are made so by discipline.
We keep the laws then, and the lawmakers,
And no woman shall seduce us. If we must lose,
Let's lose to a man, at least! Is a woman stronger than we?

Choragos.
Unless time has rusted my wits,
What you say, King, is said with point and dignity.

Haimon.
(Boyishly earnest) Father:
Reason is God's crowning gift to man, and you are right
To warn me against losing mine. I cannot say—
I hope that I shall never want to say!—that you
Have reasoned badly. Yet there are other men
Who can reason, too; and their opinions might be helpful.
You are not in a position to know everything
That people say or do, or what they feel:
Your temper terrifies them—everyone
Will tell you only what you like to hear.
But I, at any rate, can listen; and I have heard them
Muttering and whispering in the dark about this girl.
They say no woman has ever, so unreasonably,
Died so shameful a death for a generous act:
"She covered her brother's body. Is this indecent?
She kept him from dogs and vultures. Is this a crime?
Death?—She should have all the honor that we can give her!"

This is the way they talk out there in the city.

"If we must lose,
Let's lose to a man, at least!"

You must believe me:
Nothing is closer to me than your happiness.
What could be closer? Must not any son
Value his father's fortune as his father does his?
I beg you, do not be unchangeable:
Do not believe that you alone can be right.
The man who thinks that,
The man who maintains that only he has the power
To reason correctly, the gift to speak, the soul—
A man like that, when you know him, turns out empty.

It is not reason never to yield to reason!

In flood time you can see how some trees bend,
And because they bend, even their twigs are safe.
While stubborn trees are torn up, roots and all.
And the same thing happens in sailing:
Make your sheet fast, never slacken—and over you go,
Head over heels and under: and there's your voyage.
Forget you are angry! Let yourself be moved!
I know I am young; but please let me say this:
The ideal condition
Would be, I admit, that men should be right by instinct;
But since we are all too likely to go astray,
The reasonable thing is to learn from those who can
  teach.

Choragos.
You will do well to listen to him, King,
If what he says is sensible. And you, Haimon,
Must listen to your father. Both speak well.

Creon.
You consider it right for a man of my years and
  experience
To go to school to a boy?

Haimon. It is not right
If I am wrong. But if I am young, and right,
What does my age matter?

"But if I am young, and right, What does my age matter?"

Creon.
You think it right to stand up for an anarchist?

Haimon.
Not at all. I pay no respect to criminals.

Creon.
Then she is not a criminal?

Haimon.
The City would deny it, to a man.

Creon.
And the City proposes to teach me how to rule?

Haimon.
Ah. Who is it that's talking like a boy now?

Creon.
My voice is the one voice giving orders in this City!

Haimon.
It is no City if it takes orders from one voice.

Creon.
The State is the king!

Haimon. Yes, if the State is a desert.

Creon.
(Pause) This boy, it seems, has sold out to a woman.

Haimon.
If you are a woman: my concern is only for you.

Creon.
So? Your "concern"! In a public brawl with your father!

Haimon.
How about you, in a public brawl with justice?

Creon.
With justice, when all that I do is within my rights?

Haimon.
You have no right to trample on God's right.

Creon.
(Completely out of control) Fool, adolescent fool!
Taken in by a woman!

Haimon.
You'll never see me taken in by anything vile.

Creon.
Every word you say is for her!

Haimon *(quietly, darkly).* And for you.
And for me. And for the gods under the earth.

Creon.
You'll never marry her while she lives.

Haimon.
Then she must die. But her death will cause another.

Creon.
Another?
Have you lost your senses? Is this an open threat?

Haimon.
There is no threat in speaking to emptiness.

Creon.
I swear you'll regret this superior tone of yours!
You are the empty one!

Haimon. If you were not my father,
I'd say you were perverse.

Creon.
You girlstruck fool, don't play at words with me!

Haimon.
I am sorry. You prefer silence.

Creon. Now, by God—!
I swear, by all the gods in heaven above us,

You'll watch it, I swear you shall!
(To the SERVANTS*)* Bring her out!
Bring the woman out! Let her die before his eyes!
Here, this instant, with her bridegroom beside her!

Haimon.
Not here, no; she will not die here, King.
And you will never see my face again.
Go on raving as long as you've a friend to endure you.
[*Exit* HAIMON.]

Choragos.
Gone, gone.
Creon, a young man in a rage is dangerous!

Creon.
Let him do, or dream to do, more than a man can.
He shall not save these girls from death.

Choragos. These girls?
You have sentenced them both?

Creon. No, you are right.
I will not kill the one whose hands are clean.

Choragos.
But Antigone?

Creon *(somberly).* I will carry her far away
Out there in the wilderness, and lock her
Living in a vault of stone. She shall have food,
As the custom is, to absolve the State of her death.
And there let her pray to the gods of hell:
They are her only gods:
Perhaps they will show her an escape from death,
Or she may learn,
though late,
That piety shown the dead is pity in vain.
[*Exit* CREON.]

Words to Own

somberly (säm′bər·lē) *adv.:* earnestly and solemnly; in a gloomy manner.
piety (pī′ə·tē) *n.:* loyal, dutiful devotion.

North Wind Picture Archives.

Ode 3

Strophe

Chorus.
Love, unconquerable
Waster of rich men, keeper
Of warm lights and all-night vigil
In the soft face of a girl:
Sea wanderer, forest visitor!
Even the pure Immortals cannot escape you,
And mortal man, in his one day's dusk,
Trembles before your glory.

Antistrophe

Surely you swerve upon ruin
The just man's consenting heart,
As here you have made bright anger
Strike between father and son—
And none has conquered but Love!
A girl's glance working the will of heaven:
Pleasure to her alone who mocks us,
Merciless Aphrodite.°

16. Aphrodite (af′rə·dīt′ē): goddess of love and beauty.

Making Meanings
Scene 3 and Ode 3

First Thoughts

1. What is your first impression of Haimon? How does your view of him change as the scene progresses?

Shaping Interpretations

2. In this scene, Creon withstands a powerful assault on his thinking. Who makes the attack, and what effect does it have on Creon?
3. In line 29, Creon says that Antigone will probably plead "family ties" to avoid being punished for breaking the law. How has Creon completely misjudged Antigone's **character**?
4. What **metaphors** does Haimon use to argue that Creon should be more flexible? In lines 76–79 of Scene 2, Creon uses a similar argument against Antigone. At this point in the play, do you think that both Antigone and Creon should be more yielding, or do you believe that there are some principles that a person cannot compromise? Explain your opinion.
5. How do Creon's attitudes toward women seem to influence his decision about Antigone?
6. Why do you think Creon changes his mind about how to punish Antigone? How can he believe that he can absolve himself, or the state, of her death?
7. In Ode 3, the Chorus asserts that love is Haimon's **motive** in defending Antigone. What other motivation can you suggest for Haimon's actions? What support can you find in the text of the play?
8. At this point in the play, what do you think of Haimon's threat in line 119? Do you think he is serious, or do you think he is trying to pressure his father into changing his mind?

Extending the Text

9. "The State is the king!" declares Creon in line 107. "Yes," replies Haimon, "if the State is a desert." What does Haimon mean? Which contemporary figures can you think of who might express views like Creon's and Haimon's?

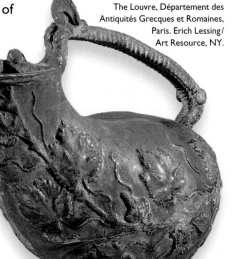

Reading Check

Suppose you are watching a serialization of this play. Write a note in which you explain to a friend the crucial developments that take place in Scene 3. Be sure to explain the **causes** of the main events in this scene and their **effects,** or results. End the letter with a P.S. that explains how you feel about what is said in Ode 3.

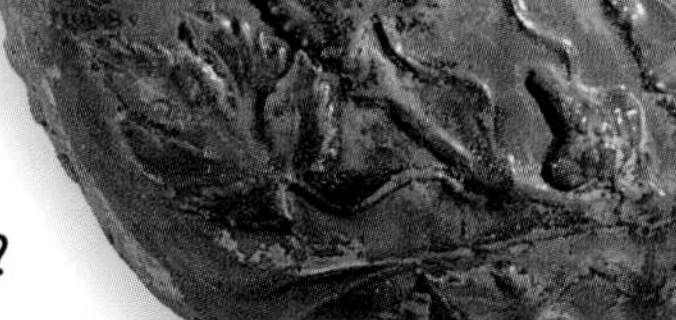

Ancient Greek perfume vase decorated with vine branches.

The Louvre, Département des Antiquités Grecques et Romaines, Paris. Erich Lessing/Art Resource, NY.

Scene 4

Choragos.
(As ANTIGONE *enters, guarded)* But I can no longer
stand in awe of this
Nor, seeing what I see, keep back my tears.
Here is Antigone, passing to that chamber
Where all find sleep at last.

Strophe 1

Antigone.
Look upon me, friends, and pity me
Turning back at the night's edge to say
Goodbye to the sun that shines for me no longer;
Now sleepy Death
Summons me down to Acheron,° that cold shore:
There is no bride song there, nor any music.

Chorus.
Yet not unpraised, not without a kind of honor,
You walk at last into the underworld;
Untouched by sickness, broken by no sword.
What woman has ever found your way to death?

Antistrophe 1

Antigone.
How often I have heard the story of Niobe,°
Tantalos'° wretched daughter, how the stone
Clung fast about her, ivy-close: and they say
The rain falls endlessly
And sifting soft snow; her tears are never done.
I feel the loneliness of her death in mine.

Chorus.
But she was born of heaven, and you
Are woman, woman-born. If her death is yours,
A mortal woman's, is this not for you
Glory in our world and in the world beyond?

Strophe 2

Antigone.
You laugh at me. Ah, friends, friends,
Can you not wait until I am dead? O Thebes,
O men many-charioted, in love with Fortune,
Dear springs of Dirce, sacred Theban grove,
Be witnesses for me, denied all pity,
Unjustly judged! and think a word of love
For her whose path turns
Under dark earth, where there are no more tears.

9. Acheron (ak′ər·än′): one of the rivers that dead souls were ferried across to reach Hades, the underworld. (Hades is also the name of the god of the underworld.)

15. Niobe (nī′ō·bə′): ancient queen of Thebes who had seven sons and seven daughters. Niobe boasted that she was superior to Leto because Leto's only children were the twins Apollo and Artemis. Offended, Leto complained to her children, who then slaughtered all of Niobe's children. Zeus turned the weeping Niobe into a column of stone. She continued to weep, however, and her tears became a stream.

16. Tantalos (tan′tə·ləs): king whose punishment in the underworld was to suffer unending hunger and thirst. Though he stood in a lake, the waters flowed away from him whenever he tried to drink. Though branches of luscious fruit hung over his head, they always remained just out of his reach.

Chorus.
You have passed beyond human daring and come at last
Into a place of stone where Justice sits.
I cannot tell
What shape of your father's guilt appears in this.

Antistrophe 2

Antigone.
You have touched it at last: that bridal bed
Unspeakable, horror of son and mother mingling:
Their crime, infection of all our family!
O Oedipus, father and brother!
Your marriage strikes from the grave to murder mine
I have been a stranger here in my own land:
All my life
The blasphemy° of my birth has followed me.

Chorus.
Reverence is a virtue, but strength
Lives in established law: that must prevail.
You have made your choice,
Your death is the doing of your conscious hand.

44. blasphemy (blas′fə·mē′): action or words showing contempt for God.

Epode°

Epode (ep′ōd′): final stanza of the ode, following the strophe and antistrophe.

Antigone.
Then let me go, since all your words are bitter,
And the very light of the sun is cold to me.
Lead me to my vigil, where I must have
Neither love nor lamentation; no song, but silence.

[CREON *interrupts impatiently.*]

Creon.
If dirges and planned lamentations could put off death,
Men would be singing forever.
(To the SERVANTS*)* Take her, go!
You know your orders: take her to the vault
And leave her alone there. And if she lives or dies,
That's her affair, not ours: our hands are clean.

Antigone.
O tomb, vaulted bride bed in eternal rock,
Soon I shall be with my own again°
Where Persephone welcomes the thin ghosts underground.

59. Soon . . . again: Antigone is looking forward to a reunion with her family. The Greeks considered the underworld a place where all dead souls wander as ghosts, or shades.

WORDS TO OWN

vigil (vij′əl) *n.:* purposeful watching and staying awake.

And I shall see my father again, and you, mother,
And dearest Polyneices—
dearest indeed
To me, since it was my hand
That washed him clean and poured the ritual wine:
And my reward is death before my time!

And yet, as men's hearts know, I have done no wrong,
I have not sinned before God. Or if I have,
I shall know the truth in death. But if the guilt
Lies upon Creon who judged me, then, I pray,
May his punishment equal my own.

Choragos. O passionate heart,
Unyielding, tormented still by the same winds!

Creon.
Her guards shall have good cause to regret their delaying.

Antigone.
Ah! That voice is like the voice of death!

Creon.
I can give you no reason to think you are mistaken.

Antigone.
Thebes, and you my fathers' gods,
And rulers of Thebes, you see me now, the last
Unhappy daughter of a line of kings,
Your kings, led away to death. You will remember
What things I suffer, and at what men's hands,
Because I would not transgress the laws of heaven.
(To the GUARDS, *simply)* Come: let us wait no longer.
[*Exit* ANTIGONE, *left, guarded.*]

WORDS TO OWN
transgress (trans·gres′) *v.:* disobey.

ODE 4

Strophe 1

Chorus.

All Danae's° beauty was locked away
In a brazen cell where the sunlight could not come;
A small room, still as any grave, enclosed her.
Yet she was a princess too,
And Zeus in a rain of gold poured love upon her.
O child, child,
No power in wealth or war
Or tough sea-blackened ships
Can prevail against untiring Destiny!

Antistrophe 1

And Dryas' son° also, that furious king,
Bore the god's prisoning anger for his pride:
Sealed up by Dionysos in deaf stone,
His madness died among echoes.
So at the last he learned what dreadful power
His tongue had mocked:
For he had profaned the revels,
And fired the wrath of the nine
Implacable sisters° that love the sound of the flute.

Strophe 2

And old men tell a half-remembered tale°
Of horror done where a dark ledge splits the sea
And a double surf beats on the gray shores:
How a king's new woman, sick
With hatred for the queen he had imprisoned,
Ripped out his two sons' eyes with her bloody hands
While grinning Ares° watched the shuttle plunge
Four times: four blind wounds crying for revenge.

Antistrophe 2

Crying, tears and blood mingled. Piteously born,
Those sons whose mother was of heavenly birth!
Her father was the god of the North Wind
And she was cradled by gales.
She raced with young colts on the glittering hills
And walked untrammeled in the open light:
But in her marriage deathless Fate found means
To build a tomb like yours for all her joy.

1. Danae (dan′ā·ē′): daughter of an ancient king of Argos. The king imprisoned Danae in a bronze (brazen) tower when he learned from an oracle that she would have a son who would kill him. Zeus fell in love with Danae and visited her in her prison as a shower of gold. When Danae gave birth to Zeus's son Perseus, the frightened king put Danae and her baby in a wooden chest and tossed them into the sea. However, Zeus saved them, and when Perseus grew up, he did (unknowingly) kill his grandfather, as prophesied.

10. Dryas' son: Lycurgos (lī·kur′gəs), ancient king of Thrace who disapproved of the worship of Dionysos and drove the god and his followers into the sea. According to some accounts, Dionysos then punished Lycurgos by driving him mad and imprisoning him in a rocky cave until he regained his sanity. Later, Zeus blinded Lycurgos as further punishment.

18. nine implacable sisters: the Muses, goddesses of literature, the arts, and the sciences. The Muses are called implacable (unbending) because once they have been offended, they no longer offer their inspiration.

19. half-remembered tale: King Phineus of Thrace imprisoned his first wife, Cleopatra, who was the daughter of Boreas, the god of the North Wind. Then the king's jealous new wife blinded Cleopatra's two sons.

25. Ares (er′ēz′): god of war and violence, who lived in Thrace.

WORDS TO OWN

wrath (rath) *n.:* intense anger.

Making Meanings
Scene 4 and Ode 4

First Thoughts

1. How does Antigone's first speech make you feel? Do you think Sophocles wants you to feel more sympathetic toward her than before, or less? Explain.

Reading Check

a. Whose fate does Antigone compare to her own?

b. What does Antigone say is the cause of her death?

c. What does Antigone look forward to in death?

d. What curse does she put on Creon?

Shaping Interpretations

2. How is Antigone's **tone** in this scene different from her tone in earlier scenes? Do you think the change results from circumstance or from a change in her character? Explain.

3. Beginning at line 25, Antigone accuses the Chorus of laughing at her and denying her "all pity." What do you think she means by pity, and how does the Chorus respond to her?

4. What does Antigone mean in line 41 when she says that her father's "marriage strikes from the grave to murder" her own marriage? How does the Chorus argue against this view in lines 45–48?

5. How do you feel about the Chorus's opinion, in lines 47–48, that Antigone is responsible for her own death?

6. In line 69, Antigone asks that Creon's punishment equal her own. What do you **predict** will happen to Creon in the final scene? Why do you think so?

7. In Antigone's last lines in the scene, what does she ask the gods to remember? What **motives** do you think she has for making this public request?

8. The side notes in Ode 4 explain **allusions** to three Greek myths. Reread those notes. What does Antigone have in common with Danae, Lycurgos, and Cleopatra? Do you think Sophocles is using this ode to condemn Antigone for her pride or to praise her courage in accepting her fate? Explain.

Extending the Text

9. In Greek **tragedies,** characters' fates are closely tied to the histories of their families. How do some people today account for their current circumstances by looking to the past?

Detail from an ancient Greek temple on the island of Siphnos (c. 525 B.C.).

Archeological Museum, Delphi. Nimatallah/Art Resource, NY.

Scene 5

Enter blind TEIRESIAS, *led by a boy. The opening speeches of* TEIRESIAS *should be in singsong contrast to the realistic lines of* CREON.

Teiresias.
This is the way the blind man comes, princes, princes,
Lock step, two heads lit by the eyes of one.

Creon.
What new thing have you to tell us, old Teiresias?

Teiresias.
I have much to tell you: listen to the prophet, Creon.

Creon.
I am not aware that I have ever failed to listen.

Teiresias.
Then you have done wisely, King, and ruled well.

Creon.
I admit my debt to you.° But what have you to say?

Teiresias.
This, Creon: you stand once more on the edge of fate.

Creon.
What do you mean? Your words are a kind of dread.

Teiresias.
Listen, Creon:
I was sitting in my chair of augury,° at the place
Where the birds gather about me. They were all achatter,
As is their habit, when suddenly I heard
A strange note in their jangling, a scream, a
Whirring fury: I knew that they were fighting,
Tearing each other, dying
In a whirlwind of wings clashing. And I was afraid.
I began the rites of burnt offering at the altar,
But Hephaistos° failed me: instead of bright flame,
There was only the sputtering slime of the fat thigh flesh
Melting: the entrails dissolved in gray smoke,
The bare bone burst from the welter. And no blaze!

This was a sign from heaven. My boy described it,
Seeing for me as I see for others.

I tell you, Creon, you yourself have brought
This new calamity upon us. Our hearths and altars

North Wind Picture Archives.

7. my debt to you: Teiresias is indirectly responsible for Creon's ascension to the throne. Teiresias helped reveal the terrible truth to Oedipus, which resulted in his exile.

11. augury (ô′gyo͞o·rē): skill of foretelling the future from signs, such as the flight of birds or the appearance of a comet.

19. Hephaistos (hē·fes′təs): god of fire and metalworking, son of Zeus and Hera.

Words to Own

calamity (kə·lam′ə·tē) *n.:* great misfortune resulting in immense loss and sorrow; disaster.

Are stained with the corruption of dogs and carrion birds
That glut themselves on the corpse of Oedipus' son.
The gods are deaf when we pray to them, their fire
Recoils from our offering, their birds of omen
Have no cry of comfort, for they are gorged
With the thick blood of the dead.
O my son,
These are not trifles! Think: all men make mistakes,
But a good man yields when he knows his course is wrong,
And repairs the evil. The only crime is pride.

Give in to the dead man, then: do not fight with a corpse—
What glory is it to kill a man who is dead?
Think, I beg you:
It is for your own good that I speak as I do.
You should be able to yield for your own good.

Creon.
It seems that prophets have made me their especial province.
All my life long
I have been a kind of butt for the dull arrows
Of doddering fortunetellers!
No, Teiresias:
If your birds—if the great eagles of God himself
Should carry him stinking bit by bit to heaven,
I would not yield. I am not afraid of pollution:
No man can defile the gods.
Do what you will,
Go into business, make money, speculate
In India gold or that synthetic gold from Sardis,°
Get rich otherwise than by my consent to bury him.
Teiresias, it is a sorry thing when a wise man
Sells his wisdom, lets out his words for hire!

Teiresias.
Ah Creon! Is there no man left in the world——

Creon.
To do what? Come, let's have the aphorism!°

Teiresias.
No man who knows that wisdom outweighs any wealth?

50. Sardis: ancient city where the first metal coins were made. The metal was a natural alloy of gold and silver.

55. aphorism (af'ə·riz'əm): short, wise, often clever saying.

WORDS TO OWN

recoils (ri·koilz') *v.:* draws back, as in fear or disgust.
defile (dē·fīl') *v.:* make dirty.

Creon.
As surely as bribes are baser than any baseness.
Teiresias.
You are sick, Creon! You are deathly sick!
Creon.
As you say: it is not my place to challenge a prophet.
Teiresias.
Yet you have said my prophecy is for sale.
Creon.
The generation of prophets has always loved gold.
Teiresias.
The generation of kings has always loved brass.
Creon.
You forget yourself! You are speaking to your king.
Teiresias.
I know it. You are a king because of me.
Creon.
You have a certain skill; but you have sold out.
Teiresias.
King, you will drive me to words that——
Creon. Say them, say them!
Only remember: I will not pay you for them.
Teiresias.
No, you will find them too costly.
Creon. No doubt. Speak:
Whatever you say, you will not change my will.
Teiresias.
Then take this, and take it to heart!
The time is not far off when you shall pay back
Corpse for corpse, flesh of your own flesh.
You have thrust the child of this world into living night,
You have kept from the gods below the child that is theirs:
The one in a grave before her death, the other,
Dead, denied the grave. This is your crime:
And the Furies° and the dark gods of hell
Are swift with terrible punishment for you.
Do you want to buy me now, Creon?
Not many days,
And your house will be full of men and women weeping,
And curses will be hurled at you from far
Cities grieving for sons unburied, left to rot
Before the walls of Thebes.

These are my arrows, Creon: they are all for you.

(To BOY*)* But come, child: lead me home.

77. Furies: three goddesses of vengeance who tormented unpunished wrongdoers, especially those who had committed crimes against their own families. The Furies had snakes entwined in their hair and drove their victims mad.

Let him waste his fine anger upon younger men.
Maybe he will learn at last
To control a wiser tongue in a better head.
[*Exit* TEIRESIAS.]

Choragos.
The old man has gone, King, but his words
Remain to plague us. I am old, too,
But I cannot remember that he was ever false.

Creon.
That is true. . . . It troubles me.
Oh it is hard to give in! but it is worse
To risk everything for stubborn pride.

Choragos.
Creon: take my advice.

Creon. What shall I do?

Choragos.
Go quickly: free Antigone from her vault
And build a tomb for the body of Polyneices.

Creon.
You would have me do this?

Choragos. Creon, yes!
And it must be done at once: God moves
Swiftly to cancel the folly of stubborn men.

Creon.
It is hard to deny the heart! But I
Will do it: I will not fight with destiny.

Choragos.
You must go yourself, you cannot leave it to others.

Creon.
I will go.
—Bring axes, servants:
Come with me to the tomb. I buried her, I
Will set her free
Oh quickly!
My mind misgives—
The laws of the gods are mighty, and a man must serve them
To the last day of his life! [*Exit* CREON.]

PAEAN°

Paean (pē′ən): hymn in praise of a god—in this case Dionysos, in whose honor the Greeks performed their plays.

Strophe 1

Choragos.
God of many names

Chorus. O Iacchos°
son
of Kadmeian Semele
O born of the Thunder!°
Guardian of the West
Regent
of Eleusis'° plain
O Prince of maenad° Thebes
and the Dragon Field° by rippling Ismenos:°

Antistrophe 1

Choragos.
God of many names
Chorus. the flame of torches
flares on our hills
the nymphs of Iacchos
dance at the spring of Castalia:°

from the vine-close mountain
come ah come in ivy:
Evohé° *evohé!* sings through the streets of Thebes

Strophe 2

Choragos.
God of many names
Chorus. Iacchos of Thebes
heavenly Child
of Semele bride of the Thunderer!
The shadow of plague is upon us:
come
with clement° feet
oh come from Parnasos°
down the long slopes
across the lamenting water

Antistrophe 2

Choragos.
Io° Fire! Chorister° of the throbbing stars!
O purest among the voices of the night!
Thou son of God, blaze for us!
Chorus.
Come with choric rapture of circling maenads
Who cry *Io Iacche!*°
God of many names!

1. Iacchos (ē′ə·kəs): another name for Dionysos.

2. Thunder: Dionysos's father was Zeus, god of thunder. His mother was the mortal Semele (sem′ə·lē′), daughter of Kadmos. Kadmos was the founder of Thebes (see note, line 5).

4. Eleusis' (e·lo͞o′sis): ancient Greek city northwest of Athens, site of secret religious festivals. **maenad** (mē′nad′): female worshiper or priestess of Dionysos. The chorus is describing the city of Thebes as a priestess.

5. Dragon Field: The oracle at Delphi had instructed Kadmos to follow a cow marked with a white full moon on each haunch and to build a city on the spot where the cow lay down to rest. Soon Kadmos saw a cow that fit this description, and he followed it until it stopped near a stream guarded by a dragon. Kadmos killed the dragon, cut off its head, and scattered its teeth in the field. Warriors sprang from these teeth and fought one another until there were only five left. With these five warriors, Kadmos founded the city of Thebes. **Ismenos** (is·mē′nəs): river near Thebes, sacred to Apollo.

8. Castalia (kas·tā′lē·ə): spring sacred to the Muses.

10. *Evohé* (ē·vō′ē): cry of joy, like "hallelujah," shouted by the worshipers at Dionysian festivals.

14. clement: mild; healing; merciful. **Parnasos** (pär·nas′əs): mountain in central Greece, sacred to Apollo and Dionysos. Castalia (see note, line 8) is located at its base.

16. Io (ī′ō): Hail! **Chorister:** choir leader.

20. *Iacche* (ē′ə·kē): another ritual cry of joy shouted by the worshipers of Dionysos. (The name *Iacchos* comes from this cry.)

Exodos°

Enter MESSENGER, *left.*

Messenger.
Men of the line of Kadmos, you who live
Near Amphion's° citadel:
I cannot say
Of any condition of human life "This is fixed,
This is clearly good or bad." Fate raises up,
And Fate casts down the happy and unhappy alike:
No man can foretell his Fate.
Take the case of Creon:
Creon was happy once, as I count happiness:
Victorious in battle, sole governor of the land,
Fortunate father of children nobly born.
And now it has all gone from him! Who can say
That a man is still alive when his life's joy fails?
He is a walking dead man. Grant him rich,
Let him live like a king in his great house:
If his pleasure is gone, I would not give
So much as the shadow of smoke for all he owns.

Choragos.
Your words hint at sorrow: what is your news for us?

Messenger.
They are dead. The living are guilty of their death.

Choragos.
Who is guilty? Who is dead? Speak!

Messenger. Haimon.
Haimon is dead; and the hand that killed him
Is his own hand.

Choragos. His father's? or his own?

Messenger.
His own, driven mad by the murder his father had done.

Choragos.
Teiresias, Teiresias, how clearly you saw it all!

Messenger.
This is my news: you must draw what conclusions you can from it.

Choragos.
But look: Eurydice, our queen:
Has she overheard us?

[*Enter* EURYDICE *from the palace, center.*]

Eurydice.
I have heard something, friends:
As I was unlocking the gate of Pallas'° shrine,

Exodos: the final, or exit, scene.

2. Amphion (am·fī′ən): ancient king of Thebes who was a son of Zeus and the husband of Niobe (see note, Scene 4, line 15). Amphion built the wall around Thebes by playing his lyre so well that he enchanted the stones into their proper places.

27. Pallas: Pallas Athena, goddess of wisdom.

For I needed her help today, I heard a voice
Telling of some new sorrow. And I fainted
There at the temple with all my maidens about me.
But speak again: whatever it is, I can bear it:
Grief and I are no strangers.°

Messenger. Dearest lady,
I will tell you plainly all that I have seen.
I shall not try to comfort you: what is the use,
Since comfort could lie only in what is not true?
The truth is always best.
I went with Creon
To the outer plain where Polyneices was lying,
No friend to pity him, his body shredded by dogs.
We made our prayers in that place to Hecate°
And Pluto,° that they would be merciful. And we bathed
The corpse with holy water, and we brought
Fresh-broken branches to burn what was left of it,
And upon the urn we heaped up a towering barrow
Of the earth of his own land.
When we were done, we ran
To the vault where Antigone lay on her couch of stone.
One of the servants had gone ahead,
And while he was yet far off he heard a voice
Grieving within the chamber, and he came back
And told Creon. And as the king went closer,
The air was full of wailing, the words lost,
And he begged us to make all haste. "Am I a prophet?"
He said, weeping, "And must I walk this road,
The saddest of all that I have gone before?
My son's voice calls me on. Oh quickly, quickly!
Look through the crevice there, and tell me
If it is Haimon, or some deception of the gods!"
We obeyed; and in the cavern's farthest corner
We saw her lying:
She had made a noose of her fine linen veil
And hanged herself. Haimon lay beside her,
His arms about her waist, lamenting her,
His love lost underground, crying out
That his father had stolen her away from him.
When Creon saw him the tears rushed to his eyes
And he called to him: "What have you done, child? Speak to me.
What are you thinking that makes your eyes so strange?
O my son, my son, I come to you on my knees!"
But Haimon spat in his face. He said not a word,
Staring—

32. Grief . . . strangers: Megareus (mə·ga′rē·əs), the older son of Eurydice and Creon, died during the Argive assault on Thebes.

39. Hecate (hek′ə·tē): goddess of sorcery and witchcraft. Offerings were left to her at crossroads, which were thought to be the best location for performing magic.

40. Pluto: another name for Hades, god of the underworld.

And suddenly drew his sword
And lunged. Creon shrank back, the blade missed; and the boy,
Desperate against himself, drove it half its length
Into his own side, and fell. And as he died
He gathered Antigone close in his arms again,
Choking, his blood bright red on her white cheek.
And now he lies dead with the dead, and she is his
At last, his bride in the houses of the dead.

[*Exit* EURYDICE *into the palace.*]

Choragos.
She has left us without a word. What can this mean?

Messenger.
It troubles me, too; yet she knows what is best,
Her grief is too great for public lamentation,
And doubtless she has gone to her chamber to weep
For her dead son, leading her maidens in his dirge.

Choragos.
It may be so: but I fear this deep silence.
[*Pause.*]

Messenger.
I will see what she is doing. I will go in.

[*Exit* MESSENGER *into the palace.*]

[*Enter* CREON *with attendants, bearing* HAIMON'S *body.*]

Choragos.
But here is the king himself: oh look at him,
Bearing his own damnation in his arms.

Creon.
Nothing you say can touch me any more.
My own blind heart has brought me
From darkness to final darkness. Here you see
The father murdering, the murdered son—
And all my civic wisdom!

Haimon my son, so young, so young to die,
I was the fool, not you; and you died for me.

Choragos.
That is the truth; but you were late in learning it.

Creon.
This truth is hard to bear. Surely a god
Has crushed me beneath the hugest weight of heaven
And driven me headlong a barbaric way
To trample out the thing I held most dear.

The pains that men will take to come to pain!

[*Enter* MESSENGER *from the palace.*]

Messenger.
The burden you carry in your hands is heavy,
But it is not all: you will find more in your house.

Creon.
What burden worse than this shall I find there?

Messenger.
The queen is dead.

Creon.
O port of death, deaf world,
Is there no pity for me? And you, Angel of evil,
I was dead, and your words are death again.
Is it true, boy? Can it be true?
Is my wife dead? Has death bred death?

Messenger.
You can see for yourself.

[*The doors are opened, and the body of* EURYDICE *is disclosed within.*]

Creon.
Oh pity!
All true, all true, and more than I can bear!
O my wife, my son!

Messenger.
She stood before the altar, and her heart
Welcomed the knife her own hand guided,
And a great cry burst from her lips for Megareus dead,
And for Haimon dead, her sons; and her last breath
Was a curse for their father, the murderer of her sons.
And she fell, and the dark flowed in through her
closing eyes.

Creon.
O God, I am sick with fear.
Are there no swords here? Has no one a blow for me?

Messenger.
Her curse is upon you for the deaths of both.

Creon.
It is right that it should be. I alone am guilty.
I know it, and I say it. Lead me in,
Quickly, friends.
I have neither life nor substance. Lead me in.

Choragos.
You are right, if there can be right in so much wrong.
The briefest way is best in a world of sorrow.

Creon.
Let it come,
Let death come quickly, and be kind to me.
I would not ever see the sun again.

Choragos.
All that will come when it will; but we, meanwhile,
Have much to do. Leave the future to itself.

Creon.
All my heart was in that prayer!

Choragos.
Then do not pray any more: the sky is deaf.

Creon.
Lead me away. I have been rash and foolish.
I have killed my son and wife.
I look for comfort; my comfort lies here dead.
Whatever my hands have touched has come to nothing.
Fate has brought all my pride to a thought of dust.

[*As* CREON *is being led into the house, the* CHORAGOS *advances and speaks directly to the audience.*]

Choragos.
There is no happiness where there is no wisdom;
No wisdom but in submission to the gods.
Big words are always punished,
And proud men in old age learn to be wise.

“There is no happiness where there is no wisdom....”

Meet the Writer

Writer, Actor, General, Politician

Sophocles (496?–406 B.C.) is generally considered the greatest of the ancient Greek playwrights. Few writers from any period have had a greater impact on drama, and few have been better loved in their own lifetimes.

A prominent citizen of Athens, Sophocles was known for his musical, poetic, and dramatic talents. He also took an active role in public life, serving as general, political leader, and priest. He is said to have been extremely handsome and graceful. At the age of about seventeen, he was the *choragos*, or chorus leader, in a dramatic celebration of Greece's victory over Persia. When he was twenty-eight, he caused a sensation by winning first prize for tragedy at the festival of Dionysos, defeating Aeschylus, the leading playwright of the day. He served as a general under Pericles. Over the next sixty-two years, Sophocles won twenty-four first prizes and seven second prizes in thirty-one competitions—the best record of any Greek playwright. Late in his life he was one of the elder statesmen who organized the recovery of Athens after its defeat at Syracuse.

Sophocles made good use of a remarkably long life, writing more than one hundred twenty tragedies, of which only seven survive. A religious conservative, he was deeply concerned with the individual's need to find a place in the existing moral and cosmic order. His plays always contain a moral lesson—usually a caution against pride and religious indifference. Sophocles was also a great technical innovator: He added a third actor to Aeschylus's original two, introduced painted sets, and expanded the size of the chorus to fifteen.

Few plays are more widely admired than Sophocles' "Theban" plays—three tragedies about King Oedipus of Thebes and his family. Sophocles wrote these plays over a forty-year period, and he actually began with the third part of the story, *Antigone*, first performed in 442 B.C. Twelve years later, Sophocles backtracked and wrote the first part of the story, *Oedipus the King*. It wasn't until the last year of his life that Sophocles wrote the middle segment, *Oedipus at Colonus*.

Perhaps the ninety-year-old playwright hoped that people would soon say of him what one of his characters says after Oedipus dies and is mysteriously carried off by the gods:

> ". . . he was taken without lamentation,
> Illness or suffering; indeed his end
> Was wonderful if mortal's ever was."

The Bettmann Archive.

Connections

A THEORY

Tragedy was first defined by the Greek philosopher Aristotle (384–322 B.C.*), and critics have been arguing about it ever since. Aristotle's definition is not a rule for what tragedy* should *be; it is a description of what he believed tragedy* was, *based on his observations of Greek drama, particularly the works of Sophocles.*

What Is a Tragic Hero?

According to Aristotle, the function of **tragedy** is to arouse pity and fear in the audience so that we may be purged, or cleansed, of these unsettling emotions. Aristotle's term for this emotional purging is the Greek word *catharsis*. Although no one is exactly sure what Aristotle meant by *catharsis,* it seems clear that he was referring to that strangely pleasurable sense of emotional release we experience after watching a great tragedy. For some reason, we usually feel exhilarated, not depressed, at the end.

According to Aristotle, a tragedy can arouse these twin emotions of pity and fear only if it presents a certain type of hero or heroine who is neither completely good nor completely bad.

Aristotle also says that the **tragic hero** should be someone "highly renowned and prosperous," which in Aristotle's day meant a member of the royalty.

> *. . . the change of fortune presented must not be the spectacle of a virtuous man brought from prosperity to adversity: For this moves neither pity nor fear; it merely shocks us. Nor again, that of a bad man passing from adversity to prosperity: For nothing can be more alien to the spirit of tragedy; . . . it neither satisfies the moral sense nor calls forth pity or fear. Nor, again, should the downfall of the utter villain be exhibited. A plot of this kind would, doubtless, satisfy the moral sense, but it would inspire neither pity nor fear; for pity is aroused by unmerited misfortune, fear by the misfortune of a man like ourselves. . . . There remains, then, the character between these two extremes—that of a man who is not eminently good and just, yet whose misfortune is brought about not by vice or depravity, but by some error or frailty. . . .*
>
> —Aristotle, *The Poetics,* translated by S. H. Butcher

Why not an ordinary working person? we might ask. The answer is simply that the hero must fall from tremendous good fortune. Otherwise, we wouldn't feel such pity and fear.

Critics have argued over what Aristotle meant by the tragic hero's "error or frailty." Is the hero defeated because of a single error of judgment, or is the cause of the hero's downfall a **tragic flaw**—a fundamental character weakness, such as destructive pride, ruthless ambition, or obsessive jealousy? In either interpretation, the key point is that the hero is on some level responsible for his or her own downfall. The hero is not the mere plaything of the gods—the helpless victim of fate or of someone else's villainy. By the end of the play, the tragic hero comes to recognize his or her own error and to accept its tragic consequences. The real hero does not curse fate or the gods. The real hero is humbled—and enlightened—by the tragedy.

Yet we, the audience, feel that the hero's punishment exceeds the crime, that the hero gets more than he or she deserves. We feel pity because the hero is a suffering human being who is flawed like us. We also feel fear because the hero is *better* than we are, and *still* he failed. What hope can there be for us?

Connections

A BIOGRAPHY

Russia's Antigone

from **Anna Akhmatova: Poet and Prophet**

Roberta Reeder

Anna Akhmatova has taken her place as one of the greatest poets and prophets of the twentieth century. At first compared with Sappho[1] because of her exquisitely lyrical love poems, Akhmatova later assumed the role of Cassandra,[2] becoming a prophetess of doom; and like Antigone, she was left behind to bury the dead and to teach us that it is an ethical imperative to remember them....

The evolution of Akhmatova's poetry represents the evolution of her personal response to the dramatic events occurring in her country. Recognition of her poetic gifts began in 1912, with her first collection of poetry, *Evening,* when Russia was already in the throes of chaos and revolution.... But World War I marked a significant change in Akhmatova's work, and soon she began to take on the role of the traditional village "Wailer": Overcome by grief, those in the village who lost someone turned to the Wailer to articulate what they felt. Then, as the dreams of the Revolution turned into a Stalinist nightmare, Akhmatova became the voice of an entire people—of the women who lost men in the apocalyptic events of this century, and her own son, who was among them....

Akhmatova never regretted her decision to remain in Russia, and watched as those who left often lost their creative urge, were misunderstood or merely ignored.

1. **Sappho** (c. 610–c. 580 B.C.): Greek poet known for her love lyrics.
2. **Cassandra:** in Greek mythology, a daughter of Priam, king of Troy. She could foretell the future, but her prophecies were never believed.

TWO POEMS

All the unburied ones

Anna Akhmatova

translated by Judith Hemschemeyer

All the unburied ones—I buried them,
I mourned for them all, but who will
  mourn for me?

I am not one of those who left the land

Anna Akhmatova

translated by Stanley Kunitz

I am not one of those who left the land
to the mercy of its enemies.
Their flattery leaves me cold,
my songs are not for them to praise.

But I pity the exile's lot.
Like a felon, like a man half-dead,
dark is your path, wanderer;
wormwood° infects your foreign bread.

But here, in the murk of conflagration,
where scarcely a friend is left to know,
we, the survivors, do not flinch
from anything, not from a single blow.

Surely the reckoning will be made after
the passing of this cloud.
We are the people without tears,
straighter than you... more proud...

8. wormwood: herb that produces a bitter oil. The word can also refer to something that produces feelings of bitterness.

Making Meanings
Scene 5, Paean, and Exodos

First Thoughts

1. How do you feel about what happens to the characters at the play's end?

Reading Check

a. What mistakes does Teiresias say Creon has made?

b. What does Teiresias predict will happen to Creon?

c. The violent **resolution** of the **plot** takes place offstage. What does the Messenger report about Antigone, Haimon, and Eurydice?

Shaping Interpretations

2. Why is it **ironic** that the prophet Teiresias is blind?

3. Why do you think Creon finally agrees to free Antigone and bury Polyneices? What lines give clues to his **motives**?

4. The Paean is recited after Creon has changed his mind but before the **plot** is **resolved**. At this point in the play, why is it appropriate for the Chorus to call on the god Dionysos to "come with clement feet"? What is the Chorus asking the god to heal?

5. In lines 32–76 of the Exodos, the Messenger says that Creon buried Polyneices first and then went to free Antigone. How do you **predict** events might have turned out if Creon had reversed the order of his tasks?

6. How would you describe the major **conflict** in *Antigone*? Is the conflict between absolute good and absolute evil, or is the conflict between opposing views of what is good? What position does Sophocles seem to take on this question?

7. Find lines from the play that you think are especially important. Then, state what you think is the main **theme** in the play—what does it reveal about human life? How do you feel about the theme?

8. At the end of this **tragedy,** Eurydice blames Creon for the disastrous turn of events. Creon accepts her curse, saying, "I alone am guilty" (line 121). What do you think of Creon's statement of sole responsibility?

9. Anna Akhmatova (1889–1966) refused to flee Russia during the years of the brutal dictatorship of Stalin. She is sometimes referred to as Russia's Antigone. (Review ***Connections*** on page 740.) Using what you learned about Akhmatova from the biography and her poems, **compare** her to Antigone. What do they have in common? How are they different?

Extending the Text

10. Many people criticize current movies and television shows for being too violent. How would you **compare** the level of violence you see in movies and television with the level of violence you witness in *Antigone*? How do you feel about having violent actions take place offstage rather than onstage?

CHOICES: Building Your Portfolio

Writer's Notebook

1. Collecting Ideas for a Cause-and-Effect Essay

Finding a topic. *Antigone* might give you a topic for the essay you'll write in the Writer's Workshop on page 752. Your focus in that essay will be to explain the possible causes of something or the possible effects of something. Think back on all the issues raised in this play, and see if they can lead you to wider issues you feel strongly about and to a topic you'd like to develop in an essay. Try gathering your ideas in cluster diagrams. Let one idea lead you to another. Ask yourself "Why did it happen?" (cause) or "What is the result?" (effect).

positive: less brutality

positive: no innocent people killed

Possible effects if capital punishment were abolished (positive and negative effects)

positive: more respect for life

negative: more prisoners

negative: fewer deterrents

Supporting an Opinion

2. Who Is the Tragic Hero?

Suppose you are a critic and you want to convince people that the true tragic hero of *Antigone* is (a) Antigone, or (b) Creon, or (c) both. Because Aristotle's theories are the ones that most people today still accept, you'll have to base your interpretation on Aristotle's view of **tragedy** and the **tragic hero** (see ***Connections*** on page 739). In a paragraph or two, present your own views, and support your opinion with details from the play. Before you begin writing, and before you make up your mind who the tragic hero is, fill out a chart like the one at the top of the next column.

	Antigone	**Creon**
Not all good or all bad?		
Downfall caused by **tragic flaw**?		
Suffers most?		
Arouses our pity and fear?		
Recognizes own error?		

Writing a Synopsis

3. Updating *Antigone*

Think about how you might update *Antigone* in a modern setting, either in the United States or in some other part of the world. What kind of figure would Creon be: an elected politician, a dictator, a business leader, a head of a family? Who would Antigone be? What would Creon's conflict with Antigone be about? Write a brief **synopsis,** or **summary,** of your modern version. (On page 690, read how the play was updated by a French playwright and set in World War II.)

CHOICES: Building Your Portfolio

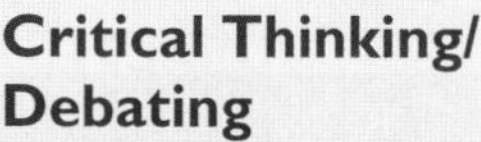

Critical Thinking/ Debating

4. Did They Act Freely?

Are the characters in this play free to make choices about their actions, or are their destinies predetermined and controlled by fate? Is Creon's fate the consequence of his own character and conduct? Is Antigone's the consequence of hers? On the other hand, are both Creon and Antigone victims of forces they cannot control? Prepare to hold a **debate** on this question of fate versus free will in *Antigone*. Your first step is to write a proposition that takes a stand on the issue. Then, form teams. The affirmative team will try to prove the proposition is true. The negative team will try to prove it is *not* true.

Comparing and Contrasting

5. Tragedy and Comedy

Antigone and *Julius Caesar* are tragedies. They tell the stories of noble people who through a series of actions suffer defeat and even death. Comedies are opposite to tragedies in structure and in characterization. In a comedy, the characters are not necessarily highborn, and they triumph over their problems. While a tragedy often ends in death, a comedy often ends with dancing or a wedding. (For more information on **comedy** and **tragedy,** see the Handbook of Literary Terms.) Choose a comedy—a movie or a play—to contrast with *Antigone*. In your essay, cite examples from both works to show how they differ.

Creative Writing/ Performance

6. Myths Onstage

The story of Oedipus is only one of many popular Greek myths. With a group of classmates, select a short Greek **myth,** and prepare an in-class **dramatization** of it. Consult resources such as Edith Hamilton's *Mythology,* the Internet, or the library. Assign each group member a role in researching, writing, producing, and performing. Will you need a narrator, or will the actions of the characters alone tell the story? Will you need costumes or props? Rehearse your play. After your performance, ask the audience for their reactions. (For help, see the Speaking and Listening Workshops on pages 750–751 and 890–891.)

VOCABULARY HOW TO OWN A WORD

WORD BANK

deference
malicious
somberly
piety
vigil
transgress
wrath
calamity
recoils
defile

Summarizing: Telling It Your Way

One of the best ways to increase your vocabulary is to use new or difficult words in sentences, either in speaking or writing. Using the words in the Word Bank, write a **summary** of *Antigone*. Not every sentence you write must contain a Word Bank word. You can use any word more than once, and you can use them in any order. Here is an example:

The play shows what can happen when people transgress the law.

Be sure to compare your summaries in class. (You might try reading them aloud.)

EXTENDING *the theme*

A LETTER

from Letter from Birmingham Jail

Martin Luther King, Jr.

April 16, 1963

Background

Dr. Martin Luther King, Jr., was arrested and jailed during the April 1963 civil rights protests in Birmingham, Alabama. While he was in prison, eight white Birmingham clergymen who considered themselves liberals wrote an open letter to the local newspaper, criticizing the demonstrations. The excerpts you will read are from King's famous reply to those clergymen.

Reading Skills and Strategies

Monitoring Your Reading: Questioning

Keep notes as you read this document. Question the text; challenge assumptions, and note where you agree with assumptions. The letter is complex and powerful. You may want to read it twice.

My Dear Fellow Clergymen:

While confined here in the Birmingham city jail, I came across your recent statement calling my present activities "unwise and untimely." Seldom do I pause to answer criticism of my work and ideas. If I sought to answer all the criticisms that cross my desk, . . . I would have no time for constructive work. But since I feel that you are men of genuine goodwill and that your criticisms are sincerely set forth, I want to try to answer your statement in what I hope will be patient and reasonable terms.

I think I should indicate why I am here in Birmingham. . . . I am in Birmingham because injustice is here. Just as the prophets of the eighth century B.C. left their villages and carried their "thus saith the Lord" far beyond the boundaries of their hometowns, and just as the apostle Paul left his village of Tarsus and carried the gospel of Jesus Christ to the far corners of the Greco-Roman world, so am I compelled to carry the gospel of freedom beyond my own hometown. Like Paul, I must constantly respond to the Macedonian call for aid.[1]

1. **Paul . . . Macedonian call for aid:** The apostle Paul traveled to Macedonia, in southeastern Europe, on a religious mission in response to a call for aid that came to him in a vision.

. . . I cannot sit idly by in Atlanta and not be concerned about what happens in Birmingham. Injustice anywhere is a threat to justice everywhere. We are caught in an inescapable network of mutuality,[2] tied in a single garment of destiny. Whatever affects one directly, affects all indirectly. Never again can we afford to live with the narrow, provincial "outside agitator" idea. Anyone who lives inside the United States can never be considered an outsider anywhere within its bounds.

"Whatever affects one directly, affects all indirectly."

You deplore the demonstrations taking place in Birmingham. But your statement, I am sorry to say, fails to express a similar concern for the conditions that brought about the demonstrations. I am sure that none of you would want to rest content with the superficial kind of social analysis that deals merely with effects and does not grapple with underlying causes. It is unfortunate that demonstrations are taking place in Birmingham, but it is even more unfortunate that the city's white power structure left the Negro community with no alternative.

In any nonviolent campaign there are four basic steps: collection of the facts to determine whether injustices exist; negotiation; self-purification; and direct action. We have gone through all these steps in Birmingham. There can be no gainsaying[3] the fact that racial injustice engulfs this community. Birmingham is probably the most thoroughly segregated city in the United States. Its ugly record of brutality is widely known. Negroes have experienced grossly unjust treatment in the courts. There have been more unsolved bombings of Negro homes and churches in Birmingham than in any other city in the nation. These are the hard, brutal facts of the case. On the basis of these conditions, Negro leaders sought to negotiate with the city fathers. But the latter consistently refused to engage in good-faith negotiation.

Then, last September, came the opportunity to talk with leaders of Birmingham's economic community. In the course of the negotiations, certain promises were made by the merchants—for example, to remove the stores' humiliating racial signs. On the basis of these promises, the Reverend Fred Shuttlesworth and the leaders of the Alabama Christian Movement for Human Rights agreed to a moratorium on all demonstrations. As the weeks and months went by, we realized that we were the victims of a broken promise. A few signs, briefly removed, returned; the others remained.

As in so many past experiences, our hopes had been blasted, and the shadow of deep disappointment settled upon us. We had no alternative except to prepare for direct action, whereby we would present our very bodies as a means of laying our case before the conscience of the local and the national community. Mindful of the difficulties involved, we decided to undertake a process of self-purification. We began a series of workshops on nonviolence, and we repeatedly asked ourselves: "Are you able to accept blows without retaliating?" "Are you able to endure the ordeal of jail?" . . .

You may well ask: "Why direct action? Why sit-ins, marches, and so forth? Isn't negotiation a better path?" You are quite right in calling for negotiation. Indeed, this is the very purpose of direct action. Nonviolent direct action seeks to create such a crisis and foster such a tension that a community which has constantly refused to negotiate is forced to confront the issue. It seeks so to dramatize the issue that it can no longer be ignored. . . .

We know through painful experience that freedom is never voluntarily given by the op-

2. **mutuality** (myo͞o'cho͞o·al'ə·tē): here, shared fate.
3. **gainsaying** (gān'sā'iŋ): denying; contradicting.

pressor; it must be demanded by the oppressed. Frankly, I have yet to engage in a direct-action campaign that was "well timed" in the view of those who have not suffered unduly from the disease of segregation. For years now I have heard the word "Wait!" It rings in the ear of every Negro with piercing familiarity. This "Wait" has almost always meant "Never." We must come to see, with one of our distinguished jurists, that "justice too long delayed is justice denied."[4]

We have waited for more than 340 years for our constitutional and God-given rights. The nations of Asia and Africa are moving with jetlike speed toward gaining political independence, but we still creep at horse-and-buggy pace toward gaining a cup of coffee at a lunch counter. Perhaps it is easy for those who have never felt the stinging darts of segregation to say "Wait." But when you have seen vicious mobs lynch your mothers and fathers at will and drown your sisters and brothers at whim; when you have seen hate-filled policemen curse, kick, and even kill your black brothers and sisters; when you see the vast majority of your twenty million Negro brothers smothering in an airtight cage of poverty in the midst of an affluent society; when you suddenly find your tongue twisted and your speech stammering as you seek to explain to your six-year-old daughter why she can't go to the public amusement park that has just been advertised on television, and see tears welling up in her eyes when she is told that Funtown is closed to colored children, and see ominous clouds of inferiority beginning to form in her little mental sky, and see her beginning to distort her personality by developing an unconscious bitterness toward white people; when you have to concoct an answer for a five-year-old son who is asking, "Daddy, why do white people treat colored people so mean?"; when you take a cross-country drive and find it necessary to sleep night after night in the uncomfortable corners of your automobile because no motel will accept you; when you are humiliated day in and day out by nagging signs reading "white" and "colored"; when your first name becomes "nigger," your middle name becomes "boy" (however old you are), and your last name becomes "John," and your wife and mother are never given the respected title "Mrs."; when you are harried by day and haunted by night by the fact that you are a Negro, living constantly at tiptoe stance, never quite knowing what to expect next, and are plagued with inner fears and outer resentments; when you are forever fighting a degenerating sense of "nobodiness"—then you will understand why we find it difficult to wait. There comes a time when the cup of endurance runs over and men are no longer willing to be plunged into the abyss of despair. I hope, sirs, you can understand our legitimate and unavoidable impatience.

You express a great deal of anxiety over our willingness to break laws. This is certainly a legitimate concern. Since we so diligently urge people to obey the Supreme Court's decision of 1954 outlawing segregation in the public schools, at first glance it may seem rather paradoxical for us consciously to break laws. One may well ask: "How can you advocate breaking some laws and obeying others?" The answer lies in the fact that there are two types of laws: just and unjust. I would be the first to advocate obeying just laws. One has not only a legal but a moral responsibility to obey just laws. Conversely, one has a moral responsibility to disobey unjust laws. I would agree with St. Augustine that "an unjust law is no law at all."

Now, what is the difference between the two? How does one determine whether a law is just or unjust? A just law is a man-made code that squares with the moral law or the law of God. An unjust law is a code that is out of harmony with the moral law. To put it in the terms of Saint Thomas Aquinas: An unjust law is a human law that is not rooted in eternal law and natural law. Any law that uplifts human personality is just. Any law that degrades human personality is unjust. All segregation statutes are unjust because segregation distorts the soul and

4. King is probably referring to a statement believed to have been made by the nineteenth-century British prime minister William Gladstone (1809–1898): "Justice delayed is justice denied."

damages the personality. It gives the segregator a false sense of superiority and the segregated a false sense of inferiority. Segregation, to use the terminology of the Jewish philosopher Martin Buber, substitutes an "I-it" relationship for an "I-thou" relationship and ends up relegating persons to the status of things. Hence segregation is not only politically, economically, and sociologically unsound, it is morally wrong and sinful. . . .

Sometimes a law is just on its face and unjust in its application. For instance, I have been arrested on a charge of parading without a permit. Now, there is nothing wrong in having an ordinance which requires a permit for a parade. But such an ordinance becomes unjust when it is used to maintain segregation and to deny citizens the First Amendment privilege of peaceful assembly and protest.

I hope you are able to see the distinction I am trying to point out. In no sense do I advocate evading or defying the law, as would the rabid segregationist. That would lead to anarchy.[5] One who breaks an unjust law must do so openly, lovingly, and with a willingness to accept the penalty. I submit that an individual who breaks a law that conscience tells him is unjust, and who willingly accepts the penalty of imprisonment in order to arouse the conscience of the community over its injustice, is in reality expressing the highest respect for law.

Of course, there is nothing new about this kind of civil disobedience. It was evidenced sublimely in the refusal of Shadrach, Meshach, and Abednego to obey the laws of Nebuchadnezzar,[6] on the ground that a higher moral law was at stake. It was practiced superbly by the early Christians, who were willing to face hungry lions and the excruciating pain of chopping blocks rather than submit to certain unjust laws of the Roman Empire. To a degree, academic freedom is a reality today because Socrates practiced civil disobedience. In our own nation, the Boston Tea Party represented a massive act of civil disobedience.

We should never forget that everything Adolf Hitler did in Germany was "legal" and everything the Hungarian freedom fighters did in Hungary was "illegal." It was "illegal" to aid and comfort a Jew in Hitler's Germany. Even so, I am sure that had I lived in Germany at the time, I would have aided and comforted my Jewish brothers. If today I lived in a Communist country where certain principles dear to the Christian faith are suppressed, I would openly advocate disobeying that country's antireligious laws.

In your statement you assert that our actions, even though peaceful, must be condemned because they precipitate violence. But is this a logical assertion? Isn't this like condemning a robbed man because his possession of money precipitated the evil act of robbery? Isn't this like condemning Socrates because his unswerving commitment to truth and his philosophical inquiries precipitated the act by the misguided populace in which they made him drink hemlock? Isn't this like condemning Jesus because his unique God-consciousness and never-ceasing devotion to God's will precipitated the evil act of crucifixion? We must come to see that, as the federal courts have consistently affirmed, it is wrong to urge an individual to cease his efforts to gain his basic constitutional rights because the quest may precipitate violence. Society must protect the robbed and punish the robber.

Although I was initially disappointed at being categorized as an extremist, as I continued to think about the matter I gradually gained a measure of satisfaction from the label. Was not Jesus an extremist for love: "Love your enemies, bless them that curse you, do good to them that hate you, and pray for them which despitefully use you and persecute you." Was not Amos an extremist for justice: "Let justice roll down like waters and righteousness like an ever-flowing stream." Was not Paul an extremist for the Chris-

5. **anarchy** (an′ər·kē): lawlessness; political disorder and violence.
6. **refusal of Shadrach, Meshach, and Abednego . . . Nebuchadnezzar:** In the Bible, three Jewish captives, Shadrach, Meshach, and Abednego, refuse the command of the Babylonian king, Nebuchadnezzar, to bow down before a golden idol and so are thrown into a fiery furnace. The fire does not harm them, and this miracle convinces Nebuchadnezzar of the error of his ways.

tian gospel: "I bear in my body the marks of the Lord Jesus." Was not Martin Luther an extremist: "Here I stand; I cannot do otherwise, so help me God." And John Bunyan: "I will stay in jail to the end of my days before I make a butchery of my conscience." And Abraham Lincoln: "This nation cannot survive half slave and half free." And Thomas Jefferson: "We hold these truths to be self-evident, that all men are created equal." So the question is not whether we will be extremists, but what kind of extremists we will be. Will we be extremists for hate or for love? Will we be extremists for the preservation of injustice or for the extension of justice? In that dramatic scene on Calvary's hill three men were crucified.[7] We must never forget that all three were crucified for the same crime—the crime of extremism. Two were extremists for immorality and thus fell below their environment. The other, Jesus Christ, was an extremist for love, truth, and goodness and thereby rose above his environment. Perhaps the South, the nation, and the world are in dire need of creative extremists.

7. **Calvary's hill . . . crucified:** reference to the crucifixion of Jesus Christ on a hill called Calvary, near Jerusalem. According to the accounts of the Gospels, two criminals were crucified there along with Jesus.

Finding Common Ground

You have now read some of what Dr. Martin Luther King, Jr., had to say about the need to fight for human dignity. As you and your group prepare to discuss his arguments, refer to your reading notes. How did Dr. King's letter affect you? Consider also the following questions:

- Do you think King believed in the necessity of laws?
- Do you think King would have supported using civil disobedience to protest any or all laws?

Discuss these questions and any other questions brought up by members of your group. See if you can reach a consensus about the relationship of the individual to the whole of society and about whether civil disobedience should be used to achieve a worthy goal.

Meet the Writer

A Matter of Conscience

Dr. Martin Luther King, Jr. (1929–1968), born in Atlanta, Georgia, became a Baptist minister like his father and was thrust into national prominence as one of the most important figures in the American civil rights movement of the mid-twentieth century. His organization of the Southern Christian Leadership Conference (SCLC) and his commitment to nonviolent protest brought him to national prominence and eventually led to his receiving the Nobel Peace Prize in 1964. In a book published the year before he died, King wrote this:

"Some years ago a famous novelist died. Among his papers was found a list of suggested plots for future stories, the most prominently underscored being this one: 'A widely separated family inherits a house in which they have to live together.' This is the great new problem of mankind. We have inherited a large house, a great 'world house' in which we have to live together—black and white, Easterner and Westerner, Gentile and Jew, Catholic and Protestant, Muslim and Hindu—a family unduly separated in ideas, culture, and interest, who, because we can never again live apart, must learn somehow to live with each other in peace."

Dr. King was assassinated while he stood on a motel balcony in Memphis, Tennessee, on April 4, 1968.

And in the Future? . . .

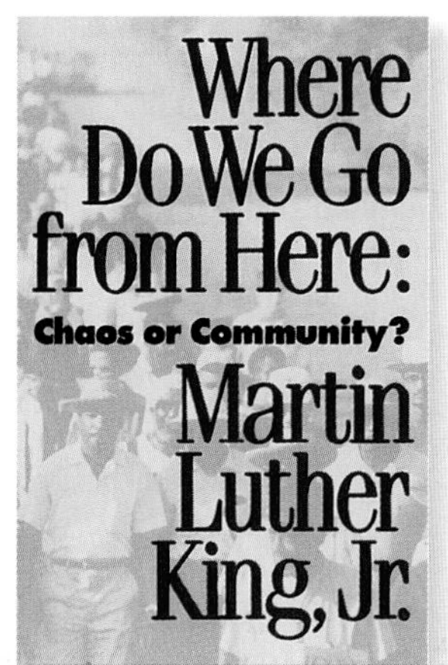

What will people have to do to make the future livable? Martin Luther King, Jr., had some realistic ideas about this question as far back as 1967. Read *Where Do We Go from Here: Chaos or Community?* (Bantam Books), and find out what the great humanitarian proposed.

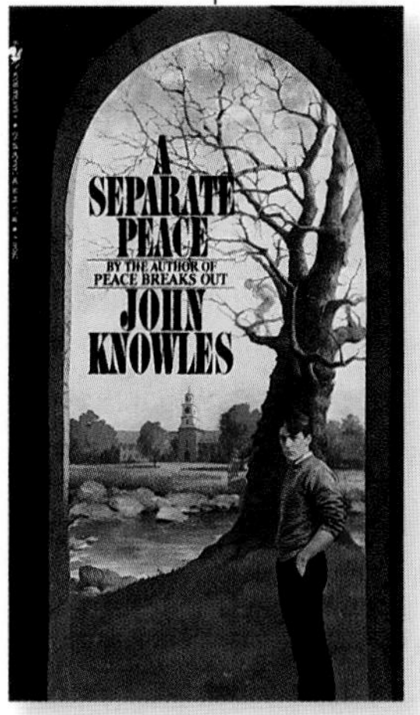

How Much Would You Do for Friendship?

How much can one act affect your life? For how many years can you carry around with you the weight of a choice that you might not make if you had it to do over again? In John Knowles's *A Separate Peace* (Bantam Books), a novel set at a boy's prep school in New England during World War II, one small action sets in motion a locomotive of a story that changes at least two lives forever. (This title is available in the HRW Library.)

Money Isn't Everything

Catherine Sloper lives in her father's house in Washington Square in New York City in the mid-nineteenth century. Her father is wealthy, Catherine is plain, and her father thinks that any young man who tries to court Catherine is simply looking for money. Catherine eventually takes control of her own life, but in a way that you might not have expected. You can read this story in various editions of *Washington Square,* a novel by Henry James. You can also see two movies based on the novel: *The Heiress* (1949) and *Washington Square* (1997).

It's Not About Whether You Win or Lose . . .

When a blue-collar genius loses a game on a TV quiz show, he suspects that his opponent—the wealthy, socially prominent Charles Van Doren—has won because the show's producers helped him to cheat. The 1994 movie *Quiz Show,* based on a compelling real-life case from the 1950s, depicts characters who confront the dishonesty within themselves and within the world at large.

Speaking and Listening Workshop

ASSIGNMENT

Prepare, organize, plan, and present an oral interpretation of a work you have read.

Three Types of Oral Performance

- **Oral interpretation:** One person reads a text aloud.
- **Choral speaking:** A group reads a text in unison or in various combinations of voices, including solo voices.
- **Reader's Theater:** A group reads a play aloud.

Chorus in the 1994 Broadway production of *Medea.*

INTERPRETING LITERATURE

When you really connect with a literary work, you can share your excitement with an audience. In an **oral interpretation,** you read aloud to express your ideas about the meaning and the beauty of a literary work.

Plan Your Interpretation

To plan and organize your interpretation, follow these steps:

1. Choose a work you understand and connect with, something likely to appeal to your audience and short enough to perform. You may interpret all or part of a **drama, poem, story,** or **nonfiction** selection (**speech, letter, journal,** or **essay**).
2. Write a brief statement of your work's **theme,** or **main idea.** Note the words or lines that help create an emotional impact.
3. Decide who the **speaker** is—the person you see and hear in your imagination as you read. Why is the speaker saying these particular words? Who might be listening?
4. Decide whether the speaker should be one person or more than one. (See the three types of oral performance at the left.) For example, the Chorus in *Antigone* speaks with great authority. If the speeches are spoken by a group, that authority becomes almost superhuman, inescapable, crushing.

Practice Performance Techniques

As you rehearse, experiment with the verbal and nonverbal techniques you'll use. Take notes on the ones that work.

1. Verbal techniques (words)

- Enunciate your words clearly, and try to say groups of related words in a single breath. If you're reading a poem, don't pause at the end of each line; follow punctuation marks instead.
- If you are doing **choral speaking,** plan which lines should be spoken as a group—and why. Experiment: Speak in unison and then try the same lines with different combinations of voices.

2. Nonverbal techniques (vocal)

You can also vary your voice in effective ways.

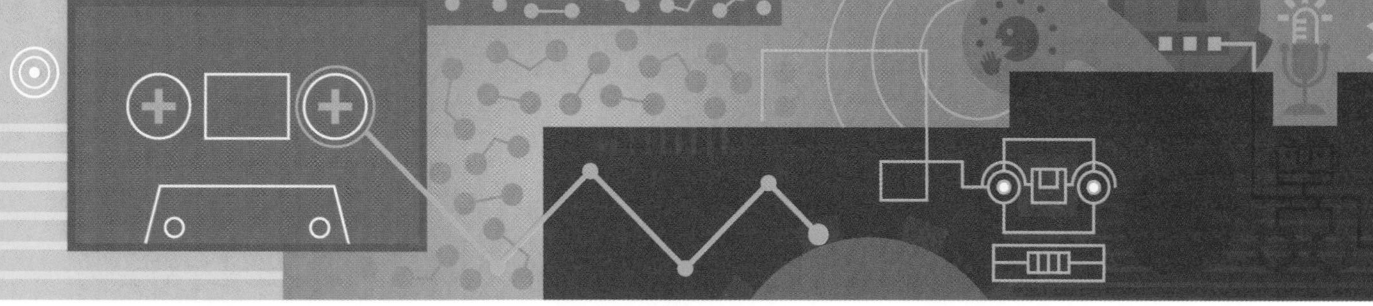

- Try out different **pitches** (high, low, middle), reading **rates** (speeds), **volumes** (loudness or softness), and **tones** (emotions such as anger, worry, or fear). Note which combinations best express the ideas and feelings you want to communicate.

3. Nonverbal techniques (body language)

- Practice **facial expressions** to reveal **emotions.**
- Decide when you will use **eye contact** to look directly at your audience, and when you want to look away.
- Choose **gestures** (hand and arm movements), **postures** (body positions), and other **movements** that seem appropriate for your speaker and the text. For example, in the Messenger's long speech about Haimon's death (pages 734–735), one interpreter might point to the cave and reenact Haimon's handling of the sword. Another might stand frozen in horror.

Reach Your Audience

You'll present your oral interpretation to a particular **audience**—perhaps your English class, a school assembly, an elementary school class, or maybe even viewers of local cable TV.

1. Who is your audience? What are their ages? Will they need some background information to understand the work? You might prepare a brief introduction, identifying the work, its author, and terms your audience needs to know. What is the occasion for presenting your interpretation? How much time will you have?
2. As you perform, tune in to your audience's responses and, if necessary, make adjustments. If you sense the audience can't hear you, speak up and enunciate more clearly. Be sure everyone can see you; the rule is, if you can see everyone, everyone can see you.
3. You can benefit from an audience critique, or evaluation, after your performance. During a critique, you might ask:

- What was your favorite part of the interpretation?
- What main idea did you get from the interpretation?
- When I perform this again, what should I change, and why?

Try It Out

Experiment with different oral interpretations of the speeches in *Antigone*, Scene 4, Strophe 2 and Antistrophe 2 (pages 723–724). First have one person read the Chorus, opposite Antigone. Then have six to eight people read the Chorus in unison. Try other combinations of voices, and discuss how each change affects the impact of the scene.

Try It Out

To explore your range of vocal expression, choose a poem to interpret. Consider "Miss Rosie" (page 535) or "Just Another Love Poem" (page 555), or use another poem of your choosing, perhaps one you've written. Decide who the speaker is and what sort of voice that person has. Which words or lines do you want to emphasize—and how? In "Miss Rosie," for instance, how would you say the line "I stand up"? Would you speak softly or loudly? Would you say it more slowly the second time?

BUILDING YOUR PORTFOLIO

Writer's Workshop

Technology HELP

See Writer's Workshop 2 CD-ROM. *Assignment: Cause and Effect.*

ASSIGNMENT

Write an essay in which you identify an issue, a situation, or an event and explain either its causes or its effects (or both).

AIM

To inform; to persuade.

AUDIENCE

Readers of your school newspaper; a broader audience. (You choose.)

Communications Handbook HELP

Taking Notes and Documenting Sources.

EXPOSITORY WRITING

CAUSE-AND-EFFECT ESSAY

Why do some teenagers smoke, despite the known health risks? What would happen if smoking were illegal? When you ask questions like these, you are analyzing causes and effects. When you explain **causes**, you try to show why something happens or has happened. When you explain **effects,** you point out what happens, has happened, or will happen as a result of something else. In this workshop, you'll help readers understand an event or situation by explaining *Why did it happen?* (its causes) or *What are the results?* (its effects).

Prewriting

WORK IN PROGRESS

1. Choose a Topic

Take another look at the topics you've listed in your Writer's Notebook. Are you still interested in the situation, issue, or event you've been working on? If not, brainstorm with a small group to come up with more ideas. Your topic may be a real-life issue or situation that interests you or one related to the plays you've read. Here are some possibilities:

- the effects of a particular law on society or your community
- the effects of technology on our schools
- the causes or effects of an act of courage or conscience
- the causes or effects of a recent trend in contemporary life
- the causes or effects of a key decision in your life

2. Analyze Causes and Effects

After you've chosen a topic, your next step is to analyze all of its possible causes or effects (or both). Consider not only the obvious causes but also the hidden ones. If you are identifying effects, consider both positive and negative ones. Brainstorm as many causes or effects as you can. To collect all your ideas, use a cluster diagram like the one at the top of the next page, which analyzes five different effects of budget cuts.

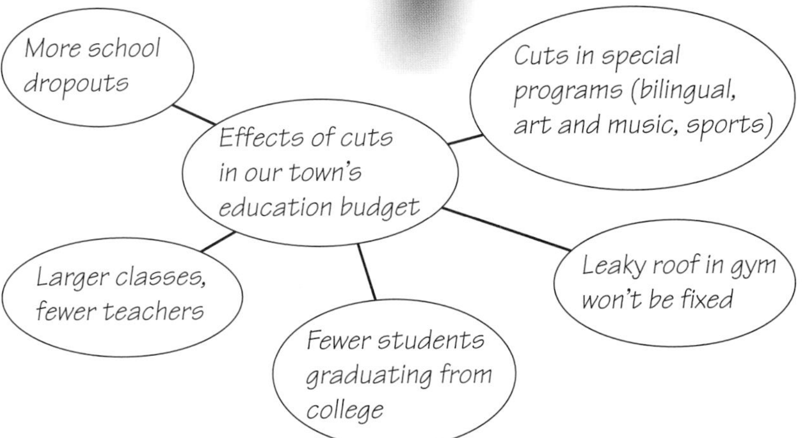

3. Elaborate: Find Evidence to Support What You Say

To give your essay credibility, you'll need to support your statements that identify causes or effects. (See the side-column list for the kinds of evidence you can use as support.) For some types of evidence (such as facts, statistics, experts' opinions, and interviews), you'll need to do research.

4. Using Persuasive Strategies

If your aim is to persuade, as in the Student Model (page 754), consider using these persuasive strategies:

- **Be logical.** Use reasons and supporting evidence.
- **Try loaded words.** See *lip service* and *vital* in the model.
- **Consider other viewpoints.** Don't assume you're right. Note others' views, and explain why you disagree.

Drafting

1. Effective Cause-and-Effect Writing

Be sure to avoid the **false-cause-and-effect fallacy**—the assumption that because one event follows another, the first is the cause of the second. (See pages 468–469 for an explanation of this and other logical fallacies.) Help readers follow your explanation by using **transitional expressions** and other words that express causality (like *therefore, as a result, consequently,* and *because*). Aim for a logical, straightforward tone, expressing your ideas as clearly and directly as you can.

Try It Out

Use a cluster diagram to analyze possible causes in answer to each question. You might brainstorm with a partner or a small group.

1. Why do young people join gangs?
2. Why is *Antigone*, written more than two thousand years ago, still popular today?

Strategies for Elaboration

Evidence for Real-Life Subjects:

- Facts, statistics, and examples
- Anecdotes about your own experiences
- Your observations
- Opinions of experts
- Interviews
- Analogies to similar situations

Evidence for Literary Subjects:

- Quotations from the work
- Analysis of the text (plot, character, theme, symbols)
- Opinions of experts
- Facts about the work and/or author

Using transitions: page 757.

2. Organize Your Essay

Here's a possible pattern of organization for your essay:

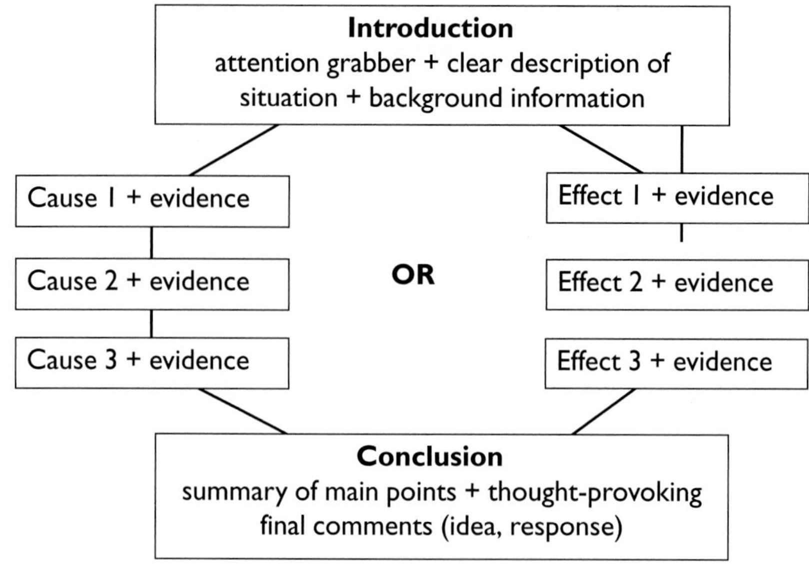

Student Model

HELPING EDUCATION BY CUTTING FUNDS?

The children of today are the future of tomorrow, and education is the tool that should be guiding the way. While our country's leaders give lip service to this idea, what they do is another story. We constantly hear of programs that are geared toward education, but politicians in the spotlight are preaching falsely. They don't truly believe in what they say. Violence in our communities has politicians concentrating on the crusade against crime. They fail to see how education, or lack of it, plays such a vital role.

Issue clearly identified. Last two sentences present thesis—lack of education causes crime.

Community colleges such as Miami-Dade can help turn people around by offering a good education at a price that most people can pay. They also help pick up, by remediation, where public schools fail. In addition, they help prepare students for four-year schools.

What's good about community colleges—their positive effects.

Yet often community colleges get overlooked in funding. They are caught in the middle. By providing additional education funding—for community colleges and other public schools—our state's leaders will see that crime in the streets will decrease. That's because people will take advantage of educational programs to get out of situations that may turn them toward crime.

Effect of funding for education: decrease in street crime.

For this plan to work, our leaders must realize that they must exercise patience and commitment. Society is in a deep hole, and things will not change overnight. The commitment must be made

Student Model (continued)

to invest in education with the knowledge that results will come years down the line. . . .

Our state government is still pouring loads of money into crime prevention and jails. Politicians are sending the message that cutting money for education is OK, as long as we fight crime.

So they build jail after jail to house criminals, many of whom committed crimes because they lacked economic opportunity. While there is no justification for crimes, lack of education contributes to the economic problems that drive many to crime.

Cause of crime: lack of education.

Yet in jail you are treated far more fairly than out. Criminals are often rewarded by being offered a college education, free medical attention, and workout facilities. Millions of dollars are wasted each year to pamper inmates who have violated our rights.

Instead of cutting the prison budgets, legislators cut education. . . .

Still, we continue to hear our government say that it is pro-education, manipulating our minds by adding some programs, then taking money behind our backs, as with the lottery funds (that are supposed to be for education). Until we do something about it, state legislators will preach education, then cut funding anyway.

Concluding paragraph—calls for action to prevent predicted effect.

—Manolo Barco
Miami-Dade Community College
Miami, Florida

Evaluating and Revising

1. Self-Evaluation

Before you share your draft with your writing group, read through it at least twice, focusing first on content and then on style.

- **Content.** Start by checking your draft against the evaluation criteria at the right. Have you stated the situation and the causes or effects clearly? Have you presented enough evidence?
- **Style.** Read your draft aloud to yourself to see if the sentences flow smoothly. Add transitions (see the Sentence Workshop on page 757), and check for fragments and run-ons.

2. Peer Review

To see how well you've stated your case, read your draft to your writing group. Ask them to focus on these questions:

- Have I presented enough evidence, and is it convincing?
- Can you follow my ideas easily?

■ *Evaluation Criteria*

A good cause-and-effect essay

1. *has an introduction that clearly identifies a situation, issue, or event and presents a thesis about its causes or effects*
2. *logically discusses one or more causes or effects*
3. *presents sufficient evidence for each cause or effect*
4. *is logically organized*
5. *has an effective conclusion*

Proofreading Tip

Ask a partner to double-check your paper, focusing on the kinds of errors you've recorded in your proofreading log.

Communications Handbook HELP

See Proofreaders' Marks.

Publishing Tip

Submit your essay to your school newspaper or to your local newspaper's op-ed page.

Revision Model

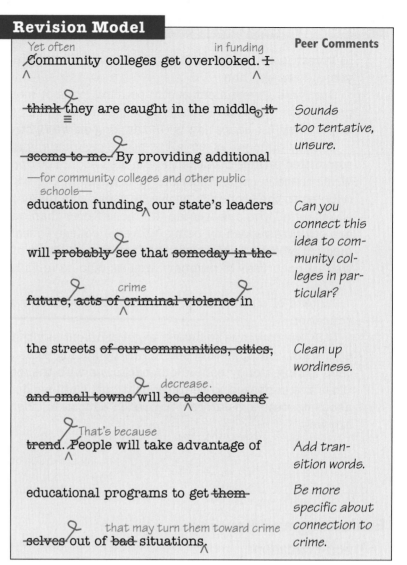

	Peer Comments
Yet often Community colleges get overlooked. in funding ~~I~~	
~~think~~ they are caught in the middle. ~~it~~	Sounds too tentative, unsure.
~~seems to me.~~ By providing additional	
education funding —for community colleges and other public schools— our state's leaders	Can you connect this idea to community colleges in particular?
will ~~probably~~ see that ~~someday in the~~	
~~future, acts of criminal violence~~ crime in	
the streets ~~of our communities, cities,~~	Clean up wordiness.
~~and small towns~~ will ~~be a decreasing~~ decrease.	
~~trend.~~ That's because People will take advantage of	Add transition words.
educational programs to get ~~them-~~	Be more specific about connection to crime.
~~selves~~ out of ~~bad~~ situations that may turn them toward crime.	

"I feed the cat nothing but veggies."

BUILDING YOUR PORTFOLIO

Sentence Workshop

USING TRANSITIONS

Words and phrases that make a transition, or connection, from one idea to another are called **transitional expressions.** Transitional expressions can indicate chronological order (*then, next, finally*), spatial order (*above, under, next to*), and relationships between ideas (*because, since, although*). Notice in the sentences that follow how transitional expressions can make ideas much more precise:

WITHOUT TRANSITIONS: Antigone died. She believed Creon's order was immoral. She refused to follow it.

WITH TRANSITIONS: Antigone died because she believed Creon's order was immoral, and so she refused to follow it.

WITH TRANSITIONS: Antigone died, for she believed Creon's order was immoral, and she consequently refused to follow it.

Here are some useful transitional expressions.

Transitional Expressions

comparing: also, similarly, too
contrasting: but, however, instead
cause and effect: as a result, so that, therefore
time: after, before, first, when
place: across, beyond, inside, into
importance: last, mainly, more important

Writer's Workshop Follow-up: Revision

Exchange with a partner the essay you've been working on for the Writer's Workshop. Read your partner's essay critically, looking especially for ideas that would be clearer if transitional expressions had been used. Remember that you have many choices when you revise sentences using transitional expressions. Experiment with the words that seem best to you.

Technology HELP

See Language Workshop CD-ROM. *Key word entry: transitional expressions.*

Try It Out

Revise the following paragraph by using transitional expressions to show more precisely how the ideas are related. Be sure to compare your revisions in class.

Tom seems stuck in the pain of his childhood. He talks about it all the time. He tells Gene and Margaret the story of his mother's funeral. He shoved his father off the funeral coach. His father was dying, and Tom sent his father oranges. Tom never saw his father again. Tom remembers his mother with fondness. He cries when he remembers her. Margaret gets irritated at Tom's old stories. She has heard them all hundreds of times. I feel sorry for Tom. He's had a hard life. He's never gotten over it.

Reading for Life

Using the Internet as a Resource

Situation

You are fascinated by people who take great risks in order to do the right thing. You've begun to do research on the Internet about India's great leader Mohandas Gandhi. Here are some strategies to use as you explore the Internet. (For more help, see Using the Internet in the Communications Handbook at the back of this text.)

- GANDHI - THE **GANDHI** HOMEPAGE A brief history of **Mohandas** K. **Gandhi** - India's greatest statesman. http://~www.maui.com/~lesslie/**gandhi**.html **GANDHI** SOUND Real Audio of Mahatma **Gandhi's** inspirational speech, "My Spiritual Message," recorded in 1925. http:/...
  --*http://www.percepticon.com/~temporal/penpalscrapbook/html...*

- Gandhi - **Gandhi** India-UK (1982) | Biography | 188 min. | Rated PG | Color Director Richard Attenborough Cast includes Ben Kingsley Candice Bergen Edward Fox John Gielgud Trevor Howard John Mills Martin Sheen Rohini Hattangandy Ian Charleson Athol Fugard...
  --*http://bertrand.bucknell.edu/home/video/movies/profiles/g...*

- **Religion: Mohandas Gandhi's grandson to preach nonviolence at Detroit...**
  Classifieds Personals Job listings Place an ad Editorials Horoscope Lottery Weather Death Notices Search Engine Back Issues Site highlights Accent Autos...
  71% *http://detnews.com/1997/detroit/9708/31/08270058.htm* (size 9.8K) Document Date: 31 Aug 1997

- **Mohandas Gandhi**
  Gandhi, Mohandas Karamchand (1869-1948). Mohandas Karamchand Gandhi was born in Poorbandar, in W India. He was the son of Karamchand Gandhi, the chief minister of Poorbandar, and his fourth wife, Putlibai, a...
  60% *http://userwww.sfsu.edu/~rsauzier/Gandhi.html* (Six 5.6K) Document Date: 2 Jan 1998

Strategies

Keep your focus in mind.
- Formulate a clear idea of the data you want to find and how you intend to use it.

Begin your search.
- Choose only those sites that look as if they will have the information you want.

Check the Uniform Resource Locator (URL).
- This is the specific address of a site. Abbreviations within the URL indicate the source of the site. Some common abbreviations are *gov* (for government), *edu* (for education), *com* (for commercial), and *org* (for organization). Data from a government source should be reliable, as should pages posted by a reputable university.

Extend your search.
- Refine your search. Use different **key words** or choose another **search engine** or subject index.

Evaluate sources.
- Consider the authority of the site or the person who authored the information. Be alert for bias, and check timeliness or currency by noticing if the site is updated regularly.

Using the Strategies

These questions refer to the Internet sites in the box above.

1. Which site has an audio component?
2. Which site offers information on a movie about Gandhi?
3. Which sites would you select for further information about Gandhi's life? Why would you choose these sites?
4. Which site would you probably not investigate further? Why?
5. To refine your search, what other key words might you use in addition to the name Mohandas Gandhi?

Extending the Strategies

Use the Internet to gather information about another historical person or event. Is anything available on Antigone?

Learning for Life

Doing the Right Thing

Problem

In *Antigone,* an individual's personal loyalties and religious beliefs conflict with her duty to obey the law. In theory, laws are passed to promote the greatest good for the greatest number. What happens when people think that a particular law is unjust or discriminatory?

Project

Identify some rules or laws within your school, community, or state that you think should be changed. Present arguments to draw attention to your concerns.

Preparation

1. With your group, choose a rule or law you all agree should be reevaluated. Think of regulations that seem poorly conceived or that treat some portion of the population unfairly or that favor some special interest group. For example, the rules in your community regarding access to public buildings may not require provision for wheelchair access, or perhaps laws limit the speed on some highways to 55 miles per hour.
2. Discuss reasons why the regulation should be changed. Why is it unfair?
3. Discuss positive aspects of the law as well. If your position seems well thought out and fair, your argument for change will be stronger.

Procedure

1. Using the group's preparation discussions as a base, formulate a reasoned argument that presents your position. Remember that your aim is to raise awareness about the issue and to persuade the public to support your efforts for change.
2. Identify the person or persons to whom you should address your protest.

Presentation

Use one of the following strategies (or another that your teacher approves):

1. Letter-Writing Campaign

Initiate a letter-writing campaign. Think of ways to encourage others to join your effort. Keep track of answers to your letters. Consider letting local papers know your results.

2. Speak Out

Write a speech to be given at a public meeting to urge the change of a rule or law. Appoint a group member to record the public's reaction to your speech. Consider reporting your results to local papers or radio stations.

3. Posters or Cartoons

Create posters or cartoons that illustrate your issues. Obtain permission to display them in public areas in your school or community.

Processing

What did you learn from this project about the difficulties in changing public policy? Write a brief reflection for your portfolio.

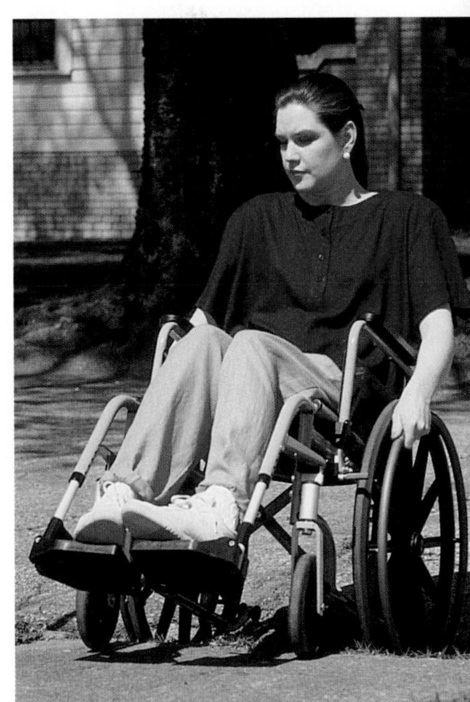

William Shakespeare

We are such stuff
As dreams are made on, and
our little life
Is rounded with a sleep.

—The Tempest
(Act IV, Scene 1)

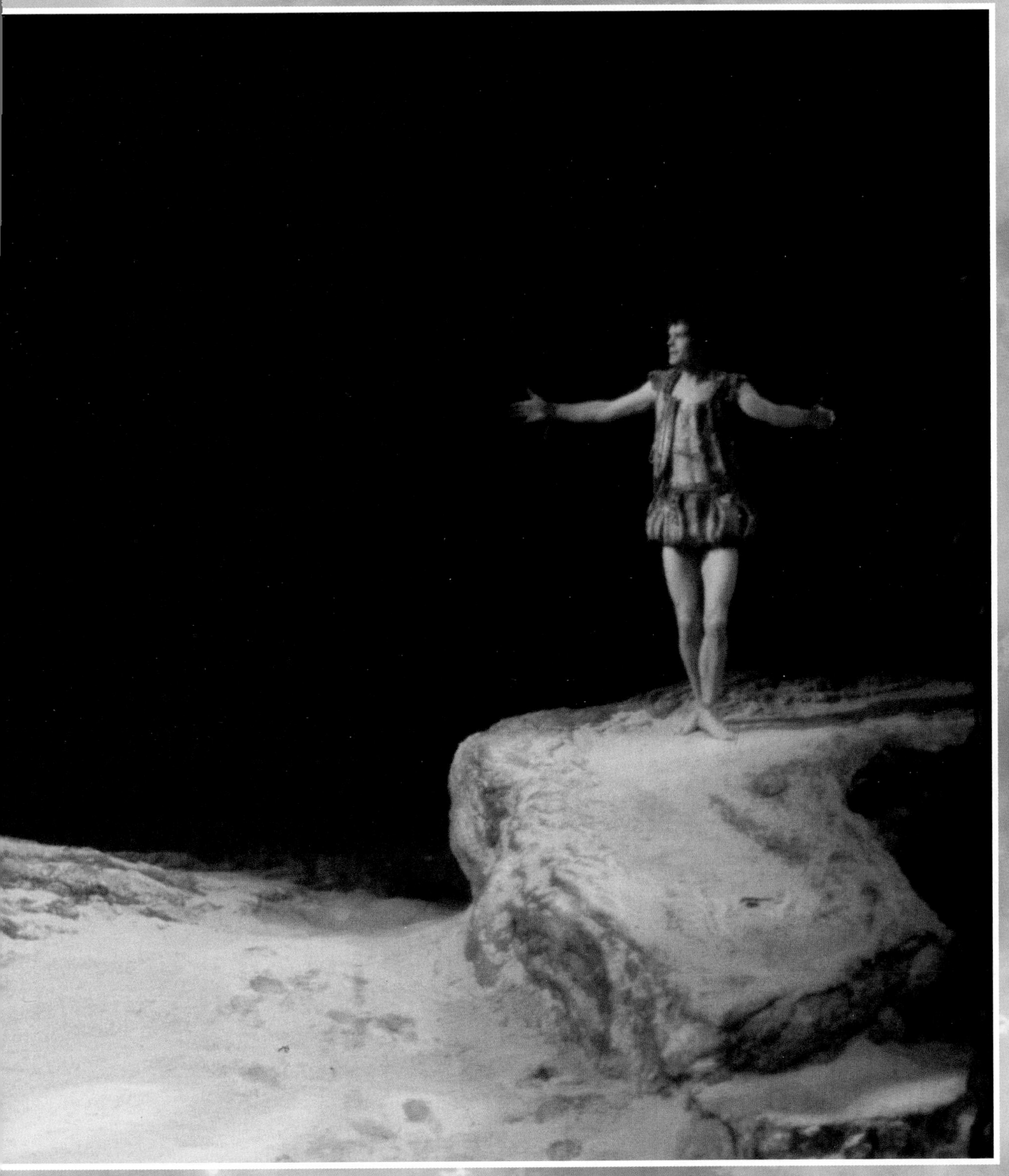

Scene from the 1974 New York Shakespeare Festival production of *The Tempest*.

William Shakespeare's Life

A Biographical Sketch

by Robert Anderson

William Shakespeare.

Popperfoto/Archive Photos.

Compared with what we know about writers today, we know very little about William Shakespeare's life. In the early 1600s, nobody realized that this actor and writer would one day become known as the world's greatest playwright and poet. In the 1600s, there were no talk show hosts to interview Shakespeare, no Sunday supplements to feature all the intimate details of his life. This neglect, however, has been corrected. By now, more material has been written about Shakespeare and his works than about any other writer in the world.

What we do know about Shakespeare comes mainly from public records. We know that he was baptized on April 26, 1564, in Stratford-on-Avon, a market town about one hundred miles northwest of London. It is assumed he was born a few days before his baptism, and so his birthday is celebrated on April 23, possibly only because he died on that date in 1616. He was one of eight children.

His father, John Shakespeare, was a merchant and a man of some importance in the town, serving at various times as alderman and "high bailiff"—the equivalent of a mayor today.

William went to the local grammar school, which was very different from grammar schools today. In those days it was rare for

Shakespeare's birthplace on Henly Street in Stratford, England.

The Photo Works/ Photo Researchers.

students to move on to a university; the Stratford grammar school provided Shakespeare and other boys of Stratford (no girls went to school) with all their formal education. What they learned in this school was Latin—Latin grammar and Latin literature, including the schoolboys' favorite—Ovid's amorous retelling of the Greek and Roman myths.

In 1582, Shakespeare married Anne Hathaway, who was eight years older than he was, and in 1583, their first child, Susanna, was born. In 1585, Anne gave birth to twins, Hamnet and Judith. Then, from 1585 until 1592, Shakespeare's history goes blank.

Many people believe that Shakespeare went to London to seek his fortune the year after the twins were born. We know that by 1592 he had become an actor and a playwright because that year a rival playwright, Robert Greene, scathingly warned other playwrights against the actor who had become a writer:

> There is an upstart crow, beautified with our feathers . . . that supposes he is as well able to bombast out a blank verse as the best of you. . . .

Greene refers to a fable in which a crow struts about in another bird's feathers—as an actor can only recite others' words. Greene was insulting an upstart, a mere actor who dared to *write*.

Actors were held in disrepute at the time. In fact, they were often lumped together with other unsavory groups: "rogues, vagabonds, sturdy beggars, and common players." Local officials frequently tried to close the theaters because they felt clerks and apprentices wasted time there (performances were in the daytime). They also felt that disease was too easily spread

Local officials frequently tried to close the theaters because they felt clerks and apprentices wasted time there.

among the audience members. In fact, the London theaters were closed for long periods during the plague years of 1592–1594.

Thus, actors sought the protection and support of noblemen with the power to speak for their rights against critical town authorities. It appears that in 1594, Shakespeare became a charter member of a theatrical group called the Lord Chamberlain's Men, which became the King's Men in 1603. (The patron of the group was none other than King James himself.) Shakespeare acted and wrote for this company until he retired to Stratford in 1612. By that time, he had written thirty-seven plays—**comedies, histories, tragedies,** and **romances**—including his tragic masterpieces *Hamlet, Othello, King Lear,* and *Macbeth.*

Glenn Close in the 1990 movie version of *Hamlet,* starring Mel Gibson.

It is sometimes difficult to fix the dates of Shakespeare's works because plays were not routinely published after production, as they generally are now. In Shakespeare's day, plays became the property of the theaters, and the theaters were not eager to have copies made available for rival theaters to use. Some of Shakespeare's plays were published during his lifetime but often in versions of dubious authenticity. It was not until 1623 that two men who had been with Shakespeare in the King's Men brought out what they called "True Original Copies" of all the plays. This volume is called the First Folio.

It is believed that *Julius Caesar* was written in 1599, because a Swiss traveler who was in England in September 1599 wrote about a visit to the Globe. The Swiss visitor was most impressed, for good reason, with the intricate and vigorous Elizabethan dancing:

> After dinner on the twenty-first of September, at about two o'clock, I went with my companions over the water, and in the strewn-roof house [the playhouse with a thatched roof] saw the tragedy of the first Emperor Julius with at least fifteen characters very well acted. At the end of the comedy they danced according to their custom with extreme elegance. Two men in men's clothes and two in women's gave this performance, in wonderful combination with each other.

Shakespeare died on April 23, 1616, at the age of fifty-two. He was buried in the Holy Trinity Church at Stratford, where his grave can still be seen today. A bequest he made in his will has attracted almost as much interest and curiosity as anything in his plays—he left his wife his "second-best bed."

The Elizabethan Stage

by Robert Anderson

The Elizabethan stage would have seemed very strange to American theatergoers of fifty or sixty years ago, who were accustomed to elaborate and realistic settings placed on a stage separated from the audience by a huge velvet curtain. This is called a proscenium stage, and though it's still more or less standard today, the newer arena stages, thrust stages, and open stages have made us much more at home with Shakespeare's theater. The use of these simpler stages that make the audience feel they're a part of the action recalls the saying that all you need for a theater is "a platform and a passion or two."

The White Hart Inn, London. Engraving.

By permission of The Folger Shakespeare Library.

As with Shakespeare's life, we have only sketchy information about the early English theaters. It appears that the wandering acting companies in England had originally set up their stages—mere platforms—wherever they could find space, often in the courtyards of inns. The audience stood around three sides of the stage, or if they paid more, they sat in chairs on the balconies surrounding the inn yard.

When James Burbage (the father of Richard Burbage, the actor who was to perform most of Shakespeare's great tragic parts) decided in 1576 to build the first permanent theater just outside the city of London, it was natural that he should duplicate the courtyard theaters in which his company had been performing. Burbage called his new playhouse simply "The Theater."

The Globe—The "Wooden O"

In 1599, the owner of the land on which Burbage had built his theater apparently decided to raise the rent. Because the theater was somewhat behind in its rent payments, the landlord threatened to take it over. On the night of January 20, 1599, James Burbage's son Cuthbert and others in the company stealthily took their theater apart timber by timber and rowed the pieces across the river, where they later reconstructed the theater and called it the Globe. This was the theater where Shakespeare's greatest plays were performed.

In *Henry V*, Shakespeare calls the theater "this wooden O."

In *Henry V*, Shakespeare calls the theater "this wooden O." It

The Globe Theater, a view of Shoreditch in 1590, by Cyril Walter Hodges. Watercolor with pen, ink, and body color (9″ × 6½″).

Courtesy Chris Beetles Ltd., London.

consisted of an open space, perhaps sixty-five feet in diameter, surrounded by a more or less circular building thirty feet high and consisting of three tiers of seats for spectators. As in the inn courtyards, the stage, which was forty feet by thirty feet and five feet off the ground, projected into the open space.

The interesting part of the stage was at the rear, where there was a small curtained inner stage, flanked by two entrances, with an upper stage above it. Stout pillars held up a narrow roof over the rear part of the stage. This was called "the Heavens." The front part of the stage was equipped with a trapdoor, which could be used for burial scenes, surprise entrances, and mysterious exits.

The Sets: Mostly Imagination

Shakespeare trusted his audience's imagination. He knew he did not need elaborate sets to re-create a battle scene or a bedroom or the Roman Forum. The audience members could do it for themselves.

Moreover, without elaborate sets to move on and off the stage, Shakespeare could change scenes with the kind of fluidity we see in movies today.

Here is how Shakespeare prompted his audience to see hundreds of horsemen (and to costume his kings) in lines from the Prologue to *Henry V*:

> . . . let us . . .
> On your imaginary forces work. . . .
> Think, when we talk of horses, that you see them
> Printing their proud hoofs i' th' receiving earth;
> For 'tis your thoughts that now must deck our kings . . .

Though Shakespeare made no attempt to use realistic settings, it appears that his kings and other characters were splendidly decked out. He also called for flags and banners and musicians, and the multilayered stage could produce special effects. Characters could be lowered from the Heavens by cranes, and there were sound effects as well. In fact, these special effects caused the destruction of the Globe. In 1613, during the battle scene of *Henry VIII,* a stagehand was lighting the fuse of a cannon. A spark flew up and started a fire in the thatched roof of the Heavens, and the theater burned down.

In yet another reversal of roles, female mezzo-soprano Tatiana Troyanos portrays Caesar in Handel's opera *Julius Caesar.*

The Bettmann Archive.

Because the plays were performed during the daytime in the open air, there was no need for stage illumination. Shakespeare had to convey the idea of night by having characters carry torches. (Today, to shoot a night scene in the daytime, movie directors use filters on their cameras to darken the scene.)

The Actors: All Males

In Shakespeare's time, all actors were male. (It wasn't until 1660, when the exiled King Charles II was restored to the English throne, and the repressive Puritan dominance ended, that women played in professional theaters.) Boys who had been recruited from the choir schools and trained professionally played the female roles. It was not too difficult to create the illusion that these boys were women. Shakespeare's plays were performed in contemporary Elizabethan costumes, and women's clothing of the day was very elaborate and concealing, with long, full skirts flowing from extremely narrow waists. Women also wore elaborate wigs and powdered their faces heavily. So, all in all, the transformation of boys into women characters was not that unbelievable.

Hooking the Audience's Attention

The Elizabethan theater was a convivial place where people arrived early, visited with friends, made new acquaintances, moved around freely, and ate and drank before and during the performance. (The occasion might have had something of the feeling of a Saturday matinee at a local shopping-mall movie theater.) Playwrights had to write scenes that would catch the attention of this audience, and many actors held their attention by vigorous and flamboyant acting. By comparison, today's movie cameras are so sensitive that sometimes all an actor has to do is think the right thoughts, and that is enough. Elizabethan actors had to do more than that since they were trying to hold the interest of three thousand restless people who were also busy eating, drinking, and talking. We get the impression that, like actors working on modern thrust or arena stages, the Elizabethan players had to keep on the move so that spectators on all three sides could catch their expressions and hear their voices.

The occasion might have had something of the feeling of a Saturday matinee at a local shopping-mall movie theater.

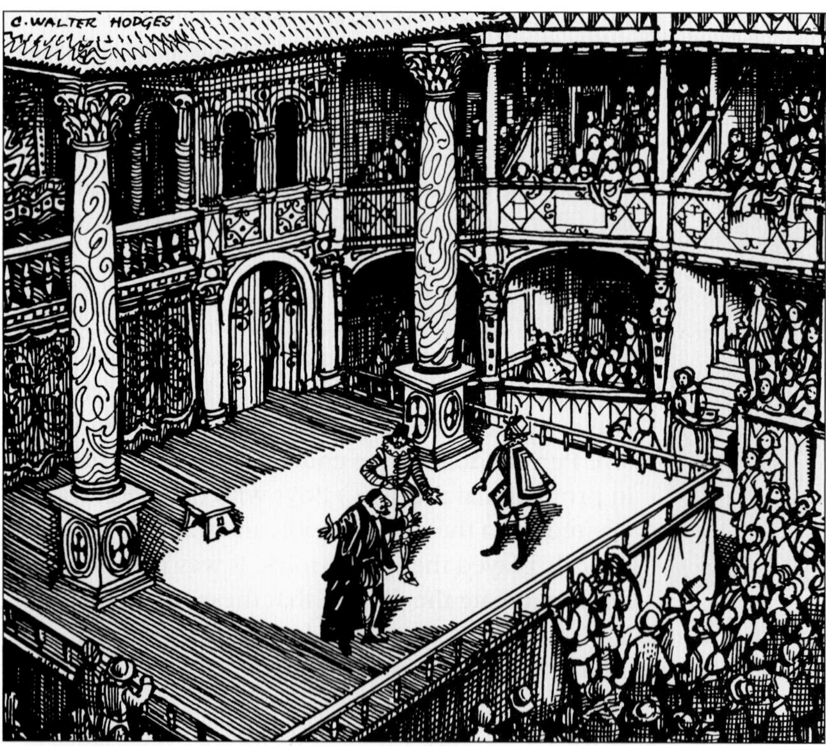

Drawing of a Globe Theater performance.

By permission of The Folger Shakespeare Library.

The Play: The Results of Violence

Assassination. The murder of a public figure is an act that can take place in a split second yet change the course of history. We've seen a number of assassinations in the twentieth century. This play is about the assassination of a Roman general and dictator who lived and died (an extremely violent death) more than two thousand years ago. Shakespeare drew his material from an ancient biographical text called *The Parallel Lives,* which first appeared under the title *The Lives of the Noble Grecians and Romans* in translation in England in 1579. This work was written by Plutarch (A.D. 46–c. A.D. 120), a Greek writer and biographer who lived close to the time of Julius Caesar. Greek and Roman history and culture had a great appeal for the English of the Elizabethan Age. They tended to see their own age mirrored in those great ancient civilizations.

Rome in Caesar's Day: Continuous War

We get the impression that the Roman world in Caesar's time was continually at war. Today, the generals of the United States Army are ultimately responsible to the president, who is their commander-in-chief. But two thousand years ago in Rome, the generals had enormous individual power. Powerful generals like Caesar moved with their plundering armies over the entire Mediterranean world. After these "private armies" subdued weaker countries, the territories were then ruled by Roman governors who exacted cruel taxes on the conquered people.

Sometimes the generals turned on one another, because they were strong men battling for power. This is what happened when the generals Caesar and Pompey clashed in the civil war that began in 49 B.C.

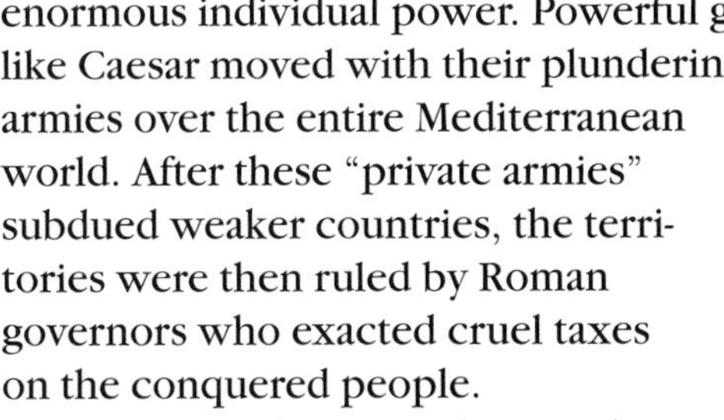

Bronze Roman helmet from Judea.

Caesar and Pompey: Jealousy and Murder

Caesar and Pompey were friends. Pompey married Caesar's daughter by his first wife. In 60 B.C., the two generals helped to bring order to a weakened government, when they, along with Crassus, formed the First Triumvirate (three-man government).

Eager for still more power and realizing that he could only achieve it with conquests and money, Caesar departed for what has been called the Gallic Wars. For eight years, he and his armies roamed Europe, subjugating France, Belgium, and parts of Holland, Germany, and Switzerland. Caesar amassed huge sums of money, which he sent back to Rome to gain favor with the people.

Caesar's daughter died in 54 B.C., and in 49 B.C. Pompey, jealous of Caesar's growing power and favor with the people, threw his weight to the Senate, which was also wary of Caesar's ambitions.

Caesar considered himself a defender of the people, but critics said that he gained the people's support with bribes and handouts. His enemies said he deprived the Romans of their liberty.

Caesar refused the Senate's order to give up his command and return to Rome as a private citizen. Instead, he marched his army on Rome, took control, and chased Pompey all the way to Egypt. There, Pompey was murdered before Caesar could capture him. Caesar lingered in Egypt for nine months, bewitched by the twenty-two-year-old Cleopatra. Establishing her on the throne of Egypt under his protection, Caesar went to Spain, where he defeated an army led by Pompey's sons.

Bust of Julius Caesar (date unknown). National Museum, Naples.

The Bettmann Archive.

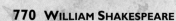

The Unconquerable God

When he returned to Rome, Caesar was invincible. He was declared dictator for ten years and saw to it that his supporters, including Brutus, became senators. As his desire for power grew obsessive, he had a statue of himself, bearing the inscription "To the Unconquerable God," erected in the Temple of Quirinus. The common people loved him; later, Caesar was declared dictator for life.

However, to a number of Romans, Caesar's ambition was deplorable. The last Roman king had been overthrown 450 years before, when the Romans set up a republican government. The idea of another king ruling the "free Romans" was unthinkable. As Caesar's arrogance and power became unbearable to certain senators, they made plans to assassinate him on March 15, 44 B.C. Shakespeare's play opens a month before the murder.

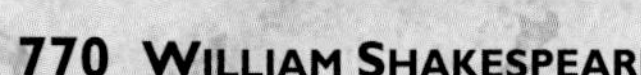

Reading Skills and Strategies

How to Read Shakespeare

Hear the Beat

As with all of Shakespeare's plays, *Julius Caesar* is written in blank verse. **Blank verse** duplicates the natural rhythms of English speech. Blank verse is unrhymed **iambic pentameter,** which means that each line of poetry in the play is built on five iambs. An **iamb** consists of an unstressed syllable followed by a stressed syllable, as in the word *prĕpare*. In this case, **pentameter** means that there are five iambs in a line. Read these lines aloud to feel the beat, or rhythm. Better yet, strike the strong and weak beats with your fingers: (Try it.)

˘ ʹ ˘ ʹ ˘ ʹ ˘ ʹ ˘ ʹ
The evil that men do lives after them,

˘ ʹ ˘ ʹ ˘ ʹ ˘ ʹ ˘ ʹ
The good is oft interrèd with their bones.

A whole play written in this pattern would become singsong. To break the monotony and alter the emphasis, Shakespeare sometimes reverses the stressed and unstressed syllables. Which syllables would you stress in the following speech? Actors don't always read speeches with the same emphasis. You'll probably find variations in reading these lines in your own group. (Read aloud.)

This was the noblest Roman of them all.
All the conspirators save only he
Did that they did in envy of great Caesar.

Shakespeare doesn't let all his characters speak in blank verse. You'll notice that the commoners speak, as we all do, in ordinary prose. (So does Brutus in his funeral oration.)

Pauses and Stops for Breath

Follow the punctuation marks, and resist the temptation to stop at the end of each line. Thus, in the first passage above, you would pause at the end of the first line and come to a full stop at the end of the second. (Try it.) In the next passage, you'd make a full stop for breath at the end of the first line but not at the end of the second line. The second line has no end punctuation, and sense requires that you move on. (Try it.) Lines that end with a punctuation mark are called **end-stopped** lines. Lines that do not end with a punctuation mark are called **run-on** lines. (For the complete meaning, you must "run on" to the next line.)

Archaic Words

One character in the play is a soothsayer. In Shakespeare's day, the word *sooth* meant "truth." We rarely use the word now. Today, we'd call such a person a fortune teller or an astrologer. Here, from *Julius Caesar*, are some other words that are now archaic.

ague: fever.

alarum: call to arms, such as a trumpet blast.

an: if.

betimes: from time to time.

fleering: flattering.

hence, whence, thence: here, where, there.

hie: hurry.

knave: servant, or person of humble birth.

moe: more. *Moe* was used to refer to number and amounts; *more,* to size.

prithee: pray thee (beg thee).

smatch: small amount.

Words with Different Meanings

The most troublesome words in Shakespeare's plays are those still in use but with different meanings. When Flavius calls the cobbler "Thou naughty knave," he seems to be merely scolding the man. However, *naughty* here means "worthless," so the sense of Flavius's line is different from what you might think. Here are other familiar words from *Julius Caesar* that had different meanings in Shakespeare's day.

closet: small room, often a private study.

exhalations: meteors.

gentle: noble. *Gentleman* once referred to a man who had a title.

ghastly: ghostly.

humor: temper or disposition.

indifferently: impartially.

just: true.

merely: wholly; entirely.

repair: go.

sad: serious.

saucy: presumptuous.

soft: slowly; "wait a minute."

wit: intelligence.

Act It Out!

Don't forget that this play was created for an ordinary audience—people just like the ones who flock to movies or to rock concerts today. To get a feel for the play as action, plan to perform as much of it as possible.

You might begin with the first scene—a brief street scene in which a group of working people encounter two military officers. Here are some suggestions for **oral interpretation:**

1. Break into small groups. Assign a part to each group member.
2. For this first scene especially, you could do **choral readings.** Again, break into groups. Each group should then split into two smaller groups. Let one small group read the commoners' lines and the other small group read the speeches of the tribunes. Then, have the groups switch roles: The commoners become the tribunes and the tribunes become the commoners.

William Shakespeare.

Drawing by David Levine. Reprinted with permission from *The New York Review of Books.* Copyright ©1978 NYREV, Inc.

As you read the scene, don't worry about the way the archaic words are pronounced. Don't worry about the poetry, either; read all the lines in the scene as if they were prose. Read for sense only: At this point, don't worry about acting out the scene.

After your reading, discuss what happens in the scene and how you feel about it. Who are these people? What is going on?

Now, give a **dramatic performance** of the scene. Some of you will be the **actors,** at least one will be the **director,** and some of you will be the **audience.** How will you set the scene? What are the characters doing as they speak? What props will you need, if any? How will you get audience feedback after your performance?

Beginnings and endings are important in Shakespeare. What did you learn from performing this opening scene?

Collection 12

AMBITION OR HONOR?

WRITING FOCUS: Analyzing and Evaluating Persuasion

Something deathless and dangerous in the world sweeps past you. . . . It is something fearful and ominous, something turbulent and to be dreaded, which distends the drama to include the life of nations as well as of men. It is an ageless warning. . . .

—John Mason Brown

Forces at work in Julius Caesar's time are still evident in the news. Wars, terrorism, mob violence, and assassinations are still problems today. People today are still swayed and even controlled by powerful and persuasive individuals and groups. How do we decide to join one group and to oppose another? What do we do when appeals to our ambition conflict with our sense of honor?

Writer's Notebook

WORK IN PROGRESS

When people talk to you, do you accept what they say, or do you evaluate their words? Think of times when people tried to persuade you to do or accept something. For each incident, note why you accepted or rejected the speaker's position. Save your notes. They'll be useful for the Writer's Workshop on page 892.

Scene from the 1953 movie version of *Julius Caesar,* directed by Joseph L. Mankiewicz.

Before You Read

THE TRAGEDY OF JULIUS CAESAR

Make the Connection

In all of Shakespeare's plays, the characters (no matter what historical period they live in) inhabit a world that is run by a just God who ultimately rewards good and punishes evil. In Shakespeare's day, people believed that the universe was essentially good and orderly. All order stemmed from the authority of God, the supreme ruler. The monarch's right to rule came from God, too, and so opposition to the anointed ruler was considered opposition to God. When the chain of authority was snapped, the Heavens would be offended, and a whole society could be plunged into disorder.

When Shakespeare wrote this play, Queen Elizabeth was old and in failing health. She had no children. When she died, what would become of the country she had ruled so peacefully for nearly forty years? Would there be a bloody struggle for the throne? Would the country slip back into the violence that had preceded Elizabeth's reign? Thus, this story of Julius Caesar had immediate connections for the Elizabethans—it tapped into their own desire for stability in government, into their dread of civil war.

Quickwrite

Before you read *Julius Caesar,* think about the Elizabethan view of the universe. How is it different from our ideas about government? Write your responses to the following statements. Do you agree? disagree? Why? Are you unsure about some of them? Are any of them disturbing?

1. Chaos results when the lawful social order is broken.
2. The best intentions of good, noble people can lead to tragedy.
3. Language is a powerful weapon, and in the hands of a skilled person, it can be used to manipulate others.
4. Violence and bloodshed can never have morally good results.
5. Orderliness and stable rule, even though dictatorial, are preferable to chaos.

"THE EVIL THAT MEN DO
LIVES AFTER THEM,
THE GOOD IS OFT INTERRÈD
WITH THEIR BONES. . . ."

Julius Caesar attributed to Donatello (c. 1386–1466). Relief. Musée du Louvre, Paris.

Giraudon/Art Resource, NY.

The Tragedy of Julius Caesar

William Shakespeare

Characters

Julius Caesar	
Octavius Caesar **Marcus Antonius** **M. Aemilius Lepidus**	triumvirs after the death of Julius Caesar
Cicero **Publius** **Popilius Lena**	senators
Marcus Brutus **Cassius** **Casca** **Trebonius** **Ligarius** **Decius Brutus** **Metellus Cimber** **Cinna**	conspirators against Julius Caesar
Flavius **Marullus**	tribunes
Artemidorus of Cnidos, a teacher of rhetoric	
A Soothsayer	
Cinna, a poet	
Another Poet	
Lucilius **Titinius** **Messala** **Young Cato** **Volumnius**	friends to Brutus and Cassius
Varro **Clitus** **Claudius** **Strato** **Lucius** **Dardanius**	servants to Brutus
Pindarus, servant to Cassius	
Calphurnia, wife to Caesar	
Portia, wife to Brutus	
Senators, Citizens, Guards, Attendants, etc.	

Scene: During most of the play, at Rome; afterward, near Sardis, and near Philippi.

Note: The text of this play is taken in entirety from the *Signet Classic Shakespeare.* The editors of the *Signet Classic Shakespeare* have refrained from making abundant changes in the text, but they have added line numbers and act and scene divisions, as well as indications of locale at the beginning of scenes.

The background photograph shows the ruins of the Roman Forum.

ACT I Scene 1. *Rome. A street.*

Enter FLAVIUS, MARULLUS, *and certain* COMMONERS *over the stage.*

Flavius.
Hence! Home, you idle creatures, get you home!
Is this a holiday? What, know you not,
Being mechanical,° you ought not walk
Upon a laboring day without the sign
Of your profession?° Speak, what trade art thou?

Carpenter. Why, sir, a carpenter.

Marullus.
Where is thy leather apron and thy rule?
What dost thou with thy best apparel on?
You, sir, what trade are you?

Cobbler. Truly, sir, in respect of a fine workman,° I am but, as you would say, a cobbler.°

Marullus.
But what trade art thou? Answer me directly.

Cobbler. A trade, sir, that, I hope, I may use with a safe conscience, which is indeed, sir, a mender of bad soles.

Flavius.
What trade, thou knave? Thou naughty knave, what trade?

Cobbler. Nay, I beseech you, sir, be not out with me: yet, if you be out, sir, I can mend you.

Marullus.
What mean'st thou by that? Mend me, thou saucy fellow?

Cobbler. Why, sir, cobble you.

Flavius.
Thou art a cobbler, art thou?

Cobbler. Truly, sir, all that I live by is with the awl:° I meddle with no tradesman's matters, nor women's matters; but withal,° I am indeed, sir, a surgeon to old shoes: when they are in great danger, I recover them. As proper men as ever trod upon neat's leather° have gone upon my handiwork.

Flavius.
But wherefore art not in thy shop today?
Why dost thou lead these men about the streets?

Cobbler. Truly, sir, to wear out their shoes, to get myself into more work. But indeed, sir, we make holiday to see Caesar and to rejoice in his triumph.

Marullus.
Wherefore rejoice? What conquest brings he home?
What tributaries° follow him to Rome,

? ***Stage direction.*** *We are on a crowded street in Rome. It is lined with statues near what is today known as the Palatine Hill (which is where the palaces, or* palatia, *were). A joyous, peaceful crowd is milling about. Two tribunes—military men—enter with the noisy mob of commoners. What tone does Flavius's first speech bring immediately to the play?*

3. mechanical: working class.

5. sign of your profession: your work clothes and tools.

10. In other words, in comparison with a skilled laborer.

11. cobbler: In Shakespeare's day the word meant both "shoemaker" and "bungler."

? **15.** *It is important in this play to watch the moods of the crowd. Do you think these commoners are afraid of the military men, or are they acting comically and boldly?*

21. awl: sharp, pointed tool for making holes in wood or leather.

23. withal: nevertheless.

25. neat's leather: leather from cattle.

33. tributaries: captives (captive enemies who have to pay "tribute," or tax, to Rome).

To grace in captive bonds his chariot wheels?
You blocks, you stones, you worse than senseless things!
O you hard hearts, you cruel men of Rome,
Knew you not Pompey?° Many a time and oft
Have you climbed up to walls and battlements,
To tow'rs and windows, yea, to chimney tops,
Your infants in your arms, and there have sat
The livelong day, with patient expectation,
To see great Pompey pass the streets of Rome.
And when you saw his chariot but appear,
Have you not made an universal shout,
That Tiber trembled underneath her banks
To hear the replication° of your sounds
Made in her concave shores?°
And do you now put on your best attire?
And do you now cull out a holiday?
And do you now strew flowers in his way
That comes in triumph over Pompey's blood?
Be gone!
Run to your houses, fall upon your knees,
Pray to the gods to intermit° the plague
That needs must light on this ingratitude.

Flavius.
Go, go, good countrymen, and, for this fault,
Assemble all the poor men of your sort;
Draw them to Tiber banks and weep your tears
Into the channel, till the lowest stream
Do kiss the most exalted shores of all.

[*Exeunt all the* COMMONERS.]

See, whe'r their basest mettle° be not moved;
They vanish tongue-tied in their guiltiness.
Go you down that way towards the Capitol;
This way will I. Disrobe the images,°
If you do find them decked with ceremonies.

Marullus.
May we do so?
You know it is the feast of Lupercal.°

Flavius.
It is no matter; let no images
Be hung with Caesar's trophies. I'll about
And drive away the vulgar° from the streets;
So do you too, where you perceive them thick.
These growing feathers plucked from Caesar's wing

? **35.** *What do you think Marullus is doing as he speaks?*

37. Pompey: Roman politician and general who was defeated by Caesar in 48 B.C. and later murdered.

46. replication: echo; copy.

47. concave shores: carved-out banks of the river.

? **52.** *How should this short line be spoken?*

54. intermit: hold back.

? **55.** *What is the key word in the last line of this speech? Why is Marullus angry at the mob?*

? ***Stage direction.*** *Pay attention to the movements of the crowd. What mood has taken over these commoners as they leave the stage? Would you have them leave in a defiant mood, or are they ashamed?*

61. basest mettle: basic substance, their "stuff."

64. images: statues.

67. Lupercal: old Roman fertility festival celebrated on February 15. In the ceremony, young men raced around the Palatine Hill (at the base of which is the Lupercal cave) and whipped bystanders with strips of goatskin. Those who were whipped were assured of fertility. The Lupercal cave is believed to be where the twins Romulus and Remus, the founders of Rome, were suckled by a wolf.

70. vulgar: common people.

Will make him fly an ordinary pitch,°
Who else would soar above the view of men
And keep us all in servile fearfulness. [*Exeunt.*]

73. an ordinary pitch: at an ordinary height.

75. *What does Flavius fear about Caesar?*

Scene 2. *A public place.*

Enter CAESAR, ANTONY (*dressed for the race*), CALPHURNIA, PORTIA, DECIUS, CICERO, BRUTUS, CASSIUS, CASCA, *a* SOOTHSAYER; *after them*, MARULLUS *and* FLAVIUS.

Stage direction. *As Caesar and his retinue enter, the crowd makes way for them. Antony is dressed for the race held on the Feast of Lupercal, which this year also celebrates Caesar's latest victory. Caesar would be richly dressed—perhaps too richly. What mood would Marullus and Flavius be in?*

Caesar.
Calphurnia!
Casca. Peace, ho! Caesar speaks.
Caesar. Calphurnia!
Calphurnia. Here, my lord.
Caesar.
Stand you directly in Antonius' way
When he doth run his course. Antonius!
Antony. Caesar, my lord?
Caesar.
Forget not in your speed, Antonius,
To touch Calphurnia; for our elders say
The barren, touchèd in this holy chase,
Shake off their sterile curse.
Antony. I shall remember:
When Caesar says "Do this," it is performed.
Caesar.
Set on, and leave no ceremony out.
Soothsayer. Caesar!
Caesar. Ha! Who calls?
Casca.
Bid every noise be still; peace yet again!
Caesar.
Who is it in the press° that calls on me?
I hear a tongue, shriller than all the music,
Cry "Caesar." Speak; Caesar is turned to hear.
Soothsayer.
Beware the ides of March.
Caesar. What man is that?
Brutus.
A soothsayer bids you beware the ides of March.
Caesar.
Set him before me; let me see his face.
Cassius.
Fellow, come from the throng; look upon Caesar.
Caesar.
What say'st thou to me now? Speak once again.

10. *This speech suggests something important about Antony. What is it?*

12. *A lot of ceremonial music and ritual have opened this scene, so our attention has been focused on Caesar and his followers. But now the soothsayer, or foreteller of the future, is suddenly visible. This is a dramatic moment, for it foreshadows what will happen. Where would you place the soothsayer? How should Caesar react to his call?*

15. press: crowd.

17. *What physical disability might this line suggest?*

18. *The ides of March are March 15. In some productions this warning is heard as an ominous and disembodied cry. In what different ways could the line be spoken?*

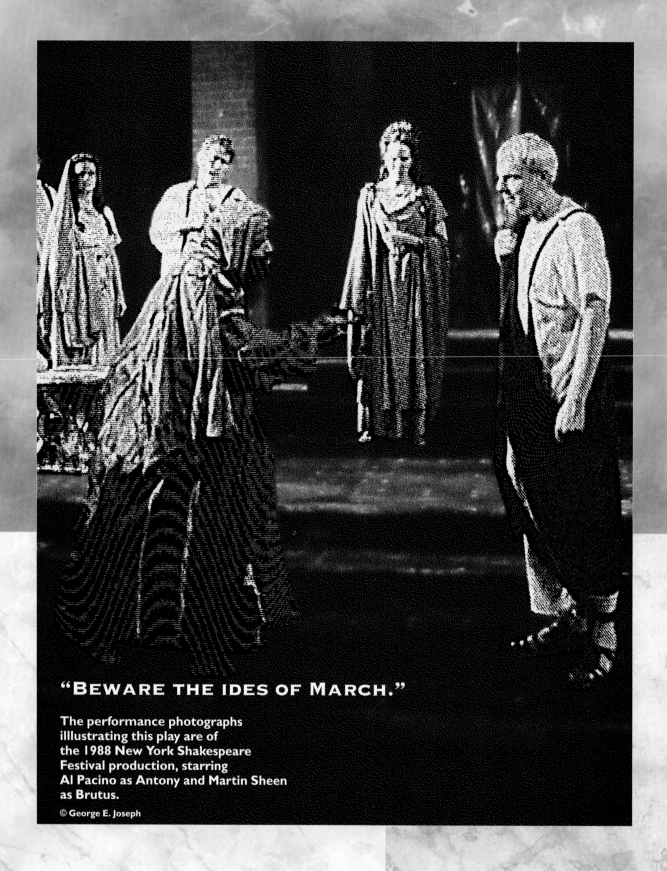

"BEWARE THE IDES OF MARCH."

The performance photographs illustrating this play are of the 1988 New York Shakespeare Festival production, starring Al Pacino as Antony and Martin Sheen as Brutus.

Soothsayer.
Beware the ides of March.
Caesar.
He is a dreamer, let us leave him. Pass.

[*Sennet.*° *Exeunt all except* BRUTUS *and* CASSIUS.]

Cassius.
Will you go see the order of the course?
Brutus. Not I.
Cassius. I pray you do.
Brutus.
I am not gamesome: I do lack some part
Of that quick spirit that is in Antony.
Let me not hinder, Cassius, your desires;
I'll leave you.
Cassius.
Brutus, I do observe you now of late;
I have not from your eyes that gentleness
And show of love as I was wont to have;
You bear too stubborn and too strange a hand°
Over your friend that loves you.
Brutus. Cassius,
Be not deceived: if I have veiled my look,
I turn the trouble of my countenance
Merely° upon myself. Vexèd I am
Of late with passions of some difference,°
Conceptions only proper to myself,
Which give some soil,° perhaps, to my behaviors;
But let not therefore my good friends be grieved
(Among which number, Cassius, be you one)
Nor construe° any further my neglect
Than that poor Brutus, with himself at war,
Forgets the shows of love to other men.
Cassius.
Then, Brutus, I have much mistook your passion,°
By means whereof this breast of mine hath buried
Thoughts of great value, worthy cogitations.°
Tell me, good Brutus, can you see your face?
Brutus.
No, Cassius; for the eye sees not itself
But by reflection, by some other things.
Cassius.
'Tis just:°
And it is very much lamented, Brutus,
That you have no such mirrors as will turn
Your hidden worthiness into your eye,

Sennet: flourish, or fanfare of trumpets announcing a ceremonial entrance or exit.

? ***Stage direction.*** *Except for Brutus and Cassius, the stage is empty for a few moments as they stand looking at the departing Caesar. The action line of the play—the assassination—begins now with Cassius's rather casual question (line 25). How should Brutus answer?*

35. You . . . hand: Cassius is comparing Brutus's treatment of him with the way a trainer treats a horse.

39. Merely: wholly.

40. passions of some difference: conflicting feelings or emotions.

42. give some soil: stain or mar.

45. construe: interpret.

? **47.** *How does Brutus explain his behavior?*

48. passion: feeling.

50. worthy cogitations: reflections of great value.

54. just: true.

That you might see your shadow.° I have heard
Where many of the best respect° in Rome
(Except immortal Caesar), speaking of Brutus,
And groaning underneath this age's yoke,
Have wished that noble Brutus had his eyes.

Brutus.
Into what dangers would you lead me, Cassius,
That you would have me seek into myself
For that which is not in me?

Cassius.
Therefore, good Brutus, be prepared to hear;
And since you know you cannot see yourself
So well as by reflection, I, your glass°
Will modestly discover to yourself
That of yourself which you yet know not of.
And be not jealous on° me, gentle Brutus:
Were I a common laughter,° or did use
To stale with ordinary oaths my love
To every new protester,° if you know
That I do fawn on men and hug them hard,
And after scandal them;° or if you know
That I profess myself in banqueting
To all the rout,° then hold me dangerous.

[*Flourish*° *and shout.*]

Brutus.
What means this shouting? I do fear the people
Choose Caesar for their king.

Cassius. Ay, do you fear it?
Then must I think you would not have it so.

Brutus.
I would not, Cassius, yet I love him well.
But wherefore do you hold me here so long?
What is it that you would impart to me?
If it be aught toward the general good,
Set honor in one eye and death i' th' other,
And I will look on both indifferently;°
For let the gods so speed me, as I love
The name of honor more than I fear death.

Cassius.
I know that virtue to be in you, Brutus,
As well as I do know your outward favor.°
Well, honor is the subject of my story.
I cannot tell what you and other men
Think of this life, but for my single self,
I had as lief° not be, as live to be
In awe of such a thing as I myself.

58. shadow: reflection (of what others think of him).

59. respect: reputation.

? **60.** *How would Cassius say the parenthetical remark?*

68. glass: mirror.

71. jealous on: suspicious of.

72. common laughter: butt of a joke; object of mockery.

74. In other words, if he swore to love everyone who came along.

76. scandal them: ruin them by gossip.

78. rout: common people, the mob.

? **78.** *What, in sum, is Cassius telling Brutus here?*

Flourish: brief, elaborate music of trumpets.

? ***Stage direction.*** *The trumpet sounds offstage, and the crowd's roar is heard again. How would Cassius and Brutus react?*

? **80.** *This is what Cassius has wanted to hear. How should he deliver this speech?*

87. indifferently: impartially; fairly.

? **89.** *Brutus could sound noble here, or he could be played as foolishly idealistic, even priggish. How would you deliver this speech?*

91. outward favor: appearance.

95. as lief: just as soon.

I was born free as Caesar; so were you:
We both have fed as well, and we can both
Endure the winter's cold as well as he:
For once, upon a raw and gusty day,
The troubled Tiber chafing with° her shores,
Caesar said to me "Dar'st thou, Cassius, now
Leap in with me into this angry flood,
And swim to yonder point?" Upon the word,
Accout'red as I was, I plungèd in
And bade him follow: so indeed he did.
The torrent roared, and we did buffet it
With lusty sinews, throwing it aside
And stemming it with hearts of controversy.°
But ere we could arrive the point proposed,
Caesar cried "Help me, Cassius, or I sink!"
I, as Aeneas,° our great ancestor,
Did from the flames of Troy upon his shoulder
The old Anchises bear, so from the waves of Tiber
Did I the tired Caesar. And this man
Is now become a god, and Cassius is
A wretched creature, and must bend his body
If Caesar carelessly but nod on him.
He had a fever when he was in Spain,
And when the fit was on him, I did mark
How he did shake; 'tis true, this god did shake.
His coward lips did from their color fly,
And that same eye whose bend doth awe the world
Did lose his luster; I did hear him groan;
Ay, and that tongue of his, that bade the Romans
Mark him and write his speeches in their books,
Alas, it cried, "Give me some drink, Titinius,"
As a sick girl. Ye gods! It doth amaze me,
A man of such a feeble temper should
So get the start of the majestic world,
And bear the palm° alone.

[*Shout. Flourish.*]

Brutus.
Another general shout?
I do believe that these applauses are
For some new honors that are heaped on Caesar.

Cassius.
Why, man, he doth bestride the narrow world
Like a Colossus,° and we petty men
Walk under his huge legs and peep about

? **97.** *This is a long and important speech. What is Cassius's chief complaint about Caesar?*

101. chafing with: raging against (the river was rough with waves and currents).

109. hearts of controversy: hearts full of aggressive feelings, or fighting spirit.

112. Aeneas (i·nē′əs): legendary forefather of the Roman people who, in Virgil's *Aeneid,* fled from the burning city of Troy carrying his old father on his back. (In many accounts of the legend, Romulus and Remus were descendants of Aeneas.)

? **118.** *How should Cassius say this last sentence?*

? **121.** *What word should be stressed here?*

131. bear the palm: hold the palm branch, an award given to a victorious general.

? **131.** *Why has Cassius told these anecdotes about Caesar? What is his point?*

136. Colossus: huge statue of Helios that was said to straddle the entrance to the harbor at Rhodes, an island in the Aegean Sea. The statue, so huge that ships passed under its legs, was one of the Seven Wonders of the Ancient World. It was destroyed by an earthquake in 224 B.C.

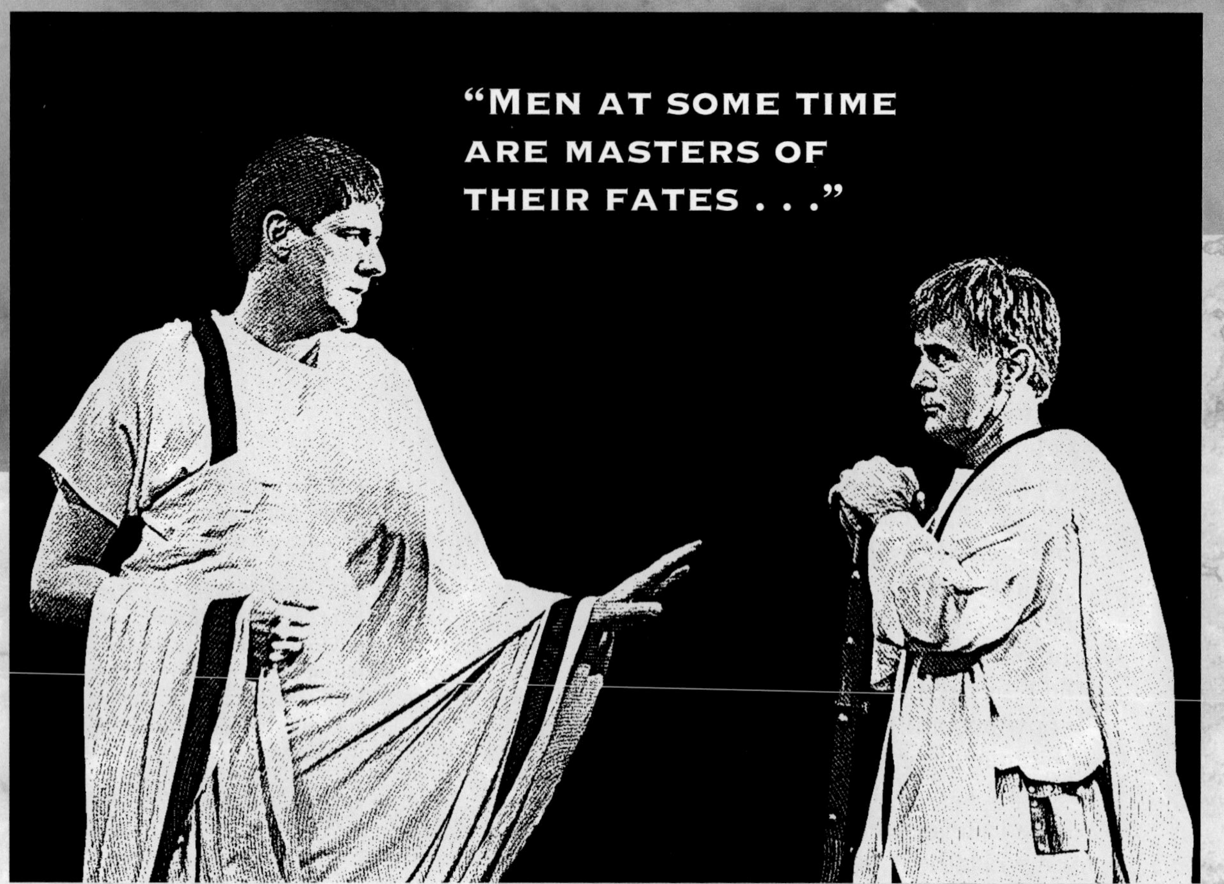
"MEN AT SOME TIME
ARE MASTERS OF
THEIR FATES . . ."

To find ourselves dishonorable graves.
Men at some time are masters of their fates:
The fault, dear Brutus, is not in our stars,°
But in ourselves, that we are underlings.
Brutus and Caesar: what should be in that "Caesar"?
Why should that name be sounded more than yours?
Write them together, yours is as fair a name;
Sound them, it doth become the mouth as well;
Weigh them, it is as heavy; conjure with 'em,
"Brutus" will start a spirit as soon as "Caesar."
Now, in the names of all the gods at once,
Upon what meat doth this our Caesar feed,
That he is grown so great? Age, thou art shamed!
Rome, thou hast lost the breed of noble bloods!
When went there by an age, since the great flood,°
But it was famed with more than with one man?
When could they say (till now) that talked of Rome,
That her wide walks encompassed but one man?
Now is it Rome indeed, and room° enough,

140. stars: Elizabethans believed that one's life was governed by the stars or constellation one was born under.

? **142.** *There is often a pause here, after the Colossus metaphor. How would Cassius say the names "Brutus" and "Caesar"?*

152. the great flood: flood sent by Zeus to drown all the wicked people on Earth. Only the faithful couple Deucalion and Pyrrha were saved.

156. Rome . . . room: a pun; both words were pronounced rōōm in Shakespeare's day.

When there is in it but one only man.
O, you and I have heard our fathers say,
There was a Brutus once that would have brooked°
Th' eternal devil to keep his state in Rome
As easily as a king.°

Brutus.
That you do love me, I am nothing jealous;
What you would work me to, I have some aim;°
How I have thought of this, and of these times,
I shall recount hereafter. For this present,
I would not so (with love I might entreat you)
Be any further moved. What you have said
I will consider; what you have to say
I will with patience hear, and find a time
Both meet° to hear and answer such high things.
Till then, my noble friend, chew upon this:
Brutus had rather be a villager
Than to repute himself a son of Rome
Under these hard conditions as this time
Is like to lay upon us.

Cassius. I am glad
That my weak words have struck but thus much show
Of fire from Brutus.

[*Enter* CAESAR *and his* TRAIN.]

Brutus.
The games are done, and Caesar is returning.

Cassius.
As they pass by, pluck Casca by the sleeve,
And he will (after his sour fashion) tell you
What hath proceeded worthy note today.

Brutus.
I will do so. But look you, Cassius,
The angry spot doth glow on Caesar's brow,
And all the rest look like a chidden° train:
Calphurnia's cheek is pale, and Cicero
Looks with such ferret° and such fiery eyes
As we have seen him in the Capitol,
Being crossed in conference by some senators.

Cassius.
Casca will tell us what the matter is.

Caesar. Antonius.

Antony. Caesar?

Caesar.
Let me have men about me that are fat,
Sleek-headed men, and such as sleep a-nights.
Yond Cassius has a lean and hungry look;

159. brooked: put up with.

161. This refers to an ancestor of Brutus who, in the sixth century B.C., helped to expel the last king from Rome and set up the Republic.

? **161.** *Why does Cassius mention Brutus's famous ancestor?*

163. aim: idea.

170. meet: appropriate.

? **177.** *According to Cassius's speech, how has Brutus delivered his previous line? Has Cassius gotten what he wants?*

? ***Stage direction.*** *Cassius and Brutus move downstage left to allow the procession (Caesar's train) to pass across the width of the backstage area to an entrance down right. In this way, the audience sees two acting areas at one time—one for the conspirators and their growing intimacy, and one for the pompous world of public ceremony. Would the two actors next speak openly, or are they already acting secretively?*

184. chidden: rebuked; corrected.

186. ferret: weasellike animal, usually considered crafty.

? **188.** *Cicero at this time is sixty-two years old, famous as a great advocate of the Republic. Though he had supported Pompey and opposed Caesar, Cicero liked Caesar personally and had nothing to do with the assassination. What does Brutus think of Cicero?*

? **190.** *Cassius and Brutus move away and we focus on Caesar, who casts a suspicious look at Cassius, now downstage left. What does Caesar's next speech tell you about Cassius's physical appearance?*

He thinks too much: such men are dangerous.

Antony.

Fear him not, Caesar, he's not dangerous;
He is a noble Roman, and well given.°

Caesar.

Would he were fatter! But I fear him not.
Yet if my name were liable to fear,
I do not know the man I should avoid
So soon as that spare Cassius. He reads much,
He is a great observer, and he looks
Quite through the deeds of men.° He loves no plays,
As thou dost, Antony; he hears no music;
Seldom he smiles, and smiles in such a sort°
As if he mocked himself, and scorned his spirit
That could be moved to smile at anything.
Such men as he be never at heart's ease
Whiles they behold a greater than themselves,
And therefore are they very dangerous.
I rather tell thee what is to be feared
Than what I fear; for always I am Caesar.
Come on my right hand, for this ear is deaf,
And tell me truly what thou think'st of him.

[*Sennet. Exeunt* CAESAR *and his* TRAIN.]

Casca.

You pulled me by the cloak; would you speak with me?

Brutus.

Ay, Casca; tell us what hath chanced today,
That Caesar looks so sad.°

Casca.

Why, you were with him, were you not?

Brutus.

I should not then ask Casca what had chanced.

Casca. Why, there was a crown offered him; and being offered him, he put it by° with the back of his hand, thus; and then the people fell a-shouting.

Brutus. What was the second noise for?

Casca. Why, for that too.

Cassius.

They shouted thrice; what was the last cry for?

Casca. Why, for that too.

Brutus. Was the crown offered him thrice?

Casca. Ay, marry,° was't, and he put it by thrice, every time gentler than other; and at every putting-by mine honest neighbors shouted.

Cassius.

Who offered him the crown?

197. well given: well disposed to support Caesar.

203. In other words, he looks through what men *do* to search out their feelings and motives.

205. sort: manner.

? **212.** *Caesar's analysis of Cassius is accurate. Why does he fear Cassius? What does the speech tell us about Caesar himself?*

? ***Stage direction.*** *As the procession leaves through an upstage portal at left, Brutus pulls on the toga of Casca as he passes. Casca is rough and sarcastic. How is his sarcasm suggested in the following lines?*

217. sad: serious.

221. put it by: pushed it aside.

228. marry: a mild oath meaning "by the Virgin Mary."

Casca. Why, Antony.

Brutus.
Tell us the manner of it, gentle Casca.

Casca. I can as well be hanged as tell the manner of it: it was mere foolery; I did not mark it. I saw Mark Antony offer him a crown—yet 'twas not a crown neither, 'twas one of these coronets°—and, as I told you, he put it by once; but for all that, to my thinking, he would fain° have had it. Then he offered it to him again; then he put it by again; but to my thinking, he was very loath to lay his fingers off it. And then he offered it the third time. He put it the third time by; and still as he refused it, the rabblement hooted, and clapped their chopt° hands, and threw up their sweaty nightcaps,° and uttered such a deal of stinking breath because Caesar refused the crown, that it had, almost, choked Caesar; for he swounded° and fell down at it. And for mine own part, I durst not laugh, for fear of opening my lips and receiving the bad air.

Cassius.
But, soft,° I pray you; what, did Caesar swound?

Casca. He fell down in the market place, and foamed at mouth, and was speechless.

Brutus.
'Tis very like he hath the falling-sickness.°

Cassius.
No, Caesar hath it not; but you, and I,
And honest Casca, we have the falling-sickness.

Casca. I know not what you mean by that, but I am sure Caesar fell down. If the tag-rag people° did not clap him and hiss him, according as he pleased and displeased them, as they use to do the players in the theater, I am no true man.

Brutus.
What said he when he came unto himself?

Casca. Marry, before he fell down, when he perceived the common herd was glad he refused the crown, he plucked me ope° his doublet° and offered them his throat to cut. An° I had been a man of any occupation,° if I would not have taken him at a word, I would I might go to hell among the rogues. And so he fell. When he came to himself again, he said, if he had done or said anything amiss, he desired their worships to think it was his infirmity. Three or four wenches,° where I stood, cried "Alas, good soul!" and forgave him with all their hearts; but there's no heed to be

? **233.** *How would Brutus respond to this news about the crown?*

237. coronets: small crowns.

239. fain: happily.

244. chopt: chapped (raw and rough from hard work and the weather).
245. nightcaps: Casca is mockingly referring to the hats of the workingmen.
247. swounded: swooned or fainted.

? **250.** *How does Casca feel about the Roman mob?*

251. soft: wait a minute.

254. falling-sickness: old term for the disease we now call epilepsy, which is marked by seizures and momentary loss of consciousness.

? **256.** *What do you think Cassius means here?*

258. tag-rag people: contemptuous reference to the commoners in the crowd.

265. plucked me ope: plucked open. **doublet:** close-fitting jacket.
266. An: if. **man of any occupation:** working man.

271. wenches: girls or young women.

taken of them; if Caesar had stabbed their mothers, they would have done no less.

Brutus.
And after that, he came thus sad away?

Casca. Ay.

Cassius.
Did Cicero say anything?

Casca. Ay, he spoke Greek.

Cassius. To what effect?

Casca. Nay, an I tell you that, I'll ne'er look you i' th' face again. But those that understood him smiled at one another and shook their heads; but for mine own part, it was Greek to me. I could tell you more news too: Marullus and Flavius, for pulling scarfs off Caesar's images, are put to silence.° Fare you well. There was more foolery yet, if I could remember it.

Cassius. Will you sup with me tonight, Casca?

Casca. No, I am promised forth.°

Cassius. Will you dine with me tomorrow?

Casca. Ay, if I be alive, and your mind hold, and your dinner worth the eating.

Cassius. Good; I will expect you.

Casca. Do so. Farewell, both. [*Exit.*]

Brutus.
What a blunt fellow is this grown to be!
He was quick mettle° when he went to school.

Cassius.
So is he now in execution
Of any bold or noble enterprise,
However he puts on this tardy form.°
This rudeness° is a sauce to his good wit,°
Which gives men stomach to disgest° his words
With better appetite.

Brutus.
And so it is. For this time I will leave you.
Tomorrow, if you please to speak with me,
I will come home to you; or if you will,
Come home to me, and I will wait for you.

Cassius.
I will do so. Till then, think of the world.°

[*Exit* BRUTUS.]

Well, Brutus, thou art noble; yet I see
Thy honorable mettle may be wrought
From that it is disposed;° therefore it is meet
That noble minds keep ever with their likes;
For who so firm that cannot be seduced?
Caesar doth bear me hard,° but he loves Brutus.

? **275.** *Casca gets very sarcastic here. What does he think of Caesar?*

286. put to silence: silenced, perhaps by being dismissed from their positions as tribunes or by being exiled.

? **286.** *Why are Marullus and Flavius silenced? What does this tell you about Caesar?*

289. forth: previously (he has other plans).

296. quick mettle: lively of disposition.

299. tardy form: sluggish appearance.

300. rudeness: rough manner.
wit: intelligence.

301. disgest: digest.

307. the world: the state of affairs in Rome.

? **308.** *Why do you think Cassius uses the respectful* you *when talking to Brutus but then switches to the familiar* thou *here?*

310. In other words, he may be persuaded against his better nature to join the conspirators.

313. bear me hard: has a grudge (hard feelings) against me.

If I were Brutus now and he were Cassius,
He should not humor° me. I will this night,
In several hands,° in at his windows throw,
As if they came from several citizens,
Writings, all tending to the great opinion
That Rome holds of his name; wherein obscurely
Caesar's ambition shall be glancèd at.°
And after this, let Caesar seat him sure;°
For we will shake him, or worse days endure. [*Exit.*]

315. humor: influence by flattery.

316. hands: varieties of handwriting.

320. glancèd at: touched on.

321. seat him sure: make his position secure.

? **322.** *What is Cassius going to write in the letters to Brutus? What does he hope these letters will accomplish?*

Scene 3. *A street.*

Thunder and lightning. Enter from opposite sides CASCA *and* CICERO.

? ***Stage direction.*** *In Shakespeare's day, other than a drum roll or "thunder sheet," there was no way to reproduce the drama of nature onstage. How might the actors themselves suggest the threatening weather?*

Cicero.
Good even, Casca; brought you Caesar home?
Why are you breathless? And why stare you so?

Casca.
Are not you moved, when all the sway of earth°
Shakes like a thing unfirm? O Cicero,
I have seen tempests,° when the scolding winds
Have rived° the knotty oaks, and I have seen
Th' ambitious ocean swell and rage and foam,
To be exalted with° the threat'ning clouds;
But never till tonight, never till now,
Did I go through a tempest dropping fire.
Either there is a civil strife in heaven,
Or else the world, too saucy° with the gods,
Incenses them to send destruction.

3. all the sway of earth: all the principles that govern Earth.

5. tempests: storms.

6. rived: split.

8. exalted with: elevated to.

12. saucy: disrespectful; presumptuous.

? **13.** *How is Casca different here from the way he was depicted earlier?*

Cicero.
Why, saw you anything more wonderful?

Casca.
A common slave—you know him well by sight—
Held up his left hand, which did flame and burn
Like twenty torches joined, and yet his hand,
Not sensible of° fire, remained unscorched.
Besides—I ha' not since put up my sword—
Against° the Capitol I met a lion,
Who glazed° upon me and went surly by
Without annoying me. And there were drawn
Upon a heap a hundred ghastly° women,
Transformèd with their fear, who swore they saw
Men, all in fire, walk up and down the streets.
And yesterday the bird of night° did sit
Even at noonday upon the market place,
Hooting and shrieking. When these prodigies°

18. not sensible of: not sensitive to.

20. Against: opposite or near.

21. glazed: stared.

23. ghastly: ghostly; pale.

26. bird of night: owl (believed to be a bad omen).

28. prodigies: extraordinary happenings.

Do so conjointly meet, let not men say,
"These are their reasons, they are natural,"
For I believe they are portentous° things
Unto the climate° that they point upon.

Cicero.
Indeed, it is a strange-disposèd time:
But men may construe things after their fashion,
Clean from the purpose° of the things themselves.
Comes Caesar to the Capitol tomorrow?

Casca.
He doth; for he did bid Antonius
Send word to you he would be there tomorrow.

Cicero.
Good night then, Casca; this disturbèd sky
Is not to walk in.

Casca. Farewell, Cicero. [*Exit* CICERO.]

[*Enter* CASSIUS.]

Cassius.
Who's there?

Casca. A Roman.

Cassius. Casca, by your voice.

Casca.
Your ear is good. Cassius, what night is this?

Cassius.
A very pleasing night to honest men.

Casca.
Who ever knew the heavens menace so?

Cassius.
Those that have known the earth so full of faults.
For my part, I have walked about the streets,
Submitting me unto the perilous night,
And thus unbracèd,° Casca, as you see,
Have bared my bosom to the thunder-stone,
And when the cross° blue lightning seemed to open
The breast of heaven, I did present myself
Even in the aim and very flash of it.

Casca.
But wherefore did you so much tempt the heavens?
It is the part° of men to fear and tremble
When the most mighty gods by tokens° send
Such dreadful heralds to astonish us.

Cassius.
You are dull, Casca, and those sparks of life
That should be in a Roman you do want,°
Or else you use not. You look pale, and gaze,
And put on fear, and cast yourself in wonder,

31. portentous: ominous.

32. climate: region or place.

? **32.** *Shakespeare often uses disorder in nature to suggest a nation's disorder. What does Casca think?*

35. Clean from the purpose: contrary to the real meaning.

? **35.** *How does the aged Cicero respond to Casca's report?*

? **43.** *Can you explain Cassius's response to the disordered night?*

48. unbracèd: with his jacket unfastened.

50. cross: jagged.

54. part: role.

55. tokens: signs.

58. want: lack.

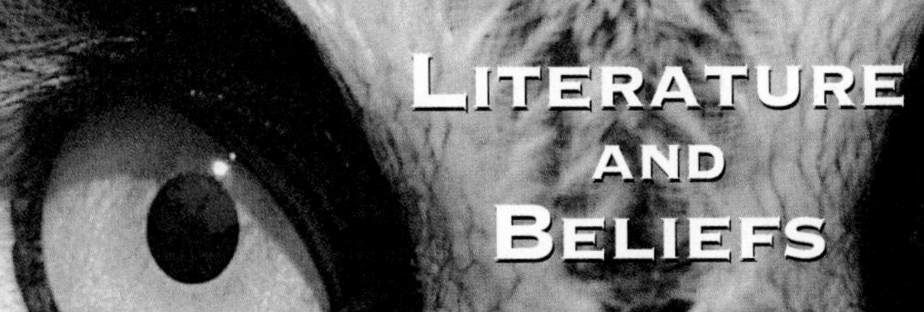

The Uses of Superstition

At the time of Julius Caesar, just about everyone believed in magic, omens, and revelations.

The Romans examined everyday occurrences for forewarnings of good and evil. For example, they believed that the sound of a distant storm or a rooster crowing in the night could affect the outcome of a personal matter or even a political event. Politicians believed so strongly in signs that they created a site in Rome's Capitol where they could consult specialists.

Many people thought that animals were the spirits of their dead ancestors. Therefore, the physical characteristics and actions of certain animals were seen as signs of protection and warning. Ravens, owls, and crows supposedly revealed signs through their calls. Other meanings were taken from the flight of eagles, vultures, and buzzards.

Animals were killed and offered as sacrifices to the gods. Their entrails were examined by a *haruspex* (hə·rus′peks′), a soothsayer who specialized in foretelling events by studying internal organs. Abnormalities—imperfections and deformities in color, shape, or position—indicated the anger of a particular god.

The commanders of Roman military fleets counted on "sacred" chickens to predict success in battle. If the chickens ate vigorously and dropped food from their beaks on the morning of battle, all would go well in combat. If the chickens did not eat, the signs were unfavorable. One commander whose sacred chickens refused to eat at sea threw them overboard. "If they won't eat, let them drink!" he said. The commander lost the battle.

The owl was considered a bad omen. Once, when an owl flew into Rome's Capitol, the Romans were so upset that they carefully scrubbed the building with water and sulfur to drive out the owl's supposed evil influences.

Solar eclipses were interpreted as supernatural and as omens of disaster. Speaking about an eclipse as a natural occurrence was against the law. Lightning was also seen as a bad omen. Even dreams were seen as messages from the gods.

As odd as all this may seem to us today, during Julius Caesar's time these superstitions were believed by everyone from the ruling classes to the common people.

To see the strange impatience of the heavens;
But if you would consider the true cause
Why all these fires, why all these gliding ghosts,
Why birds and beasts from quality and kind,°
Why old men, fools, and children calculate,°
Why all these things change from their ordinance,°
Their natures and preformèd faculties,°
To monstrous quality,° why, you shall find
That heaven hath infused them with these spirits°
To make them instruments of fear and warning
Unto some monstrous state.
Now could I, Casca, name to thee a man
Most like this dreadful night,
That thunders, lightens, opens graves, and roars
As doth the lion in the Capitol;
A man no mightier than thyself, or me,
In personal action, yet prodigious° grown
And fearful, as these strange eruptions are.

Casca.
'Tis Caesar that you mean, is it not, Cassius?

Cassius.
Let it be who it is; for Romans now
Have thews° and limbs like to their ancestors;
But, woe the while!° Our fathers' minds are dead,
And we are governed with our mothers' spirits;
Our yoke and sufferance° show us womanish.

Casca.
Indeed, they say the senators tomorrow
Mean to establish Caesar as a king;
And he shall wear his crown by sea and land,
In every place save here in Italy.

Cassius.
I know where I will wear this dagger then;
Cassius from bondage will deliver Cassius.
Therein,° ye gods, you make the weak most strong;
Therein, ye gods, you tyrants do defeat.
Nor stony tower, nor walls of beaten brass,
Nor airless dungeon, nor strong links of iron,
Can be retentive to° the strength of spirit;
But life, being weary of these worldly bars,
Never lacks power to dismiss itself.
If I know this, know all the world besides,
That part of tyranny that I do bear
I can shake off at pleasure. [*Thunder still.*°]

Casca. So can I;
So every bondman in his own hand bears
The power to cancel his captivity.

64. from quality and kind: act against their natures.
65. calculate: prophesy or try to predict the future.
66. ordinance: natural behavior.
67. preformèd faculties: natural or normal qualities.
68. monstrous quality: unnatural condition.
69. spirits: supernatural powers.

? **72.** *How might Cassius's tone of voice change here?*

77. prodigious: monstrous.

81. thews: sinews or muscles.

82. woe the while!: too bad for our times!

84. Our yoke and sufferance: our burden and our timid acceptance of it.

? **89.** *Cassius's response to this news is usually played as one of anger. What is he probably holding in his hand?*
91. Therein: in other words, in the act of suicide.

95. be retentive to: restrain.

? **100.** *What is Cassius threatening to do?*
100. still: continues.

"THEREIN, YE GODS, YOU MAKE
THE WEAK MOST STRONG . . ."

Cassius.
And why should Caesar be a tyrant then?
Poor man, I know he would not be a wolf
But that he sees the Romans are but sheep;
He were no lion, were not Romans hinds.°
Those that with haste will make a mighty fire
Begin it with weak straws. What trash is Rome,
What rubbish and what offal,° when it serves
For the base matter to illuminate
So vile a thing as Caesar! But, O grief,
Where hast thou led me? I, perhaps, speak this
Before a willing bondman; then I know
My answer must be made.° But I am armed,
And dangers are to me indifferent.

Casca.
You speak to Casca, and to such a man
That is no fleering° tell-tale. Hold, my hand.
Be factious° for redress of all these griefs,
And I will set this foot of mine as far
As who goes farthest. [*They clasp hands.*]

Cassius. There's a bargain made.
Now know you, Casca, I have moved already
Some certain of the noblest-minded Romans
To undergo with me an enterprise
Of honorable dangerous consequence;
And I do know, by this° they stay for me
In Pompey's porch,° for now, this fearful night,
There is no stir or walking in the streets,
And the complexion of the element°
In favor's like° the work we have in hand,
Most bloody, fiery, and most terrible.

[*Enter* CINNA.]

Casca.
Stand close° awhile, for here comes one in haste.

Cassius.
'Tis Cinna; I do know him by his gait;
He is a friend. Cinna, where haste you so?

Cinna.
To find out you. Who's that? Metellus Cimber?

Cassius.
No, it is Casca, one incorporate
To° our attempts. Am I not stayed for,° Cinna?

Cinna.
I am glad on't. What a fearful night is this!
There's two or three of us have seen strange sights.

106. hinds: female deer. (The word also means peasants and servants.)

109. offal: garbage, especially the parts of a butchered animal that are considered inedible or rotten.

114. My answer must be made: I must later answer for my words.

? **115.** *Does Cassius seriously mean that Casca is a willing slave of Caesar's? What reaction is he looking for?*

117. fleering: flattering.

118. Be factious: Go ahead and organize a faction, or group, opposed to Caesar.

125. by this: by this time.

126. Pompey's porch: the entrance to a theater built by Pompey.

128. complexion of the element: appearance of the sky.

129. In favor's like: in appearance is like.

? **130.** *Cassius has begun his conversation with Casca by showing him his dagger and threatening suicide as a way to free himself from bondage. At what point does the conversation shift to an altogether different method of freeing himself?*

131. close: hidden.

136. incorporate to: bound up with. **stayed for:** waited for.

Cassius.
Am I not stayed for? Tell me.

Cinna. Yes, you are.
O Cassius, if you could
But win the noble Brutus to our party——

Cassius.
Be you content. Good Cinna, take this paper,
And look you lay it in the praetor's chair,°
Where Brutus may but find it; and throw this
In at his window; set this up with wax
Upon old Brutus' statue.° All this done,
Repair° to Pompey's porch, where you shall find us.
Is Decius° Brutus and Trebonius there?

Cinna.
All but Metellus Cimber, and he's gone
To seek you at your house. Well, I will hie,°
And so bestow these papers as you bade me.

Cassius.
That done, repair to Pompey's Theater.

[*Exit* CINNA.]

Come, Casca, you and I will yet ere day
See Brutus at his house; three parts of him
Is ours already, and the man entire
Upon the next encounter yields him ours.

Casca.
O, he sits high in all the people's hearts;
And that which would appear offense in us,
His countenance,° like richest alchemy,°
Will change to virtue and to worthiness.

Cassius.
Him, and his worth, and our great need of him,
You have right well conceited.° Let us go,
For it is after midnight, and ere day
We will awake him and be sure of him. [*Exeunt.*]

? **139.** *What is Cassius's mood?*

143. praetor's chair: chief magistrate's chair; Brutus's chair.

146. old Brutus' statue: the statue of Brutus's heroic ancestor.
147. Repair: go.
148. Decius: Decimus, a relative of Brutus.
? **148.** *What is Cassius asking Cinna to do?*
150. hie: hurry.

159. countenance: approval. **alchemy:** science that was supposed to change ordinary metals into gold.

162. conceited: Cassius is punning here. The word means both "understood" and "described in an elaborate figure of speech" (called a *conceit*).

"MEN AT SOME TIME ARE MASTERS OF THEIR FATES:
THE FAULT, DEAR BRUTUS, IS NOT IN OUR STARS,
BUT IN OURSELVES,
THAT WE ARE UNDERLINGS."

—CASSIUS, ACT I, SCENE 2
(LINES 139–141)

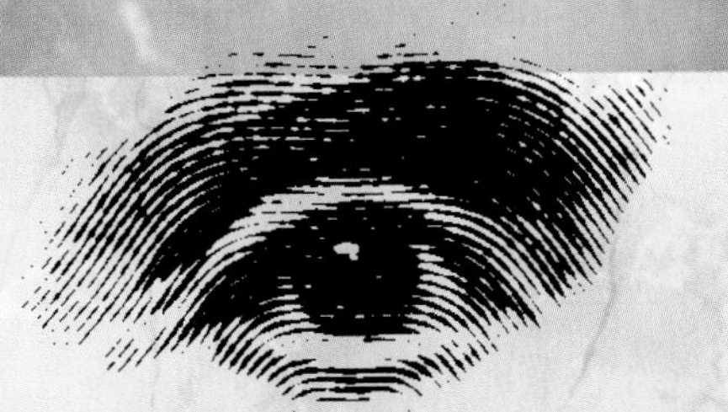

Making Meanings
Act I

First Thoughts

1. Can you think of any contemporary political leaders who are like Brutus and Cassius? Who are they?

Shaping Interpretations

2. Shakespeare uses nature to mirror the disorders in human lives. What details in Scene 3 do you think evoke a sense of danger and terror?
3. What is your impression of Cassius, the **protagonist** who drives the action in Act I? By the act's end, what steps has he taken toward his goal?
4. How would you describe the play's **conflict** as it is established in Act I?
5. A healthy republic requires a reasonably intelligent and responsive citizenry. How do the nobles in the play speak of the citizens of Rome? How do these remarks shape your feelings about the citizens?
6. How would you evaluate the **character** of Brutus? Is he strong, weak, or something in between? (Do all readers agree?)
7. Do you have conflicting feelings about Caesar during this act? Describe your impressions of his **character,** based on your responses to his speeches and actions and on what other characters say about him.

Reading Check

a. Why are the workers celebrating in Scene 1? Why does Marullus scold them?

b. What does the soothsayer tell Caesar in Scene 2? How does Caesar respond?

c. In Scene 2, how does Casca describe what happened when Caesar was offered the crown?

d. Caesar is a powerful ruler, yet he suffers from many infirmities. What are Caesar's infirmities?

e. At the end of Scene 2, what is Cassius planning to do to persuade Brutus to join the conspiracy against Caesar?

f. At the beginning of Scene 3, what do Cicero and Casca discuss? Why are they disturbed?

g. What happens to move the conspiracy plot forward at the end of Scene 3?

Extending the Text

8. Share with others some lines in this act that you think could be used to comment on current politics or politicians. (You might want to look back at your Quickwrite notes for page 774.)
9. What do you learn from this act about the moods and loyalties of the Roman people? What parallels can you draw between the Roman crowd and similar gatherings today?

Choices: Building Your Portfolio

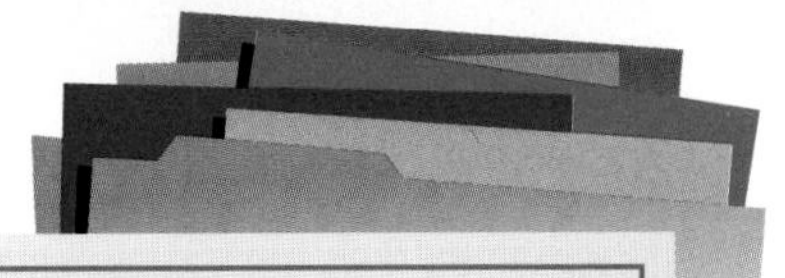

Writer's Notebook

1. Collecting Ideas for an Evaluation

Identifying persuasive techniques.

In the Writer's Workshop on page 892, you'll be asked to evaluate a piece of persuasion. **Persuasion** is the use of language to influence people to behave or think in certain ways. (For more on persuasion and its strategies, see pages 468–469.) You'll get a good idea of the power of persuasion if you examine Cassius's speeches in Act I, Scene 2, when he tries to persuade Brutus to turn against his friend and join the conspiracy against Caesar. Take notes on where the clever Cassius uses these **persuasive techniques:** specific **evidence, loaded words, repetition** for effect, appeals to self-interest. Save your notes.

Performance

2. By Their Words You Will Know Them

Cassius and Brutus are clearly going to be important figures in the play. What kind of men are they? With a partner, choose a section of their **dialogue** that reveals the character of each man. Then, prepare an **oral interpretation** of the conversation. Present your dramatic reading to the class, and be sure to ask for feedback.

Reading Skills and Strategies

Multiple Meanings: Recognizing Puns

Some people call puns juvenile humor, but Shakespeare's audiences enjoyed them. A **pun** is a word or phrase that means two different things at the same time. (Here's an old pun: "What is black and white and read all over? Answer: a newspaper.")

In the first scene of *Julius Caesar,* when the cobbler says he is a "cobbler," he plays on two meanings of the word. (In Shakespeare's day, the word could mean either "shoemaker" or "bungler.") The cobbler also puns on the meaning of *soles. Soles* refers to parts of shoes but also sounds exactly like *souls.*

Some puns are based on two meanings of a word (*cobbler*). Others involve **homophones,** words that sound alike but have different spellings and meanings (*soles/souls*).

Here are two of Shakespeare's puns in Act I:

1. ". . . all that I live by is with the awl . . ." (Scene 1, line 21)
2. ". . . I am . . . a surgeon to old shoes: when they are in great danger, I recover them." (Scene 1, lines 23–24)

Try It Out

You could map the puns used by the cobbler and show the jokes like this:

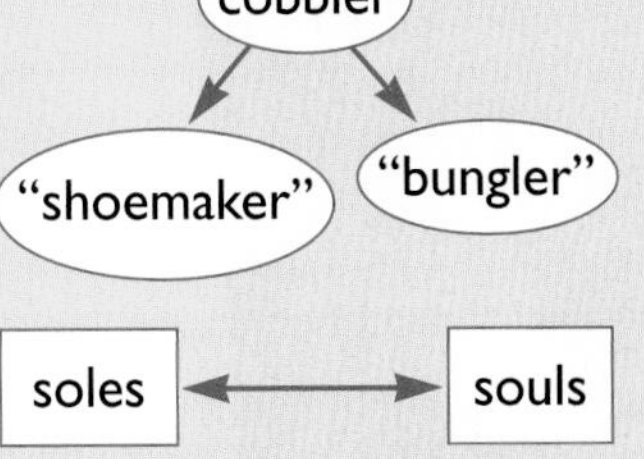

Make maps that explain the puns in the lines opposite.

Use these words to make other pun maps:

lie	flour
son	break

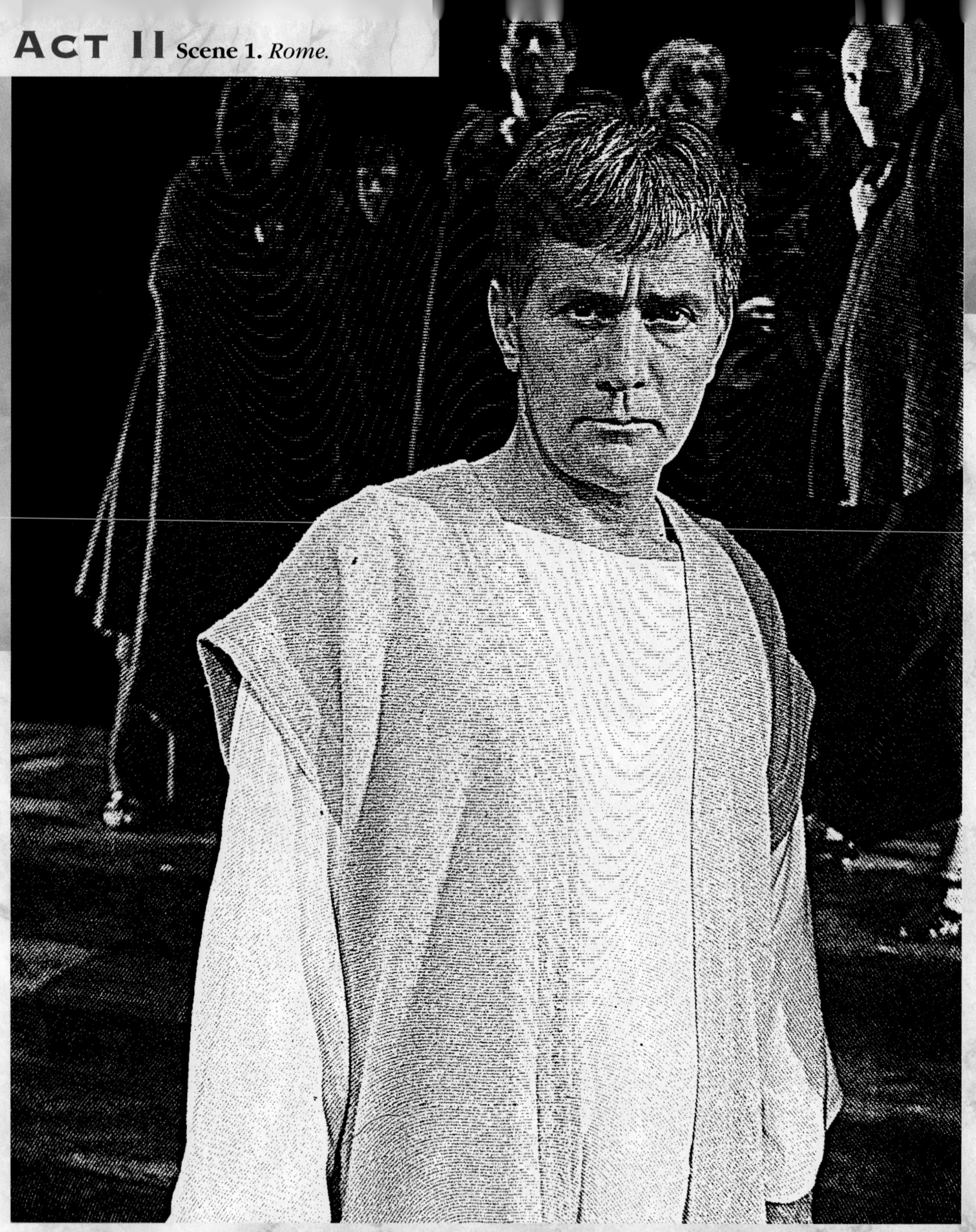

"HE WOULD BE CROWNED.
HOW THAT MIGHT CHANGE HIS NATURE,
THERE'S THE QUESTION."

Enter BRUTUS *in his orchard.*

Brutus.
What, Lucius, ho!
I cannot, by the progress of the stars,
Give guess how near to day. Lucius, I say!
I would it were my fault to sleep so soundly.
When, Lucius, when? Awake, I say! What, Lucius!

[*Enter* LUCIUS.]

Lucius. Called you, my lord?
Brutus.
Get me a taper° in my study, Lucius.
When it is lighted, come and call me here.
Lucius. I will, my lord. [*Exit.*]
Brutus.
It must be by his death; and for my part,
I know no personal cause to spurn at° him,
But for the general.° He would be crowned.
How that might change his nature, there's the question.
It is the bright day that brings forth the adder,
And that craves° wary walking. Crown him that,
And then I grant we put a sting in him
That at his will he may do danger with.
Th' abuse of greatness is when it disjoins
Remorse° from power; and, to speak truth of Caesar,
I have not known when his affections swayed°
More than his reason. But 'tis a common proof°
That lowliness° is young ambition's ladder,
Whereto the climber upward turns his face;
But when he once attains the upmost round,
He then unto the ladder turns his back,
Looks in the clouds, scorning the base degrees°
By which he did ascend. So Caesar may;
Then lest he may, prevent.° And, since the quarrel°
Will bear no color° for the thing he is,
Fashion it thus:° that what he is, augmented,
Would run to these and these extremities;
And therefore think him as a serpent's egg
Which hatched, would as his kind grow mischievous,
And kill him in the shell.

[*Enter* LUCIUS.]

Lucius.
The taper burneth in your closet,° sir.
Searching the window for a flint, I found
This paper thus sealed up, and I am sure
It did not lie there when I went to bed.

? ***Stage direction.*** *Brutus's garden often has a set of steps in the back, set in a half-circle. Below the steps is a stone bench. On the right and left are the doorways of an impressive residence. The door to the left is the servants' entrance, where Brutus directs his call to Lucius. Why is Brutus so anxious about the time?*

7. taper: candle.

? **10.** *Whom is Brutus talking about in this soliloquy?*

11. spurn at: rebel against.

12. the general: the general good.

15. craves: demands.

19. Remorse: compassion.

20. affections swayed: emotions ruled.

21. common proof: matter of common experience.

22. lowliness: humility.

26. base degrees: low rungs of the ladder; also lower government offices and lower classes of people.

28. prevent: we must prevent it. **quarrel:** argument.

29. bear no color: bear no weight.

30. Fashion it thus: state the case this way.

? **34.** *According to Brutus, who is like a serpent's egg, and why?*

35. closet: small private room; study.

[*Gives him the letter.*]

Brutus.
Get you to bed again; it is not day.
Is not tomorrow, boy, the ides of March?

Lucius. I know not, sir.

Brutus.
Look in the calendar and bring me word.

Lucius. I will, sir. [*Exit.*]

Brutus.
The exhalations° whizzing in the air
Give so much light that I may read by them.

[*Opens the letter and reads.*]

"Brutus, thou sleep'st; awake, and see thyself.
Shall Rome, &c.° Speak, strike, redress.°
Brutus, thou sleep'st; awake."

Such instigations have been often dropped
Where I have took them up.
"Shall Rome, &c." Thus must I piece it out:
Shall Rome stand under one man's awe? What, Rome?
My ancestors did from the streets of Rome
The Tarquin° drive, when he was called a king.
"Speak, strike, redress." Am I entreated
To speak and strike? O Rome, I make thee promise,
If the redress will follow, thou receivest
Thy full petition at the hand of Brutus!

[*Enter* LUCIUS.]

Lucius.
Sir, March is wasted fifteen days.

[*Knock within.*]

Brutus.
'Tis good. Go to the gate; somebody knocks.

[*Exit* LUCIUS.]

Since Cassius first did whet me against Caesar,
I have not slept.
Between the acting of a dreadful thing
And the first motion, all the interim is
Like a phantasma,° or a hideous dream.
The genius and the mortal instruments°
Are then in council, and the state of a man,
Like to a little kingdom, suffers then
The nature of an insurrection.

? ***Stage direction.*** *Whose letter is this?*

? **40.** *Does Brutus know of the soothsayer's warning?*

44. exhalations: meteors.

47. &c.: read "et cetera." **redress:** correct a wrong.

54. Tarquin: Tarquinius Superbus, the last king of Rome.

? **58.** *What actions might Brutus engage in as he reads this message? What is his tone of voice at the end?*

65. phantasma: apparition; hallucination.

66. The genius and the mortal instruments: the mind (genius) and the emotions and physical powers of the body.

[*Enter* LUCIUS.]

Lucius.
Sir, 'tis your brother° Cassius at the door,
Who doth desire to see you.

Brutus. Is he alone?

Lucius.
No, sir, there are moe° with him.

Brutus. Do you know them?

Lucius.
No, sir; their hats are plucked about their ears,
And half their faces buried in their cloaks,
That by no means I may discover them
By any mark of favor.°

Brutus. Let 'em enter. [*Exit* LUCIUS.]
They are the faction. O conspiracy,
Sham'st thou to show thy dang'rous brow by night,
When evils are most free? O, then by day
Where wilt thou find a cavern dark enough
To mask thy monstrous visage? Seek none, conspiracy;
Hide it in smiles and affability:
For if thou path, thy native semblance on,°
Not Erebus° itself were dim enough
To hide thee from prevention.

[*Enter the conspirators,* CASSIUS, CASCA, DECIUS, CINNA, METELLUS CIMBER, *and* TREBONIUS.]

Cassius.
I think we are too bold upon° your rest.
Good morrow, Brutus; do we trouble you?

Brutus.
I have been up this hour, awake all night.
Know I these men that come along with you?

Cassius.
Yes, every man of them; and no man here
But honors you; and every one doth wish
You had but that opinion of yourself
Which every noble Roman bears of you.
This is Trebonius.

Brutus. He is welcome hither.

Cassius.
This, Decius Brutus.

Brutus. He is welcome too.

Cassius.
This, Casca; this, Cinna; and this, Metellus Cimber.

Brutus.
They are all welcome.
What watchful cares° do interpose themselves
Betwixt your eyes and night?

---

70. brother: brother-in-law; Cassius is married to Brutus's sister.

72. moe: more.

76. favor: appearance.

83. In other words, if you walk (path) in your true way.

84. Erebus: dark region of the Underworld.

? ***Stage direction.*** *Describe what the stage looks like right now. From what is said of the conspirators, how would you imagine they are dressed?*

86. too bold upon: too bold in intruding on.

98. watchful cares: cares that keep you awake.

Cassius. Shall I entreat a word?

[*They whisper.*]

Decius.
Here lies the east; doth not the day break here?
Casca. No.
Cinna.
O, pardon, sir, it doth; and yon gray lines
That fret° the clouds are messengers of day.
Casca.
You shall confess that you are both deceived.
Here, as I point my sword, the sun arises,
Which is a great way growing on° the south,
Weighing the youthful season of the year.
Some two months hence, up higher toward the north
He first presents his fire; and the high east
Stands as the Capitol, directly here.
Brutus.
Give me your hands all over, one by one.
Cassius.
And let us swear our resolution.
Brutus.
No, not an oath. If not the face of men,°
The sufferance° of our souls, the time's abuse°—
If these be motives weak, break off betimes,°
And every man hence to his idle bed.
So let high-sighted tyranny range on
Till each man drop by lottery. But if these
(As I am sure they do) bear fire enough
To kindle cowards and to steel with valor
The melting spirits of women, then, countrymen,
What need we any spur but our own cause
To prick° us to redress? What other bond
Than secret Romans that have spoke the word,
And will not palter?° And what other oath
Than honesty to honesty engaged
That this shall be, or we will fall for it?
Swear priests and cowards and men cautelous,°
Old feeble carrions° and such suffering souls
That welcome wrongs; unto bad causes swear
Such creatures as men doubt; but do not stain
The even virtue of our enterprise,
Nor th' insuppressive mettle of our spirits,
To think that or our cause or our performance
Did need an oath; when every drop of blood
That every Roman bears, and nobly bears,
Is guilty of a several bastardy°

? **100.** *How would you have the actors placed on stage as Brutus and Cassius huddle and the others talk?*

104. fret: interlace.

107. growing on: tending toward.

114. If not the face of men: Our honest faces should be enough.
115. sufferance: endurance.
time's abuse: abuses of the times.
116. betimes: at once.

124. prick: urge.

126. palter: deceive.

129. cautelous: deceitful.

130. carrions: people so old or sick they are almost dead and rotting.

138. of a several bastardy: of several acts that are not truly "Roman."

If he do break the smallest particle
Of any promise that hath passed from him.

Cassius.
But what of Cicero? Shall we sound him?
I think he will stand very strong with us.

Casca.
Let us not leave him out.

Cinna. No, by no means.

Metellus.
O, let us have him, for his silver hairs
Will purchase us a good opinion,
And buy men's voices to commend our deeds.
It shall be said his judgment ruled our hands;
Our youths and wildness shall no whit appear,
But all be buried in his gravity.°

Brutus.
O, name him not! Let us not break with him,°
For he will never follow anything
That other men begin.

Cassius. Then leave him out.

Casca.
Indeed, he is not fit.

Decius.
Shall no man else be touched but only Caesar?

Cassius.
Decius, well urged. I think it is not meet
Mark Antony, so well beloved of Caesar,
Should outlive Caesar; we shall find of° him
A shrewd contriver;° and you know, his means,
If he improve° them, may well stretch so far
As to annoy° us all; which to prevent,
Let Antony and Caesar fall together.

Brutus.
Our course will seem too bloody, Caius Cassius,
To cut the head off and then hack the limbs,
Like wrath in death and envy° afterwards;
For Antony is but a limb of Caesar.
Let's be sacrificers, but not butchers, Caius.
We all stand up against the spirit of Caesar,
And in the spirit of men there is no blood.
O, that we then could come by Caesar's spirit,
And not dismember Caesar! But, alas,
Caesar must bleed for it. And, gentle friends,
Let's kill him boldly, but not wrathfully;
Let's carve him as a dish fit for the gods,
Not hew him as a carcass fit for hounds.
And let our hearts, as subtle masters do,

149. gravity: seriousness and stability.

150. break with him: break our news to him, reveal our plan.

? **152.** *Why do they decide not to ask Cicero to join them?*

? **153.** *What kind of person does Casca seem to be?*

157. of: in.

158. shrewd contriver: cunning and dangerous schemer.

159. improve: make good use of.

160. annoy: harm.

164. envy: malice.

? **170.** *How do you think the actor playing Brutus should look when he speaks this sentence?*

Stir up their servants° to an act of rage,
And after seem to chide 'em. This shall make
Our purpose necessary, and not envious;
Which so appearing to the common eyes,
We shall be called purgers,° not murderers.
And for Mark Antony, think not of him;
For he can do no more than Caesar's arm
When Caesar's head is off.

Cassius. Yet I fear him;
For in the ingrafted° love he bears to Caesar——

Brutus.
Alas, good Cassius, do not think of him.
If he love Caesar, all that he can do
Is to himself—take thought° and die for Caesar.
And that were much he should,° for he is given
To sports, to wildness, and much company.

Trebonius.
There is no fear in him;° let him not die,
For he will live and laugh at this hereafter.

[*Clock strikes.*]

Brutus.
Peace! Count the clock.

Cassius. The clock hath stricken three.

Trebonius.
'Tis time to part.

Cassius. But it is doubtful yet
Whether Caesar will come forth today or no;
For he is superstitious grown of late,
Quite from the main° opinion he held once
Of fantasy, of dreams, and ceremonies.°
It may be these apparent prodigies,°
The unaccustomed terror of this night,
And the persuasion of his augurers°
May hold him from the Capitol today.

Decius.
Never fear that. If he be so resolved,
I can o'ersway him; for he loves to hear
That unicorns may be betrayed with trees,
And bears with glasses, elephants with holes,
Lions with toils, and men with flatterers;
But when I tell him he hates flatterers,
He says he does, being then most flatterèd.
Let me work;
For I can give his humor° the true bent,
And I will bring him to the Capitol.

Cassius.
Nay, we will all of us be there to fetch him.

176. servants: the hands or the emotions.

180. purgers: healers.

180. *What does Brutus want the public, or history, to think of him?*

184. ingrafted: firmly rooted.

187. take thought: take to thinking too much and become depressed.

188. In other words, that is too much to expect of him.

190. no fear in him: nothing to fear in him.

191. *What do Brutus, Cassius, and Trebonius think of Antony?*

196. main: strong.

197. ceremonies: ceremonial rituals undertaken to determine the future, usually from the examination of signs in the entrails of slaughtered animals.

198. prodigies: disasters.

200. augurers: those who foretell the future.

210. humor: mood.

211. *According to Decius, what sort of man is Caesar? (What do you think of people like Decius?)*

Brutus.
By the eighth hour; is that the uttermost?°
Cinna.
Be that the uttermost, and fail not then.
Metellus.
Caius Ligarius doth bear Caesar hard,
Who rated° him for speaking well of Pompey.
I wonder none of you have thought of him.
Brutus.
Now, good Metellus, go along by him.°
He loves me well, and I have given him reasons;
Send him but hither, and I'll fashion him.
Cassius.
The morning comes upon 's; we'll leave you, Brutus.
And, friends, disperse yourselves; but all remember
What you have said, and show yourselves true Romans.
Brutus.
Good gentlemen, look fresh and merrily.
Let not our looks put on° our purposes,
But bear it as our Roman actors do,
With untired spirits and formal constancy.°
And so good morrow to you every one.

[*Exeunt all except* BRUTUS.]

Boy! Lucius! Fast asleep? It is no matter;
Enjoy the honey-heavy dew of slumber.
Thou hast no figures nor no fantasies°
Which busy care draws in the brains of men;
Therefore thou sleep'st so sound.

[*Enter* PORTIA.]

Portia. Brutus, my lord.
Brutus.
Portia, what mean you? Wherefore rise you now?
It is not for your health thus to commit
Your weak condition to the raw cold morning.
Portia.
Nor for yours neither. Y'have ungently, Brutus,
Stole from my bed; and yesternight at supper
You suddenly arose and walked about,
Musing and sighing, with your arms across;°
And when I asked you what the matter was,
You stared upon me with ungentle looks.
I urged you further; then you scratched your head,
And too impatiently stamped with your foot.
Yet I insisted, yet you answered not,
But with an angry wafter° of your hand
Gave sign for me to leave you. So I did,

213. uttermost: latest.

216. rated: berated; scolded.

218. him: his house.

? **221.** *How would you use lighting here to suggest the time?*

225. put on: display.

227. formal constancy: consistent good conduct.

231. figures . . . fantasies: figments of the imagination.

240. arms across: crossed arms, a sign of melancholy or depression in Shakespeare's day.

246. wafter: wave.

Fearing to strengthen that impatience
Which seemed too much enkindled, and withal°
Hoping it was but an effect of humor,°
Which sometime hath his hour with every man.
It will not let you eat, nor talk, nor sleep,
And could it work so much upon your shape
As it hath much prevailed on your condition,
I should not know you Brutus. Dear my lord,
Make me acquainted with your cause of grief.

Brutus.
I am not well in health, and that is all.

Portia.
Brutus is wise and, were he not in health,
He would embrace the means to come by it.

Brutus.
Why, so I do. Good Portia, go to bed.

Portia.
Is Brutus sick, and is it physical°
To walk unbracèd° and suck up the humors°
Of the dank morning? What, is Brutus sick,
And will he steal out of his wholesome bed,
To dare the vile contagion of the night,
And tempt the rheumy and unpurgèd air°
To add unto his sickness? No, my Brutus;
You have some sick offense within your mind,
Which by the right and virtue of my place
I ought to know of; and upon my knees
I charm° you, by my once commended beauty,
By all your vows of love, and that great vow
Which did incorporate and make us one,
That you unfold to me, your self, your half,
Why you are heavy,° and what men tonight
Have had resort to you; for here have been
Some six or seven, who did hide their faces
Even from darkness.

Brutus. Kneel not, gentle Portia.

Portia.
I should not need, if you were gentle Brutus.
Within the bond of marriage, tell me, Brutus,
Is it excepted° I should know no secrets
That appertain to you? Am I your self
But, as it were, in sort or limitation,
To keep with you at meals, comfort your bed,
And talk to you sometimes? Dwell I but in the suburbs
Of your good pleasure? If it be no more,
Portia is Brutus' harlot, not his wife.

Brutus.
You are my true and honorable wife,

249. withal: also.

250. humor: moodiness.

? **256.** *Where would Portia be standing?*

? **260.** *Some directors have Portia come too close to Brutus, physically and emotionally, and have him break away here. What would Portia's actions be?*

261. physical: healthy.

262. unbracèd: with his jacket opened. **humors:** Here the word means dampness (of the air).

266. The night was supposed to be unhealthy, since the air was not purified (purged) by the sun.

? **270.** *What clue tells us what Portia does here? Is she becoming calmer or more agitated?*

271. charm: beg.

275. heavy: depressed (heavy-hearted).

? **278.** *What is Brutus doing here?*

281. excepted: made an exception that.

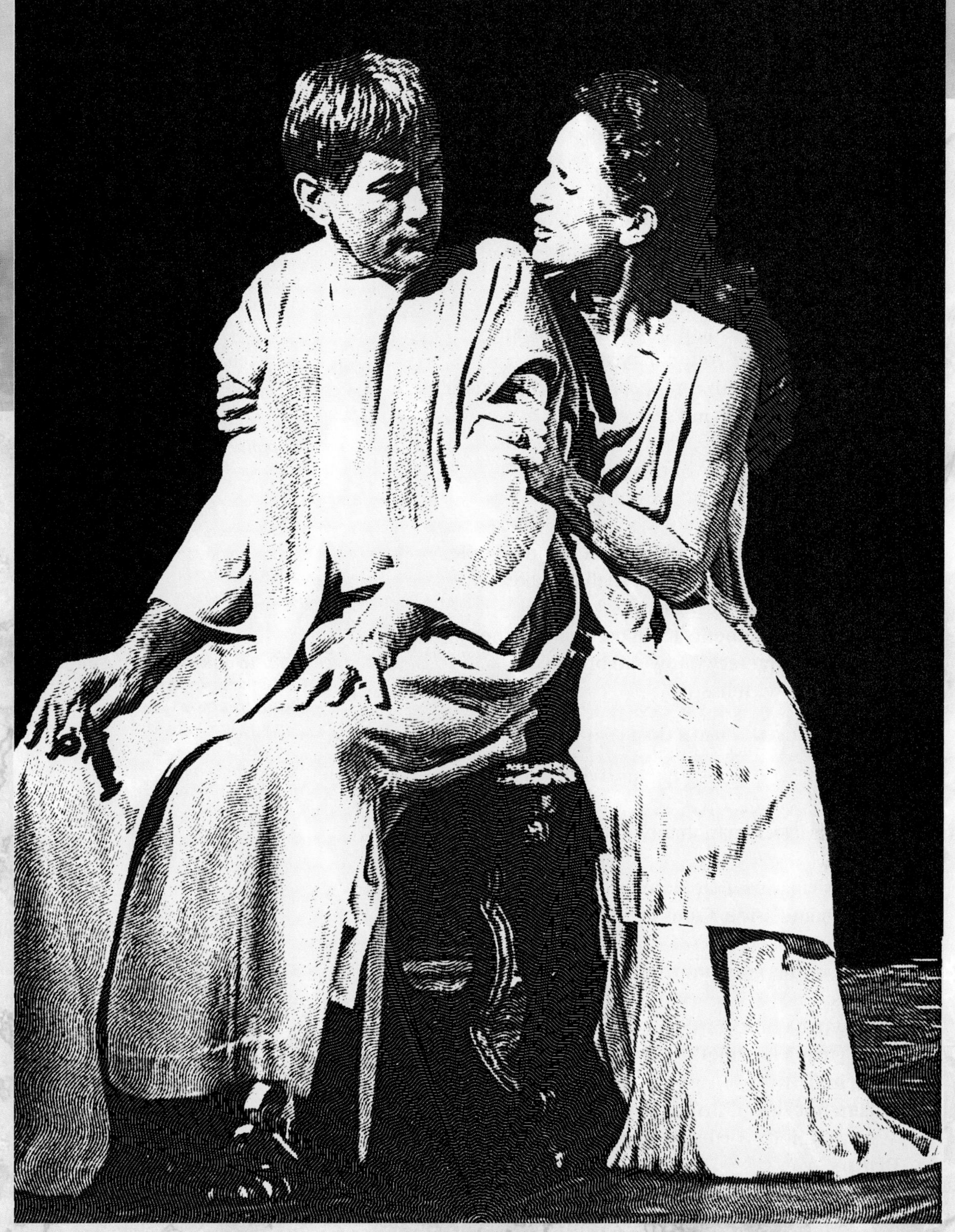

"DWELL I BUT IN THE SUBURBS
OF YOUR GOOD PLEASURE? IF IT BE NO MORE,
PORTIA IS BRUTUS' HARLOT, NOT HIS WIFE."

As dear to me as are the ruddy drops
That visit my sad heart.

Portia.
If this were true, then should I know this secret.
I grant I am a woman; but withal
A woman that Lord Brutus took to wife.
I grant I am a woman; but withal
A woman well reputed, Cato's° daughter.
Think you I am no stronger than my sex,
Being so fathered and so husbanded?
Tell me your counsels, I will not disclose 'em.
I have made strong proof of my constancy,
Giving myself a voluntary wound
Here in the thigh; can I bear that with patience,
And not my husband's secrets?

Brutus. O ye gods,
Render me worthy of this noble wife!

[*Knock.*]

Hark, hark! One knocks. Portia, go in a while,
And by and by thy bosom shall partake
The secrets of my heart.
All my engagements I will construe to thee,
All the charactery of my sad brows.°
Leave me with haste. [*Exit* PORTIA.]

[*Enter* LUCIUS *and* CAIUS LIGARIUS.]

Lucius, who's that knocks?

Lucius.
Here is a sick man that would speak with you.

Brutus.
Caius Ligarius, that Metellus spake of.
Boy, stand aside. Caius Ligarius! How?

Ligarius.
Vouchsafe° good morrow from a feeble tongue.

Brutus.
O, what a time have you chose out, brave Caius,
To wear a kerchief!° Would you were not sick!

Ligarius.
I am not sick, if Brutus have in hand
Any exploit worthy the name of honor.

Brutus.
Such an exploit have I in hand, Ligarius,
Had you a healthful ear to hear of it.

Ligarius.
By all the gods that Romans bow before,
I here discard my sickness! Soul of Rome,

295. Cato joined Pompey against Caesar and killed himself at the end to avoid living under the rule of a tyrant. He was a most respected man, famous for his integrity.

? **300.** *What does Portia suddenly do to prove her loyalty and strength of character? How do you think Brutus should respond?*

308. In other words, the meaning of all the lines written in his forehead (from worry).

313. Vouchsafe: please accept.

315. kerchief: scarf (it shows he is sick).

? **321.** *What action might he make with this line?*

"TELL ME YOUR
COUNSELS, I WILL NOT
DISCLOSE 'EM."

Brave son, derived from honorable loins,
Thou, like an exorcist, hast conjured up
My mortifièd° spirit. Now bid me run,
And I will strive with things impossible,
Yea, get the better of them. What's to do?

Brutus.
A piece of work that will make sick men whole.

Ligarius.
But are not some whole that we must make sick?

Brutus.
That must we also. What it is, my Caius,
I shall unfold to thee, as we are going
To whom° it must be done.

Ligarius. Set on° your foot,
And with a heart new-fired I follow you,
To do I know not what; but it sufficeth
That Brutus leads me on. [*Thunder.*]

Brutus. Follow me, then. [*Exeunt.*]

324. **mortifièd:** deadened.

331. **To whom:** to the house of whom. **Set on:** set off on.

Scene 2. *Caesar's house.*

Thunder and lightning. Enter JULIUS CAESAR *in his nightgown.*

Caesar.
Nor heaven nor earth have been at peace tonight:
Thrice hath Calphurnia in her sleep cried out,
"Help, ho! They murder Caesar!" Who's within?

[*Enter a* SERVANT.]

Servant. My lord?

Caesar.
Go bid the priests do present° sacrifice,
And bring me their opinions of success.°

Servant. I will, my lord. [*Exit.*]

[*Enter* CALPHURNIA.]

Calphurnia.
What mean you, Caesar? Think you to walk forth?
You shall not stir out of your house today.

Caesar.
Caesar shall forth. The things that threatened me
Ne'er looked but on my back; when they shall see
The face of Caesar, they are vanishèd.

Calphurnia.
Caesar, I never stood on ceremonies,°
Yet now they fright me. There is one within,
Besides the things that we have heard and seen,
Recounts most horrid sights seen by the watch.°

? ***Stage direction.*** *Thunder is a kind of actor in Shakespeare's plays. What mood does it evoke? Would you have this thunder sound alone, or would you have it serve as background noise for these speeches?*

5. **present** (prez′ənt): immediate.

6. **opinions of success:** opinions about the course of events.

13. **ceremonies:** again, a reference to the rituals of priests that were supposed to reveal omens of the future.

16. **watch:** watchman.

"WHEN BEGGARS DIE,
THERE ARE NO
COMETS SEEN . . ."

A lioness hath whelpèd° in the streets,
And graves have yawned, and yielded up their dead;
Fierce fiery warriors fought upon the clouds
In ranks and squadrons and right form of war,
Which drizzled blood upon the Capitol;
The noise of battle hurtled in the air,
Horses did neigh and dying men did groan,
And ghosts did shriek and squeal about the streets.
O Caesar, these things are beyond all use,°
And I do fear them.

Caesar. What can be avoided
Whose end is purposed by the mighty gods?
Yet Caesar shall go forth; for these predictions
Are to° the world in general as to Caesar.

Calphurnia.
When beggars die, there are no comets seen;
The heavens themselves blaze forth the death of princes.

Caesar.
Cowards die many times before their deaths;
The valiant never taste of death but once.
Of all the wonders that I yet have heard,
It seems to me most strange that men should fear,
Seeing that death, a necessary end,
Will come when it will come.

[*Enter a* SERVANT.]

What say the augurers?

Servant.
They would not have you to stir forth today.
Plucking the entrails of an offering forth,
They could not find a heart within the beast.

Caesar.
The gods do this in shame of cowardice:
Caesar should be a beast without a heart
If he should stay at home today for fear.
No, Caesar shall not. Danger knows full well
That Caesar is more dangerous than he.
We are two lions littered in one day,
And I the elder and more terrible.
And Caesar shall go forth.

Calphurnia. Alas, my lord,
Your wisdom is consumed in confidence.
Do not go forth today. Call it my fear
That keeps you in the house and not your own.
We'll send Mark Antony to the Senate House,
And he shall say you are not well today.
Let me, upon my knee, prevail in this.

17. whelpèd: given birth.

25. beyond all use: beyond all we are used to in our normal experience.

26. *Calphurnia can be played here as hysterical and overly emotional or as truly frightened for her husband. Which way do you think the part should be played?*

29. Are to: apply to.

31. *What does Calphurnia mean?*

37. *How does Caesar feel about death? How does his tone change when he addresses the servant?*

37. *The augurers were very important in ancient Rome. Their duty was to tell from certain signs whether some action was favored by the gods. Signs were read in the flights of birds, in thunder, in the way sacred chickens ate their food, and in the conditions of the organs of a sacrificial animal. What is Caesar's mood as he hears of the augury this morning?*

48. *Caesar could end this speech with pomposity, dignity, or even humor. How do you interpret his tone?*

54. *What is Calphurnia doing?*

Caesar.

Mark Antony shall say I am not well,
And for thy humor,° I will stay at home.

[*Enter* DECIUS.]

Here's Decius Brutus, he shall tell them so.

Decius.

Caesar, all hail! Good morrow, worthy Caesar;
I come to fetch you to the Senate House.

Caesar.

And you are come in very happy° time
To bear my greeting to the senators,
And tell them that I will not come today.
Cannot, is false; and that I dare not, falser:
I will not come today. Tell them so, Decius.

Calphurnia.

Say he is sick.

Caesar. Shall Caesar send a lie?
Have I in conquest stretched mine arm so far
To be afeard to tell graybeards the truth?
Decius, go tell them Caesar will not come.

Decius.

Most mighty Caesar, let me know some cause,
Lest I be laughed at when I tell them so.

Caesar.

The cause is in my will: I will not come.
That is enough to satisfy the Senate.
But for your private satisfaction,
Because I love you, I will let you know.
Calphurnia here, my wife, stays° me at home.
She dreamt tonight she saw my statue,°
Which, like a fountain with an hundred spouts,
Did run pure blood, and many lusty Romans
Came smiling and did bathe their hands in it.
And these does she apply for° warnings and portents
And evils imminent, and on her knee
Hath begged that I will stay at home today.

Decius.

This dream is all amiss interpreted;
It was a vision fair and fortunate:
Your statue spouting blood in many pipes,
In which so many smiling Romans bathed,
Signifies that from you great Rome shall suck
Reviving blood, and that great men shall press
For tinctures, stains, relics, and cognizance.°
This by Calphurnia's dream is signified.

56. humor: mood.

? **56.** *Here is a sudden change. Would a kiss between lines 54 and 55 explain it?*

60. happy: lucky.

? **65.** *Is Caesar angry or gentle?*

75. stays: keeps.

76. statue: pronounced here in three syllables (stat·u·a) for the meter.

80. apply for: explain as.

? **83.** *Remember what Decius is here for. We should sense his hungry absorption of Caesar's dream. How should he explain the dream—is he confident, fawning, awed, nervous?*

89. cognizance: identifying emblems worn by a nobleman's followers.

Caesar.
And this way have you well expounded it.

Decius.
I have, when you have heard what I can say;
And know it now, the Senate have concluded
To give this day a crown to mighty Caesar.
If you shall send them word you will not come,
Their minds may change. Besides, it were a mock
Apt to be rendered, for someone to say
"Break up the Senate till another time,
When Caesar's wife shall meet with better dreams."
If Caesar hide himself, shall they not whisper
"Lo, Caesar is afraid"?
Pardon me, Caesar, for my dear dear love
To your proceeding° bids me tell you this,
And reason to my love is liable.°

Caesar.
How foolish do your fears seem now, Calphurnia!
I am ashamèd I did yield to them.
Give me my robe, for I will go.

[*Enter* BRUTUS, LIGARIUS, METELLUS CIMBER, CASCA, TREBONIUS, CINNA, *and* PUBLIUS.]

And look where Publius is come to fetch me.

Publius.
Good morrow, Caesar.

Caesar. Welcome, Publius.
What, Brutus, are you stirred so early too?
Good morrow, Casca. Caius Ligarius,
Caesar was ne'er so much your enemy°
As that same ague° which hath made you lean.
What is't o'clock?

Brutus. Caesar, 'tis strucken eight.

Caesar.
I thank you for your pains and courtesy.

[*Enter* ANTONY.]

See! Antony, that revels long a-nights,
Is notwithstanding up. Good morrow, Antony.

Antony.
So to most noble Caesar.

Caesar. Bid them prepare within.
I am to blame to be thus waited for.
Now, Cinna; now, Metellus; what, Trebonius,
I have an hour's talk in store for you;
Remember that you call on me today;

? **91.** *There should be a pause here. Caesar's fate is about to be sealed. Does he seem relieved or amused?*

? **101.** *What reaction from Caesar is Decius seeking when he refers to "Caesar's wife"? How is Decius playing on Caesar's fears?*

103. proceeding: advancement.

104. liable: subordinate.

? **107.** *Suddenly Caesar changes his mind. Decius has succeeded. How would Calphurnia react now? Do you think Caesar concedes because he foolishly believes Decius, or because he heroically accepts his fate?*

? ***Stage direction.*** *What mood would the conspirators be in as they approach their victim?*

112. enemy: Ligarius had supported Pompey in the civil war and recently had been pardoned.

113. ague: fever.

? **113.** *Where else has Caesar mentioned that a character is lean?*

? **117.** *How can the actors playing Antony and Caesar establish the fact that a deep friendship exists between them?*

Be near me, that I may remember you.

Trebonius.
Caesar, I will (*aside*) and so near will I be,
That your best friends shall wish I had been further.

Caesar.
Good friends, go in and taste some wine with me,
And we (like friends) will straightway go together.

Brutus (*aside*).
That every like is not the same,° O Caesar,
The heart of Brutus earns° to think upon. [*Exeunt.*]

124. *Asides are addressed to the audience, out of hearing of the other actors. How would this aside be spoken?*

127. *What irony do you feel here? (What do we know that Caesar is ignorant of?)*

128. In other words, that those who appear to be friends are not really friends at all.

129. earns: grieves.

Scene 3. *A street near the Capitol, close to Brutus's house.*

Enter ARTEMIDORUS *reading a paper.*

Artemidorus. "Caesar, beware of Brutus; take heed of Cassius; come not near Casca; have an eye to Cinna; trust not Trebonius; mark well Metellus Cimber; Decius Brutus loves thee not; thou hast wronged Caius Ligarius. There is but one mind in all these men, and it is bent against Caesar. If thou beest not immortal, look about you: security gives way to conspiracy.° The mighty gods defend thee!

Thy lover,° Artemidorus."

Here will I stand till Caesar pass along,
And as a suitor° will I give him this.
My heart laments that virtue cannot live
Out of the teeth of emulation.°
If thou read this, O Caesar, thou mayest live;
If not, the Fates with traitors do contrive.° [*Exit.*]

7. In other words, a feeling of security gives the conspirators their opportunity.

9. lover: friend (one who loves you).

11. suitor: one who seeks a favor.

13. Out of the teeth of emulation: beyond the reach of envy.

15. contrive: plot or scheme.

Scene 4. *Another part of the street.*

Enter PORTIA *and* LUCIUS.

Portia.
I prithee, boy, run to the Senate House;
Stay not to answer me, but get thee gone.
Why dost thou stay?

Lucius. To know my errand, madam.

Portia.
I would have had thee there and here again
Ere I can tell thee what thou shouldst do there.
O constancy,° be strong upon my side;
Set a huge mountain 'tween my heart and tongue!
I have a man's mind, but a woman's might.

6. constancy: determination.

How hard it is for women to keep counsel!°
Art thou here yet?

Lucius. Madam, what should I do?
Run to the Capitol, and nothing else?
And so return to you, and nothing else?

Portia.
Yes, bring me word, boy, if thy lord look well,
For he went sickly forth; and take good note
What Caesar doth, what suitors press to him.
Hark, boy, what noise is that?

Lucius.
I hear none, madam.

Portia. Prithee, listen well.
I hear a bustling rumor like a fray,°
And the wind brings it from the Capitol.

Lucius.
Sooth,° madam, I hear nothing.

[*Enter the* SOOTHSAYER.]

Portia.
Come hither, fellow. Which way hast thou been?

Soothsayer.
At mine own house, good lady.

Portia.
What is't o'clock?

Soothsayer. About the ninth hour, lady.

Portia.
Is Caesar yet gone to the Capitol?

Soothsayer.
Madam, not yet; I go to take my stand,
To see him pass on to the Capitol.

Portia.
Thou hast some suit to Caesar, hast thou not?

Soothsayer.
That I have, lady; if it will please Caesar
To be so good to Caesar as to hear me,
I shall beseech him to befriend himself.

Portia.
Why, know'st thou any harm's intended towards him?

Soothsayer.
None that I know will be, much that I fear may chance.
Good morrow to you. Here the street is narrow;
The throng that follows Caesar at the heels,
Of senators, of praetors, common suitors,
Will crowd a feeble man almost to death.
I'll get me to a place more void,° and there
Speak to great Caesar as he comes along. [*Exit.*]

9. **counsel:** a secret.

? 9. *Is there a clue in this speech that Brutus has told Portia of the conspiracy to murder Caesar? Does the script provide an opportunity for him to tell her after their conversation in Scene 1? In "stage time" (the times at which the play's events take place), could he have told Portia of the plot?*

18. **fray:** fight.

20. **Sooth:** in truth.

37. **void:** empty.

Portia.

I must go in. Ay me, how weak a thing
The heart of woman is! O Brutus,
The heavens speed thee in thine enterprise!
Sure, the boy heard me—Brutus hath a suit
That Caesar will not grant—O, I grow faint.
Run, Lucius, and commend me to my lord;
Say I am merry; come to me again,
And bring me word what he doth say to thee.

[*Exeunt severally.*]

46. *What is Portia's state of mind? Why might she deliver line 45 after a pause?*

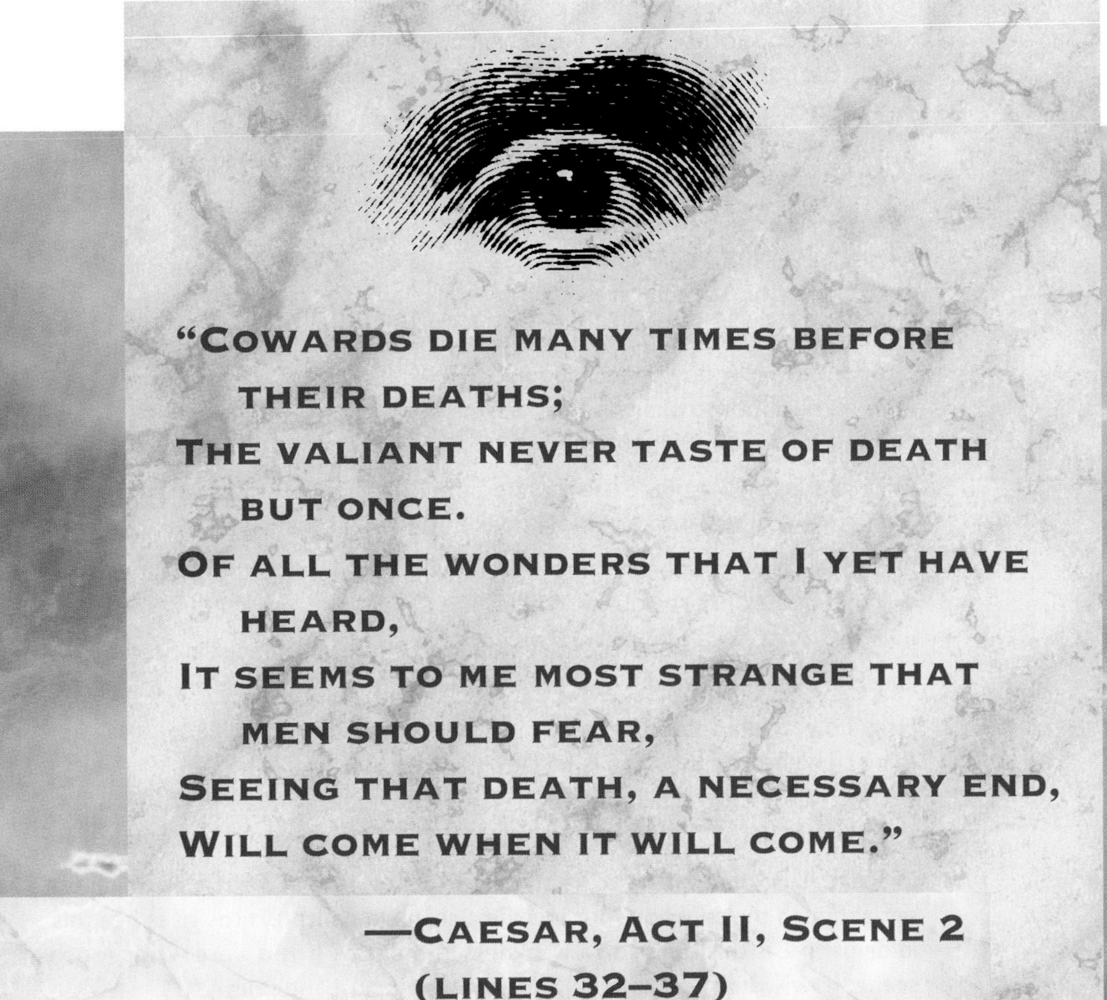

"COWARDS DIE MANY TIMES BEFORE
THEIR DEATHS;
THE VALIANT NEVER TASTE OF DEATH
BUT ONCE.
OF ALL THE WONDERS THAT I YET HAVE
HEARD,
IT SEEMS TO ME MOST STRANGE THAT
MEN SHOULD FEAR,
SEEING THAT DEATH, A NECESSARY END,
WILL COME WHEN IT WILL COME."
—CAESAR, ACT II, SCENE 2
(LINES 32–37)

Making Meanings
Act II

First Thoughts

1. We all look for principles to tell us what's right and what's wrong. What principles govern the choices Cassius and Brutus make? Do you think their choices are wise; are they "right"?

Shaping Interpretations

2. When you read rather than watch a play, you have to stage it in your imagination, to visualize the movements of characters and the sounds of voices. As you imagine Act II, tell how it compares with Act I—is the pace faster or slower? Are the characters calmer or more agitated? Which scenes make you think so?
3. Why won't Brutus swear an oath (Scene 1, lines 114–140)? What **character traits** does this speech reveal?
4. Describe the complexities of Caesar's **character.** How do you feel about him—is he a monstrous tyrant or a sympathetic man? Explain.
5. Where does Shakespeare use thunder and other storm sounds in the **setting** to suggest cosmic disorder? How does this weather make you feel?
6. Describe how Shakespeare creates and builds **suspense** during Scenes 3 and 4. What questions are you left with as the act ends?
7. Is Caesar's assassination necessary? Reread Brutus's argument in Scene 1, lines 10–34—how would you respond to it?
8. How do you feel about Portia's lament in her last speech: ". . . how weak a thing / The heart of woman is!"?

Challenging the Text

9. In Scene 4, Portia appears to know that Brutus is involved in a plot to kill Caesar, although the play does not include a scene in which Brutus gives her this information. Is this omission a weakness in the play? If you were writing such a scene, how would you have Portia react to her husband's news?

Reading Check

a. A **soliloquy** is a speech given by a character alone onstage. Look at Brutus's soliloquy at the beginning of Act II. What reasons does he give for killing Caesar?

b. Who proposes the murder of Antony? Why does Brutus oppose it?

c. What does Portia demand of her husband in Scene 1?

d. In Scene 2, what does Calphurnia try to persuade Caesar to do? Why?

e. How does Decius persuade Caesar to attend the Senate?

f. What is Portia's concern at the end of Scene 4?

CHOICES: Building Your Portfolio

Writer's Notebook

1. Collecting Ideas for an Evaluation

Critiquing a speech. One of the key tasks in evaluating a persuasive speech is determining if any parts of an argument are based on faulty reasoning. At the opening of Act II, Brutus has made up his mind to kill Caesar. The critic Mark Van Doren has said that Brutus's soliloquy is "riddled with rank fallacy. The fine man is a coarse thinker. . . ." **Fallacies** are mistakes in reasoning that lead to incorrect conclusions. Two common fallacies are **oversimplified explanations** and **hasty generalizations**—generalizations made from insufficient or bogus evidence. (For more on fallacies, see pages 468–469.) Review Brutus's first soliloquy in Scene 1. Note any fallacies in thinking that you find. Jot down explanations of why you think they are fallacies. Save your notes for the Writer's Workshop on page 892.

Performance

2. A Play-Within-a-Play

Caesar's scene with Calphurnia and later with Decius (Scene 2) is a perfect play-within-a-play. Prepare the scene for **dramatic performance.** Before you rehearse, be sure you understand the characters' motivations.

READING SKILLS AND STRATEGIES

Reading Elizabethan English

The English language classifies words as nouns, verbs, and so on. When someone mixes up the parts of speech, purists are outraged. (Today, for example, purists deplore the use of the noun *network* as a verb.) Shakespeare freely used words as different parts of speech. Here he makes a verb out of the noun *conceit:*

> You have right well conceited. . . .
>
> —Act I, Scene 3, line 162

Here he uses an adjective (*vulgar*) as a noun (we'd say "vulgar people"):

> . . . drive away the vulgar from the streets . . .
>
> —Act I, Scene 1, line 70

In some passages he omits words:

> . . . So Caesar may;
> Then lest he may, prevent. . . .
>
> —Act II, Scene 1, lines 27–28

What's understood here is ". . . prevent him from doing it."

Try It Out

Use the notes alongside the text of Act II for help with these questions.

1. In Scene 1, line 3, Brutus says he cannot "Give guess how near to day." How would you expand this phrase?
2. What word does Brutus omit after the word *general* in line 12 of Scene 1?
3. What do you think Lucius means in Scene 1, line 73, when he says the conspirators' "hats are plucked about their ears"?
4. In Scene 1, line 83, what noun does Shakespeare use as a verb?

ACT III Scene 1. *Rome. Before the Capitol.*

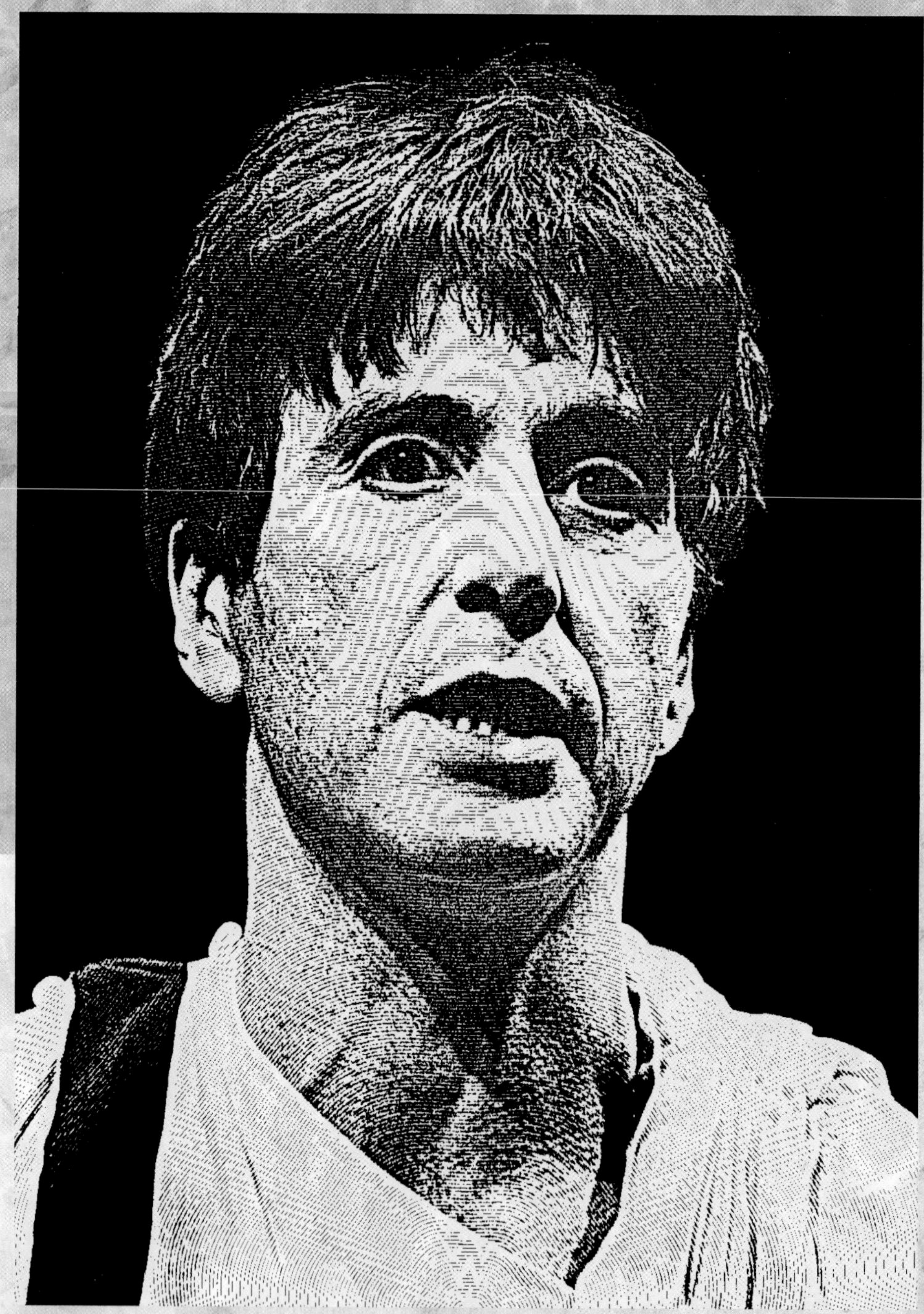

"FRIENDS, ROMANS, COUNTRYMEN, LEND ME YOUR EARS . . ."

—ANTONY, ACT III, SCENE 2 (LINE 75)

Flourish. Enter CAESAR, BRUTUS, CASSIUS, CASCA, DECIUS, METELLUS CIMBER, TREBONIUS, CINNA, ANTONY, LEPIDUS, ARTEMIDORUS, PUBLIUS, POPILIUS, *and the* SOOTHSAYER.

Caesar.
The ides of March are come.

Soothsayer.
Ay, Caesar, but not gone.

Artemidorus.
Hail, Caesar! Read this schedule.°

Decius.
Trebonius doth desire you to o'er-read,
At your best leisure, this his humble suit.

Artemidorus.
O Caesar, read mine first; for mine's a suit
That touches° Caesar nearer. Read it, great Caesar.

Caesar.
What touches us ourself shall be last served.

Artemidorus.
Delay not, Caesar; read it instantly.

Caesar.
What, is the fellow mad?

Publius. Sirrah,° give place.

Cassius.
What, urge you your petitions in the street?
Come to the Capitol.

[CAESAR *goes to the Capitol, the rest following.*]

Popilius.
I wish your enterprise today may thrive.

Cassius.
What enterprise, Popilius?

Popilius. Fare you well.

[*Advances to* CAESAR.]

Brutus.
What said Popilius Lena?

Cassius.
He wished today our enterprise might thrive.
I fear our purpose is discoverèd.

Brutus.
Look how he makes to° Caesar; mark him.

Cassius.
Casca, be sudden, for we fear prevention.°
Brutus, what shall be done? If this be known,
Cassius or Caesar never shall turn back,°
For I will slay myself.

Brutus. Cassius, be constant.°

? ***Stage direction.*** *This scene takes place on the Capitol Hill, where the Temple of Jupiter is located. A half-circle of steps is seen at the back of the stage, with a throne on top. A statue of Pompey is seen to the side—the enemy Caesar defeated in the recent civil war. Caesar walks to center stage and the others flank him. How should Caesar regard the soothsayer and Artemidorus? Should he address his first remark to the soothsayer or to the crowd in general?*

3. schedule: scroll of paper.

7. touches: concerns.

? **8.** *Is this sincerity or false humility?*

10. Sirrah: like "sir," but used to address an inferior, often intending disrespect or anger.

? **10.** *Publius speaks to Artemidorus, and the conspirators rush the petitioner away from Caesar. Whom is Cassius addressing in the next speech?*

? **13.** *Popilius speaks to Cassius. Do you think he knows about the conspiracy?*

18. makes to: makes his way toward.

19. prevention: being prevented from carrying out their deed.

21. turn back: come out alive.

22. constant: calm.

Popilius Lena speaks not of our purposes;
For look, he smiles, and Caesar doth not change.

Cassius.
Trebonius knows his time; for look you, Brutus,
He draws Mark Antony out of the way.

[*Exeunt* ANTONY *and* TREBONIUS.]

Decius.
Where is Metellus Cimber? Let him go
And presently prefer his suit to Caesar.

Brutus.
He is addressed.° Press near and second him.

Cinna.
Casca, you are the first that rears your hand.

Caesar.
Are we all ready? What is now amiss
That Caesar and his Senate must redress?

Metellus.
Most high, most mighty, and most puissant° Caesar,
Metellus Cimber throws before thy seat
An humble heart. [*Kneeling.*]

Caesar. I must prevent thee, Cimber.
These couchings° and these lowly courtesies
Might fire the blood of ordinary men,
And turn preordinance and first decree°
Into the law of children. Be not fond°
To think that Caesar bears such rebel blood
That will be thawed from the true quality°
With that which melteth fools—I mean sweet words,
Low-crookèd curtsies, and base spaniel fawning.
Thy brother by decree is banishèd.
If thou dost bend and pray and fawn for him,
I spurn thee like a cur out of my way.
Know, Caesar doth not wrong, nor without cause
Will he be satisfied.

Metellus.
Is there no voice more worthy than my own,
To sound more sweetly in great Caesar's ear
For the repealing of my banished brother?

Brutus.
I kiss thy hand, but not in flattery, Caesar,
Desiring thee that Publius Cimber may
Have an immediate freedom of repeal.°

Caesar.
What, Brutus?

Cassius. Pardon, Caesar; Caesar, pardon!
As low as to thy foot doth Cassius fall

? **26.** *Why is Trebonius getting Antony out of the way?*

29. addressed: ready.

? **29.** *What is happening near Caesar now?*

33. puissant (pyo͞o′i·sənt): powerful.

36. couchings: very low bows.

38. These were old Roman laws. Caesar warns that the laws might be changed at whim if they are not vigilant (just as the laws of children can be changed).

39. fond: so foolish as.

41. true quality: that is, firmness.

? **48.** *What is Caesar doing during this speech? What is Metellus doing in response to Caesar's words?*

? **51.** *Whom is Metellus addressing here?*

? **52.** *Brutus steps forward; notice that he uses the pronoun* thy *in an insulting way, since Caesar is not his social inferior, nor is the situation intimate. How might Caesar react to Brutus's surprising words?*

54. freedom of repeal: permission to return from exile.

To beg enfranchisement° for Publius Cimber.

Caesar.
I could be well moved, if I were as you;
If I could pray to move,° prayers would move me;
But I am constant as the Northern Star,
Of whose true-fixed and resting° quality
There is no fellow° in the firmament.
The skies are painted with unnumb'red sparks,
They are all fire and every one doth shine;
But there's but one in all doth hold his place.
So in the world; 'tis furnished well with men,
And men are flesh and blood, and apprehensive;
Yet in the number I do know but one
That unassailable holds on his rank,°
Unshaked of motion; and that I am he,
Let me a little show it, even in this—
That I was constant° Cimber should be banished,
And constant do remain to keep him so.

Cinna.
O Caesar——

Caesar. Hence! Wilt thou lift up Olympus?°

Decius.
Great Caesar——

Caesar. Doth not Brutus bootless° kneel?

Casca.
Speak hands for me!

[*They stab* CAESAR.]

Caesar.
Et tu, Brutè?° Then fall Caesar. [*Dies.*]

Cinna.
Liberty! Freedom! Tyranny is dead!
Run hence, proclaim, cry it about the streets.

Cassius.
Some to the common pulpits, and cry out
"Liberty, freedom, and enfranchisement!"

Brutus.
People, and senators, be not affrighted.
Fly not; stand still; ambition's debt is paid.

Casca.
Go to the pulpit, Brutus.

Decius. And Cassius too.

Brutus.
Where's Publius?°

Cinna.
Here, quite confounded with this mutiny.

Metellus.
Stand fast together, lest some friend of Caesar's

57. enfranchisement: restoration of the rights of citizenship.

59. pray to move: beg others to change their minds.

61. resting: changeless.

62. fellow: equal.

69. rank: position.

? **70.** *At what point in this speech would Caesar rise from his throne? The senators now rush in around Caesar and, in most productions, kneel before him. Casca has worked his way in back of Caesar.*

72. constant: firmly determined.

74. Olympus: in Greek mythology, the mountain where the gods lived.

75. bootless: in vain.

? **75.** *This line is often spoken to show Caesar's great fondness for Brutus. How else might it be spoken?*

? **76.** *What does this line mean? What is Casca doing?*

77. *Et tu, Brutè?*: Latin for "And you also, Brutus?"

? **77.** *The murder of Caesar has been staged in many ways. Low-budget productions have to worry about laundry bills for stained togas, but most productions show blood. In some productions, each dagger has attached to it a plastic capsule, which the actors break with their fingernails. In other productions, Caesar has a "blood" bag concealed under his toga. To stage the murder, directors often have the conspirators standing at different places on stage—all points to which Caesar runs in his attempt to escape. The last spot is Brutus's place. What does Caesar see as he utters his last words? Why does he say "Then fall Caesar"?*

85. Publius is a very old senator, too old to flee.

"LIBERTY, FREEDOM, AND ENFRANCHISEMENT!"

Should chance——

Brutus.
Talk not of standing. Publius, good cheer;
There is no harm intended to your person,
Nor to no Roman else. So tell them, Publius.

Cassius.
And leave us, Publius, lest that the people
Rushing on us should do your age some mischief.

Brutus.
Do so; and let no man abide° this deed
But we the doers.

[*Enter* TREBONIUS.]

Cassius.
Where is Antony?

Trebonius. Fled to his house amazed.
Men, wives, and children stare, cry out and run,
As it were doomsday.

Brutus. Fates, we will know your pleasures.
That we shall die, we know; 'tis but the time,
And drawing days out, that men stand upon.°

94. abide: take the consequences of.

100. stand upon: wait for.

Casca.
Why, he that cuts off twenty years of life
Cuts off so many years of fearing death.

Brutus.
Grant that, and then is death a benefit.
So are we Caesar's friends, that have abridged
His time of fearing death. Stoop, Romans, stoop,
And let us bathe our hands in Caesar's blood
Up to the elbows, and besmear our swords.
Then walk we forth, even to the market place,°
And waving our red weapons o'er our heads,
Let's all cry "Peace, freedom, and liberty!"

Cassius.
Stoop then, and wash. How many ages hence
Shall this our lofty scene be acted over
In states unborn and accents yet unknown!

Brutus.
How many times shall Caesar bleed in sport,
That now on Pompey's basis° lies along°
No worthier than the dust!

Cassius. So oft as that shall be,
So often shall the knot of us be called
The men that gave their country liberty.

Decius.
What, shall we forth?

Cassius. Ay, every man away.
Brutus shall lead, and we will grace his heels
With the most boldest and best hearts of Rome.

[*Enter a* SERVANT.]

Brutus.
Soft, who comes here? A friend of Antony's.

Servant.
Thus, Brutus, did my master bid me kneel;
Thus did Mark Antony bid me fall down;
And, being prostrate, thus he bade me say:
Brutus is noble, wise, valiant, and honest;
Caesar was mighty, bold, royal, and loving.
Say I love Brutus, and I honor him;
Say I feared Caesar, honored him, and loved him.
If Brutus will vouchsafe that Antony
May safely come to him and be resolved
How Caesar hath deserved to lie in death,
Mark Antony shall not love Caesar dead
So well as Brutus living; but will follow
The fortunes and affairs of noble Brutus
Thorough° the hazards of this untrod state

? **107.** *What are the conspirators doing now?*

108. market place: the Forum, center of public and commercial life in Rome.

115. basis: base (of Pompey's statue). **lies along:** stretches out.

? **118.** *These speeches can be delivered in various ways. Would you emphasize the self-righteousness of the conspirators or their idealism?*

136. Thorough: through.

With all true faith. So says my master Antony.

Brutus.

Thy master is a wise and valiant Roman;
I never thought him worse.
Tell him, so please him come unto this place,
He shall be satisfied and, by my honor,
Depart untouched.

Servant. I'll fetch him presently.°

[*Exit* SERVANT.]

Brutus.

I know that we shall have him well to friend.

Cassius.

I wish we may. But yet have I a mind
That fears him much; and my misgiving still
Falls shrewdly to the purpose.°

[*Enter* ANTONY.]

Brutus.

But here comes Antony. Welcome, Mark Antony.

Antony.

O mighty Caesar! Dost thou lie so low?
Are all thy conquests, glories, triumphs, spoils,
Shrunk to this little measure? Fare thee well.
I know not, gentlemen, what you intend,
Who else must be let blood,° who else is rank.°
If I myself, there is no hour so fit
As Caesar's death's hour, nor no instrument
Of half that worth as those your swords, made rich
With the most noble blood of all this world.
I do beseech ye, if you bear me hard,°
Now, whilst your purpled hands do reek and smoke,
Fulfill your pleasure. Live a thousand years,
I shall not find myself so apt to die;
No place will please me so, no mean of death,
As here by Caesar, and by you cut off,
The choice and master spirits of this age.

Brutus.

O Antony, beg not your death of us!
Though now we must appear bloody and cruel,
As by our hands and this our present act
You see we do, yet see you but our hands
And this the bleeding business they have done.
Our hearts you see not; they are pitiful;°
And pity to the general wrong of Rome—
As fire drives out fire, so pity pity—
Hath done this deed on Caesar. For your part,

? **137.** *What does Antony ask of Brutus?*

142. presently: immediately.

146. In other words, my misgivings or doubts are usually justified.

? **146.** *How does Cassius say this line? Notice that at this moment the play takes a turn and that the hunters now become the hunted.*

? **151.** *Where should Antony position himself? In this speech, where would you have the actor playing Antony pause? What movements or gestures would he make?*

152. Antony is punning here: "Let blood" can mean to bleed a sick person in order to cure the illness, or it can mean to shed blood (kill). **rank:** another pun—swollen with disease (and thus in need of bleeding), or swollen with power.

157. bear me hard: bear a grudge against me.

169. pitiful: full of pity.

To you our swords have leaden° points, Mark Antony:
Our arms in strength of malice, and our hearts
Of brothers' temper, do receive you in
With all kind love, good thoughts, and reverence.

Cassius.
Your voice shall be as strong as any man's
In the disposing of new dignities.°

Brutus.
Only be patient till we have appeased
The multitude, beside themselves with fear,
And then we will deliver you the cause
Why I, that did love Caesar when I struck him,
Have thus proceeded.

Antony. I doubt not of your wisdom.
Let each man render me his bloody hand.
First, Marcus Brutus, will I shake with you;
Next, Caius Cassius, do I take your hand;
Now, Decius Brutus, yours; now yours, Metellus;
Yours, Cinna; and, my valiant Casca, yours;
Though last, not least in love, yours, good Trebonius.
Gentlemen all—alas, what shall I say?
My credit° now stands on such slippery ground
That one of two bad ways you must conceit° me,
Either a coward or a flatterer.
That I did love thee, Caesar, O, 'tis true!
If then thy spirit look upon us now,
Shall it not grieve thee dearer than thy death
To see thy Antony making his peace,
Shaking the bloody fingers of thy foes,
Most noble, in the presence of thy corse?°
Had I as many eyes as thou hast wounds,
Weeping as fast as they stream forth thy blood,
It would become me better than to close
In terms of friendship with thine enemies.
Pardon me, Julius! Here wast thou bayed, brave hart;°
Here didst thou fall, and here thy hunters stand,
Signed in thy spoil and crimsoned in thy lethe.°
O world, thou wast the forest to this hart;
And this indeed, O world, the heart of thee.
How like a deer, stroken by many princes,
Dost thou here lie!

Cassius.
Mark Antony——

Antony. Pardon me, Caius Cassius.
The enemies of Caesar shall say this;
Then, in a friend, it is cold modesty.°

Cassius.
I blame you not for praising Caesar so;

173. leaden: blunt (not made of steel).

178. dignities: titles.

178. *What differences in character do Brutus and Cassius reveal here in replying to Antony?*

185. *This is a rather bold step on Antony's part. What is he doing? What is his motive?*

191. credit: reputation.

192. conceit: judge.

194. *What is Antony's position on stage now—is he standing or kneeling? Is he near the corpse or far away from it?*

199. corse: corpse.

204. Antony compares Caesar to a deer (hart) hunted down by barking (baying) hounds. "Brave hart" also is a pun on "brave heart."

206. In other words, marked with the wounds of your slaughter and reddened by your blood (compared with the river Lethe in the Underworld).

210. *Why is the imagery of the hunted deer (hart) so appropriate here? How does it make you feel about Caesar?*

213. modesty: moderation.

But what compact mean you to have with us?
Will you be pricked in number of° our friends,
Or shall we on, and not depend on you?

Antony.
Therefore I took your hands, but was indeed
Swayed from the point by looking down on Caesar.
Friends am I with you all, and love you all,
Upon this hope, that you shall give me reasons
Why, and wherein, Caesar was dangerous.

Brutus.
Or else were this a savage spectacle.
Our reasons are so full of good regard
That were you, Antony, the son of Caesar,
You should be satisfied.

Antony. That's all I seek;
And am moreover suitor that I may
Produce° his body to the market place,
And in the pulpit, as becomes a friend,
Speak in the order of his funeral.

Brutus.
You shall, Mark Antony.

Cassius. Brutus, a word with you.
(*Aside to* BRUTUS.) You know not what you do; do not consent
That Antony speak in his funeral.
Know you how much the people may be moved
By that which he will utter?

Brutus. By your pardon:
I will myself into the pulpit first,
And show the reason of our Caesar's death.
What Antony shall speak, I will protest
He speaks by leave and by permission,
And that we are contented Caesar shall
Have all true rites and lawful ceremonies.
It shall advantage more than do us wrong.

Cassius.
I know not what may fall;° I like it not.

Brutus.
Mark Antony, here, take you Caesar's body.
You shall not in your funeral speech blame us,
But speak all good you can devise of Caesar,
And say you do't by our permission;
Else shall you not have any hand at all
About his funeral. And you shall speak
In the same pulpit whereto I am going,
After my speech is ended.

Antony. Be it so;
I do desire no more.

216. pricked in number of: counted with. In counting off a list of people, the Romans would prick a hole in a wax-covered tablet.

228. Produce: take.

243. fall: befall; happen.

Brutus.
Prepare the body then, and follow us.

[*Exeunt all except* ANTONY.]

Antony.
O pardon me, thou bleeding piece of earth,
That I am meek and gentle with these butchers!
Thou art the ruins of the noblest man
That ever livèd in the tide of times.
Woe to the hand that shed this costly blood!
Over thy wounds now do I prophesy
(Which like dumb mouths do ope their ruby lips
To beg the voice and utterance of my tongue),

254. *How should Antony immediately change his tone? Whom is he talking to?*

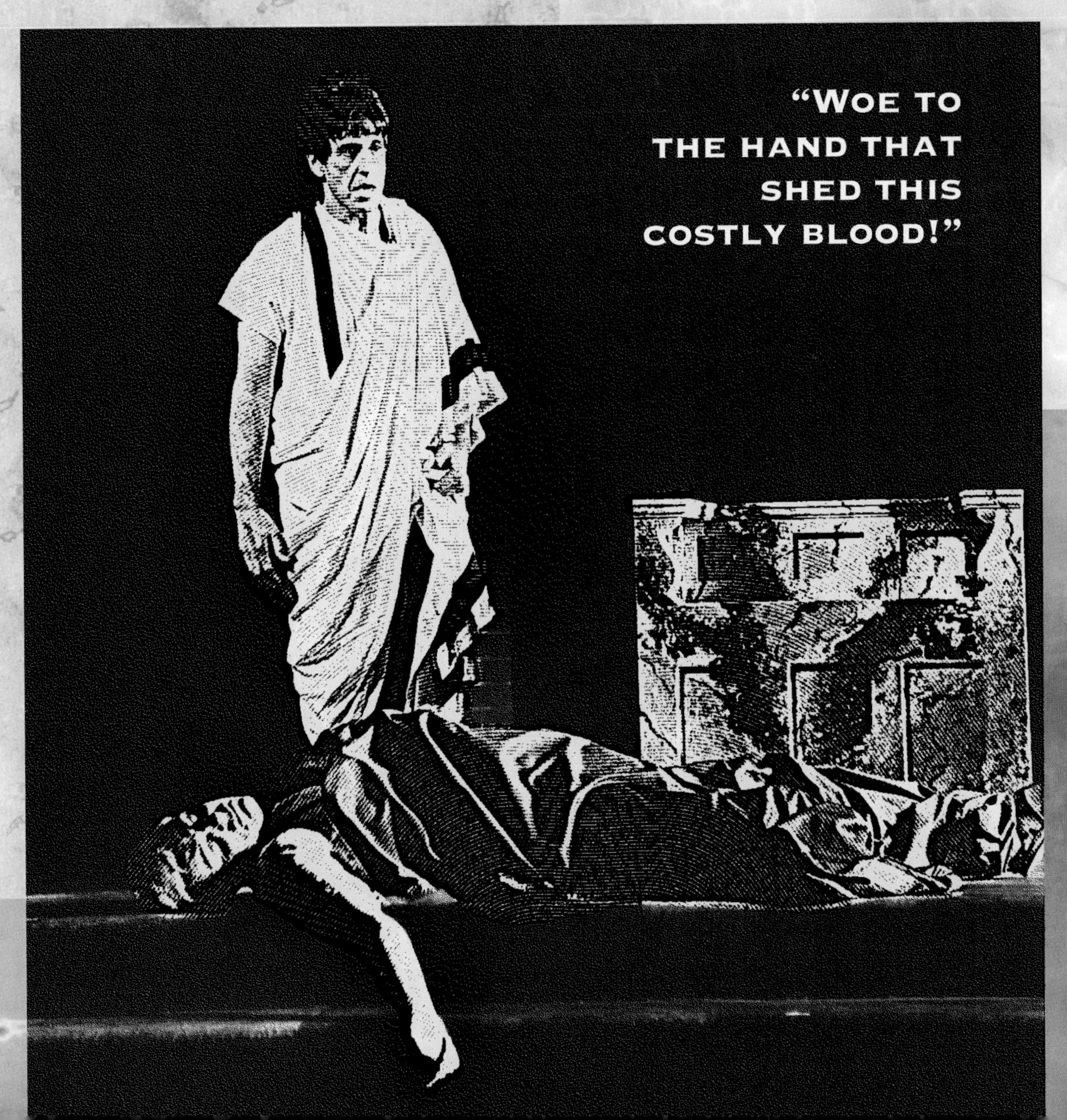
"WOE TO
THE HAND THAT
SHED THIS
COSTLY BLOOD!"

A curse shall light upon the limbs of men;
Domestic fury and fierce civil strife
Shall cumber° all the parts of Italy;
Blood and destruction shall be so in use,
And dreadful objects so familiar,
That mothers shall but smile when they behold
Their infants quartered° with the hands of war,
All pity choked with custom of fell° deeds,
And Caesar's spirit, ranging for revenge,
With Atè° by his side come hot from hell,
Shall in these confines with a monarch's voice
Cry "Havoc,"° and let slip the dogs of war,
That this foul deed shall smell above the earth
With carrion° men, groaning for burial.

[*Enter Octavius's* SERVANT.]

You serve Octavius Caesar, do you not?

Servant.
I do, Mark Antony.

Antony.
Caesar did write for him to come to Rome.

Servant.
He did receive his letters and is coming,
And bid me say to you by word of mouth—
O Caesar! [*Seeing the body.*]

Antony.
Thy heart is big;° get thee apart and weep.
Passion, I see, is catching, for mine eyes,
Seeing those beads of sorrow stand in thine,
Began to water. Is thy master coming?

Servant.
He lies tonight within seven leagues° of Rome.

Antony.
Post° back with speed, and tell him what hath
chanced.
Here is a mourning Rome, a dangerous Rome,
No Rome of safety for Octavius yet.
Hie° hence and tell him so. Yet stay awhile;
Thou shalt not back till I have borne this corse
Into the market place; there shall I try°
In my oration how the people take
The cruel issue° of these bloody men;
According to the which, thou shalt discourse
To young Octavius of the state of things.
Lend me your hand. [*Exeunt.*]

? **263.** *During this speech, some directors let us hear the offstage noise of the crowd. At what moments in this speech would the offstage cries of the mob and even other street noises be appropriate?*

264. cumber: burden.

268. quartered: butchered (cut in four parts).

269. fell: evil.

271. Atè: Greek goddess of revenge.

273. Cry "Havoc": give the signal for the devastation and disorder to begin.

275. carrion: dead and rotting.

282. big: full of grief.

? **284.** *What might Antony do to the servant to make us feel his compassion?*

286. seven leagues: about twenty-one miles.

287. Post: ride on horseback (changing horses along the way).

290. Hie: hurry.

292. try: test.

294. cruel issue: cruel deed; also, the outcome or result of cruelty.

? **297.** *Would you end this scene with Antony raising the body in his arms, or would you have him stand over it? Would the noise of the crowd be heard from offstage?*

Scene 2. *The Forum.*

Enter BRUTUS *and goes into the pulpit, and* CASSIUS, *with the* PLEBEIANS.°

Plebeians: the common people.

? ***Stage direction.*** *The Roman Forum was a busy, crowded, open area. At one end of the Forum was the Rostrum, a "pulpit" from which Rome's great public figures spoke. In stage sets, the pulpit is usually set on a semicircular platform with steps leading up to it. This scene is wild and noisy. What is Brutus's mood as he fights free of the mob and goes up to the pulpit?*

Plebeians.
We will be satisfied! Let us be satisfied!

Brutus.
Then follow me, and give me audience, friends.
Cassius, go you into the other street
And part the numbers.
Those that will hear me speak, let 'em stay here;
Those that will follow Cassius, go with him;
And public reasons shall be renderèd
Of Caesar's death.

First Plebeian. I will hear Brutus speak.

Second Plebeian.
I will hear Cassius, and compare their reasons,
When severally we hear them renderèd.

[*Exit* CASSIUS, *with some of the* PLEBEIANS.]

Third Plebeian.
The noble Brutus is ascended. Silence!

Brutus. Be patient till the last.
Romans, countrymen, and lovers, hear me for my cause, and be silent, that you may hear. Believe me for mine honor, and have respect to mine honor, that you may believe. Censure° me in your wisdom, and awake your senses,° that you may the better judge. If there be any in this assembly, any dear friend of Caesar's, to him I say that Brutus' love to Caesar was no less than his. If then that friend demand why Brutus rose against Caesar, this is my answer: Not that I loved Caesar less, but that I loved Rome more. Had you rather Caesar were living, and die all slaves, than that Caesar were dead, to live all free men? As Caesar loved me, I weep for him; as he was fortunate, I rejoice at it; as he was valiant, I honor him; but, as he was ambitious, I slew him. There is tears, for his love; joy, for his fortune; honor, for his valor; and death, for his ambition. Who is here so base, that would be a bondman?° If any, speak; for him have I offended. Who is here so rude,° that would not be a Roman? If any, speak; for him have I offended. Who is here so vile, that will not love his country? If any, speak; for him have I offended. I pause for a reply.

All. None, Brutus, none!

Brutus. Then none have I offended. I have done no more

16. **Censure:** judge.

17. **senses:** reasoning powers.

30. **bondman:** slave.

31. **rude:** rough and uncivilized.

? 35. *Notice that Brutus's speech is in prose, not poetry. What value does Brutus presume the people cherish—as he cherishes it?*

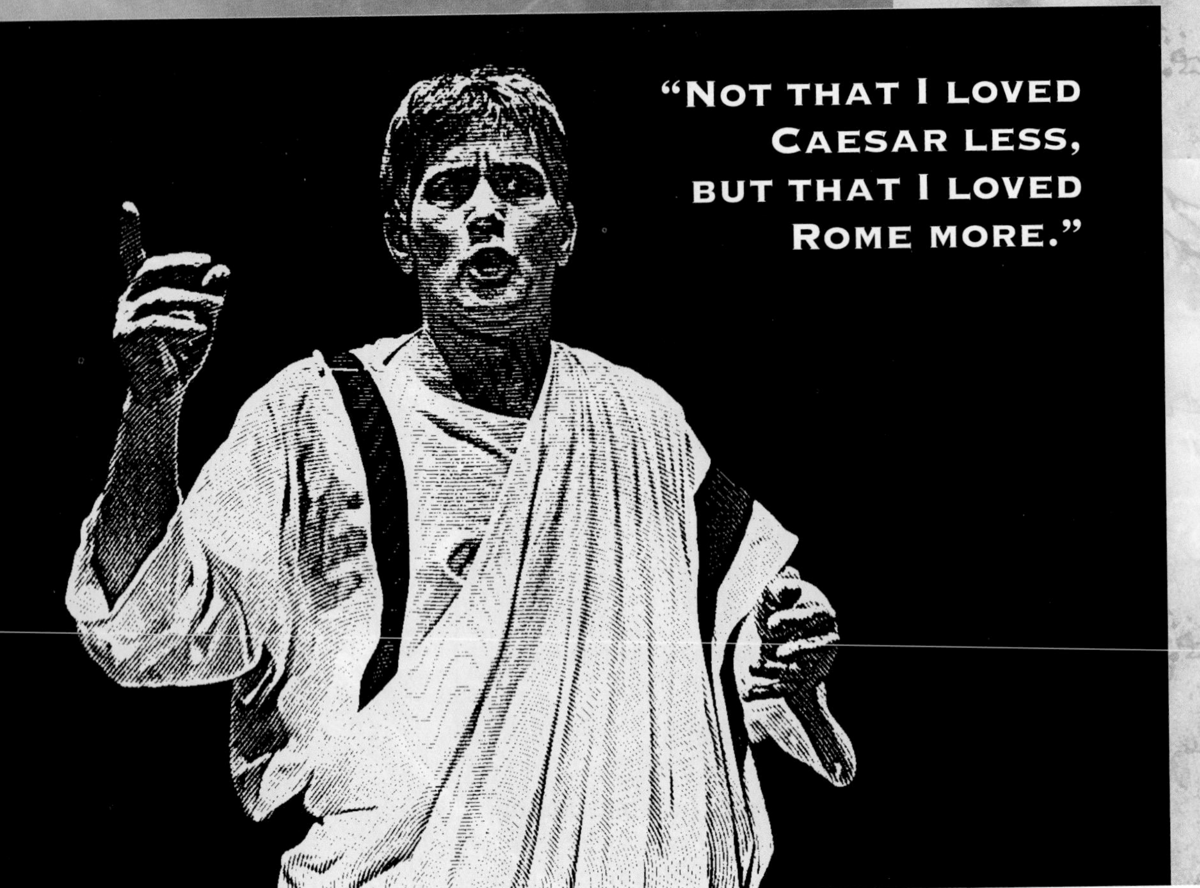
"NOT THAT I LOVED
CAESAR LESS,
BUT THAT I LOVED
ROME MORE."

to Caesar than you shall do to Brutus. The question of his death is enrolled° in the Capitol; his glory not extenuated,° wherein he was worthy, nor his offenses enforced,° for which he suffered death.

[*Enter* MARK ANTONY, *with Caesar's body.*]

Here comes his body, mourned by Mark Antony, who, though he had no hand in his death, shall receive the benefit of his dying, a place in the commonwealth, as which of you shall not? With this I depart, that, as I slew my best lover for the good of Rome, I have the same dagger for myself, when it shall please my country to need my death.

All. Live, Brutus! Live, live!

First Plebeian.
Bring him with triumph home unto his house.

Second Plebeian.
Give him a statue with his ancestors.

Third Plebeian.
Let him be Caesar.

39. In other words, there is a record of the reasons he was killed.
40. extenuated: lessened.
41. enforced: exaggerated.

Rule by the Rich

Roman politics often resembled a theatrical production, complete with performers and an audience. The Forum was the stage, the politicians were the actors, and citizens from all social classes came to watch the show. Assemblies, elections, and trials were held outdoors. Noisy crowds often booed and heckled the politicians.

With the abolition of the monarchy in 509 B.C., the Roman Republic was established. (A *republic* is a state in which power is vested in the citizens, who are entitled to vote; they elect representatives, who govern on behalf of the citizens.) Yet a huge gap continued to exist between rich and poor, and for centuries, only the rich were allowed to hold public office. Some of the wealthiest members of society were members of the Senate, which controlled Rome's domestic and foreign affairs. Not until more than two hundred years after the Roman Republic was established were a select few from the lower classes allowed to enter politics.

According to Marcus Cicero (106–43 B.C.), orator, philosopher, and senator, "the difficulty of devising policy has caused the transfer of power from a king to a group, and the ignorance and rashness of the masses have caused its transfer from the many to the few." His words affirm his belief in the ignorance of the "lower classes," a prejudice common among members of the privileged classes at the time.

The United States is a representative democracy, or a republic, in which citizens elect others to make public policy decisions for them in assemblies instead of attending the assemblies and making their own decisions, as Roman citizens did. The Roman Republic, however, was a direct democracy, not an indirect or representative one. In Rome, eligible voters could attend assemblies, vote on legislation, and elect government officials. However, Rome was the only place where voting was authorized, and so many citizens could not exercise their voting rights because they had neither the time nor the money to travel from their homes to Rome.

In Rome, legislation was proposed, formulated, and discussed by the Senate and then presented to the assemblies for approval. Because the upper classes controlled the Senate, they controlled all legislation. Even though each citizen had the right to vote on every issue, the Roman Republic wasn't an ideal democracy. Lacking the guiding principle of government of the people, for the people, and by the people, it amounted to rule by the aristocracy, which served the interests of the elite while pretending to give voice to the populace.

The background photograph shows the ruins of the Roman Forum.

R. G. Everts/Photo Researchers.

Fourth Plebeian. Caesar's better parts°
Shall be crowned in Brutus.
First Plebeian.
We'll bring him to his house with shouts and clamors.
Brutus. My countrymen——
Second Plebeian. Peace! Silence! Brutus speaks.
First Plebeian. Peace, ho!
Brutus.
Good countrymen, let me depart alone,
And, for my sake, stay here with Antony.
Do grace to Caesar's corpse, and grace his speech°
Tending to Caesar's glories, which Mark Antony
By our permission, is allowed to make.
I do entreat you, not a man depart,
Save I alone, till Antony have spoke. [*Exit.*]
First Plebeian.
Stay, ho! And let us hear Mark Antony.
Third Plebeian.
Let him go up into the public chair;°
We'll hear him. Noble Antony, go up.
Antony.
For Brutus' sake, I am beholding to you.
Fourth Plebeian.
What does he say of Brutus?
Third Plebeian. He says, for Brutus' sake,
He finds himself beholding to us all.
Fourth Plebeian.
'Twere best he speak no harm of Brutus here!
First Plebeian.
This Caesar was a tyrant.
Third Plebeian. Nay, that's certain.
We are blest that Rome is rid of him.
Second Plebeian.
Peace! Let us hear what Antony can say.
Antony.
You gentle Romans——
All. Peace, ho! Let us hear him.
Antony.
Friends, Romans, countrymen, lend me your ears;
I come to bury Caesar, not to praise him.
The evil that men do lives after them,
The good is oft interrèd with their bones;
So let it be with Caesar. The noble Brutus
Hath told you Caesar was ambitious.
If it were so, it was a grievous fault,
And grievously hath Caesar answered° it.
Here, under leave of Brutus and the rest
(For Brutus is an honorable man,

52. **better parts:** better qualities.

? 52. *Why is this cry from the mob, in lines 52–53, ironic? Has the crowd understood Brutus's motives at all?*

? 54. *What would you have Antony doing while the mob is talking? (Remember, he has brought Caesar's body to the Forum.)*

59. **grace his speech:** listen respectfully to Antony's funeral oration.

65. **public chair:** pulpit or rostrum.

? 75. *An important question: Where would you place Caesar's body so that Antony can use it most effectively? Be sure to perform this famous funeral oration. What different tones do you hear in it?*

82. **answered:** paid the penalty for.

So are they all, all honorable men),
Come I to speak in Caesar's funeral.
He was my friend, faithful and just to me;
But Brutus says he was ambitious,
And Brutus is an honorable man.
He hath brought many captives home to Rome,
Whose ransoms did the general coffers° fill;
Did this in Caesar seem ambitious?
When that the poor have cried, Caesar hath wept;
Ambition should be made of sterner stuff.
Yet Brutus says he was ambitious;
And Brutus is an honorable man.
You all did see that on the Lupercal
I thrice presented him a kingly crown,
Which he did thrice refuse. Was this ambition?
Yet Brutus says he was ambitious;
And sure he is an honorable man.
I speak not to disprove what Brutus spoke,
But here I am to speak what I do know.
You all did love him once, not without cause;
What cause withholds you then to mourn for him?
O judgment, thou art fled to brutish beasts,
And men have lost their reason! Bear with me;
My heart is in the coffin there with Caesar,
And I must pause till it come back to me.

First Plebeian.
Methinks there is much reason in his sayings.

Second Plebeian.
If thou consider rightly of the matter,
Caesar has had great wrong.

Third Plebeian. Has he, masters?
I fear there will a worse come in his place.

Fourth Plebeian.
Marked ye his words? He would not take the crown,
Therefore 'tis certain he was not ambitious.

First Plebeian.
If it be found so, some will dear abide it.°

Second Plebeian.
Poor soul, his eyes are red as fire with weeping.

Third Plebeian.
There's not a nobler man in Rome than Antony.

Fourth Plebeian.
Now mark him, he begins again to speak.

Antony.
But yesterday the word of Caesar might
Have stood against the world; now lies he there,
And none so poor to° do him reverence.

91. general coffers: public funds.

? **100.** *Remember that the crowd is pressing in on Antony. What movements or sounds would they make as Antony says things that are meant to sway their feelings?*

? **109.** *What do lines 108–109 mean? What could Antony be doing at this point, as our attention is drawn again to the crowd?*

116. dear abide it: pay dearly for it.

122. so poor to: so low in rank as to.

O masters! If I were disposed to stir
Your hearts and minds to mutiny and rage,
I should do Brutus wrong and Cassius wrong,
Who, you all know, are honorable men.
I will not do them wrong; I rather choose
To wrong the dead, to wrong myself and you,
Than I will wrong such honorable men.
But here's a parchment with the seal of Caesar;
I found it in his closet; 'tis his will.
Let but the commons hear this testament,
Which, pardon me, I do not mean to read,
And they would go and kiss dead Caesar's wounds,
And dip their napkins° in his sacred blood;
Yea, beg a hair of him for memory,
And dying, mention it within their wills,
Bequeathing it as a rich legacy

135. napkins: handkerchiefs.

"BUT HERE'S A PARCHMENT WITH THE SEAL OF CAESAR . . . 'TIS HIS WILL."

Unto their issue.°

Fourth Plebeian.
We'll hear the will; read it, Mark Antony.

All. The will, the will! We will hear Caesar's will!

Antony.
Have patience, gentle friends, I must not read it.
It is not meet you know how Caesar loved you.
You are not wood, you are not stones, but men;
And being men, hearing the will of Caesar,
It will inflame you, it will make you mad.
'Tis good you know not that you are his heirs;
For if you should, O, what would come of it?

Fourth Plebeian.
Read the will! We'll hear it, Antony!
You shall read us the will, Caesar's will!

Antony.
Will you be patient? Will you stay awhile?
I have o'ershot myself° to tell you of it.
I fear I wrong the honorable men
Whose daggers have stabbed Caesar; I do fear it.

Fourth Plebeian.
They were traitors. Honorable men!

All. The will! The testament!

Second Plebeian. They were villains, murderers! The will! Read the will!

Antony.
You will compel me then to read the will?
Then make a ring about the corpse of Caesar,
And let me show you him that made the will.
Shall I descend? And will you give me leave?

All. Come down.

Second Plebeian. Descend.

[ANTONY *comes down.*]

Third Plebeian. You shall have leave.

Fourth Plebeian. A ring! Stand round.

First Plebeian.
Stand from the hearse, stand from the body!

Second Plebeian.
Room for Antony, most noble Antony!

Antony.
Nay, press not so upon me; stand far off.

All. Stand back! Room! Bear back.

Antony.
If you have tears, prepare to shed them now.
You all do know this mantle; I remember
The first time ever Caesar put it on:
'Twas on a summer's evening, in his tent,

139. issue: children; heirs.

? **139.** *Antony says he is not going to read the will, but what has he already implied about its contents?*

? **148.** *Again, how has Antony scored his point indirectly? How could an actor play Antony in this scene to make him seem manipulative?*

152. o'ershot myself: gone farther than I intended.

? **154.** *The irony here is so obvious that an actor playing Antony must make a choice about how to say these lines: Will he continue his pretense of honoring Caesar's assassins, or will he finally drop this pose and speak with obviously scathing sarcasm?*

? **170.** *How do you visualize the placement of the actors at this point? Where is Caesar's body?*

? **173.** *Watch for clues that tell what Antony is doing for effect as he delivers this speech. What is he holding in line 172?*

That day he overcame the Nervii.°
Look, in this place ran Cassius' dagger through;
See what a rent the envious° Casca made;
Through this the well-belovèd Brutus stabbed,
And as he plucked his cursèd steel away,
Mark how the blood of Caesar followed it,
As rushing out of doors, to be resolved
If Brutus so unkindly knocked, or no;
For Brutus, as you know, was Caesar's angel.
Judge, O you gods, how dearly Caesar loved him!
This was the most unkindest cut of all;
For when the noble Caesar saw him stab,
Ingratitude, more strong than traitors' arms,
Quite vanquished him. Then burst his mighty heart;
And, in his mantle muffling up his face,
Even at the base of Pompey's statue°
(Which all the while ran blood) great Caesar fell.
O, what a fall was there, my countrymen!
Then I, and you, and all of us fell down,
Whilst bloody treason flourished over us.
O, now you weep, and I perceive you feel
The dint° of pity; these are gracious drops.
Kind souls, what weep you when you but behold
Our Caesar's vesture° wounded? Look you here,
Here is himself, marred as you see with traitors.

First Plebeian. O piteous spectacle!
Second Plebeian. O noble Caesar!
Third Plebeian. O woeful day!
Fourth Plebeian. O traitors, villains!
First Plebeian. O most bloody sight!
Second Plebeian. We will be revenged.
All. Revenge! About! Seek! Burn! Fire! Kill! Slay! Let not a traitor live!
Antony. Stay, countrymen.
First Plebeian. Peace there! Hear the noble Antony.
Second Plebeian. We'll hear him, we'll follow him, we'll die with him!
Antony.
Good friends, sweet friends, let me not stir you up
To such a sudden flood of mutiny.
They that have done this deed are honorable.
What private griefs° they have, alas, I know not,
That made them do it. They are wise and honorable,
And will, no doubt, with reasons answer you.
I come not, friends, to steal away your hearts;
I am no orator, as Brutus is;
But (as you know me all) a plain blunt man
That love my friend, and that they know full well

175. Nervii: one of the tribes conquered by Caesar, in 57 B.C.

177. envious: spiteful.

190. statue: pronounced in three syllables.

? **195.** *What is the crowd doing as Antony speaks?*

196. dint: stroke.

198. vesture: clothing.

? **199.** *What has Antony done with the body now?*

215. griefs: grievances.

? **217.** *Notice that Antony implies that reasons have not already been given. Have they?*

"HERE IS HIMSELF, MARRED AS YOU SEE WITH TRAITORS."

That gave me public leave to speak of him.
For I have neither writ, nor words, nor worth,
Action, nor utterance, nor the power of speech
To stir men's blood; I only speak right on.
I tell you that which you yourselves do know,
Show you sweet Caesar's wounds, poor poor dumb
mouths,
And bid them speak for me. But were I Brutus,
And Brutus Antony, there were an Antony
Would ruffle up your spirits, and put a tongue
In every wound of Caesar that would move
The stones of Rome to rise and mutiny.

All.
We'll mutiny.

First Plebeian. We'll burn the house of Brutus.

Third Plebeian.
Away, then! Come, seek the conspirators.

Antony.
Yet hear me, countrymen. Yet hear me speak.

All.
Peace, ho! Hear Antony, most noble Antony!

Antony.
Why, friends, you go to do you know not what:
Wherein hath Caesar thus deserved your loves?
Alas, you know not; I must tell you then:
You have forgot the will I told you of.

All.
Most true, the will! Let's stay and hear the will.

Antony.
Here is the will, and under Caesar's seal.
To every Roman citizen he gives,
To every several° man, seventy-five drachmas.°

Second Plebeian.
Most noble Caesar! We'll revenge his death!

Third Plebeian. O royal Caesar!

Antony. Hear me with patience.

All. Peace, ho!

Antony.
Moreover, he hath left you all his walks,
His private arbors, and new-planted orchards,
On this side Tiber; he hath left them you,
And to your heirs forever: common pleasures,°
To walk abroad and recreate yourselves.
Here was a Caesar! When comes such another?

First Plebeian.
Never, never! Come, away, away!
We'll burn his body in the holy place,

? **225.** *How does Antony characterize himself, as compared with Brutus? What is his motive?*

? **232.** *Again, the irony is obvious here. What is the key word in this speech?*

? **240.** *Notice how many times the mob goes to run off and how Antony pulls it back again. How do you think Antony feels about this herd of people he has so cleverly manipulated?*

244. several: individual. **drachmas:** silver coins (Greek currency).

252. common pleasures: public recreation areas.

And with the brands fire the traitors' houses.
Take up the body.

Second Plebeian. Go fetch fire.

Third Plebeian. Pluck down benches.

Fourth Plebeian. Pluck down forms, windows,° anything!

[*Exeunt* PLEBEIANS *with the body.*]

Antony.
Now let it work: Mischief, thou art afoot,
Take thou what course thou wilt.

[*Enter* SERVANT.]

How now, fellow?

Servant.
Sir, Octavius is already come to Rome.

Antony. Where is he?

Servant.
He and Lepidus are at Caesar's house.

Antony.
And thither will I straight to visit him;
He comes upon a wish. Fortune is merry,
And in this mood will give us anything.

Servant.
I heard him say, Brutus and Cassius
Are rid° like madmen through the gates of Rome.

Antony.
Belike° they had some notice of the people,
How I had moved them. Bring me to Octavius.

[*Exeunt.*]

261. forms, windows: long benches and shutters.

? **263.** *Antony is alone onstage. The noise of the mob dies off in the distance. We might in some productions see the reflection of flames and hear the sounds of rioting. How should Antony speak these lines?*

271. Are rid: have ridden.

? **271.** *What have Brutus and Cassius done?*

272. Belike: probably.

Scene 3. *A street.*

Enter CINNA *the poet, and after him the* PLEBEIANS.

Cinna.
I dreamt tonight that I did feast with Caesar,
And things unluckily charge my fantasy.°
I have no will to wander forth of doors,
Yet something leads me forth.

First Plebeian. What is your name?

Second Plebeian. Whither are you going?

Third Plebeian. Where do you dwell?

Fourth Plebeian. Are you a married man or a bachelor?

Second Plebeian. Answer every man directly.

First Plebeian. Ay, and briefly.

Fourth Plebeian. Ay, and wisely.

Third Plebeian. Ay, and truly, you were best.

2. That is, events unluckily fill his imagination (with ominous ideas).

Cinna. What is my name? Whither am I going? Where do I dwell? Am I a married man or a bachelor? Then, to answer every man directly and briefly, wisely and truly: wisely I say, I am a bachelor.

Second Plebeian. That's as much as to say, they are fools that marry; you'll bear me a bang° for that, I fear. Proceed directly.

Cinna. Directly, I am going to Caesar's funeral.

First Plebeian. As a friend or an enemy?

Cinna. As a friend.

Second Plebeian. That matter is answered directly.

Fourth Plebeian. For your dwelling, briefly.

Cinna. Briefly, I dwell by the Capitol.

Third Plebeian. Your name, sir, truly.

Cinna. Truly, my name is Cinna.

First Plebeian. Tear him to pieces! He's a conspirator.

Cinna. I am Cinna the poet! I am Cinna the poet!

Fourth Plebeian. Tear him for his bad verses! Tear him for his bad verses!

Cinna. I am not Cinna the conspirator.

Fourth Plebeian. It is no matter, his name's Cinna; pluck but his name out of his heart, and turn him going.°

Third Plebeian. Tear him, tear him!

[*They attack him.*]

Come, brands, ho! Firebrands! To Brutus', to Cassius'! Burn all! Some to Decius' house, and some to Casca's; some to Ligarius'! Away, go!

[*Exeunt all the* PLEBEIANS *with* CINNA.]

18. bear me a bang: get a blow from me.

35. turn him going: send him packing.

? **39.** *What has the mob done to the innocent poet Cinna? Try performing this chilling mob scene, perhaps using a chorus for the plebeians' lines.*

"O JUDGMENT, THOU ART FLED TO BRUTISH BEASTS,
AND MEN HAVE LOST THEIR REASON! BEAR WITH ME;
MY HEART IS IN THE COFFIN THERE WITH CAESAR,
AND I MUST PAUSE TILL
IT COME BACK TO ME."

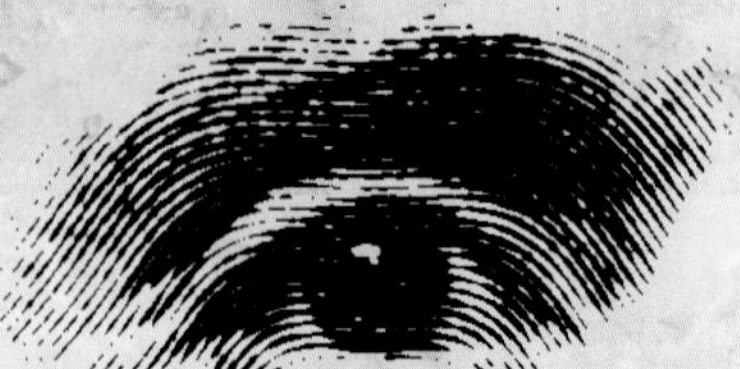

—ANTONY, ACT III, SCENE 2
(LINES 106–109)

Making Meanings
Act III

First Thoughts

1. Brutus and Antony are both persuasive speakers. Whose funeral speech comes closer to expressing your own thoughts about Caesar's death? Why?

Shaping Interpretations

2. How does Antony's speech at the end of Scene 1 (lines 254–275) indicate his intentions regarding the assassins? What could this speech **foreshadow**?
3. In his funeral oration in Scene 2, Antony holds to his agreement with Brutus and Cassius yet destroys the conspirators' reputations. How does he do this and manipulate the Roman mob?
4. Until Act III, Antony has barely figured in the play. How have others **characterized** him? Do you agree with them? Why?
5. In earlier scenes, Shakespeare *tells* about lions in the streets and people going mad. In Scene 3, with the attack on Cinna the poet, he *shows* something. What does he reveal about the psychology of a mob?
6. The third act of Shakespeare's tragedies usually contains the **turning point,** the moment when all the action of the play begins to spiral toward the **tragic ending.** Which event do you think is the turning point in this play: the assassination of Caesar or Brutus's decision to allow Antony to address the crowd? Explain.
7. Lines 111–118 of Scene 1 suggest that the conspirators' deed will be "acted over," or repeated, "many ages hence." What meaning do you think Shakespeare intended for his audience to read into these lines?

Connecting with the Text

8. How do you feel about Brutus and Antony in this act? Do you see people like Antony and Brutus today? Explain.

Reading Check

a. In Scene 1, a chance still exists that the conspiracy might be foiled. Why does Artemidorus fail to get Caesar to read his warning?

b. What petition serves as an excuse for the conspirators to gather around Caesar?

c. In Scene 1, why does Cassius argue against allowing Antony to speak at Caesar's funeral? What reasons does Brutus give for overruling him?

d. After the assassination the **protagonist** who drives the rest of the play appears. Who is this person and what does he want? How have we been prepared for his appearance?

e. What information concerning Caesar's will does Antony disclose to the crowd in Scene 2? How does the crowd react?

f. What do the plebeians do in Scene 3?

Choices: Building Your Portfolio

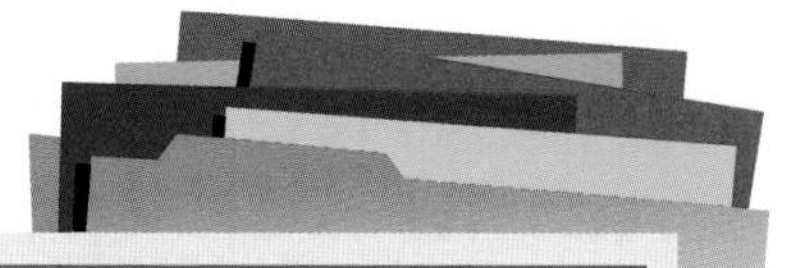

Writer's Notebook

1. Collecting Ideas for an Evaluation

Identifying emotional appeals. One of the great examples of **persuasive oratory** is found in Act III, Scene 2, lines 75–109, in which Antony, standing over Caesar's bloody corpse, completely changes the mood of the mob. Take notes on the specific **emotional appeals** Antony uses to win over his audience. Find uses of **irony, loaded words, repetition, bandwagon appeal,** and **props.** (For more on persuasion, see pages 468–469.) Save your notes.

Creative Writing

2. Behind the Scenes

Shakespeare never lets us see again the shoemaker from Act I. Suppose the shoemaker is in the crowd that listens to Brutus and Antony, carries away Caesar's body, and then kills the poet Cinna. Write a **new scene** in which the shoemaker and another character talk about what has happened on the ides of March. Perform your scene.

Reading Skills and Strategies

Paraphrasing: Your Own Words

When you **paraphrase** a passage, you express its ideas in your own words. Look at Caesar's speech and its paraphrase:

Caesar. Thy brother by decree is banishèd.
If thou dost bend and pray and fawn for him,
I spurn thee like a cur out of my way.

—Act III, Scene 1, lines 44–46

Your brother is banished by law. If you lower yourself to grovel and beg for him, I'll treat you like a dog and kick you out of my way.

Read the numbered passages below in their contexts before you paraphrase each.

1. **Antony.** That I did love thee, Caesar, O, 'tis true!
If then thy spirit look upon us now,
Shall it not grieve thee dearer than thy death
To see thy Antony making his peace,
Shaking the bloody fingers of thy foes,
Most noble, in the presence of thy corse?

—Act III, Scene 1, lines 194–199

2. **Antony.** Friends, Romans, countrymen, lend me your ears;
I come to bury Caesar, not to praise him.
The evil that men do lives after them,
The good is oft interrèd with their bones;

—Act III, Scene 2, lines 75–78

ACT IV Scene 1. *A house in Rome.*

Enter ANTONY, OCTAVIUS, *and* LEPIDUS.

Antony.
These many then shall die; their names are pricked.
Octavius.
Your brother too must die; consent you, Lepidus?
Lepidus.
I do consent——
Octavius. Prick him down, Antony.
Lepidus.
Upon condition Publius shall not live,
Who is your sister's son, Mark Antony.
Antony.
He shall not live; look, with a spot I damn him.
But, Lepidus, go you to Caesar's house;
Fetch the will hither, and we shall determine
How to cut off some charge° in legacies.
Lepidus.
What, shall I find you here?
Octavius.
Or here or at the Capitol. [*Exit* LEPIDUS.]
Antony.
This is a slight unmeritable man,
Meet to be sent on errands; is it fit,
The threefold world° divided, he should stand
One of the three to share it?°
Octavius. So you thought him,
And took his voice° who should be pricked to die
In our black sentence and proscription.°
Antony.
Octavius, I have seen more days than you;
And though we lay these honors on this man,
To ease ourselves of divers sland'rous loads,°
He shall but bear them as the ass bears gold,
To groan and sweat under the business,
Either led or driven, as we point the way;
And having brought our treasure where we will,
Then take we down his load, and turn him off,
(Like to the empty ass) to shake his ears
And graze in commons.°
Octavius. You may do your will;
But he's a tried and valiant soldier.
Antony.
So is my horse, Octavius, and for that

9. In other words, cut down on some of the expenses by changing the legacies.

14. threefold world: three parts of the Roman Empire: Europe, Asia, and Africa.
15. Antony, Octavius, and Lepidus now govern the Roman Empire as a triumvirate, or three-member ruling body.
16. voice: vote.
17. proscription: death sentence. In Roman law, a person under proscription could be killed by anyone, and the killer had no fear of murder charges being brought against him.
? **17.** *What details suggest that this triumvirate is showing signs of strain? How has Antony changed from the person we saw in Act III?*
20. divers sland'rous loads: blame that will be laid against them.
? **26.** *Who is compared to the ass?*
27. in commons: on pasture land that is commonly held, or shared by everyone.

I do appoint him store of provender.°
It is a creature that I teach to fight,
To wind, to stop, to run directly on,
His corporal motion governed by my spirit.
And, in some taste,° is Lepidus but so.
He must be taught, and trained, and bid go forth.
A barren-spirited fellow; one that feeds
On objects, arts, and imitations,
Which, out of use and staled by other men,
Begin his fashion.° Do not talk of him
But as a property.° And now, Octavius,
Listen great things. Brutus and Cassius
Are levying powers;° we must straight make head.°
Therefore let our alliance be combined,
Our best friends made, our means stretched;
And let us presently go sit in council
How covert matters may be best disclosed,
And open perils surest answerèd.

Octavius.
Let us do so; for we are at the stake,
And bayed about with many enemies;°
And some that smile have in their hearts, I fear,
Millions of mischiefs. [*Exeunt.*]

30. appoint . . . provender: allot him a supply of food.

34. in some taste: in some measure.

39. In other words, he is always behind the times.

40. property: tool.

42. levying powers: gathering armies. **straight make head:** immediately gather troops.

49. A metaphor referring to the Elizabethan sport of bearbaiting, in which a bear was chained to a stake and attacked by dogs.

Scene 2. *Camp near Sardis.*

Drum. Enter BRUTUS, LUCILIUS, LUCIUS, *and the* ARMY. TITINIUS *and* PINDARUS *meet them.*

Brutus. Stand ho!

Lucilius. Give the word, ho! and stand.

Brutus.
What now, Lucilius, is Cassius near?

Lucilius.
He is at hand, and Pindarus is come
To do you salutation from his master.

Brutus.
He greets me well.° Your master, Pindarus,
In his own change, or by ill officers,°
Hath given me some worthy cause to wish
Things done undone; but if he be at hand,
I shall be satisfied.°

Pindarus. I do not doubt
But that my noble master will appear
Such as he is, full of regard and honor.

Brutus.
He is not doubted. A word, Lucilius,
How he received you; let me be resolved.°

? ***Stage direction.*** *Several months have passed since the assassination. Brutus and Cassius are in Sardis, the capital of ancient Lydia, a kingdom in Asia Minor. Why did Brutus and Cassius flee from Rome with their armies?*

6. He . . . well: He sends greetings with a good man.

7. In other words, either from a change of feelings or because of the bad advice or the bad deeds of subordinates.

10. be satisfied: get a satisfactory explanation.

14. resolved: informed.

Lucilius.
With courtesy and with respect enough,
But not with such familiar instances,°
Nor with such free and friendly conference
As he hath used of old.

Brutus. Thou hast described
A hot friend cooling. Ever note, Lucilius,
When love begins to sicken and decay
It useth an enforcèd ceremony.
There are no tricks in plain and simple faith;
But hollow men, like horses hot at hand,°
Make gallant show and promise of their mettle;

[*Low march within.*]

But when they should endure the bloody spur,
They fall their crests, and like deceitful jades°
Sink in the trial. Comes his army on?

Lucilius.
They mean this night in Sardis to be quartered;
The greater part, the horse in general,°
Are come with Cassius.

[*Enter* CASSIUS *and his* POWERS.]

Brutus. Hark! He is arrived.
March gently on to meet him.

Cassius. Stand, ho!

Brutus. Stand, ho! Speak the word along.

First Soldier. Stand!

Second Soldier. Stand!

Third Soldier. Stand!

Cassius.
Most noble brother, you have done me wrong.

Brutus.
Judge me, you gods! Wrong I mine enemies?
And if not so, how should I wrong a brother?

Cassius.
Brutus, this sober form of yours hides wrongs;
And when you do them——

Brutus. Cassius, be content.°
Speak your griefs softly; I do know you well.
Before the eyes of both our armies here
(Which should perceive nothing but love from us)
Let us not wrangle. Bid them move away;
Then in my tent, Cassius, enlarge° your griefs,
And I will give you audience.

Cassius. Pindarus,
Bid our commanders lead their charges off
A little from this ground.

16. **familiar instances:** friendly behavior.

? 18. *What details show that a split might be taking place in the conspirators' ranks?*

23. **hot at hand:** very energetic at the start of the race.

26. **jades:** old horses.

29. **the horse in general:** all the cavalry.

? 36. *What do you picture happening on stage here?*

41. **content:** calm.

46. **enlarge:** express in greater detail.

Brutus.
Lucilius, do you the like, and let no man
Come to our tent till we have done our conference.
Let Lucius and Titinius guard our door.

[*Exeunt all except* BRUTUS *and* CASSIUS.]

Scene 3. *Brutus' tent.*

Cassius.
That you have wronged me doth appear in this:
You have condemned and noted° Lucius Pella
For taking bribes here of the Sardians;
Wherein my letters, praying on his side,
Because I knew the man, was slighted off.

Brutus.
You wronged yourself to write in such a case.

Cassius.
In such a time as this it is not meet
That every nice offense should bear his comment.°

Brutus.
Let me tell you, Cassius, you yourself
Are much condemned to have an itching palm,
To sell and mart° your offices for gold
To undeservers.

Cassius. I an itching palm?
You know that you are Brutus that speaks this,
Or, by the gods, this speech were else your last.

Brutus.
The name of Cassius honors° this corruption,
And chastisement doth therefore hide his head.

Cassius. Chastisement!

Brutus.
Remember March, the ides of March remember.
Did not great Julius bleed for justice' sake?
What villain touched his body, that did stab,
And not for justice? What, shall one of us,
That struck the foremost man of all this world
But for supporting robbers,° shall we now
Contaminate our fingers with base bribes,
And sell the mighty space of our large honors°
For so much trash as may be graspèd thus?
I had rather be a dog, and bay the moon,
Than such a Roman.

Cassius. Brutus, bait not me;
I'll not endure it. You forget yourself
To hedge me in. I am a soldier, I,

2. noted: publicly disgraced.

8. That . . . comment: That every trivial offense should be criticized.

11. mart: trade; traffic in.

? **12.** *What has Brutus accused Cassius of?*

15. honors: gives an air of respectability to.

23. supporting robbers: supporting or protecting dishonest public officials.

25. our large honors: capacity to be honorable and generous.

Older in practice, abler than yourself
To make conditions.

Brutus. Go to! You are not, Cassius.

Cassius. I am.

Brutus. I say you are not.

Cassius.
Urge° me no more, I shall forget myself;
Have mind upon your health, tempt me no farther.

Brutus. Away, slight man!

Cassius.
Is't possible?

Brutus. Hear me, for I will speak.
Must I give way and room to your rash choler?°
Shall I be frighted when a madman stares?

Cassius.
O ye gods, ye gods! Must I endure all this?

Brutus.
All this? Ay, more: fret till your proud heart break.
Go show your slaves how choleric you are,
And make your bondmen tremble. Must I budge?°
Must I observe° you? Must I stand and crouch
Under your testy humor? By the gods,
You shall digest the venom of your spleen,°
Though it do split you; for, from this day forth,
I'll use you for my mirth, yea, for my laughter,
When you are waspish.

Cassius. Is it come to this?

Brutus.
You say you are a better soldier:
Let it appear so; make your vaunting° true,
And it shall please me well. For mine own part,
I shall be glad to learn of noble men.

Cassius.
You wrong me every way; you wrong me, Brutus;
I said, an elder soldier, not a better.
Did I say, better?

Brutus. If you did, I care not.

Cassius.
When Caesar lived, he durst not thus have moved°
me.

Brutus.
Peace, peace, you durst not so have tempted him.

Cassius. I durst not?

Brutus. No.

Cassius.
What? Durst not tempt him?

Brutus. For your life you durst not.

35. Urge: goad; bully.

? **36.** *What threat is Cassius making to Brutus?*

39. choler: anger.

44. budge: defer.

45. observe: wait on.

47. spleen: fiery temper. (The spleen was believed to be the seat of the emotions.)

52. vaunting: boasting.

? **57.** *What* did *Cassius say?*

58. moved: exasperated.

Cassius.
Do not presume too much upon my love;
I may do that I shall be sorry for.

Brutus.
You have done that you should be sorry for.
There is no terror, Cassius, in your threats;
For I am armed so strong in honesty
That they pass by me as the idle wind,
Which I respect not. I did send to you
For certain sums of gold, which you denied me;
For I can raise no money by vile means.
By heaven, I had rather coin my heart
And drop my blood for drachmas than to wring
From the hard hands of peasants their vile trash
By any indirection.° I did send
To you for gold to pay my legions,
Which you denied me. Was that done like Cassius?
Should I have answered Caius Cassius so?
When Marcus Brutus grows so covetous
To lock such rascal counters° from his friends,
Be ready, gods, with all your thunderbolts,
Dash him to pieces!

Cassius. I denied you not.

Brutus.
You did.

Cassius. I did not. He was but a fool
That brought my answer back. Brutus hath rived° my heart.
A friend should bear his friend's infirmities;
But Brutus makes mine greater than they are.

Brutus.
I do not, till you practice them on me.

Cassius.
You love me not.

Brutus. I do not like your faults.

Cassius.
A friendly eye could never see such faults.

Brutus.
A flatterer's would not, though they do appear
As huge as high Olympus.

Cassius.
Come, Antony, and young Octavius, come,
Revenge yourselves alone on Cassius,
For Cassius is aweary of the world:
Hated by one he loves; braved° by his brother;
Checked like a bondman; all his faults observed,
Set in a notebook, learned and conned by rote°
To cast into my teeth. O, I could weep

75. indirection: illegal methods.

? **75.** *What do you think of Brutus's moral position here? Does it seem honorable or hypocritical?*

80. counters: coins.

84. rived: broken.

95. braved: defied.

97. conned by rote: learned by heart.

My spirit from mine eyes! There is my dagger,
And here my naked breast; within, a heart
Dearer than Pluto's mine,° richer than gold;
If that thou be'st a Roman, take it forth.
I, that denied thee gold,° will give my heart.
Strike as thou didst at Caesar; for I know,
When thou didst hate him worst, thou lovedst him
better
Than ever thou lovedst Cassius.

Brutus. Sheathe your dagger.
Be angry when you will, it shall have scope.
Do what you will, dishonor shall be humor.°
O Cassius, you are yokèd with a lamb
That carries anger as the flint bears fire,
Who, much enforcèd, shows a hasty spark,
And straight is cold again.

Cassius. Hath Cassius lived
To be but mirth and laughter to his Brutus
When grief and blood ill-tempered vexeth him?

Brutus.
When I spoke that, I was ill-tempered too.

Cassius.
Do you confess so much? Give me your hand.

Brutus.
And my heart too.

Cassius. O Brutus!

Brutus. What's the matter?

Cassius.
Have not you love enough to bear with me
When that rash humor which my mother gave me
Makes me forgetful?

Brutus. Yes, Cassius, and from henceforth,
When you are over-earnest with your Brutus,
He'll think your mother chides, and leave you so.

[*Enter a* POET, *followed by* LUCILIUS, TITINIUS, *and* LUCIUS.]

Poet.
Let me go in to see the generals;
There is some grudge between 'em; 'tis not meet
They be alone.

Lucilius. You shall not come to them.

Poet. Nothing but death shall stay me.

Cassius. How now. What's the matter?

Poet.
For shame, you generals! What do you mean?
Love, and be friends, as two such men should be;
For I have seen more years, I'm sure, than ye.

? **99.** *What is Cassius doing, and why?*

101. Pluto's mine: the riches under the earth. Pluto was the Roman god of the Underworld (akin to the Greek god Hades); Shakespeare confuses him with Plutus, god of riches.

103. that . . . gold: that *you say* denied you gold.

108. In other words, dishonor or insults will be seen merely as the result of eccentric personality traits.

? **112.** *Have Brutus's feelings changed? Why or why not?*

? **117.** *What actions could mark the change in feelings now?*

? **122.** *How could a humorous note be sounded here?*

"SHEATHE YOUR DAGGER."

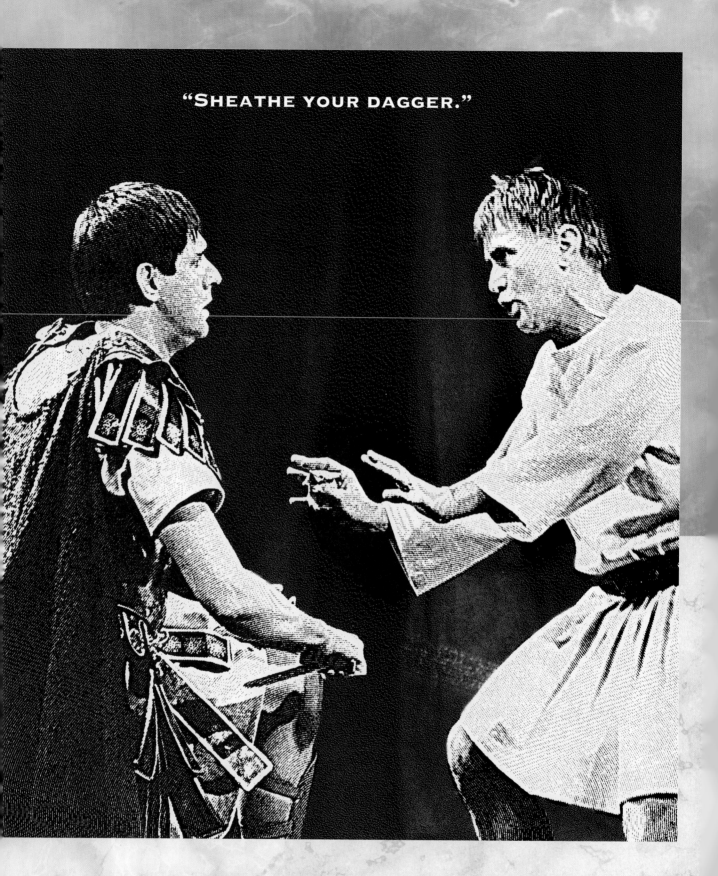

Cassius.
Ha, ha! How vilely doth this cynic° rhyme!

Brutus.
Get you hence, sirrah! Saucy fellow, hence!

Cassius.
Bear with him, Brutus, 'tis his fashion.

Brutus.
I'll know his humor when he knows his time.°
What should the wars do with these jigging° fools?
Companion,° hence!

Cassius. Away, away, be gone!

[*Exit* POET.]

Brutus.
Lucilius and Titinius, bid the commanders
Prepare to lodge their companies tonight.

Cassius.
And come yourselves, and bring Messala with you
Immediately to us. [*Exeunt* LUCILIUS *and* TITINIUS.]

Brutus. Lucius, a bowl of wine.

[*Exit* LUCIUS.]

Cassius.
I did not think you could have been so angry.

Brutus.
O Cassius, I am sick of many griefs.

Cassius.
Of your philosophy you make no use,
If you give place to accidental evils.

Brutus.
No man bears sorrow better. Portia is dead.

Cassius. Ha? Portia?

Brutus. She is dead.

Cassius.
How scaped I killing when I crossed you so?
O insupportable and touching loss!
Upon what sickness?

Brutus. Impatient of my absence,
And grief that young Octavius with Mark Antony
Have made themselves so strong—for with her death
That tidings came—with this she fell distract,°
And (her attendants absent) swallowed fire.°

Cassius.
And died so?

Brutus. Even so.

Cassius. O ye immortal gods!

[*Enter* LUCIUS, *with wine and tapers.*]

131. cynic: rude person.

134. his time: the right time to speak.
135. jigging: rhyming.
136. Companion: lower-class fellow.

? **136.** *Remember that Shakespeare himself was a "jigging fool." What is the point of this scene with the poet?*

? **144.** *This reference is to Brutus's philosophy of Stoicism, which taught that we should master our emotions, lead lives dictated by reason and duty, and submit to fate. How do you think Brutus should deliver his next shocking line?*

? **145–160.** *Who is probably more emotional in this scene—Brutus or Cassius? (Many fine actors have shown no emotion as they played Brutus in this scene.)*

153. fell distract: became distraught.
154. According to Plutarch, Portia killed herself by putting hot coals in her mouth.

Brutus.
Speak no more of her. Give me a bowl of wine.
In this I bury all unkindness, Cassius.

[*Drinks.*]

Cassius.
My heart is thirsty for that noble pledge.
Fill, Lucius, till the wine o'erswell the cup;
I cannot drink too much of Brutus' love.

[*Drinks. Exit* LUCIUS.]

[*Enter* TITINIUS *and* MESSALA.]

Brutus.
Come in, Titinius! Welcome, good Messala.
Now sit we close about this taper here,
And call in question° our necessities.

163. call in question: consider.

Cassius.
Portia, art thou gone?

Brutus. No more, I pray you.
Messala, I have here receivèd letters
That young Octavius and Mark Antony
Come down upon us with a mighty power,
Bending their expedition toward Philippi.°

168. Philippi: ancient city in northern Greece.

Messala.
Myself have letters of the selfsame tenure.°

169. tenure: tenor; meaning.

Brutus.
With what addition?

Messala.
That by proscription and bills of outlawry°
Octavius, Antony, and Lepidus
Have put to death an hundred senators.

171. bills of outlawry: lists of proscribed people.

Brutus.
Therein our letters do not well agree.
Mine speak of seventy senators that died
By their proscriptions, Cicero being one.

Cassius.
Cicero one?

Messala. Cicero is dead,
And by that order of proscription.
Had you your letters from your wife, my lord?

Brutus. No, Messala.

Messala.
Nor nothing in your letters writ of her?

Brutus.
Nothing, Messala.

Messala. That methinks is strange.

Brutus.
Why ask you? Hear you aught of her in yours?

? **179.** *A peculiar scene now takes place, in which Brutus seems again to hear for the first time the news of his wife's death. Some scholars believe that the original account of Portia's death was told in lines 179-193 and that Shakespeare later rewrote the scene, which is now lines 141-155. A production might not use both scenes. Which would you use, and why? (If a director did decide to use both scenes, how should Brutus act in the second one?)*

Messala. No, my lord.

Brutus.
Now as you are a Roman, tell me true.

Messala.
Then like a Roman bear the truth I tell,
For certain she is dead, and by strange manner.

Brutus.
Why, farewell, Portia. We must die, Messala.
With meditating that she must die once,°
I have the patience to endure it now.

Messala.
Even so great men great losses should endure.

Cassius.
I have as much of this in art° as you,
But yet my nature could not bear it so.

Brutus.
Well, to our work alive. What do you think
Of marching to Philippi presently?

Cassius.
I do not think it good.

Brutus. Your reason?

Cassius. This it is:
'Tis better that the enemy seek us;
So shall he waste his means, weary his soldiers,
Doing himself offense, whilst we, lying still,
Are full of rest, defense, and nimbleness.

Brutus.
Good reasons must of force° give place to better.
The people 'twixt Philippi and this ground
Do stand but in a forced affection;°
For they have grudged us contribution.
The enemy, marching along by them,
By them shall make a fuller number up,
Come on refreshed, new-added and encouraged;
From which advantage shall we cut him off
If at Philippi we do face him there,
These people at our back.

Cassius. Hear me, good brother.

Brutus.
Under your pardon. You must note beside
That we have tried the utmost of our friends,
Our legions are brimful, our cause is ripe.
The enemy increaseth every day;
We, at the height, are ready to decline.
There is a tide in the affairs of men
Which, taken at the flood, leads on to fortune;
Omitted,° all the voyage of their life
Is bound in shallows and in miseries.

189. once: at some time.

? **190.** *The actor playing Brutus must be careful not to make him seem cold and unfeeling. How could this scene be played to suggest Brutus's humanity, as well as his Stoicism?*

192. in art: the art of being a Stoic.

? **200.** *What plan does Cassius propose regarding Antony's forces at Philippi?*

201. of force: of necessity.

203. That is, they support us only grudgingly.

218. Omitted: neglected.

On such a full sea are we now afloat,
And we must take the current when it serves,
Or lose our ventures.

Cassius. Then, with your will,° go on;
We'll along ourselves and meet them at Philippi.

Brutus.
The deep of night is crept upon our talk,
And nature must obey necessity,
Which we will niggard with a little rest.°
There is no more to say?

Cassius. No more. Good night.
Early tomorrow will we rise and hence.

[*Enter* LUCIUS.]

Brutus.
Lucius, my gown. [*Exit* LUCIUS.]
Farewell, good Messala.
Good night, Titinius. Noble, noble Cassius,
Good night, and good repose.

Cassius. O my dear brother,
This was an ill beginning of the night.
Never come such division 'tween our souls!
Let it not, Brutus.

[*Enter* LUCIUS, *with the gown.*]

Brutus. Everything is well.

Cassius.
Good night, my lord.

Brutus. Good night, good brother.

Titinius, Messala.
Good night, Lord Brutus.

Brutus. Farewell, every one.

[*Exeunt.*]

Give me the gown. Where is thy instrument?°

Lucius.
Here in the tent.

Brutus. What, thou speak'st drowsily?
Poor knave, I blame thee not; thou art o'erwatched.°
Call Claudius and some other of my men;
I'll have them sleep on cushions in my tent.

Lucius. Varro and Claudius!

[*Enter* VARRO *and* CLAUDIUS.]

Varro. Calls my lord?

Brutus.
I pray you, sirs, lie in my tent and sleep.
It may be I shall raise you by and by

? **222.** *Where does Brutus want to fight Antony, and why?*

222. with your will: as you wish.

? **223.** *Which man seems to dominate the action now?*

226. niggard with a little rest: cheat with a short period of sleep.

? **231.** *In some productions, at this point in the scene, Brutus takes a letter out of his pocket and burns it. What letter are we to assume he is destroying, and what does his action demonstrate?*

237. instrument: probably a lute.

239. o'erwatched: exhausted.

On business to my brother Cassius.

Varro.

So please you, we will stand and watch your pleasure.°

Brutus.

I will not have it so; lie down, good sirs;
It may be I shall otherwise bethink me.

[VARRO *and* CLAUDIUS *lie down.*]

Look, Lucius, here's the book I sought for so;
I put it in the pocket of my gown.

Lucius.

I was sure your lordship did not give it me.

Brutus.

Bear with me, good boy, I am much forgetful.
Canst thou hold up thy heavy eyes awhile,
And touch thy instrument a strain or two?

Lucius.

Ay, my lord, an't please you.

Brutus. It does, my boy.

I trouble thee too much, but thou art willing.

Lucius. It is my duty, sir.

Brutus.

I should not urge thy duty past thy might;
I know young bloods look for a time of rest.

Lucius. I have slept, my lord, already.

Brutus.

It was well done, and thou shalt sleep again;
I will not hold thee long. If I do live,
I will be good to thee.

[*Music, and a song.*]

This is a sleepy tune. O murd'rous° slumber!
Layest thou thy leaden mace° upon my boy,
That plays thee music? Gentle knave, good night;
I will not do thee so much wrong to wake thee.
If thou dost nod, thou break'st thy instrument;
I'll take it from thee; and, good boy, good night.
Let me see, let me see; is not the leaf turned down
Where I left reading? Here it is, I think.

[*Enter the* GHOST *of Caesar.*]

How ill this taper burns. Ha! Who comes here?
I think it is the weakness of mine eyes
That shapes this monstrous apparition.
It comes upon° me. Art thou anything?
Art thou some god, some angel, or some devil,
That mak'st my blood cold, and my hair to stare?°

247. watch your pleasure: wait for your orders.

? ***Stage direction.*** *How could lighting be used to suggest an intimate, drowsy, and nonmilitaristic scene?*

265. murd'rous: deathlike.

266. mace: heavy club carried by public officials.

276. upon: toward.

278. stare: stand on end.

Speak to me what thou art.
Ghost.
Thy evil spirit, Brutus.
Brutus. Why com'st thou?
Ghost.
To tell thee thou shalt see me at Philippi.
Brutus. Well; then I shall see thee again?
Ghost. Ay, at Philippi.
Brutus.
Why, I will see thee at Philippi then.

[*Exit* GHOST.]

Now I have taken heart thou vanishest.
Ill spirit, I would hold more talk with thee.
Boy! Lucius! Varro! Claudius! Sirs, awake!
Claudius!
Lucius. The strings, my lord, are false.°
Brutus.
He thinks he still is at his instrument.
Lucius awake!
Lucius. My lord?
Brutus.
Didst thou dream, Lucius, that thou so criedst out?
Lucius.
My lord, I do not know that I did cry.
Brutus.
Yes, that thou didst. Didst thou see anything?
Lucius. Nothing, my lord.
Brutus.
Sleep again, Lucius. Sirrah Claudius!
(*To* VARRO.) Fellow thou, awake!
Varro. My lord?
Claudius. My lord?
Brutus.
Why did you so cry out, sirs, in your sleep?
Both.
Did we, my lord?
Brutus. Ay. Saw you anything?
Varro.
No, my lord, I saw nothing.
Claudius. Nor I, my lord.
Brutus.
Go and commend me to my brother Cassius;
Bid him set on his pow'rs betimes before,°
And we will follow.
Both. It shall be done, my lord.

[*Exeunt.*]

? **279.** *How would you "stage" the Ghost? Would you have him in military dress? In his bloodied toga? Or would you not show the Ghost at all, but merely project his voice onstage?*

289. Lucius sleepily supposes that his instrument is out of tune.

? **293.** *In one production, the ghost scene was staged so that the Ghost's words seemed to come from the mouth of the sleeping Lucius. How would this explain Brutus's question to Lucius about "crying out"?*

305. That is, lead his forces out early in the morning, ahead of Brutus and his troops.

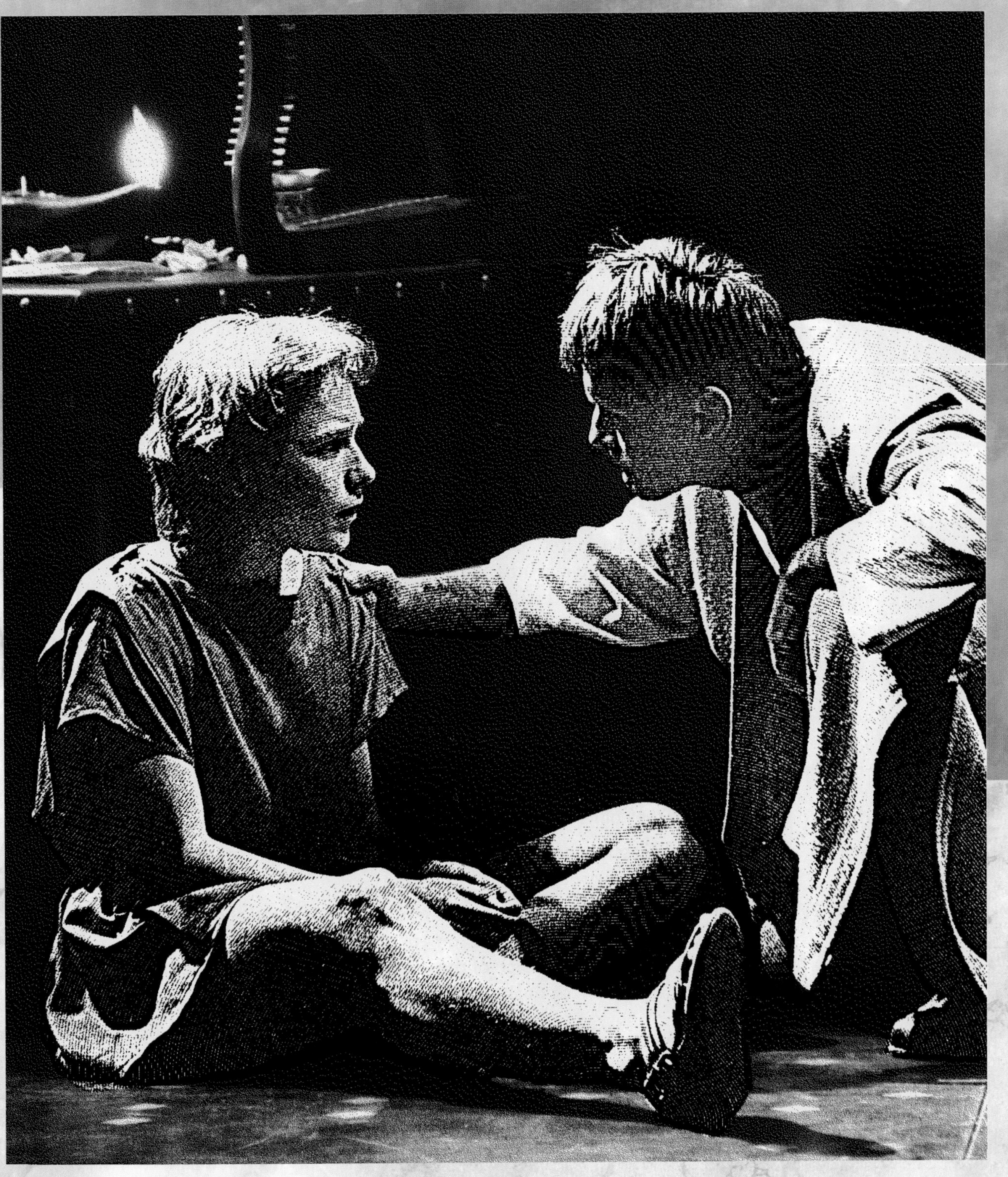

"Didst thou dream, Lucius, that thou so criedst out?"

Making Meanings
Act IV

First Thoughts

1. Whose behavior surprises you in this act? Why? How do you feel about this character now?

Shaping Interpretations

2. How is Antony **characterized** by his words and actions in Scene 1? In your opinion, is the Antony we see in this scene consistent with the Antony we saw earlier?

3. If you were staging the play, how would you let your audience know that in Scene 2 the **setting** has changed—instead of a house in Rome, the setting is now a battlefield?

4. In drama, relationships burst open under pressure and reveal certain truths. After the burst, the relationship is either renewed or ended. Brutus and Cassius have been friends throughout the play, with Cassius clearly the subordinate. In Scene 3, they quarrel. How is their **conflict** resolved? What has become of their relationship by the end of the scene?

5. **Compare and contrast** the meeting of the conspirators in Scene 3 with the meeting of the triumvirate in Scene 1. In what ways are the scenes parallel? In what ways are they different?

6. The scene with Cassius shows a harsh Brutus. What kind of Brutus appears with Lucius and the guards?

7. As the director of the play, you would have to make a decision about how to represent the Ghost. You could have someone play the Ghost, or you could just use a voice. What would each of these choices suggest about whether or not the Ghost is real? What might the Ghost represent to Brutus?

Connecting with the Text

8. Which **character** do you sympathize with most by the end of Act IV? Why?

9. In lines 141–160 of Scene 3, Brutus and Cassius display different reactions to Portia's death. Why are their reactions different? How do you feel about these men now?

10. Think about the two groups preparing for war here. Which side would you want to be on? Why?

Reading Check

a. Describe the military situation presented in Act IV. What is going on between the conspirators and the triumvirate?

b. As Scene 1 opens, what are Antony, Octavius, and Lepidus doing? What breach has opened among them?

c. Why is Brutus uneasy at the beginning of Scene 2?

d. What are the issues that cause Brutus and Cassius to quarrel in Scene 3?

e. According to Brutus, what were the reasons for Portia's death? How does he respond to her death?

f. What vision does Brutus see at the end of Act IV?

CHOICES: Building Your Portfolio

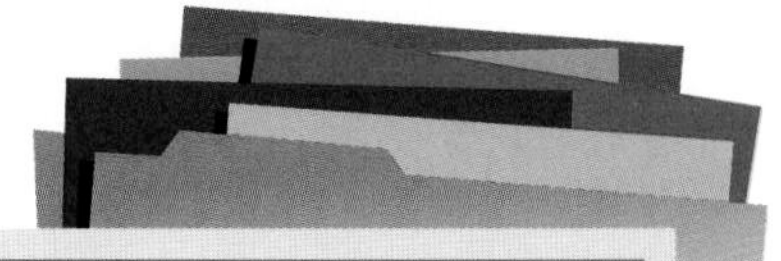

Writer's Notebook

1. Collecting Ideas for an Evaluation

Building a case and evaluating it. Try your hand at assembling **persuasive evidence** to support or refute this statement: *The conspiracy led by Brutus and Cassius was a force for good.* Review what you know from the play so far, and note all the evidence you can find that supports your point of view. Then, exchange notes with a partner, and evaluate his or her evidence. Save your notes for possible use in the Writer's Workshop assignment on page 892.

Creative Writing/ Speaking

2. A Boy's View

If you were young Lucius, what would you think about the events you've observed? How would you feel about Brutus? Write Lucius's thoughts and fears in a **journal entry**. Date the entry, and have Lucius tell where he is while writing. Read your journal aloud to the class.

READING SKILLS AND STRATEGIES

Recognizing Anachronisms

An **anachronism** (ə·nak′rə·niz′əm) (from *ana-*, "against," and *chronos,* "time") is an event or a detail that is inappropriate for the time period. For example, a car in a story about the Civil War would be an anachronism; cars had not yet been invented. In a play set in the 1920s, the word *nerd* would be an anachronism. *Nerd* wasn't used as slang until much later in the twentieth century.

Remember that *Julius Caesar* is set in 44–43 B.C., in ancient Rome. Do you see anachronisms in these passages?

1. . . . he plucked me ope his doublet and offered them his throat to cut.

—Act I, Scene 2, lines 264–266

2. Peace! Count the clock.

The clock hath stricken three.

—Act II, Scene 1, line 192

3. Look, Lucius, here's the book I sought for so;
I put it in the pocket of my gown.

—Act IV, Scene 3, lines 250–251

Try It Out

➤ Find the one word in each passage at the left that is "out of time."

➤ Suppose Shakespeare wanted to correct his errors. How could he eliminate the anachronisms?

➤ Make a class list of other situations that would be anachronistic. An example might be the conspirators' use of guns instead of daggers to kill Caesar or Brutus's receipt of a telegram telling him of Portia's death.

ACT V Scene 1. *The plains of Philippi.*

Enter OCTAVIUS, ANTONY, *and their* ARMY.

Octavius.
Now, Antony, our hopes are answerèd;
You said the enemy would not come down,
But keep the hills and upper regions.
It proves not so; their battles° are at hand;
They mean to warn us at Philippi here,
Answering before we do demand of them.

Antony.
Tut, I am in their bosoms,° and I know
Wherefore they do it. They could be content
To visit other places, and come down
With fearful bravery, thinking by this face
To fasten in our thoughts that they have courage;
But 'tis not so.

[*Enter a* MESSENGER.]

Messenger. Prepare you, generals,
The enemy comes on in gallant show;
Their bloody sign° of battle is hung out,
And something to be done immediately.

Antony.
Octavius, lead your battle softly on
Upon the left hand of the even° field.

Octavius.
Upon the right hand I; keep thou the left.

Antony.
Why do you cross me in this exigent?°

Octavius.
I do not cross you; but I will do so.

[*March. Drum. Enter* BRUTUS, CASSIUS, *and their* ARMY; LUCILIUS, TITINIUS, MESSALA, *and others.*]

Brutus.
They stand, and would have parley.

Cassius.
Stand fast, Titinius, we must out and talk.

Octavius.
Mark Antony, shall we give sign of battle?

Antony.
No, Caesar, we will answer on their charge.
Make forth, the generals would have some words.

Octavius.
Stir not until the signal.

? ***Stage direction.*** *This act is crammed with action and could be confusing to follow. As you read, you might trace in your Reader's Log the movements of the armies. What props might be used to indicate that we are now on the plains of Philippi with Antony's and Octavius's army?*

4. **battles:** armies.

7. **am in their bosoms:** know their secret thoughts.

14. **sign:** flag.

17. **even:** level.

19. **exigent:** critical moment.

? ***Stage direction.*** *The armies should be placed at opposite sides of the stage, with a kind of no man's land between them. In the next lines, notice which man in which army speaks. They are taunting one another across the short distance that separates them.*

Brutus.
Words before blows; is it so, countrymen?
Octavius.
Not that we love words better, as you do.
Brutus.
Good words are better than bad strokes, Octavius.
Antony.
In your bad strokes, Brutus, you give good words;
Witness the hole you made in Caesar's heart,
Crying "Long live! Hail, Caesar!"
Cassius. Antony,
The posture of your blows are yet unknown;
But for your words, they rob the Hybla° bees,
And leave them honeyless.
Antony. Not stingless too.
Brutus.
O, yes, and soundless too;
For you have stol'n their buzzing, Antony,
And very wisely threat before you sting.
Antony.
Villains! You did not so, when your vile daggers
Hacked one another in the sides of Caesar.
You showed your teeth like apes, and fawned like hounds,
And bowed like bondmen, kissing Caesar's feet;
Whilst damnèd Casca, like a cur, behind
Struck Caesar on the neck. O you flatterers!
Cassius.
Flatterers! Now, Brutus, thank yourself;
This tongue had not offended so today,
If Cassius might have ruled.°
Octavius.
Come, come, the cause. If arguing make us sweat,
The proof of it will turn to redder drops.
Look,
I draw a sword against conspirators.
When think you that the sword goes up again?
Never, till Caesar's three and thirty wounds
Be well avenged; or till another Caesar°
Have added slaughter to the sword of traitors.
Brutus.
Caesar, thou canst not die by traitors' hands,
Unless thou bring'st them with thee.
Octavius. So I hope.
I was not born to die on Brutus' sword.
Brutus.
O, if thou wert the noblest of thy strain,
Young man, thou couldst not die more honorable.

34. Hybla: town in Sicily famous for its honey.

47. ruled: gotten his way.

? **47.** *What is Cassius referring to?*

54. another Caesar: meaning Octavius himself.

Cassius.

A peevish schoolboy, worthless° of such honor,
Joined with a masker and a reveler.

Antony.

Old Cassius still!

Octavius. Come, Antony; away!
Defiance, traitors, hurl we in your teeth.

61. worthless: unworthy.

62. *Whom is Cassius taunting here? What does he think of this "new Caesar"?*

". . . I DRAW A SWORD AGAINST CONSPIRATORS."

If you dare fight today, come to the field;
If not, when you have stomachs.

[*Exeunt* OCTAVIUS, ANTONY, *and* ARMY.]

Cassius.
Why, now blow wind, swell billow, and swim bark!
The storm is up, and all is on the hazard.°

68. on the hazard: at risk.

Brutus.
Ho, Lucilius, hark, a word with you.

[LUCILIUS *and* MESSALA *stand forth.*]

Lucilius. My lord?

[BRUTUS *and* LUCILIUS *converse apart.*]

Cassius.
Messala.
Messala. What says my general?
Cassius. Messala,
This is my birthday; as this very day
Was Cassius born. Give me thy hand, Messala:
Be thou my witness that against my will
(As Pompey was) am I compelled to set
Upon one battle all our liberties.
You know that I held Epicurus strong,°
And his opinion; now I change my mind,
And partly credit things that do presage.°
Coming from Sardis, on our former ensign°
Two mighty eagles fell, and there they perched,
Gorging and feeding from our soldiers' hands,
Who to Philippi here consorted° us.
This morning are they fled away and gone,
And in their steads do ravens, crows, and kites
Fly o'er our heads and downward look on us
As we were sickly prey; their shadows seem
A canopy most fatal, under which
Our army lies, ready to give up the ghost.
Messala.
Believe not so.
Cassius. I but believe it partly,
For I am fresh of spirit and resolved
To meet all perils very constantly.
Brutus.
Even so, Lucilius.
Cassius. Now, most noble Brutus,
The gods today stand friendly, that we may,
Lovers in peace, lead on our days to age!
But since the affairs of men rests still incertain,
Let's reason with the worst that may befall.
If we do lose this battle, then is this
The very last time we shall speak together.
What are you then determinèd to do?
Brutus.
Even by the rule of that philosophy
By which I did blame Cato for the death

76. held Epicurus strong: believed in the philosophy of Epicurus, a philosopher of the third century B.C. who believed that omens were worthless.
78. presage: foretell.
79. former ensign: foremost flag.

82. consorted: accompanied.

? **88.** *What images in this speech suggest death and decay?*

? **92.** *Remember that the two pairs of men have been talking separately. What action should now take place onstage?*

Which he did give himself; I know not how,
But I do find it cowardly and vile,
For fear of what might fall, so to prevent
The time° of life, arming myself with patience
To stay the providence of some high powers
That govern us below.

Cassius. Then, if we lose this battle,
You are contented to be led in triumph°
Thorough the streets of Rome?

Brutus.
No, Cassius, no; think not, thou noble Roman,
That ever Brutus will go bound to Rome;
He bears too great a mind. But this same day
Must end that work the ides of March begun;
And whether we shall meet again I know not.
Therefore our everlasting farewell take.
Forever, and forever, farewell, Cassius!
If we do meet again, why, we shall smile;
If not, why then this parting was well made.

Cassius.
Forever, and forever, farewell, Brutus!
If we do meet again, we'll smile indeed;
If not, 'tis true this parting was well made.

Brutus.
Why then, lead on. O, that a man might know
The end of this day's business ere it come!
But it sufficeth that the day will end,
And then the end is known. Come, ho! Away!

[*Exeunt.*]

105. time: term, or natural span.

107. *Brutus refers again to his Stoic philosophy, which taught that he should be ruled by reason, not by emotion. What is Brutus saying about suicide?*

108. in triumph: as a captive in the victor's procession.

109. *According to this speech, what will happen to the losing armies?*

Scene 2. *The field of battle.*

Alarum.° Enter BRUTUS *and* MESSALA.

Brutus.
Ride, ride, Messala, ride, and give these bills°
Unto the legions on the other side.

[*Loud alarum.*]

Let them set on at once; for I perceive
But cold demeanor° in Octavius' wing,
And sudden push° gives them the overthrow.
Ride, ride, Messala! Let them all come down.

[*Exeunt.*]

Alarum: call to arms by drum or trumpet.

1. bills: orders.

4. cold demeanor: lack of fighting spirit.

5. push: attack.

6. *What orders has Brutus given his army?*

Scene 3. *The field of battle.*

Alarums. Enter CASSIUS *and* TITINIUS.

Cassius.
O, look, Titinius, look, the villains fly!
Myself have to mine own turned enemy.
This ensign° here of mine was turning back;
I slew the coward, and did take it° from him.

Titinius.
O Cassius, Brutus gave the word too early,
Who, having some advantage on Octavius,
Took it too eagerly; his soldiers fell to spoil,°
Whilst we by Antony are all enclosed.

[*Enter* PINDARUS.]

Pindarus.
Fly further off, my lord, fly further off!
Mark Antony is in your tents, my lord.
Fly, therefore, noble Cassius, fly far off!

Cassius.
This hill is far enough. Look, look, Titinius!
Are those my tents where I perceive the fire?

Titinius.
They are, my lord.

Cassius. Titinius, if thou lovest me,
Mount thou my horse and hide thy spurs in him°
Till he have brought thee up to yonder troops
And here again, that I may rest assured
Whether yond troops are friend or enemy.

Titinius.
I will be here again even with a thought.° [*Exit.*]

Cassius.
Go, Pindarus, get higher on that hill;
My sight was ever thick. Regard Titinius,
And tell me what thou not'st about the field.

[*Exit* PINDARUS.]

This day I breathèd first. Time is come round,
And where I did begin, there shall I end.
My life is run his compass.° Sirrah, what news?

Pindarus (*above*). O my lord!

Cassius. What news?

Pindarus (*above*).
Titinius is enclosèd round about
With horsemen that make to him on the spur;°
Yet he spurs on. Now they are almost on him.
Now, Titinius! Now some light. O, he lights too!

---

3. ensign: standard-bearer.

4. it: the flag (standard).

7. spoil: loot.

? **8.** *What have Brutus's and Cassius's armies done?*

15. In other words, dig your spurs into him to make him go at top speed.

19. even with a thought: immediately.

? **24.** *What is Cassius referring to here?*

25. is run his compass: has completed its appointed span.

? **26.** *Pindarus stands on the upper stage, suggesting that he is on the hilltop, looking over the field of battle. What does he report to Cassius, who stands below?*

29. on the spur: at top speed.

He's ta'en! (*Shout.*) And, hark! They shout for joy.

Cassius.

Come down; behold no more.
O, coward that I am, to live so long,
To see my best friend ta'en before my face!

[*Enter* PINDARUS.]

Come hither, sirrah.
In Parthia° did I take thee prisoner;
And then I swore thee, saving of° thy life,
That whatsoever I did bid thee do,
Thou shouldst attempt it. Come now, keep thine oath.
Now be a freeman, and with this good sword,
That ran through Caesar's bowels, search this bosom.
Stand not to answer. Here, take thou the hilts,
And when my face is covered, as 'tis now,
Guide thou the sword—Caesar, thou art revenged,
Even with the sword that killed thee. [*Dies.*]

37. Parthia: ancient country (corresponding to part of modern Iran) that was the site of many Roman military campaigns.
38. saving of: sparing.

? **46.** *What does Cassius have Pindarus do for him? What does he believe has happened?*

Pindarus.

So, I am free; yet would not so have been,
Durst I have done my will. O Cassius!
Far from this country Pindarus shall run,
Where never Roman shall take note of him. [*Exit.*]

[*Enter* TITINIUS *and* MESSALA.]

Messala.

It is but change,° Titinius; for Octavius
Is overthrown by noble Brutus' power,
As Cassius' legions are by Antony.

51. change: exchange of fortune.

Titinius.

These tidings will well comfort Cassius.

Messala.

Where did you leave him?

Titinius. All disconsolate,
With Pindarus his bondman, on this hill.

? **54.** *Titinius and Messala enter from the wings and do not see Cassius's body at first. What irony do we in the audience feel when we hear their conversation?*

Messala.

Is not that he that lies upon the ground?

Titinius.

He lies not like the living. O my heart!

Messala.

Is not that he?

Titinius. No, this was he, Messala,
But Cassius is no more. O setting sun,
As in thy red rays thou dost sink to night,
So in his red blood Cassius' day is set.
The sun of Rome is set. Our day is gone;
Clouds, dews, and dangers come; our deeds are done!

"THE SUN OF ROME IS SET."

Mistrust of° my success hath done this deed.

Messala.
Mistrust of good success hath done this deed.
O hateful Error, Melancholy's child,
Why dost thou show to the apt° thoughts of men
The things that are not? O Error, soon conceived,
Thou never com'st unto a happy birth,
But kill'st the mother° that engend'red thee!

Titinius.
What, Pindarus! Where art thou, Pindarus?

Messala.
Seek him, Titinius, whilst I go to meet
The noble Brutus, thrusting this report
Into his ears. I may say "thrusting" it;
For piercing steel and darts envenomèd
Shall be as welcome to the ears of Brutus
As tidings of this sight.

Titinius. Hie you, Messala,
And I will seek for Pindarus the while.

[*Exit* MESSALA.]

Why didst thou send me forth, brave Cassius?
Did I not meet thy friends, and did not they
Put on my brows this wreath of victory,
And bid me give it thee? Didst thou not hear their shouts?
Alas, thou hast misconstrued everything!
But hold thee, take this garland on thy brow;
Thy Brutus bid me give it thee, and I
Will do his bidding. Brutus, come apace,°
And see how I regarded Caius Cassius.
By your leave, gods.° This is a Roman's part:°
Come, Cassius' sword, and find Titinius' heart.

[*Dies.*]

[*Alarum. Enter* BRUTUS, MESSALA, YOUNG CATO, STRATO, VOLUMNIUS, *and* LUCILIUS.]

Brutus.
Where, where, Messala, doth his body lie?

Messala.
Lo, yonder, and Titinius mourning it.

Brutus.
Titinius' face is upward.

Cato. He is slain.

Brutus.
O Julius Caesar, thou art mighty yet!
Thy spirit walks abroad, and turns our swords

65. Mistrust of: disbelief in.

? **65.** *What does Titinius think caused Cassius to kill himself?*

68. apt: credulous; easily impressed.

71. the mother: that is to say, Cassius, who conceived the error.

87. apace: quickly.

89. He asks the gods' permission to end his life before the time they have allotted to him. **part:** role, duty.

In our own proper entrails. [*Low alarums.*]

Cato. Brave Titinius!
Look, whe'r° he have not crowned dead Cassius.

Brutus.
Are yet two Romans living such as these?
The last of all the Romans, fare thee well!
It is impossible that ever Rome
Should breed thy fellow.° Friends, I owe moe tears
To this dead man than you shall see me pay.
I shall find time, Cassius; I shall find time.
Come, therefore, and to Thasos° send his body;
His funerals shall not be in our camp,
Lest it discomfort° us. Lucilius, come,
And come, young Cato; let us to the field.
Labeo and Flavius set our battles on.
'Tis three o'clock; and, Romans, yet ere night
We shall try fortune in a second fight. [*Exeunt.*]

96. *Why does Brutus invoke Caesar's name?*

97. whe'r: whether.

101. fellow: equal.

104. Thasos: island in the Aegean Sea, near Philippi.

106. discomfort: discourage.

Scene 4. *The field of battle.*

Alarum. Enter BRUTUS, MESSALA, YOUNG CATO, LUCILIUS, *and* FLAVIUS.

Brutus.
Yet, countrymen, O, yet hold up your heads!
[*Exit, with followers.*]

Cato.
What bastard° doth not? Who will go with me?
I will proclaim my name about the field.
I am the son of Marcus Cato,° ho!
A foe to tyrants, and my country's friend.
I am the son of Marcus Cato, ho!

[*Enter* SOLDIERS *and fight.*]

Lucilius.
And I am Brutus, Marcus Brutus, I;
Brutus, my country's friend, know me for Brutus!

[YOUNG CATO *falls.*]

O young and noble Cato, art thou down?
Why, now thou diest as bravely as Titinius,
And mayst be honored, being Cato's son.

First Soldier.
Yield, or thou diest.

Lucilius. Only I yield to die.

2. bastard: low fellow.

4. Thus he is Portia's brother.

7. *Lucilius is impersonating Brutus. What are these young men doing, and why?*

There is so much that thou wilt kill me straight;°
Kill Brutus, and be honored in his death.

First Soldier.
We must not. A noble prisoner!

[*Enter* ANTONY.]

Second Soldier.
Room, ho! Tell Antony, Brutus is ta'en.

First Soldier.
I'll tell the news. Here comes the general.
Brutus is ta'en, Brutus is ta'en, my lord.

Antony.
Where is he?

Lucilius.
Safe, Antony; Brutus is safe enough.
I dare assure thee that no enemy
Shall ever take alive the noble Brutus.
The gods defend him from so great a shame!
When you do find him, or alive or dead,
He will be found like Brutus, like himself.°

Antony.
This is not Brutus, friend, but, I assure you,
A prize no less in worth. Keep this man safe;
Give him all kindness. I had rather have
Such men my friends than enemies. Go on,
And see whe'r Brutus be alive or dead,
And bring us word unto Octavius' tent
How everything is chanced.° [*Exeunt.*]

13. That is, there is so much inducement to kill me that you will surely do so right away. (Some editors have interpreted this line to mean that Lucilius is offering his captors money to kill him rather than take him prisoner.)

25. **like himself:** true to his own noble nature.

32. **chanced:** turned out.

? 32. *Not long ago, Antony was compiling a list of the enemies he was to have murdered. How does he seem to have changed?*

Scene 5. *The field of battle.*

Enter BRUTUS, DARDANIUS, CLITUS, STRATO, *and* VOLUMNIUS.

Brutus.
Come, poor remains of friends, rest on this rock.

Clitus.
Statilius showed the torchlight, but, my lord,
He came not back; he is or ta'en or slain.°

Brutus.
Sit thee down, Clitus. Slaying is the word;
It is a deed in fashion. Hark thee, Clitus.

[*Whispers.*]

Clitus.
What, I, my lord? No, not for all the world!

Brutus.
Peace then, no words.

3. According to Plutarch, Statilius volunteered to see what was happening at Cassius's camp. If all was well, he was to signal with his torchlight. He did signal but then was killed while returning to Brutus's camp.

? 5. *What is Brutus's mood?*

Clitus. I'll rather kill myself.

Brutus.
Hark thee, Dardanius. [*Whispers.*]

Dardanius. Shall I do such a deed?

Clitus. O Dardanius!

Dardanius. O Clitus!

Clitus.
What ill request did Brutus make to thee?

Dardanius.
To kill him, Clitus. Look, he meditates.

Clitus.
Now is that noble vessel° full of grief,
That it runs over even at his eyes.

Brutus.
Come hither, good Volumnius; list° a word.

Volumnius.
What says my lord?

Brutus. Why, this, Volumnius:
The ghost of Caesar hath appeared to me
Two several° times by night; at Sardis once,
And this last night here in Philippi fields.
I know my hour is come.

Volumnius. Not so, my lord.

Brutus.
Nay, I am sure it is, Volumnius.
Thou seest the world, Volumnius, how it goes;
Our enemies have beat us to the pit.°

[*Low alarums.*]

It is more worthy to leap in ourselves
Than tarry till they push us. Good Volumnius,
Thou know'st that we two went to school together;
Even for that our love of old, I prithee
Hold thou my sword-hilts whilst I run on it.

Volumnius.
That's not an office for a friend, my lord.

[*Alarum still.*]

Clitus.
Fly, fly, my lord, there is no tarrying here.

Brutus.
Farewell to you; and you; and you, Volumnius.
Strato, thou hast been all this while asleep;
Farewell to thee too, Strato. Countrymen,
My heart doth joy that yet in all my life
I found no man but he was true to me.
I shall have glory by this losing day

13. vessel: figure of speech meaning a human being.

15. list: listen to.

18. several: separate.

23. pit: trap for capturing wild animals; also, a grave.

More than Octavius and Mark Antony
By this vile conquest shall attain unto.
So fare you well at once, for Brutus' tongue
Hath almost ended his life's history.
Night hangs upon mine eyes; my bones would rest,
That have but labored to attain this hour.

[*Alarum. Cry within,* "Fly, fly, fly!"]

Clitus.
Fly, my lord, fly!

Brutus. Hence! I will follow.

[*Exeunt* CLITUS, DARDANIUS, *and* VOLUMNIUS.]

41. *What does he mean by saying that "night hangs upon" his eyes?*

"HOLD THEN MY SWORD, AND TURN
AWAY THY FACE,
WHILE I DO RUN UPON IT."

I prithee, Strato, stay thou by thy lord,
Thou art a fellow of a good respect.°
Thy life hath had some smatch° of honor in it;
Hold then my sword, and turn away thy face,
While I do run upon it. Wilt thou, Strato?

Strato.
Give me your hand first. Fare you well, my lord.

Brutus.
Farewell, good Strato—Caesar, now be still;
I killed not thee with half so good a will. [*Dies.*]

[*Alarum. Retreat. Enter* ANTONY, OCTAVIUS, MESSALA, LUCILIUS, *and the* ARMY.]

Octavius. What man is that?

Messala.
My master's man. Strato, where is thy master?

Strato.
Free from the bondage you are in, Messala;
The conquerors can but make a fire of him.
For Brutus only overcame himself,
And no man else hath honor by his death.

Lucilius.
So Brutus should be found. I thank thee, Brutus,
That thou hast proved Lucilius' saying true.

Octavius.
All that served Brutus, I will entertain them.
Fellow, wilt thou bestow° thy time with me?

Strato.
Ay, if Messala will prefer° me to you.

Octavius. Do so, good Messala.

Messala. How died my master, Strato?

Strato.
I held the sword, and he did run on it.

Messala.
Octavius, then take him to follow thee,
That did the latest service to my master.

Antony.
This was the noblest Roman of them all.
All the conspirators save only he
Did that they did in envy of great Caesar;
He, only in a general honest thought
And common good to all, made one of them.°
His life was gentle, and the elements
So mixed in him that Nature might stand up
And say to all the world, "This was a man!"

Octavius.
According to his virtue, let us use° him

45. respect: reputation.

46. smatch: trace; taste.

? **51.** *How many bodies now lie on the stage? It is important for a director of a Shakespearean tragedy to remember how many bodies are onstage. Getting rid of them is often a challenge.*

61. bestow: spend.

? **61.** *How does Octavius indicate by his words to his former enemies that the strife is finally over?*

62. prefer: recommend.

72. made one of them: joined their group.

76. use: treat.

With all respect and rites of burial.
Within my tent his bones tonight shall lie,
Most like a soldier ordered honorably.
So call the field to rest, and let's away
To part° the glories of this happy day.

[*Exeunt omnes.*]

81. part: divide.

81. *Order has been restored; healing will begin. Which actor would you have exit last?*

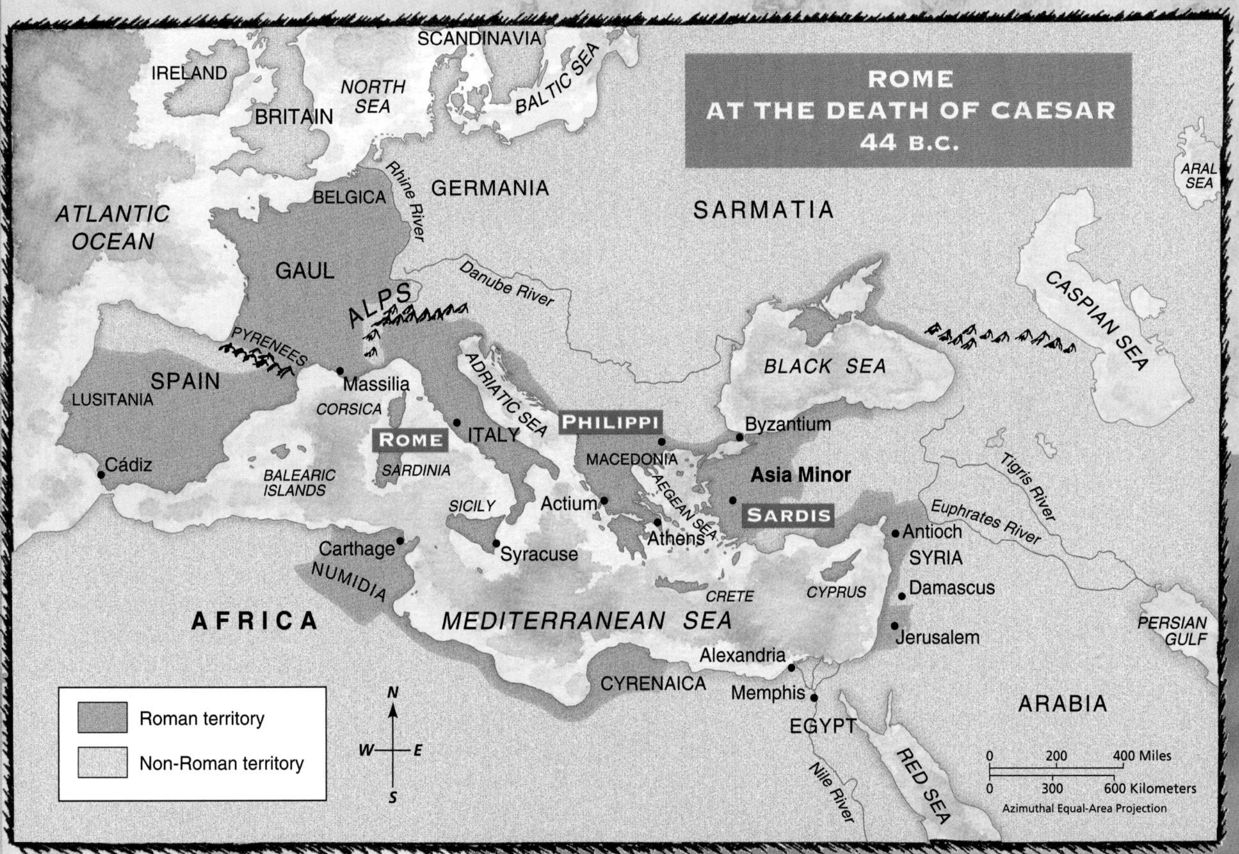

Connections | **A PLAY REVIEW**

On November 11, 1937, when Hitler and Mussolini were in power, the American director Orson Welles staged a modern-dress Julius Caesar *at the Mercury Theater in New York City. Here is John Mason Brown's review, reprinted with permission from the* New York Post.

Julius Caesar in an Absorbing Production

BY JOHN MASON BROWN

The Bettmann Archive.

The Orson Welles production of *Julius Caesar* (Mercury Theater, New York, 1937).

This is no funeral oration such as Miss Bankhead and Mr. Tearle forced me to deliver yesterday when they interred *Antony and Cleopatra.*[1] I come to praise *Caesar* at the Mercury, not to bury it. Of all the many new plays and productions the season has so far revealed, this modern-dress version of the mob mischief and demagoguery which can follow the assassination of a dictator is by all odds the most exciting, the most imaginative, the most topical, the most awesome, and the most absorbing.

The touch of genius is upon it. It liberates Shakespeare from the straitjacket of tradition. Gone are the togas and all the schoolroom recollections of a plaster Julius. Blown away is the dust of antiquity. Banished are the costumed Equity members, so ill-at-ease in a painted forum, spouting speeches which have tortured the memory of each member of the audience.

Due to Orson Welles's inspirational concept and the sheer brilliance of his staging, Shakespeare ceases at the Mercury to be the darling of the College Board of Examiners.[2] Unfettered and with all the vigor that was his when he spoke to the groundlings of his own day, he becomes the contemporary of us who are Undergroundlings. What he wrote with Plutarch in his mind, we are privileged to hear with today's headlines screaming in our eyes.

New York has already enjoyed its successful Shakespearean revivals in modern dress. There was *Hamlet*. There was *The Taming of the Shrew*. Then, under this same Mr. Welles's direction, Harlem flirted with a tantalizing, if unrealized, idea in its voodoo *Macbeth*. But these productions, vivifying as they have proven, have at their best been no more than quickening experiences *in* the theater.

The astonishing, all-impressive virtue of Mr. Welles's *Julius Caesar* is that, magnificent as it is as theater, it is far larger than its medium. Something deathless and dangerous in the world sweeps past you down the darkened aisles at the Mercury and takes possession of the proud, gaunt stage. It is something fearful and ominous, something turbulent and to be dreaded, which distends the drama to include the life of nations as well as of men. It is an ageless warning, made in such arresting terms that it not only gives a new vitality to an ancient story but unrolls in your mind's eye a map of the world which is increasingly splotched with sickening colors.

Mr. Welles does not dress his conspirators and his Storm Troopers in Black Shirts or in Brown. He does not have to. The antique Rome, which we had thought was

1. Tallulah Bankhead opened in *Antony and Cleopatra* on November 10, 1937. Mr. Brown gave the production an unfavorable review.

2. A group of academicians who set standards for college-entrance exams and for evaluating theses for advanced degrees.

securely Roman in Shakespeare's tragedy, he shows us to be a dateless state of mind. Of all the conspirators at work in the text, Mr. Welles is the most artful. He is not content to leave Shakespeare a great dramatist. He also turns him into a great anticipator. At his disposal Mr. Welles places a Time-Machine which carries him away from the past at which he had aimed and down through the centuries to the present. To an extent no other director in our day and country has equaled, Mr. Welles proves in his production that Shakespeare was indeed not of an age but for all time. After this surly modern Caesar, dressed in a green uniform and scowling behind the mask-like face of a contemporary dictator, has fallen at the Mercury and new mischief is afoot, we cannot but shudder before the prophet's wisdom of those lines which read:

"How many ages hence
Shall this our lofty scene be
acted over
In states unborn and accents
yet unknown!"[3]

To fit the play into modern dress and give it its fullest implication, Mr. Welles has not hesitated to take his liberties with the script. Unlike Professor Strunk, however, who attempted to improve upon *Antony and Cleopatra,* he has not stabbed it through the heart. He has only chopped away at its body. You may miss a few fingers, even an arm and leg in the *Julius Caesar* you thought you knew. But the heart of the drama beats more vigorously in this production than it has in years. If the play ceases to be Shakespeare's tragedy, it does manage to become ours. That is the whole point and glory of Mr. Welles's unorthodox, but welcome, restatement of it.

He places it upon a bare stage, the brick walls of which are crimson and naked. A few steps and a platform and an abyss beyond are the setting. A few steps—and the miracle of enveloping shadows, knife-like rays, and superbly changing lights. That is all. And it is all that is needed. In its streamlined simplicity this setting achieves the glorious, unimpeded freedom of an Elizabethan stage. Yet no backgrounds of the winter have been as eloquent or contributive as is this frankly presentational set. It is a setting spacious enough for both the winds and victims of demagoguery to sweep across it like a hurricane. And sweep across it they do, in precisely this fashion.

Mr. Welles's direction is as heightening as is his use of an almost empty stage. His groupings are of that fluid, stressful, virtuoso sort one usually has to journey to Russia to see. He proves himself a brilliant innovator in his deployment of his principals and his movement of his crowds. His direction, which is constantly creative, is never more so than in its first revelation of Caesar hearing the warning of the soothsayer, or in the fine scene in which Cinna, the poet, is engulfed by a sinister crowd of ruffians. Even when one misses Shakespeare's lines, Mr. Welles keeps drumming the meaning of his play into our minds by the scuffling of his mobs when they prowl in the shadows, or the herd-like thunder of their feet when they run as one threatening body. It is a memorable device. Like the setting in which it is used, it is pure theater: vibrant, unashamed, and enormously effective.

The theatrical virtues of this modern-dress *Julius Caesar* do not stop with its excitements as a stunt in showmanship. They extend to the performances. As Brutus Mr. Welles shows once again how uncommon is his gift for speaking great words simply. His tones are conversational. His manner is quiet. The deliberation of his speech is the mark of the honesty which flames within him. His reticent Brutus is at once a foil to the staginess of the production as a whole and to the oratory of Caesar and Antony. He is a perplexed liberal, this Brutus; an idealist who is swept by bad events into actions which have no less dangerous consequences for the state. His simple reading of the funeral oration is in happy contrast to what is usually done with the speech.

George Coulouris is an admirable Antony. So fresh is his characterization, so intelligent his performance that even "Friends, Romans, countrymen" sounds on his tongue as if it were a rabble-rousing harangue which he is uttering for the first time. Joseph Holland's Caesar is an imperious dictator who could be found frowning at you in this week's newsreels. He is excellently conceived and excellently projected. Some mention, however inadequate, must also be made of Martin Gabel's capable Cassius, of John Hoysradt's Decius Brutus, of the conspirators whose black hats are pluck'd about their ears, and Norman Lloyd's humorous yet deeply affecting Cinna.

It would be easy to find faults here and there: to wonder about the wisdom of some of the textual changes even in terms of the present production's aims; to complain that the whole tragedy does not fit with equal ease into its modern treatment; and to wish this or that scene had been played a little differently. But such fault-findings strike me in the case of this *Julius Caesar* as being as picayune as they are ungrateful. What Mr. Welles and his associates at the Mercury have achieved is a triumph that is exceptional from almost every point of view.

—from the *New York Post,*
November 12, 1937

3. Lines spoken by Cassius, Act III, Scene 1, lines 111–113.

Making Meanings
Act V

First Thoughts

1. How do you feel about what happens to Brutus and Cassius?

Shaping Interpretations

2. Why is it significant that Octavius delivers the play's final speech?
3. Identify at least three examples of **irony** in Scene 3, Cassius's death scene. How do these ironies make you feel?
4. Look at Scenes 3 and 5 and the dying words of Cassius and Brutus. How does each man view Caesar's murder? Do you think each man had a choice other than suicide? Explain.
5. Brutus makes two mistakes—one in Act II and one in Act III—that stem from his idealized vision of the assassination and his self-image as an "honorable man." What are these errors, and how do they lead to Brutus's downfall?
6. Describe your final view of Brutus and the choices he made. Did he misread the evidence that Caesar might become king? Should he have betrayed a friend for the public good? Was he wrong to kill the only man who could bring order out of chaos? Support your responses with evidence from the play.
7. Critics argue that Julius Caesar dominates the play (Cassius says in Act I that he "doth bestride the narrow world / Like a Colossus . . ."). How would you defend this view? How is Caesar "present" in the second half of the play?
8. In his essay *The Poetics,* Aristotle described the **tragic hero** as a person more noble than evil, whose fortunes go from good to bad (see page 739). Does Brutus fit this description, or is the tragic hero someone else, perhaps Caesar? Do you think, instead, that the play lacks a tragic hero? Defend your answer.

Extending the Text

9. Few words inspired such anxiety in the ancient Romans as the word *king.* Do you think the anxieties of Brutus and others about Caesar's potential "kingship" were justified? How do you think Shakespeare's audience, living under the strong and stable monarchy of the aging Queen Elizabeth I, might have felt about choosing between dictatorship and anarchy? How do you think American audiences of today feel about this issue? (You might want to look back at your Quickwrite notes for page 774.)

Reading Check

a. Which four characters finally confront one another in Scene 1 of Act V?

b. What are the results of the first round of battle at Philippi? In the end, who triumphs over whom?

c. What mistaken assumptions lead to Cassius's death?

d. Why does Brutus think he must commit suicide?

e. How do Antony and Octavius react to Brutus's death?

CHOICES: Building Your Portfolio

Writer's Notebook

1. Collecting Ideas for an Evaluation

WORK IN PROGRESS

State your case. A good way to begin an evaluation of a text you feel strongly about is to come up with a **thesis statement,** a clear declaration of your main idea or argument. Your thesis statement informs your audience immediately of your feelings about the text. Once this statement is clear, you can outline the main points of your essay. In the example below, the writer presents a thesis statement followed by three main points. Try to follow this model for a text you want to evaluate. Save your notes for the Writer's Workshop on page 892.

Thesis statement: In his speech to the Romans, Brutus succeeds only briefly in convincing the citizens that Caesar's murder was justified. His speech is a washout.
1. *Worst flaw is vagueness.*
2. *Uses faulty logic.*
3. *Just isn't passionate enough.*

Describing a Character

2. Updating Characters

If Cassius, Brutus, Antony, and Caesar were living today, what do you imagine their beliefs, lifestyles, and career ambitions would be? Think of yourself as a journalist, and write a brief **profile** of each of these **characters** for a national magazine.

Creative Writing

3. Extending the Story

Some contemporary writers have taken portions of older plays (or novels) and expanded on small episodes to make entirely new works of literature. Choose an episode in this play, and explain how it might be expanded into a play or story of its own. You might consider these scenes:

a. Portia's suicide
b. Caesar's last evening alive
c. the discovery of Cinna's body
d. Calphurnia's response to Caesar's murder

Supporting an Opinion

4. Responding to a Critic

In Act V, Titinius, despairing over Cassius's death, cries, "Alas, thou hast misconstrued everything!" According to the critic Marjorie Garber, "That one cry . . . might well serve as an epigraph for the whole of *Julius Caesar.*" What is your **opinion** of Garber's view? Have any characters other than Cassius fatally misunderstood actions or words? Write a response to Garber's statement. Tell whether you agree with it. Then, cite **evidence** from the text that upholds or refutes Garber's thesis.

Critical Thinking

5. Planning a Production

Reread John Mason Brown's review (see ***Connections*** on page 878). Then, with a group, plan a modern-dress version of *Julius Caesar.* Consider how you would present these elements of the play:

a. settings
b. lighting
c. props
d. music
e. sound effects
f. costumes
g. murders
h. funerals
i. battles
j. women's roles

Visual Literacy/Maps

6. Notifying the Troops

As commander of the army in Rome in 44 B.C., you must notify all troops throughout the empire of Caesar's death. Check the map on page 877, and read the legends carefully. How many runners will you send, and what routes will you assign them?

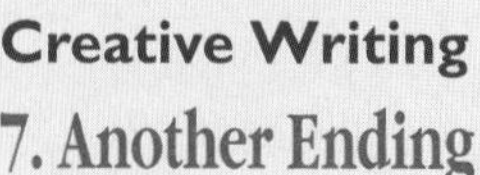

Choices: Building Your Portfolio

Creative Writing

7. Another Ending

Suppose Brutus does not die but is captured and brought before Octavius and Antony. Choose one or more partners, and use what you know about these characters to write a scene in which Brutus's fate is decided. Will the victors execute or exile Brutus, or will they carry him back to Rome in chains, as Cassius predicted? Will Brutus plead for his life? Will Antony or Octavius show mercy? Will they offer Brutus a share of the power? After you have written your new ending, consider collaborating with your partners to present your scene to your class.

Analyzing a Character

8. Critics at Large

In a brief essay, write a **character analysis** of Brutus. First, read the following critical comments. Then, become a critic yourself. Evaluate the comments and use them to help you form your own **thesis statement**. Be sure to include details from the play to elaborate and to support your statements about Brutus. You may want to consult the Writer's Workshop on page 164, Analyzing a Character.

> . . . Brutus is humorlessly good. If his duty is to know himself, his performance fails. Nobility has numbed him until he cannot see himself for his principles. When his principles are expressing themselves, they are beautiful in their clarity. . . . But when he speaks to himself he knows not who is there; he addresses a strange audience, and fumbles. . . . He is not mad or haunted or inspired or perplexed in the extreme. He is simply confused.
>
> —Mark Van Doren

> Brutus is an intellectual who can do things, who is not . . . hampered by doubts. He can do things—but he always does them wrong: His advice is invariably fatal, from the moment of the murder down to the battle of Philippi. He cannot realize that men seek their own interests, for he has never sought his own, he has lived nobly among noble thoughts, wedded to a noble wife. He is kind to his servant. Everything he does is touched with fineness.

> Yet Brutus is not frigid. He just avoids being a prig. We are able to take him to our hearts.
>
> —E. M. Forster

Critical Thinking/Art

9. A Power Line

Many readers see this as a play about power and its shifts from one faction or individual to others. Draw a **graph** tracing the shifts of power in this play. Begin with the situation in the opening scene of Act I, and follow the exchange of power through the rest of the play. You might want to illustrate your graph. Be sure to supply dates whenever you can.

Comparing and Contrasting

10. Then and Now

In *Julius Caesar*, you have seen the results of the political chaos caused by the assassination of Caesar and the battles for power that followed. Write a brief essay in which you **compare and contrast** politics today (national, state, or local) with the political scene Shakespeare described. (You may want to look back at your Quickwrite notes for page 774 for ideas.)

Memorizing Famous Passages: Making Them Yours

There are helpful techniques for memorizing, and the rewards are worth the effort. If you memorize these famous speeches now, you'll find yourself remembering them years later —and even finding occasions to *use* them.

One way to memorize speeches easily is to use the "bricklayer" method. The term means that, like a bricklayer, who lays down row upon row of bricks, an actor memorizes lines by building one line upon another.

Read the first line of a speech until you can say it without looking at it. Then, read that line and the next line until you can say the first two lines without looking at them. Continue until you can say the whole speech without looking at it. Then, you can work on your **interpretation** and **dramatic presentation**.

Try It Out

Choose at least two of the speeches below. Using the technique described at the left, memorize the speeches. Then, in a small group, **evaluate** one another's interpretations. How do they differ? Does your group have a favorite one? Also, discuss occasions in actual life when it would be appropriate to quote each speech. For example, which lines might you quote if you were a police officer assigned a dangerous beat?

1. Why, man, he doth bestride the narrow world
Like a Colossus, and we petty men
Walk under his huge legs and peep about
To find ourselves dishonorable graves.
Men at some time are masters of their fates:
The fault, dear Brutus, is not in our stars,
But in ourselves, that we are underlings.
—Act I, Scene 2, lines 135–141

2. Cowards die many times before their deaths;
The valiant never taste of death but once.
Of all the wonders that I yet have heard,
It seems to me most strange that men should fear,
Seeing that death, a necessary end,
Will come when it will come.
—Act II, Scene 2, lines 32–37

3. The evil that men do lives after them,
The good is oft interrèd with their bones;
—Act III, Scene 2, lines 77–78

4. There is a tide in the affairs of men
Which, taken at the flood, leads on to fortune;
Omitted, all the voyage of their life
Is bound in shallows and in miseries.
On such a full sea are we now afloat,
And we must take the current when it serves,
Or lose our ventures.
—Act IV, Scene 3, lines 216–222

EXTENDING *the theme*

A SPEECH

Make the Connection

Today's paper, whatever the date, will probably have an account of one or two murders. The television news will give a few minutes to them (unless the murderers or their victims are well known), and then it will move on to sports and weather. We get used to hearing about such crimes, and as long as they don't take place too close to home, we're not particularly disturbed.

Occasionally, however, someone kills several people at one time—that makes headlines. Five people dying in one violent outbreak seems even more horrible than five people murdered separately, and we want whoever is responsible to be caught, brought to justice, and punished.

The Nazi Party, during its twelve years in power in Germany, murdered not just five or ten or even one thousand people. The Nazis murdered at least eleven million people.

Quickwrite

These words by the philosopher George Santayana appear on a tablet at the entrance to the Dachau concentration camp:

"Those who cannot remember the past are condemned to repeat it."

Can you think of any societal tragedies that should not be forgotten? They may be historical or current events. What lessons should society learn from these incidents? Write briefly about one such tragedy.

Background

Two rows of Nazis in suits listened through headphones to a translation of the charges against them. Outside, the once-beautiful city of Nuremberg, Germany, lay in ruins. The twenty-two defendants were the most important Nazi leaders known to be alive after the Allied victory ended World War II in 1945. These men had helped Adolf Hitler in his plan to build a German empire and to rid Europe of those Hitler called "undesirables." Their ambition had led to the deaths of six million Jews in concentration camps and millions of others, including Polish Catholics and Gypsies.

The ambition of Robert H. Jackson (1892–1954), the U.S. Supreme Court Justice who organized the case against the Nazis, was more honorable: to hold "the first trial in history for crimes against the peace of the world." Jackson led the Allied nations (the United States, Great Britain, France, and Russia) and seventeen other countries in what he insisted would be a fair trial.

Some observers, however, have claimed that the International Military Tribunal set up to conduct the trial was acting on shaky legal grounds. These critics say that many of the Nazis' crimes were not declared illegal until after they were committed, and that individuals should not be tried for the crimes of governments.

In October 1946, after hundreds of thousands of documents, photographs, eyewitness statements, and Nazi home movies had been put into evidence, nineteen of the defendants were convicted; twelve were sentenced to death. Of these twelve, ten were hanged in a messy execution in the gymnasium of the Palace of Justice, and one swallowed poison. Another was missing and had been tried in his absence. Seven of the convicted were sentenced to long prison terms. Three were acquitted, including one who had spied for the United States and had actually been a concentration camp inmate.

You will be reading part of Jackson's opening speech to the Tribunal, delivered November 21, 1945.

"The Arrogance and Cruelty of Power"

***from* Speech at the Nuremberg Trials, November 21, 1945**

Robert H. Jackson

These side comments will help you summarize key points and draw your attention to important questions.

The privilege of opening the first trial in history for crimes against the peace of the world imposes a grave responsibility. The wrongs which we seek to condemn and punish have been so calculated, so malignant,[1] and so devastating that civilization cannot tolerate their being ignored, because it cannot survive their being repeated. That four great nations, flushed with victory and stung with injury, stay the hand of vengeance and voluntarily submit their captive enemies to the judgment of the law is one of the most significant tributes that Power has ever paid to Reason.

In opening, Jackson explains the need for this trial of major war criminals. Such evils must never be repeated, he says.

This Tribunal, while it is novel and experimental, is not the product of abstract speculations, nor is it created to vindicate[2] legalistic theories. This inquest represents the practical effort of four of the most mighty of nations, with the support of seventeen more, to utilize international law to meet the greatest menace of our times—aggressive war. The common sense of mankind demands that law shall not stop with the punishment of petty crimes by little people. It must also reach men who possess themselves of great power and make deliberate and concerted use of it to set in motion evils which leave no home in the world untouched. It is a cause of that magnitude that the United Nations will lay before Your Honors.

Jackson points out that people in power must be held responsible for their actions, especially when that power is used for evil and destructive ends.

In the prisoners' dock sit twenty-odd broken men. Reproached by the humiliation of those they have led almost as bitterly as by the desolation of those they have attacked, their personal capacity for evil is forever past. It is hard now to perceive in these men as captives the

1. **malignant:** evil; destructive.
2. **vindicate:** prove right; justify.

power by which as Nazi leaders they once dominated much of the world and terrified most of it. Merely as individuals their fate is of little consequence to the world.

What makes this inquest significant is that these prisoners represent sinister influences that will lurk in the world long after their bodies have returned to dust. We will show them to be living symbols of racial hatreds, of terrorism and violence, and of the arrogance and cruelty of power. They are symbols of fierce nationalisms and of militarism, of intrigue and war making which have embroiled Europe generation after generation, crushing its manhood, destroying its homes, and impoverishing its life. They have so identified themselves with the philosophies they conceived and with the forces they directed that any tenderness to them is a victory and an encouragement to all the evils which are attached to their names. Civilization can afford no compromise with the social forces which would gain renewed strength if we deal ambiguously or indecisively with the men in whom those forces now precariously survive.

The prisoners are important not as individuals but for what they represent.

? *What is the main thing the prisoners represent?*

What these men stand for we will patiently and temperately[3] disclose. We will give you undeniable proofs of incredible events. The catalog of crimes will omit nothing that could be conceived by a pathological[4] pride, cruelty, and lust for power. These men created in Germany, under the "Führerprinzip,"[5] a National Socialist despotism[6] equaled only by the dynasties of the ancient East. They took from the German people all those dignities and freedoms that we hold natural and inalienable rights in every human being. The people were compensated by inflaming and gratifying hatreds toward those who were marked as "scapegoats."[7] Against their opponents, including Jews, Catholics, and free labor, the Nazis directed such a campaign of arrogance, brutality, and annihilation

This section of Jackson's speech emphasizes the immoral and corrupt nature of the Nazis' actions.

? *What did their actions eventually lead to?*

3. temperately: dispassionately; in a calm, restrained way.
4. pathological: diseased; here, morally harmful or corrupt.
5. Führerprinzip (fü'rər · prin · tsēp') (German for "leader principle"): the principle vesting absolute authority in the Führer, or Nazi leader, Adolf Hitler.
6. despotism: rule by one with absolute power; tyranny.
7. scapegoats: people blamed unjustly. The Nazis used Jews, Catholics, Communists, and other groups as scapegoats for Germany's troubles after World War I.

as the world has not witnessed since the pre-Christian ages. They excited the German ambition to be a "master race," which of course implies serfdom[8] for others. They led their people on a mad gamble for domination. They diverted social energies and resources to the creation of what they thought to be an invincible war machine. They overran their neighbors. To sustain the "master race" in its war making, they enslaved millions of human beings and brought them into Germany, where these hapless[9] creatures now wander as "displaced persons." At length, bestiality and bad faith reached such excess that they aroused the sleeping strength of imperiled Civilization. Its united efforts have ground the German war machine to fragments. But the struggle has left Europe a liberated yet prostrate land where a demoralized society struggles to survive. These are the fruits of the sinister forces that sit with these defendants in the prisoners' dock. . . .

Above:
Among the Nazis on trial at Nuremberg were top leaders Hermann Goering (far left), the designated successor to Adolf Hitler, and Rudolf Hess (seated next to Goering), Hitler's deputy. The Nazis wearing headphones are listening to a German translation of the proceedings.

In general, our case will disclose these defendants all uniting at some time with the Nazi party in a plan which they well knew could be accomplished only by an outbreak of war in Europe. Their seizure of the German state, their subjugation[10] of the German people, their terrorism and extermination of dissident elements, their planning and waging of war, their calculated and planned ruthlessness in the conduct of warfare, their deliberate and planned criminality toward conquered peoples—all these are ends for which they acted in concert; and all these are phases of the conspiracy, a conspiracy which reached one goal, only to set out for another and more ambitious one. We shall also trace for you the intricate web of organizations which these men formed and utilized to accomplish these ends. We will show how the entire structure of offices and officials was dedicated to the criminal purposes and committed to the use of the criminal methods planned by these defendants and their co-conspirators, many of whom war and suicide have put beyond reach.

Jackson states that his case will focus on the conspiracy that brought about the war and its horrors, rather than on individuals' criminal behavior.

8. serfdom: servitude; bondage. Strictly speaking, a serf is someone who is compelled to work a piece of land for the benefit of the landowner and can be transferred along with the land to a new owner.
9. hapless: unfortunate; unlucky.
10. subjugation: the act of crushing or subduing.

It is my purpose to open the case, particularly under Count One of the Indictment, and to deal with the Common Plan or Conspiracy to achieve ends possible only by resort to Crimes Against Peace, War Crimes, and Crimes Against Humanity.[11] My emphasis will not be on individual barbarities and perversions which may have occurred independently of any central plan. One of the dangers ever present is that this trial may be protracted[12] by details of particular wrongs and that we will become lost in a "wilderness of single instances." Nor will I now dwell on the activity of individual defendants except as it may contribute to exposition of the common plan.

The case as presented by the United States will be concerned with the brains and authority back of all the crimes. These defendants were men of a station and rank which does not soil its own hands with blood. They were men who knew how to use lesser folk as tools. We want to reach the planners and designers, the inciters and leaders, without whose evil architecture the world would not have been for so long scourged with the violence and lawlessness, and wracked with the agonies and convulsions, of this terrible war.

? *What will the case, as presented by the United States, focus on? Whom does Jackson want to reach?*

11. **Count One of the Indictment . . . Against Humanity:** The accused were charged with four counts: crimes against peace; crimes against humanity; war crimes; and the conspiracy to commit all of these crimes.
12. **protracted:** prolonged; extended unnecessarily.

FINDING COMMON GROUND

1. With a small group of classmates, compare the passages of Jackson's speech that you found striking. Why do you think the passages you chose are important? What issues or questions do they raise?
2. Twelve of the twenty-two men tried were sentenced to hang. Some people might say that executing them on the spot when they were first captured would have saved time and trouble. Why do you think it was important to bring them to trial? Look back at your Quickwrite notes and Santayana's quote before discussing this issue in your group.
3. Jackson's opening speech addresses the crimes of power that were committed by the Nazi leaders. In your group, discuss the issue of ambition and honor:
   - Do you think that the Nazi leaders considered their actions honorable during the war? After the war?
   - Does ambition ever justify abuse of power?
4. How would you respond to those who, at the time of the Nuremberg trials, said, "Since there are no specific international laws about the Nazis' actions, we cannot justify the trials"?

All Honorable Men . . .

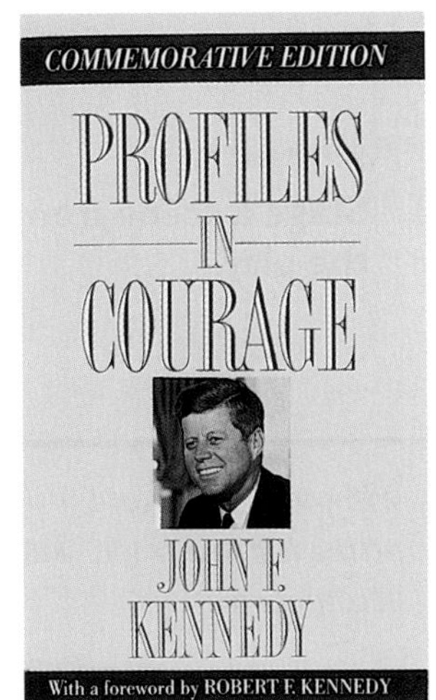

John F. Kennedy provides portraits of some courageous politicians. *Profiles in Courage* (HarperCollins) details the physical, political, and moral courage of men such as John Quincy Adams, Sam Houston, and Thomas Hart Benton. Find out how much strength, courage, and conviction are needed when people are struggling to hold a country together.

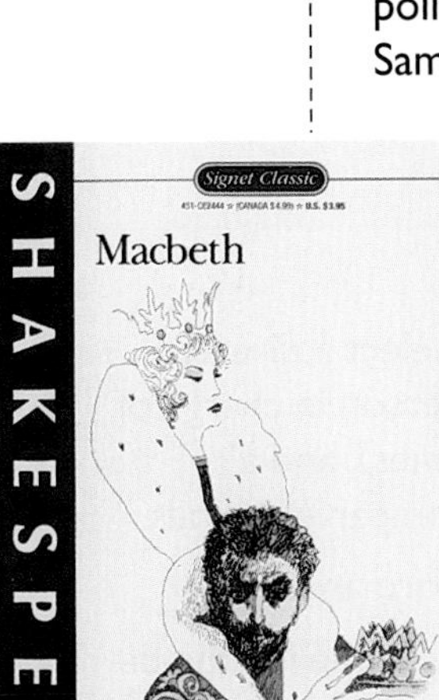

When Shall We Three Meet Again . . . ?

Julius Caesar is not the only assassinated leader featured in a Shakespearean tragedy. In 1040, a Scottish chieftain named Macbeth defeated and killed King Duncan I and seized the throne of Scotland. Shakespeare dramatized this story in his tragedy *Macbeth.* Is Macbeth motivated by ambition, or is he trying to do an honorable thing? You may find that this tale of intrigue in medieval Scotland provides shocking contrasts to *The Tragedy of Julius Caesar.* (This title is available in the HRW Library.)

You Are About to Leave Earth's Atmosphere . . .

What makes people decide to become astronauts? What qualifications must a person have to become an astronaut? How quickly can someone become a hero, and how quickly can the public forget all about that hero? In Tom Wolfe's *The Right Stuff* (Bantam Books), you'll find intriguing treatment of these and other issues relating to America's space exploration.

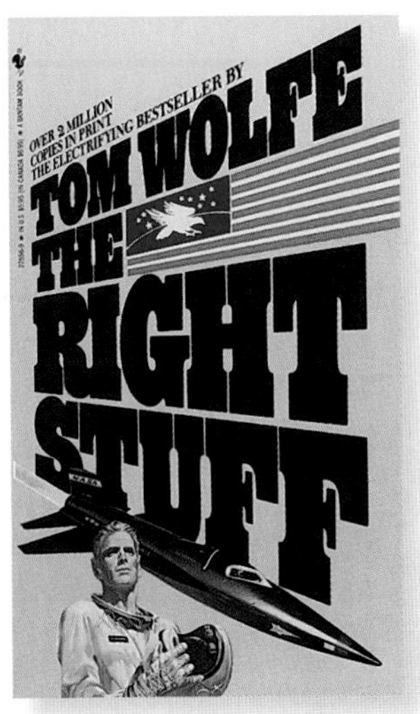

A Surprising Show of Honor

Set during World War II at the height of the Nazis' power, Thomas Keneally's novel *Schindler's List* (Touchstone) is based on a true story, including the testimony of Holocaust survivors. The title character, Oskar Schindler, is an ambitious businessman who at first uses Jews for cheap labor in his factory. After a change of heart, he saves over a thousand Jews from almost certain death.

BUILDING YOUR PORTFOLIO

Speaking and Listening Workshop

Assignment

Stage a scene from the play.

Without wonder and insight, acting is just a trade. With it, it becomes creation.

—Bette Davis

I can never remember being afraid of an audience. If the audience could do better, they'd be up here on stage and I'd be out there watching them.

—Ethel Merman

Every now and then, when you're on the stage, you hear the best sound a player can hear. It is a sound you can't get in movies or in television. It is the sound of a wonderful, deep silence that means you've hit them where they live.

—Shelley Winters

Stagecraft: Staging the Play

When you've finished *The Tragedy of Julius Caesar,* plan to perform scenes from the play. Here are some suggestions:

Getting Started

1. Break into **acting groups.** Each group should select a director, actors, a prop manager, a costume designer, a person in charge of sound effects (thunder is important in some scenes), and a prompter. You might want to give your acting companies names.
2. Each acting group should select a scene for performance.
3. Prepare **scripts** of your scene: one for each actor, one for the director, and one for the prompter. The scripts should be typed on $8\frac{1}{2} \times 11$-inch sheets of paper, with extra space between the lines.
4. The **director** and **actors** should work together to write **character analyses** of each person in the scene. Focus on these questions: What does the character want? What are the character's feelings and motives at this point in the play? What is distinct about the character?
5. The **prop person** must check the dialogue and stage directions carefully and supply all the physical properties needed by the actors: candles, torches, spears, letters, and so on.
6. The **stage designer** should sketch the set and perhaps make a shoe-box model. When you are rehearsing, be sure you know where actors are to be placed, how they should move around onstage, and where they should enter and exit.

Rehearsals

As they rehearse, actors and directors should indicate on their scripts when characters should pause, what words should be stressed, what gestures should be used. Actors might also want to note words that give them trouble. They might note what their character is feeling.

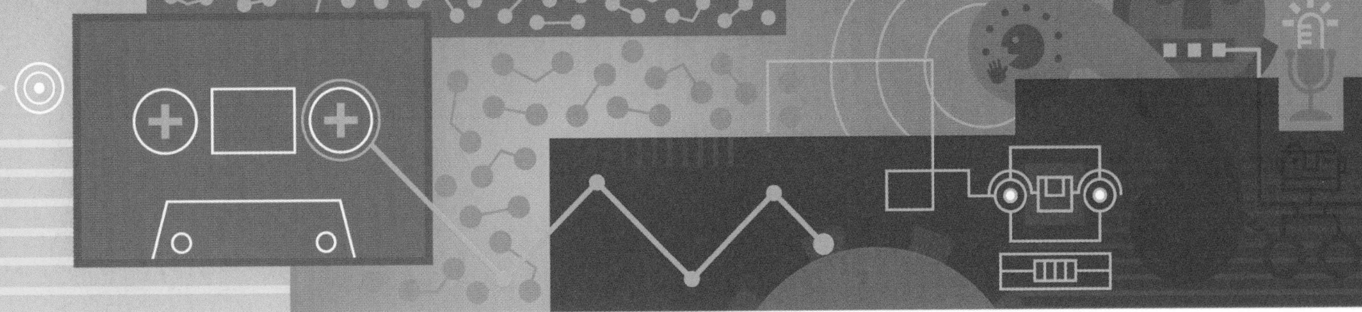

To overcome any "fear" of poetry, rewrite the lines in your scripts so they don't look like poetry. Don't change any words; just write the lines as prose. Go back to Act I, Scene 2, lines 190–198, and reread the conversation between Caesar and Antony. Then look at it here, written as prose:

Caesar. Antonius.

Antony. Caesar?

Caesar. Let me have men about me that are fat, sleek-headed men, and such as sleep a-nights. Yond Cassius has a lean and hungry look; he thinks too much: such men are dangerous.

Antony. Fear him not, Caesar, he's not dangerous; he is a noble Roman, and well given.

Caesar. Would he were fatter! But I fear him not. . . .

With a partner, read both versions aloud. Which version seems easier to read?

Finding a Scene

Choose a scene that you think you would *enjoy* playing. Here are some suggestions:

- Act I, Scene 2: large cast; big speeches for Cassius
- Act II, Scene 1: large cast; big speeches for Brutus
- Act II, Scene 2: requires special effects—thunder and lightning
- Act II, Scene 4: small cast; important scene for Portia
- Act III, Scene 1: the assassination; large cast; complex stage movement
- Act III, Scene 2: the great funeral orations; high-powered acting

BIZARRO © 1995 by Dan Piraro. Reprinted with permission of Universal Press Syndicate.

BUILDING YOUR PORTFOLIO

Writer's Workshop

Technology HELP

See Writer's Workshop 2 CD-ROM. *Assignment: Evaluation.*

ASSIGNMENT

Write an essay in which you analyze the techniques used in persuasive writing and evaluate their effectiveness.

AIM

To persuade; to inform.

AUDIENCE

Readers of your school newspaper; a broader audience. (You choose.)

PERSUASIVE WRITING

ANALYZING AND EVALUATING PERSUASION

You're confronted with persuasive speaking and writing every day—when you read a newspaper editorial that tries to change your opinion, listen to a candidate who tries to win your vote, or watch a TV commercial that tries to get you to spend your money. Your ability to **analyze and evaluate persuasion**—the skill you'll practice in this Writer's Workshop—will prove an invaluable tool.

Prewriting

WORK IN PROGRESS

1. Find a Subject

Mark Antony's funeral speech in Act III of *The Tragedy of Julius Caesar* would make an excellent focus for your essay. If you prefer another topic, there are many other pieces of persuasive writing you could use, such as those suggested below:

- one of the other persuasive speeches in the play. Be sure to check your Writer's Notebook for ideas. (The model essay on page 895 analyzes and evaluates Brutus's funeral oration.)
- one of the nonfiction selections in Collection 7 of this book.
- a famous speech—for example, "I Have a Dream" by Martin Luther King, Jr., or the excerpt from Robert H. Jackson's "Speech at the Nuremberg Trials" (page 885).
- a recent topical political speech or a newspaper editorial.

2. Gather Your Data

Whether you've chosen to analyze a piece of persuasive writing or a speech, your approach will be the same. You'll **analyze** your subject—take it apart to see how it works. First, identify the writer's **audience** and **purpose.** Then, consider what **persuasive techniques** the writer uses to appeal to this audience. (For a discussion of these techniques, see pages 468–469.) Remember that persuasion may achieve its purpose by appealing to the audience's reason, emotions, or both. Gather your ideas in a chart like the one that follows:

The history
of the written
word is rich and
Page 1

Audience and Purpose	
Audience (the people the writer is trying to persuade)	
Purpose (what the writer wants the audience to do or believe)	
Persuasive Techniques	
Logical appeals (reasons, facts, statistics, examples, expert testimony, etc.)	
Faulty reasoning (hasty generalizations, either/or reasoning, false cause and effect, etc.)	
Emotional appeals (loaded words, glittering generalities, bandwagon appeal, testimonials, etc.)	

3. Establish Your Criteria

Before you can evaluate a piece of writing, you must set up **criteria,** or standards, by which to judge its effectiveness. With one or more partners, brainstorm to come up with a list of features of good persuasive writing. Here are some questions you should ask when you evaluate persuasion:

- Is there a clear statement of the writer's **position,** or **opinion**?
- Does the writer provide convincing **reasons** to support his or her position?
- Are the reasons supported by sufficient **evidence**?
- Does the argument contain any **logical fallacies**? (See pages 468–469.)
- Does the writer use **emotional** appeals? (See page 469.) Does the writer appeal chiefly to reason or to emotions?
- Is there a strong and effective **conclusion**?

Useful Words for Evaluating Persuasive Writing
Positive words: *good, excellent, powerful, moving, convincing, persuasive, logical, strong, coherent, incisive, on target*
Negative words: *weak, disorganized, vague, unconvincing, illogical, incoherent, deceptive, manipulative, wordy, evasive*

Try It Out

In Act I, Scene 2, Cassius tries to turn Brutus against Caesar. What kind of appeal (logical or emotional) does Cassius use as he speaks to Brutus in the following lines?

1. . . . I was born free as Caesar; so were you:
We both have fed as well, and we can both
Endure the winter's cold as well as he. . . .

2. He had a fever when he was in Spain,
And when the fit was on him, I did mark
How he did shake; 'tis true, this god did shake.
His coward lips did from their color fly. . . .

Give It a Grade

To help determine your evaluation of a work, try giving it an overall rating.

- You could use a letter grade (as in the introductory paragraph of the Model on page 895) or a number rating from 1 to 10 (10 being the highest).
- You could use one rating for logical appeals (reasons and sufficient evidence) and another rating for skillful use of emotional appeals.

Language Handbook HELP

See Quotation Marks, pages 1054–1056.

Sentence Workshop HELP

Parallel structure: page 897.

4. State Your Case!

Work on your **thesis statement,** your essay's main idea. Try stating it in the clearest words possible. Be sure to cite the work and its author, and make clear what your **evaluation** is.

EXAMPLE
Roger Rosenblatt's excellent essay "The Man in the Water" convinced me that unselfishness and heroism still exist today.

5. Elaborate: Support Your Position

You've analyzed the work (your chart) and established your position (your thesis statement). Now it's time to outline your **argument.** Begin by choosing the two or three persuasive techniques (or other points you analyzed in your chart) that you think are the most important in the work. These will be the **reasons** for your evaluation, and you'll develop each one in its own paragraph. It's a good idea to state each reason directly in a topic sentence: for example, "The most serious flaw in Brutus's speech is that he is too vague."

Next, you'll need to assemble sufficient and convincing **evidence** to support each reason: **quotations** from the text and **specific references** to the text. (In the model essay on page 895, notice that the writer has included act and scene numbers.)

Drafting

When writing your draft, write freely and fully to get all your ideas on paper. When you draft, don't be too concerned about structure or organization. Often, you'll discover new ideas while you draft. Once you have collected all your thoughts, you can begin to polish and order them.

You might think about using the following pattern of organization for your essay:

1. **Paragraph 1:** Introductory paragraph, including a **thesis statement** presenting your overall evaluation of the work. (Paragraphs 2–4 will offer **evidence** to **support** your evaluation.)
2. **Paragraphs 2–4:** Analysis and evaluation of the persuasive techniques used in the work. Discuss each technique and cite as examples passages and evidence from the text.
3. **Paragraph 5:** Concluding paragraph. Summarize your main points, or restate the **main idea.**

Model

Brutus's Funeral Speech

When Brutus speaks to the Romans, he has two purposes. His first (and surely more important) purpose is to convince his listeners that Caesar's murder was justified. His second purpose is to introduce Mark Antony. Brutus gets a "D–" grade on his speech, while Antony walks away with an "A+." Brutus's speech is practically a failure.

Introductory paragraph. Identifies Brutus's two purposes.

Thesis statement.

The most serious flaw in Brutus's speech is that his "evidence" is too vague. This is the essence of Brutus's argument: You know that I am an honorable man. (Is it honorable to assassinate a leader for the reasons Brutus offers?) I loved Caesar as much as you did, but Caesar was a threat to Rome because he was ambitious. Brutus is vague about Caesar's "crimes"; he never tells exactly how Caesar was ambitious or why his ambition was bad. In fact, the word *ambitious* is a poor choice because it has favorable connotations as well as negative ones. For example, we admire someone for being ambitious and striving to achieve a high goal. Yet Brutus assumes that ambition is all bad. He doesn't give any convincing evidence to prove that Caesar deserved to die.

Topic sentence: Worst flaw is lack of evidence. Analyzes (summarizes) main points of argument. Cites specific instance of vagueness.

Last sentence restates paragraph's main idea.

Brutus's logic is faulty also. As part of his justification of Caesar's murder, he says, "Had you rather Caesar were living, and die all slaves, than that Caesar were dead, to live all free men?" (Act III, Scene 2, lines 23–24). This is an example of the either-or fallacy, one kind of faulty reasoning. Brutus says that only two positions are possible: Either Caesar is allowed to live and all Rome is in slavery, or Caesar is killed and all Rome is free. In reality, there are many other possibilities between these two extremes. Why should we believe Brutus anyway? He doesn't substantiate either of the claims he makes: Why does Caesar alive mean slavery? Why does Caesar dead mean freedom?

Topic sentence: faulty logic. Cites specific instance of faulty logic. Identifies fallacy and explains why it is a fallacy.

Again, cites lack of evidence.

Brutus uses a powerful emotional appeal when he appeals to his listeners' patriotism, but it's not enough to justify Caesar's murder. He says, "Who is here so rude, that would not be a Roman? . . . Who is here so vile, that will not love his country?" (Act III, Scene 2, lines 31–33). He pauses for effect, knowing full well that no one will publicly admit to being unpatriotic. *Vile,* of course, is a loaded word, and it's "vile" not to love one's country.

Topic sentence: emotional appeal.

Gives example of a loaded word.

If we had only Brutus's speech in this act, we'd probably think it wasn't bad. He is very sincere. Yet Brutus is far less passionate and thus far less convincing to the mob than Antony is. Brutus doesn't use any of the persuasive devices that Antony uses. He also ignores Rule 1 of Persuasive Speaking: Nobody believes anybody without proof. Brutus is vague and illogical, and his appeal to patriotism isn't enough to save his speech. Brutus may or may not be an honorable man, but he is certainly a terrible orator.

Cites some good points about speech. Compares Brutus's speech to Antony's. Summarizes main points of essay. Strong clincher sentence.

Evaluating and Revising

1. On Your Own

Before sharing your draft with your writing group, go over it twice on your own. Check first for content; then check for form.

- **Content.** Does your thesis statement clearly express your evaluation? Have you given reasons and evidence to support your position? Have you cited passages from the text?
- **Form.** Keep your writing trim and tight. Have you included a clear topic sentence in each paragraph? Does each paragraph cover only one main idea? Be sure to check paragraph organization and sentence structure.

2. Peer Review

Give copies of your draft to the members of your writing group. Ask them to consider the following questions about your essay:

- Does the essay analyze the piece of writing to show clearly how it works?
- Does the essay contain convincing examples?
- Does the evaluation seem logical, fair-minded, and objective?

Revision Model

	Peer Comments
Brutus uses a powerful emotional appeal when he appeals to his listeners'. patriotism, but it's not enough to justify Caesar's murder.	What is the emotional appeal, and does it work?
He says, "Who is here so rude, that would not be a Roman? . . . Who is here so vile, that will not love his country?" (Act III, Scene 2, lines 31–33).	How can a reader find this quotation?
He pauses for effect, knowing full well that no one will publicly admit to being unpatriotic. Vile, of course, is a loaded word, and It's "vile" not to love one's country.	Can you make the connection clearer?

■ ***Evaluation Criteria***

A good analysis and evaluation

1. *contains a thesis statement that states the writer's evaluation*
2. *contains reasons and evidence that support the writer's evaluation*
3. *analyzes the elements of the text*
4. *cites passages to support the writer's evaluation*
5. *contains a concluding paragraph that summarizes or restates the thesis*

Proofreading Tips

- Skim your paper, looking for the kinds of errors you've recorded in your Proofreading Log.
- Check all quotations for accuracy and correct punctuation.

Communications Handbook HELP

See Proofreaders' Marks.

Publishing Tip

Get together with classmates who have written about the same work. Share your papers and compare your evaluations.

BUILDING YOUR PORTFOLIO

Sentence Workshop

PARALLEL STRUCTURE

When you use related items in a sentence, you should express those items in the same grammatical structure. For example, you would match a word with a word, a phrase with a phrase, and a clause with a clause. This kind of balance in writing is called **parallel structure.** Be particularly alert for the use of parallel structure whenever you use a coordinating conjunction (*and, but, or, nor, for, so, yet*). The examples of parallel structure in these passages from *Julius Caesar* are underscored.

1. . . . Let's kill him boldly, but not wrathfully; . . .

   —Act II, Scene 1, line 172

2. The torrent roared, and we did buffet it
   With lusty sinews, throwing it aside
   And stemming it with hearts of controversy.

   —Act I, Scene 2, lines 107–109

3. . . . As / Caesar loved me, I weep for him; as he was fortunate, I rejoice at it; as he was valiant, I honor him; but, as he was ambitious, I slew him.

   —Act III, Scene 2, lines 24–27

4. Write them together, yours is as fair a name;
   Sound them, it doth become the mouth as well;
   Weigh them, it is as heavy; . . .

   —Act I, Scene 2, lines 144–146

Note that in the first example, two words, adverbs, are matched in parallel structure. In the second example, the parallel structures are participial phrases. In the third example, each item consists of a dependent clause and an independent clause. The fourth example has three parallel imperative clauses.

Writer's Workshop Follow-up: Proofreading

Review your essay analyzing and evaluating persuasion. For any sentence that has faulty parallel structure, choose a way to correct it. Decide to make each item a word, a phrase, or a clause; then, rewrite the sentence.

Technology HELP

See Language Workshop CD-ROM. *Key word entry: parallel structure.*

Try It Out

Look at the following passages in *Julius Caesar,* and identify the use of parallel structure in each one. Then, write five passages of your own, modeling them after these passages from the play. For example, here's a new passage modeled on the first passage opposite: *Let's hide them swiftly, but not carelessly.*

1. Act II, Scene 1, lines 203–206
2. Act II, Scene 2, line 84
3. Act III, Scene 1, line 33
4. Act III, Scene 1, line 45
5. Act III, Scene 2, line 76

Reading for Life

Recognizing Persuasive Techniques in Advertisements

Situation

After reading *Julius Caesar,* you have a better appreciation of methods of persuasion. Now you are interested in analyzing advertisements to see how they attempt to persuade readers.

Psst! Heard the BUZZ?
SAVE $$$$
JOIN THE BUZZARDS! BE CURRENT!
BUZZ MAGAZINE
Subscribe to Buzz Magazine today and you'll know the latest about your favorite stars. Our HOT magazine includes personal stories as well as photos you'll want for your own walls. Sign up now at our special low price and save megabucks over the newsstand price. For only $31.00, you can receive the next 12 buzz-packed issues. Buy them on the newsstand and you'll pay $51.00. Can you use $20? Of course you can!
An extra-special offer.
Get an autographed picture of your favorite star. (You tell us who it is, we'll get the picture.) Just mail the coupon below along with your check or money order. Subscribe now, while the offer lasts.

Strategies

Notice the purpose of the advertisement. To whom is it directed?

- To what audience is the ad directed? (Teens, seniors, families, women, single men?)
- What do the advertisers want you to do? Most ads are designed to convince you to buy something, but political ads may try to persuade you to take some action.

Identify the persuasive techniques.

- **Testimonials** use this line of reasoning: "If celebrities use it, it must be good for you."
- Advertisements may make **logical appeals,** using reasons, facts, and statistics, but look closely. The reasons are often not valid, and facts and statistics may be used in a misleading way.
- Ads often use **faulty reasoning,** such as **hasty generalizations, false analogies,** and **either/or reasoning.** An example of either/or reasoning is "Buy now or miss this once-in-a-lifetime chance."
- Many ads make **emotional appeals,** which include the use of **loaded words** and the **bandwagon appeal.** Loaded words might include, for example: *best, finest, outstanding, most effective, breakthrough, clinically tested, guaranteed, favorite, foremost, exclusive, clean, wholesome,* and *greatest.* When ads use the bandwagon appeal, they try to persuade you to join "everybody" or a "select group" in buying the product. (You'll find other examples of persuasive techniques on pages 468–469.)

Using the Strategies

1. To whom is the ad on this page directed?
2. What does it want you to do?
3. What persuasive techniques can you identify in the ad?
4. What might be two valid reasons for *not* subscribing to this magazine?
5. In a free-enterprise system, advertising is important. What guidelines would you propose advertisers follow?

Extending the Strategies

Bring a variety of ads into the classroom and critique them. Look for ads in newspapers, magazines, on television, or on the Internet.

Learning for Life

Finding Honor

Problem

This collection focuses on ambition and honor. Ambition is fairly easy to define, but who can say exactly what honor is? How does an honorable person behave? How does the concept of honor apply to modern life?

Project

Create guidelines for honorable behavior—at school, at work, in personal relationships, and in politics.

Preparation

1. Meet with a small group to try to pin down what honor means. Besides checking dictionary definitions, list the things an honorable person does and doesn't do.
2. Apply your definition to the specific behavior of people famous or unknown, real or fictional. Would you call "the man in the water" in Rosenblatt's essay (page 471) honorable? Was Mark Antony honorable? Brainstorm a list of people you'd call honorable.
3. Identify and discuss some real-life situations that test one's sense of honor. Here are two.
   - What would you do if you saw a friend cheating on a test?
   - What would you do if a grocery store clerk mistakenly gave you $10 extra change?

Procedure

1. Join a small group that will focus on one of these areas: school, business, politics, or personal life. How does the concept of honor apply to this area of life?
2. Develop an "honor code," a list of statements describing honorable behavior, for the area your group has chosen. (For example: An honorable person keeps promises.) After discussing all the proposed statements, include only those that everyone has agreed to. Reaching agreement is called developing a consensus.

Presentation

Use one of the following formats (or another that your teacher approves):

1. A Press Conference
With your group, hold a press conference announcing the publication of your honor code. Read and distribute copies of the code, and then answer questions from the press (your classmates).

2. A Skit with an Open Ending
With a group, act out a real-life situation that might test a person's sense of honor. Leave the ending open, and lead a class discussion based on the skit.

3. Gallery of Honor
Create a Gallery of Honor in your school or community. Display photographs and/or drawings of honorable people, past and present, famous and unknown. Under each person's likeness, include a statement about why the person has been selected.

Processing

What did you learn from this project about the role of honor in modern life? What did you learn about working with a group to reach a consensus? Write a brief reflection for your portfolio.

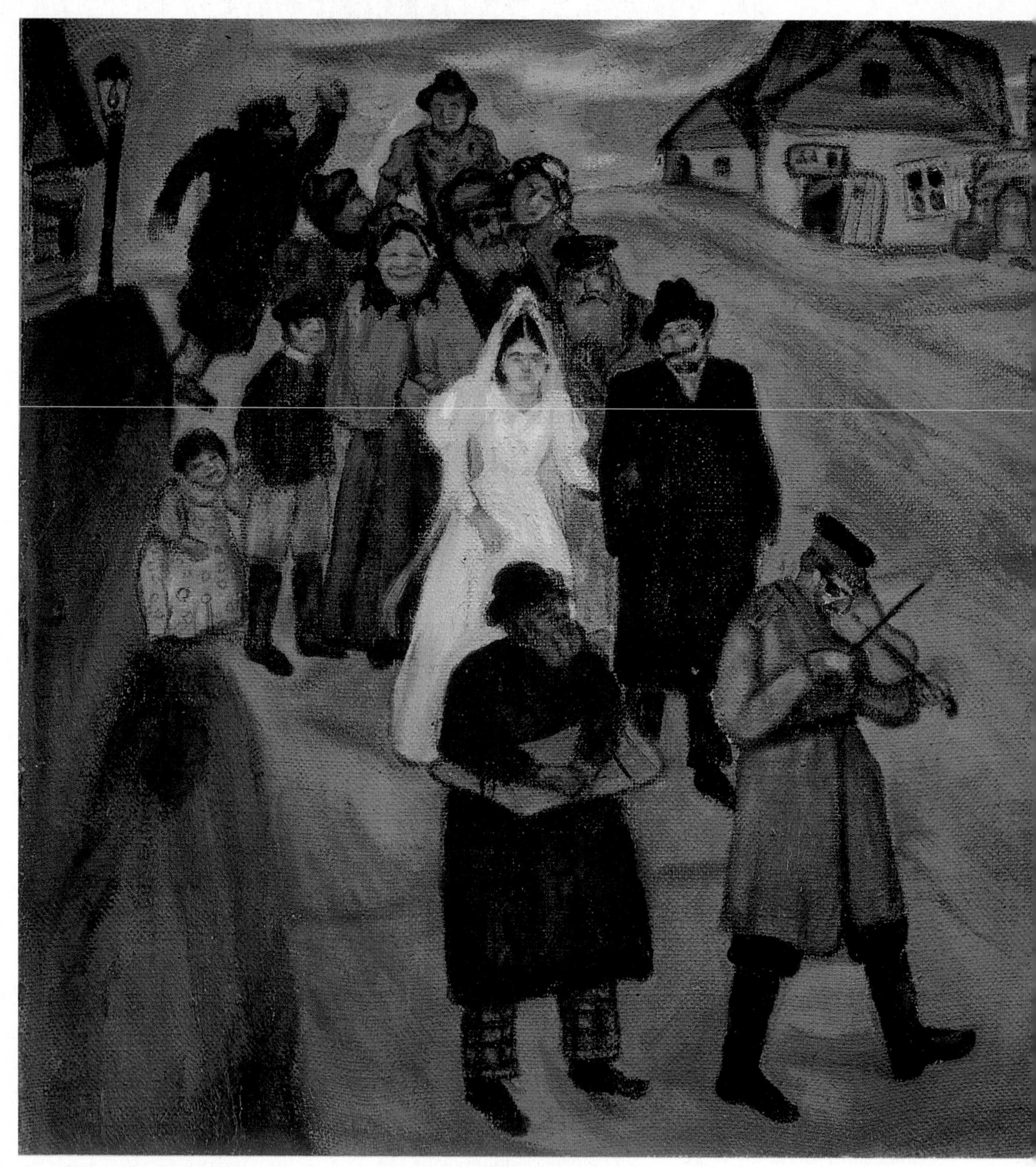

The Wedding (1909) by Marc Chagall. Oil on canvas.

Private Collection, Zurich, Switzerland. Erich Lessing/Art Resource, NY.

Traditions!

Readings in World Literature

Tevye: ***A fiddler on the roof. Sounds crazy, no? But in our little village of Anatevka, you might say every one of us is a fiddler on the roof, trying to scratch out a pleasant, simple tune without breaking his neck. It isn't easy. You may ask, why do we stay up here if it's so dangerous? We stay because Anatevka is our home. And how do we keep our balance? That I can tell you in a word—tradition!***

—from **Fiddler on the Roof**

Collection 13

SOURCES OF WISDOM

Writing Focus: Supporting a Generalization

Who are we? How should we live? What, in the long run, really matters? People in all societies have searched for the wisdom to answer these questions. Their speculations, found in their literature and in their religious texts, might help you in your own quest for the meaning of this gift called life.

But where shall wisdom be found?

—Job 28:12

Writer's Notebook

WORK IN PROGRESS

Think about the question that opens this collection. What do you think wisdom is? What is the difference between wisdom and knowledge? What, in your experience, makes a person wise? Do you know people who have found wisdom? Write down some thoughts about wisdom, as you interpret the word. Save your notes for possible use in the Writer's Workshop on page 986.

The Bible

by David Adams Leeming

In Western cultures, the Bible is important as a sacred book and as a chronicle of history. As a work of literature, it has had a profound influence on every aspect of people's imaginative lives. Writers like Ernest Hemingway, Walt Whitman, Emily Dickinson, Martin Luther King, Jr., and James Baldwin have been influenced by the Bible—not only by its themes but also by its rhythms and language.

Literature is not the only art form indebted to the Bible. It is virtually impossible to visit an art museum without seeing works that reflect Biblical themes or events: Adam and Eve's expulsion from the Garden of Eden, David's slaying of Goliath, the birth of Jesus, the Last Supper, the Crucifixion. Biblical **allusions**, or references, abound in everyday language, too. A person who helps another is called a good Samaritan. A mass movement of holiday travelers from the city is called an exodus. A particularly tough job requires the patience of Job.

It is important to understand that the Bible is two different books to two different religions. The Hebrew Bible is made up of many books that contain narratives, poems, historical records, prophecies, and laws. The first five books of the Hebrew Bible are called the Torah (Hebrew for "teaching" or "law"); they are also known as the Five Books of Moses or the Pentateuch (Greek for "five books"). The Torah together with the other most sacred texts of Judaism (the books of the prophets and other "writings") is known by the Hebrew acronym Tanakh.

The early Christians were Jews, and so they considered the Hebrew Bible their sacred text also, but they did not believe that it contained the complete story of God's relationship with His people. Thus, the Hebrew Bible became the first part of the Christian Bible. The second part, the New Testament, includes four Gospels, which are accounts of the life and teachings of Jesus. The Gospels are followed by historical accounts of the early days of the Christian Church and the Book of Revelation (a vision of the end of time). The Gospels were first written down between A.D. 50 and 150 in Koine Greek, the everyday "international" language of the Middle East at that time.

Writing of the Dead Sea Scrolls (detail) (1967) by Shraga Weil. Serigraph (15¾″ × 24½″).

Courtesy Pucker/Safrai Gallery, Boston, Massachusetts.

Before You Read

ABRAHAM AND ISAAC

Background

This account of Abraham and his son Isaac occurs near the middle of the Book of Genesis, the first book of the Bible. (In Hebrew this book is called *Bereshit*, which means "in the beginning.") The poignant narrative about Abraham's near sacrifice of Isaac is thought to have been written in the eighth century B.C., perhaps around the time of Homer.

Abraham—a name meaning "the father of many"—was the patriarch of the ancient Hebrews. He lived during one of the periods of migration in the Middle East, probably during the nineteenth century B.C. According to the Book of Genesis, God ordered Abraham to journey from his home in Mesopotamia to Canaan (later named Palestine by the Greeks). Then, God made a promise to Abraham:

"I will give unto thee, and to thy seed after thee, the land wherein thou art a stranger, all the land of Canaan, for an everlasting possession; and I will be their God."

Despite the promise that the land of Canaan would belong to his descendants, Abraham and his wife, Sarah, remained childless.

One day when Abraham was ninety-nine years old and Sarah was ninety, three angels disguised as men visited Abraham. When Sarah overheard one of the visitors say that she would bear a child within a year's time, she laughed to herself, believing that she and Abraham were far too old to conceive a child. Then a miracle happened: Sarah did bear a child, a son whom God told them to name Isaac (which means "laughter"). Through this one child, Abraham's covenant, or agreement, with God would be fulfilled:

". . . walk before me, and be thou perfect. And I will make my covenant between me and thee, and will multiply thee exceedingly, . . . and thou shalt be a father of many nations, . . . and kings shall come out of thee. And I will establish my covenant between me and thee and thy seed after thee in their generations, for an everlasting covenant. . . ."

What would happen if Isaac were to die young?

Reading Skills and Strategies

Dialogue with the Text

Much is left out of this spare, dramatic story. As you read, jot down questions that the story doesn't answer.

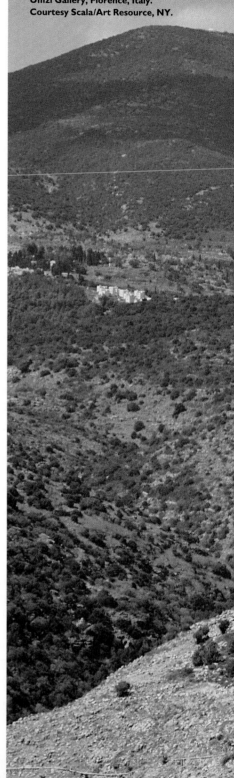

The Sacrifice of Isaac **(c. 1603–1604) by Caravaggio. Oil on canvas.**

Uffizi Gallery, Florence, Italy. Courtesy Scala/Art Resource, NY.

Abraham and Isaac

Tanakh: A New Translation by the Jewish Publication Society

Some time afterward, God put Abraham to the test. He said to him, "Abraham," and he answered, "Here I am." And He said, "Take your son, your favored one, Isaac, whom you love, and go to the land of Moriah,[1] and offer him there as a burnt offering on one of the heights that I will point out to you." So early next morning Abraham saddled his ass and took with him two of his servants and his son Isaac. He split the wood for the burnt offering, and he set out for the place of which God had told him. On the third day Abraham looked up and saw the place from afar. Then Abraham said to his servants, "You stay here with the ass. The boy and I will go up there; we will worship and we will return to you."

Abraham took the wood for the burnt offering and put it on his son Isaac. He himself took the firestone and the knife, and the two walked off together. Then Isaac said to his father Abraham, "Father!" And he answered, "Yes, my son." And he said, "Here are the firestone and the wood; but where is the sheep for the burnt offering?" And Abraham said, "God will see to the sheep for His burnt offering, my son." And the two of them walked on together.

They arrived at the place of which God had told him. Abraham built an altar there; he laid out the wood; he bound his son Isaac; he laid him on the altar, on top of the wood. And Abraham picked up the knife to slay his son. Then an angel of the Lord called to him from heaven: "Abraham! Abraham!" And he answered, "Here I am." And he said, "Do not raise your hand against the boy, or do anything to him. For now I know that you fear God, since you have not withheld your son, your favored one, from Me."

When Abraham looked up, his eye fell upon a ram, caught in the thicket by its horns. So Abraham went and took the ram and offered it up as a burnt offering in place of his son. And Abraham named that site *Adonai-yireh,*[2] whence the present saying, "On the mount of the Lord there is vision."

The angel of the Lord called to Abraham a second time from heaven, and said, "By Myself I swear, the Lord declares: Because you have done this and have not withheld your son, your favored one, I will bestow My blessing upon you and make your descendants as numerous as the stars of heaven and the sands on the seashore; and your descendants shall seize the gates of their foes. All the nations of the earth shall bless themselves by your descendants, because you have obeyed My command." Abraham then returned to his servants, and they departed together for Beer-sheba; and Abraham stayed in Beer-sheba.

—Genesis 22:1–19

1. **land of Moriah:** According to tradition, this is Mount Moriah, a hill in Jerusalem.
2. ***Adonai-yireh*** (a'dō·nī' yēr·e'): Hebrew for "the Lord will see" or "the Lord will provide."

Connections | **A Poem**

This poem was written by the young British poet Wilfred Owen during World War I. Owen fought in the war and was killed in action at the age of twenty-six, just one week before the war ended. Think about how Owen's poem relates to the brutal, bloody war he died in and to the Biblical account of Abraham and Isaac you have just read.

The Parable of the Old Man and the Young

Wilfred Owen

So Abram rose, and clave° the wood, and went,
And took the fire with him, and a knife.
And as they sojourned both of them together,
Isaac the firstborn spake and said, My father,
Behold the preparations, fire and iron,
But where the lamb for this burnt offering?
Then Abram bound the youth with belts and
    straps,
And builded parapets and trenches there,
And stretchèd forth the knife to slay his son.
When lo! an angel called him out of heaven,
Saying, Lay not thy hand upon the lad,
Neither do anything to him. Behold,
A ram, caught in a thicket by its horns;
Offer the Ram of Pride instead of him.
But the old man would not so, but slew his son—
And half the seed of Europe, one by one.

1. **clave** (archaic form of *cleaved*): split with an ax.

Making Meanings
Abraham and Isaac

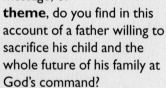

First Thoughts

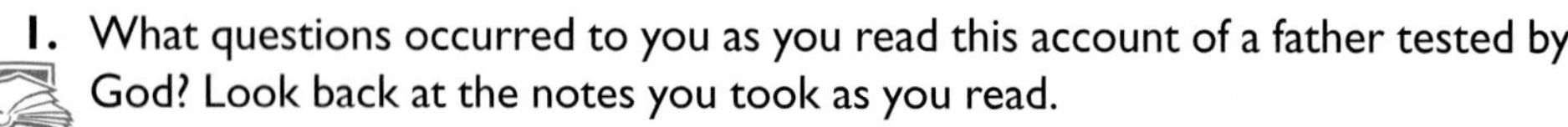

1. What questions occurred to you as you read this account of a father tested by God? Look back at the notes you took as you read.

Shaping Interpretations

2. In the ancient days of Abraham, human sacrifice was sometimes practiced. If you had lived at that time, how do you think you might have interpreted this story?
3. Isaac was a miraculous baby. He was the firstborn of parents in their nineties. How does this account describe a second miraculous "birth" for Isaac?
4. What does Isaac represent to Abraham? What might have been the long-term results if Abraham had sacrificed Isaac? Name two possibilities.

Extending the Text

5. Who are the "old man" and the "young" in the poem by Wilfred Owen (see *Connections* on page 907)? **Contrast** the poem's **characters** with those in the Biblical story.

Choices: Building Your Portfolio

Writer's Notebook

1. Collecting Ideas for an Essay Supporting a Generalization

WORK IN PROGRESS

Stating a theme. What general message, or **theme**, do you find in this account of a father willing to sacrifice his child and the whole future of his family at God's command?

Write a sentence or two that sums up the story's overall meaning as you see it. Save your notes.

Research/ Expository Writing

2. What's in a Name?

God told Sarah and Abraham to name their son Isaac, which means "laughter." The name refers to Sarah's response when the angels told her, in her ninetieth year, that she was to bear a son. Hebrew names are often rich in meaning, often symbolic. Use a dictionary to find out what the following Biblical names mean. If you can, explain why each name is appropriate.
Adam • Eve • Sarah • Jonah • Noah • Ruth • Joseph • Joshua

Speaking/Listening

3. Onstage

In the Middle Ages, people loved to act out Biblical stories. **Dramatize** the story of Abraham and Isaac. "Open up the story," just as the medieval playwrights did. (They added **dialogue** and **scenes** as father and son climb the mountain and prepare the fire.) Consider adding Sarah, Isaac's mother, to the story, too. What might she say and do? You could even add music if you wish. Present your play to an audience.

Before You Read

PSALM 23

Background

The Book of Psalms is an anthology of Hebrew poetry written over a span of several centuries. Traditionally, almost half of the 150 psalms were attributed to King David (c. 1040–970 B.C.). Some Biblical scholars, however, believe that most of the psalms were written much later than David's time, and a few might even have been written earlier.

The word *psalm* derives from the Greek word *psalmos,* which means "a plucking of strings." Originally, the psalms were chanted by a choir and a cantor, or solo singer. They were accompanied by stringed instruments, cymbals, and, on High Holy Days, the flute. The psalms might also have been chanted antiphonally—that is, by different voices or groups of voices alternately addressing one another. (This device would explain the shift in speakers that seems to occur in some of the psalms.)

The Hebrew name for the Book of Psalms is *Tehillim,* which means "praise songs." Although many of the psalms are songs of praise and thanks to God, the collection also includes personal meditations, laments, battle songs, and even a marriage ode. Like most ancient Hebrew poetry, the psalms are written in unrhymed, usually unmetered verse, and the **rhythm** is created through **parallelism** (see pages 914 and 915).

Psalm 23 is one of the most famous passages in the Bible. It is frequently read at funeral services. As you read the psalm, think about what kind of consolation it might offer people.

Biblical Musicians, the Harpists (1975) by Shraga Weil. Serigraph (25″ × 17½″).

Courtesy Pucker/Safrai Gallery, Boston, Massachusetts.

This translation of Psalm 23 is from the King James Version of the Bible, which was commissioned by James I of England and published in 1611. It is written in the language used during William Shakespeare's time.

Psalm 23

King James Bible

The Lord is my shepherd; I shall not want.
He maketh me to lie down in green pastures:
He leadeth me beside the still waters.
He restoreth my soul:
He leadeth me in the paths of righteousness for his name's sake.
Yea, though I walk through the valley of the shadow of death,
I will fear no evil: for thou art with me;
Thy rod and thy staff they comfort me.
Thou preparest a table before me in the presence of mine enemies:
Thou anointest my head with oil; my cup runneth over.
Surely goodness and mercy shall follow me all the days of my life:
And I will dwell in the house of the Lord for ever.

Shepherd of Qumran (1965) by Shraga Weil. Color lithograph (24½″ × 17½″).

Courtesy Pucker/Safrai Gallery, Boston, Massachusetts.

Before You Read

To Every Thing There Is a Season

Background

The Book of Ecclesiastes (Kohelet in Hebrew) is a collection of poetry and wisdom. *Ecclesiastes* is a Greek word meaning "a speaker before an assembly." *Kohelet* may mean "a debater" or "a wise man who preaches to the young," or it may be the name of the person who wrote the book. Some scholars believe that the book is actually a collection of extracts from a sage's notebook.

For many years, people believed that King Solomon wrote Ecclesiastes in his old age (and that he wrote the sensual Song of Songs in his youth). Now, based on the type of Hebrew used in the book, scholars think that Ecclesiastes was written in about the third century B.C., more than six hundred years after King Solomon died.

Whoever wrote the book seems to have had a skeptical view of the world. Human existence is a series of struggles, the writer seems to say. Life proceeds in long cycles, and death is inevitable. The only valid intellectual stance is to recognize that the ways of God are unknowable. The best we can do is live moderately and accept what comes.

Few books of the Bible have had more of an impact on modern thinking than Ecclesiastes. Its questions about the purpose of human existence have appealed to such twentieth-century writers as Jean-Paul Sartre and Albert Camus. Its style has colored the work of writers as diverse as Walt Whitman and Ernest Hemingway. The verses from Chapter 3 that follow have even found their way into popular music.

Ecclesiastes, like the Book of Ruth and the Song of Songs, is one of the five festival scrolls in the Hebrew Bible. It is read during the autumn harvest festival of Sukkot. Why do you think the following passage might be especially appropriate for a harvest celebration?

Month of April, leaf from the calendar in a book of hours by Simon Bening (Flemish, early 16th century). Watercolor on parchment.

Victoria and Albert Museum, London. Courtesy Art Resource, NY.

To Every Thing There Is a Season

King James Bible

To every thing there is a season,
And a time to every purpose under the heaven:
A time to be born, and a time to die;
A time to plant, and a time to pluck up that which is planted;
A time to kill, and a time to heal;
A time to break down, and a time to build up;
A time to weep, and a time to laugh;
A time to mourn, and a time to dance;
A time to cast away stones, and a time to gather stones together;
A time to embrace, and a time to refrain from embracing;
A time to get, and a time to lose;
A time to keep, and a time to cast away;
A time to rend,° and a time to sew;
A time to keep silence, and a time to speak;
A time to love, and a time to hate;
A time of war, and a time of peace.

—Ecclesiastes 3:1–8

13. rend: tear.

Making Meanings
Psalm 23
To Every Thing There Is a Season

First Thoughts

1. Can you see why people have found comfort in these two poems? How do you respond to them? Jot down words and phrases that describe your feelings.

Shaping Interpretations

2. What are the two central **metaphors** of Psalm 23? (The first one is directly stated in line 1, and the second is implied in lines 9 and 10.) By implication, what is the **speaker** compared to in each metaphor?
3. How does the poet **extend** the first metaphor through line 8 of Psalm 23?
4. In the Middle East it was a sign of hospitality to pour a small amount of oil onto a guest's head (because he would be dusty from traveling or from working in the fields). What other **images** of hospitality do you find in Psalm 23?
5. In the passage from Ecclesiastes, what do you think the phrase "a time to cast away stones" means? What does "gather stones together" mean? What modern **figures of speech** would you use to express these ideas?
6. When do you think it might be appropriate "to lose" rather than "to get"? Can you suggest when it is best "to keep silence" and when it is best "to speak"?

Extending the Text

7. Look at the world around you. In terms of "To Every Thing There Is a Season," what "time" is it? Give examples to support your opinion.

Challenging the Text

8. The poem from Ecclesiastes says that there is "a time to kill," "a time to hate," and "a time for war." How can these be reconciled with the commandments "Thou shalt not kill" and "Love thy neighbor as thyself"? Explain your views.

Month of December, Book of Hours (1530), Flanders.

The Walters Art Gallery, Baltimore. (MS W.425.f.12)

CHOICES: Building Your Portfolio

Writer's Notebook

1. Collecting Ideas for an Essay Supporting a Generalization

Stating a general idea. What wisdom about life and death, joys and sorrows do you think is expressed in Psalm 23 and in Ecclesiastes? Take one of these poems and write a statement of what the text as a whole says to you. To support your **generalization**, find the most important line in each poem, as you see it. Save your notes for possible use in the Writer's Workshop on page 986. (The notes below focus on Psalm 8, which is not in this collection.)

WORK IN PROGRESS

In general, this psalm says that God is so powerful that it is a mystery why He is so generous to the human race.
Key line: 9.

Art Research/ Expository Writing

2. Eternal Images

Some of the world's greatest artists have been inspired by the Bible. Research one of the following artists or an artist of your choice, and write a brief essay about how the Bible influenced the artist's imagination. Try to find reproductions of works by the artist. Present your research to the class in a **multimedia presentation**, if possible.

- Michelangelo (Italian)
- Leonardo da Vinci (Italian)
- Albrecht Dürer (German)
- Rembrandt (Dutch)
- Peter Paul Rubens (Flemish)
- El Greco (Spanish)
- Horace Pippin (American)

Speaking/Listening

3. Hearing the Texts

Parallelism is what gives ancient Hebrew poetry its rhythm. **Parallelism** is the use of two or more words, phrases, or sentences that have the same grammatical structure. Parallelism can also involve the repetition of an idea in slightly different words. (For more on parallelism, see page 915 and the Handbook of Literary Terms.)

Prepare Psalm 23 or the passage from Ecclesiastes for **oral presentation**. You'll have to find the parallel structure in each piece and let that structure guide your interpretation. You can present each text in a single voice, in several alternating voices, or in a chorus. Many variations are possible. For example:

Voice 1: A time to be born,
Voices 1 and 2: and
Voice 2: a time to die;
Voice 1: A time to plant,
Voices 1 and 2: and
Voice 2: a time to pluck up that which is planted; . . .

Try all possibilities before you decide which presentation sounds the most dramatic. Be sure to ask for feedback from your audience. Does *hearing* the texts make them more powerful?

Music

4. Words to Music

Several composers and songwriters have set these Biblical poems to music. The most famous is probably Pete Seeger's folk song "Turn! Turn! Turn!," inspired by the verses from Ecclesiastes and recorded in the late 1960s by the rock group The Byrds. Choose one of the two Biblical poems, and set it to music: ballad music, folk, rock, rap—whatever seems appropriate. If you wish, work with a partner to present your musical version, either live or on tape, to the class.

GRAMMAR LINK **MINI-LESSON**

Language Handbook HELP

See Using Parallel Structure, pages 1044–1045.

Technology HELP

See Language Workshop CD-ROM. *Key word entry: parallel structure.*

Watch for Parallel Structure

Parallel structure is not just an element of style. If you use compound structures—if you combine several ideas into one sentence—you must be sure your combinations are balanced. When your sentence parts are out of balance, you've made an error. Here is a part of Ecclesiastes (lines 3–5) that a writer has rewritten with faulty parallel structure.

NOT PARALLEL A time to be born, and for death;

A time to plant, and for plucking up that which is planted;

There is a time to kill, and also for healing.

Here is another sentence rewritten from Ecclesiastes that contains faulty parallel structure. It is followed by three correct sentences. Notice that correct parallel structure is based on balancing a noun with a noun, a phrase with a phrase, a clause with a clause.

NOT PARALLEL There's a time for war and to make peace. [combines a prepositional phrase and an infinitive phrase]

PARALLEL There's a time for war and a time for peace. [two nouns followed by prepositional phrases]

There's a time for war, and there's a time for peace. [two clauses]

There's a time to make war and a time to make peace. [two nouns followed by infinitive phrases]

Try It Out

Edit the following passage to correct its faulty parallel structure. To test your editing, read the revised passage aloud. Sometimes faulty parallel structure shows up in awkward rhythms that you will be able to hear when you read the sentences aloud.

Modern novels sometimes have the names of Biblical books as their titles—for example, Leon Uris's novel *Exodus* and *Song of Solomon*, a novel by Toni Morrison. Other works make references to the Bible in their titles. Ingmar Bergman's movie *Through a Glass Darkly* is an example of this and so does George Cukor in his movie *Adam's Rib*. When I hear "I Have a Dream," I can't help thinking of the Bible and hope for the future.

Shepherds and sheep. Bas-relief from a portal of the Cathedral of Notre-Dame (1194–1240), Chartres, France.

Giraudon/Art Resource, NY.

Before You Read

THE PARABLE OF THE PRODIGAL SON

Background

This parable is from the Gospel of Luke—one of the New Testament's four Gospels, or books describing the life and teachings of Jesus. Luke was a physician who accompanied the apostle Paul on his missionary journeys. Scholars believe that his Gospel was written around A.D. 90.

Over the centuries many writers have made allusions to this well-known parable. An **allusion** is a reference to a work of literature, a person, a thing, or an event that the reader is expected to recognize. Allusions to the Bible are common in Western culture.

As you read this parable and the three poems that draw allusions to it, think about the word *prodigal. Prodigal* means "recklessly wasteful" or "extravagant." It also means "lavish" or "abundant." How can these different meanings be applied to both the son and the father?

Elements of Literature

Parables: Story Lessons

A **parable** is a short, simple story with a moral lesson. Jesus, like other Jewish teachers of his time, often told such stories. The message of a parable is not always crystal clear—parables are told to make us think.

> A **parable** is a very brief story about ordinary events and human characters that teaches a moral lesson about life.
>
> *For more on Parable, see the Handbook of Literary Terms.*

THE PARABLE OF THE PRODIGAL SON

New English Bible

There was once a man who had two sons, and the younger said to his father, "Father, give me my share of the property." So he divided his estate between them. A few days later the younger son turned the whole of his share into cash and left home for a distant country, where he squandered it in reckless living. He had spent it all, when a severe famine fell upon that country and he began to feel the pinch.

So he went and attached himself to one of the local landowners, who sent him on to his farm to mind the pigs. He would have been glad to fill his belly with the pods that the pigs were eating; and no one gave him anything. Then he came to his senses and said, "How many of my father's paid servants have more food than they can eat, and here am I, starving to death! I will set off and go to my father and say to him, 'Father, I have sinned, against God and against you; I am no longer fit to be called your son; treat me as one of your paid servants.'"

So he set out for his father's house. But while he was still a long way off, his father saw him, and his heart went out to him. He ran to meet him, flung his arms round him, and kissed him. The son said, "Father, I have sinned, against God and against you; I am no longer fit to be called your son."

The Return of the Prodigal Son (1773) by Pompeo Batoni. Oil on canvas (173 cm x 122 cm).

Kunsthistorisches Museum, Gemaeldegalerie, Vienna. Courtesy Erich Lessing/Art Resource, NY.

The Return of the Prodigal Son (1619) by Guercino.
Kunsthistorisches Museum, Vienna, Austria.

But the father said to his servants, "Quick! fetch a robe, my best one, and put it on him; put a ring on his finger and shoes on his feet. Bring the fatted calf and kill it, and let us have a feast to celebrate the day. For this son of mine was dead and has come back to life; he was lost and is found." And the festivities began.

Now the elder son was out on the farm; and on his way back, as he approached the house, he heard music and dancing. He called one of the servants and asked what it meant. The servant told him, "Your brother has come home, and your father has killed the fatted calf because he has him back safe and sound."

But he was angry and refused to go in. His father came out and pleaded with him; but he retorted, "You know how I have slaved for you all these years; I never once disobeyed your orders; and you never gave me so much as a kid,° for a feast with my friends. But now that this son of yours turns up, after running through your money with his women, you kill the fatted calf for him."

"My boy," said the father, "you are always with me, and everything I have is yours. How could we help celebrating this happy day? Your brother here was dead and has come back to life, was lost and is found."

—Luke 15:11–32

°**kid:** young goat.

The Prodigal

Elizabeth Bishop

The brown enormous odor he lived by
was too close, with its breathing and thick hair,
for him to judge. The floor was rotten; the sty°
was plastered halfway up with glass-smooth dung.
Light-lashed, self-righteous, above moving snouts,
the pigs' eyes followed him, a cheerful stare—
even to the sow° that always ate her young—
till, sickening, he leaned to scratch her head.
But sometimes mornings after drinking bouts
(he hid the pints behind a two-by-four),
the sunrise glazed the barnyard mud with red;
the burning puddles seemed to reassure.
And then he thought he almost might endure
his exile yet another year or more.

But evenings the first star came to warn.
The farmer whom he worked for came at dark
to shut the cows and horses in the barn
beneath their overhanging clouds of hay,
with pitchforks, faint forked lightnings, catching light,
safe and companionable as in the Ark.°
The pigs stuck out their little feet and snored.
The lantern—like the sun, going away—
laid on the mud a pacing aureole.°
Carrying a bucket along a slimy board,
he felt the bats' uncertain staggering flight,
his shuddering insights, beyond his control,
touching him. But it took him a long time
finally to make his mind up to go home.

3. sty: pen for pigs.

7. sow: adult female pig.

20. ark: In the story of the flood in the Bible, the ark was the boat in which Noah, his family, and two of every kind of creature survived.

23. aureole: illuminated area around the sun or a light when seen in a mist; also, the halo or radiance encircling the head or body of a holy person in religious paintings.

The Prodigal

Sara Henderson Hay

They made a feast in the banquet hall,
And the calf was slain for the prodigal.
And here I sit, while the last guests linger,
With a robe on my back, and a ring on my finger.

Well, home calls somehow, the whole world through,
And its threshold portal is a dream come true,
And the glow of the home hearth is beautiful to see
When one has been a vagrant, in a Far Country.

Oh it's not much fun to be swine herd keeping,
And to bed with the hard earth is cold enough sleeping,
And after the husks were gone, I fasted—
But Oh, my friends—while the money lasted!

The Father

Sara Henderson Hay

Well, he's come home, this younger son of mine.
But something in his penitence betrays
He had been guardian of fouler swine,
Before those latter days. . . .

For there's a furtive something sliding under
His speech; he sits and twists his ring around
And stares at it. My son was lost—I wonder,
Is he so truly found?

Oh I am glad I did not hesitate
To run and clasp him hard in my embrace.
Still, it was rather more than fortunate
He could not see *my* face.

Making Meanings

The Parable of the Prodigal Son

First Thoughts

1. Do you think the father in the Biblical story is fair? Explain your feelings.

Shaping Interpretations

2. The word *prodigal* does not appear in the story at all; it was added to the title in later translations. In what ways is the younger son *prodigal* with money? How is the father *prodigal* with his love?
3. What about the elder son? Some critics say that he represents those people who can't accept God's goodness. How could this interpretation be explained? What people in life today remind you of this elder son?
4. What would you say is the moral lesson of this **parable**? How do you feel about its message?

Connecting with the Text

5. How do you feel about the value placed on forgiveness in this parable? How easy or difficult would it be to live according to this message? Compare your responses with those of your classmates.

Choices: Building Your Portfolio

Writer's Notebook

1. Collecting Ideas for an Essay Supporting a Generalization

WORK IN PROGRESS

Stating a generalization. Modern writers allude to this Biblical parable in their own unique ways. **Compare and contrast** Bishop's and Henderson Hay's **allusions** to the parable. (See *Connections* on pages 919–920.) What generalizations can you make about each portrayal of the son and the father? Save your notes.

Research/ Expository Writing

2. Biblical Archaeology

Exciting archaeological finds related to the Bible have been made in the Middle East. With a small group, look in an encyclopedia or on the Internet for information on the Dead Sea Scrolls. Then, assign topics to group members for further research. When all your material is assembled, decide on a focus for your essay. Finally, assign writers to present your findings.

Art

3. Set Designer Needed

Imagine you are the set designer for a dramatization of the story of the prodigal son. (A famous ballet based on the story was choreographed by George Balanchine.) Sketch three sets for the play. Go back to the text to find details for your sets. What tone or atmosphere do you want to set in each scene? Will you set the story in Biblical times, or will it take place today?

Before You Read

THE GREATEST OF THESE IS CHARITY

Background

This portion of a letter written around A.D. 50–52 by a man named Paul is one of the world's most famous writings on love. Paul was an apostle who preached the gospel of Christianity on missionary journeys throughout the Mediterranean world. After his visits, he wrote many letters, urging people to be faithful, correcting them when he thought they were doing wrong, and helping them deal with various problems and theological questions. To Paul, the Corinthian church, made up mostly of poor people, posed special problems because the port city of Corinth, in Greece, was notorious for its immorality.

Quickwrite

The King James Bible uses the word *charity* in this letter; later translators use the word *love*. Are love and charity the same? How important is each in human life? Quickwrite for several minutes.

The Greatest of These Is Charity

King James Bible

The citizens of Corinth had written to Paul asking him to clarify some of the rules and practices of Christians, especially concerning marriage and idolatry. In Paul's reply, he addresses these and other problems and, in this well-known passage, emphasizes the importance of charity—that is, love.

Though I speak with the tongues of men and of angels, and have not charity, I am become as sounding brass, or a tinkling cymbal.

And though I have the gift of prophecy, and understand all mysteries, and all knowledge; and though I have all faith, so that I could remove mountains, and have not charity, I am nothing.

And though I bestow all my goods to feed the poor, and though I give my body to be burned, and have not charity, it profiteth me nothing.

Charity suffereth long, and is kind; charity envieth not; charity vaunteth[1] not itself, is not puffed up,

Doth not behave itself unseemly, seeketh not her own, is not easily provoked, thinketh no evil;

Rejoiceth not in iniquity,[2] but rejoiceth in the truth;

Beareth all things, believeth all things, hopeth all things, endureth all things.

Charity never faileth: but whether there be prophecies, they shall fail; whether there be tongues, they shall cease; whether there be knowledge, it shall vanish away.

For we know in part, and we prophesy[3] in part.

But when that which is perfect is come, then that which is in part shall be done away.

When I was a child, I spake as a child, I understood as a child, I thought as a child: but when I became a man, I put away childish things.

For now we see through a glass, darkly; but then face to face: now I know in part; but then shall I know even as also I am known.

And now abideth faith, hope, charity, these three; but the greatest of these is charity.

—I Corinthians 13:1–13

1. **vaunteth** (archaic form of *vaunts*): boasts; brags.
2. **iniquity:** lack of righteousness or justice; wickedness.
3. **prophesy** (verb form of the noun *prophecy*): predict; here, with divine guidance.

Making Meanings
The Greatest of These Is Charity

First Thoughts

1. Do you agree that charity (love) is the greatest of human qualities? If not, what do you consider the greatest quality?

Shaping Interpretations

2. Beginning with the fourth verse, Paul uses a series of **verbs** to describe what a loving person *does* and *does not* do. Find these verbs, and list them in a chart like the one shown here. What are their modern forms? What verbs could you add?

Charity	
Does	Does Not
suffereth long	envieth

Connecting with the Text

3. What people can you name who display love or charity in the way Paul describes it? Explain why your choices are good ones.

Challenging the Text

4. More recent translations of the Bible have changed the word *charity* to *love*. (The original word in Greek, the language Paul wrote in, was *agape* [ag′ə·pē].) What is the difference between *charity* and *love* in modern English? (Check your Quickwrite notes.) Now, read the letter again. Substitute the word *love* for *charity*, and see if you detect a difference in emotional impact.

Choices: Building Your Portfolio

Writer's Notebook

1. Collecting Ideas for an Essay Supporting a Generalization

WORK IN PROGRESS

Finding support. In his last verse, Paul clearly states the **thesis**, or general truth, he is proposing: "The greatest of these [faith, hope, charity] is charity." He has done more than assert what he values, however; he has given examples, made comparisons, and offered reasons to support his beliefs. Make a statement about a personal quality or a way of living that you value highly. Then, list examples and reasons to back up your statement. Save your notes.

Creative Writing

2. A Letter on Love

Write to someone you love, or might love, very much—perhaps a parent or grandparent or the person you'll marry some day or a child to whom you'll have much to say in the future. Tell that person what you believe about love.

Creative Writing

3. Love Is . . .

Write your own description of love. Follow Paul's structure: Tell what love is, what it does, and what it does not do.

Besser a guter soineh aider a shlechter freint.
Better a good enemy than a bad friend.
(Yiddish)

Is maith an scéalaí an aimsir.
Time is a great storyteller.
(Irish)

Haz bien, y no mires a quien.
Do good, without caring to whom.
(Spanish)

Didactic Literature: Teaching Lessons

Probably every society that has ever existed on Earth has told stories to teach its people how to live and how not to live. Writings like these, which are primarily aimed at teaching or instructing, are called **didactic** works.

Both the Bible (which contains the sacred scripture of Judaism and Christianity) and the Koran (the sacred scripture of Islam) include didactic texts written to fulfill the most serious of instructive purposes. They ask and answer profound questions about the meaning of life, what happens after death, how we should worship God, and how we should live our everyday lives.

Other didactic writings are less profound; some of them are immensely practical, even cynical.

Didactic writings make use of a variety of forms. Two of the most popular teaching forms are the anecdote and the parable. (A parable from the New Testament is on page 916.) A **parable** is a very brief story that teaches by means of **comparison**. The teacher telling the parable draws the story's action from familiar situations: a lost coin, a traveler attacked by thieves, a problem son. The listeners have to infer the comparison the teacher is making. The message is not always easy to understand—parables are told to make us think.

Taoist teachers in China (see page 931) and Sufi masters from Persia (see page 927) teach by means of anecdotes. Like parables, **anecdotes** are brief stories that contain familiar characters, settings, and actions that teach a lesson about living. The lesson of the anecdote often has to be inferred by the listener.

Another popular didactic form is the brief, wise saying called the **aphorism** or **maxim**. America's Benjamin Franklin liked to write aphorisms on the value of thrift, hard work, and the simple life. Laotzu, the Chinese philosopher thought to have founded Taoism in the sixth century (see page 931), also used maxims.

The **beast fable** is a narrative form that teaches its lessons through talking animals. Beast fables appeared in India long ago, well before the sixth century B.C. They were probably collected in the fifth century A.D. or earlier in a story cycle known as the *Panchatantra* (see page 940). Beast fables were later used by Aesop in ancient Greece, by La Fontaine in France, and even by the American humorist James Thurber in the twentieth century (see page 944). Beast fables are still alive and well today: Think, for example, of Disney's *The Lion King*.

OMOITATSU HI GA KICHINICHI.
THE DAY YOU MAKE YOUR DECISION TO DO SOMETHING IS A LUCKY DAY.
(JAPANESE)

Odò kì í sàn k'ó gbàgbé isun rè.
However far the stream flows, it never forgets its source.
(Yoruba)

Before You Read

THE KORAN

Background

The Koran (also spelled Qur'an) is the sacred scripture of Islam. Muslims (followers of Islam) believe that the Arabic text was revealed by God to the prophet Mohammed. The prophet was born in Mecca, in what is now Saudi Arabia, about A.D. 570 and began to preach there around 613. Devout Muslims throughout the world shape their lives and societies according to the Koran's teachings.

The book consists of 114 chapters, or *suras*. The two suras that follow emphasize the mercy of the one God (Allah) as well as the rewards that await those who obey Allah's laws.

Reading Skills and Strategies

Monitoring Your Reading: Rereading

You might find **rereading** necessary for these short but complex suras. Try this strategy: After you read each sura, note what you think it is saying. Then, reread it. Have your thoughts changed? Finally, read it a third time. Now you should know what the text says to you.

go.hrw.com
LEO 10-13

from The Koran

translated by N. J. Dawood

Daylight

In the Name of Allah,
the Compassionate, the Merciful

By the light of day, and by the fall of night, your Lord has not forsaken you, nor does He abhor you.

The life to come holds a richer prize for you than this present life. You shall be gratified with what your Lord will give you.

Did He not find you an orphan and give you shelter?

Did He not find you in error and guide you?

Did He not find you poor and enrich you?

Therefore do not wrong the orphan, nor chide away the beggar. But proclaim the goodness of your Lord.

—Sura 93

Comfort

In the Name of Allah,
the Compassionate, the Merciful

Have We not lifted up your heart and relieved you of the burden which weighed down your back?

Have We not given you high renown?

Every hardship is followed by ease. Every hardship is followed by ease.

When your task is ended, resume your toil, and seek your Lord with all fervor.

—Sura 94

Making Meanings
The Koran

First Thoughts

1. How would these passages help people during difficult times?

Shaping Interpretations

2. Did you **reread** the suras? How did your understanding of the suras change with each reading?
3. In the passage "Daylight," what message about God is given to believers? What have believers been promised, and what is expected of them?
4. In the passage "Comfort," what assurances have been offered to believers? What is asked of them?
5. Like other sacred texts, these passages from the Koran are meant to be recited. The word *Koran* comes from the Arabic for "recite" and "recitation." Today the sacred words of the Koran are still recited in Arabic by devout Muslims. Point out **parallel structures** in these suras that make them especially suitable for recitation.

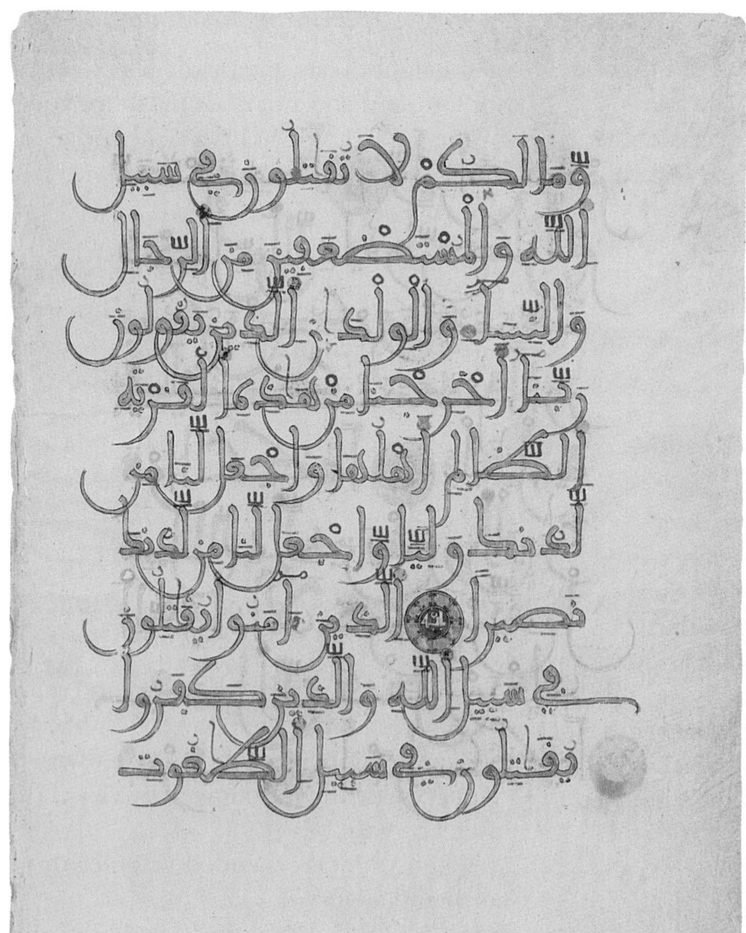

Koran leaf of Sura 4:72–73, written in the Maghrebi dialect of Arabic (14th century). Ink, colors, and gold on parchment ($10\frac{1}{4}'' \times 8\frac{9}{16}''$).

The Metropolitan Museum of Art, Rogers Fund 1937 (37.21). Photograph © 1992 The Metropolitan Museum of Art.

Before You Read

SAYINGS OF SAADI

Background

Saadi, a thirteenth-century teacher who wrote in Persian, was a Sufi, a member of a mystical branch of Islam. He lived in a time of great upheaval in the Islamic world, with Mongols invading from the east and Crusaders coming from the west. Like mystics of other faiths, Sufis believe that knowledge of God can be gained by experiencing a spiritual transformation and by renouncing worldly possessions and achievements. Saadi, however, was a down-to-earth mystic, and his writing offers practical ethical advice in simple and direct language. Saadi's collection of didactic tales in verse is called the *Gulistan,* or *The Rose Garden.*

go.hrw.com
LEO 10-13

from Sayings of Saadi

translated by Idries Shah

Relative

A lamp has no rays at all in the face of the sun;
And a high minaret even in the foothills of a
mountain looks low.

Information and Knowledge

However much you study, you cannot know
without action.
A donkey laden with books is neither an
intellectual nor a wise man.
Empty of essence, what learning has he—
Whether upon him is firewood or book?

The Thief and the Blanket

A thief entered the house of a Sufi, and found nothing there. As he was leaving, the dervish perceived his disappointment and threw him the blanket in which he was sleeping, so that he should not go away empty-handed.

The Destiny of a Wolf Cub

The destiny of a wolf cub is to become a wolf, even if it is reared among the sons of men.

MAKING MEANINGS

SAYINGS OF SAADI

Shaping Interpretations

1. Paraphrase—restate in your own words—each of these sayings of Saadi. Compare your paraphrases with those of your classmates. Have you read the sayings the same way? Are different interpretations possible?

Extending the Text

2. Could you apply any of these old sayings to situations or people today? Explain.

Before You Read

THE RUBÁIYÁT

Background

Omar Khayyám (1048–1131), whose full name was Ghias uddin Abul Fath Omar ibn Ibrahim al-Khayyám, was a noted Persian mathematician and astronomer from Nishapur.

The *rubá'i* is an old and complex literary form that Persian poets have long favored for expressing their thoughts on a variety of subjects. Omar Khayyám composed his collection of self-contained **rhymed quatrains**, or *rubáiyát*, over an extended period. Many years after his death, Khayyám's poems were moderately popular in Persia (now Iran), but they gained worldwide fame when an English poet named Edward FitzGerald (1809–1883) translated them in the 1850s. In his English version, FitzGerald freely rearranged the order of Khayyám's verses and adapted the **imagery** and even the philosophy, making his translation a near reinvention of the original.

As you read, think about whether Khayyám was an optimist or a pessimist about human life.

go.hrw.com

LEO 10-13

from The Rubáiyát

Omar Khayyám

translated by Edward FitzGerald

7

Come, fill the Cup, and in the fire of Spring
Your Winter-garment of Repentance fling:
The Bird of Time has but a little way
To flutter—and the Bird is on the Wing.

12

A Book of Verses underneath the Bough,
A Jug of Wine, a Loaf of Bread—and Thou
Beside me singing in the Wilderness——
Oh, Wilderness were Paradise enow!°

4. **enow** (ē·nou'): archaic form of *enough.*

13

Some for the Glories of This World; and some
Sigh for the Prophet's Paradise to come;
Ah, take the Cash, and let the Credit go,
Nor heed the rumble of a distant Drum!

24

Ah, make the most of what we yet may spend,
Before we too into the Dust descend;
Dust into Dust, and under Dust to lie
Sans° Wine, sans Song, sans Singer, and—sans End!

4. **sans:** French for "without."

71

The Moving Finger writes; and, having writ,
Moves on: nor all your Piety nor Wit
Shall lure it back to cancel half a Line,
Nor all your Tears wash out a Word of it.

Humay and Humayun in a garden. Leaf from *Jami at-Tawarikh (Compendium of Histories)* by Rashid ad-Din, Fadl Allah (c. 1400). Persia (now Iran), early Timurid period. Colors and gilt on paper (19¼″ × 12⁹⁄₁₆″).

MAKING MEANINGS
THE RUBÁIYÁT

First Thoughts

1. How do you feel about the philosophy of life described in this translation of *The Rubáiyát*? Find some specific lines you agree or disagree with.

Shaping Interpretations

2. In verse 12, what does the speaker say is enough (*enow*) for him?
3. In what ways is verse 13 like the writings of Saadi (page 927)? In what ways is it different?
4. Verse 24 is a good example of a *rubá'i* with a twist at the end. What is the speaker saying about life and death? What do you make of the last words?
5. What do you think the Moving Finger is in verse 71?

Extending the Text

6. The outlook on life expressed in FitzGerald's translation of *The Rubáiyát* is sometimes called *carpe diem*, Latin for "seize the day" (or, roughly, "eat, drink, and be merry, for tomorrow we die"). Do people today have this philosophy? Explain.

CHOICES: Building Your Portfolio

Writer's Notebook

1. Collecting Ideas for an Essay Supporting a Generalization

WORK IN PROGRESS

Making a generalization. The selections here are brief, but they reveal very definite points of view about life. These points of view are not always stated directly; often they are implied—the reader is supposed to **infer** the meaning.

Write a statement that sums up the beliefs about human life that underlie any of these selections: from the Koran, from Saadi, or from Khayyám (as translated by FitzGerald). If you see dramatic **contrasts**, make a generalization about the differences in the texts. Save your notes for possible use in the Writer's Workshop on page 986.

Speaking/ Presenting Research

2. Being a Researcher

Research begins with questions. What questions do you have about the Koran, Saadi's sayings, or *The Rubáiyát*? For example, you might want to know how close FitzGerald's translation of *The Rubáiyát* is to the original. Generate a list of questions about these texts, and identify sources, including the Internet, that might help you find answers. Be sure to evaluate your sources. Tell the class about your experiences doing research.

Art

3. Adding Art

The Rubáiyát has been translated into almost every modern language and has often been illustrated. Illustrate one of the quatrains from the poem, and display your class's drawings.

Before You Read

TAOIST ANECDOTES / TAO TE CHING

Background

Laotzu (loʊ′dzu), who was born in China around 571 B.C., is considered the founder of the Chinese philosophy called Taoism (doʊ′iz′m). Few facts are known about him, but legend has it that when Laotzu retired from government service, he wrote the collection of sayings and poems called the *Tao Te Ching* (doʊ′ de jing′), or *The Way and Its Power.* The word *Tao* refers to the mysterious "way" or "path" of the universe.

Elements of Literature

Paradox: A Seeming Contradiction

Taoism, like many philosophies and religions, uses paradoxes to express aspects of life that are mysterious, surprising, or difficult to describe. A **paradox** is a seeming contradiction that is also somehow true. A paradox may be a situation or a statement. For example, in *Romeo and Juliet*, Juliet says, "Parting is such sweet sorrow" when Romeo is leaving her. This paradox is true because the parting kisses are sweet but the leave-taking itself is sad.

A **paradox** is a statement or a situation that seems to be a contradiction but that reveals a truth.

For more on Paradox, see the Handbook of Literary Terms.

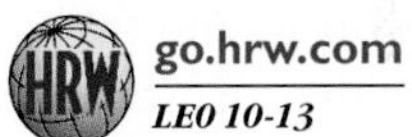

go.hrw.com
LEO 10-13

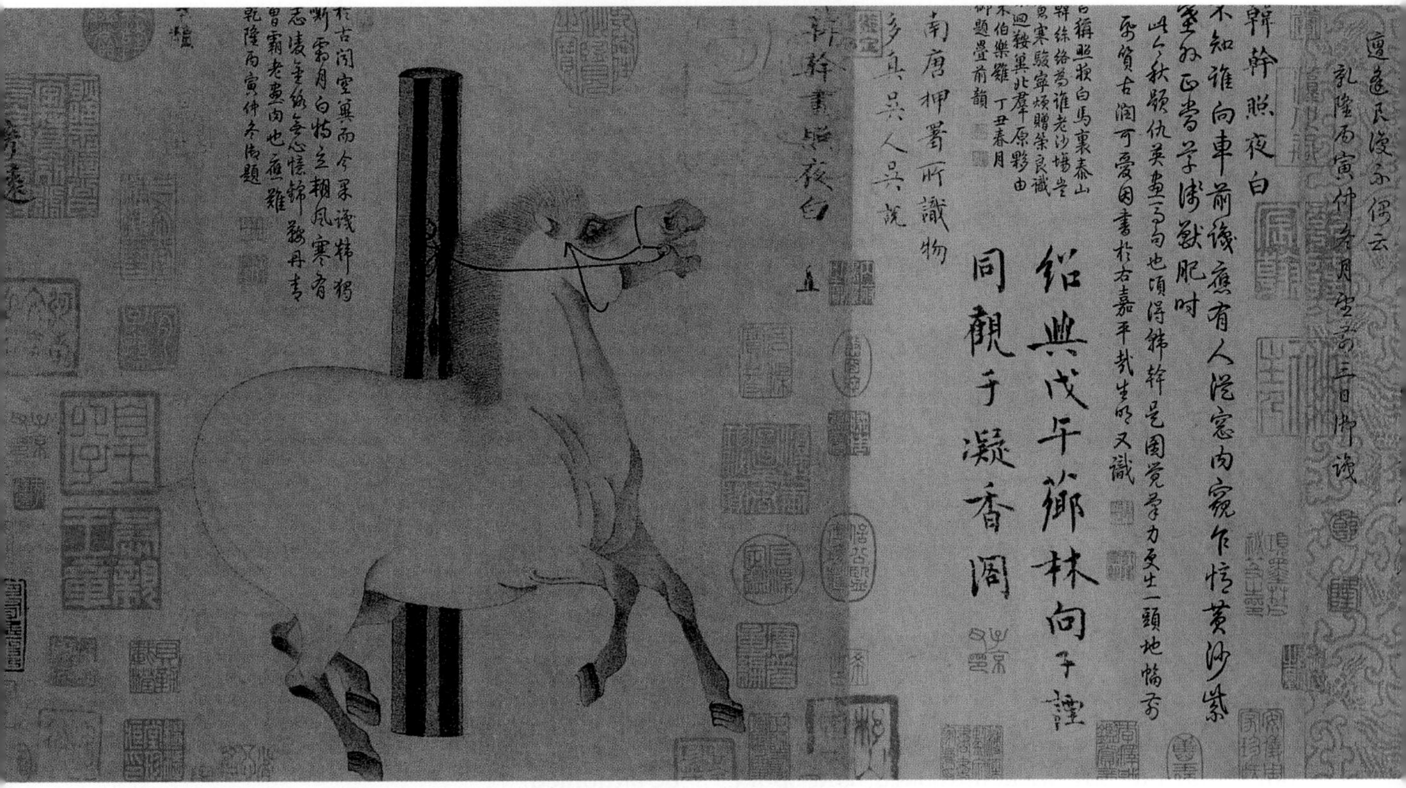

Night-Shining White (detail), attributed to Han Kan (active c. 740–756). China, Tang dynasty (A.D. 618–906). Hand scroll; ink on paper (13⅜″ × 12⅛″).

The Metropolitan Museum of Art, Purchase, The Dillon Fund Gift, 1977 (1977.78).

Taoist Anecdotes

translated by Moss Roberts

Wagging My Tail in the Mud

The hermit poet Chuang Tzu was angling in the River Pu. The king of Ch'u sent two noblemen to invite Chuang to come before him. "We were hoping you would take on certain affairs of state," they said. Holding his pole steady and without looking at them, Chuang Tzu said, "I hear Ch'u has a sacred tortoise that has been dead three thousand years, and the king has it enshrined in a cushioned box in the ancestral hall. Do you think the tortoise would be happier wagging its tail in the mud than having its shell honored?" "Of course," replied the two noblemen. "Then begone," said Chuang Tzu. "I mean to keep wagging my tail in the mud."

—Chuang Tzu

Laotzu. Detail from *Lord of the Southern Dipper.* Chinese Taoist fresco.
The Granger Collection, New York.

The Missing Ax

A man whose ax was missing suspected his neighbor's son. The boy walked like a thief, looked like a thief, and spoke like a thief. But the man found his ax while he was digging in the valley, and the next time he saw his neighbor's son, the boy walked, looked, and spoke like any other child.

—Lieh Tzu

The Lost Horse

A man who lived on the northern frontier of China was skilled in interpreting events. One day, for no reason, his horse ran away to the nomads across the border. Everyone tried to console him, but his father said, "What makes you so sure this isn't a blessing?" Some months later his horse returned, bringing a splendid nomad stallion. Everyone congratulated him, but his father said, "What makes you so sure this isn't a disaster?" Their household was richer by a fine horse, which the son loved to ride. One day he fell and broke his hip. Everyone tried to console him, but his father said, "What makes you so sure this isn't a blessing?"

A year later the nomads came in force across the border, and every able-bodied man took his bow and went into battle. The Chinese frontiersmen lost nine of every ten men. Only because the son was lame did the father and son survive to take care of each other. Truly, blessing turns to disaster, and disaster to blessing: The changes have no end, nor can the mystery be fathomed.

—Lui An

Wang Hsi-chih Watching Geese (detail) by Ch'ien Hsüan (c. 1235–before 1307). Hand scroll; ink and color on paper ($9\frac{1}{8}'' \times 36\frac{1}{2}''$).

from the Tao Te Ching

Laotzu
translated by Stephen Mitchell

8

The supreme good is like water,
which nourishes all things without trying to.
It is content with the low places that people disdain.
Thus it is like the Tao.

In dwelling, live close to the ground.
In thinking, keep to the simple.
In conflict, be fair and generous.
In governing, don't try to control.

In work, do what you enjoy.
In family life, be completely present.

When you are content to be simply yourself
and don't compare or compete,
everybody will respect you.

11

We join spokes together in a wheel,
but it is the center hole
that makes the wagon move.

We shape clay into a pot,
but it is the emptiness inside
that holds whatever we want.

We hammer wood for a house,
but it is the inner space
that makes it livable.

We work with being,
but non-being is what we use.

67

Some say that my teaching is nonsense.
Others call it lofty but impractical.
But to those who have looked inside themselves,
this nonsense makes perfect sense.
And to those who put it into practice,
this loftiness has roots that go deep.

I have just three things to teach:
simplicity, patience, compassion.
These three are your greatest treasures.
Simple in actions and in thoughts,
you return to the source of being.
Patient with both friends and enemies,
you accord with the way things are.
Compassionate toward yourself,
you reconcile all beings in the world.

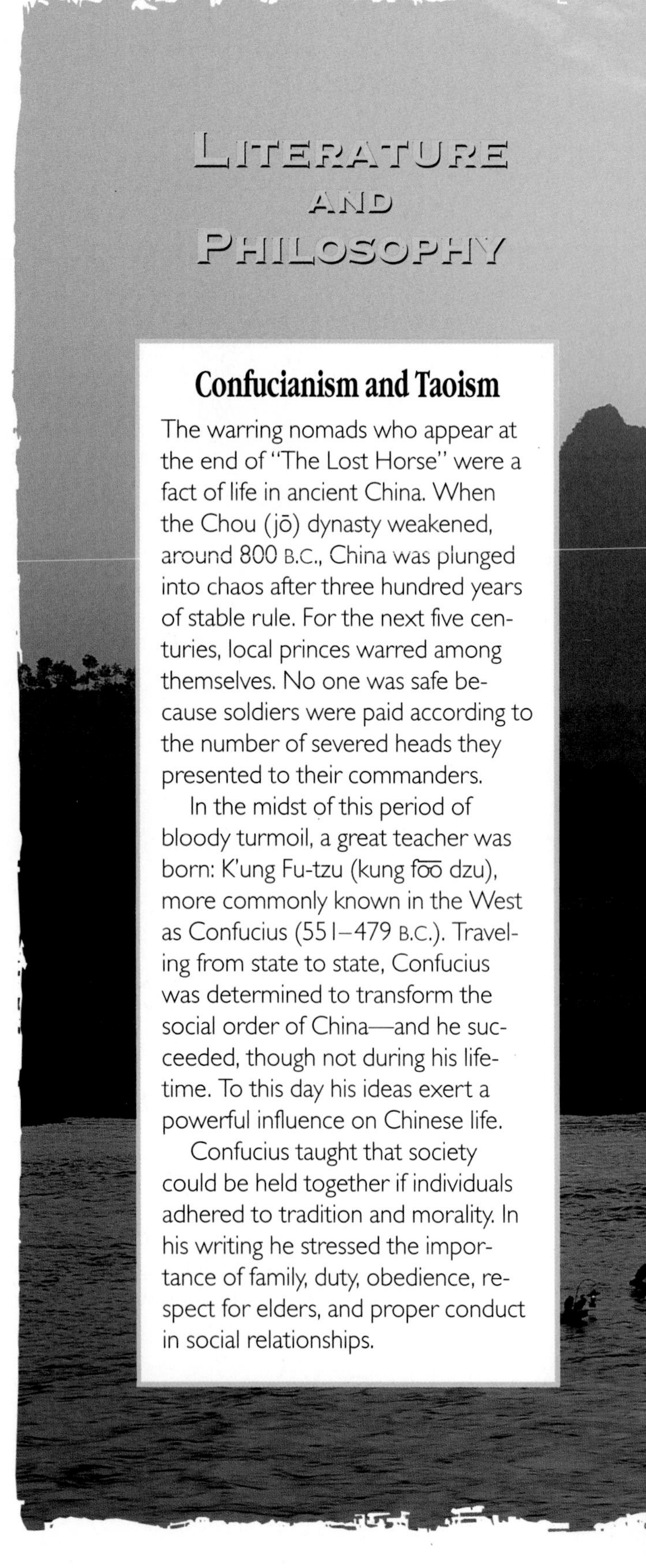

LITERATURE AND PHILOSOPHY

Confucianism and Taoism

The warring nomads who appear at the end of "The Lost Horse" were a fact of life in ancient China. When the Chou (jō) dynasty weakened, around 800 B.C., China was plunged into chaos after three hundred years of stable rule. For the next five centuries, local princes warred among themselves. No one was safe because soldiers were paid according to the number of severed heads they presented to their commanders.

In the midst of this period of bloody turmoil, a great teacher was born: K'ung Fu-tzu (kung fo͞o dzu), more commonly known in the West as Confucius (551–479 B.C.). Traveling from state to state, Confucius was determined to transform the social order of China—and he succeeded, though not during his lifetime. To this day his ideas exert a powerful influence on Chinese life.

Confucius taught that society could be held together if individuals adhered to tradition and morality. In his writing he stressed the importance of family, duty, obedience, respect for elders, and proper conduct in social relationships.

Where there's nobility of spirit,
there's beauty of character.

Where there's beauty of character,
there's a harmonious home.

Where there's a harmonious home,
there's an orderly nation.

Where there's an orderly nation,
there's peace in the world.

—Confucius, from *The Great Learning*

As Confucianism spread and transformed Chinese society, a looser, more mystical philosophy, called Taoism, rose up to challenge it. In fact, the conflict between these two great philosophies has given shape to Chinese culture. We know very little about Taoism's legendary founder, Laotzu—his name simply means "the old master." Scholars disagree on when he lived and even who he was. The traditional view is that Laotzu was born around 571 B.C.; no one knows when he died. Confucius supposedly met the old sage and came away bewildered by his ideas but full of respect for him. According to tradition, Laotzu's only written expression of his philosophy is a short, mystical book called the *Tao Te Ching* (dou′ de jing′), or *The Way and Its Power*. It is an exploration of the *Tao*—the mysterious "way" or "path" of the universe.

Though the two philosophies have much in common, Taoism differs from Confucianism on many basic points. Taoists object to the Confucian stress on duty, social hierarchy, and materialism. They also reject the Confucian emphasis on status and getting ahead in the world. Instead, Taoists value humility and simplicity—"doing by not doing," freedom from desire. While Confucianism focuses on relationships among people, Taoism stresses the relationship between people and nature. Most significant, Taoists see the world as fluid, as being made up of counterbalanced opposites flowing in and out of each other. This belief is embodied in the yin and yang symbol, the constantly spinning wheel of the universe that has come to symbolize Taoism itself. (Literally, *yin* means the "dark side" and *yang* means the "sunny side" of the hill.)

Another important difference is that Confucians distinguish between proper and improper social conduct, whereas Taoists believe that nothing is fixed; nothing is what it seems at first glance. In "The Missing Ax," the boy at first is a thief, and then he's not. In "The Lost Horse," the runaway horse is a disaster and then a blessing and then a disaster again—but ultimately the horse leads to salvation.

MAKING MEANINGS
TAOIST ANECDOTES
TAO TE CHING

First Thoughts

1. What lines from these Taoist writings do you find most relevant to life today?

Shaping Interpretations

2. What does "Wagging My Tail in the Mud" reveal about Chuang Tzu's values? What does he prize in life and what does he reject?
3. What does "The Missing Ax" teach about the danger of distrust? How could the story have meaning for us today?
4. Do you agree with the observation made in "The Lost Horse" about life's changing fortunes? Explain your response.
5. According to passage 8 from the *Tao Te Ching,* how is the Tao like water? What other concrete image can you think of that might represent the Tao?
6. Passage 11 in the *Tao Te Ching* uses **paradoxes** to teach that nothing is what it seems to be. Explain the paradox of a clay pot.
7. What do you think of the values the teacher treasures in passage 67? How do these **compare** with what people value today?

CHOICES: Building Your Portfolio

Writer's Notebook

1. Collecting Ideas for an Essay Supporting a Generalization

Paraphrasing a message. A **paraphrase** is a restatement of a text, using other words. A paraphrase is often useful in critical writing, when you want to restate a difficult or complex text using simpler language of your own. A paraphrase can often help you pinpoint difficulties you have with a text. Try your hand at paraphrasing one or more of these Taoist texts. Save your notes.

WORK IN PROGRESS

Creative Writing

2. What Would He Say?

Create an imaginary **dialogue** between Laotzu and a contemporary high school student in which the student asks for the philosopher's advice. Focus the dialogue on a concrete situation involving school, work, or relationships, and be sure that Laotzu's advice is in harmony with his beliefs. Role-play your dialogue with a partner.

Speaking/Listening

3. Telling an Anecdote

Think of an experience in life that taught someone a lesson. Recall exactly what happened and what the person learned. Practice telling the story aloud, including any colorful **details**, humorous **dialogue**, or surprising **twists**. Be sure your anecdote makes a clear point, whether you state it directly or imply it. Tell your anecdote to the class. Ask the audience for feedback: Did your listeners get your point?

Before You Read

ZEN PARABLES

Background

Who was Buddha? Buddha (in Sanskrit the name means "enlightened one") was a reformer of the Hindu religion. He is thought to have been born in Nepal about 563 B.C. and to have died in 483 B.C. His given name was Siddhartha, and his family name was Gautama. Born to a rich family, Siddhartha lived in luxury until, at age twenty-nine, he saw four signs that changed his life: an aged man, a sick man, a corpse, and a wandering religious beggar. The first three signs revealed to him the suffering in the world; in the beggar, he saw his own destiny.

Buddhism, with its ethical commandments and way of life that calls for renunciation of desire, established a strong position in China and later in Korea and Japan.

Zen Buddhism. Over the centuries, a number of schools and subsects of Buddhism developed, each emphasizing a different path to the same goal. Zen Buddhism, for example, stresses the importance of meditation and self-discipline. Unlike many other religions, Zen has no sacred scripture, no prescribed rituals, no grand temples. It is essentially a meditative practice designed to give followers a direct experience of their own inner natures. When Zen was introduced in Japan in A.D. 1191, its emphasis on self-mastery appealed to the warrior class, or samurai, who protected the feudal aristocracy. Today Zen is practiced by ordinary people in both the East and the West to discover spiritual meaning and to relieve stress.

go.hrw.com
LEO 10-13

Woman Visiting a Shrine (c. 1800) by Suzuki Harunobu. Japanese print.

Zen Parables

translated by Paul Reps

Muddy Road

Tanzan and Ekido were once traveling together down a muddy road. A heavy rain was still falling.

Coming around a bend, they met a lovely girl in a silk kimono and sash, unable to cross the intersection.

"Come on, girl," said Tanzan at once. Lifting her in his arms, he carried her over the mud.

Ekido did not speak again until that night, when they reached a lodging temple. Then he no longer could restrain himself. "We monks don't go near females," he told Tanzan, "especially not young and lovely ones. It is dangerous. Why did you do that?"

"I left the girl there," said Tanzan. "Are you still carrying her?"

The Thief Who Became a Disciple

One evening, as Shichiri Kojun was reciting sutras,° a thief with a sharp sword entered, demanding either his money or his life.

Shichiri told him: "Do not disturb me. You can find the money in that drawer." Then he resumed his recitation.

A little while afterward, he stopped and called: "Don't take it all. I need some to pay taxes with tomorrow."

The intruder gathered up most of the money and started to leave. "Thank a person when you receive a gift," Shichiri added. The man thanked him and made off.

A few days afterward, the fellow was caught and confessed, among others, the offense against Shichiri. When Shichiri was called as a witness, he said: "This man is no thief, at least as far as I am concerned. I gave him the money and he thanked me for it."

After he had finished his prison term, the man went to Shichiri and became his disciple.

° **sutras** (so͞o′trəz): Buddhist (or Hindu) scriptures.

Making Meanings
Zen Parables

First Thoughts

1. Were the lessons of these two **parables** immediately clear to you? Why or why not? What did they "teach" you?

Shaping Interpretations

2. In "Muddy Road," what do you think Tanzan means when he asks Ekido if he is "still carrying" the girl?
3. How would you state the implied **moral** of "Muddy Road"? Discuss a situation in someone's life today in which this lesson would apply.
4. Why do you think the thief became a disciple of Shichiri Kojun? What did he learn?

Choices: Building Your Portfolio

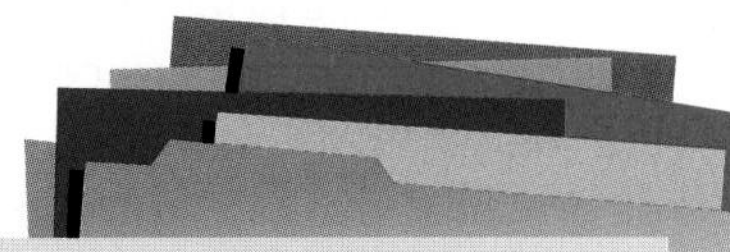

Writer's Notebook

1. Collecting Ideas for an Essay Supporting a Generalization

Finding supporting details. *Zen teaches people to renounce desire and to be open to enlightenment.* List details in the parables you've just read that illustrate this statement. Save your notes.

Creative Writing

2. A Modern Parable

Update one of these Zen parables, keeping the same **moral** but making the **characters**, **setting**, and **action** more contemporary. Begin by stating your moral.

Comparing and Contrasting

3. Two Thief Stories

Reread the anecdote by Saadi called "The Thief and the Blanket" (page 927). **Compare and contrast** Saadi's story with the Zen parable "The Thief Who Became a Disciple." Consider especially the **characters**, **themes**, and **morals** of the anecdotes.

Creative Writing

4. Haiku

Haiku poetry reflects certain emphases in Zen philosophy. Japanese haiku have a definite structure: three lines and a total of seventeen syllables (five syllables each in lines 1 and 3 and seven syllables in line 2).

Haiku bring together **images** of two dissimilar objects. The writer wants us to share the impression of a fleeting moment and then experience *satori*—enlightenment.

Below is a haiku by a famous Zen master. It brings together a poor child on Earth and the distant moon.

Write some haiku about a moment when you saw two dissimilar things brought together.

> Poverty's child—
> he starts to grind the rice
> and gazes at the moon.
>
> —Matsuo Bashō (1644–1694)

Before You Read

THE TIGER, THE BRAHMAN, AND THE JACKAL

Background

One of the most widely translated story collections in the world, the *Panchatantra* (five *tantras*, or books) is made up of **fables** originally created and recited by Hindu priests in ancient India. When written down in Sanskrit in the fifth century A.D. or sometime before, the individual stories were placed within a "frame" story in which a priest is trying to teach statecraft to three stupid princes. The central value that unites all the stories is the need for worldly or practical wisdom to attain success. The Brahman in this tale is a member of the highest, or priestly, class of Hindu society, but he is neither rich nor powerful.

Kalpa Sūtra and *Kalakācāryakathā*. Prākrit manuscript on 123 leaves with colophon. Gujarat, Rajputana, India (15th century), Jain (Svetambara).

Courtesy of the Freer Gallery of Art, Smithsonian Institution, Washington, D.C. (23.3).

Maharaja Umed Singh of Kotah Shooting a Tiger (c. 1790). Gouache on paper.

Victoria and Albert Museum, London. Courtesy Art Resource, NY.

go.hrw.com
LEO 10-13

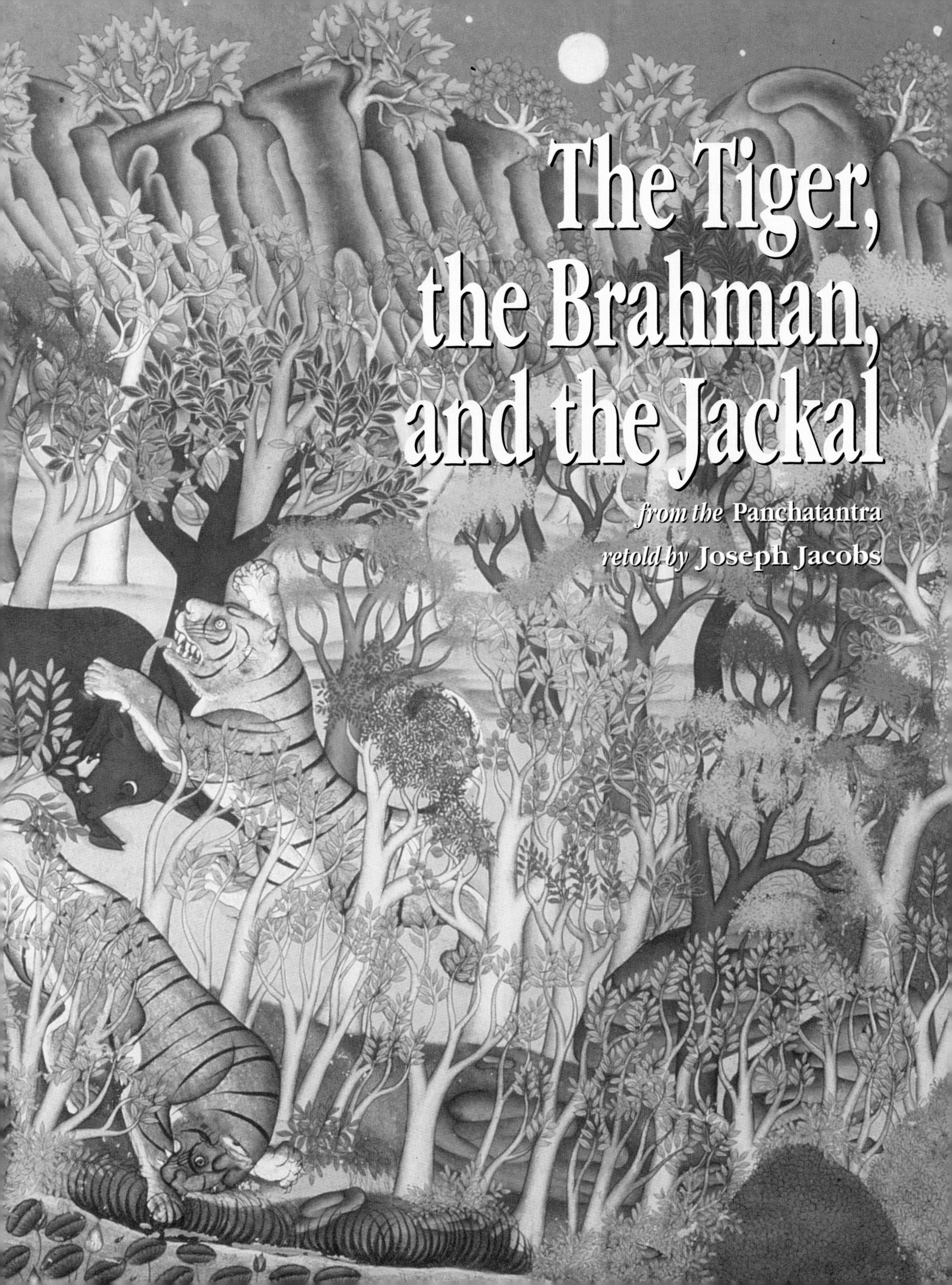

The Tiger, the Brahman, and the Jackal

from the Panchatantra

retold by Joseph Jacobs

Once upon a time, a tiger was caught in a trap. He tried in vain to get out through the bars, and rolled and bit with rage and grief when he failed.

By chance a poor Brahman came by.

"Let me out of this cage, oh, pious one!" cried the tiger.

"Nay, my friend," replied the Brahman mildly, "you would probably eat me if I did."

"Not at all!" swore the tiger with many oaths; "on the contrary, I should be forever grateful and serve you as a slave!"

Now when the tiger sobbed and sighed and wept and swore, the pious Brahman's heart softened, and at last he consented to open the door of the cage. Out popped the tiger, and seizing the poor man, he cried, "What a fool you are! What is to prevent my eating you now, for after being cooped up so long, I am just terribly hungry!"

In vain the Brahman pleaded for his life; the most he could gain was a promise to abide by the decision of the first three things he chose to question as to the justice of the tiger's action.

So the Brahman first asked a pipal tree° what it thought of the matter, but the pipal tree replied coldly: "What have you to complain about? Don't I give shade and shelter to everyone who passes by, and don't they in return tear down my branches to feed their cattle? Don't whimper—be a man!"

Then the Brahman, sad at heart, went farther afield till he saw a buffalo turning a well wheel; but he fared no better from it, for it answered: "You are a fool to expect gratitude! Look at me! While I gave milk, they fed me on cottonseed and oil cake, but now I am dry they yoke me here and give me refuse as fodder!"

The Brahman, still more sad, asked the road to give him its opinion.

"My dear sir," said the road, "how foolish you are to expect anything else! Here am I, useful to everybody, yet all, rich and poor, great and small, trample on me as they go past, giving me nothing but the ashes of their pipes and the husks of their grain!"

On this the Brahman turned back sorrowfully, and on the way he met a jackal, who called out: "Why, what's the matter, Mr. Brahman? You look as miserable as a fish out of water!"

The Brahman told him all that had occurred. "How very confusing!" said the jackal, when the recital was ended; "would you mind telling me over again, for everything has got so mixed up?"

"What a fool you are! What is to prevent my eating you now, for after being cooped up so long, I am just terribly hungry!"

The Brahman told it all over again, but the jackal shook his head in a distracted sort of way and still could not understand.

°**pipal tree:** Indian fig tree.

"It's very odd," said he, sadly, "but it all seems to go in at one ear and out at the other! I will go to the place where it all happened, and then perhaps I shall be able to give a judgment."

So they returned to the cage, by which the tiger was waiting for the Brahman and sharpening his teeth and claws.

"You've been away a long time!" growled the savage beast, "but now let us begin our dinner."

"*Our* dinner!" thought the wretched Brahman, as his knees knocked together with fright; "what a remarkably delicate way of putting it!"

"Give me five minutes, my lord!" he pleaded, "in order that I may explain matters to the jackal here, who is somewhat slow in his wits."

The tiger consented, and the Brahman began the whole story over again, not missing a single detail and spinning as long a yarn as possible.

"Oh, my poor brain! oh, my poor brain!" cried the jackal, wringing its paws. "Let me see! how did it all begin? You were in the cage, and the tiger came walking by——"

"Pooh!" interrupted the tiger, "what a fool you are! *I* was in the cage."

"Of course!" cried the jackal, pretending to tremble with fright; "yes! I was in the cage—no I wasn't—dear! dear! where are my wits? Let me see—the tiger was in the Brahman, and the cage came walking by—no, that's not it, either! Well, don't mind me, but begin your dinner, for I shall never understand!"

"Yes, you shall!" returned the tiger, in a rage at the jackal's stupidity; "I'll *make* you understand! Look here—I am the tiger——"

"Yes, my lord!"

"And that is the Brahman——"

"Yes, my lord!"

"And that is the cage——"

"Yes, my lord!"

"Give me five minutes, my lord!" he pleaded, "in order that I may explain matters to the jackal here, who is somewhat slow in his wits."

"And I was in the cage—do you understand?"

"Yes—no—Please, my lord——"

"Well?" cried the tiger impatiently.

"Please, my lord!—how did you get in?"

"How!—why in the usual way, of course!"

"Oh, dear me!—my head is beginning to whirl again! Please don't be angry, my lord, but what is the usual way?"

At this the tiger lost patience and, jumping into the cage, cried: "This way! Now do you understand how it was?"

"Perfectly!" grinned the jackal, as he dexterously shut the door, "and if you will permit me to say so, I think matters will remain as they were!"

Connections A FABLE

Here is a modern ***fable****. Notice how American these animal characters are.*

The Scotty Who Knew Too Much

James Thurber

Several summers ago there was a Scotty who went to the country for a visit. He decided that all the farm dogs were cowards because they were afraid of a certain animal that had a white stripe down its back. "You are a pussycat and I can lick you," the Scotty said to the farm dog who lived in the house where the Scotty was visiting. "I can lick the little animal with the white stripe, too. Show him to me." "Don't you want to ask any questions about him?" said the farm dog. "Naw," said the Scotty. "*You* ask the questions."

So the farm dog took the Scotty into the woods and showed him the white-striped animal and the Scotty closed in on him, growling and slashing. It was all over in a moment and the Scotty lay on his back. When he came to, the farm dog said, "What happened?" "He threw vitriol," said the Scotty, "but he never laid a glove on me."

A few days later the farm dog told the Scotty there was another animal all the farm dogs were afraid of. "Lead me to him," said the Scotty. "I can lick anything that doesn't wear horseshoes." "Don't you want to ask any questions about him?" said the farm dog. "Naw," said the Scotty. "Just show me where he hangs out." So the farm dog led him to a place in the woods and pointed out the little animal when he came along. "A clown," said the Scotty, "a pushover," and he closed in, leading with his left and exhibiting some mighty fancy footwork. In less than a second the Scotty was flat on his back, and when he woke up the farm dog was pulling quills out of him. "What happened?" said the farm dog. "He pulled a knife on me," said the Scotty, "but at least I have learned how you fight out here in the country, and now I am going to beat *you* up." So he closed in on the farm dog, holding his nose with one front paw to ward off the vitriol and covering his eyes with the other front paw to keep out the knives. The Scotty couldn't see his opponent and he couldn't smell his opponent and he was so badly beaten that he had to be taken back to the city and put in a nursing home.

MORAL: *It is better to ask some of the questions than to know all the answers.*

Making Meanings
The Tiger, the Brahman, and the Jackal

First Thoughts

1. Do the animal characters in the Hindu **fable** remind you of any people you know or read about in the news?

Shaping Interpretations

2. "The Tiger, the Brahman, and the Jackal" is structured around questions, a pattern repeated throughout the *Panchatantra*. What question is asked three times? Who asks it and of whom, and what answers are received?
3. In a fable, the animal characters usually represent human types. What kind of person do you think the tiger represents? the Brahman? the jackal?
4. What lesson in worldly wisdom do you think the tiger's behavior demonstrates? the jackal's?
5. What does the jackal achieve and how does he do it? What qualities do you think the fable writer admires about the jackal? Do you share his view?
6. What kinds of real-life people do the characters in Thurber's fable (see ***Connections*** on page 944) remind you of?

Choices: Building Your Portfolio

Writer's Notebook

1. Collecting Ideas for an Essay Supporting a Generalization

WORK IN PROGRESS

Writing an opinion. Write a general statement, giving your opinion of the effectiveness of using animal stories to teach practical lessons. Then, list reasons and cite examples to support your opinion. Save your notes.

Creative Writing

2. Fables for Your Time

Thurber's collection of fables is called *Fables for Our Time.* Write some **fables** or **anecdotes** of your own called *Teaching Stories for the Twenty-first Century.* Who or what will be your characters? Where will your stories be set? What lessons will you teach? You might find some ideas in the **maxims** cited on page 924. Or you might invent some twists on these old maxims to make them apply to life today.

Drawing

3. Turn It into a Toon

Like fables, cartoons and animated films frequently have animal characters. (Modern-day tricksters include Bugs Bunny and Wile E. Coyote, Road Runner's adversary.) Present "The Tiger, the Brahman, and the Jackal" as a cartoon strip. In order to tell the story in a limited number of frames, you will have to eliminate most of the words and any nonessential action.

If Stones Could Talk

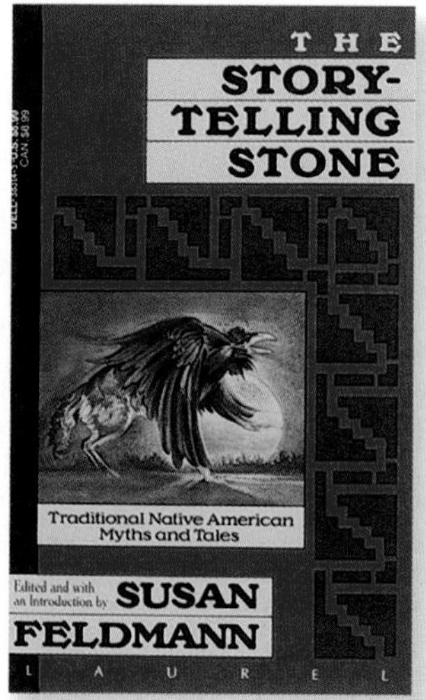

According to a Seneca tale, a talking stone told the first stories about things that happened long ago. You'll meet this storytelling stone as well as the tricksters Raven and Coyote, the woman who fell from the sky, and the girl who wished to marry stars in *The Story-Telling Stone* (Laurel), a collection of Native American myths and folk tales edited by Susan Feldmann.

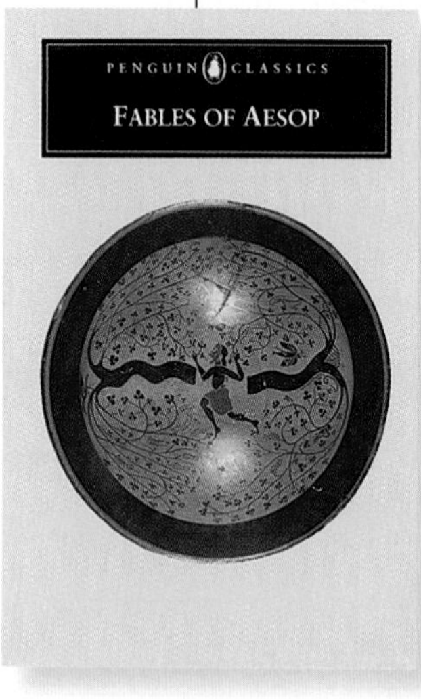

Sour Grapes and Swan Songs

Aesop wrote his fables, short tales that teach us how to live, long ago in ancient Greece, but they're still very much alive in our language. You'll discover the origin of such common expressions as "Look before you leap," "sour grapes," and "the boy who cried wolf" in *Fables of Aesop* (Penguin), S. A. Handford's translation of 207 fables.

Wisdom of Arab Villages

Inea Bushnaq took her tape recorder to Palestinian villages to capture stories told by old women on winter nights, by professional storytellers in the marketplace, and by Bedouins of the desert in a storytelling tradition as filled with treasure as Aladdin's cave. The stories in *Arab Folktales* (Pantheon) range from supernatural, animal, and moral tales to stories of wit and wisdom and tales about rascals and fools.

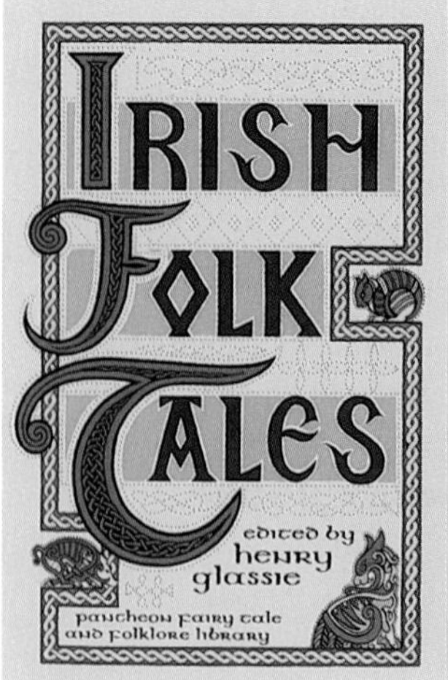

The Irish Storytellers

Sample *Irish Folk Tales,* edited by folklorist Henry Glassie (Pantheon), and you'll see why the Irish are known as gifted storytellers. Ghost stories, tall tales, mysteries, humorous tales, and bits of Irish history—each of the stories in this collection gives the storyteller's name and the date and place of the telling.

Collection 14

FINDING OUR HEROES

WRITING FOCUS: Supporting a Generalization

We have not even to risk the adventure alone, for the heroes of all time have gone before us.

—Joseph Campbell

Writer's Notebook

Our heroes tell us who we want to be. They tell what matters to us. List some of the men and women you consider heroes, and tell why you admire them. Then write a general statement about what you think your list reveals about *you*. Save your notes.

Where can we hope to find heroes for our times? The superheroes in stories of our childhood battled against tremendous odds. Yet superior strength and magical powers gave them victories that mortal men and women can never hope to win. Today a hero may be a world leader, someone of great spiritual depth, a neighbor who works to help others, a person whom only you admire. Who are your heroes?

Astronaut and teacher Christa McAuliffe in training, Houston, 1985.

The Literature of Romance: Where Good Always Triumphs

by **David Adams Leeming**

During the Middle Ages, a new form of literature, called the **romance,** developed in France and spread like a firestorm throughout Europe. The stories are called romances because they were first told in Old French and Provençal, which are Romance languages (languages derived from Roman, the popular form of Latin).

Romances began in the twelfth century as popular narratives about the adventures of knights and other heroes. This was long before the age of paperbacks—or of any printed material, for that matter. Troubadours, or minstrels—wandering story singers who were probably illiterate—used to collect the stories and recite them for people as they traveled from town to town. By the fourteenth century, the romances had been taken over by the upper classes. Gradually, as the old oral storytellers disappeared, the romances were passed on as written stories, polished and professional.

The primary purpose of romances was to celebrate the ideals of **chivalry,** the code of behavior the medieval knight was supposed to follow. He was to be brave, honorable, loyal, pious, generous in his treatment of foes, and ready to help the weak and protect women.

The Hero's Quest: Something of Value

The world of romance was—and still is today—an ideal world of exaggeration and wish fulfillment, a world where the forces of good always triumph over the forces of evil.

The typical plot of a romance consists of a series of marvelous adventures that include many magical or supernatural events. The hero's adventures usually assume the form of a **quest,** a long, perilous journey in search of something of value: a kingdom, the rescue of a maiden, the destruction of a devouring beast, a treasure trove.

Joseph Campbell, the author of *The Hero with a Thousand Faces,* writes that the hero's journey underlies the literature of all cultures. Typically, the **hero** leaves the safety of home to cross into strange lands where he must prove that he has the wit, will, and strength to survive. During his quest, the hero comes into conflict with a host of adversaries—evil knights, monsters, and dragons—that he must fight or outsmart. He may be aided in his quest by a faithful companion or by a magic weapon. He often has a mysterious connection to the world of nature and is sometimes aided by animals. (In the modern quest trilogy *The Lord of the Rings* by J. R. R. Tolkien, the hero is aided by trees.) By the end of a typical romance, the hero has passed all the tests, suffered losses, gained what he sought, and earned a measure of wisdom. In its purest form, the hero's quest is a struggle between good and evil. Interpreted metaphorically, the quest is a journey into and out of the evil side of human nature.

Smaug the evil dragon guards his hoard of gold. Illustration from *The Hobbit* by J.R.R. Tolkien. HarperCollins Publishers Ltd.

Romances: Still Alive and Well

Descendants of these old romances are in our books and movies today. Western novels and movies, science fiction and fantasy, adventure tales like those about Indiana Jones, mysteries, even some computer and video games use elements of the old romances. In today's romances, good is still pitted against evil, but the modern hero confronts twentieth-century monsters. He (or she) still has incredible luck and strength, but the supernatural powers have disappeared. Still, the solitary hero triumphs "by dint of love and bravery," as the old romances put it.

Western novels and movies especially have helped to satisfy Americans' appetite for romance. Like the medieval knight, the lone cowboy imposes law and order on a violent society. Tough but possessing a certain nobility, the cowboy hero appears in time of need, riding faster and shooting straighter than anyone else. He bravely faces down the evil threatening the security of a town, and, finally triumphant, he rides off, still alone, into the sunset. The same hero type will show up in the next movie.

Kate Mulgrew as Kathryn Janeway in *Star Trek: Voyager.*

Something New: The Women Step Up (or Out)

More and more romances today portray women boldly going where no female had gone before. In the old romances, women were usually cast as betrayers, seducers, victims, or rewards. Today, especially in science fiction and fantasy, women pursue the hero's journey; they go on their own quests, take risks, and slay their own dragons. The latest *Star Trek* series for television shows our descendants, both male and female, journeying to star lands together. And in the twenty-fourth century, according to *Star Trek,* a courageous and brilliant scientist, Kathryn Janeway, is the captain of the U.S.S. *Voyager.* Now a woman leads a heroic quest to battle the forces of intergalactic evil.

But no matter who the questing hero is, our romance stories continue to reveal our dreams of what an ideal human community should be. Whether they were written yesterday or will be written tomorrow, romances continue to show us the best that humans are capable of.

Before You Read

The Sword in the Stone

Make the Connection

Yesterday's Heroes and Today's

We often fail, at least at first, to recognize heroes, but heroes may be anywhere—even in our own neighborhoods, even in our own homes.

Quickwrite

Jot down five or six qualities that you associate with the word *hero*.

Background

Legendary heroes like King Arthur are born in dangerous times, when they are most needed. Here is the background of Arthur's birth. King Uther of England, who was unmarried, loved Igraine (ē·grān′), who was another man's wife.

LETH OUTE THIS SWERD OF THIS STON

In disguise, the king deceived Igraine into thinking he was her husband. Arthur was the child born to Igraine as a result of this trick.

The wise man Merlin knew the baby was in danger because many men wanted Uther's throne. To protect the infant, Merlin took the baby to a knight, Sir Ector, and his wife and asked them to bring Arthur up with their own son, Kay.

King Uther died, and Arthur stayed with his foster family. No one knew Arthur's true identity, which would be revealed when he completed a task that only the rightful king could perform. Merlin was to arrange Arthur's test.

The character of King Arthur is probably based on a sixth-century Celtic warlord. This chieftain, who lived in Wales, led his people to victory against Saxon invaders. He was said to have been fatally wounded in battle and buried in the abbey of Glastonbury in England, where a gravestone can still be seen bearing his name.

The legend of King Arthur as we know it today emerged gradually. As storytellers over the ages told and retold popular tales about a great chief who mysteriously disappeared and promised to return, characters and details were changed and added.

Even today, Arthur lives. For example, T. H. White's novel based on the Arthurian legends, *The Once and Future King,* became a best-seller and the basis of the long-running Broadway musical *Camelot* (1960). Arthur and his knights appeared in a parody—the hilarious British movie *Monty Python and the Holy Grail* (1975). You can see Arthur in the comics, too—in Hal Foster's *Prince Valiant.* There are even computer games retelling Arthur's story. The great knight has now entered the computer age.

Perhaps Arthur continues to live in the imagination because he represents the leader who will return in a time of darkness to save his people. In all ages, people seem to need such hope.

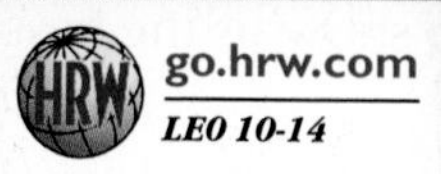

THE SWORD IN THE STONE

from **Le Morte Darthur**
Sir Thomas Malory
retold by **Keith Baines**

D ANVYLD IS RIGHTWYS KYNGE BORNE

During the years that followed the death of King Uther, while Arthur was still a child, the ambitious barons fought one another for the throne, and the whole of Britain stood in jeopardy. Finally the day came when the Archbishop of Canterbury, on the advice of Merlin, summoned the nobility to London for Christmas morning. In his message the archbishop promised that the true succession to the British throne would be miraculously revealed. Many of the nobles purified themselves during their journey, in the hope that it would be to them that the succession would fall.

The archbishop held his service in the city's greatest church (St. Paul's), and when matins[1] were done, the congregation filed out to the yard. They were confronted by a marble block into which had been thrust a beautiful sword. The block was four feet square, and the sword passed through a steel anvil which had been struck in the stone and which projected a foot from it. The anvil had been inscribed with letters of gold:

WHOSO PULLETH OUTE THIS SWERD OF THIS STONE AND ANVYLD IS RIGHTWYS KYNGE BORNE OF ALL BRYTAYGNE

The congregation was awed by this miraculous sight, but the archbishop forbade anyone to touch the sword before Mass had been heard. After Mass, many of the nobles tried to pull the sword out of the stone, but none was able to, so a watch of ten knights was set over the sword, and a tournament proclaimed for New Year's Day, to provide men of noble blood with the opportunity of proving their right to the succession.

Sir Ector, who had been living on an estate near London, rode to the tournament with Arthur and his own son Sir Kay, who had been recently knighted. When they arrived at the tournament, Sir Kay found to his annoyance that his sword was missing from its sheath, so he begged Arthur to ride back and fetch it from their lodging.

Arthur found the door of the lodging locked and bolted, the landlord and his wife having left for the tournament. In order not to disappoint his brother, he rode on to St. Paul's, determined to get for him the sword which was lodged in the stone. The yard was empty, the guard also having slipped off to see the tournament, so Arthur strode up to the sword and, without troubling to read the inscription, tugged it free. He then rode straight back to Sir Kay and presented him with it.

Sir Kay recognized the sword and, taking it to Sir Ector, said, "Father, the succession falls to me, for I have here the sword that was lodged in the stone." But Sir Ector insisted that they should all ride to the churchyard, and once there, bound Sir Kay by oath to tell how he had come by the sword. Sir Kay then admitted that Arthur had given it to him. Sir Ector turned to Arthur and said, "Was the sword not guarded?"

Arthur pulling the sword out of the stone. Detail from a French manuscript (c. 1290).

Bibliothèque Nationale de France, Paris.

"It was not," Arthur replied.

"Would you please thrust it into the stone again?" said Sir Ector. Arthur did so, and first Sir Ector and then Sir Kay tried to remove it, but both were unable to. Then Arthur, for the second time, pulled it out. Sir Ector and Sir Kay both knelt before him.

"Why," said Arthur, "do you both kneel before me?"

"My lord," Sir Ector replied, "there is only one

1. **matins** (mat′'nz): morning prayers.

man living who can draw the sword from the stone, and he is the true-born king of Britain." Sir Ector then told Arthur the story of his birth and upbringing.

"My dear father," said Arthur, "for so I shall always think of you—if, as you say, I am to be king, please know that any request you have to make is already granted."

Sir Ector asked that Sir Kay should be made royal seneschal,[2] and Arthur declared that while they both lived it should be so. Then the three of them visited the archbishop and told him what had taken place.

All those dukes and barons with ambitions to rule were present at the tournament on New Year's Day. But when all of them had failed, and Arthur alone had succeeded in drawing the sword from the stone, they protested against one so young, and of ignoble blood, succeeding to the throne.

The secret of Arthur's birth was known to only a few of the nobles surviving from the days of King Uther. The archbishop urged them to make Arthur's cause their own; but their support proved ineffective. The tournament was repeated at Candlemas[3] and at Easter, with the same outcome as before.

Finally, at Pentecost,[4] when once more Arthur alone had been able to remove the sword, the commoners arose with a tumultuous cry and demanded that Arthur should at once be made king. The nobles, knowing in their hearts that the commoners were right, all knelt before Arthur and begged forgiveness for having delayed his succession for so long. Arthur forgave them and then, offering his sword at the high altar, was dubbed first knight of the realm. The coronation took place a few days later, when Arthur swore to rule justly, and the nobles swore him their allegiance.

2. **royal seneschal** (sen′ə·shəl): person in charge of the king's household. This was a powerful and respected position.
3. **Candlemas:** Christian festival that honors the purification of the Virgin Mary after the birth of Jesus. It falls on February 2.
4. **Pentecost:** Christian festival celebrated on the seventh Sunday after Easter, commemorating the descent of the Holy Spirit upon the Apostles.

Meet the Writer

A Master of Escape

We know only a little about the life of **Sir Thomas Malory** (1405?–1471). His title indicates that he was a knight, and we know that he was a soldier and a member of Parliament for a brief time. We also know that he spent most of the last twenty years of his life in prison, accused of some very unchivalrous crimes: assault, extortion, cattle rustling, poaching, jail breaking, plundering an abbey, and "waylaying the Duke of Buckingham." Malory pleaded innocent to all charges, and it is likely that he was framed by political enemies. (It is also possible that Malory was something of a rogue.) During those miserable years in jail, Malory wrote his great romance.

The twelfth-century world of chivalrous knights in shining armor was almost as foreign to Malory as it is to us today. The invention of gunpowder and the rise of the middle class had already broken down the feudal order. While Malory scribbled heroic tales in a dank jail cell, English political and social life was in a state of turmoil that no amount of chivalry seemed likely to cure. Perhaps Malory yearned for a return to chivalry, to a simpler way of life with established codes of behavior. He might also have been trying to create a romantic escape from the grim realities of his personal life.

(For another knightly adventure from Malory's *Le Morte Darthur,* see page 964.)

Connections A REFLECTION

"The Magic Happened"

John Steinbeck

The American novelist John Steinbeck (1902-1968), author of The Grapes of Wrath, Of Mice and Men, *and* The Pearl, *was nine years old when he first read an abridged version of Malory's King Arthur tales.*

Books were printed demons—the tongs and thumbscrews of outrageous persecution. And then, one day, an aunt gave me a book and fatuously ignored my resentment. I stared at the black print with hatred, and then, gradually, the pages opened and let me in. The magic happened. The Bible and Shakespeare and *Pilgrim's Progress* belonged to everyone. But this was mine— It was a cut version of the Caxton *Morte d'Arthur* of Thomas Malory. I loved the old spelling of the words—and the words no longer used. Perhaps a passionate love for the English language opened to me from this one book. I was delighted to find out paradoxes—that *cleave* means both "to stick together" and "to cut apart"; that *host* means both "an enemy" and "a welcoming friend"; that *king* and *gens* (people) stem from the same root. For a long time, I had a secret language—*yclept* and *hyght, wist*—and *accord* meaning "peace," and *entente* meaning "purpose," and *fyaunce* meaning "promise.". . . But beyond the glorious and secret words—"And when the chylde is borne lete it be delyvered to me at yonder privy posterne uncrystened"—oddly enough I knew the words from whispering them to myself. The very strangeness of the language dyd me enchante, and vaulted me into an ancient scene.

King Arthur. Detail from tapestry of the Nine Worthies (c. 1490).

Historisches Museum, Basel, Switzerland. Courtesy Art Resource, NY.

And in that scene were all the vices that ever were—and courage and sadness and frustration, but particularly gallantry—perhaps the only single quality of man that the West has invented. I think my sense of right and wrong, my feeling of noblesse oblige, and any thought I may have against the oppressor and for the oppressed came from this secret book. It did not outrage my sensibilities as nearly all the children's books did. It did not seem strange to me that Uther Pendragon wanted the wife of his vassal and took her by trickery. I was not frightened to find that there were evil knights, as well as noble ones. In my own town there were men who wore the clothes of virtue whom I knew to be bad. In pain or sorrow or confusion, I went back to my magic book. Children are violent and cruel—and good—and I was all of these—and all of these were in the secret book.

MAKING MEANINGS For CHOICES activities, see page 970.

First Thoughts

1. If you were illustrating this part of Arthur's story, what scene would be your focus?

Shaping Interpretations

2. According to the critic Northrop Frye, "The hero of **romance** moves in a world in which the ordinary laws of nature are slightly suspended." What elements of magic appear in this tale that move it out of the realm of the ordinary?

3. In the typical **romance**, the hero's origins are mysterious. He is frequently raised in obscurity before taking his rightful place as leader. How does the story of Arthur reflect this pattern? Why do you think people so enjoy these stories of the supposed underdog being the real hero?

4. In what other ways does Arthur, even as a young boy, resemble the typical romance **hero**? How does Sir Kay, his foster brother, show signs that he is definitely *not* heroic material?

Reading Check

Make a **time line** showing the **main events** that take place in this part of Arthur's story. Start with the death of King Uther. End with Arthur's coronation. Compare your time line with a classmate's and discuss any differences.

Connecting with the Text

5. What heroic values does this story teach? Do any of these values seem important to you today? Be sure to refer to your Quickwrite notes.

Extending the Text

6. "The magic happened" for John Steinbeck at the age of nine when he first read Malory (see ***Connections*** on page 954). Think of a book, movie, or TV show that made a strong, almost "magical," impression on you at a young age. Explain its impact.

"Robin Hood and his mother on their way to Nottingham Fair" (1917). Illustration by N.C. Wyeth.

The Granger Collection, New York.

Before You Read

THE ROUND TABLE

Make the Connection

Is That All There Is?

The next selection, a scene from the musical *Camelot*, shows Arthur at another critical time in his life. He's several years older than he was when he pulled the sword from the stone. His beautiful wife, Guenevere, believes him to be the most splendid king who ever sat on any throne, and everyone agrees that he's the greatest warrior in England. Yet Arthur feels there's something missing.

Quickwrite

What do you think drives most lawmakers and rulers today? A desire to do good? Ambition? In a few sentences, write your thoughts on this question.

Background

Camelot is based on T. H. White's novel *The Once and Future King*, which is a modernized retelling of Malory's legends. White took many liberties with Malory's stories. For example, in White's novel, Merlin educates the future king by turning Arthur into various animals so that he can see the world from different perspectives. When he flies as a bird, for example, he realizes how silly the boundaries are that separate people.

Galahad being introduced to the Company of the Round Table. Italian manuscript (c. 1370–1380). King Arthur, wearing a crown, is on the opposite side of the table, the third figure from the top.

Bibliothèque Nationale de France, Paris. Courtesy Art Resource, NY.

"Suppose we create a *new* order of chivalry?"

The Round Table *from* Camelot

Alan Jay Lerner *and* Frederick Loewe

Scene: ARTHUR'S *study*.
Time: *Early evening*.

At rise: GUENEVERE *is at a tapestry easel working with needle and thread.* ARTHUR *is standing next to her.*

Arthur (*heatedly*). You cannot deny the facts! Did I or did I not pledge to you five years ago that I would be the most splendid king who ever sat on any throne?
Guenevere. You did.
Arthur. And in five years, have I become the most splendid king who ever sat on any throne?
Guenevere. You have.
Arthur. Rubbish! I have not, and you know it well. I'm nothing of what I pledged to you I would be. I'm a failure, and that's that.
Guenevere. Arthur, it's not true. You're the greatest warrior in England.
Arthur. But for what purpose? Might isn't always right, Jenny.
Guenevere. Nonsense, dear, of course it is. To be right and lose couldn't possibly be right.
Arthur (*thinking*). Yes. Might and right, battle and plunder. That's what keeps plaguing me. Merlyn used to frown on battles, yet he always helped me win them. I'm sure it's a clue. If only I could follow it. I'm always walking down a winding, dimly lit road, and in the distance I see the outline of a thought. Like the shadow of a hill. I fumble and stumble, and at last I get there; but when I do, the hill is gone. Not there at all. And I hear a small voice saying: "Go back, Arthur, it's too dark for you to be out thinking."
Guenevere. My poor love. Let me see you do it. Walk out loud.
Arthur. All right. (*He crosses to the end of the stage.*) Proposition: It's far better to be alive than dead.

The Pierpont Morgan Library/Art Resource, NY.

Guenevere and Arthur receiving the magic chessboard. From *Le Roman de Lancelot du Lac* (early 14th century), northern France.

Guenevere. Far better.

Arthur (*taking a step forward*). If that is so, then why do we have battles, where people can get killed?

Guenevere (*chews on it a moment*). I don't know. Do you?

Arthur. Yes. Because somebody attacks.

Guenevere (*sincerely*). Of course. That's very clever of you, Arthur. Why do they attack?

[ARTHUR *leaves "the road" and comes to her.*]

Arthur. Jenny, I must confess something I've never told you before, for fear you would not believe me.

Guenevere. How silly, Arthur, I would never not believe you.

Arthur. You know Merlyn brought me up, taught me everything I know. But do you know how?

Guenevere. How?

Arthur. By changing me into animals.

Guenevere. I don't believe it.

Arthur. There, you see? But it's true. I was a fish, a bobolink, a beaver, and even an ant. From each animal he wanted me to learn something. Before he made me a hawk, for instance, he told me that while I would be flying through the sky, if I would look down at the earth, I would discover something.

Guenevere. What did you discover?

Arthur. Nothing. Merlyn was livid. Yet tonight, on my way home, while I was thinking, I suddenly realized that when you're in the sky looking down at the earth, there are no boundaries. No borders. Yet that's what somebody always attacks about. And you win by pushing them back across something that doesn't exist.

Guenevere. It *is* odd, isn't it?

Arthur. Proposition: We have battles for no reason at all. Then why? Why?

Guenevere. Because knights love them. They adore charging in and whacking away. It's splendid fun. You've said so yourself often.

Arthur. It *is* splendid fun. (*Steps forward*) But that doesn't seem reason enough. (*He steps back.*)

Guenevere. I think it is. And from a woman's point of view, it's wonderfully exciting to see your knight in armor riding bravely off to battle. Especially when you know he'll be home safe in one piece for dinner.

Arthur. That's it! It's the armor! I missed that before. Of course! Only knights are rich enough to bedeck themselves in armor. They can declare war when it suits them, and go clodhopping about the country slicing up peasants and foot soldiers, because peasants and foot soldiers are not equipped with armor. All that can happen to a knight is an occasional dent. (*He takes a long run to the fireplace.*) Proposition: Wrong or right, they have the might, so wrong or right, they're always right—and that's wrong. Right?

Guenevere. Absolutely.

Arthur (*excitedly*). Is that the reason Merlyn helped me to win? To take all this might that's knocking about the world and do something with it. But what?

Guenevere. Yes, what?

[ARTHUR *sighs with resignation.*]

Arthur. It's gone. I've thought as hard as I can,

and I can walk no further. (*He walks around and sits on the chaise longue.*) You see, Jenny? I'm still not a king. I win every battle and accomplish nothing. When the Greeks won, they made a civilization. I'm not creating any civilization. I'm not even sure I'm civilized. . . .

Guenevere (*tenderly*). Dear Arthur. You mustn't belabor yourself like this. Let us have a quiet dinner, and after, if you like, you can stroll again.

Arthur. Bless you. (*He takes her hand, kisses her, rises and moves to exit. Then he stops and turns.*) Jenny, suppose we create a *new* order of chivalry?

Guenevere. Pardon?

Arthur. A new order, a new order, where might is only used for right, to improve instead of destroy. And we invite all knights, good or bad, to lay down their arms and come and join. Yes! (*Growing more and more excited*) We'll take one of the large rooms in the castle and put a table in it, and all the knights will gather at the table.

Guenevere. And do what?

Arthur. Talk! Discuss! Make laws! Plan improvements!

Guenevere. Really, Arthur, do you think knights would ever want to do such a peaceful thing?

Arthur. We'll make it a great honor, very fashionable, so that everyone will want to be in. And the knights of my order will ride all over the world, still dressed in armor and whacking away. That will give them an outlet for wanting to whack. But they'll whack only for good. Defend virgins, restore what's been done wrong in the past, help the oppressed. Might for right. That's it, Jenny! Not might is right. Might *for* right!

Guenevere. It sounds superb.

Arthur. Yes. And civilized. (*Calls*) Page! (*To* GUENEVERE) We'll build a whole new generation of chivalry. Young men, not old, burning with zeal and ideals. (*The* PAGE *enters.*) Tell the heralds to mount the towers. And to have their trumpets. And assemble the Court in the yard. Send word there is to be a proclamation.

Page. Yes, Your Majesty! (*He exits.*)

Guenevere. Arthur, it will have to be an awfully large table! And won't there be jealousy? All your knights will be claiming superiority and wanting to sit at the head.

Arthur. Then we shall make it a round table so there is no head.

Guenevere (*totally won*). My father has one that would be perfect. It seats a hundred and fifty. It was given to him once for a present, and he never uses it.

Arthur (*suddenly doubting*). Jenny, have I had a thought? Am I at the hill? Or is it only a mirage?

[*The* PAGE *enters.*]

Page. The heralds await, Your Majesty. Shall I give the signal, Your Majesty?

Arthur. No, wait. I may be wrong. The whole idea may be absurd. If only Merlyn were here! He would have known for certain. (*Disparagingly*) Knights at a table . . .

Guenevere (*correcting him*). A round table.

Arthur (*corrected*). Round table. Might for right, a new order of chivalry, shining knights gallivanting around the countryside like angels in armor, sword-swinging apostles battling to snuff out evil! Why, it's naive . . . it's adolescent . . . it's juvenile . . . it's infantile . . . it's folly . . . it's . . . it's . . .

Guenevere. It's marvelous.

Arthur. Yes, it is. It's marvelous. Absolutely marvelous. (*To the* PAGE) Page, give the signal.

Page. Yes, Your Majesty. (*He exits.*)

Arthur (*sings*).

We'll send the heralds riding through the
  country;
Tell ev'ry living person far and near . . .

Guenevere (*interrupting him*).

That there is simply not
In all the world a spot
Where rules a more resplendent king than here
In Camelot.

[*The heralds appear in the towers and sound their horns.* ARTHUR *embraces* GUENEVERE *and goes to the window to make his proclamation.*]

Dim out

LITERATURE AND ENTERTAINMENT

American Musical Theater

The musical is America's contribution to the theater. Europe developed its grand operas for the upper classes; America created the musical for everyone.

Musical theater took an important turn in the 1920s. It happened with *Show Boat* (music by Jerome Kern and book and lyrics by Oscar Hammerstein). *Show Boat* was the first musical in which songs and dances were integrated into the plot. *Show Boat* was also a uniquely American show: It is based on an American novel by Edna Ferber, and it is set on the great Mississippi River. It also deals frankly with racial themes, and its music is based on folk songs and spirituals.

Show Boat was followed by some of the most successful musicals in theater history, many of them written by the team of Richard Rodgers and Oscar Hammerstein II: *Oklahoma!* (1943), *Carousel* (1945), *South Pacific* (1949), and *The King and I* (1951).

The first musical to use rock music was *Hair* (1967), the high-spirited hippie-era hit. Another milestone is the exuberant rock opera *Rent* (1996), an update of Puccini's opera *La Bohème*. To pop-rock, salsa, gospel, and reggae beats, *Rent's* struggling artists and lost young people sing powerfully of love, loss, and hope.

Scene from the Broadway production of *Show Boat*.

Frederick Loewe and Alan Jay Lerner.

Meet the Writer and Composer

Happy-Ever-Aftering

Alan Jay Lerner (1918–1986) and **Frederick Loewe** (1904–1988) collaborated on five musicals—Lerner writing the lyrics and the script, Loewe composing the music. They are probably best known for four Broadway hits: *Brigadoon* (1947); *Paint Your Wagon* (1951); *My Fair Lady* (1956), based on George Bernard Shaw's *Pygmalion;* and *Camelot* (1960).

Lerner, whose father founded a chain of clothing stores, inherited a fortune but chose the musical theater for his career while he was still a child. (He began to compose music for poems when he was eleven.) In 1942, while working as a freelance writer, he met Loewe in New York City.

Born in Vienna, Austria, the son of a famous operetta tenor, Loewe had been a child prodigy at the piano. When he was thirteen, he was a concert pianist with major European orchestras. At twenty-three, Loewe immigrated to the United States, but he had difficulty earning a living from music until he and Lerner began their twenty-year collaboration. *Camelot* was the last musical they did together.

In his autobiography, *The Street Where I Live,* Lerner wrote:

" I believe it is the idealism expressed in the concept of the Round Table that accounts for the indestructibility of the Arthurian legend. Stripped of its tales of derring-do, its magic, love potions, and medieval trimmings and trappings, there lie buried in its heart the aspirations of mankind, and if Arthur lived at all, he was a light in the Dark Ages. If Arthur is pure fantasy, it is even more significant. "

Making Meanings For Choices activities, see page 970.

First Thoughts

1. At the beginning of the scene from *Camelot,* how did you respond to the king's feelings of failure and disappointment? How common do you think such feelings are among lawmakers and rulers today? Refer to your Quickwrite notes.

Reading Check

Suppose you were the director of this scene and you wanted to review it for the two actors. **Summarize** the **main events** as told through the **dialogue,** or conversation, between Arthur and Guenevere.

Shaping Interpretations

2. According to Guenevere, why do knights battle even when there's no reason for war? Is this true of the military today, or are things very different now?
3. Why does Arthur want a *round* table?

Extending the Text

4. Arthur is establishing a new order of chivalry in which might fights for right. Do you think might is always used for right today? Talk about it.
5. Suppose Arthur were the political and military leader of a great country such as the United States today. How successful do you think his visions would be?
6. Do you agree with Gary in the cartoon below? What do *you* think is the difference between a hero and a celebrity?

Challenging the Text

7. Based on Guenevere's lines in this scene, what do you think is the writer's attitude toward her? Do you think Guenevere would have been portrayed differently if *Camelot* had been written today? Why or why not?

"Very good, Gary: 'A hero is a celebrity who did something real.'"

Before You Read

The Tale of Sir Launcelot du Lake

Make the Connection

Quests and Tests

Like a true knight, Sir Launcelot goes off in search of tests to prove his courage. The knightly quest typically involves saving maidens, slaying dragons, and battling less noble persons. Adventure is the call; heroism, the role.

Quickwrite

Jot down your ideas about how someone in today's world proves his or her heroism.

Background

Of the one hundred and fifty knights who sat at the Round Table, Sir Launcelot was King Arthur's favorite—and the bravest and mightiest, too. Although devoted to Arthur, Launcelot fell in love with Arthur's wife, Queen Gwynevere. This caused great suffering for the unfortunate trio. In this tale, as Launcelot goes searching for adventure, he runs into Morgan le Fay, Arthur's evil half-sister. Famous for her enchantments, Morgan is continually plotting to destroy Arthur and his followers.

go.hrw.com

LEO 10-14

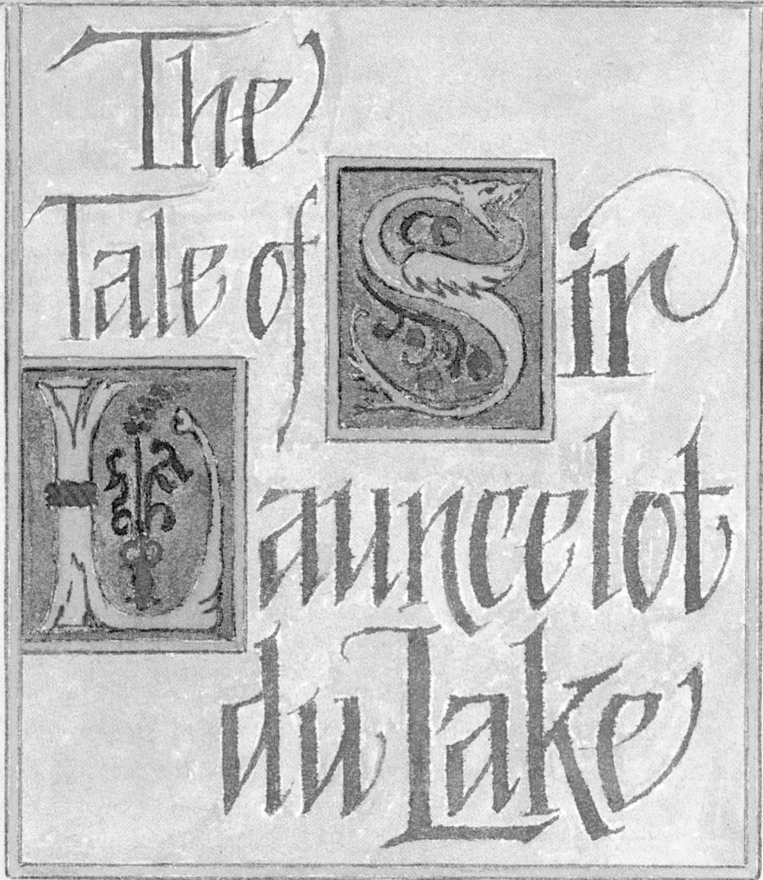

"Of all his knights one was supreme."

from **Le Morte Darthur**

Sir Thomas Malory

***retold by* Keith Baines**

When King Arthur returned from Rome he settled his court at Camelot, and there gathered about him his knights of the Round Table, who diverted themselves with jousting[1] and tournaments. Of all his knights one was supreme, both in prowess at arms and in nobility of bearing, and this was Sir Launcelot, who was also the favorite of Queen Gwynevere, to whom he had sworn oaths of fidelity.[2]

1. **jousting:** form of combat between two knights on horseback. Each used a long lance to try to knock the other from his horse.
2. **fidelity:** loyalty; devotion.

One day Sir Launcelot, feeling weary of his life at the court, and of only playing at arms, decided to set forth in search of adventure. He asked his nephew Sir Lyonel to accompany him, and when both were suitably armed and mounted, they rode off together through the forest.

At noon they started across a plain, but the intensity of the sun made Sir Launcelot feel sleepy, so Sir Lyonel suggested that they should rest beneath the shade of an apple tree that grew by a hedge not far from the road. They dismounted, tethered their horses, and settled down.

"Not for seven years have I felt so sleepy," said Sir Launcelot, and with that fell fast asleep, while Sir Lyonel watched over him. . . .

While Sir Launcelot still slept beneath the apple tree, four queens started across the plain. They were riding white mules and accompanied by four knights who held above them, at the tips of their spears, a green silk canopy, to protect them from the sun. The party was startled by the neighing of Sir Launcelot's horse and, changing direction, rode up to the apple tree, where they discovered the sleeping knight. And as each of the queens gazed at the handsome Sir Launcelot, so each wanted him for her own.

"Let us not quarrel," said Morgan le Fay. "Instead, I will cast a spell over him so that he remains asleep while we take him to my castle and make him our prisoner. We can then oblige him to choose one of us for his paramour."[3]

Sir Launcelot was laid on his shield and borne by two of the knights to the Castle Charyot, which was Morgan le Fay's stronghold. He awoke to find himself in a cold cell, where a young noblewoman was serving him supper.

"What cheer?" she asked.

"My lady, I hardly know, except that I must have been brought here by means of an enchantment."

"Sir, if you are the knight you appear to be, you will learn your fate at dawn tomorrow." And with that the young noblewoman left him. Sir Launcelot spent an uncomfortable night but at dawn the four queens presented themselves and Morgan le Fay spoke to him:

"Sir Launcelot, I know that Queen Gwynevere loves you, and you her. But now you are my prisoner, and you will have to choose: either to take one of us for your paramour, or to die miserably in this cell—just as you please. Now I will tell you who we are: I am Morgan le Fay, Queen of Gore; my companions are the Queens of North Galys, of Estelonde, and of the Outer Isles. So make your choice."

"A hard choice! Understand that I choose none of you, lewd sorceresses that you are; rather will I die in this cell. But were I free, I would take pleasure in proving it against any who would champion you that Queen Gwynevere is the finest lady of this land."

"So, you refuse us?" asked Morgan le Fay.

"On my life, I do," Sir Launcelot said finally, and so the queens departed.

Sometime later, the young noblewoman who had served Sir Launcelot's supper reappeared.

"What news?" she asked.

"It is the end," Sir Launcelot replied.

"Sir Launcelot, I know that you have refused the four queens, and that they wish to kill you out of spite. But if you will be ruled by me, I can save you. I ask that you will champion my father at a tournament next Tuesday, when he has to combat the King of North Galys, and three knights of the Round Table, who last Tuesday defeated him ignominiously."

"My lady, pray tell me, what is your father's name?"

"King Bagdemagus."

"Excellent, my lady, I know him for a good king and a true knight, so I shall be happy to serve him."

"May God reward you! And tomorrow at dawn I will release you, and direct you to an abbey which is ten miles from here, and where the good monks will care for you while I fetch my father."

"I am at your service, my lady."

3. paramour (par′ə·moor′): sweetheart; from Old French, meaning "with love." Today the term refers to an illicit lover.

As promised, the young noblewoman released Sir Launcelot at dawn. When she had led him through the twelve doors to the castle entrance, she gave him his horse and armor, and directions for finding the abbey.

"God bless you, my lady; and when the time comes I promise I shall not fail you."

Sir Launcelot rode through the forest in search of the abbey, but at dusk had still failed to find it, and coming upon a red silk pavilion, apparently unoccupied, decided to rest there overnight, and continue his search in the morning.

He had not been asleep for more than an hour, however, when the knight who owned the pavilion returned, and got straight into bed with him. Having made an assignation[4] with his paramour, the knight supposed at first that Sir Launcelot was she, and taking him into his arms, started kissing him. Sir Launcelot awoke with a start, and seizing his sword, leaped out of bed and out of the pavilion, pursued closely by the other knight. Once in the open they set to with their swords, and before long Sir Launcelot had wounded his unknown adversary so seriously that he was obliged to yield.

The knight, whose name was Sir Belleus, now asked Sir Launcelot how he came to be sleeping in his bed, and then explained how he had an assignation with his lover, adding:

"But now I am so sorely wounded that I shall consider myself fortunate to escape with my life."

"Sir, please forgive me for wounding you; but lately I escaped from an enchantment, and I was afraid that once more I had been betrayed. Let us go into the pavilion and I will staunch your wound."

Sir Launcelot had just finished binding the wound when the young noblewoman who was Sir Belleus' paramour arrived, and seeing the wound, at once rounded in fury on Sir Launcelot.

"Peace, my love," said Sir Belleus. "This is a noble knight, and as soon as I yielded to him he treated my wound with the greatest care." Sir Belleus then described the events which had led up to the duel.

"Sir, pray tell me your name, and whose knight you are," the young noblewoman asked Sir Launcelot.

"My lady, I am called Sir Launcelot du Lake."

"As I guessed, both from your appearance and from your speech; and indeed I know you better than you realize. But I ask you, in recompense for the injury you have done my lord, and out of the courtesy for which you are famous, to recommend Sir Belleus to King Arthur, and suggest that he be made one of the knights of the Round Table. I can assure you that my lord deserves it, being only less than yourself as a man-at-arms, and sovereign of many of the Outer Isles."

"My lady, let Sir Belleus come to Arthur's court at the next Pentecost.[5] Make sure that you come with him, and I promise I will do what I can for him; and if he is as good a man-at-arms as you say he is, I am sure Arthur will accept him."

Launcelot Enters a Tournament

As soon as it was daylight, Sir Launcelot armed, mounted, and rode away in search of the abbey, which he found in less than two hours. King Bagdemagus' daughter was waiting for him, and as soon as she heard his horse's footsteps in the yard, ran to the window, and, seeing that it was Sir Launcelot, herself ordered the servants to stable his horse. She then led him to her chamber, disarmed him, and gave him a long gown to wear, welcoming him warmly as she did so.

King Bagdemagus' castle was twelve miles away, and his daughter sent for him as soon as she had settled Sir Launcelot. The king arrived with his retinue[6] and embraced Sir Launcelot, who then described his recent enchantment,

4. **assignation** (as′ig·nā′shən): appointment, often made secretly.

5. **Pentecost** (pen′ti·kôst): Christian holiday that falls seven weeks after Easter.

6. **retinue** (ret′′n·yo͞o′): servants; attendants serving someone of importance.

and the great obligation he was under to his daughter for releasing him.

"Sir, you will fight for me on Tuesday next?"

"Sire, I shall not fail you; but please tell me the names of the three Round Table knights whom I shall be fighting."

"Sir Modred, Sir Madore de la Porte, and Sir Gahalantyne. I must admit that last Tuesday they defeated me and my knights completely."

"Sire, I hear that the tournament is to be fought within three miles of the abbey. Could you send me three of your most trustworthy knights, clad in plain armor, and with no device, and a fourth suit of armor which I myself shall wear? We will take up our position just outside the tournament field and watch while you and the King of North Galys enter into combat with your followers; and then, as soon as you are in difficulties, we will come to your rescue, and show your opponents what kind of knights you command."

This was arranged on Sunday, and on the following Tuesday Sir Launcelot and the three knights of King Bagdemagus waited in a copse, not far from the pavilion which had been erected for the lords and ladies who were to judge the tournament and award the prizes.

The King of North Galys was the first on the field, with a company of ninescore knights; he was followed by King Bagdemagus with fourscore knights, and then by the three knights of the Round Table, who remained apart from both companies. At the first encounter King Bagdemagus lost twelve knights, all killed, and the King of North Galys six.

With that, Sir Launcelot galloped on to the field, and with his first spear unhorsed five of the King of North Galys' knights, breaking the backs of four of them. With his next spear he charged the king, and wounded him deeply in the thigh.

"That was a shrewd blow," commented Sir Madore, and galloped onto the field to challenge Sir Launcelot. But he too was tumbled from his horse, and with such violence that his shoulder was broken.

Sir Modred was the next to challenge Sir Launcelot, and he was sent spinning over his horse's tail. He landed head first, his helmet became buried in the soil, and he nearly broke his neck, and for a long time lay stunned.

Finally, Sir Gahalantyne tried; at the first encounter both he and Sir Launcelot broke their spears, so both drew their swords and hacked vehemently at each other. But Sir Launcelot, with mounting wrath, soon struck his opponent a blow on the helmet which brought the blood streaming from eyes, ears, and mouth. Sir Gahalantyne slumped forward in the saddle, his horse panicked, and he was thrown to the ground, useless for further combat.

Sir Launcelot took another spear, and unhorsed sixteen more of the King of North Galys' knights, and with his next, unhorsed another twelve; and in each case with such violence that none of the knights ever fully recovered. The King of North Galys was forced to admit defeat, and the prize was awarded to King Bagdemagus.

That night Sir Launcelot was entertained as the guest of honor by King Bagdemagus and his daughter at their castle, and before leaving was loaded with gifts.

"My lady, please, if ever again you should need my services, remember that I shall not fail you."

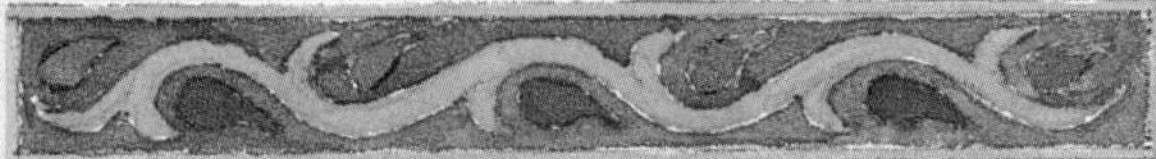

Arthur's kingdom thrived while the Round Table existed, but "might for right" did not last. Several knights told King Arthur about the relationship between his wife and Launcelot. Gwynevere was judged guilty of adultery and sentenced to burn at the stake. At the last moment, Launcelot, charging through the guards, snatched Gwynevere from the flames and took her back to his castle. The resulting hostility between Arthur and Launcelot split the knights' allegiance. Thus, sexual immorality brought an end to the fellowship of the Round Table.

Connections A PERSONAL ESSAY

Where I Find My Heroes

Oliver Stone

Oliver Stone became a movie director after serving in the Vietnam War. His films include Born on the Fourth of July *(1989),* JFK *(1991), and* Nixon *(1995).*

It's not true that there are no heroes anymore—but it is true that my own concept of heroism has changed radically over time. When I was young and I read the Random House biographies, my heroes were always people like George Washington and General Custer and Abraham Lincoln and Teddy Roosevelt. Men, generally, and doers. Women—with the exception of Clara Barton, Florence Nightingale, and Joan of Arc—got short shrift. Most history was oriented toward male heroes.

But as I've gotten older, and since I've been to war, I've been forced to reexamine the nature of life and of heroism. What is true? Where are the myths?

The simple acts of heroism are often overlooked—that's very clear to me not only in war but in peace. I'm not debunking all of history: Crossing the Delaware *was* a magnificent action. But I am saying that I think the meaning of heroism has a lot to do with evolving into a higher human being. I came into contact with it when I worked with Ron Kovic, the paraplegic Vietnam vet, on *Born on the Fourth of July.* I was impressed by his life change, from a patriotic and strong-willed athlete to someone who had to deal with the total surrender of his body, who grew into a non-violent and peaceful advocate of change in the Martin Luther King, Jr., and Gandhi tradition. So heroism *is* tied to an evolution of consciousness. . . .

Since the war, I've had children, and I'm wrestling now with the everyday problems of trying to share my knowledge with them without overwhelming them. It's difficult to be a father, to be a mother, and I think that to be a kind and loving parent is an act of heroism. So there you go—heroes are everyday, common people. Most of what they do goes unheralded, unappreciated. And that, ironically, *is* heroism: not to be recognized.

Who is heroic? Scientists who spend years of their lives trying to find cures for diseases. The teenager who says no to crack. The inner-city kid who works at McDonald's instead of selling drugs. The kid who stands alone instead of joining a gang, which would give him an instant identity. The celebrity who remains modest and treats others with respect, or who uses his position to help society. The student who defers the immediate pleasure of making money and finishes college or high school. People who take risks despite fears. People in wheelchairs who don't give up. . . .

We have a lot of corruption in our society. But we mustn't assume that everything is always basely motivated. We should allow for the heroic impulse—which is to be greater than oneself, to try to find another version of oneself, to grow. That's where virtue comes from. And we must allow our young generation to strive for virtue, instead of ridiculing it.

MAKING MEANINGS

First Thoughts

1. If you were producing a movie of this tale, whom would you cast as Launcelot? Why?

> **Reading Check**
>
> You are Sir Launcelot, reporting to King Arthur about your adventures. Using the first-person, briefly **summarize** the **main events** that befell you on your journey.

Shaping Interpretations

2. Identify at least three of Launcelot's actions that are worthy of a chivalric **hero.** What, if anything, does he do that seems unheroic?

3. Based on this tale, what **character traits** did this medieval culture value in its heroes? **Compare and contrast** these qualities with your own ideas about heroes. (Where do your own ideas about heroes come from?) Be sure to refer to your Quickwrite notes.
4. A **romance** usually includes these motifs: adventure, quests, wicked adversaries, even magic (see pages 948–949). Describe the typical elements of a romance that you find in this tale. Are any of these motifs found in movies or TV shows today?
5. The Arthurian stories are not prim; they are full of violence, betrayals, romantic intrigues, and even comedy. Did you find any of these elements in the tales in this collection? Cite details from the text in your response.

Extending the Text

6. Do you think Oliver Stone (see ***Connections*** on page 968) would consider Launcelot heroic? Why? What do you think of Stone's ideas about heroes?
7. In his essay (see ***Connections*** on page 968), Stone says "most history was oriented toward male heroes." If he's right, why do you think this is so? Is the situation changing?

"He rode his way with the queen unto Joyous Gard" by N.C. Wyeth. Illustration from *The Boy's King Arthur* (1917).

CHOICES: Building Your Portfolio

Writer's Notebook

1. Collecting Ideas for Supporting a Generalization

Finding your ideas. In a television interview about modern-day heroes, Joseph Campbell, a professor of mythology (who died in 1987), and Bill Moyers, a journalist, exchanged some thought-provoking ideas. At one point, Moyers said: *"We seem to worship celebrities today, not heroes."* Campbell remarked at another time: *"The big problem of any young person's life is to have models to suggest possibilities."* Think about these two comments. Both are **generalizations**, or broad statements that apply to many cases. Freewrite for a few minutes, exploring your feelings about what they say. Then, formulate a generalization of your own, sparked by these comments or by the Arthurian tales you've read. Cite **evidence** that could be used to support your generalization. Save your notes for possible use in the Writer's Workshop on page 986.

Generalization: It's not true that people were more heroic in the past.

Evidence:
1. It's hard to be a true hero today because the media digs up dirt on everyone.
2. People today don't see heroes right under their noses.

Comparing and Contrasting

2. Knights and Cowboys

John Steinbeck, who was captivated by Malory's tales as a boy (see ***Connections*** on page 954), once compared the Arthurian legends to the American western. The settings and the weapons are different, he said, but the types of characters, stories, and themes are similar. In a brief essay, **compare and contrast** the knightly stories and American westerns.

Viewing/Representing

3. Medieval Media

Pretend that the mass media had been invented in the twelfth century. With a group, create a **TV or radio newscast**, with interviews, that reports one of these events:

a. On New Year's Day, an unknown kid pulls a sword from a stone.

b. There is fierce fighting at a tournament. Sir Launcelot emerges victorious.

Research/Literature and History

4. Stay Tuned for More About Arthur

What became of Gwynevere and Morgan le Fay? What special powers did Merlin have? What eventually happened to him? How did knights move around with such heavy armor? With a partner or group, generate a list of Arthur-related questions. Then, research answers, using print and Internet sources. Report your findings to the class.

Creative Writing

5. Star Quests

Write a **heroic romance** set in the future or on another planet. (Think of *Star Wars*, *Star Trek* and other sci-fi epics.) Invent a hero (who could be an alien) and give your hero a mysterious or obscure childhood. Determine the focus of your hero's quest, the nature of the enemy, the settings encountered, the trials faced, and the end of the quest. If you prefer, tell your story in the form of a screenplay. In any case, be sure to elaborate with vivid descriptive details.

Language Link MINI-LESSON

A Changing Language: English Word Origins

All languages change over time. English vocabulary, grammar, spelling, and pronunciation have changed a great deal since the fifteenth century, when Malory wrote in the Midland dialect then spoken in London. For example, consider the **derivation** and the original **meaning** and **spelling** of *worship:* When Malory called a brave knight "a knight of much worship," he meant "a knight well-known for his worth." In Old English, the word for this concept was *weorthscipe*, or *worthship*, that is, "worthy of honor, dignity, or rank." Gradually the word acquired religious connotations and lost its secular meaning, as well as its *th* sound. Today the meaning of *worship* is almost wholly religious.

Although the written form of Malory's Midland dialect looks quite different from today's English, by reading the words aloud and doing some intelligent guessing, you can understand their meanings.

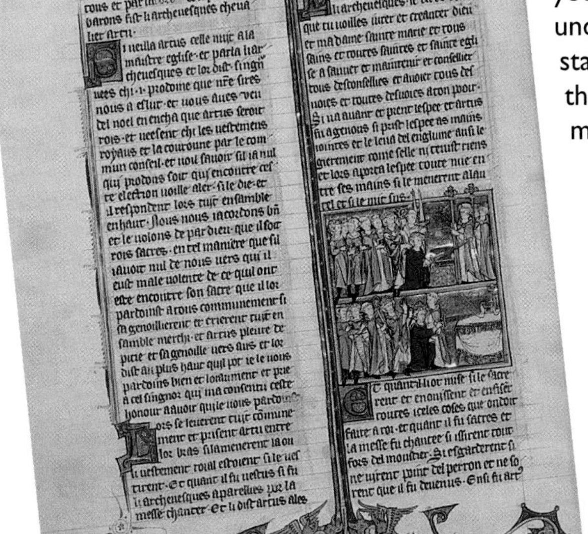

Page from a French manuscript (c. 1290), showing Arthur pulling the sword out of the stone.

Bibliothèque Nationale de France, Paris.

Try It Out

Suppose you want to translate Malory into modern English for a new edition of *Le Morte Darthur.* Translate the following passage into the kind of English spoken in the United States today. Before you tackle the job of translating, read the passage aloud. Then research your guesses in a dictionary. Do you find the Middle English spelling listed as part of the word's etymology, or **origin**?

"A, Launcelot!" he sayd, "thou were hede of al Crysten knyghtes! And now I dare say," sayd syr Ector, "thou sir Launcelot, there thou lyest, that thou were never matched of erthely knyghtes hande. And thou werre the curtest knyght that ever bare shelde! And thou were the truest frende to thy lover that ever bestrade hors, and thou were the trewest lover of a synful man that ever loved woman, and thou were the kyndest man that ever strake with swerde. And thou were the godelyest persone that ever cam among prees of knyghtes, and thou was the mekest man and the jentyllest that ever ete in halle among ladyes, and thou were the sternest knyght to thy mortal foo that ever put spere in the reeste."

—Sir Thomas Malory

Before You Read

SUNDIATA: AN EPIC OF OLD MALI

Make the Connection

Setting Out

From King Arthur to Luke Skywalker, heroes are known for their obscure starts in life. Born in mysterious, often disadvantaged circumstances, they must prove themselves before they set out on their perilous journeys to become the heroes they were born to be. One of the most remarkable childhoods belongs to Sundiata, the Lion King, hero of an epic from Mali, in Africa. At the age of seven, Sundiata could not walk, rarely spoke, and did not play with other children. How could this poor child ever become a king and hero?

Quickwrite

Think of an example from real life or literature of someone who started out as the underdog and succeeded in doing something that others thought he or she would never accomplish. Write about that person's experience as an underdog.

Background

Two strangers bring a maiden named Sogolon to the king of the Islamic country of Mali. They promise that if he takes her as his second wife (he already has one wife, who is the queen mother), she will bear a son who will make Mali into a powerful empire. The king marries Sogolon, and Sundiata is born to them.

Elements of Literature

Epic: A Superhero's Story

One of the oldest literary forms, the **epic,** contains myth, legend, and history and is strongly rooted in one society. Oral historians, called griots (grē′ōz) in Africa, recited the African epic of *Sundiata*, passing it down from generation to generation before it was written down. We know that Sundiata was a real person, a thirteenth-century leader who founded the empire of Mali in West Africa. Much of what is told in this epic, as in all epics, is not meant to be "true history." In performing the story of Sundiata, the griots not only celebrated the hero's life but also instructed and inspired their listeners to adopt his purpose in life: to confront and conquer evil wherever he found it.

An **epic** is a long narrative work that relates the deeds of a larger-than-life hero who embodies the values of a particular society.

For more on the Epic, see the Handbook of Literary Terms.

go.hrw.com
LEO 10-14

God has
his mysteries,
which none
can fathom.

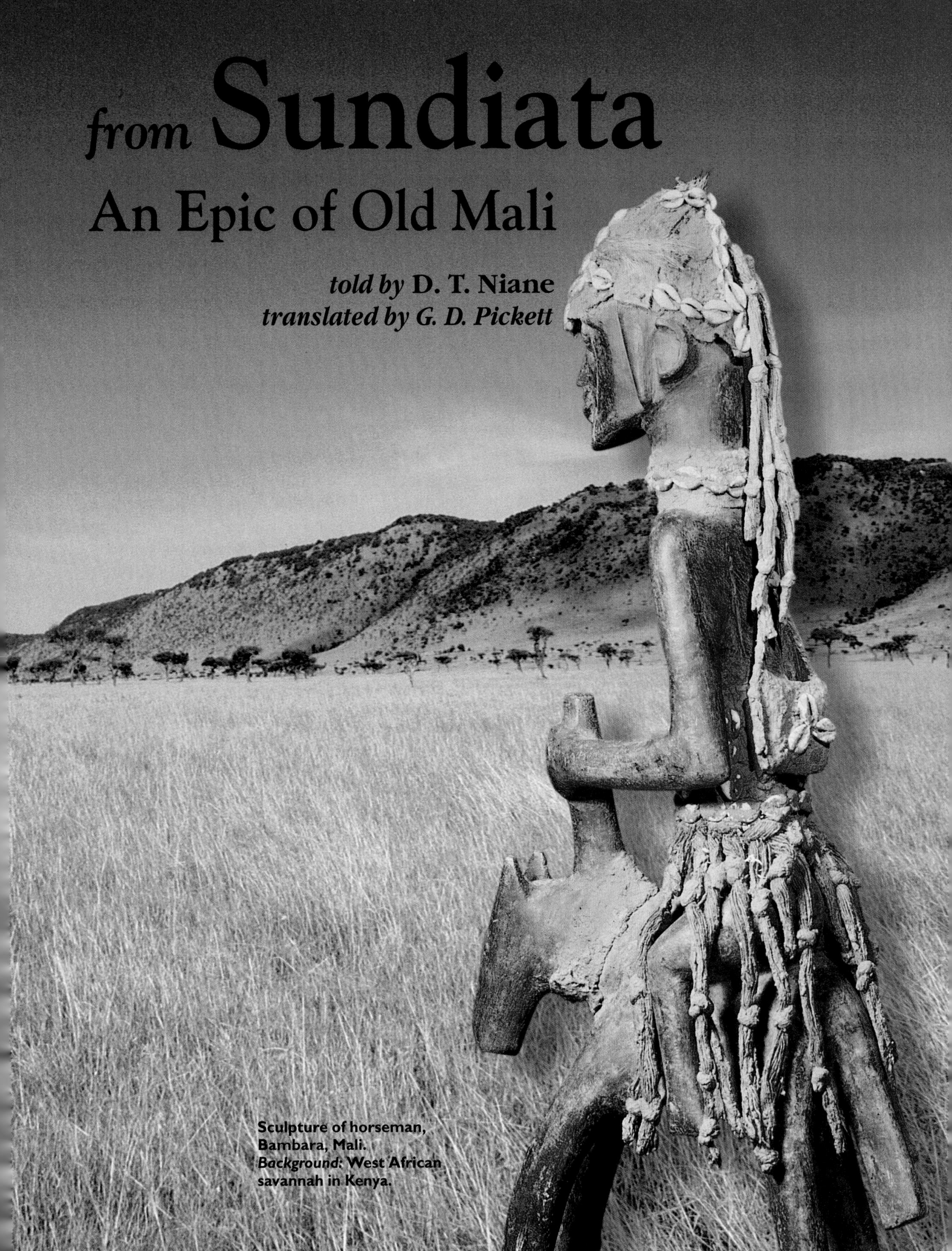

from Sundiata

An Epic of Old Mali

told by **D. T. Niane**

translated by G. D. Pickett

Sculpture of horseman, Bambara, Mali.
***Background:* West African savannah in Kenya.**

Main Characters

Maghan Sundiata: the hero of the epic. He is also called **Sogolon Djata, Mari Djata,** and **Djata.**

Sogolon Kedjou: Sundiata's mother, usually referred to as **Sogolon.**

King Maghan Kon Fatta: Sundiata's father, the king of Mali. He is also called **Naré Maghan.**

Sassouma Bérété: the queen mother; the first wife of the king.

Dankaran Touman: Sassouma Bérété's son. He is King Maghan Kon Fatta's successor and Sundiata's half brother.

Balla Fasséké: Sundiata's griot.

Gnankouman Doua: the king's griot, father of Balla Fasséké.

Farakourou: master blacksmith and a soothsayer, or fortuneteller.

Nounfaïri: Farakourou's father, also a master blacksmith and a soothsayer.

When this selection opens, Sundiata is three. It continues four years later, when he is seven. By this time, Sundiata has accepted Balla Fasséké as his griot and has finally said his first words.

God has his mysteries, which none can fathom. You, perhaps, will be a king. You can do nothing about it. You, on the other hand, will be unlucky, but you can do nothing about that either. Each man finds his way already marked out for him, and he can change nothing of it.

Sogolon's son had a slow and difficult childhood. At the age of three he still crawled along on all fours, while children of the same age were already walking. He had nothing of the great beauty of his father, Naré Maghan. He had a head so big that he seemed unable to support it; he also had large eyes, which would open wide whenever anyone entered his mother's house. He was taciturn and used to spend the whole day just sitting in the middle of the house. Whenever his mother went out, he would crawl on all fours to rummage about in the calabashes[1] in search of food, for he was very greedy.

Malicious tongues began to blab. What three-year-old has not yet taken his first steps? What three-year-old is not the despair of his parents through his whims and shifts of mood? What three-year-old is not the joy of his circle through his backwardness in talking? Sogolon Djata (for it was thus that they called him, prefixing his mother's name to his), Sogolon Djata, then, was very different from others of his own age. He spoke little and his severe face never relaxed into a smile. You would have thought that he was already thinking, and what amused children of his age bored him. Often Sogolon would make some of them come to him to keep him company. These children were already walking, and she hoped that Djata, seeing his companions walking, would be tempted to do likewise. But nothing came of it. Besides, Sogolon Djata would brain the poor little things with his already strong arms, and none of them would come near him anymore.

The king's first wife was the first to rejoice at Sogolon Djata's infirmity. Her own son, Dankaran Touman, was already eleven. He was a fine and lively boy, who spent the day running about the village with those of his own age. He had even begun his initiation in the bush.[2] The king had had a bow made for him, and he used

1. **calabashes** (kal′ə·bash′əz): dried, hollowed gourds used as containers.

2. **initiation in the bush:** It is customary for West African boys, at around the age of twelve, to go into the bush with their elders to learn tribal lore in preparation for the rite of circumcision. After this, they are fully initiated adult members of the tribe.

Words to Own

taciturn (tas′ə·tʉrn′) *adj.:* usually silent and uncommunicative.

malicious (mə·lish′əs) *adj.:* mischievous; mean; intending to cause harm.

infirmity (in·fʉr′mə·tē) *n.:* weakness; physical defect.

to go behind the town to practice archery with his companions. Sassouma was quite happy and snapped her fingers at Sogolon, whose child was still crawling on the ground. Whenever the latter happened to pass by her house, she would say, "Come, my son, walk, jump, leap about. The jinni[3] didn't promise you anything out of the ordinary, but I prefer a son who walks on his two legs to a lion that crawls on the ground." She spoke thus whenever Sogolon went by her door. The innuendo would go straight home, and then she would burst into laughter, that diabolical laughter which a jealous woman knows how to use so well.

Her son's infirmity weighed heavily upon Sogolon Kedjou; she had resorted to all her talent as a sorceress to give strength to her son's legs, but the rarest herbs had been useless. The king himself lost hope. . . .

[*Four years pass and Sundiata is seven.*]

Sogolon Kedjou and her children lived on the queen mother's leftovers, but she kept a little garden in the open ground behind the village. It was there that she passed her brightest moments looking after her onions and gnougous.[4] One day she happened to be short of condiments and went to the queen mother to beg a little baobab leaf.

"Look you," said the malicious Sassouma, "I have a calabash full. Help yourself, you poor woman. As for me, my son knew how to walk at seven, and it was he who went and picked these baobab leaves. Take them, then, since your son is unequal to mine." Then she laughed derisively with that fierce laughter which cuts through your flesh and penetrates right to the bone.

Sogolon Kedjou was dumbfounded. She had never imagined that hate could be so strong in a human being. With a lump in her throat, she left Sassouma's. Outside her hut Mari Djata, sitting on his useless legs, was blandly eating out of a calabash. Unable to contain herself any longer, Sogolon burst into sobs and, seizing a piece of wood, hit her son.

"Oh son of misfortune, will you never walk? Through your fault I have just suffered the greatest affront of my life! What have I done, God, for you to punish me in this way?"

Mari Djata seized the piece of wood and, looking at his mother, said, "Mother, what's the matter?"

"Shut up, nothing can ever wash me clean of this insult."

"But what, then?"

"Sassouma has just humiliated me over a matter of a baobab leaf. At your age her own son could walk and used to bring his mother baobab leaves."

"Cheer up, Mother, cheer up."

"No. It's too much. I can't."

"Very well, then, I am going to walk today," said Mari Djata. "Go and tell my father's smiths to make me the heaviest possible iron rod. Mother, do you want just the leaves of the baobab, or would you rather I brought you the whole tree?"

"Ah, my son, to wipe out this insult, I want the tree and its roots at my feet outside my hut."

Balla Fasséké, who was present, ran to the master smith, Farakourou, to order an iron rod.

Sogolon had sat down in front of her hut. She was weeping softly and holding her head between her two hands. Mari Djata went calmly back to his calabash of rice and began eating again as if nothing had happened. From time to time he looked up discreetly at his mother, who was murmuring in a low voice, "I want the whole tree in front of my hut, the whole tree."

All of a sudden a voice burst into laughter behind the hut. It was the wicked Sassouma telling one of her serving women about the scene of humiliation, and she was laughing loudly so that

Words to Own

innuendo (in′yo͞o·en′dō′) *n.:* hint, usually implying something negative.
diabolical (dī′ə·bäl′ə·kəl) *adj.:* cruel; wicked; devilish.
derisively (di·rī′siv·lē) *adv.:* with scorn or contempt.
affront (ə·frunt′) *n.:* insult.
smiths *n.:* blacksmiths; people who make metal tools.

3. **jinni:** supernatural being believed to appear as a human or animal and to influence human affairs.
4. **gnougous** (noo′goos): part of an edible plant.

Sogolon could hear. Sogolon fled into the hut and hid her face under the blankets so as not to have before her eyes this heedless boy, who was more preoccupied with eating than with anything else. With her head buried in the bedclothes, Sogolon wept, and her body shook violently. Her daughter, Sogolon Djamarou, had come and sat down beside her, and she said, "Mother, Mother, don't cry. Why are you crying?"

Mari Djata had finished eating, and dragging himself along on his legs, he came and sat under the wall of the hut, for the sun was scorching. What was he thinking about? He alone knew.

The royal forges[5] were situated outside the walls, and over a hundred smiths worked there. The bows, spears, arrows, and shields of Niani's[6] warriors came from there. When Balla Fasséké came to order the iron rod, Farakourou said to him, "The great day has arrived, then?"

"Yes. Today is a day like any other, but it will see what no other day has seen."

The master of the forges, Farakourou, was the son of the old Nounfaïri, and he was a soothsayer like his father. In his workshops there was an enormous iron bar wrought by his father, Nounfaïri. Everybody wondered what this bar was destined to be used for. Farakourou called six of his apprentices and told them to carry the iron bar to Sogolon's house.

When the smiths put the gigantic iron bar down in front of the hut, the noise was so frightening that Sogolon, who was lying down, jumped up with a start. Then Balla Fasséké, son of Gnankouman Doua, spoke.

"Here is the great day, Mari Djata. I am speaking to you, Maghan, son of Sogolon. The waters of the Niger can efface the stain from the body, but they cannot wipe out an insult. Arise, young lion, roar, and may the bush know that from henceforth it has a master."

The apprentice smiths were still there, Sogolon had come out, and everyone was watching Mari Djata. He crept on all fours and came to the iron bar. Supporting himself on his knees and one hand, with the other hand he picked up the iron bar without any effort and stood it up vertically. Now he was resting on nothing but his knees and held the bar with both his hands. A deathly silence had gripped all those present. Sogolon Djata closed his eyes, held tight; the muscles in his arms tensed. With a violent jerk he threw his weight onto the bar and his knees left the ground. Sogolon Kedjou was all eyes and watched her son's legs, which were trembling as though from an electric shock. Djata was sweating, and the sweat ran from his brow. In a great effort, he straightened up and was on his feet at one go—but the great bar of iron was twisted and had taken the form of a bow!

Then Balla Fasséké sang out the "Hymn to the Bow," striking up with his powerful voice:

Take your bow, Simbon,
Take your bow and let us go.
Take your bow, Sogolon Djata.

When Sogolon saw her son standing, she stood dumb for a moment; then suddenly she sang these words of thanks to God, who had given her son the use of his legs:

Oh day, what a beautiful day,
Oh day, day of joy;
Allah Almighty, you never created a finer day.
So my son is going to walk!

Standing in the position of a soldier at ease, Sogolon Djata, supported by his enormous rod, was sweating great beads of sweat. Balla Fasséké's song had alerted the whole palace; people came running from all over to see what had happened, and each stood bewildered before Sogolon's son. The queen mother had rushed there, and when she saw Mari Djata standing up, she trembled from head to foot. After recovering his breath, Sogolon's son

5. **forges:** places where metal is heated and shaped into tools.
6. **Niani's:** of the town where King Maghan and the others live.

Words to Own

heedless *adj.:* careless; not paying attention.
efface (ə·fās′) *v.:* rub out; erase.

dropped the bar and the crowd stood to one side. His first steps were those of a giant. Balla Fasséké fell into step, and pointing his finger at Djata, he cried:

> Room, room, make room!
> The lion has walked;
> Hide, antelopes,
> Get out of his way.

Behind Niani there was a young baobab tree, and it was there that the children of the town came to pick leaves for their mothers. With all his might the son of Sogolon tore up the tree and put it on his shoulders and went back to his mother. He threw the tree in front of the hut and said, "Mother, here are some baobab leaves for you. From henceforth it will be outside your hut that the women of Niani will come to stock up."

After the events related in this selection from the epic, the queen mother plots to have Sundiata killed. Sundiata escapes into exile and journeys from one kingdom to the other until he finds refuge with the king of Mema, who makes him his heir.

When Sundiata is eighteen years old, the people of Mali beg him to return. He raises an army, and with supernatural help from the same blacksmith-magician who aided him before, he defeats his enemies and unites the kingdom. Under Sundiata's rule, Mali, the "Bright Country," becomes one of the most powerful empires in Africa. Its rulers control the salt and gold trades and dominate western Sudan from about A.D. *1200 to* A.D. *1500.*

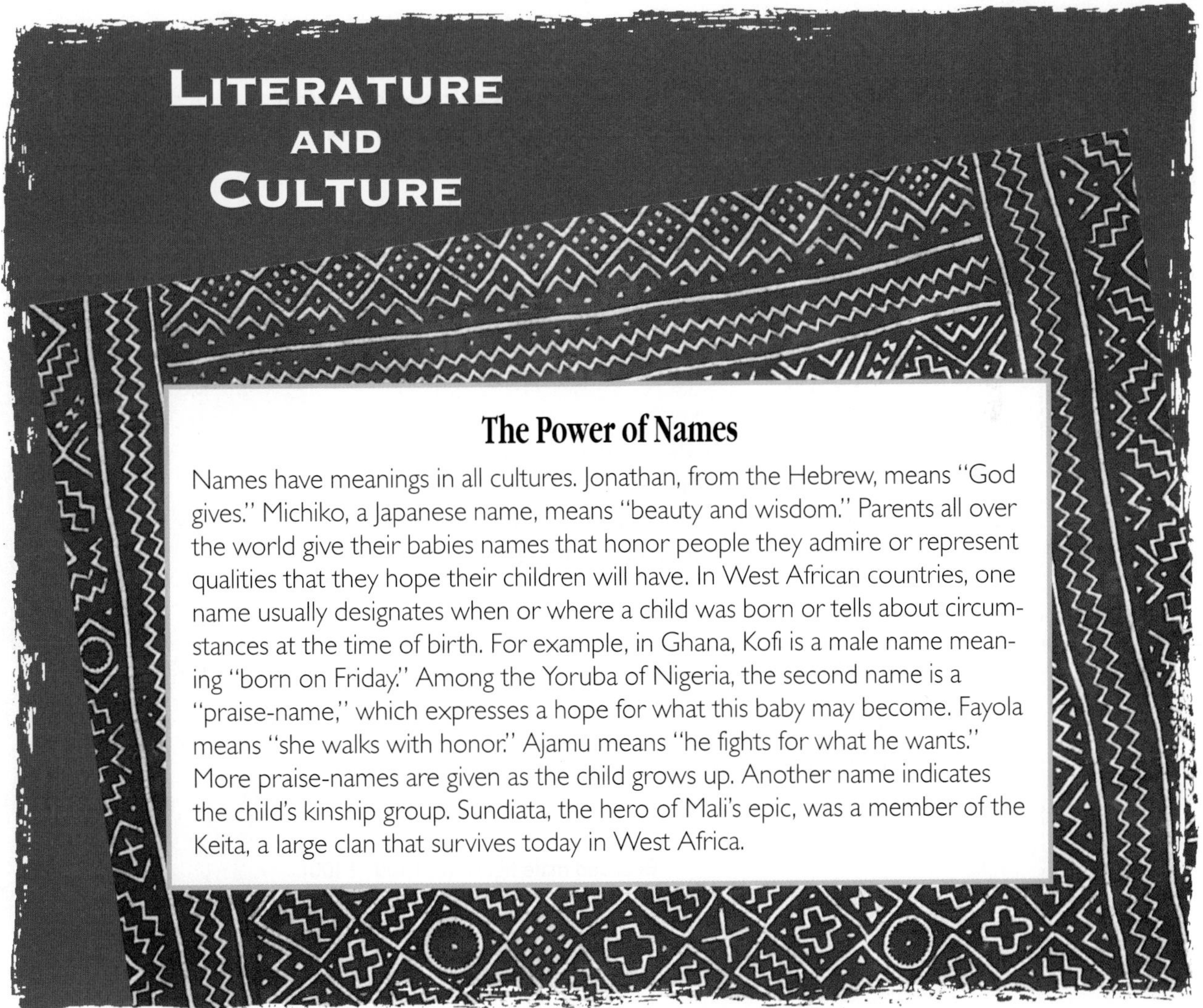

Literature and Culture

The Power of Names

Names have meanings in all cultures. Jonathan, from the Hebrew, means "God gives." Michiko, a Japanese name, means "beauty and wisdom." Parents all over the world give their babies names that honor people they admire or represent qualities that they hope their children will have. In West African countries, one name usually designates when or where a child was born or tells about circumstances at the time of birth. For example, in Ghana, Kofi is a male name meaning "born on Friday." Among the Yoruba of Nigeria, the second name is a "praise-name," which expresses a hope for what this baby may become. Fayola means "she walks with honor." Ajamu means "he fights for what he wants." More praise-names are given as the child grows up. Another name indicates the child's kinship group. Sundiata, the hero of Mali's epic, was a member of the Keita, a large clan that survives today in West Africa.

Making Meanings

First Thoughts

1. What other stories that you've read or heard does this tale remind you of?

Shaping Interpretations

2. What **character traits** help Sundiata to overcome his problems? What similarities can you find between his childhood and Arthur's?

3. The belief that everything that happens has been decreed by God is fundamental to many religions, including Islam. What clues can you find that Sundiata's way has already been marked for him? Who helps carry out Sundiata's destiny?

4. How does this **epic** combine elements of magic with elements that appear to be grounded in historical reality?

5. What social values of Old Mali does this epic suggest? What seems to be the general attitude toward women in this culture?

6. Scholars think that griots often performed the epic of Sundiata for the army of Mali before it went into battle. What effect do you think hearing the epic might have had on that audience? Which passages might have been especially aimed at that audience?

Bambara mask. Mali.

Connecting with the Text

7. Why do you think readers and audiences throughout the world like stories about underdogs who triumph over their foes? How do you feel about such stories? Be sure to review your Quickwrite notes.

Extending the Text

8. Some people feel that children with low self-esteem often have no heroes. Do you agree or disagree? Could Sundiata be a positive role model for a child with low self-esteem? Discuss your ideas.

Reading Check

Make a **time line** showing the major events in Sundiata's life as you know them from the Background on page 972 and from the episode narrated here. Compare your time lines in class, and add or subtract events until you feel you have them all. Discuss (and agree on as a class) which events are the major ones, and circle them on the time line.

Bearded male figure (c. 1300–1400). Djenné sculpture (38.1 cm). South-central Mali.

Founders Society Purchase, Eleanor Clay Ford Fund for African Art. Photograph ©1995 The Detroit Institute of Arts.

CHOICES: Building Your Portfolio

Writer's Notebook

1. Collecting Ideas for Supporting a Generalization

Making a generalization. Make a generalization about the Sundiata epic you just read. You might focus on the idea of fate, the belief in magic, or the role of women in Old Mali. Find details from the epic to support your general statement. Save your notes for the Writer's Workshop assignment on page 986.

Generalization:
Idea of fate extremely important in Old Mali.

Supporting details:
Opening paragraph: No one can fathom God's mysteries.
Character can't do anything about being king.

Oral Interpretation / Art

2. More Epic Tales

Most cultures have their own epics. Find out enough about one of these epics to **summarize** the hero's story or to retell an exciting adventure:

- *Odyssey* (Greece)
- *Epic of Gilgamesh* (Babylonia)
- *Beowulf* (England)
- *Mahabharata* (India)
- *The Tale of the Heike* (Japan)

Make your oral version rich in detail with clear, vivid descriptions of the characters and events. You might even work with a partner to retell and illustrate one of the hero's adventures as a children's book.

Research / Informative Report

3. African Kingdoms

Use the resources of your school and public libraries or the Internet to find out about one African kingdom of your choice. Focus on the period from about A.D. 300 to A.D. 1600. After you've decided on a kingdom to research, divide up the work with others interested in the same culture. Here are areas that group members may want to focus on: history, religion, art, music, daily life, economics, the political system, and the country or countries that occupy the area in Africa today. Prepare a written group report as well as a visual presentation, and share your findings with the rest of the class.

Performance / Dramatic Interpretation

4. Sundiata Onstage

With a group, script a scene from *Sundiata.* Select a scene that has some dramatic interest and action. In your **script,** tell when and where your scene is **set** and which **characters** will appear in it. Be sure to provide **stage directions** telling what the characters are thinking and how they are speaking—even how they are moving. After you've written the scene, perform it for the class. (Maybe you'll want to do what Lerner and Loewe did for the Arthurian legends and make *Sundiata* into a musical.)

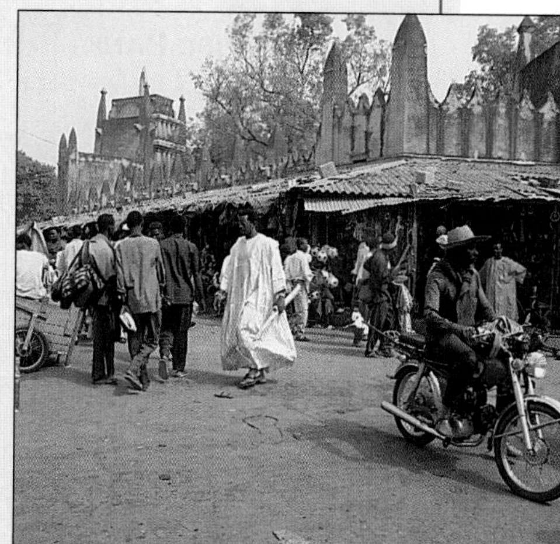

Bamako, Mali.

Grammar Link — Mini-Lesson

Commas and Appositives

Language Handbook HELP

See Appositives: page 1036.

Technology HELP

See Language Workshop CD-ROM. *Key word entry: commas.*

An **appositive** is a noun or pronoun placed next to another noun or pronoun to identify or explain it.

> "He had nothing of the great beauty of his father, **Naré Maghan.**"

Appositives that are **not essential** to the meaning of a sentence, such as the name of Sundiata's father above, are set off by commas. After all, Sundiata has only one father. If you take away his name, the meaning of the sentence will still be clear. Now try reading this sentence without the play's title:

> William Shakespeare wrote his play ***Romeo and Juliet*** around 1594.

Shakespeare didn't write only one play; he wrote many. Therefore, this appositive is **essential** to the meaning of the sentence. Essential appositives are not set off with commas.

Whenever you use an appositive, check to see if it's essential or nonessential. If the meaning is clear without the appositive, set it off with commas. If the meaning is *not* clear, don't use commas.

Try It Out

As an editor, it's your job to add commas for nonessential appositives in the following passage. Exchange your edited version with a partner. Do you agree on where to use commas?

> France's great epic *The Song of Roland* is based on a real incident that happened in 778 to Charlemagne the king of the Franks. His army was attacked on the way through Spain by the Basques, the inhabitants of the region. The epic's hero Roland makes some bad decisions. He can't believe that his real enemy is Ganelon his stepfather. Roland stupidly rejects the advice of his best friend Oliver.

Vocabulary — How to Own a Word

Word Bank

taciturn
malicious
infirmity
innuendo
diabolical
derisively
affront
smiths
heedless
efface

What to Do When You Get Stuck: Look at Context

The words in the Word Bank are defined in notes in the text, but what if they weren't? Look back at the text, and see if there are **clues** in the surrounding sentences (the **context**) that would tell you what each word means. Record your findings for each word in a chart like the one below. Also indicate the words that have no context clues.

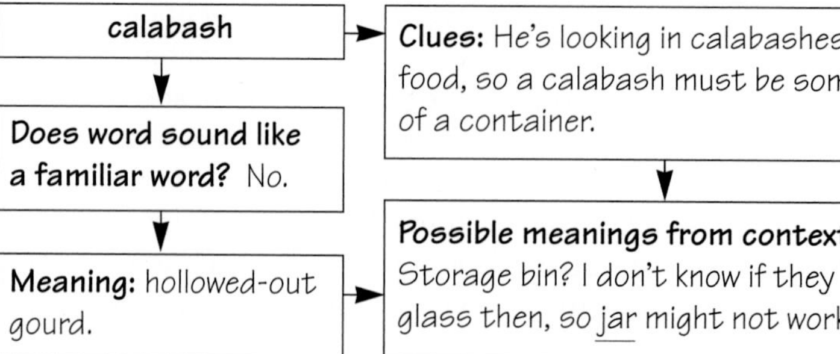

calabash
Clues: He's looking in calabashes for food, so a calabash must be some kind of a container.
Does word sound like a familiar word? No.
Possible meanings from context: Jar? Storage bin? I don't know if they had glass then, so jar might not work.
Meaning: hollowed-out gourd.

EXTENDING *the theme*

A PHOTO ESSAY

STAR TREK Galactic Heroes

". . . to explore strange new worlds, to seek out new life and new civilization, to boldly go where no one has gone before."

Quickwrite

Since the original TV series in 1966, *Star Trek* has riveted fans with its appealing intergalactic heroes and villains. What part do you think TV shows and movies such as *Star Trek* play in providing role models for today's young people?

The starship *Enterprise* and the crew of *Star Trek: The Next Generation.*

Boldly Going, Going, Going . . .

BY CHARLES STRUM

Thirty-one years ago Neil Armstrong was just another NASA astronaut, and a Moon walk—the Armstrong original as well as the Michael Jackson knockoff—had not yet been imagined. But Kirk, Spock, and Bones were becoming real heroes of the 23rd century, and this one, too.

They are heroes still, as are Picard and Sisko and now Janeway, commanders of a Federation starship maintaining course through a fourth decade, a fourth television incarnation, eight movies (a ninth is on the way), and deeper into popular culture, if that is possible. Their exploration of the galaxy, now a 24th-century phenomenon, is 350 episodes along, with no end in sight. It's as if science fiction had finally come up with a perpetual-entertainment machine.

Ratings are steady, demographics the same. All systems go.

How can this be? Can Paramount keep this going forever? Ask Rick Berman, Brannon Braga, Ira Steven Behr, and Jeri Taylor. From their offices in Los Angeles, they write and produce what *Star Trek's* originator, Gene Roddenberry, once characterized as "'Wagon Train' to the stars."

"It's distinctly American," said Mr. Braga, who is co-executive producer of *Star Trek: Voyager,* the latest version of the original 1966 series. "It's all about the frontier. Yet another level is probably the fact that we have basically conquered the frontier. Now we're offering a new frontier. A group of very individualistic heroes driving in their car down the intergalactic highway."

But that alone might not explain why generations of viewers maintain such a strong, almost personal link to the *Star Trek* franchise, a kind of brand loyalty impervious to the television fashion of the moment. Mr. Braga and his colleagues agree on several points: the oft-cited sense of hope, a sense of family, and the need for heroes. . . .

Ms. Taylor, too, thinks the starship odyssey has provided viewers the heroes people desperately crave but don't find much anymore.

"Sports figures have feet of clay," she said. "Politicians and royalty are faulted and flawed. I think, as a people, we are desperately scanning to find those larger-than-life people with values and beliefs that give us something to steer toward."

—from *The New York Times,*
November 30, 1997

Star Trek crews: the original *Star Trek* TV series (top), *Star Trek: Deep Space Nine* (middle), and *Star Trek: Voyager* (bottom).

Top: STAR TREK: ORIGINAL SERIES ©1966 by Paramount Pictures. *Middle:* STAR TREK: DEEP SPACE NINE ©1993 by Paramount Pictures. *Bottom:* STAR TREK: VOYAGER ©1995 by Paramount Pictures. All Rights Reserved. Courtesy of Paramount Pictures.

On *Star Trek* and Heroes: An Interview

I believe that one of the reasons for the popularity of *Star Trek* is that it has accessed some deeply felt needs among people of the late 20th century. And again I will go back to that mythic connotation—stories of heroes, stories of a quest, stories of a search for something better, facing the unknown, facing dangers, fighting monsters, conquering or befriending them. Those are very ancient kinds of stories and tales that were once held very dear by people. In the modern day we have lost track or sight of those kinds of enduring myths and rituals, and I think that on an unconscious level *Star Trek* and certainly other kinds of literary experiences help us to access them once again.

—Jeri Taylor (former *Star Trek* producer), from a 1996 interview

Star Trek at the Movies

Chief DeFalco: Heading sir?
Captain Kirk: Out there . . . thataway.
—*Star Trek: The Motion Picture* (1979)

Picard: Someone once told me that time was a predator that stalked us all our lives. I rather believe that time is a companion who goes with us on the journey and reminds us to cherish every moment, because it will never come again. What we leave behind is not as important as how we've lived. After all, Number One, we're only mortal.
Riker: Speak for yourself, sir. I plan to live forever.
—*Star Trek: Generations* (1994)

Riker: Someone once said, "Don't try to be a great man. Just be a man, and let history make its own judgment."
Cochrane: That's rhetorical nonsense. Who said that?
Riker: You did, ten years from now.
—*Star Trek: First Contact* (1996)

The Cardassian, Gul Dukat, from *Star Trek: Deep Space Nine* (top); Riker and Picard from *Star Trek: The Next Generation* (bottom).

Star Trek and Literature

Cultural memory sweeps through the starship *Enterprise.* No matter how far the crew members venture into strange and uncharted worlds, they carry with them layer upon layer of common stories. These stories include not only past episodes but literary borrowings. Plots and characters revolve around everything from Shakespeare to *Beowulf* to Homer to Sherlock Holmes. Literature is a thread that ties the crew's past to its present, allowing familiar territory to accompany them on their heroic exploits.

Geordi, Dr. Pulaski, and Data (dressed as Sherlock Holmes), from *Star Trek: The Next Generation.*

FINDING COMMON GROUND 

Get together in a small group to talk about the photo essay. You might start by comparing your Quickwrite notes. If you need help getting your discussion underway, consider these questions:

1. How important do you think TV and movies are in providing heroic role models for children and young people? Give some examples.
2. Do you agree with Jeri Taylor that we seek to learn values and beliefs from larger-than-life heroes? Do you think, instead, that life-size heroes—ordinary people who do admirable things—are better models?
3. What do you like or dislike most about the original *Star Trek* TV series, the spin-off TV series, and the *Star Trek* movies? How would you explain their immense popularity?
4. If *Star Trek* movies and TV shows were all that survived from our time, what might archaeologists in the year 3000 conclude about our society's heroes and values?

See if your group can reach a consensus on any of these questions, and compare your conclusions with those of your classmates.

From Guinevere's Point of View

Persia Woolley's *Child of the Northern Spring* (Poseidon) gives Guinevere her chance to tell the King Arthur legend. Richly detailed and romantic, this fascinating novel is the first in a trilogy that takes Guinevere from childhood to middle age.

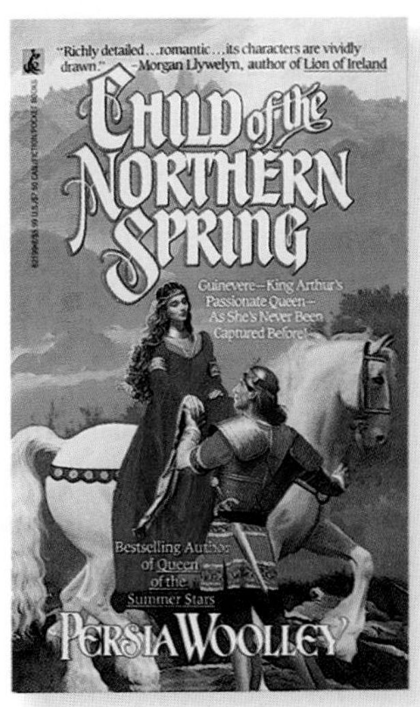

A Perilous Quest

In *The Lord of the Rings* (Ballantine), a three-part modern fantasy by J.R.R. Tolkien, the free people of Middle-Earth unite to battle the forces of evil. The first part, *The Fellowship of the Ring*, tells how Frodo and a small but courageous band of companions take the Ring of Power to Mount Doom, the only place it can be destroyed.

The Final Ordeal

Arthur Ashe looks back on his life and recounts his battle with AIDS in the inspiring *Days of Grace: A Memoir* (Knopf). Ashe recalls his childhood in the segregated South, his career as a tennis champion, his fight against heart disease, and his active opposition to injustice. Some of the most moving parts of the book describe his devotion to his religion and his family.

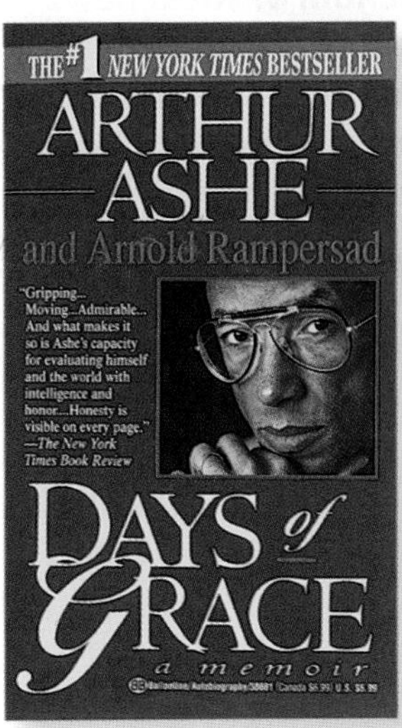

Models to Live By

In *Rosey Grier's All-American Heroes* (Master Media), the former football star and current social activist profiles the lives of thirty men and women from diverse cultural backgrounds who overcame hardships to reach their goals in politics, music, law, education, medicine, publishing, and television. Grier bases his biographies on in-depth interviews that provide not only insights into his subjects' achievements but also interesting career information.

Writer's Workshop

ASSIGNMENT

Write an essay in which you state a generalization (a main idea or thesis) and then support it with details, such as facts, examples, reasons, and anecdotes.

AIM

To inform.

AUDIENCE

Your teacher and classmates; readers of your school or local newspaper; readers of a national magazine for young people. (You choose.)

EXPOSITORY WRITING

SUPPORTING A GENERALIZATION

Each of the stories and poems in Collection 13 offers some wise advice about how to live. When you stated the **theme** of each story or poem, you stated it as a **generalization**—a broad statement that takes into account all the details in the text, not just one.

Generalizations help people make sense of the world. Just think how complicated life would be if we couldn't make generalizations about natural laws (wet climates produce lush foliage) or about people (everyone wants to be loved). In this workshop, you'll write an essay that begins with a generalization based on information you've gathered about a topic. Then you'll back up your generalization with specific **supporting details.**

Prewriting

WORK IN PROGRESS

1. Tailor a Topic

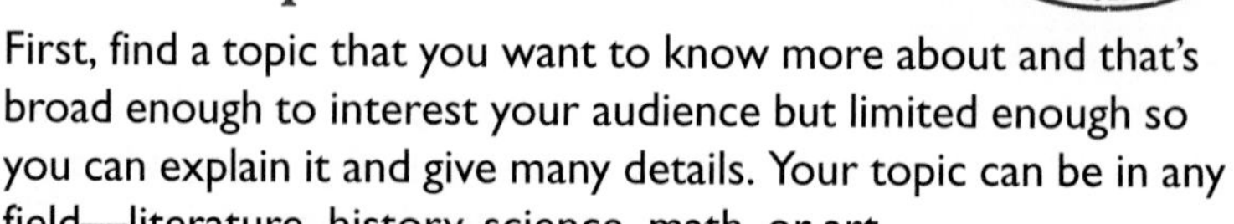

First, find a topic that you want to know more about and that's broad enough to interest your audience but limited enough so you can explain it and give many details. Your topic can be in any field—literature, history, science, math, or art.

- Look through your Writer's Notebook for Collections 13 and 14. You should have some notes on generalizations there. See if any generalizations about wisdom and heroes appeal to you.
- If you are not satisfied with your notes, glance through current magazines. Choose a broad topic that really interests you. Then narrow it. (See the Try It Out activity on page 987.)

2. Generate a Generalization

After you've narrowed your topic, write down ideas that you may want to explore in your paper. Choose one of these ideas for your **generalization**—the main idea or thesis of your essay. Your generalization will make a statement that the rest of your essay will support. State your generalization in a complete declarative sentence. Let's say your limited topic is Dr. Martin Luther

Communications Handbook HELP

See Taking Notes and Documenting Sources.

The history
of the written
word is rich and
Page 1
Once upon a time

King, Jr., as a hero. Here are three possible generalizations on that topic:

- Dr. Martin Luther King, Jr., helped millions gain their civil rights.
- Religious beliefs directed Dr. Martin Luther King, Jr.'s life and work.
- Dr. Martin Luther King, Jr., is a perfect example of a twentieth-century hero.

3. Gather Details to Elaborate

Once you have decided on your generalization, back it up and elaborate with facts, statistics, definitions, examples, quotations, reasons, opinions, or descriptive details. (You may need to do some research in the library or on the Internet.) You may also want to elaborate by telling an anecdote, a brief account of an incident, or you may want to tell of your own involvement in your topic.

4. Impose Order

Here are some methods for organizing details in a paragraph or in your essay as a whole:

- **Deductive method:** Start big—with a topic sentence or a generalization—and then do the small stuff. Develop your topic sentence or generalization with specific supporting details.
- **Inductive method:** Start small—with details or a story or an anecdote—and then pull all your details together with a topic sentence or generalization at the end.
- **Chronological order:** If you're telling about a sequence of events (the history of the Montgomery bus boycott, for instance, or a sit-in protest that you witnessed), chronological order is the best way to organize your details.
- **Comparison and contrast:** If you want to compare two heroes (Gandhi and King, for example) or two legendary figures (such as King Arthur and Launcelot) or two of anything, this is the logical order to use.
- **Order of importance:** For emphasis, you might begin with the least important detail or point and end with the most important. Readers tend to remember best what they read last.

Try It Out

Think of several different ways to limit each broad topic. Then, make each of your limited topics even more limited.

EXAMPLE

Broad Topic: Women who do great things
↓
Limited Topic: Women who fight in wars
↓
More Limited: Women who fought in the Civil War

1. Scientists who have made major contributions to humanity
2. Unknown heroes who work quietly and without publicity
3. Ways society teaches young people
4. Influence of TV
5. Computers in modern life

Try It Out

Think of three different ways to begin your essay. Write these three different introductions, and ask several classmates to vote on the winner. Choose the introduction you like best or the one that seems to work best for your paper. Then try writing three different conclusions.

Sentence Workshop HELP

Revising sentence fragments: page 991.

Language/Grammar Link HELP

Parallel structure: page 915.
Word origins: page 971.
Appositives: page 980.

Drafting

Start by just writing. Turn your ideas into sentences and paragraphs, and keep going till your first draft is down on paper or in an electronic document. Only then should you go back and edit for content and organization.

1. The Introduction

Your introduction should usually be no more than one paragraph. An effective introduction

- grabs the audience's attention
- states the generalization or topic clearly
- makes the audience feel that the topic is important

Here are some ways to begin: with a definition, an anecdote, a quotation, an unusual piece of information, or a question.

2. The Body

The body of your paper will contain the supporting evidence you've researched, chosen, and arranged. Each paragraph should develop a major point, which may be stated in a topic sentence; all these points should relate to the generalization made at the beginning of the essay. Transitional words and phrases (*first, second, next*) help your readers follow the order of your ideas.

3. The Conclusion

Wind up your essay by summarizing and emphasizing your main idea. You might end with a personal observation, as the writer of the Student Model does in her final sentence.

Fox Trot.

Student Model

WOMEN IN THE CIVIL WAR

Women have accomplished many great things. One thing that makes me proud is their contribution to the American Civil War. Their participation in the war was a giant leap for women and society. Women had many important jobs during that stressful time, including cooking for the soldiers, nursing the wounded, spying, and fighting in the war effort.	*Generalization. Narrows her topic. Gives a reason. Four specific examples.*
One of the most important jobs women had was cooking for the soldiers. It was a dangerous job. Many of the camps where the soldiers stayed were close to the battlefields, and some camps were attacked. Despite the danger, women were dedicated to helping their brothers, husbands, sons, and fathers. Women were so desperate to see their loved ones that they risked their lives for them. Supplies were short, and women had to use what little provisions they got. Women worked in hard, stressful, unhealthy conditions. Cooking for the soldiers was important yet deadly.	*Topic sentence considers first example. Uses deductive order. Summarizes and emphasizes her main point.*
Nursing and caring for the wounded were difficult tasks. The women worked hard despite the conditions. Nurses were always in demand, and there was never enough room. The Civil War was the bloodiest war in American history; there was an infinite need for doctors and nurses. Nurses often carried out the roles of doctors as well. They had to help with surgery, give medications, and do other jobs doctors did. Nurses and doctors worked under terrible conditions, and they never had enough supplies.	*Second example begins new paragraph. Gives reasons. Concrete detail. Specific examples. Paragraph has a strong ending.*
Many women were brave enough to spy and fight in the war. Over four hundred women disguised themselves as men and fought in the Civil War. Francis Clalin, Kady Brownell, Eliza Wilson, Loreta Velazquez, Sarah Edmonds, Harriet Tubman, Rose O'Neal Greenhow, and Belle Boyd spied and fought. (Women spies were able to decode enemy messages much faster than the men.) The women who served got little recognition, yet they helped to affect the outcome of the war. It has been stated that had the women not fought, the outcome of the American Civil War would have been different from what it was.	*Third topic sentence (and third major point). Includes facts—in particular, names that can be verified.*
Women had so many roles during our Civil War. Cooking, nursing, spying, and fighting in the Civil War were only a few of the roles they played. So many women dedicated their lives to helping the war effort. Those women make me proud.	*Summarizes, restates main points. Repeats some words the writer started with. A strong ending.*

—Laren Cuprill
Manhasset High School
Manhasset, New York

■ ***Evaluation Criteria***

A good essay that supports a generalization

1. *states the generalization or topic clearly in the introduction*
2. *develops one major point in each paragraph of the body*
3. *relates all major points to the generalization or topic*
4. *contains specific details that support the major point of each paragraph*
5. *is arranged in an order that is easy to follow*
6. *restates the generalization in the conclusion*

Proofreading Tip

Use an index card to focus on one line at a time.

Communications Handbook HELP

See Proofreaders' Marks.

Publishing Tip

The Student Model in this workshop first appeared in a magazine of young people's writing. Find addresses for such magazines (print or on-line) and send your essay.

Evaluating and Revising

1. Peer Review

Exchange first drafts with a classmate or work in a small group to evaluate one another's papers. Using the Evaluation Criteria as a guide, let the writer know what you like about the work as well as where you think it can be improved.

2. Self-Evaluation

If you have time, put your paper aside for a day or so. Then, look at your work and the comments about it, and make whatever changes you think will improve your essay.

Revision Model

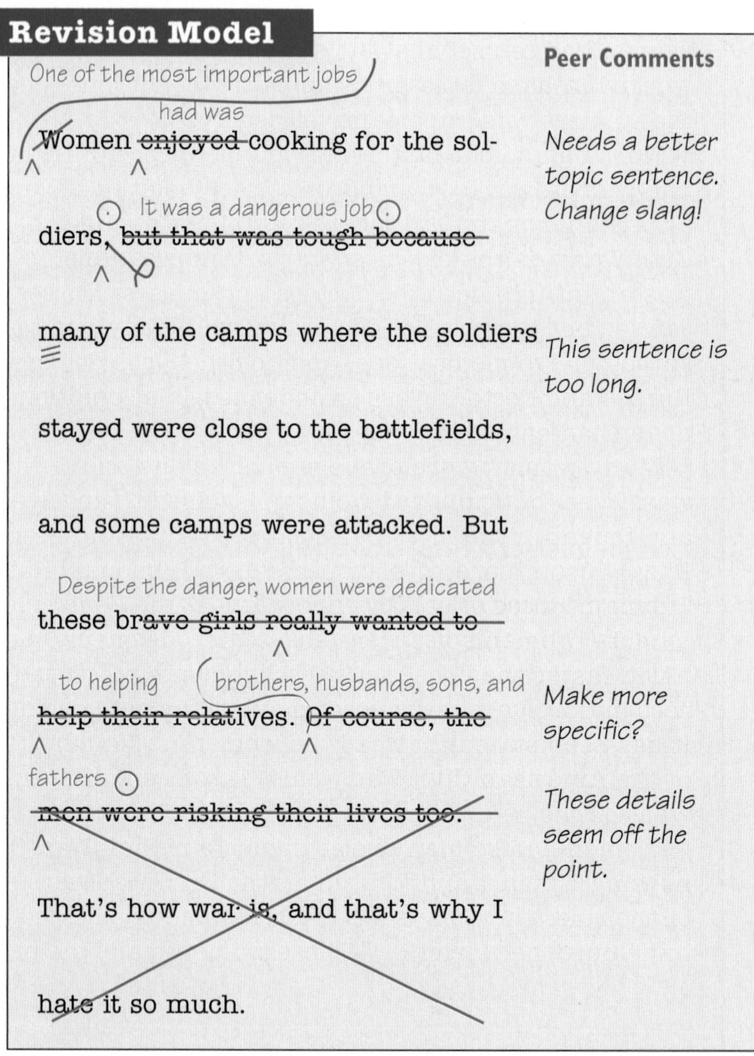

Peer Comments

One of the most important jobs / had was

Women ~~enjoyed~~ cooking for the soldiers, ~~but that was tough because~~ It was a dangerous job.

Needs a better topic sentence. Change slang!

many of the camps where the soldiers stayed were close to the battlefields, and some camps were attacked. But

This sentence is too long.

these br~~ave girls really wanted to~~ Despite the danger, women were dedicated ~~help their rela~~tives. to helping brothers, husbands, sons, and ~~Of course, the men were risking their lives too.~~ fathers.

Make more specific?

~~That's how war is, and that's why I hate it so much.~~

These details seem off the point.

BUILDING YOUR PORTFOLIO

Sentence Workshop

Revising Sentence Fragments

A **sentence fragment** is a piece of a sentence. A fragment looks like a sentence because it has a capital letter at the beginning and a period, question mark, or exclamation point at the end. A fragment is therefore difficult to spot.

To qualify as a complete sentence, a group of words must have both a subject and a verb and must also express a complete thought. A sentence satisfies *all three* of these requirements.

FRAGMENT	Rode to the tournament. [The subject is missing.]
SENTENCE	Arthur rode to the tournament.
FRAGMENT	The weapons from there. [The verb is missing.]
SENTENCE	The weapons came from there.
FRAGMENT	Whenever anyone entered the churchyard. [This fragment has a subject and a verb, but it does not express a complete thought because it is introduced by a subordinating conjunction, the word *whenever*.]
SENTENCE	Cheers went up whenever anyone entered the churchyard.

You should always avoid fragments when you write formal papers or answers to essay questions. Fiction or plays are another matter: There, sentence fragments are often used by professional writers for emphasis or to make dialogue more realistic.

Writer's Workshop Follow-up: Proofreading

When you revise your writing, look for sentence fragments masquerading as complete sentences. If you suspect that a group of words does *not* express a complete thought, see if it fulfills the three conditions listed above. In particular, watch for groups of words introduced by subordinating conjunctions—words like *after, because, before, if, unless, when.* Remember: When you write a formal paper, as a general rule, use only complete sentences.

Language Handbook HELP

See Sentence or Sentence Fragment, page 1038; Clauses, pages 1036-1037.

Technology HELP

See Language Workshop CD-ROM. *Key word entry: sentence fragments.*

Try It Out

Turn the following notes into sentences. Exchange your sentences with a partner to be sure you did not include any dread "frags."

> Mali founded by the Mandinka people. Also called the Malinke or Mandingo. Great empires long ago in West Africa—Mali, Songhai, and Ghana. Many of the people of Mali converted to Islam. In the eleventh century when Islamic armies conquered Mali.

Find a passage written by a professional writer that combines complete sentences with at least one fragment.

1. Copy the example you find, and circle every fragment.
2. Rewrite the passage, eliminating every fragment.
3. Write one sentence explaining why you think the writer used fragments.

Reading for Life

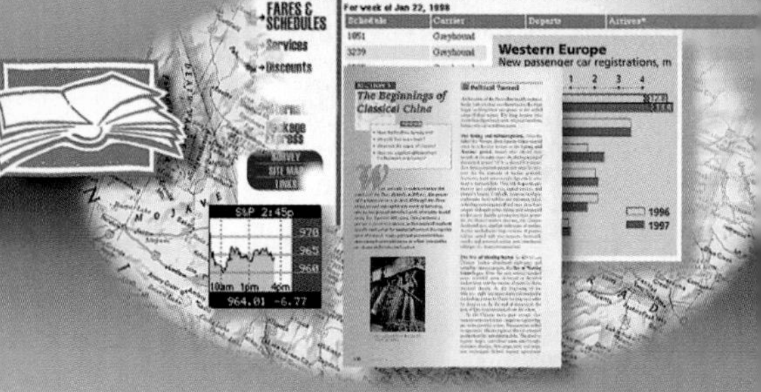

Comparing Movie or Play Reviews: Yours and the Pro's

Situation

Suppose you've recently seen the movie *The X-Files: Fight the Future,* and you are curious to know how a professional critic's review compares to your own responses. Part of a critic's review appears in the box.

Strategies

Be aware of the reviewer's criteria.

- Is the emphasis on subject matter, plot, characterization, or message? Is the focus on the acting, the directing, or special effects? Does the reviewer mention cinematography or stage design? What criteria matter to you?

Examine the support.

- Are statements of opinion backed up by strong reasons and relevant details from the work?
- Does the critic reveal bias?

Look for insights and oversights.

- Does the reviewer refer to other movies or plays to make his or her points? Are these references useful?
- Does the critic offer you any new insights into the work? If so, do they make you reconsider your opinion?
- Does the reviewer overlook any points you consider important?

Clarify or defend your views.

- If you could discuss your response to the movie or play with the critic, what would you say?

> ***The X-Files***
>
> **ROGER EBERT**
>
> As pure movie, *The X-Files* more or less works. As a story, it needs a sequel, a prequel, and Cliff Notes. I'm not sure even the filmmakers can explain exactly what happens in the movie, and why. It doesn't make much difference if you've seen every episode of the TV series, or none: The film is essentially self-contained, and that includes its enigmas. X-philes will probably be as puzzled at the end as an infrequent viewer like myself.
>
> Puzzled, but not dissatisfied. Like *Mission: Impossible*, this is a movie that depends on surface, on mystery, on atmosphere, on vague hints and murky warnings. Since the underlying plot is completely goofy, it's probably just as well it's not spelled out. . . . Instead, producer-writer Chris Carter, who conceived the TV series, reassembles his basic elements in a glossy extravaganza that ends, apparently, with humankind facing precisely the same danger it did at the beginning. . . .
>
> Much has been made of the fact that *The X-Files* is not so much a film based on a TV series as a continuation of that series in film form. The movie feeds out of last season and into next one. No final answers are therefore provided about anything; it's as if, at the end of *Casablanca*, the airplane circled around and landed again. But I liked the way the movie looked, and the unforced urgency of Mulder and Scully, and the way the plot was told through verbal puzzles and visual revelations, rather than through boring action scenes.
>
> And it was a relief to discover that the guys in the Black Helicopters are just as clueless as the rest of us.
>
> —*Chicago Sun Times*
>
> *©1998*

Using the Strategies

1. In his review of the movie *The X-Files,* what features does Roger Ebert focus on?
2. Does he support his opinions effectively? Explain your judgment.
3. Does he refer to other movies? If he does, are his references useful?
4. If you've seen the movie *The X-Files,* explain why you agree or disagree with Ebert's opinions.

Extending the Strategies

Find a review of a movie, TV show, or play you've seen recently, and use these strategies to compare your response with the critic's.

Learning for Life

Lessons for Our Time

Problem

Many of the wisdom and hero stories of traditional literature give us pointed, sometimes profound lessons about how to conduct our lives. How can traditional literature help us deal with contemporary problems?

Project

With a group, find pieces of traditional literature that seem to contain a lesson for our time. Update one of these pieces by retelling it in a modern setting and situation.

Preparation

1. Look over the selections in Collections 13 and 14. You might also explore legends, myths, and proverbs from various cultures; Aesop's fables; and fairy tales and folk tales. Choose four or five selections to update.
2. Discuss how you might draw an **analogy,** or comparison, between the selection and a modern situation. For example, a proverb advises, "Waste not, want not." What might that mean to a company buying computer equipment? What might it mean to people concerned about the environment?

Procedure

1. Brainstorm to gather a list of issues facing people today—issues that elicit strong opinions and different solutions.
2. Match at least three of the issues to an appropriate piece of traditional literature—one of the ones you've selected as having a lesson for our time.
3. Form small groups to plan an updated version of one of these selections, applying it to a modern situation or issue.

Presentation

Use one of the following formats (or another that your teacher approves):

1. The Play's the Thing

Develop a short play or skit with a modern setting. Remember to make the payoff, or moral, the climax of the skit. Consider presenting an evening of such skits, charging a small admission fee, and donating the profits to a charity or nonprofit organization.

2. Modern Mottoes

Create banners, bumper stickers, or posters that apply a piece of traditional literature to a modern issue—for example, "Just as it's a good idea not to count your chickens before they've hatched, it's a good idea not to . . ."

3. Tell It to the Kids

With at least one artist on your team, create a children's book or comic book that updates a proverb, fable, or hero tale. You could instead record a reading of your children's story. You might donate the finished books and tapes to a day-care center, an elementary school, or the children's ward of a hospital.

Processing

Discuss these questions with a group of classmates: What did you learn from doing this project? What was your favorite part? your least favorite? What do you think is the best way to preserve traditional literature and pass it on to our descendants?

RESOURCE CENTER

HANDBOOK OF LITERARY TERMS

For more information about a topic, turn to the page(s) in this book indicated on a separate line at the end of the entries. For example, to learn more about *Alliteration,* turn to pages 305 and 589.

On another line are cross-references to entries in this handbook that provide closely related information. For instance, at the end of *Alliteration* are cross-references to *Assonance* and *Rhythm.*

ALLITERATION **Repetition of the same or similar consonant sounds in words that are close together.** Although alliteration most often consists of sounds that begin words, it may also involve sounds that occur within words:

> Where the quail is whistling betwixt the
> woods
> and the wheat-lot.
>
> —Walt Whitman, from "Song of Myself"

See pages 305, 589.
See also *Assonance, Rhythm.*

ALLUSION **Reference to a statement, person, place, event, or thing that is known from literature, history, religion, myth, politics, sports, science, or the arts.** Can you identify the literary allusion in the following cartoon? If not, turn to page 823.

See page 128.

"Et tu, Baxter?"

ANACHRONISM (ə·nak′rə·niz′əm) **Event or detail that is inappropriate for the time period.** For example, the chiming clock in *Julius Caesar* (Act II, Scene 1) is an anachronism—they had not yet been invented.

See page 861.

ANALOGY **Comparison made between two things to show how they are alike.** In "The Man in the Water" (page 471), the writer draws an analogy between a man's struggle to stay alive in freezing water and a battle against "an implacable, impersonal enemy."

See also *Metaphor, Simile.*

ANECDOTE **Very brief account of a particular incident.** Like **parables,** anecdotes are often used by philosophers and teachers of religion to point out truths about life.

See pages 354, 924.
See also *Fable, Folk Tale, Parable.*

ASIDE **In a play, words spoken by a character directly to the audience or to another character but not overheard by others onstage.** In Act II, Scene 4 (page 815) of *Julius Caesar,* Trebonius and Brutus speak ominous asides that Caesar cannot hear.

See page 815.

ASSONANCE **Repetition of similar vowel sounds followed by different consonant sounds in words that are close together.** Like alliteration, assonance creates musical and rhythmic effects:

> And so all the night-tide, I lie down by the side,
> Of my darling, my darling, my life and my bride
>
> —Edgar Allan Poe, from "Annabel Lee"

See also *Alliteration, Rhythm.*

ATMOSPHERE **Mood or feeling in a work of literature (also called *mood*).** Atmosphere is usually created through descriptive details and evocative language. In "The Pit and the Pendulum" (page 289), Edgar Allan Poe creates a dizzying atmosphere of horror.

See pages 50, 172.
See also *Setting.*

AUTHOR **The writer of a literary work.** Authors may speak in their own voice, as they do in an **autobiography** or **essay,** or convey their ideas about life and people through fiction. The **speaker** in a poem may be the author or a fictional character.

See also *Autobiography, Speaker.*

AUTOBIOGRAPHY **An account by a writer of his or her own life.** "Hair" (page 345) is a selection from a famous autobiography by Malcolm X. "By Any Other Name" by Santha Rama Rau (page 321) and "Lessons of Love" by Judith Ortiz Cofer (page 158) are examples of short autobiographical essays.

See pages 343, 353.
See also *Biography.*

BALLAD **Song or song-like poem that tells a story.** Ballads often tell stories that have tragic endings. Most ballads have a regular pattern of **rhythm** and **rhyme** and use simple language and repetition. Generally they have a **refrain**—lines or words repeated at regular intervals. **Folk ballads** (such as "Bonny Barbara Allan" on page 565) were composed by unknown singers and passed on orally for generations before being written down. **Literary ballads** and some country-and-western songs imitate folk ballads.

See page 564.

BIOGRAPHY **An account of a person's life written or told by another person.** A classic American biography is Carl Sandburg's multi-volume work about Abraham Lincoln. Today, biographies of writers, actors, sports stars, and TV personalities are often best-sellers.

See also *Autobiography.*

BLANK VERSE **Poetry written in unrhymed iambic pentameter.** *Blank verse* means that the poetry is unrhymed. *Iambic pentameter* means that each line contains five iambs; an **iamb** is a type of **metrical foot** that consists of an unstressed syllable followed by a stressed syllable (˘ ʹ). Blank verse is the most important metrical form in English dramatic and epic poetry and the major verse line in Shakespeare's plays. One reason blank verse has been popular, even with some modern poets, is that it combines the naturalness of unrhymed verse and the structure of metrical verse.

> When I see birches bend to left and right
> Across the line of straighter darker trees,
> I like to think some boy's been swinging them.
>
> —Robert Frost, from "Birches"

See page 771.
See also *Iambic Pentameter, Meter.*

CHARACTER **Individual in a story, poem, or play.** A character always has human traits, even if the character is an animal, as in Aesop's fables or James Thurber's "The Scotty Who Knew Too Much" (page 944). In myths, the characters are divinities or heroes with superhuman powers, such as the hero Sundiata in *Sundiata* (page 973). Most characters are ordinary human beings, however.

A writer can reveal a character's personality by

1. telling us directly what the character is like (generous, deceitful, timid, and so on)
2. describing how the character looks and dresses
3. letting us hear the character speak
4. letting us listen to the character's inner thoughts and feelings
5. revealing what other people think or say about the character
6. showing the character's actions

The first method listed above is called **direct characterization:** The writer tells us directly what the character is like. The other five methods are **indirect characterization**. We have to put clues together to figure out what a character is like, just as we do in real life when we are getting to know someone.

A **static character** does not change much in the course of a story. A **dynamic character,** on the other hand, changes in some important ways as a result of the story's action. **Flat characters** have only one or two personality traits and can be summed up in a single phrase. In contrast, **round characters** are complex and have many different traits.

See pages 51, 110–111, 119, 132, 196, 631.
See also *Protagonist.*

COMEDY In general, a story that ends happily. The hero or heroine of a comedy is usually an ordinary character who overcomes a series of obstacles that block what he or she wants. Many comedies have a boy-meets-girl (or girl-meets-boy) plot, in which young lovers must face figures from the older generation who do not want them to marry. At the end of such comedies, the lovers marry, and everyone celebrates the renewal of life and love, as in Shakespeare's play *A Midsummer Night's Dream*. In structure and characterization a comedy is the opposite of a **tragedy.**

In a serious literary work, a humorous scene is said to provide **comic relief.**

See pages 365, 743.
See also *Tragedy.*

CONFLICT Struggle or clash between opposing characters, forces, or emotions. In an **external conflict,** a character struggles against an outside force, which may be another character, society as a whole, or something in nature. In "Trap of Gold" (page 249), Wetherton struggles against a huge mass of rock that threatens to collapse and bury him.

An **internal conflict** is a struggle between opposing needs, desires, or emotions within a single character. Jing-mei in Amy Tan's "Two Kinds" (page 95) struggles between her desire to please her mother and her need to be herself. Many works, especially longer ones, contain both internal and external conflicts, and an external conflict often leads to internal problems.

See pages 32–33, 34, 69, 630–633.

CONNOTATIONS All the meanings, associations, or emotions that a word suggests. For example, an expensive restaurant might advertise its delicious "cuisine" rather than its delicious "cooking." *Cuisine* and *cooking* have the same **denotation** (literal meaning): "prepared food." However, *cuisine,* a word from French, has connotations of elegance and sophistication; *cooking,* a plain English word, suggests the plainness of everyday food.

See pages 68, 181, 467, 520.
See also *Diction, Tone.*

COUPLET Two consecutive lines of poetry that form a unit, often emphasized by rhythm or rhyme. Since the Middle Ages the couplet has been used to express a completed thought or to provide a sense of closure, as in this final speech from Shakespeare's play *Julius Caesar:*

> So call the field to rest, and let's away,
> To part the glories of this happy day.

See page 560.

DESCRIPTION Type of writing intended to create a mood or an emotion or to re-create a person, a place, a thing, an event, or an experience. Description uses **images** that appeal to the senses, helping us imagine how a subject looks, sounds, smells, tastes, or feels. Description is used in fiction, nonfiction, drama, and poetry.

See also *Imagery.*

DIALECT Way of speaking that is characteristic of a particular region or group of people. A dialect may have a distinct vocabulary, pronunciation system, and grammar. In the United States the dialect used in formal writing and spoken by most TV and radio announcers is known as standard English. This is the dialect taught in schools, and you'll find its rules in the handbook that begins on page 1021. To bring characters to life, writers often use dialects.

See pages 131, 971.

DIALOGUE Conversation between two or more characters. Dramas are made up of dialogue, which is also important in novels and stories and in some poems and nonfiction.

See page 109.

DICTION Writer's or speaker's choice of words. Diction is an essential element of a writer's **style**. A writer can choose words that are simple or flowery (*clothing/apparel*), modern or old-fashioned (*dress/frock*), general or specific (*pants/designer jeans*). Writers choose words for their connotations (emotional associations) as well as their literal meanings, or denotations.

See pages 80, 112.
See also *Connotations, Tone.*

DIDACTIC LITERATURE Writing that aims primarily to teach. Sacred texts (such as the Bible and the Koran) of the major world religions contain didactic literature. Other types of didactic literature include brief wise sayings, called aphorisms or maxims, and anecdotes, fables, parables, and folk tales.

See page 924.
See also *Anecdote, Fable, Folk Tale, Parable.*

DRAMA Story that is written to be acted for an audience. The action of a drama is driven by a character who wants something and who takes steps to get it. The major elements of a dramatic plot are **exposition, complications, climax,** and **resolution**.

See pages 628–629, 630–634, 685–687, 765–768.

EPIC Long narrative poem that relates the great deeds of a larger-than-life hero who embodies the values of a particular society. Most epics include elements of myth, legend, folklore, and history; their tone is serious and their language grand. Epic heroes undertake quests to achieve something of tremendous value to themselves or their society. Homer's *Odyssey* and *Iliad* and Virgil's *Aeneid* are the best-known epics in the Western tradition. The great epic of India is *The Mahabharata;* Japan's is *The Tale of the Heike;* and Mali's is *Sundiata* (page 973).

See page 972.

ESSAY Short piece of nonfiction that examines a single subject from a limited point of view. Most essays can be classified as personal or formal. A **personal essay** (sometimes called **informal**) is generally subjective, revealing a great deal about the writer's personality and feelings. Its tone is conversational, sometimes even humorous.

A **formal essay** is usually serious, objective, and impersonal in tone. Because formal essays are often written to inform or persuade, they are expected to be factual, logical, and tightly organized.

See pages 409, 416–417, 470, 479.

EXPOSITION Type of writing that explains, gives information, or clarifies an idea. Exposition is generally objective and formal in tone (as in a magazine article on nutrition).

Exposition is also the term for the first part of a plot (also called the **basic situation**), which presents the main characters and their conflicts.

See page 408.
See also *Plot.*

FABLE Brief story in prose or verse that teaches a moral, or a practical lesson about life. The characters of most fables are animals that behave and speak like humans. Some of the most popular fables are those attributed to Aesop, who was supposed to have been a slave in ancient Greece. Other widely read fables are those in the *Panchatantra* (page 941), ancient Indian tales about the art of ruling wisely.

See page 924.
See also *Anecdote, Folk Tale, Parable.*

FIGURE OF SPEECH Word or phrase that describes one thing in terms of another and that is not meant to be understood on a literal level. Figures of speech, or **figurative language,** always involve some sort of imaginative comparison between seemingly unlike things. The most common are the **simile** ("My heart is like a singing bird"), the **metaphor** ("Life's but a walking shadow"), and **personification** ("Death has reared himself a throne").

See pages 307, 506–507, 512, 515.
See also *Metaphor, Personification, Simile, Symbol.*

FLASHBACK Scene in a movie, play, short story, novel, or narrative poem that interrupts the present action of the plot to show events

that happened at an earlier time. The story "The Bet" (page 210) opens with a long flashback to a party held fifteen years before the story's present action.

FOIL Character who serves as a contrast to another character. Writers use a foil to emphasize differences between two characters. In *Julius Caesar,* the solemn, self-controlled Octavius is a foil for the excitable, impetuous Antony.

FOLK TALE Anonymous traditional story originally passed down orally from generation to generation. Folk tales are told in every culture, and similar tales are told throughout the world. Many of these stories have been written down—sometimes retold in a literary way and sometimes recorded in the words of oral storytellers. Scholars draw a sharp distinction between folk tales and myths. **Myths,** unlike folk tales, are stories about humans and gods and are basically religious in nature. Examples of folk tales are fairy tales, fables, legends, ghost stories, tall tales, anecdotes, and even jokes. Folk tales tend to travel, so you'll often find the same plot surfacing in several cultures. For example, there are said to be nine hundred versions of the folk tale about Cinderella.

See also *Anecdote, Fable, Myth, Tall Tale.*

FORESHADOWING The use of clues to hint at events that will occur later in the plot. Foreshadowing arouses the reader's curiosity and increases **suspense**. In Act I of *Julius Caesar* (page 777), references to violent disturbances in the heavens foreshadow the turbulence and violence that will soon occur in the human world.

See pages 146, 630.
See also *Plot, Suspense.*

FREE VERSE Poetry that does not have a regular meter or rhyme scheme. Poets writing in free verse try to capture the natural rhythms of ordinary speech. To create musical effects, they may use **alliteration, assonance, internal rhyme,** and **onomatopoeia**. They also often repeat words or grammatical structures.

> Women sit or move to and fro, some old,
> some young,
> The young are beautiful—but the old are
> more beautiful than the young.
>
> —Walt Whitman, "Beautiful Women"

See pages 558–559, 607.
See also *Alliteration, Assonance, Meter, Onomatopoeia, Rhythm.*

HAIKU Japanese verse form consisting of three lines and usually seventeen syllables (five in the first line, seven in the second, and five in the third). The writer of a haiku uses association and suggestion to describe a particular moment of discovery or enlightenment. A haiku often presents an image of daily life that relates to a particular season. Many modern American poets (such as William Carlos Williams, Amy Lowell, Ezra Pound, Richard Wright, and Gary Snyder) have tried to capture the spirit of haiku, though they have not always followed the form strictly.

See page 939.

HYPERBOLE Figure of speech that uses exaggeration to express strong emotion or create a comic effect. Writers often use hyperbole (hī·pʉr′bə·lē), also called **overstatement,** to intensify a description or to emphasize the essential nature of something. If you say that a limousine is as long as an ocean liner, you are using hyperbole.

IAMBIC PENTAMETER Line of poetry made up of five iambs. An **iamb** is a metrical foot consisting of an unstressed syllable followed by a stressed syllable, as in *dĕný* and *ĕxpéct.*

See pages 592, 771.
See also *Blank Verse, Meter.*

IDIOM Expression peculiar to a particular language that means something different from the literal meaning of the words. "It's raining cats and dogs" and "We heard it straight from the horse's mouth" are idioms of American English. One of the difficulties of translating a work from another language is translating idioms.

See page 534.

IMAGERY Language that appeals to the senses. Imagery is used in all types of writing but is especially important in poetry. Most images are visual—that is, they create in the reader's mind pictures that appeal to the sense of sight. Imagery may also appeal to the senses of sound, smell, touch, and taste, as in the following lines about winter. (*Saw* in line 2 is a wise saying; *crabs* in line 5 are crab apples; and to *keel* is to cool by stirring.)

When all aloud the wind doth blow,
  And coughing drowns the parson's saw,
And birds sit brooding in the snow,
  And Marian's nose looks red and raw,
When roasted crabs hiss in the bowl,
Then nightly sings the staring owl—Tu whit,
Tu-who, a merry note,
While greasy Joan doth keel the pot.

—William Shakespeare,
from *Love's Labor's Lost*

See pages 42, 208, 234, 418, 430, 548–549.

INVERSION Reversal of normal word order in a sentence. The normal word order in an English sentence is subject-verb-complement (if there is a complement). Modifiers are usually placed immediately before or after the word they modify. Poets use inversion to give emphasis and variety and to create rhymes or accommodate a meter.

Open here I flung the shutter, when, with
  many a flirt and flutter,
In there stepped a stately Raven of the
  saintly days of yore;
Not the least obeisance made he; not a
  minute stopped or stayed he. . . .

—Edgar Allan Poe, from "The Raven"

See pages 275, 563.

IRONY Contrast or discrepancy between expectation and reality. In **verbal irony** a speaker says one thing but means the opposite. In Shakespeare's *Julius Caesar,* Antony uses verbal irony during his funeral oration for Caesar. When he insists that "Brutus is an honorable man," he means precisely the opposite.

In **situational irony** what actually happens is the opposite of what is expected or appropriate. In Tim O'Brien's story "Where Have You Gone, Charming Billy?" (page 197), we feel a strong sense of irony when Paul Berlin is overcome with laughter upon being told of the death of his fellow soldier, Billy Boy Watkins.

Dramatic irony occurs when the reader or the audience knows something important that a character does not know. In "The Cold Equations" by Tom Godwin (page 9), when Marilyn mischievously asks what her punishment will be, she expects simply to be fined; we know that her fate will be much graver.

See pages 194–195, 389, 456.
See also *Tone.*

LYRIC POETRY Poetry that expresses a speaker's emotions or thoughts and does not tell a story. The term *lyric* comes from ancient Greece, where such poems were recited to the accompaniment of a stringed instrument called a lyre. Most lyric poems are short, and they imply, rather than state directly, a single strong emotion. A. E. Housman's "Loveliest of Trees" (page 520) and John Masefield's "Sea Fever" (page 591) are lyric poems.

See page 550.
See also *Sonnet.*

MAGIC REALISM Style of fiction, commonly associated with contemporary Latin American writers, in which fantasy and reality are casually combined, producing humorous and thought-provoking results. "A Very Old Man with Enormous Wings" (page 223), in which an old, winged, humanlike creature lands in a poor family's backyard, is an example of magic realism.

See page 222.

METAPHOR Figure of speech that makes a comparison between two unlike things without using a connective word such as *like, as, than,* or *resembles.* Some metaphors, such as Gerard Manley Hopkins's comparison "I am soft sift / In an hourglass," are **direct**. (If he had written, "I am *like* soft sift . . . ," he would have been using a **simile**.) Other metaphors are

implied, such as the one in Walt Whitman's lines "O Captain! my Captain! our fearful trip is done, / The ship has weather'd every rack, the prize we sought is won." The images imply a comparison between a captain commanding his ship and a president leading his country (in this case, the president was Lincoln).

An **extended metaphor** is developed over several lines or throughout an entire poem. Langston Hughes uses an extended metaphor comparing life to a stairway in his poem "Mother to Son" (page 508).

A **mixed metaphor** is the inconsistent combination of two or more metaphors. Mixed metaphors are usually unintentional and often humorous: "It's no use closing the barn door after the milk has been spilled."

See pages 507, 508, 552.
See also *Analogy, Figure of Speech, Personification, Simile, Symbol.*

METER A generally regular pattern of stressed and unstressed syllables in poetry. To indicate the metrical pattern of a poem, we mark the stressed syllables with the symbol (′) and the unstressed syllables with the symbol (˘). Analyzing the metrical pattern of a poem in this way is called **scanning** the poem, or **scansion** (skan′shən).

Meter is measured in units called feet. A **foot** usually consists of one stressed syllable and one or more unstressed syllables. Here are examples of the standard feet in English poetry:

1. **iamb** (iambic): an unstressed syllable followed by a stressed syllable, as in *fŏrgét, dĕcéive.* This line from "The Eagle" by Alfred, Lord Tennyson, has four iambic feet:

   ˘ ′ ˘ ′ ˘ ′ ˘ ′
   The wrinkled sea beneath him crawls

2. **trochee** (trochaic): a stressed syllable followed by an unstressed syllable, as in *lístĕn, lónelÿ.* This line from William Shakespeare's *Macbeth* is in trochees:

   ′ ˘ ′ ˘ ′ ˘ ′ ˘
   Double, double, toil and trouble

3. **anapest** (anapestic): two unstressed syllables followed by one stressed syllable, as in *ŭndĕrstánd, lŭnchĕonétte.* This line from "The Destruction of Sennacherib" by George Gordon, Lord Byron, is in anapests:

   ˘ ˘ ′ ˘ ˘ ′ ˘ ˘ ′ ˘ ˘ ′
   The Assyrian came down like the wolf on the fold

4. **dactyl** (dactylic): One stressed syllable followed by two unstressed syllables, as in *éxcĕllĕnt, témpĕrăte.* This extract from Shakespeare's *Macbeth* contains dactyls:

   ˘ ′ ˘ ˘ ′ ˘ ˘
   . . . you murdering ministers . . .

5. **spondee** (spondaic): Two stressed syllables, as in *héartbéat* and *fóotbáll.* This foot is used for emphasis, as in these lines from *Leaves of Grass* by Walt Whitman:

   ˘ ′ ˘ ′ ′
   Come up here, bard, bard,
   ˘ ′ ˘ ′ ′
   Come up here, soul, soul. . . .

A metrical line is named for the type of foot and the number of feet in the line. (*Dimeter* is two feet, *trimeter* three feet, *tetrameter* four feet, and *pentameter* five feet.) Thus a line of five iambs is called *iambic pentameter;* a line of four trochees is *trochaic tetrameter.*

See pages 558–559, 564, 590.
See also *Blank Verse, Iambic Pentameter.*

MOOD *See* Atmosphere.

MYTH Traditional story that is rooted in a particular culture, is basically religious, and usually serves to explain a belief, a ritual, or a mysterious natural phenomenon. Most myths grew out of religious rituals; almost all of them involve the influence of gods on human affairs. Every culture has its own mythology. For centuries the myths of ancient Greece and Rome were influential in the Western world.

See pages 687, 688–689.

NARRATION Type of writing that tells about a series of related events. Narration can be long (an entire book) or short (a brief anecdote). Narration is most often found in fiction, drama, and narrative poetry (such as epics and ballads), but it also is used in nonfiction works (such as biographies and essays).

See page 408.

NONFICTION Prose writing that deals with real people, things, events, and places. The most popular forms are biography and autobiography.

Essays, newspaper stories, magazine articles, historical accounts, scientific reports, and even personal diaries and letters are also nonfiction.

See pages 338, 339, 353, 416–417.

NOVEL Long fictional prose narrative, usually of more than fifty thousand words. In general, the novel uses the same basic literary elements as the short story **(plot, character, setting, theme,** and **point of view)**, but these elements are usually more fully developed in the novel. Many novels have several subplots, for instance. Some modern novels are basically character studies, with only the barest plot. Others concentrate on setting, tone, or even language itself.

ONOMATOPOEIA (än′ō·mat′ō·pē′ə) **Use of a word whose sound imitates or suggests its meaning.** *Buzz, splash,* and *bark* are examples of onomatopoeia. In poetry, onomatopoeia reinforces meaning and creates evocative and musical sound effects.

See page 589.

PARABLE Brief story that teaches a lesson about life. A parable has human characters, and its events are drawn from the stuff of everyday life. Parables usually illustrate moral or religious lessons. A fable, in contrast, usually has animal characters and teaches a practical lesson about how to succeed in life.

See pages 916, 924.
See also *Anecdote, Fable, Folk Tale.*

PARADOX A statement or a situation that seems to be a contradiction but that reveals a truth. Paradoxes are designed to make readers stop and think. They often express aspects of life that are mysterious, surprising, or difficult to describe. Jorge Luis Borges is noted for his use of paradoxes, as in "The Book of Sand" (page 44).

See page 931.

PARALLELISM Repetition of words, phrases, or sentences that have the same grammatical structure or that state a similar idea. Parallelism, or **parallel structure,** helps make lines rhythmic and memorable and heightens their emotional effect:

> Bring me my bow of burning gold!
> Bring me my arrows of desire!
> Bring me my spear! O clouds, unfold!
> Bring me my chariot of fire!
>
> —William Blake, from "Jerusalem"

See pages 909, 915.

PARODY Imitation of a work of literature, art, or music for amusement or satirical purposes. Parodies often use exaggeration or inappropriate subject matter to make a serious work seem ridiculous. "Mending Test" by Penelope Bryant Turk (page 528) is a parody of Robert Frost's "Mending Wall" (page 526).

PERSONIFICATION Type of metaphor in which a nonhuman thing or quality is talked about as if it were human. In the example below, trees are personified as women throwing off their robes.

> The trees are undressing, and fling in many places—
> On the gray road, the roof, the window sill—
> Their radiant robes and ribbons and yellow laces.
>
> —Thomas Hardy, from "Last Week in October"

See pages 507, 568.
See also *Figure of Speech, Metaphor.*

PERSUASION Type of writing designed to change the way a reader or listener thinks or acts. Persuasive writing can be found in speeches, newspaper editorials, essays, articles, and advertisements. Persuasion uses language that appeals to reason, to the emotions, or to both.

See pages 455, 467, 468–469.

PLOT Series of related events that make up a story or drama. Plot is "what happens" in a story, novel, or play. A story map (see next page) shows the bare bones of a story's plot.

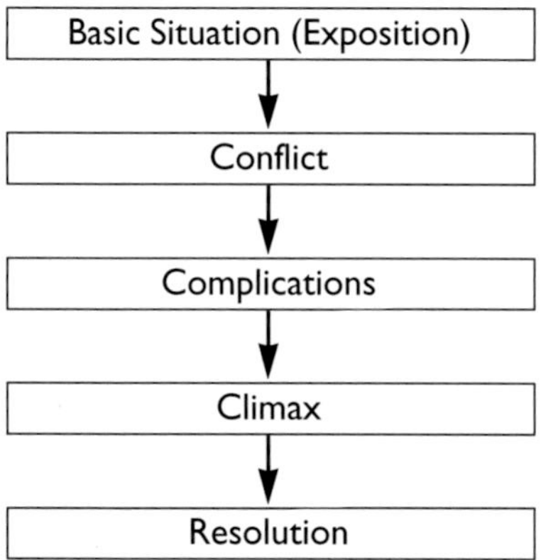

The **climax** is the most intense moment in the plot, the moment at which something happens that reveals how the conflict will turn out. In the **resolution,** or denouement (dā'nōō·män'), all the problems in the story are resolved, and the story is brought to a close.

See pages 32–33, 52.

POETRY **Type of rhythmic, compressed language that uses figures of speech and imagery to appeal to the reader's emotions and imagination.** The major forms of poetry are the **lyric,** the **epic,** and the **ballad.** Though poetry is one of the oldest forms of human expression, it is extremely difficult to define. Here is how Gary Snyder, a contemporary American poet, "defines" poetry:

> There's a freedom of mind, imagination, language, spirit that is granted you in poetry. It's the singing voice. It's the dancing body that is not in prose.

See pages 502, 503, 506–507, 558–559, 588–589.
See also *Ballad, Epic, Lyric Poetry.*

POINT OF VIEW **Vantage point from which a writer tells a story.** The three main points of view are omniscient, third-person limited, and first-person.

In the **omniscient** (or "all-knowing") **point of view,** the narrator plays no part in the story but can tell us what all the characters are thinking and feeling as well as what is happening in other places. For example, in "Through the Tunnel" (page 277), the storyteller can tell us what both Jerry and his mother are thinking and feeling.

In the **third-person limited point of view,** the narrator, who plays no part in the story, zooms in on the thoughts and feelings of one character. In "The Cold Equations" by Tom Godwin (page 9), we know the pilot's thoughts and feelings, but the emotions of the young stowaway are revealed only through her words and the pilot's observations.

In the **first-person point of view,** the narrator (using the first-person pronoun *I*) is a character in the story. When we read a story told in the first person, we hear and see only what the narrator hears and sees. We may have to interpret what the narrator says, because a first-person narrator may or may not be objective, honest, or perceptive. Alice Munro's "Boys and Girls" (page 53) is told from the first-person point of view of a girl just entering adolescence. She reveals her own turbulent thoughts and feelings, but we see the other characters in the story only through her eyes.

See pages 262–263, 264, 276, 308.

PROTAGONIST **Main character in fiction or drama.** The protagonist is the character we focus our attention on, the person who sets the plot in motion. The character or force that blocks the protagonist is called the **antagonist**. Most protagonists are rounded, dynamic characters who change in some important way by the end of the story, novel, or play. The antagonist is often, but not always, the villain in a story. Similarly, the protagonist is often, but not always, the hero.

See page 119.
See also *Character.*

PUN **Play on the multiple meanings of a word or on two words that sound alike but have different meanings.** Many jokes and riddles are based on puns. ("When is a doctor most annoyed?" Answer: "When he runs out of patients.") Shakespeare was one of the greatest punsters of all time. In Antony's speech to the conspirators after Caesar's murder in Act III (page 826), Antony puns on the expression "to let blood." Doctors used to draw, or let, blood from sick people to cure them; murderers also "let blood."

See page 797.

REFRAIN **Repeated word, phrase, line, or group of lines.** Though refrains are usually associated with poetry and songs, they are sometimes used in prose, especially in speeches. Refrains create rhythm and may also build suspense or emphasize important words or ideas.

See page 564.

RHYME **Repetition of accented vowel sounds and all sounds following them in words that are close together in a poem.** *Heart* and *start* rhyme, as do *plaster* and *faster.* The most common type of rhyme, **end rhyme,** occurs at the ends of lines.

> When she I loved looked every day
> Fresh as a rose in June,
> I to her cottage bent my way,
> Beneath the evening moon.
>
> —William Wordsworth,
> from "Strange Fits of Passion Have I Known"

The pattern of rhymed lines in a poem is called its **rhyme scheme**. You indicate a rhyme scheme by giving each new end rhyme a new letter of the alphabet. For example, the rhyme scheme in Wordsworth's stanza is *abab.*

Internal rhymes occur within lines.

> The warm sun is failing, the bleak wind is
> wailing,
> The bare boughs are sighing, the pale flowers
> are dying . . .
>
> —Percy Bysshe Shelley,
> from "Autumn: A Dirge"

Words that sound similar but do not rhyme exactly are called **approximate rhymes** (or **half rhymes, slant rhymes,** or **imperfect rhymes**). The approximate rhymes at the ends of lines in this stanza from a poem about war keep the reader off balance and even uneasy, in keeping with the poem's subject:

> Let the boy try along this bayonet blade
> How cold steel is, and keen with hunger of
> blood;
> Blue with all malice, like a madman's flash;
> And thinly drawn with famishing for flesh.
>
> —Wilfred Owen, from "Arms and the Boy"

See pages 588–589, 598.

RHYTHM **Musical quality in language, produced by repetition.** Rhythm occurs naturally in all forms of spoken and written language. Poems written in **meter** create rhythm by a strict pattern of stressed and unstressed syllables. Writers can also create rhythm by repeating grammatical structures, by using pauses, by varying line lengths, and by balancing long and short words or phrases.

See pages 305, 558–559.
See also *Alliteration, Assonance, Meter.*

ROMANCE **Centuries ago, in France and England, a romance was a verse narrative about the adventures of a hero who undertakes a quest for a high ideal.** The tales of King Arthur are typical romances. The term *romance* later came to mean any story set in a world of wish fulfillment, with larger-than-life characters having superhuman powers. Romances usually involve a series of adventures that end with good triumphing over evil. Fairy tales and western movies are often built on the old romance plots and use the characters typical of romance literature. Movies like *Star Wars* also owe something to the plots and characters of the old romances.

See page 955.

SATIRE **Type of writing that ridicules human weakness, vice, or folly in order to bring about social reform.** Satires often try to persuade the reader to do or believe something by showing the opposite view as absurd—or even as vicious and inhumane. One of the favorite techniques of the satirist is **exaggeration**—overstating something to make it look worse than it is.

See pages 195, 456.
See also *Hyperbole, Irony.*

SETTING **Time and place of a story or play.** Setting can function in several ways in a story. It can provide atmosphere, as the repellent pit setting does in Edgar Allan Poe's "The Pit and the Pendulum" (page 289). Setting may provide conflict in a story, as it does in Tim O'Brien's "Where Have You Gone, Charming Billy?" (page 197). One of the most important functions of setting is to reveal character. In Alice Walker's

"Everyday Use" (page 70), the narrator's home helps show us who she is and what her life is like.

See pages 50–51, 172, 248.
See also *Atmosphere.*

SHORT STORY Short piece of narrative fiction. Edgar Allan Poe (see page 302), who lived and wrote during the first half of the nineteenth century, is often credited with writing the first short stories. He defined the short story (which he called the "prose tale") as a narrative that can be read in a single sitting and that creates a "single effect."

See pages 2, 3.

SIMILE Figure of speech that makes a comparison between two seemingly unlike things by using a connective word such as *like, as, than,* or *resembles.* Here is a simile that creates a dramatic visual image; like any good figure of speech, Hardy's simile is original and vivid:

> The Roman Road runs straight and bare
> As the pale parting-line in hair
>
> —Thomas Hardy, from "The Roman Road"

See pages 506–507.
See also *Analogy, Figure of Speech, Metaphor.*

SOLILOQUY Long speech in which a character who is alone on stage expresses private thoughts or feelings. The soliloquy (sə·lil′ə·kwē), especially popular in Shakespeare's day, is an old dramatic convention. Near the beginning of Act II in *Julius Caesar* (page 799), Brutus's speech in which he decides to join the conspiracy against Caesar is a soliloquy.

See page 799.

SONNET Fourteen-line lyric poem, usually written in iambic pentameter. There are two major types of sonnets. The **Italian sonnet,** also called the **Petrarchan sonnet,** is named after the fourteenth-century Italian poet Francesco Petrarch, who popularized the form. The Petrarchan sonnet has two parts: an eight-line **octave** with the rhyme scheme *abbaabba,* and a six-line **sestet** with the rhyme scheme *cdecde.* The octave usually presents a problem, poses a question, or expresses an idea, which the sestet then resolves, answers, or drives home. A modern variation on the Italian sonnet, by E. E. Cummings, can be found on page 552. Like many sonnets, Cummings's poem is about love.

The other major sonnet form is called the **Shakespearean sonnet,** or the **English sonnet**. It has three **quatrains** (four-line units) followed by a concluding **couplet** (a two-line unit). The three quatrains often express related ideas or examples; the couplet sums up the poet's conclusion or message. The most common rhyme scheme for the Shakespearean sonnet is *abab cdcd efef gg.* A Shakespearean sonnet—also about love—can be found on page 561.

See page 560.
See also *Lyric Poetry.*

SPEAKER The voice that is talking to us in a poem. Sometimes the speaker is the same as the poet, but the poet may also create a different voice, speaking as a child, a woman, a man, a nation, an animal, or even an object.

See pages 522, 574.

STANZA Group of consecutive lines that form a single unit in a poem. A stanza in a poem is something like a paragraph in prose: It often expresses a unit of thought. A stanza may consist of only one line or of any number of lines beyond that. A. E. Housman's "Loveliest of Trees" (page 520) consists of three four-line stanzas, or **quatrains,** each expressing a unit of thought.

See also *Sonnet.*

SUSPENSE The uncertainty or anxiety we feel about what is going to happen next in a story. Writers often create suspense by dropping hints or clues foreshadowing something—especially something bad—that is going to happen later. In Louis L'Amour's "Trap of Gold" (page 249), details at the beginning of the story make us feel anxious and uncertain about Wetherton's fate. Will he stop digging in time, or will he be crushed?

See pages 8, 630–631.
See also *Foreshadowing, Plot.*

SYMBOL Person, place, thing, or event that stands both for itself and for something beyond itself. Many symbols have become so widely recognized that they are **public symbols:** In Western cultures, for example, most people recognize the heart as a symbol of love and the snake as a symbol of evil. Writers often invent new, personal symbols. For example, in this mysterious poem, "The Sick Rose," what might the rose and the worm symbolize?

O Rose, thou art sick!
The invisible worm,
That flies in the night,
In the howling storm,
Has found out thy bed
Of crimson joy:
And his dark secret love
Does thy life destroy.

—William Blake

See pages 288, 306–307, 515, 516.
See also *Figure of Speech.*

TALL TALE An outrageously exaggerated and obviously unbelievable humorous story. In pre-TV days, the tall tale was a kind of oral entertainment. In the Southwest, cowboys sat around their campfires telling stories about Pecos Bill, who invented the lariat, rode a bucking Kansas tornado, and dug the Rio Grande river. Other tall tale heroes include the Northwest logger Paul Bunyan (and Babe, his gigantic blue ox), the Pennsylvania steel man Joe Magarac, and the New England fisherman Captain Stormalong. Tall tales were told about real-life figures, too, such as Tennessee frontiersman Davy Crockett and sharpshooter Annie Oakley.

A modern **urban tall tale**—perennially rumored to be true—tells of a baby pet alligator someone flushed down a toilet in New York City. The result, according to this tale, is that monster alligators populate the sewers beneath the city.

See *Folk Tale.*

THEME The central idea or insight revealed by a work of literature. A theme is not the same as a work's subject, which can usually be expressed in a word or two: old age, ambition, love. The theme is the message the writer wishes us to discover *about* that subject. There is no single correct way to express a theme, and sometimes a work has several themes. Many works have ambiguous themes; that is, they have no clear single meaning but are open to a variety of interpretations, even opposing ones.

Although a few stories, poems, and plays have themes that are stated directly, most themes are implied. The reader must piece together all the clues the writer has provided to arrive at a discovery of the work's total meaning. Two of the most important clues to consider are the way the main character has changed and the way the conflict has been resolved.

See pages 182–183, 196, 209, 307, 526.

TONE The attitude a writer takes toward the reader, a subject, or a character. Tone is conveyed through the writer's choice of words and details. For example, Tim O'Brien's story "Where Have You Gone, Charming Billy?" (page 197) is ironic in tone. A. E. Housman's poem "Loveliest of Trees" (page 520) is tender and almost sad.

See pages 184, 344, 352, 530, 603.
See also *Connotations, Diction, Irony.*

TRAGEDY Play, novel, or other narrative, depicting serious and important events, in which the main character comes to an unhappy end. In a tragedy, the main character is usually dignified and courageous and often high ranking. This character's downfall may be caused by a **tragic flaw** (a serious character weakness) or by forces beyond the hero's control. The tragic hero usually wins self-knowledge and wisdom, even though he or she suffers defeat, possibly even death. Shakespeare's *The Tragedy of Julius Caesar* (page 775) and Sophocles' *Antigone* (page 691) are tragedies. Tragedy is distinct from **comedy,** in which an ordinary character overcomes obstacles to get what he or she wants. At the end of most comedies, the characters are all happily integrated into society (comedies often end with weddings). Tragedies often end with death or separation or alienation.

See pages 686, 739.

READING STRATEGIES

Whether you're looking for information or reading for pleasure, you can become a more effective reader by practicing the following six strategies.

PREVIEWING AND SETTING A PURPOSE

Before you read, **preview** the text by looking at its title, table of contents, headings, and illustrations. A preview will help you determine the genre of the text (whether it is fiction or nonfiction, for example), whether you should read it carefully or quickly, and whether you should take notes or rely on your memory.

Your **purpose for reading** will help you decide how quickly to read and what to focus on. If, for example, you're reading to be entertained, you might read quickly to find out what happens next. If, however, you're reading to appreciate the writer's craft, to find models for your writing, to make a decision, or to take an action, you will read more carefully. It's important to establish your purpose—whether it is to enjoy, interpret, or learn from the text—before you begin to read. Then you can select the reading rate and strategy that suit your purpose.

A good reader knows that different methods of reading work best in different situations. If, for instance, you want an overview of a nonfiction article, try **skimming,** reading rapidly to identify main ideas. If you're looking for a detail, try **scanning,** searching for specific information by glancing over the text and looking for key words. Skimming and scanning are reading techniques that can save you time and effort. If you're reading to appreciate the writer's craft or discover information, try **active reading,** interacting with the text by drawing on your background, making predictions and inferences, and monitoring and modifying your reading strategies appropriately.

USING YOUR BACKGROUND

Before they read something, good readers see whether they can draw on their experiences to find a connection to the text. Good readers also use their background knowledge *as* they read. If, for example, you are reading "R.M.S. *Titanic*" (page 390) and you know something about the sinking of the *Titanic,* you can use that information as you read. You can keep track of your knowledge on a KWL chart like this one:

K	W	L
What I already **know**	What I **want** to know	What I **learned**

In the K column, list what you already know about the *Titanic.* For example, you might know that the ship was supposed to be unsinkable, but it sank when it hit an iceberg. Next, in the W column, list what you want to know. You might want to know how the crew responded to the emergency. Then, after you read, fill in the L column with what you learned about the *Titanic.*

MAKING PREDICTIONS

Good readers make predictions by previewing the text and guessing what it is about. As they read, they may even jot down hunches about what will happen next. Then they adjust their predictions as they continue to read. This process makes reading like solving a puzzle. Try plotting your predictions in a chart like this one:

Overall prediction: This selection is about ________________

Prediction 1: ________________

Prediction was correct: ________________

Prediction needs adjustment: ________________

[etc.]

MAKING INFERENCES

An **inference** is a guess based on evidence. You make inferences about a literary work based on evidence in the text and your own experiences. In "The First Seven Years" (page 120), Malamud doesn't tell you anything about how Miriam feels toward Sobel. You must infer her feelings from what she says and does and from what Sobel says when he tells her father about his love for Miriam. When reading, record your inferences on a chart like this one:

Inference 1: ____________________

Evidence in the text: ____________________

Personal experience: ____________________

[etc.]

Here are some clues to look for when making inferences about aspects of literature:

- **Character.** Look at a character's speech, actions, thoughts, and appearance. What do others think and say about the character?
- **Tone (the writer's attitude).** Look at the writer's choice of words and details.
- **Theme.** Look at the turning point in a story. How do the main characters change? What do they learn?

Conclusions and generalizations are types of inferences. A **conclusion** is a judgment based on a consideration of evidence. For example, when you piece together details about an object in a poem and decide that the object is a symbol, you're drawing a conclusion. A **generalization** is a broad statement based on specific examples; it extends beyond a particular text to the world at large. When you're exploring the theme of a literary work, you're formulating a generalization.

MONITORING YOUR READING STRATEGIES

When you're having trouble understanding a text, stop and try one or more of these helpful techniques:

1. **Rereading.** Go back to the last point you understood, and find where you lost the thread.
2. **Reading on.** Keep reading to see whether context clues or additional information clears things up.
3. **Asking questions.** Ask *who, what, where, when, why,* and *how* questions about everything in the text. These questions force you to think about what you're reading.
4. **Using resources.** Use a dictionary or other reference works to figure out difficult passages.

CHECKING YOUR COMPREHENSION

When you finish reading a text, check your understanding by creating a **summary,** a short restatement of the important ideas and details in a work. There are many ways to summarize; the one you choose should depend on the genre of the text. For a short story, use a story map like this one:

Story Map

Basic situation:
Setting:
Main character:
His or her problem:
Main events or complications:
Climax:
Resolution:

For a poem, try a **paraphrase.** In a paraphrase you express every idea, line by line, in your own words. Here is a paraphrase of A. E. Housman's "Loveliest of Trees" (page 520):

> The speaker thinks the cherry tree is the most beautiful kind, and it is blooming now at Easter. The trees are full of white blossoms. The speaker is twenty years old. Thus, if he lives to be seventy, he has only fifty years left. He thinks fifty years is not much time to look at the beauty of spring, so he's going to make sure he appreciates the cherry trees hung with white blossoms that now remind him of snow (old age?).

For a work of nonfiction, make an **outline** that shows the **main ideas** and **supporting details:**

I. Main idea
    A. Supporting detail
        1. Supporting detail
            a. Supporting detail

STUDY SKILLS

USING A DICTIONARY

Use a dictionary to find the precise meaning and usage of words. The elements of an entry are explained below.

1. **Entry word.** The entry word shows how the word is spelled and divided into syllables. It may also show capitalization and variant spellings.
2. **Pronunciation.** Phonetic symbols and diacritical marks show how to pronounce the entry word. A key to these symbols and marks usually appears on every other page.
3. **Part-of-speech label.** This label tells how the entry word is used. When a word can be used as more than one part of speech, definitions are grouped by part of speech. The sample entry shows definitions of *increase* as an intransitive verb (*vi.*), as a transitive verb (*vt.*), and as a noun.
4. **Other forms.** Sometimes the spellings of plural forms of nouns, principal parts of verbs, and comparative and superlative forms of adjectives and adverbs are shown.
5. **Word origin.** A word's origin, or **etymology** (et′ə·mäl′ə·jē), shows where the word comes from. *Increase* comes from the Middle English *encresen,* which comes from the Old French *encreistre,* which comes from the Latin *increscere.* This oldest known source is from the prefix *in-* and the word *crescere,* "to grow."
6. **Definitions.** If a word has more than one meaning, the meanings are numbered or lettered.
7. **Special-usage labels.** These labels identify special meanings or special uses of the word. Here, *Archaic* indicates an outdated meaning.
8. **Examples.** Phrases or sentences show how the entry word is used.
9. **Related word forms.** Other forms of the entry word are listed. Usually these are created by the addition of suffixes.
10. **Synonyms and antonyms. Synonyms** (words similar in meaning) and **antonyms** (words opposite in meaning) may appear at the end of the entry.

A dictionary is available as a book or as part of a word-processing program or as a site on the World Wide Web.

Sample Dictionary Entry

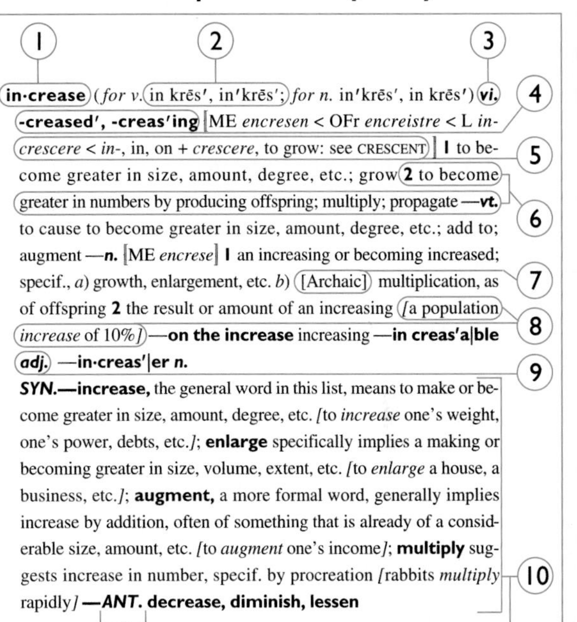

in·crease (*for v.* in krēs′, in′krēs′; *for n.* in′krēs′, in krēs′) ***vi.*** **-creased′, -creas′ing** [ME *encresen* < OFr *encreistre* < L *increscere* < *in-*, in, on + *crescere*, to grow: see CRESCENT] **1** to become greater in size, amount, degree, etc.; grow **2** to become greater in numbers by producing offspring; multiply; propagate ***—vt.*** to cause to become greater in size, amount, degree, etc.; add to; augment ***—n.*** [ME *encrese*] **1** an increasing or becoming increased; specif., *a)* growth, enlargement, etc. *b)* [Archaic] multiplication, as of offspring **2** the result or amount of an increasing [*a population increase* of 10%] **—on the increase** increasing **—in·creas′a|ble** ***adj.*** **—in·creas′|er *n.***

SYN.*—increase,** the general word in this list, means to make or become greater in size, amount, degree, etc. [to *increase* one's weight, one's power, debts, etc.]; **enlarge** specifically implies a making or becoming greater in size, volume, extent, etc. [to *enlarge* a house, a business, etc.]; **augment,** a more formal word, generally implies increase by addition, often of something that is already of a considerable size, amount, etc. [to *augment* one's income]; **multiply** suggests increase in number, specif. by procreation [rabbits *multiply* rapidly] ***—ANT. **decrease, diminish, lessen**

Webster's New World Dictionary of American English, Third College Edition.

USING A THESAURUS

A **thesaurus** is a collection of synonyms. There are two kinds of thesauruses. The first, in the style of *Roget's Thesaurus,* groups words in categories. Here's how to use it: In the index, look up the word that conveys your general meaning. For instance, under *change,* you might find *reverse, adjust,* and *convert.* Choose the subentry closest to the meaning you have in mind. In this case, suppose you choose *adjust.* In the body of the text, look up the number that follows the subentry *adjust.* There you will find synonyms of *adjust.*

The second kind of thesaurus presents words in alphabetical order, as in a dictionary. See below.

Sample Thesaurus Entry

commencement, *n.* **1.** [A beginning] —*Syn.* genesis, start, initiation; see **origin 1.**
2. [Graduation ceremony] —*Syn.* convocation, graduation, commencement exercises, services; see **celebration 1, 2, ceremony 2, graduation.**

©1997 Webster's New World Thesaurus, Third Edition.

READING MAPS, CHARTS, AND GRAPHS

Types of Maps

Physical maps illustrate the natural landscape of an area, using shading, lines, and color to show landforms and elevation. **Political maps** show political units, such as states and nations. They usually show borders and capitals and other major cities. The map on page 877, which shows Rome in 44 B.C., at the death of Caesar, is a political map. **Special-purpose maps** present specific information, such as the ancient ruins of southern Mexico (identified by the triangular symbol in the map below).

How to Read a Map

1. **Determine the focus of the map.** The map's title and labels tell you its focus—its subject and the geographical area it covers.
2. **Study the legend.** The **legend,** or **key,** explains the symbols, lines, and colors used in the map.
3. **Check directions and distances.** Maps often include a compass rose, a diagram that shows north, south, east, and west. If there isn't one, assume that north is at the top, west to the left, and so on. Many maps also include a scale that relates distances on the map to actual distances.
4. **Look at the larger context.** The **absolute location** of any place on earth is given by its **latitude** (the number of degrees north or south of the equator, which is 0 degrees latitude) and its **longitude** (the number of degrees east or west of the **prime meridian,** or 0 degrees longitude). Some maps also include **locator maps,** which show the area depicted in relation to a larger area.

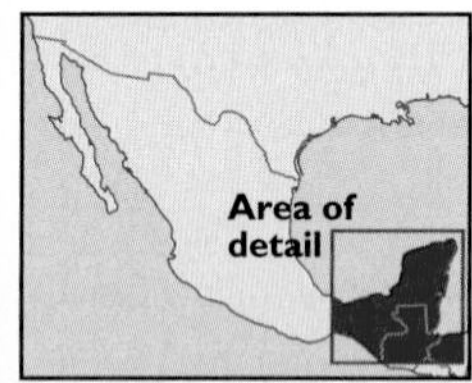

SOUTHERN MEXICO

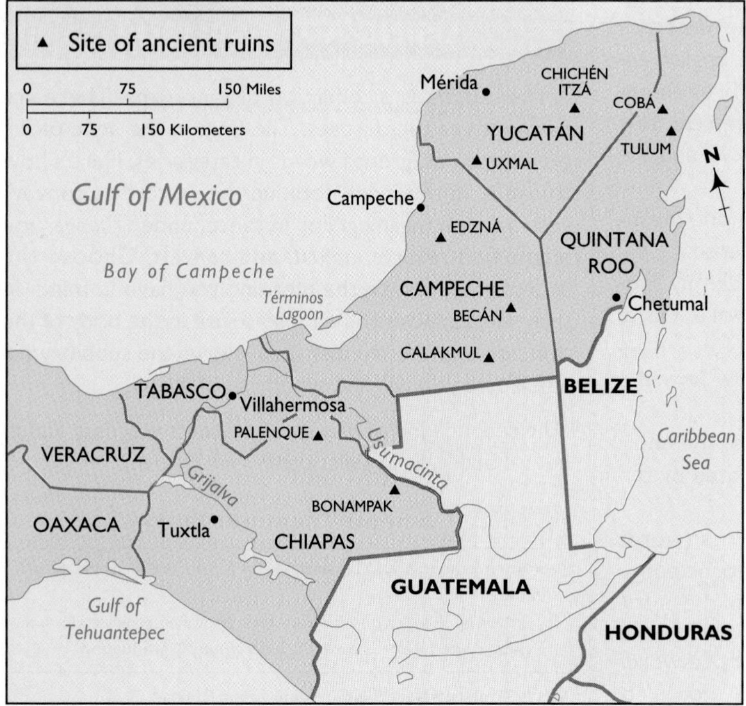

Types of Charts and Graphs

Flowcharts show a sequence of events or steps in a process. See page 657 for an example. **Time lines,** like the one on page 386, display historical events in chronological order (the order in which they happened). **Tables** categorize information and organize it in columns and rows so it is easy to find and compare. A table appears on page 364.

Line graphs generally show changes in quantity over time. In such graphs, dots showing the quantity at certain times are connected to create a line. **Bar graphs** usually compare quantities within categories. **Pie graphs,** or **circle graphs,** show proportions by dividing a circle into different-sized sections, like slices of a pie.

How to Read a Chart or a Graph

1. **Read the title.** The title will tell you the subject and purpose of the chart or graph.
2. **Read the headings and labels.** These will help you determine the type of information presented.
3. **Analyze the details.** Read numbers carefully. Note increases or decreases. Look for the direction or order of events and trends and for relationships.

RESEARCH STRATEGIES

When you're looking for information, where should you begin? First you might create a research plan that outlines the topics you want to explore or the questions you want to answer. Then you can begin your search for print and nonprint resources that might be relevant to your plan. When doing research, do not rely solely on one source; instead, consult as many reliable sources as possible. The following research strategies can help you find resources in your school's media center, in your local library, or on a home computer that is linked to the Internet.

USING A MEDIA CENTER OR LIBRARY

Library Catalogs

To find information in a library, start by looking in the catalog. Most libraries record their holdings in an **on-line,** or **computer, catalog.**

On-line catalogs vary from library to library. With some you begin by searching for resources by **title, author,** or **subject.** With others you simply enter **key words** relating to the subject you're researching. With either system, when you enter the relevant information in response to the on-screen prompts, a new screen will display a list of materials or subject headings that relate to your request. When you find an item you want to examine, write down the title, author, and **call number,** the code of numbers and letters that shows you where to find the item on the library's shelves.

Some libraries still use **card catalogs.** A card catalog is a collection of index cards arranged in alphabetical order. Every item in the library is cataloged by title and author. Nonfiction is also cataloged by subject.

Other Library Resources

Every library has a **reference section** containing materials you can use only in the library.

These materials include encyclopedias; yearbooks; biographical, scientific, and other dictionaries; almanacs; atlases; and **indices,** extensive lists of books, magazines, or newspapers arranged by author, title, and subject. Two useful book indices are *Books in Print* and *The Reader's Catalog.* Many reference works appear in print and various electronic formats.

Electronic Databases **Electronic databases** are large collections of information that you can access at a computer terminal. Among the types of information stored on databases are statistics, biographical data, museum collections, indices, and back (not current) issues of magazines.

There are two kinds of electronic databases. **On-line databases** are accessed at a computer terminal that is connected to a modem. The modem allows the computer to communicate with other computers via telephone lines. **Portable databases** are available on magnetic tape, diskette, or CD-ROM.

A **CD-ROM** (compact disc–read-only memory) is played on a computer with a CD-ROM player. CD-ROMs can store not only text but also sound, pictures, and video clips. If you were to look up the civil rights movement on a CD-ROM devoted to American history, you might see a video clip of a speech being delivered by Martin Luther King, Jr., or Malcolm X.

Periodicals Most libraries have a collection of periodicals and resources you can use to find information in them. To find up-to-date magazine or newspaper articles on a topic, look in an electronic index such as *InfoTrac* or *EBSCO.* Some electronic indices provide a summary, or **abstract,** of articles. Others provide the entire text, which you can read on screen or print out. The *Readers' Guide to Periodical Literature* is a useful print index of articles that have appeared in hundreds of magazines. Back issues of periodicals may be stored in print form or on **microfilm** (a reel of film), **microfiche** (a sheet of film), or **CD-ROM.**

Audiovisual Resources Most libraries have collections of books on tape, videos, CDs, and so on.

USING THE INTERNET

The **Internet** is a worldwide electronic network that connects millions of computers and computer networks. The Net can provide up-to-the-minute information on a vast range of topics. Institutions sharing information on the Net include libraries, universities, museums, news media, and government agencies. Resources available include **e-journals,** periodicals found only on-line. You can reach the Net through Internet service providers (ISPs) or on-line information providers, such as America Online and Prodigy. To use the Internet to do research, explore the options described below.

E-Mail

E-mail is an electronic message sent over a computer network. On the Internet you can use e-mail to contact institutions, businesses, and individuals. When you e-mail institutions such as museums and nonprofit organizations, you may be able to consult **experts** on the topic you're researching. You can also use e-mail to chat about various issues with students around the world.

Electronic Forums

Internet forums, or **newsgroups,** enable you to discuss and debate various subjects. You can post a question to a forum and get a response from someone who may (or may not) know something about the topic.

The World Wide Web

The easiest way to conduct research on the Internet is through the World Wide Web. On the Web, information is stored in colorful, easy-to-access files called **Web pages.** A Web page may contain text, graphics, images, sounds, and even video clips.

Using a Web Browser You view Web pages with a **Web browser,** a program for accessing information on the Web. Every page on the Web has its own address, called a **URL,** or Uniform Resource Locator. If you know the URL of a Web page you want to go to, just enter it in the location field on your browser. See the figure below.

Hundreds of millions of Web pages are connected by **hyperlinks** that enable you to jump from one page to another. These links are often signaled by underlined or colored words or images, or both, on your computer screen. With hundreds of millions of linked Web pages, how do you find the information you want?

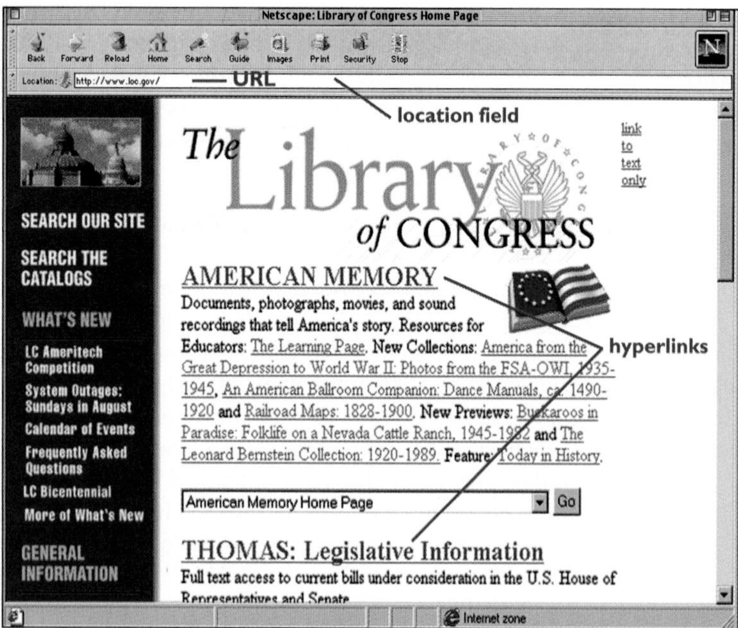

Using a Web Directory If you're just beginning to look for a research topic, click on a **Web directory,** a list of topics and subtopics created to help you find Web sites. Use a directory as you would a giant index. Begin with a broad category, such as Literature. Then, work your way down through the subtopics, from perhaps Latino: Literature to Latino: Authors, until you find a Web page that looks promising, such as one on Sandra Cisneros.

Using a Search Engine If you already have a well-defined topic and you are looking for specifics, try using a **search engine,** a software tool that locates information on the Web. To use a search engine, enter a **search term,** a key word or several key words. The search engine will return a list of Web pages containing your search term. The list will also include the first few lines of each page. A search term like the name Tyler can produce thousands of results, or **hits,** including information on President John Tyler and the city of Tyler, Texas. If you're looking for material on the author Anne Tyler, most of these thousands of hits will be irrelevant. It's important, therefore, to refine, or tailor, your search.

Refining a Key Word Search Searches using more than one key word generally provide more focused results. Most search engines allow you to use **search operators** to create a string of key words. Common search operators include the capitalized words AND, OR, NOT, ADJ (adjacent), and NEAR. Use these operators to narrow or broaden the scope of your search. Here's how the operators work. Let's assume, for example, that you're looking for material on the writer Anne Tyler. You might use this search term:

Anne ADJ Tyler AND novels NOT Texas

This more focused search term yields pages that contain the words *Anne, Tyler,* and *novels* but nothing about Texas, thus eliminating references to the city of Tyler, Texas. Now, suppose you want to learn about Japanese poetry. If your first search yields only information about haiku, you can expand the range by using OR:

haiku OR tanka

The chart below explains various search operators.

Doing a Phrase Search Exact phrases often produce better results than single words or strings of key words. If you're looking up Greek tragedy, for example, a search made with the unlinked key words *Greek* and *tragedy* could yield thousands of pages about Greek islands, Greek restaurants, and any recent tragedies in the news. On the other hand, a search using the exact phrase "Greek tragedy," signaled by quotation marks, will yield only pages containing that phrase.

Knowing Your Search Engine Not all search engines operate in the same way. Some have rules about using uppercase and lowercase letters. Others require a plus sign or a minus sign between key words rather than the operator AND or NOT. Others require that you enter exact phrases within quotation marks. Yet others provide a list of options that enable you to search by exact phrases, individual words, and so on. Because the rules governing search engines are constantly changing, read the on-line help information before you begin a search on any engine.

EVALUATING THE CREDIBILITY OF WEB SOURCES

Since anyone can publish a Web page, it's important to evaluate your sources. By examining the top-level domain in the URL of a source, you can learn about where the Web site is housed.

COMMON SEARCH OPERATORS AND WHAT THEY DO	
AND	Demands that both terms appear on the page; narrows search
+	Demands that both terms appear on the page; narrows search
OR	Yields pages that contain either term; widens search
NOT	Excludes a word from consideration; narrows search
–	Excludes a word from consideration; narrows search
NEAR	Demands that two words be in proximity; narrows search
ADJ	Demands that two words be in proximity; narrows search
" "	Demands the exact phrase; narrows search

top-level domain

```
http://www.loc.gov
```

Once you know where the Web site is housed (in this case, a government agency), you'll be in a better position to evaluate the information you find there. See the chart below for a list of common top-level domains and what they stand for.

In evaluating any source, also consider the following criteria:

Authority Who is the author, and what are his or her qualifications? Trust established sources, such as the *Encyclopaedia Britannica*'s or the Library of Congress's Web site, but not an individual's home page.

Accuracy Is the information reliable? Does the author cite sources? Check information from one site against information from two other sites or print sources.

Objectivity What is the author's **bias,** or perspective? Does the provider of the information have a hidden motive or a special interest? You don't have to discard information from sources that do, but you should take the bias into consideration.

Currency How current is the information? At the bottom of a site's home page, look for the date on which the page was created or revised. If you need current information, reject dated sources.

Coverage How well does a Web site cover the topic? Could you find better information in a reference book?

TAKING NOTES AND DOCUMENTING SOURCES

Whenever you paraphrase someone's ideas or quote a source in a research paper, you must acknowledge that source.

Preparing Source Cards

1. For every source, record the publication data on a 3- × 5-inch index card or in a computer file.
2. Assign each source a number, and note it at the top right of the card or computer entry. Later, when you're taking notes, you can label them by source number instead of author and title.
3. Record the publication data. Specific information about books, videos, Web sites, and other sources appears on pages 1015–1017. Follow the format of the **works cited** list, described on page 1015.
4. Note the library call number or the URL.

Sample Source Card

4

Sophocles. Antigone. Translated by R. C. Jebb. Internet Classics Archive. Ed. Daniel C. Stevenson. April 1998. MIT Program in Writing and Humanistic Studies. 16 March 1999 <http://classics.mit.edu/classics/Sophocles/antigone.body.html>.

The criteria opposite have been adapted from the Web site "Evaluating Web Resources" at http://www.widener.edu/libraries.html (select "Evaluating Web Resources"), which complements the book *Web Wisdom: How to Evaluate and Create Quality Information on the Web* by Jan Alexander and Marsha Ann Tate of Widener University, Chester, PA.

COMMON TOP-LEVEL DOMAINS AND WHAT THEY STAND FOR	
.edu	Educational institution. Site may publish scholarly work or the work of elementary, high school, or college students.
.gov	Government body. Information should be reliable.
.org	Usually a nonprofit organization. If the organization promotes culture (as a museum does), information should be reliable; if it advocates a cause, information may be biased.
.com	Commercial enterprise. Information should be evaluated carefully.
.net	Organization offering Internet services.

Here's where to find the appropriate publication data, such as the name of the publisher and the copyright date, for different types of sources:

- **Books.** See the title and copyright pages.
- **Portable electronic databases.** Look at the start-up screen, accompanying printed material, such as the package or a package insert, or the disc.
- **On-line sources.** Look at the beginning or end of the document or in a separate electronic file. On a Web page, look for a link with the word *About.*

Taking Notes

After examining your sources, start taking notes.

1. Use 4- × 6-inch index cards or a separate computer file. Never put notes from more than one source on the same card or on the same page in a file.
2. Write an identifying word or phrase in the upper left and the source number in the upper right of each card or page.
3. **Quote, summarize,** or **paraphrase** your source. If you quote it, be sure to use quotation marks.
4. Note the page number or numbers of the source, if any, in the lower right of the card or page.

Citing Sources

Parenthetical Citations One way to let your readers know what sources you are paraphrasing or quoting is to use **parenthetical citations.** A parenthetical citation consists of the author's last name and a page number enclosed in parentheses. (For unnumbered Web pages, include just the author or, if no author is identified, the title.) If in your text you make clear which work you are referring to—by stating the author's name or the author and title—include only the page number in the parenthetical citation. Here are some rules for the placement of citations and longer quotes:

1. Place a citation as close as possible to the material it documents. If possible, place it at the end of a sentence.
2. Place a citation after the closing quotation marks and before the end punctuation mark.

   EXAMPLE In her book Edgar Allan Poe, Bettina Knapp says that Poe's "inner emotions were encompassed in the mood he created, in the music of the words" (46).
3. If a quotation consists of four lines or more, set it off by indenting each line ten spaces from the left margin. Don't use quotation marks. Insert the citation in parentheses one space after the end punctuation mark.

List of Works Cited A **works cited** list must appear at the end of your report. It should contain complete citations for every source you used to write your paper. On page 1016 you will find citations of electronic sources in the Modern Language Association (MLA) style. The chart on page 1017 has sample citations of print and audiovisual sources.

GUIDELINES FOR PREPARING A WORKS CITED LIST

- At the top of a new page, center the title *Works Cited* (or *Bibliography*).
- Alphabetize your sources by author's last name. If no author is named, alphabetize the source by the first word in the title, ignoring *A, An,* and *The.*
- If two or more sources are by the same author, use the author's full name in the first entry only. For the other entries, type three dashes in place of the name, followed by a period and the rest of the citation.

  EXAMPLE Chekhov, Anton Pavlovich. The Kiss and Other Stories. Trans. R.E.C. Long. Freeport, NY: Books for Libraries P, 1972.

  ---. The Chekhov Omnibus: Selected Stories. Trans. Constance Garnett; revised with additional material by Donald Rayfield. Rutland, VT: C. E. Tuttle, 1994.
- Double-space the list, and begin each entry at the left margin. If an entry is longer than one line, indent the succeeding lines five spaces.

Formatting Electronic-Source Citations

Writing entries for electronic sources for a works cited list is not always easy, because on-line sources are constantly changing and many do not provide all the publication information that the format requires. For instance, many Web pages don't identify an author. In such cases, include in your citation whatever relevant publication information is available.

The format for citing electronic sources depends on (1) whether the source is on-line or portable, and (2) whether the source has a print version or stands alone.

Listed below are the elements required for the citation of various kinds of electronic sources. These citations are based on the Modern Language Association (MLA) style. Note that most elements likely to be included are listed, but many citations will not include every element (for instance, a source may not have an editor).

Source from a Computer Network, such as the World Wide Web, with a Print Version

Author's Last Name, First Name. "Title of Document, Article, or Part of a Work." Title of Print Source. Print Publication Information. Title of Project, Database, Periodical, or Site. Date of Electronic Publication. Name of Sponsoring Institution. Date Information Was Accessed. <URL> [or] Name of On-line Service or Network.

Note: If an electronic address, or URL, breaks onto a second line, divide the address immediately after one of the slash marks within it or after a dot. Do not use a hyphen or any other mark of punctuation to divide the address.

EXAMPLE Poe, Edgar Allan. "The Pit and the Pendulum." The Unabridged Edgar Allan Poe. Philadelphia: Running, 1983. Electronic Text Center. Jan. 1995. 745–757. U of Virginia. 22 Apr. 1998 <http://etext.lib.virginia.edu/modeng/modengP.browse.html>.

Source from a Computer Network, such as the World Wide Web, with No Print Version

Author's Last Name, First Name. "Title of Document, Article, or Part of a Work." Title of Project, Database, Periodical, or Site. Date of Electronic Publication. Name of Sponsoring Institution. Date Information Was Accessed. <URL> [or] Name of On-line Service or Network.

EXAMPLE Wozniak, Rhonda. "A Place for Miracles." Titanic Library. 1997. RMS Titanic, Inc. 27 Jan. 1998 <http://www.titanic-online.com/library/index.html>.

CD-ROM with a Print Version Not Published Periodically

Author's Last Name, First Name. "Title of Document, Article, or Part of a Work." Title of Print Source. Print Publication Information. Database Title. Edition, Release, or Version. Publication Medium [use the term *CD-ROM, Diskette,* or *Magnetic tape*]. City of Electronic Publication: Electronic Publisher, Electronic Publication Date.

EXAMPLE "Julius Caesar." Encyclopaedia Britannica. 15th ed. 1995. Britannica CD. Home ed., version 2.02. CD-ROM. Chicago: Encyclopaedia Britannica, 1995.

CD-ROM with No Print Version and Not Published Periodically

Author's Last Name, First Name. "Title of Document, Article, or Part of a Work." Title of Work. Database Title. Edition, Release, or Version. Publication Medium [use the term *CD-ROM, Diskette,* or *Magnetic tape*]. City of Electronic Publication: Electronic Publisher, Electronic Publication Date.

EXAMPLE "The African-American Experience." American Journey: History in Your Hands. CD-ROM. Woodbridge, CT: Primary Sources Media, 1996.

Formatting Print and Audiovisual Citations

This chart shows sample entries for various kinds of print and audiovisual sources according to the *MLA Handbook for Writers of Research Papers,* fourth edition.

STANDARD REFERENCE WORKS	
Encyclopedia article	Danson, Lawrence. "Shakespeare, William." Academic American Encyclopedia. 1997 ed.
Biographical dictionary	"Shakespeare, William." Merriam-Webster's Biographical Dictionary. 1995 ed.
BOOKS	
Book with one author	Vendler, Helen. The Art of Shakespeare's Sonnets. Cambridge: Harvard UP, 1997.
Book with two or more authors	Dollimore, Jonathan, and Alan Sinfield. Political Shakespeare: Essays in Cultural Materialism. Ithaca: Cornell UP, 1994.
Book with one editor	Rowse, A. L., ed. The Annotated Shakespeare. New York: Potter, 1978.
Book with two or more editors	Campbell, Oscar James, and Edward G. Quinn, eds. The Reader's Encyclopedia of Shakespeare. New York: Crowell, 1966.
SELECTIONS FROM BOOKS	
Selection from book of works by one author	Furtwangler, Albert. "Brutus." Assassin on Stage: Brutus, Hamlet, and the Death of Lincoln. Urbana: U of Illinois P, 1991. 13–30.
Selection from book of works by two or more authors	Sprague, A. C., and J. C. Trewin. "Additions to the Text." Shakespeare's Plays Today: Some Customs and Conventions of the Stage. London: Sidgwick and Jackson, 1970. 51–65.
Selection from book of works with one or more editors	Shakespeare, William. "Sonnet 107." Shakespeare's Sonnets. Ed. Louis B. Wright and Virginia LaMar. New York: Washington Square P, 1967. 107.
ARTICLES FROM MAGAZINES, NEWSPAPERS, AND JOURNALS	
Magazine article	Simon, J. "Julius Caesar Review." New York Magazine 22 Apr. 1991: 77.
Newspaper article	Wells, Stanley. "Brutissimo." Times Literary Supplement 22 Nov. 1991: 18.
OTHER SOURCES	
Telephone interview	Sutphin, Andrea. Telephone interview. 17 Apr. 1999.
Sound recording	Shakespeare, William. Julius Caesar. Performed by Sir Ralph Richardson et al. Harper Audio, 1991.
Radio or TV program	NBC Nightly News. NBC. WNBC, New York. 8 July 1999.
Film, filmstrip, or videotape	Julius Caesar. By William Shakespeare. Prod. BBC Television. Videocassette. Time-Life Video, 1978.

WRITING FOR LIFE

COMPOSING BUSINESS LETTERS

The ability to write clear and effective letters, memos, and résumés can help you greatly, whatever career you choose. Follow these guidelines whenever you write a business letter:

1. **Use formal, standard English.** The tone of your letter should be polite and respectful.
2. **Be clear.** Explain your purpose clearly. Include all the necessary information, but be as brief as possible.
3. **Use the correct format.** Type, print, or write neatly on white 8 1/2- × 11-inch paper. Follow the **block form** (shown below).

Sample Business Letter (Block Format)

3500 Aransas Street Corpus Christi, TX 78411 September 11, 1999	**Heading** Your street address Your city, state, and ZIP code Date you write the letter
Ms. Angela Mendez Director of Community Relations Nueces County Juvenile Justice Center 2310 Gollihar Street Corpus Christi, TX 78415	**Inside Address** Name, title, and address of the person you are writing to. Use a title (for example, *Mr., Ms., Mrs., Dr.*) with the person's name, and put his or her business title after the name.
Dear Ms. Mendez:	**Salutation (greeting)** Use *Dear* followed by the person's title and last name and a colon. If the letter isn't addressed to a specific person, use a business title.
Six students in my English class at Fay High School would like to visit juvenile court on Tuesday, October 1, as part of our research project on the juvenile justice system. Do we need permission to attend court sessions? If so, please tell me how to obtain permission. You can reach me at my home address above or by phone at 512-555-9102. Thank you for your help.	**Body** Your message. If the body contains more than one paragraph, leave a blank line between paragraphs.
Sincerely yours,	**Closing** Use *Yours truly* or *Sincerely yours* followed by a comma.
Sarah Sikes Sarah Sikes	**Signature** Type or print your name, leaving space for your signature. Sign your name in ink.

Strategies for Taking Tests

When you begin a test, scan it quickly and count the items. Then, decide how to budget your time. Here are some sample questions and specific strategies for answering five common kinds of test questions:

Multiple-choice questions ask you to select a correct answer from a number of choices. For example:

1. A **rhymed couplet** is
- **A** fourteen lines of iambic pentameter
- **B** two lines with end rhymes
- **C** eight rhyming lines in two stanzas
- **D** lines with no rhyme or meter

HOW TO COMPLETE MULTIPLE-CHOICE ITEMS

- Make sure you understand the question before you examine the choices.
- Look for a **qualifier** (a word that limits a statement) such as *not* or *always,* which might help you eliminate some choices.
- Read all the choices before selecting an answer. Eliminate choices you know are incorrect.
- Think carefully about the remaining choices, and select the one that makes the most sense.

True/false questions require you to decide whether a statement is true or false. For example:

1. T F In a short story the **climax** occurs when the main character is introduced.

HOW TO COMPLETE TRUE/FALSE ITEMS

- Read the statement carefully. If any part of the statement is false, the whole statement is false.
- Check for a qualifier such as *always* or *never.* A statement is true only if it is always true.

Matching questions require you to match items in one list with items in a second list. For example:

Directions: Match each item in the left-hand column with its definition in the right-hand column.

___**1.**	Shakespearean sonnet	**A**	group of eight rhyming lines in a sonnet
___**2.**	couplet	**B**	English sonnet
___**3.**	octave	**C**	two rhyming lines in a sonnet

HOW TO COMPLETE MATCHING ITEMS

- Read the directions carefully. Not all the items in one column may be used, or items may be used more than once.
- Scan the columns. First, match items you are sure of. Then, match items you are less sure of.
- For the remaining items, make your best guess.

Analogy questions require you to recognize the relationship between a pair of words and then identify another pair with a similar relationship. For example:

Directions: Select the pair of words that best completes the analogy.

1. OAK : TREE ::
- **A** wheel : car
- **B** page : read
- **C** bicycle : vehicle
- **D** world : round

HOW TO COMPLETE ANALOGY ITEMS

- Identify the relationship in the first pair. (In the example an *oak* is a type of *tree.*)
- Express the analogy in a statement or question. ("An *oak* is a kind of *tree.* In what other pair is the first item a kind of the second item?")
- Select the pair of words that have the same relationship as the first pair. (A *bicycle* is a kind of *vehicle.*)

These are some common relationships in analogies: a thing to its cause; a thing to the whole it belongs to; a thing to its opposite, or a word to its antonym.

Essay questions ask you to think critically about material you have learned and to express your understanding in one paragraph or more.

HOW TO ANSWER ESSAY QUESTIONS

- Scan the questions quickly. If you have a choice, decide which questions you can answer best. See how much time you have to spend on each.
- Find the key verb in each question. See the chart below for explanations of what to do in response to different directives.
- Make notes or a simple outline on scratch paper, organize your ideas logically, and write a thesis statement expressing your main idea.
- Revise as you write to tighten and clarify.
- Proofread for mistakes in spelling, mechanics, and usage. See the proofreaders' chart below.

ESSAY QUESTIONS

Key Verb	Task	Sample Question
analyze	Take something apart to see how it works.	Analyze the central character in "The Pit and the Pendulum."
discuss	Examine something in detail.	Discuss the conflict between Jing-mei and her mother in "Two Kinds."
explain	Give reasons for something.	Explain why Julius Caesar is killed.
interpret	Give the meaning or significance of something.	How do you interpret the wall in "Mending Wall"?

Proofreaders' Marks

Symbol	Example	Meaning
≡	Forty-second street (s underlined with ≡)	Capitalize lowercase letter.
/	Tina's Uncle (U struck with /)	Lowercase capital letter.
^	the capital ^of Texas	Insert.
℘	Where's the the beef? (second "the" deleted)	Delete.
⁀ ‿	a good camp ground (space closed)	Close up space.
∿	recieve (ie transposed)	Change order (of letters or words).
¶	¶ "What's happening?" I asked.	Begin new paragraph.
⊙	Stay calm⊙	Add period.
^,^	Well^,^ it's done.	Add comma.

1 The Parts of Speech

PART OF SPEECH	DEFINITION	EXAMPLES
NOUN	Names person, place, thing, or idea	father, singers, U2, crew, valley, poem, "With All Flags Flying," age, wisdom
PRONOUN	Takes place of one or more nouns or pronouns	
Personal	Refers to one(s) speaking (first person), spoken to (second person), spoken about (third person)	I, me, my, mine, we, us, our, ours you, your, yours he, him, his, she, her, hers, it, its, they, them, their, theirs
Reflexive	Refers to subject and directs action of verb back to subject	myself, ourselves, yourself, yourselves, himself, herself, itself, themselves
Intensive	Refers to and emphasizes noun or another pronoun	(See Reflexive.)
Demonstrative	Refers to specific one(s) of group	this, that, these, those
Interrogative	Introduces question	what, which, who, whom, whose
Relative	Introduces subordinate clause and refers to noun or pronoun outside clause	that, which, who, whom, whose
Indefinite	Refers to one(s) not specifically named	all, any, anyone, both, each, either, everybody, many, none, nothing
ADJECTIVE	Modifies noun or pronoun by telling *what kind, which one, how many,* or *how much*	**a young, self-assured** officer; **a Mexican** tradition; **a suspenseful horror** story; **many** passengers
VERB	Shows action or state of being	
Action	Expresses physical or mental activity	read, dance, fly, care, pretend, argue
Linking	Connects subject with word identifying or describing it	appear, be, seem, become, feel, look, smell, sound, taste
Helping (Auxiliary)	Helps another verb express time	be, have, may, can, shall, will, would
ADVERB	Modifies verb, adjective, or adverb by telling *how, when, where,* or *to what extent*	drives **carefully,** spoke **loudly, very** old, **almost** ready, coming **here tomorrow**
PREPOSITION	Relates noun or pronoun to another word	across, between, into, near, of, on, with, aside from, instead of, next to
CONJUNCTION	Joins words or word groups	
Coordinating	Joins words or word groups used in same way	and, but, for, nor, or, so, yet

(continued)

PART OF SPEECH	DEFINITION	EXAMPLES
Correlative	A pair of conjunctions that joins parallel words or word groups	both . . . and, either . . . or, neither . . . nor, not only . . . but (also)
Subordinating	Begins subordinate clause and connects it to independent clause	as though, because, if, since, so that, than, when, where, while
INTERJECTION	Expresses emotion	hooray, yikes, ouch, wow

Determining Parts of Speech

The way a word is used in a sentence determines the word's part of speech. Many words can be used as different parts of speech.

EXAMPLES

The wolf came **near.** [adverb]
All their **near** relations were with them. [adjective]
At least all of them would be **near** each other. [preposition]
Finally, the bus would **near** the camp. [verb]

The room was filled with **light.** [noun]
Let's **light** some candles. [verb]
A **light** snowfall covered the trees. [adjective]

What did you say? [pronoun]
I don't know **what** time it is. [adjective]
What! I won the contest! [interjection]

Have you ever been there **before**? [adverb]
Before they all died out, dinosaurs ruled the earth for millions of years. [conjunction]
The moon rose **before** sunset. [preposition]

Avoiding Overused Words

The adverbs *really, too, so,* and *very* are often overused. To keep your writing lively and interesting, replace those inexact, overused words with adverbs such as these: *completely, definitely, especially, entirely, extremely, generally, largely, mainly, mostly, particularly, rather,* and *unusually.*

Try It Out

For each of the following sentences, replace the words *really, too, so,* and *very* with more lively adverbs. Use a different adverb in each sentence.

1. This is a very intriguing poem.
2. E. E. Cummings really can be a commentator on writing.
3. Some critics feel that he is too clever.
4. Punctuation can be so expressive.
5. Isn't this fact really overlooked?

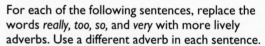

2 Agreement

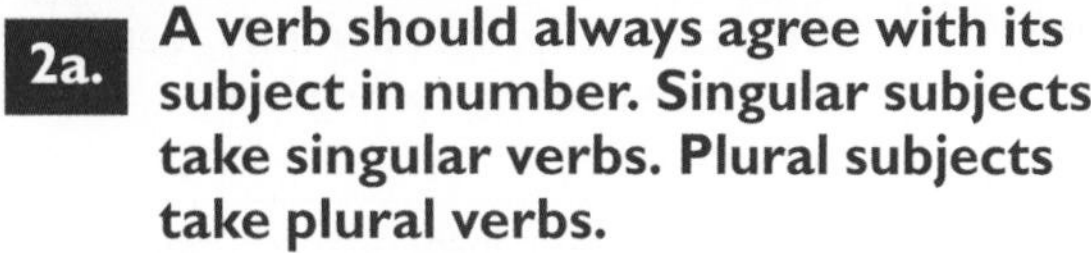

AGREEMENT OF SUBJECT AND VERB

2a. A verb should always agree with its subject in number. Singular subjects take singular verbs. Plural subjects take plural verbs.

SINGULAR Her **father has** an accident while working.
PLURAL **They have moved** to Florida.

SINGULAR **She was staying** home from school.
PLURAL Her **brothers were** back at school the next day.

Some word-processing programs can identify problems in subject-verb agreement. If you have access to such a program, use it to help you search for errors when you are proofreading your writing. If you are not sure whether a problem found by the program is truly an error, check rules 2a–2n in this section of the Language Handbook.

2b. **The number of the subject is not changed by a phrase following the subject.**

SINGULAR **Friends** of the girl **are** sympathetic.
PLURAL **Tears,** absent in the day, **fall** at night.

SINGULAR The **aim** of her stories **is** to express truth.
PLURAL The **words** of their mother **reassure** them.

For more about kinds of phrases, see Part 6: Phrases.

The number of the subject is not changed by a negative construction following the subject.

EXAMPLE
Miami, not the Florida Keys, **is** their home.

The number of the subject is also not affected when it is followed by a phrase beginning with *as well as, along with, in addition to,* or a similar expression.

EXAMPLE
The **teacher,** as well as her students, **looks** forward to spring break.

2c. **The following indefinite pronouns are singular: *anybody, anyone, anything, each, either, everybody, everyone, everything, neither, nobody, no one, nothing, one, somebody, someone, something.***

EXAMPLES
One of her mother's friends **asks** about him.
Somebody in the class **does** not **use** commas.

2d. **The following indefinite pronouns are plural: *both, few, many, several.***

EXAMPLES
Both of the boys **want** to stay.
Several of the students **offer** explanations.

2e. **The indefinite pronouns *all, any, most, none,* and *some* are singular when they refer to singular words and are plural when they refer to plural words.**

SINGULAR **Most** of the garden still **needs** to be weeded.
PLURAL **Most** of the plants also **need** to be watered.

SINGULAR **All** of the kitchen **was** clean.
PLURAL **All** of them **begin** to cry.

2f. **A *compound subject,* which is two or more subjects that have the same verb, may be singular, plural, or either.**

(1) Subjects joined by *and* usually take a plural verb.

EXAMPLES
Eddie and **Lee sleep.**
Jean and her **mother talk** in the car.

A compound subject that names only one person or thing takes a singular verb. Also, a compound noun used as a subject usually takes a singular verb.

EXAMPLES
Jean's **friend** and **classmate was** Nancy Dryer.
Has law and order been restored yet?

(2) Singular subjects joined by *or* or *nor* take a singular verb.

EXAMPLES
Eddie or **Jean washes** dishes.
Neither **Mother** nor **Eddie wants** to return to Indiana.

(3) When a singular subject and a plural subject are joined by *or* or *nor,* the verb agrees with the subject nearer the verb.

EXAMPLES
Neither the plot nor the **characters were** too complex.
Neither the characters nor the **plot was** too complex.

If such a construction sounds awkward, revise the sentence to give each part of the subject its own verb.

EXAMPLE
The **plot wasn't** too complex, and neither **were** the **characters.**

2g. ***Don't* and *doesn't* must agree with their subjects.**

With the subjects *I* and *you* and with plural subjects, use *don't* (*do not*).

EXAMPLES
I **don't** agree.
You **don't** sound well.
Some people **don't** listen.

With other subjects, use *doesn't* (*does not*).

EXAMPLES
She **doesn't** bring a lunch.
It **doesn't** matter.
Jean **doesn't** sleep well.

2h. **A *collective noun* (such as *club, family,* or *swarm*) is singular in form but names a group of persons or things. A collective noun takes a singular verb when the noun refers to the group as a unit. However, a collective noun takes a plural verb when the noun refers to the parts or members of the group.**

SINGULAR The family **is** going home. [family = a unit]
PLURAL The family **are** getting into the van. [family = individual family members]

Collective Nouns

army	club	flock	public
assembly	committee	group	squad
audience	crew	herd	staff
band	crowd	jury	swarm
choir	faculty	majority	team
chorus	family	number	troop
class	fleet	pair	wildlife

2i. **A verb agrees with its subject, not with its predicate nominative.**

SINGULAR The best **part** of her lunch **is** the **cheese and crackers.**
PLURAL The **cheese and crackers are** the best **part** of her lunch.

2j. **A verb agrees with its subject even when the verb precedes the subject, as in sentences beginning with *here* or *there* and in questions. Contractions such as *here's* and *there's* are used only with subjects that are singular in meaning.**

SINGULAR Here **is** [*or* **here's**] my **locker.**
PLURAL Here **are** the **lockers.**

SINGULAR Where **is** [*or* **where's**] the school **bus**?
PLURAL Where **are** your gym **clothes**?

2k. **An expression of an amount (a length of time, a statistic, or a fraction, for example) is singular when the amount is thought of as a unit or when it refers to a singular word. However, such an expression is plural when the amount is thought of as many parts or when it refers to a plural word or more than one word.**

SINGULAR **Twenty-five cents is** the amount Dad gave my brother.
PLURAL **Twenty-five cents were** jingling in his pocket.

SINGULAR **One half** of the class **has** finished.
PLURAL **One half** of the students **are** still working.

NOTE Use a singular verb when the expression *the number* comes before a prepositional phrase. Use a plural verb when the expression *a number* comes before a prepositional phrase.

SINGULAR **The number** of students **has** increased.
PLURAL **A number** of students **have** transferred.

2l. **The title of a creative work (such as a book, song, film, or painting) or the name of an organization, a country, or a city (even if it is plural in form) takes a singular verb.**

EXAMPLES
"Boys and Girls" was written by Alice Munro.
The **United States is voting** in favor of the measure.
Wichita Falls is in Texas, not Kansas.

2m. **Some nouns that are plural in form are singular in meaning.**

Nouns that always take singular verbs include

civics	gymnastics	measles	news
electronics	mathematics	molasses	physics

EXAMPLE
Mathematics is my favorite course.

Some nouns that end in *–s,* such as the following ones, take a plural verb even though they refer to single items.

binoculars	pants	shears	Olympics
eyeglasses	pliers	shorts	scissors

EXAMPLE
The **scissors are** in the sewing basket.

2n. **Subjects preceded by *every* or *many a* take singular verbs.**

EXAMPLES
Many a child **wants** a dog.
Every student **has** a dream.

AGREEMENT OF PRONOUN AND ANTECEDENT

A pronoun usually refers to a noun or another pronoun, which is called the pronoun's ***antecedent.***

2o. A pronoun agrees with its antecedent in number and gender. Singular pronouns refer to singular antecedents. Plural pronouns refer to plural antecedents.

A few singular pronouns indicate gender:

Feminine—*she, her, hers, herself*
Masculine—*he, him, his, himself*
Neuter—*it, its, itself*

EXAMPLES

The **man** had made the choice **himself.** [singular, masculine]
His **daughter** wanted **her** father to stay with **her.** [singular, feminine]

2p. A singular pronoun is used to refer to *anybody, anyone, anything, each, either, everybody, everyone, everything, neither, nobody, no one, nothing, one, somebody, someone,* or *something.* The gender of any of these pronouns is determined by the gender of the pronoun's antecedent.

EXAMPLE

Each of the boys brought **his** uniform.

When the antecedent could be either masculine or feminine, use both the masculine and the feminine pronoun forms connected by *or.*

EXAMPLE

Not **everyone** gets a chance to know **his or her** grandparents.

2q. A singular pronoun is used to refer to two or more singular antecedents joined by *or* or *nor.*

EXAMPLES

Tim or **Jason** will read **his** poem next.
Did **Heidi** or **Lynn** read **hers** yet?

If a sentence sounds awkward when antecedents are of different genders, revise it.

AWKWARD Neither **Eric nor Sue** finished **his or her** part.
REVISED **Eric** didn't finish **his** part, and **Sue** didn't finish **hers** either.

Avoiding the *His or Her* Construction

When the antecedent of a pronoun could be either masculine or feminine, you can avoid using the awkward *his or her* construction by revising the sentence.

AWKWARD Bill or Eva will bring his or her recorder.
REVISED Bill will bring his recorder, or Eva will bring hers.
REVISED Bill or Eva will bring a recorder.

Try It Out

Revise each of the following sentences to eliminate the *his or her* construction.

1. Ask Joseph or Victoria to loan us his or her copy.
2. Anyone who is late must take his or her test later.
3. Does everyone have a theme for his or her paper?
4. Mark or Ellen can explain his or her own drawing.
5. Will Otis or Dee read his or her essay in assembly?

2r. A plural pronoun is used to refer to two or more antecedents joined by *and.*

EXAMPLES

The **man** and his **granddaughter** have a good relationship despite the difference in **their** ages.
My **father** and my **brother** have **their** fishing licenses with **them.**

2s. The number of a relative pronoun (such as *who, whom, whose, which,* or *that*) depends on the number of its antecedent.

EXAMPLES

He is one **man who** insists on deciding **his** own fate. [*Who* refers to the singular noun *man.* Therefore, the singular form *his* is used to agree with *who.*]
Many who are growing old make **their** homes there. [*Who* refers to the plural pronoun *many.* Therefore, the plural form *their* is used to agree with *who.*]

For more about relative pronouns in adjective clauses, see page 1037.

3 USING VERBS

THE PRINCIPAL PARTS OF VERBS

3a. **The four *principal parts* of a verb are the *base form,* the *present participle,* the *past,* and the *past participle.***

BASE FORM	use	sing
PRESENT PARTICIPLE	using	singing
PAST	used	sang
PAST PARTICIPLE	used	sung

COMMON REGULAR VERBS			
BASE FORM	**PRESENT PARTICIPLE**	**PAST**	**PAST PARTICIPLE**
ask	(is) asking	asked	(have) asked
happen	(is) happening	happened	(have) happened
plan	(is) planning	planned	(have) planned
try	(is) trying	tried	(have) tried
use	(is) using	used	(have) used

COMMON IRREGULAR VERBS			
BASE FORM	**PRESENT PARTICIPLE**	**PAST**	**PAST PARTICIPLE**
be	(is) being	was, were	(have) been
begin	(is) beginning	began	(have) begun
bring	(is) bringing	brought	(have) brought
catch	(is) catching	caught	(have) caught
drink	(is) drinking	drank	(have) drunk
drive	(is) driving	drove	(have) driven
eat	(is) eating	ate	(have) eaten
fall	(is) falling	fell	(have) fallen
find	(is) finding	found	(have) found
freeze	(is) freezing	froze	(have) frozen
go	(is) going	went	(have) gone
have	(is) having	had	(have) had
keep	(is) keeping	kept	(have) kept
lead	(is) leading	led	(have) led
pay	(is) paying	paid	(have) paid
ride	(is) riding	rode	(have) ridden
shake	(is) shaking	shook	(have) shaken
sing	(is) singing	sang	(have) sung
steal	(is) stealing	stole	(have) stolen
swim	(is) swimming	swam	(have) swum
swing	(is) swinging	swung	(have) swung
tear	(is) tearing	tore	(have) torn

All verbs form the present participle by adding *–ing* to the base form. All verbs, however, do not form the past and past participle in the same way.

3b. **A *regular verb* forms its past and past participle by adding *–d* or *–ed* to the base form.**

3c. **An *irregular verb* forms its past and past participle in some other way than by adding *–d* or *–ed* to the base form.**

NOTE The examples in the chart include *is* and *have* in parentheses to show that helping verbs (forms of *be* and *have*) are used with the present participle and past participle forms.

Drop the final silent e after a consonant in the base form of a verb before adding *–ing* to form the present participle and *–ed* to form the past participle.

PRESENT PARTICIPLE
spare + ing = spar**ing**
outline + ing = outlin**ing**

PAST PARTICIPLE
spare + ed = spar**ed**
outline + ed = outlin**ed**

For more about correct spelling when adding suffixes to words, see pages 1059–1060.

NOTE If you are not sure about the principal parts of a verb, look in a dictionary. Entries for irregular verbs give the principal parts. If no principal parts are listed, the verb is a regular verb.

TENSE

3d. The *tense* of a verb indicates the time of the action or state of being that is expressed by the verb.

Every English verb has six tenses: *present, past, future, present perfect, past perfect,* and *future perfect.* The tenses are formed from the verb's principal parts.

Past	*Present*	*Future*
existing or happening in the past	existing or happening now	existing or happening in the future

Past Perfect	*Present Perfect*	*Future Perfect*
existing or happening before a specific time in the past	existing or happening sometime before now	existing or happening before a specific time in the future

Each of the six tenses has an additional form called the ***progressive form.*** The progressive form expresses a continuing action or state of being. It consists of the appropriate tense of *be* followed by the verb's present participle. For the perfect tenses, the progressive form also includes one or more helping verbs.

Present Progressive	am, are, is singing
Past Progressive	was, were singing
Future Progressive	will (shall) be singing
Present Perfect Progressive	has, have been singing
Past Perfect Progressive	had been singing
Future Perfect Progressive	will (shall) have been singing

3e. Each of the six tenses has its own special uses.

(1) The ***present tense*** is used mainly to express an action or a state of being that is occurring now.

EXAMPLES
Tara **knows** the answer.
Can you **hear** the music?

The present tense is also used

- to show a customary or habitual action or state of being
- to express a general truth—something that is always true
- to make historical events seem current (such use is called the ***historical present***)
- to discuss a literary work (such use is called the ***literary present***)
- to express future time

EXAMPLES
He **works** here. [customary action]
Basketball **entertains** millions. [general truth]
The Roman Empire **falls.** [historical present]
The poem **describes** Flick. [literary present]
We **leave** on vacation next week. [future time]

(2) The ***past tense*** is used to express an action or a state of being that occurred in the past but is not occurring now.

EXAMPLES
Flick once **scored** almost four hundred points.
We **remembered** his kindness.

A past action or state of being can also be shown with the verb *used to* followed by the base form.

EXAMPLE
My brother **used to ride** his bike to school.

(3) The ***future tense*** (formed with *will* or *shall* and the verb's base form) is used to express an action or a state of being that will occur.

EXAMPLES
Probably, he **will stay** in town.
We **will read** Maya Angelou's poem next.

(4) The ***present perfect tense*** (formed with *have* or *has* and the verb's past participle) is used to express an action or a state of being that occurred at some indefinite time in the past.

EXAMPLES
Her poems **have commented** on many situations.
She **has published** widely.

The present perfect tense is also used to express an action or a state of being that began in the past and continues into the present.

EXAMPLE
We **have lived** in the same house for nearly nine years.

(5) The ***past perfect tense*** (formed with *had* and the verb's past participle) is used to express an action or a state of being that was completed in the past before some other past action or event.

EXAMPLES
Other people remembered what he **had accomplished.** [The accomplishing occurred before the remembering.]
I **had driven** for hours, and I arrived on time. [The driving occurred before the arriving.]

(6) The ***future perfect tense*** (formed with *will have* or *shall have* and the verb's past participle) is used to express an action or a state of being that will be completed in the future before some other future occurrence.

EXAMPLES
After tonight, I **will have seen** the film twice.
Next Tuesday, we **will have lived** here two years.

3f. Do not change needlessly from one tense to another.

INCONSISTENT	Her family packed up and moves.
CONSISTENT	Her family **packed** up and **moved.**
CONSISTENT	Her family **packs** up and **moves.**
INCONSISTENT	They marry and finally bought a house.
CONSISTENT	They **married** and finally **bought** a house.
CONSISTENT	They **marry** and finally **buy** a house.

Using Appropriate Verb Tenses

Using different verb tenses is often necessary to show the order of events that occur at different times.

NONSTANDARD
I wished that I wrote that poem.

STANDARD
I **wished** that I **had written** that poem. [Since the action of writing was completed before the action of wishing, the verb should be *had written,* not *wrote*.]

Try It Out 

For each of the following sentences, correct the verb tenses to show the order of events.

1. After the clock had struck eight, Mr. Leonard Mead had gone for a walk.
2. For years, he had enjoyed the cool air and only occasionally has had trouble from roaming dogs.
3. Nothing had moved on the street for an hour, and now he has heard no sounds.
4. While he was walking, a police car has approached him.
5. A voice had told him to stop, and he does so.

ACTIVE AND PASSIVE VOICE

3g. A verb in the *active voice* expresses an action done by its subject. A verb in the *passive voice* expresses an action received by its subject.

ACTIVE VOICE	Dick Fool Bull **told** his story.
PASSIVE VOICE	The story **was told** by Dick Fool Bull.
ACTIVE VOICE	The holy man **instructed** them.
PASSIVE VOICE	They **were instructed** by the holy man.

3h. Use the passive voice sparingly.

The passive voice is not any less correct than the active voice, but it is less direct, less forceful, and less concise. As a result, a sentence in the passive voice can be wordy and sound awkward or weak.

AWKWARD PASSIVE	Instructions were given to them by the holy man.
ACTIVE	The holy man gave them instructions.

The passive voice is useful, however, in certain situations:

1. when you do not know the performer of the action

   EXAMPLE
   The First National Bank **was robbed** last night.

2. when you do not want to reveal the performer of the action

   EXAMPLE
   Police **were notified.**

3. when you want to emphasize the receiver of the action

   EXAMPLE
   Already, seven suspects **have been questioned.**

Some software programs can identify verbs in the passive voice. If you use such a program, keep in mind that it can't tell why you have used the passive voice. If you did so for a good reason, you may want to leave the verb in the passive voice.

4 Using Pronouns

CASE

Case is the form that a noun or pronoun takes to indicate its use in a sentence. In English, there are three cases: *nominative, objective,* and *possessive.*

The form of a noun is the same for both the nominative case and the objective case. For the possessive case, however, a noun changes its form, usually by adding an apostrophe and an s to most singular nouns and only an apostrophe to most plural nouns.

NOMINATIVE **Dick Fool Bull** told his story.
OBJECTIVE The events at Wounded Knee greatly affected **Dick Fool Bull.**
POSSESSIVE **Dick Fool Bull's** story made me think.

Most personal pronouns, however, have a different form for each case.

The Nominative Case

4a. A subject of a verb is in the nominative case.

EXAMPLES
They knew that **he** was sincere. [*They* is the subject of *knew; he* is the subject of *was.*]
Has **he** or **she** visited Wounded Knee? [*He* and *she* are the subjects of *has visited.*]

4b. A predicate nominative is in the nominative case.

A ***predicate nominative*** follows a linking verb and explains or identifies the subject of the verb.

EXAMPLES
One of the witnesses was my **uncle.** [*Uncle* follows *was* and identifies the subject *one.*]
The narrators will be **Larry** and **I.** [*Larry* and *I* follow *will be* and identify the subject *narrators.*]

Expressions such as *It's me, That's him,* and *Could it have been her?* are examples of informal usage. Avoid using such expressions in formal speaking and writing.

The Objective Case

4c. A direct object of a verb is in the objective case.

A ***direct object*** follows an action verb and tells *whom* or *what.*

EXAMPLES
I haven't met **her** yet. [*Her* tells *whom* I haven't met yet.]
They made **shirts** and painted **them.** [*Shirts* tells *what* they made, and *them* tells *what* they painted.]

PERSONAL PRONOUNS			
SINGULAR			
	NOMINATIVE	**OBJECTIVE**	**POSSESSIVE**
FIRST PERSON	I	me	my, mine
SECOND PERSON	you	you	your, yours
THIRD PERSON	he, she, it	him, her, it	his, her, hers, its
PLURAL			
	NOMINATIVE	**OBJECTIVE**	**POSSESSIVE**
FIRST PERSON	we	us	our, ours
SECOND PERSON	you	you	your, yours
THIRD PERSON	they	them	their, theirs

Notice in the chart that *you* and *it* are the only personal pronouns that have the same forms for the nominative and the objective cases. Notice also that only third-person singular pronouns indicate gender.

For more information about possessive pronouns, see page 1064.

4d. An indirect object of a verb is in the objective case.

An ***indirect object*** comes before a direct object and tells *to whom* or *to what* or *for whom* or *for what.*

EXAMPLES

The vision had given **them** hope. [*Them* tells *to whom* hope was given.]
Tell **me** another story. [*Me* tells *for whom* the story is told.]

4e. An object of a preposition is in the objective case.

An ***object of a preposition*** comes at the end of a phrase that begins with a preposition.

EXAMPLES

The sight of the baby and **her** haunts the narrator.
For **us,** such a sight is difficult to imagine.

SPECIAL PRONOUN PROBLEMS

4f. The pronoun *who* (*whoever*) is in the nominative case. The pronoun *whom* (*whomever*) is in the objective case.

NOMINATIVE **Who** was Sitting Bull? [*Who* is the subject of *was.*]

OBJECTIVE With **whom** was he traveling? [*Whom* is the object of *with.*]

When choosing between *who* and *whom* in a subordinate clause, do not be misled by a word outside the clause. Be sure to base your choice on how the pronoun functions in its own subordinate clause.

NOMINATIVE Do you know **who** the bean eaters are? [*Who* is the predicate nominative identifying the subject of the subordinate clause *who the bean eaters are.* The entire subordinate clause serves as the direct object of *do know.*]

OBJECTIVE Perhaps Gwendolyn Brooks was acquainted with the people **whom** she wrote about. [*Whom* is the object of *about.* The entire subordinate clause *whom she wrote about* serves as an adjective modifying *people.*]

In spoken English, the use of *whom* is becoming less common. In written English, however, you should distinguish between *who* and *whom.*

INFORMAL **Who** did you see at the dance?
FORMAL **Whom** did you see at the dance?

Using *Whom*

Frequently, *whom* is left out of a subordinate clause.

EXAMPLE

The poet [**whom**] I like best is Emily Dickinson. [*Whom* is the unstated direct object of ***like.***]

Leaving out *whom* in such cases tends to make writing sound more informal. In formal situations, it is generally better to include *whom.*

Try It Out 

Revise each of the following sentences to include *whom.*

1. Has anyone identified the person Dickinson was writing about in that poem?
2. In this poem, she presents herself as a woman conflict has divided into heart and mind.
3. Did she, in fact, forget the man she loved?
4. The Dickinson we know from literary legend seems both shy and eloquent.
5. Was there someone she might have told of her feelings?

4g. An appositive is in the same case as the noun or pronoun to which it refers.

An ***appositive*** is a noun or pronoun placed next to another noun or pronoun to identify or explain it.

NOMINATIVE They, **Lacy and she,** played the sisters. [The appositive, *Lacy and she,* is in the nominative case because it identifies the subject, *they.*]

OBJECTIVE The sisters were played by them, **Lacy and her.** [The appositive, *Lacy and her,* is in the objective case because it identifies *them,* the object of a preposition.]

Sometimes the pronouns *we* and *us* are used with noun appositives.

EXAMPLES

We actors like to pretend. [The pronoun is in the nominative case because it is the subject of *like.*]
Pretending is fun for **us** actors. [The pronoun is in the objective case because it is the object of the preposition *for.*]

For more information about appositives, see page 1036.

4h. **A pronoun following *than* or *as* in an incomplete construction is in the same case as it would be if the construction were completed.**

Notice how the meaning of each of the following sentences depends on the pronoun form in the incomplete construction.

NOMINATIVE I liked Kim more than **he** [did].
OBJECTIVE I liked Kim more than [I liked] **him.**

NOMINATIVE You called me more than **he** [called me].
OBJECTIVE You called me more than [you called] **him.**

Clear Pronoun Reference

4i. **A pronoun should refer clearly to its antecedent.**

(1) Avoid an ***ambiguous reference,*** which occurs when a pronoun can refer to any one of two or more antecedents.

AMBIGUOUS Dee talked to Mama while she was eating. [*She* can refer to either Mama or Dee.]
CLEAR While **Mama** was eating, Dee talked to **her.**

(2) Avoid a ***general reference,*** which occurs when a pronoun refers to a general idea rather than to a specific antecedent.

GENERAL Dee insisted on having the quilt. This did not surprise Maggie. [*This* has no specific antecedent.]
CLEAR That Dee insisted on having the quilt did not surprise Maggie.
CLEAR Maggie was not surprised that Dee insisted on having the quilt.

(3) Avoid a ***weak reference,*** which occurs when a pronoun refers to an implied antecedent.

WEAK She made quilts, but it was more than a hobby. [No antecedent is given for *it.*]
CLEAR Making quilts was more than a hobby for her.

(4) Avoid an ***indefinite reference,*** which occurs when a pronoun (such as *you, it,* or *they*) refers to no particular person, place, thing, or idea.

INDEFINITE In that museum, they display fine quilts. [*They* has no antecedent in the sentence.]
CLEAR That museum displays fine quilts.

The indefinite use of *it* is acceptable in familiar expressions such as *It is snowing, It seems as though . . . ,* and *It's late.*

5 Using Modifiers

A ***modifier*** is a word or group of words that limits the meaning of another word or group of words. The two kinds of modifiers are adjectives and adverbs, both of which may consist of a word, a phrase, or a clause.

ONE-WORD MODIFIERS

Adjectives

5a. **Use an *adjective* to limit the meaning of a noun or pronoun.**

EXAMPLES
Maggie was also a **skilled** quilter. [*Skilled* limits the meaning of the noun *quilter.*]
Arrogant and **grasping,** she forfeited the quilts. [*Arrogant* and *grasping* limit the meaning of the pronoun *she.*]

Adverbs

5b. **Use an *adverb* to limit the meaning of a verb, an adjective, or another adverb.**

EXAMPLES
Suddenly, Mama made her decision. [*Suddenly* limits the meaning of the verb *made.*]
Mama was **not** talkative. [*Not* limits the meaning of the adjective *talkative.*]
She **quite** abruptly gave the quilts to Maggie. [*Quite* limits the meaning of the adverb *abruptly.*]

NOTE Some modifiers can function as adjectives or as adverbs, depending on the word or words they modify.

ADJECTIVE That's a **hard** job.
ADVERB We worked **hard.**

Using Adjectives and Adverbs

Adjectives often follow linking verbs. Adverbs often follow action verbs. You can tell whether a verb is a linking or an action verb by replacing it with a form of *seem.* If the substitution makes sense, the original verb is a linking verb and should be followed by an adjective. If the substitution does not make sense, the original verb is an action verb and should be followed by an adverb.

ADJECTIVE Behind the mist, the sun appeared dim. [*The sun seemed dim* makes sense. In this case, *appeared* is a linking verb.]

ADVERB From behind the mist, the sun appeared suddenly. [*The sun seemed suddenly* doesn't make sense. In this case, *appeared* is an action verb.]

Try It Out 

For each of the following sentences, choose the correct modifier in parentheses.

1. The collard greens tasted (*delicious, deliciously*).
2. He looked (*suspicious, suspiciously*) at the dish.
3. That car is (*noisy, noisily*).
4. She looked around (*quick, quickly*) and took photos.
5. Maggie's hands were (*cold, coldly*).

COMPARISON OF MODIFIERS

5c. The forms of modifiers change to show comparison.

The three degrees of comparison are *positive, comparative,* and *superlative.*

(1) Most one-syllable modifiers form the comparative and superlative degrees by adding *–er* and *–est.*

(2) Some two-syllable modifiers form their comparative and superlative degrees by adding *–er* and *–est.* Other two-syllable modifiers form the comparative and superlative degrees by using *more* and *most.*

(3) Modifiers of more than two syllables form the comparative and superlative degrees by using *more* and *most.*

(4) To show decreasing comparisons, all modifiers form their comparative and superlative degrees with *less* and *least.*

(5) Some modifiers form the comparative and superlative degrees in other ways.

POSITIVE	COMPARATIVE	SUPERLATIVE
rude	ruder	rudest
happy	happier	happiest
skillful	more skillful	most skillful
quickly	more quickly	most quickly
artistic	more artistic	most artistic
carefully	more carefully	most carefully
ripe	less ripe	least ripe
safely	less safely	least safely

Drop the final silent e before adding *–er* or *–est.*

EXAMPLES
safe + er = saf**er**
ripe + est = rip**est**

For more information about correct spelling when adding suffixes to words, see pages 1059–1060.

The following pairs of modifiers are frequently confused: *bad, badly* and *good, well.* For discussions of the correct uses of these modifiers, see page 1062.

POSITIVE	COMPARATIVE	SUPERLATIVE
bad	worse	worst
good/well	better	best
little	less	least
many/much	more	most

5d. **Use the comparative degree when comparing two things. Use the superlative degree when comparing more than two.**

COMPARATIVE Maggie was **more respectful** than Dee.
I liked this story **better** than that one.

SUPERLATIVE Is this the **best** story of the ones you've read?
Which of the three poems was the **least complex?**

5e. **Include the word *other* or *else* when comparing one thing with others in the same group.**

ILLOGICAL This image is more vivid than any in the poem. [This image is in the poem. Logically, this image cannot be more vivid than itself.]

LOGICAL This image is more vivid than any **other** in the poem.

ILLOGICAL Rita understands plot better than everyone does. [*Everyone* includes Rita. Logically, she cannot understand better than she herself does.]

LOGICAL Rita understands plot better than everyone **else** does.

5f. **Avoid a *double comparison*—the use of both *–er* and *more* (or *less*) or both *–est* and *most* (or *least*) to modify the same word.**

EXAMPLES

Alice Walker, **better** [*not* more better] known as the author of *The Color Purple,* wrote this story.

The test was **easier** [*not* more easier] than I thought it would be.

5g. **Be sure your comparisons are clear.**

UNCLEAR The traffic here is faster than Detroit. [This sentence incorrectly compares traffic with a city.]

CLEAR The traffic here is faster than **traffic in** Detroit.

State both parts of an incomplete comparison if there is any chance of misunderstanding.

UNCLEAR I see her more than Mark.

CLEAR I see her more than Mark **sees her.**

CLEAR I see her more than **I see** Mark.

PLACEMENT OF MODIFIERS

5h. **Avoid using a *dangling modifier*—a modifying word or word group that does not sensibly modify any word or word group in the same sentence.**

You may correct a dangling modifier

- by adding a word or words that the dangling modifier can sensibly modify
- by adding a word or words to the dangling modifier
- by rewording the sentence

DANGLING To understand Shakespeare's plays, some knowledge of his vocabulary is necessary.

CLEAR To understand Shakespeare's plays, **readers** need some knowledge of his vocabulary.

DANGLING While studying for the math test, my phone rang incessantly.

CLEAR While **I was** studying for the math test, my phone rang incessantly.

DANGLING After giving an example of a simile, our next task was to create one.

CLEAR **Our tasks were to give an example of a simile and then to create one.**

5i. **Avoid using a *misplaced modifier*—a modifying word or word group that sounds awkward or unclear because it seems to modify the wrong word or word group.**

To correct a misplaced modifier, place the modifying word or word group as near as possible to the word you intend it to modify.

MISPLACED Sunglasses hid her face on her nose.

CLEAR Sunglasses **on her nose** hid her face.

MISPLACED A scrap from a uniform was part of the quilt that had been worn during the Civil War.

CLEAR A scrap from a uniform **that had been worn during the Civil War** was part of the quilt.

MISPLACED Made from pieces of old clothing, Dee held the quilts.

CLEAR Dee held the quilts **made from pieces of old clothing.**

6 PHRASES

6a. **A *phrase* is a group of related words that is used as a single part of speech and does not contain both a verb and its subject.**

VERB PHRASE	have been writing
PREPOSITIONAL PHRASE	with you and me

For information about placement of modifying phrases, see page 1033.

PREPOSITIONAL PHRASES

6b. **A *prepositional phrase* begins with a preposition and ends with the *object of the preposition,* a word or word group that functions as a noun.**

EXAMPLES
They were covered **with golden fur.** [The noun *fur* is the object of the preposition *with.*]
According to John Steinbeck, coyotes can be pests. [The noun *John Steinbeck* is the object of the preposition *according to.*]

(1) A prepositional phrase that modifies a noun or pronoun is called an ***adjective phrase.***

An adjective phrase tells *what kind* or *which one.*

EXAMPLES
The stories **of American Indians** sometimes feature coyotes. [*Of American Indians* modifies *stories,* telling *what kind.*]
Stories **about coyotes** depict them as tricksters. [*About coyotes* modifies *stories,* telling *which ones.*]

An adjective phrase generally follows the word it modifies. That word may be the object of another preposition.

EXAMPLE
Did you see the film **about the coyotes of the desert**? [*Of the desert* modifies *coyotes,* the object of the preposition *about.*]

More than one adjective phrase may modify the same noun or pronoun.

EXAMPLE
The sight **of them through the scope** made Steinbeck think. [*Of them* and *through the scope* modify the noun *sight.*]

(2) A prepositional phrase that modifies a verb, an adjective, or an adverb is called an ***adverb phrase.*** An adverb phrase tells *when, where, how, why,* or *to what extent.*

EXAMPLES
In a moment, he reached for his rifle. [*In a moment* modifies *reached,* telling *when.*]
The coyotes were not far **from him.** [*From him* modifies *far,* telling *where.*]
They were not dangerous **to him.** [*To him* modifies *dangerous,* telling *how* they were dangerous.]

An adverb phrase may come before or after the word it modifies.

EXAMPLES
To me, this was a wonderful story.
This was a wonderful story **to me.**

More than one adverb phrase may modify the same word.

EXAMPLE
In 1962, John Steinbeck received the Nobel Prize **at age sixty.** [Both *in 1962* and *at age sixty* modify *received.*]

VERBALS AND VERBAL PHRASES

A ***verbal*** is a form of a verb used as a noun, an adjective, or an adverb. A ***verbal phrase*** consists of a verbal and its modifiers and complements. Three kinds of verbals are *participles, gerunds,* and *infinitives.*

Participles and Participial Phrases

6c. **A *participle* is a verb form that can be used as an adjective. A *participial phrase* consists of a participle and all the words related to the participle.**

(1) ***Present participles*** end in *–ing.*

EXAMPLES
It was certainly an **embarrassing** moment. [The present participle *embarrassing* modifies the noun *moment.*]
Hammering loudly, Sobel took out his frustration in hard work. [The participial phrase *hammering loudly* modifies *Sobel.* The adverb *loudly* modifies the present participle *hammering.*]

(2) Most ***past participles*** end in *–d* or *–ed*. Others are irregularly formed.

EXAMPLES

The **injured** player did not return. [The past participle *injured* modifies the noun *player*.]

Feld, **dazzled by Max's college education,** thinks that the boy is a good match for Miriam. [The participial phrase modifies the noun *Feld*. The adverb phrase *by Max's college education* modifies the past participle *dazzled*.]

Read aloud, the story entertained the kindergarten class. [The participial phrase modifies the noun *story*. The adverb *aloud* modifies the past participle *read*.]

Do not confuse a participle used as an adjective with a participle used as part of a verb phrase.

ADJECTIVE What are **fighting** fish?
VERB PHRASE They **are fighting.**

Gerunds and Gerund Phrases

6d. A *gerund* is a verb form ending in *–ing* that is used as a noun. A *gerund phrase* consists of a gerund and all the words related to the gerund.

SUBJECT **Reading** was Sobel's pastime. [The gerund *reading* is the subject of *was*.]

DIRECT OBJECT She didn't like **speaking in class.** [The gerund phrase *speaking in class* is the direct object of the verb *did like*. The prepositional phrase *in class* modifies the gerund *speaking*.]

PREDICATE NOMINATIVE The best part was **winning the match.** [The gerund phrase *winning the match* is the predicate nominative identifying the subject *part*. *Match* is the direct object of *winning*.]

OBJECT OF A PREPOSITION After **waiting for two years,** Sobel can propose to Miriam. [The gerund phrase *waiting for two years* is the object of the preposition *after*. The prepositional phrase *for two years* modifies *waiting*.]

A noun or pronoun should be in the possessive form when preceding a gerund.

EXAMPLES

Sobel's pounding bothered Feld because it interfered with **his** daydreaming.

Do not confuse a gerund with a present participle used as an adjective or as a part of a verb phrase.

EXAMPLE

Meddling, Feld was **arranging** for Max and Miriam to go out. [*Meddling* is a present participle modifying *Feld*. *Arranging* is part of the verb phrase *was arranging*.]

Infinitives and Infinitive Phrases

6e. An *infinitive* is a verb form, usually preceded by *to*, that can be used as a noun, an adjective, or an adverb. An *infinitive phrase* consists of an infinitive and all the words related to the infinitive.

NOUN **To have friends** is important. [The infinitive phrase *to have friends* is the subject of *is*. *Friends* is the direct object of the infinitive *to have*.]

Maggie did not want **to argue with Dee.** [The infinitive phrase *to argue with Dee* is the object of the verb *did want*. The prepositional phrase *with Dee* modifies the infinitive *to argue*.]

Dee's plan was **to take the quilts.** [The infinitive phrase *to take the quilts* is the predicate nominative identifying the subject *plan*. *Quilts* is the direct object of the infinitive *to take*.]

ADJECTIVE Her refusal **to answer questions** puzzled him. [The infinitive phrase *to answer questions* modifies the noun *refusal*. *Questions* is the direct object of the infinitive *to answer*.]

ADVERB We were ready **to go to the game.** [The infinitive phrase *to go to the game* modifies the adjective *ready*. The prepositional phrase *to the game* modifies the infinitive *to go*.]

Do not confuse an infinitive with a prepositional phrase that begins with *to*.

EXAMPLE

Eric went **to the gym** [prepositional phrase] **to meet Clint** [infinitive phrase]**.**

Sometimes the *to* of the infinitive is omitted.

EXAMPLES

Would you help me [to] proofread this?
You need not [to] make the corrections.

6f. **An infinitive may have a subject, in which case it forms an *infinitive clause.***

EXAMPLE

He asked **the teacher to excuse him.** [The infinitive clause *the teacher to excuse him* is the direct object of the verb *asked. The teacher* is the subject of the infinitive *to excuse. Him* is the direct object of the infinitive.]

For more about clauses, see Part 7: Clauses.

Avoiding Split Infinitives

A ***split infinitive*** occurs when a word is placed between the *to* and the verb in an infinitive. Although split infinitives are commonly used in informal speaking and writing, you should avoid using them in formal situations.

SPLIT It was better to just mind his own business.

REVISED It was better just **to mind** his own business.

Try It Out

Revise each of the following sentences to eliminate the split infinitive.

1. Mrs. Johnson liked to sometimes tell jokes that nobody understood.
2. Ken pretended to not know the answers.
3. She began to suddenly smile at him.
4. Clint wanted to right away escape.
5. To simply take the next train was the boys' advice.

Appositives and Appositive Phrases

6g. **An *appositive* is a noun or pronoun placed beside another noun or pronoun to identify or explain it. An *appositive phrase* consists of an appositive and its modifiers.**

EXAMPLES

Janet Frame, **a resident of New Zealand,** wrote the essay. [The appositive phrase *a resident of New Zealand* identifies the subject *Janet Frame.*]

Have you seen *The Maltese Falcon,* **one of Humphrey Bogart's most famous films**? [The appositive phrase *one of Humphrey Bogart's most famous films* explains the direct object *The Maltese Falcon.*]

Who wrote the poem **"Mother to Son"**? [The appositive *"Mother to Son"* identifies the direct object *poem.*]

An appositive phrase usually follows the noun or pronoun it refers to. For emphasis, however, it may come at the beginning of a sentence.

EXAMPLE

A big brother all my life, I rushed to help the little girl who reminded me of my sister.

Appositives and appositive phrases are usually set off by commas. However, some appositives are necessary to identify or explain a noun or pronoun and therefore should not be set off by commas.

EXAMPLES

My cousin **Jim** lives in Alaska. [The appositive is not set off by commas because it is necessary to tell which of the writer's cousins lives in Alaska.]

My cousin**, Jim,** lives in Alaska. [The appositive is set off by commas because the writer has only one cousin, and the appositive is not necessary.]

7 Clauses

7a. **A *clause* is a group of words that contains a verb and its subject and is used as part of a sentence.**

SENTENCE Lichens are small, rootless plants that are composed of both fungi and algae.

CLAUSE Lichens are small, rootless plants. [complete thought]

CLAUSE that are composed of both fungi and algae [incomplete thought]

KINDS OF CLAUSES

7b. **An *independent* (or *main*) *clause* expresses a complete thought and can stand by itself as a sentence.**

EXAMPLES

His cousin had an apartment, and **Shorty roomed there.**

When his hair was long enough, **he got it conked.**

7c. **A *subordinate* (or *dependent*) *clause* does not express a complete thought and cannot stand alone.**

EXAMPLE
When his hair was long enough, he got it conked.

Subordinate clauses can be used as adjectives, adverbs, or nouns.

7d. **An *adjective clause* is a subordinate clause that modifies a noun or a pronoun.**

An adjective clause, which usually follows the word it modifies, usually begins with a ***relative pronoun***—*who, whom, whose, which,* or *that.* Besides introducing an adjective clause, a relative pronoun has its own function within the clause.

EXAMPLES
Alex Haley, **who helped write this story,** wrote *Roots*. [The adjective clause modifies *Alex Haley. Who* serves as the subject of *helped*.]
Malcolm X, **whose life touched many,** was an extraordinary man. [The adjective clause modifies the noun *Malcolm X. Whose* serves as an adjective modifying *life*.]

A relative pronoun may sometimes be left out of an adjective clause.

EXAMPLE
Was lye one of the ingredients [that] **he used**?

Occasionally an adjective clause begins with the relative adverb *where* or *when.*

EXAMPLES
That was the time **when it started to burn.**
Sores formed in the places **where the congolene remained.**

Depending on how it is used, an adjective clause is either essential or nonessential. An ***essential clause*** provides information that is necessary to the meaning of a sentence. A ***nonessential clause*** provides additional information that can be omitted without changing the meaning of a sentence. A nonessential clause is always set off by commas.

ESSENTIAL	Students **who are going to the track meet** can take the bus at 7:45 A.M.
NONESSENTIAL	Austin Stevens, **whose mother is a pediatrician,** plans to study medicine.

For more information about punctuating essential and nonessential clauses, see page 1051.

7e. **An *adverb clause* is a subordinate clause that modifies a verb, an adjective, or an adverb.**

An adverb clause, which may come before or after the word it modifies, tells *how, when, where, why, to what extent* (*how much*), or *under what condition.* An adverb clause begins with a ***subordinating conjunction,*** such as *although, because, if, so that,* or *when.*

EXAMPLES
Because he wanted to transform himself, he submitted to the pain. [The adverb clause modifies *submitted,* telling *why*.]
If he touched the jar, it felt hot. [The adverb clause modifies *felt,* telling *under what condition*.]
He was amazed **when he saw himself in the mirror.** [The adverb phrase modifies the verb *was amazed,* telling *when*.]
Malcolm X may be more famous today **than he was during his lifetime.** [The adverb clause modifies *famous,* telling *to what extent*.]

7f. **A *noun clause* is a subordinate clause used as a subject, a predicate nominative, a direct object, an indirect object, or an object of a preposition.**

The words commonly used to begin noun clauses include *that, what, whether, who,* and *why.*

SUBJECT	**What he had** was especially strong determination.
PREDICATE NOMINATIVE	Potatoes and other ingredients were **what they used** in making the stew.
DIRECT OBJECT	Who could have guessed **where his desire for transformation would take him**?
INDIRECT OBJECT	His story gives **whoever listens** the benefit of his experience.

The word that introduces a noun clause may or may not have a function within the noun clause.

EXAMPLES
Later, he regretted **what he had done.** [*What* is the direct object of *had done*.]
He believed **that the practice of conking was demeaning.** [*That* has no function in the clause.]

Sometimes the word that introduces a noun clause is not stated, but its meaning is understood.

EXAMPLE
He is a **man** [whom] **you should respect.**

Revising Short, Choppy Sentences

Although short sentences can be effective, it's usually a good idea to alternate between shorter sentences and longer ones. Often, you can combine short sentences by changing some of them into subordinate clauses and inserting them in other sentences.

CHOPPY Malcolm X had a troubled youth. He landed in jail. There, he changed his life completely.

REVISED Malcolm X, who had a troubled youth, landed in jail, where he changed his life completely.

Try It Out

The following paragraph consists mostly of short sentences. Revise the paragraph by changing some of these sentences into subordinate clauses and then combining them with other sentences and clauses to create longer, smoother sentences.

[1] Many people are slaves to fashion. [2] They worry about their hair. [3] Some people have straight hair. [4] They want curly hair. [5] Some people have curly hair. [6] They want straight hair. [7] They spend millions of dollars. [8] That money might be put to better use. [9] These people discover something. [10] Their appearance can't change who they really are.

8 Sentence Structure

SENTENCE OR SENTENCE FRAGMENT?

8a. **A *sentence* is a group of words that contains a subject and a verb and that expresses a complete thought.**

A sentence should begin with a capital letter and end with a period, a question mark, or an exclamation point. A group of words that either does not have a subject and a verb or does not express a complete thought is called a ***sentence fragment.***

FRAGMENT While his father was getting the wagon.
SENTENCE While his father was getting the wagon, the boys got ready.

FRAGMENT Their father up early on Saturday morning.
SENTENCE Why was their father up early on Saturday morning?

FRAGMENT What fun!
SENTENCE What fun that was!

FRAGMENT Meeting on Friday to make plans.
SENTENCE We are meeting on Friday to make plans.

For information on how to correct fragments, see pages 1041–1042. For more information about capitalizing and punctuating sentences, see page 1046 and page 1050.

SUBJECT AND PREDICATE

8b. **A sentence consists of two parts: the subject and the predicate. The *subject* tells *whom* or *what* the sentence is about. The *predicate* tells something about the subject.**

In the following examples, all the words labeled *subject* make up the ***complete subject,*** and all the words labeled *predicate* make up the ***complete predicate.***

SUBJECT	PREDICATE
They	rode in the wagon.

SUBJECT	PREDICATE
A maze of streets and alleys	led to the dump.

PREDICATE	SUBJECT	PREDICATE
Doesn't	Brian's car	have a tape deck?

The Simple Subject

8c. **The *simple subject* is the main word or group of words that tells *whom* or *what* the sentence is about.**

EXAMPLES

The railroad **crossing** south of 86th Street was noisy. [The complete subject is *the railroad crossing south of 86th Street.*]

The gifted **Hugo Martinez-Serros** wrote "Distillation." [The complete subject is *the gifted Hugo Martinez-Serros.*]

The Simple Predicate

The *simple predicate*, or *verb*, is the main word or group of words that tells something about the subject.

EXAMPLES

He **ran** faster and faster up the hill. [The complete predicate is *ran faster and faster up the hill*.]

Have you ever **had** such a wild ride on a sled before? [The complete predicate is *have ever had such a wild ride on a sled before*.]

In this book, the term *subject* refers to the simple subject and the term *verb* refers to the simple predicate unless otherwise noted.

The Compound Subject and the Compound Verb

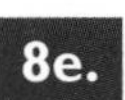

A *compound subject* consists of two or more subjects that are joined by a conjunction and have the same verb.

EXAMPLES

He and his **brothers** were frightened.

Were the **boys or** their **father** hurt?

A *compound verb* consists of two or more verbs that are joined by a conjunction and have the same subject.

EXAMPLES

They **ran** to the shack **and hid** inside.

Pa **protected** them **but was pelted** with hail himself.

A sentence may have a compound subject and a compound verb.

EXAMPLE

Both my **aunt** and my **uncle have** nice cars but rarely **drive** anywhere.

Finding the Subject of a Sentence

To find the subject of a sentence, ask "Who?" or "What?" before the verb.

(1) The subject of a sentence is never in a prepositional phrase.

EXAMPLES

Piles of rotten garbage stood before them. [What stood? *Piles* stood, not *garbage*, which is the object of the preposition *of*.]

In the trash hid **rats.** [What hid? *Rats* hid. *Trash* is the object of the preposition *in*.]

(2) The subject of a sentence expressing a question usually follows the verb or part of the verb phrase. Questions often begin with a verb, a helping verb, or a word such as *what, when, where, how,* or *why*.

Turning the question into a statement may help you find the subject.

QUESTION Is hail dangerous to people?
STATEMENT **Hail** is dangerous to people.

(3) The word *there* or *here* is never the subject of a sentence.

EXAMPLES

There is the **tarp.** [What is there? A *tarp* is.]

Here is your **water.** [What is here? *Water* is.]

(4) The subject of a sentence expressing a command or request is always understood to be *you* although *you* may not appear in the sentence.

EXAMPLE

[**You**] Pay attention to his metaphors. [Who is to pay attention? *You* are.]

The subject of a command or request is *you* even when the sentence contains a ***noun of direct address,*** a word naming the one or ones spoken to.

EXAMPLE

Ed, [**you**] please explain this story's ending.

COMPLEMENTS

A *complement* is a word or group of words that completes the meaning of a verb.

Three kinds of complements are *subject complements* (*predicate nominative* and *predicate adjective*), *direct objects,* and *indirect objects.*

The Subject Complement

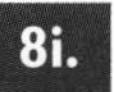

A *subject complement* is a word or a word group that completes the meaning of a linking verb and that identifies or modifies the subject.

(1) A ***predicate nominative*** is a noun or pronoun that follows a linking verb and identifies the subject of the verb.

EXAMPLES

Their father was a powerful **man.** [*Man* identifies the subject *father*.]

Was the author the youngest **son**? [*Son* renames the subject *author*.]

(2) A ***predicate adjective*** is an adjective that follows a linking verb and modifies the subject of the verb.

EXAMPLES

Was their father **strong**? [The adjective *strong* modifies the subject *father*.]

The wagon was **sturdy** and **large.** [The adjectives *sturdy* and *large* modify the subject *wagon*.]

A subject complement may precede the subject and the verb.

PREDICATE ADJECTIVE How **glad** they were to have the tarp!

For more information about the different kinds of verbs, see page 1021.

The Direct Object and the Indirect Object

8j. A *direct object* is a noun or pronoun that receives the action of a verb or that shows the result of the action. The direct object tells *whom or what* after a transitive verb.

EXAMPLES

Ice covered the **ground.** [covered what? *ground*]

How he admires his **father** and **mother**! [admires whom? *father* and *mother*]

8k. An *indirect object* is a noun or pronoun that precedes the direct object and usually tells *to whom or for whom* (or *to what* or *for what*) the action of the verb is done.

EXAMPLES

They brought their **mother** sacks of food. [brought sacks for whom? *mother*]

He had given the **wheels** and **gears** some grease. [had given grease to what? *wheels* and *gears*]

CLASSIFYING SENTENCES BY PURPOSE

8l. Sentences may be classified as *declarative, imperative, interrogative,* or *exclamatory*.

(1) A ***declarative sentence*** makes a statement. It is followed by a period.

EXAMPLE

They gazed out over the city**.**

(2) An ***imperative sentence*** makes a request or gives a command. It is usually followed by a period. A very strong command, however, is followed by an exclamation point.

EXAMPLES

Let me know when you are free**.** [request]

Be careful not to fall**.** [mild command]

Hurry**!** [strong command]

(3) An ***interrogative sentence*** asks a question. It is followed by a question mark.

EXAMPLE

What is the high point of the action**?**

(4) An ***exclamatory sentence*** expresses strong feeling. It is always followed by an exclamation point.

EXAMPLE

Watch out**!**

For more information about end punctuation for sentences, see page 1050.

CLASSIFYING SENTENCES BY STRUCTURE

8m. Sentences may be classified as *simple, compound, complex, or compound-complex*.

(1) A ***simple sentence*** has one independent clause and no subordinate clauses.

EXAMPLES

Warehouses and markets sent all of their refuse to the dump.

Look at this!

(2) A ***compound sentence*** has two or more independent clauses but no subordinate clauses.

EXAMPLES

A shack had sheltered them, but then the wind tore its roof off.

The lightning diminished; the storm was over.

The children were afraid; however, Pa calmed them.

NOTE Do not confuse a compound sentence with a simple sentence that has a compound subject or a compound predicate.

COMPOUND PREDICATE **He**(S) **rose**(V) and **stretched**(V) his arms.

COMPOUND SENTENCE **Pa**(S) **rose**(V), and **he**(S) **stretched**(V) his arms.

(3) A ***complex sentence*** has one independent clause and at least one subordinate clause.

EXAMPLES

After they got home, they unloaded the wagon. [The subordinate clause is *after they got home;* the independent clause is *they unloaded the wagon.*]

As he ran, sweat darkened the shirt that he was wearing. [The subordinate clauses are *as he ran* and *that he was wearing.*]

 For information about independent clauses and subordinate clauses, see Part 7: Clauses.

(4) A ***compound-complex sentence*** contains two or more independent clauses and at least one subordinate clause.

EXAMPLE

When the boys were ready, they piled in the wagon, and Pa slipped into the harness. [The independent clauses are *they piled in the wagon* and *Pa slipped into the harness.* The subordinate clause is *when the boys were ready.*]

 For information about using varied sentence structure and improving sentence style, see Part 10: Writing Effective Sentences.

Varying Sentence Structure

To keep readers interested in your ideas, evaluate your writing to see whether you have used a variety of sentence structures. Then, use revising techniques to vary the structure of your sentences.

Try It Out 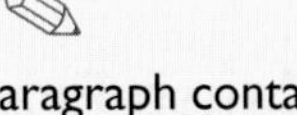

The following paragraph contains only simple sentences. Revise the paragraph to create a variety of sentence structures.

[1] Many people immigrate to the United States. [2] Some bring children along. [3] These children often face enormous difficulties. [4] Many do not have the same cultural background as the other students at their new schools. [5] The young immigrants may not speak English. [6] They do not know the customs of their new home. [7] Yet, their parents have high hopes for them. [8] The children try to fulfill those hopes. [9] Millions of immigrants have done so. [10] Somehow these children adapt to life in the United States.

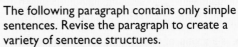

9 WRITING COMPLETE SENTENCES

SENTENCE FRAGMENTS

9a. Avoid using sentence fragments.

A ***sentence*** is a word group that has a subject and a verb and expresses a complete thought. A ***sentence fragment*** is a word group that does not have the basic parts of a complete sentence.

To find out whether a word group is a complete sentence or a sentence fragment, use this simple three-part test. If you answer no to any of these questions, the word group is a fragment.

1. Does the group of words have a subject?
2. Does it have a verb?
3. Does it express a complete thought?

SUBJECT MISSING Was her dancing partner. [*Who* was her dancing partner?]

SENTENCE **Geraldo** was her dancing partner.

VERB MISSING Marin at the hospital. [*What* did she do at the hospital?]

SENTENCE Marin **waited** at the hospital.

NOT A COMPLETE THOUGHT When she was asked. [*What happened* when she was asked?]

SENTENCE **She could not give his full name** when she was asked.

Phrase Fragments

A ***phrase*** is a group of words that does not have a subject and a verb.

FRAGMENT Attending many dances.

SENTENCE She enjoyed **attending many dances.**

FRAGMENT To wonder about him.

SENTENCE His family began **to wonder about him.**

FRAGMENT	Living far away from him.
SENTENCE	**Living far away from him,** they will never know his fate.

FRAGMENT	A writer of Mexican heritage.
SENTENCE	Sandra Cisneros, **a writer of Mexican heritage,** wrote this story.

FRAGMENT	In green pants and a fancy shirt.
SENTENCE	Marin danced with the boy **in green pants and a fancy shirt.**

Subordinate Clause Fragments

A ***clause*** is a group of words that has a subject and a verb. An ***independent clause*** expresses a complete thought and can stand on its own as a sentence.

INDEPENDENT CLAUSE She found her voice.

However, a ***subordinate clause*** does not express a complete thought and can't stand by itself as a sentence.

FRAGMENT	When Sandra Cisneros found her point of view.
SENTENCE	**When Sandra Cisneros found her point of view,** she found her voice.

RUN-ON SENTENCES

9b. Avoid run-on sentences.

A ***run-on sentence*** is two or more complete sentences that are run together as one. Because a reader cannot tell where one idea ends and another begins, run-on sentences can be confusing.

There are two kinds of run-ons. In the first kind, called a ***fused sentence,*** the sentences have no punctuation at all between them.

RUN-ON He had no papers on him no one knew his identity.

In the other kind of run-on, called a ***comma splice,*** only a comma separates the sentences from one another.

RUN-ON He had no papers on him, no one knew his identity.

Revising Run-on Sentences

There are several ways that you can revise run-on sentences. Usually, the easiest way is to make two separate sentences. However, if the two thoughts are closely related and equally important, you may want to make a compound sentence. Here are three ways to make a compound sentence out of a run-on.

1. You can use a comma and a coordinating conjunction—*and, but, or, yet, for, so,* or *nor.*

   REVISED He had no papers on him**, and** no one knew his identity.

2. You can use a semicolon.

   REVISED He had no papers on him**;** no one knew his identity.

3. You can use a semicolon and a ***conjunctive adverb***—a word such as *therefore, instead, also, meanwhile, still, nevertheless,* or *however.* Follow a conjunctive adverb with a comma.

   REVISED He had no papers on him**; consequently,** no one knew his identity.

10 WRITING EFFECTIVE SENTENCES

SENTENCE COMBINING

Inserting Words

10a. Combine short sentences by inserting a key word from one sentence into another sentence.

Sometimes you can simply insert a key word without changing its form. In many cases, however, you will need to change the form of the key word in some way before you can insert it smoothly into another sentence.

ORIGINAL	Abioseh Nicol is a writer. He is from Africa.
COMBINED	Abioseh Nicol is an **African** writer.

ORIGINAL	You will read one of his stories. It involves a mystery.
COMBINED	You will read one of his **mystery** stories.

When you change the form of a key word, you often need to add an ending that makes the word an adjective or an adverb. Usually the ending is *–ed, –ing,* or *–ly.* For information about the correct spelling of words when adding suffixes, see pages 1059–1060.

Inserting Phrases

10b. Combine closely related sentences by taking a phrase from one sentence and inserting it in another sentence.

Prepositional Phrases

A ***prepositional phrase,*** a preposition with its object, can usually be inserted into another sentence without changing the phrase. All you have to do is leave out some of the words in one of the sentences.

ORIGINAL Nicol studied in Africa and abroad. He studied at Cambridge.

COMBINED Nicol studied in Africa and abroad **at Cambridge.**

Participial Phrases

A ***participial phrase*** contains a participle and words related to the participle. The entire phrase acts as an adjective, modifying a noun or a pronoun. Sometimes, you can insert a participial phrase just as it is. At other times, you can change the verb from one sentence into a participle and insert it in the other sentence.

ORIGINAL Bola's son came to visit. He was wearing a scarf around his neck.

COMBINED Bola's son came to visit, **wearing a scarf around his neck.**

ORIGINAL He showed Asi a necklace. The necklace bore a gold locket.

COMBINED He showed Asi a necklace **bearing a gold locket.**

Appositive Phrases

An ***appositive phrase*** is placed next to a noun or pronoun to identify or explain it. Sometimes you can combine sentences by changing one of the sentences to an appositive phrase.

ORIGINAL Meji was Bola's only son. He was Asi's father.

COMBINED Meji, **Bola's only son,** was Asi's father.

Using Compound Subjects and Compound Verbs

10c. Combine sentences by making compound subjects and compound verbs.

Look for sentences that have the same subject or the same verb. Then, make the subject, verb, or both compound by using a coordinating conjunction.

ORIGINAL Meji went for a walk. Asi went with him. [same verb with different subjects]

COMBINED **Meji and Asi** went for a walk. [compound subject]

ORIGINAL He came for a visit. He could not stay long. [same subject with different verbs]

COMBINED He **came** for a visit **but could** not **stay** long. [compound verb]

ORIGINAL Bola slept. So did Asi. The next day, they learned of Meji's death. [same verb (*slept*) with different subjects and plural subject (*they*) that refers to the same two subjects with a different verb]

COMBINED **Bola and Asi slept and learned** the next day of Meji's death. [compound subject and compound verb]

Creating a Compound Sentence

10d. Combine sentences by creating a compound sentence.

A ***compound sentence*** is two or more simple sentences linked by

- a comma and a coordinating conjunction

  or
- a semicolon

  or
- a semicolon and a conjunctive adverb

ORIGINAL Asi was Meji's daughter. She lived with Bola.

COMBINED Asi was Meji's daughter**, but** she lived with Bola. [comma and coordinating conjunction]

Asi was Meji's daughter**;** she lived with Bola. [semicolon]

Asi was Meji's daughter**; however,** she lived with Bola. [semicolon and conjunctive adverb]

For more information about compound sentences, see pages 1040, 1042, and 1051.

Using Compound Sentences

Before linking two thoughts in a compound sentence, make sure that the thoughts are closely related to one another and equally important. Otherwise, you may confuse your readers.

UNRELATED IDEAS The spirit of Africa is noble. This story takes place in a village.

CLOSELY RELATED IDEAS The spirit of Africa is noble, and this story depicts that nobility.

Try It Out 

Most of the following pairs of sentences can be combined into a compound sentence. Combine each pair of sentences that have closely related ideas. If a pair of sentences contains unrelated ideas, write *unrelated.*

1. Some people love ghost stories. Other people do not.
2. Spirits can help people. Spirits can harm people.
3. Meji is a friendly ghost. He is kind to his family.
4. He helps his mother. She is grateful for his visit.
5. Did you like the story? When did you know about Meji?

Creating a Complex Sentence

10e. **Combine sentences by creating a complex sentence.**

A ***complex sentence*** includes one independent clause and one or more subordinate clauses.

 See pages 1036–1038 and 1042 for more about independent and subordinate clauses.

Adjective Clauses

You can change a sentence into an adjective clause by inserting *who, whom, which,* or *that* in place of the subject. Then you can use the adjective clause to give information about a noun or a pronoun in another sentence.

ORIGINAL Musa attended the service. Musa was the village's magician.

COMBINED Musa, **who was the village's magician,** attended the service.

Adverb Clauses

You can turn a sentence into an adverb clause by placing a subordinating conjunction (such as *after, if, although, because, when,* or *where*) at the beginning of the sentence. Then you can use the clause to modify a verb, an adjective, or an adverb in another sentence.

ORIGINAL Bola had suffered greatly. She did not regret her choice.

COMBINED **Although Bola had suffered greatly,** she did not regret her choice.

Noun Clauses

You can make a sentence into a noun clause and insert it into another sentence, using it just as you would use a noun. You can create a noun clause by inserting a word such as *that, how, what,* or *who* at the beginning of a sentence. When you place the noun clause in the other sentence, you may have to change or remove some words or revise the sentence in other ways.

ORIGINAL Asi knew about the locket. Did the mourners believe how?

COMBINED Did the mourners believe **how Asi knew about the locket**? [The word *how* introduces the noun clause, which becomes the object of the verb *believe*.]

IMPROVING SENTENCE STYLE

Using Parallel Structure

10f. **Use the same form to express equal ideas.**

Using the same form for equal ideas creates balance in a sentence. For example, you balance a noun with a noun, a phrase with the same type of phrase, and a clause with a clause. This balance is called ***parallel structure.***

NOT PARALLEL I like reading, writing, and to draw. [two gerunds and an infinitive]

PARALLEL I like **reading, writing,** and **drawing.** [three gerunds]

NOT PARALLEL Some of these stories are funny, entertaining, and teach me a lot. [two adjectives and a complete predicate]

PARALLEL Some of these stories are **funny, entertaining,** and **educational.** [three adjectives]

NOT PARALLEL I knew that an airplane had crashed but not about the passenger's heroic rescue. [a clause and a phrase]

PARALLEL I knew **that an airplane had crashed** but not **that a passenger had made a heroic rescue.** [two clauses]

Revising Stringy Sentences

10g. Avoid using stringy sentences.

A ***stringy sentence*** usually has too many independent clauses strung together with coordinating conjunctions like *and* or *but*. Since all the ideas are treated equally, the reader has trouble seeing how they are related. To fix a stringy sentence, you can break the sentence into two or more sentences or turn some of the independent clauses into subordinate clauses or phrases.

STRINGY The water was freezing cold, and a few survivors clung to some wreckage, and a helicopter came, but it could only take one person at a time, and one man let the others go first.

REVISED Although the water was freezing cold, a few survivors clung to some wreckage. A helicopter came, but it could only take one person at a time. One man let the others go first.

Revising Wordy Sentences

10h. Avoid using wordy sentences.

Extra words and unnecessarily difficult words clutter your writing and make it hard to follow. Compare the following sentences.

WORDY I wonder if you would be so kind as to take the time to enlighten me as to the current weather conditions in the immediate vicinity.

IMPROVED What's the weather?

Avoiding Wordy Sentences

Here are three tips for avoiding wordy sentences.

- Don't use complicated words where simple ones will do.
- Don't repeat yourself unless repetition is absolutely necessary.
- Don't use more words than you need to.

WORDY The rescuers were brave men who bravely risked death to rescue the injured.

REVISED The rescuers bravely risked death to save the injured.

Try It Out

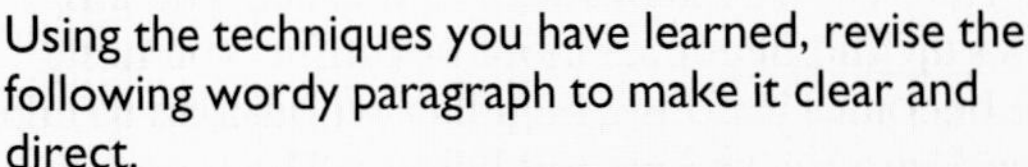

Using the techniques you have learned, revise the following wordy paragraph to make it clear and direct.

[1] Roger Rosenblatt attests to the fact that he wrote "The Man in the Water" in less time than it takes for an hour to pass. [2] However, any piece composed in this manner may be—and often, as practical experience indicates, is—flawed. [3] This possible eventuality Rosenblatt admits. [4] Writers, consequently, who are not far along in years should eschew procrastination, remembering one thing. [5] Rosenblatt has spent many, many years, decades even, editing, revising, and learning to perfect his skills.

Varying Sentence Structures

10i. Vary the structure of your sentences.

Using a variety of sentence structures makes your writing livelier. Instead of using all simple sentences, you can use a mix of simple, compound, complex, and compound-complex sentences.

ALL SIMPLE SENTENCES

I visited a friend on her grandparents' farm. I was about ten years old at the time. There wasn't much room in the farmhouse. My friend and I begged hard. We got to sleep in the hayloft in the barn. It was wonderful. We lay awake at night. We counted shooting stars. We told each other our dreams and our hopes for the future.

VARIED SENTENCE STRUCTURE

When I was about ten years old, I visited a friend on her grandparents' farm. Because there wasn't much room in the farmhouse and because we begged hard, my friend and I got to sleep in the hayloft in the barn. It was wonderful. We counted shooting stars as we lay awake at night, and we told each other our dreams and our hopes for the future.

Varying Sentence Beginnings

10j. Vary the beginnings of your sentences.

The basic structure of an English sentence is a subject followed by a verb. But following this pattern all the time can make your writing dull. Compare the following paragraphs.

SUBJECT-VERB PATTERN

The young girl's mother dies. Her father remarries. His new wife is beautiful but cruel. The girl grows up and becomes more beautiful. The new wife becomes jealous. She tells a woodsman to take the girl into the woods and kill her. The woodsman cannot bring himself to do so. He lets her go. The girl discovers a house in the forest. The house is inhabited by seven tiny men.

VARIED SENTENCE BEGINNINGS

After the young girl's mother dies, her father remarries. Although beautiful, his new wife is cruel. As the girl grows up and becomes more beautiful, the new wife becomes jealous. "Take the girl into the woods and kill her," she tells a woodsman. Unable to bring himself to do so, the woodsman lets the girl go. In the forest, the girl discovers a house inhabited by seven tiny men.

You can use the methods given in the chart to vary sentence beginnings.

VARYING SENTENCE BEGINNINGS
SINGLE-WORD MODIFIERS
Courageously, the man remained behind. [adverb]
Cautious, the copilot doubted an instrument reading. [adjective]
Iced, the plane's wings were dangerous. [participle]
Laughing, they dismissed their fear. [participle]
PHRASES
With haste, the rescue team rushed to the river. [prepositional phrase]
Writing of the incident, Roger Rosenblatt says that people must fight back against nature. [participial phrase]
To operate safely, wings must be clear of ice. [infinitive phrase]
SUBORDINATE CLAUSES
Because no one knew the hero's name, all people could identify with him. [adverb clause]
When Lenny Skutnik saw the injured woman, he dragged her to shore. [adverb clause]

11 CAPITALIZATION

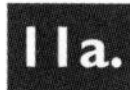

11a. Capitalize the first word in every sentence.

EXAMPLES
This poem has no title.
Does the author say why?

(1) Capitalize the first word of a direct quotation.

EXAMPLE
Roger answered, "**Y**es, I believe she does."

(2) Traditionally, the first word of a line of poetry is capitalized.

EXAMPLES
He turned his face to the wall;
She turned her back upon him;
—Anonymous, "Bonny Barbara Allan"

11b. Capitalize the first word both in the salutation and in the closing of a letter.

EXAMPLES
Dear Ann, **D**ear Sir: **S**incerely, **Y**ours truly,

11c. Capitalize the pronoun *I* and the interjection *O*.

The interjection *O* is always capitalized. The common interjection *oh* is not capitalized unless it is the first word in a sentence.

EXAMPLES
"'**O** Father, **O** Father, go dig my grave'" is a line from "Bonny Barbara Allan."
The play was a hit, but, **oh,** how nervous **I** was.

11d. Capitalize proper nouns and proper adjectives.

A ***common noun*** is a general name for a person, place, thing, or idea. A ***proper noun*** names a particular person, place, thing, or idea. ***Proper adjectives*** are formed from proper nouns. Common nouns are not capitalized unless they begin a sentence, begin a direct quotation, or are included in a title.

COMMON NOUNS	poet nation
PROPER NOUNS	Shakespeare Sioux
PROPER ADJECTIVES	Shakespearean sonnet Sioux art

In proper nouns with more than one word, do *not* capitalize

- articles (*a, an, the*)
- short prepositions (those with fewer than five letters, such as *at* and *with*)
- coordinating conjunctions (*and, but, for, nor, or, yet*)
- the sign of the infinitive (*to*)

EXAMPLES
Attila the Hun
"The Tale of the Sands"

Notice in the second example above that these words are capitalized if they are the first word in a proper noun.

(1) Capitalize the names of persons and animals.

GIVEN NAMES	Oliver	Gwendolyn	Tomás
SURNAMES	Brown	Furuya	Muñoz
ANIMALS	Big Red	Bambi	Wildfire

Descriptive names and nicknames also should be capitalized.

EXAMPLES
Ivan the Terrible Old Glory

Abbreviations such as *Ms., Mr., Dr.,* and *Gen.* should always be capitalized. Capitalize the abbreviations *Jr.* (*junior*) and *Sr.* (*senior*) after a name, and set them off with commas.

EXAMPLES
Is Gen. Daniel James, Jr., still on active duty?

Capitalization is part of the spelling for names with more than one word. Always check the spelling of such a name with the person whose name it is, or look in a reference source.

EXAMPLES
La Croix Du Pont McEwen O'Connor

(2) Capitalize geographical names.

TYPE OF NAME	EXAMPLES	
Towns and Cities	Rio de Janeiro	St. Louis
Counties, Townships, and Parishes	Osceola County Hayes Township	East Baton Rouge Parish Brooklyn Borough
States	North Dakota	Hawaii
Countries	Mexico	United States of America
Continents	North America	Asia
Islands	Cayman Islands	Isle of Man
Mountains	Mesabi Range	Camelback Mountain
Other Land Forms and Features	Cape Horn Angel Falls	Death Valley Dismal Swamp
Bodies of Water	Dead Sea	Lake of the Woods
Parks	Williams Park	Cedar Point Primitive Area
Regions	New England the South	Bermuda Triangle the Corn Belt
Roads, Streets, and Highways	Interstate 4 Route 66	West First Street North Tenth Street

☞ The abbreviations of names of states are always capitalized. For more about using and punctuating such abbreviations, see page 1050.

NOTE Words such as *north, western,* and *southeast* are not capitalized when they indicate direction.

EXAMPLES
western Iowa
driving south

NOTE In a hyphenated number, the second word begins with a lowercase letter.

EXAMPLE
Forty-second Street

(3) Capitalize the names of organizations, teams, business firms, institutions, buildings and other structures, and government bodies.

TYPE OF NAME	EXAMPLES	
Organizations	B'nai B'rith	Chess Club
Teams	Los Angeles Lakers	New England Patriots
Business Firms	Apple Computer, Inc.	Walgreen Company
Institutions	Lakes High School	Cedars Hospital
Buildings and Other Structures	Empire State Building the Alamo	Oak Mall London Bridge
Government Bodies	Congress	House of Commons

NOTE Capitalize words such as *democratic* and *republican* only when they refer to a specific political party.

EXAMPLES

The new leaders promised to establish democratic elections.

Was Abraham Lincoln a Republican?

(4) Capitalize the names of historical events and periods, special events, holidays and other calendar items, and time zones.

TYPE OF NAME	EXAMPLES	
Historical Events and Periods	Industrial Revolution War on Poverty	Battle of Camlan Paleozoic Era
Special Events	Interscholastic Debate Tournament Spring Fling	
Holidays and Other Calendar Items	Sunday Election Day	Memorial Day Yom Kippur
Time Zones	Central Daylight Time (CDT) Eastern Standard Time (EST)	

NOTE Do not capitalize the name of a season unless the season is personified or is used as part of a proper noun.

EXAMPLES

Soon, summer will be here.

Striding across the fields, Summer scorched the crops.

Are you going to the Summer Spectacular at the lake?

(5) Capitalize the names of nationalities, races, and peoples.

EXAMPLES

Greek, Caucasian, African Americans, Asian, Cherokee, Hispanic, Viking, Roman

The words *black* and *white* may or may not be capitalized when they refer to races.

(6) Capitalize the brand names of business products.

EXAMPLES

Cadillac, Teflon, Kleenex, Lee

Do not capitalize a common noun that follows a brand name.

EXAMPLES

Cadillac convertible, Teflon pan

(7) Capitalize the names of ships, trains, aircraft, spacecraft, monuments, awards, and planets, stars, and other heavenly bodies.

TYPE OF NAME	EXAMPLES	
Ships and Trains	*Californian* *City of New Orleans*	
Aircraft and Spacecraft	*Air Force One* *Vanguard II*	
Monuments and Memorials	Statue of Liberty Tomb of the Unknowns	
Awards	Distinguished Flying Cross Academy Award	
Planets, Stars, and Other Heavenly Bodies	Saturn Orion 51 Pegasi	Betelgeuse Little Dipper Milky Way

NOTE Do not capitalize the words *sun* and *moon*. Do not capitalize the word *earth* unless it is used along with the capitalized names of other heavenly bodies.

11e. Do *not* capitalize the names of school subjects, except for languages or course names followed by a number.

EXAMPLES
You need not take **a**rt or a **f**oreign **l**anguage, but you must take **E**nglish, **c**ivics, and **M**athematics II.

11f. Capitalize titles.

(1) Capitalize the title of a person when it comes before the person's name.

EXAMPLES
President Taft   **P**rofessor Hayakawa

Do not capitalize a title that is used alone or following a person's name, especially if the title is preceded by *a* or *the*.

EXAMPLES
Was the **r**everend at the concert?
When did Cleopatra become **q**ueen of Egypt?

When a title is used alone in direct address, it is usually capitalized.

EXAMPLES
Hurry, **D**octor!   Pardon me, **S**ir [*or* sir]?

(2) Capitalize words showing family relationship when used with a person's name but *not* when preceded by a possessive.

EXAMPLES
my **m**other   **A**untie Em   **D**ad   your **f**ather

(3) Capitalize the first and last words and all important words in titles of books, periodicals, poems, stories, essays, speeches, plays, historical documents, movies, radio and television programs, works of art, musical compositions, and cartoons. Unimportant words in a title are

- articles: *a, an, the*
- short prepositions (fewer than five letters): *of, to, for, from, in, over,* and so on.
- coordinating conjunctions: *and, but, so, nor, or, yet, for*

TYPE OF TITLE	EXAMPLES	
Books	*Spoon River Anthology*	*Travels with Charley*
Periodicals	*Family Computing*	*Horse and Pony*
Poems	"The Power of a Poem"	"What the Mirror Said"
Stories	"Life Is Sweet at Kumansenu"	"The Bet"
Essays and Speeches	"Where I Find My Heroes"	Gettysburg Address
Plays	*Antigone*	*I Never Sang for My Father*
Historical Documents	Declaration of Independence	Emancipation Proclamation
Movies	*Dances with Wolves*	*The Bear*
Radio and Television Programs	*Dinosaurs!*	*Home Improvement*
Works of Art	*View of Toledo*	*David*
Musical Compositions	"Greensleeves"	*La Mer*
Cartoons	*Calvin and Hobbes*	*The Neighborhood*

(4) Capitalize the names of religions and their followers, holy days and celebrations, holy writings, and specific deities.

TYPE OF NAME	EXAMPLES		
Religions and Followers	Judaism	Baptist	Taoist
Holy Days and Celebrations	Passover	Ramadan	Lent
Holy Writings	Bible	Upanishads	Koran
Specific Deities	Brahma	God	Allah

The word *god* is not capitalized when it refers to the gods of mythology. The names of such gods are capitalized, however.

EXAMPLE
The Egyptian **g**od of the sun was **R**a.

Revising Capitalization

You may notice that various publications differ in the way they use capital letters. Nevertheless, making sure your own capitalization agrees with the rules and guidelines presented in this part of the Language Handbook will help you communicate clearly with nearly any audience.

Try It Out

Revise the capitalization in the following sentences.

1. Have you read the story "What happened during the ice storm"?
2. I asked, "isn't this a Prince Tennis Racket?"
3. That is professor John Luís nickol Bell, jr.
4. Most of the Senators were already present.
5. I'm taking Shop II and Home Economics.

12 PUNCTUATION

END MARKS

End marks—periods, question marks, and exclamation points—are used to indicate the purpose of a sentence.

12a. A statement (or declarative sentence) is followed by a period.

EXAMPLE

Butterflies can symbolize rebirth**.**

12b. A question (or interrogative sentence) is followed by a question mark.

EXAMPLES

Who drew this picture of a butterfly**?** Did you**?**

12c. An exclamation (or exclamatory sentence) is followed by an exclamation point.

EXAMPLE

What a great idea**!**

12d. A command or request (or imperative sentence) is followed by either a period or an exclamation point.

When an imperative sentence makes a request, it is followed by a period. When an imperative sentence makes a command or shows strong feeling, an exclamation point is used.

EXAMPLES

Let me see it**.**
Be quiet**!**

12e. An abbreviation is usually followed by a period.

If a statement ends with an abbreviation, do not use an additional period as an end mark. However, do use a question mark or an exclamation point if one is needed.

EXAMPLES

Abraham lived around the nineteenth century B.C**.**
Was the story written in the eighth century B.C.**?**

TYPE OF ABBREVIATION	EXAMPLES
Personal Names	A. E. Housman Hanson W. Baldwin
Organizations and Companies	Assn. Co. Inc. Corp. Ltd.
Titles Used with Names	Mr. Ms. Mrs. Jr. Dr.
Times of Day	A.M. P.M.
Years	B.C. (written after the date) A.D. (written before the date)
Addresses	Ave. St. Blvd. Hwy.
States	Calif. Mass. Tex. N. Dak.

NOTE Two-letter state abbreviations without periods are used only when the ZIP Code is included.

EXAMPLE

Cincinnati, OH 45233

NOTE Usually, abbreviations are capitalized only if the words they stand for are capitalized. If you are unsure about capitalizing an abbreviation or using periods with it, look in a dictionary.

Abbreviations for government agencies and official organizations and some other frequently used abbreviations are written without periods. Abbreviations for most units of measure are usually written without periods, especially in science books.

EXAMPLES
CPR, FM, IQ, TV, USAF, cm, km, lb, ml, rpm
EXCEPTION
To avoid confusion with the word *in,* use *in.* for *inch.*

COMMAS

12f. Use commas to separate words, phrases, or clauses in a series.

EXAMPLE
Three major forms of poetry are the lyric**,** the epic**,** and the ballad.

(1) If all items in a series are joined by *and* or *or,* do not use commas to separate them.

EXAMPLE
They need firestone **and** some sticks **or** twigs.

NOTE Some words—such as *bread and butter, rod and reel,* and *table and chairs*—are used in pairs and may be considered one item in a series.

EXAMPLE
My waders, tackle box, **rod and reel,** and bait are already in the boat.

(2) As a rule, independent clauses in a series are separated by semicolons. Short independent clauses, however, may be separated by commas.

EXAMPLE
God called**,** Abraham answered**,** and Isaac obeyed.

12g. Use commas to separate two or more adjectives preceding a noun.

EXAMPLE
What a strange**,** awesome**,** dramatic story this is!

When the last adjective in a series is thought of as part of the noun (as in a compound noun), the comma before the adjective is omitted.

EXAMPLE
These are great short stories.

NOTE The comma may be omitted before a coordinating conjunction that joins the last two items in a series if the meaning is clear without the comma. However, using the comma is never wrong, and many writers prefer always to do so. Follow your teacher's instructions on this point.

12h. Use commas before *and, but, or, nor, for, so,* and *yet* when they join independent clauses.

EXAMPLE
Abraham raised his hand**, but** an angel called to him.

You may omit the comma before *and, but, or,* or *nor* if the clauses are very short and there is no chance of misunderstanding.

For more information about using coordinating conjunctions to join independent clauses, see pages 1040–1041 and 1043.

12i. Use commas to set off nonessential clauses and nonessential phrases.

A ***nonessential*** (or ***nonrestrictive***) clause or phrase adds information that is not needed to understand the main idea in the sentence.

NONESSENTIAL CLAUSE Isaac**, who was Abraham's son,** was spared. [Omitting the clause would not change the main idea of the sentence.]

When a clause or phrase is necessary to the meaning of a sentence, the clause or phrase is ***essential*** (or ***restrictive***), and commas are *not* used.

ESSENTIAL PHRASE The blessings **given to Abraham** were numerous. [Omitting the clause would change the meaning of the sentence.]

For more information about phrases and clauses, see Part 6: Phrases and Part 7: Clauses.

12j. Use commas after certain introductory elements.

(1) Use commas after words such as *next* and *no* and after introductory interjections such as *why* and *well.*

EXAMPLE
Yes, Wilfred Owen wrote that poem.

(2) Use a comma after an introductory participial phrase.

EXAMPLE
Drawing from the Bible, Owen updated its message.

(3) Use a comma after one long introductory prepositional phrase or two or more short introductory prepositional phrases.

EXAMPLE
At the end of Owen's poem, the son is slain.

(4) Use a comma after an introductory adverb clause.

EXAMPLE
When the angel speaks, the father ignores it.

12k. Use commas to set off elements that interrupt a sentence.

EXAMPLE
The thief**, in fact,** later became a disciple.

(1) Appositives and appositive phrases are usually set off by commas.

EXAMPLE
Shichiri**, a man of his word,** denied any theft.

(2) Words used in direct address are set off by commas.

EXAMPLE
What**, David,** is the meaning of this parable?

(3) Parenthetical expressions are set off by commas. ***Parenthetical expressions*** are side remarks that add minor information or that relate ideas to each other.

EXAMPLE
It is**, I believe,** about generosity.

12l. Use commas in certain conventional situations.

(1) Use a comma to separate items in dates and addresses.

EXAMPLES
My sister was born in Akron**,** Ohio**,** on May 7**,** 1991.
Leon's new address is 945 Oak Drive**,** Covington**,** KY 41011.

(2) Use a comma after the salutation of a friendly letter and after the closing of any letter.

EXAMPLES
Dear Aunt Hazel**,** Sincerely yours**,**

(3) Use a comma after a name followed by an abbreviation such as *Jr., Sr.,* or *M.D.* Follow such an abbreviation with a comma unless it ends the sentence.

EXAMPLE
My report is about Martin Luther King**,** Jr.

12m. Do not use unnecessary commas.

Too much punctuation is just as confusing as not enough punctuation, especially in the case of commas.

CONFUSING	A man thought that a boy, who was a neighbor, was a thief, but, then, the man found, to his surprise, that he was wrong.
CLEAR	A man thought that a boy who was a neighbor was a thief, but then the man found to his surprise that he was wrong.

SEMICOLONS

12n. Use a semicolon between independent clauses in a sentence if they are not joined by *and, but, or, nor, for, so,* or *yet.*

EXAMPLE
The tiger was in a cage**;** a Brahman let him out.

Similarly, a semicolon can take the place of a period to join two sentences that are closely related.

TWO SIMPLE SENTENCES	The man opened the door**.** Then the tiger jumped out.
ONE COMPOUND SENTENCE	The man opened the door**;** then the tiger jumped out.

12o. Use a semicolon between independent clauses joined by a conjunctive adverb or a transitional expression.

EXAMPLES
The tiger thought the jackal was stupid**; however,** it was the jackal who outsmarted the tiger.
The tiger was angry**; in fact,** he yelled at the jackal.

Notice in the two examples above that a comma is placed after the conjunctive adverb and the transitional expression.

Commonly Used Conjunctive Adverbs

besides	indeed	nevertheless	then
consequently	instead	next	therefore

Commonly Used Transitional Expressions

as a result	for instance	in fact
for example	in addition	in other words

12p. Use a semicolon (rather than a comma) before a coordinating conjunction to join independent clauses that contain commas.

EXAMPLE
The tree, buffalo, and road were no help**;** but the jackal was.

12q. Use a semicolon between items in a series if the items contain commas.

EXAMPLE
We visited Lima, Peru**;** Rome, Italy**;** and Oslo, Norway.

COLONS

12r. Use a colon to mean "note what follows."

(1) In some cases, a colon is used before a list of items, especially after the expressions *the following* and *as follows*.

EXAMPLE
Discuss the following elements of the story**:** theme, plot, and conflict.

NOTE Do not use a colon before a list that follows a verb or a preposition.

INCORRECT Additional figures of speech are: image, symbol, and metaphor.
CORRECT Additional figures of speech are image, symbol, and metaphor.

(2) Use a colon before a long, formal statement or a long quotation.

EXAMPLE
An angel spoke this message to Abraham**:** "Because you have done this and have not withheld your son, your favored one, I will bestow My blessing upon you and make your descendants as numerous as the stars."

12s. Use a colon in certain conventional situations.

(1) Use a colon between the hour and the minute.

EXAMPLES
7**:**30 A.M. 3**:**10 P.M.

(2) Use a colon between chapter and verse when referring to passages from the Bible.

EXAMPLES
Genesis 1**:**1 John 3**:**10–16

(3) Use a colon between a title and a subtitle.

EXAMPLE
"Nisei Daughter**:** The Second Generation"

(4) Use a colon after the salutation of a business letter.

EXAMPLES
Dear Ms. Ash**:** Dear Sir**:**
To Whom It May Concern**:**

Using Punctuation

In speaking, your tone and pitch, your pauses in your speech, and your gestures and expressions all help make your meaning clear. In writing, marks of punctuation signal these verbal and nonverbal cues.

Try It Out 

Correct any errors in punctuation in each of the following sentences.

1. Do you know about: Camelot, Arthur, and the sword Excalibur?
2. The sword the mighty Excalibur was in a stone.
3. Did anyone, in the region, pull the sword out.
4. No no one could; until Arthur did.
5. Aren't knights, and ladies, and magic in the tales?

13 PUNCTUATION

ITALICS

When writing or typing, indicate italics by underlining. If your composition were to be printed, the typesetter would set the underlined words in italics, *like this.*

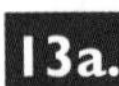

13a. Use underlining (italics) for titles of books, plays, long poems, films, periodicals, works of art, recordings, long musical works, television series, trains, ships, aircraft, and spacecraft.

TYPE OF TITLE	EXAMPLES
Books	*Tales of King Arthur* *Silent Dancing*
Plays	*Macbeth* *A Raisin in the Sun*
Long Poems	*Odyssey* *Evangeline*
Films	*Pocahontas* *Free Willy*
Periodicals	*Life* *The New York Times*

The words *a, an,* and *the* written before a title are italicized only when they are part of the official title. The official title of a book appears on the title page. The official title of a newspaper or periodical appears on the masthead, which is usually found on the editorial page.

EXAMPLES
***The** Wall Street Journal*
the *Miami Herald*

TYPE OF TITLE	EXAMPLES
Works of Art	*Christina's World* *Discobolos*
Recordings	*Into the Light* *The Bridge*
Long Musical Works	*Treemonisha* *Swan Lake*
Television Series	*Ancient Mysteries* *Avonlea*
Trains and Ships	*Orange Blossom Special* *Titanic*
Aircraft and Spacecraft	*Hindenburg* *Voyager 2*

For examples of titles that should be placed in quotation marks rather than being italicized, see page 1055. For information about capitalizing titles, see page 1049.

If you use a personal computer, you can probably set words in italics yourself.

13b. Use underlining (italics) for words, letters, and figures referred to as such and for foreign words not yet part of English vocabulary.

EXAMPLES
There is only one *r* in *Kari.*
Put six *0*'s after that *5.*
Hawaiians say *aloha oe* as both a greeting and a farewell.

If you are not sure whether or not to italicize a foreign word or phrase, look it up in a current dictionary.

QUOTATION MARKS

13c. Use quotation marks to enclose a *direct quotation*—a person's exact words.

EXAMPLES
I asked, "Where does Gabriel García Márquez get his ideas?"
"Apparently, from everywhere," answered Eric.

Do not use quotation marks for ***indirect quotations,*** which are rewordings of direct quotations.

DIRECT She said, "I'll call them later."
INDIRECT She said she will call them later.

An interrupting expression is not a part of a quotation and therefore should never be inside quotation marks.

EXAMPLE
"Let's go," Larry whispered, "right now."

When two or more sentences by the same speaker are quoted together, use only one set of quotation marks.

EXAMPLE
Al said, "Cassius was right. The fault is not in the stars."

13d. A direct quotation begins with a capital letter.

EXAMPLE
Ms. Wells asked, "**W**ho is Cassius?"

If a direct quotation is obviously a fragment of the original quotation, it should begin with a lowercase letter.

EXAMPLE
Cassius is described as having "**a** lean and hungry look."

13e. When a quoted sentence is divided into two parts by an interrupting expression, the second part begins with a lowercase letter.

EXAMPLE
"The film version," he said, "**w**as great."

If the second part of a quotation is a new sentence, the second part begins with a capital letter.

EXAMPLE
"I enjoy seeing a stage play," Paul commented**.** "**I**t's more interesting."

13f. **A direct quotation is set off from the rest of the sentence by commas or by a question mark or an exclamation point.**

EXAMPLES

"I have to leave now," Alison said, "so that I will be on time."

"Wow!" he cried. "Wasn't that a great speech?"

13g. **When used with quotation marks, other marks of punctuation are placed according to the following rules.**

(1) Commas and periods are always placed inside the closing quotation marks.

EXAMPLES

After "Secrets," we will read "Candles."

(2) Semicolons and colons are always placed outside the closing quotation marks.

EXAMPLES

I've finally decided to title my paper "Caesar's March"; it's done now.

Study the following in "First Lesson": rhyme, meter, and image.

(3) Question marks and exclamation points are placed inside closing quotation marks if the quotation is a question or an exclamation; otherwise, they are placed outside.

EXAMPLES

"Jennifer," Mr. Finn asked, "can you give us an example?"

Is the good in people really "oft interrèd with their bones"?

After lunch, the principal said, "All classes for the rest of the day are canceled"!

I shouted, "Hooray!"

13h. **When you write dialogue (a conversation), begin a new paragraph every time the speaker changes.**

EXAMPLE

"Hey, I've got a great idea! Why don't we do our own modern version of *Julius Caesar*?" suggested Matt.

"What do you mean?" Ben replied. "We'd wear business suits and stuff?"

Matt seemed surprised and said, "Well, no, but that's a good idea."

"It sure is," Paula commented. "What were *you* thinking, Matt?"

"Well, let me explain."

13i. **When a quoted passage consists of more than one paragraph, put quotation marks at the beginning of each paragraph and at the end of the entire passage. Do not put quotation marks after any paragraph but the last.**

EXAMPLE

"On Saturday, March 24," read the press release, "Hills High School will present *The Tragedy of Julius Caesar*.

"Tickets will be available at the box office. Advance tickets can be purchased by contacting the school at 555-0915.

"The performance will begin at 7 P.M. The box office will open at 6 P.M."

13j. **Use single quotation marks to enclose a quotation within a quotation.**

EXAMPLE

He asked, "What is the main theme in the story 'The Man to Send Rain Clouds'?"

13k. **Use quotation marks to enclose titles of articles, short stories, essays, poems, songs, individual episodes of TV shows, chapter titles, and other parts of books and periodicals.**

TYPE OF TITLE	EXAMPLES
Short Stories	"The Cold Equations" "Secrets"
Poems	"We Real Cool" "Those Winter Sundays"
Essays	"A 'Piercing' Issue" "The Lowest Animal"
Articles	"What About Diets?" "Saving the Whales"
Songs	"Ave Maria" "If I Had a Hammer"
TV Episodes	"The Sure Thing" "Monarch in Waiting"
Chapters and Parts of Books and Periodicals	"Medieval Life" "Guide to the Dictionary" "All in a Day's Work"

For information about titles of works that are italicized, see pages 1053–1054.

13l. Use quotation marks to enclose slang words, technical terms, and other special uses of words.

EXAMPLES

I'm fresh out of "long green."

She "birdied" (shot one under par on) the sixth hole.

Using Quotations from Interviews

Whenever you conduct an interview, always ask permission to quote the person, and use the person's *exact* words. When quoting someone's exact words, be sure to enclose them in quotation marks.

Try It Out 

You are a reporter for your school paper and have just conducted an interview with a local actor, Mr. Thespian, who is playing the role of Mark Antony in *The Tragedy of Julius Caesar.* Use the following quotations from Mr. Thespian to write a paragraph or two for your article. Be sure to use at least four direct quotations.

1. "Acting is more than playing dress-up."
2. "To learn to act is to learn to live."
3. "The plot of *Julius Caesar* is enacted all over the world every day."
4. "The main thing is to be able to see—no, to feel—events from anyone's point of view."
5. "Antony loved Rome and Caesar, as the people did."

14 PUNCTUATION

APOSTROPHES

Possessive Case

14a. The *possessive case* of a noun or pronoun shows ownership or relationship. To form the possessive case of a singular noun, add an apostrophe and an *s*.

EXAMPLES

Malamud**'s** story a shoemaker**'s** problem

Add only an apostrophe if the added *s* will make the noun hard to pronounce.

EXAMPLES

Sophocles' play Ms. Fuentes' class

14b. To form the possessive case of a plural noun ending in *s*, add only the apostrophe.

EXAMPLES

shoes' soles fathers' hopes

To form the possessive case of a plural noun that does not end in *s*, add an apostrophe and an *s*.

EXAMPLES

children**'s** dreams mice**'s** tails

14c. Possessive pronouns do not require an apostrophe.

EXAMPLES

Whose book is that?

That opinion is **yours.**

The dog chased **its** own tail.

 For more information about possessive pronouns, see Tips for Writers on page 1064.

14d. Indefinite pronouns in the possessive case require an apostrophe and an *s*.

EXAMPLES

nobody**'s** fault another**'s** help

14e. In compound words, names of organizations and businesses, and word groups showing joint possession, only the last word is possessive in form.

EXAMPLES

father-in-**law's** shop Cattle **Company's** corrals

Mom and **Dad's** car United **Way's** volunteers

14f. When two or more persons possess something individually, each name is possessive in form.

EXAMPLES

Pat **Mora's** and Audre **Lorde's** poems

Contractions

14g. Use an apostrophe to show where letters, words, or numerals have been omitted in a contraction.

EXAMPLES

she will . . . she**'ll**
who is . . . who**'s**
is not . . . is**n't**
1992 . . . **'92**
I am . . . I**'m**
Bill has . . . Bill**'s**
were not . . . were**n't**
of the clock . . . o**'**clock

EXCEPTION

will not . . . **won't**

HYPHENS

14h. Use a hyphen to divide a word at the end of a line.

EXAMPLE

At first, Feld did not consider the assistant shoe-maker suitable for his daughter.

When you divide a word at the end of a line, keep in mind the following rules.

1. Do not divide one-syllable words.
   gasped [*not* gas-ped]
2. Divide a word only between syllables.
   frag-ment [*not* fra-gment]
3. Words with double consonants may usually be divided between those two consonants.
   drum-mer
4. Usually, a word with a prefix or a suffix may be divided between the prefix or suffix and the base word (or root).
   pre-judge, fall-ing
5. Divide a hyphenated word only at a hyphen.
   mother-in-law [*not* moth-er-in-law]
6. Do not divide a word so that one letter stands alone.
   elec-tricity [*not* e-lectricity]

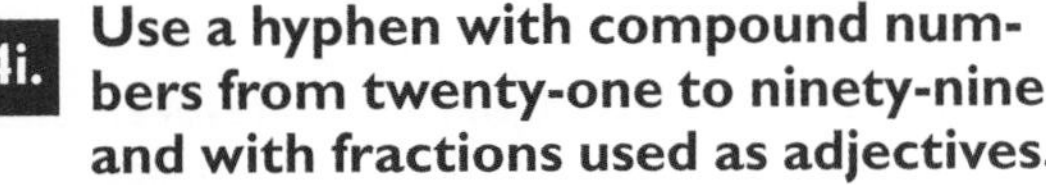

14i. Use a hyphen with compound numbers from twenty-one to ninety-nine and with fractions used as adjectives.

EXAMPLES

thirty-five years
one-half pound [*One-half* is an adjective modifying *pound*.]
one half of the flour [*Half* is a noun modified by the adjective *one*.]

14j. Use a hyphen with the prefixes *ex–*, *self–*, and *all–*; with the suffix *–elect;* and with all prefixes before a proper noun or proper adjective.

EXAMPLES

ex-wife all-star self-employed
governor-elect pro-American

14k. Hyphenate a compound adjective when it precedes the noun it modifies.

EXAMPLES

a **well-designed** engine
an engine that is **well designed**

a **world-famous** skier
a skier who is **world famous**

Do not use a hyphen if one of the modifiers is an adverb ending in *–ly*.

EXAMPLE

a **partly finished** research paper

Some compound adjectives are always hyphenated, whether they precede or follow the words they modify.

EXAMPLES

an **up-to-date** dictionary
a dictionary that is **up-to-date**

a **self-reliant** person
a person who is **self-reliant**

If you are unsure about whether a compound adjective should always be hyphenated, look up the word in a current dictionary.

DASHES

14l. Use a dash to indicate an abrupt break in thought or speech or an unfinished statement or question.

EXAMPLES

Jim**—**Tim, I mean**—**will show us his video.
"But, I'm**—**" Tim began and then stopped.

14m. Use a dash to mean *namely, that is, in other words,* and similar expressions that introduce an explanation.

EXAMPLES

I know who wrote that story**—**Ray Bradbury.
No, Arthur C. Clarke**—**he wrote *2001: A Space Odyssey***—**was the author.

Using Dashes Sparingly

In general, avoid using dashes in formal writing, and don't overuse them in any case. When you evaluate your writing, make sure you haven't used dashes unnecessarily or in place of commas, semicolons, colons, or end marks. Using dashes only for special emphasis will make them more effective.

Try It Out 

Revise the following sentences to eliminate the dashes.

1. Mark Twain—by the way—is widely recognized as a master of humor.
2. His essay—"The Lowest Animal"—is quite amusing.
3. Will you—Michael—comment on Twain's theme in this story?
4. Twain—whose real name was Samuel Clemens—preferred to write under a pen name.
5. What or who—as he sees it—is the lowest animal?

PARENTHESES

14n. Use parentheses to enclose explanatory or additional information.

EXAMPLES

Richard Burton (as Mark Antony) appears in *Cleopatra*.
Emily Dickinson (1830–1886) was a unique person.
Fill in the application carefully. (Use a pen.)
After reading the story (it was great), I ate.

15 SPELLING

UNDERSTANDING WORD STRUCTURE

Many English words are made up of word parts from other languages or earlier forms of English.

NOTE Some word parts have alternate spellings. The spelling used in a particular word is influenced by how the word sounds. If you try pronouncing "televidion," for example, you'll see why *–vis–*, not *–vid–*, is the form used in *television*.

Roots

The ***root*** is the part of the word that carries the word's core meaning. Other word parts can be added to a root to create many different words.

ROOTS	MEANINGS	EXAMPLES
–aud–, –audit–	hear	audible, auditorium
–anthrop–	human	anthropology, misanthrope
–biblio–	book	bibliography, bibliophile
–chron–	time	chronological, synchronize
–vid–, –vis–	see	evident, television

Prefixes

A ***prefix*** is a word part that is added before a root. When a prefix is added to a root, the new word combines the meanings of the prefix and the root.

PREFIXES	MEANINGS	EXAMPLES
bi–	two	bimonthly, bisect
mis–	badly, not, wrongly	misfire, misspell
re–	back, again, backward	revoke, reflect
tra–, trans–	across, beyond	traffic, transport
un–	reverse of, not	untrue, unfold

Suffixes

A ***suffix*** is a word part that is added after a root. Often, adding a suffix to a word changes the word's part of speech as well as its meaning.

SUFFIXES	MEANINGS	EXAMPLES
–dom	state, rank, condition	freedom, wisdom
–en	cause to be, become	deepen, darken
–ful	full of, marked by	thankful, hopeful
–ly	characteristic of, like	friendly, cowardly
–ness	quality, state	softness, shortness

SPELLING RULES

ie and *ei*

15a. Write *ie* when the sound is long e, except after c.

EXAMPLES
bel**ie**f achi**e**ve th**ie**f gr**ie**f
dec**ei**ve rec**ei**ve c**ei**ling conc**ei**t

EXCEPTIONS
l**ei**sure prot**ei**n **ei**ther s**ei**ze

15b. Write *ei* when the sound is not long e.

EXAMPLES
h**ei**fer r**ei**n b**ei**ge w**ei**ght

EXCEPTIONS
v**ie**w anc**ie**nt pat**ie**nt fr**ie**nd

–cede, –ceed, and *–sede*

15c. Only one English word ends in *–sede: supersede.* Only three words end in *–ceed: exceed, proceed,* and *succeed.* Most other words with this sound end in *–cede.*

EXAMPLES
ac**cede** inter**cede** re**cede**
con**cede** pre**cede** se**cede**

Adding Prefixes

15d. When a prefix is added to a word, the spelling of the original word remains the same.

EXAMPLES
bi + monthly = **bi**monthly
un + natural = **un**natural
re + edit = **re**edit

Adding Suffixes

15e. When the suffix *–ness* or *–ly* is added to a word, the spelling of the original word remains the same.

EXAMPLES
careful + ly = careful**ly**
kind + ness = kind**ness**

EXCEPTIONS
Words ending in y usually change the *y* to *i* before *–ness* and *–ly:*
shady + ness = shad**iness** busy + ly = bus**ily**

Most one-syllable adjectives ending in *y* follow rule 15e.

EXAMPLES
coy + ness = coy**ness** shy + ly = shy**ly**

15f. Drop the final silent e before adding a suffix that begins with a vowel.

EXAMPLES
tape + ing = tap**ing**
eliminate + ed = eliminat**ed**

EXCEPTIONS
Keep the final silent e

- in words ending in *ce* or *ge* before a suffix that begins with *a* or *o:*
  peac**eable**, knowledg**eable**, courag**eous**, outrag**eous**
- in *dye* and *singe* before *–ing:*
  dy**eing**, sing**eing**
- in *mile* before *–age:*
  mil**eage**

15g. Keep the final silent e before adding a suffix that begins with a consonant.

EXAMPLES
care + less = care**less** ease + ment = ease**ment**

EXCEPTIONS
argue + ment = argu**ment** nine + th = nin**th**
true + ly = tru**ly** whole + ly = whol**ly**

15h. **When a word ends in *y* preceded by a consonant, change the *y* to *i* before any suffix except one beginning with *i*.**

EXAMPLES
hurry + ed = hurr**ied**
hardy + ness = hard**iness**

EXCEPTIONS

1. some one-syllable words:
   shy + ness = shy**ness** sky + ward = sky**ward**
2. *lady* and *baby* with suffixes:
   lady**like** lady**ship** baby**hood**

15i. **When a word ends in *y* preceded by a vowel, simply add the suffix.**

EXAMPLES
survey + ed = survey**ed**
gray + est = gray**est**

EXCEPTIONS
day + ly = da**ily** say + ed = sa**id**

15j. **When a word ends in a consonant, double the final consonant before a suffix that begins with a vowel only if the word**

- **has only one syllable or is accented on the last syllable**

and

- **ends in a *single* consonant preceded by a *single* vowel.**

EXAMPLES
wrap + ing = wra**pping**
occur + ence = occu**rrence**

Forming Plurals of Nouns

15k. **To form the plurals of most English nouns, simply add *–s*.**

SINGULAR	ship	pan	horse	piano
	blacksmith	Johnson		
PLURAL	ships	pans	horses	pianos
	blacksmiths	Johnsons		

15l. **To form the plurals of other nouns, follow these rules.**

(1) If the noun ends in *s, x, z, ch,* or *sh,* add *–es.*

SINGULAR	guess	fox	buzz
	peach	wish	Hernandez
PLURAL	guess**es**	fox**es**	buzz**es**
	peach**es**	wish**es**	Hernandez**es**

NOTE Proper nouns also usually follow rule 15l.

EXAMPLES
the Jones**es** the Sánchez**es**

(2) If the noun ends in *y* preceded by a consonant, change the *y* to *i* and add *–es.*

SINGULAR	fly	city	quality	puppy
PLURAL	fl**ies**	cit**ies**	qualit**ies**	pupp**ies**

EXCEPTIONS
The plurals of proper nouns: the Darc**ys**, the Lac**ys**

(3) If the noun ends in *y* preceded by a vowel, add *–s.*

SINGULAR	key	boy	journey	Momaday
PLURAL	key**s**	boy**s**	journey**s**	Momaday**s**

(4) For some nouns ending in *f* or *fe,* add *–s.* For other such nouns, change the *f* or *fe* to *v* and add *–es.*

EXAMPLES

thief	hoof	belief	roof
thie**ves**	hoo**ves**	belief**s**	roof**s**

(5) If the noun ends in *o* preceded by a vowel, add *–s.*

SINGULAR	curio	rodeo	kangaroo	Julio
PLURAL	curio**s**	rodeo**s**	kangaroo**s**	Julio**s**

(6) If the noun ends in *o* preceded by a consonant, add *–es.*

SINGULAR	potato	echo	torpedo
	hero	veto	tomato
PLURAL	potato**es**	echo**es**	torpedo**es**
	hero**es**	veto**es**	tomato**es**

EXCEPTIONS
Some common nouns ending in o preceded by a consonant, especially musical terms, and some proper nouns form the plural by adding only *–s.*

SINGULAR	taco	hairdo	alto	piano
	photo	Latino	Sakamoto	
PLURAL	taco**s**	hairdo**s**	alto**s**	piano**s**
	photo**s**	Latino**s**	Sakamoto**s**	

NOTE Some nouns that end in *o* preceded by a consonant have two plural forms.

SINGULAR	**PLURAL**
zero	zero**s** *or* zero**es**

(7) The plurals of some nouns are formed irregularly.

SINGULAR	foot	man	tooth	child
PLURAL	f**ee**t	m**e**n	t**ee**th	child**ren**

(8) Some nouns have the same form in both the singular and the plural.

SINGULAR AND PLURAL	deer	Chinese	species
	Sioux	series	aircraft

(9) If a compound noun is written as one word, form the plural by adding *–s* or *–es* to the end of the compound.

SINGULAR	ballgame	background	housefly
PLURAL	ballgame**s**	background**s**	housefl**ies**

(10) If a compound noun is hyphenated or written as two words, make the main noun plural. The ***main noun*** is the noun that is modified.

SINGULAR	mother-in-law	runner-up
PLURAL	mother**s**-in-law	runner**s**-up

A few compound nouns form the plural in irregular ways.

SINGULAR	go-between sixteen-year-old	mix-up
PLURAL	go-between**s** sixteen-year-old**s**	mix-up**s**

Whenever you're not sure about the plural form of a compound noun, check a recent dictionary.

(11) Some nouns borrowed from Latin and Greek form the plural as they do in the original language.

SINGULAR	**PLURAL**
analysis	analys**es**
crisis	cris**es**
datum	dat**a**
phenomenon	phenomen**a**

Some nouns borrowed from other languages have two plural forms.

SINGULAR	**PLURAL**
cactus	cactus**es** *or* cact**i**
index	index**es** *or* indi**ces**
antenna	antenna**s** *or* antenna**e**

(12) To form the plurals of numerals, most capital letters, symbols, and words used as words, add either an *–s* or an apostrophe and an *–s*.

EXAMPLES

These *R*'**s** [*or Rs*] look like *K*'**s** [*or Ks*].
Erase these *&*'**s** [*or &'s*] and write *and***s** [*or and's*].
These *1*'**s** [*or 1s*] look like *7*'**s** [*or 7s*].

Using both an apostrophe and an *s* is never wrong. Therefore, if you have any doubt about whether or not to use the apostrophe, use it.

Using Apostrophes in Spelling

To prevent confusion, it is a good idea to get in the habit of using both an apostrophe and an *–s* to form the plurals of lowercase letters, certain capital letters, and some words used as words.

EXAMPLES

These *i*'**s** should be *e*'**s**. [Without an apostrophe, the plural of *i* would look like *is*.]
My sister always gets all A'**s**. [Without an apostrophe, the plural of *A* would look like *As*.]

Try It Out

For each of the following sentences, insert apostrophes where appropriate.

1. These #s are known as "pound signs."
2. People sometimes mistake *tos* for *toos*.
3. The *3*s in this column should be omitted.
4. I've spelled these *toes* with *w*s instead of *e*s.
5. These *I*s mean "incomplete."

16 Glossary of Usage

The Glossary of Usage is an alphabetical list of words, expressions, and special terms with definitions, explanations, and examples. Some of the examples have specific labels. *Standard* or *formal* usages are appropriate in serious writing and speaking, such as compositions and speeches. *Informal* words and expressions are standard English usages generally appropriate in conversation and in everyday writing such as personal letters. *Nonstandard* usages do not follow the guidelines of standard English.

a lot Always write the expression *a lot* as two words. *A lot* may be used as a noun meaning "a large number or amount" or as an adverb meaning "a great deal; very much." Avoid using *a lot* in formal writing.

EXAMPLES

Ray Bradbury writes **a lot** of science fiction. [noun]
Your last draft is **a lot** more interesting. [adverb]

among See **between, among.**

and etc. The abbreviation *etc.* (*et cetera*) means "and other things." Do not use *and* with *etc.*

EXAMPLE
They sell CDs, videos, **etc.** [*not* and etc.]

anyways, anywheres Use these words (and others like them, such as *everywheres, nowheres,* and *somewheres*) without the final *s.*

EXAMPLES
She didn't like the piano **anyway** [*not* anyways].
They couldn't find the Grail **anywhere** [*not* anywheres].

as See **like, as.**

as if See **like, as if.**

at Do not use *at* after *where.*

NONSTANDARD Where was the pendulum at?
STANDARD **Where** was the pendulum?

bad, badly *Bad* is an adjective. *Badly* is an adverb. In standard English, only the adjective form, *bad,* should follow a linking verb, such as *feel, see, hear, taste,* or *smell,* or forms of the verb *be.*

EXAMPLE
Does that conk solution smell **bad** [*not* badly]?

The expression *feel badly* has become acceptable in informal situations, but use *feel bad* in formal speaking and writing.

being as, being that Use *since* or *because* instead of these expressions.

EXAMPLE
Because [*not* being as] they were Japanese, they were sent to Manzanar.

beside, besides *Beside* is a preposition that means "by the side of" or "next to." As a preposition, *besides* means "in addition to" or "other than." As an adverb, *besides* means "moreover."

EXAMPLES
People stood **beside** the coop.
Who **besides** Brutus was in this group? [preposition]
His wings were dirty; **besides,** he was almost toothless. [adverb]

between, among Use *between* when you are referring to two things at a time, even though they may be part of a group consisting of more than two.

EXAMPLES
She walked **between** her mother and father.
I couldn't decide which of the ten poems to study because there were so many differences **between** them. [Although there are more than two poems, each one is being compared separately with each of the others.]

Use *among* when you are thinking of a group rather than of separate individuals.

EXAMPLE
There were conflicts **among** the passengers on the raft. [The passengers are thought of as a group.]

bust, busted Avoid using these words as verbs. Use a form of either *burst* or *break,* depending on the meaning.

EXAMPLES
The airtight compartments **burst** [*not* busted].
A torrent of water **broke** [*not* busted] the doors.

could of See **of.**

done *Done* is the past participle of *do.* Avoid using *done* for *did,* which is the past form of *do* and which does not require a helping verb.

NONSTANDARD The captain done all that he could do.
STANDARD The captain **did** all that he could do.
STANDARD The captain **had done** all that he could do.

etc. See **and etc.**

everywheres See **anyways, anywheres.**

fewer, less *Fewer* tells "how many"; it is used with plural nouns. *Less* tells "how much"; it is used with singular nouns.

EXAMPLES
We have **fewer** students in class this year.
There is **less** emphasis on symbolism in this poem than in that one.

good, well *Good* is an adjective. *Well* may be used as an adjective or an adverb. Never use *good* to modify a verb; instead, use *well* as an adverb meaning "capably" or "satisfactorily."

EXAMPLE
Leslie Marmon Silko writes **well** [*not* good].

Feel good and *feel well* mean different things. *Feel good* means "feel happy or pleased." *Feel well* simply means "feel healthy."

EXAMPLES
I didn't feel **well** that day.
Helping others always makes me feel **good** about myself.

had of See **of.**

had ought, hadn't ought Unlike other verbs, *ought* is not used with *had.*

NONSTANDARD Her mother had ought to come out of her room; she hadn't ought to stay in there so long.
STANDARD Her mother **ought** to come out of her room; she **ought not** to stay in there so long.

he, she, it, they Do not use an unnecessary pronoun after the subject of a clause or a sentence. This error is called the ***double subject.***

NONSTANDARD Gary Soto he writes stories and poems.
STANDARD Gary Soto writes stories and poems.

hisself, theirselves Avoid using these words for *himself* and *themselves.*

EXAMPLES
Phillip said that he would put up his tent **himself** [*not* hisself] and that they could put up their tents **themselves** [*not* theirselves].

imply, infer *Imply* means "suggest indirectly." *Infer* means "interpret" or "draw a conclusion [from a remark or an action]."

EXAMPLES
This language **implies** a symbolic meaning.
From this metaphor, we may **infer** his deep fear.

it See **he, she, it, they.**

kind of, sort of Avoid using these terms in formal situations. Instead, use *somewhat* or *rather.*

INFORMAL Edgar Allan Poe's stories can be kind of scary.
FORMAL Edgar Allan Poe's stories can be **somewhat** [*or* **rather**] scary.

kind of a, sort of a In formal situations, omit the *a.*

INFORMAL What kind of a rhyme scheme does it have?
FORMAL What **kind of** rhyme scheme does it have?

kind(s), sort(s), type(s) Use *this* or *that* with the singular form of each of these nouns. Use *these* or *those* with the plural form.

EXAMPLES
This kind of guitar is less expensive than **those kinds.**

learn, teach *Learn* means "acquire knowledge." *Teach* means "instruct" or "show how."

EXAMPLE
If you will **teach** me, I will **learn.**

leave, let *Leave* means "go away" or "depart from." *Let* means "allow" or "permit." Avoid using *leave* for *let.*

EXAMPLES
Let [*not* leave] her stay if she wants.
They **let** [*not* left] the children go first.

less See **fewer, less.**

like, as In informal English, the preposition *like* is often used as a conjunction meaning "as." In formal English, use *like* to introduce a prepositional phrase, and use *as* to introduce a subordinate clause.

EXAMPLES
This song sounds **like** the other one.
She should do **as** her mother says.

like, as if In formal situations, *like* should not be used for the compound conjunction *as if* or *as though.*

EXAMPLE
It looked **as if** [*not* like] the crew would see them.

might of, must of See **of.**

nowheres See **anyways, anywheres.**

of *Of* is a preposition. Do not use *of* in place of *have* after verbs such as *could, should, would, might, must,* and *ought* [*to*]. Also, do not use *had of* for *had.*

NONSTANDARD They should of signaled.
STANDARD They **should have** [*or* **should've**] signaled.

Do not use *of* after other prepositions such as *inside, off,* or *outside.*

EXAMPLES
Hundreds jumped **off** [*not* off of] the ship.
What's **inside** [*not* inside of] survival kits?

off of See **of.**

ought See **had ought, hadn't ought.**

ought to of See **of.**

she See **he, she, it, they.**

some, somewhat In formal situations, do not use *some* to mean "to some extent." Instead, use *somewhat.*

INFORMAL Your advice helped some.
FORMAL Your advice helped **somewhat.**

somewheres See **anyways, anywheres.**

sort(s) See **kind(s), sort(s), type(s)** and **kind of a, sort of a.**

sort of See **kind of, sort of.**

teach See **learn, teach.**

than, then *Than* is a conjunction used in comparisons. *Then* is an adverb meaning "at that time" or "next."

EXAMPLES
I liked "Everyday Use" better **than** that story.
Had you heard of Langston Hughes **then**?
I wrote a thesis statement; **then** I made an outline.

them *Them* should not be used as an adjective. Use *those.*

EXAMPLE
I like **those** [*not* them] Stephen King novels.

then See **than, then.**

this, that, these, those See **kind(s), sort(s), type(s).**

try and Use *try to,* not *try and.*

EXAMPLE
He would **try to** [*not* try and] send a message.

type(s) See **kind(s), sort(s), type(s).**

way, ways Use *way,* not *ways,* in referring to a distance.

INFORMAL The sisters walked a long ways to school.
FORMAL The sisters walked a long **way** to school.

well See **good, well.**

what Use *that,* not *what,* to introduce an adjective clause.

EXAMPLE
The poem **that** [*not* what] I studied was "George Gray."

when, where Do not use *when* or *where* to begin a definition.

NONSTANDARD A "stanza" in poetry is when lines are grouped to form a unit.
STANDARD A "stanza" in poetry is a group of lines that form a unit.

where Do not use *where* for *that.*

EXAMPLES
I read **that** [*not* where] Alice Walker is speaking here.
Roger saw on TV **that** [*not* where] the mayor has been reelected.

where . . . at See **at.**

who, which, that The relative pronoun *who* refers to persons only; *which* refers to things only; *that* may refer to either persons or things.

EXAMPLES
Isn't Louis L'Amour the man **who** [*or* **that**] writes westerns? [person]
Arthur's sword, **which** is called Excalibur, is legendary. [thing]
The psalm **that** I memorized is beautiful. [thing]

would of See **of.**

Using Contractions and Possessive Pronouns

Do not confuse contractions with possessive pronouns.

POSSESSIVE PRONOUNS	CONTRACTIONS
This one is **theirs.**	**There's** [There is] Lana.
Their bus is here.	**They're** [They are] on the bus.
Your turn is next.	**You're** [You are] next.
Whose book is this?	**Who's** [Who is] your partner?
What is **its** title?	**It's** [It is] time to eat.

Try It Out

Proofread the following sentences, and correct each error in the use of contractions and possessive pronouns.

1. Whose it's author?
2. Are you done with you're report on they're lives?
3. Their here to see who's name was chosen.
4. Paul, your late, and theirs your ride.
5. They're team won, and its about time, too.

GLOSSARY

The glossary below is an alphabetical list of words found in the selections in this book. Use this glossary just as you use a dictionary—to find out the meanings of unfamiliar words. (Some technical, foreign, and more obscure words in this book are not listed here but instead are defined for you in the footnotes that accompany many of the selections.)

Many words in the English language have more than one meaning. This glossary gives the meanings that apply to the words as they are used in the selections in this book. Words closely related in form and meaning are usually listed together in one entry (for instance, *ineffable* and *ineffably*), and the definition is given for the first form.

The following abbreviations are used:

adj.	adjective
adv.	adverb
n.	noun
v.	verb
pl.	plural

Each word's pronunciation is given in parentheses. A guide to the pronunciation symbols appears at the bottom of each right-hand glossary page.

For more information about the words in this glossary or for information about words not listed here, consult a dictionary.

abate (ə·bāt') *v.:* let up; lessen; decrease.
abhor (ab·hôr') *v.:* detest; hate.
abiding (ə·bīd'iŋ) *adj.:* continuing; lasting.
abrasive (ə·brā'siv) *adj.:* **1.** scraping; rubbing; wearing away. **2.** irritating; harsh.
absolve (ab·zälv') *v.:* free from guilt, blame, or responsibility.
abyss (ə·bis') *n.:* bottomless gulf or pit; profound depth.
accentuation (ak·sen'cho͞o·ā'·shən) *n.:* emphasis; heightening of the effect of something.
accessible (ak·ses'ə·bəl) *adj.:* capable of being approached or entered.
accordance (ə·kôrd''ns) *n.:* agreement; conformity.
acrid (ak'rid) *adj.:* sharp or bitter in smell or taste.
admonish (ad·män'ish) *v.:* warn; caution against specific faults.
admonition (ad'mə·nish'ən) *n.:* scolding; warning.
adulation (a'jo͞o·lā'shən) *n.:* intense admiration.
affluent (af'lo͞o·ənt) *adj.:* wealthy; prosperous.
affront (ə·frunt') *n.:* insult.
allegiance (ə·lē'jəns) *n.:* loyalty or devotion.
alleviate (ə·lē'vē·āt') *v.:* reduce; make easier to bear or deal with.
allude (ə·lo͞od') *v.:* refer to casually or indirectly.
amiable (ā'mē·ə·bəl) *adj.:* having a friendly disposition; good-natured.
anguish (aŋ'gwish) *v.:* feel great suffering from worry, grief, or pain; distress. **—anguished** *v.* used as *adj.*
annihilate (ə·nī'ə·lāt') *v.:* destroy; demolish.
antipathy (an·ti'pə·thē) *n.:* feeling of hatred; powerful and deep dislike.
apex (ā'peks') *n.:* highest point; top.
appall (ə·pôl') *v.:* horrify. **—appalled** *v.* used as *adj.*
apparition (ap'ə·rish'ən) *n.:* figure that appears mysteriously; ghost.
appease (ə·pēz') *v.:* satisfy; pacify.
append (ə·pend') *v.:* attach or affix; add as a supplement.
appraise (ə·prāz') *v.:* examine with the aim of estimating the value.
appreciable (ə·prē'shə·bəl) *adj.:* enough to be observed; noticeable; measurable.
apprehension (ap'rē·hen'shən) *n.:* dread; fear of a future event.
arbitrary (är'bə·trer'ē) *adj.:* based on whim or personal preference rather than reason. **—arbitrarily** *adv.*
arch (ärch) *adj.:* clever; crafty; sarcastic.
archive (är'kīv') *n.:* place where material having documentary interest is kept; records.
ascertain (as'ər·tān') *v.:* find out with certainty; determine.
askew (ə·skyo͞o') *adv.:* to one side; crookedly.
aspiration (as'pə·rā'shən) *n.:* strong desire or ambition.

at, āte, cär; ten, ēve; is, īce; gō, hôrn, look, to͞ol; oil, out; up, fur; ə *for unstressed vowels, as* a *in* ago, u *in* focus; ' *as in* Latin (lat''n); chin; she; zh *as in* azure (azh'ər); thin, *the*; ŋ *as in* ring (riŋ)

assertion (ə·sur′shən) *n.:* statement maintaining or defending rights or claims.
assimilation (ə·sim′ə·lā′shən) *n.:* process of becoming absorbed into the prevailing culture.
atrocious (ə·trō′shəs) *adj.:* evil; brutal; very bad.
attain (ə·tān′) *v.:* gain through effort; accomplish; reach.
attest (ə·test′) *v.:* **1.** declare to be true or genuine. **2.** serve as proof of; demonstrate.
audible (ô′də·bəl) *adj.:* capable of being heard.
augment (ôg·ment′) *v.:* increase in size or quantity. **—augmented** *v.* used as *adj.*
auspicious (ôs·pish′əs) *adj.:* of good omen; favorable.
austere (ô·stir′) *adj.:* **1.** having a severe look or manner. **2.** plain; lacking luxury.
avaricious (av′ə·rish′əs) *adj.:* greedy.
avert (ə·vurt′) *v.:* **1.** turn away. **2.** prevent.

Baroque (bə·rōk′) *adj.:* of or like a style of classical music noted for intricate melody.
bearings (ber′iŋz) *n. pl.:* **1.** position or direction determined by relation to known points. **2.** awareness of one's position.
beatific (bē′ə·tif′ik) *adj.:* angelic; displaying delight or kindliness.
belabor (bē·lā′bər) *v.:* **1.** spend too much time and effort on. **2.** scold.
belligerent (bə·lij′ər·ənt) *adj.:* quarrelsome; ready to fight.
benign (bi·nīn′) *adj.:* favorable or harmless.
bequeath (bē·kwēth′) *v.:* leave to another person in a will; hand down; pass on.
bereaved (bē·rēvd′) *adj.:* sad or lonely because of the death of a loved one.
bewilder (bē·wil′dər) *v.:* confuse hopelessly; puzzle. **—bewildered** *v.* used as *adj.*
bibliophile (bib′lē·ə·fīl′) *n.:* book lover or collector.
boisterous (bois′tər·əs) *adj.:* noisy and unruly; rowdy.

cache (kash) *n.:* **1.** safe place for storing or hiding things. **2.** anything stored or hidden in such a place.
cadence (kad′′ns) *n.:* rhythmic flow of sound; beat.
cajole (kə·jōl′) *v.:* coax with flattery, soothing words, or promises.
calamity (kə·lam′ə·tē) *n.:* great misfortune resulting in immense loss and sorrow; disaster.
caliber (kal′ə·bər) *n.:* quality or ability; worth.
callous (kal′əs) *adj.:* hardened; unfeeling; pitiless.
callousness (kal′əs·nis) *n.:* hardheartedness; lack of feeling for other people.
caprice (kə·prēs′) *n.:* sudden notion or desire.
cataclysm (kat′ə·kliz′əm) *n.:* disaster; sudden, violent event.
cavernous (kav′ər·nəs) *adj.:* deep-set and hollow, like a cave.
cessation (se·sā′shən) *n.:* ceasing or stopping.
chronic (krän′ik) *adj.:* constant; lasting a long time or recurring often.
circuitous (sər·kyo͞o′ət·əs) *adj.:* roundabout; indirect. **—circuitously** *adv.*
clamor (klam′ər) *v.:* cry out; ask.
cleave (klēv) *v.:* split. **—cleaving** *v.* used as *adj.*
clench (klench) *v.:* close tightly. **—clenched** *v.* used as *adj.*
coagulate (kō·ag′yo͞o·lāt′) *v.:* gel into a soft, semisolid mass; clot. **—coagulated** *v.* used as *adj.*
complacent (kəm·plā′sənt) *adj.:* self-satisfied; smug.
composure (kəm·pō′zhər) *n.:* calmness of manner; self-control.
comprehensive (käm′prē·hen′siv) *adj.:* including all of the relevant details.
compulsion (kəm·pul′shən) *n.:* irresistible impulse; compelling force.
compulsory (kəm·pul′sə·rē) *adj.:* required; enforced.
conceivable (kən·sēv′ə·bəl) *adj.:* capable of being imagined or believed.
concussion (kən·kush′ən) *n.:* powerful shock or impact.
confound (kən·found′) *v.:* **1.** cause to feel confused. **2.** mix up or lump together carelessly. **—confounded** *v.* used as *adj.*
conjecture (kən·jek′chər) *n.:* theory or prediction based on guesswork. —*v.:* guess.
connivance (kə·nī′vəns) *n.:* act of scheming in an underhanded or sneaky way.
conspicuous (kən·spik′yo͞o·əs) *adj.:* obvious or easy to see.
contemplative (kən·tem′plə·tiv′) *adj.:* thoughtful.
contingent (kən·tin′jənt) *n.:* group forming part of a larger group.
contort (kən·tôrt′) *v.:* twist out of shape.
contrition (kən·trish′ən) *n.:* regret or sense of guilt at having done wrong.
contrivance (kən·trī′vəns) *n.:* artificial arrangement; invention, plan, or mechanical device.
conviction (kən·vik′shən) *n.:* **1.** state or appearance of being convinced. **2.** strong belief.
convivial (kən·viv′ē·əl) *adj.:* having to do with a feast or festive activity; sociable.
corroborate (kə·räb′ə·rāt′) *v.:* support; uphold the truth of.

cow (kou) *v.:* make timid or submissive by frightening; intimidate. **—cowed** *v.* used as *adj.*
cower (kou′ər) *v.:* draw back or huddle in fear. **—cowering** *v.* used as *adj.*
coy (koi) *adj.:* pretending innocence or shyness.
crestfallen (krest′fôl′ən) *adj.:* disheartened; dejected; humbled.
crucial (kro͞o′shəl) *adj.:* extremely important; decisive.
curtness (kurt′nəs) *n.:* briefness, especially to the point of rudeness.

dally (dal′ē) *v.:* **1.** waste time; loiter. **2.** deal with lightly or carelessly.
dank (daŋk) *adj.:* uncomfortably damp; moist and chilly.
dawdle (dôd′′l) *v.:* waste time; linger.
debunk (dē·buŋk′) *v.:* expose the false claims or pretensions of someone or something.
decrepitude (dē·krep′ə·to͞od′) *n.:* state of being broken down by old age or long use.
deduce (dē·do͞os′) *v.:* reason or conclude based on known facts or principles; infer.
deference (def′ər·əns) *n.:* courteous respect.
defile (dē·fīl′) *v.:* make dirty.
deft (deft) *adj.:* skillful in a quick and sure way.
degenerate (dē·jen′ər·āt′) *v.:* decline or become lowered morally or culturally. **—degenerating** *v.* used as *adj.*
deign (dān) *v.:* lower oneself to do something thought to be beneath one's dignity.
delegate (del′ə·gāt′) *v.:* assign or entrust power or authority to a person.
delirious (di·lir′ē·əs) *adj.:* **1.** raving incoherently as from mania. **2.** wildly excited.
deliverance (di·liv′ər·əns) *n.:* state of being freed; rescue or release.
delude (di·lo͞od′) *v.:* mislead; fool; deceive.
demean (dē·mēn′) *v.:* lower in status or character; humble. **—demeaning** *v.* used as *adj.*
denizen (den′ə·zən) *n.:* inhabitant or occupant.
deplore (dē·plôr′) *v.:* condemn as wrong; disapprove of.
depravity (dē·prav′ə·tē) *n.:* corruption; wickedness.
derisive (di·rī′siv) *adj.:* **1.** mocking. **2.** scornful or contemptuous. **—derisively** *adv.*
designation (dez′ig·nā′shən) *n.:* distinguishing name or title.
deteriorate (dē·tir′ē·ə·rāt′) *v.:* worsen.
deviate (dē′vē·āt′) *v.:* turn from a set course or direction; diverge.
devious (dē′vē·əs) *adj.:* **1.** roundabout; indirect. **2.** deceitful.
dexterous (deks′tər·əs) *adj.:* showing skillful use of the hands. **—dexterously** *adv.*
diabolical (dī′ə·bäl′ə·kəl) *adj.:* cruel; wicked; devilish.
diffuse (di·fyo͞os′) *adj.:* not focused; scattered.
diligent (dil′ə·jənt) *adj.:* steady, careful, and hard-working. **—diligently** *adv.*
diminished (də·min′isht) *adj.:* made smaller; lessened; reduced.
dire (dīr) *adj.:* **1.** dreadful; terrible. **2.** urgent.
discern (di·zurn′) *v.:* recognize; perceive.
disconsolate (dis·kän′sə·lit) *adj.:* so unhappy that nothing will comfort.
discord (dis′kôrd′) *n.:* **1.** disagreement; conflict. **2.** harsh or confused noise.
discordant (dis·kôrd′′nt) *adj.:* clashing; not in harmony.
discourse (dis·kôrs′) *v.:* **1.** converse; talk; confer. **2.** speak formally and at length on a topic.
discreet (di·skrēt′) *adj.:* careful about what one says or does.
disdain (dis·dān′) *n.:* feeling that someone or something is unworthy; treating as unworthy.
disillusionment (dis′i·lo͞o′zhən·mənt) *n.:* disappointment or bitterness resulting from the loss of ideals; disenchantment.
disparage (di·spar′ij) *v.:* discredit; speak badly of. **—disparaging** *v.* used as *adj.*
disperse (di·spurs′) *v.:* break up and move in different directions; scatter.
disposition (dis′pə·zish′ən) *n.:* nature; temperament.
disrepute (dis′ri·pyo͞ot′) *n.:* bad reputation; disgrace.
dissipate (dis′ə·pāt′) *v.:* break up and scatter; disperse.
dividend (div′ə·dend′) *n.:* gift of something extra; bonus.
doctrine (däk′trin) *n.:* principle; teaching; belief.
dubious (do͞o′bē·əs) *adj.:* doubtful; not sure.

ebb *v.:* lessen or weaken. *—n.:* flow of water away from the land as the tide falls.
eclipse (i·klips′) *v.:* **1.** cover over; darken. **2.** outshine; surpass.
edict (ē′dikt′) *n.:* official order; decree.

---

at, āte, cär; ten, ēve; is, īce; gō, hôrn, look, to͞ol; oil, out; up, fur; ə *for unstressed vowels, as* a *in* ago, u *in* focus; ′ *as in* Latin (lat′′n); chin; she; zh *as in* azure (azh′ər); thin, *the*; ŋ *as in* ring (riŋ)

---

efface (ə·fās′) *v.:* rub out; erase.
elect (ē·lekt′) *v.:* choose.
elitism (ā·lēt′iz′əm) *n.:* belief that one belongs to a group that is better than others.
eloquent (el′ə·kwənt) *adj.:* fluent and persuasive; clearly expressive.
emaciated (ē·mā′shē·āt′id) *adj.:* abnormally thin, usually because of disease or starvation.
embodiment (em·bäd′i·mənt) *n.:* concrete form or expression of an idea or a quality.
eminent (em′ə·nənt) *adj.:* distinguished; outstanding; remarkable. **—eminently** *adv.*
encompass (en·kum′pəs) *v.:* contain; include.
endeavor (en·dev′ər) *v.:* try; make a serious attempt; strive.
enthrall (en·thrôl′) *v.:* hold as if in a spell; fascinate.
entreat (en·trēt′) *v.:* ask earnestly; beg.
enunciate (ē·nun′sē·āt′) *v.:* pronounce words clearly and distinctly.
envelop (en·vel′əp) *v.:* cover completely; surround.
esteem (e·stēm′) *v.:* have great regard for; respect. **—esteemed** *v.* used as *adj.*
ethereal (ē·thir′ē·əl) *adj.:* light and delicate; unearthly.
eulogy (yo͞o′lə·jē) *n.:* formal speech praising a person who has recently died.
evoke (ē·vōk′) *v.:* draw forth or call up a reaction or mental image.
exacerbate (eg·zas′ər·bāt′) *v.:* increase; aggravate.
exact (eg·zakt′) *v.:* force payment of.
exasperation (eg·zas′pər·ā′shən) *n.:* great irritation or annoyance.
executor (eg·zek′yo͞o·tər) *n.:* person who carries out the provisions of a will.
exertion (eg·zʉr′shən) *n.:* effort; use of strength or power.
exhilarate (eg·zil′ə·rāt′) *v.:* make cheerful or lively; stimulate. **—exhilarated** *v.* used as *adj.*
expend (ek·spend′) *v.:* use or use up.
exuberant (eg·zo͞o′bər·ənt) *adj.:* in good spirits; full of life.

fabricate (fab′ri·kāt′) *v.:* make; build; construct.
fathom (fa*th*′əm) *v.:* get to the bottom of; understand thoroughly.
fecund (fē′kənd) *adj.:* fertile; producing abundantly.
fervent (fʉr′vənt) *adj.:* intense; earnest. **—fervently** *adv.*
fiasco (fē·äs′kō) *n.:* complete failure.
filial (fil′ē·əl) *adj.:* pertaining to or due from a son or a daughter.
flail (flāl) *v.:* wave wildly.
flamboyant (flam·boi′ənt) *adj.:* showy or ornate; extravagant.
fleeting (flēt′iŋ) *adj.:* passing quickly; not lasting.
flotsam (flät′səm) *n.:* odds and ends; floating pieces of a ship or its cargo.
fluidity (flo͞o·id′ə·tē) *n.:* gracefulness of movement; liquidlike flow.
forbear (fôr·ber′) *v.:* refrain from; avoid doing or saying by keeping oneself in check. **—forbearing** *v.* used as *adj.*
foreboding (fôr·bōd′iŋ) *n.:* feeling that something bad is about to happen.
frivolous (friv′ə·ləs) *adj.:* **1.** not properly serious; silly. **2.** of little value or importance.
fume (fyo͞om) *v.:* show anger or annoyance.
furtive (fʉr′tiv) *adj.:* **1.** acting as if trying not to be seen. **2.** done secretly.
futile (fyo͞ot′′l) *adj.:* useless; ineffective. **—futilely** *adv.*

gallantry (gal′ən·trē) *n.:* nobility of behavior or spirit; heroic courage.
gallivant (gal′ə·vant′) *v.:* go about in search of amusement or excitement.
galvanize (gal′və·nīz′) *v.:* stimulate; excite.
garble (gär′bəl) *v.:* confuse; mix up. **—garbled** *v.* used as *adj.*
glower (glou′ər) *v.:* glare; stare angrily.
gnarled (närld) *adj.:* roughened; hardened and twisted.
goad (gōd) *n.:* device that gives a sharp electric shock, used to drive cattle. —*v.:* prod into action.
grapple (grap′əl) *v.:* struggle; try to cope.
grievous (grēv′əs) *adj.:* serious; severe.

heedless (hēd′lis) *adj.:* careless; not paying attention.
hemorrhage (hem′ər·ij′) *v.:* bleed heavily.
herald (her′əld) *v.:* introduce or announce; publicize. **—heralding** *v.* used as *n.*
homage (häm′ij) *n.:* respect; honor; reverence.
hurtle (hʉrt′′l) *v.:* move swiftly and forcefully.
hyperactive (hī′pər·ak′tiv) *adj.:* abnormally active; very lively.

illiterate (il·lit′ər·it) *adj.:* ignorant; uneducated; not knowing how to read or write.
illumination (i·lo͞o′mə·nā′shən) *n.:* lighting up; supplying of light.
illusory (i·lo͞o′sə·rē) *adj.:* not real; based on false ideas.
imminent (im′ə·nənt) *adj.:* likely to happen soon; impending.

immutable (im·myo͞ot'ə·bəl) *adj.:* unchangeable; never changing or varying.
impassive (im·pas'iv) *adj.:* not feeling or showing emotion. **—impassively** *adv.*
impede (im·pēd') *v.:* hold back or block, as by an obstacle. **—impeded** *v.* used as *adj.*
impediment (im·ped'ə·mənt) *n.:* obstacle; something that slows or prevents movement or progress.
imperative (im·per'ə·tiv) *adj.:* absolutely necessary; urgent.
imperceptible (im'pər·sep'tə·bəl) *adj.:* not clear or obvious to the senses or the mind; too slight or gradual to be noticeable.
impertinence (im·purt''n·əns) *n.:* insult; disrespectful act or remark.
implacable (im·plā'kə·bəl) *adj.:* relentless; not affected by attempts at change.
implore (im·plôr') *v.:* ask seriously; beg for.
impose (im·pōz') *v.:* place or set as by authority.
incessant (in·ses'ənt) *adj.:* never ceasing; continual. **—incessantly** *adv.*
incongruous (in·käŋ'gro͞o·əs) *adj.:* not suitable; not what would reasonably be expected.
inconsolable (in'kən·sōl'ə·bəl) *adj.:* unable to be comforted; brokenhearted.
incredulous (in·krej'o͝o·ləs) *adj.:* disbelieving; skeptical.
increment (in'krə·mənt) *n.:* small increase.
indeterminate (in'dē·tur'mi·nit) *adj.:* not decided or known; uncertain.
indiscriminate (in'di·skrim'i·nit) *adj.:* not making careful choices or distinctions; random. **—indiscriminately** *adv.*
induce (in·do͞os') *v.:* persuade; lead on.
ineffable (in·ef'ə·bəl) *adj.:* indescribable; inexpressible. **—ineffably** *adv.*
ineptitude (in·ep'tə·to͞od') *n.:* clumsiness; inefficiency.
inevitable (in·ev'i·tə·bəl) *adj.:* unavoidable; certain to happen.
inexorable (in·eks'ə·rə·bəl) *adj.:* incapable of being changed or stopped. **—inexorably** *adv.*
infinite (in'fə·nit) *adj.:* endless.
infinitesimal (in'fin·i·tes'i·məl) *adj.:* too small to be measured.
infirmity (in·fur'mə·tē) *n.:* weakness; physical defect.
ingenious (in·jēn'yəs) *adj.:* made or done in a clever or inventive way.
ingenuous (in·jen'yo͞o·əs) *adj.:* trusting; innocent; tending to believe too readily.
inherent (in·hir'ənt) *adj.:* existing as a necessary part of something.
inhibition (in'hi·bish'ən) *n.:* holding back or keeping from some action.
innocuous (in·näk'yo͞o·əs) *adj.:* harmless.
innuendo (in'yo͞o·en'·dō') *n.:* hint, usually implying something negative.
inquisitive (in·kwiz'ə·tiv) *adj.:* questioning; curious.
insolence (in'sə·ləns) *n.:* bold disrespect.
insular (in'sə·lər) *adj.:* **1.** isolated from one's surroundings, like an island. **2.** narrow-minded.
insuperable (in·so͞o'pər·ə·bəl) *adj.:* incapable of being overcome or passed over.
insurrection (in'sə·rek'shən) *n.:* rebellion; revolt; rising up against authority.
intact (in·takt') *adj.:* kept together; not broken up.
inter (in·tur') *v.:* put in a grave or tomb; bury.
intermittent (in'tər·mit''nt) *adj.:* appearing or occurring from time to time.
internment (in·turn'mənt) *n.:* confinement, as of prisoners during war.
intimidate (in·tim'ə·dāt') *v.:* make afraid; daunt.
intuitive (in·to͞o'i·tiv) *adj.:* having or perceiving without conscious reasoning.
inure (in·yo͝or') *v.:* make accustomed to something difficult or painful. **—inured** *v.* used as *adj.*
ironic (ī·rän'ik) *adj.:* opposite of what is expected.
irreconcilable (i·rek'ən·sīl'ə·bəl) *adj.:* cannot be brought into agreement.
irrelevant (ir·rel'ə·vənt) *adj.:* not relating to the subject. **—irrelevantly** *adv.*
irrevocable (ir·rev'ə·kə·bəl) *adj.:* irreversible; incapable of being canceled or undone.

jeopardize (jep'ər·dīz') *v.:* endanger.

labyrinth (lab'ə·rinth') *n.:* **1.** maze. **2.** complicated, confusing arrangement.
lament (lə·ment') *v.:* **1.** say with regret or sorrow. **2.** mourn or grieve for; regret deeply.
lethargy (leth'ər·jē) *n.:* **1.** abnormal drowsiness; great lack of energy. **2.** dull or indifferent state.
listless (list'lis) *adj.:* having no energy or interest. **—listlessly** *adv.*

at, āte, cär; ten, ēve; is, īce; gō, hôrn, lo͝ok, to͞ol; oil, out; up, fur; ə *for unstressed vowels, as* a *in* ago, u *in* focus; ' *as in* Latin (lat''n); chin; she; zh *as in* azure (azh'ər); thin, *the*; ŋ *as in* ring (riŋ)

lithe (līth) *adj.:* flexible and graceful.

livid (liv′id) *adj.:* bruised; black-and-blue.

loom (lo͞om) *v.:* appear as through mist, especially in a large, awesome form.

lucid (lo͞o′sid) *adj.:* **1.** clearheaded; not confused; understandable. **2.** bright and shining.

lugubrious (lə·go͞o′brē·əs) *adj.:* sad or mournful, often in an exaggerated way.

luminous (lo͞o′mə·nəs) *adj.:* glowing; giving off light.

magnanimous (mag·nan′ə·məs) *adj.:* generous; noble.

malevolent (mə·lev′ə·lənt) *adj.:* wishing evil or harm to others; malicious; mean.

malicious (mə·lish′əs) *adj.:* mischievous; mean; intending to cause harm.

manifest (man′ə·fest′) *v.:* **1.** appear; become evident. **2.** show or reveal.

mesmerize (mez′mər·īz′) *v.:* spellbind; hypnotize; fascinate. **—mesmerizing** *v.* used as *adj.*

mettle (met′'l) *n.:* quality of character, especially high quality; courage.

minion (min′yən) *n.:* helper who is too eager to please.

minute (mī·no͞ot′) *adj.:* small; tiny.

mirth (murth) *n.:* joyfulness, particularly when marked by laughter.

misanthropy (mis·an′thrə·pē) *n.:* hatred or mistrust of people.

mollify (mäl′ə·fī′) *v.:* soothe; pacify.

moor (moor) *v.:* hold in place, as by cable or rope.

mull (mul) *v.:* ponder; think deeply about. **—mulled** *v.* used as *adj.*

multitude (mul′tə·to͞od′) *n.:* large number.

mutilate (myo͞ot′'l·āt′) *v.:* damage; injure.

myopic (mī·äp′ik) *adj.:* nearsighted.

myriad (mir′ē·əd) *adj.:* countless; of a highly varied nature.

nebulous (neb′yə·ləs) *adj.:* vague; ill-defined.

negligent (neg′lə·jənt) *adj.:* careless; neglectful or indifferent. **—negligently** *adv.*

neuter (no͞ot′ər) *adj.:* neither male nor female; neutral.

nonchalant (nän′shə·länt′) *adj.:* showing no interest or concern; indifferent. **—nonchalantly** *adv.*

nondescript (nän′di·skript′) *adj.:* uninteresting; lacking in recognizable qualities.

notorious (nō·tôr′ē·əs) *adj.:* famous, usually in an unfavorable sense.

numinous (no͞o′mə·nəs) *adj.:* deeply spiritual or mystical.

obsequious (əb·sē′kwē·əs) *adj.:* overly attentive and respectful.

ominous (äm′ə·nəs) *adj.:* suggesting something bad is going to happen. **—ominously** *adv.*

omnipotence (äm·nip′ə·təns) *n.:* all-powerfulness; limitless power.

opaque (ō·pāk′) *adj.:* not letting light pass through; not transparent or translucent.

oppressive (ə·pres′iv) *adj.:* hard to endure; causing great discomfort.

oration (ō·rā′shən) *n.:* formal public speech.

pallid (pal′id) *adj.:* pale; lacking in color.

palpitate (pal′pə·tāt′) *v.:* throb; quiver; tremble.

paradoxical (par′ə·däks′i·kəl) *adj.:* seemingly full of contradictions.

paramount (par′ə·mount′) *adj.:* supreme; dominant.

paraplegic (par′ə·plē′jik) *adj.:* incapable of function or movement in the lower half of the body.

pedantic (pi·dant′ik) *adj.:* putting undue attention on trivial points of scholarship. **—pedantically** *adv.*

peevishness (pēv′ish·nes) *n.:* irritability; impatience.

pensive (pen′siv) *adj.:* dreamily thoughtful.

perceptible (pər·sep′tə·bəl) *adj.:* capable of being observed. **—perceptibly** *adv.*

perfunctory (pər·fuŋk′tə·rē) *adj.:* not exerting much effort; unconcerned.

perpetual (pər·pech′o͞o·əl) *adj.:* continual; constant.

perplex (pər·pleks′) *v.:* confuse; puzzle. **—perplexed** *v.* used as *adj.*

pertinent (purt′tə·nənt) *adj.:* having some connection with the subject.

pervade (pər·vād′) *v.:* spread or become dominant throughout.

perversity (pər·vur′sə·tē) *n.:* stubborn opposition; rejection of what is considered right or good.

piety (pī′ə·tē) *n.:* loyal, dutiful devotion.

pique (pēk) *v.:* cause resentment in; displease by treating inconsiderately. **—piqued** *v.* used as *adj.*

pit (pit) *v.:* place in competition.

pittance (pit′'ns) *n.:* small, barely sufficient amount or share.

placid (plas′id) *adj.:* calm; undisturbed. **—placidly** *adv.*

plaintive (plān′tiv) *adj.:* sad; expressing sorrow.

plausibility (plô′zə·bil′i·tē) *n.:* believability; apparent trustworthiness; seeming honesty.

pliant (plī′ənt) *adj.:* **1.** easily bent; pliable. **2.** adaptable; compliant.

poignant (poin′yənt) *adj.:* emotionally touching; evoking pity or compassion.

poise (poiz) *v.:* balance; get in position. **—poised** *v.* used as *adj.*
pomposity (päm·päs′ə·tē) *n.:* self-importance; pretentiousness.
ponder (pän′dər) *v.:* think deeply.
ponderous (pän′dər·əs) *adj.:* heavy and slow-moving.
portal (pôrt′'l) *n.:* doorway or gate, especially a large, impressive one.
posterity (päs·ter′ə·tē) *n.:* descendants or all future generations.
potent (pōt′'nt) *adj.:* powerful; effective; convincing.
precarious (prē·ker′ē·əs) *adj.:* in danger of falling down; unstable; dependent on chance or circumstances.
precipitate (prē·sip′ə·tət) *adj.:* hurried; unexpected. **—precipitately** *adv.*
precipitous (prē·sip′ə·təs) *adj.:* steep.
preclude (prē·klo͞od′) *v.:* prevent; make impossible.
prelude (prel′yo͞od′) *n.:* preliminary part; opening; introduction to main part.
pretentious (prē·ten′shəs) *adj.:* making claims to some distinction or importance.
prodigy (präd′ə·jē) *n.:* child of highly unusual talent or genius.
profound (prō·found′) *adj.:* very deep.
profuse (prō·fyo͞os′) *adj.:* plentiful; abundant; given freely.
promontory (präm′ən·tôr′ē) *n.:* peak of high land that juts out into a body of water.
prostrate (präs′trāt′) *adj.:* **1.** lying flat. **2.** helpless; overcome; lying with the face downward to show devotion or submission.
providential (präv′ə·den′shəl) *adj.:* fortunate; like something caused by a divine act.
provincial (prō·vin′shəl) *adj.:* belonging to a certain, usually rural, province; narrow-minded; unsophisticated.
proximity (präks·im′ə·tē) *n.:* nearness.
prudence (pro͞od′'ns) *n.:* cautiousness; sound judgment.

quagmire (kwag′mīr′) *n.:* **1.** wet, boggy ground. **2.** difficult position.
qualm (kwäm) *n.:* **1.** uneasiness or doubt; misgiving. **2.** twinge of conscience.
quaver (kwā′vər) *n.:* quivering or shaky quality in voice or tone.
quell (kwel) *v.:* quiet; subdue.
quizzical (kwiz′i·kəl) *adj.:* puzzled; questioning.

rationale (rash′ə·nal′) *n.:* fundamental reasons or logical basis for something.
recoil (ri·koil′) *v.:* draw back in fear, surprise, or disgust.
recrimination (ri·krim′ə·nā′shən) *n.:* accusation against an accuser; countercharge.
refrain (ri·frān′) *v.:* hold back; keep oneself from doing something.
regimen (rej′ə·mən) *n.:* regulated system of diet or exercise for the improvement and maintenance of health.
regressive (ri·gres′iv) *adj.:* moving backward or returning to an earlier or less advanced condition.
relentless (ri·lent′lis) *adj.:* **1.** not yielding; harsh. **2.** persistent.
remand (ri·mand′) *v.:* send back, order to go back.
reminiscence (rem′ə·nis′əns) *n.:* act of remembering experiences.
remote (ri·mōt′) *adj.:* distant.
renounce (ri·nouns′) *v.:* give up, especially by formal statement; reject.
renowned (ri·nound′) *adj.:* having a great reputation; famous.
repellent (ri·pel′ənt) *adj.:* causing distaste or dislike; disgusting.
repertoire (rep′ər·twär′) *n.:* all the musical selections that a musician is prepared to perform or teach.
repressive (ri·pres′iv) *adj.:* severely controlling; preventing natural expression.
reproach (ri·prōch′) *n.:* blame; expression of disapproval.
repugnant (ri·pug′nənt) *adj.:* distasteful; offensive.
repulse (ri·puls′) *n.:* driving back; repelling.
resolve (ri·zälv′) *v.:* **1.** break up into separate parts. **2.** decide.
respective (ri·spek′tiv) *adj.:* relating individually to each of two or more things.
resplendent (ri·splen′dənt) *adj.:* dazzling; shining brightly; splendid.
reverence (rev′ər·əns) *n.:* attitude or display of deep respect.
reverie (rev′ər·ē) *n.:* daydreaming; state of being absorbed in thought.

at, āte, cär; ten, ēve; is, īce; gō, hôrn, look, to͞ol; oil, out; up, fʉr; ə *for unstressed vowels, as* a *in* ago, u *in* focus; ′ *as in* Latin (lat′'n); chin; she; zh *as in* azure (azh′ər); thin, *the*; ŋ *as in* ring (riŋ)

revoke (ri•vōk′) *v.:* withdraw or take away, as a privilege; cancel.
rifle (rī′fəl) *v.:* search thoroughly or in a rough manner. **—rifling** *v.* used as *n.*
riposte (ri•pōst′) *n.:* sharp, swift response or retort.

sanctified (saŋk′tə•fīd′) *adj.:* blessed; made holy.
sate (sāt) *v.:* fill; satisfy.
sauciness (sô′sē•nəs) *n.:* pertness; liveliness.
scathing (skā′*th*iŋ) *adj.:* harsh; cutting or sarcastic. **—scathingly** *adv.*
scruple (skrōō′pəl) *v.:* hesitate because of feelings of guilt.
sedate (si•dāt′) *adj.:* calm and dignified. **—sedately** *adv.*
self-degradation (self′deg′rə•dā′shən) *n.:* tendency to destroy or weaken one's moral character and self-respect.
senile (sē′nīl′) *adj.:* mentally impaired, especially as the result of old age.
sententious (sen•ten′shəs) *adj.:* trite and moralizing. **—sententiously** *adv.*
sidle (sīd′′l) *v.:* move sideways, especially in a shy or sneaky manner.
skirt (skʉrt) *v.:* **1.** pass around rather than through. **2.** miss narrowly; avoid.
smith (smith) *n.:* blacksmith; person who makes metal tools.
solicitude (sə•lis′ə•tōōd′) *n.:* care or concern for other people.
somber (säm′bər) *adj.:* earnest and solemn; gloomy. **—somberly** *adv.*
sordid (sôr′did) *adj.:* dirty; cheap; shameful; tainted.
spasmodic (spaz•mäd′ik) *adj.:* having or resembling involuntary muscle twitches or spasms; sudden and violent.
specter (spek′tər) *n.:* frightening figure; ghost.
speculate (spek′yōō•lāt′) *v.:* think; guess.
spoils (spoilz) *n.:* **1.** loot; goods gotten through special effort. **2.** items taken by force by the victors in a war.
squander (skwän′dər) *v.:* spend or use wastefully.
stark (stärk) *adj.:* **1.** harsh; severe. **2.** sharply outlined or defined.
stealthy (stel′thē) *adj.:* secret; artfully sly. **—stealthily** *adv.*
stellar (stel′ər) *adj.:* **1.** of the stars or a star. **2.** outstanding or excellent.
stench (stench) *n.:* offensive smell.
stilted (stil′tid) *adj.:* artificially formal; pompous.
stricken (strik′ən) *adj.:* heartbroken; affected by or suffering from something painful or distressing.
suave (swäv) *adj.:* smoothly gracious or polite; socially polished and refined.
subdue (səb•dōō′) *v.:* **1.** conquer; overcome. **2.** make less intense.
sublime (sə•blīm′) *adj.:* majestic; grand; outstanding. **—sublimely** *adv.*
subsidiary (səb•sid′ē•er′ē) *n.:* company owned and controlled by another company.
succumb (sə•kum′) *v.:* yield; submit; give way.
superlative (sə•pʉr′lə•tiv) *adj.:* supreme; better than all others.
supple (sup′əl) *adj.:* easily bent; flexible.
supplicate (sup′lə•kāt′) *v.:* appeal humbly and earnestly, as if in prayer. **—supplicating** *v.* used as *adj.*
supplication (sup′lə•kā′shən) *n.:* humble appeal or request.
surreptitious (sur′əp•tish′əs) *adj.:* stealthy; sneaky. **—surreptitiously** *adv.*
susceptible (sə•sep′tə•bəl) *adj.:* easily affected emotionally; easily influenced.
swagger (swag′ər) *n.:* bold, arrogant strut.

taciturn (tas′ə•tʉrn′) *adj.:* usually silent and uncommunicative.
taut (tôt) *adj.:* **1.** tightly stretched. **2.** tense.
telescope (tel′ə•skōp′) *v.:* slide or collapse into one another, like the sections of a collapsible telescope.
telltale (tel′tāl′) *adj.:* revealing what is meant to be kept secret.
temper (tem′pər) *v.:* moderate by mixing with something else. **—tempered** *v.* used as *adj.*
temperate (tem′pər•it) *adj.:* moderate; not extreme.
tenacious (tə•nā′shəs) *adj.:* holding firmly; persistent; stubborn. **—tenaciously** *adv.*
tentative (ten′tə•tiv) *adj.:* **1.** uncertain; hesitant. **2.** not definite or final.
tenuous (ten′yōō•əs) *adj.:* weak; slight.
tepid (tep′id) *adj.:* neither hot nor cold.
terse (tʉrs) *adj.:* using few words; concise. **—tersely** *adv.*
throng (thrôŋ) *n.:* crowd; multitude. —*v.:* crowd upon in large numbers.
topical (täp′i•kəl) *adj.:* having to do with current topics or events.
torrent (tôr′ənt) *n.:* violent, forceful rush.
transcend (tran•send′) *v.:* go beyond the limits of.
transformation (trans′fər•mā′shən) *n.:* change or conversion in appearance or form.
transgress (trans•gres′) *v.:* disobey.

transition (tran • zish′ən) *n.:* passing from one condition, form, or stage to another.

translucent (trans • lo͞o′sənt) *adj.:* partially transparent.

traverse (trə • vʉrs′) *v.:* cross.

tribulation (trib′yo͞o • lā′shən) *n.:* misery or suffering; affliction.

tumultuous (to͞o • mul′cho͞o • əs) *adj.:* **1.** violent; greatly agitated or disturbed. **2.** wild, noisy, and confused.

ulterior (ul • tir′ē • ər) *adj.:* beyond what is expressed; unrevealed.

uncouth (un • ko͞oth′) *adj.:* crude; uncultured.

undaunted (un • dônt′id) *adj.:* not hesitating in the face of fear or discouragement.

unfaltering (un • fôl′tər • iŋ) *adj.:* not weakening or wavering. **—unfalteringly** *adv.*

unfurl (un • fʉrl′) *v.:* open or unroll, as a flag or banner.

unrequited (un • ri • kwīt′id) *adj.:* not returned or paid back.

unscrupulous (un • skro͞o′pyə • ləs) *adj.:* not restrained by ideas of right and wrong.

unseemly (un • sēm′lē) *adj.:* not decent or proper.

untenable (un • ten′ə • bəl) *adj.:* incapable of being defended, maintained, or occupied.

untrammeled (un • tram′əld) *adj.:* not confined or shackled; free.

unutterable (un • ut′ər • ə • bəl) *adj.:* inexpressible; indescribable.

usher (ush′ər) *v.:* escort.

vain (vān) *adj.:* without success; fruitless. **—vainly** *adv.*

valid (val′id) *adj.:* meeting the requirements of established standards.

vanquish (vaŋ′kwish) *v.:* conquer or defeat in battle.

vehement (vē′ə • mənt) *adj.:* violent; having intense feeling. **—vehemently** *adv.*

vigil (vij′əl) *n.:* purposeful watching and staying awake.

violate (vī′ə • lāt′) *v.:* fail to show proper respect for.

vitriol (vi′trē • ôl) *n.:* venom; sharpness or bitterness of feeling.

vivacity (vi • vas′ə • tē) *n.:* liveliness of spirit.

vivify (viv′ə • fī′) *v.:* **1.** give life to. **2.** make more lively, active, or striking.

wanton (wän′tən) *adv.:* careless, often with deliberate malice. **—wantonly** *adv.*

waver (wā′vər) *v.:* show doubt or uncertainty about what to do.

wizened (wiz′ənd) *adj:* wrinkled and dried up.

wrath (rath) *n.:* intense anger.

wrench (rench) *v.:* suddenly and violently twist or jolt.

writhe (rīth) *v.:* make twisting movements; squirm.

zealous (zel′əs) *adj.:* fervent; devoted. **—zealously** *adv.*

zenith (zē′nith) *n.:* point directly overhead in the sky; highest point.

at, āte, cär; ten, ēve; is, īce; gō, hôrn, look, to͞ol; oil, out; up, fʉr; ə *for unstressed vowels, as* a *in* ago, u *in* focus; ′ *as in* Latin (lat′′n); chin; she; zh *as in* azure (azh′ər); thin, *the*; ŋ *as in* ring (riŋ)

ACKNOWLEDGMENTS

For permission to reprint copyrighted material, grateful acknowledgment is made to the following sources:

Lily Lee Adams: "The Friendship Only Lasted a Few Seconds" by Lily Lee Adams from *Connections,* newsletter of the William Joiner Center at University of Massachusetts, Boston, Spring 1990. Copyright © 1990 by Lily Lee Adams.

Addison Wesley Longman Ltd.: From "Childhood" and from "The Lion's Awakening" from *Sundiata: An Epic of Old Mali* by D. T. Niane, translated by G. D. Pickett. Copyright © 1960 by Présence Africaine; English translation copyright © 1965 by Longman Group Ltd.

Rose A. Adkins: From "Reporting the Details of Life" by Rose A. Adkins from *Writer's Digest,* March 1993. Copyright © 1993 by Rose A. Adkins.

Robert Anderson: *I Never Sang for My Father* by Robert Anderson. Includes slight author's adaptations. Copyright © 1968 by Robert Anderson.

Andrews and McMeel Publishing: "Daddy Doll Under the Bed—June 21, 1981" from *Forever, Erma* by Erma Bombeck. Copyright © 1996 by the Estate of Erma Bombeck. All rights reserved.

Arte Público Press: From "The Looking Glass Shame" (retitled "Lessons of Love") from *Silent Dancing: A Partial Remembrance of a Puerto Rican Childhood* by Judith Ortiz Cofer. Copyright © 1990 by Judith Ortiz Cofer. Published by Arte Público Press—University of Houston, Houston, TX, 1990. From "Distillation," slightly adapted from *The Last Laugh and Other Stories* by Hugo Martínez-Serros. Copyright © 1988 by Hugo Martínez-Serros. Published by Arte Público Press—University of Houston, Houston, TX, 1988. "A Voice" and "Señora X No More" from *Communion* by Pat Mora. Copyright © 1991 by Pat Mora. Published by Arte Público Press—University of Houston, Houston, TX, 1991. "Same Song" from *Borders* by Pat Mora. Copyright © 1986 by Pat Mora. Published by Arte Público Press—University of Houston, Houston, TX, 1986.

David Askia-Forbes: "Dark Symphony" by David Askia-Forbes from *Phoenix,* vol. XVII, no. 1, May 1993. Copyright © 1993 by David Askia-Forbes. Published by Gonzaga College High School, Washington, D.C.

Angel Bagley: "I Want to Be Somebody" by Angel Bagley from *Rites of Passage, a Literary Magazine, 1991–1992.* Copyright © 1992 by Angel Bagley. Published by Thomas Jefferson High School, Portland, OR.

Erika L. Banick: "Just Another Love Poem" by Erika Banick from *Creations Literary/Art Magazine,* vol. XIV (*Spirit: The Human Experience*), 1991–1992. Copyright © 1992 by Erika L. Banick. Published by Warren Township High School, Gurnee, IL.

Bantam Books, a division of Bantam Doubleday Dell Publishing Group, Inc.: "Trap of Gold" from *War Party* by Louis L'Amour. Copyright 1951 by Popular Publications, Inc.

Virginia Barber Literary Agency, Inc.: "Boys and Girls" from *Dance of the Happy Shades* by Alice Munro. Copyright © 1968 by Alice Munro. Originally published by McGraw Hill Ryerson. All rights reserved.

Manolo Barco: From "Helping education by cutting funds?" by Manolo Barco from *Miami Herald,* April 15, 1995. Copyright © 1995 by Manolo Barco.

Belles Lettres: From "Lucille Clifton," an interview by Naomi Thiers, from *Belles Lettres,* Summer 1994. Copyright © 1994 by Belles Lettres.

Susan Bergholz Literary Services, New York: "Liberty" by Julia Alvarez. Copyright © 1996 by Julia Alvarez. First published in *Writer's Harvest 2,* edited by Ethan Canin, published by Harcourt Brace and Company, 1996. All rights reserved. From comments about *Names/Nombres* by Julia Alvarez. Copyright © 1985 by Julia Alvarez. First published in *Nuestro,* March 1985. All rights reserved. From "Alvarez, Julia 1950–" from *Contemporary Authors.* Copyright © 1980 by Julia Alvarez. Published by Gale Research. All rights reserved. "Geraldo No Last Name" from *The House on Mango Street* by Sandra Cisneros. Copyright © 1991 by Sandra Cisneros. Published by Vintage Books, a division of Random House, Inc., and in hardcover by Alfred A. Knopf. All rights reserved.

Bilingual Press/Editorial Bilingüe, Arizona State University, Tempe, AZ: "Tony Went to the Bodega but He Didn't Buy Anything" from *Trumpets from the Islands of Their Eviction* by Martín Espada. Copyright © 1987 by Bilingual Press/Editorial Bilingüe.

David Blow: From "Her Heart Belongs to 'Father'" by Marya Mannes from *The New York Times,* November 15, 1970.

BOA Editions, Ltd., 260 East Ave., Rochester, NY 14604: "miss rosie" from *good woman: poems and a memoir 1969–1980* by Lucille Clifton. Copyright © 1987 by Lucille Clifton.

The Book Report, Inc.: From "Exclusive TBR Interview with Frank McCourt" by Jesse Kornbluth from "Author Transcripts," Online, World Wide Web, September 11, 1998. Available at http://www.bookwire.com/TBR/transcripts.article$3259.

Brandt & Brandt Literary Agents, Inc.: "By the Waters of Babylon" from *The Selected Works of Stephen Vincent Benét.* Copyright © 1937 by Stephen Vincent Benét; copyright renewed © 1964 by Thomas C. Benét, Stephanie P. Mahin, and Rachel Benét Lewis. Published by Holt, Rinehart & Winston, Inc. From "You Are Now Entering the Human Heart" by Janet Frame. Copyright © 1969 by Janet Frame. Originally appeared in *The New Yorker.*

Broadside Press: From *Report from Part One* by Gwendolyn Brooks. Copyright © 1972 by Gwendolyn Brooks. Published by Broadside Press, Detroit.

Gwendolyn Brooks: "The Bean Eaters" and "We Real Cool" from *Blacks* by Gwendolyn Brooks. Copyright © 1991 by Gwendolyn Brooks. Published by Third World Press, Chicago, 1991.

Curtis Brown, Ltd.: "R.M.S. Titanic" by Hanson W. Baldwin from *Harper's Magazine,* January 1934. Copyright © 1933 by Hanson W. Baldwin.

Calyx Books: "VI. Nisei Daughter: The Second Generation" from "Proud upon an Alien Shore" by Rose Furuya Hawkins from *The Forbidden Stitch,* edited by Shirley Geok-Lin Lim. Copyright © 1989 by Rose Furuya Hawkins. Published by Calyx Books, 1989.

Cambridge University Press: Genesis 29:15–30 (retitled "Jacob and Rachel") and Luke 15:11–32 (retitled "The Parable of the Prodigal Son") from *The New English Bible.* Copyright © 1961, 1970 by Oxford University Press and Cambridge University Press.

Carnegie Mellon University Libraries, Special Collections, Pittsburgh, PA: "The Father" and "The Prodigal" from *A Footing on This Earth* by Sara Henderson Hay. Copyright © 1966 by Sara Henderson Hay. Published by Doubleday, a division of Bantam Doubleday Dell Publishing Group, Inc.

Don Congdon Associates, Inc.: "The Pedestrian" by Ray Bradbury from *The Reporter,* August 7, 1951. Copyright © 1951 by the Fortnightly Publishing Co.; copyright renewed © 1979 by Ray Bradbury. From "Drunk and in Charge of a Bicycle" from *The Stories of Ray Bradbury.* Copyright © 1981 by Ray Bradbury. From *Zen in the Art of Writing* by Ray Bradbury. Copyright © 1990 by Ray Bradbury. Published by Capra Press. Quotes by Ray Bradbury from "An Exclusive Interview with Ray Bradbury" by Frank Roberts from *Writer's Digest,* vol. 47, no. 2, February 1967. Copyright © 1967 by Ray Bradbury.

Lauren Cuprill: "Women in the Civil War" by Lauren Cuprill from *Voices of Youth,* April/May 1994. Copyright © 1994 by Voices of Youth: Educational Goals Study Group.

The Dallas Morning News: From "Alice in Wonderland" by Toni Y. Joseph from *The Dallas Morning News,* May 27, 1992. Copyright © 1992 by The Dallas Morning News.

Darhansoff & Verrill Literary Agency: "I Am Not One of Those Who Left the Land . . ." from *Poems of Akhmatova* by Anna Akhmatova, translated by Stanley Kunitz and Max Hayward. Copyright © 1967, 1968, 1972, 1973 by Stanley Kunitz and Max Hayward.

Delacorte Press/Seymour Lawrence, a division of Bantam Doubleday Dell Publishing Group, Inc.: "Where Have You Gone, Charming Billy?" slightly adapted from *Going After Cacciato* by Tim O'Brien. Copyright © 1975, 1976, 1977, 1978 by Tim O'Brien. From *If I Die in a Combat Zone, Box Me Up and Ship Me Home* by Tim O'Brien. Copyright © 1973 by Tim O'Brien.

Annie Dillard and Blanche C. Gregory, Inc.: "Is There Really Such a Thing as Talent?" by Annie Dillard from *Seventeen®,* June 1979. Copyright © 1979 by Annie Dillard.

Barbara Sande Dimmitt: From "The Education of Frank McCourt" by Barbara Sande Dimmitt from *Reader's Digest,* November 1997. Copyright © 1997 by Barbara Sande Dimmitt.

Doubleday, a division of Bantam Doubleday Dell Publishing Group, Inc.: From "My Words Will Be There" by Audre Lorde from *Black Women Writers (1950–1980),* edited by Mari Evans. Copyright © 1984 by Mari Evans. Quotes by Naomi Shihab Nye and Quincy

Troupe from *The Language of Life: A Festival of Poets* by Bill Moyers. Copyright © 1995 by Public Affairs Television, Inc., and David Grubin Productions, Inc.

Dutton, a division of Penguin Putnam Inc.: From "The Book of Sand" from *The Book of Sand* by Jorge Luis Borges, translated by Norman Thomas di Giovanni. Translation copyright © 1971, 1975, 1976, 1977 by Emece Editores, S.A., and Norman Thomas di Giovanni. "The Destiny of a Wolf-Cub," "Information and Knowledge," "Relative," and "The Thief and the Blanket" from "Sayings by Saadi" from *The Way of the Sufi* by Idries Shah. Copyright © 1968 by Idries Shah.

Dutton Signet, a division of Penguin Putnam Inc.: "The Tale of Sir Launcelot du Lake" and "The Sword in the Stone" from *Le Morte D'Arthur* by Sir Thomas Malory, translated by Keith Baines. Translation copyright © 1962 by Keith Baines; copyright renewed © 1990 by Francesca Evans. Introduction copyright © 1962 by Robert Graves; copyright renewed © 1990 by Beryl Graves. Footnotes from *Julius Caesar* by William Shakespeare, edited by William and Barbara Rosen. Introduction and footnotes copyright © 1987 by William Rosen and Barbara Rosen.

The Ecco Press: From "A Letter to the José Zárate Family in Mexico from Patricia Zárate" (retitled "Hello Papa, . . .") from *Between the Lines,* edited and translated by Larry Siems. Copyright © 1992 by Larry Siems.

Farrar, Straus & Giroux, Inc.: "The Prodigal" from *The Complete Poems 1927–1979* by Elizabeth Bishop. Copyright © 1979, 1983 by Alice Helen Methfessel. From "For the Union Dead" from *For the Union Dead* by Robert Lowell. Copyright © 1959 by Robert Lowell; copyright renewed © 1987 by Harriet Lowell, Caroline Lowell, and Sheridan Lowell. "The First Seven Years" from *The Magic Barrel* by Bernard Malamud. Copyright © 1950, 1958 and renewed © 1977, 1986 by Bernard Malamud. "A Storm in the Mountains" from *Stories and Prose Poems* by Alexander Solzhenitsyn, translated by Michael Glenny. Translation copyright © 1971 by Michael Glenny. From "Introduction" from *The Acts of King Arthur and His Noble Knights* by John Steinbeck, edited by Chase Horton. Copyright © 1976 by Elaine Steinbeck.

David Flanagin: Quote by Jeri Taylor from "On *Star Trek,* Literature, and Writing" by David Flanagin from *Studying Star Trek.* Copyright © 1995 by David Flanagin. Available at http://www.hputx.edu/Academics/English/jeritay2.htm.

Gale Research: From "Barry Holstun Lopez" from *Contemporary Authors, New Revision Series,* vol. 23, edited by Deborah A. Straub. Copyright © 1988 by Gale Research.

Isabella Gardner Trust: From "Summer Remembered" from *The Looking Glass* by Isabella Gardner. Copyright © 1961 by The University of Chicago Press.

Tom Godwin and Scott Meredith Literary Agency, 845 Third Avenue, New York, NY 10022: From *The Cold Equations* by Tom Godwin. Copyright 1954 by Tom Godwin.

The Griffith Institute, Ashmolean Museum: From Howard Carter's personal diaries of the first excavation season in the tomb of Tutankhamen, Sunday, November 26, 1922. Copyright © by The Griffith Institute. Available at http://www.ashmol.ox.ac.uk/gri/4sea1not.html.

Hanging Loose Press: "Sonnet for Heaven Below" from *Correspondence Between the Stonehaulers* by Jack Agüeros. Copyright © 1991 by Jack Agüeros.

Harcourt Brace & Company: "Antigone" from *Sophocles: The Oedipus Cycle, an English Version* by Dudley Fitts and Robert Fitzgerald. Copyright 1939 by Harcourt Brace & Company; copyright renewed © 1967 by Dudley Fitts and Robert Fitzgerald. CAUTION: All rights, including professional, amateur, motion picture, recitation, lecturing, performance, public reading, radio broadcasting, and television are strictly reserved. Inquiries on all rights should be addressed to Harcourt Brace & Company, Permissions Department, Orlando, FL 32887-6777. From "Julius Caesar" from *Two Cheers for Democracy* by E. M. Forster. Copyright 1951 by E. M. Forster; copyright renewed © 1979 by Donald Parry. From "June 1936" (letter to her mother) from *The Diary of Anaïs Nin,* vol. II, by Anaïs Nin. Copyright © 1967 by Harcourt Brace & Company. From "Wanderin'" from *The American Songbag* by Carl Sandburg. Copyright 1927 by Harcourt Brace & Company; copyright renewed © 1955 by Carl Sandburg. "Everyday Use" from *In Love & Trouble: Stories of Black Women* by Alice Walker. Copyright © 1973 by Alice Walker.

HarperCollins Publishers, Inc.: From *An American Childhood* by Annie Dillard. Copyright © 1987 by Annie Dillard. From *Pilgrim at Tinker Creek* by Annie Dillard. Copyright © 1974 by Annie Dillard. "The supreme good is like water" (#8), "Some say that my teaching is nonsense" (#67), and "We join spokes together in a wheel" (#11) from *Tao Te Ching by Lao Tzu, A New English Version,* with foreword and notes by Stephen Mitchell. Translation copyright © 1988 by Stephen Mitchell. "A Very Old Man with Enormous Wings" from *Leaf Storm and Other Stories* by Gabriel García Márquez, translated by Gregory Rabassa. Copyright © 1971 by Gabriel García Márquez. From "The Lowest Animal" from *Letters from the Earth by Mark Twain,* edited by Bernard DeVoto. Copyright 1938, 1944, 1946, © 1959, 1962 by the Mark Twain Company; copyright renewed © 1990 by HarperCollins Publishers, Inc. "By Any Other Name" from *Gifts of Passage* by Santha Rama Rau. Copyright 1951 and renewed © 1979 by Santha Rama Rau. Originally appeared in *The New Yorker.*

Harvard University Press and the Trustees of Amherst College: "Heart! We will forget him!," "The Moon was but a chin of gold," "This is the land the sunset washes," and from "This is my letter to the world" from *The Poems of Emily Dickinson,* edited by Thomas H. Johnson. Copyright © 1951, 1955, 1979, 1983 by the President and Fellows of Harvard College. Published by The Belknap Press of Harvard University Press, Cambridge, MA.

David Higham Associates Limited: "Life Is Sweet at Kumansenu" from *The Truly Married Woman and Other Stories* by Abioseh Nicol. Published by Oxford University Press.

Hill and Wang, a division of Farrar, Straus & Giroux, Inc.: From "Vachel Lindsay" from *The Big Sea* by Langston Hughes. Copyright © 1940 by Langston Hughes; copyright renewed © 1968 by Arna Bontemps and George Houston Bass.

Henry Holt and Company, Inc.: From "Acquainted with the Night" and "Stopping by Woods on a Snowy Evening" from *The Poetry of Robert Frost,* edited by Edward Connery Lathem. Copyright 1951, © 1956 by Robert Frost; copyright 1923, 1928, © 1969 by Henry Holt and Company, Inc. "Loveliest of trees, the cherry now" from "A Shropshire Lad"—Authorized Edition—from *The Collected Poems of A. E. Housman.* Copyright 1939, 1940, © 1965 by Henry Holt and Company, Inc.; copyright © 1967, 1968 by Robert E. Symons.

Garrett Hongo: Comment on "The Legend" by Garrett Hongo. Copyright © 1997 by Garrett Hongo.

Houghton Mifflin Company: From Foreword and from "Shikata Ga Nai" (retitled "It Can't Be Helped") from *Farewell to Manzanar* by James D. Houston and Jeanne Wakatsuki Houston. Copyright © 1973 by James D. Houston. All rights reserved. From "Meeting-House Hill" from *What's O'Clock* from *The Complete Poetical Works of Amy Lowell.* Copyright © 1955 by Houghton Mifflin Company; copyright renewed © 1983 by Houghton Mifflin Company, Brinton P. Roberts, and G. D'Andelot Belin, Esq. All rights reserved. "Courage" from *The Awful Rowing Toward God* by Anne Sexton. Copyright © 1975 by Loring Conant, Jr., Executor of the Estate of Anne Sexton. All rights reserved.

The Hudson Review: From "Interview with Anne Sexton" by Patricia Marx from *The Hudson Review,* vol. XVII, no. 4, Winter 1965–66. Copyright © 1966 by The Hudson Review, Inc.

Janklow & Nesbit Associates: From "Why I Write" by Joan Didion. Copyright © 1976 by Joan Didion. First published in *The New York Times Book Review,* December 6, 1976.

Jewish Museum in Prague: "The Butterfly" by Pavel Friedmann from *I Have Not Seen a Butterfly Around Here.* Published by Jewish Museum in Prague, 1993.

The Jewish Publication Society: Genesis 22:1–19 from *Tanakh: A New Translation of the Holy Scriptures.* Copyright © 1985 by The Jewish Publication Society.

The Heirs to the Estate of Martin Luther King, Jr., c/o Writers House, Inc. as agent for the proprietor: From "An Experiment in Love" from *A Testament of Hope: The Essential Writings of Martin Luther King, Jr.,* edited by James Washington. Copyright © 1963 by Martin Luther King, Jr.; copyright renewed © 1991 by Coretta Scott King. "Chapter VI: The World House" from *Where Do We Go from Here: Chaos or Community?* by Martin Luther King, Jr. Copyright © 1967 by Martin Luther King, Jr. From "Letter from Birmingham Jail" from *Why We Can't Wait* by Martin Luther King, Jr. Copyright © 1963 by the Estate of Martin Luther King, Jr.; copyright renewed © 1991 by Coretta Scott King.

Stephen King and TV Guide® Magazine: From "Now You Take 'Bambi' or 'Snow White'—That's Scary" by Stephen King from *TV Guide® Magazine,* June 13, 1981. Copyright © 1981 by News America Publications, Inc.

Alfred A. Knopf, Inc.: From *Death Comes for the Archbishop* by Willa Cather. Copyright 1926, 1927 by Willa Cather. "What Happened During the Ice Storm" from *The One-Room Schoolhouse* by Jim Heynen. Copyright © 1993 by Jim Heynen. "The Legend" from *The River of Heaven* by Garrett Hongo. Copyright © 1988 by Garrett

Hongo. "Mother to Son," "Epigram," and "Theme for English B" from *Collected Poems* by Langston Hughes. Copyright © 1994 by the Estate of Langston Hughes. "Through the Tunnel" from *Stories* by Doris Lessing. Copyright © 1978 by Doris Lessing. "Gracious Goodness" and from "Some Collisions Bring Luck" from *Circles on the Water* by Marge Piercy. Copyright © 1982 by Marge Piercy. "Ex-Basketball Player" from *The Carpentered Hen and Other Tame Creatures* by John Updike. Copyright © 1982 by John Updike.

Ted Kooser: "Abandoned Farmhouse" from *A Local Habitation and a Name* by Ted Kooser. Published by Solo Press.

The Estate of Alan Jay Lerner: Act I, Scene 3 (retitled "The Round Table"), from *Camelot* by Alan Jay Lerner and Frederick Loewe. Copyright © 1960, 1961 and renewed © 1988 by Alan Jay Lerner and Frederick Loewe. CAUTION: Professionals and amateurs are hereby warned that *Camelot,* being fully protected under the Copyright Laws of the United States of America, the British Empire, including the Dominion of Canada, and all other countries of the Berne and Universal Copyright Conventions, is subject to royalty. All rights, including professional, amateur, motion picture, recitation, lecturing, public reading, radio and television broadcasting, and the rights of translation into foreign languages, are strictly reserved. Particular emphasis is laid on the question of readings, permission for which must be secured in writing.

Liveright Publishing Corporation: "since feeling is first" from *Complete Poems, 1904–1962* by E. E. Cummings, edited by George J. Firmage. Copyright 1926, 1954, © 1991 by the Trustees for the E. E. Cummings Trust; copyright © 1985 by George James Firmage. "Those Winter Sundays" from *Angle of Ascent: New and Selected Poems* by Robert Hayden. Copyright © 1966 by Robert Hayden.

Sterling Lord Literistic, Inc.: From "A Presentation of Whales" from *Crossing Open Ground* by Barry Lopez. Copyright © 1988 by Barry Lopez.

Los Angeles Times: From "Baca: A Poet Emerges from Prison of His Past" by Beth Ann Krier from *Los Angeles Times,* February 15, 1989. Copyright © 1989 by the Los Angeles Times.

Macmillan General Reference USA, a division of Ahsuog, Inc.: From *Webster's New World™ College Dictionary,* Third Edition. Copyright © 1988, 1991, 1994, 1996, 1997 by Simon & Schuster, Inc.

Hilary Masters: From *Across Spoon River* by Edgar Lee Masters. Copyright 1936 by Edgar Lee Masters; copyright renewed © 1964 by Ellen Coyne Masters. Originally published by Farrar & Rinehart.

McCall's Magazine: "Where I Find My Heroes" by Oliver Stone from *McCall's Magazine,* November 1992. Copyright © 1992 by Gruner & Jahr USA Publishing.

Merlyn's Pen, Inc.: "Jurassic Park" review by Matthew Harry from *Merlyn's Pen,* February 5, 1994. Copyright © 1994 by Merlyn's Pen, Inc. First appeared in *Merlyn's Pen: The National Magazines of Student Writing.* "Ocean Beach Childhood" by Ann Marie Hoppell from *Merlyn's Pen,* February/March 1994. Copyright © 1994 by Merlyn's Pen, Inc. All rights reserved.

Jeffrey Meyers: "Foe of Walls," letter to the editor by Jeffrey Meyers from *The New York Times,* April 27, 1995. Copyright © 1995 by Jeffrey Meyers.

Pat Mora: Comment on "A Voice" by Pat Mora. Copyright © 1997 by Pat Mora.

National Book Foundation: From "National Book Awards Acceptance Speech" by John Updike, 1982.

National Council of Teachers of English: "Mending Test" by Penelope Bryant Turk from *English Journal,* January 1993. Copyright © 1993 by the National Council of Teachers of English.

New Directions Publishing Corp.: "I Am Offering This Poem" from *Immigrants in Our Own Land & Selected Early Poems* by Jimmy Santiago Baca. Copyright © 1982 by Jimmy Santiago Baca.

New Rivers Press: "Aunt Fannie Fixes Bison Bourguignon" and "Dedication" from *Iron Woman: Poems* by Diane Glancy. Copyright © 1990 by Diane Glancy. Published in 1990 by New Rivers Press, 420 N. 5th St., #910, Minneapolis, MN 55401.

New York Post: "'Julius Caesar' in an Absorbing Production" by John Mason Brown from *New York Post,* November 12, 1937. Copyright 1937 by New York Post.

The New York Times Company: From "No News from Auschwitz" by A. M. Rosenthal from *The New York Times,* August 31, 1958. Copyright © 1958 by The New York Times Company. From "Love and Age: A Talk with García Márquez" by Marlise Simons from *The New York Times Book Review,* April 7, 1985. Copyright © 1985 by The New York Times Company. From "In Georgia's Swept Yards, a Dying Tradition" by Anne Raver from *The New York Times,* August 8, 1993. Copyright © 1993 by The New York Times Company. From "Appearances Are Destructive" by Mark Mathabane from *The New York Times,* August 26, 1993. Copyright © 1993 by The New York Times Company. From "Melting Pot Still Bubbles at I.S. 237" by Charisse Jones from *The New York Times,* June 12, 1994. Copyright © 1994 by The New York Times Company. From chart "Teen-Agers and Sex Roles" (The New York Times/CBS News Poll) from *The New York Times,* July 11, 1994. Copyright © 1994 by The New York Times Company. "Lunar Legacy" (Editorial) from *The New York Times,* July 20, 1994. Copyright © 1994 by The New York Times Company. "A Test of Honor" by Owen Robinson from *The New York Times,* September 30, 1997. Copyright © 1997 by the New York Times Company. From "Boldly Going, Going, Going . . ." by Charles Strum from *The New York Times,* November 30–December 6, 1997. Copyright © 1997 by The New York Times Company. From "Havana Journal: A Sentimental Journal to La Casa of Childhood" by Mirta Ojito from *The New York Times,* February 3, 1998. Copyright © 1998 by The New York Times Company. From "Blazing an Unconventional Trail to a New Theory of Immunity" by Claudia Dreifus from *The New York Times,* June 14, 1998. Copyright © 1998 by The New York Times Company.

92nd Street YM-YWHA, New York, NY 10128: Quote by A. M. Rosenthal from "A. M. Rosenthal Speaks His Mind" by Brian Scott Lipton. Copyright © 1995 by 92nd Street Y. First appeared in the *92nd Street Y Review,* February 1995.

W. W. Norton & Company, Inc.: From *Don Quixote: A Norton Critical Edition: The Ormsby Translation, Revised* by Miguel de Cervantes, edited by Joseph Jones and Kenneth Douglas. Copyright © 1981 by W. W. Norton & Company, Inc. From "Camelot" from *The Street Where I Live* by Alan Jay Lerner. Copyright © 1978 by Alan Jay Lerner. "Hanging Fire" from *The Black Unicorn* by Audre Lorde. Copyright © 1978 by Audre Lorde. From *Mrs. Stevens Hears the Mermaids Singing* by May Sarton. Copyright © 1965 by May Sarton. From "Still Just Writing" by Anne Tyler from *The Writer on Her Work,* edited by Janet Sternburg. Copyright © 1980 by Janet Sternburg.

Christian O'Connor: "I Wish I Had Said" by Christian O'Connor from *Phoenix,* vol. XVI, no. 1, May 1992. Copyright © 1992 by Christian O'Connor. Published by Gonzaga College High School, Washington, D.C.

Pantheon Books, a division of Random House, Inc.: From "The Ghost Dance at Wounded Knee" by Dick Fool Bull from *American Indian Myths and Legends,* edited by Richard Erdoes and Alfonso Ortiz. From "A Lost Childhood" (retitled "The Power of a Poem") from *Life for Me Ain't Been No Crystal Stair* by Susan Sheehan. Copyright © 1993 by Susan Sheehan. "Wagging My Tail in the Mud" by Chuang Tzu, "The Missing Axe" by Lieh Tzu, and "The Lost Horse" by Lui An from *Chinese Fairy Tales and Fantasies,* edited and translated by Moss Roberts. Copyright © 1979 by Moss Roberts.

Paramount Pictures: Quotes from *Star Trek: Original Series.* Copyright © 1966 by Paramount Pictures. All rights reserved. From *Star Trek: The Motion Picture.* Copyright © 1979 by Paramount Pictures. All rights reserved. From *Star Trek: Generations.* Copyright © 1994 by Paramount Pictures. All rights reserved. From *Star Trek: First Contact.* Copyright © 1996 by Paramount Pictures. All rights reserved.

Penguin Books Ltd.: "Daylight" and "Comfort" from *The Koran,* translated by N. J. Dawood. Copyright © 1956, 1959, 1966, 1968, 1974, 1990 by N. J. Dawood. Published by Penguin Classics, 1956, Fifth Revised Edition, 1990.

G. P. Putnam's Sons, a division of The Putnam Publishing Group: "Two Kinds" from *The Joy Luck Club* by Amy Tan. Copyright © 1989 by Amy Tan.

Random House, Inc.: Excerpt (retitled "Hair") from *The Autobiography of Malcolm X* by Malcolm X, with the assistance of Alex Haley. Copyright © 1964 by Alex Haley and Malcolm X; copyright © 1965 by Alex Haley and Betty Shabazz.

Marian Reiner: "Inside a Poem" from *It Doesn't Always Have to Rhyme* by Eve Merriam. Copyright © 1964, 1992 by Eve Merriam.

Luis Rodríguez: From "Over There in East L.A." by Luis Rodríguez from *L.A. Weekly,* I, 33, July 20–26, 1979, p. 6. Copyright © 1979 by Luis Rodríguez.

Russell & Volkening, Inc., as agents for Anne Tyler: "With All Flags Flying" by Anne Tyler. Copyright © 1971 by Anne Tyler. Originally appeared in *Redbook,* June 1971.

Jim Sagel and Publishers Weekly®: From "Sandra Cisneros," an interview by Jim Sagel, from *Publisher's Weekly,* vol. 238, no.15, March 29, 1991. Copyright © 1991 by Publishers Weekly.

Scribner, a division of Simon & Schuster: From "Last Years" from *A. E. Housman: The Scholar-Poet* by Richard Perceval Graves. Copyright © 1979 by Richard Graves. From *Angela's Ashes* by Frank McCourt. Copyright © 1996 by Frank McCourt.
The Society of Authors as the Literary Representative of the Estate of John Masefield: "Sea Fever" from *Poems* by John Masefield. Published by Macmillan Publishing Company, New York, 1953.
St. Martin's Press, Incorporated: From Prologue from *Anna Akhmatova: Poet and Prophet* by Roberta Reeder. Copyright © 1994 by Roberta Reeder.
Amy Tan and Sandra Dijkstra Literary Agency: From "Mother Tongue" by Amy Tan. Copyright © 1990 by Amy Tan. First appeared in *The Threepenny Review.*
Rosemary A. Thurber and the Barbara Hogenson Agency: "The Scotty Who Knew Too Much" from *Fables for Our Time* by James Thurber. Copyright © 1940 by James Thurber; copyright © 1968 by Rosemary A. Thurber. Published by HarperCollins Publishers.
Time Inc.: "The Man in the Water" by Roger Rosenblatt from *Time,* January 26, 1982. Copyright © 1982 by Time Inc. From "The Unknown Rebel" by Pico Iyer from *Time,* April 13, 1998. Copyright © 1998 by Time Inc.
Brian Trusiewicz: From "Virtuality" by Brian Trusiewicz from *Voices of Youth,* September/October 1993. Copyright © 1993 by Brian Trusiewicz.
Charles E. Tuttle Company, Inc.: "Muddy Road" and "The Thief Who Became a Disciple" from *Zen Flesh, Zen Bones,* compiled by Paul Reps. Copyright © 1957 by Charles E. Tuttle Company, Inc. Published by Charles E. Tuttle Company, Inc., Rutland, Vermont, and Tokyo, Japan.
Universal Press Syndicate, an Andrews McMeel Universal Company: From review of *The X-Files* by Roger Ebert from the *Chicago Sun-Times,* 1998. Copyright © 1998 by Universal Press Syndicate.
University of Pittsburgh Press: "The Bass, the River, and Sheila Mant" from *The Man Who Loved Levittown* by W. D. Wetherell. Copyright © 1985 by W. D. Wetherell.
University Press of New England: "Moons" from *The Stone Harp* by John Haines. Copyright © 1971 by John Haines. Published by Wesleyan University Press. "The Wrestlers" from *A Summer Life* by Gary Soto. Copyright © 1990 by University Press of New England.
U.S. News & World Report: Quotes by Alice Walker from "The Craft of Survival" by Alvin P. Sanoff from *U.S. News & World Report,* June 3, 1991. Copyright © 1991 by U.S. News & World Report.
Charles Van Doren: From *Shakespeare* by Mark Van Doren. Copyright © 1953 by Mark Van Doren.
Viking Penguin, a division of Penguin Putnam Inc.: From *Travels with Charley* by John Steinbeck. Copyright © 1961, 1962 by The Curtis Publishing Co.; copyright © 1962 by John Steinbeck; copyright renewed © 1990 by Elaine Steinbeck, Thom Steinbeck, and John Steinbeck IV.
Villard Books, a division of Random House, Inc.: From *Into Thin Air* by Jon Krakauer. Copyright © 1997 by Jon Krakauer.
Vintage Books, a division of Random House, Inc.: "How sad that I hope . . . ," "Should the world of love . . . ," and "Since my heart placed me . . ." from *The Ink Dark Moon: Love Poems* by Ono No Komachi and Izumi Shikibu, translated by Jane Hirshfield and Mariko Aratani. Copyright © 1990 by Jane Hirshfield and Mariko Aratani.
Melissa Wafer: "La Profesora" by Melissa Wafer from *Pegasus,* Literary-Arts Publication, vol. XVIII, 1991. Copyright © 1991 by Melissa Wafer. Published by Half Hollow Hills High School, Dix Hills, NY.
David Wagoner: "Tumbleweed" from *Collected Poems 1956–1976* by David Wagoner. Copyright © 1976 by Indiana University Press.
Warner Bros. Publications Inc., Miami, FL 33014: From lyrics to "The Round Table" from *Camelot* by Alan Lerner and Frederick Loewe. Copyright © 1960, 1961 and renewed © 1988 by Alan Jay Lerner (ASCAP) & Frederick Loewe (ASCAP). All rights administered by Chappell & Co. (ASCAP). All rights reserved.
Kristen J. Wells: "Now and Then" by Kristi Wells from *Pegasus,* 1991. Copyright © 1991 by Kristi Wells. Published by Brookwood High School, Snellville, GA.
W. D. Wetherell: From "A Trout for Celeste" from *Vermont River* by W. D. Wetherell. Copyright © 1984 by W. D. Wetherell.
The Yale Herald, Inc.: Quote by Annie Dillard from "Ideas are tough; irony is easy" from *The Yale Herald,* October 4, 1996. Copyright © 1996 by The Yale Herald, Inc.
Jennifer Yu: "A 'Piercing' Issue" by Jennifer Yu from *Creations, Literary/Art Magazine,* vol. XV (*Milestones: Celebrations of Life*), 1992–93. Copyright © 1993 by Jennifer Yu. Published by Warren Township High School, Gurnee, IL.
Zephyr Press: From "All the Unburied Ones . . ." from *The Complete Poems of Anna Akhmatova,* vol. II, translated by Judith Hemschemeyer, edited by Roberta Reeder. Translation copyright © 1983, 1984, 1985, 1986, 1987, 1988, 1989 by Judith Hemschemeyer.
William K. Zinsser: From "Nonfiction as Literature" from *On Writing Well,* Fifth Edition, by William Zinsser. Copyright © 1976, 1980, 1985, 1988, 1990, 1994 by William K. Zinsser.

SOURCES CITED

Quotes by Jon Krakauer from "False Summit" from *Outside,* May 1997. Published by Mariah Media, Santa Fe, NM, 1997.
Quote by Jon Krakauer from "The Top of the World" by Mary Voboril from *Newsday,* May 14, 1997. Published by Newsday, Melville, NY, 1997.
Quote by Frank McCourt from "From 'Ashes' to Stardom" by Malcolm Jones, Jr., from *Newsweek,* August 25, 1997. Published by Newsweek.

PICTURE CREDITS

The illustrations on the Contents pages are picked up from pages in the textbook. Credits for those illustrations can be found either on the textbook page on which they appear or in the listing below.

Page xxii, British Museum. Erich Lessing/Art Resource, NY; 4–5, Walter Geiersperger/Index Stock Photography; 5, 6, Stephen John Krasemann/Photo Researchers, Inc.; 7, Movie Still Archives; 8–9, (background) Paul Ambrose/FPG International; 8, Joe Sohm/The Stock Market; 9, (top right) WY/The Image Bank, (center) John Lei/OPC; 11, (background) NASA/FPG International, (inset) John Lei/OPC; 13, (top) Stephen Simpson/FPG International, (bottom) Jon Davison/The Image Bank; 16, Aram Gesar/The Image Bank; 20, Al Giddings Images, Inc.; 22, (background) Chris Butler/Science Photo Library/Photo Researchers, Inc., (inset) John Lei/OPC; 24–25, 27, Stephen Simpson/FPG International; 28, NASA; 34, Kirchoff/Wohlberg; 35, (top) Burton McNeely/The Image Bank; 35 (bottom), 37, Gerald Brimacombe/The Image Bank; 38, Burton McNeely/The Image Bank; 40, François Camoin; 47, UPI/Corbis; 52–53, (background) Martin Coleman/Picture Perfect; 52 (top) Bryan Peterson/The Stock Market, (middle) T. Eggers/The Stock Market, (bottom) John Skye Chalmers/The Stock Market; 53, (center) Preston Lyon/Index Stock Imagery, (right) Steve Smith/FPG International; 54, Bill Binzen/The Stock Market; 57, (background) Grant Heilman Photography, (left) John Skye Chalmers/The Stock Market, (right) © SuperStock Inc.; 58, Jeff Lowenthal/Woodfin Camp & Associates; 61, (background) Thomas Hovland/Grant Heilman Photography, (inset) Bryan Peterson/The Stock Market; 63, (background) Picture Perfect, (left) Preston Lyon/Index Stock Imagery, (top right) Philip Little/Picture Perfect, (bottom right) Steve Smith/FPG International; 65, (left) John Henley/The Stock Market, (right) Paul Simcock/The Image Bank; 69, 71, 72, 73, 75, Phoebe Beasley (1943–), courtesy of the artist; 76, ©Anthony Barboza; 79, Jeffrey Markowitz/Sygma; 81, Art Wolfe/Tony Stone Images; 82, Erich Hartmann/Magnum Photos, Inc.; 84, (top left) *Black Ice* book cover © 1991 by Lorene Cary. Vintage Books/Random House, (bottom left) *A Tale of Two Cities,* by Charles Dickens, book cover. Penguin UK, (top right) *Fahrenheit 451* book cover © 1953 by Ray Bradbury. Donna Diamond/Ballantine Books/Random House, (bottom right) *Dune* book cover © 1965 by Frank Herbert. John Schoener/Penguin/Putnam; 104, Reuters/Corbis; 105, 106, Suzanne DeChillo/New York Times Pictures; 112–113, Donald Johnston/Tony Stone Images; 115, ©1994 Rubén Guzmán; 119, 120 (background), Victoria and Albert Museum, London/Art Resource, New York; 127, © Nancy Crampton; 140, Hugo Martinez-Serros; 146–147, (top) Lorentz Gullachsen/Tony Stone Images, (bottom) Robin Smith/Tony Stone Images; 147, (inset) Betty Press/Woodfin Camp & Associates; 148, By The Women of Burkina Faso/Courtesy of The Museum for African Art, New York; 149, A. E. Zuckerman/PhotoEdit; 150 (background), (top right), Marc and Evelyne Bernheim/Woodfin Camp & Associates; 151, By The Women of Burkina Faso/Courtesy of The Museum for African Art, New York; 153, (left) Betty Press/Woodfin Camp & Associates, (right) University of Cambridge/Department of Biochemistry, Cambridge, England; 155, A. E. Zuckerman/PhotoEdit; 157 (bottom right), 158, 160, 161, Richard Hutchings/PhotoEdit; 162, Arte Público Press/University of Houston; 163, (left) From *Fences,* by August Wilson. Copyright © 1986 by August Wilson. Used by permission of Dutton Signet, a division of Penguin Putnam Inc., (top right) From *The Pigman* (jacket cover), by Paul Zindel. Copyright Cover Art © 1983 by John Thompson. Used by permission of Bantam Books, a division of Bantam Doubleday Dell Publishing Group, Inc., (bottom right) Used by permission of HarperCollins Publishers; 171, © Alex Stewart/The Image Bank; 177, Topham/The Image Works; 184–185, (background) © Kunio Owaki/The Stock Market; 185, ©Larry Allan/Bruce Coleman, Inc.; 189, José Antonio Velasquez, *San Antonio de Orient,* 1957, Art Museum of the Americas, OAS; 190, © Theo Westenberger/Liaison International; 196–197, Philip Jones Griffiths/Magnum Photos, Inc.; 200, Mary Ann Hemphill/Photo Researchers, Inc.; 202–203, Dirck Halstead/Liaison International; 203, Philip Jones Griffiths/Magnum Photos, Inc.; 204, Tim O'Brien/AP/Wide World Photos; 205, Paul S. Conklin/Uniphoto; 206, James Pickerell/Black Star; 213, Stewart Cohen/Tony Stone Images; 218, ITAR–TASS/Sovfoto; 225, 226 (background and inset), 227, 228, 229, Art by Sergio Bustamante/all photographs copyright Clint Clemens. All rights reserved; 230, Ulf Andersen/Liaison International; 231, Sepp Seitz/Woodfin Camp & Associates; 238, George Braziller, Inc.; 239, (left) Cover, from *Lord of the Flies,* by William Golding. Copyright 1954 by William Gerald Golding, renewed 1982. Used by permission of Coward-McCann, Inc., a division of Penguin Putnam Inc., (top right) From *Alice's Adventures in Wonderland and Through the Looking Glass* (jacket cover), by Lewis Carroll. Copyright. Used by permission of Bantam Books, a division of Bantam Doubleday Dell Publishing Group, Inc., (bottom right) From *Jane Eyre,* by Charlotte Brontë. Copyright © 1960 by New American Library. Used by permission of Dutton Signet, a division of Penguin Putnam Inc./Cover art from Victoria and Albert Museum/Art Resource, New York; 246, Greg MacGillivray, producer and director; 248–249, H. Beebower/SharpShooters; 251, 254, 256 (insets), Bartee/Stock Imagery; 251, 254, 256, North Wind Picture Archives; 257, (top) Nancy Wilson/Sygma, (bottom) From *The High Graders* (jacket cover), by Louis L'Amour. Copyright. Used by permission of Bantam Books, a division of Bantam Doubleday Dell Publishing Group, Inc.; 258, (background) © PhotoDisc, Inc. 1998, (inset) Lee Boltin Picture Library; 259, North Wind Picture Archives; 264, 265, 266, 267, 268, 269, 270, 271, © PhotoDisc, Inc. 1998; 272, Culver Pictures, Inc.; 276–277, (top) M. Rubio/West Stock; 277, Jerry Jones/Photo Researchers, Inc.; 279, (left) John Neubauer/PhotoEdit, (right) M. Rubio/West Stock; 283, Andy Sacks/Tony Stone Images; 284, UPI/Corbis; 285, (left) John Neubauer/PhotoEdit; 285 (right), 286, M. Rubio/West Stock; 289, Mary Evans Picture Library; 291, Claire Hayden/Tony Stone Images; 295, 299, Mary Evans Picture Library; 302, Corbis; 308, Arthur Tilley/FPG International; 316, Fewblatt/Sygma; 317, Jean-Claude LeJeune/Stock, Boston; 321, Copyright © 1977 by Santha Rama Rau. Reprinted by permission of William Morris Agency, Inc., on behalf of the author; 324, Ilene Perlman/Stock, Boston; 326, Elliott Erwitt/Magnum Photos, Inc.; 327, (top left) Cover, Jasper Francis Cropsey, *Greenwood Lake,* 1875. National Museum of American Art, Washington, D.C./Art Resource, New York/HarperPerennial/HarperCollins, (bottom left) From *Incidents in the Life of a Slave Girl,* by Harriet A. Jacobs. Copyright 1987 by the President and Fellows of Harvard College. Reprinted by permission of Harvard University Press, (top right) © 1986 by Bascove/Collier Books/Macmillan Publishing, (bottom right) From *The Hot Zone* (jacket cover), by Richard Preston. Copyright 1994. Used by permission of Doubleday, a division of Bantam Doubleday Dell Publishing Group, Inc.; 335, © SuperStock; 338, Mike Mathers/Photo Researchers, Inc.; 340–341, Courtesy Frank Romero; 343, Courtesy Michael Escoffery; 344, 345, From *Malcolm: The Life of a Man Who Changed Black America,* by Bruce Perry, © 1991 Station Hill Press, Barrytown, NY; 349, Copyright Indigo Gallery 1991, photo, Bruce Mathews; 350, Photofest; 351, Jerry Jacka Photography; 355, UPI/Corbis; 359, (left) Barbara Hall, (right) Howard Ikemoto; 362, UPI/Corbis; 365, 366, 367, 368, 369, 370, 371 (background), Corbis; 367, (inset) From *Angela's Ashes,* by Frank McCourt. ©1996 by Frank McCourt. Reproduced by permission of Scribner's, a division of Simon & Schuster. All rights reserved; 371, Bebeto Matthews/AP/Wide World Photos; 379, (top left) Gary Soto, cover of *A Summer Life,* © 1990 by University Press of New England, (bottom left) Cover of *The Flame Trees of Thika,* by Elspeth Huxley (Penguin Books, 1962), cover artwork by Francesca Pelizzoli. Reproduced by permission of Penguin Books Ltd., (top right) Cover of *David Copperfield,* by Charles Dickens (Penguin Books, 1985). Reproduced by permission of Penguin Books Ltd., (bottom right) From *The Pigman and Me* (jacket cover), by Paul Zindel. Copyright © 1991. Used by permission of Bantam Books, a division of Bantam Doubleday Dell Publishing Group, Inc.; 387, © Eric Meola/The Image Bank; 388–389, (background) Telegraph Colour Library/FPG International; 388, (left) Courtesy Ken Marschall Collection, (center) Titanic Historical Society, Redondo Beach, CA, (right) The Illustrated London News Picture Library; 389, (inset) Sygma; 390–391, © 1992 Ken Marschall, from *Titanic: An Illustrated History,* Madison Press Books, Toronto; 393, (background) Color Box/FPG International, (upper left) Reproduced by courtesy of White Star Publications, (lower right) The Illustrated London News Picture Library; 394, (background) Color Box/FPG International, (top) Hulton Deutsch Collection, London, (bottom) Titanic Historical Society, Redondo Beach, CA; 397, (background) Color Box/FPG International, (top) Titanic Historical Society, Redondo Beach, CA, (bottom) Corbis; 398–399, © 1992 Ken Marschall, from *Titanic: An Illustrated History,* Madison Press Books, Toronto; 403, AP/Wide World Photos; 404–405, (background) Color Box/FPG International; 404, (left) UPI/Corbis, (top right) The Illustrated London News Picture Library, (bottom right) AP/Wide World Photos; 405, (left) Titanic Historical Society, Redondo Beach, CA; 406, Everett Collection; 409, Kenneth Garrett/FPG International; 410–411, Sovfoto; 410, 412 (top), Donor, Marta Elkana/Courtesy U.S. Holocaust Memorial Museum, Washington, D.C.; 412, (bottom) Arnold Kramer/U.S. Holocaust Memorial Museum, Washington, D.C.; 413, AP/Wide World Photos; 419, (background) © Gordon Wiltsie/Alpenimage Ltd., (top) © Ed Viesturs/Ethereal, Inc., (bottom) © Caroline Mackenzie/Woodfin Camp & Associates; 420–421, © Neal Beidleman/Woodfin Camp & Associates; 422–423, (background) © Gordon Wiltsie/Alpenimage Ltd.; 424, © Neal Beidleman/Woodfin Camp & Associates; 427, Scott Fischer/Woodfin Camp & Associates; 428–429, (background) © Gordon Wiltsie/Alpenimage Ltd.; 429, (bottom) © Andrew Eccles/Outline Press; 433, Ozzie Tollefson/American Society of Mammalogists; 434–435, Richard Ellis/Photo Researchers, Inc.; 435, Michael S. Thompson/Comstock; 438, David C. Tomlinson/Tony Stone Images; 441, Michael S. Thompson/Comstock; 445, AGE FotoStock/© SuperStock Inc.; 446, AP/Wide World Photos; 447, (top left) From *Eyes on the Prize: America's Civil Rights Years,* by Juan Williams, introduction by Julian Bond. Copyright © 1987 by Blackside, Inc. Used by permission of Viking Penguin, a division of Penguin Putnam Inc., (bottom left) © 1994 by Pathways Productions, Inc., (top right) Wendell Minor/Vintage Books/Random House, (bottom right) From *The Crucible,* by Arthur Miller. Copyright 1952, 1953, 1954, renewed 1980, 1981, 1982 by Arthur Miller. Used by permission of Viking Penguin, a division of Penguin Putnam Inc.; 454, © SuperStock Inc.; 463, Corbis; 466, Courtesy *Voices of Youth;* 470–471, 472–473, Terry Ashe/Liaison International; 474, Liaison International; 475, Bernard Gotfryd/Woodfin Camp & Associates; 479, Tomek Sikora/The Image Bank; 480–481, Classics International Entertainment; 483, Randy Duchaine/The Stock Market; 485, Joe Travers/Liaison International; 489, Stuart Franklin/Magnum Photos, Inc.; 491, (top left) Cover of *Silent Spring.* Copyright © 1962 by Rachel L. Carson, renewed 1990 by Roger Christie. Reprinted by permission of Houghton Mifflin Company. All rights reserved, (top right) From cover of *Animal Farm,* by George Orwell. Copyright © 1950 by New American Library on cover. Used by permission of Dutton Signet, a division of Penguin Putnam Inc., (bottom left) From *All I Really Needed to Know I Learned in Kindergarten,* by Robert Fulghum. Copyright © 1986, 1988 by Robert L. Fulghum. Reprinted by permission of Villard Books, a division of Random House, Inc., (bottom right) Burt Glinn/Magnum Photos, Inc./Vintage International/Random House; 499, © SuperStock Inc.; 502, AP/Wide World Photos; 505, Masao Mukai/Photonica; 510, Griff Davis/Black Star; 512, Richard Nowitz; 513, © Nancy Crampton; 515, Leonard Freed/Magnum Photos, Inc.; 517, National Museum of American Art, Washington, D.C./Art Resource, New York; 518, (top) Fred Ward/Black Star, (bottom) Kosti Ruohomaa/Black Star; 521, (top) Corbis, (bottom) Library of Congress; 524, Courtesy of Hilary Masters; 526–527, 528, Fred M. Dole/f/Stop Pictures; 530–531, (background) Koichi Eda/Photonica; 532–533, (background) Jim Ballard/Tony Stone Images; 533, (inset) Charles Wright; 540, © Nancy Crampton; 545, By permission of the Houghton Library, Harvard University; 546, © SuperStock Inc.; 551, Red Crane Books; 554, (background) Miyoko Komine/Photonica, (inset) Brown Brothers, (signature) By permission of the Houghton Library, Harvard University; 555, © Michael A. A. Keller/The Stock Market; 560–561, (background) Kaoru Mikami/Photonica; 564–565, (background) J. Nakamichi/Photonica; 566, Hans Reinhard/Photo Researchers, Inc.; 568–569, Joanie Schwarz; 574–575, Dennie Cody/FPG International; 575, ©Layle Silbert; 578, © 2000 Estate of Pablo Picasso/Artists Rights Society (ARS), New York /Scala/Art Resource, New York; 579, Corbis; 587, Ron Chapple/FPG International; 590–591, Harold Sund/The Image Bank; 590, UPI/Corbis; 592, © PhotoDisc, Inc. 1998; 594, © Nancy Crampton; 596, M. P. Kahl/Photo Researchers, Inc.; 599, © Janet Century; 600, UPI/Corbis; 604, Arte Público Press/University of Houston; 605, 606, (background) Koichi Eda/Photonica; 606, (bottom) © LaVerne Harrell Clark; 607, 608–609, Charlyn Zlotnik/Woodfin Camp & Associates; 609, (bottom) Katherine Gilbert Espada; 610, Steve McCurry/Magnum Photos, Inc.; 612, Denver Public Library/Western History Collection; 613, Nebraska State Historical Society; 616, Courtesy Richard Erdoes; 617 (top left) Woodcut by Mary F. Rhinelander/Little, Brown & Company, (bottom left) Algonquin Books/Workman Publishing Company, Inc., (top right) © 1982 by Edward Gorey/Harcourt Brace, (bottom right) "Above the Clouds at Sunrise" by Frederick Church/Ballantine Books/Random House; 625, © SuperStock Inc.; 626–627, T. Charles Erickson; 628, Courtesy Robert Anderson; 629, © Nancy Crampton; 630, (right) PLAYBILL® cover, printed by permission of PLAYBILL Incorporated. PLAYBILL® is a registered trademark of PLAYBILL Incorporated, New York, NY; 632, The Kobal Collection; 635, Photofest; 636–637, Martha Swope © Time Inc.; 638, PLAYBILL® cover, printed by permission of PLAYBILL Incorporated. PLAYBILL® is a registered trademark of PLAYBILL Incorporated, New York, NY; 639, Martha Swope © Time Inc.; 645, The Kobal Collection; 648, 656, 663, 665, 677 (top), Martha Swope © Time Inc.; 677, (bottom) Michael Quackenbush/The Image Bank; 688–689, (background) Will and Deni McIntyre/Photo Researchers, Inc.; 690–691, 692, 699, 701, 709, Martha Swope © Time Inc.; 715, Gian Berto Vanni/Art Resource, New York; 719, 721, 725, 730, 737, Martha Swope © Time Inc.; 744, UPI/Corbis; 749, (left) from *A Separate Peace* (jacket cover), by John Knowles. Copyright © 1959 by John Knowles. Used by permission of Bantam Books, a division of Bantam Doubleday Dell Publishing Group, Inc., (top right) *Where Do We Go From Here?* by Martin Luther King, Jr. © 1967 by Martin Luther King, Jr. Reprinted by permission of Beacon Press, Boston. Cover art by Flip Schulke, (bottom right) National Gallery of London/Oxford University Press; 750, ©Joan Marcus; 759, (top) © SuperStock Inc., (bottom) Billy Brown, copyright © 1994 Comstock; 760–761, © George E. Joseph; 764, Photofest; 768, The Shakespeare Centre Library, Stratford-on-Avon, England; 769, Erich Lessing/Art Resource, New York; 773, Photofest; 776, © SuperStock Inc.; 784, © George E. Joseph; 791, Rod Planck/Photo Researchers, Inc.; 793, © George E. Joseph; 798, Martha Swope © Time Inc.; 807, 809, 811, 820, 824, 829, 832, 836, 839, 852, 859, 864–865, 870, 875, © George E. Joseph; 877, Mike Reagan; 878, Corbis; 886–887, FPG International; 889, (left) From *Macbeth,* by William Shakespeare. Copyright © 1963, renewed 1991 by Sylvan Barnet for introduction and annotations. Used by permission of Dutton Signet, a division of Penguin Putnam Inc., (top right) Courtesy of the John F. Kennedy Library/HarperPerennial, a division of HarperCollins Publishers, (bottom right) From *The Right Stuff* (jacket cover), by Tom Wolfe. Copyright ©1979 by Tom Wolfe. Used by permission of Bantam Books, a division of Bantam Doubleday Dell Publishing Group, Inc.; 899, © SuperStock Inc.; 902–903, Courtesy Pucker/Safrai Gallery, Boston, MA; 904–905, 906–907, Israel Talby/Woodfin Camp & Associates; 907, (lower right) Photri; 911, Art Resource, New York; 915, Giraudon/Art Resource, New York; 918, Erich Lessing/Art Resource, New York; 919, Alix Coleman/Grant Heilman Photography; 920, Grant Heilman Photography; 934–935, Lindsay Hebberd/Woodfin Camp & Associates; 935, (inset) Corbis; 941, © SuperStock Inc.; 946, (top left) EDIMEDIA/Penguin UK, (bottom left) From *Irish Folktales,* by Henry Glassie, editor. Copyright © 1985 by Henry Glassie. Reprinted by permission of Pantheon Books, a division of Random House, Inc., (top right) From *The Story Telling Stone* (jacket cover), by Susan Feldman, editor. Copyright 1965. Used by permission of Dell Books, a division of Bantam Doubleday Dell Publishing Group, Inc., (bottom right) From *Arab Folktales,* by Inea Bushnaq. Copyright © 1986 by Inea Bushnaq. Reprinted by permission of Pantheon Books, a division of Random House, Inc.; 947, NASA; 948–949, (background) Gabe Palmer/The Stock Market; 949, (top) Copyright ©1966 by J.R.R. Tolkien, by permission of Frank Richard Williamson and Christopher Reuel Tolkien, executors of the Estate of the late John Ronald Reuel Tolkien, (bottom) Photofest; 950–951, IPA/The Image Works; 961, Photofest; 962, (background) *Camelot,* words by Alan Jay Lerner and Frederick Loewe, copyright © 1960, 1961 by Alan Jay Lerner and Frederick Loewe. Copyright renewed. Chappell & Co., owner of publication and allied rights throughout the world. International copyright secured. All rights reserved, (top) The Kobal Collection; 969, Reprinted with the permission of Atheneum Books for Young Readers, an imprint of Simon & Schuster Children's Publishing Division, from *The Boy's King Arthur,* by Sidney Lanier, illustrated by N. C. Wyeth. Copyright 1917, 1924 Charles Scribner's Sons, copyright renewed 1945 N. C. Wyeth and 1952 John Lanier, David Lanier, and Sterling Lanier; 972–973, Simon Wilkinson/The Image Bank; 973, From the collection of Pierre Verité, Paris/André Held; 977, 978, Marc and Evelyne Bernheim/ Woodfin Camp & Associates; 979, Betty Press/Woodfin Camp & Associates; 985, (top left) Cover from *The Fellowship of the Ring,* by J.R.R. Tolkien, cover art by Michael Herring. Copyright © 1955, 1965 by J.R.R. Tolkien; copyright renewed © 1982 by Christopher R. Tolkien, Michael H. R. Tolkien, John F. R. Tolkien, and Priscilla M.A.R. Tolkien, (bottom left) Mastermedia Limited: Jacket Cover from *Rosey Grier's All American Heroes,* by Roosevelt "Rosey" Grier, cover design by Antler & Baldwin, Inc. Copyright © 1993 by Roosevelt "Rosey" Grier, (top right) Reprinted with the permission of Simon & Schuster from *Child of the Northern Spring,* by Persia Woolley. Copyright © 1987 by Simon & Schuster, (bottom right) Ballantine Books, a division of Random House, Inc.; Jacket Cover from *Days of Grace: A Memoir,* by Arthur Ashe and Arnold Rampersad. Copyright © 1993 by Joanne Moutoussamy-Ashe and Arnold Rampersad; 993, © SuperStock Inc.; 1012, Portions copyright Netscape Communications Corporation, 1998. All rights reserved. Netscape, Netscape Navigator, and the Netscape N logo are registered trademarks of Netscape in the United States and other countries.

Borders for Speaking and Listening Workshops and for Sentence Workshops, Troy Vis; borders for Elements of Literature features and for Writer's Workshops, Paul Kazmercyk.

In Writers Workshops, Macintosh window elements and icons © 1984 Apple Computer, Inc. All rights reserved. Used with the permission of Apple Computer, Inc.

Border for Reading Skills and Strategies, (background) Art Montes de Oca/FPG International, (left) Copyright 1998, USA TODAY. Reprinted with permission, (right) Copyright 1998 Netscape Communications Corp. Used with permission. All rights reserved. This electronic file or page may not be reprinted or copied without the express written permission of Netscape. Netscape Communications Corporation has not authorized, sponsored, or endorsed or approved this publication and is not responsible for its content. Netscape and Netscape Communications corporate logos are trademarks and trade names of Netscape Communications Corporation. All other product names and/or logos are trademarks of their respective owners.

INDEX OF SKILLS

LITERARY TERMS

The boldface page numbers indicate an extensive treatment of the topic.

READING AND CRITICAL THINKING

LANGUAGE (GRAMMAR, USAGE, AND MECHANICS)

VOCABULARY AND SPELLING

WRITING

SPEAKING, LISTENING, AND VIEWING

RESEARCH AND STUDY

CROSSING THE CURRICULUM

INDEX OF ART

FINE ART AND CRAFTS

ILLUSTRATIONS

MAPS

CARTOONS

INDEX OF AUTHORS AND TITLES

Page numbers in italic type refer to the pages on which author biographies appear.